THE PARENTS' RESOURCE ALMANAC

THE PARENTS' RESOURCE ALMANAC

Where to write, who to call,
what to buy, and how to find out
everything you need to know.

BETH DeFRANCIS

BOB ADAMS, INC.
Holbrook, Massachusetts

Published by Bob Adams, Inc.
260 Center Street, Holbrook, MA 02343

ISBN: 1-55850-396-X (hardcover)
ISBN: 1-55850-394-3 (paperback)

Printed in the United States of America.

J I H G F E D C B A (hardcover)
J I H G F E D C B A (paperback)

Library of Congress Cataloging-in-Publication Data
DeFrancis, Beth.
    The parents' resource almanac : where to write, who to call, what to buy, and how
to find out everything you need to know / Beth DeFrancis
      p.   cm.
    Includes index.
    ISBN 1-55850-396-X — ISBN 1-55850-394-3 (pbk.)
    1. Parenting—United States—Handbooks, manuals, etc. 2. Parenting—United States—
Bibliography. 3. Children—Services for—United States—Directories. 4. Child rearing—United
States—Handbooks, manuals, etc. I. Title.
    HQ755.8.D43   1994
    649'.1'02573—dc20   94-15476
                                           CIP

This publication is designed to provide accurate and authoritative information with regard to the
subject matter covered. It is sold with the understanding that the publisher is not engaged in ren-
dering legal, accounting, or other professional advice. If legal advice or other expert assistance is
required, the services of a competent professional person should be sought.
—From a *Declaration of Principles* jointly adopted by a Committee of the American Bar
Association and a Committee of Publishers and Associations

COVER DESIGN: Barry Littmann

*This book is available at quantity discounts for bulk purchases.
For information, call 1-800-872-5627.*

For Michael and Paula

Table of Contents

Acknowledgments

Although many people worked hard to make this book possible, I owe special thanks to my agent, Bill Adler, Jr., who recognized the value of this project and took the steps necessary to help turn it into a book.

Literally hundreds of others played an important role by returning my phone calls, sending materials (promptly), and otherwise passing along valuable pieces of the parenting resource puzzle. "Thanks" to all of you who looked things up, popped packages in the mail, and cheerfully pointed me in the right direction when I was off course.

I'd also like to thank Brandon Toropov, Angela Miccinello, Christopher Ciaschini, Susan Beale, Rick Dey, and the many individuals who worked behind the scenes to turn my manuscript into a bound book in record time.

The information on children's radio programming would not have been possible without independent producer Jamie Deming and the people of the Children's Music Network in Boston, who shared with me their unique, ongoing research in this field. Numerous producers and program directors also offered advice, though I must single out P. J. Swift, producer of "Pickleberry Pie" in Santa Cruz, California, for sharing both her insider's information and her contagious enthusiasm. A special thank-you as well to the staff at the municipal and county libraries of Baltimore, Boston, Cleveland, Denver, Des Moines, Houston, Newark and Paterson (New Jersey), Providence, Seattle, Springfield (Missouri), Topeka, West Oahu (Hawaii), Wilmington, and Washington, D.C.

Others who graciously offered assistance include Linda McKenney, the Education Coordinator at Northern Virginia F.A.C.E. (Families Adopting Children Everywhere), and the helpful staff members at the Association of Science-Technology Centers and the American Symphony Orchestra League.

Many thanks, also, to the dedicated librarians who helped me locate materials in the Alexandria Library System, the Arlington County Public Library, and the Fairfax County Public Library. The staff at the Library of Congress were also most helpful.

I owe special thanks to my friend Molly Cameron who helped out in a number of ways. Molly taught me how to take full advantage of library databases (one of her areas of expertise); compiled the Fitness, Exercise, and Sports chapter of the book; and offered words of encouragement when I was inundated. She also entertained my two children on numerous occasions so that I was free to work, uninterrupted during the final stages of the book. Others who helped care for my energetic (i.e., demanding) son and daughter during the duration of the project include Donna and Cordell Cassens, who tended to my infant for one morning a week during the peak of her separation anxiety, and Robin Rathbun, a neighbor who kindly offered to watch both of my children (along with her own) one afternoon a week.

Finally *The Parents' Resource Almanac* would not have been the same book were it not for the help of my husband, Marc. He made phone calls, converted disks, mailed letters, edited my writing, and conducted all the research for the radio section of the book. Marc also took the kids away for extended visits to "grandma's and grandpa's," so that I could work in a quiet house. To him, I am most grateful.

Introduction

Although parenthood is a joy, it is also an exercise in endurance. When your baby is screaming, your toilet is backing up, your school-age child is bleeding after jumping off the back of the couch, and dinner is burning in the oven, the situation calls on all of your physical and emotional reserves. Despite your fatigue, you act. You turn off the oven, grab your baby, head to the medicine chest for a box of bandages, and throw all of your clean towels on the bathroom floor. You call the plumber, kiss your child's boo-boo, and phone for a pizza.

While there have been days when I felt I did little more than keep my children out of harm's way, there have been many others when we reached higher plateaus. I think of the times we imitated cheetahs at the zoo, the cakes my enterprising son "invented," the paper airplanes we launched from the top of the jungle gym. Stories read aloud have stimulated not only my kids' imaginations but mine too. Music and dancing have improved our moods, and family trips have cleared our minds.

While I'd like to take the credit for all that has gone well, I owe much of it to the many people (parents, pediatricians, and child development experts) who have shared what they've learned about raising children over the years. Well before I began researching this book, I found myself sifting through magazine articles, reading recommended parenting books, and sharing how-to tips with other moms and dads. When I grew concerned (alarmed, actually) about my first-born's high energy level, I picked up a copy of T. Berry Brazelton's *Infants and Mothers* and was reassured that my son was in fact normal. When discipline became an issue, I found numerous articles and books by Penelope Leach most helpful. Wise words from Burton White,

Louise Bates Ames, and other experts have also helped me better understand, and parent, my children.

While there are few books that accurately describe parenthood itself (only experience can teach that), in recent years thousands of resources have emerged to help moms and dads escort their sons and daughters through childhood. The main purpose of *The Parents' Resource Almanac* is to guide parents through this labyrinth of information so they can find the very best books, magazines, products, and services as the need arises.

Since it would be impossible to describe *all* parenting resources in a single volume, I turned to the experts for their viewpoints and tried to ensure that the major voices on all major issues were included here. In some areas, the experts are in disagreement, and the entries in this book reflect their differing opinions. For example, there are some who believe television can be a powerful learning tool, while others believe it should be banned from the home altogether; both views are represented among the resources listed. On the other hand, nearly all early childhood education experts agree that there is little value in pushing preschoolers to read, so under this topic I did not list the small handful of authors who encourage parents to teach infants their ABCs. In both cases, as throughout the book, it was expert consensus that dictated which resources would be included in this guide. Throughout *The Parents' Resource Almanac*, you'll find that my listings generally expand on current ways of thinking.

While child-rearing experts often have strong opinions, they also understand the realities parents face today and the difficulties they have in doing the "ideal" thing. When it comes to childcare, for example, Brazelton and many other experts agree that parents provide the best care for their own children. Nevertheless, they acknowledge that this is not always possible and offer valuable advice for parents who work outside the home and must choose some form of alternative care. And while most pediatricians advocate breast milk as the ideal food for infants, many of them offer advice on bottle feeding for moms who, for whatever reason, choose not to nurse their babies.

In this book, you'll find descriptions of free and inexpensive materials, books, periodicals, associations, businesses, computer software, radio programs, videotapes and cassettes, mail order catalogs, and much more. The sources for my selections included dozens of review journals, recommendations from experts, suggestions from parents, and innovative offerings gleaned from many media sources. I also tapped databases, delved into the Library of Congress holdings, pored over mail-order catalogs, and logged-in many miles visiting bookstores and libraries.

To assist you in locating specific information, entries are alphabetized by type of resource under specific topic headings, and a detailed contents page appears at the beginning of each chapter. In appendix I, you'll find contact information for the most frequently mentioned associations.

I have done everything in my power to ensure accuracy in *The Parents' Resource Almanac*. Nevertheless, any book of this size is bound to contain an occasional error, as well as some out-of-date listings. The offices of even the largest associations can pick up and move overnight, phone numbers can change, periodicals can shut down, and services can transform or cease to exist. To keep such errors to a minimum, I confirmed the information by making hundreds of phone calls, sending postcards (when I couldn't find a phone number), double-checking entries against my source materials, and using the most current library directories and databases. If you do discover an error as you try to obtain a listed resource, keep in mind that the book often gives more than one way to track it down. For example, if a phone number has changed, you can call information for the city or town given in the mailing address. If an address is wrong, try calling the phone number listed. (Where a phone number is omitted, it is usually because the organization preferred not to list it; where an address is omitted, it's because the contact source is better able to handle telephone requests.) If all else fails, you can consult the current edition of a standard library directory such as the *Encyclopedia of Associations* (Gale Research, Inc.) or *Ulrich's International Periodicals Directory* (R. R. Bowker). In addition, related organizations are usually happy to point callers in the right direction.

You'll notice that I have generally not included prices for books, videotapes, or other products listed. The exceptions to this rule occur only when a resource is very expensive, when you have to mail your money with your request, or when the price is otherwise relevant. I omitted the prices because they change so frequently and can vary between stores, catalogs and other purvey-ors. If you want to purchase an item, you can easily find out the current price by contacting the listed sources.

This book should become a jumping-off point for your own explorings as you discover the parenting style that works best for you. In the fall of 1993, I watched my own kindergartner get on the school bus for the first time in his life. As the enormous yellow vehicle took him out into the bigger world, I was surprised to feel tears forming in my eyes. As he waved good-bye through the window, I thought, "Go share your enthusiasm, honey, and remember what we've taught you," and hoped that I had done my job well in preparing him.

On some level, I think we all realize that our role as parents is limited—that our kids come into our lives with certain tendencies, temperaments, and ways of being that nothing in our parenting approach can ever change. Somewhere in my research, I read that parents often blame themselves more than they should when things go wrong and take more credit than they should when things go right. Perhaps our biggest challenge is to learn when to step back and when to step in—and to enjoy our children along the way.

— *Beth DeFrancis*
Arlington, Virginia
May 1994

THE PARENTS'
RESOURCE
ALMANAC

Chapter 1

Child Development:
Understanding Your Baby's and Child's Physical, Emotional, Cognitive, and Social Development

---

GENERAL RESOURCES

Free and Inexpensive Resources

A Beginner's Bibliography. An annotated materials list for parents, teachers, and others who want to learn more about how young children grown and learn. Includes recent and classic books, brochures, and periodicals about child development and early childhood education and child development. Among the book titles are *Ages and Stages*, *The Magic Years*, and *The Learning Child*. Available for 50¢ from the National Association for the Education of Young Children (see appendix I for contact information).

Off to a Sound Start. By J. B. McCracken. A brochure explaining what happens during the first year of life, with helpful tips for parents and caregivers. Includes a chart listing developmental milestones (language development, motor skills, self-awareness, interest in others, etc.). Available for 50¢ from the National Association for the Education of Young Children (see appendix I for contact information).

Patterns of Growth. A free booklet describing patterns of physical growth in children. Available from the Human Growth Foundation, 7777 Leesburg Pike, Falls Church, Virginia 22043. Phone: 703/883-1773 or 1/800-451-6434.

Your Child's Growth: Developmental Milestones. Parents can use this handy developmental checklist, prepared by the American Academy of Pediatrics, to gauge "normal" stages of development in children three months to six years old. Ask your pediatrician for a copy or send a self-addressed, stamped envelope to American Academy of Pediatrics, "Developmental Milestones" (see appendix I for contact information).

Books

Ages and Stages. By Karen Miller. Telshare, 1985. 153 pages. Offers an account of the stages of physical, emotional, and intellectual development of children (from birth through age eight), along with suitable activities at each stage. Includes a sampling of homemade items to foster emerging skills.

Babyhood. By Penelope Leach. Second edition, revised and expanded. Alfred A. Knopf, 1991. 413 pages. Traces the sequence of changes that take place from infancy through toddlerhood. Explores physical patterns (eating, sleeping, and eliminating), body control (rolling, crawling, walking), language development (gurgling, babbling, talking), learning, and playing. Draws on research findings from around the globe, and contains a bibliography of more than two hundred reports associated with child development. Rather than telling parents what to do with their baby, this book explains what your baby *will do* during the first few years of life.

Baby Journal. By Matthew Bennett. Meadowbrook, 1993. 36 pages. Offers month-by-month guidelines for new parents. Lists developmental milestones and gives tips on topics such as touching and putting a baby to sleep. Doubles as a diary of your child's first year of life.

Babywatching. By Desmond Morris. Crown, 1991. 214 pages. Babies are aware of far more than we think, according to this book by a zoologist and author of the international bestseller *The Naked Ape.* Explores babies' senses (sight, sound, smell, touch, taste), answers dozens of commonly asked questions ("Why do babies cry?" "Do babies dream?" "What makes a baby laugh?" "Why does a baby have a softspot on his head?" "How soon do the baby's teeth appear?" "Why are babies swaddled?" "Why do babies like to sleep with a treasured possession?" "Why do most mothers cradle their babies in their left arms?"), and shares insights on how newborns learn.

Child Behavior. By Louise Bates Ames, Frances L. Ilg, Sidney M. Baker, and Gesell Institute of Human Development. Revised edition. HarperCollins, 1992. 368 pages. This classic guide shows how child behavior develops in patterned and predictable ways. Explains cycles of behavioral change, including periods of equilibrium and disequilibrium. Describes stages of development in children from infancy through age ten, including a discussion of typical behavioral difficulties (eating behavior, fears, brothers and sisters, etc.).

Childhood. By Melvin Konner. Little, Brown, 1991. 451 pages. Filled with accounts from children and families in Japan, Brazil, West Africa, the United States, and elsewhere around the globe, this book takes readers on a journey through the childhood years—from conception and birth through adolescence. Includes a discussion of language in play and imagination, learning and teaching, and moral development, among other topics. Examines research findings behind the "nature versus nurture" controversy and offers new evidence for the importance of biology in explaining the experience and development of children. Companion volume to the nine-hour public television series by the same name.

Childhood and Adolescence: A Psychology of the Growing Person. By L. Joseph Stone and Joseph Church. Random House, 1984. 638 pages. An introductory textbook on child development, now in its fifth edition.

Childhood and Society. By E. Erikson. W. W. Norton, 1950. 445 pages. Written by one of the leading figures in the field of psychoanalysis and human development, this classic explores the relationships between child-rearing practices and the growth of personality and character in the young child.

A Child's World. By Diane Papalia and Sally Wendkos Olds. Fourth edition. New York: McGraw-Hill, 1987. 640 pages. Widely used as a college text, this book summarizes research findings and information on child development from conception through adolescence.

Diary of a Baby. By Daniel N. Stern, M.D. Basic Books, 1990. 165 pages. Written as a diary, this book sheds light on what a baby sees, feels, and experiences from infancy through age four. Alternates sections representing the baby's own voice with explanatory text. Endorsed by T. Berry Brazelton.

The Earliest Relationship: Parents, Infants, and the Drama of Early Attachment. By T. Berry Brazelton and Bertrand G. Cramer. Addison-Wesley, 1990. 251 pages. Combines insights on mother/infant interaction with research on infant development.

First Feelings: Milestones in the Emotional Development of Your Baby and Child from Birth to Age Four. By Stanley Greenspan and Nancy Thorndike Greenspan. Viking, 1985. 247 pages. Helps parents recognize key stages of a child's emotional growth. The six stages of growth outlined involve not only the baby's feelings but how those feelings are communicated. Also looks at the differences in parenting styles and attitudes, and discusses how these can help—or hinder—a child's development. Also by Stanley Greenspan: *Playground Politics: Understanding the Emotional Life of the School-Age Child* (Addison-Wesley, 1993).

The First Three Years of Life. By Burton L. White. New and revised edition. Prentice-Hall, 1991. 384 pages. A phase-by-phase guide to the mental, physical, social, and emotional development of infants and toddlers. Recognizes the role of the parent in the child's development, and offers advice in areas such as discipline, toilet training, purchasing toys, and the nurturing of intelligence. Explores substitute child care, the benefits of breastfeeding, professional testing, and other relevant topics as well. Other books by White include *Educating the Infant and Toddler* (Lexington Books, 1990) and *Human Infants* (Prentice-Hall, 1971).

The First Twelve Months of Life: Your Baby's Growth Month by Month. By Theresa Caplan. Revised and updated. Putnam, 1993. 302 pages. An updated version of the bestseller by Frank Caplan, this book explores motor, auditory, and visual development, as well as growth in language, cognitive, and social skills during the first year of life. Includes growth charts and photographs. Also available: *The Second Twelve Months of Life: A Kaleidoscope of Growth* and *The Early Childhood Years: The Two to Six Year Old* (Bantam Books), both by Frank Caplan and Theresa Caplan.

The Gesell Institute of Human Development Series. By Louise Bates Ames and others. Delacorte Press. These books contain descriptions of children's behavior at each age. Also discusses children's health, individuality, appropriate disciplinary measures, and other age-specific topics. Suggests toys and books for children, as well as resources for parents. Books in the series include the following:

Your One-Year-Old: The Fun-Loving, Fussy 12-24-Month-Old
Your Two-Year-Old: Terrible or Tender
Your Three-Year-Old: Friend or Enemy
Your Four-Year-Old: Wild and Wonderful
Your Five-Year-Old: Sunny and Serene
Your Six-Year-Old: Loving and Defiant
Your Seven-Year-Old: Life in a Minor Key
Your Eight-Year-Old: Lively and Outgoing
Your Nine-Year-Old: Thoughtful and Mysterious
Your Ten-to-Fourteen-Year-Old

The Growing Years: A Guide to Your Child's Emotional Development from Birth to Adolescence. By the New York Hospital/Cornell Medical Center Department of Psychiatry with Mark Rubinstein, M.D. Simon and Schuster, 1989. 386 pages. Divided into four stages of growth—newborn, toddler, preschool, and school age—this book discusses the biological and emotional changes unique to each stage of a child's life. Offers advice on common problems and addresses complex issues such as day care and single parenting. Each section concludes with a "Consultation" (a roster of frequently asked questions, with answers by experts from the Cornell University Medical College).

The Importance of Being Baby. By Bertrand G. Cramer; translated by Gillian Gill. Addison-Wesley/ Lawrence, 1992. 203 pages. A child psychiatrist discusses "the scripts parents write and the roles babies play." Describes the ways that parents transmit their expectations in every gesture they make toward their babies (some match the fantasy, others don't). Shows how parents can learn to see and enjoy the *real* child.

Infants and Mothers: Differences in Development. By T. Berry Brazelton, M.D. Revised edition. Delacorte Press/Seymour Lawrence, 1983. 302 pages. Revised edition. A classic work by the renowned child development expert, this book guides parents through the first twelve months of their child's life. Brazelton has chosen three representative babies—one "quiet," one "average," and one "active"—to demonstrate individual differences and reassure parents that their young charges are developing normally. The book reads like a diary, taking readers on a personal journey through the daily lives of infants and mothers: eating (feedings), social interaction, play, mobility, language acquisition, and sleeping patterns are all explored. Offers advice and commentary throughout the book. See also listing for *Toddlers and Parents: Declaration of Independence.*

Magical Child. By Joseph Chilton Pearce. Penguin Books, 1992 (first published in 1977). 256 pages. Expanding on the ideas of child psychologist Jean Piaget, Pearce traces the growth of the mind-brain from birth to adulthood. Argues that children from the moment of birth have only one concern: to learn all that there is to learn about the world. Emphasizes the importance of child's play and questions current thinking on childrearing and childhood education. Shows how parents can help restore the creative intelligence that, the author believes, is the birthright of every child. [Note: *In Raising a Magical Child*, a sixty-minute audiocassette, Pearce answers questions about his work during a question-and-answer session with Phylicia Rashad (of "The Cosby Show"). This cassette is available from Music for Little People, (see chapter 27 for contact information).]

Piaget Primer: How a Child Thinks. By Dorothy Singer and T. Revenson. New American Library, 1978. 148 pages. Offers a practical introduction to the thought and theories of the world's foremost authority on child development. Explains how children play, use language, and process information. [Note: More ambitious parents might want to work their way through Piaget's original classic, *The Origins of Intelligence in Children* (International Universities Press, 1952).]

To Listen to a Child: Understanding the Normal Problems of Growing Up. By T. Berry Brazelton, M.D. New edition. Addison-Wesley/Lawrence, 1992. 192 pages. Helps parents better understand their child's developmental needs and offers guidelines for dealing with common problems (fears in small children, discipline, sleep, etc.). Explores each issue from two points of view—the child's and the parent's.

Toddlers and Parents: Declaration of Independence. By T. Berry Brazelton, M.D. Revised edition. Delacorte Press/Seymour Lawrence, 1989. 249 pages. As with his classic *Infants and Mothers* (see separate listing), Brazelton has chosen representative children (in this case toddlers) to demonstrate individual differences and guide parents through the specific challenges of childrearing. In this revised edition, Brazelton emphasizes the special strains on working parents, the role of fathers, and the needs of toddlers in day-care centers.

Touchpoints: Your Child's Emotional and Behavioral Development. By T. Berry Brazelton, M.D. Addison-Wesley, 1992. 469 pages. A general reference book highlighting developmental milestones during the first six years of life. Part One follows each of the "touchpoints" (universal spurts of development and trying periods of regression) from the prenatal visit through the first three years of life. Part Two covers common behavioral and emotional challenges (listed in alphabetical order) during the first six years. (For information on Brazelton's videotapes by the same name, see "Videotapes" listed under "Meeting Basic Needs" in chapter 3.)

What to Expect the First Year. By Arlene Eisenberg, Heidi E. Murkoff, and Sandee E. Hathaway, B.S.N. Workman, 1989. 671 pages. Explains, month-by-month, what parents can expect during the first year of life. Each chapter explains what your baby may be doing that month (cooing, smiling, rolling over, crawling, etc.), what to expect during routine checkups, and what parents may be concerned about (for example, spitting up, sleeping problems, and ear pulling; the book addresses these issues in a question/answer format). In addition, this work includes a first-aid guide, a primer on everyday care, guidelines on selecting the right physician, information on family travel, safety tips, and other valuable information.

Your Baby and Child: From Birth to Age Five. By Penelope Leach. New edition, revised and expanded. Alfred A. Knopf, 1989. 553 pages. Examines what happens within your child from the moment of birth until he or she is ready for school. Explores the various stages of development (mental, physical, and emotional); explains how to feed, bathe, and otherwise care for your child; and offers guidance in coping with common troublespots such as teething, tantrums, and sleeping problems. This popular guidebook also sheds light on the learning process and explains how parents can help make the most of their child's play time. A special reference section provides a quick guide to medical matters such as colds, head injuries, allergic reactions, and hospital admission.

Your Child's Growing Mind. By Jane Healy. Doubleday, 1987. 324 pages. Describes how children learn from birth to adolescence and how parents can help in the process. Discusses brain development, intelligence, memory, language development, and academic learning. Offers an indictment of early pressures to teach children to read.

Periodicals

American Baby. Cahners Publishing Co., 475 Park Avenue South, New York, New York 10016. Phone: 212/689-3600. A monthly magazine for expectant and new parents with an emphasis on the physical and mental well-being of the baby and mother. (Note: A special issue of the magazine called *First Year of Life* is offered to new mothers through hospitals. This issue covers babies' growth and development during the first twelve months of life. The advisory board for this special issue includes Burton L. White, Ph.D., Lawrence Balter, Ph.D., and Alvin N. Eden, M.D., F.A.A.P., among other experts. If you haven't received a copy and would like one, contact *American Baby* for information on how to obtain one.)

The Brown University Child and Adolescent Behavior Letter. 205 Governor Street, Providence, Rhode Island 02906. Phone: 401/831-6020. Reports on current research and trends in the field of child development. Offers insights on the problems of children and adolescents growing up. Information comes from experts in the field, professional journals, and the publication's editorial board. Primarily for professionals in the field. 8 pages. Issued monthly. $77 for an annual subscription.

The Center for Parent Education Newsletter. Center for Parent Education, 81 Wyman Street, Waban, Massachusetts 02168. A bimonthly newsletter featuring articles on topics and issues in early childhood development (birth to age three). Includes quotations; resource listings; announcements of upcoming events; and reviews of books, toys, films, and videotapes. Although geared toward professionals, this publication offers insights for parents as well. Available by subscription.

Child Development. See Society for Research in Child Development, listed under "Associations."

Growing Child. Dunn and Hargitt, Inc., P.O. Box 620, Lafayette, Indiana 47902. Phone: 1/800-927-7289. This newsletter for parents follows a child's development month-by-month from birth to age six (there are separate editions for each age group). Explains what babies and young children are like at each age, and what they need from adults. Discusses topics such as crying, feeding, language development, and the importance of play. Back issues are available. Comes with a supplement, *Growing Parent*, that addresses the concerns adults have about their roles and responsibilities as parents, spouses, and family members. (Note: The *Growing Up* newsletter picks up where *Growing Child* leaves off, covering the physical, behavioral, and academic development of children in kindergarten through high school. However, *Growing Up* is marketed directly to schools and is issued in the form of reproducible masters for teachers to send home with their students.)

Growing Child Research Review. Dunn and Hargitt, Inc., P.O. Box 620, Lafayette, Indiana 47902. Phone: 1/800-927-7289. Provides news, recent research findings, and expert opinions on child development-related topics in the areas of education, psychology, mental health, and medicine. Of interest to parents and professional educators. Issued monthly.

Growing Together. Dunn and Hargitt, Inc., P.O. Box 620, Lafayette, Indiana 47902. Phone: 1/800-927-7289. A newsletter for parents who have young children in day care. Discusses a child's growth and development. Covers topics such as academics, activities, social skills, and parenting. Issued monthly.

The In Between Years. P.O. Box 575, Orono, Maine 04473. A newsletter for parents and caregivers of ten- to fourteen-year-olds. Provides information, strategies, and advice about growth and development, education, health family ties, and other concerns of young adolescents and their parents. Published four times during the school year (September, November, February, and May).

Your Child Now. Phone: 1/800-777-0987. A four-page supplement bound into regular issues of *Child* magazine. Subscribers submit their child's date of birth, and the magazine sends inserts geared to the specific age of the child (children). These monthly supplements offer parenting advice, milestone charts, physical and cognitive developmental tests, and suggestions for appropriate toys. If you have an infant, you'll receive month-by-month supplements; if you have a one-, two-, or three-year-old, you'll receive supplements geared to your child's yearly developmental stages. (If you have two or more young children, you can request more than one insert.) Prepared under the guidance of Lewis Lipsitt, Ph.D., the founding director of the Child Study Center at Brown University and editor of *The Child and Adolescent Behavior Letter*.

Videotape

Infant Development: A First Year Guide to Growth and Learning. Johnson and Johnson, 1989. Running time: 45 minutes. Child psychiatrist Stanley Greenspan and pediatrician T. Berry Brazelton discuss a baby's physical, emotional, and intellectual development during the first year. Comes with a quick-reference video guidebook. Available by mail from the ICEA Bookcenter, ICEA, P.O. Box 20048, Minneapolis, Minnesota 55420. Phone: 1/800-624-4934.

Mail Order Catalog

Modern Learning Press. Programs for Education, P.O. Box 167, Department 323, Rosemont, New Jersey 08556. Phone: 1/800-627-5867. Offers books and related materials based on the developmental principles of Dr. Arnold Gesell, founder of the Child Study Center at Yale University. The works presented in the catalog take into account the child's stage of development, exploring topics in education, parent/child communication, physical and emotional development, discipline, and the importance of childhood. Although the catalog is compiled for developmental educators, many of the resources are equally useful to parents who want to better understand—and enjoy—their children. Includes The Gesell Institute of Human Development series, by Louise Bates Ames and others (see lising under "Books").

Associations

Association for Childhood Education International (ACEI). 11501 Georgia Avenue, Suite 315, Wheaton, Maryland 20902. Phone: 301/942-2443 or 1/800-423-3563. A professional organization for those involved in the education of children from infancy through early adolescence. Although ACEI's publications are targeted at education professionals, many of them will be of interest to parents. Produces a publications catalog that lists many titles on child development and childhood education. Titles include *Early Adolescents: Understanding and Nurturing Their Development, Childhood Education,* and *Personalizing Care with Infants, Toddlers, and Families.* (For more information on ACEI, see "Associations" listed under "Teaching: Approaches and Techniques" in chapter 13.)

Bank Street College of Education. 610 West 112th Street, New York, New York 10025. Phone: 212/875-4400. Founded in 1916, the Bank Street College of Education conducts programs of research and consultation, and develops curriculum and educational materials to benefit children. Bank Street College offers graduate programs for educators and early childhood specialists; operates a demonstration school for children ages three to thirteen that serves as a working model of the college's approach to learning and teaching; and runs a nonprofit child-care center that offers a training site for the college's graduate students studying infant/parent development, early childhood education, or special education. Educators, psychologists, and child development experts are on the staff. (For more information on Bank Street, see "Associations" listed under "Teaching: Approaches and Techniques" in chapter 13.)

The Early Childhood Development Center. 163 East Ninety-seventh Street, New York, New York 10029. Phone: 212/360-7872. Contact: Nina R. Lief, M.D. The aim of this center is to help mothers and fathers enjoy and derive a sense of satisfaction from their roles as parents and to help them guide their children toward healthy emotional and social development. Offers programs, sessions, and discussions to help parents understand their child's development—and the importance of parent-child interaction in this process. The center has developed a series of paperback books based on its parenting curriculum. *The First Year of Life, The Second Year of Life,* and *The Third Year of Life* (Walker and Company, 1991) explore stages of development in young children, child-rearing issues, and parenting concerns. These books are available through bookstores (or check your public library).

The Gesell Institute of Human Development. 310 Prospect Street, New Haven, Connecticut 06511. Phone: 203/777-3481. Conducts research and sponsors lectures, seminars, and workshops on early childhood development. Provides educational and psychological counseling and assessment services. Publishes research results in books, monographs, and professional journals. Books available directly from the institute include *Child Behavior, Don't Push Your Preschooler*, and the human development series by Louise Bates Ames and others (see The Gesell Institute of Human Development series, listed under "Books," for more information).

National Association for the Education of Young Children (NAEYC). 1509 Sixteenth Street, N.W., Washington, D.C. 20036-1426. Phone: 202/232-8777 or 1/800-424-2460. Fax: 202/328-1846. Offers resources and services to early childhood professionals, parents, and policymakers about child development and early education. Publishes *Young Children*, a bimonthly membership journal offering early childhood research, theory, and practice. Also publishes the *Early Childhood Research Quarterly* (members receive a reduced subscription rate). Offers brochures, books, videos, posters, and information kits as well. While many of these publications are intended for teachers and child care providers, others are directed at parents. Available publications are described in NAEYC's early childhood resources catalog. (For more information on NAEYC, see "Associations" listed under "Teaching: Approaches and Techniques in chapter 13.)

Society for Research in Child Development. University of Chicago Press, 5720 Woodlawn Avenue, Chicago, Illinois 60637. Phone: 312/702-7470. An interdisciplinary society of professionals, including pediatricians, educators, nutritionists, psychologists, sociologists, and statisticians. Works to encourage and support research in child development. Periodicals include *Child Development*, a bimonthly journal containing original articles written by specialists in various fields, including medicine, psychology, and sociology (in *Educating the Infant and Toddler* (Lexington Books, 1990), author Burton White says, "This is the best journal available for professionals in the field . . . . It receives many new reports of research on young children, and the editors do an excellent job of selecting the cream of the crop."), and *Child Development Abstracts and Bibliography*, a tri-annual journal containing abstracts and reviews of research literature selected from books, journals, and reports on the growth and development of children. Also publishes detailed research studies and findings in the area of child development.

Southern Association of Children under Six. P.O. Box 5403, Brady Station, Little Rock, Arkansas 72215-5403. Phone: 501/663-0353. An association of parents, educators, child-care providers, researchers, and others concerned about the well-being of young children. Explores contemporary issues in child development and early childhood education. Sponsors conferences and conducts workshops. Publishes books, pamphlets, and position papers exploring child development and early childhood education. Also issues *Dimensions*, a quarterly journal for those interested in young children.

Zero to Three National Center for Clinical Infant Programs. 2000 Fourteenth Street North, Suite 380,

Arlington, Virginia 22201-2500. Phone: 703/528-4300. A national organization dedicated to promoting the physical, emotional, cognitive, and social development of infants and toddlers (birth to age three). Works to expand awareness of the importance of the earliest years of life for human development; translate research into policy and practice; nurture new leadership; and enable others to work more effectively on behalf of infants, toddlers, and their families. Educates policymakers and the general public on the complex needs of infants, toddlers, and their families through publications, seminars, and conferences; offers training programs and materials that enable professionals to share expertise and learn new approaches to promote the optimal health and development of zero- to three-year-olds; and provides technical assistance to administrators to improve the effectiveness of services for infants, toddlers, and their families. Publishes the *Zero to Three* bulletin, designed to keep instructors, parents, researchers, policymakers, and practitioners abreast of current research and clinical findings, public policy developments, publications, training opportunities, and financial resources on topics related to infants, toddlers, and their families. (The journal offers an index, which groups by topic the articles and reviews of publications that appeared in *Zero to Three* from September 1980 through June 1992.)

Research Centers

Dozens of research centers across the country (many of which are affiliated with colleges and universities) are dedicated to the study of infant and child development. The following are among the more prominent:

Brown University Center for the Study of Human Development. Box 1938, Providence, Rhode Island 02912. Phone: 401/421-8241. Studies human development and behavior, including abilities of infants, learning behavior of newborn and older children, risk-taking behavior in children, and effectiveness of behavior modification programs. Also coordinates and sponsors research relating to normal child development and behavior at the university.

Institute of Child Development, University of Minnesota. 51 East River Road, Minneapolis, Minnesota 55455-0345. Phone: 612/624-0526. Studies various aspects of child development, including socialization and personality, learning and cognition, attention and perception, and language. Research results are published in journals and reports.

The National Institute of Child Health and Human Development. Office of Research and Reporting, Building 31, Room 2A32, Bethesda, Maryland 20892. Phone: 301/496-5133. Conducts and sponsors research on the normal processes of growth and development upon which the health of both children and adults depends. Also strives to find out what causes developmental abnormalities and disease, how these might be prevented, and how they can be treated. Topics under study include the physical and behavioral adaption of the newborn, child nutrition, the development of the immune system, learning and cognitive development, developmental disabilities, and family and household structure. Call the Office of Research Reporting for information on research topics, programs, and publications for professional and lay audiences.

Yale University Child Study Center. P.O. Box 3333, New Haven, Connecticut 06510. Phone: 203/785-5759. Created in 1991 by Dr. Arnold Gesell, one of America's most influential leaders in child development, the Child Study Center provides clinical consultation and treatment for children and adolescents with mental, emotional, and developmental problems (there is a special concern for those with biological and pervasive developmental disorders). The center also conducts scientific research, trains professionals, and helps shape social policy concerning children. A nonprofit, academic department within Yale University and the School of Medicine.

LANGUAGE DEVELOPMENT

Books

Baby Talk, Parent Talk: Understanding Your Baby's Body Language. By Sirgay Sanger. Doubleday, 1990. 159 pages. Shows how babies communicate through body language, long before they begin to use words. Using black and white photographs and descriptive text, this book helps parents understand what infants are "saying" with their eyebrows, mouths, hands, and other communicative parts. Suggests that parents talk to their baby in ways that seem natural to them and that their child responds to. Offers advice and guidelines.

Growing Up with Language: How Children Learn to Talk. By Naomi S. Baron. Addison-Wesley, 1992. 269 pages. Written by a linguistics professor, this book takes readers on a journey through language acquisition, showing how children master the ability to express themselves—and how parents play a key role in this remarkable process. Baron has chosen three representative children and their families to show the variety in language-learning styles among children and the different approaches parents use in the process. Guides parents through various stages of development and explains how parents can help instill a love of language in their children. Includes additional resources such as books, forums, and organizations.

Language Games to Play with Your Child. By Allyssa McCabe, Ph.D. Fawcett Columbine, 1987. 264 pages. A collection of 103 games that can help parents enhance their child's language skills. A statement of the game's purpose, instructions for playing it, and game variations are included in each entry. Based on the belief that good reading, writing, and communication skills begin with language skills.

Talking from Infancy: How to Nurture and Cultivate Early Language Development. By W. Fowler. Brookline Books, 1991. 236 pages. Provides games and exercises to help adults stimulate and encourage children's language development. Includes guidelines and detailed instructions for using these language-enrichment activities. Also discusses the central role of language in learning and the stages of language acquisition.

Videotape

Baby Talk. WGBH, PBS. Running time: 60 minutes. From the award-winning NOVA television series, this videotape takes viewers on a journey through the process of language development, from infant crying to adult speech. Available from Schoolmasters (see chapter 27 for contact information).

Helpline

The American Baby Helpline. Phone: 1/900-860-4888 (twenty-four-hour-a-day helpline operating seven days a week. The cost is 95¢ per minute). Prerecorded messages offer expert advice on a variety of baby-related topics. For information on language development in babies (six months to eighteen months), call the above number, then dial code "38."

Association

American Speech-Language Hearing Association. 10801 Rockville Pike, Rockville, Maryland 20852.

Phone: 1/800-638-TALK. A professional organization. If you think your child may have a hearing problem or if you are concerned about your child's language development, this association can refer you to a licensed audiologist (who will test your child's hearing) or a speech and language pathologist (who will evaluate your child's language development) in your area. Issues journals dealing with language acquisition, including the *Journal of Speech and Hearing Research*.

Baby's Growth and Development
From *Infant Care*, produced by the Health Resources and Services Administration, U.S. Department of Health and Human Services.

Here are some of the things you can usually expect your baby to do in the first year of life:

By about 6 weeks

- Holds head off of bed for a few moments while lying on stomach
- Follows an object with eyes for a short distance
- Pays attention to sounds
- Makes a few vocal sounds other than crying
- Looks at your face
- Smiles when you smile or play with him or her
- Moves arms and legs in an energetic manner

By about 5 months

- Holds head upright while lying on stomach
- Holds head steady when held in a sitting position
- Laughs, squeals, and babbles
- Turns to your voice
- Rolls over
- Follows with eyes from side to side
- Recognizes parents
- Brings hands together in front of body

- Reaches for and holds objects
- Passes object from one hand to other
- Begins to chew
- Stretches out arms to be picked up
- Smiles by him or herself

By about 8 months

- Sits without support when placed in sitting position
- Takes part of weight on own legs when held steady
- Creeps (pulls body with arm and leg kicks)
- Starts to make recognizable sounds ("baa" or "daa")
- Responds to "no" and his or her name
- Grasps object off flat surface
- Feeds crackers to self
- Looks around for the source of new sounds

By about 10 months

- Gets into sitting position on own
- Stands, holding on
- Crawls
- Picks up small object with thumb and fingers
- Tries to get an object that is out of reach
- Pulls back when you put a toy in his or her hand
- Drinks from a cup when it is held
- Plays peek-a-boo
- Uses voice to get attention

By about 12 months

- Brings together two toys held in hands
- Imitates your speech
- Uses "Dada" or "Mama" to mean a specific person
- Plays pat-a-cake
- Can walk holding onto something
- Finds one object under another
- Waves bye-bye
- Understands simple words and phrases ("come here")

Soon after baby's first birthday

- Stands alone, then walks alone
- Scribbles with a pencil or crayon
- Drinks from a cup by self
- Uses a spoon (spills a little!)
- Plays with ball on the floor
- Can say 2–3 words (may not be clear)

Don't worry if your baby is different—each baby develops in his or her own way. However, if you notice large variations from what you might expect, or have other concerns, ask your doctor or clinic staff.

Chapter 2

Individual Differences in Children

PERSONALITY AND TEMPERAMENT

Books

The Developing Child: Using Jungian Type to Understand Children. By Elizabeth Murphy. Consulting Psychologists Press, 1992. 155 pages. This resource is designed to help adults develop positive, healthy relationships with children of all psychological types (based on Carl G. Jung's "type" theory).

The Difficult Child. By Stanley Turecki, M.D. Revised edition. Bantam Books, 1989. 258 pages. This book helps parents with temperamentally difficult children (those who defy, whine, complain, throw tantrums, don't listen) understand their child's behavior; respond when conflicts arise; discipline effectively in a supportive atmosphere; cope with the special demands of a difficult infant; get support from schools, doctors, and other parents; and lessen the strain on the entire family. The author points out that the most difficult children can also be the most enthusiastic and creative. Offers guidelines to help parents release their child's positive potential and enjoy parenting more everyday.

Gifts Differing. By Isabel Briggs Myers (with Peter B. Myers). Consulting Psychologists Press, 1980. 217 pages. Based on observations of people throughout a lifetime, the author offers insights on how behavior reflects psychological type as measured by the Myers-Briggs Type Indicator. My-ers believes that each of the sixteen types outlined in the book has its own strengths and that understanding and using these can lead to fulfillment. Discusses type as it relates to early learning, individual learning styles, and motivation for type development in children.

Infants and Mothers: Differences in Development. By T. Berry Brazelton, M.D. Revised edition. Delacorte Press/Seymour Lawrence, 1983. 302 pages. A classic work by the renowned child development expert, this book guides parents through the first twelve months of their child's life. Brazelton has chosen three representative babies—one "quiet," one "average," and one "active"—to demonstrate individual differences and reassure parents that their young charges are developing normally. Also by Brazelton: *Toddlers and Parents: Declaration of Independence.* (For more information on either of these titles, see "Books" listed under "General Resources" in chapter 1.)

Inner World of Childhood. By Frances Wickes. Third edition. Sigo Press, 1988. 295 pages. Written by a respected Jungian, this book provides insights on children of each psychological type. Includes an introduction by Carl G. Jung.

Know Your Child. By Stella Chess, M.D., and Alexander Thomas, M.D. Basic Books, 1989. 416 pages. At the center of this book is the authors' finding that children have recognizable individual differences, or temperaments, right from the start. Shows how parents can avoid problems by matching their own expectations and attitudes to their child's temperament, a match known as "goodness of fit." Offers information and advice to help parents understand and enjoy their children from infancy through adolescence.

Living With the Active Alert Child: Groundbreaking Strategies for Parents. By Linda Budd, Ph.D. Revised edition. Parenting Press, 1993. 272 pages. Offers advice to parents whose children are highly active (and typically bright, controlling, and fearful at the same time). Suggests parenting strategies to help make life with these challenging children less frustrating and more enjoyable.

Nature's Thumbprint: The New Genetics of Personality. By Peter Neubauer, M.D., and Alexander Neubauer. Addison-Wesley, 1990. 223 pages. Explores the range of inborn inclinations upon which personality is later built. Shows how our genes affect the way we react to the world, interact with it, and behave in many situations. Based on Peter Neubauer's fifty years of clinical practice as a psychoanalyst and research, and on studies of identical twins.

One of a Kind. By LaVonne Neff. Multnomah, 1988. 197 pages. Focuses on psychological types in children, based on Carl G. Jung's theory, and explains how to make the most of your child's uniqueness. Provides many practical and amusing examples from the author's observations of families. Topics include parenting styles, discipline, school success, and religious education.

Raising Your Spirited Child: A Guide for Parents Whose Child Is More. By Mary Sheedy Kurcinka.

Is Your Child a "Type T"?

Type Ts are thrill seekers who push aside rules to push the limits of their imagination—whirling dervishes engaged in frequent acts of derring-do. The April 1992 issue of *Parenting* magazine reported on recent research suggesting that this personality trait may emerge in children born with a "sluggish arousal system," a part of the brain-nerve complex that affects alertness and motivation. According to the new theory, these children must compensate for their built-in numbness by stirring up an extraordinary amount of stimulation. As the *Parenting* editors put it, "Type-T youngsters must create a whirlwind in order to feel a breeze."

HarperCollins, 1992. 302 pages. Offers support and suggests strategies to help parents better understand and care for a "spirited" child (i.e., one who is more intense, persistent, perceptive, and sensitive). Describes individual characteristics and discusses specific parenting techniques that can help parents teach their child to accept their unique temperament but also find ways to make it easier for the child to get along in the world.

Raising Your Type A Child: How to Help Your Child Make the Most of an Achievement-Oriented Personality. By Steven Shelov and John Kelly. Simon and Schuster, 1991. 224 pages. Explains how to help your child make the most of an achievement-oriented personality.

The Shy Child. By Philip G. Zimbardo and Shirley Radl. McGraw-Hill,

1981. 261 pages. Based on research conducted at Stanford University and tested by the Stanford Shyness Clinic, this book explores the causes of shyness and explains what can be done to minimize it. Discusses parenting styles that encourage self-confidence in a child and offers guidance in dealing with problems associated with shyness.

Association

Center for Applications of Psychological Type, Inc. 2815 Northwest Thirteenth Street, Suite 401, Gainsville, Florida 32609. Phone: 904/375-0160. Fosters an understanding of—and promotes constructive use of—personality differences in children and adults. Encourages practical applications of Carl G. Jung's theory of psychological types. (The theory states that variations in behavior that appear to be random are actually consistent and orderly if one understands differences in the ways people process information and make decisions.) Disseminates information on the work of Isabel Briggs Myers, who created the Myers-Briggs Type Indicator (MBTI) for determining psychological type and the Murphy- Meisgeier Type Indicator for Children. Conducts training programs, offers consultations, and maintains a library. Publishes books, papers, research reports, training exercises, and other materials. Offers a free publications catalog, which includes many books of interest to parents and teachers.

BIRTH ORDER AND ONLY CHILDREN

Books

Birth Order. By C. Ernst and J. Angst. Springer-Verlag, 1985. 340 pages. Describes how order of birth influences the development of personality.

The Birth Order Book. By Kevin Leman. Dell Publishing, 1992. Explains how birth order affects children's behavior.

The Only Child: Being One, Loving One, Understanding One, Raising One. By Darrell Sifford. Harper and Row, 1990. 221 pages. The author, an only child herself, draws from case studies and interviews with psychologists to come up with a unique picture of the only child. Discusses both the blessings and burdens inherent in growing up in the spotlight. Offers guidelines for parents.

Parenting an Only Child. By Susan Newman. Doubleday, 1990. 239 pages. Explores the joys and challenges of raising an only child. Offers advice on avoiding common pitfalls, such as overindulgence and the urge to raise a superchild.

Your Second Child. By Joan Solomon Weiss. Summit Books, 1981. 286 pages. Offers a detailed look at the impact of the second child on the family and provides advice on how to handle the second born.

Understanding Baby's Growth and Development

From *Infant Care*, produced by the Health Resources and Services Administration, U.S. Department of Health and Human Services.

How Your Baby Reacts

Babies differ from each other in many ways. They may be big or small, fast growing or slow growing, early developers or late developers, brown-eyed or blue-eyed. One of the most important ways in which babies differ is in their temperament—the usual way they react to you, to other people, and to things around them. You and your family will find it much easier to understand, to take care of, to teach, and to enjoy your baby if you pay attention to how your baby reacts.

There are many ways in which young babies differ from each other in how they act or behave. No one knows to what extent these differences are inherited or whether they develop in the first weeks of life. Probably both play a part in making your baby an individual. These are some of the kinds of behavior you may look for in your child:

Activity Level

- How much does your baby move around?

- Does your baby wiggle all around the crib or stay in one place?

- When you change baby's diaper or clothes, do you have trouble because of constant wiggling, or does your baby lie quietly and let you work?

Normal babies may be very active, very inactive, or somewhere in between. Your job in caring for a very active baby will be different from caring for a very inactive one. If you believe that all babies should be active, you may be unhappy about an inactive baby. If you think all babies should stay still while being dressed or bathed, you may think that an active baby is "bad" or that all the activity is due to your improper care. Don't blame yourself or the baby. It is just the way some babies are made.

If your baby is super-active, you may just choose to enjoy the activity, or you may want to behave in a more soothing and gentle way to encourage your infant to slow down a little.

If your baby is very inactive, you may want to take more initiative in playing, moving about, and rewarding baby when he or she reacts.

Regularity

- How regular are your baby's habits?

- Does your baby always awaken at about the same time, get hungry at about the same time, take naps and nurse at about the same time?

- Does your baby eat and drink about the same amount each morning?

- Does this vary slightly each day or is it completely unpredictable?

If your infant is very regular, it is unusual. If your baby's habits are very irregular, you will have to be prepared for changes every day. Or, you may want to set a schedule for your baby rather than going entirely by what he or she seems ready for. Of course, you can't feed an infant who isn't hungry, or force sleep on an infant who isn't ready to sleep. But, you can feed your baby before he or she cries a long time from hunger, and you can put the baby down for a quiet time or for sleep even though your infant doesn't appear very tired. All of this takes time and patience. Don't push it—ease into it. It's better to be flexible rather than frustrated or angry if it doesn't work well.

Adaptability

- How long does it take your baby to get used to new situations or to changes?

- When you changed from sponge bathing to a bath, was it accepted immediately, or did it take 6 or 7 tries before it was really accepted?

- If your baby fusses the first time you put a cap on his or her head, is there an objection every time you try, or is it accepted quickly?

High or low "adaptability" is neither good nor bad. The child who resists change may take longer to become comfortable with it. If helped to become comfortable with it, a child will gradually learn to cope with changes.

Approach or Withdrawal

- How does your baby usually react the first time to new people, new toys, and new activities?

- Does your baby reach out for them and seem pleased, or shy away and fuss?

"Approach and withdrawal" differ from adaptability. They describe a baby's first reaction to something new rather than the length of time or number of tries it takes to get used to it. A baby who immediately reaches out for something may seem easier to deal with at first. But a baby who withdraws slightly from a new situation may be much easier to keep out of trouble and danger when he or she is a little older. Again, neither reaction is good or bad, but if you recognize how your baby acts, it may be easier for you to respond.

Sensitivity

Is your baby aware of slight noises or slight differences in temperature, in tastes, or in different types of clothing?

- Do bright lights or sunlight make your child uncomfortable?

- Does your baby let you know every time the diapers are wet or soiled or ignore them?

A very sensitive baby may seem to make your job more difficult at first. Some infants who notice small differences are fast learners and you can enjoy that. Any baby may be very sensitive in some areas (such as touch or hearing) but not in others.

Extreme insensitivity to sounds may be caused by poor hearing, not temperament. You should tell your doctor or clinic if your baby does not seem to notice or react to your voice or other sounds by 3 to 6 months.

Intensity of Reaction

- How strong or violent are your child's reactions when pleased or displeased?

When pleased, some children laugh and wiggle all over, while others just smile. When displeased, some children scream loudly and immediately, while others frown and fuss quietly.

If your baby reacts very strongly and intensely, you may want to help him or her regulate those reactions. You can help an intense baby learn that loudness and activity are not necessary to get a response. Such a child's active way of showing pleasure may make up for some of the loud crying when showing disappointment or discomfort. Usually, if you respond before your baby gets really "wound up," it will help with this intensity.

Distractibility and Attention Span

Some babies will keep on sucking—no matter what happens—during a feeding. Others will stop and pay attention to a door opening or someone entering the room. A toy will keep some hungry babies quiet for several minutes; others will keep demanding to be fed. Some will turn to any new sound or sight while they are busy playing; others will continue to play.

You may want to feed your baby in a quiet place if your child is distractible, and to give just one or two toys at any one time.

- How long will your baby stick with something?

Some babies will continue to try difficult tasks, even if you try to stop them. Others give up quickly. Some will keep watching a mobile above the crib for 10 or 15 minutes; others turn to something else after a few minutes. "Attention span" means how long babies stick with something on their own, not how easy it is to distract them with something new or different.

You will be pleased when your child keeps doing things you like, and unhappy when he or she keeps on doing things that upset you. You will want to be firm and patient and use distraction to get a persistent child to change activities. You will want to encourage and praise a non-persistent child for sticking with a useful activity.

Pleasant or Unpleasant Mood

- How much of the time is your baby friendly, pleasant, joyful, as compared to unpleasant, crying, fussy, or unfriendly?

This means not just the first reaction to new situations, or to the times of actual hunger or discomfort, but the way your baby is during most of the day. Your baby's mood may be expressed quietly with a frown or a whimper, or with a smile and a twinkling eye. Or it may be a loud scream or a deep laugh.

A baby with an unpleasant mood can be difficult for anyone. You must remember that your baby's general fussiness does not necessarily mean that you are doing anything wrong. However, you will want to reassure yourself that you are doing what you can to soothe and comfort the baby and that the baby is not suffering.

Such an infant may wear you out very quickly. You may need more recreation and more time away from the baby. You may have to learn to ignore some of the crying and fussing once you have made sure your child really doesn't need anything at the moment and has no reason to be uncomfortable. If you feel stressed, you may want to talk with your doctor about ways of dealing with your baby. Don't take your frustrations out on the baby.

The Need for Patience

While no single trait of behavior makes a baby hard to cope with, babies with certain combinations of traits are certainly much harder to care for.

For example, a baby who demonstrates irregularity, withdrawal from new situations, slow adaptability, negative mood, and intense reactions will need a great deal of your patience. You will need more time away from your infant and more help from your partner, family, and others.

Such a baby will especially need your signs of approval and affection at those times when he or she is comfortable and cooperative. But even such a fussy baby will likely become less difficult, in which case you can have the satisfaction of knowing that your patient efforts have worked. If you feel that your baby is not getting better, you should talk to your doctor or clinic staff.

If both parents pay attention to how your baby reacts, you both will be better prepared to give your child the kind of help that is most needed. By taking the time to understand your baby's personality, you will be much more certain that what you are doing is right.

GENDER DIFFERENCES

Books

Beginning Equal: A Manual about Nonsexist Childrearing for Infants and Toddlers. Women's Action Alliance, 1983. 241 pages. This manual contains workshop materials and background readings for parents and caregivers of children (birth to three years) for identifying and reducing sex-role stereotyping. Available from the Women's Action Alliance, Inc., 370 Lexington Avenue, Suite 603, New York, New York 10017. Phone: 212/532-8330.

Boys & Girls: Superheroes in the Doll Corner. By Vivian Gussin Paley. University of Chicago Press, 1984. 116 pages. Reporting on the play patterns and fantasies of a group of kindergartners with whom she worked as a teacher, Vivian Gussin Paley leads her readers to conclude that boys and girls do, in fact, behave differently. The children's own conversations, stories, play-acting, and scuffles are interwoven with Paley's observations and accounts of her attempts to alter the children's stereotyped play.

Boys Will Be Boys: Breaking the Link Between Masculinity and Violence. By Myriam Miedzian. Doubleday, 1991. 354 pages. The values of the masculine mystique (toughness, dominance, repression of empathy, and extreme competitiveness) play a major role in criminal and domestic violence, the author of this book argues. She explores the psychology of masculinity in our society and makes concrete recommendations on how we might change the way we socialize boys in order to create a more harmonious world.

The Gesell Institute's Child from One to Six: Evaluating the Behavior of the Preschool Child. By Louise Bates Ames, Clyde Gillespie, Jacqueline Haines, and Frances L. Ilg. Harper and Row, 1979. 228 pages. Chapter 12 addresses sex and group differences in performance. Includes charts showing girl/boy differences in response to Gesell developmental tests. Out of print but available at many libraries.

Girls and Boys: The Limits of Nonsexist Childrearing. By Sara Bonnett Stein. Charles Scribner's Sons, 1983. 208 pages. Drawing from research findings in fields such as psychology, sociobiology, and anthropology, Stein examines gender differences and the role they have played in the development and survival of the human species. Discusses gender at each stage of development. Offers advice to parents who are determined to raise nonsexist children, despite the fact that girls still spend their time dressing dolls while boys continue to push around toy trucks and play with toy pistols.

Human Sexuality. By Zella Luria, Ph.D., Susan Friedman, and Mitchel Rose. John Wiley, 1987. 752 pages. This textbook explores various aspects of human sexuality, including gender differences and gender-segregated play.

Raising a Son: Parents and the Making of a Healthy Man. By Don Elium and Jeanne Elium. Beyond Words Publishing, 1992. 244 pages. Addresses the unique challenges parents face in raising boys. Discusses what being male is all about and the specific developmental changes in a boy's life, from infancy through young adulthood. Offers parenting advice accordingly.

Rituals for Our Times: Celebrating, Healing, and Changing Our Lives and Our Relationships. By Evan Imber-Black, Ph.D., and Janine Roberts, Ed.D. HarperCollins, 1992. 331 pages. Points out how family rituals can encourage gender stereotypes. (For more information on *Rituals for Our Times,* see "Books" listed under "Family Rituals and Traditions" in chapter 3.)

Periodicals

For Adults

Equal Play. Women's Action Alliance, 370 Lexington Avenue, Suite 603, New York, New York 10017. Phone: 212/532-8330. Fourteen separate back issues of this resource magazine are available for purchase. These issues explore educational equity for children and feature ideas and model programs for nonsexist childrearing and teaching. "Positive and Negative Aspects of Toys," "Beginning Equal," and "Sex Equity in Sport" are among the available issues. Contact the Women's Action Alliance for a complete listing.

Journal of Genetic Psychology. Heldref Publications, 1319 Eighteenth Street, N.W., Washington, D.C. 20036-1802. Phone: 202/296-6267. A refereed journal exploring various topics in genetic psychology, including gender differences and the roles of male and female characters in children's literature.

Sex Roles. Plenum Publishing, 233 Spring Street, New York, New York 10013-1578. Phone: 212/620-8000. Publishes original research articles and theoretical manuscripts concerned with the basic processes underlying gender role socialization in children and its consequences. Published twenty-four times a year.

Gender-Specific Magazines for Children

American Girl. Pleasant Company, 8400 Fairway Place, P.O. Box 620190, Middleton, Wisconsin 53562-0190. Phone: 1/800-845-0005 (for subscriptions). A magazine for girls who aren't quite ready to become teenagers. Contains stories about girls of the past, as well as the present, along with nonfiction, puzzles, games, paper dolls, sports tips, party plans, and contributions from kids. From the makers of the immensely popular "American Girl" book and doll series. For ages seven to twelve. Issued six times annually.

Boys Life. Boy Scouts of America, 1325 West Walnut Hill Lane, P.O. Box 152079, Irving, Texas 75015-2079. "The Magazine for All Boys," produced by the Boy Scouts of America. Includes fiction and features exploring topics such as ultra-fast trains, lost treasure, sports figures, heroic deeds, and American history. Comic strips, riddles, and other fun fillers are included as well. For ages eight to sixteen. Issued monthly.

Hopscotch: The Magazine for Girls. P.O. Box 1292, Saratoga Springs, New York 12866. This magazine contains light fiction, nonfiction, games, crafts, and activities for girls between the ages of six and twelve. Central characters in the stories and articles are girls and exemplary women. Avoids topics such as romance and cosmetics (topics deemed to be more appropriate for young adults).

New Moon: The Magazine for Girls and Their Dreams. P.O. Box 3587, Duluth, Minnesota 55803-3587. Phone: 218/728-5507. Celebrates the special qualities in girls and encourages them to dream big. Each issue has a special theme (inventing, for example). Includes challenging puzzles, games, folktales and other stories, articles, etc. Includes "Ask A Girl," an advice column for and by girls. Published bimonthly.

Videotape

NOVA: Secrets of the Sexes. WGBH, PBS. Running time: 60 minutes. A program from the award-winning television series, this videotape provides an eye-opening look at the sex roles we teach our children. Available from Schoolmasters (see chapter 27 for contact information).

Associations

American Association of University Women Educational Foundation. 1111 Sixteenth Street, N.W., Washington, D.C. 20036. Phone: 202/785-7700 or 1/800-225-9998 (for publications list and orders). Among the publications available from this foundation are *Shortchanging Girls, Shortchanging America* (a nationwide poll conducted on girls and self-esteem), and *How Schools Shortchange Girls: A Study of Major Findings on Girls and Education* (girls receive significantly less attention from teachers than boys and are often not encouraged to pursue higher levels of learning in math and science, among other findings).

Organization for Equal Education of the Sexes. P.O. Box 438, Blue Hill, Maine 04614. Phone: 207/374-2489.

Works to ensure equal educational opportunities for all students, regardless of sex. Disseminates information, promotes the sharing of ideas, and maintains a library of nonsexist curricula. Members include parents, students, educators, and others working to ensure sex-equity in education.

Women's Action Alliance. 370 Lexington Avenue, Room 603, New York, New York 10017. Phone: 212/532-8330. Among its various activities, the Women's Action Alliance seeks to create a nonsexist environment for school-aged children. Conducts research, initiates development projects, distributes educational materials, and offers training and technical assistance. Manages a computer equity project, which encourages school-age girls to make greater use of computers. Another project seeks to help girls in their early teens develop a positive body image. Publishes books, manuals, informational brochures, and other materials. Call or write for a publications catalog.

CREATIVITY, TALENT, AND GIFTEDNESS

Books

Awakening Your Child's Natural Genius. By Thomas Armstrong, Ph.D. Jeremy P. Tarcher, 1991. 268 pages. Armstrong argues that every child is a genius, and explains how parents can help their child realize his or her true gifts. Discusses "giftedness," including Howard Gardner's theory of seven intelligences (logical-mathematical, musical, bodily-kinesthetic, linguistic, spatial, interpersonal, and intrapersonal). Describes various teaching approaches that can help children make the most of their talents and abilities. (For more information on this book,

see "Books" listed under "Preparing Your Child for School Success" in chapter 13.)

Books for the Gifted Child (volumes 1 and 2). Volume 1 by Barbara H. Baskin and Karen H. Harris; volume 2 by Paula Hauser and Gail A. Nelson. R. R. Bowker, 1980 (volume 1); 1988 (volume 2). 263 pages (volume 1); 244 pages (volume 2). A selection guide to help parents, teachers, and librarians choose quality fiction and nonfiction titles for gifted children. Introductory chapters offer guidelines on identifying the gifted and understanding their needs.

How Is Your Child Smart

According to Harvard psychologist Howard Gardner, there are at least seven different kinds of intelligence. Summarized below, these include:

Bodily-Kinesthetic Intelligence. Children who are gifted in this area learn best when they're in motion (either working with their hands or moving their bodies). They often excel in—and achieve better understanding through—creative movement, drama, role-playing, hands-on activities, and involvement in sports.

Interpersonal (Social) Intelligence. Kids with interpersonal gifts learn by doing things with others. They're often good at communicating, mediating conflict, and understanding other people's feelings.

Intrapersonal Intelligence. A child who in intrapersonal has a strong sense of self. Such children do well when given the freedom to pursue their own interests or develop their own activities.

Linguistic (Verbal) Intelligence. Children with high linguistic intelligence learn quickly by listening, speaking, and reading. They are often motivated by books, audio recordings, word games, engaging discussion, and informal writing.

Logical-Mathematical. Kids who are strong in this area think in terms of concepts. They explore patterns and relationships by experimenting with their environment. Often, you'll find these youngsters working on logic puzzles, winning at chess or checkers, are searching for answers to philosophical questions.

Musical Intelligence. Children who are musically gifted learn well through rhythm and melody. They come to a quicker understanding when something is sung, tapped out, or played on an instrument.

Spatial Intelligence. Children with spatial intelligence think visually. They learn through pictures, images, color, and metaphor. Building with blocks, reading maps and charts, hearing vivid stories, or putting together jigsaw puzzles or among the spatially-gifted child's preferred activities.

Bringing Out the Best: A Resource Guide for Parents of Young Gifted Children. By J. Saunders with Pamela Espeland. Free Spirit Publishing, 1991. 240 pages. Offers guidelines on promoting creativity and intellectual development in young, gifted children. Explains how to tell if your child is gifted and how to choose the right school for exceptionally bright/talented youngsters. Suggests dozens of creative activities for parents and children to do together.

Developing Talent in Young People. Edited by Benjamin S. Bloom. Ballantine, 1985. 558 pages. Reveals the results of a University of Chicago study to determine how and why 120 extraordinary men and women (including concert pianists, Olympic swimmers, and research neurologists) achieved the highest levels of accomplishment in their chosen fields. Explores in detail each of the crucial stages of talent development and shows that the quality of support and instruction that children receive from their parents and teachers is central to the process. Raises questions about earlier views of special gifts and innate aptitudes as necessary prerequisites of talent development.

Frames of Mind: The Theory of Multiple Intelligence. By Howard Gardner. Basic Books, 1985. 464 pages. In this award-winning book, Gardner presents his theory on seven difference kinds of intelligence: logical-mathematical, musical, bodily-kinesthetic, linguistic (verbal), spatial, interpersonal (social), and intrapersonal (highly developed sense of self).

Gifted Children: A Guide for Parents and Teachers. By Virginia Z. Ehrlich. Prentice-Hall, 1982. 201 pages. Answers questions commonly asked about gifted children (preschool through college age). Discusses the various characteristics of gifted children, standardized tests, and the roles that parents and teachers play in the life of the gifted children.

Gifted Children Growing Up. By Joan Freeman. Heinemann, 1991. 256 pages. Based on a British study conducted over a sixteen-year period, this book paints a vivid picture of the lives of gifted young people from a variety of backgrounds. The research was based on in-depth interviews with the children themselves.

Growing Up Creative: Nurturing a Lifetime of Creativity. By Teresa Amabile. Crown, 1989. 212 pages. Explains how to recognize and foster creativity in children. Describes techniques and hands-on exercises that can help parents and teachers keep creativity alive at home and at school. The author points out that, paradoxically, creativity is often destroyed when grown-ups attempt to foster it through reward and encouragement. Internal motivation is key, according to the author.

In Their Own Way: Discovering and Encouraging Your Child's Personal Learning Style. By Thomas Armstrong, Ph.D. Jeremy P. Tarcher, 1987. 211 pages. Shows how children are individuals with distinct personal learning styles (linguistic, logical-mathematical, spatial, musical, bodily-kinesthetic, interpersonal, and intrapersonal). Includes a list of resources (publications and organizations) for each of the distinct styles of learning described in the book.

The Joys and Challenges of Raising a Gifted Child. By Susan K. Golant, M.A. Prentice-Hall, 1991. 244 pages. Explains how to create a rich and nurturing environment for a gifted child, including how to obtain the best schooling, how to avoid over-scheduling or pushing your child, how to handle problems with peers, and how to help the gifted child thrive socially and emotionally—not just academically. Discusses intelligence, precociousness, giftedness, and creativity and offers current information on IQ and other intelligence tests.

Parents' Guide to Raising a Gifted Child: Recognizing and Developing Your Child's Potential. By James Alvino and the editors of *Gifted Children Monthly*. Little, Brown, 1985. 325 pages. A book about raising and educating gifted children. Provides guidelines for parents to help determine—and nurture—individual giftedness. Outlines ways to help children develop critical thinking, research skills, and creativity. Recommends books, toys, games, and computer programs for gifted children.

The Passionate Mind: Bringing Up an Intelligent and Creative Child. By Michael Schulman. The Free Press, 1991. 352 pages. This book focuses on intellectual achievement in its broadest sense, encompassing curiosity, imagination, creativity, concentration, problem-solving ability, and aesthetic sensitivity. Concept learning, reading, computation, and test-taking skills are dealt with as part of a general program to support and stimulate a child's natural passion for learning. Offers practical ways to enhance abilities at every stage of development.

Your Child's Growing Mind. By Jane Healy. Doubleday, 1987. 324 pages. Describes how children learn from birth to adolescence and how parents can help in the process. Discusses brain development, intelligence, memory, language development, and academic learning. Offers an indictment of early pressures to teach children to read.

Periodicals

For Adults

Creative Child and Adult Quarterly. National Association for Creative Children and Adults, 8080 Springvalley Drive, Cincinnati, Ohio 45236. Phone: 513/631-1777. A journal dedicated to helping readers understand and apply research on creativity. Contains career interviews; research summaries; reviews; and views regarding gifted, talented, creative individuals (children and adults). Promotes the use of creative problem solving as a means of reducing the problems of the world. Issued quarterly.

Gifted Child Quarterly. National Association for Gifted Children. 1155 Fifteenth Street, N.W., No. 1002, Washington, D.C. 20005. Phone: 202/785-4268. For parents and teachers interested in better educational options for the gifted and talented. Articles explore curriculum and educational theory and policy. Also pro-

vides news of recent events concerning gifted children.

The Gifted Child Today. Prufrock Press, P.O. Box 8813, Waco, Texas 76714-8813. Offers suggestions and advice for those working with the gifted, including parents and teachers. Issued bimonthly.

Journal for the Education of the Gifted. Circulation Manager, University of North Carolina Press, P.O. Box 2288, Chapel Hill, North Carolina 27515-2288. Committed to the analysis and communication of knowledge and research on the gifted and talented, this journal offers a presentation of theory and practice for parents as well as educators. Issued quarterly.

Journal of Creative Behavior. 1050 Union Road, Buffalo, New York 14224. Phone: 716/675-3181. Fax: 716/675-3209. Issued quarterly by the Creative Education Foundation, this publication contains articles on giftedness, creativity in the arts and the sciences, ways to develop creative curricula and to foster creative productivity, and reviews of the literature on creativity and problem solving.

Understanding Our Gifted. Open Space Communications, Inc., P.O. Box 18268, Boulder, Colorado 80308. Phone: 303/444-7020. Designed to help parents, teachers, psychologists, pediatricians, and others better understand gifted children in order to increase their potential for happiness. Issued bimonthly.

By and For Kids

Creative Kids. P.O. Box 6448, Mobile, Alabama 36660. (Editorial offices: 350 Weinacker Avenue, Mobile, Alabama 36604.) Written by and for children ages eight to eighteen, this magazine contains articles, music, poetry, puzzles, photography, activities, and cartoons. For creative kids, including budding artists, writers, musicians, photographers, and inventors. Issued eight times annually.

Mail Order Catalogs

Catalog of Creative Resources. Creative Education Foundation, 1050 Union Road, Buffalo, New York 14224. Phone: 716/675-3181. Fax: 716/675-3209. Contains a wide variety of books on creativity, including guided imagery, intuition, innovative thinking, and problem solving. *Growing Up Creative* by Teresa M. Amabile, *How Can We Create Thinkers?* by Marylou Dantonio, and *Flow: The Psychology of Optimal Experience* by Mihaly Csikszentmihalyi are among the titles listed. Audiocassettes are offered for sale as well.

The Gifted Child Today Catalog. GCT, Inc., 314-350 Weinacker Avenue, P.O. Box 6448, Mobile, Alabama 36660-0448. Approved by the Parents' Choice Foundation, this catalog contains activity books, teachers' manuals, creative-thinking and problem-solving guides, magazines, and other publications for those who work with gifted children.

Zephyr Press. 3316 North Chapel Avenue, P.O. Box 66006, Tucson, Arizona 85728-6006. Phone: 602/322-5090. Mail order distributor for many books and tapes on the topics of creative thinking, hands-on learning, and the education of multiple intelligences. Although many of the materials are designed for use in the classroom, parents who want to help challenge their children will find the catalog useful as well.

Associations

American Association for Gifted Children. c/o Talent Identification Program, Duke University, One West Duke Building, Campus Drive, Durham, North Carolina 27708. Phone: 919/684-3847. Works to help gifted children reach their full potential and use their talents to benefit others. Conducts programs that encourage public understanding of the special needs of the gifted and talented. Maintains a database of information services. Publishes a periodic newsletter. Also issues guides for parents, grandparents, and others dealing with gifted children.

The Association for the Gifted. Council for Exceptional Children, 1920 Association Drive, Reston, Virginia 22091. Phone: 703/620-3660. A division of the Council for Exceptional Children. Works to stimulate interest in program development for gifted children. Publishes *Journal for the Education of the Gifted* (see listing under "Periodicals"). Also publishes *Update*, a bimonthly bulletin, as well as monographs. (For more information on the Council for Exceptional Children, see separate listing.)

Association for Gifted and Talented Students. Northwestern State University, Natchitoches, Louisiana 71497. Phone: 318/357-4572. Serves parents, educators, and others interested in meeting the social and educational needs of gifted and talented students. Conducts research, monitors legislation, and develops extracurricular programs for the gifted and talented. Publishes *Gifted-Talented Digest*, a quarterly publication that includes material written by gifted students.

Council for Exceptional Children. 1920 Association Drive, Reston, Virginia 22091. Phone: 703/620-3660. Professional organization dedicated to improving the quality of education for all exceptional children, both handicapped and gifted. Maintains the most complete collection of special-education literature in the world through its Department of Information Services and the ERIC Clearinghouse on Disabilities and Gifted Education (see listing under "Government Resources"). A number of publications are available through their catalog. (See also the separate listing for The Association for the Gifted, a division of the Council for Exceptional Children.)

Creative Education Foundation. 1050 Union Road, Buffalo, New York 14224. Phone: 716/675-3181. Fax: 716/675-3209. Encourages creativity in learning and decision making. Offers training programs, promotes research on the creative processes of children and adults, and maintains a library. Periodicals include *Creativity in Action*, issued monthly, and the *Journal of Creative Behavior*, issued quarterly (see listing under "Periodicals"). Also produces a series of minibooks, papers on creativity, and the *Catalog of Creative Resources*, which lists and describes books, courses, and cassettes on the creative process (titles of interest to parents include Thomas Armstrong's *Awakening Your Child's Natural Genius* and Teresa Amabile's *Growing Up Creative*—see listings under "Books").

Gifted Child Society. 190 Rock Road, Glen Rock, New Jersey 07452. Phone: 201/444-6530. This parent-advocacy group provides educational enrichment and support services for gifted children and their families. Services include workshops, programs for preschoolers, clinical services, remediation for school-age children, seminars, and conferences. Also sponsors competitions and bestows awards. Publications include a semiannual newsletter and advocacy packets, such as "How to Help Your Gifted Child."

The Johns Hopkins University Center for Talented Youth. 3400 North Charles Street, Baltimore, Maryland 21218. Phone: 410/516-0337. Provides parents and teachers with information on gifted programs. Offers a variety of publications. Conducts talent searches for extremely bright children at the fifth, sixth, and seventh grade levels.

National Association for Creative Children and Adults. 8080 Springvalley Drive, Cincinnati, Ohio 45236. Phone: 513/631-1777. Provides workshops and conferences on creativity, conducts research, and promotes the role of the arts in creative education. Publishes The *Creative Child and Adult Quarterly* (see listing under "Periodicals" for more information). Other publications include books, brochures, monographs, and a periodic newsletter.

National Association for Gifted Children. 1155 Fifteenth Street, N.W., No. 1002, Washington, D.C. 20005. Phone: 202/785-4268. Advocacy organization dedicated to the needs of the gifted. Helps create interest in programs for the gifted. Seeks to further educate gifted children and enhance their potential creativity. Members include librarians, teachers, university personnel, administrators, and parents. Distributes information to teachers and parents on the development of gifted children. Publishes an academic journal, *Gifted Child Quarterly* (see listing under "Periodicals"). Also publishes *Communique*, a quarterly newsletter that reports on federal legislative action and describes new educational material for the gifted. For information on resources for the gifted in your state, send a self-addressed, stamped envelope along with the name of the state.

National Association of Private Schools for Exceptional Children. 1522 K Street, N.W., Suite 1032, Washington, D.C. 20005. Phone:

202/408-3338. Acts as a national voice for private schools working with exceptional children (gifted or disabled). Provides a forum for the exchange of ideas and information. Informs parents and the public of special services available to exceptional students, and works to match exceptional children with the programs that best meet their needs. Publications include *National Issues Service*, a monthly publication reporting on legislative updates, and *NAPSEC News*, a quarterly newsletter containing news on member facilities and statements of association positions.

World Council for Gifted and Talented Children. Lamar University, P.O. Box 10034, Beaumont, Texas 77710. Phone: 409/880-8046. Fosters the international exchange of information on programs and research for gifted and talented children and promotes educational programs for these children. Assists other countries in developing appropriate programs for the gifted and talented. Publishes *Gifted International*, a semiannual journal, and *World Gifted*, a quarterly newsletter.

Government Resource

ERIC Clearinghouse on Disabilities and Gifted Education. Council for Exceptional Children, 1920 Association Drive, Reston, Virginia 22091-1589. Phone: 703/264-9474. This clearinghouse provides information on all aspects of the education and development of children with disabilities and special gifts, including identification, assessment, intervention, and enrichment, both in special settings and within the mainstream. Managed by the U.S. Department of Education, the Educational Resources Information Center (ERIC) is a nationwide information network designed to provide users with ready access to education literature.

CHILDREN WITH DISABILITIES

Free and Inexpensive Resources

Everyone Is Able: Exploding the Myth of Learning Disabilities. Edited by Susannah Sheffer. Holt Associates, 1987. 15 pages. This booklet contains a collection of stories by parents and specialists on learning disabilities that challenge prevailing opinions on learning disabilities. Available from John Holt's Book and Music Store (see chapter 27 for contact information).

Pocket Guide to Federal Help for Individuals with Disabilities. Produced by the U.S. Department of Education, this guide describes benefits and services available to individuals with disabilities and to parents or guardians of children with disabilities. Explains how to make use of the available resources. To order a copy of the revised edition (published in 1993), contact the Clearinghouse on Disability Information, Office of Special Education and Rehabilitative Services, Switzer Building, Room 3132, Washington, D.C. 20202-2425. Phone: 202/205-8241 or 202/205-8723 (publications).

Books

ADHD/Hyperactivity: A Consumer's Guide. By Michael Gordon, Ph.D. GSI Publications, 1990. 192 pages. For parents and teachers, this book describes, in easy-to-understand language, the identification and treatment process for one of the most common, and yet most difficult to understand, childhood problems.

Believe the Heart: Our Dyslexic Days. By Elizabeth Fleming. Strawberry Hill Press, 1984. 160 pages. The author of this book tells the story of six people who are hereditary dyslexics (herself and her five children), all of whom have gone on to success. Points out that dyslexia needs to be recognized as a hidden strength. Offers advice on parenting dyslexic children.

Creative Play Activities for Children with Disabilities. By Lisa Rappaport Morris and Linda Schulz. Second edition. Human Kinetics, 1989. 217 pages. Designed for parents and teachers, this book describes 250 games to help children with special needs (physical, emotional, and mental) grow through play. Includes activities for children from infancy through age ten.

Eagle Eyes: A Child's Guide to Paying Attention. By Jeanne Gehret, M.A. Verbal Images Press, 1991. 40 pages. An inspiring tale of a young boy who learns to recognize and control his Attention Deficit Disorder (ADD). By the end of the story, his family has learned to appreciate his special way of seeing the world. For children ages six to ten.

Help Me to Help My Child. By Jill Bloom. Little, Brown, 1990. 324 pages. A sourcebook for parents of learning disabled children. Offers an overview of available information and resources plus a step-by-step plan of action to assist parents in getting the help their child needs and deserves.

Helping the Child Who Doesn't Fit In. By Stephen Nowicki, Jr., Ph.D., and Marshall P. Duke, Ph.D. Peachtree Publishers, 1992. 192 pages. A guide to the puzzle of social rejection and its relationship to nonverbal language. Discusses Dyssemia, a learning disability that prevents children from properly using or understanding nonverbal communication. For parents, teachers, and caregivers.

How It Feels to Live with a Physical Disability. By Jill Krementz. Simon and Schuster, 1992. 176 pages. Portrays twelve children with various physical disabilities, including dwarfism, paralysis, and spasticity.

Language Learning Disabilities: A New and Practical Approach for Those Who Work with Children and Their Families. By Sophie L. Lovinger, Mary Ellen Brandell, and Linda Seestedt-Stanford. Continuum, 1991. 180 pages. Written in nontechnical language, this book provides information on auditory, speech, and language development and disabilities. Offers insights on how those with language learning disabilities process information, and how parents, teachers, and others can help them resolve learning and social difficulties.

Learning Disabilities: A Family Affair. By Betty Osman, Ph.D. Warner Books, 1988. Shows how to recognize early signs and symptoms of learning disabilities and suggests ways to make life easier for the entire family. Stresses the importance of parent/teacher cooperation and discusses major areas of concern: retention, special classes, homework, and the use of resource rooms. Offers guidance on social development, including ways to help children with learning disabilities make and keep friends and ways to improve relations with siblings.

The Learning Mystique: A Critical Look at "Learning Disabilities." By Gerald Coles. Pantheon Books, 1987.

330 pages. Challenges the prevailing idea that learning problems are biological in origin. Scrutinizes the evidence on which school and clinical practices are built and argues that the neurological explanations have never been scientifically substantiated. Argues that school failure cannot be separated from the learning environment and must be seen (and treated) as the product of interaction between social and family relationships, individual behavior, and different kinds of neurological function (not dysfunction).

The Magic Feather: The Truth about Special Education. By Bill Granger and Lori Granger. Dell Publishing, 1986. 251 pages. Offers advice on how to fight the mislabeling of children as "disabled" or "handicapped," how to help children overcome school difficulties, and how to ensure a future full of promise instead of certain failure. The authors discuss ways to improve the school system and work with teachers to help children get the most from their education. Suggests medical reasons for many learning problems—hearing and vision problems in particular—many of which are easily treated.

Maybe You Know My Kid. By Mary Cahill Fowler. Carol Publishing, 1993. 222 pages. A parent's guide to identifying, understanding, and helping your child with attention deficit hyperactivity disorder.

The Misunderstood Child: A Guide for Parents of Children with Learning Disabilities. By Larry Silver, M.D. McGraw-Hill, 1984. 212 pages. A step-by-step guide to becoming what the author calls "an informed consumer and assertive advocate" for your learning-disabled child. Explains the causes and symptoms of learning disabilities and the social and school problems that can accom-

pany them. Discusses the evaluation process, as well as treatment procedures—and the important role parents play in the process.

Negotiating the Special Education Maze. By Winifred Anderson, Stephen Chitwood, and Deidre Hayden. Woodbine House, 1990. 269 pages. Offers a step-by-step guide to the special education system. Includes information about early intervention laws and services, plus a chapter on career education for older children.

No One to Play With: The Social Side of Learning Disabilities. By Betty Osman, Ph.D., with Henriette Blinder. Academic Therapy, 1989. Identifies and offers solutions to the social problems that children with learning disabilities face.

A Parents' Guide to Attention Deficit Disorders. By Lisa J. Bain with the Children's Hospital of Philadelphia. Dell, 1991. 216 pages. This comprehensive guide for parents is designed to help foster a better understanding of Attention Deficit Disorder (ADD). Drawing on the expertise of professionals from Philadelphia's Children's Hospital and its affiliates, the book covers the history, possible causes, diagnosis, and treatment (behavior therapy, medication, etc.) of ADD. Also covers issues of family stress and home-school relationships. Lists support groups and organizations specializing in the disorder.

Portraying Persons with Disabilities (Fiction). By Debra Robertson. **Portraying Persons with Disabilities (Nonfiction).** By Joan Brest Friedberg, June B. Mullins, and Adelaide Weir Sukiennik. R. R. Bowker, 1992. 482 pages (fiction); 385 pages (nonfiction). Each of these volumes offers an annotated bibliography of books for children and teenagers. Fiction annotations identify specific impairments and plot themes related to featured characters who are disabled. The nonfiction volume includes reference books on disabilities plus introductory essays. Each volume groups titles by broad disability categories.

A Reader's Guide: For Parents of Children with Mental, Physical, or Emotional Disabilities. By Cory Moore. Third edition. Woodbine House, 1990. 248 pages. An annotated bibliography listing more than one thousand books and other resources on disabilities.

Succeeding against the Odds: Strategies and Insights from the Learning Disabled. By Sally L. Smith. Jeremy P. Tarcher, 1991. 304 pages. Written by an experienced educator of children and adults with learning disabilities, this book presents stories of adults whose childhoods were shaped by their learning problems. The author blends these stories with her own experiences as a teacher, showing how learning disabled individuals can be encouraged to work from their strengths and can soar to any height when they receive the support they need.

To a Different Drumbeat. By P. Clarke, H. Kofsky, and J. Lauruol. Anthroposophic Press, 1989. 240 pages. A practical guide to parenting children with special needs, including those with visual and hearing difficulties, developmental delays, learning disabilities, physical handicaps, etc. Written by the parents of children with special needs.

Understanding the Alpha Child at Home and School. By Jack L. Fadely and Virginia N. Hosler. Charles C. Thomas, 1979. 238 pages. Argues that many children labeled learning disabled need to be recognized as "alpha children" with a different but not necessarily disabled pattern of neurological organization.

Why Is My Child Having Trouble at School? By Barbara A. Nowick, Ph.D., and Maureen M. Arnold, Ph.D. Villard Books, 1991. 259 pages. An action guide to learning disabilities, for parents of school-aged children. Describes the neurological basis for learning disabilities and helps parents recognize common signs, cope with the day-to-day stresses, and become their learning disabled child's most important advocate.

Your Child Has a Disability: A Complete Sourcebook of Daily and Medical Care. By Mark L. Batshaw. Little, Brown, 1991. 345 pages. Discusses the diagnosis and possible causes of disabilities. Provides practical information on specific syndromes and diseases, forms of treatment, and the legal, social, and educational decisions that parents must make. Written by a pediatrician who works with children with developmental disabilities.

Periodicals

Ability. P.O. Box 4140, Irvine, California 92716-9919. Explores topics of interest to individuals with disabilities and those who live/work with them. "Reading by the Colors: Dyslexia and Other Learning Dysfunctions" and "Who's Covered under the Americans with Disabilities Act?" are examples of articles featured. Also included are listings of national and regional support centers. Issued six times annually.

Disability Rag. Box 145, Louisville, Kentucky 40201. Phone: 502/459-5343. Addresses disability concerns. Encourages more aids for the disabled, such as wheelchair ramps. Advocates equal access to all jobs. Issued six times a year.

Disabled Outdoors Magazine. 2052 West Twenty-third Street, Chicago, Illinois 60608. Phone: 708/358-4160. A quarterly publication for people of all ages with all types of disabilities. Covers camping, fishing, horseback riding, snow and water skiing, and other sports. Contains information on new products and services, organizations, places to go, and state laws concerning outdoor recreational activities.

Exceptional Children. See Council for Exceptional Children, under "Associations."

Exceptional Parent: Parenting Your Child with a Disability. Psy-Ed Corp., 1170 Commonwealth Avenue, Boston, Massachusetts 01234-4646. Phone: 1/800-247-8080. A magazine for parents of children with all kinds of disabilities. Contains articles on handling special-needs children, updates on legislation for disabled children, and information on equipment that can help disabled children move about and be more comfortable. Issued nine times annually.

Kaleidoscope: International Magazine of Literature, Fine Arts, and Disabilities. United Disability Services, 326 Locust Street, Akron, Ohio 44398-0202. Contains fiction, poetry, and visual arts related to disabilities. Also included are photo essays, book reviews, interviews, critical essays, and personal-experience narratives. Each issue focuses on a different theme. Issued semiannually.

Their World. National Center for Learning Disabilities, 99 Park Avenue, 6th Floor, New York, New York 10016. Phone: 212/687-7211. Annual magazine covering various aspects of learning disabilities, including diagnosis and disabilities in preschoolers. Also explores specific disabilities such as dyslexia. Includes book reviews. (For more information on the National Center for Learning Disabilities, see listing under "Associations.")

Videotapes

Attention Deficit Hyperactivity Disorder: What Can We Do? By Russell A. Barkley. A Guildford Press Video. Running time: 36 minutes. By a leading authority on Attention Deficit Hyperactivity Disorder (ADHD), this videotape offers an overview of the most effective approaches to treating the problems associated with ADHD. Comes with a manual detailing treatments for the disorder, including counseling and education, parent training in child behavior management skills, medication, and other treatments. Available from Childswork/Childsplay (see chapter 27 for contact information).

Understanding Learning Disabilities: How Difficult Can This Be. Running time: 70 minutes. Available from the Connecticut Association for Children with Learning Disabilities, 18 Marshall Street, South Norwalk, Connecticut 06854. Phone: 203/838-5010.

Why Won't My Child Pay Attention? Running time: 76 minutes. This lecture on tape by psychologist Sam Goldstein sheds light on Attention Deficit Hyperactivity Disorder. Offers pointers and advice for parents whose children have a short attention span, are impulsive, frequently become over-aroused, and/or have difficulty delaying gratification. Available from the Neurology, Learning, and Behavior Center, 670 East 3900 South, Suite 100, Salt Lake City, Utah 84107.

Mail Order Catalogs

Childswork/Childsplay. Center for Applied Psychology, Inc., P.O. Box 1586, King of Prussia, Pennsylvania

19406. Phone: 1/800-962-1141. A catalog addressing the mental health needs of children and their families through play. Includes a selection of books on learning disabilities for children and adults. Also offers games, toys, and books to help children develop self-esteem, understand their feelings, and control their behavior.

Descriptive Video Service (DVS) Home Video. WGBH, 125 Western Avenue, Boston, Massachusetts 02134. Phone: 617/492-2777. A video service for visually impaired children and adults. Adds descriptive narration between scenes to help "viewers" better understand and appreciate classics such as Disney's *Alice in Wonderland*, *101 Dalmations*, and *Dumbo*. Contact DVS for a mail order catalog of available videos.

Funtastic Therapy Catalog. Phone: 1/800-531-3176. A catalog filled with games, balls, blocks, and other toys that are both fun and therapeutic for children with learning differences, attention problems, or developmental delays.

Jesana Ltd.: A Very Special Catalogue. Phone: 1/800-443-4728. This catalog contains toys, play structures, therapeutic equipment, software programs, and other products for children with disabilities.

Kapable Kids. P.O. Box 250, Bohemia, New York 11716. Phone: 1/800-356-1564. This catalog contains toys, tapes, and learning tools for children with different abilities, including those with special needs. Included in the selection are mobiles, throw-and-catch toys, boardgames, and puzzles. Many of the products have been specially adapted.

Love Publishing Company/Catalog of Books. 1777 South Bellaire Street, Denver, Colorado 80222. Phone: 303/757-2579 or 303/757-6912. Of-

Oppenheim Toy Portfolio.

By Joanne Oppenheim. This review of toys includes products that can be adjusted or adapted to provide play opportunities for children with special needs. Contact: Oppenheim Toy Portfolio, 40 East Ninth Street, New York, New York 10003. Phone: 212/598-0502. [Also available: A book based on the *Oppenheim Toy Portfolio* called *The Best Toys, Books and Videos for Kids*, by Joanne Oppenheim and Stephanie Oppenheim (HarperCollins, 1993), which describes a variety of quality toys and books for children with special needs. Includes a resource listing as well.]

fers a variety of books on educating exceptional children. Although most of the titles are intended for teachers, parents will find insightful materials as well. *Exceptional Children in Today's Schools*, *Free Appropriate Public Education (The Law and Children with Disabilities)*, and *Academic and Developmental Learning Disabilities* are among the books (all of which are described in detail) that can be ordered from Love Publishing Company.

Special Clothes for Special Children. P.O. Box 4220, Alexandria, Virginia 22303. Phone: 703/683-7343. Free catalog features special clothing for children with physical disabilities.

Woodbine House. 5615 Fishers Lane, Rockville, Maryland 20852. Phone: 301/468-8800 or 1/800-843-7323. Publishes a variety of books to help parents and teachers of children with disabilities. Among the many titles featured in this publisher's catalog are *Negotiating the Special Education Maze: A Guide for Parents and Teachers* by Winifred Anderson, Stephen Chitwood, and Deidre Hayden; *Differences in Common: Straight Talk on Mental Retardation, Down Syndrome, and Life* by Marilyn Trainer; *Children with Cerebral Palsy: A Parents' Guide* edited by Elaine Geralis; *Children with Tourette Syndrome: A Parents' Guide* edited by Tracy Haerle; *Babies with Down Syndrome: A New Parents' Guide* edited by Karen Stray-Gundersen; *The Language of Toys: Teaching Communication Skills to Special-Needs Children* by Sue Schwartz, Ph.D., and Joan E. Heller Miller, Ed.M.; and *A Reader's Guide: For Parents of Children with Mental, Physical, or Emotional Disabilities* by Cory Moore. Other books in the Woodbine House special-needs collection cover children with visual impairments, children with Fragile X Syndrome, and "Topics in Down Syndrome"—a new series that explores nutrition and fitness for children with down syndrome, communication skills in these children, and other topics.

Associations

Association for Children and Adults with Learning Disabilities. 4156 Library Road, Pittsburgh, Pennsylvania 15234. Phone: 412/341-1515. Provides general information on learning disabilities. Local chapters (there are more than nine hundred) make referrals to physicians and treatment centers. Produces a resource listing of publications for sale, as well as films that can be rented.

The Association for Retarded Citizens (The Arc). 500 East Border Street, Suite 300, Arlington, Texas 76010. Phone: 817/261-6003. Serves parents, professionals, and others interested in individuals with mental retardation. Promotes research, services, and public understanding of mentally retarded persons and their families. Offers support for parents of children with mental retardation and other developmental disabilities. Offers a book called *How to Provide for Their Future*, as well as *A Family Handbook on Future Planning.*

Center for Family Support. 386 Park Avenue South, New York, New York 10016. Phone: 212/481-1082. A service agency that offers support and assistance to families with retarded children. Provides consultation services, counseling, and in-home aid. Sponsors parents' groups.

Children with Attention-Deficit Disorder (CHADD). 499 Northwest Seventieth Avenue, Suite 308, Plantation, Florida 33317. Phone: 305/587-3700. Members of this national organization include parents and professionals with an interest in attention-deficit disorders (characterized by deficits in attention span and impulse control, often accompanied by hyperactivity). Provides support services, offers educational programs, and disseminates information. Publishes *Chadder*, a bimonthly newsletter. Produces booklets and brochures, as well as a guide for teachers.

Council for Exceptional Children. 1920 Association Drive, Reston, Virginia 22091. Phone: 703/620-3660. Professional organization dedicated to improving the quality of education for all exceptional children, both gifted and disabled. Maintains the most complete collection of special-education literature in the world through its Department of Information Services and the ERIC Clearinghouse on Handicapped and Gifted Children. Publishes *Exceptional Children*, a bimonthly journal exploring topics of interest to parents with special-needs children. Issues a publications catalog.

Early Childhood Direction Center/Center on Human Policy. New York State Education Department, Division of Program Development, Room 1066, Albany, New York 12234. Phone: 518/474-5804. The center offers information, support, and referrals for families of young disabled children. Its goal is to promote the integration of persons with disabilities into the mainstream of society. Call for a catalog of publications.

Educational Equity Concepts. 114 East Thirty-second Street, New York, New York 10016. Phone: 212/725-1803. This nonprofit organization supplies educational materials that show children with disabilities in positive roles. Will provide a list of bias-free books and toys upon request. Also operates the National Clearinghouse on Women and Girls with Disabilities, a computerized system for identifying programs that provide services for girls and women with disabilities.

Federation for Children with Special Needs. 95 Berkeley Street, Suite 104, Boston, Massachusetts 02116. Phone: 617/482-2915 or 1/800-331-0688. Coalition of parents' organizations acting on behalf of children and adults with developmental disabilities (mental as well as physical). Among its various activities, the federation conducts workshops, training programs, and parent consultations. Offers information on special education laws and resources. Maintains library. Periodicals include *Coalition Quarterly*, issued three times annually, and *Newsline*, a newsletter issued five times annually.

IBM Special Needs Information Referral Center. P.O. Box 2150, Atlanta, Georgia 30301-2150. Phone: 1/800-426-2133 or 1/800-284-9482 (TDD). Will refer parents with disabilities to agencies that supply information on assistive technology (equipment that can help disabled parents better care for their children).

Learning Disabilities Association of America. 4156 Library Road, Pittsburgh, Pennsylvania 15234. Phone: 412/341-1515. Fax: 412/344-0224. Works to improve the education of children who have learning disabilities. Offers referral services. Provides assistance to state and local groups. Membership includes parents of children with learning disabilities, as well as interested professionals. Provides information on tutors, learning centers, and independent living programs. Maintains a library. Publishes *Learning Disabilities*, a semiannual journal, as well as a bimonthly newsletter (*LDA Newsbriefs*). Also offers a variety of pamphlets and other informational material covering a range of learning disabilities, including dyslexia. Write for a publications catalog.

Let's Play to Grow. 8610 Contree Road, Laurel, Maryland 20708. Phone: 301/776-8054 or 202/673-7166. An inclusive network of playgroups across the United States for children with special needs.

National Association of Private Schools for Exceptional Children. See "Associations" listed under "Creativity, Talent, and Giftedness" in this chapter.

National Center for Learning Disabilities. 99 Park Avenue, 6th Floor, New York, New York 10016. Phone: 212/687-7211. National organization promoting increased public awareness of learning disabilities. Provides referrals and makes resources available to parents, professionals, and volunteers working with the learning disabled. Develops programs and provides services for learning disabled children. Publishes *Their World*, a magazine. (For more information, see listing under "Periodicals.")

National Easter Seal Society. 70 East Lake Street, Chicago, Illinois 60601. Phone: 312/726-6200. Establishes and conducts programs that serve people with disabilities. Sponsors activities involving advocacy, research, public education, government relations, and resource development. Offers physical, occupational, and language therapies, training programs, and recreational activities. Publishes a variety of informational materials including *Computer-Disability News*, a quarterly publication containing news and information on computer use for people with disabilities. Issues a publications catalog as well.

National Fathers Network. The Merrywood School, 16120 North East Eighth Street, Bellevue, Washington 98008. Phone: 206/747-4004 or 206/282-1334. Puts fathers of children with special needs in contact with support groups located around the country. Publishes a free, quarterly newsletter written for and by dads.

The National Information Clearinghouse for Infants with Disabilities and Life-threatening Conditions. Center for Developmental Disabilities, University of South Carolina, Benson Building, 1st Floor, Columbia, South Carolina 29208. Phone: 1/800-922-9234. Helps parents of infants with disabilities and life-threatening conditions identify services available both nationally and in their area. The clearinghouse also produces fact sheets on disability terminology, community resources, the roles of professionals, family involvement in medical decision making,

and other topics. Offers abstracted bibliographies on topics related to the care of infants with disabilities, including ethical, legal, and nursing issues.

National Lekotek Center. 2100 Ridge Avenue, Evanston, Illinois 60201. Phone: 1/800-366-PLAY. Offers play-centered programs and toy lending library services for children with special needs. Contact Lekotek to locate the center nearest you.

National Parent Network on Disabilities. 1600 Prince Street, Suite 115, Alexandria, Virginia 22314. Phone: 703/684-6763. Promotes the needs of children with severe disabilities and keeps an eye on policies that affect them.

Orton Dyslexia Society. Chester Building, Suite 382, 8600 LaSalle Road, Baltimore, Maryland 21286-2044. Phone: 301/296-0232 or 1/800-ABC-D123. A nonprofit, professional organization for those interested in the study, treatment, and prevention of the specific language disability known as dyslexia (characteristics may include a delayed ability to use spoken language, difficulty in learning or remembering printed words, difficulty in finding the "right" word in speaking, and the reversal of orientation of letters or sequence of letters in words). Named for Dr. Samuel T. Orton, a pioneer in the field. Staff members at this nonprofit organization will help parents locate tutors and local centers where your child can be tested for dyslexia. Publishes *Perspectives on Dyslexia*, a quarterly newsletter, as well as *Annals of Dyslexia*, an annual journal. Also publishes monographs and issues reprints of papers.

Parents Helping Parents. 535 Race Street, Suite 140, San Jose, California 95126. Phone: 408/288-5010. An organization of parents, professionals, and others working to help families with special-needs children, including those with physical, mental, emotional, or learning disabilities. Among its various programs, Parents Helping Parents offers support services, including education, information, and training to decrease the feeling of isolation parents of special-needs children experience and to help them gain a sense of control over their lives. Publishes *Special Addition*, a bimonthly newsletter containing association news, updates on legislation and medical findings, and a calendar of events. Also publishes books, information packets, and brochures.

Pediatric Projects. P.O. Box 1880, Santa Monica, California 90406. Phone: 213/828-8963. This nonprofit organization offers products for exceptional children, including teddy bears designed with a variety of ailments and disabilities. Also produces a newsletter listing medically oriented books and toys for both children and adults.

Sibling Information Network. University of Connecticut, 991 Main Street, East Hartford, Connecticut 06108. Phone: 203/282-7050. A university-affiliated program serving families, teachers, social workers, and others interested in the welfare of siblings of children with disabilities and issues related to families of individuals with disabilities. Acts as a clearinghouse for information and services.

Special Needs PTA (SEPTA). Unites parents whose children have disabilities ranging from mild dyslexia to severe physical impairments. Many of these groups (there are nearly three hundred across the country) function independently of regular school-based PTAs. Parents interested in forming a SEPTA should contact their state or local PTA representative or send a self-addressed, stamped envelope to the National PTA (see appendix I for contact information).

Special Olympics. 1350 New York Avenue, N.W., Suite 500, Washington, D.C. 20005-4709. Phone: 202/628-3630. Inquire about competitive sports for children with disabilities. Training begins as early as age five; competition starts at age eight.

Winners on Wheels (WOW). 2842 Business Park Avenue, Fresno, California 93727-1328. Phone: 209/292-2171. A national program for children in wheelchairs, offering social and learning opportunities.

Government Resources

Clearinghouse on Disability Information. U.S. Department of Education, Office of Special Education and Rehabilitative Services (OSERS), Switzer Building, Room 3132, Washington, D.C. 20202-2425. Phone: 202/205-8241 or 202/205-8723 (publications). Responds to inquiries, provides referrals, and disseminates information about services for individuals with disabilities at the national, state, and local levels. Publications include a seasonal newsletter, *OSERS News in Print*, which details federal activities affecting children and adults with disabilities, and a booklet called *A Summary of Existing Legislation Affecting Persons with Disabilities* (a history and description of relevant federal laws enacted through 1991). Also offers the *Pocket Guide to Federal Help for Individuals with Disabilities* (see listing under "Free Resource").

ERIC Clearinghouse on Disabilities and Gifted Education. See "Government Resource" listing under "Creativity, Talent, and Giftedness" in this chapter.

National Information Center for Children and Youth with Disabilities, P.O. Box 1492, Washington, D.C. 20013. Phone: 202/416-0300 or 1/800-999-5599. This federally supported clearinghouse provides information and referrals to assist parents, educators, caregivers, advocates, and others in helping children and youth with disabilities to become participating members of the community. Fights for educational rights of learning disabled children. Offers parents training programs and disseminates information. Refers families to camps for children with special needs. Publications include free newsletters, booklets, information packets, and other print materials. Offers a free publications list.

The National Institutes of Health. Office of the Director, Editorial Operations Branch, Office of Communications, Bethesda, Maryland 20892. Phone: 301/496-4000 (main number) or 301/496-4143 (publications department). The National Institutes of Health seeks to improve the health and well being of Americans by conducting and supporting biomedical research. Offers a free publications list that combines works issued by the individual institutes, centers, and offices (publications in these lists are divided into two broad categories: "For Health Professionals" and "For the General Public"). These publications are generally available to the public free of charge upon written request. Contact the institutes for their complete list.

The following institutes conduct research on disabilities.

The National Institute of Child Health and Human Development. Office of Research and Reporting, Building 31, Room 2A32, Bethesda, Maryland 20892. Phone: 301/496-5133. Conducts and sponsors research on the processes of growth and development on which the health of both children and adults depends. Strives to find out what causes developmental abnormalities and disease, how these might be prevented, and how they can be treated. Topics under study include the physical and behavioral adaption of the newborn, the development of the immune system, learning and cognitive development, and developmental disabilities. Call the Office of Research Reporting for information on research topics, programs, and publications for professional and lay audiences.

National Institute of Neurological Disorders and Stroke. Building 31, Room 8A06, Bethesda, Maryland 28092. Phone: 301/496-5751. Conducts and supports fundamental and applied research on human neurological disorders such as epilepsy, muscular dystrophy, and head and spinal cord injuries. Offers a variety of free publications written for the general public, including *Tourette Syndrome*, *Cerebral Palsy*, and *Epilepsy*.

National Institute on Deafness and Other Communication Disorders. Building 31, Room 3C35, Bethesda, Maryland 20892. Phone: 301/496-7243. TDD: 301/402-0252. Conducts and supports research and training on disorders of hearing and other communication processes, including diseases affecting hearing, balance, voice, speech, language, taste, and smell. Offers a variety of free publications written for the general public, including *Update on Stuttering* and *Update on Developmental Speech and Language Disorders*.

Specific Disabilities (organizations)

Following is a partial listing of organizations that provide information on specific disabilities. More listings can be found in the *Directory of Associations* (Gale, published annually) and *Who to Call* by Daniel Starer (William Morrow, 1992). For more information on physical disabilities, see chapter 6.

Down's Syndrome

Association for Children with Down's Syndrome, Inc. 2616 Martin Avenue, Bellmore, New York 11710. Phone: 516/221-4700.

National Down Syndrome Congress. 1800 Dempster Street, Park Ridge, Illinois 60068-1146. Phone: 312/823-7550 or 1/800-232-6372.

National Down Syndrome Society. 666 Broadway, New York 10012. Phone: 1/800-221-4602.

Dyslexia

Orton Dyslexia Society. Chester Building, Suite 382, 8600 LaSalle Road, Baltimore, Maryland 21286-2044. Phone: 301/296-0232 or 1/800-ABC-D123.

Epilepsy

Epilepsy Foundation of America. 4351 Garden City Drive, Landover, Maryland 20785. Phone: 301/459-3700 or 1/800-332-1000.

Fetal Alcohol Syndrome

Fetal Alcohol Syndrome Network. 158 Rosemont Avenue, Coatesville, Pennsylvania 19320. Phone: 215/384-1133.

Fragile X Syndrome

National Fragile X Foundation. 1441 York Street, Suite 215, Denver, Colorado 80206. Phone: 303/333-6155 or 1/800-688-8765.

Hearing Impairment

Alexander Graham Bell Association for the Deaf. 3417 Volta Place, N.W., Washington, D.C. 20007-2778. Phone: 202/337-5220.

American Society for Deaf Children. 814 Thayer Street, Silver Spring, Maryland 20910. Phone: 301/585-5400.

Better Hearing Institute. P.O. Box 1840, Washington, D.C. 20013. Phone: 1/800-327-9355.

Neurological Disorders

Child Neurology Society. 475 Cleveland Avenue, North, Suite 225, St. Paul, Minnesota 55104-5051. Phone: 612/625-7466.

Rare Disorders

National Organization for Rare Disorders. 100 Route 37, P.O. Box 8923, New Fairfield, Connecticut 06812-1783. Phone: 1/800-999-6673 or 203/746-6518.

Reye's Syndrome

National Reye's Syndrome Foundation. 426 North Lewis, P.O. Box 829, Bryan, Ohio 43506. Phone: 419/636-2679 or 1/800-233-7393 (24-hour hotline) or 1/800-231-7393 (in Ohio).

Stuttering

National Center for Stuttering. 200 East Thirty-third Street, New York, New York 10016. Phone: 212/532-1460 or 1/800-221-2483.

Stuttering Foundation of America. P.O. Box 11749, Memphis, Tennessee 38111-0749. Phone: 1/800-992-9392.

Tourette Syndrome

Tourette Syndrome Association. 42-40 Bell Boulevard, Bayside, New York 11361. Phone: 718/224-2999 or 1/800-237-0717.

Visual Impairment/Blindness

American Foundation for the Blind, Inc. 15 West Sixteenth Street, New York, New York 10011. Phone: 212/620-2000 or 1/800-232-5463.

Blind Children's Fund. 230 Central Street, Auburndale, Massachusetts 02166. Phone: 617/332-4014.

National Association for Parents of the Visually Impaired. P.O. Box 180806, Camden, New York 13316. Phone: 315/245-3442 or 1/800-562-6265.

National Society to Prevent Blindness. 500 East Remington Road, Schaumburg, Illinois 60173. Phone: 1/800-331-2020.

Parents and Cataract Kids. 179 Hunter's Lane, Devon, Pennsylvania 19333. Phone: 215/721-9131 or 215/293-1917.

Chapter 3

Parenting: Approaches and Techniques

GENERAL RESOURCES

Books

The Anxious Parent: How to Overcome Your Fears about Discipline, Toilet Training, Feeding and Sleeping Difficulties, Separation, Sibling Rivalry, and Other Childhood Problems. By Dr. Michael Schwartzman. Simon and Schuster, 1992. 352 pages. Drawing on his clinical practice and his own observations as a parent, Dr. Michael Schwartzman explains the origins of unnecessary parental anxiety. Reveals how our own experiences as children affect the decisions we make as parents adversely. Offers a "program for change" to help parents overcome these destructive anxiety reactions.

Babywatching. By Desmond Morris. Crown, 1991. 214 pages. What comforts a baby? What makes a baby laugh? How often does a baby feed? Why do babies like to sleep with a treasured possession? What is a spoiled baby? How soon can babies be toilet trained? In this book, zoologist Desmond Morris answers these and dozens of other commonly asked questions. (For more information on *Babywatching*, see "Books" listed under "General Resources" in chapter 1.)

Between Parent and Child. By Dr. Haim Ginott. Avon Books, 1969. 256 pages. Provides insights and offers information on self-esteem, discipline, anger, parent/child communication, and other important topics.

Focuses on the child's feelings and offers child-sensitive advice. More than five million copies in print.

Caring for Your Baby and Young Child: Birth to Age 5. Steven P. Shelow, M.D., F.A.A.P., editor-in-chief; Robert E. Hannemann, M.D., F.A.A.P., associate medical editor. Bantam, 1991. 676 pages. Developed by the American Academy of Pediatrics, this reference book addresses common parenting concerns, as well as childhood medical problems. The first portion of the book, which is arranged according to the child's age, offers information on growth and development, basic care (feeding, sleeping, toilet training, etc.), behavior, and general health. Special sections on safety and child care are also included. The second portion of the book is an encyclopedic guide to recognizing and solving health problems. Includes information on common infectious diseases, disabilities, musculoskeletal problems, skin problems, chronic conditions and diseases (including AIDS), and commonly used medications. Instructions for dealing with medical emergencies are also contained in this guide. A special section on family issues covers adoption, divorce, sibling rivalry, child abuse and neglect, single parent households, and stepfamilies. Also available: *Caring for Your Adolescent: Ages 12 to 21.* (Note: *Caring for Your School-Age Child: Ages 5 to 12* is scheduled for publication in 1995. This volume will serve as a health reference, as well as a guide to the complex developmental issues of the middle years. Will cover nutrition, physical fitness, immunizations, sports participation, and injury prevention. Will also discuss school readiness; gifted and disabled students; developmental stages; behavioral problems such as depression, school avoidance, and running away; issues such as friendships, sibling rivalry, and gender differences; family issues; and how to cope with moving, divorce, death, and stepfamilies.)

Childhood's Future. By Richard Louv. Houghton Mifflin, 1991. 420 pages. Based on interviews with parents, educators, children, and others, the author concludes that the ties that used to bind neighbors, communities, learning institutions, and government with children are gone. Louv's goal is to "reweave the web," to reconnect young and old, schools and families, and so forth. Challenges government to encourage family-friendly workplaces. Counsels parents to reach out to other parents for support. Emphasizes the importance of children in our society's future.

Children: The Challenge. By Rudolf Dreikurs with Vicki Solz. Penguin, 1990 (first published in 1964). 335 pages. Based on a lifetime of experience with children, child psychiatrist Rudolf Dreikurs presents a program that teaches parents how to cope with the common childhood problems that occur from toddlerhood through the preteen years. A popular book, with more than 500,000 copies in print. Other books by Rudolf Dreikurs include *The Challenge of Parenthood* and *The New Approach to Discipline: Logical Consequences* (with Loren Grey).

Different and Wonderful: Raising Black Children in a Race-Conscious Society. By Darlene Powell Hopson and Derek S. Hopson. Prentice-Hall, 1990. 241 pages. Explores the sometimes tough, sometimes unspoken challenges that face middle class African-American family today. Takes readers through each stage of the child's life, offering tools to assist parents in raising healthy, well-adjusted children—without sacrificing family values or ethnic pride.

Dr. Spock's Baby and Child Care. By Benjamin Spock, M.D., and Michael B. Rothenberg, M.D. Sixth edition. Simon and Schuster, 1992. 832 pages. First published in 1946, *Dr. Spock's Baby and Child Care* has been translated into thirty-nine languages and has sold more than forty million copies worldwide. This new edition has new and expanded sections exploring topics such as breastfeeding; working and parenting; single parenting; traveling with children; and talking to your child about sex, AIDS, and other difficult topics. In addition to health topics such as childhood illnesses and immunization schedules, this book covers daily care, child safety, physical and emotional development, day care and school-related issues, behavioral problems, and other parenting challenges. By the same author: *Dr. Spock on Parenting* (Simon and Schuster, 1988), which addresses the challenges parents face in a changing world, including finding reliable child care and the new role of the father. Also discusses feeding, family relationships, sleep problems, behavioral problems, discipline, and divorce.

The Essential Partnership: How Parents and Children Can Meet the Emotional Challenges of Infancy and Childhood. By Stanley Greenspan, M.D. Viking Penguin, 1990. 256 pages. Explains how a healthy parent/child partnership can help turn the predictable problems of a child's emotional development into challenges that can be met and overcome. Shows how parents can use an exercise called "floor time" to help the child work through negative emotions. Anger, aggression, fear, discipline, self-esteem, temper tantrums, sibling rivalry, separation anxiety, sexuality, competitiveness, and other parental concerns are addressed and related to the developmental stages through which children pass from infancy to age five.

Experts Advise Parents. Edited by Eileen Shiff. Delacorte, 1987. 370 pages. Recognized child-care authorities offer parenting advice and address common child-rearing problems. Chapters cover self-esteem, father-infant bonding, common sleep problems, school readiness, effective discipline, and other important topics. Each is written by a separate author (Dorothy Corkille Briggs, M.S.; Richard Ferber, M.D.; and Louise Bates Ames, Ph.D.; among others). Includes a developmental checklist that lists typical behaviors (social, linguistic, cognitive, and physical) for children from birth to age ten. Particularly useful for parents who don't have the time to read the whole books written by the contributing experts.

Familyhood: Nurturing the Values That Matter. By Lee Salk. Simon and Schuster, 1992. 206 pages. Affirms the strength of the American family and offers guidelines on raising children with a strong set of values.

Family Living series. Children's Television Workshop. Prentice-Hall. A series of books produced by the Children's Television Workshop, creators of "Sesame Street." Titles in the series include *Parents' Guide to Understanding Discipline: Infancy through Preteen, Parents' Guide to Raising Kids Who Love to Learn: Infant to Grade School, Parents' Guide to Feeding Your Kids Right: Birth through Teen Years,* and *Raising Kids in a Changing World.* Another book in the series—*Parents' Guide to Raising Responsible Kids: Preschool through Teen Years*—won a *Child* magazine Book Award for Excellence in Family Issues for 1992. Experts in child development, health, and communication—including Louise Bates Ames (founder of the Gesell Institute of Human Development) and Hannah Nuba (director of the New York Public Library Early Childhood Resource and Information Center)—have served on the advisory panel for this series.

A Good Enough Parent: A Book on Child Rearing. By Bruno Bettelheim. Alfred A. Knopf, 1987. 377 pages. In this classic, Bruno Bettelheim sums up the results of his lifelong effort to understand what is involved in successful childrearing. At the center of the book is the author's belief that children should not be raised to be successful in the eyes of the world but, rather, to be satisfied with themselves. Discusses the relationship between parent and child, the development of selfhood, and the child as a part of the larger community.

The Growing Years: A Guide to Your Child's Emotional Development from Birth to Adolescence. By the New York Hospital/Cornell Medical Center Department of Psychiatry with Mark Rubinstein, M.D. Simon and Schuster, 1989. 386 pages. Offers advice on common problems such as weaning, toilet training, temper tantrums, childhood fears, sibling rivalry, discipline, and peer pressure.

The Magic Years. By Selma H. Fraiberg. Charles Scribner's Sons, 1959. 305 pages. This classic work takes parents on a journey into the mind of a young child, showing how he confronts the world and learns to cope with it. Discusses common fears, feeding, fantasy, gender differences, and other topics. Helps parents understand and handle problems that arise during various stages of development. Recipient of the *Child* magazine Book Award for

excellence in family issues. Over a million copies in print.

The Measure of Our Success: A Letter to My Children and Yours. By Marian Wright Edelman. Beacon Press, 1992. 97 pages. In this bestselling book, the founder and president of the Children's Defense Fund shares the values she relied on in raising her own three sons, including honesty, hard work, self-reliance, self-confidence, and social responsibility. Winner of the Child magazine Book Award for Excellence in Family Issues.

The Mother's Almanac. By Marguerite Kelly and Elia Parsons. Revised edition. Doubleday, 1992. 392 pages. Offers friendly advice on dozens of topics, including child-proofing, craft projects for kids, and videotapes worth viewing. Written by two mothers and updated to address the various changes that have occurred in family life since its first publication (with sections on divorce, child care, and more).

The Mother's Almanac II: Your Child from Six to Twelve. By Marguerite Kelly. Doubleday, 1989. 408 pages. The sequel to *The Mother's Almanac*, this book covers the joys, challenges, and changes that take place during the elementary school years. Divided into three parts: (1) The Child (including the child's body, mind, spirit, needs, and worries); (2) The Family (relationships, time spent together, traditions, and family stress such as moving, divorce, and death); and (3) The World (school, friendships, and good times). Offers advice, information, and interesting things to do with your six- to twelve-year-old.

Parent and Child: Getting through to Each Other. By Lawrence Kutner, Ph.D. William Morrow, 1991. 248 pages. Lawrence Kutner, whose "Parent and Child" column is syndicated in over three hundred newspapers nationwide, offers advice on dealing with the often vexing problems of childrearing.

Parenting by Heart: How to Connect with Your Kids in the Face of Too Much Advice, Too Many Pressures, and Never Enough Time. By Ron Taffel, Ph.D. Addison-Wesley, 1991. 302 pages. Reminds parents to trust their natural instincts and offers tips based on real-life situations. Examines basic parenting myths ("the myth of the 'in-charge' parent," "the myth of quality time," "the myth of the fair parent," etc.) and offers a framework for new ways of thinking.

Parenting "Keys" series. Barron's Educational Series. A series of guides exploring various aspects of parenthood and childhood, written by qualified professionals. Available through bookstores or directly from the publisher (phone: 1/800-645-3476). Books in this ongoing series include:

> Keys to Becoming a Father
> Keys to Breast Feeding
> Keys to Calming the Fussy Baby
> Keys to Childhood Illnesses
> Keys to Children's Nutrition
> Keys to Children's Sleep Problems
> Keys to Child Safety and Care of Minor Childhood Injuries
> Keys to Choosing Child Care
> Keys to Dealing with Childhood Allergies
> Keys to Dealing with Stuttering
> Keys to Disciplining Your Young Child
> Keys to Investing for Your Child's Future
> Keys to Parenting a Child with Attention Deficit Disorder
> Keys to Parenting a Child with Down Syndrome
> Keys to Parenting Twins
> Keys to Parenting Your One-Year-Old

> Keys to Parenting Your Teenager
> Keys to Parenting Your Two-Year-Old
> Keys to Preparing and Caring for Your Newborn
> Keys to Preparing and Caring for Your Second Child

Parenting Young Children. By Don Dinkmeyer, Gary D. McKay, and James S. Dinkmeyer. Random House, 1990. 157 pages. Offers parenting strategies and advice based on the S.T.E.P. (Systematic Training for Effective Parenting) program. For parents of children under age six. Other books by the same author/s include: *The Effective Parent, The Parents Handbook,* and *Raising a Responsible Child.* (See also listing for S.T.E.P. under "Parenting Classes.")

"Parents Book" series. By the *Parents* magazine editors. Ballantine. A series of books exploring various topics of interest to parents. Titles include the following:

> Parents Book for New Fathers
> Parents Book for Raising a Healthy Child
> Parents Book for the Toddler Years
> Parents Book for Your Baby's First Year
> Parents Book of Baby Names
> Parents Book of Breastfeeding
> Parents Book of Childhood Allergies
> Parents Book of Child Safety
> Parents Book of Discipline
> Parents Book of Infant Colic
> Parents Book of Pregnancy and Birth
> Parents Book of Toilet Teaching

P.E.T.—Parent Effectiveness Training. By Thomas Gordon, Ph.D. New American Library, 1975. 334 pages. Provides step-by-step guidelines for raising cooperative, responsible children, based on Dr. Thomas Gordon's Parent Effectiveness Training program. By the same author: *P.E.T. in Action* (Wyden Books, 1976), which draws on the real-life experiences of P.E.T. graduates, explaining what really happens when parents apply P.E.T. in the home.

Practical Parenting Tips. By Vicki Lansky. Meadowbrook, 1982. 168 pages. A bestseller by the author of more than twenty-five parenting books. Offers 1,500 practical ideas from hundreds of experienced parents, including tips on child-proofing, bathtub safety, doing the laundry, etc. Also available: *Practical Parenting Tips for the School Age Years* (Bantam Books, 1985).

The Preschool Years: Family Strategies that Work—From Experts and Parents. By Ellen Galinsky and Judy David. Ballantine, 1991. 504 pages. Based on questions that emerged during hundreds of seminars conducted by the authors, this guide provides information on child and parent development, models for solving problems, and insight into the conflicts between parents and preschoolers. Discipline, sexuality, moral and social development, temperament, routines (eating, sleeping, toilet training, etc.), family relationships, schools, and child care are among the topics explored. From the Bank Street College of Education.

Raising Baby Right: A Guide for Avoiding the 20 Most Common Mistakes New Parents Make. By Charles E. Schaefer, Ph.D., and Theresa Foy DiGeronimo, M.Ed. Prince Paperbacks, 1992. 112 pages. This paperback describes the mistakes parents frequently make (misreading their baby's temperament, trying to be "perfect" parents, trying to raise superbabies, "putting" a baby to sleep, feeding to soothe, and so forth). By drawing attention to these misguided (but good-intentioned) child-rearing techniques, this book directs parents toward more fruitful methods and approaches.

Raising Black Children. By James P. Comer, M.D., and Alvin F. Poussaint, M.D. Penguin Group, 1992. 436 pages. In this guide, two African-American child psychiatrists focus on the special concerns of black parents. They address hundreds of common concerns, paying special attention to the challenges of building self-esteem and coping with often unconscious racism in our society. The book has a question-and-answer format, with chapters arranged according to the age of the child—the infant, the preschool child, the school-aged child, and the adolescent. Includes a recommended reading list.

Traits of a Healthy Family: Fifteen Traits Commonly Found in Healthy Families by Those Who Work with Them. By Dolores Curran. Harper San Francisco, 1985. Discusses the traits commonly found in well-adjusted families and describes ways that they can be encouraged. Based on the author's survey of teachers, doctors, and other professionals who work with parents and children.

We Have a Problem: A Parent's Sourcebook. By Jane Marks. American Psychiatric Press, 1992. 449 pages. Features a compilation of columns by Jane Marks originally published in *Parents* magazine. Explores a wide range of topics, including divorce, school problems, and substance abuse. Each real-life problem is described by concerned parents, then followed by solutions from qualified counselors.

What Every Baby Knows. By T. Berry Brazelton. Addison-Wesley, 1987. 274 pages. Presents five families as they address important child-rearing issues with renowned pediatrician T. Berry Brazelton. Crying, sleep, discipline, childhood fears and fantasies, sibling rivalry, early learning, and separation and divorce are among the topics explored. Based on the Lifetime cable television series (see listing under "Television Programs"). (Note: For other titles by T. Berry Brazelton, see book listings under "General Resources" in chapter 1.)

Whole Child/Whole Parent. By Polly Berrien Berends. Harper and Row, 1987. 360 pages. Offers practical suggestions for new parents, as well as spiritual guidance. Explores discipline, creativity, child-proofing, child's play, and other topics in chapters such as "Spirit," "Freedom," and "Unity." Includes annotated booklists, mail order catalogs, and other resources.

Your Baby and Child: From Birth to Age Five. By Penelope Leach. New edition, revised and expanded. Alfred A. Knopf, 1989. 553 pages. Examines what happens within your child from the moment of birth until he or she is ready for school. Explores the various stages of development (mental, physical, and emotional); explains how to feed, bathe, and otherwise care for your child; and offers guidance in coping with common trouble spots such as teething, tantrums, and sleeping problems. This popular guidebook also sheds light on the learning process and explains how parents can help make the most of their child's play time. A special reference section provides a quick guide to medical matters such as colds, head injuries, allergic reactions, and hospital admission. (Note: Penelope Leach's television series, "Your Baby and Child," can be viewed on Lifetime cable television. See listing under "Television Programs" for more information.)

Your Child's Health: The Parent's Guide to Symptoms, Emergencies, Common Illnesses, Behavior, and School Problems. By Barton D. Schmitt, M.D., F.A.A.P. Bantam, 1991.

672 pages. Designed to help parents ensure the physical and emotional well-being of their children. In addition to health topics (baby care, nutrition, medicine, illness, disease, etc.), this book covers child behavior, exploring topics such as sleep, discipline, temper tantrums, sibling rivalry, toilet-training basics, homework problems, and television. Recipient of the *Child* magazine Book Award for excellence in family issues.

Your Growing Child: From Babyhood through Adolescence. By Penelope Leach. Alfred A. Knopf, 1986. 732 pages. An A-to-Z compendium of information and advice for parents. Explains how to help your child feel safe and confident; how to teach appropriate behavior; what to do when a child cheats, lies, or steals; how to cope with toilet training and bed-wetting; how to deal with sibling rivalry; how to handle temper tantrums; and how to deal with the fears and anxieties that children experience from babyhood through adolescence. Explores more than one hundred broad topics, which are listed alphabetically. The index at the back of the book assists readers in their search for specific information.

Periodicals

American Baby. Cahners Publishing Co., 475 Park Avenue South, New York, New York 10016. Phone: 212/689-3600. Monthly magazine covering pregnancy, child care, and parenting. Offers advice on topics such as health and safety, toilet training, and traveling with children. Also provides information on baby products, including clothing and furniture. Issued monthly.

Baby Talk. Parenting Unlimited, Inc., 636 Sixth Avenue, New York, New York 10011. Phone: 212/989-8181. Magazine covering baby care and the challenges of being a new parent. Health, food and nutrition, stages of development, safety, and travel are among the topics explored. Issued monthly.

Birth to Three and Beyond. 3411 Willamette Street, Eugene, Oregon 97405. Phone: 503/484-4401. A newsletter covering topics of interest to families with young children, including everyday care, discipline, and nutrition. Issued bimonthly.

Child. P.O. Box 3176, Harlan, Iowa 51593-0367. Phone: 1/800-777-0222. Slick magazine targeted toward educated, high-income families. Feature articles exploring various aspects of parenting (discipline, building self-esteem, etc.), as well as columns and reviews. Issued ten times annually.

Children Today. Administration for Children and Families, 370 L'Enfant Promenade, S.W., 7th Floor, Washington, D.C. 20447. Reports on child development findings; health and welfare; and federal, state, and local services for children. Includes feature articles, book reviews, summaries of new research, reports, and resources. An interdisciplinary journal for professionals, para-professionals, and others whose daily jobs and interests are in children, youth, and families. Issued bimonthly. Subscriptions available through the U.S. Government Printing Office (see appendix B for contact information).

Christian Parenting Today. Good Family Magazine, Box 3850, Sisters, Oregon 97759. Phone: 503/549-8261. A bimonthly parenting magazine written from a Christian perspective.

Family Fun. See "Periodical" listed under "Activities and Projects for Kids" in chapter 16.

Growing Parent. Dunn and Hargitt, Inc., 22 North Second Street, Lafayette, Indiana 47902. Phone: 317/423-2624. A monthly newsletter focusing on the issues, problems, and choices parents face as their children grow. Offers information, inspiration, and advice.

Mothering. P.O. Box 1690, Santa Fe, New Mexico 87504. Phone: 1/800-827-1061 (subscriptions and customer service). Publishes a variety of feature articles exploring various aspects of parenting. Offers practical advice on topics such as birthing, breastfeeding, self-esteem, family policy, and alternative education. Most articles conclude with resource listings for those seeking additional information. Each issue of *Mothering* contains a current list of available back issues, along with a listing of feature articles contained within. Here is a sampling of subjects covered: Sexuality (issue 41); Value of Crying (issue 62); The Truth About Diapers (issue 67); Working Fathers (issue 67); Speaking Is An Addiction (issue 69); and Helping Children Communicate Their Feelings (issue 69). Each issue of *Mothering* contains a current list of available back issues, which can be purchased for $3.00 each.

Mothers Resource Guide. Stork Deliveries, P.O. Box Box 38, South Milwaukee, Wisconsin 53172. Phone: 1/800-886-1550. Published quarterly, this guide lists hundreds of resources for mothers, including support groups, hotlines, publications, businesses, and mail order catalogs. Topics include childbirth and pregnancy, education, health, mental health, parent support, and children with special needs.

Parenting. Time, Inc., Ventures, 301 Howard Street, 17th Floor, San Francisco, California 94105. Phone: 1/800-635-2665 (subscriptions). Both informative and entertaining, this magazine offers feature articles on care and feeding, child behavior and development, parenting tactics, current events, health, exercise and fitness, education, family travel, activities for children, and other topics of interest to parents (including adoptive, single, and stepparents). Also contains news items, opinion columns, essays, and reviews of the latest books, videotapes, software, and television programs.

Parents. 685 Third Avenue, New York, New York 10017. Phone: 1/800-727-3682. A popular magazine containing articles on child development, parenting approaches and techniques (toilet teaching, discipline, building self-esteem, etc.), health, safety, activities and crafts, family life, work options, and other topics of interest to parents. Also contains news items on health, child care, and fitness; reviews of children's books and other media; and questions and answers on health and family topics.

Parent's Digest. Ladies' Home Journal, 100 Park Avenue, New York, New York 10017. Each issue contains articles adapted from books written by child-care experts (pediatricians, child development specialists, children's rights activists, etc.), as well as some new material and reprinted feature articles. Explores topics such as discipline, day care, health and safety, family policy, family activities, and child development. Also contains columns, recipes, photo essays, and resource listings. Recipient of the Parents' Choice seal of approval.

Parent-to-Parent. P.O. Box 85324, Burlington, Ontario L7R 4K5, Canada Phone: 416/335-3549. A bimonthly magazine that deals with the psychological relations between parents and children (from tots to teens). Includes articles written by parents, as well as professionals.

Practical Parenting. King's Reach Tower, Stamford Street, London SE1 9LS. Phone: 071-261-5058. Fax: 071-261-5366. Produced in England, this popular magazine explores various aspects of baby and child care, including articles on childbirth, health and safety, education, family life, family cookery (including recipes), buying baby and child-care products, activities for children, and more. Includes quick parenting tips and additional resource listings.

Priority Parenting. Tamra B. Orr, P.O. Box 1793, Warsaw, Indiana 46581-1793. Phone: 219/268-1415. A 20-page monthly magazine designed to encourage and support parents who believe in natural child care. Each issue explores a different topic (home birth, family beds, child-led breastfeeding, family nutrition, peaceful homes, etc.). Includes editorials, personal experiences, poetry, excerpts from parenting professionals, and resource listings. Reviews books, tapes, and videos as well. Sample issue available for $2.00.

Sesame Street Parents' Guide. Children's Television Workshop, One Lincoln Plaza, New York, New York 10023. Phone: 212/595-3456. A supplement to *Sesame Street Magazine*, this guide helps parents of preschoolers expand on themes explored in the television series. In addition to family-oriented features on health, safety, learning opportunities, and other topics, this publication includes the "Practical Parenting" column by Vicky Lansky. Approved by Parents' Choice. Issued ten times a year.

Shop Talk. P.O. Box 64211, Lubbock, Texas 79424-4211. A newsletter offering a collection of parenting experiences written by its readers. Each issue covers one aspect of parenting. Traveling with children, learning at home, childhood friendships, and children's fears are examples of topics discussed. Issued bimonthly.

More than fifty back issues are available for $2.00 each. Titles/topics include the following:

All Night Long
Being a Mother
Birth
Birth Attendants
Child Care
Children and Their Friends
Children at Birth
Children's Fears
Circumcision
Cooking for a Family
Cooking with Children
Couple Relationships
Dads
Death of a Child
Discipline
Family Finances
Family Planning
Finding a Birth Attendant
Grandparents
Homebirth
How Children Learn
Immunizations
Learning at Home
Mother's Self-Esteem
Mothers at Home
Moving with Children
Naps (Part 1)
Naps (Part 2)
Nursing
Nursing in Public
Nursing More Than One
Pets
Potty Training
Pregnancy
Shopping with Children
Sibling Relationships
Sleeping Together/Nursing Beyond Infancy
Social Needs
The Family Bed
The Food We Eat
Traveling with Children
Two-Year-Olds
Vaginal Birth after Caesarean
Weaning (Part 1)
Weaning (Part 2)
When Parents Disagree

Working Mother. See "Periodicals" listed under "Work Options for Parents" in chapter 11.

Videotapes

For Adults

Parenting Tapes. This issue of the *Children's Video Report* contains reviews of fifteen quality videotapes for parents, with subjects ranging from bringing a newborn home to disciplining an older child. Single copies of this issue are available for $5.00. Contact *Children's Video Report*, 370 Court Street, #76, Brooklyn, New York 11231-4331. Phone: 718/935-0600. (Request issue #4 in volume 5.)

For Children

You Can Choose! series. Live Wire Video. This award-winning series of videotapes is designed to teach elementary school-age children lessons that contribute to high self-esteem, self-discipline, good decision-making, a sense of responsibility, and the ability to get along with others. *You Can Choose* combines comedy, drama, music, peer-education, role modeling, and a lively format that challenges young viewers. Each program in the series presents a dramatic skit depicting a real problem, which is eventually resolved by children. Tapes in the series (which can be purchased separately or as a collection) include (1) Cooperation, (2) Being Responsible, (3) Dealing with Feelings, (4) Saying No, (5) Doing the Right Thing, (6) Dealing with Disappointment, (7) Appreciating Yourself, (8) Asking for Help, (9) Being Friends, and (10) Resolving Conflicts. Available from Live Wire Video, 3315 Sacramento Street, San Francisco, California 94118. Phone: 415/564-9500 or 1/800-359-KIDS.

Audiocassettes

How to Be the Parent You Always Wanted to Be. By Adele Faber and Elaine Mazlish. This portable "parenting workshop," by the authors of the bestselling *Siblings without Rivalry* and *How to Talk So Kids Will Listen, and Listen So Kids Will Talk* is designed to help parents deal with children's strong emotions (as well as their own), set reasonable limits, express anger in appropriate ways, and resolve family conflicts. Contains two fifteen-minute audiocassettes plus a sixty-seven-page exercise workbook. Available from Childswork/-Childsplay (see chapter 27 for contact information).

The S.T.E.P. Audio Handbook. By American Guidance Service. Explains the basic concepts of S.T.E.P. (Systematic Training for Effective Parenting). Offers parenting techniques and suggestions for improving family communication. Explains how to help children learn to make their own decisions and deal with the consequences. On two cassettes. Available from the American Guidance Service. Phone: 1/800-328-2560.

Mail Order Catalogs

Cambridge Parenting and Family Life. This video catalog contains a wide selection of videotapes on parenting skills and techniques, child safety, health, child development, newborn care, breastfeeding, and related topics. Although the catalog is designed primarily for teachers, libraries, and media centers, parents with children from infancy through the teen years can find good tapes at reasonable prices ($29.95 and up) as well. For a copy, contact Cambridge Parenting, P.O. Box 2153, Department PA5, Charleston, West Virginia 25328-2153. Phone: 1/800-468-4227.

Childswork/Childsplay. Center for Applied Psychology, Inc., P.O. Box 1586, King of Prussia, Pennsylvania 19406. Phone: 1/800-962-1141. A collection of unique and hard to find products (toys, games, and books, primarily) "designed to teach children the values, self-confidence, and the courage they need to face the future, while retaining the fun and adventure of childhood." Items featured in this catalog (most created by educators and mental health professionals) include boardgames designed to help children better understand their feelings and fears, teach appropriate behavior, encourage cooperation, and promote self-esteem; dolls and playsets that encourage children to express themselves through imaginative play; and books (for children as well as adults) addressing common problems and concerns (handling bullies, behavioral problems, school success, divorce, learning disabilities, etc.). Parents can also join the Childswork Book Club and receive the quarterly Book Club News offering a wide range of books on helping children (parenting books, self-help books for children, therapeutic stories, and professional books on child psychology, among others).

Creative Parenting. Parenting Press, Inc., P.O. Box 75267, Seattle, Washington 98125. Phone: 1/800-992-6657. This catalog contains a collection of parenting books by respected authors such as Vicki Lansky, Elizabeth Crary, and Adele Faber and Elaine Mazlish. Also contains books to help children understand their feelings, solve problems, and develop self-esteem.

Family Communications. 4802 Fifth Avenue, Pittsburgh, Pennsylvania 15213. Phone: 412/687-2990. Fax: 412/687-1226. Originally formed as the production company for *Mr. Roger's Neighborhood*, this nonprofit company now offers a wide range of materials in a variety of media for children, parents, and professionals. Their product brochure is full of books (for both parents and children), audiocassettes, videotapes, activity kits, toys, and gifts. "Mister Rogers' First Experience Books" address common concerns of children: *The New Baby, Going to Day Care, Going to the Potty, Going to the Doctor, Making Friends, Moving, Going to the Hospital, When a Pet Dies, Going to the Dentist,* and *Going on an Airplane.* Each offers an inexpensive way for parents and children to explore "first experiences" together. A book and cassette titled *If We Were All the Same* helps children understand that it's human differences that make each individual special. Videocassettes help children understand the importance of communicating feelings, the difference between what is real and what is imagined, the value of love, and the joy of music. Books for adults include *Mister Rogers Talks with Parents, Mister Rogers' How Families Grow, Mister Rogers Talks with Families About Divorce,* and *Mister Rogers' Playbook: Insights and Activities for Parents and Children. Mister Rogers' Plan and Play Book,* which describes dozens of easy-to-do activities, is designed to complement the television program. This book also includes descriptions of each of the televisions programs, words to many of the songs, and a section with recipes and how-to information. Miniature neighborhood trolleys, shoelaces, duffle bags, sweatshirts, puppets, and backpacks are among the other items listed in this brochure.

Imprints. Birth and Life Bookstore, 7001 Alonzo Avenue, N.W., P.O. Box 70625, Seattle, Washington 98107-0625. Phone: 206/789-4444 or 1/800-736-0631 (orders only). A review newsletter and mail order catalog rolled into one, from the Birth and Life Bookstore. Each issue includes in-depth reviews of books on pregnancy, childbirth, and parenting. Review titles have included *Crying Baby, Sleepless Nights* by Sandy Jones; *How to Avoid Your Parents' Mistakes When You Raise Your Children* by Claudette Wassil-Grimm, and *The Nature of Birth and Breastfeeding* by M. Odent. Also includes brief descriptions of hundreds of other books on parenthood, toilet teaching, sleeping habits, child health and safety, child development, education, and other topics. Audiocassettes, videotapes, and informational brochures are also available by mail from the Birth and Life Bookstore.

Practical Parenting Catalogue: Vicki Lansky's Books by Mail. Practical Parenting, 18326 Minnetonka Boulevard, Deephaven, Minnesota 55391. Phone: 1/800-255-3379 or 612/475-3527 (customer service). Fax: 612/475-1505. Through this mail order service, parents can purchase all of the books penned by parenting expert Vicki Lansky. *Practical Parenting Tips* (over 1,500 helpful hints for the first five years), *Trouble-Free Travel with Children, Getting Your Child to Sleep, Feed Me I'm Yours, Games Babies Play, Baby Proofing Basics, Toilet Training,* and *100 Ways to Tell Your Child "I Love You"* are among the books featured in the catalog. Also offers a fold-up potty seat adapter, T-shirts that say "I'm the Big Brother" and "I'm the Big Sister," and perfect-for-your pocket song books (the words of favorite tunes) that sell for just $1.00. An eighty-four-page book called *The Best of Vicki Lansky's Practical Parenting Newsletter* (currently in its ninth year of publication) is free with orders over $20.

Parenting Classes

Active Parenting. A nationwide parenting education network. Check with local schools, churches, synagogues, or social service organizations to find out if the classes are offered in your community. Alternatively, you can call the Family Resource Coalition (see appendix I for contact information) for tips on locating parent education classes in your area.

Parent Effectiveness Training (PET). Phone: 1/800-628-1197. Teaches parents how to eliminate the power struggles that prevent effective communication. Call the above number for a directory of certified instructors in your state.

S.T.E.P. (Systematic Training for Effective Parenting). More than two million parents have participated in S.T.E.P. classes, which help moms and dads discover new ways to handle problems, build their child's self-confidence, set limits, and increase cooperation. The classes are offered through many adult education centers, as well as preschools and elementary schools. For information on groups near you—or on starting up a S.T.E.P. group—contact American Guidance Service, Publishers Building, Circle Pines, Minnesota 55014-1796. Phone: 1/800-328-2560. (Note: A videotape and print parenting course—designed to teach groups the basics of S.T.E.P.—is available as well. This three-part package covers early childhood, the middle years, and adolescence. Contact the American Guidance Service for more information.)

Helplines

The American Baby Helpline. Phone: 1/900-860-4888 (twenty-four-hour-a-day helpline operating seven days a week. The cost is 95¢ per minute). Prerecorded messages offer expert advice on a variety of baby-related topics. Following is a partial listing of available topics. A complete listing of topics can be found in a current issue of *American Baby* magazine (see listing under "Periodicals").

Birth to Six Months
Bathing (code 22)
Sleep problems (code 23)
Burping your baby (code 24)
Is baby eating enough? (code 25)
Taking baby outdoors (code 26)
Colic (code 27)
Pacifiers (code 28)
Understanding baby's cries (code 29)
Taking baby's temperature (code 30)
Giving solid foods (code 31)
Giving medicine (code 32)

Six to Eighteen Months
Immunization (code 33)
Weaning (code 34)
Treating a cold (code 35)
Diarrhea (code 36)
Finding a baby-sitter (code 37)
Language development (code 38)
Average height and weight (code 39)
Early discipline (code 40)

Eighteen Months to Three Years
Discipline without spanking (code 41)
First friends (code 42)
Nightmares (code 43)
Toilet training (code 44)
Bedtime problems (code 45)
Early learning (code 46)
Treating injuries (code 47)
Preparing for a sibling (code 48)
Finding a preschool (code 49)

Bright Beginnings Warmline. Phone: 412/641-4546 (Monday through Friday, 9 a.m. to 9 p.m., eastern standard time). A parent-support service of the Parental Stress Center at Magee-Womens Hospital in Pittsburgh. Trained volunteers will answer questions from concerned parents having to do with tantrums, sleep problems, bedwetting, and other topics.

Parenting Hotline. Phone: 1/900-535-MOMS (the cost is $1.95 for the first minute and 95¢ for each additional minute). A service of *Parenting* magazine and the National Parenting Center. Callers can select the age group of their choice (pregnancy, newborns, infants, toddlers, preschool, preteen, or adolescence) then choose a topic from the ever-changing menu. Child experts such as Penelope Leach, Thomas Armstrong, and Vicki Lansky can then be heard on prerecorded messages addressing topics such as bottlefeeding, ear infections, learning to read, and much more. Topics change daily. Alternatively, parents can leave a personalized question and will receive a written reply.

Parents Helpline. Phone: 1/900-903-KIDS. *Parents* magazine has set up a 900 number (the cost is 95¢ per minute) so that parents can receive prerecorded advice on various topics twenty-four hours a day. Following is a partial listing of available topics. A complete listing of topics can be found in *Parents* magazine (see listing under "Periodicals").

> Aggressive toddlers (code 02)
> Bed-wetting (code 05)
> Burping your baby (code 09)
> Hiccup cures (code 26)
> Hyperactivity (code 27)
> Nap-time tips (code 31)
> Potty accidents (code 33)
> Separation anxiety (code 36)
> Sleeping through the night (code 37)
> Starting to talk (code 39)
> Stopping the pacifier (code 40)

> Teething (code 43)
> Temper tantrums (code 44)
> Thumb sucking (code 45)
> Toilet teaching (code 53)

Parents Stressline. Phone: 1/800-421-0353 (Monday through Friday, 8:30 a.m. to 5:00 p.m., pacific standard time). A service of Parents Anonymous, a nonprofit program for parents who fear they will abuse their children. Trained staff members will help diffuse feelings of anger and hostility and refer callers to mental health professionals and community resources, when appropriate.

Television Programs

The American Baby TV Show. This thirty-minute program airs Sunday mornings at 11:00 a.m. (eastern standard time) on the Family Channel (FAM). This show explores various aspects of your young child's physical and emotional well-being. New format includes audience participation.

The Healthy Kids TV Show. Hosted by model and mother Kim Alexis, this cable television series provides parents and caregivers of children, newborn to age five, with current information on various aspects of children's health. Programs have explored crying and colic, sleep problems, childhood fears, sibling rivalry, separation and stranger anxiety, breast and bottlefeeding, toy safety, and playtime with baby, among many other topics. Produced by Cahners Childcare Group in association with the American Academy of Pediatrics, this thirty-minute program airs Sunday mornings at 11:30 a.m. (eastern standard time) on the Family Channel (FAM). Program guides are available from the Healthy Kids Show, 475 Park Avenue South, New York, New York 10016.

Dealing with Stress

Being a parent is the most demanding job in the world, yet most of us train "on the job." When things are going well, savor the moment. Give your child hugs and plenty of praise. Be generous with pats on the back for yourself and the other adults in your life, and don't be afraid to admit mistakes—your child will respect your honesty.

Sometimes things will not go well. You may feel stressed, overwhelmed. The way you deal with these times is important. Even young children can be helped to understand how you're feeling if you tell them. Tension relievers can help. Try some of these:

- Tell your child you need a break.

- Count to ten. Go to another room or outside for a few minutes. If your child is an infant or toddler, put him in a safe place first.

- Go into another room, close the door and let it out—cry or scream. For ten minutes, do whatever relaxes you best.

- Lie on the couch, put your feet up, and place a cool cloth on your eyes and forehead. Take a couple of deep breaths and think of a peaceful scene. Lie there for at least five minutes.

- Call someone who cares about you and understands what you're going through. Tell what's bothering you and get the support you need.

- If your children take naps, use that quiet time to pamper yourself. Take a bubble bath, read a book or listen to music with your eyes closed.

- Change your daily routine. Take a walk, visit a friend, watch a special program on television.

- Do something physical. Physical activity is good for you and your children. It lets off steam, and often it's free.

—From *Children: Virginia's Greatest Resource*, developed by the Virginia Department of Social Services, the National Committee for Prevention of Child Abuse (Virginia Chapter), and Parents Anonymous of Virginia, Inc.

What Every Baby Knows. Hosted by T. Berry Brazelton, this television program explores topics such as crying, sleep, discipline, childhood fears and fantasies, sibling rivalry, early learning, and separation and divorce. Presents the pediatrician in action, and the problems of real families. Can be viewed on Lifetime cable television. Check your program guide for times.

Your Baby and Child. Based on Penelope Leach's bestselling book (see listing under "Books"), this half-hour program explores topics such as sleep, bonding, spoiling, discipline, toilet training, and other issues of interest to parents of babies, toddlers, and preschoolers. Can be viewed on Lifetime cable television. Check your program guide for times.

Your Child Six to Twelve with Dr. Kyle Pruett. A parenting show focusing on older children, hosted by the author of *The Nurturing Father* and clinical professor of psychiatry at the Yale Child Study Center. This half-hour show answers parents' questions about self-esteem, peer pressure, morality, and more. Can be viewed on Lifetime cable television. Check your program guide for times.

Radio Program

The Parent's Journal. Hosted by Bobbie Conner, this highly acclaimed radio program covers a wide range of parenting topics, including newborn care, parent/teacher communication, and teaching racial equality to kids. Produced by Livy Morris Productions, this one-hour, weekly program currently airs on more than 110 public radio stations across the country. Call (or tune-in) to your local public broadcasting station to find out whether/when they air it.

PARENT SUPPORT: SERVICES AND RESOURCES

Book

Starting and Operating Support Groups: A Guide for Parents. By the Family Resource Coalition. Family Resource Coalition, 1992. 22 pages. A booklet for parents who are thinking of starting up a support group, produced by the Family Resource Coalition in cooperation with the American Self-Help Clearinghouse. Defines support groups, gives tips for planning meetings, and offers guidelines on maintaining a healthy group. Also contains advice from parents who have started up or run support groups. Appendices include sample flyers and meeting handouts, as well as a resource directory of publications and national organizations. Available from the Family Resource Coalition (see appendix I for contact information).

Associations

Depression after Delivery. P.O. Box 1282, Morrisville, Pennsylvania 19067. Phone: 215/295-3994. A nonprofit organization that supports women who are suffering from post-

partum depression. Serves as a national clearinghouse on postpartum depression. Distributes a quarterly newsletter.

Family Resource Coalition. 200 South Michigan Avenue, Suite 1520, Chicago, Illinois 60604. Phone: 312/341-0900. Fax: 312/341-9361. A coalition of family support professionals and others concerned with parenting, child development, and family issues. Seeks to improve the quality of family resource programs and to educate public, government, and corporate leaders on the needs of families. Conducts a resource and referral service for parents. Provides information on finding or starting up parents' groups. By calling or writing, you can get a list of the existing groups in your areas as well as a packet of information on how to start a group. Offers books and other resources materials, including *Starting and Operating Support Groups: A Guide for Parents* (see listing under "Books"). Also publishes the Family Resource Coalition *Report*, a quarterly exploring family policy, health and education issues, program design, and other topics (adoption, work and family, rural families, intergenerational programs, etc.). Produces a catalog that lists and describes available publications and services.

La Leche League International. See "Associations" listed under "Breastfeeding" in chapter 8.

MOPS (Mothers of Preschoolers) International, Inc. Phone: 303/733-5353. Founded in 1973, MOPS is a nonprofit, national support group with a Christian focus. Chapters across the country hold small discussion groups and regular group meetings (usually in churches of various denominations) that offer instruction on child rearing, marriage, home from a biblical perspective, and other topics. Individual groups also help mothers find encouragement and acceptance from other mothers, provide opportunities for women to volunteer in the group, and run preschool programs with planned activities and Christian teaching for children. Publishes a quarterly newsletter called *Connections*, which offers support and resource information.

Mothers Matter. 171 Wood Street, Rutherford, New Jersey 07070. Phone: 201/933-8191. Offers educational seminars and workshops designed to help mothers exchange ideas, find support, meet their own needs for personal growth, and increase their enjoyment of parenting. Seminars, which consist of five two-hour sessions (including one addressing the concerns of fathers), are primarily held in New York, New Jersey, Connecticut, and Pennsylvania, although the founder, Kay Willis, sometimes takes her seminars on the road.

National Association of Mother's Centers. 336 Fulton Avenue, Hempstead, New York 11550. Phone: 1/800-645-3828 or 516/486-6614. The parent organization for a national, nonprofit network of Mothers' Centers across the country. Mothers' Centers offer a place where mothers can come together for support, education, and professional training. They offer baby-sitting cooperatives, social activities, and educational programs on the developmental needs of children. They also conduct research on issues related to motherhood and help develop services to meet the needs of local mothers and families. The overall goal of these groups is to support and validate the important work of mothering.

New Parents' Network. 2827 North Cherry Avenue, Tucson, Arizona 85719. Phone: 602/327-1451. Computer bulletin board access number: 602/326-9345 (for those with a computer and a modem). This nonprofit organization operates a national computer bulletin board system that offers parenting information, guidelines on safety and poison control, product recall news, and information on social services and government agencies of interest to parents. Also allows parents the opportunity to share experiences and questions with each other.

Postpartum Support, International. 927 North Kellogg Avenue, Santa Barbara, California 93111. Phone: 805/967-7636. Aims to increase awareness of mental health related to childbearing. Offers educational programs and encourages research and the formation of support groups. Publishes *PSI News*, a quarterly.

For an additional listing of parent support groups, refer to "Parents at Home" in chapter 11.

MEETING BASIC NEEDS: CARING FOR YOUR INFANT AND YOUNG CHILD

Free and Inexpensive Resources

Better Baby Series. Pennypress. A series of four- to eight-page pamphlets discussing topics of interest to expecting and new mothers. Titles in the series include "A Working Mother Can Breastfeed When . . .," "The First Days after Birth: Care of Mother and Baby," "The Circumcision Decision," "The New Parent—Postpartum Adjustment," and "Siblings, Birth, and the Newborn." Four-page pamphlets are 50¢; eight-page pamphlets are $1.00. The series is available from Moonflower Birthing Supply Ltd., 2810 Wilderness Place, #D, Boulder, Colorado 80301. Phone: 303/440-5566 or 1/800-462-4784.

Off to a Sound Start. By J. B. McCracken. What can we expect our baby to learn during the first year of life? How will we know what our baby wants? What can we do to get our baby off to a sound start? Answers to these three basic questions can be found in this brochure. Includes a chart listing developmental milestones during baby's first twelve months. Available for 50¢ from the National Association for the Education of Young Children (see appendix I for contact information).

Books

The Baby Book: Everything You Need to Know about Your Baby from Birth to Age Two. By William Sears, M.D., and Martha Sears, R.N. Little Brown, 1993. 689 pages. A comprehensive guide to child care during the first two years of life. Among the many chapters are "Getting Attached—What It Means," "Get-

ting the Right Start With Your Newborn," "Bodywearing—the Art and Science of Carrying Your Baby," and "Caring for Your Baby's Bodily Needs" (diapering, cord care, bathing, a discussion of pacifiers and thumbsucking, and more). Also discusses breastfeeding, bottlefeeding, stages of development, nighttime parenting (including getting your baby to sleep), keeping baby safe and healthy, and working and parenting. The sections on bonding and pacifiers/thumbsucking are insightful, as are many other portions of the book.

Baby Skin. By Nelson Lee Novick, M.D. Clarkson Potter, 1991. 180 pages. A guide to infant and child skin care, written by a dermatologist. The first portion of the book covers basic care, including bathing, shampooing, diapering, and sun protection. Describes available cleansing products. The second part of the book covers skin problems (diagnosis and treatment), including rashes, eczemas, bug bites, moles, infections, and melanomas. Also covers hair and nail problems.

Caring for Your Baby and Young Child: Birth to Age 5. Steven P. Shelow, M.D., F.A.A.P., editor-in-chief; Robert E. Hannemann, M.D., F.A.A.P., associate medical editor. Bantam, 1991. 676 pages. From the American Academy of Pediatrics, this book discusses the basic care of infants, babies, toddlers, and preschoolers. Arranged according to the child's age, the first portion of the book offers information and advice on feeding, sleeping, bathing, diapering, toilet training, and other topics of daily importance. (For more information on this book, see "Books" listed under "General Resources" in this chapter.)

Dr. Spock's Baby and Child Care. By Benjamin Spock, M.D., and Michael B. Rothenberg, M.D. Sixth edition. Simon and Schuster, 1992. 832 pages. Offers information and advice on bathing, diapering, equipment and clothing, toilet teaching, sleeping, feeding, health care, safety, and other aspects of child care (from infancy through adolescence). Discusses common concerns (colic, teething, sleeping problems, childhood illnesses, separation anxiety, whining, aggression, sibling rivalry, stealing, lying, etc.), stages of development, and parenting approaches and techniques (discipline, talking about sex, children's emotional needs, and so forth). (For more information on *Dr. Spock's Baby and Child Care*, see "Books" listed under "General Resources" in this chapter.)

Infant Care. By the U.S. Department of Health and Human Services. U.S. Public Health Service, 1989. 109 pages. Offers tips on feeding, bathing, diapering, dressing, protecting, nurturing, and otherwise caring for your baby during the first year of life. Includes a chapter on how to prepare for baby's arrival (selecting a doctor, equipment you'll need, choosing diapers, etc.), as well as chapters on basic care, growth and development, health, safety, and first aid. One of the federal government's all time bestsellers. Available from the Superintendent of Documents (see appendix B for ordering information). Request S/N 017-091-00241-0 when ordering.

What to Expect the First Year. By Arlene Eisenberg, Heidi E. Murkoff, and Sandee E. Hathaway, B.S.N. Workman, 1989. 671 pages. A first-year child-care manual from the authors of *What to Expect When*

You're Expecting. Includes a section called "The Baby Care Primer," which offers practical advice on bathing, burping, diapering, dressing, carrying, and otherwise caring for babies. (For more information on *What to Expect the First Year*, see "Books" listed under "General Resources" in chapter 1.)

Your Baby and Child: From Birth to Age Five. By Penelope Leach. New edition, revised and expanded. Alfred A. Knopf, 1989. 553 pages. Explains how to feed, bathe, dress, and otherwise care for your baby and young child. (For more information on this book, see "Books" listed under "General Resources" in this chapter.)

Periodicals

American Baby. Cahners Publishing Co., 475 Park Avenue South, New York, New York 10016. Phone: 212/689-3600. A monthly magazine for expectant and new parents with an emphasis on the physical and mental well-being of baby and mother. Covers topics in health, safety, and basic care (feeding, bathing, and otherwise caring for an infant). Offers advice on topics such as health and safety, toilet training, and traveling with children. Also provides information on baby products, including clothing and furniture. Issued monthly.

Baby Talk. Parenting Unlimited, Inc., 636 Sixth Avenue, New York, New York 10011. Phone: 212/989-8181. Magazine covering baby care and the challenges of being a new parent. Health, safety, food and nutrition, stages of development, and traveling with children are among the topics explored. Issued monthly.

Birth to Three and Beyond. 3411 Willamette Street, Eugene, Oregon 97405. Phone: 503/484-4401. A newsletter covering topics of interest to families with young children, including everyday care, discipline, and nutrition. Issued bimonthly.

Ready for Baby. The Parenting Group, 25 West Forty-third Street, New York, New York 10036. Phone: 212/840-4200. An annual guide to baby care and baby products, produced in cooperation with the International Childbirth Education Association. Offers advice on bathing, feeding, dressing, and otherwise caring for a baby during the first year of life. Articles also cover health, safety, travel, stages of development, buying baby equipment, and survival tactics for new moms and dads.

Videotapes

Baby Basics. Vida Health Communications. Running time: 110 minutes. Meant for first-time parents, this videotape discusses daily care of the infant, feeding, baby's sleeping and crying, general health, safety, growth, and development. Talks about the newborn at birth, the first days at home, and self-care (postpartum). Includes demonstrations and diagrams.

Caring for Your Newborn with Dr. Benjamin Spock. VidAmerica. Running time: 111 minutes. Dr. Spock talks with new parents about everyday concerns of raising a baby and demonstrates care techniques. Bathing, feeding, fever, and comforting are among the topics covered.

Infant Health Care. Johnson and Johnson. Running time: 45 minutes. A video guide for new parents, covering daily care. Also explains how to recognize signs of common illness in infants. Comes with a quick-reference video guidebook. Available by mail from the ICEA Bookcenter, ICEA, P.O. Box 20048, Minneapolis, Minnesota 55420. Phone: 1/800-624-4934.

Touchpoints. Goodtimes Home Video. Three cassettes. Created and hosted by T. Berry Brazelton, this series guides new parents through the early stages of their child's life. Volume one covers pregnancy, birth, and the first weeks of life; volume two covers the first month through the first year; volume three covers age one through toddlerhood. Bonding, cognitive and motor development, teething, sibling rivalry, discipline, and toilet training are some of the topics the renowned pediatrician touches upon. *Parenting* magazine says these videos are "the most practical and intelligent baby care guide available for home viewing." Available from ConsumerVision. Phone: 1/800-756-8792. (For information on Brazelton's book by the same name, see "Books" listed under "General Resources" in chapter 1.)

What Every Baby Knows series. IVE. Running time: 60 minutes each. Each video in this four-part series focuses on a specific topic. Parents of newborns will be interested in "Most Common Questions about Newborns," which offers reassuring advice from T. Berry Brazelton. Other tapes in the series include "On Being a Father," "The Working Parent," and "A Guide to Pregnancy and Childbirth."

Your Baby: A Video to Care and Understanding. With Penelope Leach. Sidney Place Communications, 1989. Running time: 75 minutes. Demonstrates techniques of everyday care. Explains what baby needs in a variety of situations during the first three months of life.

Mail Order Catalogs

Baby Basics. 4809 Avenue N, Brooklyn, NY 11234. Phone: 718/531-3992. Among the items offered for sale in this catalog are baby carriers, cloth diapers, baby toiletries (talc-free powder and all-natural moisturizers), lambskins (including car seat covers), 100% organic cotton clothing for babies, and a variety of products for nursing mothers.

Hand in Hand. Catalogue Center, Route 26, RR 1, Box 1425, Oxford, Maine 04270-9711. Phone: 1/800-872-9745. Baby strollers, safety devices, feeding products, clothes organizers, and books and toys for tots are among the items offered for sale in this attractive catalog.

Moonflower Natural Parenting Catalog. 2810 Wilderness Place, #D, Boulder, Colorado 80301. Phone: 303/440-5566 or 1/800-462-4784. A new mail order catalog from Moonflower, containing baby carriers, safety products, baby blankets, lambskins, cotton diapers and covers, and a fanny-style diaper bag (among many other items). Moonflower also produces a birthing supply catalog and a gift catalog for mothers and midwives.

The Natural Baby Catalog. 114 West Franklin, Suite S, Pennington, New Jersey 08534. Phone: 609/737-2895. This catalog contains all-natural products such as Tom's of Maine baby shampoo and toothpaste and Weleda Calendula baby soap and baby oil; a potty chair, high chair, and hand-made cradle (each made from solid wood); bedding; clothes (including hats and booties); baby-safe stuffed animals; infant carriers; American-made lambskin rugs; wooden toys; and books (some for children, others for adults). Also contains homeopathic medicines and other health-care products, as well as items for mom (a breast pump kit, nursing pads, nursing bras and nightgowns, and reusable cloth menstrual pads). Offers diapering products as well.

One Step Ahead. P.O. Box 517, Lake Bluff, Illinois 60044. Phone: 1/800-274-8440. This catalog contains "thoughtfully selected products to help with baby . . . every step of the way." Within these pages, you'll find top-name diaper covers, cotton flannel diapers, bedding, feeding accessories, toilet teaching aids, health care products, bathing items, safety devices, travel accessories, and toys.

The Perfectly Safe Catalog. See listing under "Mail Order Catalogs" in chapter 7.

The Right Start. Right Start Plaza, 5334 Sterling Center Drive, Westlake Village, California 91361. Phone: 1/800-548-8531. Recipient of the Parents' Choice Approval Award, this catalog contains scores of items to help parents through the first few years of their child's life. Includes portable cribs, changing tables, diapering products (diaper covers and the Kooshies® all-in-one diaper, for example), feeding accessories (bottle warmers, baby food carousels, travel sipper cups, thermal travel bags, bottle drying racks, etc.), bedding, breast pumps, safety items (gates, electric outlet plates, and a fire escape ladder, for example), health-care products, bicycle seats and safety helmets, backpacks and front packs, strollers, toilet training items, and toys (both indoor and outdoor).

Sassy. 1534 College S.E., Grand Rapids, Michigan 49507. Phone: 616/243-0767. Fax: 616/243-1042. This catalog contains MAM feeding accessories (fork and spoon sets, feeding bowls, dinner sets, bottles, sipper cups, nipples, a breast pump, portable highchair, and baby food carousel), as well as pacifiers, comb and brush sets, potties, bathing items (an inflatable baby bath and sit 'n' splash bath seat), and health care products (a warm mist vaporizer, emergency medical treatment handbook, and a kit containing a thermometer, nasal aspirator, pill case, infant nail clippers, and oral medicine syringe). Sassy products are also sold through retail outlets such as Toys 'R' Us, Wal-Mart, JC Penney, Giant Foods, and Child World.

For other suppliers of baby and child care products, see Juvenile Products, appendix A. The "Product Listing by Category" index will be especially useful to those in search of specific products.

Association

American Academy of Pediatrics. 141 Northwest Point Boulevard, P.O. Box 927, Elk Grove Village, Illinois 60009-0927. Phone: 708/228-5005 or 1/800-433-9016. An organization of forty-four thousand pediatricians dedicated to the health, safety, and well-being of infants, children, adolescents, and young adults. While the academy primarily serves pediatricians and other health professionals, many of its publications are geared toward parents and are available through pediatric offices. Available brochures include *Diaper Rash*, which discusses the causes and prevention of diaper rash; *A Guide to Children's Dental Health*, offering practical advice on everything from teething to thumb sucking; and *Newborns: Care of the Uncircumcised Penis*, which offers guidelines on caring for the uncircumcised penis. Ask your pediatrician for a copy of any of these brochures or send a self-addressed, stamped envelope to the academy. Include the name of the brochure on the envelope. (The academy cannot fulfill requests that do not include a return envelope.) (For more information on the American Academy of Pediatrics, see "Associations" listed under "General Resources" in chapter 6.)

MULTIPLES (TWINS, TRIPLETS, AND BEYOND)

Books

Keys to Parenting Twins. By Karen Kerkhoff Gromada and Mary C. Hurlburt. Barrons, 1992. 181 pages. Covers various aspects of parenting twins, including questions to ask the obstetrician, information on family adjustments, the different bonding process, issues of individuality, and the twins' changing relationships as they mature, among other topics.

Make Room for Twins. By Terry Pink Alexander. Bantam, 1987. 408 pages. A guide to pregnancy, delivery, and the childhood years (infancy through age five). Topics covered include equipment for baby and baby, identifying and encouraging individual differences, development during the first five years, and managing a household with twin occupants.

Periodicals

Double Feature. Parents of Multiple Births Association of Canada, Inc., 4981 Highway No. 7 E, Unit 12A, Suite 161, Markham, Ontario, Canada L3R 1N1. Phone: 416/513-7506. A newsletter for parents of twins, triplets, and quadruplets. Covers issues of special interest to parents of multiples. Issued quarterly. Includes articles written by parents and professionals in the fields of health and education.

Double Talk. Karen Kerkhoff Gromada, Box 412, Department ND, Amelia, Ohio 45102. Phone: 513/231-8946. Contains news items and feature articles of interest to parents of twins, triplets, etc., and professionals who deal with multiples and their families. Also includes book reviews, interviews, child care tips, and product information. Issued quarterly.

MOTC's Notebook. National Organization of Mothers of Twins Clubs, Inc., P.O. Box 23188, Albuquerque, New Mexico 87192-1188. Phone: 505/275-0955. Contains reports on recent research, general articles of interest to mothers of twins, and news of interest to organization members. Issued quarterly.

The Triplet Connection. P.O. Box 99571, Stockton, California 95209. Phone: 209/474-0885. A newsletter providing information for families who are either expecting or already have triplets, quadruplets, or quintuplets. Issued quarterly.

Twin Services Reporter. Twin Services, P.O. Box 10066, Berkeley, California 94709. Phone: 510/524-0863. Offers information and advice concerning the care and development of multiples (twins, triplets, quadruplets, and quintuplets). Explores the challenge of breastfeeding multiples, twin relationships, and other topics. Issued quarterly. Price is included in agency membership (contact Twin Services for more information).

Twins Magazine. Twins Customer Service, P.O. Box 12045, Overland Park, Kansas 66282-2045. Phone: 913/722-1090 or 1/800-821-5533. A national magazine offering support and information about giving birth and rearing multiples (twins, triplets, etc.).

Associations

Center for the Study of Multiple Birth. 333 East Superior Street, Suite 464, Chicago, Illinois 60611. Phone: 312/266-9093. A research foundation concerned with the study of multiple birth and the care of multiple birth children. Operates a mail order book business for parents of multiples. Serves as a resource center.

National Organization of Mothers of Twins Clubs. National Organization of Mothers of Twins Clubs, Inc., P.O. Box 23188, Albuquerque, New Mexico 87192-1188. Phone: 505/275-0955. Makes information about twins available to the public. Maintains an ongoing bibliography of books on caring for twins. Also publishes *MOTC's Notebook* (see listing under "Periodicals").

The Triplet Connection. P.O. Box 99571, Stockton, California 95209. Phone: 209/474-0885. A support group for parents and expectant parents of triplets or large multiple births. Offers information on twin care, including breastfeeding, clothing, and medical care. Publishes *The Triplet Connection* (see listing under "Periodicals").

Twins Foundation. P.O. Box 6043, Providence, Rhode Island 02940-6043. Phone: 401/274-TWIN. Gathers and disseminates information on twins and research on twins. Compiles statistics and offers research assistance. Publishes *The Twins Letter*, a quarterly newsletter.

TOPIC-BY-TOPIC: A PARENTING COMPENDIUM

Bonding and Attachment

Books

The Earliest Relationship. By T. Berry Brazelton and Bertrand G. Cramer. Addison-Wesley/Lawrence, 1990. 251 pages. Explores mother-infant interaction, integrating recent research findings on infant development.

Mother-Infant Bonding: A Scientific Fiction. By Diane E. Eyer. Yale University Press, 1992. 237 pages. Traces the history of "the bonding myth," which has led mothers to believe that they must be physically close to their infants immediately after birth in order for the future parent/child relationship to develop properly. Explains the lack of validity in early studies of mother/infant bonding and discusses its continuing popularity.

On Becoming a Family: The Growth of Attachment. By T. Berry Brazelton. Revised edition. Delacorte, 1992. 217 pages. Traces the process of attachment as it develops throughout pregnancy and beyond birth.

Parent-Infant Bonding. By Marshall H. Klaus and John Kennell. Mosby, 1982. 314 pages. A standard on parent-infant bonding and attachment. Marshall Klaus, a distinguished neonatologist, is also the author of *The Amazing Newborn* and other works.

Bonding—Myth and Fact

Many people give the term "bonding" a literal meaning. They fear that any parent who fails to touch her child within the first few hours of birth may suffer permanent alienation. However, there is little evidence to support this popular belief. In fact, for the past thirty or forty years and until very recently, most parents who gave birth in hospitals had no early contact with their newborns, yet almost all of them bonded with—became emotionally attached to—their children.

The Amazing Newborn (Addison-Wesley: 1985), Dr. Marshall Klaus and Phyllis Klaus write that "The process of becoming attached to one's infant occurs at different times for different people. For some parents, it develops during pregnancy; for other parents, it happens during the first moments after birth; and for many others, not until they are home from the hospital taking care of their infants for the first time alone. Fully 40 percent of perfectly normal mothers take a week or longer to feel the baby is truly theirs."

Crying

Inexpensive Resource

When Babies Cry. This pamphlet, from La Leche League International, helps mothers understand why babies cry and offers helping hints for soothing one who is. Available for 50¢ from La Leche League International (see appendix I for contact information).

Books

Crying: The Mystery of Tears. By William H. Frey II. Harper and Row, 1985. 204 pages. In researching the biochemical aspects of crying, the author of this book found a difference in the chemical consistency of emotional tears and irritant tears (those caused by onions, dust particles, etc.) Believes that crying serves an important purpose. "Crying it out," he believes, may literally be a way the human body rids itself of stress-induced chemicals.

Crying Babies, Sleepless Nights. By Sandy Jones. Revised edition. Harvard Common Press, 1992. 162 pages. Explains why babies cry and what parents can do to soothe them. Disagrees with those who feel crying is good for a baby and criticizes programs that promise magic cures for infant crying and night waking. Feels that the baby's need for attention is reasonable and that many popular strategies discourage a parent's instinctive response.

The Crying Baby. By Sheila Kitzinger. Viking Penguin, 1989. 294 pages. Explains why babies cry, how parents feel about it (usually not very good), and what they can do about it.

Keys to Calming the Fussy Baby. By William Sears, M.D. Barrons, 1991. 170 pages. Offers pediatric advice on dealing with fussy babies. Part of the Parenting Keys series.

The Self-Calmed Baby: A Revolutionary New Approach to Parenting Your Infant. By William Sammons, M.D., with a foreword by T. Berry Brazelton. Little, Brown, 1989. 254 pages. Based on the theory that every baby is capable of calming himself, this book explains how parents can help their infants achieve independence. Talks about the importance of learning how to interpret and respond to baby's signals; demonstrates how very young children are capable of using techniques to protect themselves from an oftentimes overstimulating environment.

Helpline

The American Baby Helpline. Phone: 1/900-860-4888 (twenty-four-hour-a-day helpline operating seven days a week. The cost is 95¢ per minute). Prerecorded messages offer expert advice on a variety of baby-related topics. For advice on "understanding baby's cries" dial the above number, then code "29."

Diapering

Free and Inexpensive Resources

All about Diapering. A diapering booklet available from Biobottoms (see listing under "Cloth Diapers").

Shows how to diaper a baby using cloth diapers, offers guidelines on preventing diaper rash, and provides tips on making diapering time pleasurable. Strongly advocates the use of

Keeping Your Baby Clean

Baby Powder. Many pediatricians discourage the use of talc. When accidentally inhaled, it can cause potentially serious health problems, including pneumonia. If you decide to use power, very gently shake a small amount onto your hands (away from the baby's face) and apply it very carefully.

Laundry Detergent. Avoid detergents containing bleach, dyes, perfumes, and fabric softeners, since they can irritate sensitive skin. Ivory Snow or Dreft are among the recommended choices.

Shampoos. Choose a mild, no-tears shampoo such as Johnson's tear-free baby shampoo or Mennen's hypoallergenic formula.

Soaps. Ones recommended by leading dermatologists for baby's sensitive skin include Basis, fragrance-free Dove, and fragrance-free Neutrogena.

Wipes. Many brands contain alcohol and other drying agents that can harm baby's skin. Use a washcloth—or look for alcohol- and fragrance-free brands.

Bathing Tips

From *Infant Care*, produced by the U.S. Department of Health and Human Services.

During the first week, before the umbilical cord has fallen off and the navel heals, wash your baby with a cloth and warm water. Baby's face and diaper area require frequent washing—food, urine and bowel movements can irritate the skin. The rest of his or her body may need washing only several times a week.

After the first week or two, you may find it more convenient to give your baby a bath in a plastic tub or dishpan. To get ready:

- Bring your basin or dishpan containing an inch or two of warm (not hot) water into a warm room.

- Place the basin on a table or counter top of convenient height. Check with your hand to be sure the water is not too hot.

- Place a small towel or diaper in the bottom of the basin to keep your baby from slipping.

- Gather a bar of mild soap, a wash cloth, and a towel.

Now that you are ready, follow these steps:

- Hold your baby with one hand for safety.

- Wash baby's head and face first while the water and wash cloth are cleanest. You don't need soap for the face.

- Use your hand to lather the rest of baby's body with soap. Wash your girl's labia and your boy's penis just as you wash any other part of their bodies.

- You may find it easier to wash your baby on the table on a towel, and use the tub only for rinsing.

- Rinse your baby thoroughly with the wash cloth—at least two rinsings.

- Wrap your baby in a towel and pat dry.

- Give your baby a hug!

Here is more advice:

- Never, never leave the baby alone in the water for any reason whatsoever. The bath is never safe, no matter how little water you may use.

- If the telephone or doorbell rings, or your 2-year-old hollers, wrap your baby (soap and all) in a towel and put the baby under your arm. If there is a real crisis or emergency, you can put the baby in a safe place where he or she cannot fall (out of reach of pets and children) such as a playpen or on the floor.

- Always check the water temperature with your hand. Hot water, even from the tap, can cause scalds and burns! If you aren't sure how hot is safe, ask your doctor or clinic.

- Don't try to clean the ears, nose, navel, genitals or anus with cotton-tipped sticks. Anything you can't clean with a corner of a wash cloth doesn't need cleaning.

- Don't use a special disinfectant soap unless your doctor tells you to. Plain soap is best. Too much soap can be almost as irritating to the skin as dirt or soiled diapers.

- Wash baby's hair with a non-irritating baby shampoo about once a week, or more frequently if your baby has a scaly, waxy head rash ("cradle cap")

- Bathe the soft spot on baby's head just as you do the rest of the head.

cloth diapers. Points out why disposable diapers are an environmental hazard. For a copy, call 1/800-766-1254.

Diaper Rash. A brochure produced by the American Academy of Pediatrics explaining what causes—and how to prevent—diaper rash. Ask your pediatrician for a copy or send a self-addressed, stamped envelope to American Academy of Pediatrics, "Diaper Rash" (see appendix I for contact information).

Is Your Baby Wet?

Diaper Check is a monitor that measures moisture through a baby's clothes and displays it on an LCD. Available from Diaper Check. Phone: 1/800-322-7638.

Cloth Diapers

Baby Bunz and Co. P.O. Box 1717, Sebastopol, California 95473. Phone: 707/829-5347 or 1/800-676-4559. Specializes in Nikky diaper covers and natural baby products. This catalog also includes 100 percent cotton layettewear, blankets, wooden rattles, and more.

Babyworks. 11725 Northwest West Road #2, Portland, Oregon 97229. Phone: 503/645-4349 or 1/800-422-2910. This catalog contains velcro diaper covers in many styles (including wool and cotton), Bumkins® all-in-ones, training pants, flushable cotton liners, prefolded and no-folds diapers, unbleached diapers, diaper bags, baby washcloths, natural baby cream and powder, waterproof sheets, and other related products. The catalog also offers guidelines for washing cloth diapers and suggestions for a diapering layette.

Biobottoms. P.O. Box 6009, Petaluma, California 94953. Phone: 1/800-766-1254. Sells an assortment of Biobottom diaper covers (made from lamb's wool), 100 percent cotton diaper covers, cloth diapers (including some that are undyed, unbleached, and unprocessed), Rubber Duckies® (pull-on or velcro-closing pants), cotton liners, and training pants, as well as diaper bags, specially formulated detergent for diaper covers, a soiled diaper squeezer, portable potty, and the *Once Upon a Potty*

doll and book set. Also offers a free diapering booklet, "All about Diapering" (see listing under "Free and Inexpensive Resources"), and runs the "Diapering Smart-line" (call 1/800-766-1254 for information on cloth versus single-use diapers).

Bumpkins® Family Products. Phone: 602/254-2626. Offers an all-in-one diaper, combining diaper and cover in one garment. Also sells waterproof diaper covers (along with contoured diapers that fit inside these covers), waterproof pull-on pants, and waterproof diaper totes for carrying clean or dirty diapers on outings. Call for a product brochure and a list of mail order companies and retail outlets that carry these products.

Diaperaps. P.O. Box 3050, Granada Hills, California 91344. Phone: 1/800-477-3424. Product list includes diaper covers, waterproof pull-on pants, training pants, nighttime pants, and diapers (prefolded, contoured, and doublers), all invented by a mother.

Family Clubhouse. 6 Chiles Avenue, Asheville, North Carolina 28803. Phone: 1/800-876-1574. Offers Nikky and Family Clubhouse diaper covers in cotton, cotton terry, and polyester fabrics; diapers (contoured and prefolds); diaper liners; diaper doublers; and training pants. Also sells unbleached, undyed cottonwear, including crib sheets and receiving blankets.

Nikky. Phone: 1/800-67-NIKKY. Offers velcro-close diaper covers in cotton, wool, or polyester; contoured diapers to fit Nikky covers; and a cover with a built-in diaper. Also sells training pants, shorts with built-in training pants, T-shirts that match covers, and bedwetter pants that look like underwear (for children ages three to fifteen). Nikky covers are

The Case for Cloth Diapers

Although first introduced to parents only twenty-five years ago, disposable diapers have virtually replaced cloth diapers and now dominate the market. However, disposables are far from an ideal choice. Critics point out not only environmental drawbacks to disposables but health and economic drawbacks as well. Here is a brief sampling of the arguments that have been most often raised in favor off cloth diapers.

Economics

The following cost comparison appeared in the January 1994 issue of *The Natural Baby Catalog.*

Disposables 12 per day at 22 cents each = $79/month

Cloth (Through Diaper Service) $10/week for service + 24 covers at $11 each = $49/month

Cloth (Laundered at Home) 60 diapers + 24 covers at $11 each + 2 half-washloads/week = $19/month

Environmental Benefit

The effect of disposable diapers on our resources and environment is considerable; more than 800 million pounds of paper is used up each year to produce disposables, which in turn cannot be recycled and must be incinerated or buried in landfills. According to a 1972 study by the U.S. Environmental Protection Agency, a significant amount of polio and intestinal viruses survive in disposables long after they are discarded. Cloth diapers, of course, solve those problems.

On the negative side, the frequent laundering of cloth diapers can have harmful effects on the environment as well, particularly if bleach or non-biodegradable detergents are used.

Health Benefit

Disposables may cause rashes far more often than cloth diapers. A study of one-month-olds reported in the September 1979 issue of the *Journal of Pediatrics* found that among babies wearing disposables, 54 percent developed rashes and 16 percent had severe rashes, whereas among babies wearing cloth, only 18 percent had any rashes and none had severe rashes.

It is still unclear why disposables lead to more rashes. Allergic reactions to chemicals used in their construction might be one explanation, or it might be the lack of air circulation and greater warmth typically caused by disposables. Or it might simply be that babies wearing disposables are changed less often than other babies because there are fewer signals when the diaper is wet.

available from a variety of sources, including the Natural Baby Catalog (for contact information, see chapter 27, "Mail Order Catalogs") and Family Clubhouse (see separate listing).

The R. Duck Company, Inc. 650 Ward Drive, Suite H, Santa Barbara, California 93111. Phone: 1/800-422-DUCK (3825). Sells the original Rubber Duckie® pull-on diaper covers and Wrap Ups® diaper covers with velcro closures. Sizes from preemie to thirty-five-plus pounds. Catalog also contains bibs, aprons, rainwear, and more. Company established in 1983 by a mother of three.

Other Suppliers: Diapers, diaper covers, and diapering accessories can also be purchased from One Step Ahead, The Right Start, and The Natural Baby Catalog (see chapter 27 for contact information). See also: Diaper Bags, Diaper Covers/Wraps, Diaper Pails, Diapers (Cloth), and Diaper Stackers listed in the "Product Listing by Category" in appendix A.

Toilet Teaching

Some signs of readiness:

- Your child understands what the potty is used for.
- She wants to accompany you to the toilet.
- She asks you to change her diaper when it's wet or dirty.
- She stays dry for longer periods of time and wakes up dry after naps.
- She lets you know when she's urinating or having a bowel movement.
- She wants to wear a pair of underwear.

Free and Inexpensive Resources

Developing Toilet Habits. Part of Ross Laboratories' Growth and Development series, this booklet offers parents guidance on toilet training their children. Discusses readiness, how to begin, washing up afterwards, and related topics. Ross Laboratories, makers of Similac® and Isomil® provides this booklet to health care professionals as an aid in counseling patients. Ask your physician for a copy.

Toilet Training. Brochure explaining when it is (and isn't) appropriate to begin toilet training. Also explains a step-by-step training process. Available from the American Academy of Pediatrics. Ask your pediatrician for a copy or send a self-addressed, stamped envelope to American Academy of Pediatrics, "Toilet Training" (see appendix I for contact information).

Books

The Growing Years: A Guide to Your Child's Emotional Development from Birth to Adolescence. By the New York Hospital/Cornell Medical Center Department of Psychiatry with Mark Rubinstein, M.D. Simon and Schuster, 1989. 386 pages. Covers toilet training of boys and girls, fear of toilet training, readiness, and other aspects. (For more information on *The Growing Years*, see "Books" listed under "General Resources" in this chapter.)

No More Diapers! By J. G. Brooks, M.D., and members of the staff of the Boston Children's Hospital. Revised edition. Delta/Lawrence, 1991. This two-part guide (one section for girls, another for boys) shows how two children (Johnny and Susie) learn to use the potty and how they feel (good!) after mastering the task.

Once upon a Potty (His and Hers). By Alona Frankel. Barron's, 1980 and 1984. 43 pages. A child's introduction to the potty and its use. Also available: (1) The books plus anatomically correct dolls with their own toy potties and (2) his and her videotapes based on the bestselling books, thirty minutes in length. These items are available from Hand in Hand (see chapter 27 for contact information).

Parents Book of Toilet Teaching. By Joanna Cole. Ballantine, 1983. 127 pages. Explains how to ease the transition from diapers to underwear, how to alleviate stress and reinforce success, how to talk to your child about the potty, and what to do about bedwetting.

Toilet Learning: The Picture Book Technique for Children and Parents. By Alison Mack. Little, Brown, 1983. 109 pages. A book in two parts, including the "Parents' Guide to Toilet Learning" and an illustrated "Child's Guide to Toilet Learning." A unique approach.

Toilet Training: A Practical Guide to Daytime and Nighttime Training. By Vicki Lansky. Revised and updated. Bantam, 1993. 107 pages. Helpful advice on readiness, rewards, choosing a potty seat, and dealing with accidents and regression. Complete with an expanded section on bedwetting. Information on diaper and toilet training products is also included.

Your Baby and Child: From Birth to Age Five. By Penelope Leach. New edition, revised and expanded. Alfred A. Knopf, 1989. 553 pages. Explains how to decide on the right time for introducing the potty, and offers advice on going about it. (For more information on *Your Baby and Child,* see "Books" listed under "General Resources" in this chapter.)

Your Child's Health: The Parent's Guide to Symptoms, Emergencies, Common Illnesses, Behavior, and School Problems. By Barton D. Schmitt, M.D., F.A.A.P. Bantam, 1991. Discusses toilet-training readiness, the training process, and prevention of problems. Also explores toilet-training resistance. (For more information on *Your Child's Health,* see "Books" listed under "General Resources" in this chapter.)

Videotapes

It's Potty Time. Learning through Entertainment, Inc. Running time: 28 minutes. A musical video that uses easy-to-understand language, child actors, and sing-along songs to inspire and inform soon-to-be potty users (and their parents). Approved by the Duke University Medical Center. Recommended for children ages 2 and up.

Once upon a Potty (for Him and Her). See listing under "Books."

Helpline

Parents Helpline. Phone: 1/900-903-KIDS. *Parents* magazine has set up a 900 number (the cost is 95¢ per minute) so that parents can receive advice on various topics twenty-four hours a day. Enter the number "33" after dialing the main number for information on potty "accidents." Enter the number "53" for information on toilet teaching.

Helpful Tip: If your child wets his bed at night, you can remove the odor in the sheets and blankets by taking them outdoors to dry. Since there is no bacteria in urine, wet bedding does not present a health risk.

Toilet Teaching Aids

Portable Potty. A potty seat that fits all standard toilets and can be folded up and taken along on trips. Has protective covers over the hinges to prevent pinching and a locking system for stability. Available from Hand in Hand (see chapter 27 for contact information).

Tinkle Targets. Packages that encourage boys to aim more carefully. Contains forty-five flushable targets with cows, cats, dogs, fish, and other animals printed on them. They float on water until hit directly. Available from Hand in Hand (see chapter 27 for contact information).

Two-Stage Toilet Trainer. Serves as both a potty seat and toilet trainer. During stage one, the seat sits low to the ground. Later, the top portion fits over a standard size toilet, while the lower part serves as a stepping stool to get up there (with handles for support). Available from The Right Start Catalog (see chapter 27 for contact information).

Additional Toilet Teaching Aids. See "Toilet Training Items," listed in the "Product Listing by Category" in appendix A.

Bed-Wetting (Concerns as Your Child Grows Older)

Books

For Adults

Caring for Your Baby and Young Child: Birth to Age 5. Steven P. Shelov, M.D., F.A.A.P., editor-in-chief; Robert E. Hannemann, M.D., F.A.A.P., associate medical editor. Bantam, 1991. 676 pages. Offers information and advice concerning bedwetting. (For more information on *Caring for Your Baby and Young Child,* see "Books" listed under "General Resources" in this chapter.)

The Growing Years: A Guide to Your Child's Emotional Development from Birth to Adolescence. By the New York Hospital/Cornell Medical Center Department of Psychiatry with Mark Rubinstein, M.D. Simon and Schuster, 1989. 386 pages. Explores the causes of bed-wetting and explains how to handle it. (For more information on *The Growing Years,* see "Books" listed under "General Resources" in this chapter.)

Toilet Training: A Practical Guide to Daytime and Nighttime Training. By Vicki Lansky. Revised and updated. Bantam, 1993. 107 pages. This revised edition includes an expanded section on bed-wetting. (For more information on this book, refer to "Books" listed under "Toilet Teaching.")

Your Baby and Child: From Birth to Age Five. By Penelope Leach. New edition, revised and expanded. Alfred A. Knopf, 1989. 553 pages. Discusses the problem of bed-wetting and offers reassuring advice. (For more information on *Your Baby and Child,* see "Books" listed under "General Resources" in this chapter.)

Your Child's Health: The Parent's Guide to Symptoms, Emergencies, Common Illnesses, Behavior, and School Problems. By Barton D. Schmitt, M.D., F.A.A.P. Bantam, 1991. 672 pages. Explains the characteristics and causes of bed-wetting, and offers guidance on handling it. Discusses bed-wetting alarms, as well as other techniques for staying dry all night. (For more information on *Your Child's Health*, see "Books" listed under "General Resources" in this chapter.)

Your Growing Child: From Babyhood through Adolescence. By Penelope Leach. Alfred A. Knopf, 1986. 732 pages. Discusses various aspects of bed-wetting. Explains how to protect/wash the bedding, when to seek help for a child who still wets the bed, and what kind of help is available. Describes enuresis alarms and drugs for bed-wetting, along with other methods of treatment. (For more information on *Your Growing Child*, see "Books" listed under "General Resources" in this chapter.)

For Children

Dry All Night: A Picture Book Technique that Stops Bedwetting. By Alison Mack. Little, Brown, 1989. 174 pages. offers a step-by-step program for curing bed-wetting in school-aged children, with separate sections for parent and child.

Sammy the Elephant and Mr. Camel. By Joyce C. Mills, Ph.D. Magination Press, 1988. 48 pages. A fable to help children overcome bed-wetting while enhancing their self-esteem. For ages four to eight.

For Children Who Soil

Clouds and Clocks: A Story for Children Who Soil. By Matthew Galvin, M.D. Magination Press, 1989. 48 pages. A story designed to reduce feelings of anxiety and helplessness children feel when they soil. For ages four to eight.

Helpline

Parents Helpline. Phone: 1/900-903-KIDS. *Parents* magazine has set up a 900 number (the cost is 95¢ per minute) so that parents can receive advice on various topics twenty-four hours a day. Dial the main number then enter the number "05" for information on bed-wetting.

Sleep Patterns and Problems

Books

Getting Your Baby to Sleep . . . And Back to Sleep. By Vicki Lansky. Revised edition. The Book Peddlers, 1991. 131 pages. Explains how to "read" your baby's sleep patterns, how to gently alter your baby's feeding and sleeping schedule to suit your own, and how to coax a night waker back to sleep. Discusses the pros and cons of sharing a bed with your baby, and the advantages and disadvantages of having your baby "cry it out." Offers tips for parents of infants, toddlers, and preschoolers.

Healthy Sleep Habits, Happy Child. By Marc Weissbluth, M.D. Fawcett Columbine, 1987. 288 pages. Written by the director of the Sleep Disorders Center at Children's Memorial Hospital, this book offers a step-by-step program for establishing good sleep habits. Reveals common mistakes parents make to get their children to sleep; analyzes ways to get children to fall asleep according to their internal clocks; and explores the different sleep needs for different temperaments—from quiet babies to active toddlers. Includes guidelines for infancy through the growing years. Reference section includes many related articles published in medical journals.

Helping Your Child Sleep through the Night: A Guide for Parents of Children from Infancy to Age Five. By Joanne Cuthbertson and Susie Schevill. Doubleday, 1985. 246 pages. A guide that explains how parents can "teach" their children to get a good night's sleep. Also discusses colic, bed-wetting, nightmares, and other sleep-related problems, and offers advice accordingly.

The Sleep Book for Tired Parents. By Rebecca Huntley. Parenting Press, 1991. 102 pages. Describes the various ways to approach sleep problems so that parents are free to choose their own course of action. Includes worksheets to help parents assess their needs and establish a program.

Solve Your Child's Sleep Problems. By Richard Ferber, M.D. Simon and Schuster, 1985. 251 pages. Explains how to train babies to fall asleep on their own. Offers a systematic approach to solving sleep problems.

Winning Bedtime Battles: How to Help Your Child Develop Good Sleep Habits. By Charles E. Schaefer, Ph.D., with Theresa Foy DiGeronimo. Carol Publishing, 1992. 169 pages. Offers guidance on getting your children (ages two to ten) to sleep. Tells parents how they can find out why their children won't go to sleep–and how to use that information to develop healthy sleep habits. Also discusses overtiredness, separation anxiety, fear of the dark, sleep disorders, setting a bedtime hour, and other sleep-related topics.

On Cosleeping

The Family Bed: An Age-Old Concept in Child Rearing. By Tine Thevenin. Revised edition. Avery, 1987. 176 pages. Classic on co-sleeping arrangements. Explores the benefits and explains how families in other cultures (past and present) have shared beds for centuries.

Nighttime Parenting: How to Get Your Baby and Child to Sleep. By William Sears, M.D. New American Library, 1987. 203 pages. Helps parents understand children's sleeping patterns. Endorses cosleeping arrangements. Questions the "cry it out" approach to solving sleep problems and offers alternative solutions.

Three in a Bed: The Healthy Joys and Remarkable Benefits of Sharing Your Bed with Your Baby. By Deborah Jackson. Avon, 1992. 230 pages. Explains how cosleeping arrangements can eliminate sleep problems.

Videotape

Helping Your Baby Sleep through the Night. Lancaster Productions. Running time: 30 minutes. A four-night program for babies (between two and five months). Explains what parents can do to eliminate feedings in the middle of the night, with an emphasis on encouraging self-soothing.

Helplines

The American Baby Helpline. Phone: 1/900-860-4888 (twenty-four-hour-a-day helpline operating seven days a week. The cost is 95¢ per minute). Prerecorded messages offer expert advice on a variety of baby-related topics. For advice on sleep problems (during the first six months) dial the above number, then code "23"; for advice on bedtime problems (during eighteen months to three years), dial code "45."

Parents Helpline. Phone: 1/900-903-KIDS. *Parents* magazine has set up a 900 number (the cost is 95¢ per minute) so that parents can receive advice on various topics twenty-four hours a day. Dial the main number then enter the number "37" for information on sleeping through the night. For nap-time tips, enter the number "31."

Association

Association of Sleep Disorder Centers. 1610 Fourteenth Street, Suite 300, Rochester, Minnesota 55901. Phone: 507/287-6006. Offers a listing of sleep disorder clinics around the country, many of which offer pediatric advice. (Consider calling your nearest clinic if all other efforts to modify your child's poor sleeping patterns have failed.)

Bedtime Stories, Lullabies, and Other "Go-to-Sleep" Aids

Books

Asleep, Asleep. By Mirra Ginsburg. Illustrated by Nancy Tafuri. Greenwillow. 24 pages. Contains lyrical text and soothing watercolors that can help lull babies, toddlers, and preschoolers (as well as their parents) to sleep.

Goodnight Moon. By Margaret Wise Brown. HarperCollins (1947). 32 pages. A classic go-to-sleep book, now available in a variety of forms, including a gift set version that comes with a soft, stuffed bunny; a sturdy board book for the very young; and a book and cassette version. *The Runaway Bunny*, by the same author, also makes for a comforting bedtime story.

Audiocassettes

Baby's Bedtime. By Judy Collins. Stories to Remember. Running time: 42 minutes. An award-winning tape that helps lull babies to sleep. Includes twenty-seven lullabies sung by Judy Collins to the music of Ernest Troost.

Dreamland. By Scott Fitzgerald. The Nature Recordings Reference Series. Running time: 39 minutes. Includes Beethoven's "Moonlight Sonata" and other classical themes combined with sounds of crickets, rolling waves, and other "songs" from nature. Available from Hand in Hand (see chapter 27 for contact information).

G'night Wolfgang. Running time: 45 minutes. For children of all ages, this recording features twelve lullabies played by pianist Ric Louchard as they were written by Mozart, Bach, Satie, Beethoven, and Schumann. Available on cassette or compact disc from Music for Little People (see chapter 27 for contact information).

Imagine Yourself to Sleep Tapes. By Bett Sanders and Chuck Cummings. Audio Outings. Two volumes. Running time: 60 minutes. Designed to relax children and help them slip into a peaceful sleep. Includes the soothing nature sounds of gentle rain, babbling brooks, and other relaxing noises. Suggests that young listeners imagine themselves as a bird flying over a house, a bouncing ball that comes to rest on a beach, or a horse trotting through a meadow. Available from The Children's Small Press Collection (see chapter 27 for contact information).

Lullaby Magic. By Joanie Bartels. Discovery Music. Running time: 50 minutes. Features songs on one side and instrumentals on the other. Also includes the lyrics to each lullaby. One in a series of tapes that have received The Parents' Choice Honors. Available from The Right Start Catalog (see chapter 27 for contact information).

Rock a Bye Baby. By Scott Fitzgerald. The Nature Recordings Reference Series. Running time: 52 minutes. Includes sounds of brooks flowing, birds singing, and waves breaking, together with lullabies played on an assortment of gentle-sounding instruments. Available from Hand in Hand (see chapter 27 for contact information).

Spoiling

Books

The Growing Years: A Guide to Your Child's Emotional Development from Birth to Adolescence. By the New York Hospital/Cornell Medical Center Department of Psychiatry with Mark Rubinstein, M.D. Simon and Schuster, 1989. 386 pages. Discusses "spoiling" as it relates to infants, toddlers, preschoolers, and school-age children. Addresses some aspects in a question/answer format, including excessive gift buying. (For more information on *The Growing Years*, see "Books" listed under "General Resources" in this chapter.)

Spoiled Rotten: Today's Children and How to Change Them. By Fred G. Gosman. Bashford and O'Neill, 1990. 196 pages. The author argues that parents need to give their children more love and fewer material "things," to effectively discipline for misbehavior, and to remind our kids that although they are exceedingly important, the earth still revolves around the sun. [Note: This book is also available on cassette (Random House Audiobooks, 1992).]

Your Baby and Child: From Birth to Age Five. By Penelope Leach. New edition, revised and expanded. Alfred A. Knopf, 1989. 553 pages. Addresses "spoiling" as it relates to babies and children. (For more information on *Your Baby and Child*, see "Books" listed under "General Resources" in this chapter.)

Your Child's Health: The Parent's Guide to Symptoms, Emergencies, Common Illnesses, Behavior, and School Problems. By Barton D. Schmitt, M.D., F.A.A.P. Bantam, 1991. 672 pages. Explains how to avoid spoiling a child. (For more information on *Your Child's Health*, see "Books" listed under "General Resources" in this chapter.)

Self-Esteem

Free Resource

Leading Children to Self-Esteem. A PTA brochure explaining how to help build children's and teens' self-esteem. For a free copy, send a self-addressed, business-size envelope along with your request to the National PTA (see appendix I for contact information).

Books

Beyond Self-Esteem: Developing a Genuine Sense of Human Values. By Nancy Curry and John N. Johnson. National Association for the Education of Young Children, 1990. 177 pages. How do young children really develop self-esteem? The authors point out that it take much more than indiscriminate praise. Explores the common myths about developing self-esteem and explains how children develop a genuine sense of self-worth. This publication is part four in a monograph series produced by the National Association for the Education of Young Children (see appendix I for contact information).

How to Develop Self-Esteem in Your Child: 6 Vital Ingredients. By Bettie B. Youngs, Ph.D. Fawcett Columbine, 1991. 280 pages. Explains how parents can help unleash potential and empower children to meet life's challenges with confidence. Outlines positive steps parents can take to create an environment that successfully develops their child's sense of self.

The Magic of Encouragement: Nurturing Your Child's Self-Esteem. By Stephanie Marston. William Morrow, 1990. 252 pages. Describes techniques for nurturing self-esteem in children and creating more fulfilling family relationships.

101 Ways to Make Your Child Feel Special. By Vicki Lansky. Contemporary Books, 1991. 108 pages. Contains creative ideas to help parents enhance their child's self-esteem.

The Psychology of Self-Esteem. By Nathaniel Branden, Ph.D. Bantam, 1983. A guide to understanding the concept of self-esteem. Explains what it is, why we need it, and what happens if it isn't there.

Self Esteem: A Family Affair. By Jean Illsley Clarke. Harper San Francisco, 1985. 280 pages. Explains the ways in which self-esteem nourishes both parents and children. Suggests

> ### What Is Self-Esteem?
>
> High self-esteem is not a noisy conceit. It is a quiet sense of self-respect, a feeling of self-worth. When you have it deep inside, you're glad you're you. Conceit is but whitewash to cover low self-esteem. With high self-esteem you don't waste time and energy impressing others; you already know you have value.
> —From *Your Child's Self Esteem*, by Dorothy Corkille Briggs (Doubleday, 1975).

ways to help self-esteem flourish using theory and techniques based on transactional analysis. Provides worksheets.

Your Child's Self Esteem. By Dorothy Corkill Briggs. Doubleday, 1975. 360 pages. Tells parents how they can build a strong sense of self-worth in their children. Offers step-by-step guidelines for raising responsible, productive, happy children.

Dealing with Emotions

Feelings

Books

For Children

Dealing with Feelings (series). By Elizabeth Crary. Parenting Press, 1992. 30 pages each. A series of books that help children handle their feelings and make appropriate decisions about expressing them. For children (ages four through eight) and adults to read together. Titles in this series include *I'm Mad, I'm Frustrated*, and *I'm Proud*.

Double-Dip Feelings: Stories to Help Children Understand Emotions. By Barbara S. Cain, M.S.W. Magination Press, 1990. 32 pages. Explores the mixed emotions that children often feel: happy (and sad) when they move to a new house and have their own room; joyous (and a bit sad) when there's a new baby in the house; proud (and scared) on the first day of school. Shows how feelings can be expressed in non-threatening ways. For children ages three to seven.

Good Times, Bad Times. By Priscilla Galloway. Women's Press, 1993. 32 pages. What makes children feel good? (Playing in the bathtub, bedtime stories, and dinner out on payday are examples.) What makes children feel lousy? (Bran flakes for breakfast and wearing boots in the rain.) A book about positive and negative feelings, for ages four to eight.

Why Do Kids Need Feelings? A Guide to Healthy Emotions. By Monte Elchoness. Monroe Press, 1992. 92 pages. This is the dream journey of a young boy named Daniel and his guide, Noitome (backwards spelling of *emotion*), who meet a variety of characters who help them learn how to use their feelings to work out problems and enjoy their lives. For children ages eight to thirteen.

Game

The Mad Sad Glad Game. A game designed to help teach children about their feelings and the feelings of others. During the game, players are asked to match emotions to situations. Comes with two decks of "feeling" cards (one for beginners, one for more advanced players). For three to six players (adult participation is recommended). A good resource for helping children who have difficulty handling emotions, used by professional therapists. Available from Playfair Toys (see chapter 27 for contact information).

Anger

Free Resource

Dealing with the Angry Child. From the National Institute of Mental Health, this two-page informational sheet offers practical advice to help children learn to channel and direct their anger to constructive ends. For ordering information, request a copy of the free *Consumer Information Catalog*, available from the Consumer Information Center, P.O. Box 100, Pueblo, Colorado 81002.

Books

Love and Anger: The Parental Dilemma. By Nancy Samalin with Catherine Whitney. Viking Penguin, 1991. 242 pages. Explores what parents typically say and do to their children when they are angry—and offers constructive alternatives. Proposes that parents stop berating themselves when they get angry; instead, parents should remember that this emotion is a human one. The secret, as parents, is to limit our actions when we feel enraged.

Managing and Understanding Parental Anger. By Harriet Barrish, Ph.D. and I. J. Barrish. Westport, 1989. 64 pages. Part of the Coping Parent series.

Aggression

Books

For more information on the following titles, see "Books" listed under "General Resources" in this chapter.

Caring for Your Baby and Young Child: Birth to Age 5. Steven P. Shelow, M.D., F.A.A.P., editor-in-chief; Robert E. Hannemann, M.D., F.A.A.P., associate medical editor. Bantam, 1991. 676 pages. "Anger, Aggression, and Biting" is one of the topics listed in the A-to-Z compendium that makes up the second portion of the book. Ag-

Dealing with the Angry Child
From *Dealing with the Angry Child* (the National Institute of Mental Health).

Handling children's anger can be puzzling, draining, and distressing for adults. In fact, one of the major problems in dealing with anger in children is the angry feelings that are often stirred up in us. It has been said that we as parents, teachers, counselors, and administrators need to remind ourselves that we were not always taught how to deal with anger as a fact of life during our own childhood. We were led to believe that to be angry was to be bad, and we were often made to feel guilty for expressing anger.

It will be easier to deal with children's anger if we get rid of this notion. Our goal is not to repress or destroy angry feelings in children—or in ourselves—but rather to accept the feelings and to help channel and direct them to constructive ends.

Parents and teachers must allow children to feel *all* their feelings. Adult skills can then be directed toward showing children acceptable ways of expressing their feelings. Strong feelings cannot be denied, and angry outbursts should not always be viewed as a sign of serious problems; they should be recognized and treated with respect.

To respond effectively to overly aggressive behavior in children we need to have some ideas about what may have triggered an outburst. Anger may be a defense to avoid painful feelings; it may be associated with failure, low self-esteem, and feelings of isolation; or it may be related to an anxiety about situations over which the child has no control.

Angry defiance may also be associated with feelings of dependency, and anger may be associated with sadness and depression. In childhood, anger and sadness are very close to one another and it is important to remember that much of what an adult experiences as sadness is expressed by a child as anger.

Before we look at specific ways to manage aggressive and angry outbursts, several points should be highlighted:

■ We should distinguish between anger and aggression. Anger is a temporary emotional state caused by frustration; aggression is often an attempt to hurt a person or to destroy property.

■ Anger and aggression do not have to be dirty words. In other words, in looking at aggressive behavior in children, we must be careful to distinguish between behavior that indicates emotional problems and behavior that is normal.

In dealing with angry children, our actions should be motivated by the need to protect and to teach, not by a desire to punish. Parents and teachers should show a child that they accept his or her feelings, while suggesting other ways to express the feelings. An adult might say, for example, "Let me tell you what some children would do in a situation like this . . . ." It is not enough to tell children what behaviors we find unacceptable. We must teach them acceptable ways of coping. Also, ways must be found to communicate what we expect of them. Contrary to popular opinion, punishment is not the most effective way to communicate to children what we expect of them.

gressiveness in toddlers is covered earlier on in this volume from the American Academy of Pediatrics.

The Growing Years: A Guide to Your Child's Emotional Development from Birth to Adolescence. By the New York Hospital/Cornell Medical Center Department of Psychiatry with Mark Rubinstein, M.D. Simon and Schuster, 1989. 386 pages. Covers various aspects of child aggression and bullying.

Parent and Child: Getting through to Each Other. By Lawrence Kutner, Ph.D. William Morrow, 1991. 248 pages. Talks about aggressive children, bullies, and the acts of teasing and taunting, and offers advice to concerned parents.

The Preschool Years: Family Strategies that Work—From Experts and Parents. By Ellen Galinsky and Judy David. Ballantine, 1991. 504 pages. Discusses bullying by other children—and how to best deal with it.

Your Baby and Child: From Birth to Age Five. By Penelope Leach. New edition, revised and expanded. Alfred A. Knopf, 1989. 553 pages. Covers physical anger and aggression and offers suggestions for dealing with them.

Your Child's Health: The Parent's Guide to Symptoms, Emergencies, Common Illnesses, Behavior, and School Problems. By Barton D. Schmitt, M.D., F.A.A.P. Bantam, 1991.

672 pages. Explains what to do when one child hurts another.

Helpline

Parents Helpline. Phone: 1/900-903-KIDS. *Parents* magazine has set up a 900 number (the cost is 95¢ per minute) so that parents can receive advice on various topics twenty-four hours a day. Dial the main number then enter the number "02" for information on aggressive toddlers.

For Older Children Who Are Bullied

Bully on the Bus. By Carl W. Bosch. Parenting Press, 1988. 58 pages. Part of "The Decision Is Yours" series, where readers choice their own endings. In this book, a fifth-grade bully named Nick has been picking on you. You don't want to fight, but you don't want your friends to think you're a chicken. What can you do? The decision is yours. For children in grades five and up.

Why Is Everybody Always Picking on Me: A Guide to Handling Bullies. By Terrence Webster-Doyle. Atrium Society Publications, 1991. 133 pages. Part of the Education for Peace series, this book contains stories and activities to help children learn effective, non-violent ways to deal with bullies (and keep their self-confidence intact). For children in grades five and up.

Tantrums

Free Resource

Temper Tantrums: A Normal Part of Growing Up. Guidelines available from the American Academy of Pediatrics. Ask your pediatrician for a copy or send a self-addressed, stamped envelope to: American Academy of Pediat-

rics, "Temper Tantrums" (see appendix I for contact information).

Books

For more information on the following titles, see "Books" listed under "General Resources" in this chapter.

Caring for Your Baby and Young Child: Birth to Age 5. Steven P. Shelow, M.D., F.A.A.P., editor-in-chief; Robert E. Hannemann, M.D., F.A.A.P., associate medical editor. Bantam, 1991. 676 pages. Explains how to prevent and cope with temper tantrums in young children.

The Essential Partnership. By Stanley Greenspan, M.D. Viking Penguin, 1990. 256 pages. Discusses temper tantrums and ways of dealing with them.

Your Baby and Child: From Birth to Age Five. By Penelope Leach. New edition, revised and expanded. Alfred A. Knopf, 1989. New edition, revised and expanded. 553 pages. Describes tantrums in young children and offers advice for handling them.

Helpline

Parents Helpline. Phone: 1/900-903-KIDS. *Parents* magazine has set up a 900 number (the cost is 95¢ per minute) so that parents can receive advice on various topics twenty-four hours a day. Dial the main number then enter the number "44" for information on temper tantrums.

Fears (Nightmares, etc.)

Free Resource

Your Child's Fears. A booklet that helps parents understand their child's fears. Describes symptoms of fear, what parents can do about it, and common fears at various stages of development. Produced by Ross Laboratories for health care professionals as an aid in counseling parents. Ask your pediatrician for a copy.

Books

For Adults

Monsters under the Bed and Other Childhood Fears. By Stephen Garber, Ph.D., Marianne Daniels Garber, Ph.D., and Robyn Freedman Spizman. Villard Books, 1993. 374 pages. Explains how to help your child overcome anxieties, fears, and phobias. Includes a selected reading list for parents and children on specific topics.

Taming Monsters, Slaying Dragons: The Revolutionary Family Approach to Overcoming Childhood Fears and Anxieties. By Joel Feiner, M.D., and Graham Yost. William Morrow, 1988. 296 pages. Covers fears, phobias, and anxieties in children. Individual chapters focus on the normal fears of every child's development, fears caused by stresses within the family (divorce, remarriage), and fears born out of external forces (unemployment, natural disasters, and racism). Reveals how parents sometimes unconsciously sustain, and even encourage, fears and offers guidelines to help parents recognize unhealthy family patterns.

Things that Go Bump in the Night: How to Help Your Children Overcome Their Natural Fears. By Paul Warren and Frank Minirth. Thomas Nelson, 1992. 284 pages. Two doctors from the Minirth/Meier Clinic help parents understand and cope with the natural fears of childhood.

When Your Child Is Afraid. By Dr. Robert Schachter and Carole McCauley. Simon and Schuster, 1989. 284 pages. Helps parents identify and deal with their children's fears. Offers strategies that can be used to reassure a fearful child. Arranged in part by children's ages, from infancy through adolescence, so that parents can easily research and prepare for the

Is Your Child Afraid?

Like adults, children often hide their feelings, and even a child's troubling fear can go unnoticed by his family. Children do not want to look foolish or appear weak. Nevertheless, as a parent you can keep an eye open for certain clues that may indicate an underlying fear. The following list is derived from *Taming Monsters, Slaying Dragons: The Revolutionary Family Approach to Overcoming Childhood Fears and Anxieties,* by Joel Feiner, M.D., and Graham Yost (William Morrow, 1988).

You child may be harboring a fear if she/he exhibits:

- Changes in activity level and concentration
- A surge or drop in appetite
- An increase or decrease in the child's talkativeness
- Regression to a younger stage of behavior
- Disturbed sleep
- Changes in physical movement or coordination
- Obsessions and compulsions
- Panic
- Psychosomatic complaints

Avoidance, for example, of dogs, school, elevators, or even certain rooms in the house.

typical fears of their children's group. Addresses common fears young children encounter. Describes symptoms and offers parenting advice.

For Children

The Blammo-Surprise! Book: A Story to Help Children Overcome Fears. By Stephen R. Lankton, MSW. Magination Press, 1988. 48 pages. A book to help children overcome their fears, big and small, through their own positive thinking. Using the story of a young child who is afraid of the circus, this book offers visualization techniques and strategies to help children cope with their fears, whatever they may be (strangers, animals, loud noises, nightmares, etc.). For ages four to eight.

There's a Nightmare in My Closet. By Mercer Mayer. Dial Press, 1968. 31 pages. When the boy finally musters up the courage to attack the enormous green-spotted Nightmare, it begins to cry like a baby. Suddenly the creature is no longer scary. For children in preschool through third grade.

There's Something in My Attic. By Mercer Mayer. Dial Books, 1988. 32 pages. In this story, a young girl decides to find out—once and for all— what's causing the strange noises in the attic. Flashlight and lasso in hand, she bravely confronts a creature who, it turns out, has been stealing her toys. The creature is more frightened than she is! For children in preschool through third grade.

Where the Wild Things Are. By Maurice Sendak. HarperCollins. 48 pages. Tells the story of Max, who leaves home after being sent to his room without supper, and travels to the land of the Wild Things. Although he becomes king of the horrific creatures who reside there, he eventually decides that where he really wants to be is home. While some grown-ups feel this book is too frightening for children, others feel that the story deals with the essential dilemma of young children—the struggle between dependence and independence. The inherent need children have to confront and conquer their fears has made this book a classic. Winner of the Caldecott Medal in 1964.

Helpline

The American Baby Helpline. Phone: 1/900-860-4888 (twenty-four-hour-a-day helpline operating seven days a week. The cost is 95¢ per minute). Prerecorded messages offer expert advice on a variety of baby-related topics. For advice on nightmares dial the above number, then code "43."

Game

Not So Scary Things. Developed by a psychologist and a pediatrician, this boardgame allows children to safely act out common fears (of being alone in the dark, monsters, thunderstorms, etc.). When players land on "scary" or "courage" spots, they pick up a card to act out (the card might say "hiss like a snake," or "show how to look a bully straight in the eye"). Includes seventy-two activities that help inspire confidence, promote creativity, and encourage strength. For two to four players, ages four to eight. Available from Animal Town (see chapter 27 for contact information).

Separation Anxiety

Inexpensive Resource

So Many Goodbyes: Ways to Ease the Transition between Home and Groups for Young Children. A brochure explaining how families and teachers can work together to help children feel secure in their adjustment to a new child care or school arrangement. Available for 50¢ from the National Association for the Education of Young Children (see appendix I for contact information).

Books

For Adults

Attachment and Loss. By John Bowlby, M.D. Basic Books, 1983, 1982. 425 pages (*Attachment*) and 492 pages (*Loss*). Two separate volumes describe Bowlby's scientific approach to the human behaviors of attachment to mother and loss of mother. These writings form the basis for many subsequent writings on separation anxiety. First published in 1969 as one volume.

The Continuum Concept. By Jean Liedloff. Addison-Wesley, 1985. 256 pages. Offers insights on the essential needs of infants, including the instinctive need to be held and the need to move freely within a secure environment once creeping and crawling take place. Also shows that benefits of keeping children of all ages near adult activity. Based on a study of primitive tribes, where separation anxiety and other childhood fears common in modern cultures are virtually nonexistent.

The Essential Partnership. By Stanley Greenspan, M.D. Viking Penguin,

1990. 256 pages. Discusses separation anxiety at various stages of development. (For more information on *The Essential Partnership*, see "Books" listed under "General Resources" in this chapter.)

The Growing Years: A Guide to Your Child's Emotional Development from Birth to Adolescence. By the New York Hospital/Cornell Medical Center Department of Psychiatry with Mark Rubinstein, M.D. Simon and Schuster, 1989. 386 pages. Explores separation anxiety in toddlers, preschoolers, and school-age children. Suggests ways to ease children's fear of separation. (For more information on *The Growing Years*, see "Books" listed under "General Resources" in this chapter.)

Separation. Edited by K. Jervis. Photographs by J. Berlfein. Revised edition. National Association for the Education of Young Children, 1992. 52 pages. Through a series of photographs and suggestions, this book helps parents and children cope with separation difficulties. Available from the National Association for the Education of Young Children (request publication #230). (For contact information, see appendix I).

Stress

Books

Childhood Stress: How to Raise a Healthier, Happier Child. By Barbara Kuczen, Ph.D. Dell Publishing, 1987. 394 pages. Provides practical solutions for children from toddlers through teens. Describes techniques designed for parents to use in helping their children cope with a wide variety of stressors they encounter at school, at home, and among friends.

Stress and Your Child. By Ruth Arent, M.S.W. Prentice-Hall, 1984. 254

Your Baby and Child: From Birth to Age Five. By Penelope Leach. New edition, revised and expanded. Alfred A. Knopf, 1989. 553 pages. Discusses separation and stranger anxieties at various stages of development. (For more information on *Your Baby and Child*, see "Books" listed under "General Resources" in this chapter.)

For Children

Into the Great Forest: A Story for Children away from Parents for the First Time. By Irene Wineman Marcus and Paul Marcus. Magination Press, 1992. 32 pages. A fairy tale dream to help children better understand and cope with their feelings (often mixed emotions) when they're away from their parents for the first time (at camp, school, etc.). For children ages three to seven.

Helpline

Parents Helpline. Phone: 1/900-903-KIDS. *Parents* magazine has set up a 900 number (the cost is 95¢ per minute) so that parents can receive advice on various topics twenty-four hours a day. Dial the main number then enter the number "36" for information on separation anxiety.

pages. A parents' guide to the symptoms, strategies, and benefits of stress.

Stress in Children: How to Recognize, Avoid and Overcome It. By Bettie B. Youngs. Arbor House, 1985. 170 pages. The author examines the growing problem of stress in children and offers parents and other concerned adults information and guidance to help children overcome this often debilitating condition.

The Stress-Proof Child: A Loving Parent's Guide. By Antoinette Saunders, Ph.D., and Bonnie Remsberg.

Holt, Rinehart, and Winston, 1985. 228 pages. Offers guidance on teaching children how to relax.

Audiocassette

Magic Island: Relaxation for Kids. By Betty Mehling. An audiotape for children offering exercises to help reduce stress. For more information, write Magic Island California Publications, P.O. Box 8014-PS, Calabasas, California 91302.

Social Interaction

Parent/Child Communication

Books

Between Parent and Child. By Dr. Haim Ginott. Avon Books, 1976. 256 pages. Offers insight and advice on parent/child communication. (For more information on *Between Parent and Child*, see "Books" listed under "General Resources" in this chapter.)

How to Talk So Kids Will Listen and Listen So Kids Will Talk. By Adele Faber and Elaine Mazlish. Avon Books, 1982. 242 pages. Helps parents acquire the skill necessary to communicate effectively with their children. Based on the work of the late child psychologist Dr. Haim Ginott, which demonstrates how effective interaction with children enables them to identify their feelings and solve their own problems.

Videotape and audiocassette versions of *How to Talk* also available. Audiocassette: An abridged version of the book is available on a one-hour cassette from Nightingale-Conant Audio (1987). Can be ordered from Chinaberry (see chapter 27 for contact information). Videotapes: A series of six 30-minute video programs based on the book can be ordered from the Modern Learning Press (see chapter 27 for contact information).

Kids Can Cooperate: A Practical Guide to Teaching Problem Solving. By Elizabeth Crary. Parenting Press, 1984. 112 pages. This book offers guidelines to help parents teach their children cooperation and problem-solving skills. Includes sample dialogues and activities that encourage listening, recognizing feelings, and thinking of alternatives in order to avoid arguments and eliminate conflicts. By the same author: *Pick Up Your Socks* and *Without Spanking or Spoiling: A Practical Approach to Toddler and Preschool Guidance.*

Parent and Child: Getting through to Each Other. By Lawrence Kutner, Ph.D. William Morrow, 1991. 248 pages. "Arguing with children is as much a part of being a parent as nurturing them," according to the author. Offers advice on avoiding power struggles, explains the benefits of verbal sparring matches, and offers practical advice on effective communication. (For more information on *Parent and Child*, see "Books" listed under "General Resources" in this chapter.)

Raising Kids Who Can. By Amy Lew, Ph.D., and Betty Lou Bettner. Connexions Press, 1990. 120 pages. Explains how scheduling regular family meetings can help children learn how to cooperate, communicate, and become responsible. It also helps them feel connected, capable, and confident.

Talking to Your Child about a Troubled World. By Lynne S. Dumas. Random House, 1992. 335

pages. Guides parents in approaching difficult subjects—AIDS, sexual abuse, divorce, war, etc.—with their children. Provides parents with the tools and language they need to address these important issues.

Tough Questions: Talking Straight with Your Kids about the Real World. By Sheila Kitzinger and Celia

Sibling Relationships

Books

Between Brothers and Sisters: A Celebration of Life's Most Enduring Relationship. By Adele Faber and Elaine Mazlish. Putnam, 1989. 192 pages. An inspirational book of poetry and photographs on brother/sister relationships.

He Hit Me First: When Brothers and Sisters Fight. By Louise Bates Ames with Carol Chase Haber and The Gesell Institute of Human Development. Warner Books, 1989. 190 pages. Offers insights on sibling rivalry and advice on what parents can do about it. Explains what parents can expect from their children's sibling relationships at each stage of development from eighteen months to sixteen years of age.

Keys to Preparing and Caring for Your Second Child. By Meg Zweiback, R.N. Barron's Education Series, 1991. 160 pages. Offers advice on handling the special challenges of raising two. Part of the Parenting Keys series.

Raising Cain: How to Help Your Children Achieve a Happy Sibling Relationship. By Herbert S. Strean, D.S.W., and Lucy Freeman. Facts on File, 1988. 175 pages. Explains how parents can help their children accentuate the positive aspects of sibling relationships and minimize the negative feelings of jealousy and resentment. Explores the sources of sibling

Kitzinger. The Harvard Common Press, 1991. 306 pages. Encourages parents to communicate openly with their children, exploring hard-to-talk-about topics such as sex, birth, death, religion, and prejudice.

rivalry; the effects of birth order, age difference, and family size; and how the relationships of parents influence those of their children.

The Sibling Bond. By Stephen P. Bank and Michael D. Kahn. Basic Books, 1982. 363 pages. Two clinical psychologists offer a theory on the ways in which siblings attach, shape each other's identities, and affect the course of each other's lives.

Siblings without Rivalry. By Adele Faber and Elaine Mazlish. Avon Books, 1988. 219 pages. Describes methods for handling sibling problems. Explains why comparisons among siblings are devastating, how to intervene (if at all) when conflicts occur, and the importance of allowing your children to express their feelings. Also available on a one-hour audiocassette from Chinaberry (see chapter 27 for contact information).

Helpline

The American Baby Helpline. Phone: 1/900-860-4888 (twenty-four-hour-a-day helpline operating seven days a week. The cost is 95¢ per minute). Prerecorded messages offer expert advice on a variety of baby-related topics. For advice on preparing your young child for a sibling, dial the above number, then code "48."

The New Baby in the House

Books for Children

My Baby Brother. By Harriet Hains. Dorling Kindersley, 1992. 22 pages. Designed to help the very young welcome a new brother or sister, at a time when the older child may be feeling threatened by the baby's arrival. Contains full color photographs, illustrations, and sturdy pages (not quite a board book, but close).

The New Baby. By Fred Rogers. G. P. Putnam's Sons, 1985. 31 pages. Part of the Mister Rogers Neighborhood "First Experiences" series, this book explains what it's like to have a new baby brother or sister. Sometimes it's fun; sometimes it makes you feel grumpy. Contains full-color photos and simple text.

Videotape

Hey, What about Me? Kidvidz (Price Stern Sloan Video). Running time: 25 minutes. Winner of the American Film Institute Award for Children's Educational Programming, this videotape helps children ages two to six adjust to a new baby in the house. Helps the older child know what to expect and deal with his or her feelings about the baby. Offers games, lullabies, and bouncing rhymes for the older and younger child to share.

Friendships

Books

For Adults

Children's Friendships. By Zick Rubin, Ph.D. Harvard University Press, 1980. 165 pages. Offers an introduction to the psychology of the child's social world. Helps readers understand how friendships develop, how the child's conception of friendship changes with cognitive development, and how individuals become popular

Includes original songs that dramatize a child's feelings about the baby.

New Baby Collection

The New Baby Collection. This collection includes baby dolls (Caucasian, African-American, or Asian) with companion pop-up books that show how to care for a newborn. The book (*Our New Baby*, by Pleasant T. Rowland) includes a zipper to zip, a ribbon to tie, and a stuffed toy to squeak for the new baby. In rhyming text, the book describes basic care from the first morning feeding to the evening's last lullaby. Clothes and accessories can be purchased separately for the dolls. These items include doll's bunting, knit sweaters and sweatshirts, party and play clothes, socks and shoes, a changing table, a stroller, a carrier, and a doll's diaper bag (complete with a terry wash mitt and towel, make-believe lotion and baby powder, extra diapers, a changing pad, and bottles of milk and orange juice that magically disappear when baby is fed). Dolls and books may also be purchased separately. For toddlers and preschoolers (babies, too). Available from the Pleasant Company, Department 8401, Box 497, Middleton, Wisconsin 53562. Phone: 1/800-845-0005. Ask for a copy of their free mail order catalog.

or unpopular and how this affects the child. Answers questions on why children form cliques, adopt stereotypes, and exclude members of the opposite sex in the years just before puberty.

Helping Kids Make Friends. By Holly S. Stocking, Diana Arezzo, and Shelley Leavitt. Argus, 1979. 95 pages. Explains how grownups can help children develop the social skills and gain the confidence they need to make friends.

Playgroups

The Playgroup Handbook.

By Nancy Towner Butterworth and Laura Peabody Broad. St. Martin's Press, 1991. 336 pages. Offers step-by-step guidelines for organizing a playgroup, including lists of organizations to contact for information. Also contains more than two hundred suggestions on crafts and activities for young children who participate in playgroups.

For Children

I Want to Play. By Elizabeth Crary. Parenting Press, 1982. 32 pages. Part of "The Children's Problems Solving" series, where young readers make their own decisions and see the consequences. *I Want to Play* allows children to decide how Danny can get someone to play with him. For children ages four to eight.

Making Friends. By Fred Rogers. G. P. Putnam's Sons, 1987. 32 pages. By Fred Rogers of "Mister Rogers' Neighborhood," this book is designed to help preschoolers understand what friendship is all about. Part of the "First Experiences" series.

Audiocassette

Getting Along. This sixty-minute cassette has songs, animal stories, and activities to help kids work and play together in a cooperative manner. Topics include sharing, taking turns, individual differences, and more. Comes with a sixty-three-page

book. Available from Chaselle, Inc. (see chapter 27 for contact information).

Videotapes

Alan and Naomi. Columbia TriStar, 1992. Running time: 95 minutes. The story about a friendship that develops between a fourteen-year-old Jewish boy and a French girl living in Brooklyn during World War II. The girl, who was traumatized by the Nazis before coming to America, had been unable to speak to anyone, until she met Alan. Rated PG. For ages eight and up.

Mark Twain and Me. Disney, 1991. Running time: 93 minutes. Based on the true story of the close friendship that developed between the author (in his later years) and an eleven-year-old girl. Shows how people of different ages can benefit from each other's company. For children ages six and up.

Stand By Me. Columbia TriStar, 1986. Running time: 87 minutes. A coming-of-age story about a group of twelve-year-olds who set out on foot to search for a missing boy and, along the way, discover the true value of friendship. For parents who aren't offended by the language, the film is appropriate for ages ten to adult (twelve-year-olds, in particular).

Helpline

The American Baby Helpline. Phone: 1/900-860-4888 (twenty-four-hour-a-day helpline operating seven days a week. The cost is 95¢ per minute). Pre-recorded messages offer expert advice on a variety of baby-related topics. For advice on "first friends," dial the above number, then code "42."

Imaginary Friends

Books

The House of Make Believe: Children's Play and the Developing Imagination. By Dorothy G. Singer, Ed.D., and Jerome L. Singer, Ph.D. Harvard University Press, 1990. 330 pages. Discusses the role of imaginary playmates in children's lives. Explores the connection between imaginative play in childhood and the development of long-term creativity in adults.

Your Child at Play: Three to Five Years. By Marilyn Segal, Ph.D., and Don Adcock, Ph.D. Newmarket Press, 1986. 218 pages. One in a series of books exploring indoor and outdoor play through the various stages of a child's development. One chapter is devoted to imaginary friends—explains what they are (distinguishing between "imaginary" and "invisible" friends), what purpose they serve, and how parents should treat these "friends."

Attachments to dolls, stuffed animals and invisible friends give children genuine experiences with loving, caring, protecting, and sharing. At the same time, parents can benefit from a child's attachment to an imaginary friend. The friend helps the child reveal his or her feelings and provides a nonthreatening way to handle difficult situations, and to communicate values
—From *Your Child at Play: Three to Five Years* (Newmarket Press, 1986)

Setting Limits

Quick Tips

- Criticize the action, not the child.
- Praise good behavior.
- Give your child responsibilities; show trust.
- Acknowledge your child's feelings.
- Set a good example.

Free and Inexpensive Resources

Discipline: A Parent's Guide. A PTA brochure presenting helpful tips, such as praising a child for good behavior, setting limits and enforcing them, and avoiding nagging and power struggles. For a free copy, send a self-addressed, stamped, business-size envelope along with your request to the National PTA (see appendix I for contact information).

Helping Children Learn Self-Control. A brochure describing basic techniques to help children develop self-discipline. Available for 50¢ from the National Association for the Education of Young Children (see appendix I for contact information).

Discipline vs. Conformity

Parents sometimes confuse discipline with conformity. But as many childhood experts point out, it is not a blind willingness to conform that one wishes to instill in children. As Dr. Stan Katz writes in *Success Trap* (Dell, 1991), "We all need to be disciplined enough to survive within the general rules of society, respecting the boundaries between ourselves and others while upholding our rights as individuals. Discipline is about setting and observing our own limits so that we can lead safe, productive, fulfilling lives. It is about initiative, perseverance, and faith rather than blind compliance. Discipline fosters creativity; conformity deadens."

Love and Learn: Discipline for Young Children. A brochure describing positive approaches to discipline (for example, offering choices, stating rules clearly, respecting children's feelings, and having reasonable expectations). Describes typical difficulties and suggests positive solutions. Includes a recommended reading list. Available for 50¢ from the National Association for the Education of Young Children (see appendix I for contact information).

Books

Beyond Discipline: Parenting that Lasts a Lifetime. By Edward R. Christophersen, Ph.D. Westport Publishers, 1990. 152 pages. Rather than focus on behavior modification techniques, this book suggests ways that parents can help their children develop life long coping skills, self-esteem, and independence. Offers guidelines on teaching self-control, redirecting inappropriate behavior, and encouraging independent play. For parents with children from infants to adolescents. By the same author: *Little People: Guidelines for Commonsense Child Rearing* (Westport Publishers, 1988).

Child Behavior. By Louise Bates Ames, Frances L. Ilg, Sidney M. Baker, and the Gesell Institute of Hu-

man Development. Revised edition. HarperCollins, 1992. 360 pages. This classic guide shows how child behavior develops in a patterned and predictable way. Advises parents to use "developmental techniques" in disciplining children, that is, to adapt their techniques to their child's abilities, interests, and weaknesses at whatever stage of development he or she has reached. Offers specific advice on common behavioral problems in children through the age of ten.

Dare to Discipline. By James Dobson. Tyndale House, 1987 (36th printing). 228 pages. More than a million copies in print. Points out the importance of setting limits and inhibiting defiant behavior within a framework of love and affection. Based on the idea that children *need* consistent discipline.

Discipline: A Sourcebook of 50 Failsafe Techniques for Parents. By James Windell, M.A. Collier Books, 1991. 206 pages. Offers parents an inventory of effective discipline skills and techniques (for example, offering choices, using humor, defining limits, and so forth). Includes approaches for children of every age.

For Your Own Good: Hidden Cruelty in Child-Rearing and the Roots of Violence. By Alice Miller.

Farrar, Straus, Giroux, 1983. 284 pages. A study on the origins of violence. Argues that the root causes of violence are consequences of our misguided childrearing practices.

A Good Enough Parent: A Book on Child Rearing. By Bruno Bettelheim. Alfred A. Knopf, 1987. 377 pages. Offers insight on discipline, based on the author's lifelong work studying children and child-rearing practices. See chapter 9, "About Discipline," and chapter 10, "Why Punishment Doesn't Work." (For more information on *A Good Enough Parent*, see "Books" listed under "General Resources" in this chapter.)

Good Kids, Bad Behavior: Helping Children Learn Self-Discipline. By Peter Williamson, Ph.D. Simon and Schuster, 1991. 256 pages. Argues that misbehavior has a natural place in children's lives—that it is the way they learn about their world. Once parents understand that their child's misbehavior is purposeful, they can approach discipline constructively— as a teaching process rather than a punishing one.

The Growing Years: A Guide to Your Child's Emotional Development from Birth to Adolescence. By the New York Hospital/Cornell Medical Center Department of Psychiatry with Mark Rubinstein, M.D. Simon and Schuster, 1989. 386 pages. Discusses discipline (distinguishing it from punishment) and limit-setting. Includes general principles and offers guidance for specific behavioral problems. (For more information on *The Growing Years*, see "Books" listed under "General Resources" in this chapter.)

Holding Time: How to Eliminate Conflict, Temper Tantrums, and Sibling Rivalry and Raise Happy, Loving, Successful Children. By Martha G. Welch, M.D. Simon and Schuster, 1988. 254 pages. Presents a parenting approach whereby parents hold their children, firmly, until negative emotions subside. Welch draws from research on primate and infant bonding in building her case for this technique.

How to Help Children with Common Problems. By Charles E. Schaefer, Ph.D., and Howard L. Millman, Ph.D. NAL-Dutton, 1989. Covering early childhood through adolescence, this guide explains the practical steps parents can take in dealing with problems such as insecure behaviors, antisocial behavior, sexual misbehavior, habit disorders, and other problems. Lists a variety of parenting strategies for each. A section on preventive parenting highlights child-rearing techniques that can avert or minimize behavior problems. Lists professional resources and suggests additional reading materials.

Loving Your Child Is Not Enough. By Nancy Samalin. Penguin Books, 1987. 226 pages. Explores the art of effective discipline using nonpunitive techniques.

Parents' Guide to Understanding Discipline: Infancy through Preteen. Children's Television Workshop. Prentice-Hall, 1990. Part of a series of books produced by the Children's Television Workshop, creators of "Sesame Street." This guide advocates "authoritative parenting," which means setting firm and consistent limits while being warm and respectful toward the child. Explains how to handle difficult behavior at various stages of development, offers strategies for teaching consistent behavior, and explains how to express anger without harming your child's self-esteem. Among the fourteen chapters are "When Parents Disagree on Discipline," "Dealing With Anger—Yours and Your Kids' " and "Discipline by Other Care Givers." (For more information on the "Family Living" series, see "Books" listed under "General Resources" in this chapter.)

Parents, Please Don't Sit on Your Kids: A Parent's Guide to Nonpunitive Discipline. By Clare Cherry. Lake Publishers, 1985. 187 pages. Offers alternatives to punishment, including modeling correct behavior, having rational discussions (as opposed to screaming matches), and pointing out consequences. Offers guidelines on passing along values (trust, respect, and caring for others). For parents of preschoolers through fourth grade.

Positive Discipline. By Jane Nelsen, Ed.D. Ballantine, 1987. 232 pages. The author—a psychologist, educator, and mother—believes that children misbehave when they feel thwarted in their need to belong and in their need for love and attention. Explains that parents who show their children compassion and understanding will encourage self-respect, self-discipline, cooperation, good behavior, and problem-solving skills. Offers a practical program for achieving this.

Raising Good Kids: A Developmental Approach to Discipline. By Louise Bates Ames, Ph.D. Dell Publishing, 1992. 127 pages. This renowned author defines discipline not as punishment but as teaching. Provides an overview of children's development, explains what children tend to be like at different ages (from eighteen months to ten years and after), and offers a variety of discipline techniques that work well at each stage. Also explains how to make rules that take into account individual differences in temperament. Includes separate chapters on fighting between brothers and sisters and discipline in day care and nursery school.

Spare the Child: The Religious Roots of Punishment and the Psychological Impact of Physical Abuse. By Philip Greven. Random House, 1992. 263 pages. Explores the religious roots of corporal punishment in America and its consequences. Highlights biblical passages ("He that spareth his rod hateth his son: but he that loveth him chasteneth him betimes," "the rod and reproof give wisdom: but a child left to himself bringeth his mother to shame," and so forth) which, the author explains, have served as primary guides to childrearing and discipline for centuries.

Stop Struggling with Your Child: Quick-Tip Parenting Solutions that Will Work for You and Your Kids Ages 4–12. By Evonne Weinhaus and Karen Friedman. HarperCollins, 1991. 188 pages. Offers sensible solutions to help build positive parent/child relationships, reduce conflict, and promote self-esteem.

Teaching Children Self-Discipline . . . at Home and at School. By Thomas Gordon. Random House, 1989. 258 pages. Explains why punitive methods of discipline don't work, and advances a workable alternative based on cooperation. Draws on published research findings as well as his own experience as a clinical psychologist.

The Time-Out Solution: A Parent's Guide for Handling Everyday Behavior Problems. By Lynn Clark, Ph.D. Contemporary Books, 1989. 187 pages. Discusses in detail the "time out" method of discipline. Includes tips for using time out with two children, time out away from home, and lists of common mistakes people make when using this technique (and how to correct them).

A Very Practical Guide to Discipline with Young Children. By Grace Mitchell. Telshare, 1982. 160 pages. Written by an educator, this guide to discipline takes into account the child's limitations and point of view.

When Your Child Drives You Crazy. By Eda LeShan. St. Martin's Press, 1985. 393 pages. Written by an educator and family counselor, this book tells parents how to cope with the crisis—and find time for the pleasures—of raising a child. Explains how to read behavior and spot the hidden agenda. Explains why children need tears as well as laughter.

Who's in Control? Dr. Balter's Guide to Discipline without Combat. By Dr. Lawrence Balter with Anita Shreve. Poseidon Press, 1989. 187 pages. Explains how parents can learn to direct their children, set a good example, anticipate problems, distract the child's attention, and intervene when appropriate—rather than lose control and lash out at the child. Contains age-appropriate strategies and techniques—from infancy through the preteen years—for teaching children empathy, motivation, and self-control.

Without Spanking or Spoiling: A Practical Approach to Toddler and Preschool Guidance. By Elizabeth Crary. Revised edition. Parenting Press, 1992. Helps parents to recognize and attain their goals as parents without overindulging, verbally attacking, or spanking their toddlers and preschoolers. By the same author: *Kids Can Cooperate: A Practical Guide to Teaching Problem Solving* and *Pick Up Your Socks*.

Your Baby and Child: From Birth to Age Five. By Penelope Leach. New edition, revised and expanded. Alfred A. Knopf, 1989. 553 pages. Examines the concept of "discipline." Explains how parents can help their children behave appropriately. Explores problems of behavior and offers practical advice. (For more information on *Your Baby and Child*, see "Books" listed under "General Resources" in this chapter.)

Your Child's Health: The Parent's Guide to Symptoms, Emergencies, Common Illnesses, Behavior, and School Problems. By Barton D. Schmitt, M.D., F.A.A.P. Bantam, 1991. 672 pages. Explains the goals of discipline (protect your child; teach right from wrong) and describes various techniques, including "time-out." (For more information on *Your Child's Health*, see "Books" listed under "General Resources" in this chapter.)

The Art of Discipline

No two parents set limits in the same fashion, and no two kids are cast from the same mold. The "right" way to discipline is the way that works well for you and your child. While a quiet "time out" may work well with one child, another might simply refuse to sit in the chair or go to the designated room. When deciding on disciplinary approaches, keep in mind the child's age and temperament, and be willing to modify your technique to fit the circumstances.

Some Terms, Tools, and Techniques

Communication. Words are powerful tools, but keep in mind that yelling, shouting, screaming, ranting, and raving are counterproductive. Reasoning with the child, reaching compromises, and offering (making) choices are examples of positive communication techniques.

"Consequences." A way of either increasing good behavior or decreasing inappropriate behavior (frequently used the latter way as a disciplinary measure). Parents using this approach might calmly explain to their child (before calamity strikes) that there will be consequences if inappropriate behavior (unwillingness to cooperate, for example) persists. Ideally, parents then follow through with a "consequence" related to the child's action (for example, if the child keeps taking apart his baby sister's "busy box" with a toy screwdriver, a parent might explain that they are taking the tool away for a specified period of time). Some parents teach their children the "logical consequences" of their actions (for example, they ask their child (repeatedly) to put her bike away. She never does, and the chain eventually rusts (or someone steals the bike)

Developmental Techniques. Understanding how your child's behavior changes with the passing of time—and what disciplinary approaches are the most effective at different ages and stages of development.

Distraction. Steer attention away from negative activity (such as banging on a breakable glass with a metal spoon) to something more acceptable (like banging on a metal pot with a wooden spoon).

Extinction. A disciplinary technique whereby parents systematically ignore their child when he breaks a rule. Used primarily for annoying behavior (like whining), rather than dangerous or destructive behavior (*Dare to Discipline* and *Caring for Your Baby and Child: Birth to Age 5* discuss this technique).

Holding Time. Using this technique, parents hold their child, firmly, until his emotions are discharged. Parents accept the feelings the child expresses, whatever they may be, and continue until everyone is feeling better.

Modeling Behavior. Demonstrating behavior you want your child to learn. By behaving in a certain fashion, parents make it clear that they value such behavior. (*A Good Enough Parent* discusses the importance of modeling behavior.)

Punishment. Many child-rearing experts distinguish between discipline and punishment and believe that the latter should be avoided. Here are a few wise words on the topic, written by a child development specialist: "Is discipline really about telling children what to do and punishing them when they don't do it? To me, it is, rather, about helping children grow into people who will one day do as they should and behave as they ought when there's nobody around to tell, supervise, or punish them." [From "Instead of Spanking," by Penelope Leach, *Parenting* magazine (December/January 1992).]

Rewards. Positive reinforcement. Appropriate and effective in certain situations, but proceed with caution. Keep the child's age in mind when offering "incentives" for good behavior; make sure the reward more or less matches the child's performance; and remember that rewards don't have to be material—and shouldn't be eatable (linking good behavior to tasty treats can contribute to life-long eating problems). Remember, too, that a job well done is often rewarding enough. Hugs and kisses from proud parents are icing on the cake.

Structure the Environment. Make your home child-friendly by keeping dangerous or valuable objects out of your child's reach. Baby-proof, so you don't find yourself saying "no" too often, thereby allowing your child to explore freely—and learn in the process.

Time-Out. The child is asked to sit in a chair, go to her room, or otherwise be isolated for a specified period of time. A popular disciplinary measure, although some child-care experts feel it is emotionally harmful since it requires the temporary withholding of love and attention. Advocates of the time-out approach see it as a gentle alternative to physical punishment. (*The Time-Out Solution* explains how this technique works. For those interested in the opposing view, see "The Disadvantage of Time-Out," by Aletha Solter, in *Mothering* magazine (Fall 1992). To find out how to order back issues of *Mothering*, see listing under "Magazines and Newsletters" under "General Resources" in this chapter.)

Withholding Privileges. A common approach with school-aged children. Most effective when the privilege being withheld is related to the child's behavior. A word of caution: If you opt for this technique, keep in mind that the withholding of a privilege (like television) can make it seem even more appealing in the child's mind.

Hotline

The American Baby Helpline. Phone: 1/900-860-4888 (twenty-four-hour-a-day helpline operating seven days a week. The cost is 95¢ per minute). Prerecorded messages offer expert advice on a variety of baby-related topics. For advice on early discipline (children six to eighteen months), dial the above number, then code "40"; for advice on discipline without spanking (children eighteen months to three years), dial code "41."

Manners

Books

For Adults

Miss Manners' Guide to Rearing Perfect Children. By Judith Martin. Viking Penguin, 1985. 405 pages. A book devoted to the subject of civilizing the young (from prekindergarten through postgraduation). Includes a complete course in table manners; etiquette for christenings, birthday parties, and family gatherings; appropriate courses of action for special situations (including bullying, rudeness, name-calling, unwillingness to share, etc.); and much more. Written in question and answer format ("Dear

Where Good Manners Come From

Often the first thing that comes to mind when asked to define manners is a set of Politeness Rules—which fork to use, when to blow your nose. But true manners are not about rule-knowledge—they are a well-developed habit of being considerate toward others.

Children, however, are naturally self-centered, aren't they? As the authors of the *Parents' Guide to Raising Kids Who Love to Learn* (from the Children's Television Workshop, published by Prentice-Hall, 1989) put it, "Children are notoriously egocentric, so even simple niceties, such as waiting their turn in conversation, go against the grain. On the other hand, children also show an early awareness of the feelings of others." Parents can build on this early awareness.

The *Parents' Guide* quotes Dr. Laura Dittman, a child development expert from the University of Maryland, who explains it this way: "Even before the age of two, children will become silent and very concerned when another child is unhappy. That concern for other people's feelings is the substratum of manners."

Miss Manners" letters, followed by "Gentle Reader" responses).

Raising a Confident Child. By Joanne Oppenheim, Betty Boegehold, and Barbara Brenner. Pantheon Books, 1984. 256 pages. Offers suggestions on teaching the importance of manners and preparing your child to be a guest (or a host). Explains how parents can help their children enjoy the process of becoming a social being and an independent member of the community.

For Children

Manners. By Aliki. Greenwillow Books, 1990. 38 pages. A book to help children understand what manners are all about. Demonstrates both good and bad behavior in various situations (at the table, on the phone, in a public place, etc.) and encourages readers to distinguish between the two.

Videotape

Lamb Chop in the Land of No Manners. A&M Video. Running time: 47 minutes. This Shari Lewis production shows children ages four to six how a reasonable set of rules makes it easier for people to live together. Using animation and live action, the popular Lamb Chop can reinforce parents' efforts to teach children basic etiquette.

Game

The Good Behavior Game. A boardgame designed to help teach children the importance of sharing, being polite, cooperating, and other "good" behaviors. In the version for nonreaders (ages four to six), players acquire tokens when they land on positive behaviors but lose them when they land on negative ones. In the version for readers (ages seven to twelve), players must answer questions about appropriate behaviors to acquire tokens. Available from Childswork/Childsplay (see chapter 27 for contact information).

Patience: Helping Your Child Learn to Wait

Books

For Adults

Child Potential: Fulfilling Your Child's Intellectual, Emotional and Creative Promise. By Theodore Isaac Rubin, M.D. Continuum, 1990. 299 pages. This book offers ways to help parents fulfill their child's emotional, intellectual, and creative promise. Includes a section on the postponement of gratification, including ways to help teach children how to wait.

For Children

I Can't Wait. By Elizabeth Crary. Parenting Press, 1982. 32 pages. Part of "The Children's Problems Solving" series, where young readers make their own decisions and see the consequences. A book to help children learn how to wait, with no right or wrong answers. For children ages four to eight.

Activities that Teach Children How to Wait

"Why can't you learn how to wait?" This familiar question—perhaps really a whine—is as exasperating for our children to hear as it is for us to repeat. Far better to guide your child into enjoyable activities that can teach the virtue of waiting well by rewarding it naturally. The following list of patience-rewarding activities is based on suggestions in *Child Potential: Fulfilling Your Child's Intellectual, Emotional and Creative Promise.* (Continuum Publishing Co., 1990), by Theodore Isaac Rubin, M.D.

- Go fishing. For all but the expert angler, fishing is 90 percent waiting. Rubin writes that fishing "aids in the experience of tranquillity."

- Learning how to make things that require hours or days—rather than minutes—to complete. Knitting and building with erector sets are just two examples. Your child can use the finished product—or just show it off.

- Put together a truly challenging jigsaw puzzle. Watch as the full picture reveals itself.

- Build collections and watch them grow: coins, stamps, rocks, butterflies, bottle caps, favorite magazine pictures.

- Save money. If it's your child's allowance or lemonade-stand earnings, the fattening piggy bank gains a special importance.

- Engage in any activity that depends on acquiring a skill over time and becomes increasingly enjoyable. Virtually all sports fit this category, as well as many games and crafts.

Habits

Books

Good Kids/Bad Habits. By Charles E. Schaefer, Ph.D., and Theresa Foy Digeronimo, M.Ed. Prince Paperbacks, 1993. 113 pages. Addresses nail biting, hair pulling, thumb sucking, and other habits in children, and offers step-by-step guidelines to help children (from tots to teens) give them up.

Your Growing Child: From Babyhood through Adolescence. By Penelope Leach. Alfred A. Knopf, 1986. 732 pages. Discusses habits such as thumb sucking, nail-biting, nose picking, and masturbation. Explains when and why such habits occur and how parents should handle them. (For more information on *Your Growing Child*, see "Books" listed under "General Resources" in this chapter.)

Beyond the Basics: Teaching Responsibility and Passing Along Values

Responsibility

Books

Parents Guide to Raising Responsible Kids: Preschool through Teen Years. Children's Television Workshop. Prentice-Hall, 1991. 216 pages. Part of the Children's Television Workshop's "Family Living" series, this book offers information and advice on raising confident, capable kids. Winner of a *Child* magazine Book Award for Excellence in Family Issues for 1992.

Pick Up Your Socks . . . and Other Skills Growing Children Need! By Elizabeth Crary. Parenting Press, 1990. 108 pages. A guide to raising responsible children. Discusses the difference between obedience and responsibility, the skills children need to be responsible (and how to help build those skills), and how to help children become independent, among other topics. By the same author: *Kids Can Cooperate: A Practical Guide to Teaching Problem Solving* and *Without Spanking or Spoiling: A Practical Approach to Toddler and Preschool Guidance.*

Raising a Responsible Child: Practical Steps to Successful Family Relationships. By Don Dinkmeyer and Gary D. McKay, M.A. Simon and Schuster, 1973. 256 pages. Offers practical steps to develop responsibility in children. By the authors of many books based on the S.T.E.P. (Systematic Training for Effective Parenting) program, including *The Effective Parent, The Parents Handbook, PREP for Effective Family Living, Parenting Teenagers,* and *Parenting Young Children* (for more information on these titles, see "Books" under "General Resources" in this chapter). (Note: see also S.T.E.P. listing under "Parenting Classes" under "General Resources" in this chapter.)

Raising Self-Reliant Children in a Self-Indulgent World. By H. Stephen Glenn and Jane Nelson, Ed.D. Prima Publishing and Communications, 1988. 243 pages. Offers insights and helpful steps for parents and teachers to aid children in becoming capable and self-reliant. Points out the value of risk-taking, which gives children a chance to develop confidence and life skills.

Teach Your Child Decision Making. By Maurice Elias and John Clabby. Doubleday, 1987. 343 pages. Shows parents how they can teach their children to solve everyday problems and make sound decisions. Suggests activities to help children get into the habit of thinking through projects.

Morality

Books

Bringing Up a Moral Child. By Michael Schulman, Ph.D., and Eva Mekler. Addison-Wesley, 1985. 362 pages. Shows how the family provides the ideal setting for teaching morals. The authors do not dictate which moral values should be taught; instead, they show parents how to teach children their own values, using games, role-playing, and other techniques.

The Moral Life of Children. By Robert Coles. Atlantic Monthly Press, 1986. 302 pages. Presents the drawings and voices of children of varying origins and ages facing every kind of moral challenge. Explores the moral reactions of children to life at school, at home, on the streets, and elsewhere. Other books by Robert Coles include *The Political Life of Children* and *The Spiritual Life of Children* (see listing under "Books" under "Religion/Spirituality" in this chapter).

When Your Child Lies

Books

The Growing Years: A Guide to Your Child's Emotional Development from Birth to Adolescence. By the New York Hospital/Cornell Medical Center Department of Psychiatry with Mark Rubinstein, M.D. Simon and Schuster, 1989. 386 pages. Discusses child's lies, including those of toddlers, preschoolers, and school-age children. Explores the reasons for lying and offers advice for each age group. (For more information on *The Growing Years*, see "Books" listed under "General Resources" in this chapter.)

Telling Lies: Clues to Deceit in the Marketplace, Politics, and Marriage. By Paul Ekman, Ph.D. W. W. Norton, 1992. 366 pages. Examines how and when people lie and tell the truth. Discusses lies between parent and child and points out that the severity of punishment is one of the factors that influences whether children lie or confess transgressions.

Why Kids Lie: How Parents Can Encourage Truthfulness. By Paul Ekman, Ph.D. Scribner, 1989. 206 pages. Explains why children lie (to avoid punishment, to avoid hurting someone else's feelings, to win admiration, etc.) and how lies differ at various stages of development. Offers advice on the best responses to the situations that cause children to lie.

Your Baby and Child: From Birth to Age Five. By Penelope Leach. New edition, revised and expanded. Alfred A. Knopf, 1989. 553 pages. Offers advice to parents whose children stretch the truth. (For more information on *Your Baby and Child*, see "Books" listed under "General Resources" in this chapter.)

When Your Child Steals

Books

Bringing Up a Moral Child. By Michael Schulman, Ph.D., and Eva Mekler. Addison-Wesley, 1985. Explains the reasons for stealing—and how parents should deal with it. (For more information on this book see "Books" listed under "Morality" in this chapter.)

Your Baby and Child: From Birth to Age Five. By Penelope Leach. New edition, revised and expanded. Alfred A. Knopf, 1989. 553 pages. Discusses stealing and advises parents not to make it a moral issue at preschool age. (For more information on *Your Baby and Child*, see "Books" listed under "General Resources" in this chapter.)

Sexuality

Free and Inexpensive Resources

How to Talk to Your Child about Sex. Offers tips on talking to children (ages one through ten) about sex. Explains why it's important that you initiate conversations about sex rather than wait for them to ask questions. Also available: *How to Talk to Your Preteen and Teen about Sex* and *How to Talk To Your Teens and Children about Aids*. For a free copy of any of these brochures, send a self-addressed, business-size envelope along with your request to the National PTA (see appendix I for contact information).

Sex Education: A Bibliography. A listing of educational materials for children, adolescents, and their families. Available from the American Academy of Pediatrics. Ask your pediatrician for a copy or send a self-addressed, stamped envelope to American Academy of Pediatrics (see appendix I for contact information).

Books

For Adults

The Growing Years: A Guide to Your Child's Emotional Development from Birth to Adolescence. By the New York Hospital/Cornell Medical Center Department of Psychiatry with Mark Rubinstein, M.D. Simon and Schuster, 1989. 386 pages. Discusses sex education for boys and girls, masturbation, and the parents sexuality (and the child's response to it). (For more information on *The Growing Years*, see "Books" listed under "General Resources" in this chapter.)

Raising Sexually Healthy Children: A Loving Guide for Parents, Teachers, and Caregivers. By Lynn Leight, R.N. Rawson Associates, 1988. 284 pages. Reveals a system for raising sexually healthy children in a sexually sophisticated word. Covers nudity, masturbation, explicit media, fantasy, flirting, and other topics. Offers tips on how to get children to talk openly about their deepest concerns. Outlines how youngsters develop sexually—from toddler to teen. Includes a list of seventy-five questions parents can ask themselves to help them decide which values they wish to convey to their children.

Talking with Your Child about Sex: Questions and Answers for Children from Birth to Puberty. By Mary Calderone and James Ramey. Random House, 1982. 133 pages. Presents the questions your son or daughter is likely to ask at each stage of development, and answers that will make sense to your children and help you, as a parent, be more responsive to their concerns.

For Children

Asking about Sex and Growing Up: A Question and Answer Book for Boys and Girls. By Joanna Cole. Morrow Junior Books, 1988. 90 pages. Using a question-and-answer format, this book discusses how girls' and boys' bodies differ, what happens to people's bodies during adolescence, what happens during masturbation and intercourse, preventing unwanted pregnancy, and other topics of interest to preadolescents. For ages eight through twelve.

How Babies Are Made. By Andrew Andry and Steven Schepp. Little, Brown, 1984. 88 pages. A frank explanation of reproduction, complete with tasteful paper sculpture illustrations. For ages three to ten.

The What's Happening to My Body? Book for Girls and **The What's Happening to My Body? Book for Boys.** By Lynda Madaras. Revised editions. Newmarket Press, 1988. 269 and 251 pages. These two books are designed to help children and parents better understand the physical and emotional changes of puberty. Each discusses the stages of puberty, changes in the body, sexual attitudes, birth control, and related topics (including information on AIDS and sexually transmitted diseases). For children ages nine to fifteen.

What's Inside? Baby. By Alexandra Parsons. Dorling Kindersley, 1992. 16 pages. For children interested in how babies grow inside their mothers,

this book contains simple text and full-color photographs with cut-aways that reveal what's inside. Opens with photos of a pregnant woman and the fetus growing inside her uterus. Also contains photos of a pregnant dog, pony, porcupine, crocodile, and other animals—and the life developing inside them. (The *process* of conception is not covered here.) For ages three to seven years.

Where Did I Come From? By Peter Mayle. Carol Publishing, 1973. 48 pages. Offers a humorous, explicit presentation of the human reproduction process. For ages four to seven.

Videotapes

The Miracle of Life. Random House Home Video. Running time: 60 minutes. Remarkable close-up photography shows the earliest stages of human life, magnified 500,000 times. Narrated by June Lockhart (of the long-running television series "Lost in Space"), this video presents the process of fertilization and cell division in full color. For ages eight to adult.

What Kids Want to Know about Sex and Growing Up. Children's Television Workshop. Running time: 60 minutes. Created for families with kids ages eight to twelve, this video program offers information on puberty, sex, and reproduction in easy-to-understand language. Addresses safety, peer pressure, love, relationships, and responsibility. Packaged with a free twenty-four-page parent's guide.

Religion/Spirituality

Books

For Adults

Do Children Need Religion? How Parents Today Are Thinking about the Big Questions. By Martha Fay. Pantheon Books, 1993. 237 pages. Explores questions about religion's benefits and limitations.

Gently Lead: How to Teach Your Children about God While Finding Out for Yourself. By Polly Berrien Berends. HarperCollins, 1991. 172 pages. A collection of poems, commentaries, stories, anecdotes, and dialogues for parents, both in and out of organized religion, who are concerned with being responsive to the awakening sprituality of their children. By the author of *Whole Child/Whole Parent.*

The Spiritual Life of Children. By Robert Coles. Houghton Mifflin, 1990. 358 pages. In this book, which is part of "The Inner Lives of Children" trilogy, children speak out and depict their views on the nature of God's wishes, the devil, heaven and hell, faith, and skepticism. Brings readers the words and colorful pictures of Christian, Muslim, Jewish, and secular children. Other books in the author's trilogy: *The Political Life of Children* and *The Moral Life of Children* (for more information on the latter, see listing under "Books" under "Morality").

For Children

A Child's First Bible. By Sandol Stoddard. Dial, 1991. 96 pages. An adaptation featuring easy-to-understand language and colorful drawings for young children (ages three to six). Approved by Protestant, Catholic, and Jewish scholars.

My Friends' Beliefs: A Young Reader's Guide to World Religions. By Hiley Ward. Walker and Company, 1988. 183 pages. Offers easy-to-understand insights into the history, rituals, and leaders of the world's major religions. Intended for children ages twelve and up, although parents with younger children can read it themselves and pass along their findings. Illustrated with black-and-white photographs.

What Is God? By Etan Boritzer. Firefly Books, 1990. 32 pages. This book can assist parents who aren't quite sure how to talk about God with their children. Discusses many beliefs and religions, rather than one specific one. Talks about how Christians, Muslims, Buddhists, Jews, and others regard God and how differences in beliefs can cause conflict. Also points out the similarities among various religions. Helps bring God down to a level that children can understand. For children in grades one through seven.

Newsletter

Bringing Religion Home. Claretian Publication, 205 West Monroe Street, Chicago, Illinois 60606. Phone: 1/800-328-6515 or 312/236-7782. Offers parents support and encouragement in the religious education of their children. Offers advice on prayer and spiritual problems, as well as family and moral issues. Also reviews books. Issued monthly.

Raising Happy Children

Books

Back to the Family. By Ray Guarendi. Villard Books, 1990. 254 pages. One hundred American families answer the question, "What makes a happy family?" Time spent together, open communication, and effective discipline are among the topics explored.

Celebrate Your Child: The Art of Happy Parenting. By Richard Carlson. New World Library, 1992. 192 pages. For parents who want to help their children achieve lifelong happiness. Explains how to teach children to use their imaginations and to think positively about themselves and their world.

Flow: The Psychology of Optimal Experience. By Mihaly Csikszentmihalyi. Harper and Row, 1990. 303 pages. What makes people feel most happy? For a child, it might be putting the last block on a tower she has built; for a short-order cook, it might be placing a slice of cheese on a juicy hamburger patty. In this bestselling book, the author presents a theory of "optimal experience" based on the concept of *flow*—the state in which people are so involved in an activity that nothing else seems to matter. Based on information supplied by thousands of contented people from all walks of life living on various parts of the planet (and, on occasion, in paradise).

If You're Afraid of the Dark, Remember the Night Rainbow. By Cooper Edens. Green Tiger Press, 1991. Helps remind parents and children that every cloud has a silver lining; every problem has a solution. Teaches the important lesson of resilience. For parents as well as children.

Traits of a Healthy Family: Fifteen Traits Commonly Found in Healthy Families by Those Who Work with Them. By Dolores Curran. Harper San Francisco, 1985. In the author's survey of teachers, doctors, and other professionals who work with parents and children, the ability to communicate effectively emerged as the most highly rated quality in healthy families. (For more information on *Traits of a Healthy Family*, refer to "Books" listed under "General Resources" in this chapter.)

Family Rituals and Traditions

Books

Family Traditions: Celebrations for Holidays and Everyday. By Elizabeth Berg. Reader's Digest Association, 1992. 287 pages. Offers hundreds of ideas for creating rituals and meaningful family activities. Talks about the importance of rituals, routine activities, and family practices, pointing out how they add richness to our lives.

Mrs. Sharp's Traditions. By Sarah Ban Breathnach. Simon and Schuster, 1990. 224 pages. Contains nostalgic suggestions for recreating the family celebration and seasonal pastimes of the Victorian home. Offers tips on making daily events (mealtimes, bathtime, bedtime) memorable, as well as suggestions for special events (birthdays, "family night," etc.) and seasonal celebrations. Includes historical tidbits, recipes, and illustrations.

Rituals for Our Times: Celebrating, Healing, and Changing Our Lives and Our Relationships. By Evan Imber-Black, Ph.D., and Janine Roberts, Ed.D. HarperCollins, 1992. 331 pages. This book points out how meaningful rituals serve as anchors, providing stability for children and a sense of connectedness. Contains first-person stories and examples of rituals to help readers enhance the meaning of their own traditions, old and new.

Chapter 4

Inspiration for Parents

Books

Daily Affirmations for Parents. By Tian Dayton. Health Communications, 1992. 366 pages. Tells parents how to nurture their children and renew themselves during the ups and downs of parenthood.

The Joy of Parenthood. By Jan Blaustone. Meadowbrook Press, 1993. 102 pages. A collection of insightful quotations offering inspiration and encouragement for parents.

Meditations for New Mothers. By Beth Wilson Saavedra. Workman, 1992. 314 pages. A reassuring book of meditations. Addresses the doubts, conflicts, emotions, anxieties, and wonders of living with a newborn.

Meditations for Parents Who Do Too Much. By Jonathon and Wendy Lazear. Simon and Schuster, 1993. Meditations to help parents recharge their batteries and meet daily challenges. Gently reminds mothers and fathers to slow down, pay attention to their children, and recapture the joys and rewards of parenthood.

Today's Gift: Daily Meditations for Families. HarperSanFrancisco, 1984. 400 pages. A collection of inspiring quotes, messages, and thought-provoking questions to be shared among family members.

Chapter 5

Grandparents and Grandchildren

RESOURCES FOR GRANDPARENTS

Book

Grandparent Power! By Arthur Kornhaber with Sondra Forsyth. Crown, 1994. Explains how to strengthen the vital connection among grandparents, parents, and children.

Videotape

Grandparenting. Running time: 30 minutes. Veryl Rosenbaum, psychoanalyst and author, explores the importance of grandparents in today's families. Contains interviews with grandparents who discuss the various facets of family life today, including the contributions they make as members of the third generation. Available from Cambridge Parenting, P.O. Box 2153, Department PA5, Charleston, West Virginia 25328-2153. Phone: 1/800-468-4227.

Association

The Foundation for Grandparents. Box 326, Cohassett, Massachusetts 02025. This nonprofit organization works to enhance intergenerational relations. Organizes Grandparents Conferences, which bring together grandparents and grandchildren from around the country, along with experts in the field of intergenerational relations. Publishes a quarterly newsletter called *Vital Connections*.

TRAVELING TOGETHER

Associations

Grandtravel. Phone: 1/800-247-7651. Located in Chevy Chase, Maryland, this travel agency specializes in trips for grandparents and grandchildren. Washington, D.C., Colonial Williamsburg, and the coast of Maine are among their domestic destinations.

Vistatours. Phone: 1/800-248-4782. Offers trips for grandparents and grandchildren. Destinations include Nevada, New England, and South Dakota.

RESOURCES FOR GRANDCHILDREN

Books

Dear Annie. By Judith Caseley. Greenwillow, 1991. 32 pages. Annie saves all the warm letters and cards sent to her by her grandfather (beginning when she was born). When she's old enough, she dictates and writes her own replies. When Annie brings in her shoe-box full of grandpa's letters for show-and-tell, her classmates decide they want pen pals, too. For children ages five to eight.

Grandma and Grandpa Are Special People. By Barbara Kay Polland. Celestial Arts, 1984. 80 pages. Children describe all the things that make their grandmas and grandpas special (evening walks and raisin cookies included). For children ages five to eight.

Granpa. By John Burningham. Random House, 1992. This picture book focuses on the relationship between a young girl and her grandpa as they share special times together (tending a garden, caring for a sick teddy bear, etc.). Contains award-winning illustrations by John Burningham. For children ages four and up. (See listing under "Videotapes" as well.)

Me and My Grandma and **Me and My Grandpa.** Checkerboard Press, 1992. 26 pages each. For the very young, these photo board books feature babies and grandparents cuddling, playing, and otherwise engaged. For ages six months to three years.

Not the Piano, Mrs. Medley! By Evan Levine. Orchard Books, 1991. 32 pages. Mrs. Medley and her grandson Max set off for the beach one day. Oh, but they might need a radio, hats, boots, a Monopoly game, a table and chairs, and . . . . They make a series of trips back to the house to collect these items. Although Mrs. Medley finally realizes how silly they've been (in thinking they need all these things), they realize they forgot one important thing—their bathing suits! For children ages four to seven.

A Visit to Grandma's. By Nancy Carlson. Viking, 1991. Tina discovers that grandparents aren't all "old" when she visits her grandma in Florida. There she finds out her granny does aerobics, drives a shiny red sports car, and concocts wacky health shakes. For children ages three to eight.

Videotapes

Grandmother and Leslie. WTTW Chicago; distributed by Perennial

Education, Inc. Running time: 29 minutes. Part of the "Look at Me" series, this video presents a day's worth of activities shared by a grandmother and her grandchild. Explores the interaction and relationship between the two.

Granpa. Sony Music Video Enterprises. Running time: 30 minutes. Based on the children's book by John Burningham, this video shows how a young girl and her grandfather share a fun-filled day. Includes the voices of Peter Ustinov and Sarah Brightman. Distributed by Sony Music Video Enterprises and Baker and Taylor Video.

Software

Just Grandma and Me. Broderbund. CD-ROM, IBM, Macintosh. In this story by Mercer Mayer, Little Critter and his grandma go to the beach, where they have a series of exciting adventures. With myriad hidden "buttons" to discover on each page, children can spend countless hours exploring. Click on a chimney and it puffs out smoke; click on Little Critter and he talks to Grandma; click on a nest and you wake the baby bird. When children click on a word or text, it is highlighted and spoken by the computer (you can choose English, Spanish, or Japanese). Designed for computers with CD-ROM drives. For children ages three to eight.

Chapter 6

Health:
Your Child's Physical and Mental Health

GENERAL RESOURCES

Free and Inexpensive Resources

The American Academy of Pediatrics—Health Brochures. A variety of free health-related brochures are available from the American Academy of Pediatrics. Many of these are described under "Specific Topics in Health" (see Immunization, Circumcision, Drug Abuse, etc.). Others include *Allergies in Children*, which provides information on major and minor allergic reactions, and *Tobacco Abuse*, which discusses the harmful effects of passive smoking on children, points out the dangers of smokeless tobacco to adolescents, and encourages adult smokers to break the habit. You can ask your pediatrician for a copy of either of these or send a self-addressed, stamped envelope to American Academy of Pediatrics, "Name of brochure" (see appendix I for contact information).

Pediatric Referrals. In addition to health brochures, the American Academy of Pediatrics provides free listings of AAP member pediatricians and subspecialists (immunologists and pediatric neurologists, for example) located in specific parts of the country. To receive a listing of those in your area (or the areas to which you will be traveling), send a self-addressed, stamped business-size envelope, along with the names of the cities or towns for which you would like to receive a listing of pediatricians and, if applicable, the type of specialist(s) you are seeking to American Academy of Pediatrics, Pediatrician Referral (see appendix I for contact information).

Consumer Information Catalog. Many free and low-cost publications on various aspects of health are listed in the federal government's *Consumer Information Catalog*. Titles include *Getting a Second Opinion* (answers questions you might have and includes a toll-free number for locating specialists) and *Headaches* (explains possible causes and treatments of headaches). For a free copy of the catalog, write *Consumer Information Catalog*, P.O. Box 100, Pueblo, Colorado 81002.

Health Tips: What to Do for Childhood Emergencies and Illnesses. A free booklet covering twenty-one pediatric health problems ranging from animal bites and burns to sprains and teething. Also explains how to prevent common childhood illnesses and injuries, when to treat them at home, and when to call a doctor or ambulance. Available from Children's National Medical Center, 111 Michigan Avenue, N.W., Washington, D.C. 20010-2970. Phone: 202/939-4500.

Keeping Healthy: Parents, Teachers, and Children. A brochure offering tips on ways to keep children in early childhood programs healthy. Available for 50¢ from the National Association for the Education of Young Children (see appendix I for contact information).

What Parents Need to Know about Chickenpox. A free brochure, available with a self-addressed, stamped business envelope from the National Foundation for Infectious Diseases, c/o Health Information Services, P.O. Box 1486, North Wales, Pennsylvania 19454.

Books

The American Medical Association Family Medical Guide. Edited by Jeffrey R. M. Kunz, M.D. Random House, 1987. 832 pages. Includes descriptions of hundreds of common physical and mental illnesses. Also covers preventive measures, symptoms and self-diagnosis, and caring for the sick at home.

The Available Pediatrician: Every Parent's Guide to Common Childhood Illnesses. By Ralph Berberich, M.D., and Ann Parker, M.D. Pantheon Books, 1988. 239 pages. Based on questions parents most frequently ask their pediatricians, this book offers guidance on coping with routine illnesses. Tells parents how to recognize and deal with childhood ailments such as colds, fevers, chicken pox, and appendicitis. Explains when to call the doctor and when to treat at home (and how). Includes sections on sound health habits and preventive measures, immunization, and home safety.

Caring for Your Baby and Young Child: Birth to Age 5. Steven P. Shelow, M.D., F.A.A.P., editor-in-chief; Robert E. Hannemann, M.D., F.A.A.P., associate medical editor. Bantam Books, 1991. 676 pages. From the American Academy of Pediatrics, this reference book covers general health (pediatric visits, immunizations, and preventive measures) as well as medical problems. The second portion of the book is an A-to-Z compendium of medical problems including common infectious diseases, disabilities, musculoskeletal problems, skin problems, chronic conditions and diseases (including AIDS), and commonly used medications. Instructions for dealing with medical emergencies are also contained in this guide. Also available: *Caring for Your Adolescent: Ages 12 to 21.* (For more information on *Caring for Your Baby and Young Child,* see "Books" listed under "General Resources" in chapter 3.)

Child Care/Parent Care. By Marilyn Heins, M.D., and Anne M. Seiden, M.D. Doubleday, 1987. 905 pages. Written by a pediatrician and a psychiatrist (both of whom are experienced mothers), this extensive volume covers child safety (including steps to take during emergencies), preventive health, illness, medical treatment, choosing a health practitioner, and caring for a sick child at home. Also covers hygiene, child development, parenting approaches and techniques (including discipline), and the future of parenting in our society. Offers advice to parents on personal care as well.

Childhood Symptoms: Every Parent's Guide to Childhood Illnesses. By Edward R. Brace and John P. Pacanowski, M.D., F.A.A.P. Revised edition. (Revised by Ed Weiner.) HarperPerennial, 1992 (first published in 1985). 338 pages. A parent's guide to the signs and symptoms of illnesses and other problems that can affect infants, children, and adolescents. Divided into two A-to-Z sections, the first describing more than 175 specific diseases, disorders, and conditions; the second covering health concerns, complaints, symptoms, and problems (including abdominal pain, bed-wetting, circumcision, compulsive behavior, masturbation, nightmares, spitting up, stuttering, and scores of others).

Dr. Spock's Baby and Child Care. By Benjamin Spock, M.D., and Michael B. Rothenberg, M.D. Sixth edition. Simon and Schuster, 1992. 832 pages. Revised and updated for the 90s, this classic bestseller offers information and advice on the problems of infancy (jaundice, diarrhea, rashes, etc.), childhood illness (ear infections, allergies, chicken pox, colds, and more serious medical problems such as tuberculosis and heart murmurs), and first aid (for cuts, burns, head injuries, choking, poisonings, and so forth). Also covers common behavioral problems and everyday care and feeding.

How to Raise a Healthy Child . . . In Spite of Your Doctor. By Robert S. Mendelsohn, M.D. Ballantine, 1987. 304 pages. Provides parents with the information they need to make informed decisions about their child's health. What are the warning signs that indicate your child needs the help of a physician? Why are pediatricians so quick to prescribe medicine? And at what point does medical intervention do more harm than good? This book addresses such questions.

Mayo Clinic Family Health Book. David E. Larson, editor-in-chief. William Morrow, 1990. 1,392 pages. A massive volume offering descriptions of medical conditions, symptoms, and treatments, including information on more than 1,000 diseases. Also covers wellness, first aid procedures, and the health care system in general. (Note: For information on a CD-ROM version of the *Mayo Clinic Family Health Book*, see listing under "Computer Access to Health Information.")

The Mothercare Guide to Child Health. By Penny Stanway. Prentice-Hall, 1989. 224 pages. A reference guide to childhood symptoms, illnesses, and diseases. Covers anemia, colic, breathing difficulties, earaches, diarrhea, diaper rash, influenza, tetanus, tummy aches, and many other health topics.

The New American Encyclopedia of Children's Health. By Robert Hoekleman, Noni MacDonald, and David Baum. NAL-Dutton, 1991. 288 pages. Offers step-by-step guidelines for childhood health problems. Explains how to recognize them and how to react to them.

The New Child Health Encyclopedia. By the Boston Children's Medical Center. Delacorte Press, 1987. 740 pages. Designed as an easy reference for use in situations involving a child's health and safety: emotional and physical, emergencies and everyday questions, common ailments and serious diseases. Divided into four parts: (1) Keeping Children Healthy; (2) Finding Health Care for Children; (3) Emergencies; and (4) Diseases and Symptoms.

The Parents' Guide to Baby and Child Medical Care. Edited by Terril H. Hart. Revised edition. Meadowbrook Press, 1991. 241 pages. Contains updated information on more than 150 common children's illnesses, injuries, and emergencies, including illustrated treatment procedures. A description of the problem, advice on when to get professional help, and a listing of symptoms are included with each entry.

The Parent's Pediatric Companion. By Gilbert Simon, M.D., and Marcia Cohen. William Morrow, 1985. 378 pages. Explains the physical and behavioral conditions that are part of the natural growth and development of a healthy child from birth through adolescence. Organized in three parts: The Newborn, The Preschooler, and The Older Child. Each part includes a description of the physical changes that normal growth produces during that stage of life, a discussion of problems that can arise, and guidelines for parents on what to do.

Safe and Healthy: A Parent's Guide to Children's Illnesses and Accidents. By William Sears, M.D. La Leche League International, 1989. 239 pages. Guides parents through childhood illnesses and explains what to do in case of an accident. From La Leche League's Growing Family Series.

The Self-Help Sourcebook: Finding and Forming Mutual Aid Self-Help Groups. By the American Self-Help Clearinghouse staff. Fourth edition. St. Clares-Riverside Medical Center, 1992. 222 pages. Provides information on support groups to help individuals and families deal with physical and emotional challenges (managing cancer, parenting a child with disabilities, etc.). Includes a listing of toll-free help lines, as well as guidelines on how to start up a support group. Available from the American Self-Help Clearinghouse, St. Clares-Riverside Hospital, 25 Pocono Road, Denville, New Jersey 07834. Phone: 201/625-7101.

Should I Call the Doctor? A Comprehensive Guide to Understanding Your Child's Illnesses and Injuries. By Christine A. Nelson, M.D., and Susan Pescar. Warner Books, 1986. 742 pages. A guide to child health care from birth through adolescence, including quick reference advice on childhood injuries and illnesses. Explains how to safeguard against accidents, recognize the symptoms of serious illnesses and injuries, evaluate your child's medical condition, treat your child at home, and know when to see a doctor.

Take Charge of Your Child's Health: A Guide to Recognizing Symptoms and Treating Minor Illnesses at Home. By George Wootan, M.D., and Sarah Verney. Crown, 1992. 349 pages. Intended to help save parents unnecessary trips to the pediatrician, this book shows you how to take into account your child's history and symptoms, and then diagnose and treat common illnesses using remedies you have at home. Also explains how to choose, evaluate, and get what you want from a doctor.

Taking Care of Your Child: A Parent's Guide to Medical Care. By Robert H. Pantell, M.D., Donald M. Vickery, M.D., and James F. Fries, M.D. Addison-Wesley, 1990. 525 pages. A manual to help parents make wise decisions regarding medical care for their children Offers advice on a wide range of health-related topics including prenatal nutrition. Explains how to diagnose illness, when and how to treat your child at home, and when to call the doctor.

Testing and Your Child: What You Should Know about 150 of the Most Common Medical, Educational, and Psychological Tests. By Virginia E. McCullough. Penguin Books, 1992. 334 pages. This book includes descriptions of a variety of medical tests (Apgar, cultures, skeletal screening, blood tests, asthma tests, etc.). Each entry includes information on who must administer the test (and under what conditions), what the test tests for and what it cannot reveal, what preparation is required, what affects scoring, and what follow-up testing might be recommended. Also includes full descriptions of developmental, psychological, and educational tests.

What to Expect the First Year. By Arlene Eisenberg, Heidi E. Murkoff, and Sandee E. Hathaway, B.S.N. Workman Publishing, 1989. 671 pages. Includes guidelines for selecting the right physician and explains what to do when your baby is sick. Lists common childhood illnesses, explaining the symptoms, the cause and transmission of, treatment for, and preventive measures. Also contains sections on low-birthweight infants and babies with specific problems (malformations, autism, down syndrome, etc.). A first aid guide for parents is included as well. (For more information on *What to Expect the First Year*, see "Books" listed under "General Resources" in chapter 1.)

When Do I Call the Doctor? By Loraine Stern, M.D. Doubleday, 1993. 274 pages. A guide to more than two hundred major and minor childhood medical concerns, including headaches, hiccups, swollen glands, swimmer's ear, bed-wetting, rashes, ringworm, middle ear infection, habits (such as nail biting and thumb sucking), and scarlet fever. Each entry offers an overview of the problem

and guidelines on treatment (including advice on when to call your pediatrician). Explains whether or not the "problem" is normal (or at least common) in children. Health concerns of the newborn are treated in a separate section. Comes with a children's emergency and first-aid pull-out chart.

Your Child: A Medical Guide. By the editors of *Consumer Guide* with Ira J. Chasnoff, M.D. Beekman House, 1983. 384 pages. An illustrated reference guide containing current information on the common illnesses, diseases, disorders, and other problems of infancy and childhood. Arranged alphabetically, with a special emergency reference section containing step-by-step instructions for dealing with life-threatening situations. Available from The Right Start (see chapter 27 for contact information).

Your Child's Health: The Parents' Guide to Symptoms, Emergencies, Common Illnesses, Behavior, and School Problems. By Barton D. Schmitt, M.D., F.A.A.P. Revised edition. Bantam, 1991. 672 pages. Winner of the *Child* magazine book award for excellence in family issues, this guide explains how to keep your child healthy, how to handle medical emergencies and injuries, how to recognize and treat common symptoms and illnesses, how to prevent and solve behavioral problems, and how to care for newborns. Also discusses normal growth and development and family issues, such as child care arrangements and the impact that divorce has on children. Also by Barton Schmitt: *Pediatric Telephone Advice* (Little, Brown, 1980).

Your Child's Symptoms: A Parent's Guide to Understanding Pediatric Medicine. By Bruce Taubman. Simon and Schuster, 1992. 384 pages. Describes common signs of childhood illnesses, the course they take, and how to treat them. Also explains how to evaluate pediatricians and deal with medical professionals. Winner of *Child* magazine's 1992 award for excellence in family issues.

Your Growing Child: From Babyhood through Adolescence. By Penelope Leach. Alfred A. Knopf, 1986. An A-to-Z compendium of vital information for parents. Accidents, allergy, bedwetting, colds, coughs, croup, eating disorders, headaches, pain and pain control, rabies, ringworm, tetanus, thrush, tonsils, vomiting, warts, and whooping cough are some of the health topics explored in this comprehensive volume. (For more information on *Your Growing Child*, see "Books" listed under "General Resources" in chapter 3.)

Periodicals

Children's Health

American Baby. Cahners Publishing Co., 475 Park Avenue South, New York, New York 10016. Phone: 212/689-3600. A monthly magazine for expectant and new parents with an emphasis on the physical and mental well-being of baby and mother. Covers topics in health, safety, and basic care (feeding, bathing, etc.). Issued monthly.

Child Health Alert. P.O. Box 338, Newton Highlands, Massachusetts 02161. Phone: 617/237-3310. This six-page newsletter surveys current developments affecting children's health. Contains features on health-related topics (infections, cholesterol, caffeine's effect on kids, and controlling head lice are examples), based on analysis and interpretation of articles published in professional journals. Also offers information on safety, including listings of product recalls. Issued monthly.

For Quick and Easy Temperature Taking

Thermoscan Instant Thermometer. Using this ear thermometer, parents can get an accurate temperature read in just one second. Simply place in your child's ear and press the button. To order, contact Thermoscan at 1/800-EAR-SCAN.

Healthy Kids. Approved by the American Academy of Pediatrics, *Healthy Kids (Birth-10)* covers safety and health issues. Nutrition, fitness, common illnesses, child development, and learning opportunities are among the topics explored. Published by Cahners Publishing (475 Park Avenue South, New York, NY 10016) and available, free of charge, through pediatric offices. (Order forms are also available from the American Academy of Pediatric's division of public education. Phone: 1/800-336-6348.)

Pediatric Report's Child Health Newsletter. Box 155, 71 Hope Street, Providence, Rhode Island 02906-2062. An eight-page newsletter written by pediatricians for parents, educators, child care providers, and health professionals. Offers child health updates and easy-to-understand summaries of research findings reported in medical journals. Issued monthly.

Pediatrics. 141 Northwest Point Boulevard, P.O. Box 927, Elk Grove Village, Illinois 60009-0927. Phone: 708/228-5505 or 1/800-433-9016. Monthly journal of the American Academy of Pediatrics containing technical articles of interest to specialists in the field. However, according to *Magazines for Libraries* (R. R.

Bower), parents and other professionals working with children will also be interest in updates on topics such as nutrition, breastfeeding, genetic research, vitamins, and car safety. Each article is abstracted to make browsing easier.

Pediatrics for Parents. P.O. Box 1069, Bangor, Maine 04402-1069. Phone: 207/942-7334. A monthly newsletter containing a variety of health-related articles. Covers topics such as allergies, colic, and hay fever. Includes a section on toy recalls as well. Write or call for a free sample copy.

Family Health

American Health. RD Publications, a subsidiary of the Reader's Digest Association, 28 West 23rd Street, New York, New York 10010. Phone: 1/800-365-5005. Covers various aspects of health, including medicine, nutrition, fitness and sports, beauty, mental health, and health-related consumer issues, such as insurance coverage. Includes summaries of research findings, health facts, and feature articles, as well as resource listings. Issued ten times annually.

The Edell Health Letter. P. O. Box 57812, Boulder, Colorado 80322-7812. This monthly newsletter offers colorful summaries of research findings reported in medical journals. Food and nutrition, exercise, and psychology are among the topics covered.

FDA Consumer. Food and Drug Administration, Rockville, Maryland 20857. The official magazine of the U.S. Food and Drug Administration (FDA) the consumer protection agency responsible for food, drugs, medical devices, and related products. Covers topics such as children's vaccinations, new medicines, prescription and nonprescription drugs, diet and nutrition, food safety, and

other health-related topics. Also reports on FDA research and agency rulings. Issued ten times a year. [For a subscription, contact the Superintendent of Documents, U.S. Government Printing Office (see appendix B for address and phone number).]

Harvard Health Letter. P.O. Box 420300, Palm Coast, Florida 33142-0300. Phone: 1/800-829-9045. An eight-page newsletter covering current health concerns. Each issue contains one or two feature articles, as well as summaries of research findings from professional journals. Topics have included postpartum depression, human gene therapy for children, and food irradiation.

Health. P.O. Box 56863, Boulder, Colorado 80322-6863. Phone: 1/800-274-2522. This magazine explores various aspects of health, including nutrition, safety, fitness, medicine, mental health, environmental health, and health-related consumer issues. Drawing from recent research findings, the magazine aims to provide timely information in an entertaining fashion. Issued bimonthly.

Mayo Clinic Health Letter. Mayo Foundation for Medical Education and Research, 200 First Street, S.W., Rochester, Minnesota 55905. Phone: 1/800-333-9038. An eight-page newsletter containing "reliable information for a healthier life." Each issue includes a cover story (topics have included the common cold, the health benefits of walking, and blood cholesterol levels), along with shorter items examining various aspects of health and safety. Back issues are available (write for a listing of these).

Medical Abstracts Newsletter. P.O. Box 2170, Teaneck, New Jersey 07666. Billed as a "direct pipeline to the latest breakthroughs in health care," this newsletter summarizes articles from 150 professional medical journals. Covers breakthroughs in medicine, disease, pediatrics, obstetrics, gynecology, psychiatry, and other areas. Written to inform the layperson about current research in medicine. Issued monthly.

Prevention. Rodale Press, 33 East Minor Street, Emmaus, Pennsylvania 18098. Phone: 215/967-5171. A monthly magazine emphasizing a healthy lifestyle with a special emphasis on the prevention of illness. Includes information on children's health and healthy parenting strategies. Topics explored include nutrition, medicine, exercise, and mental health.

University of California, Berkeley. Wellness Letter: The Newsletter of Nutrition, Fitness, and Stress Management. P.O. Box 420148, Palm Coast, Florida 32142. An eight-page newsletter published in association with the University of California School of Public Health. Contains current health information with an eye on wellness and informed medical consumerism. Covers medicine, nutrition, sports and exercise, environmental issues, and stress management. Issued monthly.

Medical/Professional Journals

American Journal of Diseases of Children. See American Medical Association, under "Associations."

American Journal of Public Health. See American Public Health Association, under "Associations."

The Journal of Pediatrics. Mosby, Inc., Journal Subscription Services, 11830 Westline Industrial Drive, St. Louis, Missouri 63146. Phone: 314/872-8370 or 1/800-453-4351.

Journal of the American Medical Association. See American Medical Association, under "Associations."

The Lancet. Lancet Ltd., 46 Bedford Square, London WC1B 3SL, England. Phone: 44-71-436-4981 (North American Edition: 428 East Preston Street, Baltimore, Maryland 21202. Phone: 410/528-4000).

The New England Journal of Medicine. P.O. Box 9150, Waltham, Massachusetts 02254. Phone: 617/734-9800 or 1/800-843-6356.

Hotlines

Below is a sampling of health-related helplines. Many others can be found in *Who to Call*, by Daniel Starer (William Morrow) and the *National Healthlines Directory (Toll-free Numbers)*, compiled by the staff of Herner and Company (available from Information Resources Press, 1110 North Glebe Road, Suite 550, Arlington, Virginia 22201). In addition, the National Health Information Center provides a list of toll-free numbers for health information. For a copy, send $1.00 to the center, P.O. Box 1133, Washington, D.C. 20013-1133.

The American Baby Helpline. Phone: 1/900-860-4888 (twenty-four-hour-a-day helpline operating seven days a week. The cost is 95¢ per minute). Prerecorded messages offer expert advice on a variety of baby-related topics. After dialing the main number, callers enter a two-digit code number indicating their topic of choice. Below is a partial listing of available topics. A complete listing of topics can be found in a current issue of *American Baby* magazine (see "Periodicals" listed under "General Resources" in chapter 3).

Colic (27)
Diarrhea (36)
Giving medicine (32)
Immunization (33)
Taking baby outdoors (26)
Taking baby's temperature (30)

Treating a cold (35)
Treating injuries (47)

Ask-A-Nurse. Phone: 1/800-535-1111. For parents whose children develop an unusual medical symptom late at night or on weekends (when most doctor's offices are closed), this hotline can put callers in touch with a registered nurse who will answer health questions and provide referrals to physicians who will accept your medical insurance. More than two hundred hospitals in states across the country take part in the Ask-A-Nurse program. To find out if there is an Ask-A-Nurse hotline in your area, call the toll-free number listed above using a touch-tone phone.

Headaches Hotline. National Headache Foundation. Phone: 1/800-843-2256 (9:00 a.m. to 5:00 p.m., central standard time). Parents concerned about a child's headaches can call the National Headache Foundation's toll-free number to ask general questions. (Parents can receive more detailed information by sending a self-addressed, stamped envelope along with a note explaining their child's symptoms, including when and under what circumstances the headaches occur.)

Health Helpline. Phone: 1/800-336-4797 (Monday through Friday, 9:00 a.m. to 5:00 p.m., eastern standard time). A service of the National Health Information Center (P.O. Box 1133, Washington, D.C. 20013-1133). Provides information on AIDS, cancer, health insurance, alcohol and other drug abuse, and asthma and allergies. Also informs callers where they can get a copy of a pamphlet on free health care, by government information specialist Matthew Lesko.

Parenting Hotline. Phone: 1/900-535-MOMS (the cost is $1.95 for the first minute and 95¢ for each additional minute). A service of *Parenting* magazine and the National Parenting Center. Callers can select the age group of their choice (pregnancy, newborns, infants, toddlers, preschool, preteen, or adolescence) then choose a topic from the ever-changing menu. Child experts such as Penelope Leach, Thomas Armstrong, and Vicki Lansky can then be heard on prerecorded messages addressing topics such as ear infections, congestion, child obesity, and much more. Topics change daily. Alternatively, parents can leave a personalized question and will receive a written reply.

Parents Helpline. *Parents* magazine has set up a 900 number (the cost is 95¢ per minute) so that parents can receive advice on various topics, including child safety, twenty-four hours a day. Dial 1/900-903-KIDS, then enter the two numbers next to the topic of your choice. (In case of technical difficulties, call 1/800-253-3688.) Here is a partial listing of available topics. (A complete listing of topics can be found in the most recent issue of *Parents* magazine, available at most newsstands.)

Allergies, Pets, and Kids (01)
Babies' Coughs and Sneezes (03)
Biting (06)
Chicken Pox (11)
Colds and Flu (52)
Colic and Its Causes (14)
Constipated Babies (15)
Day Care and Colds (16)
Diaper Rash (18)
Diarrhea (19)
Ear Infections (20)
Earwax Buildup (21)
Fever and Illness (22)
Head Lice (25)
Hiccup Cures (26)
Nosebleeds (61)
Obese Kids (32)
Secondhand Smoke (35)
Teething (43)
Thumb Sucking (45)

Television

The American Baby TV Show. This 30-minute program airs Sunday mornings at 11:00 a.m. (eastern/pacific time) on the Family Channel (FAM). This show explores various aspects of your young child's physical and emotional well-being. New format includes audience participation.

The Healthy Kids TV Show. Hosted by model and mother Kim Alexis, this cable television series provides parents and caregivers of children, newborn to age five, with current information on various aspects of children's health. Programs have explored ear infections, vision, first aid, dental care, and allergies, among many other topics. Produced by Cahners Childcare Group in association with the American Academy of Pediatrics, this thirty-minute program airs Sunday mornings at 11:30 a.m. (eastern/pacific time) on the Family Channel (FAM). Program guides are available from the Healthy Kids Show, 475 Park Avenue South, New York, New York 10016.

Computer Access to Health Information

Interactive Computer System

Healthtouch. A health care computer system with terminals in seven hundred locations across the country. Users can simply touch a computer screen to gain access to health information, including health facts, nutrition guidelines, and preventive health care advice. Produced by the American Academy of Pediatrics. Call 1/800-825-3742 to find out if there is a system in your area.

Software

Mayo Clinic Family Health Book. Mayo Clinic Interactive Ventures. A CD-ROM version of the book (see listing under "Books"), which can be used with Macintosh computers or computers that use Microsoft Windows software. This interactive edition, which sells for $99.95, includes everything offered in the book plus sound and animation (including animation of medical procedures).

The Pediatric Advisor. Clinical Reference Systems, Ltd. A computer software program by Barton D. Schmitt, M.D., F.A.A.P., which can be used with a Macintosh or PC-MS/DOS compatible computer. Provides advice for parents on over six hundred infant, child, and adolescent health problems. Available for $395 from Clinical Reference Systems. Phone: 1/800-237-8401 or 303/220-1661.

Databases

Directory of Online Healthcare Databases. A guide to dozens of online healthcare databases, available for $38 by calling 503/471-1627.

Medline. A database of 3,600 medical journals, which can be used by anyone with a personal computer, a modem, and an inexpensive software package such as Grateful Med. For more information, call 1/800-638-8480.

Health Data Brokers

The Health Resource Inc. 209 Katherine Drive, Conway, Arkansas 72032. Phone: 501/329-5272. This service offers information on specific medical problems. Provides individualized research reports, including current treatment procedures. The fee for this services ranges from $85 (for short reports ranging from 20 to 25 pages) to $225 (for reports ranging from 50 to 150 pages). There is a shipping charge as well.

Planetree Health Resource Center. California Pacific Medical Center. Phone: 415/923-3680. Provides information packets on specific illnesses, which include book excerpts, magazine articles, and material pulled from health databases.

Associations

American Academy of Pediatrics. 141 Northwest Point Boulevard, P.O. Box 927, Elk Grove Village, Illinois 60009-0927. Phone: 708/228-5005 or 1/800-433-9016. An organization of forty-four thousand pediatricians dedicated to the health, safety, and well-being of infants, children, adolescents, and young adults. While the academy primarily serves pediatricians and other health professionals, many of its publications are geared toward parents and are available through pediatric offices.

Single copies of educational brochures can be ordered free of charge directly from the American Academy of Pediatrics (AAP) (see listing under "Free and Inexpensive Resources").

Together with the Cahners Childcare Group, AAP participates in the production of "The Healthy Kids TV Show" (see listing under "Television").

Offers a series of child care books written by AAP members, including *Caring for Your Baby and Young Child: Birth to Age 5* (for more information, see listing under "Books").

Publishes *Pediatrics*, a professional journal issued monthly (see listing under "Periodicals" for more information). Also publishes *Pediatrics in Review*, the academy's continuing education journal, and the monthly membership newspaper *AAP News*. Periodically publishes manuals on such topics as infectious diseases, school health, and hospital care.

American Council on Science and Health. 1995 Broadway, New York, New York 10028-5860. Phone:

212/362-7044. A consumer education association promoting scientifically balanced evaluation of nutrition, chemicals, lifestyle factors, the environment, and human health. Founded in 1978, the council now has a board of two hundred scientists, physicians, and policy advisors. Publishes *Priorities: For Long Life and Good Health*, a quarterly publication covering fitness, nutrition, health hazards, safety, and other health-related topics. Also publishes research reports.

American Health Foundation. 320 East Forty-third Street, New York, New York 10017. Phone: 212/953-1900. Promotes preventive medicine, conducts research, and offers screening and intervention services. Produces public health education programs, including "Know Your Body," which includes curriculum material with teachers' guides for children in kindergarten through sixth grade. Plans Child Health Day, which helps focus the nation's attention on the importance of children's health.

American Medical Association. 515 North State Street, Chicago, Illinois 60610. Phone: 312/464-4818. Professional association of physicians. Represents the medical profession before congress and government agencies. Maintains a lending library, and disseminates information to association members, as well as the general public. Publishes a variety of medical journals, including the *Journal of the American Medical Association* and the *American Journal of Diseases of Children*.

American Public Health Association. 1015 Fifteenth Street, N.W., Washington, D.C. 20005. Phone: 202/789-5600. Seeks to promote and protect public health. Works to establish standards, including uniform practices and procedures. Conducts research and produces reports on findings (one report published by this association found that infection was more easily transmitted through the use of cloth diapers). Also produces periodicals, including the *American Journal of Public Health*, a refereed journal covering current aspects of public health, including health factors in the workplace. Issued monthly, it contains reports of original research and evaluations.

Association of Maternal and Child Health Programs. 2001 L Street, N.W., Suite 308, Washington, D.C. 20036. Phone: 202/775-0436. An association for individuals involved in the administration of state and regional maternal and child health care programs or programs for children with special health needs. Informs decision makers and others in the public and private sectors, as well as the general public on the health care needs of mothers and children. Recommends child health policies, and assists those involved in child health care services. Committees include Health of School Age Children, Early Childhood Health and Development, and Children with Special Needs.

Emily Anderson Family Learning Center. Phoenix Children's Hospital. Phone: 602/239-2867 or 602/239-6902. At this resource lab, parents of children with AIDS, leukemia, diabetes, epilepsy, and other medical problems can educate themselves by watching videotapes and reading textbooks. They can also use dolls to practice home health-care procedures such as cardiopulmonary resuscitation (CPR), injections, and breathing techniques. While parents learn more about their child's illness, their child can read books about kids with ailments like their own. Doctors and families across the country are considering opening similar centers in their communities.

Human Growth Foundation. 7777 Leesburg Pike, Falls Church, Virginia 22043. Phone: 703/883-1773 or 1/800-451-6434. A union of families and individuals working to help medical science better understand the process of growth. Supports growth research, disseminates information, and presents educational programs to families and physicians. Offers a growth chart and a variety of free brochures for parents concerned about the physical growth of their children.

International Child Health Foundation. American City Building, P.O. Box 1205, Columbia, Maryland 21044. Phone: 301/596-4514. Addresses major health issues which affect children and their mothers, particularly in developing countries and medically underserved regions of the United States. Develops and encourages the use of inexpensive medical technologies. Conducts educational programs and workshops on disease prevention and simple medical treatments. Publishes the quarterly *International Child Health Foundation Newsletter*, which contains research summaries and information on foundation activities.

National Association of Pediatric Nurse Associates and Practitioners. 1101 Kings Highway North, No. 206, Cherry Hill, New Jersey 08034. Phone: 609/667-1773. Seeks to improve the quality of infant and child health care, and works to make health care services more accessible. Provides a forum for the continuing education of members. Publishes the *Journal of Pediatric Health Care*, a bimonthly containing news on legislation, literature abstracts, book reviews, and product information.

Also publishes *Pediatric Nurse Practitioner*, a bimonthly newsletter.

National Center for Education in Maternal and Child Health. Phone: 703/524-7802. Funded by the Office of Maternal and Child Health, U.S. Department of Health and Human Services, this organization provides education and information services for parents and professionals who have maternal and child health interests. Refers parents to appropriate hotlines and organizations. Produces newsletters, bibliographies, resources guides, brochures, and directories, including *Reaching Out: A Directory of National Organizations Related to Maternal and Child Health* and *Starting Early: A Guide to Federal Resources in Maternal and Child Health* (both published annually). Will send a publications catalog upon request.

National Council on Patient Information and Education. 666 Eleventh Street, N.W., Suite 810, Washington, D.C. 20001. Phone: 202/347-6711. Council members include health care organizations, federal agencies, voluntary health agencies, and consumer groups. Works to improve the dialogue between consumers and health care providers and to increase the availability of information about prescription medicines. Offers a variety of informational materials, including a quarterly newsletter, the *Directory of Prescription Drug Information and Education Programs and Resources*, and a free brochure, *A Parent's Guide to Medicine Use By Children* (see "Free and Inexpensive Resources," listed under "Prescription and Nonprescription Drugs" in this chapter).

National Foundation for Infectious Diseases. 4733 Bethesda Avenue, Suite 750, Bethesda, Maryland 20814. Phone: 301/656-0003. Supports research into the causes of—and cures for—infectious diseases; educates professionals and the general public on infectious diseases. Publishes *Double Helix*, a bimonthly newsletter covering research, education, legislation, and prevention of infectious diseases. Other publications include a free brochure, *What Parents Need to Know about Chickenpox* (see listing under "Free and Inexpensive Resources").

National Maternal and Child Health Clearinghouse. Phone: 703/821-8955. Funded by the Office of Maternal and Child Health, U.S. Department of Health and Human Services, this organization collects and disseminates information on maternal and child health, primarily from materials developed by the U.S. Department of Health and Human Services. Produces an annual publications catalog.

The People's Medical Society. 462 Walnut Street, Allentown, Pennsylvania 18102. Phone: 215/770-1670 or 1/800-624-8773. Consumer advocate for better and less expensive medical treatment. Promotes preventive health care, self-care, and alternative health care procedures, and addresses major policy issues. Publishes *People's Medical Society Newsletter*, a bimonthly membership publication covering topics of interest to medical consumers, including health insurance, consumer rights, medical treatments, product safety, finding capable physicians, and the health care system as a whole. Includes excerpts from society publications. Also produces health bulletins, bibliographies, and other informational materials, including a pamphlet called *A Parents' Rights Guide*, containing general information on your child's health and your legal rights.

Government Agencies

Agency for Health Care Policy and Research. P.O. Box 8547, Silver Spring, Maryland 20907. Phone: 1/800-358-9295 (Monday through Friday, 9:00 a.m. to 5:00 p.m., eastern standard time). A component of the Public Health Service, the goals of this agency are to promote high-quality health care; increase access to care; and to improve the way health services are organized, delivered, and financed. Conducts research and offers a variety of free health-related publications and reprints, including *Insuring the Children: A Decade of Change* (a reprint from *Health Affairs*) and *Checkup on Health Insurance Choices*, a booklet demystifying health insurance (see "Health Insurance" listed under "Free and Inexpensive Resources"). The agency anticipates adding more consumer-oriented publications in the future (currently, the majority of its offerings are targeted at professionals).

Centers for Disease Control and Prevention. Public Health Service, U.S. Department of Health and Human Services, Atlanta, Georgia 30333. Phone: 404/639-3286. Works with partners throughout the nation and around the world to monitor health, detect and investigate health problems, conduct research to enhance prevention, develop and advocate sound public health policies, implement prevention strategies, promote healthy behaviors, and foster safe and healthful environments. Centers and programs of CDC include the following:

> **Epidemiology Program Office.** Works to provide domestic and international epidemiologic, communication, and statistical support, and trains experts in epidemiology.

International Health Program Office. Works to strengthen the capacity of other nations to reduce disease, disability, and death.

National Center for Chronic Disease Prevention and Health Promotion. Works to prevent death and disability from chronic diseases and promote healthy personal behaviors.

National Center for Environmental Health. Works to prevent death and disability due to environmental factors.

National Center for Health Statistics. Monitors the health of the American people, the impact of illness and disability, and factors affecting health and the nation's health care system. Collects statistics on health nationwide, including the average size of newborns (they're getting bigger!).

National Center for Infectious Diseases. Works to prevent and control unnecessary disease and death caused by infectious diseases of public health importance.

National Center for Injury Prevention and Control. Works to prevent and control nonoccupational injuries, both those that are unintentional and those that result from violence.

National Center for Prevention Services. Works to prevent and control vaccine-preventable diseases, human immunodeficiency virus (HIV) infection, sexually transmitted diseases, tuberculosis, dental diseases, and the introduction of diseases from other countries.

National Institute for Occupational Safety and Health. Works to prevent workplace-related injuries, illnesses, and premature death caused by trauma; toxic chemicals, dusts, and radiation; musculosketal and psychological stressors; noise; and other occupational hazards.

Public Health Practice Program Office. Works to improve the effectiveness of public health delivery systems in promoting health and preventing disease.

National Health Information Center, Office of Disease Prevention and Health Promotion. P.O. Box 1133, Washington, D.C. 20013-1133. The National Health Information Center can help individuals locate health information, publications, or programs, using its database of over 1,100 health information resources. In addition, the center offers a variety of government-sponsored health publications, including a list of toll-free numbers for health information (available for $1.00). Write for a copy of the center's free publications list. Also operates a health hotline (1/800-336-4797), which provides information on AIDS, cancer, health insurance, asthma and allergies, health insurance, and alcohol and other drug abuse. A service of the Office of Disease Prevention and Health Promotion, Public Health Service, U.S. Department of Health and Human Services.

The National Institute of Child Health and Human Development. Office of Research and Reporting, Building 31, Room 2A32, Bethesda, Maryland 20892. Phone: 301/496-5133. Conducts and sponsors research on the normal processes of growth and development upon which the health of both children and adults depends. Also strives to find out what causes developmental abnormalities and disease, how these might be prevented, and how they can be treated. Topics under study include the physical and behavioral adaption of the newborn, child nutrition, the development of the immune system, learning and cognitive development, developmental disabilities, and family and household structure. Call the Office of Research Reporting for information on research topics, programs, and publications for professional and lay audiences.

National Institutes of Health. Office of the Director, Editorial Operations Branch, Office of Communications, Bethesda, Maryland 20892. Phone: 301/496-4000 (main number) or 301/496-4143 (publications department). The National Institutes of Health seeks to improve the health and well-being of Americans by conducting and supporting biomedical research. Includes the following institutes:

> The National Cancer Institute
> National Eye Institute
> National Heart, Lung, and Blood Institute
> National Institute of Allergy and Infectious Diseases
> National Institute of Arthritis and Musculoskeletal and Skin Diseases
> National Institute of Child Health and Human Development (see separate listing)
> National Institute on Deafness and Other Communication Disorders
> National Institute of Dental Research
> National Institute of Diabetes and Digestive and Kidney Diseases
> National Institute of Environmental Health Sciences
> National Institute of General Medical Sciences
> National Institute of Mental Health

National Institute of Neurological Disorders and Stroke
National Institute on Aging
National Institute on Alcohol Abuse and Alcoholism
National Institute on Drug Abuse

The National Institutes of Health produces a free publications list that combines works issued by the individual institutes, centers, and offices (publications in these lists are divided into two broad categories: "For Health Professionals" and "For the General Public"). Under the National Heart, Lung, and Blood Institute, for example, you will find *Parents Guide*

– Cholesterol in Children. The National Institute of Allergy and Infectious Diseases offers *Allergic Diseases: Medicine for the Public* and *The Immune System: How It Works.* Under the National Institute of Child Health and Human Development, you will find *Facts about Anorexia Nervosa; New Faces of AIDS: A Maternal and Pediatric Epidemic;* and *Pregnancy Basics (What You Need to Know and Do to Have a Good Healthy Baby).* These publications are generally available to the public free of charge upon written request. Contact the institutes for their complete list.

FOR CHILDREN: TOOLS TO HELP KIDS UNDERSTAND DOCTOR'S VISITS

Books

My Doctor. By Harlow Rockwell. Macmillan, 1973. 24 pages. Combines simple text and detailed illustrations to help young children overcome their fear of visiting the doctor. For children ages two to six.

When I See My Doctor. By Susan Kuklin. Bradbury Press, 1988. 32 pages. Assures young children that a visit to the doctor's office isn't so bad. Combines simple words and full-color photographs, presenting a real-life picture. For children ages three to eight.

Toys

Doctor's Office. This play kit contains realistic medical equipment for pint-sized doctors. Among the dozens of pieces are an eye chart, bandages, appointment cards, and a stethoscope that really works. Comes in a cardboard medicine cabinet for easy storing. Available from Toys to Grow On (see chapter 27 for contact information).

Hospital Playsets. Highly detailed playsets, complete with patients, medical professionals, and healthcare equipment (tiny surgical tools, crutches, removable casts, etc.). Three separate sets available (Operating Room, Ambulance, and Hospital Room) for hours of imaginative play. Available from Childswork/Childsplay (see chapter 27 for contact information).

PRESCRIPTION AND NONPRESCRIPTION DRUGS

Free and Inexpensive Resources

Buying Medicine? Help Protect Yourself Against Tampering. Explains how to make sure the medicine you buy has not been tampered with. Published in 1992 by the Food and Drug Administration. For ordering information, write for a copy of the free *Consumer Information Cata-*

log, available from the Consumer Information Center, P.O. Box 100, Pueblo, Colorado 81002.

Kids Aren't Just Small Adults. Offers guidelines on giving nonprescription medicine to children. Published in 1992 by the Food and Drug Administration. For ordering information, write for a copy of the free *Consumer Information Catalog*, available from the Consumer Information Center, P.O. Box 100, Pueblo, Colorado 81002.

A Parent's Guide to Medicine Use by Children. A brochure explaining how to talk to your child, health professional, and child care provider about administering medicine. Available from the National Council on Patient Information and Education, 666 Eleventh Street, N.W., Suite 810, Washington, D.C. 20001. Send a self-addressed, stamped, business-size envelope along with your request.

RX to OTC. Offers information on prescription medications that have become available over-the-counter. Published in 1991 by the Food and Drug Administration. For ordering information, write for a copy of the free *Consumer Information Catalog*, available from the Consumer Information Center, P.O. Box 100, Pueblo, Colorado 81002.

Books

The Complete Drug Reference. By the United States Pharmacopeial Convention. Consumer Reports Books, 1992. 1,656 pages. This enormous volume covers hundreds of available drugs, offering dosage information, directions for use, possible side effects, and colored illustrations for easy identification. Includes listings of brand names and long lists of the medication's contraindications—the medical conditions

under which the use of a particular drug is unadvisable.

The Essential Guide to Prescription Drugs. By James W. Long. HarperPerennial, 1994. 1,156 pages. Large compendium covering hundreds of available drugs. Each entry describes the benefits and possible risks; explains how the drug works; offers precautions for use; and provides dosage information, guidelines to follow while taking the drug, and advisability of use during pregnancy or while breastfeeding. Also mentions the availability of generic forms and provides information on brand names.

The New Pediatric Guide to Drugs & Vitamins. By Edward R. Brace and Kenneth N. Anderson. Body Press, 1987. 287 pages. Presents drug profiles for more than 240 commonly used prescription and over-the-counter medications prescribed for children. Arranged alphabetically, each entry explains how the drug works, why it's used, and how it's administered. Also gives correct dosage and explains side effects and interactions with other drugs. A section on vitamins is included as well.

The Parent's Guide to Pediatric Drugs. By Ruth McGillis Bindler, R.N., M.S., Yvonne Tso, R. Ph., M.S., and Linda Berner Howry, R.N., M.S. Harper and Row, 1986. 313 pages. A guide to prescription and over-the-counter drugs for children from infancy through adolescence. Divided into chapters discussing parts of the body (the eye, the ear, the stomach and intestines, the heart and lungs, etc.). For more than 125 generic drugs and 700 brand-name products, this guide explains why the drug is used, how it is administered, unintended side effects, possible drug and food interactions, contraindications to the use of the drug, proper storage instructions, and the amount of time needed for the drug to work.

The Pill Book Guide to Children's Medications. By Michael D. Mitchell, M.D., with Marvin S. Eiger, M.D. Bantam, 1990. 277 pages. A guide to more than two hundred prescriptions and over-the-counter drugs for young children. Each profile explains when the drug is recommended and when natural methods work better; how dosage should be adjusted for age and weight; common side effects and what to do about them; and cautions and warnings, including how to recognize a drug allergy. Also contains a list of items that should be in every home medicine chest; a discussion of the immunization controversy; guidelines on preventing accidental poisonings (and what to do, should they occur); and advice on how to overcome a child's resistance to medication. A chapter on drugs and the nursing infant, by Eiger, coauthor of *The Complete Book of Breastfeeding*, is also included.

Periodical

Drug Facts and Comparisons. 111 West Port Plaza, Suite 400, St. Louis, Missouri 63146. Phone: 1/800-223-0554. Issued monthly, this publication covers prescription and over-the-counter drugs, including cost and brand comparisons and information on adverse side effects. $180.00 for first-time subscribers ($149 for subscription renewals).

Associations

Council on Family Health. 420 Lexington Avenue, New York, New York 10017. Phone: 212/210-8836. An association of manufacturers of prescription and over-the-counter medications. Provides information on proper use of medications, safety, and other family health concerns. Offers "Ten Guides to Proper Medicine Use," a free Health Emergency Chart for first aid in the home, and emergency telephone stickers to keep handy numbers for the family doctor, pharmacy, and poison control centers. Send a self-addressed, stamped envelope for stickers and brochures.

National Council on Patient Information and Education. See "Associations" listed under "General Resources" in this chapter.

HOSPITAL CARE: WHEN YOUR CHILD NEEDS SPECIAL MEDICAL ATTENTION

Free and Inexpensive Resources

For Adults

Hospital Tips for Parents. A free information sheet for parents whose children are in the hospital, available from the Association for the Care of Children's Health, 7910 Woodmont Avenue, Suite 300, Bethesda, Maryland 20814.

Preparing Your Child for a Repeated or Extended Hospital Stay. A brochure for parents with a child who requires extended hospital care, available for $1.00 plus a self-addressed, stamped envelope from the Association for the Care of Children's Health, 7910 Woodmont Avenue, Suite 300, Bethesda, Maryland 20814.

Your Child Goes to the Hospital. A brochure for parents, available for $1.00 plus a self-addressed, stamped envelope from the Association for the Care of Children's Health, 7910 Woodmont Avenue, Suite 300, Bethesda, Maryland 20814.

For Children

What Will They Do to Me in the Hospital? This free pamphlet is designed to help children understand what will happen during their stay at a major medical facility. Available from the National Mental Health Association, 1021 Prince Street, Alexandria, Virginia 22314.

Books

A Hospital Story: An Open Family Book for Parents and Children Together. By Sara Bonnett Stein. Photography by Doris Pinney. Walker, 1985. 47 pages. A book to help parents help their children overcome their fear of hospitals. For parents and youngsters (ages four to eight) to read together.

Videotapes

For Children

The Before Tour: An Operation Preparation Video. Slim Goodbody. Running time: 15 minutes. Helps prepare children (ages six to ten) for the experience of surgery. Recommended by the American Academy of Pediatrics and approved by Parents' Choice. Available at libraries or directly from Slim Goodbody Corporation, 27 West Twentieth Street, Suite 1207, New York, New York 10011. Phone: 212/254-3300.

Sesame Street Visits the Hospital. Children's Television Workshop. Running time: 30 minutes. Young viewers (ages three to six) follow Big Bird on a trip to the hospital where the endearing *Sesame Street* character discovers that it isn't such a scary place after all—that it's full of people working to make him feel better. Includes information on various aspects of hospital life.

Associations

Association for the Care of Children's Health. 7910 Woodmont Avenue, Suite 300, Bethesda, Maryland 20814. Phone: 301/654-6549. An association of parents, pediatricians, social workers, and others concerned about the emotional and social needs of children in pediatric settings. Promotes family-centered care policies and practices in health, early intervention, education, and social services. Offers a variety of free and low-cost pamphlets and brochures, including *Your Child Goes to the Hospital* and *Preparing Your Child for a Repeated or Extended Hospital Stay* (see listings under "Free and Inexpensive Resources"). Also publishes a directory of parents throughout North America who will help people locate qualified medical care in their city. Offers a book list as well.

Children in Hospitals. c/o Barbara Popper, Federation for Children with Special Needs, 95 Berkeley Street, Suite 104, Boston, Massachusetts 02116. Phone: 617/482-2915. Offers education and support for parents coping with the hospitalization of a child. Works to minimize the trauma involved in a child's hospitalization. Encourages hospitals to adopt flexible visiting policies. Publishes a quarterly newsletter, together with the *CIH Consumer Directory of Hospitals*, issued twice a year.

PREMATURE BABIES

Associations

Intensive Caring Unlimited. 910 Bent Lane, Philadelphia, Pennsylvania 19118. Phone: 215/233-6994. Offers services to parents with a baby in intensive care, including over-the-phone advice from trained counselors who have had similar experiences with their own children. Members receive *Intensive Caring Unlimited*, a bimonthly newsletter covering prematurity, hospitalization, developmental delays, grieving, and general parenting topics.

IVH Parents. P.O. Box 56-1111, Miami, Florida 33256-1111. Phone: 305/232-0381. Offers support services to parents with children who have had an intraventricular hemorrhage (bleeding in the brain common in babies born weighing less than three pounds). Also offers services to professionals who work with such children. Provides over-the-phone counseling and produces a newsletter for members.

La Leche League. P.O. Box 1209, Franklin Park, Illinois 60131-8209. Phone: 1/800-LA-LECHE. Offers advice to mothers who choose to breastfeed their premature baby. Provides a twenty-eight-page booklet called "Breastfeeding Your Premature Baby," available for $1.95.

Parent Care Inc. 9041 Colgate Street, Indianapolis, Indiana 46268-1210. Phone: 317/872-9913. An organization of parents and professionals working to improve the neonatal intensive care unit experience for infants, families, and caregivers. Offers support group referrals and disseminates information. Members receive *News Brief*, a quarterly newsletter containing articles on neonatal intensive care. Many books and tapes are available for purchase.

Parents Helping Parents. 535 Race Street, Suite 140, San Jose, California 95126. Phone: 408/288-5010. An organization of parents, professionals, and others working to help families with special-needs children, including those born prematurely. Among its various programs, Parents Helping Parents offers support services, including education, information, and training to decrease the feelings of isolation parents of special-needs children experience and to help then gain a sense of control over their lives. Publishes *Special Addition*, a bimonthly newsletter containing association news, updates on legislation and medical findings, and a calendar of events. Also publishes books, information packets, and brochures.

Parents of Preemies Inc. P.O. Box 5183, Arlington, Virginia 22205. Phone: 301/253-6534. Links parents of premature babies with other parents who have had a premature baby with the same medical conditions. Members also receive a monthly newsletter.

ALTERNATIVE MEDICINE

Books

The Encyclopedia of Alternative Health Care. By Kristin Gottschalk Olsen. Pocket Books, 1990. 325 pages. An introductory guide to new choices in healing from acupuncture to yoga.

Everybody's Guide to Homeopathic Medicines. By Stephen Cummings, M.D., and Dana Ullman, M.P.H. Revised and expanded edition. Jeremy P. Tarcher, 1991. 336 pages. This family homeopathic guidebook explains how to select the correct homeopathic remedy for various ailments and injuries. (Homeopathy is a branch of medicine that uses plant- and mineral-based remedies to stimulate the body's natural disease-fighting powers.

Homeopathic Medicine for Children and Infants. By Dana Ullman, M.P.H. Jeremy P. Tarcher, 1992. 256 pages. Introduces the principles of homeopathy and explains how to use the medicines effectively. Contains information on homeopathic theory, common ailments, and common remedies, including dosage information.

Natural Child Care: A Complete Guide to Safe and Effective Herbal Remedies and Holistic Health Strategies for Infants and Children. By Maribeth Riggs. Crown, 1989. 300 pages. This holistic guide to child health covers colds, fevers, sore throats, allergies, and other ailments. Includes nutritional guidelines for strengthening immune systems and explains how parents can involve their children in their own care.

Natural Medicine for Children. By Julian Scott, Ph.D. William Morrow, 1990. 130 pages. A guide to herbs, homeopathy, massage, and other alternative remedies for children from birth to age twelve. Not intended as a replacement for orthodox medicine, the author also explains when it's important to see a medical practitioner. Covers many childhood ailments, including diaper rash, earaches, chicken pox, and behavioral problems.

Your Healthy Child: A Guide to Natural Health Care for Children. By Alice L. Duncan. Jeremy P. Tarcher, 1990. 294 pages. A guide to natural health care for children, including an A-to-Z compendium of illnesses and appropriate therapies (herbal remedies, nutritional therapy, acupressure, etc.).

Mail Order Catalogs

Dr. Possum. P.O. Box 4183, Mountain View, California 94040. Phone: 1/800-827-4086. Includes a selection of homeopathic remedies and home-treatment products.

Homeopathy. Homeopathic Educational Services, 2124 Kittredge Street, Berkeley, California 94704. Phone: 510/649-0294 or 1/800-359-9051 (orders only). This mail-order catalog contains introductory books, cassettes, videotapes, homeopathic medicines (for children and adults), and software programs, among other items. The "Kids' Kit" contains seven of the most common individual remedies for pediatric problems (chamomile, calendula, belladonna, etc.) and comes with an instruction booklet for their use. The catalog also describes what homeopathy is, and lists associations that support homeopathy and offer information on it.

The Natural Baby Catalog. 114 West Franklin, Suite S, Pennington, New Jersey 08534. Phone: 609/737-2895. This catalog contains homeopathic medicines and other health-care products, in addition to diapering products, all-natural baby cleansers, clothing, and other items.

Self Care Catalog. 5850 Shellmound Street, Emeryville, California 94662-0813. Phone: 1/800-345-3371. Contains a variety of products for those who believe they are primarily responsible for their own health. Among the items of interest to parents are the CribCuddle Heartbeat Hammock (a sleeping device for infants that simulates the rhythm of the heartbeat and attaches to crib rails); Family Earscope (for monitoring your child's ears and detecting infection); and the *Ear Book* (a parents' guide to ear problems). This catalog also contains exercise equipment and videotapes, pain-relief devices, sleep and bath products, home safety items, and personal care products. Sprinkled with health updates on topics such as the health benefits of friendship and recent findings on nutrition.

Associations

American Institute of Homeopathy. 1585 Glencoe Street, Suite 44, Denver, Colorado 80220-1338. Phone: 303/829-6059. A professional society of medical doctors, osteopaths, and dentists practicing homeotherapeutics. Promotes research and quality homeopathic health care. Publishes *Homeopathy Notes,* a monthly newsletter, and the *Journal of the American Institute of Homeopathy,* issued quarterly.

Committee for Freedom of Choice in Medicine. 1180 Walnut Avenue, Chula Vista, California 92011. Phone: 619/429-8200 or 1/800-227-4473. Informs the public, physicians, and healers of new techniques in alternative medicine. Makes referrals to consumers looking for a doctor. Publishes books, pamphlets, brochures, reprints, and a quarterly magazine called *Choice.* Also offers videotapes and audiocassettes.

International Foundation for Homeopathy. 2366 Eastlake Avenue East, #301, Seattle, Washington 98102. Phone: 206/324-8230. Members include professionals and laypersons interested in homeopathy. Promotes homeopathy and provides the public with information on this method of treatment. Will help individuals find a homeopathic practitioner in their area. Publishes a bimonthly magazine containing information on case histories and clinical advances.

The National Center for Homeopathy. 801 North Fairfax, Suite 306, Alexandria, Virginia 22314. Phone: 703/548-7790. Promotes the art of healing according to the natural laws of homeopathy. Facilitates the study of homeopathy, funds scientific research in the field, and sponsors introductory courses in homeopathy. Publishes *Homeopathy Today,* a monthly newsletter for members, as well as the *Directory of Homeopathic Practitioners* (issued biennially).

SPECIAL TOPICS IN HEALTH

AIDS (Acquired Immunodeficiency Syndrome)

Free and Inexpensive Resources

How to Talk with Your Kids about AIDS. A step-by-step pamphlet produced by the Sex Information and Education Council of the United States (SIECUS). Offers language parents can use in discussing AIDS with children from preschoolers to teenagers. For a free copy of this publication, send a self-addressed, stamped envelope along with your request to SIECUS, 130 West Forty-second Street, Suite 2500, New York, New York 10036.

Tips on Preventing AIDS. Explains how AIDS is spread and offers prevention tips. Produced by the Food and Drug Administration. For ordering information, write for a copy of the free *Consumer Information Catalog*, available from the Consumer Information Center, P.O. Box 100, Pueblo, Colorado 81002.

Books

For Adults

AIDS-Proofing Your Kids: A Step-by-Step Guide. By Loren E. Acker, Bram C. Goldwater, and William H. Dyson, M.D. Beyond Words Publishing, 1992. 150 pages. Suggests ways to help parents help their children protect themselves against the AIDS virus. Available from Beyond Words Publishing (phone: 1/800-284-9673).

For Children

Children and the AIDS Virus. By Rosemarie Hausherr. Clarion Books, 1989. 48 pages. Uses reassuring text and photographs to help children ages five to twelve better understand AIDS and deal with their fear of the disease.

Does AIDS Hurt? Educating Young Children About AIDS. By Marcia Quackenbush and Sylvia Villarreal. Network Publications, 1988. 149 pages. For children ages six to ten. Available from ETR Associates by calling 1/800-321-4407.

My Friend . . . and AIDS. By Sharon Schilling and Marc Mossburg. A Way with Words, 1988. 66 pages. A story about a friendship between two children, one of whom has been infected with the AIDS virus. For children ages six to nine. Available from Good News Printing and Advertising (phone: 303/841-5497).

Hotline

The National AIDS Hotline. 1/800-342-AIDS. Operated by the Centers for Disease Control and Prevention, this hotline offers callers medical information and referrals twenty-four hours a day. If your child asks you a question you can't answer, dial this number.

Associations

National Pediatric HIV Resource Center. Children's Hospital of New Jersey, 15 South Ninth Street, Newark, New Jersey 07107. Phone: 201/268-8251.

Pediatric AIDS Coalition. c/o American Academy of Pediatrics, 601 Thirteenth Street, N.W., Suite 400 North, Washington, D.C. 20005. 202/347-8600.

Care of the Asthmatic Child
From *More than Snuffles: Childhood Asthma*, a reprint from *FDA Consumer Magazine*, produced by the Food and Drug Administration.

Many factors can trigger an asthma "flare" in a susceptible child, but the most common are allergens, colds, flu, and other respiratory infections. Exercise is also a common trigger in children, as well as adults.

Irritants such as perfumes, cigarette smoke, wood smoke, hair sprays, paint odors, cotton or wood dust, industrial chemicals and fumes, and outdoor pollution may also bring on an attack. Cold air and changes in the weather, in which winds sweep in from other areas carrying irritants, pollution or different pollens, often cause a flare. A cough, shout or laugh may stimulate the vagus nerve that leads to the lungs, and cause an attack.

Allergies play a part in triggering attacks in a large percentage of children with asthma. Some of the most common offenders are animal dander, pollen, mold, ragweed, house dust, bacteria, dust mites, fungi, and animal and human skin fragments. Certain foods, such as chocolate, shellfish, milk, orange juice, eggs, nuts and peanut butter, along with foods or drugs containing sulfites and other preservatives, can also trigger attacks. Some children may develop severe bronchospasm from aspirin and nonsteroidal anti-inflammatory drugs such as ibuprofen, naproxen and piroxicam.

A recent study performed at the National Jewish Center for Immunology and Respiratory Medicine in Denver, Colorado, found that children with severe asthma suffer from depression and guilt feelings, often have problems in school, and limit their normal activities because of the disease. Asthma's damage extends to the family, whose lifestyles are often affected. When the cost of medication and devices is added in, it can be seen that severe chronic asthma can be a burden on the family.

Doctors advise parents of asthmatic children whose attacks are allergy-related to help the child avoid the allergen whenever possible, which means that sometimes the family pet must go or more rigorous dust-control measures must be instituted. With unavoidable allergens, allergy shots given year-round are helpful in most cases. Moving to another area to escape allergens is not recommended unless the new area is given a trial in all seasons of the year. It is quite possible that after a "honeymoon" period in the new area, the child may begin to react to local allergens.

Since asthma attacks can happen anytime, anywhere, parents of children with asthma need to communicate with school personnel if their children must take medicine at designated times or use devices such as inhalers. Unfortunately, many teenagers try to ignore asthma symptoms at school because they don't want to be seen using an inhaler, especially before sports activities. The result is often out-of-control asthma.

Parents should see that the child eats a nutritious diet, including plenty of fluids, has adequate rest and exercise, and is knowledgeable about factors that will set off an episode.

To avoid reliance on emergency rooms and hospitals, parents and child need to be alert to the early signs of asthma and have a definite medical regimen to follow when an attack begins. Medications should be taken exactly as prescribed. A supportive and sympathetic doctor, who can provide the parents with an asthma prevention plan as well as care for acute episodes, is a necessity.

Children with well-controlled asthma should be encouraged to take part in exercises or sports activities. Besides increasing lung capacity, exercise improves breathing and may eliminate or lessen the severity of asthma attacks. An added bonus: Doing what other children can do increases self-esteem. In 1984, 66 of the U.S. Olympic competitors had been diagnosed as having exercise-induced asthma. Forty-one of those athletes won medals in the games.

Pediatric AIDS Foundation. 1311 Colorado Avenue, Santa Monica, California 90404. Phone: 310/395-9051.

Sunburst National AIDS Project. 148 Wilson Hill Road, Petaluma, California 94952. Phone: 707/769-0169.

Asthma

Free and Inexpensive Resources

Asthma: What Every Parent Should Know. Available from the Asthma and Allergy Information Center, this brochure offers general information on asthma. Also available is *The U.S. Pollen Predictor*, a brochure identifying, by region, peak pollen periods for various types of plants, as well as two brochures on airborne allergens. To order, call 1/800-727-5400. (For more information about the Asthma and Allergy Information Center, see listing under "Associations.")

Captain Wonderlung. A coloring/activity book designed to encourage asthmatic children to do breathing exercises. Available from the American Academy of Pediatrics. Ask your pediatrician for a copy or send a self-addressed, stamped envelope to American Academy of Pediatrics, "Captain Wonderlung" (see appendix I for contact information).

More than Snuffles: Childhood Asthma. By Evelyn Zamula. A four-page reprint from *FDA Consumer Magazine* examining the symptoms, causes, and treatment of this common chronic disease. Produced in 1991 by the Food and Drug Administration. For ordering information, write for a copy of the free *Consumer Information Catalog*, available from the Consumer Information Center, P.O. Box 100, Pueblo, Colorado 81002.

Associations

American Allergy Association. P.O. Box 7273, Menlo Park, California 94026. Phone: 415/322-1663.

Asthma and Allergy Foundation of America. 1717 Massachusetts Avenue, Suite 305, Washington, D.C. 20036. Phone: 202/265-0265

Asthma and Allergy Information Center. Phone: 1/800-727-5400. Provides information, including a list of organizations that can steer parents to local asthma and allergy specialists. Produces several free brochures

(see listings under "Free and Inexpensive Resources").

Mothers of Asthmatics. 10875 Main Street, Suite 210, Fairfax, Virginia 22030. Phone: 703/385-4403.

Circumcision

Free Resource

Newborns: Care of the Uncircumcised Penis. From the American Academy of Pediatrics, this brochure offers advice on caring for the uncircumcised penis. Ask your pediatrician for a copy or send a self-addressed, stamped envelope to American Academy of Pediatrics, "Care of the Uncircumcised Penis" (see appendix I for contact information).

Books

Circumcision: *Mothering* **Special Edition.** Edited by Vicki Stamler and Barrett Flascher Dunn. Revised edition. *Mothering* magazine, 1988. 32 pages. Contains reprints of articles on circumcision appearing in *Mothering* magazine from 1976 to 1988. Personal accounts from parents, research findings, and resources are included. Can be ordered directly from *Mothering* magazine (P.O. Box 1690, Santa Fe, New Mexico 87504. Phone: 1/800-827-1061).

Dr. Spock's Baby and Child Care. By Benjamin Spock, M.D., and Michael B. Rothenberg, M.D. 6th edition. Simon and Schuster, 1992. 832 pages. Provides a brief history of circumcision and discusses recent research findings. Although Spock believes there is no solid medical evidence to support routine circumcision ("some parents may choose circumcision for religious reasons," he says, but "in other cases, I recommend leaving the foreskin the way

> ### The American Academy of Pediatrics' Policy Statement:
>
> The academy says that circumcision has potential medical benefits and advantages, as well as inherent disadvantages and risks. Therefore, the academy recommends that the decision to circumcise is one best made by parents in consultation with their physician. Factors affecting the parents' decision include esthetics, religion, cultural attitudes, social pressures, and tradition. Physicians should explain and discuss the benefits and risks of circumcision with parents, and informed consent should be obtained before the procedure is performed.

Nature meant it to be"), his treatment of the subject is even-handed. Explains the importance of genital hygiene, whether the penis is circumcised or not. (For more information on *Dr. Spock's Baby and Child Care*, see "Books" listed under "General Resources.")

Your Child's Health: The Parents' Guide to Symptoms, Emergencies, Common Illnesses, Behavior, and School Problems. By Barton D. Schmitt, M.D., F.A.A.P. Revised edition. Bantam, 1991. 672 pages. Discusses the pros and cons of circumcision, including the benefits and risks. Believes that this is a parental decision, not a medical decision. Includes a section on "Circumcision Care and Problems" and "Foreskin Care and Problems." (For more information on *Your Child's Health*, see "Books" listed under "General Resources."]

Association

National Organization of Circumcision Information Resource Centers. P.O. Box 2512, San Anselmo, California 94979. Phone: 415/488-9883. An umbrella organization for circumcision information centers. Seeks to educate professionals and the public about routine infant circumcision, a surgical procedure that the organization feels may not be medically indicated. Hopes to end the practice of routine infant circumcision. Publishes a semiannual newsletter and offers a brochure called *Circumcision. Why?*

Ear Infections

Books

Childhood Ear Infections: What Every Parent and Physician Should Know about Prevention, Home Care, and Alternative Treatment. By Michael A. Schmidt. North Atlantic, 1990. 250 pages. This book defines middle ear infections and describes various methods of treatment, including alternative methods such as diet, acupressure, homeopathy, and herbal remedies. Explains the drawbacks of indiscriminate use of antibiotics and how to determine which children will benefit from standard treatment.

Ear Infections in Your Child. By Kenneth Grundfast, M.D., and Cynthia J. Carney. Warner Books, 1989. 283 pages. Offers an overview of the most common medical problem among young children. Discusses its causes, standard treatment, and prevention.

Hotline

Hearing Helpline. Phone: 1/800-EAR-WELL. Will send callers free brochures on the diagnosis, prevention, and treatment of hearing loss in infants and children. The Better Hearing Institute, which sponsors the Helpline, will also provide a list of hearing specialists in your zip code area.

Health-Care Product

Earlight. Dr. Dedo's Family. Allows parents to presceen their child's ears before problems develop. Comes with an illustrated guidebook developed by ear specialists. Available from Hand in Hand (see chapter 27 for contact information).

Health Insurance

Free and Inexpensive Resources

Checkup on Health Insurance Choices. A booklet demystifying health insurance, including definitions of Health Maintenance Organizations (HMOs), Preferred Provider Organizations (PPOs), and other terms. Includes a worksheet to help readers evaluate their insurance options. Available from the Agency for Health Care Policy and Research, Publications Clearinghouse, P.O. Box 8547, Silver Spring, Maryland 20907.

Phone: 1/800-358-9295 (Monday through Friday, 9:00 a.m. to 5:00 p.m., eastern standard time).

Guidelines for Your Family's Health Insurance. From the American Academy of Pediatrics, this brochure discusses the three major types of health insurance and explains how to budget for insurance and medical care. Ask your pediatrician for a copy or send a self-addressed, stamped envelope to American Academy of Pediatrics, "Your Family's Health Insurance" (see appendix I for contact information).

Fact:

More than 37 million Americans have no health insurance.

Hotline

National Insurance Consumer Helpline. Phone: 1/800-942-4242. Will answer consumers' questions about health insurance, including those having to do with claim disputes.

Immunization

Free and Inexpensive Resources

Haemophilus Influenzae Type b: What Parents Need to Know. Describes the different vaccines available to protect against meningitis, epiglottitis, and other serious diseases associated with Haemophilus Influenzae Type b. Ask your pediatrician for a copy or send a self-addressed, stamped envelope to American Academy of Pediatrics, "Haemophilus Influenzae Type b" (see appendix I for contact information).

Health Record and Immunization Chart. Provides a place for keeping your child's health information and a handy chart on when your child should receive various immunizations. Available from Metropolitan Insurance Company, Health and Safety Education (16UV), Box HR, One Madison Avenue, New York, New York 10010. Send your name and address along with your request.

Hepatitis B: What Parents Need to Know. This brochure provides information on the disease and explains the American Academy of Pediatric's immunization recommendation and

schedule. Ask your pediatrician for a copy or send a self-addressed, stamped envelope to American Academy of Pediatrics, "Hepatitis B" (see appendix I for contact information).

Immunization Schedule. A reminder form for parents from the American Academy of Pediatrics. Includes the academy's immunization schedule, along with recommendations on the vaccine for the Haemophilus Influenzae infection. Ask your pediatrician for a copy or send a self-addressed, stamped envelope to American Academy of Pediatrics, "Immunizations Schedule" (see appendix I for contact information).

Vaccinations for Children. Recommended schedules of vaccinations for children are available from the Centers for Disease Control and Prevention, Public Health Service, U.S. Department of Health and Human Services, Atlanta, Georgia 30333. Phone: 404/639-3286 (main number) or 404/639-8225 (National Immunization Program).

Books

Vaccinations: *Mothering* Special Edition. *Mothering* magazine. Santa Fe, 1989. 50 pages. This booklet contains reprints of seventeen articles, together with letters and resources that have appeared in *Mothering* magazine on the controversy regarding immunization. Also features parents' accounts of their own experiences. Formerly titled *Immunization.* Can be ordered directly from *Mothering* magazine or from the Birth and Life Bookstore, 7001 Alonzo Avenue, N.W., P.O. Box 70625, Seattle, Washington 98107-0625. Phone: 206/789-4444 or 1/800-736-0631 (for orders).

Hotline

National Immunization Campaign Hotline. Phone: 1/800-525-6789. Will answer questions concerning the immunization of children.

WHEN THERE IS NO CURE

Terminally-Ill Children

Associations

Brass Ring Society. 314 South Main Street, Ottawa, Kansas 66067.

Children's Wish Foundation International. 8215 Roswell Road, Building 200, Suite 100, Atlanta, Georgia 30350. Phone: 404/393-9474.

MAGIC Foundation. 770 Alexandria Drive, Naperville, Illinois 60565. Phone: 708/369-1605.

Make-a-Wish Foundation of America. 100 West Clarendon, Suite 2200, Phoenix, Arizona 85013. Phone: 602/279-9474.

When a Child Dies

Book

Empty Cradle, Broken Heart: Surviving the Death of Your Baby. By Deborah L. Davis, Ph.D. Fulcrum Publishing, 1991. 232 pages. This book helps grieving parents to deal with the loss of their baby due to miscarriage, stillbirth, or infant death. Guides them along the path to emotional recovery. Available from La Leche League International (see appendix I for contact information).

Associations

The Compassionate Friends, Inc. National Headquarters, P.O. Box 3696, Oakbrook, Illinois 60522-3696. Phone: 708/990-0010. This organization offers support to parents and siblings after the death of a child. Helps them work through the grieving process and works to foster their physical and emotional health. Provides free brochures on a variety of topics. Will refer callers to a local chapter.

SHARE: Pregnancy and Infancy Loss Support, Inc. St. Joseph's Health Center, 300 First Capitol Drive, St. Charles, MO 63301. Phone: 314/947-5000. Offers information and support to families after the death of a child due to miscarriage, stillbirth, perinatal death, or sudden infant death syndrome. Offers educational packets on a variety of topics;

provides referrals to support groups across the country.

SIDS (Sudden Infant Death Syndrome) Alliance. 10500 Little Patuxent Parkway, Suite 420, Columbia, Maryland 21044. Phone: 1/800-221-SIDS. Offers a variety of literature, including a general information packet. Will refer callers to a local SIDS chapter.

Unite, Inc., Grief Support. 7600 Central Avenue, Philadelphia, Pennsylvania 19111-2499. Phone: 215/728-3777. This groups provides information and support to parents who have experienced the death of a baby during pregnancy or shortly after birth. Publishes a bimonthly newsletter and acts as an information clearinghouse.

DENTAL CARE: TAKING CARE OF YOUR CHILD'S TEETH

Free and Inexpensive Resources:

A Guide to Children's Dental Health. Offers practical advice on everything from teething to thumb sucking. Available from the American Academy of Pediatrics. Ask your pediatrician for a copy or send a self-addressed, stamped envelope to American Academy of Pediatrics, "A Guide to Children's Dental Health" (see appendix I for contact information).

One Tooth. A brochure for children explaining how they can take proper care of their teeth. Write to The Sugar Association, 1101 Fifteenth Street, N.W., Suite 600, Washington, D.C. 20005.

Prevent Baby Bottle Tooth Decay. Free guidelines, available from the National Institute of Dental Research, Public Inquiries Office, Bethesda, Maryland 20892. Write for a copy. (Other free publications from the institute include *A Healthy Mouth for You and Your Baby* and *Rx for Sound Teeth*).

Books

For Adults

The Mount Sinai Medical Center Family Guide to Dental Health. By Jack Klatell, Andrew Kaplan, and Gray Williams, Jr. Macmillan, 1991. 416 pages. A general guide to family dental care, covering care of the teeth and gums, diseases that affect the mouth, and routine and special procedures at the dental office.

Protecting Our Children's Teeth: A Guide to Quality Dental Care from Infancy through Age Twelve. By Malcolm S. Foster. Insight Books, 1992. 275 pages. Written by a pediatric dentist, this book explains what to expect and what to do for a child's teeth at various ages. Describes healthy oral hygiene practices (including advice on choosing a toothbrush and toothpaste). Answers a variety of commonly asked questions and offers practical advice.

For Children

Brush Them Bright. By Patricia Quilan. Hyperion Books for Children, 1992. 24 pages. A story about Thomas, a boy who learns how to brush his teeth. Helps children ages three to seven learn how to brush their teeth in five easy steps. Comes with a toothbrush and fourteen "remember-to-brush" stickers.

Going to the Dentist. By Fred Rogers. Putnam, 1989. 32 pages. Helps preschoolers understand what it's like to go to the dentist.

First Trip to the Dentist:

The American Academy of Pediatrics recommends making the first trip to the pediatric dentist at age three, unless your child has a gum problem, mouth injury, improper positioning of teeth, or other conditions that warrant prompt attention.

My Dentist. By Harlow Rockwell. Greenwillow Books, 1975. 32 pages. Helps preschoolers understand what it's like to visit a dentist. Combines easy-to-understand text and detailed illustrations.

When I See My Dentist. By Susan Kuklin. Bradbury Press, 1988. 32 pages. Using reassuring words and full-color photographs, this book helps young children understand routine dental check-ups. For children ages three to eight.

Associations

American Academy of Pediatric Dentistry. 211 East Chicago Avenue, Suite 1036, Chicago, Illinois 60611. Phone: 312/337-2169. Professional society of dentists whose practice is limited to children, as well as teachers and researchers in pediatric dentistry. Seeks to advance the specialty of pediatric dentistry through practice, education, and research. Will provide the names of pediatric dentists in your areas, as well as the names of hospitals and universities with pediatric-dentistry departments. Publications include the bi-monthly journal *Pediatric Dentistry*, as well as a bimonthly newsletter and the *American Academy of Pediatric Dentistry–Membership Roster*.

American Association of Orthodontists. 401 North Lindbergh Boulevard, St. Louis, Missouri 63141. Phone: 314/993-1700 or 1/800-222-9969. Professional society of orthodontists working to advance orthodontics through research, public information programs, continuing education for members, and cooperation with other health groups. Publications include the *American Association of Orthodontists Membership Directory*. (If your child needs braces, this list can put you in touch with an orthodontist in your area.)

American Dental Association. 211 East Chicago Avenue, Chicago, Illinois 60611. Phone: 312/440-2500. Encourages the improvement of public dental health, inspects and accredits dental schools, and conducts research programs. Produces dental health education materials used in the United States. Sponsors National Children's Dental Health Month. Also publishes the *American Dental Directory*, an annual listing of dentists in the United States.

American Society of Dentistry for Children. 211 East Chicago Avenue, Suite 1430, Chicago, Illinois 60611. Phone: 312/943-1244. A society of specialists and general practitioners interested in dentistry for children. Conducts education and research programs. Publishes the *Journal of Dentistry for Children*, a refereed journal issued bimonthly. Contains news about children's dental health concerns.

MENTAL HEALTH

Free Resource

A Consumer's Guide to Mental Health Services. Answers commonly asked questions, helps identify warning signals, discusses various treatments, and lists resources for help and information. Revised in 1992 by the National Institute of Mental Health. For ordering information, write for a copy of the free *Consumer Information Catalog*, available from the Consumer Information Center, P.O. Box 100, Pueblo, Colorado 81002.

Books

For Adults

A Parent's Guide to Child Therapy. By Richard Bush. Delacorte Press, 1980. 340 pages. Offers a comprehensive introduction to the subject of child therapy. Explains when, where, and how to get help.

Playing for Real. By Richard Bromfield, Ph.D. Penguin Books, 1992. 240 pages. A child therapist explores the world of play therapy and the inner worlds of children. Shares the stories of young patients struggling with a wide variety of problems (severe anxiety, attention-deficit disorder, the trauma of incest, etc.). Offers overviews of both children's emotional development and the techniques of play therapy. Explains how psychotherapy can heal childhood traumas and help troubled children grow into healthy adults.

Testing and Your Child: What You Should Know about 150 of the Most Common Medical, Educational, and Psychological Tests. By Virginia E. McCullough. Penguin Books, 1992. 334 pages. This book includes descriptions of a variety of psychological tests. Each entry includes information on who must administer the test (and under what conditions), what the test tests for and what it cannot reveal, what preparation is required, what affects scoring, and what follow-up testing might be recommended. Also includes full descriptions of developmental, psychological, and educational tests.

When Your Child Needs Help: A Parent's Guide to Therapy for Children. By Norma Doft, Ph.D., with Barbara Aria. Harmony Books, 1992. 224 pages. How can parents distinguish between mere "growing pains" and more serious problems requiring therapeutic treatment? What should parents expect from their child's therapy? What will the process be like? This book addresses these questions. The author takes readers on a tour of the therapy playroom, following the cases of four children. Along the way, she offers insights for parents whose children are showing signs of emotional distress. While emphasizing the important role of the professional therapist in evaluating and treating troubled children, the author reveals how informed, confident parents can not only participate in their child's therapy, but also speed it along.

When Your Child Needs Testing: What Parents, Teachers, and Other Helpers Need to Know about Psychological Testing. By Milton F. Shore, Patrick J. Brice, and Barbara G. Love. Crossroad, 1992. 192 pages. Offers an overview of psychological testing for parents and others with little background in psychology. Explains the beneficial insights that testing can provide, describes basic testing procedures, and explains how to follow up on test results. Includes a list of psychological tests, a glossary of terms, and an annotated bibliography.

For Children

A Child's First Book about Play Therapy. By Jane Annunziata and Marc Nemiroff. American Psychological Association, 1990. 60 pages. Explains how children can talk about their emotions within the context of play.

Psychology for Kids: 40 Fun Tests that Help You Learn about Yourself. By Jonni Kincher. Free Spirit Publishing, 1990. 151 pages. Helps children learn more about their temperaments, styles of communication, and general outlooks on life. Tested on children, these exercises are meant to enhance the process of self-discovery and help take the mystery out of psychology. For children ages ten and up.

Periodical

The Family Therapy Networker. Subscription Service, 8528 Bradford Road, Silver Spring, Maryland 20901. Phone: 301/589-6536. Although this bimonthly magazine is targeted at mental health professionals, it contains articles that might interest families undergoing therapy. Back issues are available. (Topics covered include "Cries and Whispers: The Haunting Legacy of Family Secrets," "Bringing Up Baby: Family Therapy Rediscovers Its Youngest Clients," "The Postmodern Family: Staying Afloat in the Cultural Soup," and "Illness in the Family: Will Systems Thinking Revolutionize Medical Treatment?," along with many others.)

Mail Order Catalog

Childswork/Childsplay. Center for Applied Psychology, Inc., P.O. Box 1586, King of Prussia, Pennsylvania 19406. Phone: 1/800-962-1141. This catalog contains products developed by mental health professionals and educators that are designed to teach children coping skills, self-confidence, and values through play. Includes boardgames, toys, audiocassettes, and books.

Associations

American Academy of Child and Adolescent Psychiatry. 3615 Wisconsin Avenue, N.W., Washington, D.C. 20016. Phone: 202/966-7300. Fax: 202/966-2891. A professional society of physicians with training in child and adolescent psychiatry. Parents concerned about their child's behavior (an inability to focus on anything, withdrawal from relationships, chronic sleep problems, and so forth) can call this organization for referrals. Publishes a quarterly newsletter containing research updates and statistics, as well as the bimonthly *Journal of the AACAP.*

American Association for Marriage and Family Therapy. 1100 Seventeenth Street, N.W., 10th Floor, Washington, D.C. 20036. Phone: 202/452-0109 or 1/800-374-2638. Professional society of marriage and family therapists. Will provide a free list of qualified mental health professionals in your area. Also offers *A Consumer's Guide to Marriage and Family Therapy,* which includes questions to ask before selecting a therapist.

American Mental Health Counselors Association. 5999 Stevenson Avenue, Alexandria, Virginia 22304. Phone: 703/823-9800. An association of professional counselors employed in mental health services, as well as students in the field. Works to deliver quality mental health services to children, adolescents, adults, and families. A division of the American Association for Counseling and Development.

American Psychiatric Association. 1400 K Street, N.W., Washington, D.C. 20005. Phone: 202/682-6000. A society of psychiatrists working to further the study of mental disorders, including preventive measures and treatment. Assists in formulating programs to meet mental health needs. Publishes books, pamphlets, periodicals, and a membership directory.

American Psychological Association. 1200 Seventeenth Street, N.W., Washington, D.C. 20036. Phone: 202/955-7600. A professional society of psychologists, working to advance psychology as a science, a profession, and as a means of promoting human welfare. Provides information and referrals to the public on mental health, learning disabilities, and other topics. The association produces the PsycINFO database, the most comprehensive index to psychological literature available. Publishes a variety of journals exploring various aspects of psychology.

Federation of Families for Children's Mental Health. 1021 Prince Street, Alexandria, Virginia 22314-2971. Phone: 703/684-7710. Offers information and advocacy for families with children who have severe emotional disabilities.

National Association of Social Workers. 750 First Street, N.E., Suite 700, Washington, D.C. 20002. Phone: 202/408-8600. An association of social workers, as well as students in the field. Advocates strong public social policies through advocacy and political action, offers continuing education opportunities, and conducts research. Publishes a variety of books and periodicals, including *Social Work*, a bimonthly journal examining current social problems such as child abuse, dual-income families, single parenthood, and homelessness. Offers a publications catalog.

National Mental Health Association. 1021 Prince Street, Alexandria, Virginia 22314. Phone: 703/684-7722 or 1/800-969-NMHA. Consumer advocacy organization working to promote mental health and fight mental illness. Provides educational materials on mental health and conducts public education on mental illnesses. Produces a quarterly tabloid covering association and legislative news, mental health trends, and recent research. Offers a free pamphlet for children, *What Will They Do to Me In the Hospital* (see "Free and Inexpensive Resources" listed under "Hospital Care" in this chapter).

DRUG ABUSE

Free and Inexpensive Resources
Alcohol: Your Child and Drugs. From the American Academy of Pediatrics, this brochure explains the developmental damage that can occur to children and emphasizes parent-child communication as one of the best ways of preventing this problem. Ask your pediatrician for a copy or send a self-addressed, stamped envelope to American Academy of Pediatrics, "Alcohol: Your Child and Drugs" (see appendix I for contact information).

Cocaine: Your Child and Drugs. From the American Academy of Pediatrics, this brochure discusses the dangers of cocaine and alerts parents to the warning signs of cocaine

Drug Education

From *Growing Up Drug Free: A Parent's Guide to Prevention*, published by the U.S. Department of Education.

Preschoolers

Drug education may seem unnecessary for preschoolers, but the attitudes and habits learned early can have an important bearing on the decisions children make later.

Three- and four-year-olds are not yet ready to learn complex facts about alcohol and other drugs, but they can learn the decision-making and problem-solving skills that they will need to refuse alcohol and other drugs later. Remember that children in this age group are not able to listen quietly for very long; they are more interested in doing things for themselves.

It's tempting for busy parents to do things *for* young children because it's quicker and easier. With a little planning, however, you can use the learn-by-doing approach to teach your preschooler how to make decisions. Let your child pick from a range of options that are acceptable to you. When the choice is made, make sure your child sticks with it.

Suggested Activities

- Set aside regular times when you can give your child your full attention. Playing together, reading a book, and taking a walk are special times that help to build strong bonds of trust and affection between you and your child.

- Point out to your child poisonous and harmful substances that can be found in your home. Household products such as bleach, lye, and furniture polish all have warning labels that you can read to your child. Keep all household products that could harm a small child away from the place you store foods and out of your child's reach.

- Explain how medicine can be harmful if used incorrectly. Teach your child not to take anything from a medicine bottle unless you give it to the child yourself or specify someone else who can give it, such as a babysitter or grandparent.

- Provide guidelines that teach your child what kind of behavior you expect. Teach your child the basic rules of how to get along with other children: Play fair. Share toys. Tell the truth. Treat others the way you want them to treat you.

- Encourage your child to follow instructions. For example, invite your child to help you cook; following a recipe—measuring ingredients, cracking eggs, kneading dough—can help children have fun while learning about step-by-step procedures. Playing simple board games with your child can give practice in following instructions and rules.

- Take advantage of opportunities to use play as a way to help your child handle frustrating situations and solve simple problems. A tower of blocks that continuously collapses can drive a child to tears. You can offer a few suggestions to keep the tower up, but at the same time you should ask your child what he or she thinks is the best way to do it. Turning a bad situation into a success reinforces a child's self-confidence.

- To help your child learn decision making in a practical way, lay out some clothing from which the child can select what he or she wishes to wear. Don't worry if the choices don't quite match. Let your child know that you think he or she is able to make good decisions.

Kindergarten–Grade 3

Five- to nine-year-olds usually feel good about themselves. They like growing up, and they generally like school and all the new opportunities it provides. They still think and learn primarily by experience, and they don't have a good understanding of things that will happen in the future. Fact and fantasy mingle easily; the world is seen as the child wishes it to be, and not as it actually is. Children of this age need rules to guide their behavior and information to make good choices and decisions.

Discussions about alcohol and other drugs must be in the here and now, and related to people and events the child knows about. Most children are very interested in how their bodies work, so discussions should focus on maintaining good health and avoiding things that might harm the body.

Adults are very important both as teachers and as role models. Children are generally trusting, and they believe that the decisions adults make for them are right. Helping your child know whom to trust is important. They need to understand that just because someone tells them to do something, it is not always right to do it. By the end of the third grade, your child should understand:

- what an illicit drug is, why it is illegal, what it looks like, and what harm it can do;

- how foods, poisons, medicines, and illicit drugs differ;

- how medicines may help during illness, when prescribed by a doctor and administered by a responsible adult, but also how medicines are drugs that can be harmful if misused;

- why it is important to avoid unknown and possibly dangerous objects, containers, and substances;

- which adults, both at school and outside, you want your child to rely on for answers to questions or help in an emergency;

- which foods are nutritious and why exercise is important;

- what the school and home rules are about alcohol and other drug use; and

- how using alcohol and other drugs is illegal for all children.

Suggested Activities

- Children in this age group need to understand the family's rules. You can explain the need for rules by talking about traffic safety rules and school rules with which your child is already familiar.

- Emphasize the importance of good health by talking about things people do to stay healthy, such as brushing teeth after each meal, washing hands, eating good foods, getting plenty of rest and sleep. You can use this discussion to contrast the harmful things that people do, such as taking drugs, smoking, or drinking to excess.

- Discuss how TV advertisers try to persuade children to buy their products, including high-sugar/additives-loaded cereals, candy bars, and toys named after characters in cartoon shows that children find appealing.

- Discuss illnesses with which your child is familiar and for which prescription drugs are often necessary. Many children have had strep throat, ear infections, flu, and colds. Discussing such illnesses can help your child understand the difference between medicine and illicit drugs.

- Practice ways to say no with your child. Describe situations that may make your child feel uncomfortable: being invited to ride a bike where you do not allow your child to go, for example, or being offered medicine or other unfamiliar substances. Give your child some responses to use in these situations.

- Develop a "helpers" file of people your child can rely on. Put together a phone list of relatives, family friends, neighbors, teachers, religious leaders, and the police and fire departments. Illustrate the list with photos. Talk with your child about the kind of help each person on the list could provide in case of various unexpected situations, such as being approached by strangers or losing a house key.

Grades 4–6

This is a period of slowed physical growth when typically a lot of energy goes into learning. Children 10 to 12 years old love to learn facts, especially strange ones, and they want to know how things work and what sources of information are available to them.

Friends—a single best friend or a group of friends—become very important. What children this age are interested in or will be committed to often is determined by what the group thinks. Children's self-image is determined in part by the extent to which they are accepted by peers, especially popular peers. As a result, a lot of "followers" are unable to make independent decisions and choices.

This age is perhaps the most important time for parents to focus on increased efforts at drug prevention. These late elementary school years are crucial to decisions about the use of alcohol and other drugs. The greatest risk for starting to smoke comes in the sixth and seventh grades. Research shows that the earlier youngsters begin to use alcohol and other drugs, the more likely they are to have real trouble.

Your child will need a clear no-use message, factual information, and strong motivation to resist pressures to try alcohol and other drugs and to reinforce the determination to remain drug free. Appropriate new information could include:

■ ways to identify specific drugs, including alcohol, tobacco, marijuana, inhalants, and cocaine in their various forms;

■ the long- and short-term effects and consequences of use;

■ the effects of drugs on different parts of the body, and the reasons why drugs are especially dangerous for growing bodies; and

■ the consequences of alcohol and other illegal drug use to the family, society, and the user.

Suggested Activities

■ Create special times when you are available to talk to your child. Try to give your child undivided attention. A walk together, dinner in a quiet place, or a visit to the ice cream parlor after a movie are some ways to make talking together a little easier.

■ Encourage your child to participate in wholesome activities that will allow the child to form new friendships and have fun. Sports, scouts, religious-sponsored youth programs, and community-sponsored youth organizations are excellent ways for children to meet others of their own age.

■ Teach your child to be aware of how drugs and alcohol are promoted. Discuss how children are bombarded with messages—from TV, song lyrics, billboards, and advertisements—that using alcohol and other drugs is very glamorous. Clearly separate the myths from the realities of alcohol and other drug use.

■ Continue to practice ways to say no with your child, emphasizing ways to refuse alcohol and other drugs. It is not uncommon for sixth graders to be offered beer and cigarettes and to know other children who smoke and drink alcohol.

■ Ask your child to scan the morning newspaper and to circle any article that has to do with alcohol and other drug use. No doubt there will be articles about drug-related murders, strife in other countries due to drug trafficking, and alcohol-related auto accidents. Talk with your child about the tremendous loss of lives and resources because of the use of alcohol and other drugs.

■ Make friends with the parents of your child's friends so that you can reinforce one another's efforts in teaching good personal and social habits. A neighborhood social gathering, sporting event, or school assembly are good places to meet.

abuse. Ask your pediatrician for a copy or send a self-addressed, stamped envelope to American Academy of Pediatrics, "Cocaine: Your Child and Drugs" (see appendix I for contact information).

Growing Up Drug Free: A Parent's Guide to Prevention. A guide to show parents what children should know about drugs, including alcohol and tobacco, at each age level. Published by the U.S. Department of Education. For ordering information, write for a copy of the free *Consumer Information Catalog*, available from the Consumer Information Center, P.O. Box 100, Pueblo, Colorado 81002.

Marijuana: Your Child and Drugs. From the American Academy of Pediatrics, this brochure reviews the effects of marijuana and explains how it affects learning ability and scholastic performance. Ask your pediatrician for a copy or send a self-addressed, stamped envelope to American Academy of Pediatrics, "Marijuana: Your Child and Drugs" (see appendix I for contact information).

Young Children and Drugs: What Parents Can Do. This popular brochure tells parents how to reduce the chances their children will ever get involved with drugs. For a free copy, send a self-addressed, stamped business-size envelope to the National PTA (see appendix I for contact information).

Associations

American Council for Drug Education. 204 Monroe Street, Rockville, Maryland 20850. Phone: 301/294-0600 or 1/800-488-3784. Provides information on drug use, reviews scientific findings, develops media campaigns, publishes books and a newsletter, and offers films and curriculum materials for preteens.

National Clearinghouse for Alcohol and Drug Information. Box 2345, Rockville, Maryland 20852. Phone: 301/468-2600 or 1/800-729-6686. A resource for alcohol and other drug information. Carries a variety of publications dealing with alcohol and other drug abuse.

SPECIFIC ILLNESSES, DISEASES, AND BIRTH DEFECTS: A GUIDE TO ASSOCIATIONS, CENTERS, AND FOUNDATIONS

Following is a list of organizations that provide information on specific illnesses, diseases, and physical handicaps. More listings can be found in the *Directory of Associations* (Gale), updated annually, and *Who to Call* by Daniel Starer (William Morrow). Alternatively, you can order a list of public and private sources of information by writing to the Resource Information Guide, P.O. Box 990297, Redding, California 96099 (the cost is $17.25). The National Health Information Center will also refer callers to appropriate organizations (see listing under "Government Agencies"). If you need information on a rare disease or disorder, you can contact the National Organization for Rare Disorders (203/746-6518 or 1/800-999-6673).

Anorexia/Bulimia

American Anorexia/Bulimia Association. 418 East Seventy-Sixth Street, New York, New York 10021. Phone: 212/734-1114.

Bulimia/Anorexia Self-Help. Phone: 314/768-3292 or 1/800-227-4785.

National Association of Anorexia Nervosa and Associated Disorders. Box 7, Highland Park, Illinois 60035. Phone: 708/831-3438.

Arthritis

Arthritis Foundation/American Juvenile Arthritis Organization. 1314 Spring Street, N.W., Atlanta, Georgia 30309. Phone: 404/872-7100 or 1/800-283-7800 (information hotline).

Birth Defects

March of Dimes Birth Defects Foundation. 1275 Mamaroneck Avenue, White Plains, New York 10605. Phone: 914/428-7100.

Blood Disorders

Children's Blood Foundation. 333 East Thirty-eighth Street, #210, New York, New York 10016. Phone: 212/297-4336.

Cancer

American Cancer Society, Inc. 1599 Clifton Road, N.E., Atlanta, Georgia 30329. Phone: 1/800-227-2345 (response line).

Candlelighters Childhood Cancer Foundation. 7910 Woodmont Avenue, Suite 460, Bethesda, Maryland 20814. Phone: 301/657-8401.

Leukemia Society of America, Inc. 733 Third Avenue, New York, New York 10017. Phone: 212/573-8484.

National Cancer Care Foundation. 1180 Avenue of the Americas, New York, New York 10036. Phone: 212/221-3300.

Parents of Kids with Cancer. 81 Eastside Circle, Petaluma, California 94954. Phone: 707/763-7967.

Cerebral Palsy

United Cerebral Palsy Association, Inc. UCP Research and Educational Foundation, 7 Penn Plaza, Suite 804, New York, New York 10001. Phone: 212/268-6655 or 1/800-872-1827.

Cleft Lip and Palate

American Cleft Palate Association. 1218 Grandview Avenue, Pittsburgh, Pennsylvania 15211. Phone: 412/481-1376.

Cleft Palate Parents' Council. 28 Cambria Road, Syosset, New York 11791. Phone: 516/679-5135.

Prescription Parents, Inc. P.O. Box 426, West Roxbury, Massachusetts 02132. Phone: 617/527-0878.

Cystic Fibrosis

Cystic Fibrosis Foundation. 6931 Arlington Road, Room 200, Bethesda, Maryland 20814. Phone: 301/951-4422 or 1/800-344-4823.

Diabetes

American Diabetes Association, Inc. P.O. Box 25757, Alexandria, Virginia 22314. Phone: 703/549-1500 or 1/800-232-3472.

Juvenile Diabetes Foundation International. 432 Park Avenue South, 16th Floor, New York, New York 10016. Phone: 212/889-7575 or 1/800-223-1138.

Digestive Disorders

Digestive Disease National Coalition. 711 Second Street, N.E., Suite 200, Washington, D.C. 20002. Phone: 202/544-7497.

National Digestive Diseases Information Clearinghouse. Box NDDIC, 9000 Rockville Pike, Bethesda, Maryland 20892. Phone: 301/468-6344.

Epilepsy

Epilepsy Foundation of America.
4351 Garden City Drive, Landover,
Maryland 20785. Phone: 301/459-
3700 or 1/800-332-1000.

Fetal Alcohol Syndrome

Fetal Alcohol Syndrome Network.
158 Rosemont Avenue, Coatesville,
Pennsylvania 19320. Phone: 215/384-
1133.

Heart Disease

American College of Cardiology.
9111 Old Georgetown Road, Bethesda, Maryland 20814. Phone:
301/897-5400.

**Council on Cardiovascular Dis-
ease in the Young.** American Heart
Association National Center, 7272
Greenville Avenue, Dallas, Texas
75231. Phone: 214/373-6300.

Hemophilia

National Hemophilia Foundation.
110 Greene Street, Suite 406, New
York, New York 10012. Phone:
212/219-8180.

Kidney Disease

National Kidney Foundation, Inc.
30 East Thirty-third Street, Suite
1100, New York, New York 10016.

Phone: 212/889-2210 or 1/800-622-
9010.

Liver Disease

American Liver Foundation. 998
Pompton Avenue, Cedar Grove, New
Jersey 07009. Phone: 201/256-2550
or 1/800-223-0179.

Children's Liver Foundation, Inc.
14245 Ventura Boulevard, Suite 201,
Sherman Oaks, California 91423.
Phone: 818/906-3021.

Lung Disease

American Lung Association. 1740
Broadway, New York, New York
10019. Phone: 212/315-8700.

Multiple Sclerosis

**National Multiple Sclerosis Soci-
ety.** 733 Third Avenue, New York,
New York 10017. Phone: 212/986-
3240 or 1/800-624-8236.

Muscular Dystrophy

Muscular Dystrophy Association.
810 Seventh Avenue, New York, New
York 10019. Phone: 212/586-0808.

Scoliosis

Scoliosis Association, Inc. P.O. Box
811705, Boca Raton, Florida 33481-
1705. Phone: 407/994-4435.

TOP MEDICAL CENTERS FOR PEDIATRICS

Children's Hospital. Boston. Phone:
617/735-6000.

Children's Hospital Medical Center.
Cincinnati. Phone: 513/559-4200.

**Children's Memorial Medical Cen-
ter.** Chicago. Phone: 312/880-4000.

Johns Hopkins Children's Center.
Baltimore. Phone: 410/955-2000.

Mount Sinai Medical Center. New
York City. Phone: 212/241-6500.

New England Medical Center. Boston. Phone: 617/956-5000.

New York University (NYU) Medical Center. New York City. Phone: 212/263-7300.

University of California at San Francisco (UCSF) Medical Center. Phone: 415/476-1000.

Yale–New Haven Hospital. New Haven, Connecticut. Phone: 203/785-4242.

THE AMERICAN ACADEMY OF PEDIATRICS: WHERE WE STAND

Following are summaries of some of the American Academy of Pediatrics' child and adolescent health policy statements.

Acquired Immune Deficiency Syndrome (AIDS) – The AAP recommends that most children infected with the AIDS virus should be allowed to attend school and day care in an unrestricted manner, with the approval of their physician. Mandatory screening of children for AIDS should not be undertaken. The AAP also says the nation's schools should immediately initiate AIDS education programs in kindergarten through twelfth grade, with candid emphasis in later grades. Athletes infected with HIV (the AIDS virus) should be allowed to participate in competitive sports, the AAP says. Also, routine HIV testing for athletes is not recommended.

Auto Safety – All 50 states require that children ride in safety seats. The AAP also urges that all newborns discharged from hospitals be brought home in infant car safety seats. The AAP established car-seat guidelines for low-birth weight infants, which include riding in a rear-facing seat and supporting the infant with ample padding. A convertible safety seat is recommended as a child gets older.

Breastfeeding – The benefits of breastfeeding are so numerous that pediatricians strongly encourage the practice. Human milk is nutritionally superior to formulas for the content of fats, cholesterol, protein, and iron. In addition, there is evidence that human milk confers protection against infections.

Choking – The AAP recommends the abdominal thrust technique (Heimlich maneuver) for treatment of a choking child, except in infants younger than one year old. For infants under one year, the AAP says that back blows and chest thrusts, if needed, are still the best treatment for choking to avoid injury to the abdominal organs.

Cholesterol Testing – Regular elective cholesterol testing is suggested for children older than two years of age whose parents or grandparents have a history of premature (before age fifty-five) cardiovascular disease or whose parents have a cholesterol level above 240mg/dl. Factors that weigh against universal cholesterol testing include the imperfect tracking of blood cholesterol values from childhood to adulthood and the possibility of unwarranted anxiety and unnecessary dietary restrictions from false-positive results. The academy opposes universal testing because of the lack of standardization of testing. In addition, a single blood cholesterol level in children may not reflect day-to-day and seasonal variations and could result in unnecessary dietary treatment of a large number of children.

Diet – For a variety of reasons human milk represents the best source of nutrition for most infants during the first months of life. Because whole cow's milk contains inadequate concentrations of certain important ingredients, including iron, the AAP recommends that infants be fed breast milk or iron-fortified infant formula for the first 12 months of life. Skim or low fat milk is not recommended in the first 2 years of life because of the high protein and electrolyte content and low calorie density of these milks.

Introducing Solid Foods

To meet the nutritional needs of growing children, the AAP recommends that appropriate solid foods should be added to their diets between 4 and 6 months of age.

Restrictive Diets

The AAP contends that there is no compelling evidence to make recommendations concerning modification of the diet during the first two decades of life, without first assessing effects on growth and development. Diets that avoid extremes are safe for children with no special vulnerability. Current trends toward a decreased consumption of saturated fats, cholesterol and salt and increased intake of polyunsaturated fats should be followed with moderation. Fat intake should not be restricted in children younger than age 2.

Drug-Exposed Infants – The most appropriate way to prevent intrauterine drug exposure is to educate women of childbearing age about the hazards of drugs to fetuses and to encourage drug avoidance. The AAP does not advocate universal screening for illicit drugs of either mothers or infants.

Drug treatment programs should be made readily available to pregnant women and to women anticipating and/or at risk for pregnancy.

DTP Vaccine – The academy believes that children should receive the DTP (diphtheria-tetanus-pertussis) vaccine at two, four, and six months of age with booster doses at 15-18 months and prior to school entry 4-6 years. The AAP recommends using the acellular pertussis vaccine for the fourth and fifth doses of this immunization, as studies have shown fewer minor adverse reactions. As an alternative, the HbOC-DTP combination vaccine may be used at 2, 4, and 6 months with a booster dose at 15 months to protect against diptheria, tetanus, pertussis, and *Haemophilus influenza* type b infections.

Firearm Safety – The academy believes handguns, deadly air guns, and assault weapons should be banned. The AAP also recommends regulation of handgun ammunition, reduction of the number of privately owned handguns, and placing restrictions on handgun ownership. It also recommends product liability actions and public and parent education.

Formulas – Because whole cow's milk contains inadequate concentrations of certain important ingredients, including iron, the AAP recommends that infants be fed breast milk or iron-fortified infant formula during the first 12 months of life. Since the AAP believes that direct advertising of infant formula to mothers will inevitably decrease the incidence of breast-feeding, and thereby impair the health of infants in the U.S., the AAP has for many years recommended that infant formula companies refrain from advertising their products to the general public.

Hepatitis B – The academy now recommends immunization of all infants for hepatitis B. The first dose should be given to newborns before hospital discharge, the second dose at one to two months of age, and the third dose at six to eighteen months of age. Infants not vaccinated at birth should receive three doses of hepatitis B vaccine by eighteen months of age.

Hib Vaccine – The AAP recommends that all children receive *Haemophilus influenza* type b (Hib) conjugate vaccine beginning at 2 months of age. As an alternative, the DTP-HbOC combination vaccine is also recommended at 2, 4, and 6 months with a booster dose at 12–15 months for protection against diphtheria, tetanus, pertussis and *Haemophilus influenzae* type b infections. As an option for the 15 month booster dose, the acellular pertussis (DTaP) vaccine can be used in conjunction with any Hib conjugate vaccine. Implementation of any of these schedules could eliminate most cases of Hib diseases, including meningitis.

Immunization – The AAP continues efforts to ensure that every child receives age-appropriate vaccination. The AAP has recommended that Congress and the administration focus on ways in which systematic barriers to immunization can be reduced and encourage improvement of data collection on children's immunization status.

Lead Poisoning – Lead causes serious impairments to children at relatively low levels of exposure–the effects of which are largely irreversible. The AAP supports broadbased, routine lead screening of children, as well as restored funding for a national program to screen for lead and to remove lead hazards from the environment.

Measles Vaccine – The AAP recommends two doses of a combined measles-mumps-rubella (MMR) vaccine. The first dose should be given at 15 months of age and the second to children 11–12 years old or older, except where public health authorities require otherwise. The aim is to increase immunization in unvaccinated preschool-age children in high risk areas with the first dose and to prevent the spread of measles in schools and colleges by giving all children routine second doses later in life.

Pediatric Emergency Services – Children have unique medical needs in emergency situations. The AAP advocates regional Emergency Medical Service (EMS) systems so optimal care can be provided. These systems are being developed to organize care at the community level to be sure children with emergency problems, illnesses, or injuries are transported to facilities as quickly and as safely as possible.

Religious Exemptions – The AAP says statutes that permit denial of medical care to children on the grounds of their parents' religious beliefs should not exist. The AAP urges state legislatures and regulatory agencies to remove religious exemption clauses and treat all parents and caretakers of children equally by state and federal laws. When parental practices have potentially harmful consequences for the child, the AAP says state intervention may be warranted.

Smoking – During pregnancy: Many studies have now shown that if a woman smokes during pregnancy, the birth weight and growth during the first year of her child's life is reduced. The range of indisputable effects runs from depressed breathing movements during fetal life to cancer, respiratory disorders, and heart disease in later years. The AAP's message is clear—don't smoke when pregnant.

Passive smoking: Children of parents who smoke have more respiratory infections, bronchitis, pneumonia, and reduced pulmonary function than children of nonsmokers. The AAP supports legislation that would prohibit smoking in public places frequented by children. The AAP also supports a complete ban on tobacco advertising, harsher warning labels on cigarette packages, and increasing the cigarette excise tax.

Sports and Fitness — Because American children do not perform well on fitness tests, the AAP urges schools to maintain, if not increase, physical education programs. Programs should emphasize aerobic and "lifetime" activities such as bicycling, swimming, tennis and running, and decrease time spent on football, basketball, and baseball—traditional school sports that are not particularly fitness-enhancing. Also, the AAP does not support structured infant exercise programs.

Substance Abuse — Alcohol is the drug most often abused by the largest number of children and adolescents. The academy supports a ban on alcohol advertising or equal time for counter advertising. The AAP has helped to develop legislation that would require all print and broadcast advertisements for alcoholic beverages to include health and safety messages.

Sudden Infant Death Syndrome — After evaluating data indicating an association between SIDS and infants who sleep on their stomachs, the AAP recommends that healthy infants, when being put down to sleep, be placed on their side or back. The AAP says that despite common beliefs, there is no evidence that choking is more frequent among infants

lying supine (on their backs) when compared to other positions. In some circumstances, there are still good reasons for placing certain infants on their stomachs for sleep. Parents are encouraged to discuss their individual circumstances with their pediatrician.

Surrogate Motherhood — The academy believes surrogate parenting arrangements should be considered a tentative, preconception adoption agreement in which the surrogate mother is the sole decision maker until after she gives birth to the infant. After birth, applicable local adoption rules and practices should be followed, the AAP says. The interests of the children involved should be the most important consideration for judging surrogate arrangements.

Swimming — The AAP feels that there is little justification for infant swimming programs. It is unlikely that these infants can be made "water safe"—in fact, parents can develop a false sense of security if they think their infant can "swim" a few strokes. Organized group swimming should be reserved for children more than three years of age.

Television —TV advertising and programming can adversely affect learning and behavior of children and adolescents and detract from time spent reading or using other active learning skills. TV also contributes substantially to obesity. The AAP therefore recommends that TV viewing by children be limited to 1-2 hours per day.

The primary goal of commercial children's TV is to sell products to children. Young children cannot distinguish between programs and commercials, and they often don't understand that commercials are designed to sell products. TV also conveys unrealistic messages regarding drugs, alcohol and tobacco, and portrays misleading sex roles and unrealistic sexuality. The AAP also supports legislative efforts to improve children's programming content and promote more constructive viewing.

Vitamins — Normal, healthy children receiving a normal diet do not need vitamin supplementation over and above the recommended dietary allowances.

Chapter 7

Child Safety

GENERAL RESOURCES

Free and Inexpensive Resources

General Safety

Consumer Product Safety Commission. Offers more than fifty safety-related booklets (free of charge), including *For Kids Sake: Think Toy Safety* and *Bicycle Safety: Sprocket Man* (a comic book for kids). Other booklets cover baby-proofing basics, poison prevention, fire safety, pool safety, safety in the nursery, etc. For more information, contact the Consumer Product Safety Commission, Office of Information and Public Affairs, 5401 West Bard Avenue, Bethesda, Maryland 20816. Phone: 301/504-0580.

Holiday Safety. Safety tips for the holidays, including Christmas tree decorating. Send a self-addressed, stamped envelope to the National Safe Kids Campaign, 111 Michigan Avenue, N.W., Washington, D.C. 20010-2970.

Keeping Danger Out of Reach. For a copy of this guide containing home safety tips, write Aetna Life and Casualty, 151 Farmington Avenue, Hartford, Connecticut 06156. (Note: Aetna Life and Casualty offers other safety-related publications as well, including *Poisoning: How to Protect Your Kids.*)

Making Your Child's Home Safer. A fold-out pamphlet containing tips on child-proofing your home. One in a series of reports for parents from the Fisher-Price, Family Alert Program. To request a free copy, call 1/800-635-2440 or write Fisher-Price, Family Alert Program, P.O. Box 7, East Eurora, New York 14052.

Safe and Sound for Baby. A free guide to baby-product safety, use, and selection. Covers child car seats, changing tables, cribs, crib toys and pacifiers, infant bedding, carriers, highchairs, and more. Also discusses household dangers, including electrocution, suffocation, and strangulation. For a copy, send a self-addressed, stamped envelope along with your request to the Juvenile Products Manufacturers Association, Two Greentree Centre, Suite 225, P.O. Box 955, Marlton, New Jersey 08053.

Choking

Choking Prevention and First Aid. Guidelines for parents produced by the American Academy of Pediatrics in consultation with the American Trauma Society. Ask your pediatrician for a copy or send a self-addressed, stamped envelope to American Academy of Pediatrics, "Choking Prevention and First Aid" (see appendix I for contact information).

Reducing Choking Risks. A pamphlet explaining how to eliminate choking risks from your child's environment. To order a free copy, call 1/800-635-2440 or write Fisher-

Price, Family Alert Program, P.O. Box 7, East Eurora, New York 14052.

Crib Safety

Crib Safety Brochure. Available from the Juvenile Products Manufacturers Association, Two Greentree Centre, Suite 225, P.O. Box 955, Marlton, New Jersey 08053. Send a self-addressed, stamped envelope and request the JPMA crib safety brochure.

Fire Safety

Fire Safety. For a copy of this publication, send a self-addressed, stamped envelope to Metropolitan Life Insurance Company, Health and Safety Educational Division, One Madison Avenue, New York, New York 10010.

Playground Safety

Playground Safety. Guidelines available from the American Academy of Pediatrics. Ask your pediatrician for a copy or send a self-addressed, stamped envelope to American Academy of Pediatrics, "Playground Safety" (see appendix I for contact information).

Playgrounds: Safe and Sound. This brochure provides information on injury prevention related to playground equipment, surfacing materials, supervision of children, and awareness of developmentally appropriate playground environments. Available for 50¢ from the National Association for the Education of Young Children (see appendix I for contact information).

Play It Safe! A guide to playground safety, published by the American Academy of Orthopaedic Surgeons (AAOS). For a copy, send a self-addressed, stamped, business-size envelope to "Play It Safe," AAOS, P.O. Box 2058, Des Plains, Illinois 60017.

What Toys Can a Baby Choke On?

To find out, order the "No-Choke Test Tube," a small cylinder designed to measure whether or not specific toys can be choked on. Send $1.00 (check or cash) to Toys to Grow On, P.O. Box 17, Long Beach, California 90801. Be sure to include your mailing address on your request slip.

Sun Protection

Sunproofing Your Baby. Offers guidelines to help protect your baby from the sun's harmful rays. To receive a free copy, send a stamped, self-addressed, business-size envelope to the Skin Cancer Foundation, Box 561, Department SBT, New York, New York 10156.

Sunscreens. For a list of sunscreens that meet standards established by the Skin Cancer Foundation, send a self-addressed, stamped envelope to the Skin Cancer Foundation, P.O. Box 561, New York, New York 10156.

Books

For Adults

The American Red Cross First Aid and Safety Handbook. By Kathleen A. Handal, M.D., and the American Red Cross. Little, Brown, 1992. 321 pages. Not just for use in emergencies, this handbook describes precautions you can take to make your home (and life) safer. Covers first aid techniques and preventive measures.

Baby Proofing Basics. By Vicki Lansky. The Book Peddlers, 1991. Handbook for creating a safe environment for your baby and young child. Seven chapters include "Baby Proofing Room by Room," "Outdoor Safety,"

Fire! (How to Escape from Your Home)

Would you know how to get your family out safely if there was a fire in your home? Now is the time to plan your home escape routes (before the unthinkable happens). Here are a few guidelines:

- Bring all family members together and sketch a simple floor plan of your home.

- Plan two ways out of each room in the house. The first way out should be the door (if it's not blocked by smoke or fire); the second way out might be another door or a window.

- Check all doors and windows and make sure they can be opened easily. In a two-story building, plan your escape through a window onto a roof or porch, if possible. If you must use an escape ladder, make sure everyone knows how to use it.

- Choose a special location outside your home where all family members will meet.

- Be sure everyone in the family clearly understands the planned escape routes (primary and alternate).

- If you haven't done so already, install smoke detectors on each level and also outside each sleeping area. Test these weekly. Family members who sleep with their doors closed should be able to hear the alarms (make sure they can).

- Have a fire drill at least every six months. Have family members practice using both escape routes (out the door, plus the alternate route you have chosen).

Never use an elevator to escape from a burning building. If you live in an apartment building, take the stairs. If fire blocks your exit, close your door and cover all cracks where smoke could enter. Immediately call the fire department—even if fire fighters are already at the building—and tell them exactly where you are. Wave a sheet or towel from the window to help the fire fighters find you.

"Travel," "Safety in Play" (toys, arts, and crafts), "Special Times" (birthdays, Halloween, and other holidays), "Childproofing Your Child" (mealtime, clothing, pets, etc.), and "Poison Prevention."

Baby-Safe Houseplants and Cut Flowers: A Guide to Keeping Children and Plants Safely under the Same Roof. By John Alber and Delores Alber. Genus Books, 1990. 186 pages. Describes and illustrates dozens of dangerous household plants, offers guidelines on eliminating the risks of plant poisonings, and explains what to do if a child eats a plant. Includes a buyer's guide to selecting safe house plants.

The Childwise Catalog: A Consumer Guide to Buying the Safest and Best Products for Your Children. By Jack Gillis and Mary Ellen

R. Fise. Third edition. HarperPerennial, 1993. 470 pages. Endorsed by Dr. Benjamin Spock and other child experts, this comprehensive guide contains practical information to help parents and other caregivers make wise decisions when purchasing car safety seats, cribs, strollers, diapers, gates, highchairs, beds, clothing, and dozens of other items. The first three chapters cover products and services for infants, toddlers, and preschoolers, with proceeding chapters covering child care, health, travel, and safety. The safety section explains how to childproof your home (room by room); stay safe outside the home (when shopping, on the playground, around swimming pools, etc.); be aware of environmental hazards; and teach your child safety and simple emergency procedures. The book also includes lists of associations, government agencies, publications, child-product manufacturers, and mail order catalogs.

Guide to Baby Products: Consumer Reports Books. By Sandy Jones with Werner Freitag and the Editors of Consumer Reports Books. 3rd revised edition. Consumers Union, 1991. 334 pages. Offers advice on buying almost every conceivable baby product, including backpacks, bassinets, cradles, breastfeeding and bottlefeeding equipment, changing tables, safety seats, mattresses, clothing, diapers, baby foods, gates and other safety devices, highchairs, playpens, swings, strollers, toys, decorative items, and nursery accessories. Provides detailed safety information and guidelines on how to avoid hidden hazards. *Consumer Reports'* brand-name ratings, price guidelines, comparative tables, and recall information are also contained in this reliable guidebook.

Healthy Homes, Healthy Kids: Protecting Your Children from Everyday Environmental Hazards. By Joyce M. Schoemaker, Ph.D., and Charity Y. Vitale, Ph.D. Island Press, 1991. 221 pages. This book helps parents locate and eliminate household environmental hazards such as lead, radon, asbestos, and electromagnetic fields. Also explains how to purge pesticides from products, curb contaminants in water, and choose safe household cleaning products. Each section lists additional sources of information such as associations, government agencies, publications, and safe product suppliers.

The New Child Health Encyclopedia. By the Boston Children's Medical Center. Delacorte Press, 1987. 740 pages. Designed as an easy reference for use in situations involving a child's health and safety: emotional and physical, emergencies and everyday questions, common ailments and serious diseases. Divided into four parts: (1) "Keeping Children Healthy"; (2) "Finding Health Care for Children"; (3) "Emergencies"; (4) "Diseases and Symptoms."

Parents™ Book of Child Safety. By David Laskin. Ballantine, 1991. 290 pages. A guide to keeping children (from birth through grade school) safe both inside and outside the home. Includes information on home child-proofing, selecting children's products, evaluating child-care facilities, and outdoor play. Contains instructions on cardiopulmonary resuscitation (CPR) and other emergency procedures as well.

The Perfectly Safe Home. By Jeanne Miller. Simon and Schuster, 1991. 284 pages. Explains how to create a safe environment for your child and offers guidelines for general safety practices and procedures. Evaluates available safety devices, gives specific child-proofing instructions, and explains how to eliminate household toxins and other hazards from the home. Valuable appendices list harmful plants and household products, certified regional poison centers, and statistics on accidental injuries and deaths, as well as books and other resources on child safety. The author, Jeanne Miller, is president of Perfectly Safe, Inc., which produces a catalog highlighting carefully tested child safety products (see listing under "Mail Order Catalogs" for more information).

Safe from the Start. By Joanna Cole and Stephanie Calmenson. Facts On File, 1989. 204 pages. The safety advice in this volume was reviewed by the National Safety Council. Includes everyday safety tips, a guide to choosing baby products, and a step-by-step guide to child-proofing your home. Cowritten by former school teachers Stephanie Calmenson and Joanna Cole (the author of *The Magic School Bus* series).

Safe Kids: A Complete Child-Safety Handbook and Resource Guide for Parents. By Vivian Kramer Fancher. John Wiley, 1991. 209 pages. Covers household safety, basic first aid, travel and recreational safety, child-care safety (including selecting a caregiver and evaluating day-care facilities), and more. Resource listings, included in each chapter, explain where readers can find more information on specific topics. Free and low-cost pamphlets and posters are listed here, along with recommended books, associations, products, and programs.

Saving Children. By Modena Wilson, et al. Oxford University Press, 1991. 247 pages. A guide to injury prevention.

A Sigh of Relief: The First-Aid Handbook for Childhood Emergencies. By Martin I. Green. Bantam, 1993. Completely revised and updated. First-aid handbook containing step-by-step, illustrated instructions for treating common childhood injuries such as burns, bee stings, and broken bones. The beginning of the book is devoted to accident prevention, covering home safety, toy safety, bicycle safety, car safety, water safety, hiking and camping safety, and other areas of concern. Also provides a handy sheet for jotting down all of your emergency telephone numbers.

Who to Call: The Parent's Source Book. By Daniel Starer. William Morrow, 1992. 654 pages. This directory lists hundreds of important phone numbers for parents concerned about the safety and well-being of their children. The safety section lists associations, agencies, and research centers that disseminate information on air, automobile, fire, food, gun, home, school, swimming, recreational, and environmental safety. Names, addresses, phone numbers, and descriptions of resources are all contained in this large volume.

Your Baby and Child: From Birth to Age Five. By Penelope Leach. New edition, revised and expanded. Alfred A. Knopf, 1989. 553 pages. In the back of this child-care classic, parents will find a quick guide to medical emergencies such as choking, smothering, electric shock, head injuries, sunburn, and poisoning. Includes an extensive list of first aid supplies every parent should have on hand, safety tips for avoiding accidents (and treatment procedures should they occur). The section called "Accidents A-Z: First Aid and Safety Tips" offers concise guidelines on many avoidable injuries.

Household Poisons

Every thoughtful parent makes the effort to remove from his child's reach any household liquid or powder that is obviously poisonous. But not all poisons are obvious. A few handfuls of vitamin tablets can do a lot of harm to a toddler. The following list of dangerous items, derived from *Baby Proofing Basics* by Vicki Lansky (1991), may be a reminder that, if you are in doubt, keep it out (of the way).

Kitchen Items
Alcoholic beverages
Dishwasher detergent
Oven cleaner
Vitamins

Bathroom Items
After-shave lotion
Aspirin
Acetaminophen
Baby powder
Cosmetics
Drain cleaner
Hair spray
Iodine
Laxatives
Mouthwash
Perfume
Toilet bowl cleaner

Laundry/Closet Items
Ammonia
Bleach

Boric acid
Cleaning solvents
Detergents
Furniture polish
Lamp oil

Bedroom/Office Items
Correction fluid
Mothballs
Room deodorizer
Tobacco

Garage/Basement/Attic Items
Anti-freeze
Fertilizer
Gasoline
Insecticides
Mercury batteries
Motor oil
Paint
Paint thinner
Weed killer
Windshield washer solution

For Children

Dinosaurs, Beware! By Marc Brown and Stephen Krensky. Little, Brown, 1982. Uses a group of dinosaurs to help teach children basic safety rules, including tips on fire safety and telephone manners. Winner of the 1982 Notable Book Award from the American Library Association.

Kids to the Rescue! By Maribeth and Darwin Boelts, Parenting Press, 1992. 71 pages. Teaches children how to recognize danger and how to "think smart" in an emergency. Explains how to give basic first aid and how to get help. For children ages four to twelve.

Videotapes

Baby Alive. Action Films and Video. Running time: 65 minutes. Produced in cooperation with the American Academy of Pediatrics, this videotape offers valuable information on the safety of children from infancy through age five. Medical experts, together with Phylicia Rashad of *The Cosby Show*, offer step-by-step guidelines for the prevention and treatment of potential life-threatening situations including drowning, poisoning, choking, bleeding, and head injuries. Teaches the Heimlich Maneuver, CPR, and aid for cuts and burns. Also covers child-proofing the home and selecting safe nursery products.

First Aid: The Video Kit. CBS/Fox Company. Running time: 95 minutes. Developed under the auspices of the American Red Cross, this video shows you what to do in case of an emergency. Explains how to prevent shock, how to apply CPR, and how to handle crises such as poisonings, burns, and fractures.

How to Save Your Child or Baby. Activideo. Running time: 40 minutes. Demonstrates CPR, the Heimlich maneuver, and choking rescue procedures for babies and children (infants through age eight). Developed using the latest American Heart Association standards. 20th Annual U.S. Film and Video Festival Award Winner. Available from One Step Ahead (see chapter 27 for contact information).

Kid Safe. Activideo. Running time: 30 minutes. Produced for grade-school children, this videotape explains how to handle emergencies—and how to prevent them from happening. Explains first-aid techniques, how to call 911, how to prevent fires and what to do if they occur, and how to

find out who's at the door before answering it.

Kids for Safety. Monterey Home Video. Running time: 25 minutes. A guide to bicycle, fire, and personal safety. Available from Schoolmasters (see chapter 27 for contact information).

Mr. Baby Proofer. Bogner. Running time: 30 minutes. This home-safety video demonstrates basic baby-proofing techniques.

The Ouchless House. Cambridge Educational. Running time: 30 minutes. Hosted by Toria Tolley, a CNN anchorwoman, this videotape focuses on accident prevention. Covers household baby-proofing, as well as car seat and automobile safety.

Strong Kids, Safe Kids. Paramount. Running time: 42 minutes. A family guide for protecting children against sexual abuse and other dangerous situations. Hosted by Henry Winkler and a cast of cartoon characters, including the Smurfs and Yogi Bear. For ages four to adult.

Think First and Stay Safe. Running time: 30 minutes. Part of the Child Lures Prevention Program, this videotape addresses child sexual abuse. For more information on the Child Lures Prevention Program, which includes a twenty-page guide for parents and guardians, send a self-addressed, stamped, business-size envelope to American Academy of Pediatrics, "Child Lures Prevention Program," Department MTM, P.O. Box 927, Elk Grove Village, Illinois 60009.

Safety Kit

Safety Synergy Kit. Approved by Parents' Choice, this child-proofing kit comes with a child-proofing checklist, a product guide and cata-

Crib Safety Checklist

From *Infant Care*, produced by the Health Resources and Services Administration, U.S. Department of Health and Human Services.

- Side slats of a crib should be less than $2\frac{3}{8}$ inches apart (so baby can't get caught between them)

- Other openings—such as decorative cutouts—should be avoided

- Corner posts should be less than $\frac{5}{8}$ inch high above the rails; take off any that are higher (so that baby's clothing cannot catch on taller posts)

- When the mattress is in the crib, the crib side in the raised position should be at least 20 inches above the mattress surface

- The mattress should fit snugly—you shouldn't be able to get more than two fingers between the mattress and the crib side (so baby can't become wedged between them and get hurt)

- Bumper pads should fit around the entire crib, and tie or snap into place in at least 6 places (after they are tied, trim off excess straps so baby won't chew or be caught in them)

- Remove bumper pads when baby learns to pull up to a standing position (so baby won't use them to try to crawl out)

- Never use any type of thin plastic—such as trash bags—as mattress covers (plastic film can cling to baby's face and smother him or her)

- Remove and destroy all plastic wrapping materials, tying plastic in knots first (children can suffocate if they play with plastic)

- An old painted crib should be stripped of paint (*not* sanded); re-paint with only high quality household enamel paint—do not use old paint—and check the label to make sure it is lead-free; let paint dry thoroughly (old paint may have enough lead to poison a baby who chews on his or her crib)

You may find that a portable mesh crib is easier to handle than a wooden one. If you choose a crib with mesh sides, be sure to keep all of the sides raised because they can form a hazardous pocket when lowered.

log, and health and safety inserts on conducting a family fire drill, stocking and maintaining your medicine cabinet, poisonous plants, and more. Sells for $9.95. Available from Safety by Design, Ltd., P.O. Box 4312, Great Neck, New York 11023.

Mail Order Catalogs

One Step Ahead. P.O. Box 517, Lake Bluff, Illinois 60044. Phone: 1/800-274-8440. Security gates, outlet protectors, sharp corner guards, and an additional baby monitor receiver that will work with your existing set are among the safety devices highlighted in this catalog. Also included are toys, products for feeding and bathing, nursery furnishings, storage containers, diapering products, travel devices, and more.

The Perfectly Safe Catalog. 7245 Whipple Avenue, N.W., North Canton, Ohio 44720. Phone: 1/800-837-KIDS. Every item in this sixty-plus page catalog is carefully evaluated and systematically tested. In addition to more common child-proofing devices such as gates, bath mats, cabinet latches, and electrical-outlet safety plates, this company offers unusual items such as a car-seat sun screen, a microwave radiation-leak detector, and a cool-touch electronic toaster designed to prevent small fingers from being burned. You can also order the Comprehensive Home Safety Kit which contains popular safety items plus a copy of *The Perfectly Safe Home*, a 284-page book full of home-safety information and helpful suggestions (see listing under "Books"). In addition to items designed to prevent accidents, this catalog lists educational toys and computer software for kids. Colorful photographs of available items make it easier for parents to make wise purchasing decisions. Thoughtfully designed and well-organized by topic.

The Right Start. Right Start Plaza, 5334 Sterling Center Drive, Westlake Village, California 91361. Phone: 1/800-LITTLE-1 (twenty-four hours a day). Recipient of the Parents' Choice Approval Award, this catalog offers well-designed health and safety products, along with toys, bedding and bath items, feeding and travel accessories, books, videotapes, audiocassettes, and other items to make the job of parenting just a bit easier. Items for sale in this quality catalog are primarily for babies, toddlers, and preschoolers (or the parents of the aforementioned). Repeat customers and admirers of this catalog's products may want to join The Right Start's Silver Rattle Club™ and receive 20 percent off all orders placed for a full year. The annual fee for club membership is $50.

Associations

American Academy of Pediatrics. 141 Northwest Point Boulevard, P.O. Box 927, Elk Grove Village, Illinois 60009-0927. Phone: 708/228-5005 or 1/800-433-9016. An organization of forty-four thousand pediatricians dedicated to the health, safety, and well-being of infants, children, adolescents, and young adults. While the academy primarily serves pediatricians and other health professionals, many of its publications are geared toward parents and are available through pediatric offices.

Through The Injury Prevention Program (TIPP), the Academy offers guidelines for parents covering many aspects of safety, including: poison prevention, water safety, life jackets and life preservers, bicycle safety, crib safety, home playground equipment, and other topics. Ask your pediatrician for copies of these guidelines.

The Shopping Guide for Car Seats, an annually updated guide, compares the features of more than sixty different car seats. Also explains how to use safety seats correctly. Ask your pediatrician for a copy of this guide.

Single copies of other brochures, such as "Choking Prevention and First Aid" and "Playground Safety" can be ordered free of charge directly from the American Academy of Pediatrics (see listings under "Free and Inexpensive Resources").

In addition, books and videotapes covering safety topics can be ordered from the Academy. For example, a three-hundred-page manual called *Injury Control for Children and Youth* covers sources of injuries to children, explains their causes, and offers steps for their prevention (the cost is $40 to non-members). Videotapes available from the academy include *Baby Alive* (see listing under "Videotapes") and *Bicycle Safety Camp* (see videotape listing under "Biking" in chapter 9).

American Red Cross. National Headquarters, 431 Eighteenth Street, N.W., Washington, D.C. 20006. Phone: 202/737-8300. Headquarters for local and regional chapters of the American Red Cross, many of which offer free and low-cost information and programs on health and safety. Ask your local chapter for information on first aid, CPR, fire prevention, and water safety.

Juvenile Products Manufacturers Association (JPMA). Two Greentree Centre, Suite 225, P.O. Box 955, Marlton, New Jersey 08053. Among its various activities, this trade association certifies baby products that meet safety standards established by the American Society for Testing and Materials. Standards have been developed for highchairs, play yards, walkers, carriages and strollers, gates and enclosures, full-size cribs, and portable hook-on chairs. In the future, standards may be developed for other products as well.

To become JPMA certified, a product must be tested by an independent testing facility. If the product passes the tests, JPMA then allows the manufacturer to label it with a JPMA Certified mark. (Look for this mark on a product or its package for added assurance that the manufacturer designed and built it with safety in mind.)

Offers a variety of safety-related publications, including *JPMA's Directory of Certified Products* and the booklet *Safe and Sound for Baby* (see listing under "Free and Inexpensive Resources"). Write to JPMA at the above address for more information on safety.

National Child Safety Council. 4065 Page Avenue, P.O. Box 1368, Jackson, Michigan 49204. Phone: 517/764-6070. Provides educational materials on child-safety to schools, agencies, and individuals. Produces manuals, pamphlets, and posters covering bicycle safety, substance abuse, crime prevention, and general child safety.

National Safe Kids Campaign®. 111 Michigan Avenue, N.W., Washington, D.C. 20010-2970. Phone: 202/939-4993. A long-term effort to prevent unintentional injury. Seeks to raise public awareness of child injury prevention and to help develop community-based programs to create safer environments for children. Advocates stronger child-safety laws. Safe Kids Campaign coalitions around the country (one hundred state and local) are comprised of individuals, associations, and institutions interested in creating safer homes and neighborhoods for children.

Offers printed information on child safety, including fire safety, burn prevention strategies, safety-seat protection, and childhood injury prevention (guidelines on playground safety, for example). Publishes the *Childhood Injury Prevention Quarterly*, containing information on injury prevention programs and research throughout the country. Includes case studies, interviews, and research summaries. Periodically publishes *Safe Kids Are No Accident: A Fire Safety Magazine for Kids*.

National Safety Council. 1121 Spring Lake Drive, Itasca, Illinois 60143-3201. Phone: 1/800-621-7619. Promotes accident prevention. Provides a forum for the exchange of ideas, strategies, and techniques regarding safety and health practices.

Produces brochures, booklets, manuals, and posters on all aspects of safety, including accident prevention, lead poisoning, transportation safety, occupational illnesses, substance abuse, fire prevention, and toxic substances. Publishes dozens of periodicals, including *Family Safety and Health*, a quarterly magazine covering health and safety both inside and outside the home, and *School Safety World Newsletter*, a quarterly covering school safety, including security policies and employee protection. Other periodicals cover industrial and occupational safety.

Cosponsors, together with Johnson and Johnson, "Safe Kids Are No Accident," an educational campaign to help prevent child injuries

Government Agency

Consumer Product Safety Commission. Office of Information and Public Affairs, 5401 West Bard Avenue, Bethesda, Maryland 20816. Phone: 301/504-0580. (For information on recalls, or to file a complaint, call the Consumer Product Safety Hotline at 1/800-638-CPSC.) Helps protect the public from risks of injury associated with consumer products, including cribs, playpens, strollers, and other products designed for babies and children. Collects information on consumer product-related injuries and maintains an injury information clearinghouse, requires manufacturers to report defects in

products that could create safety hazards, assists in the development of voluntary standards, and establishes, where appropriate, mandatory consumer product standards. If a product is hazardous, the CPSC has the authority to require the manufacturer to correct it, or to recall the product. Issues daily news releases on safety topics. Offers more than fifty safety-related booklets (free of charge), including *For Kids Sake: Think Toy Safety* and *Bicycle Safety: Sprocket Man* (a comic book for kids). Other booklets cover poison prevention, fire safety, pool safety, safety in the nursery, etc.

American Association of Poison Control Centers–Certified Regional Poison Centers (as of March 1994)

If a certified regional poison center is not listed for your area, check the emergency listings in your telephone book (usually found in the front of the book). If you can't find a number there, call 911.

Alabama
Regional Poison Control Center. The Children's Hospital of Alabama, 1600 Seventh Avenue, South, Birmingham, Alabama 35233-1711. Emergency numbers: 205/939-9201 or 205/933-4050. Alabama only: 1/800-292-6678.

Arizona
Arizona Poison and Drug Information Center. Arizona Health Sciences Center, Room #3204-K, 1501 North Campbell Avenue, Tucson, Arizona 85724. Emergency numbers: 602/626-6016. Arizona only: 1/800-362-0101.

Samaritan Regional Poison Center. Teleservices Department, 1441 North Twelfth Street, Phoenix, Arizona 85006. Emergency number: 602/253-3334.

Keeping Your Baby Safe

From *Infant Care*, produced by the Health Resources and Services Administration, U.S. Department of Health and Human Services.

Safety and injury prevention. Babies born healthy are more likely to get hurt or die from accidents than from illness. Accidental injuries can cause severe handicaps. *You can prevent almost all accidents by knowing what your baby is able to do and making sure it is done in a safe way.*

Use the following checklist to be sure your home is safe:

Birth to 4 Months

What the baby can do:

- Eat, sleep, cry, plan, smile.
- Roll off a flat surface, wiggle a lot.

Babies at this age need complete protection all of the time.

Safety Checklist

Bath

- Turn thermostat on your hot water heater down to below 120 degrees F.
- Check bath water temperature with your hand to avoid burns.
- Keep one hand on baby at all times in bath. Never leave baby alone in the bath.

Falls

- Never turn your back on a baby who is on a table, bed, or chair.
- Always keep crib sides up.
- If interrupted, put your baby in the crib, under your arm, or on the floor.
- Do not leave baby in an infant seat on a table or counter unattended.

Burns

- Put screens around hot radiators, floor furnaces, stoves, or kerosene heaters.
- Don't let caregivers smoke when they are caring for your baby.
- Don't hold your baby when you are drinking a hot beverage.
- Don't leave a filled coffee or tea cup on a placemat or near a table edge where it could be pulled down.
- Be sure that foods, bottles, and bath water are not too hot. Test before using.

- Avoid heating baby food or formula in a microwave oven—it can get "hot spots."

In Crib, Bassinet, Carriage, or Playpen

- Be sure bars are close enough so that your baby can't slide through or get stuck ($2\frac{3}{8}$ inches at most).

- Be sure the mattress fits the crib snugly so your baby can't slip between the mattress and the sides of the crib.

- Don't use a pillow.

- Select toys that are too large to swallow, too tough to break, with no small breakable parts and no sharp points or edges.

- Keep pins, buttons, coins, and plastic bags out of reach.

- Never put anything but things a baby can eat or drink in a baby bottle, baby food jar, or baby's dish. Someone might feed it to the baby.

- Don't use a harness or straps in the crib.

- Toys or mobiles that hang by a string should be out of baby's reach and should never be strung across the crib.

In Motor Vehicle

- Always use your car safety seat in the infant position (semi-reclining and facing rearward) for your baby when traveling in a motor vehicle.

- The safest place for an infant is in the rear seat of a car, correctly secured into a car safety seat.

- Adults cannot hold on to a baby in even a minor crash. The child is torn from the adult's arm—even if the adult is buckled up.

- Not all models of car safety seats fit all cars. Use a seat that is convenient for you to install; install it in the car according to the instructions and use it each and every time your child rides in the car.

- Safety seats must *always* be anchored to the car with the car's manual lap belt exactly as specified by the manufacturer.

- Automatic safety belts are not designed, and should not be used, to install safety seats in a car. For cars without manual lap belts in the front, the safety seat must be installed in the rear.

- Whenever a child safety seat is involved in a crash it must be replaced.

- For the best protection, use the seat only for the length of one child's growth through childhood.

- Never use plastic feeder stands, car beds, pillows, or cushions that are not certified for use in cars.

Other

- Never put a loop of ribbon or cord around your baby's neck to hold a pacifier or for any other reason.
- Do not put necklaces, rings, or bracelets on babies.
- Take all toys and small objects out of the crib or playpen when your baby is asleep or unsupervised.

Supervision

- Don't leave your baby alone with young children or with pets.
- Have the telephone numbers of physician, rescue squad, and poison control center posted near your telephone.

Household

- Teach your older children how and when to call "911," the emergency telephone number.
- Install smoke detectors if you do not already have them. Keep a small fire extinguisher out of children's reach in the kitchen.

4 to 7 Months

What baby can do:

- Move around quickly
- Put things in mouth
- Grasp and pull things

Babies at this age will need more time out of the crib.

Safety Checklist

- Recheck the Birth to 4 Months list.
- Never leave your baby on the floor, bed, or in the yard without watching constantly.
- Fence all stairways, top and bottom. Do not use accordion-style expandable baby gates that can strangle.
- Don't tie toys to crib or playpen rails—a baby can strangle in the tapes or string.
- Keep baby's crib away from drapery or venetian blind cords that can strangle.
- Never use a mesh playpen or crib that has holes in the mesh—baby's head can get caught.

- Baby-proof all rooms where the child will play by removing matches, cigarette lighters, cigarette butts, other small objects, breakable objects, sharp objects, and tables or lamps that can be pulled over.

- Cover all unused electric outlets with safety caps or tape.

- Keep high chairs, playpens, and infant seats away from stoves, work counters, radiators, furnaces, kerosene heats, electrical outlets, electric cords, draperies, and venetian blind cords.

- Always use restraining straps on a highchair and do not leave your baby unattended in one.

- Keep cans, bottles, spray cans, and boxes of all cleansers, detergents, pesticides, bleaches, liquor, and cosmetics out of reach.

- Never put a poisonous household product into a food jar, bottle, or soft drink can. Someone may swallow it or feed it to the baby.

- Do not use old paint that might have been made before February 1978—it could contain lead. If a toy or crib is old and needs repainting, remove the old paint completely (with a chemical—do not sand) and paint it with safe lead-free household paint (check the label). Let it dry thoroughly to avoid fumes.

- If your house is old and has any chipping paint or plaster, repair it (don't sand it) and cover it with wallpaper or safe, new paint. If there is chipped paint or plaster in halls or other places you can't repair, have it tested for lead by the health department. If it contains lead, cover it with wallpaper or fabric, or put furniture in front of it to keep it out of reach.

8 to 12 Months

What baby can do:

- Move fast.

- Climb on chairs and stairs.

- Open drawers and cupboards.

- Open bottles and packages.

At this point, your baby needs more opportunity to explore *while you are watching*.

Safety Checklist

- Recheck the Birth to 4 Months list.

- Recheck the 4 to 7 Months list.

- If you use a toy chest or trunk, make sure it has a safety hinge (one that holds the lid open) or remove the lid.

- Baby-proof all cupboards and drawers that can possibly be reached and opened. Remove all small objects and sharp objects, breakables, household products that might poison, plastic bags, and foods that might cause choking (small foods such as nuts, raisins, or popcorn).

- Keep hot foods and hot beverages, hot pots and pans out of your baby's reach. Turn pot or pan handles toward the back of the stove.

- Don't use a dangling table cloth; it can be pulled and everything on it can crash on your baby and the floor.

- Keep medicines and household products (such as bleach, oven and drain cleaners, paint solvents, polishes, waxes) that might poison in a locked cabinet. Try to buy items in child resistant containers.

- Keep young children out of the bathroom unless you are watching. They can drown in a few inches of water (including the toilet or buckets filled with water).

- Be very careful when you or someone else in the family is sick. Medicines are likely to be out of their usual safe place, and your baby may want to imitate you by eating them.

- Keep medicines separate from household products and household products separate from food.

- Never give medicine in the dark. Turn on the light and read the label—every time.

- Avoid overexposure to the sun which can lead to sunburn. Use sunscreens on advice from your doctor or clinic staff.

- Keep diaper pails tightly closed and out of reach.

- Get 1 ounce of Ipecac Syrup from the druggist and keep it on the medicine shelf to treat poisoning. Use as directed.

- Keep a close watch for moving machinery (lawnmowers, cars backing up) when your baby is outdoors.

- Car safety seat can be used in the toddler position with the child sitting up and facing forward when baby is about 20 pounds at about 9 months of age.

- Never leave your baby alone in a child safety seat in a car.

- During hot weather, cover your child safety seat with a towel if your car is parked in the hot sun to avoid burning your child.

California
Fresno Regional Poison Control Center of Fresno Community Hospital and Medical Center. 2823 Fresno Street, Fresno, California 93721. Emergency numbers: 209/445-1222 or 1/800-346-5922.

San Diego Regional Poison Center. UCSD Medical Center, 200 West Arbor Drive, San Diego, California 92103-8925. Emergency numbers: 619/543-6000. In 619 area code only: 1/800-876-4766.

San Francisco Bay Area Regional Poison Control Center. San Francisco General Hospital, 1001 Potrero Avenue, Building 80, Room 230, San Francisco, California 94110. Emergency number: 1/800-523-2222.

Santa Clara Valley Medical Center Regional Poison Center. 750 South Bascom Avenue, San Jose, California 95128. Emergency numbers: 408/299-5112. California only: 1/800-662-9886.

University of California, Davis, Medical Center Regional Poison Control Center. 2315 Stockton Boulevard, Sacramento, California 95817. Emergency numbers: 916/734-3692. Northern California only: 1/800-342-9293.

Colorado
Rocky Mountain Poison and Drug Center. 645 Bannock Street, Denver, Colorado 80204. Emergency number: 303/629-1123.

District of Columbia
National Capital Poison Center. Georgetown University Hospital, 3800 Reservoir Road, N.W., Washington, D.C. 20007. Emergency number: 202/625-3333.

Florida
The Florida Poison Information Center at Tampa General Hospital. P.O. Box 1289, Tampa, Florida 33601. Emergency numbers: 813/253-4444 (in Tampa) or 1/800-282-3171 (in Florida).

Georgia
Georgia Poison Center. Grady Memorial Hospital, 80 Butler Street, S.E., P.O. Box 26066, Atlanta, Georgia 30335-3801. Emergency numbers: 404/616-9000. Georgia only: 1/800-282-5846.

Indiana
Indiana Poison Center. Methodist Hospital of Indiana, 1701 North Senate Boulevard, P.O. Box 1367, Indianapolis, Indiana 46206-1367. Emergency numbers: 317/929-2323. Indiana only: 1/800-382-9097.

Maryland
Maryland Poison Center. 20 North Pine Street, Baltimore, Maryland 21201. Emergency numbers: 410/528-7701. Maryland only: 1/800-492-2414.

National Capital Poison Center. Georgetown Hospital, 3800 Reservoir Road, N.W., Washington, D.C. 20007. Emergency number: 202-625-3333.

Massachusetts
Massachusetts Poison Control System. 300 Longwood Avenue, Boston, Massachusetts 02115. Emergency numbers: 617/232-2120 or 1/800-682-9211.

Michigan
Poison Control Center. Children's Hospital of Michigan, 3901 Beaubien Boulevard, Detroit, Michigan 48201. Emergency number: 313/745-5711.

Minnesota
Hennepin Regional Poison Center. Hennepin County Medical Center, 701 Park Avenue, Minneapolis, Minnesota 55415. Emergency numbers: 612/347-3141. Petline: 612/337-7387. TDD: 612/337-7474.

Missouri
Cardinal Glennon Children's Hospital Regional Poison Center. 1465 South Grand Boulevard, St. Louis, Missouri 63104. Emergency numbers: 314/772-5200 or 1/800-366-8888.

Montana
Rocky Mountain Poison and Drug Center. 645 Bannock Street, Denver, Colorado 80204. Emergency number: 303/629-1123.

Nebraska
The Poison Center. 8301 Dodge Street, Omaha, Nebraska 68114. Emergency numbers: 402/390-5555 (Omaha) or 1/800-955-9119 (Nebraska).

New Jersey
New Jersey Poison Information and Education System. 201 Lyons Avenue, Newark, New Jersey 07112. Emergency number: 1/800-962-1253.

New Mexico
New Mexico Poison and Drug Information Center. University of New Mexico, Albuquerque, New Mexico 87131-1076. Emergency numbers: 505/843-2551. New Mexico only: 1/800-432-6866.

New York
Hudson Valley Poison Center. Nyack Hospital, 160 North Midland Avenue, Nyack, New York 10960. Emergency numbers: 914/353-1000 or 1/800-336-6997.

Long Island Regional Poison Control Center. Winthrop University Hospital, 259 First Street, Mineola, New York 11501. Emergency numbers: 516/542-2323, -2324, -2325, -3813.

New York City Poison Control Center. N.Y.C. Department of Health, 455 First Avenue, Room 123, New York, New York 10016. Emergency numbers: 212/340-4494 or 212/POISONS. TDD: 212/689-9014.

Ohio
Central Ohio Poison Center. 700 Children's Drive, Columbus, Ohio 43205-2696. Emergency numbers: 614/228-1323, 614/461-2012, or 1/800-682-7625. TTY: 614/228-2272.

Cincinnati Drug and Poison Information Center and Regional Poison Control System. 231 Bethesda Avenue, M.L. 144, Cincinnati, Ohio 45267-0144. Emergency numbers: 513/558-5111. Ohio only: 1/800-872-5111.

Oregon
Oregon Poison Center. Oregon Health Sciences University, 3181 Southwest Sam Jackson Park Road, Portland, Oregon 97201. Emergency numbers: 503/494-8968. Oregon only: 1/800-452-7165.

Pennsylvania
Central Pennsylvania Poison Center. University Hospital, Milton S. Hershey Medical Center, Hershey, Pennsylvania 17033. Emergency number: 1/800-521-6110.

Pittsburgh Poison Center. 3705 Fifth Avenue at DeSoto Street, Pittsburgh, Pennsylvania 15213. Emergency number: 412/681-6669.

The Poison Control Center Serving the Greater Philadelphia Metropolitan Area. One Children's Center, Philadelphia, Pennsylvania 19104-4303. Emergency number: 215/386-2100.

Rhode Island
Rhode Island Poison Center. 593 Eddy Street, Providence, Rhode Island 02903. Emergency number: 401/277-5727.

Texas
North Texas Poison Center. 5201 Harry Hines Boulevard, P.O. Box 35926, Dallas, Texas 75235. Emer-

gency numbers: 214/590-5000. Texas Watts: 1/800-441-0040.

Texas State Poison Center. The University of Texas Medical Branch, Galveston, Texas 77550-2780. Emergency numbers: 409/765-1420 (in Galveston); 713/654-1701 (in Houston).

Utah
Utah Poison Control Center. 410 Chipeta Way, Suite 230, Salt Lake City, Utah 84108. Emergency numbers: 801/581-2151. Utah only: 1/800-456-7707.

Virginia
Blue Ridge Poison Center. Box 67, Blue Ridge Hospital, Charlottesville, Virginia 22901. Emergency numbers: 804/924-5543 or 1/800-451-1428.

National Capital Poison Center. Georgetown University Hospital, 3800 Reservoir Road, N.W., Washington, D.C. 20007. Emergency number: 202/625-3333.

West Virginia
West Virginia Poison Center. 3110 MacCorkle Avenue, S.E., Charleston, West Virginia 25304. Emergency numbers: 304/348-4211. West Virginia only: 1/800-642-3625.

Wyoming
The Poison Center. 8301 Dodge Street, Omaha, Nebraska 68114. Emergency numbers: 402/390-5555 or 1/800-955-9119.

A TOPIC-BY-TOPIC LISTING OF ASSOCIATIONS

Abduction
See Missing Children.

Auto Safety
Center for Auto Safety. 2001 S Street, N.W., Suite 410, Washington, D.C. 20009. Phone: 202/328-7700. Auto and highway safety advocacy organization.

National Highway Traffic Safety Administration. Phone: 1/800-424-9393. Call for information on child safety seats, school bus safety, and auto safety defects and recalls.

Child Abuse
Child Help USA. 6463 Independence Avenue, Woodland Hills, California 91370. Phone: 818/347-7290. Runs the National Child Abuse Hot Line (see separate listing).

International Society for Prevention of Child Abuse and Neglect.

1205 Oneida Street, Denver, Colorado 80220. Phone: 303/321-3963.

National Child Abuse Hot Line. Phone: 1/800-422-4453 (1/800-4-ACHILD). Crisis intervention and professional counseling services. Makes referrals; provides literature. Explains how to report child abuse.

National Clearinghouse on Child Abuse and Neglect Information. Department of Health and Human Services. Phone: 1/800-394-3366 or 703/385-7565. Offers free materials.

National Committee for the Prevention of Child Abuse. 332 South Michigan Avenue, Suite 1600, Chicago, Illinois 60604. Phone: 312/663-3520 or 1/800-835-2671 (publications only). Offers information and free materials on parental stress and child abuse, and a catalog of materials.

Parents Anonymous. 520 South Lafayette Park Place, Suite 316, Los Angeles, California 90057. Phone: 213/388-6685. A network of parent-support groups offering services to stressed-out parents who are at risk of abusing their children.

Crib Safety

Danny Foundation. P.O. Box 680, Alamo, California 94507. Phone: 1/800-83-DANNY. A crib-safety awareness group.

Fire Prevention and Safety

International Association of Fire Chiefs, Inc. 1329 Eighteenth Street, N.W., Washington, D.C. 20036-6516. Phone: 202/833-3420. Offers free pamphlets on fire prevention.

National Fire Protection Association. Batterymarch Park, P.O. Box 9101, Quincy, Massachusetts 02269-9101. Phone: 617/770-3000. Offers a catalog of literature on fire safety.

National Institute for Burn Medicine. 909 East Ann Street, Ann Arbor, Michigan 48104. Phone: 313/769-9000. Works to prevent burn injuries and to improve the survival rate of burn victims. Distributes pamphlets on burns and burn prevention.

Injury Prevention/Recreational Safety

The American Academy of Orthopaedic Surgeons. 222 South Prospect Avenue, Park Ridge, Illinois 60068-4058. Phone: 708/823-7186 or 1/800-824-BONES. Available publications include free guidelines on playground safety.

Bicycle Federation of America. 1818 R Street, N.W., Washington, D.C. 20009. Phone: 202/332-6986. Provides information on bicycle safety.

Bicycle Helmet Safety Institute. 4611 Seventh Street, South, Arlington, Virginia 22204-1419. Phone:

703/486-0100. Promotes the use of helmets for bicyclists.

National Head and Spinal Cord Injury Prevention Program. American Association of Neurological Surgeons, 22 South Washington Street, Suite 100, Park Ridge, Illinois 60068. Phone: 708/692-9500. A public service program created by the American Association of Neurological Surgeons and the Congress of Neurological Surgeons. Provides prevention education on head and spine injuries to young people throughout North America.

National Society to Prevent Blindness. 500 East Remington Road, Schaumburg, Illinois 60173. Phone: 708/843-2020. Offers information on eye injury prevention and first aid for eye emergencies.

National Water Safety Congress. c/o Mac Wimbish, 2101 North Frontage Road, Vicksburg, Mississippi 39180-5191. Promotes swimming, boating, and scuba safety. Publishes the *Water Safety Journal.*

The Skin Cancer Foundation. 245 Fifth Avenue, Suite 2402, New York, New York 10016. Phone: 212/725-5176. Offers a free guide to sensible sun protection for children.

Sporting Goods Manufacturers Association. 200 Castlewood Drive, North Palm Beach, Florida 33408. Phone: 407/842-4100. Provides information concerning safety and product standards.

For a topic-by-topic listing of sports and recreation associations turn to chapter 9. Many of them will provide safety guidelines upon request.

Lead Poisoning

Alliance to End Childhood Lead Poisoning. 600 Pennsylvania Avenue, S.E., Suite 100, Washington,

Book Tie-Ins

It's My Body. By L. Freeman. Parenting Press, 1983. 24 pages. Using language that minimizes embarrassment and doesn't cause unnecessary fear, this book introduces young children to the dangers of sexual abuse. Emphasizes the importance of self-reliance and communication. Designed to be read to children (preschool through the early elementary years) by a grown-up.

Protect Your Child from Sexual Abuse. By Janie Hart-Rossi. Parenting Press, 1984. 24 pages. A how-to guide for parents, offering information and activities to help teach children how to resist uncomfortable touching.

D.C. 20003. Phone: 202/543-1147. Fax: 202/543-4466. A public interest organization working to eliminate lead poisoning in children.

Lead Information Clearinghouse. Phone: 1/800-LEAD-FYI. Offers information on preventing lead poisoning; maintains a listing of state and local agencies where you can obtain additional information.

Missing Children

Adam Walsh Child Resource Center. 11911 U.S. Highway 1, Suite 301, North Palm Beach, Florida 33408. Phone: 407/775-7191. Provides public information and referral services. Offers support services for families of missing and exploited children. Seeks to change legislation at the state and federal level for the protection of victimized children and their families.

Child Find of America. P.O. Box 277, New Paltz, New York 12561. Phone: 914/255-1848. Offers information and education programs to help prevent child abduction. Works to locate missing children through investigation, photo distribution, public information, and other means. Operates a twenty-four-hour hotline (1/800-426-5678).

Find the Children. 11811 West Olympic Boulevard, Los Angeles, California 90064. Phone: 310/477-6721. Educates parents and children on child safety. Supports safety legislation. Assists families and law-enforcement officials in locating missing children.

National Center for Missing and Exploited Children. 2101 Wilson Boulevard, Suite 550, Arlington, Virginia 22201. Phone: 703/235-3900. Assists parents and law enforcement officials in preventing child exploitation and in locating missing children. Serves as a national clearinghouse for information on effective legislation directed at the protection of children. Operates a toll-free hotline (1/800-843-5678) to collect and disseminate information on sightings of children.

Product Safety

American Society for Testing and Materials (ASTM). 1916 Race Street, Philadelphia, Pennsylvania 19103-1187. Phone: 215/977-9679. Establishes test standards for products (including items for children), materials, and services.

Consumer Product Safety Commission. Office of Information and Public Affairs, 5401 West Bard Avenue, Bethesda, Maryland 20816.

Phone: 301/504-0580 or 1/800-638-CPSC (Safety Hotline). Helps protect the public from risks of injury associated with consumer products. (For more information, see listing under "Government Agency.")

Juvenile Products Manufacturers Association (JPMA). Two Greentree Centre, Suite 225, P.O. Box 955, Marlton, New Jersey 08053. Certifies baby products that meet safety standards established by the American Society for Testing and Materials. (For more information, see listing under "Associations.")

Toy Manufacturers of America, Inc. 200 Fifth Avenue, Suite 740, New York, New York 10010. Phone: 212/675-1141. Provides information on toy safety.

School Safety

National Alliance for Safe Schools. P.O. Box 30177, Bethesda, Maryland 20824. Phone: 301/907-7888.

Sexual Abuse

Parents against Molesters. P.O. Box 3557, Portsmouth, Virginia 23701. Phone: 804/363-2549. Promotes awareness and prevention of child molestation. Offers community self-help services, including counseling and film presentations for schools and civic groups.

Parents United International. 232 East Gish Road, San Jose, California 95112. Phone: 408/453-7616. A group of individuals and families who have experienced child sexual molestation. Offers assistance and support, including professional counseling and group sessions for children. Conducts educational programs; offers publications and other informational materials.

Chapter 8

Food and Nutrition

BREASTFEEDING

Free and Inexpensive Resources

Breastfeeding Education Materials. The following pamphlets are among many available from La Leche League International (see appendix I for contact information). Each is available for 50¢.

Breastfeeding Does Make a Difference. A pamphlet filled with facts on breastfeeding.

The Breastfeeding Father. An introduction to breastfeeding for fathers, explaining why the father's support is crucial to successful breastfeeding.

Can Breastfeeding Become the Cultural Norm? Takes a look at breastfeeding beliefs and practices in the United States—and how they affect breastfeeding mothers.

Does Breastfeeding Take Too Much Time? Written for breastfeeding mothers who are considering weaning or feeling overwhelmed with the job of caring for a young child.

How to Handle a Nursing Strike. Suggests ways to help nursing mothers persuade their babies to give up their nursing strikes (and understand the possible reasons behind them).

Increasing Your Milk. Describes the process of milk production and explains what the new mother can expect as her body adjusts. Also discusses factors that contribute to a low milk supply.

Positioning Your Baby at the Breast. A step-by-step guide to positioning your baby at the breast.

Sore Nipples. Recommends treatment of sore and cracked nipples. Includes step-by-step illustrations of latch-on; emphasizes the importance of proper positioning.

When You Breastfeed Your Baby. Offers instructions for the early days and weeks of breastfeeding. Includes guidelines on nipple care, manual expression, feeding frequency, and more.

Other La Leche League pamphlets include *Breastfeeding the Chronically Ill Child* (75¢), *Practical Hints for Working and Breastfeeding, Nutrition and Breastfeeding, Breastfeeding Twins* (75¢), *Nipple Confusion: Overcoming and Avoiding This Problem, Breastfeeding after a Caesarean Birth,* and *Breastfeeding and Fertility.*

La Leche League International also offers low-cost booklets and packets (prices range from 75¢ to $1.95), including *The Diabetic Mother and Breastfeeding, Breastfeeding Your Premature Baby, Breastfeeding with Breast Implants, A Mother's Guide to Milk Expression and Breast Pumps, Nursing Your Adopted Baby, Legal Rights of Breastfeeding Mothers, USA Scene*, and other titles (request a copy of La Leche's free mail-order catalog for a complete listing).

Nursing: The First Two Months. A 96-page excerpt from *The Nursing Mother's Companion* by Kathleen Huggins, R.N., M.S. (published by The Harvard Common Press; see listing under "Books"). This informative booklet is provided as a service by Mead Johnson Nutritionals and is available free of charge from participating hospitals and physicians.

Books

Breastfeeding and the Working Mother. By Diane Mason and Diane Ingersoll. St. Martin's Press, 1986. 212 pages. Offers breastfeeding strategies for mothers who work outside the home, including the option of part-time nursing.

Bestfeeding: Getting Breastfeeding Right for You. By Mary Renfrew, Chloe Fisher, and Suzanne Arms. Celestial Arts, 1990. 240 pages. Explains the benefits and joys of breastfeeding. Explains how to get off to the right start (including information on latch-on and positioning) and how to remedy problems should they arise. Also explains different cultural attitudes toward breastfeeding.

Breastfeeding Success for Working Mothers. By Marilyn Grams, M.D. National Capital Resources, 1985. 156 pages. Written by a working mother, this book offers personal tips

> ### More Support for Breastfeeding Mothers
>
> *Mothering* magazine contains many news items and feature articles exploring various aspects of breastfeeding. Back issues are available. Contact: *Mothering*, P.O. Box 1690, Santa Fe, New Mexico 87504. Phone: 1/800-827-1061 (subscriptions and customer service).

that can help make breastfeeding and working outside the home compatible. Covers the basics of breastfeeding, the return to work while nursing, and various crises that may crop up (along with advice on ending them).

Breastfeeding Your Baby. By Sheila Kitzinger. Alfred A. Knopf, 1989. 160 pages. Covers the scientific, emotional, and practical aspects of breastfeeding. Includes photographs.

The Complete Book of Breastfeeding. By Marvin S. Eiger, M.D., and Sally Wendkos Olds. Revised edition. Workman Publishing, 1987. 318 pages. Explains why breastfeeding is beneficial, answers commonly asked questions, covers the scientific and medical aspects of lactation, and addresses the roles of the father and other family members in the breastfeeding process. Problems while breastfeeding, working outside the home while nursing, and "special situations" that result from premature birth or the birth of twins, for example, are all covered in this popular volume. A step-by-step guide on expressing and storing milk can be found at the back of the book.

Mothering Your Nursing Toddler. By Norma Jane Bumgarner. La Leche League International, 1983. 208

pages. This book offers advice and support to mothers who breastfeed beyond the first year. While this practice is considered normal elsewhere around the globe, mothers in the United States face special challenges and obstacles, many of which are addressed in this book.

The Nursing Mother's Companion. By Kathleen Huggins, R.N., M.S. Revised edition. Harvard Common Press, 1990. 220 pages. Endorsed by Marian Tompson, cofounder of La Leche League, and many others, this illustrated book guides mothers through the breast-feeding process. Preparations to make during pregnancy, survival tactics during the first days and weeks of breastfeeding, and nursing babies as they grow older are all addressed in this guide. Includes resource listings such as associations and companies that rent breast pumps.

Nursing Your Baby. By Karen Pryor and Gale Pryor. Revised edition. Pocket Books, 1991. 416 pages. Updated for the '90s, this classic guide includes information on relactation, working mothers, and the effects of drugs and alcohol on breastfeeding.

Only Mothers Know: Patterns of Infant Feeding in Traditional Cultures. By Dana Raphael and Flora Davis. Greenwood Press, 1985. 159 pages. Explores the ways in which women in various countries feed their babies.

The Womanly Art of Breastfeeding. By La Leche League International. Fifth revised edition. NAL-Dutton, 1991. 446 pages. A basic how-to book from La Leche League International, *The Womanly Art of Breastfeeding* has offered advice and answered questions about breastfeeding for two generations and has sold more than a million copies. Note: An audiocassette edition of this book is also available. This two-tape set (180 minutes) is available from La Leche League International, P.O. Box 1209, Franklin Park, Illinois 60131-8209. Phone: 708/451-1891.

The Working Woman's Guide to Breastfeeding. By Nancy Dana and Anne Price. Meadowbrook, 1987. 130 pages. Offers practical advice for working mothers. Explains how to plan maternity leave, how to pump and store breast milk, and much more. Nancy Dana and Anne Price are also the authors of *Successful Breastfeeding*, a practical guide for nursing mothers, also published by Meadowbrook (1985).

Other Books of Interest

Child of Mine: Feeding with Love and Good Sense. By Ellyn Satter, R.D. Expanded edition. Bull Publishing, 1986. 463 pages. A book about feeding and the feeding relationship. Chapters include "Breastfeeding Versus Bottle Feeding," "The Milk Feeding," and "Breastfeeding How-to."

Eat Well, Lose Weight While Breastfeeding. By Eileen Behan, R.D. Random House, 1992. 208 pages. Written by a registered dietician, this book shows how to shed pounds while keeping your baby properly nourished. Includes a complete diet (along with recipes) and reshaping plan (along with exercises). Provides special diets for women who are anemic, allergic, or diabetic.

Guide to Baby Products: Consumer Reports Books. By Sandy Jones with Werner Freitag and the Editors of Consumer Reports Books. 3rd revised edition. Consumers Union, 1991. 333 pages. Chapter 5 evaluates breast pumps (hand-operated, battery-operated, and electric), nipples, and nursing bras. Additional sources of information and medical aspects of breastfeeding are also contained in this guide produced by Consumers Union, a reputable nonprofit organization.

Jane Brody's Nutrition Book. By Jane Brody. Bantam, 1987. Contains more than 500 pages on healthy eating and sound nutrition. Offers eating guidelines for pregnant and nursing women.

Of Cradles and Careers: A Guide to Reshaping Your Job to Include a Baby in Your Life. By Kaye Lowman. La Leche League International, 1984. 300 pages. A La Leche League International Book, *Of Cradles and Careers* contains stories of women who have pioneered changes in the American workplace to made them more responsive to the needs of mothers and babies. Includes personal accounts from mothers who continued to breastfeed while working outside the home. Practical hints on pumping and storing milk, guidelines for self-care, and listings of additional resources are all contained in the chapter on breastfeeding.

Working and Caring. By T. Berry Brazelton, M.D. Addison-Wesley, 1985. 197 pages. Offers sensible advice to working parents, including professional couples and single mothers. Follows three different families as they grapple with important issues such as childcare and feeding options. Addresses the special challenges breastfeeding mothers face when they return to work.

Videotapes

Breastfeeding: A Special Relationship. Eagle Video Productions. Running time: 25 minutes. Intended for inexperienced parents, this video covers the latch-on process, breastfeeding positions, engorgement and sore nipples, and returning to work.

What about Cabbages?

Though much folklore about breastfeeding may have a sound basis in experience, some folklore is more unhelpful than wise, including the many admonitions on what *not* to eat. According to the editors of *Parenting* magazine (see their June/July 1992 "Mothercare" column), "There's no strict list of foods that nursing mothers must swear off. Women have been warned for generations to stay away from onions, garlic, broccoli, cabbage, and anything spicy, or suffer the consequences of a colicky, gassy baby. In fact, each baby responds differently to these foods, and the only way of knowing whether a particular item will cause trouble is by trial and error."

Available from La Leche League International (see appendix I for contact information).

Breastfeeding: The Art of Mothering. Alive Productions Ltd. Running time: 40 minutes. A video guide to breastfeeding, written by a nurse lactation consultant, a pediatrician, and a nurse childbirth educator. Approved by the American Academy of Pediatrics (AAP). Available from the American Academy of Pediatrics, Publications Department (see appendix I for contact information).

Breastfeeding Your Baby: A Mother's Guide. Medela. Running time: 60 minutes. Produced in cooperation with the La Leche League, this video explains the advantages of breastfeeding and offers advice on techniques. Addresses common problems and offers solutions. Available from La Leche League International (see appendix I for contact information). (Note: An excerpt from this videotape, *Breastfeeding Your Baby: Positioning*, is also available. This fifteen-minute tape demonstrates various nursing positions.)

Hotline

La Leche League Hotline. 1/800-LALECHE. Trained volunteers answer questions and offer information and support on breastfeeding. They will also refer you to local chapters.

Mail Order Catalogs

Be Healthy, Inc., Catalog. 51 Saltrock Road, Baltic, Connecticut 06330. Phone: 203/822-8573 or 1/800-433-5523. A catalog for expectant and new parents, containing breast pumps, shields, and herbal remedies, along with books, videotapes, and audiocassettes to help new parents relax, learn, and enjoy their new baby.

Bosom Buddies. P.O. Box 6138, Kingston, New York 12401. Phone: 914/338-2038. This illustrated catalog features products for nursing mothers, including a wide selection of bras, comfortable clothing with concealed openings, and accessories such as breast pumps and pads.

Boyston, Inc. 2606 Thirty-seventh Avenue, N.E., Minneapolis, Minnesota 55421-3633. Phone: 612/788-0180. Mail order service offering a variety of nursing bras.

ICEA Bookmarks. ICEA Bookcenter, P.O. Box 20048, Minneapolis, Minnesota 55420. Phone: 612/854-8660. A mail order catalog from the International Childbirth Education Association listing dozens of titles on breastfeeding. Also lists videotapes

and informational pamphlets on nursing.

Imprints. Birth and Life Bookstore, 7001 Alonzo Avenue, N.W., P.O. Box 70625, Seattle, Washington 98107-0625. Phone: 206/789-4444. A free mail-order catalog and review newsletter offering many books and pamphlets on breastfeeding.

La Leche League International Catalog. See La Leche League International, listed under "Associations."

Moonflower Birthing Supply Ltd. 2810 Wilderness Place, #D, Boulder, Colorado 80301. Phone: 303/440-5566 or 1/800-462-4784. In addition to midwife supply items (cord clamps, scales, and such), this mail order catalog also features items of interest to breastfeeding mothers, including videotapes, audiocassettes, books and pamphlets, breast pumps, and washable breast pads. General books on parenting are featured as well. The Better Baby Series pamphlets, published by Pennypress, are also available through this company. Topics in the series include "A Working Mother Can Breastfeed When . . ." and "Babies and Jobs: Concerns and Choices."

Motherwear. Box 114M, Northampton, Massachusetts 01061. Phone: 1/800-950-2500. Designed to make nursing and nurturing easier for mothers, this free forty-page catalog features breast pumps, milk coolers, nursing bras, and clothing items such as dresses, shirts, and nightgowns. Also lists diapering supplies, natural baby care products, baby carriers, car seat covers, books, tapes, and a sixteen-page newsletter called *Parenting from the Heart.*

Breast-Pump Rental Companies

Emeda/Egnell, Inc. Phone: 1/800-323-8750. Will direct callers to a rental station in their area. Recommends lactation consultants as well.

Medela, Inc. Phone: 1/800-TELL-YOU. (If you live in Alaska, Illinois, or Hawaii, call 815/363-1166.) Will refer callers to a rental station in their area. Also recommends lactation consultants.

Associations

Human Lactation Center. 666 Sturges Highway, Westport, Connecticut 06880. Phone: 203/259-5995. Conducts research on lactation and supports educational efforts around the globe. Provides consultation services in the areas of infant and maternal nutrition, feeding practices, and food policy. Publishes *The Lactation Review*, issued periodically. Also produced *Only Mothers Know: Patterns of Infant Feeding in Traditional Cultures* (see listing under "Books").

International Lactation Consultant Association. 201 Brown Avenue, Evanston, Illinois 60202-3601. Phone: 708/260-8874. An association of lactation consultants, health professionals, and institutions interested in breastfeeding and lactation. Works to increase awareness of breastfeeding and lactation and encourages education and research in these areas. Publishes the *Journal of Human Lactation*, a quarterly containing research findings, scientific articles, association news, and reviews. Also publishes brochures, papers, and journal supplements.

La Leche League International. 9616 Minneapolis Avenue, P.O. Box 1209, Franklin Park, Illinois 60131-8209. Phone: 708/455-7730. Hotline: 1/800-LA-LECHE. Offers information and support to breastfeeding mothers and those who are interested in the option. Upon request, this organization will refer you to one of its local groups (located in all fifty states and dozens of

---

**For Your Child
A Toy that Gets the
Message Across**

You can order breastfeeding dolls from Milk & Honey, a company based in Bloomington, Indiana. The rag doll sets include the mother doll, the baby doll, a front/back baby carrier, and a flannel receiving blanket. You can choose skin tone (white, tan, or brown) and hair color (black, brown, blonde, auburn, or yellow). For more information, write Milk and Honey, P.O. Box 1315, Bloomington, Indiana 47402.

---

countries around the globe).

Produces a variety of useful publications including *Practical Hints for Working and Breastfeeding, The Womanly Art of Breastfeeding,* and *Legal Rights of Breastfeeding Mothers: USA Scene.* Pamphlets exploring specific breastfeeding challenges include *Nursing Your Adopted Baby, The Diabetic Mother and Breastfeeding,* and *Breastfeeding the Baby with Down's Syndrome.* Publishes *New Beginnings,* a bimonthly journal containing articles on breastfeeding, nutrition, parenting, and family life. Also offers a free resource catalog full of books, pamphlets, posters, videotapes, breastfeeding pumps, and other items for breastfeeding mothers.

Nursing Mothers Counsel. P.O. Box 50063, Palo Alto, California 94303. Phone: 415/591-6688. A breastfeeding support group based in California with branches around the country. Lends an ear and offers assistance, including home visits, to nursing mothers.

BOTTLEFEEDING

Free and Inexpensive Resources

Feeding Baby: A Guide for New Parents. A booklet containing information on formula feeding, breastfeeding, and the introduction of solid foods. Explains how to prepare formula, how often to feed, how much to feed, and why cow's milk should be avoided during the first year. Also discusses burping, spitting up, and different types of nipples. Produced by Mead Johnson Nutritionals, makers of Enfamil® and ProSobee®, and available free of charge from your physician or hospital.

Feeding Baby: Nature and Nurture. This four-page pamphlet compares milk- and soy-based formulas and explores the dangers of confusing soy beverages with soy-based formulas. Produced in 1990 by the Food and Drug Administration. For ordering information, request the free *Consumer Information Catalog*, available from the Consumer Information Center, P.O. Box 100, Pueblo, Colorado 81002.

Food Sensitivity: Your Milk- or Food-Sensitive Infant. Talks about cow's-milk and soy allergies in infants, as well as other food sensitivities. Explains how to identify a food allergy—and what you can do about it. Produced as a service by Ross Laboratories, makers of Similac®, Isomil®, and Alimentum®. Available from your physician or hospital.

Books

The Baby Book: Everything You Need to Know about Your Baby from Birth to Age Two. By William Sears, M.D., and Martha Sears, R.N. Little, Brown, 1993. 689 pages.

Among the many chapters in this guide to child care are "Bottlefeeding with Safety and Love" (chapter 10), which discusses concerns about formulas, choosing a formula (including various types), and preparing formula. Also addresses the questions "how much?" and "how often?" and offers general bottlefeeding tips.

Caring for Your Baby and Young Child: Birth to Age Five. Steven P. Shelow, M.D., F.A.A.P., editor-in-chief; Robert E. Hannemann, M.D., F.A.A.P., associate medical editor. Bantam, 1991. 676 pages. Includes sections on bottlefeeding and breastfeeding. Describes the advantages of each. Offers guidelines for choosing a formula, preparing formula, and feeding amounts and schedules. Also discusses the feeding process.

Child of Mine: Feeding with Love and Good Sense. By Ellyn Satter, R.D. Expanded edition. Bull Publishing, 1986. 463 pages. A book about feeding and the feeding relationship. Chapters include "Breastfeeding versus Bottle Feeding" and "The Milk Feeding."

Dr. Spock's Baby and Child Care. By Benjamin Spock, M.D., and Michael B. Rothenberg, M.D. Pocket Books, 1992. 832 pages. This classic bestseller, revised and updated for the 90s, explains how to mix formula, how to give the bottle, and when to wean to a cup. Also explains what to do if your baby is a poor nurser, why bottles in bed should be avoided, and how to avoid common feeding problems. Dr. Spock believes that "scheduled feedings" (as opposed to "on-demand feedings") can help parents who want or need structure and predictability in their lives.

Bottlefeeding

From *Infant Care,* produced by the Health Resources and Services Administration, U.S. Department of Health and Human Services.

If for some reason you cannot or choose not to breastfeed your baby, bottlefeeding of infant formulas is a good substitute. Formula comes in many different packages and sizes including ready-to-use form, liquid concentrate and dry powder. The ready-to-use form needs no added water and is the most expensive, and powder is the cheapest choice. You will need to carefully follow the directions on the container for the type you choose. You may want to ask your doctor or clinic staff to recommend a specific brand, and choose a formula with iron unless there are medical reasons why you should not. If someone else will be feeding your baby, make sure they know exactly how to prepare the formula. Adding water when you don't need it and not adding water when you do can hurt your baby.

Once you have chosen and brought home the formula, follow these easy steps to prepare it to feed your baby:

- Always wash your hands before preparing baby formula and bottles to prevent infection.

- Use bottles, caps and nipples that have been washed in clean water and dishwashing soap or detergent, or in the dishwasher if you have one. (You may wash them with the family dishes.) If you wash them by hand, use a bottle brush. Squeeze water through the nipple holes to be sure that they are open. Rinse well to remove all detergent, and let them stand in a rack to dry. (Check the package to see if they should be boiled before you use them the first time.)

- When you are ready to feed your baby, clean the top of the formula can (if the formula you've chosen is canned) with soap and water. Rinse.

- Open the can with a clean punch-type opener.

- Using the directions that came with the formula, pour it into the bottle. Mix it with water if it is a concentrate or powder. Use only fresh water directly from the cold water tap.

- Put on the nipple and cap.

- No warming is necessary. Babies can take cold formula, although they may prefer it warm when they are very young.

- Try to feed your baby with the formula within 30 minutes of the time you make it. If it isn't used up within about an hour, throw it away and start again with a clean bottle.

- Keep any opened can of liquid formula covered in the refrigerator (powdered formula does not need to be kept cold until it is mixed with water).

If you bottlefeed your baby:

- Don't feed formula that has been left at room temperature in a nursing bottle or open can for more than an hour, or in the refrigerator for more than 2 days. (Germs can multiply rapidly in warm milk.)

- Don't feed any formula without first reading instructions on the container. Some formulas are sold ready to feed and should not have water added to them. Powdered formulas and concentrated liquid formulas need to be prepared differently. Be sure you know how your formulas should be prepared.

- Don't give baby vitamins or iron if you are using a prepared infant formula with iron, unless these are specifically prescribed by your doctor and you have told him or her that you are using a formula that contains iron.

- Don't leave a bottle containing formula—or anything else—with your baby to calm or help him or her sleep. Your baby's teeth are developing and milk, formula, juices or other liquids that remain in your baby's mouth can lead to cavities. In addition, propping a bottle may result in baby choking or developing an ear infection.

- If you are concerned about your baby's bowel habits or spitting up, don't expect to change them by changing from one brand of formula to another. It is best to ask your doctor before making changes in formula for these reasons.

How to bottlefeed:

- Hold your baby close to you in your arms, with the head a little higher than the rest of the body.

- Tilt the bottle to be sure that milk is in the nipple. Touch the nipple next to the baby's mouth and the baby will turn and grasp the nipple. Hold the bottle so that it sticks straight out at a right angle to the baby's mouth.

- The nipple's holes should be large enough so that milk drops slowly (about one drop per second) from the bottle when it is held with the nipple down.

- You should see air bubbles entering the bottle as the baby drinks (except when using plastic-lined bottles that collapse as the bottle empties). If no air bubbles appear, milk will stop flowing. Check to see that the cap is not on too tight.

■ Halfway through the bottle and again when your baby is finished eating, burp your baby on your shoulder by patting him or her gently on the back until you hear a burp. (Another way is to hold your baby face down on his or her stomach in your lap over your hand or knee and pat his or her back.) Your baby will usually burp up some air and often a little of the formula.

How often to feed:
Feed your baby when he or she seems hungry. Most babies will fall into a pattern of 6 to 8 feedings about 3 to 5 hours apart. It is easier and better to get to a regular schedule by working from the baby's own timing, than by just deciding to feed at certain times whether the baby is hungry or not. You will soon by able to tell from your baby's crying and fussing what his or her needs are.

After a few weeks, most babies will begin to sleep through one of the feedings. Most parents prefer to skip the night feeding rather than a daytime feeding. If your baby sleeps through a daytime feeding, wake and feed at the usual time so that the baby—hopefully—will give up one of the nighttime feedings.

How much to feed:
Don't worry about how much is taken at a single feeding; most babies will have times when they just aren't hungry and other times when they take more than you expect. If your baby is growing at a satisfactory rate, he or she is probably getting the right amount .

Most babies, after the first few days, take 2 to 3 ounces of milk each day for each pound of their body weight. Most bottlefed babies want 6 or 7 feedings each day. For a 7-pound baby, this would mean 14 to 21 ounces of formula a day (2½ to 3½ ounces in each 6 or 7 feedings).

You might begin by offering 3 ounces in each bottle. When your baby begins to empty the bottle completely at 2 or 3 feedings a day, add an additional 1 ounce to the bottle. Stay a little ahead of the baby and let the baby decide how much to take. If your baby takes much more or less than 2 to 3 ounces per pound per day, talk with your doctor or clinic staff.

Guide to Baby Products: Consumer Reports Books. By Sandy Jones with Werner Freitag and the Editors of Consumer Reports Books. Third revised edition. Consumers Union, 1991. 333 pages. Chapter 5 evaluates bottlefeeding equipment such as nipples, formula, bottles, and heating units. Also describes the basic types of formula and explains why its unsafe to heat bottles in microwave ovens.

Hotlines

Formula Hotline. For information on formula, you can call Gerber's toll-free formula hotline: 1/800-828-9119 (from 8 a.m. to 5 p.m., central standard time). For general information on care and feeding, you can call Gerber's other hotline—1/800-4-GERBER.

Parents Helpline. *Parents* magazine has set up a 900 number (the cost is

95¢ per minute) so that parents can receive advice on various topics, including bottlefeeding and breastfeeding, twenty-four hours a day. Dial 1/900-903-KIDS, then enter the two numbers next to the topic of your choice:

Babies' Weight Gain (04)
Bottle Water vs. Tap Water (07)
Burping Your Baby (09)
Giving Up the Bottle (24)
Tap-Water Safety (41)

Associations

Formula. P.O. Box 39051, Washington, D.C. 20016. Phone: 703/527-7171. Works to ensure that all infant formula is safe and nutritionally complete. Collects information from parents whose children have suffered physical and learning disabilities as a result of having been fed formula lacking essential components, and strives to prevent such occurrences from happening again. Played a key role in the passage of the Infant Formula Act, which sets nutrient standards for infant formulas and requires routine testing by formula producers.

National Center for Nutrition and Dietetics. 216 West Jackson Boulevard, Suite 800, Chicago, Illinois 60606-6995. Phone: 312/899-0040. Public education initiative of the American Dietetic Association and its foundation. Builds awareness of the importance of good nutrition and promotes healthy lifestyles. Will refer callers to registered dietitians for nutrition-related advice, including guidelines on using infant formulas.

FOOD AND NUTRITION FOR CHILDREN: TOTS TO TEENS

"Am I offering my preschooler too many snacks?" "Is my toddler getting enough calcium (she hates milk)?" "Is my 3rd grader eating too many fast food burgers and fries?" These are just some of the questions that concerned parents ask.

The following resources will help answer these (and other) questions and provide general guidelines and advice on feeding infants, babies, toddlers, preschoolers, and elementary-school-aged children. (For specific information on breastfeeding and bottlefeeding, turn to previous sections.)

Free and Inexpensive Resources

Baby Foods. The American Council on Science and Health offers a booklet on the nutritional value of all kinds of baby food, from homemade to commercially prepared. For a copy of "Baby Foods—A Report by the ACSH," send $3.25 along with your request to the American Council on Science and Health, 1995 Broadway, 16th Floor, New York, New York 10023.

Cholesterol and Your Family's Health. Citizens for Public Action on Blood Pressure and Cholesterol, Inc., has developed a colorful fold-out brochure listing low-fat, low-cholesterol food choices and preparation tips for family meals. To order, send $3.00 along with your request to Citizens for Public Action on Blood Pressure and Cholesterol, Inc., 7200 Wisconsin Avenue, Suite 1002, Bethesda, Maryland 20814. Phone: 301/907-7790.

Cooking without Your Salt Shaker, a guide to salt-free food preparation. For a copy, contact a local chapter of the American Heart Association. The publication sells for $5.00.

Quick Tips: Sound Advice from Food and Nutrition Experts

■ Parents should offer their children healthy food *choices*. They can't (or shouldn't) make them eat, but they can offer nutritious (and tasty) options. Research indicates that children will eat what they need—and as much as they need—when given good food to select from.

■ Children don't need a balanced diet *every day*. Instead, parents should take a look at what their children eat during a ten-day period. One day it might be megadoses of peanut butter; the next day it might be bread, spaghetti, watermelon, or peas. Over time, children will typically take in the essential nutrients that their bodies need.

■ Food variety is important, but don't be overly concerned about a young child's food jags (say, a 3½-week stretch when your son eats nothing but yogurt or cereal). Such phases are common in young children and will eventually pass (if they don't, you may want to seek further advice).

■ Keep meals simple: spaghetti and meatballs, a lean burger and corn, a plain pizza with some raw veggies on the side. Kids tend to like foods more when they're kept separate (they usually aren't crazy about one-dish meals).

■ Don't try to force your child to eat certain foods. If your pre-schooler doesn't touch her green beans on Monday, try giving her a small portion again on Friday. According to studies, the more she's exposed to a particular food, the more likely she is to taste it, and, who knows . . . maybe even like it!

■ Never make dessert a reward. If you say to your child, "Eat three more brussel sprouts and then you can have a slice of apple pie," you're confirming his belief that sweets are more desirable than vegetables. (Would you say to your child, "If you eat all of your ice cream, you can have a broccoli spear?" Probably not.)

■ Snacks provide a significant portion of a toddlers daily calorie intact (20 to 25 percent, according to nutritionists). Therefore, it makes sense to think of snacks as small meals and offer foods that pack a nutrient-laden punch: fruit, yogurt, or peanut butter on celery, for example.

■ If your toddler doesn't like milk, give her yogurt (an excellent source of calcium); if your preschooler doesn't like spinach, feed her watermelon (an excellent source of vitamins A and C); if your 3rd grader won't touch green beans, try bananas and pears instead.

■ Is your child healthy? Growing well? Alert? Enthusiastic? If so, you're probably doing something right.

The Eating Smart Fast-Food Guide, available from the Center for Science in the Public Interest, is designed to help families make healthy fast-food choices. Using this guide, parents can find out the fat, sugar, sodium, and calorie content of more than 250 fast foods. For a copy, send $3.95 along with your request to: Publications, Center for Science in the Public Interest, 1875 Connecticut Avenue, N.W., Suite 300, Washington, D.C. 20009.

Eating Well Can Help Your Child Learn Better. This brochure explains how good nutrition promotes health, which in turn helps children learn. Offers guidelines for parents. Includes a nutritional chart listing basic nutrients, what they do, and the foods that contain them. For a free copy, send a self-addressed, stamped, business-size envelope along with your request to the International Reading Association (see appendix I for contact information).

Fast Food and the American Diet. A report on fast foods published by the American Council on Science and Health. Includes addresses of popular food chains for those who would like to write for complete nutrition information on their products. To order a copy, send $2.00 along with your request to the American Council on Science and Health, 47 Maple Street, Summit, New Jersey 07901.

Feeding Kids Right Isn't Always Easy. Offers advice to help parents and caregivers deal with childrens' eating behavior problems. Also contains tips to help make mealtime more pleasant. Ask your pediatrician for a copy or send a self-addressed, stamped envelope to American Academy of Pediatrics, "Feeding Kids Right" (see appendix I for contact information).

Food Guide Pyramid. According to the U.S. Department of Agriculture's new food group chart, your daily diet should look like a pyramid—with a lot of breads and cereals at the base and only a few fats, oils, and sweets at the top. This 30-page booklet explains how to use this concept to eat right and maintain a healthy weight. For ordering information on *The Food Guide Pyramid,* request the most recent issue of the free *Consumer Information Catalog,* available from the Consumer Information Center, P.O. Box 100, Pueblo, Colorado 81002.

Growing Up Healthy—Fat, Cholesterol, and More. Contains general guidelines on health and eating for children two to six years of age. Ask your pediatrician for a copy or send a self-addressed, stamped envelope to: American Academy of Pediatrics, "Growing Up Healthy" (see appendix I for contact information).

Making Snacking a Healthy Habit and **Pleasing Picky Eaters' Taste Buds** are just two of the many free brochures offered by The Sugar Association, Inc. Write: The Sugar Association, Inc., 1101 Fifteenth Street, N.W., Suite 600, Washington, D.C. 20005.

Nourishing and Nurturing Two-Year-Olds. Fact sheets on feeding and nutrition for toddlers, prepared by Cornell University. To order, write Distribution Center, 7 Research Park, Cornell University, Ithaca, New York 14850. Enclose a check or money order for $1.75 (made payable to Cornell University) along with your request.

Nutritional Parenting: How to Get Your Child Off Junk Foods and Into Healthy Eating Habits, by Sara Sloan. An informative pamphlet available from Keats Publishing Company, 27 Pine Street, Box 876, New

Canaan, Connecticut 06840. Available for $1.95.

Nutritive Value of Foods. From the Human Nutrition Information Service, United States Department of Agriculture. Lists the nutritive values of commonly used foods: beverages, dairy products, eggs, fats and oil, fish and shellfish, fruits and fruit juices, grain products, legumes, nuts, seeds, meat and meat products, mixed dishes, fast foods, poultry and poultry products, soups, sauces and gravies, sugars and sweets, vegetables and vegetable products, and miscellaneous items. Produced by the U.S. Department of Agriculture's Human Nutrition Information Service. May be purchased from any U.S. Government Printing Office bookstore or from the Superintendent of Documents, U.S. Government Printing Office, Washington, D.C. 20401. Inquire about price. (See appendix B for ordering information.)

Organizing for Better School Meals, published by the Center for Science in the Public Interest, contains tips for working with the school system to improve food quality. To order, send $8.00 ($7.00 plus $1.00 shipping and handling charge) to Publications, Center for Science in the Public Interest, 1875 Connecticut Avenue, N.W., Suite 300, Washington, D.C. 20009.

Right from the Start: ABC's of Good Nutrition for Young Children. This free brochure contains information on essential nutrients, child-size portions, the basic food groups, and snack foods. Ask your pediatrician for a copy or send a self-addressed, stamped envelope to American Academy of Pediatrics, "Right from the Start" (see appendix I for contact information).

Sodium Scoreboard is a colorful poster that lists the sodium content

---

Your Local Supermarket

Many supermarket chains offer free information on food and nutrition. For example, Safeway shoppers can pick up pamphlets and brochures on feeding babies, nutrition during pregnancy, and food additives (among many other food-related topics). Safeway also produces a bi-monthly mini-magazine called *Foods Unlimited*, which contains tips on healthy eating, recipes, and more. Giant has a program called "Healthy Start . . . Food to Grow On," which promotes healthful food choices and eating habits for children ages two to six. As part of the program, Giant stores have a "Kids' Corner," where there are food-related activity sheets for kids, as well as brochures for parents. Check your local supermarket for similar freebies.

---

of more than 250 everyday food items. Available for $3.95 from the Center for Science in the Public Interest, 1875 Connecticut Avenue, N.W., Suite 300, Washington, D.C. 20009.

What's To Eat? Healthy Foods for Hungry Children. This brochure contains suggestions for healthy meals that are tasty and easy to prepare. Also contains information on fast foods and microwave-oven safety. Ask your pediatrician for a copy or send a self-addressed, stamped envelope to American Academy of Pediatrics, "What's To Eat?" (see appendix I for contact information).

Uncle Sam's Information Service

Many free and low-cost publications on food and nutrition are available from the federal government's Consumer Information Center. For a free copy of their most recent publications catalog, write Consumer Information Center, P.O. Box 100, Pueblo, Colorado 81002.

Here's a list of other free fact sheets, pamphlets and booklets you can order:

A Food Guide for the First Five Years. National Livestock and Meat Board, 444 N. Michigan Avenue, Chicago, Illinois 60611.

Baby's 1st Foods, Healthy Feeding Plan and **Keeping Baby's Food Safe.** Gerber Products Company, 445 State Street, Fremont, Michigan 49413. 1/800-4-GERBER.

Good Eaters—Not Tiny Tyrants: Feeding Children Ages 3–5 and **Healthy Eating During the 'Tween Years: The Independent 6- to 12-Year-Old.** American Dietetic Association, 430 N. Michigan Avenue, Chicago, Illinois 60611. (Send $1 postage.)

Heart Healthy Cookbook. Send a self-addressed, stamped envelope along with your request to Heart Healthy Cookbook, Idaho Potato Commission, P.O. Box 1068, Boise, Idaho 83701.

Kids and Food: Starting a Lifetime of Healthy Eating. Baylor College of Medicine, P.O. Box 130567, Houston, Texas 77219.

Lean Toward Health. American Dietetic Association, National Center for Nutrition and Dietetics, 216 West Jackson Boulevard, Chicago, Illinois 60606.

Living Fit and **Cholesterol Reduction.** Mazola Nutrition/Health Information Service, Box 307, Department CL, Coventry, Connecticut 06238.

Books

Child of Mine: Feeding With Love and Good Sense. By Ellyn Satter. Expanded edition. Bull Publishing, 1986. 463 pages. A book about feeding and the feeding relationship. Offers advice on presenting wholesome food and guidelines on solving some of the nutritional problems of childhood. Chapters include (1) History of Child Feeding, (2) Nutrition for Pregnancy, (3) Breastfeeding Versus Bottle Feeding, (4) Calories and Normal Growth, (5) the Milk Feeding, (6) Breastfeeding How-to, (7) Introduction of Solid Foods to the Infant Diet, (8) Feeding the Toddler, (9) Diarrhea, (10) Regulation of Food Intake, (11) Obesity, and (12) the Feeding Relationship.

Dr. Eden's Healthy Kids: The Essential Diet, Exercise, and Nutrition Program. By Alvin N. Eden, M.D. New American Library, 1987. 285 pages. Written by a pediatrician, this book provides life-extending diet and exercise programs for children (infants through adolescents) based on research findings about cholesterol, salt, sugar, and essential minerals, as well as new discoveries about exercise and obesity. Offers specific fitness recommendations for both overweight and normal-weight children. Counsels parents on what to feed their children and how to get them hooked for life on good eating and exercise.

The Fast Food Guide. By Michael Jacobson, Ph.D., and Sarah Fritschner.

Nutritive Values of Some Favorite Foods

From *Nutritive Value of Foods*, produced by the Human Nutrition Information Service, United States Department of Agriculture.

Apple Juice (bottled or canned), one cup
115 calories; trace fat; 0 cholesterol; 2 milligrams vitamin C; trace vitamin A; 0.9 milligrams iron; 17 milligrams calcium; trace protein.

Orange Juice (canned, unsweetened), one cup
105 calories; trace fat; 0 cholesterol; 86 milligrams vitamin C; 440 IU* vitamin A; 1.1 milligrams iron; 20 milligrams calcium; 1 gram protein.

Froot Loops, one cup
110 calories; 1 gram fat; 0 cholesterol; 15 milligrams vitamin C; 1,250 IU* vitamin A; 4.5 milligrams iron; 3 milligrams calcium; 2 grams protein.

Rice Krispies, one cup
110 calories; trace fat; 0 cholesterol; 15 milligrams vitamin C; 1,250 IU* vitamin A; 1.8 milligrams iron; 4 milligrams calcium; 2 grams protein.

French Toast, home recipe, one slice
155 calories; 7 grams fat; 112 milligrams cholesterol; trace vitamin C; 110 IU* vitamin A; 1.3 milligrams iron; 72 milligrams calcium; 6 grams protein.

Hamburger, one sandwich, 4 ozs.
445 calories; 21 grams fat; 71 milligrams cholesterol; 1 milligram vitamin C; 160 IU* vitamin A; 4.8 milligrams iron; 75 milligrams calcium; 25 grams protein.

Milk chocolate candy, 1 oz.
145 calories; 9 grams fat; 6 milligrams cholesterol; trace vitamin C; 30 IU* vitamin A; 0.4 milligrams iron; 50 milligrams calcium; 2 grams protein.

Cucumber with peel, 8 small (1¾-inch diameter) slices
5 calories; trace fat; 0 cholesterol; 1 milligram vitamin C; 10 IU* vitamin A; 0.1 milligram iron; 4 milligrams calcium; trace protein.

Carrot, whole, 7½ by 1⅛ inch, without crowns and tips, scraped
30 calories; trace fat; 0 cholesterol; 7 milligrams vitamin C; 20,250 IU* vitamin A; 0.4 milligrams iron; 19 milligrams calcium; 1 gram protein.

French Fries, 10 strips 2 to 3½ inches long, frozen, fried in vegetable oil
160 calories; 8 grams fat; 0 cholesterol; 5 milligrams vitamin C; 0 vitamin A; 0.4 milligrams iron; 10 milligrams calcium; 2 grams protein.

Peanut Butter, one tablespoon
95 calories; 8 grams fat; 0 cholesterol; 0 vitamin C; 0 vitamin A; 0.3 milligrams iron; 5 milligrams calcium; 5 grams protein.

Frankfurter, one**
145 calories; 13 grams fat; 23 milligrams cholesterol; 12 milligrams vitamin C; 0 vitamin A; 0.5 milligrams iron; 5 milligrams calcium; 5 grams protein.

Yogurt, plain, 8 oz. container, made with lowfat milk
145 calories; 4 grams fat; 14 milligrams cholesterol; 2 milligrams ascorbic acid; 150 IU* vitamin A; 0.2 milligrams iron; 415 milligrams calcium; 12 grams protein.

* IU = International units

** According to *The Food Book* (Dell Publishing, 1987), one Oscar Meyer beef frank has 145 calories, 14 grams of fat; 27 milligrams of cholesterol, and 5 grams of protein and supplies the following U.S. Recommended Daily Allowance (USRDA): protein, 11%; vitamin C, 18%; iron, 3%. As with many other foods, the nutritive value of frankfurters varies widely.

In 1913 the Coney Island Chamber of Commerce banned the term "hot dog" because they feared people would believe the sausage was actually made from ground canine.
— From *The Food Book*, Dell Publishing, 1987.

Second edition. Workman Publishing, 1991. 348 pages. Helps consumers make informed choices among the hamburgers, chicken nuggets, french fries, and shakes produced by McDonalds, Roy Rogers, and other fast food chains. Contains nutrition charts, quick-reference ratings, and other useful information.

Fat-Proofing Your Children. By Vicki Lansky. Bantam, 1988. 256 pages. A comprehensive guide for parents who want to raise healthy, slim children—and keep them that way. Provides information on children's physical development and nutritional needs, and offers advice to parents at every stage, from infancy to young adulthood. Includes sidebars such as "Whole-Wheat Baking" and "A Sugar Primer." Other books by the author—a nationally known authority on parenting—include *Feed Me! I'm Yours* and *The Taming of the C.A.N.D.Y. Monster.*

Guide to Baby Products: Consumer Reports Books. By Sandy Jones with Werner Freitag and the Editors of Consumer Reports Books. 3rd revised edition. Consumers Union, 1991. 333 pages. Featured for the first time in this edition are nutritional tables for dozens of baby food brands. Also evaluates items such as cups, bibs, warmers, and eating utensils. Offers advice on preparing homemade baby food and guidelines on reducing choking risks.

How to Get Your Kid to Eat . . . But Not Too Much. By Ellyn Satter. Bull Publishing, 1987. 396 pages. In the early chapters, Satter explains what works, and what doesn't, with feeding. The middle section of the book—Feeding as Your Child Grows—explains, in concrete detail, *how* to feed children from infancy through adolescence. The final section is devoted to special feeding problems.

Jane Brody's Nutrition Book. By Jane Brody. Revised and updated. Bantam, 1987. 552 pages. A guide to good eating for better health and weight control by The *New York Times* columnist. More than five hundred pages on healthy eating and sound nutrition. Includes chapters on eating during pregnancy, feeding your baby, and "child feeding in the junk food generation." Also includes charts, healthy recipes, details on nutrients, and the lowdown on items such as salt, sugar, and caffeine.

Kidfood. By Lisa Tracy. Dell Publishing, 1989. 324 pages. Tells parents how to meet recommended daily allowances of essential nutrients for children of all ages (infancy through the teen years). Includes eating games that end power struggles, a step-by-step system for introducing new foods, strategies for feeding finicky eaters, tips for eating out, and much more. Contains a collection of easy recipes with strong kid-appeal.

Nutrition in Infancy and Childhood. By Peggy Pipes and Christine Trahms. 5th edition. Mosby—Year Book, 1993. 429 pages. An introductory textbook on childhood nutrition (infants through adolescents). Covers nutrition and growth, nutrient needs, managing mealtime behavior, the development of food patterns, and eating disorders, among other topics.

A Restaurant Survival Guide for Parents

The following survival tips for successfully dining out with your children are drawn from Vicki Lansky's *Fat-Proofing Your Children* (Bantam Books, 1988).

- Choose a restaurant where children are welcome. Available high chairs with booster seats are a good sign that this is the case.

- Look for places that offer healthy menu choices.

- Try to go out at a time when the kids are accustomed to eating, but avoid restaurants when they are most heavily trafficked.

- Unless you have nerves of steel, avoid restaurants that feature loud music.

- Avoid small tables, since you'll want to leave your child lots of elbow room to amuse himself before and after eating. A booth can be ideal.

- Bring along puzzles, small cars, crayons, and coloring books—anything your child can enjoy while you're waiting.

- A kids' menu is nice, but see if it goes beyond the usual burgers-hotdogs-fishsticks-fries offering. Best of all is an option to choose child-size portions from the regular menu.

- Don't press to hard to get the kids to clean their plates. (It's not worth it in public!)

- Do not, of course, promise dessert as a reward.

Parents' Guide to Feeding Your Kids Right. Children's Television Workshop. Prentice-Hall, 1989. 211 pages. This book explains how children's nutritional needs change according to age and individual growth patterns; how to solve common eating problems; and why it's easier than parents think to feed kids right, from infancy through the teen years. Includes consumer tips and growth charts.

Videotape

CNN's Eating Healthy for Kids. Running time: 20 minutes. CNN's registered dietitian and journalist, Carolyn O'Neil, hosts this video featuring advice from experts on what families should know about making healthy food choices for children. Available from Turner Educational Services, Inc. Call 1/800-344-6219 to order by check, Visa, or Mastercard.

Hotlines

Beech-Nut Nutrition Hotline. Dial 1/800-523-6633, Monday–Friday from 9 a.m. to 5 p.m., eastern standard time. Your call will be answered by Beech-Nut representatives who have been trained to answer questions about baby food. Advice on child development from nutritionists, pediatricians, and other specialists is also available on recorded messages.

Consumer Nutrition Hotline. Dial 1/800-366-1655, Monday–Friday from 9 a.m. to 4 p.m., central standard time. Registered dieticians and nutritionists will answer your questions. During off-hours, the hotline has prerecorded messages on topics such as food safety and eating well while traveling. This service is provided by the National Center for Nutrition and Dietetics, the public-education arm of the American Dietetic Association.

Food Allergies. Phone: 1/800-YES-RELIEF. The Food Allergy Center will provide callers with information to help them determine whether or not an ailment is food-related—and what treatments are available.

Gerber Consumer Information Service. Dial 1/800-443-7237, twenty-four hours a day, seven days a week. Calls are answered by experienced mothers who give information on feeding and caring for babies.

Parents Helpline. *Parents* magazine has set up a 900 number (the cost is 95¢ per minute) so that parents can receive prerecorded advice on various topics 24 hours a day. Dial 1/900-903-KIDS, then enter the two numbers next to the topic of your choice:

> Babies' Weight Gain (04)
> Bottle Water versus Tap Water (07)
> Burping Your Baby (09)
> Feeding Toddlers (46)
> Food Allergies (23)
> Giving Up the Bottle (24)
> Obese Kids (32)
> Starting Solids (38)

FEEDING THE FAMILY

Some Parent-Friendly Cookbooks

The Baby Cookbook. By Karin Knight, R.N., and Jeannie Lumley. Revised edition. William Morrow and Company, 1992. 352 pages. A complete guide to nutrition, feeding, and cooking for babies six months to two years plus two hundred nutritious family meals that babies and toddlers can share. Includes nutrient and growth charts, menus, and cautionary advice on salt, sugar, and processed foods. Discusses in detail important nutrients: proteins, fats, fiber, carbohydrates, vitamins, and minerals. In the section called "Mirabai's Diary from Six Months to Her Second Birthday," parents can gain insights into early eating/feeding patterns beginning with the introduction of solid foods.

Baby Let's Eat. By Rena Coyle with Patricia Messing. Workman Publishing, 1987. 128 pages. How to feed your baby like the rest of the family. One hundred easy recipes for wholesome meals and snacks you can all enjoy together. With complete nutritional guidelines for children ages six months to three years.

The Complete New Guide to Preparing Baby Foods. By Sue Castle. Revised edition. Bantam, 1992. 385 pages. Everything you need to know about feeding your infant and toddler with over one hundred low-cost, high nutrition foods and simple recipes. Tells when different foods should be introduced (for example, cooked potatoes at seven months cooked sweet peppers at eight months; cooked cauliflower at nine months). Explains how to buy and store different foods, and gives a nutritional summary on scores of foods. Chapters include "Equipment for Easy Cooking" and "How to Be a Smart Shopper."

Creative Lunch Box. By Ellen Klavan. Crown, 1991. 112 pages. This book features one hundred easy-to-prepare, nutritious, and inviting meals for your child's lunch box. Includes recipes for salads, sandwiches, drinks, desserts, and more. Illustrated.

The Healthy Baby Meal Planner. By Annabel Karmel. Simon and Schuster, 1992. 192 pages. Mom-tested, child-approved recipes for your baby and toddler. The author's advice: aim for fresh food, and keep animal fat, sugar, and salt to a minimum. Recipes include Fruity Swiss Muesli, Bang Bang Chicken, and Nursery Fish Pie. The book is arranged by age group (The Best First Food for Baby, Weaning, Four to Six Months, Six to Nine Months, and Toddlers), and each chapter begins with a brief, informative overview. Delightfully illustrated with pineapples, broccoli, cucumbers, and other friendly-faced fruit and vegetables.

Once Upon a Recipe. By Karen Greene. New Hope Press, 1989. 96 pages. Over fifty recipes in all, including Frog Prince Tortilla Pie, Tinker Bell's Raspberry Buns, Old Lady in a Shoe Box Lunch, Baloo's Mint Brownies, and Aesop's Fabled Chicken. All natural and nutritious. "A handsome book . . . . There are lots of tie-ins with children's literature and the recipes are all very nutritious . . . ." The *New York Times*.

Earth's Best

Parents who don't have time to prepare their own baby foods (or, for whatever reason, choose to purchase already-prepared food) might try the Earth's Best baby foods—100 percent organically-grown fruits, vegetables, grains, yogurts, and juices. These products are available from Hand in Hand, Route 26, R.R. I, Box 1425, Oxford, Maine 04270-9711. Phone: 1/800-872-9745. (Note: The minimum baby food order is a case of twenty-four jars and at least six jars of a flavor. Hand in Hand's mail order catalog lists some three dozen items from which to choose, including brown rice cereal, sweet potato and chicken, winter squash, and pears and rasberries.)

The Penny Whistle Lunch Box Book. By Meredith Brokaw and Annie Gilbar. Simon and Schuster, 1991. 96 pages. Offers creative suggestions for nutritious and good tasting lunch box fare, including everything from soup to sandwiches.

FUN WITH FOOD

Books

Dinner's Ready Mom. By Helen Gustafson. Celestial Arts, 1986. 80 pages. With this book, children ages eight to fourteen can learn to cook dinner for the entire family. Contains forty recipes written in easy-to-understand language and organized in a format that kids can follow.

Elliot's Extraordinary Cookbook. By Christina Bjork and Lena Anderson. Translated by Joan Sandin. R&S Books, 1990. 59 pages. Elliot loves to cook. Luckily, his upstairs neighbor knows all about food because she used to be a cook on a boat. So she invites Elliot upstairs, where he discovers the wonders of food and the pleasure of cooking. He learns how to grow bean sprouts; finds out who discovered tea; makes his own butter, cheese, and ice cream; and investigates what's healthy and what's not healthy. He finds out about protein, carbohydrates, and even the workings of the small intestine ("where does all the food go?"). Recipes include after school snacks, breads, Parisian hamburgers, and other delights.

Fanny at Chez Panisse. By Alice Waters with Bob Carrau and Patricia Curtan. Illustrated by Ann Arnold. HarperCollins, 1992. 133 pages. This book tells the story a nine-year-old girl and her restaurant adventures (written in Fanny's own voice). Includes easy family recipes as well.

Foodworks. By the Ontario Science Centre. Addison-Wesley, 1987. 90 pages. More than one hundred science activities and interesting facts about food and healthy eating. Teaches kids how food travels through the body; how to make ice cream, cheese, and chocolate bars; and how to play fun food games. Also explores the history of the noodle, gives the inside story on popcorn and soda pop, and explains what Ferdinand Magellan fed his hungry crew. For ages six and up.

Kids Cook! By Sarah and Zachary Williamson. Williamson Publishing, 1992. 157 pages. A children's cookbook written by kids. Teaches kids how to help with the family cooking and have fun in the process. More than 150 recipes, including breakfast sundaes, veggie shells, and roast beef subs. For ages eight and up.

Kids Cooking: A Very Slightly Messy Manual. By the editors of Klutz Press. Klutz Press, 1987. 88 pages. This stain-resistant cookbook is full of fun recipes for kids ages six to twelve. In addition to standard kid fare, the book contains recipes for giant soap bubbles (using a coat hanger), peanut butter popcorn, and other delights. Comes with colorful measuring spoons. For ages four and up.

Kitchen Fun. By the editors of *OWL* and *Chickadee* magazines. Little, Brown, 1988. 32 pages. With this activity book, kids can learn how to make a fish pizza, turn walnut shells into magnets, and prepare palatable ice puppets. Supplies are mainly kitchen materials.

Kitchen Fun for Kids: Healthy Recipes and Nutrition Facts for 7- to 12-Year-Old Cooks. By Laura Hill and Michael Jacobson. Henry Holt, 1991. 136 pages. Written by a nutrition activist and a registered dietician, this book offers solid advice for kids interested in the cooking process. Includes sections on safety, nutrition, and kitchen basics. Lists necessary tools for each recipe. "How to" section at the beginning of the book explains how to crack an egg, how to grate cheese, and so forth. For children in grades two through seven.

Mudpies to Magnets: A Preschool Science Curriculum. By Robert A. Williams, Robert E. Rockwell, and Elizabeth A. Sherwood. Gryphon House, 1987. 160 pages. One chapter, called "Science to Grow On: Health and Nutrition," includes experiments such as "Good and Juicy" (cutting up fruit and vegetables, putting them in a blender, tasting them); "Little Bitty Butter Beaters" (how to make butter in jars); and "Orange You Glad You're Not All Alike" (tasting and comparing orange fruits and vegetables such as oranges, carrots, pumpkin, and melon). Individual entries list words that parents/teachers can use to encourage language development, a list of things needed for the experiment, a description of how to do the activity and what will probably happen as a result, and suggestions for extending the activity.

My First Cookbook. By Angela Wilkes. Alfred A. Knopf, 1989. 48 pages. This large-format book contains photographs of materials needed and completed products (so real-looking you'll be tempted to pick them off the page) and easy-to-follow, step-by-step directions. Dishes range from cheesy potato boats to chocolate truffles. The companion volume, *My First Baking Book*, uses the same method to teach kids about baking. For children in grades three through seven.

The Please Touch Cookbook. Please Touch Museum for Children. Edited by Bonnie Brook. Silver Press, 1990. 64 pages. Compiled by the Please Touch Museum for Children, this cookbook includes a variety of easy-to-assemble recipes, along with food facts and experiments. For ages three to seven.

Science Experiments You Can Eat. By Vicki Cobb. Harper and Row, 1972. 127 pages. Readers learn how to turn a kitchen into a chemistry lab and, in the process, produce a variety of delectable eatables. For ages eight to fourteen. Also available: *More Science Experiments You Can Eat.*

Videotapes

Kids Get Cooking. Kidvidz (Price Stern Sloan Video). Running time: 30 minutes. A kid's video guide to food and cooking, endorsed by the National Education Association. Combines cooking, kitchen safety tips, and science information with jokes, music, and animated puppetry. Hosted by children. For ages five to twelve. Comes with an activity guide.

Kids' Kitchen (Cookies, Volume 1). Auntie Lee's Kitchen. Running time: 23 minutes. A video demonstrating cookie-baking skills to children. Takes young viewers through the basic procedures of mixing and measuring, showing how to make drop cookies, chocolate brownies, and other treats. Comes with printed recipes. For children ages six to nine. Write: Kids' Kitchen, P.O. Box 25503, Portland, Oregon 97225.

My First Cooking Video. Sony. Running time: 50 minutes. Based on *My First Cook Book*, this videotape shows young chefs (ages five and up) how to create fun things to eat, including picture pizzas, animal breads, and other tasty items.

Club

Cook It! Club. Created by HearthSong, the *Cook It! Club* offers children ages eight to fourteen a series of cooking lessons by mail. Each month, subscribers receive fun recipes, along with the tools required to make them. Each lesson has a theme (soups, cookies, etc.) Available from HearthSong. Phone: 1/800-325-2502.

Associations

American College of Nutrition. 722 Robert E. Lee Drive, Wilmington, North Carolina 28412-0927. Phone: 919/452-1222. Provides education on developments in the field of nutrition. Stimulates the exchange of information between nutrition scientists and physicians interested in applying research findings to the care of patients. Publishes the *Journal of the American College of Nutrition*, a bimonthly journal containing peer-reviewed articles.

American Council on Science and Health. 1995 Broadway, 16th Floor, New York, New York 10023-5860. Provides consumers with scientific evaluations of food. Publishes *Priorities: For Long Life and Good Health*, a quarterly consumer magazine. Also publishes scientific papers, consumer update booklets, and research reports on health risks and benefits associated with public health and environmental issues. Produces documentary films as well.

American Dietetic Association. 216 West Jackson Boulevard, Suite 800, Chicago, Illinois 60606. Phone: 312/899-0040. A professional organization of dietetic professionals and registered dietitians. Provides a variety of member services including career guidance. Publishes the *Journal of the American Dietetic Association*, a monthly journal containing news, articles, research findings, abstracts, and a list of new publications. See also National Center for Nutrition and Dietetics, the public education initiative of the American Dietetic Association and its foundation.

American Heart Association. 7320 Greenville Avenue, Dallas, Texas 75231. Phone: 214/373-6300. Fax: 214/706-1341. Works to reduce premature death and disability from stroke and cardiovascular diseases. Supports research, education, and community service programs. Publishes a variety of periodicals, including *Circulation, Circulation Research, Cardiovascular Nursing*, and *Stroke–A Journal of Cerebral Circulation*. Also produces guides, cookbooks, informational pamphlets, and brochures.

American School Food Service Association. 1600 Duke Street, 7th Floor, Alexandria, Virginia 22314. Phone: 1/800-877-8822. Provides information on school food programs and legislation dealing with child nu-

trition. Members are involved in school food service or related activities in public and private schools, pre-schools, colleges, and universities. Publishes *ASFSA Legislative News*, a bimonthly newsletter covering regulatory and legislative issues regarding child nutrition. Also publishes *School Food Service Journal*, a monthly journal containing current news and trends, articles on management and equipment, media reviews, a calendar of events, and information on legislative and regulatory developments.

Americans for Safe Food. c/o Roger Blobaum, 1875 Connecticut Avenue, N.W., Suite 300, Washington, D.C. 20009-5728. Phone: 202/332-9110. Fax: 202/265-4954. A project of the Center for Science in the Public Interest. Seeks to increase the availability of contaminant-free foods; promotes the use of alternative agriculture. Operates an information clearinghouse. Publishes *Safe Food Action*, a quarterly newsletter, as well as reports on model state programs.

Center for Science in the Public Interest. 1875 Connecticut Avenue, N.W., Suite 300, Washington, D.C. 20009-5728. Phone: 202/332-9110. Fax: 202/265-4954. A consumer group concerned with food, nutrition, agriculture, alcohol, and other health issues. Produces educational materials and attempts to influence policy decisions related to American health and diet. Publishes books, reports, research papers, brochures, catalogs, posters, computer software, videotapes, and slide charts. Also publishes *Nutrition Action Healthletter*, a newsletter covering food and nutrition. Articles have included "Getting Your Vitamins" and "Frozen Novelties: The Dove Bar's Revenge."

Child Nutrition Forum. 1875 Connecticut Avenue, N.W., Washington, D.C. 20009. Phone: 202/986-2200. A coalition of nutrition organizations. Compiles information on national child nutrition policies and serves as a liaison between organizations that support effective federal food programs for children. Committees include Child Care Food, School Lunch and Breakfast, and Women, Infants, and Children. Publishes information on school lunches, national child nutrition policies, and the federal budget process.

Feingold Association of the United States. P.O. Box 6550, Alexandria, Virginia 22306. Phone: 703/768-3287. Believes that symptoms such as overactivity, sleeping problems, and learning disabilities can be alleviated by a program developed by Ben Feingold, M.D., which eliminates preservatives and synthetic colors and flavors from the diet. Gathers and disseminates information; offers educational services for children and adults. Publishes a newsletter for members called *Pure Facts* (issued ten times a year), as well as books and pamphlets. Videotapes are also available.

Food & Nutrition Board of the National Academy of Sciences—Institute of Medicine. 2101 Constitution Avenue, N.W., Washington, D.C. 20418. 202/334-2138. Supports research on food, nutrition, and health (as it relates to food and nutrition). The board is part of the Institute of Medicine, established in 1970 by the National Academy of Sciences, which, by congressional charter, serves as an adviser to the federal government. Publishes studies based on the research of eminent nutrition scientists and food experts. Recent topics explored include nutrition during pregnancy, the nation's diet (and how to improve it), and advances made in the nutrition sciences. Call or write for the National Academy Press' publications catalog.

Testing Children for Cholesterol Levels

The National Cholesterol Education Program has issued guidelines on the testing of children over the age of two for cholesterol levels: If either parent has a blood cholesterol level of 240 or above, of if a parent or grandparent had cardiovascular disease before the age of fifty-five, then children over age two should be tested.

Food Research and Action Center. See National Anti-Hunger Coalition.

Mothers and Others for Pesticide Limits. c/o Natural Resources Defense Council, 1350 New York Avenue, N.W., Suite 300, Washington, D.C. 20005. Phone: 202/783-7800. Publishes a quarterly newsletter alerting parents to pesticide-related legislation. Also available: *For Our Kids' Sake*, a handbook on how to protect your child against pesticides ($7.95).

National Academy of Sciences. See Food and Nutrition Board of the National Academy of Science—Institute of Medicine.

National Anti-Hunger Coalition. 1319 F Street, N.W., Suite 500, Washington, D.C. 20004. Phone: 202/393-5060. Educates the public on domestic hunger and issues affecting federal food policy. Seeks to improve accessibility to federal food programs and to increase food program benefits. Affiliated with the Food Research and Action Center. Call or write for information on federal food programs for low-income families.

National Center for Nutrition and Dietetics. 216 West Jackson Boulevard, Suite 800, Chicago, Illinois 60606-6995. Phone: 312/ 899-0040. Public education initiative of the American Dietetic Association and its foundation. Builds awareness of the importance of good nutrition and promotes healthy lifestyles. Will refer callers to registered dietitians for nutrition-related advice. Provides information on food and nutrition through a series of free informational brochures, an extensive research library, and a consumer nutrition hotline (see listing under "Hotlines"). Individuals can become Friends of the Center by contributing $35 a year. Friends receive a quarterly newsletter and discounts on library services. See also: American Dietetic Association.

National Coalition Against the Misuse of Pesticides. 701 E Street, S.E., Washington, D.C. 20003. Phone: 202/543-5450. Creates public awareness of health, environmental, and economic problems caused by pesticides. Monitors governmental activities and works to improve legislation and regulation concerning pesticide control. Promotes alternatives. Provides consumer information on pesticides and alternatives to their use. Publishes a variety of periodicals. Also produces pamphlets such as *Pesticide Safety: Myths and Facts*. Write for a list of publications.

National Dairy Council. 6300 North River Road, Rosemont, Illinois 60018. Phone: 708/696-1020. Offers information on nutrition research, particularly concerning the nutritional value of milk and its various products. Publications include the *Dairy Council Digest*, a bimonthly newsletter containing current nutrition research findings.

Natural Food Associates. P.O. Box 2010, Atlanta, Texas 75551. Phone: 214/796-3612. Informs the public about the value of natural, chemical-free food and exposes the dangers of chemical contamination. Conducts demonstrations on organic gardening, composting, and other natural techniques. Operates a bookstore offering books on nutrition, natural food, and organic farming. Publishes *Natural Food and Farming*, a monthly magazine, and *Natural Food News*, a monthly newspaper. Book catalogs are available as well.

Nutrition Education Association. P.O. Box 20301, 3647 Glen Haven, Houston, Texas 77225. Phone: 713/665-2946. Educates the public on the importance of good nutrition. Encourages research in nutrition, and sponsors nutrition study groups. Offers a home study course on nutrition emphasizing the importance of good eating habits in preventing and curing disease. Offers publications about fighting cancer through nutrition, including *Switchover! The Anti-Cancer Cooking Plan for Today's Parents and Their Children* and *Crackdown on Cancer with Good Nutrition.*

Nutrition for Optimal Health Association. P.O. Box 380, Winnetka, Illinois 60093. Phone: 312/835-5030. Promotes good nutrition as a means of achieving and maintaining optimal health. Distributes information on the science of good nutrition, hosts educational seminars, and offers cooking classes. Maintains an audio- and videotape library. Publishes a cookbook, *Cooking for the Health of It.*

Pesticide Action Network/North America Regional Center. 965 Mission Street, No. 514, San Francisco, California 94103. Phone: 415/541-9140. Coalition of organizations and individuals involved with issues concerning pesticide use. Promotes alternatives to pesticide use in agriculture and acts as a network for pesticide action groups at the local, state, and national levels. Distributes reports, manuals, booklets, and other materials on pesticides issues.

Price-Pottenger Nutrition Foundation. P.O. Box 2614, LaMesa, California 91944-2614. Phone: 619/582-4168. Conducts programs to increase public awareness of the importance of good nutrition. Members are educators in the field of nutrition. Maintains a library and resource file, and distributes books, pamphlets, reprints, films, slides, and videotapes on nutrition.

Society for Nutrition Education. 1700 Broadway, Suite 300, Oakland, California 94612. Phone: 415/444-7133. Society of nutrition educators from the fields of medicine, public health, dietetics, home economics, and education. Promotes nutritional well-being for the general public. Produces and sells educational publications and films, including the *Journal of Nutrition Education*, a bimonthly journal containing research reports, book reviews, and employment opportunity listings.

The Sugar Association, Inc. 1101 Fifteenth Street, N.W., Suite 600, Washington, D.C. 20005. Phone: 202/785-1122. Disseminates information on sucrose. Represents the interests of processors and refiners of beet and cane sugar. Maintains a library and publishes *On Your Mark*, a quarterly newsletter (first copy free; 20¢ for additional copies) on nutrition and fitness emphasizing recent developments concerning sugar and health. Also publishes special reports on topics of interest to sugar users and producers.

Government Agencies

The following agency will answer general questions on nutrition:

Food and Nutrition Information Center. National Agricultural Library, Room 304, 10301 Baltimore Road, Beltsville, Maryland 20705-2351. Phone: 301/504-5414. This center answers questions and offers publications and audiovisual materials on such topics as nutrition, food service management, food technology, and nutrition for adolescents, particularly teenage mothers. Publications are geared toward consumers, educators, and professionals.

Other offices to contact include:

Nutrition Data Research. Human Nutrition Information Service, U.S. Department of Agriculture, Federal Building, Room 321, 6505 Belcrest Road, Hyattsville, Maryland 20782. Phone: 301/436-8491 (or -8498).

Nutrition Education Division. Food and Nutrition Information Service, National Agricultural Library, 10301 Baltimore Road, Beltsville, Maryland 20705-2351. Phone: 301/436-5090.

For information on food labeling and manufacturing practices contact:

Office of Consumer Affairs, Food and Drug Administration. H.T.E. 88, 5600 Fishers Lane, Rockville, Maryland 20857. Phone: 301/443-5006. The Food and Drug Administration answers consumers' inquiries and supplies information and publications concerning food labeling, food safety, and manufacturing practices.

Chapter 9

Fitness, Exercise, and Sports

Free and Inexpensive Resources

Better Health through Fitness. Available from the American Academy of Pediatrics, this brochure describes the concept of physical fitness and includes a fitness activity chart. For a free copy, send a self-addressed, stamped, business-size envelope to American Academy of Pediatrics, "Better Health through Fitness" (see appendix I for contact information).

Developmentally Appropriate Physical Education Practices for Children. A position statement of the National Association for Sport and Physical Education developed by the Council on Physical Education for Children. Available for $1.50. Phone: 1/800-321-0789.

Fit Kids. This brochure includes tips on how to help children stay active. For a copy, send $1.00 and a self-addressed, stamped, business-size envelope to The Melpomene Institute, 1010 University Avenue, St. Paul, Minnesota 55104. Phone: 612/642-1951.

Healthy Growing Up. Twenty-four lessons teaching children to eat right, stay fit, and feel good about themselves. Complements established health and fitness curricula, but useful for parents with an interest in children's fitness. Available free of charge (except for shipping and handling) from McDonald's Educational Resource Center, P.O. Box 8002, St. Charles, Illinois 60174-8002. Phone: 1/800-627-7646.

Kids in Action. The first section of this free fifteen-page booklet contains descriptions and pictures of twenty-one exercises you can do with your two- to six-year-old. The next section describes the President's Council on Physical Fitness and Sports' test for measuring the fitness of children six to seventeen. Available from the President's Council on Physical Fitness and Sports, 701 Pennsylvania Avenue, N.W., Suite 250, Washington, D.C. 20004. Phone: 202/272-3421.

A Nation of Winners Video. The President's Council on Physical Fitness and Sports. Running time: 28 minutes. This videotape introduces the Presidential Sports Award and, through inspirational stories, seeks to motivate people from six years of age and above to engage in regular physical activity. A copy of the tape may be obtained on a free-loan basis from A Nation of Winners, Walter J. Klein Company, Ltd., Box 472087, Charlotte, North Carolina 28247-2087.

Parent's Guide to Girls' Sports. A booklet available for $3.00 from the Women's Sports Foundation, 342 Madison Avenue, Suite 728, New York, New York 10173. Phone: 212/972-9170 or 1/800-227-3988.

Sports and Your Child. Available from the American Academy of Pediatrics, this brochure includes information on the age-appropriateness of different activities. For a free copy, send a self-addressed, stamped, business-size envelope to American Academy of Pediatrics, "Sports and Your Child" (see appendix I for contact information).

Walking for Exercise and Pleasure. An overview of walking as a means to physical fitness and recreational pleasure. Discusses the benefits of walking; includes sample warm-up and conditioning exercises. Available for $1.00 from Superintendent of Documents, P.O. Box 371954, Pittsburgh, PA 15250-7954. Phone: 202/783-3238 (request S/N 017-001-00447-2).

Books

General Fitness and Exercise

Arnold's Fitness for Kids Ages Birth to 5: A Guide to Health, Exercise, and Nutrition. By Arnold Schwarzenegger with Charles Gaines. Doubleday, 1993. 101 pages. Explains how to work with your young child and get her prepared for a lifetime of fitness. Describes motor milestones for the first five years and play exercises to do with your child at each stage of development. Also offers nutritional guidelines, sports and fitness programs outside the home, and ideas on how to set up a good outside play area to help build skills.

Arnold's Fitness for Kids Ages 6 to 10: A Guide to Health, Exercise, and Nutrition. By Arnold Schwarzenegger with Charles Gaines. Doubleday, 1993. 120 pages. Discusses nutrition, exercise, family fitness, and physical education at school. Shows aerobic exercises and games, motor skills drills, and exercises to help increase flexibility, strength, and endurance. Also offers suggestions for less athletically inclined children.

Family Fitness Handbook. By Bob Glover and Jack Shepherd. Penguin Books, 1989. 417 pages. Includes guidelines for physical fitness programs in your child's school, suggestions for imaginative fitness games, family fitness evaluation tests, and information on lifetime aerobic fitness activities such as walking, hiking, running, biking, and swimming.

Fitness from Six to Twelve. By Bonnie Prudden. Ballantine, 1987. 464 pages. A comprehensive fitness and exercise manual covering basic exercise regimes, tumbling fun and flexibility exercises, myotherapy (a trigger point treatment for sore muscles and poor posture), and setting up a garage or basement gym. Also

covers the basics of specific sports such as swimming, dance, tennis, skiing, figure skating, and riding.

Give Your Kids a Sporting Chance: A Parents' Guide. By Kevin S. Spink, Ph.D. Summerhill Press, 1988. 117 pages. Offers practical advice on how to help make your child's athletic experiences positive. Discusses how your expectations affect your children, how to know if your child has "star" potential, and letting your child exit from a sport. Kid athletes are quoted throughout, providing some surprising insights into children's feelings about sports.

Good Sports: A Concerned Parent's Guide to Little League and Other Competitive Youth Sports. By Rick Wolff. Dell, 1993. 226 pages. Covers the psychological aspects of competitive sports. Explains how to build your child's self-esteem and encourage good sportsmanship. Also included are specifics on how much pressure to place on children, comments not to make, when to interfere (or take a child out of a game), alternatives to established leagues, and working with the athletically gifted child.

Great Games for Young People. By Marilee A. Gustafson, Sue K. Wolfe, and Cheryl L. King. Human Kinetics Books, 1991. 138 pages. Offers 68 sport games to substitute for the same old drills. The game finder at the front cross-references each game according to the skill (throwing, running, kicking, dodging, shooting, catching, passing, dribbling, stick handling, etc.). For children in grades four and up.

Healthy Kids for Life. By Dr. Charles T. Kuntzleman. Simon and Schuster, 1988. 222 pages. Describes the "Feelin' Good" fitness program, a plan of simple exercises and healthy eating. Emphasizes vigorous aerobic activities the whole family can enjoy together (biking, running, swimming, calisthenics, and others). Explains how to first get an idea of your family's overall fitness; learn how to set fitness goals; and build endurance, muscle fitness, and flexibility.

Ideas for Action: Award Winning Approaches to Physical Activity. Sporting Goods Manufacturers Association, 1993. 288 pages. In this manual, teachers share detailed outlines of their successful fitness programs. The book includes developmentally appropriate activities for elementary-, middle school-, and secondary school-age children. Offers information on fitness goals based on guidelines developed by the National Association for Sport and Physical Education. Includes a listing of organizations and corporations that will provide information on their fitness programs.

Kid Fitness: A Complete Shape-up Program from Birth through High School. By Kenneth H. Cooper, M.D., M.P.H. Bantam, 1991. 367 pages. Describes a complete diet and exercise program for children, customized for different fitness levels, from the physically unfit to the athletically gifted. Explains how to foster smart eating habits to protect your children from obesity, cancer, and heart disease. Includes drawings of exercises. Comes with recipes and menus.

Kidsports: A Survival Guide for Parents. By Nathan J. Smith, M.D., Ronald E. Smith, and Frank L. Smoll. Addison-Wesley, 1983. 229 pages. Offers guidelines to help parents make informed decisions about their children's participation in sports. Discusses the psychology of the young athlete, choosing a sport program and equipment, conditioning, nutrition, sports injuries, girls in sports, and parents as coaches.

Moms and Dads, Kids and Sports. By Pat McInally. Charles Scribners Sons, 1988. 238 pages. In a question/answer format, this author writes about getting in shape, mental preparation for a game, young athletes' frustrations and injuries, and sports psychology topics. Explains how deeply involved you and your child should become in sports, what to do about your child wanting to practice all the time, and what to do if your son or daughter decides to quit altogether.

Parents' Guide to Kids and Sports. By Lee Schreiber. Little, Brown, 1990. 138 pages. Offers practical information on a wide variety of sports. Discusses costs, required equipment, sports injuries, girls in sports, and parental involvement. Addresses psychological issues such as sports pressure, quitting a sport, and the reluctant athlete. Includes resource listings (places to turn for additional information).

Sports. By Tim Hammond. Eyewitness Books. Alfred A. Knopf, 1988. 64 pages. Offers a pictorial history and description of the rules and equipment of the world's most popular sports.

The Sports-Confident Child: A Parents' Guide to Helping Children. By Chris Hopper. Pantheon Books, 1988. 255 pages. When should my child play sports? How should I select a sports program? How can I tell which sports best suit my child? What is the best way to teach sports skills to her? When should she get out of a sport? This book will help parents with these and other questions.

Sportswise: An Essential Guide for Young Athletes. By Lyle J. Micheli, M.D. Houghton Mifflin, 1990. 300 pages. Offers advice on preventing injuries, building overall health fitness, and creating safe sports programs.

Includes chapters on problems facing female school athletes and balancing sports with the classroom.

Sports Without Pressure: A Guide for Parents and Coaches of Young Athletes. By Eric Margenau. Gardner Press, 1991. 143 pages. Covers the stages of a child's development and the types of sports and activities that may be most suitable for various age groups. Includes advice on the role of parents in their child's athletic development.

Starting Right: Suzy Prudden's Fitness Program for Children 5–11. By Suzy Prudden and Joan Meijer-Hirshland. Doubleday, 1988. 167 pages. Prudden defines fitness, offers guidelines to evaluate a child's fitness, and describes how to build an exercise program. Photographs show stretches and exercises for each muscle group, including warm-up and cool-down exercises. Describes what one school system did to turn a failing physical education program into a winning one.

Suzy Prudden's Exercise Program for Young Children. By Suzy Prudden. Workman, 1983. 191 pages. Offers exercises to do with infants and young children (from four weeks to four years) to increase balance; eye-hand coordination; and strength in the arms, legs, back, and chest.

Sport-By-Sport

Baseball: Just for Kids

Baseball. By Ray Broekel. A New True Book. Childrens Press, 1983. 48 pages. With large type and color photos, this book takes children through amateur and professional baseball, team uniforms, the playing field, innings, strikes and balls, National and American League teams, infielders, outfielders, the umpire, pitcher, catcher, and more.

Batter Up! By Neil Johnson. Scholastic, 1990 32 pages. A kid's-eye view of playing on a baseball team. Follow Nick through his first season.

The Kids' World Almanac of Baseball. By Thomas G. Aylesworth. Revised edition. World Almanac, 1993. 273 pages. Because baseball is as much a spectator sport as it is a participant sport, this book seems a natural for budding young baseball aficionados. Includes baseball history, biographies, records, quotes, information on the teams, and more facts and trivia.

Know Your Game: Baseball. By Marc Bloom. Scholastic, 1991. 64 pages. In addition to describing baseball rules and specific skills, this children's sport book offers advice on setting goals and having fun. Lists major league teams by division. Contains a glossary.

Make the Team: Baseball. By Mark Crose. A Sports Illustrated for Kids Book. Little, Brown, 1991. 123 pages. Following a chapter on the history and basics of baseball, kids can learn about batting, pitching, catching, infield and outfield, and the team itself.

Basketball: Just for Kids

Basketball, Play Like a Pro. By James Allen. Troll Associates, 1990. 64 pages. For young would-be players, this book contains illustrations and accompanying text describing exercises and basketball skills. Shows the court and positions and discusses regulation play and sportsmanship.

I Can Be a Basketball Player. By Kathy Henderson. Childrens Press, 1991. 31 pages. This book takes children through the game of basketball. Shows what the game is (using action color photos) and describes basic positions and skills required. Includes a picture dictionary.

Biking: Just for Kids

Wheels! The Kids' Bike Book. By Megan Stine. A Sports Illustrated for Kids Book. Little, Brown, 1990. 84 pages. Explains the basics of bicycling—how to choose a good bike, how to keep it running smoothly, and how to fix it if it breaks. Also contains tips for bike touring and road racing and listings of recommended books and biking organizations to contact for additional information. Fun facts about cycling, full-color photographs, and bicycle quizzes and puzzles are included as well.

Fishing: Just for Kids

The Kids' Book of Fishing. By Michael J. Rosen. Workman, 1991. 96 pages. A guide for parents and children. Offers easy-to-understand information on a popular pastime. Comes with a mini-tackle box complete with hooks, a sinker, bobber, and fishing line.

Football: Just for Kids

Football. By Sue Boulais. Bancroft-Sage, 1992. 48 pages. A basic guide to the field, players and positions, football equipment, playing the game, learning football skills, and getting and staying in shape for football.

Football, Play Like a Pro. By James Allen. Troll Associates, 1990. 64 pages. Teaches children about football positions and offensive and defensive play. Photographs show drills and how to play touch football.

Foxtail: Just for Fun!

The Foxtail Book. By the editors of Klutz Press and Mike Gallaghan, inventor. Klutz Press, 1991. 75 pages. A foxtail is a ball with a nylon tail, by which you can throw or catch it. (A foxtail is included with the book.) Using pictures, the book describes basic catches and throws and shows games such as "straight up baseball,"

Psss . . . A Fun Game:

Fishin' Time. A board game for fishermen, fisherwomen, and fisherkids. Players choose a launch site and search for perch, northern pike, muskie, and other fish in a freshwater lake. Winning requires a combination of strategy and good luck. Comes with game board, fish playing pieces, a fishing license, and life vest cards. Available from World Wide Games, P.O. Box 517, Colchester, Connecticut 06415-0517. Phone: 1/800-243-9232.

"spud," "tennis tail," and "stay put 21."

Gymnastics: Just for Kids

Gymnastics: A Step-by-Step Guide. By Carey Huber. Be the Best Series. Troll Associates, 1990. 64 pages. Complete with illustrations and step-by-step instructions, this book takes young readers through flexibility and stretching exercises; vaulting; and work on the balance beam, parallel bars, and floor. Discusses safety and the history of gymnastics as well.

Make the Team: Gymnastics for Girls. By Steve Whitlock for the U.S. Gymnastics Federation. A Sports Illustrated for Kids Book. Little, Brown, 1991. 127 pages. Offers tips on getting started (including choosing a program). Covers vaulting, uneven parallel bars, the balance beam, rhythmic gymnastics, floor exercises, and competing in a gymnastics meet. Discusses safety as well.

Hockey: Just for Kids

Hockey: The Book for Kids. By Brian McFarlane. Kids Can Press,

1990. 95 pages. An introduction to hockey for kids. Covers warm-up exercises, choosing equipment, hockey talk, hockey greats, and some fun extras such as how to make a hockey scrapbook. Explains what coaches look for in a player.

Jumping Rope: Just for Kids

Anna Banana: 101 Jump-Rope Rhymes. By Joanna Cole. William Morrow, 1989. 64 pages. A compilation of classic rhymes for jumping rope. Also includes instructions for jump-rope games. Also by Joanna Cole (with Stephanie Calmenson): *Miss Mary Mack: And Other Children's Street Rhymes.*

Skateboarding

Rad Boards. By Ron King. A Sports Illustrated for Kids Book. Time, 1991. 83 pages. With this book, kids can learn about skateboarding, snowboarding, and bodyboarding. Describes basic equipment, moves (toe turns, linking turns), tricks, stunts, and competitions. Explains where to go with their rad boards.

Thrasher: the Radical Skateboard Book. By Kevin J. Thatcher and Brian Brannon. Random House, 1992. 67 pages. Illustrated with photographs, this book shows just what you can do with a skateboard. Discusses street terrain, ramps, and skating on solid cement; outlines basic moves. Also covers the buying and maintenance of skateboards and safety equipment and skateparks in the United States and Canada.

The Ultimate Skateboard Book. By Albert Cassorla. Running Press, 1988. 128 pages. Using this book, children can bone up on the history of skateboarding; learn how to choose the right equipment; and find out about vertical moves, advanced freestyle, and slides in skateboarding. Also covers skateboarding contests.

Skating

In-Line Skating: A Complete Guide for Beginners. By George Sullivan. Cobblehill Books, 1993. 48 pages. An introductory guide to in-line skating, covering moves, safety gear, equipment, and more.

Skiing

Kids on Skis. By I. William Berry. Charles Scribner's Sons, 1980. 231 pages. A guide to family skiing and children's equipment, instruction, and clothing. Explains how to pick ski schools and evaluate ski lessons. Includes a teaching/learning syllabus on the "Skill Approach to Teaching," with descriptions of class levels and specific skill teaching at each level.

Soccer: Just for Kids

Make the Team, Soccer: A Heads Up Guide to Super Soccer. By Richard J. Brenner. A Sports Illustrated for Kids Book. Little, Brown, 1990. 127 pages. Designed as a complete course in the game, this book includes descriptions and pictures of soccer skills and drills. Tells kids how to make the most of free kicks, corner kicks, and goal kicks; mark their opponents on defense; head the ball accurately; and work with their teammates.

Soccer. By Jane Mersky Leder. Bancroft-Sage, 1992. 48 pages. Offers an introduction to the game of soccer, covering basic skills and soccer action.

Soccer, Play Like a Pro. By Anthony Venture. Troll Associates, 1990. 64 pages. Covers drills, skills, the field, positions, tips on regulation play, equipment, and a brief history of the game.

Spalding Youth Soccer. By Paul Harris. Masters Press, 1992. 111 pages. Illustrated with photographs, this book covers basic soccer skills and moves, including dribbling, passing, and juggling. Offers information on soccer rules, the youth soccer parent, refereeing, coaching, and more.

Swimming

Make the Team: Swimming and Diving. By Charles Carson. A Sports Illustrated for Kids Book. Little, Brown, 1991. 123 pages. Offers guidelines on developing better swim strokes and dives, training on dry land, starting out right in races, and doing your best at swimming and diving meets.

Swimming: A Step-by-Step Guide. By Gene Dabney. Troll Associates, 1990. 64 pages. Takes children through the basics of swimming and floating. Covers the crawl, backstroke, breast stroke, and the butterfly.

Teach Your Child to Swim: From Infants to 10 Years. By Eva Bory. Simon and Schuster, 1993. 142 pages. Offers guidelines, tips, and techniques for teaching children to swim, from games in the bathtub for the very young to competitive swimming for older children. Illustrates teaching techniques with photographs and describes each skill step-by-step. Emphasizes the importance of praise and patience.

Tennis

Teaching Your Child Tennis. By Bob Huang and Arthur Shay. Contemporary Books, 1979. 71 pages. Provides beginning and intermediate drills for serves, grips, and strokes. Discusses tennis rules and scoring.

Walking

Dayhiker: Walking for Fitness, Fun and Adventure. By Robert S. Wood. Ten Speed Press, 1991. 144 pages. A guide to short hikes and walking trips through cities, suburbs, the woods, and the country side. Talks about hiking with children, reading the weather, walking techniques, traveling light, and trail manners.

Yoga

Yoga for Children. By Mary Stewart and Kathy Phillips. Simon and Schuster, 1992. 128 pages. Provides simple movements and games you and your kids can do together to help them grow strong and flexible. The basic program includes warm-up, action, games, winding down, being quiet, and lying flat.

Sports Equipment Catalogs

Back to Basics Toys. 2707 Pittman Drive, Silver Spring, Maryland 20910-1807. Phone: 1/800-356-5360. Offers a collection of active play and sports gear for children.

Childcraft. P.O. Box 29149, Mission, Kansas 66201-9149. Phone: 1/800-631-5657. Many pages in the Childcraft toy catalog are devoted to sports and active play equipment (pogo sticks, a golf set, a mini-trampoline, big bouncy balls, skates, skis, a polo set, and more).

Constructive Playthings. 1227 East 119th Street, Grandview, Missouri 64030. Phone: 816/761-5900; 1/800-832-0572. This toy catalog includes active play equipment such as a baseball glove and ball, tumbling mat, soccer set, junior golf set, tunnel, indoor gym-house, and child-size basketball rimboard.

Just for Kids. P.O. Box 29141, Shawnee, Kansas 66201-9141. Phone: 1/800-654-6963. This catalog includes a section on sports, where you can find clothing, athletic shoes, skates, a junior golf set, a pogo stick, elbow and knee pads, an adjustable volleyball net, an archery set, and more (offerings vary with the seasons).

Lakeshore Learning Materials. 2695 East Dominquez Street, Carson, California 90749. Phone: 1/800-421-5354 or 310/537-8600. Produces a toy and equipment catalog oriented

Fitness and Children
The following facts and statistics come from the *Youth Fitness Fact Sheet*,
President's Council on Physical Fitness and Sports.

■ 55 percent of girls ages 6–17 and 25 percent of boys 6–12 cannot do one pullup.

■ Only 32 percent of 6- to 17-year-olds meet the minimum standards for cardiovascular fitness, flexibility, and abdominal and upper-body strength.

■ 40 percent of children ages 5–8 show at least one heart disease risk factor such as physical inactivity, obesity, elevated cholesterol, or high blood pressure.

■ American children have become fatter since the 1960s.

■ Youth fitness in the United States has not improved in the last ten years, and in some cases has declined.

toward schools and teachers, but great for parents too. Many pages are devoted to active play equipment, including balance and coordination toys (balance boards, burlap jumping sacks, play mats, etc.); movement activities equipment (a rainbow parachute, game hoops, and bean bag sets); and playspace equipment (indoor and outdoor, including slides, snap-together houses, and elaborate climbing structures).

Passon's Sports. P.O. Box 49, Jenkintown, Pennsylvania 19046. Phone: 1/800-523-1557. An A-to-Z catalog of sports equipment for all ages, including balls, nets, paddles, rackets, tumbling aids, and swingsets.

Toys to Grow On. P.O. Box 17, Long Beach, CA 90801. Phone: 310/603-8890 or 1/800-542-8338 (ordering); 1/800-874-4242 (customer service). This toy catalog devotes several pages to indoor and outdoor sports equipment and climbing toys.

Periodicals

International Gymnast. P.O. Box 2450, Oceanside, California 92051. Phone: 619/722-0030. For both the serious competitor and gym class enthusiast, this magazine includes training tips, interviews with top gymnasts, and up-to-date information on competitions. Issued ten times annually.

KidSports. P.O. Box 8488, Coral Springs, Florida 33075. Phone: 1/800-938-5588. "The Official Sports Magazine for Kids." Offers advice and encouragement from professional athletes. Covers track and field, baseball, tennis, soccer, and many other sports. Puzzles and posters are included. For children ages eight to fourteen. Issued bimonthly.

Soccer Jr. P.O. Box 420442, Palm Coast, Florida 32142-9744. Phone: 1/800-829-5382. In addition to articles on soccer stars, this magazine features playing tips, new soccer games, and practice drills. Also contains puzzles, cartoons, and equipment reviews. Issued bimonthly.

Sports Illustrated for Kids. P.O. Box 830609, Birmingham, Alabama 35283-0609. Phone: 1/800-992-0196. Profiles professional athletes and kids involved in sports. One issue told readers about a sportscaster camp for kids and an all-kids rodeo. Issued monthly.

Some Worthwhile Magazine Articles

"Answers To Keeping Kids Fit," *Parents*, November 1992.

"Are Girls and Boys Equally Fit?" *Working Mother*, May 1992.

"Boost Your Child's Immunity," *Working Mother*, March 1992.

"Children Say Having Fun Is Number One," *USA Today*, September 10, 1990.

"Children's Sports: Fun Outranks Winning," *Philadelphia Inquirer*, August 30, 1991.

"Fathers and Their Athletic Children: A Fragile Partnership," *Rockland Journal-News* (White Plains, New York), June 16, 1991.

"Field of Dreams: Little League's Not So Little Anymore," *Sport*, September 1989.

"Fitness for the Fun of It," *Parenting*, September 1992.

"Fitness Report," *Parents Digest*, Spring 1993.

"Frisky Fitness," *Parenting*, May 1993.

"Getting Physical (Three- and Four-Year-Olds)," *Parents*, June 1993.

"Going for Broke," *Parenting*, April 1993.

"Helping to Develop Confidence in Sports Activities," The *New York Times*, July 4, 1991.

"How to Foster Self-Esteem," The *New York Times Magazine*, April 28, 1991.

"Is Your Child Ready for Team Sports?" *Parents*, May 1991.

"It's a Kids' Game," *Hartford Courant*, April 10, 1991.

"Karate?! Yes!" *Healthy Kids: 4-10 Years*, Fall 1992.

"Kids in Sports: Pushed Too Hard?" *Scholastic News*, March 15, 1991.

"A Little League Coach Shares His Secrets," The *New York Times*, August 24, 1991.

"Make Feeling Fit Fun," *Working Mother*, January 1992.

"The Making of a Good Sport," *Working Mother*, April 1992.

"A Program For Kids: Success-Oriented Physical Education," *Childhood Education*, Spring 1993.

"Put Me In, Coach! The Pros and Cons of Team Sports for Kids," *Healthy Kids: 4-10 Years*, Spring/Summer 1993.

"Soccer Smarts," *Family Fun*, September/October 1992.

"Stress-Free Little League," *Sports Illustrated*, August 22, 1988.

"Touch All the Bases," *USA Today*, April 18, 1991.

"Whose Game Is It, Anyway?" *Parents*, October 1991.

"Why Don't the Kids Seem to Be Having Fun in Little League? The Deterrent Is the Adults," *Newsweek*, May 22, 1989.

"Why Young People Play . . . Or Quit," *Scholastic Coach*, September 1991.

"Working Out a Strategy to Shape Up Flabby Kids," *USA Today*, August 7, 1991.

"The Worry over Weight," *Working Mother*, October 1992.

"Your Child Athlete," *Living Well/Family File*, Spring 1992.

Videotapes

General Fitness and Exercise

American Junior Workout. Kids Klassics. Running Time: 29 minutes. An aerobic exercise tape for children, demonstrating warm-up, cool-down, and the workout in between.

Fun House Fitness: The Fun House Funk, Ages 7 and Older. Warner Home Video. Running time: 45 minutes. This videotape features J. D. Roth demonstrating dance and exercise routines designed to help children develop balance, coordination, agility, endurance, and strength.

Fun House Fitness: The Swamp Stomp, Ages 3-7. Warner Home Video. Running time: 40 minutes. A play-along program for children ages three through seven. Designed to help develop motor skills, including balance, coordination, agility, endurance, and strength.

Kids in Motion: An Interactive Creative Movement Program. Playhouse Video. Running time: 66 minutes. Uses dance, music, poetry, and imaginative game play to help children gain a better understanding of their bodies and themselves. Title song is by the Temptations.

Leslie Sansone's Walk Aerobics for Kids. PPI Entertainment Group/Paradise Video. Running time: 36 minutes. A segmented aerobic workout for children. Viewers can do individual segments or complete the entire tape (depending on their attention span and energy level).

A National of Winners Video. See listing under "Free and Inexpensive Resources."

Sing, Stretch and Shape Up: 11 Video Songs. Golden Music Video. Running time: 30 minutes. Join Casey Rabbit, Albert Possum, and their friend Omar Owl as they explore new ways to move like different animals while listening to music. Encourages kids to use their imaginations while participating in the exercise workout.

Tip Top with Suzy Prudden. Warner Home Video. Running time: 53 minutes (volume 1); 39 minutes (volume 2). Fitness expert Suzy Prudden calls on young viewers to join her as she works her way through a series of exercises and warm-up activities. (Volume 1 is for children ages three to six; volume 2 is for ages seven to ten.)

Workout with Mommy and Me. Today Home Entertainment. Running time: 22 minutes. Fitness expert Barbara Peterson David works out with her daughter. Demonstrates imaginative exercises for parents to do with children ages three and up. Includes lots of jumping and tumbling.

Sport-By-Sport

Baseball

Fielding for Kids. Running time: 30 minutes. Demonstrates the fundamentals of fielding: how to approach the ground ball, track down the fly, and throw with speed and accuracy. Available from Schoolmasters Video, 745 State Circle, P.O. Box 1941, Ann Arbor, Michigan 48106. Phone: 1/800-521-2832.

Hitting for Kids. Running time: 30 minutes. Offers demonstrations and advice on hitting. Available from Schoolmasters Video, 745 State Circle, P.O. Box 1941, Ann Arbor, Michigan 48106. Phone: 1/800-521-2832.

Pitching for Kids. Running time: 30 minutes. Demonstrates the basics of pitching. Available from Schoolmasters Video, 745 State Circle, P.O. Box 1941, Ann Arbor, Michigan 48106. Phone: 1/800-521-2832.

Teaching Kids Baseball with Jerry Kindall. ESPN Home Video. Running time: 75 minutes. Shows parents and coaches how to teach children the fundamentals and techniques of baseball.

Basketball

Teaching Kids Basketball with John Wooden. ESPN Home Video. Running time: 75 minutes. Starts with the basics of passing, dribbling, and rebounding; continues with segments on youth injury, conditioning tips, and coordination drills.

Biking

Bicycle Safety Camp. Actividey. Running time: 25 minutes. Endorsed by the American Academy of Pediatrics, this videotape teaches children the importance of bicycle safety—why they need to wear a helmet, how to use turn signals, and making sure there are no motor vehicles coming or going before crossing driveways or streets. Young riders (ages five to ten) learn these lessons and others by watching others their own age spend a day at a bicycle safety camp. This video is available from the American Academy of Pediatrics (see appendix I for contact information).

Bowling

Teaching Kids Bowling with Gordon Vadakin. ESPN Home Video. Running time: 75 minutes. Champion bowler and youth coach Gordon Vadakin shows you how to teach your kids the right techniques and the proper attitudes for bowling.

Football

Teaching Kids Football with Bo Schembechler. ESPN Home Video. Running time: 75 minutes. For parents and coaches, this videotape explains how to teach children the basics of football. Covers blocking, receiving, passing, tackling, kicking, and punting. Provides warm-up techniques, conditioning exercises, and injury prevention guidelines.

Golf

Teaching Kids Golf with the Ben Sutton Golf School. ESPN Home Video. Running time: 75 minutes. Experts use computer graphics, props, and drills to demonstrate the basics of golf.

Skiing

Teaching Children to Ski. Professional Ski Instructors Association of America. Running time: 30 minutes. An instructional videotape for parents showing the methods for teaching children (ages six to ten) to ski. Available from Back to Basics Toys, 2707 Pittman Drive, Silver Spring, Maryland 20910. Phone: 1/800-356-5360.

Teaching Kids Skiing with Hank Kashiwa. ESPN Home Video. Running time: 60 minutes. Explains how to help make your child's first downhill ski experience safe and fun. Provides parents with advice on preparation, proper techniques, and equipment.

Soccer

Soccer Fun-Damentals. Morris Video. Running time: 30 minutes. In this videotape, Shep Messing teaches individual and team skills to children of all ages. Covers warm-up exercises, dribbling, juggling, and practice games.

Teaching Kids Soccer with Bob Gansler. ESPN Home Video. Running time: 75 minutes. For parents and coaches, this tape shows how to teach kids basic soccer skills. Demonstrates ball lifting and control, dribbling, passing, heading, and shooting. Offers drills for each skill. Discusses incorrect tendencies and offers recommendations for correcting them.

Swimming

Becoming Water Safe with Rita Curtis. The Video Studio. Designed to teach parents how to teach their children to swim and to help swimming instructors improve their teaching techniques. For work with students of all ages.

Swim Lessons for Kids. SwimSafe Fundamentals. Running time: 40 minutes. Approved by the American Academy of Pediatrics and the director of the Council for National Cooperation in Aquatics, this videotape offers a simple method for parents to teach their children (ages three to twelve) to swim. Includes guidelines on teaching breathing and floating techniques and various swim strokes, including the crawl and backstroke. Also covers survival skills. Comes with a booklet containing illustrations and additional guidelines. Available from the American Academy of Pediatrics (see appendix I for contact information).

Teaching Kids Swimming with John Naber. ESPN Home Video. Running time: 40 minutes. Coach John Naber shares his personal teaching methods to help you teach your child to swim with confidence and enthusiasm.

Tennis

Teaching Kids Tennis with Nick Bollettieri. ESPN Home Video. Running time: 75 minutes. Shows parents how to teach their children the game of tennis. Once children learn how to hit the ball, they can move on to forehand and backhand techniques, volleying, and serving.

Associations

General Fitness and Exercise

Amateur Athletic Union (AAU), Carrier Youth Sports Programs. 3400 West Eighty-sixth Street, P.O. Box 68207, Indianapolis, Indiana 46268. Phone: 317/872-2900. Sponsors training and competition for nearly two dozen different sports. Holds the Junior Olympic Games

each summer (sixteen games for ages eight to eighteen). Publishes an annual directory of AAU officials, a newsletter, and sports manuals.

American Alliance for Health, Physical Education, Recreation, and Dance. 1900 Association Drive, Reston, Virginia 22091. Phone: 703/476-3400. Maintains an information and referral service for students, educators, and instructors of athletics, dance, and recreation. Programs include the health-related fitness test and educational program for school children (Physical Best) and the National Youth and Children Fitness Study. Publishes *Fitting It*, a monthly newsletter on fitness and nutrition for eleven- and twelve-year-olds.

American Fitness Association. 820 Hillside Drive, Long Beach, California 90815. Phone: 310/596-8660. Offers clinics and seminars and makes referrals to the public. Provides children's services and maintains a speakers bureau and a hall of fame. Publishes a number of directories and periodicals, including *Who's Who in Sports and Fitness.*

American Sports Education Institute. 200 Castlewood Drive, North Palm Beach, Florida 33408. Phone: 407/842-3600. Promotes and sponsors amateur sports in many local communities through their United States Sports Boosters Clubs of America. Call the national office for information on Booster Clubs in a particular community.

Direction in Sports. 600 Willshire Boulevard, Suite 320, Los Angeles, California 90017. Phone: 213/627-9861. Offers programs based on the belief that the teaching and coaching of one's peers can counteract destructive behavior and low self-esteem and stimulate academic achievement in children.

Institute for Aerobics Research. 12330 Preston Road, Dallas, Texas 75230. Phone: 214/239-7223. This institute studies the relationship between health and living habits and promotes participation in aerobic exercise. Provides training programs and consulting services to schools, agencies, and corporations.

National Association for Sport and Physical Education. 1900 Association Drive, Reston, Virginia 22091. Phone: 703/476-3410. Provides information to the public on the value of physical education and sports participation, conducts research in sports-related areas, and offers sports training seminars and competitions. Produces a publications catalog (although geared toward physical education teachers, many of the publications can also be used by parents).

National Association of Police Athletic Leagues. 200 Castlewood Drive, Suite 400, North Palm Beach, Florida 33408. Phone: 407/844-1823. Offers coeducational instruction and competition in a variety of sports (from baseball to Tae Kwan Do) for children ages eight to eighteen. For information on a local league, consult your telephone directory, or call the national office.

National Fitness Foundation. 2801 Northeast Fiftieth Street, Oklahoma City, Oklahoma 73111. Phone: 405/424-5266. Works to increase participation in exercise and sports activities by Americans of all ages. Promotes, facilitates, and sponsors fitness research. Sponsors youth fitness summer camps.

North American Youth Sports Institute. P.O. Box 957, Kernersville, North Carolina 27285. Phone: 919/784-4926. Offers training, education, consulting, and support services to youth agencies, corporations, and education groups. Maintains a library on sport recreation education.

President's Council on Physical Fitness and Sports. 701 Pennsylvania Avenue, N.W., Suite 250, Washington, D.C. 20004. Phone: 202/272-3421. Established to promote an interest in overall physical fitness, the council sponsors the Physical Fitness Award program for kids ages six to seventeen and the Presidential Sports Award Program for anyone age six and above.

Sporting Goods Manufacturers Association. 200 Castlewood Drive, North Palm Beach, Florida 33408. Phone: 407/842-4100. Manufacturers of athletic clothing, footwear, and sporting goods. Seeks to increase sports participation.

YMCA Youth Sports. YMCA of the USA. 101 North Wacker Drive, Chicago, Illinois 60606. Phone: 312/977-0031 or 1/800-USA-YMCA (872-9622). Conducts sports programs for both elementary and secondary school children. Check your local telephone directory for local programs or call the toll-free number for referrals.

Sport-By-Sport

Archery

Junior Olympic Archery Development. One Olympic Plaza, Colorado Springs, Colorado 80909. Phone: 719/578-4576. Part of the National Archery Association, Junior Olympic Archery Development encourages youthful participation in the sport. Call for local programs for the seven- to seventeen-year-old.

National Field Archery Association. 31497 Outer 1-10, Redlands, California 92373. Phone: 714/794-2133. Runs schools and tournaments. Supports the preservation of game and the natural environment.

Has a special committee on youth and conducts the Junior Bowhunter Program. Publishes a bimonthly magazine.

Baseball

American Amateur Baseball Congress. P.O. Box 467, Marshall, Michigan 49068. Phone: 616/781-2002. Serves as an information clearinghouse and a governing body for amateur baseball in the United States, Canada, and Puerto Rico. Sponsors annual tournaments, including one for children ages twelve and under.

Babe Ruth Baseball. P.O. Box 5000, 1770 Brunswick Avenue, Trenton, New Jersey 08638. Phone: 609/695-1434. Runs baseball programs for children from six to eighteen, including annual "World Series" games and workshops.

George Khoury Association of Baseball Leagues. 5400 Meramec Bottom Road, St. Louis, Missouri 63128. Phone: 314/849-8900. An association of supervised softball and baseball leagues for girls and boys age seven and up, supported by churches and community groups.

Little League Baseball, Inc. P.O. Box 3485, Williamsport, Pennsylvania 17701. Phone: 717/326-1921. Offers a wide network of leagues for children between the ages of six and eighteen.

Pony Baseball. 300 Clare Drive, Washington, Pennsylvania 15301. Phone: 412/225-1060. Has six baseball leagues divided by age group. Pony Baseball also has a softball league for girls.

Biking

Bicycle Federation of America. 1818 R Street, N.W., Washington, D.C. 20009. Phone: 202/332-6986. Serves as an information clearinghouse. Fosters the growth and safety of recreational biking, runs training programs, and helps local groups form bicycling programs. Publishes a newsletter called *Pro Bike News*, as well as the *Pro Bike Directory*.

Rails-to-Trails Conservancy. 1400 Sixteenth Street, N.W., Suite 300, Washington, D.C. 20036. Phone: 202/797-5400. A nonprofit organization that has helped transform more than five thousand miles of old, unused railroad tracks into a national network of bicycle, hiking, and cross-country ski trails. Publishes a periodic directory listing converted railways serving as trails. Also publishes *Trailblazer*, a quarterly newsletter exploring issues, trends, and legislation dealing with the conversion of railroad lines into trails. Contact this organization to find the nearest trail or to help out in this family-friendly cause.

Bowling

Young American Bowling Alliance. 5301 South Seventy-sixth Street, Greendale, Wisconsin 53129. Phone: 414/421-4700. An alliance of bowling leagues for children and youth (including the pee wee leagues for three- to seven-year-olds and the tenpin leagues for people under twenty-two). Conducts the National Junior Bowling Championships and the National Collegiate Bowling Championships. Publishes *New YABA World*, with articles about youthful bowlers. Distributes rule books, teaching aids, videotapes, and other materials.

Fencing

U.S. Fencing Association. 1750 East Boulder Street, Colorado Springs, Colorado 80909. Phone: 719/578-4511. Organizes age-level fencing instruction and competition (there is an eleven-and-under division). Conducts junior training camps and sponsors educational activities such as the Junior Development Program. Publishes rule books, educational pamphlets, a quarterly magazine, and a semiannual directory.

Field Hockey

U.S.A. Junior Field Hockey Association. 1750 East Boulder Street, Colorado Springs, Colorado 80909. Phone: 719/578-4567. Part of the U.S.A. Field Hockey Association, the Junior Association encourages safe, enjoyable, and inexpensive participation in field hockey among children six to thirteen.

Fishing

American Bass Association. 886 Trotters Trail, Wetumpka, Alabama 36092. Phone: 205/567-6035. Runs the National Youth Program of fishing programs for children, including those who are disabled or underprivileged. Offers information on conservation and sponsors fishing contests.

American Casting Association. 1739 Praise Boulevard, Fenton, Missouri 63026. Phone: 314/225-9443. Promotes youth involvement in fishing. Offers training clinics and runs tournaments. Publishes *Creel*, a bimonthly bulletin.

Bass Incorporated. c/o Wayne Goble, Anglers for Clean Water, P.O. Box 17141, Montgomery, Alabama 36141-0141. Phone: 205/272-9530. Promotes an interest in fishing. Works to enhance fishery resources through management, conservation, and other environmental measures. Sponsors children's services.

Football

Pop Warner Football. 920 Town Center, Suite I-25, Langhorn, Pennsylvania 19047. Phone: 215/752-2691. Office for youth leagues with teams arranged by age and weight.

Gymnastics

U.S. Gymnastics Federation. 201 South Capitol, Suite 300, Indianapolis, Indiana 46225. Phone: 317/237-5050. Offers a competitive gymnastics program (five different skill levels) and encourages recreational participation in the sport. Publishes *USA Gymnastics*, a monthly magazine, and several handbooks, including *National Compulsory Routines*.

Handball

United States Handball Association. 930 North Benton Avenue, Tucson, Arizona 85711. Phone: 602/795-0434. Although mainly for collegiate players, this organization also oversees tournaments for children and teenagers. Publishes *Handball*, a bimonthly magazine, and the *Annual Guide and Directory*.

Horsemanship

American Horse Shows Association. 220 East Forty-second Street, Suite 409, New York, New York 10017. Phone: 212/972-2472. Hosts competitions and oversees the rules and regulations of horseback riding at both junior and adult levels. Publishes educational pamphlets, a rule book, and the monthly magazine *Horse Show*.

Camp Horsemanship Association. P.O. Box 188, Lawrence, Michigan 49064. Phone: 616/674-8074. Offers riding programs, instructor certification programs, and an information and referral service to ensure that children and other students receive safe training. Publishes a membership directory and the *Riding Instructors Manual*.

Harness Horse Youth Foundation. 14950 Greyhound Court, Suite 210, Carmel, Indiana 46032. Phone: 317/848-5132. This foundation works to increase youth participation in harness racing through 4-H programs, training camps, internships, and a scholarship program. Publishes the *Directory to Equine Schools and Colleges* and *Studying the Standardbreed* (a 4-H project book).

Horsemanship Safety Association. 120 Ohio Avenue, Madison, Wisconsin 53704. Phone: 608/244-8547. Teaches proper horsemanship to instructors and students. Maintains a library. Publishes a quarterly newsletter and a variety of manuals on horsemanship.

United States Pony Clubs, Inc. 893 South Matlack Street, Suite 110, West Chester, Pennsylvania 19382-4913. Phone: 215/436-0300. These clubs work to build character and develop leadership through participation in equestrian activities. Sponsors competitions for riders under twenty-one, runs an overseas exchange program, and maintains a resource library for member clubs. Publishes the *Pony Club Handbook*.

Ice Skating

Amateur Skating Union of the United States. 1033 Shady Lane, Glen Ellen, Illinois 60137. Phone: 708/790-3230 or 1/800-634-4766. For anyone (age six and up) who wants to participate in speed skating. Conducts seminars and training programs at the local level. Publishes a handbook.

Ice Skating Institute of America. 355 West Dundee Road, Buffalo Grove, Illinois 60089-3500. Phone: 708/808-SKAT. An association of skaters, ice skating instructors, rink owners, and industry suppliers. Publishes a bimonthly newsletter covering ice skating news, events, and other information for members. Also publishes *Recreational Ice Skating*, a quarterly magazine for figure, hockey, and speed skaters.

U.S. Figure Skating Association. 20 First Street, Colorado Springs, Colorado 80906. Phone: 719/635-5200. Oversees the rules and regulations of amateur figure skating, manages competitions, and selects team members for international tournaments. Has clubs throughout the United States for toddlers and up. Offers information and referrals. Publishes an annual rulebook and the magazine *Skating*. (Call for information on clubs in your area.)

Martial Arts

American Amateur Karate Foundation. 1930 Wilshire Boulevard, Suite 1208, Los Angeles, California 90057. Phone: 213/483-8261. Governs the rules and standards of karate as practiced in the United States. Runs a summer training program and oversees competitions. Answers questions from the public.

United States Judo Association. 19 North Union Boulevard, Colorado Springs, Colorado 80909. Phone: 719/633-7750. Through its National Judo Institute, this association trains instructors and students, operates a summer camp, and offers a scholarship program. Also hosts a national annual tournament, and publishes a number of handbooks and periodicals.

United States Tae Kwon Do Union. 1750 East Boulder Street, Colorado Springs, Colorado 80909. Phone: 719/578-4632. Runs an instructional competitive program for youth ranging in age from two to seventeen. Competition includes a Junior Olympics. Publishes a handbook.

Racquet Sports

American Platform Tennis Association. Box 901, Upper Montclair, New Jersey 07043. Phone: 201/744-1190. Sponsors a junior program for eighteen-year-olds and under. Publishes a newsletter, a rulebook, an informational booklet, and a tournament schedule.

U.S. Table Tennis Association. 1750 East Boulder Street, Colorado Springs, Colorado 80909. Phone: 719/578-4583. Offers a youth program through educational institutions and boys' and girls' clubs. Conducts a competitive program, organized by age, which culminates in a Junior Olympics. Publications include instructional booklets and the monthly *Table Tennis Topics*. Also produces films.

Roller Skating

U.S. Amateur Confederation of Roller Skating. P.O. Box 6579, Lincoln, Nebraska 68506. Phone: 402/483-7551. Offers information on roller skating clubs across the country (for all ages). Oversees rules and regulations for roller skating competitions. Publishes an annual directory.

Running and Walking

Road Runners Club of America. c/o Henley Gibble, 629 South Washington Street, Alexandria, Virginia 22314. Phone: 703/836-0558. Offers information on Run for Your Life, a "fun run" program for both children and adults. Sponsors races nationwide. Publishes a runner's handbook.

The Rockport Company. 72 Howe Street, Marlborough, Massachusetts 01752. Phone: 508/485-2098. Provides free information and booklets on walking for fitness.

Skiing

American Ski Association. P.O. Box 480067, Denver, Colorado 80248. Phone: 303/825-0153 or 1/800-525-SNOW. An association of recreational skiers. Arranges skiing excursions and travel for members. Offers discounts on lift tickets, accommodations, equipment, and transportation to ski areas. Publishes

American Skier, a quarterly covering developments and issues that affect the sport. Also publishes a ski directory.

Cross Country Ski Areas Association. 259 Bolton Road, Winchester, New Hampshire 03470. Phone: 603/239-4341. Promotes cross-country skiing in North America. Compiles and distributes information concerning developments in the cross country ski industry.

National Brotherhood of Skiers. 1525 East Fifty-third Street, Suite 408, Chicago, Illinois 60615. Phone: 312/955-4100. Promotes winter sports among minorities, with an emphasis on youth. Publishes the *Skier's Edge* magazine and *NBS Ski Club Guide* (a directory).

Rails-to-Trails Conservancy. 1400 Sixteenth Street, N.W., Suite 300, Washington, D.C. 20036. Phone: 202/797-5400. A nonprofit organization that has helped transform more than five thousand miles of old, unused railroad tracks into a national network of bicycle, hiking, and cross-country ski trails. Publishes a periodic directory listing converted railways serving as trails.

United States Skiing. P.O. Box 100, Park City, Utah 84060. Phone: 801/649-9090. Recognized by the U.S. Olympic Committee as the official governing organization for skiing in the United States. Will answer questions and make referrals on a wide range of subjects. Publishes the magazine *Ski Racing*.

Soccer

American Youth Soccer Organization. P.O. Box 5045, Hawthorne, California 90251. Phone: 213/643-6455. Runs competitions (organized by age) for those under nineteen. Publishes *The ABC's of AYSO—Parents' Handbook*.

National Soccer League. 4534 North Lincoln Avenue, Chicago, Illinois 60625. Phone: 312/275-2850. Promotes the development and growth of soccer. Sponsors international games. Offers children's services. Publishes a directory.

Soccer Association for Youth, Soccer-USA. 5945 Ridge Avenue, Cincinnati, Ohio 45213. Phone: 513/351-7291. Oversees soccer competitions for six- to eighteen-year-olds (organized by age but carefully mixed according to ability levels to ensure fair play). Publishes the *Parents Guide to Soccer* (issued annually), as well as a number of periodicals and handbooks.

U.S. Youth Soccer Association. 2050 North Plano Road, Suite 100, Richardson, Texas 75082. Phone: 214/235-4499. A youth division of the U.S. Soccer Federation, the Youth Association seeks to develop and promote the game for children ages five to nineteen. Runs clinics and competitions. Publishes the *U.S. Youth Soccer Association–National Directory*, as well as handbooks, manuals, and a newspaper containing tips for parents. Also produces videotapes.

Softball

Amateur Softball Association of America. 2801 Northeast Fiftieth Street, Oklahoma City, Oklahoma 73111-7203. Phone: 405/424-5266. A national agency for softball in the United States, this group sponsors research, clinics, and competitions. Coordinates a Junior Olympics. Maintains a reference library. Publishes a newsletter, an official guide and rulebook, and a catalog.

Cinderella Softball League, Inc. P.O. Box 1411, Corning, New York 14830. Phone: 607/937-5469. Promotes softball for girls. Runs several leagues for girls up to eighteen years old. Publishes a rulebook and a newsletter.

U.S. Slo-Pitch Softball Association. 3935 South Crater Road, Petersburg, Virginia 23805. Phone: 804/732-4099. Has a youth division. Publishes a rulebook, a newsletter, and a softball almanac.

Surfing

National Scholastic Surfing Association. P.O. Box 495, Huntington Beach, California 92648. Phone: 213/592-2285. For students from sixth grade through college, this association maintains a training camp, runs an international exchange program, and publishes a newsletter called *Surflines*.

Swimming

U.S. Swimming, Inc. 1750 East Boulder Street, Colorado Springs, Colorado 80909. Phone: 719/578-4578. Runs instructional programs for children ages five and up. Sponsors competitions and selects members for the national team. Publishes the *United States Swimming Directory*.

Tennis

American Tennis Association. P.O. Box 3277, Silver Spring, Maryland 20918-9998. Phone: 301/681-4832. For African Americans interested in tennis. Runs special training programs for youth and holds an annual tournament.

Black Tennis and Sports Foundation. 1893 Amsterdam Avenue, New York, New York 10032. Provides help for African-American and minority youth interested in athletics, including tennis, skating, and gymnastics. Organizes tennis teams, competitions, and educational projects.

Junior Tennis Foundation. 550 Mamaroneck Avenue, Harrison, New York 10528. Phone: 914/698-0414. Encourages general interest in tennis.

Provides free tennis clinics for under-privileged children of all creeds and races, and undertakes research on tennis teaching.

Youth Tennis League. 9704 Ashby Road, Fairfax, Virginia 22031. Promotes and fosters the sport of tennis for youth.

Exercise Programs

Discovery Zone. 205 North Michigan Avenue, Chicago, Illinois 60601. Phone: 312/616-3800. A national network of indoor playgrounds designed by fitness experts for kids twelve and under. Offers programs and sessions emphasizing physical fitness (developing coordination, agility and flexibility, endurance, and balance) and social/conceptual skills (encouraging imagination and creativity and developing self-esteem). More than ninety locations nationwide, with more being added every week. Offers fitness and movement programs for children from six months to five years and "fitplay" sessions for all children. Some locations offer parties and playgroup packages. Call for locations near you.

Gymboree. Gymboree Corporation, Parent Child Classes, 700 Airport Boulevard, Suite 200, Burlingame, California 94010. Phone: 415/579-0600 or 1/800-227-3900. A nationally franchised exercise program for the very young (infants through age two). Basic classes include Cradlegym (zero to three months), Babygym (three to twelve months), and Gymboree I (ten to sixteen months), II (twelve to thirty months), and III (two-year-olds).

Consult your phone directory for local classes, or call the headquarters for a listing for your area.

Playorena. Playorena, Inc., 125 Mineola Avenue, Roslyn Heights, New York 11577. Phone: 516/621-7529. Nationally franchised exercise and recreational programs for three- to thirty-six-month-olds. Classes include: Hello World (three to eleven months), Toddlers (thirteen to twenty-four months), and Runners (eighteen to thirty-six months).

Presidential Sports Award Program. The President's Council on Physical Fitness and Sports offers the Presidential Sports Award to individuals who exercise consistently over time. Recently opened to children ages six and above, the award can be earned for sixty-eight separate categories, ranging from aerobic dance to wrestling. (There is also a "family fitness" category.) For program brochures and additional information, contact Presidential Sports Award, P.O. Box 68207, Indianapolis, Indiana 46268-0207. Phone: 317/872-2900.

President's Challenge. A physical fitness testing program of the President's Council on Physical Fitness and Sports. Developed for children ages six to seventeen, the program includes five separate fitness components (a one mile run/walk, curl-ups, the V-sit and reach, pull-ups, and the shuttle run). For information, contact President's Challenge, Poplars Research Center, 400 East Seventh Street, Bloomington, Indiana 47405. Phone: 1/800-258-8146.

Putting It All Together: Tips from the Pros

Putting it all together will mean different things for different families, but all the fitness pros—Arnold Schwarzenegger, Bonnie and Suzy Prudden, Bob Glover, and others—agree that children need, and indeed love, to move. The following suggestions might help you get started, but you will probably want to add your own ideas to the list.

- Plan some kind of physical activity for each day. To help make this work and make it fun, try:
  — Keeping a calendar of physical activity.
  — Turning off the TV; let your child choose a "break from television" day. If you make this seem special, she'll think it's a treat.

- Start walking places. For instance, walk with your child to school. You can plan a nature walk or play counting or rhyming games if the walk seems "too boring." Or if there is a younger child, let the older ones pull him in a wagon or push the stroller.

- Have a family Olympics, or maybe a neighborhood Olympics. Try to keep the competitive spirit down though, by awarding every child a prize. (See listings under "Books" for some ideas on non-competition.)

- The older school-age child may want to set personal goals and keep records. Some children love the idea of having a special notebook set aside for this.

- Active chores can be a fitness boost. Let your child help rake leaves; older kids may want to mow the lawn (with supervision).

- Consider participating in an organized sport with your child. Call the local YMCA/YWCA or a scouting troop to find out about parent-child teams.

- Hardy enough to plan a sports vacation? Maybe everybody would be totally jazzed by a ski trip at Christmas break or a walking tour of the moors in England. The point is not where you go, but that you impress your child with the fact that an active lifestyle is fun and adventurous.

- Plan a bike trip with the family or friends. Or you might make your child the coolest kid on the block by having a biking birthday party (bike to a nearby park and have the rest of the party there).

- Join the YMCA or YWCA. They have family events, or your child can take swimming or some other instruction while you work out.

- Just playing a game of tag is aerobic exercise for everybody, and there are few kids who will say no to a romp in the yard. Freeze tag is a good variation, or "sports freeze tag," which involves freezing in a sports pose (a baseball player swinging a bat, a gymnast on the balance beam).

- Have your child act out the movements of her favorite animal for a little aerobic fun.

- Let your child ride her bike alongside you if you like to jog or walk for exercise.

- Don't forget to be silly. Make working out fun. One fitness expert says her fitness class attendees balked at floor work but would do a dozen sit-ups during a Halloween theme class. She had them pretend they were Dracula rising from his coffin to shout, "I vant to drink your blood."

Chapter 10

Grooming and Clothes for Kids

GROOMING

Books

Braids and Bows: A Book of Instruction. By Anne Akers Johnson and Robin Stoneking. Klutz Press, 1992. 73 pages. A how-to book on braiding and tying hair in almost every imaginable style. Contains full-color photographs, illustrations, and step-by-step instructions. Comes with a box full of ribbons, elastic bands, barrettes, and other hair accessories. For ages six and up (with or without an adult's help).

Bringing Out Their Best: A Parent's Guide to Healthy Good Looks for Every Child. By Wende Devlin Gates. Bantam, 1992. 246 pages. Provides information and ideas to help parents bring out their child's natural beauty. Discusses the care of skin, teeth, and hair (including guidelines for a basic home haircut), as well as fashion, diet and nutrition, body image, exercise, and fitness.

CLOTHING

Mail Order Catalogs

After the Stork. 1501 Twelfth Street, N.W., Albuquerque, Mew Mexico 87104. Phone: 1/800-333-KIDS. This catalog offers a variety of comfortable kids clothes at outlet prices. Includes cotton fashions of all kinds (from tee shirts to overalls), layette items, school fashions, jackets, sweats, socks, and underwear. Sizes from newborn to children's size 14.

Biobottoms. P.O. Box 6009, Petaluma, California 94953. Phone: 1/800-766-1254. In addition to diaper covers, cloth diapers, and diaper accessories, this company sells clothing for children (sizes range from 3 months to children's 18/20) in 100 percent cotton and cotton/lycra combinations. For babies, there are snap-crotch outfits for quick diapering and a wide variety of sun bonnets. For older children, there are bike shorts, soccer pants, pull-on tees, sweatshirts, and more. Animals and floral patterns are popular, as are solid, primary colors. Biobottoms also sells shoes, socks, and belts. For more information, see listing under "Diapering."

Brights Creek. Bay Point, Hampton, Virginia 23653. Phone: 1/800-285-4300. Fax: 1/800-677-8687. This mail order catalog contains colorful clothing for kids (sizes from newborn through children's 16) at affordable prices. Items for newborns and infants include stretchies, bodysuits, drawstring gowns, caps, bibs, hooded cardigans, and long-sleeved coveralls. For older offspring (toddlers, preschoolers, and elementary school age kids), there are dresses, skirts, shirts, pants, overalls, shorts, bathing suits, jackets, and other items in cotton, polyester, and combination fabrics. Tie die, solid colors, floral designs and sports, super hero, and animal motifs are among the available patterns. Also sells belts, hats, socks, and shoes (sneakers, sandals, and dress shoes).

Children's Wear Digest. 31333 Agoura Road, Westlake Village, California 91361-4639. Phone: 1/800-242-KIDS. This catalog offers the latest in children's fashions. Earthlings' 100 percent organically grown cotton dresses and natural leggings; Tom and Jerry's pajamas in prehistoric (dinosaur) prints; Guess Kid's coordinates; Canoli Kids' 100 percent cotton flannel button-front dresses; Lyka Bear's wildlife coordinates (animal tops, shorts, pants, and caps);

and Sara's Prints 100 percent cotton short sets are just a few of the offerings. Children's sizes 2 through 16.

CW. One Clifford Way, Asheville, North Carolina 28810-1000. Phone: 1/800-633-3485. Offers durable clothing for girls, sizes 4 to 6X and 7 to 14. Specializes in colorful casual wear for school and play.

Hanna Andersson. 1010 Northwest Flanders, Portland, Oregon 97209. Phone: 1/800-222-0544. This catalog contains 100 percent cotton clothing of "Swedish quality" for babies and children from 6 to 110 pounds (uses metric sizes with conversion charts). Offers layette items in combed cottons and equally comfortable fabrics (including snapsuits, hooded towels, receiving blankets, hooded drawstring coverups, etc.), as well as pants, shirts, dresses, overalls, sun hats, jackets, shoes, socks, suspenders, belts, and other accessories. Also offers a selection of casual clothing for mothers.

Just for Kids. P.O. Box 29141, Shawnee, Kansas 66201-9141. Phone: 1/800-654-6963. Catalog full of kids clothing, accessories, and toys, many based on popular children's characters like Barney, Batman, and Barbie. The summer 1993 catalog offered bathing suits, sandals, hooded coverups, shorts, and sun hats, along with sand play sets, kid-sized beach chairs, inflatable pool racers, "bubble blasters," and a kid-size pool. Offers clothes for play, sports, and school, as well as sleepwear and rainwear. Shoes, socks, and hats are available as well. Sizes from children's 4 to 14.

Patagonia Kids. 1609 West Babcock Street, P.O. Box 8900, Bozeman, Montana 59715. Phone: 1/800-336-9090. An environmentally conscious mail order catalog printed on recycled paper and woven around ecologic themes. Specializes in outdoor clothing made from synthetic materials such as Synchilla® pile (a warm-as-wool, lightweight fabric that washes well). Jackets, coveralls, pants, and baby buntings are among the items made from these materials. Also sells shirts, pants, sweatsuits, and shorts made from 100 percent cotton, cotton/nylon, and cotton/rayon blends. One percent of sales are pledged to preservation and restoration of the natural environment.

Richman Cotton Company. 529 Fifth Street, Santa Rosa, California 95401. Phone: 707/575-8924 or 1/800-992-8924. A no-frills catalog full of affordable cotton items for babies and children, including snappies, crawlers, bubble pants, infant tanks, canvas aprons, pants, dresses, and jumpers. Also offers cloth diapers, Rubber Duckies® pull-on pants and wrap-up covers, and training pants. A small selection of books and tapes (for children and grown-ups), as well as toys and craft kits are listed too.

Fun Books for Kids

Getting Dressed. By Vicki Cobb. J. B. Lippincott, 1989. 31 pages. Presents simple historical background on the things that fasten our clothes—elastic, buttons, zippers, and sticky tapes. For children ages five to eight.

Keeping Clean. By Vicki Cobb. J. B. Lippincott, 1989. 32 pages. Most of us wash our face, brush our teeth, and comb our hair at least once a day, almost without thinking. But how does the water get into the bathtub? Who discovered soap and how is it made? And why is a brush better than a comb for getting out tangles? In this book for children, Vicki Cob explains in colorful detail how soap, toothpaste, and water help keep us clean and healthy. Imparts the importance of good hygiene in a lighthearted way. For children ages five to eight.

Chapter 11

Work and Child Care Options

CHILD CARE

General Resources

Free and Inexpensive Resources

Child Care Action Campaign (Information Guides). The Child Care Action Campaign offers a variety of information guides on child care (a partial listing follows). Up to three of these guides are available, free of charge, to nonmembers. Simply send a self-addressed, stamped, business-size envelope along with your request to Child Care Action Campaign, 330 Seventh Avenue, 17th Floor, New York, New York 10001. Phone: 212/239-0138.

Here is a partial listing of available guides:

Child-Care Policy
1. Current Child Care Legislation
2. Is Day Care Good for Children?
3. Facts about the Child Care Crisis

4. Where Are the Dollars for Child Care?
5. Do Criminal Record Checks Protect Children?

Child-Care Advocacy
6. How Civic Organizations Can Help Resolve the Child Care Crisis
7. How to Advocate for Child Care: A Guide for Parents
8. Local Governments and Child Care

Employers and Child Care
9. Speaking with Your Employer about Child Care Assistance
10. Employer Supported Child Care: Current Options and Trends
11. Examples of Corporate Involvement
12. Examples of Union Involvement

Information for Parents

13. Care for Your Child: Making the Right Choice
14. Family Day Care
15. School Age Child Care
16. How to Use the Federal Child Care Tax Credit
17. Questions and Answers about Infant and Toddler Care
18. Infectious Disease and Child Care
19. Finding Good Child Care: A Checklist
20. Finding and Hiring a Qualified In-Home Caregiver
21. Temporary Care for the Mildly Sick Child
22. Dealing with Sexual Abuse: A Guide for Parents

Child Care: What's Best for Your Family. This brochure explains what to look for in a day-care facility. Includes a detachable checklist for on-site inspections. Available from the American Academy of Pediatrics. Ask your pediatrician for a copy or send a self-addressed, stamped envelope to American Academy of Pediatrics, "Child Care: What's Best for Your Family" (see appendix I for contact information).

Early Childhood Program Accreditation: A Commitment to Excellence. A brochure for parents describing the accreditation process of the National Association for the Education of Young Children. Stresses its role in assuring high quality in early childhood programs. Available for 50¢ from the National Association for the Education of Young Children (see appendix I for contact information).

Finding the Best Care for Your Infant or Toddler. A brochure that helps parents make informed choices about the options for caring for infants and toddlers. Available for 50¢ from the National Association for the

Education of Young Children (see appendix I for contact information).

Getting the Most Out of Day Care. A free brochure available by writing Lysol Day-Care Brochure, P.O. Box 5440-N, Westbury, New York 11592-5440.

How to Choose a Good Early Childhood Program. A brochure explaining what to look for in a good program for your child. Available for 50¢ from the National Association for the Education of Young Children (see appendix I for contact information).

Selecting a Safe Day-Care Center. Free information packet available by contacting the National Safe Kids Campaign, 111 Michigan Avenue, N.W., Washington, D.C. 20010-2970.

What Are the Benefits of High Quality Programs? A brochure identifying research demonstrating that quality early childhood programs have lasting benefits for children, families, and society and are a cost-effective investment in our future. Available for 50¢ from the National Association for the Education of Young Children (see appendix I for contact information).

Where Your Child Care Dollars Go. A brochure explaining why child-care costs can seem high. Stresses the links between staff compensation and high-quality programs. Available for 50¢ from the National Association for the Education of Young Children (see appendix I for contact information).

Books

For Adults

Caring for Our Children. By the American Academy of Pediatrics with the American Public Health Association. 400 pages. A set of 981 national health and safety standards for out-of-home child-care programs. Addresses the needs of infants, toddlers, preschoolers, and school-age children through age twelve and provides information on such topics as food services, health policies, staffing, and age-appropriate activities. The development of the standards was funded by the U.S. Department of Health and Human Services. If your local library or child care center does not have a copy, you can order one from APHA Publication Sales, Department 5037, Washington, D.C. 20061-5073. Phone: 202/789-5636. The cost is $50 plus $7 shipping and handling.

Child Care that Works: How Families Can Share Their Lives with Child Care and Thrive. By Ann Muscari and Wenda Wardell Morrone. Doubleday, 1989. 256 pages. Offers advice to help parents make child care work. Explains how to share parenting effectively; build a trusting relationship with a caregiver; handle emergencies; resolve conflicts when they arise; and build a strong sense of family, even if your child spends more waking hours with others.

Choosing Child Care: A Guide for Parents. By Stevanne Auerbach. E.P. Dutton, 1981. 116 pages. Offers step-by-step advice for parents in search of quality child care. Includes a checklist to use in evaluating each type of facility and specific questions to ask of staff. Explains how to interview prospective baby-sitters as well.

The Complete Guide to Choosing Child Care. By Judith Berezin. Random House, 1990. 258 pages. From the National Association of Child Care Resource and Referral Agencies in cooperation with Child Care, Inc., this book discusses in-home care, family day care, child care centers, after-school care, and safety factors to consider when selecting child care. Offers checklists for making a choice

and important questions to ask caregivers. Includes a state-by-state listing of agencies that can help parents find quality child care.

Nothing but the Best: Making Daycare Work for You and Your Child. By Diane Lusk and Bruce McPherson. William Morrow, 1992. 383 pages. Not about how to choose day care—but how to live with it. Includes discussions of separation, toilet training, social life, curriculum, and teachers (caregivers).

The Parents' Guide to Daycare. By Jo Ann Miller. Bantam, 1986. 245 pages. A guide on how to select and evaluate child-care facilities, with an emphasis on health and safety. Also offers advice on making day care a positive experience. Includes tips on how to help your child adjust to separation, how to avoid morning and pickup hassles, and how to communicate effectively with the caregiver.

Sharing the Caring. By Amy Dombro. Simon and Schuster, 1991. 159 pages. Explains how to find the right child care and make it work for you and your child.

Who Cares for America's Children? Edited by Cheryl D. Hayes, John L. Palmer, and Martha J. Zaslow. National Academy Press, 1990. 362 pages. Drawing on existing data and research on trends in work, family, and child care, this book concludes that current child-care policies and programs in the United States are inadequate to meet current demands and projected future needs. Recommends research priorities and specific policy goals to ensure high-quality accessible care. Highlights a set of short-term priorities for immediate action.

For Children

Growing in Day Care. By Lynnrae and Steven Francis. Photographs by

Mark Bowers. Francis Family Publishing, 1991. Two family child-care providers use real-life photographs to follow one child as he plays, learns, and grows under their care. For children ages one to four (whether in home- or center-based care).

Mommy Don't Go. By Elizabeth Crary. Parenting Press. 32 pages. Part of "The Children's Problem Solving Series"—a collection of interactive picture books that invite young children to make their own decisions in difficult situations and see the possible consequences. Several alternatives are given for each issue, and there are no right or wrong answers. *Mommy Don't Go* is designed to help children (ages three to eight) cope with their feelings when a parent needs to leave. (Other books in the series include *I Can't Wait, My Name Is Not Dummy, I'm Lost, I Want It,* and *I Want to Play.*)

Periodicals

Child. P.O. Box 3176, Harlan, Iowa 51593-0367. Phone: 1/800-777-0222. Frequently contains feature articles on child care options and family-friendly work arrangements. Targeted at parents who have the financial resources to provide their children with quality products and services.

Working Mother. Customer Service Manager, P.O. Box 5239, Harlan, Iowa 51593-0739. Phone: 1/800-876-9414. This magazine contains news items and feature articles of interest to working mothers, including many on child-care options. Has published features which list and describe the best states for child care, the best day-care centers around the country, and the best after-school programs. Also publishes an annual list of family-friendly companies (each listing includes information on the company's child-care facilities and/or assistance programs, family leave policies, and work options—flextime, part time, job sharing, etc.).

Videotapes

The Daycare Dilemma. Childcare Concepts. Running time: 45 minutes. What should parents look for in a day-care center? This videotape offers guidelines to help parents evaluate centers, including the staff, regulations, safety procedures, and disciplinary measures. Includes a checklist for parents visiting centers and a discussion of the child's adjustment by a child psychologist. Available from PlayFair Toys (see chapter 27 for contact information).

Safe and Sound: Choosing Quality Child Care. Carle Media. Running time: 56 minutes. Narrated by Meredith Baxter-Birney, this video offers guidelines on finding good child care, including discussions of licensing and accreditation, health and safety, separation and attachment, and the importance of child/caregiver interaction, among other topics. Comes with a forty-six-page resource guidebook.

Helplines

Child Care Aware Resource Referral Line. Phone: 1/800-424-2246. Will refer parents to resource and referral agencies that provide information on child care in their area. These agencies are located throughout the United States (some of them require a modest fee for their services).

Child Care Information Service. National Association for the Education of Young Children. Phone: 1/800-424-2460. Provides information on various types of child-care programs and refers callers to child-care resources. Explains where parents can find accredited early-education programs in their area.

Dial a Nanny. Phone: 1/800-942-2278. Operated by Mother's Helper, a national nanny-placement agency. Will help callers locate a nanny. Charges a placement fee.

Associations

American Business Collaboration for Quality Dependent Care. Phone: 1/800-253-5264, ext. 4283. Coalition of 137 businesses working to improve child- and elder-care options around the country. Funds child-care projects such as provider training, child-care facility expansion, and school vacation programs. Participants include American Express, AT&T, Eastman Kodak, and Johnson & Johnson. If you think your employer might be interested in joining the coalition, call the above number for more information.

AuPair/Homestay USA. Experiment in International Living, 1015, Fifteenth Street, N.W., Suite 750, Washington, D.C. 20005. Phone: 202/408-5380. Since its inception in 1986, AuPair/Homestay USA has placed more than nine thousand *au pairs* with U.S. host families. Screens young women and men from other countries who provide child care in exchange for room, board, and family living in this country. Offers an information packet to families interested in hosting an *au pair*.

Au Pair in America. American Institute for Foreign Study, 102 Greenwich Avenue, Greenwich, Connecticut 06830. Phone: 203/869-9090 or 1/800-727-2437. Screens young women and men from other countries who provide child care in exchange for room, board, and family living in this country. Offers information on hosting an *au pair* in your home.

Child Care Action Campaign. 330 Seventh Avenue, 17th Floor, New York, New York 10001. Phone: 212/239-0138. A national advocacy organization working to increase and improve child-care services across the country. Analyzes existing services and identifies gaps. Works with communities in developing plans for quality child-care programs. Alerts the public on legislative action and child-care regulations in various states. Publishes a bimonthly newsletter on innovations in the field of child care for working parents and a variety of free information guides (see listings under "Free and Inexpensive Resources").

Child Care Employee Project. 6536 Telegraph Avenue, Suite A201, Oakland, California 94609. Phone: 510/653-9889. An advocacy group that seeks to improve salaries, working conditions, and the status of child-care providers. Is conducting a campaign to secure decent wages for child-care workers. Plans a "Worthy Wage Day" each year to encourage people to talk about the problem and work on viable solutions. Encourages parent involvement in this cause. Issues *Child Care Employee News,* a quarterly newsletter. Offers a packet of materials about the campaign and information about community efforts across the country.

Child Care Law Center. 22 Second Street, 5th Floor, San Francisco, California 94105. Phone: 415/495-5498. Produces *The Family Day Care Zoning Advocacy Guide,* which includes a state-by-state listing of child-care resource and referral agencies. These agencies can provide information on local child-care services and also help challenge local zoning laws that make if difficult for family child-care providers to take care of children in their homes.

The Family Day Care Advocacy Project. Children's Foundation, 725 Fifteenth Street, N.W., Suite 505, Washington, D.C. 20005. Phone: 202/347-3300. Provides Information and training for family day-care providers, advocates, and support groups. Publishes annually the *Directory of Family Day Care Associations and Support Groups,* which lists more than 1,000 groups across the country involved in family day care issues. Also publishes *The Family Day Care Licensing Study,* a state-by-state listing of family day-care regulations. Also offers fact sheets, handbooks, and a quarterly newsletter, *Family Day Care Bulletin,* which provides updates on legislation, insurance, zoning, and other topics related to family day care.

International Nanny Association. P.O. Box 26522, Austin, Texas 78755. Phone: 512/454-6462. Nonprofit association promoting in-home professional child care. Members include placement agencies, training programs, and nannies interested in upgrading the profession. Publishes a state-by-state directory of placement agencies that specialize in helping parents find live-in care. Also offers a directory of more than sixty nanny schools offering classes in child development, nutrition, safety, family relations, and play/learning activities for children.

National Association for Family Day Care. 725 Fifteenth Street, N.W., Suite 505, Washington, D.C. 20005. Phone: 202/347-3356 or 1/800-359-3817. Promotes high standards for all child-care operations. Offers a national voice for caregivers who provide child care services in a home setting. Runs an accreditation program. Will refer callers to an accredited provider in their area (if there is one) and also put them in touch with any local family day-care association. Members include parents, advocates,

---

The Nanny Kit

This kit offers information on finding and screening a live-in caregiver, determining legal obligations, and drawing up a contract. Organized in a loose-leaf binder, the kit includes general guidelines (written in straightforward text), sample forms, letters, and more. Available for $30 from a California-based nanny placement agency. For more information or to order a copy, call: 1/800-NANNY4U.

---

and providers of family day-care services.

National Association for the Education of Young Children (NAEYC). 1509 Sixteenth Street, N.W., Washington, D.C. 20036-1426. Phone: 202/232-8777 or 1/800-424-2460. Fax: 202/328-1846. A nonprofit professional organization of more than eighty thousand members dedicated to improving the quality of services provided to young children and their families. Provides educational opportunities and resources to promote the professional development of those working for and with young children. Works to increase public knowledge and support for high quality early childhood programs, including those at day-care centers and in family child-care homes. Offers advice and information on child-care programs (see Child Care Information Service, listed under "Helplines"). Offers an accreditation program. Available publications are described in NAEYC's early childhood resources catalog (see listing under "Mail Order Catalogs").

National Association of Child Care Resource and Referral Agencies (NACCRRA). P.O. Box 40246, Washington, D.C. 20016. Phone: 202/393-5501. A national membership organization of local child-care resource and referral agencies in all fifty states. Promotes the development, maintenance, and expansion of quality child care across the country, exercising policy leadership and promoting the growth and development of member agencies and services. Through its "Child Care Aware," campaign, NACCRRA seeks to help parents recognize and choose quality child care. As part of the campaign, the association operates a toll-free hotline to help parents locate local resource and referral agencies and services (see listing under "Helplines"). Another project designed for parents is *The Complete Guide to Choosing Child Care,* a book published by Random House as a joint venture between NACCRRA and Child Care, Inc., a resource and referral agency in New York City (see listing under "Books" for more information).

National Association of Hospital Affiliated Child Care Programs. Methodist Hospital Child Care Center, 2210 Joliet Avenue, Lubbock, Texas 79410. Phone: 806/792-9398. Fax: 919/990-6725. Hospital child-care programs typically offer evening and weekend child care. They sometimes have slots for the general public as well. Check with hospitals in your area or contact this association.

National Coalition for Campus Child Care. P.O. Box 258, Cascade, Wisconsin 53011. Phone: 414/528-7080. Promotes child-care centers on college campuses. Offers information on organizing and operating these centers. Offers a list of campus child-care facilities, as well as books and bibliographies. Also issues a semiannual newsletter.

School-Age Child Care Project. Wellesley College, Center for Research on Women, Wellesley, Massachusetts 02181. Phone: 617/431-1453. Committed to promoting and enhancing the development of child-care programs and services for children ages five through twelve, before and after school. Handles requests for information about school-age child care startup, development, and assessment. Publications include the *SACC Newsletter,* which reports on programs across the country, lists resources and upcoming conferences, and reviews books. Also offers a booklet called *When School's Out and Nobody's Home* and the book *School-Age Child Care: An Action Manual for the 90s* (published by Auburn House). Ask for the brochure listing available publications.

Baby-Sitter Training

Training Program

Safe Sitter. 1500 North Ritter Avenue, Indianapolis, Indiana 46219-3095. A national training program for children ages eleven to thirteen. Currently, more than 350 Safe Sitter courses are offered across the country, with fees ranging from $5 to $40. Write to Safe Sitter to find out about a class in your area—or to start your own Safe Sitter program.

Videotape

Supersitters. By Lee Salk. Running time: 30 minutes. Developed for parents to train their baby-sitters right in their own home and provide them with the information they will need

Finding Quality After-School Care for Your Child

The following advice comes from a pamphlet produced by Project Home Safe, a national initiative on latchkey children that was sponsored by American Home Economics Association and Whirlpool Foundation.

Your child's school day ends at 3:00 p.m., but your work day isn't over until 5:00 p.m. How will your child be cared for between the time he or she leaves school and the time you get home?

It's up to you to decide how to best answer that question. Although many children take care of themselves in their own homes after school, it's often better for them to be supervised by an adult.

Your Choices

Have you considered:

- **Changing your work schedule** so that you could be home when your child returns from school? Some employers allow flexible work hours or job sharing.

- **Hiring a friend, neighbor or relative** to care for your child in your home?

- **Arranging with neighbors** to have your child go to their home after school?

If none of the situations above is possible or suitable, you'll want to find a good child-care program for the times that school is not in session. Two options are:

- **A Family Day-Care Home**—where someone cares for a few children in her or his home.

- **A Child-Care Center**—where one or more staff care for a larger number of children. Many are located in schools, churches and community centers, as well as in child-care facilities.

Where to Look

Many local agencies and organizations have after-school programs for school-age children. You might check first with your local school district. Many schools offer before- and after-school care, sometimes called extended-day programs. Also, see if your employer has a program to help employees find school-age child care.

Other resources for finding out what's available in your community are:

- The Yellow Pages of your telephone book. Check the listings under "Child Care."

- Child-Care Referral Services. These groups, also listed in the yellow pages, will give you names of programs near you. Some referral services charge fees, others are free.

- The Licensing Division of your State Human or Social Services Department. This government agency can tell you where to find state-licensed programs in your area.

- Local churches, Community Centers or Civic Groups. Groups like the YM/YWCA or your local library may sponsor or know about after-school programs.

- Friends, Neighbors or Parents of Your Child's Classmates. They may tell you not only about programs they know of, but also their own experiences with these programs.

to provide good child care. Comes with an emergency care manual, medical release forms, and more. Approved by Parents' Choice. Available from the ICEA Bookcenter, International Childbirth Education Association, P.O. Box 20048, Minneapolis, Minnesota 55420. Phone: 1/800-624-4934.

Grandparents Raising Grandchildren

Programs

The Brookdale Grandparent Caregiver Information Project. Phone: 510/643-6427. Among its offerings, this group issues a free newsletter offering updates on family-related legislation and listings of resources for grandparents who provide care for their grandchildren.

Grandparents Raising Grandchildren. P.O. Box 104, Colleyville, Texas 76034. Phone: 313/646-7191. Will help grandparents who are the primary caregivers for their children's children find or start a local support group. For more information, send a self-addressed, stamped envelope (58¢ postage).

Resources for Employers (and Employees)

Book

DCAP Handbook: A How-to Manual for Employers and Employees on the Dependent Care Assistance Program. Published by the Massachusetts Public Interest Research Group Education Fund, this handbook explains how employers can set up dependent-care accounts, which offer working parents significant tax savings on child-care expenses. To order a copy, call 617/292-4800.

Database

The Human Resource Information Network. A database containing information on more than seventy thousand child-care centers and family-care homes across the country. Those who have access to the network simply key in the age of their child, their geographical location, and the type of care they are looking for. The database will call up a list of possibilities. The network also provides profiles on local schools, job openings, and other information of interest to working parents. If your company does not yet subscribe, perhaps you can put in a recommendation that they begin to (an annual subscription costs $950). For more information, call 1/800-421-8884 or fax 317/872-2059.

Mail Order Catalog

Childhood Resources Catalog. From the National Association for the Education of Young Children, this catalog describes books, brochures, videotapes, posters, information kits, and other materials for teachers, child-care providers, parents, and others interested in early education programs. Some of the titles described within include:

The Demand and Supply of Child Care in 1990
Employer-Assisted Child Care Resource Guide
Family Day Care: Out of the Shadows and Into the Limelight

Information Kit on Employer-Assisted Child Care

Keeping Current in Child Care Research: An Annotated Bibliography

Quality in Child Care: What Does Research Tell Us?

What Is Quality Childcare?

For a copy of the catalog, contact the National Association for the Education of Young Children (see appendix I for contact information).

Government Agency

Administration for Children and Families. Department of Health and Human Services, 370 L'Enfant Promenade, S.W., Washington, D.C. 20447. Phone: 202/401-9215. Administers a variety of programs to help low-income families obtain child-care services. *Assistance is available at the state level* through the following four programs:

At-Risk Child Care. Gives states the option of providing child care to low-income working families who are not receiving AFDC (Aid to Families with Dependent Children); who need child care in order to work; and who would be at risk of becoming dependent on AFDC if they did not receive child-care assistance. States may provide child care in the following ways:

- Directly;
- By arranging care through providers;

- By providing cash or vouchers in advance to the family;
- By reimbursing the family; or
- By adopting other arrangements as the state agency deems appropriate.

The Child Care and Development Block Grant. Government funds are made available to states, Indian tribes, and territories to provide grants, contracts, and certificates for child-care services for low-income families. To be eligible, a family must need child care because a parent is working or attending a training or educational program (or because the family receives or needs to receive protective services).

Child Care for AFDC Recipients. Title IV-A Child Care provides funds for applicants and recipients of Aid to Families with Dependent Children through the AFDC and Job Opportunities and Basic Skills Training (JOBS) programs. This financial support allows these individuals to pursue employment or work training and approved education that will help them become economically self-sufficient.

Transitional Child Care. Transitional child care continues child-care assistance for up to twelve months after a recipient stops receiving AFDC as a result of increased work hours or higher wages.

Latchkey Children

Free and Inexpensive Resources

Child Alone. This twenty-four-page pamphlet discusses home-alone safety, as well as safety to and from school. Latchkey care, strangers, traffic, and recreation are among the topics explored. Available for $1.20 by contacting the National Safety Coun-

cil, 1121 Spring Lake Drive, Itasca, Illinois 60143. Phone: 1/800-621-7619.

Kids with Keys . . . Parents with Jobs . . . Who's in Charge? This brochure offers practical advice for parents considering leaving their children in self-care for part of the day. Offers options and what kids who stay home alone need to know. For a free copy, send a self-addressed, stamped business-size envelope along with your request to the National PTA (see appendix I for contact information).

Books

For Adults

The Handbook for Latchkey Children and Their Parents. By Lynette and Thomas Long. Arbor House, 1983. 316 pages. Describes the latchkey phenomenon and suggests ways for parents to make the best of this sometimes less-than-ideal option. Offers advice on relieving the unspoken fears and special stresses placed on latchkey children. Explains how to teach your child to become self-sufficient and prepare your child for an emergency. Currently out of print (check your local library).

Latchkey Kids: Unlocking Doors for Children and Their Families. By Bryan E. Robinson, Bobbie H. Rowland, and Mick Coleman. Lex-

ington Books, 1986. 220 pages. Suggests measures that families, schools, businesses, and government can take to address the needs of latchkey children. Points out that there are workable latchkey arrangements as well as harmful ones. Contains case studies. Offers alternatives such as after-school hotlines and extended day programs at public schools.

For Children

Alone After School. By H. L. Swan and V. Houston. Prentice-Hall, 1985. 200 pages. A self-care guide for latchkey children and their parents.

On My Own. By Lynette Long. Acropolis Books, 1984. 160 pages. A self-care book for kids on their own. Includes more than one hundred different activities for eight- to twelve-year-olds.

School's Out. By Joan M. Bergstrom. Revised edition. Ten Speed Press, 1990. 330 pages. A resource to help elementary school children make good use of their out-of-school time.

WORK OPTIONS FOR PARENTS

Books

General

The Best Jobs In America—For Parents Who Want Careers and Time for Children Too. By Susan Bacon Dynerman and Lynn O'Rourke Hayes. Rawson Associates, 1991. 243 pages. Provides negotiating tips and suggests strategies for parents in search of flexible work options and family-friendly work environments. Discusses work options such as flextime, job sharing, telecommuting, shortened work weeks, and extended parental leave. Offers tools to use in presenting your case to a skeptical

boss. Case studies show that it's possible to balance work and family, when employers are flexible. Concludes with profiles of twenty-five companies that allow work flexibility. Also contains a resource guide listing national associations, as well as state-by-state listings.

Companies that Care. By Hal Morgan and Kerry Tucker. Simon and Schuster, 1991. 351 pages. The authors present profiles of family-friendly companies across the country, including information on family policies, workplace flexibility, childcare assistance, and family-support programs.

Children at Home Alone

From *Children: Virginia's Greatest Resource,* developed by the Virginia Department of Social Services, the National Committee for Prevention of Child Abuse (Virginia Chapter), and Parents Anonymous of Virginia, Inc.

There is no magic age when a child is ready to stay by himself. All children are different, but a child under eight should never be left alone. To help you make a decision, consider the following:

- How does the child feel about the situation?

- Look at his age in relationship to his maturity, behavior, and judgment.

- What are the responsibilities your child will be left with?

- Will he be able to handle those responsibilities?

- How long will he/she be left alone? The first few times should be quite short. You will be able to stay away longer once he feels more confident about his safety.

- What are the safety risks if your child is alone? (fires, accidents, burglaries, etc.)

- Can your child say no to peer pressure if friends encourage him to break rules in your absence?

Whether children are at home every day after school or once in a while when parents need to run errands, the experience can be made safer and more fun with some of the following tips:

- Remove fire hazards and install smoke detectors. Hold fire drills with each child "practicing" what he is to do and where he is to go.

- Teach the children basic first aid and have a first aid kit available.

- Have the children rehearse emergency (911) calls giving their full address and directions if necessary.

- It is important that ground rules be established. This avoids confusion about what you expect and adds to the child's own sense of security. Careful planning can help ensure physical safety and emotional well-being for your child.

- Review safety rules, such as not playing with matches, knives, or scissors.

- Have a clear understanding about use of ovens, stoves, and other appliances.

- Instruct children not to tell callers they are alone. They should say that the parent is busy and offer to take a message. If a call seems suspicious, they should call the parent or another adult.

- Warn children never to allow strangers into the house.

- Encourage the child to discuss feelings about being alone. If a child seems afraid, help him to talk about it and help him feel safe.

- Set up an emergency plan with a relative, friend, or neighbor who may be unable to care for your child but would be willing to be called by the child for advice and reassurance in "small emergencies" when the parent is unavailable by phone.

- When you leave, post the house address and important phone numbers near the telephone.

- Establish a daily routine in which your child calls you or the designated person when he arrives home.

- If your child comes home after school, give him/her keys and an attractive key chain. The keys should be carried out of sight so that the child isn't easily identified as one on his own.

- Provide at-home projects and materials as well as juice and nutritious snacks.

- Arrange some after school activities such as clubs, scouts, sports, or library. If you need help with transportation, make arrangements to trade weekend driving or sitting.

- Afterward, praise your child for doing a good job. You may be pleasantly surprised at how readily and how well he assumes responsibility when prepared and given the opportunity.

Downshifting: Reinventing Success on a Slower Track. By Amy Saltzman. HarperCollins, 1991. 238 pages. Drawing on in-depth interviews with sociologists, career consultants, human resource specialists, and professionals themselves, the author demonstrates how it is possible to find professional fulfillment and happiness on a slower track.

The Job-Sharing Handbook. By Barney Olmsted and Suzanne Smith. Penguin, 1983. 199 pages. A basic guide to an increasingly popular work option. Includes case studies of job-sharing arrangements in a variety of fields. Offers advice on negotiating salaries and benefits, along with worksheets on dividing workloads and assessing partner compatibility.

Juggling: The Unexpected Advantages of Balancing Career and Home for Women and Their Families. By Faye Crosby, Ph.D. The Free Press, 1991. 269 pages. The author argues that women who juggle home and work—who concurrently play different life roles—are more likely to escape from the worst aspects of any one role and, as a result, be less prone than other women to depression. Argues that children benefit from the working mother's increased sense of well-being.

More Work for Mother: The Ironies of Household Technology from the Open Hearth to the Microwave. By Ruth Schwartz Cowan. Basic Books, 1983. 257 pages. Taking a look at technology in the home, the author shows how mothers' workloads have actually *increased* with the introduction of each new invention designed to save time. "Time-saving" inventions such as electric ovens, vaccuum cleaners, and washing machines have led to higher expectations and a higher standard of living (gourmet meals, spotless floors, and clean clothes daily). This, in turn, has led to a dramatic increase in the number of hours women are required to spend on housework.

Of Cradles and Careers: A Guide to Reshaping Your Job to Include a Baby in Your Life. By Kaye Lowman. New American Library, 1985. 267 pages. A La Leche League International book, *Of Cradles and Careers* contains stories of women who have pioneered changes in the American workplace to make them more responsive to the needs of mothers and babies. Explores various work options (including part-time work, job sharing, and self-employment), choices in child care, and the balance between working and parenting.

The Overworked American: The Unexpected Decline of Leisure. By Juliet B. Schor. HarperCollins, 1991. 247 pages. Shows how the demands of employers and the addictive nature of consumption have led to increasingly long work hours in the United States. Discusses the time squeeze at home, the insidious cycle of work-and-spend (and the steps we might take to change this cycle), and the options we have as a society to make time for play and pleasure.

The Part-Time Solution: The New Strategy for Managing Your Career while Managing Motherhood. By Charlene Canape. Harper and Row, 1990. 278 pages. Includes information and guidance on various part-time work options, including job sharing.

The Second Shift: Working Parents and the Revolution at Home. By Arlie Hochschild, Ph.D., and Anne Machung. Viking, 1989. 309 pages. A study documenting the dual burden of responsibility that the typical working wife and mother bears.

Sequencing. By Arlene Rossen Cardozo. Macmillan, 1989. 332 pages. Mothers do not need to choose between their careers and their children according to this book. Rather, they can view their life as a sequence of phases, staying home while their children are young and returning to the workforce when their children are no longer as dependent. Outlines the change in thinking that allows women with children and careers to have it all—but not all at once.

Working and Caring. By T. Berry Brazelton, M.D. Addison-Wesley, 1985. 197 pages. Offers advice to working parents, including professional couples and single mothers. Follows three different families as they grapple with important issues such as child-care arrangements and family leave policies. Brazelton goes one step further in recommending national policies to help make America better suited to meet the needs of working parents and their offspring.

The Working Mother's Guilt Guide: Whatever You're Doing, It Isn't Enough. By Mary C. Hickey and Sandra Salmans. Viking Penguin, 1992. 150 pages. Takes a humorous look at the occupational hazards of working motherhood.

Working Parent—Happy Child. By Caryl Waller Krueger. Abingdon Press, 1990. 317 pages. Explains how parents can successfully combine working and parenting. Offers guidelines to help balance job and family.

Your Rights in the Workplace. By Dan Lacey with the editors of Nolo

Press. Nolo Press, 1992. A book on workplace rights, including sections on the rights of pregnant women, maternity leave, health care insurance, and parents' workplace rights. Discusses federal and state laws. Suggests ways to balance work and family.

Bargaining for Family Benefits
Bargaining for Family Benefits: A Union Members Guide. By the Coalition of Labor Union Women. Although this booklet is targeted at union members who want family benefits written into their contracts, it can also be useful to nonunion employees seeking to create more family-friendly work environments. Outlines current develops concerning family leave, flexible work options, child care, and parents' benefits. Offers case studies in flexible workplaces for parents, as well as negotiating tools for persuading bosses to develop profamily policies. Available for $5.00 from the Coalition of Labor Union Women, 15 Union Square, New York, New York 10003. Phone: 212/242-0700.

For Children
A Million Moms and Mine. Explores the advantages and disadvantages of having a working mother, from an elementary-school child's point of view. Touches upon the often conflicting emotions children experience when their mom works outside the home. Written and illustrated by and for children (ages seven to twelve) as part of the national Women's Work program (Liz Claiborne's public-arts project addressing women's issues). To order a copy, contact Liz Clairborne Women's Work, P.O. Box 726, Department A, Radio City Station, New York, New York 10101.

Periodicals
Work and Family Life. 6211 West Howard, Niles, Illinois 60714. Phone: 202/265-1282 or 1/800-676-2838. A monthly newsletter that focuses on balancing work and family life, produced by the Bank Street College of Education. Discusses topics related to parenting, child care, marriage, and work, including nutrition, health, and family finances. Offers suggestions for making time with children more rewarding.

Working Mother. Customer Service Manager, P.O. Box 5239, Harlan, Iowa 51593-0739. Phone: 1/800-876-9414. Targeted at mothers who juggle work and family, this magazine contains news items and articles on work options (flextime, part time, job sharing, etc.), office savvy, child care, family leave policy, etc. Also contains articles on parenting, child development, health and safety, and other topics of interest to parents (whether they work outside the home or not).

Hotline
Job Survival Hotline. Phone: 1/800-522-0925 (toll-free hotline operating Monday through Friday, 10:00 a.m. to 4:00 p.m., eastern standard time). Operated by 9to5, an advocacy organization for working women and their families, this hotline offers answers to questions concerning maternity benefits, family leave, flexible work options, discrimination, and other workplace issues. (For more information on 9to5, see listing under "Associations.")

Associations
The Association of Part-Time Professionals. Crescent Plaza, Suite 216, 7700 Leesburg Pike, Falls Church, Virginia 22043. Phone: 703/734-7975. Promotes flexible work alterna-

tives, including part-time work, job sharing, and home-based work. Offers career counseling, as well as a job referral service. Advocates equitable compensation and benefits for part-time employees. Offers information on negotiating part-time employment and benefits. Publishes *Working Options*, a monthly newsletter providing information on trends, topics, and developments relating to flexible work alternatives. Also offers a forty-one-page selected bibliography on flexible work options and the *Part-Timer's Resource Kit,* containing information on alternative work schedules, answers to frequently asked questions, and a resource listing.

Catalyst. 250 Park Avenue South, New York, New York 10003. Phone: 212/777-8900. A national nonprofit organization working to promote positive change for women (including working mothers) in the workplace. Conducts research and provides consultation services (primarily to businesses). Offers publications covering flexible work options.

Families and Work Institute. 330 Seventh Avenue, 14th Floor, New York, New York 10001. Phone: 212/465-2044. Fax: 212/465-8637. Conducts studies and offers educational programs on business, government, and community efforts to help families balance their work and family responsibilities. Has created the Family-Friendly Index which can be used by large companies to compare their work-family policies—child-care provisions, work schedules, etc.— with those of other large companies. Provides information on work/family consultants, who can advise companies on child care and flexible work schedules for their employees. Offers a variety of publications, including *The Corporate Reference Guide to Work-Family Programs,* which evaluates corporate family-friendliness.

> **The "Mommy Track"**
>
> A term created by the media to describe a work option for working mothers proposed by Felice Schwartz in an article for the *Harvard Business Review.* In the article, Schwartz argues that women are more expensive for employers because of their childrearing responsibilities. She recommends that employers identify the minority of women who put their careers first (and offer them opportunities for advancement) and suggests that women who want more time for their families be offered flexible schedules, including part-time work, job sharing, and flextime. Working mothers who choose such options would be taken off the fast track and asked to accept a lower rate of pay.

Labor Force Participation of Dual-Earner Couples and Single Parents and *Productivity Effects of Workplace Child Care Centers* are also among the institute's offerings.

National Federation of Business and Professional Women's Clubs, Inc. 2012 Massachusetts Avenue, N.W., Washington, D.C. 20036. Phone: 202/293-1100. Encourages public- and private-sector responsiveness to the needs of working women on issues such as child care and pay equality. Publishes *National Business Woman,* a bimonthly paper containing associations news along with articles exploring issues such as pay equity.

New Ways to Work. 149 Ninth Street, San Francisco, California 94103. Phone: 415/552-1000. Offers

Some Work Options for Parents

The Compressed Work Week. A full week's work is completed in less than five days (for example, four ten-hour days or three twelve-hour days)

Flextime. Rather than work from 9:00 to 5:00, flextime workers might work from 7:00 to 3:00, 8:00 to 4:00, or other hours, depending on the employer's policies.

Home-Based Businesses. Self-employment can eradicate commuting hassles and allow parents more time with their children.

Job Sharing. When two people share the same job. One employee might work Mondays and Wednesdays, the other Tuesdays, Thursdays, and Fridays.

Part-Time Work. Working thirty or fewer hours a week.

Taking Your Child to Work. Some employers allow new parents to bring their babies to work with them.

Telecommuting. Working for an outside employer in the privacy of one's home. Computers, modems, fax machines, and other technology make this possible.

Temporary/Seasonal Work. Work accomplished within a specific time frame (days, weeks, months). Can be taken on as schedules allow (or as pocketbooks dictate), with no long-term commitment required.

information and support to individuals and organizations interested in new work options, including job sharing, flextime, and compressed work weeks. Provides information on work/family consultants who can advise companies on child care and flexible work schedules for their employees. Publishes a variety of materials on flexible workplace benefits, including resource guides for professionals in the fields of education, health care, and law. Also publishes *Work Times,* a quarterly newsletter.

9to5, National Association of Working Women. 614 Superior Avenue, N.W., Room 852, Cleveland, Ohio 44113. Phone: 216/566-9308 or 1/800-522-0925 (toll-free hotline). A grassroots advocacy organization for working women and their families.

Among its various activities, 9to5 conducts research and produces studies on family leave policy, maternity benefits, flexible work options, and other workplace issues. Operates a toll free "job survival hotline" (see listing under "Hotlines" for more information).

Women Employed. 22 West Monroe Street, Chicago, Illinois 60603. Phone: 312/782-3902. Works to improve job opportunities for women. Conducts advocacy efforts on equitable pay and family leave, among other areas. Analyzes government programs and employer policies that affect women. Recommends public and corporate policy changes.

Help from the Government

The Women's Bureau. U.S. Department of Labor, 200 Constitution Avenue, N.W., Washington, D.C. 20210. Phone: 1/800-827-5335. Maintains the Work and Family Issues Clearinghouse—a source of information on work options (flextime, part-time, job sharing, etc.), child-care arrangements, and policy. Can provide information to help working parents secure flexible benefits in the workplace. Offers a publications catalog.

PARENTS AT HOME FULL-TIME

Mothers at Home

Books

Discovering Motherhood. Edited by Heidi L. Brennan, Pamela M. Goresh, and Catherine H. Myers. Mothers at Home, 1991. 82 pages. A collection of essays, poems, advice, and resources for at-home mothers (or those who would like to be at home). Breastfeeding, adoption, and family finances are among the topics explored.

The Heart Has Its Own Reasons: An Inspirational Resource Guide for Mothers Who Choose to Stay Home with Their Young Children. By Mary Ann Cahill. New American Library, 1983. 340 pages. This La Leche League International publication acknowledges the importance of parent/child togetherness and offers advice on saving and earning money at home while raising children. Currently out of print (check your local library).

Home by Choice. By Brenda Hunter, Ph.D. Multnomah Press, 1991. 233 pages. For mothers who choose to stay home full-time with their children (and for those who are contemplating this option), this book offers advice to help maximize the season of childrearing. Addresses the devaluation of motherhood by the media and explains how at-home mothers can respond. Discusses the psychological factors behind a mother's choice to return to work or stay home and explains what future career success an at-home mother can hope to achieve. Calls for mothers to come home—both physically and emotionally.

A Mother's Work. By Deborah Fallows. Houghton Mifflin, 1985. 243 pages. Discusses the importance of parents in the lives of children and the respectable (if not respected) position of at-home mother. Offers an overview of child-care options in the United States. Describes in detail the all-too-frequent benign neglect of children placed in day-care centers. Written by a mother who chose to set aside her career in linguistics in order to raise her two sons at home.

No Place Like Home. By Linda Weltner. William Morrow, 1988. 288 pages. A collection of essays on being at home (raising children, entertaining guests, managing family life, etc.). Explores the joys, as well as the challenges.

Sequencing. By Arlene Rossen Cardozo. Macmillan, 1989. 332 pages. Mothers do not need to choose between their careers and their children according to this book. Rather, they can view their life as a sequence of phases, staying home while their children are young and returning to the workforce when their children are no longer as dependent. Outlines the change in thinking that allows women with children and careers to have it all—but not all at once.

Staying Home: From Full-Time Professional to Full-Time Parent. By Darcie Sanders and Martha M. Bullen. Little, Brown, 1992. 239 pages. Offers advice to mothers taking a hiatus from their professional careers in order to rear their children full-time. Explains how to make the transition; how to create a new self-image; how to find support groups; and how to help influence public policy on families, work life, and child care. Also discusses work options for at-home mothers (home-based businesses, community work, etc.).

Staying Home Instead: Alternatives to the Two-Paycheck Family. By Christine Davidson. Revised edition. Macmillan, 1992. For parents who are tired of juggling home, family, and work, this book takes a look at other alternatives, including part-time work, job sharing, and home-based businesses.

Associations

FEMALE (Formerly Employed Mothers at the Leading Edge). P.O. Box 31, Elmhurst, Illinois 60126. Phone: 708/941-3553. A national support and advocacy group for mothers taking time out from paid employment to raise their children at home. More than forty chapters nationwide. Issues *FEMALE Forum*, a monthly newsletter featuring personal accounts of life at home, interviews, book reviews, and more. Also offers chapter start-up materials.

Home by Choice. P.O. Box 103, Vienna, Virginia 22183. Phone: 703/242-2063. A national Christian organization for mothers who choose to be at home. Refers mothers to local support groups and offers assistance in starting one up. Issues a bimonthly newsletter.

(The National) MOMS Club. 814 Moffatt Circle, Simi Valley, California 93065. Phone: 805/526-2725. The MOMS (Moms Offering Moms Support) Club is a nonprofit organization for mothers who choose to stay home with their children full-time or part-time. Fifty groups, located in more than twenty states across the country, provide support by conducting meetings, organizing local playgroups, and arranging babysitting co-ops. Chapters also participate in child-related community service work such as fund-raising events for children's shelters. Publishes a newsletter highlighting club events, as well as a how-to manual on starting up a local chapter.

Mothers at Home. 8310-A Old Courthouse Road, Vienna, Virginia 22182. Phone: 703/827-5903. A nonprofit organization devoted to the support of mothers who choose (or would like to choose) to be at home to nurture their families. Serves as a forum for the exchange of information among members. Conducts research, compiles statistics, sponsors seminars, and provides information at congressional hearings. Publishes *Welcome Home*, a monthly magazine aimed at boosting the morale and image of mothers at home. Approved by Parents' Choice, this publication includes stories of mothers' struggles and successes, articles on parenting, essays about the memorable moments and humorous episodes, analyses of public policy, and reviews of available resources.

Mothers' Home Business Network. P.O. Box 423, East Meadow, New York 11554. Phone: 516/997-7394. Publishes a quarterly newsletter, *Homeworking Mothers*. Offers information, advice, and support to mothers who choose to work at home so they can earn income and remain the primary caregivers for their children. Publication offerings include *Kids and Career: New Ideas and Options for Mothers* and *Mothers' Home Businesspages: A Resource Guide for Homeworking Mothers.*

Fathers at Home

Books

Being a Father—Family, Work and Self. Edited by Anne Pedersen and Peggy O'Mara. John Muir, 1990. 161 pages. From *Mothering* magazine, this book offers insights for men who want to share the parenting of their children equally. Through personal accounts, men here illuminate the struggles, frustrations, and joys of modern fatherhood. Balancing work and family life, coparenting after divorce, fathers as sons, and sexuality are among the topics explored.

Between Father and Child. By Ronald F. Levant and John Kelly. Viking, 1989. 236 pages. Shows how fathers can strengthen the relationships they have with their children. Drawing on the experiences of fathers who participated in the Fatherhood Project at Boston University, the author presents solutions to common problems that arise between fathers and their children. Conflict resolution, opening channels of communication, addressing difficult subjects (such as sex and drugs), and better understanding of how children think and feel are all addressed in this book.

The Birth of a Father. By Martin Greenberg, M.D.. Continuum, 1985. 198 pages. Provides a first-person account of a young doctor's experience of becoming a father, as well as practical advice on parenting. Family bonding, the tyranny of an infant's crying, and solutions to parent burnout are among the topics explored. Also discusses the ways in which fathers fall in love with their offspring.

Fatherhood Today: Men's Changing Role in the Family. Edited by Phyllis Bronstein and Carolyn Pape Cowan. John Wiley, 1988. 364 pages. In this book, leading experts in pediatrics, psychology, sociology, and social work describe research on the changing role of fathers in today's American family. Discusses how the age of a father affects his approach to parenting; the changes men undergo with fatherhood; and the role the father plays in his children's development. Includes a section on programs to help fathers adjust to their role as a parent.

The Father's Almanac. By S. Adams Sullivan. Revised edition. Doubleday, 1992. 391 pages. This sourcebook offers hundreds of ideas and suggestions for hands-on dads. Diapering, discipline, rough-house play, computers, television, and rainy-day activities are among the topics explored. The new edition also discusses the deepening involvement of fathers in the lives of their young children.

Fathers, Sons, and Daughters. Edited by Charles S. Scull, Ph.D. Jeremy P. Tarcher, 1992. 262 pages. A collection of poems, stories, and essays exploring the emerging meanings of fatherhood. Among the many contributors are Bill Cosby, Sherwood Anderson, and Robert Bly.

Finding Time for Fathering. By Mitch Golant, Ph.D., and Susan Golant, M.A. Fawcett Columbine, 1992. 288 pages. Explains how fathers can share more of their lives with their children—in work, chores, and play.

Discusses child development and parenting approaches. Suggests dozens of father/child activities. Also discusses the role of the father in the family (past and present), the father's influence on a child's development, and the formation of the father/child bond.

The Nurturing Father. Kyle Pruett, M.D. Warner Books, 1987. 322 pages. Reveals the significant benefits for children whose fathers are actively involved in their care: in self-esteem, sexual identity, cognitive development, and social relatedness. Introduces readers to stay-at-home fathers and to the children they are raising. Challenges long-held assumptions about paternal nurturing.

Staying Home: From Full-Time Professional to Full-Time Parent. By Darcie Sanders and Martha M. Bullen. Little, Brown, 1992. 239 pages. Much of the information and advice provided for full-time mothers will be equally useful to full-time fathers. Discusses work options for parents at home (telecommuting, home-based businesses, etc.). Includes a section on how to help influence public policy on families, work life, and child care. (See "Books" listed under "Mothers at Home" for more information.)

Staying Home Instead: Alternatives to the Two-Paycheck Family. See "Books" listed under "Mothers at Home."

Periodical

Full-Time Dads. Big Daddy Publications, P.O. Box 577, Cumberland Center, Maine 04021. A bimonthly journal targeted at stay-at-home dads. Feature articles cover a wide range of topics, including family finances and parent/child communication. Includes book reviews, an events calendar, and a forum for readers. Sample copies are available for $5.00 (annual subscriptions cost $26.00).

Association

Fatherhood Project. c/o Families and Work Institute, 330 Seventh Avenue, 14th Floor, New York, New York 10001. Phone: 212/268-4846. Fax: 212/465-8637. Encourages the development of new options for male involvement in childrearing. Serves as a national clearinghouse for information on programs that encourage father-participation. Conducts research on innovative programs and policies supporting men in nurturing roles.

Chapter 12

Life Changes and Family Options

MOVING

Resource Packet

Smooth Moves for Families with Kids: Resources to Help Your Family Adjust to Relocation. One of Parent Action's "Short Cuts" resource packets, which contain brochures, fact sheets, check lists, and recent articles to help families cope with transition or crisis. For a copy of "Smooth Moves for Families with Kids," send $1.60 along with your request to Parent Action, 2 North Charles Street, Suite 960, Baltimore, Maryland 21201. Phone: 410/727-3687.

Resources for Children

Books

Gila Monsters Meet You at the Airport. By Marjorie W. Sharmat. Illustrated by Byron Barton. Macmillan, 1980. 32 pages. A young boy's preconceived notions of life in the West make him apprehensive about the family's move from the East. He then meets a boy who has fears in the opposite direction. For children ages four to nine. Note: A Reading Rainbow selection, *Gila Monsters Meet You at the Airport* is also available on videocasette. To order a copy of the *Gila Monsters* program, contact GPN, University of Nebraska-Lincoln, P.O. Box 80669, Lincoln, Nebraska 68501-0669. Phone: 402/472-1785.

I'm Not Moving, Mama! By Nancy White Carlstrom. Macmillan, 1990. 32 pages. Mouse keeps telling Mama why he refuses to move from their cozy home. While Mama continues to pack up the family belongings, she explains why she can't leave Mouse behind, offering assurance that their new home will be just fine. For ages three to six.

Moving. By Fred Rogers. Putnam Publishing Group, 1987. 32 pages. Part of the "First Experience Books" series by the host of "Mister Roger's Neighborhood." Designed to lessen the younger child's fear of the unknown and encourage parents and children to talk together about feelings and concerns. Illustrated with full-color photographs.

Stars for Sarah. By Ann Turner. HarperCollins, 1991. 32 pages. Lying awake in bed one night, Sarah worries about moving to a new house. Her mom comes and reassures her that some things will, indeed, change, but the most important things will remain the same. For children ages four to eight.

Videotape

Let's Get a Move On! Kidvidz. A Price Stern Sloan Video. Running time: 30 minutes. A child's video guide to the family move. Designed to make the transition as painless as possible. Winner of the Parents' Choice Honor Award. For ages four to ten.

LOSS (DEATH, GRIEF)

Books

For Adults

Books to Help Children Cope with Separation and Loss. By Joanne E. Bernstein and Masha K. Rudman. R. R. Bowker, 1988. Volume 3. An annotated bibliography of books for children ages three to sixteen. Included are more than six hundred books that focus on themes of separation and loss. Each entry includes a review of the book's plot and themes, along with bibliographic information.

The Grieving Child: A Parent's Guide. By Helen Fitzgerald. Simon and Schuster, 1992. 207 pages. Offers practical advice for helping a child cope with the death of a parent or loved one. Offers guidance on visiting the seriously ill or dying; using language appropriate to the child's age level; selecting useful books about death; handling especially difficult situations, including murder and suicide; and deciding whether a child should attend a funeral.

Talking about Death: A Dialogue between Parent and Child. By Earl A. Grollman. Third edition. Beacon Press, 1991. 128 pages. A guide to help parents talk about death with a child. The first portion of the book can be read by school-age children. The second part is a guide for the parent. Includes a listing of resources.

Tough Questions: Talking Straight with Your Kids about the Real World. By Sheila Kitzinger and Celia Kitzinger. Harvard Common Press, 1991. 306 pages. Encourages parents to communicate openly with their children, exploring hard-to-talk-about topics such as sex, birth, death, religion, and prejudice.

For Children

Charlotte's Web. By E. B. White. HarperCollins, (1952). 184 pages. E. B. White tells the tale of the innocent pig, Wilbur, who is saved from slaughter by his spider friend, Charlotte. A rich story about the cycle of life (and the fear of death). A Newbery Honor book. For ages eight and up.

How It Feels when a Parent Dies. By Jill Krementz. Alfred A. Knopf, 1988. 128 pages. Children of different ages and backgrounds describe how it feels when a parent dies. For middle readers.

I'll See You in My Dreams. By Mavis Jukes. Alfred A. Knopf, 1993. 40 pages. As a girl prepares to visit her seriously ill uncle, she imagines being a skywriter and flying over his bed with a message of love (and a final farewell).

Nana Upstairs and Nana Downstairs. By Tomie dePaola. Putman Publishing Group, 1973. 32 pages. As an adult, Tommy remembers his frequent visits as a child to the house of his energetic grandmother ("Nana Downstairs") and his bedridden great-grandmother ("Nana Upstairs"), both of whom he loved a great deal. Even now Tommy can see his Nanas' spirits in the form of shooting stars. For children in grades one through three.

On the Wings of a Butterfly: A Story about Life and Death. By Marilyn Maple, Ph.D. Parenting Press, 1992. 32 pages. A story about a young girl with a terminal illness who befriends a caterpillar about to transform into a butterfly. The two discover they have something in common and support each other through their changes. For children in grades one through six.

The Tenth Good Thing about Barney. By Judith Viorst. Atheneum, 1971. 32 pages. When a cat named Barney dies, his young owner struggles to think of good things about his pet. In the process, he tackles the issues of life and death. For children in kindergarten through fourth grade.

When a Pet Dies. By Fred Rogers. Putnam Publishing Group, 1988. 32 pages. In clear language, this book talks about what happens when a pet dies. Part of the "First Experience Books" series by the host of "Mister Roger's Neighborhood." For ages four to eight.

ADOPTION

Books

For Adults

Adoption: A Handful of Hope. By Suzanne Arms. Celestial Arts, 1989. 436 pages. Using case studies, the author shows what adoption means to those involved in the process (the children, adoptive parents, and women who plan to have their babies adopted). Sheds light on the adoption process and shows how it can be improved. Describes how open adoption has changed families' lives during the past decade.

The Adoption Resource Book. By Lois Gilman. Third edition. Harper Perennial, 1992. 421 pages. Offers an overview of domestic and foreign adoption, including details about agencies, home studies, paperwork, and legal issues. Offers information to help couples or individuals investi-gate adoption alternatives and arrange for and complete successful adoptions. Includes listings of nearly one thousand domestic agencies, along with the names and addresses of parent groups, exchanges, and public service offices.

The Adoption Resource Guide. By Julia L. Posner. Child Welfare League of America, 1990. 754 pages. Includes profiles of licensed adoption agencies across the country. Tells prospective parents the cost of the placement service, how long the waiting period is, the ages of children placed, and whether the agency does placements in other states or internationally. Also describes policies on one-parent adoptions and other nontraditional arrangements. Available from the Child Welfare League of America, 440 First Street, N.W., Suite 310, Washington, D.C. 20001. Phone: 202/638-2952.

Thinking About Adopting?

Adopting a child is a complicated matter, requiring much thought before-hand and many tough decisions throughout the process. Be sure at the outset to take the time to examine your own motives and needs. In *The Adoption Resource Book* (Third edition, Harper Collins, 1992), author Lois Gilman asks, "Is adoptive parenthood or even parenthood itself what you really want? Your own feelings will influence the type of child you seek and will have a direct impact on the child you raise." The following list of questions to reflect on is adapted from Gilman's book.

- How important is it for you to be a parent?

- Is it important to you to experience your own pregnancy?

- How important is it for you to parent an infant?

- Are you confident you can offer a child a healthy family life?

- Have you already considered alternative ways, beside adoption, by which you could in effect be a parent?

- If you have a fertility problem, how have you addressed it?

- Are you grieving over a list child?

- How would you describe your ideal "fantasy child"?

- How do you feel about parenting a child who is not biologically related to you?

- What are your fears about being an adoptive parent?

- What risks are you willing to take?

- Can you love a child for what she or he is, rather than for what you hope the child will become? Can you accept a child who is very different from yourself?

- What do you imagine you would do if your adopted child turned out to have unusual needs you hadn't anticipated?

- Your adopted child is definitely going to wonder about his or her genetic parents and think about how they relinquished him or her. Are you willing to explore these issues together with the child?

- How does your spouse feel about each of these issues? How do other members of your family feel? How important to you are the feelings about adoption that your extended family may have?

- Do you have the perseverance to adopt a child?

Are Those Kids Yours? By Cheri Register. The Free Press, 1991. 240 pages. Offers answers to central questions about international adoption. Addresses ethical issues inevitably raised by adoption across lines of culture, race, and social class.

The Private Adoption Handbook.
By Stanley B. Michelman and Meg
Schneider with Antonio Van Der Meer.
Dell Publishing, 1990. 228 pages. A
book for prospective parents who
choose to bypass adoption agencies
and find a birth mother on their own.

Report on Foreign Adoption. International Concerns Committee for
Children. 160 pages. Issued annually,
this report lists agencies that arrange
foreign adoptions, as well as a country-by-country overview of adoption.
Available from the International Concerns Committee for Children, 911
Cypress Drive, Boulder, Colorado
80303. Phone: 303/494-8333.

For Children

The Day We Met You. By Phoebe
Koehler. Bradbury Press, 1990. 40
pages. An introduction to adoption
for very young children. Combines illustrations with a few simple words
to express the warm feelings behind
each action on the day adoptive parents first meet their child. For children from birth to age five.

A Forever Family. By Roslyn Banish
with Jennifer Jordan-Wong. Harper-
Collins, 1992. 44 pages. This book
explains what it feels like to be
adopted. Written from the perspective of an adopted eight-year-old who
first lived with her biological parents
and then in foster homes. For ages
four to twelve.

How It Feels to Be Adopted. By Jill
Krementz. Alfred A. Knopf, 1988.
128 pages. Nineteen youngsters explain how it feels to be adopted, including the good parts and the
not-so-good parts. Recommended for
older children.

Mulberry Bird. By Anne B. Brodzinsky. Perspectives Press, 1986. 48
pages. A story about a mother bird
who decides to place her baby bird
up for adoption. Helps explains why

a mother might plan adoption for her
child. For children ages four to
twelve.

**Through Moon and Stars and
Night Skies.** By Ann Turner. Harper-
Collins, 1992. 32 pages. A Reading
Rainbow selection, this book describes a young boy's journey
"through moon and stars and night
skies" to his new home in America.
At first he's frightened, but then he
begins to recognize things from the
pictures he was sent—his new house,
the dog, and the faces of his new parents. For children ages two to ten.

Periodicals

**OURS: The Magazine of Adoptive
Families.** Adoptive Families of America, 3333 North Highway 100, Minneapolis, Minnesota 55422. Phone:
612/535-4829. A ninety-six-page
magazine for adoptive families, issued six times a year.

Roots and Wings. P.O. Box 638,
Chester, New Jersey 07930. "For families and friends touched by adoption," this magazine contains
features, advice, reviews, and columns. Issued quarterly.

Videotape

**Adoption: Two Different Kinds of
Love.** Family Matters Productions.
Running time: 80 minutes. Offers a
clear picture of the independent
adoption process, including the emotions and feelings that go along with
it. Includes interviews with birth
mothers and adopting couples. Available from Family Matters Productions, 8383 Wilshire Boulevard, Suite
750, Beverly Hills, California 90211.
Phone: 1/800-321-2138.

Mail Order Catalogs

Adoption Book Catalog. Tapestry
Books, P.O. Box 359, Ringoes, New

Jersey 08551-0359. Phone: 908/806-6695 or 1/800-765-2367. This catalog lists and describes a wide variety of books on adoption for both children and adults. Offers books on open adoption, international adoptions, special-needs adoptions, adopting older children, and many other special areas of interest, as well as general titles on adoption, the adoption process, and raising adopted children. Also included are fiction and nonfiction titles for children of all ages.

Adoptive Parenting Resources. See Adoptive Families of America, listed under "Associations."

Associations

Adoptive Families of America. 3333 North Highway 100, Minneapolis, Minnesota 55422. Phone: 612/535-4829. A nonprofit organization providing problem-solving assistance and information about the challenges of adoption to members of adoptive and prospective adoptive families. Seeks to create opportunities for successful adoptive placement and promotes the health and welfare of children without permanent families. Has 275 adoptive parent support groups worldwide. Maintains a twenty-four-hour-a-day helpline. Provides information on adoption leave and companies that offer it. Will direct prospective parents to local resources. Publishes a bimonthly called *Ours* (for more information, see listing under "Periodicals"). Offers the fifty-six-page *How-to-Adopt Information Packet,* containing information on adoption agencies, independent adoption, national organizations, and adoptive parent support groups. Also issues Adoptive Parenting Resources, a mail order catalog that lists and describes dozens of books and cassettes for parents, families, and children.

American Academy of Adoption Attorneys. P.O. Box 33053, Washington, D.C. 20033-0053. Offers a state-by-state directory of adoption attorneys (names, addresses, and phone numbers are also listed alphabetically). Write for a copy.

American Adoption Congress. 1000 Connecticut Avenue, N.W., Suite 9, Washington, D.C. 20036. Phone: 202/483-3399. Serves as a public information center on adoption and related issues. Also conducts research, develops educational programs, and sponsors conferences. Refers members to local adoption services, search services, and support groups. Available publications include an annual legislative update and a bibliography. Also publishes *Decree* (issued quarterly).

Committee for Single Adoptive Parents. P.O. Box 15084, Chevy Chase, Maryland 20825. Phone: 202/966-6367. An organization of single persons who have adopted or wish to adopt children. Offers assistance. Provides information on legislation and research related to single-person adoption. Produces a directory of adoption agencies that will accept single-person applications.

Families Adopting Children Everywhere (F.A.C.E.). P.O. Box 28058, Northwood Station, Baltimore, Maryland 21239. Phone: 410/488-2656. Offers support services to adoptive parents and their families. Disseminates information concerning adoption. Advocates children's rights. Conducts research programs. Publishes *FACE Facts,* a bimonthly magazine covering adoption issues. Also produces *The FACE Adoption Resource Manual,* which lists adoption agencies and other resources.

International Concerns Committee for Children. 911 Cypress Drive, Boulder, Colorado 80303. Phone:

303/494-8333. Helps those interested in adopting children from foreign countries. Although this is not a child placement agency, the committee helps educate prospective parents on the adoption process, informs them on the availability of "waiting children" in the United States and abroad, and provides personal counseling for adoptive parents. Disseminates information by adoption experts. Offers the *Report on Foreign Adoption,* which lists agencies that arrange foreign adoptions, as well as a country-by-country overview of adoption (for more information, see listing under "Books").

National Adoption Center. 1500 Walnut Street, #701, Philadelphia, Pennsylvania 19102. Phone: 215/735-9988 or 1/800-862-3678 (1/800-TO-ADOPT). Promotes adoption opportunities for children with special needs, including minority, handicapped, and older children, as well as sibling groups. Provides information on adoption, including updates on adoption leave and companies that offer it. Offers matching referral services for children and potential adoptive parents and maintains computerized listings of both children and prospective parents. Operates the National Adoption Network linking states, adoption agencies, and other interested groups. Publishes *National Adoption Center News,* a semiannual newsletter. Also produces brochures, pamphlets, a bibliography, films, and videotapes.

National Adoption Information Clearinghouse. 11426 Rockville Pike, Suite 410, Rockville, Maryland 20852. Phone: 301/231-6512. Fax: 301/984-8527. Answers questions about adoption and provides referrals to adoption experts. Issues fact sheets, brochures, and reports covering a wide range of adoption topics. Also publishes directories listing adoption agencies, support groups,

training programs, and crisis pregnancy centers (the NAIC publication and services catalog contains a complete list of titles). Maintains full-text copies of every state's adoption laws and all federal laws concerning adoption. Offers a catalog of audiovisual materials on adoption, as well. Maintains a three thousand volume library.

National Foster Parents Association, Information and Services Office, 226 Kitts Drive, Houston, Texas 77024. Phone: 713/467-1850. Seeks to identify and help meet the needs of children in foster care and those who care for them. Works to improve the foster parenting image. Encourages mandatory parenting skills training. Informs foster parents of their legal rights. Offers assistance to state and local foster parent associations. Publishes *National Advocate,* a bimonthly tabloid covering legislation and issues related to foster care.

North American Council on Adoptable Children. 1821 University Avenue, Suite N-498, St. Paul, Minnesota 55104. Phone: 612/644-3036. Serves as clearinghouse for information on adoption. Believes that every child has a right to a permanent, loving home. Provides assistance to state and local child advocacy efforts. Sponsors annual Adoption Awareness Month. Publishes *Adoptalk Newsletter,* a quarterly newsletter for members, as well as other materials on adoption.

Resolve, Inc. National Office, 1310 Broadway, Somerville, Massachusetts 02144-1731. Phone: 617/623-0744. Offers support, counseling, and referrals to those experiencing problems of infertility and others striving to build a family. Issues a starter kit, called "Exploring Adoption," for prospective parents investigating that option (the kit contains fact sheets and a newsletter). Offers a variety of materials on various aspects of infertility.

STEPFAMILIES

Resource Packet

Yours, Mine, Ours: Resources for Building a Successful Stepfamily. One of Parent Action's "Short Cuts" resource packets, which contain brochures, fact sheets, check lists, and recent articles to help families cope with transition or crisis. For a copy of "Yours, Mine, Ours," send $2.25 along with your request to Parent Action, 2 North Charles Street, Suite 960, Baltimore, Maryland 21201. Phone: 410/727-3687.

Books

For Adults

Living in Step. By Ruth Roosevelt and Jeannette Lofas. McGraw-Hill, 1977. 192 pages. This book explores the many issues facing stepparents, and offers practical advice. The authors are stepparents themselves.

Making Peace in Your Stepfamily. By Harold H. Bloomfield, M.D., with Robert Kory. Hyperion, 1993. 284 pages. A guide to stepfamily life. Offers exercises, case studies, and techniques to deal with stepfamily conflicts and problems.

The Stepfamily: Living, Loving and Learning. By E. Einstein. Macmillan, 1982. 210 pages. Offers information and advice on how stepfamilies can realize their potential for happiness. Examines each family member's role within the context of the group. Shows how stepfamilies can overcome some of the more common stresses.

Stepmothers: Keeping It Together with Your Husband and His Kids. By Merry Bloch Jones and Jo Ann Schiller. Carol Publishing Group, 1992. 188 pages. The dozens of stepmothers interviewed for this book present a true-to-life picture of life in a stepfamily. In recounting their experiences, these women describe daily life, changes in routines and lifestyles, discipline, and other important issues. Offers encouragement, guidance, and support.

For Children

The Boys and Girls Book about Stepfamilies. By Dr. Richard A. Gardner. Creative Therapeutics, 1985. 180 pages. Helps children living in stepfamilies face the challenges with realistic expectations and develop coping skills. Assures them that things will be all right. For children ages six to twelve.

My Mother Got Married (and Other Disasters). By Barbara Park. Alfred A. Knopf, 1989. 128 pages. A story about a boy who eventually learns to accept his stepfamily. For children in grades three to seven.

Sam Is My Half Brother. By Lizi Boyd. Puffin Books, 1992. 32 pages. A story about a young girl who discovers how good it feels to help care for her new half brother. For children ages four to nine.

Talking about Stepfamilies. By Maxine B. Rosenberg. Bradbury Press, 1990. 160 pages. In this book, children and adults from different families explain what it feels like to be part of a stepfamily (whether the family came about because of divorce, a first-time marriage, or the death of a spouse). For children in grades four to seven.

What Am I Doing in a Stepfamily? By Claire Berman. Lyle Stuart, 1982. 48 pages. Written for children who have a parent remarrying, this book offers straightforward information and reassurance that things will work out. For ages six to ten.

Periodical

Life in Step. 7 South Lincoln Street, Hinsdale, Illinois 60521. A quarterly newsletter focusing on solutions to adjustment problems in stepfamilies. A free sample copy is available with a self-addressed, stamped, business-size envelope.

Associations

The Stepfamily Association of America. 215 Centennial Mall South, Suite 212, Lincoln, Nebraska 68508. Phone: 402/477-7837. Offers a support network and serves as a national advocate for stepparents and their children. Works to improve the quality of life for stepfamilies. Provides educational services. Publishes *Stepfamilies,* a quarterly. Also produces books, a bibliography of books, research reports, and articles covering issues of importance to stepfamilies.

The Stepfamily Foundation. 333 West End Avenue, New York, New York 10023. Phone: 212/877-3244 or 1/800-SKY-STEP. Gathers and disseminates information on stepfamilies and stepfamily relationships. Offers over-the-phone counseling and makes referrals. Publishes *Step News,* a quarterly newsletter. Also offers books, pamphlets, audiocassettes, and videotapes on common stepfamily concerns.

GAY AND LESBIAN PARENTS

Book

The Lesbian and Gay Parenting Handbook. By April Martin, Ph.D. HarperCollins, 1993. 395 pages. Drawing on interviews with families and experts and her own personal and professional experience, psychologist April Martin walks readers through the many issues involved in forming and nurturing a lesbian or gay family, including the decision to parent (or not to parent); different options for creating a family (including adoption, surrogacy, and artificial insemination); legal considerations; relationships and communications within the family; the needs of the children; etc. Includes a detailed resource section with listings of organizations and parenting groups.

Association

Gay and Lesbian Parents Coalition International. P.O. Box 50360, Washington, D.C. 20091. A coalition of lesbian and gay parenting groups across the country. Provides information, education, and support services. Sponsors an annual conference for gay and lesbian parents and their children. Publishes a newsletter for gay parents, as well as a publication for their children. Also offers bibliographies for gay and lesbian families.

DIVORCE

Resource Packet

Separation and Divorce: Resources for Revival. One of Parent Action's "Short Cuts" resource packets, which contain brochures, fact sheets, check lists, and recent articles to help families cope with transition or crisis. For a copy of "Separation and Divorce," send $4.25 along with your request to Parent Action, 2 North Charles Street, Suite 960, Baltimore, Maryland 21201. Phone: 410/727-3687.

Books for Adults

For the Sake of the Children. By Kris Kline and Stephen Pew. Prima Publishing, 1992. 250 pages. Explains how to share your children with your ex-spouse, in spite of your anger.

Growing Up with Divorce: Helping Your Child Avoid Immediate and Later Emotional Problems. By Neil Kalter. Fawcett Columbine, 1991. 416 pages. Offers strategies for parents and professionals to help children cope with their anxiety, anger, and confusion, and avoid emotional problems that may arise immediately or develop over the years.

Helping Children Cope with Divorce. By Edward Teyber, Ph.D. Free Press, 1992. 221 pages. An experienced clinician, the author shares his own observations on divorce, along with research findings regarding the effects of divorce on children. Offers advice for parents and children alike. Winner of the 1992 *Child* Magazine Book Award for Excellence in Family Issues.

Mom's House, Dad's House. By Isolina Ricci. Macmillan, 1982. 270 pages. A book about shared custody, and how to make it work.

The Parent's Book about Divorce. By Richard A. Gardner, M.D. Second edition. Creative Therapeutics, 1991. 385 pages. Written by one of the country's leading experts on divorce, this book offers guidance and advice.

Second Chances: Men, Women, and Children a Decade after Divorce. By Judith Wallerstein and Sandra Blakeslee. Ticknor and Fields, 1989. 329 pages. An account of the long-term emotional, economic, and psychological effects of divorce on children and adults, based on a ten-year longitudinal study.

Talking to Your Child about a Troubled World. By Lynne S. Dumas. Random House, 1992. 335 pages. Guides parents in approaching difficult subjects—AIDS, sexual abuse, divorce, war, etc.—with their children. Provides parents with the tools and language they need to address these important issues.

Vicki Lansky's Divorce Book for Parents. By Vicki Lansky. NAL-Dutton, 1991. 250 pages. Helps parents guide children through divorce. Explains how to tell the children, how to handle the holidays, and how to keep your ex-spouse from becoming an ex-parent. Dating, "divorce-speak," and other topics are also addressed.

Resources for Children

Books

At Daddy's on Saturdays. By Linda W. Girard. Illustrated by Judith Friedman. A. Whitman, 1987. 32 pages. At first Katie was sad and angry when her dad moved out. But with reassurance from mom, she learns to accept her father's absence and looks forward to her weekly visits at his new home. For ages four to ten.

The Dinosaurs Divorce: A Guide for Changing Families. By L. K. Brown and M. Brown. Little, Brown, 1988. 32 pages. A book to help children understand, accept, and cope with divorce, presented in a nonthreatening (and often amusing) way using a cast of dinosaurs. For children from preschool through grade three.

The Divorce Workbook. By Sally B. Ives, David Fassler, and Michele Lash. Waterfront Books, 1985. 160 pages. Contains candid thoughts from children who have gone through their parents' divorce or separation. Illustrated, with occasional handwritten passages from kids. Describes divorce, marriage, and separation. Asks young readers how they might express anger and sorrow, and encourages them to respond on the pages. For children ages four to twelve.

How It Feels when Parents Divorce. By Jill Krementz. Alfred A. Knopf, 1988. 128 pages. Girls and boys from ages eight to sixteen talk about divorce in their own families.

Game

My Two Homes. A boardgame designed to help children understand and accept divorce. Comes with two sets of playing cards ("Factual" and "Situational") to help children better understand divorce and learn positive coping skills. For two to six players, ages six to twelve. Available from Childswork/Childsplay (for contact information, see chapter 27).

Newsletter

K.I.D.S. Express. P.O. Box 782, Littleton, Colorado 80160-0782. A newsletter about divorce that encourages children to explore and express their feelings. Includes an advice column,

letters from other children whose parents are divorced, and activities that help teach coping skills. Issued monthly.

Associations

Joint Custody Association. 10606 Wilkins Avenue, Los Angeles, California 90024. Phone: 310/475-5352. Provides information on joint custody. Assists parents, counselors, and others in implementing joint custody practices. Surveys court decisions and their consequences.

Mothers without Custody. P.O. Box 27418, Houston, Texas 77227-7418. Phone: 713/840-1622. An association of women living apart from one or more of their minor children. Helps establish local self-help groups. Offers support to women exploring their child custody options.

Parents Sharing Custody. 420 South Beverly Drive, Suite 100, Beverly Hills, California 90212-4410. Phone: 310/286-9171. An association of parents sharing custody of children after divorce. Educates parents on maintaining their parental roles and works to protect the rights of children.

Parents without Partners. See "Associations" listed under "Single Parenting."

United Fathers of America. 595 City Drive, Suite 202, Orange, California 92668. Phone: 714/385-1002. Offers information, counseling, and support services to individuals whose families are disrupted due to divorce. Monitors legislation on custody and divorce. Conducts research. Seeks to establish equal rights for fathers with regard to child custody and to provide the best possible environment for the child.

Women on Their Own. See "Associations" listed under "Single Parenting."

SINGLE PARENTING

Inexpensive Resource

Parenting on Your Own. A set of fourteen pamphlets for single parents published by the University of Illinois, in conjunction with the U.S. Department of Agriculture Extension Service. Covers issues such as time management and the sharing of parenting responsibilities. The set is available for $3.00 from Robert Hughes, University of Illinois, 115 Child Development Lab, 1105 West Nevada, Urbana, Illinois 61801.

Books

For Adults

Operating Instructions. By Anne Lamott. Pantheon Books, 1993. 240 pages. A single mother chronicles the first year of her son's life.

Positive Discipline for Single Parents. By Jane Nelson, Cheryl Erwin, and Carol Delzer. Prima Publishing, 1993. 196 pages. A guide to help single parents raise children who are responsible, respectful, and resourceful.

The Single Mother's Book. By Joan Anderson. Peachtree Publisher, 1990. 352 pages. A practical guide to managing your children, career, home, finances, and everything else.

Single Parents by Choice. By Naomi Miller, Ph.D. Insight Books, 1992. 239 pages. This book investigates the reasons behind the intentionally decision men and women make to become single parents. Takes a look at four separate groups of single parents, including single adoptive mothers and fathers, divorced parents who have decided not to remarry, single biological mothers, and gay and lesbian parents.

For Children

The Boys and Girls Book about One-Parent Families. By Dr. Richard A. Gardner. Creative Therapeutics, 1983. 122 pages. Reassures children in single-parent families that things will work out. Helps them face the challenge with realistic expectations and develop coping skills. For children ages six to twelve.

My Kind of Family: A Book for Kids in Single Parent Homes. By Michele Lash, Sally Ives Laughridge, and David Fassler. Waterfront Books, 1990. 208 pages. Written from the young child's perspective, this book is about single-parent homes and the people who live in them. Explores the various reasons why children might live in a single-parent family, including death, divorce, guardianship, or birth outside of marriage. Encourages kids to confront their feelings and ask questions. Provides space for children to express their own thoughts and ideas. For ages of five and twelve.

Associations

National Organization of Single Mothers. P.O. Box 68, Midland, North Carolina 28107-0068. Phone: 704/888-KIDS. Helps new members form or join local support groups. Publishes *SingleMOTHER,* a bimonthly newsletter offering information and advice, plus tips that can save single mothers time and money. (For a free sample copy, send a self-addressed, business-size envelope with 52¢ postage.)

Parents without Partners. 8807 Colesville Road, Silver Spring, Maryland 20910. Phone: 301/588-9354. Membership organization made up of 145,000 single parents. Offers education and referral services. Organizes social events for single parents. Conducts research on topics associated with single parenthood. Publishes *The Single Parent,* a bimonthly magazine.

Single Mothers by Choice. P.O. Box 1642, Gracie Square Station, New York, New York 10028. Phone: 212/988-0993. An organization of single professional women who either have or are considering having children outside of marriage. Offers support and information to women who are considering adoption as single parents. Also provides information on artificial insemination and other routes to conception.

Single Parent Resource Center. 141 West Twenty-eighth Street, New York, New York 10001. Phone: 212/947-0227. Offers a start-up manual for single parents who would like to or-

ganize a support group. Working to establish a network of local single parent groups so that such groups will have a collective political voice.

Unwed Parents Anonymous. P.O. Box 44556, Phoenix, Arizona 85064. Phone: 602/952-1463. Offers support to unwed parents. Provides information and advice on childrearing, child care, relationships, finances, and other issues affecting parent and child. Issues a variety of informational pamphlets.

Women on Their Own. P.O. Box 1026, Willingboro, New Jersey 08046. Phone: 609/871-1499. Offers information, referral services, and support to single, divorced, separated, or widowed women raising children on their own. Also conducts workshops and seminars. Produces a periodic newsletter, as well as a membership directory.

CHILD SUPPORT

Associations

American Child Support Collection Association. Children's Services, P.O. Box 691067, San Antonio, Texas 78269. Phone: 1/800-729-2445. A national network of professional agencies that specialize in child support collection. Will put callers in touch with the nearest agency.

Association for Children for Enforcement of Support. 723 Phillips Avenue, Suite 216, Toledo, Ohio 43612. Phone: 1/800-537-7072. A nonprofit agency that offers advice on obtaining child support. Offers a handbook called *How to Collect Child Support,* as well as an information packet. Will put callers in touch with their local chapter (there are 250 across the country).

National Child Support Advocacy Coalition. P.O. Box 4629, Alexandria, Virginia 22303. Phone: 908/828-2901. Affiliates of this organization conduct workshops on starting the collection process, obtaining a support order (a legal document ordering a parent to supply support), and shopping for legal assistance. Active in more than thirty states across the country.

Government Resources

Office of Child Support Enforcement. Administration for Children and Families, U.S. Department of Health and Human Services, 370 L'Enfant Promenade, S.W., Fourth Floor, Washington, D.C. 20447. The goal of this federal program, carried out by state and local Child Support

Enforcement (CSE) offices, is to ensure that children are financially supported by both of their parents. The program helps parents locate an absent parent for child support enforcement, establish paternity if necessary, determine child support obligations, and enforce child support orders (legal documents ordering a parent to provide support). To learn how to apply for enforcement services, parents should contact their local CSE office. In most states, CSE offices are listed under the human services agency in the local government section of the telephone directory. If you cannot find a listing, you can call the human services agency information operator, who should be able to give you the number, or contact your state CSE agency (see listing that follows). (For more information on the Child Support Enforcement Program, you can write to the Office of Child Support Enforcement at the address listed above.)

Alabama. Phone: 205/242-9300.
Alaska. Phone: 907/276-3441.
Arizona. Phone: 602/252-0236.
Arkansas. Phone: 501/682-8398.
California. Phone: 916/654-1556.
Colorado. Phone: 303/866-5998.
Connecticut. Phone: 203/566-3053.
Delaware. Phone: 302/421-8300.
District of Columbia. Phone: 202/724-5610.
Florida. Phone: 904/488-9900.
Georgia. Phone: 404/894-4119.
Hawaii. Phone: 808/587-3712.

Idaho. Phone: 208/334-5710.
Illinois. Phone: 217/782-1366.
Indiana. Phone: 317/232-4894.
Iowa. Phone: 515/281-5580.
Kansas. Phone: 913/296-3237.
Kentucky. Phone: 502/564-2285.
Louisiana. Phone: 504/342-4780.
Maine. Phone: 207/289-2886.
Maryland. Phone: 410/333-3979.
Massachusetts. Phone: 617/621-4200.
Michigan. Phone: 517/373-7570.
Minnesota. Phone: 612/296-2499.
Mississippi. Phone: 601/354-0341.
Missouri. Phone: 314/751-4301.
Montana. Phone: 406/444-4614.
Nebraska. Phone: 402/471-9125.
Nevada. Phone: 702/885-4744.
New Hampshire. Phone: 603/271-4426.
New Jersey. Phone: 609/588-2361.
New Mexico. Phone: 505/827-7200.
New York. Phone: 518/474-9081.
North Carolina. Phone: 919/571-4120.
North Dakota. Phone: 701/224-3582.
Ohio. Phone: 614/752-6561.
Oklahoma. Phone: 405/424-5871.
Oregon. Phone: 503/378-5439.
Pennsylvania. Phone: 717/787-3672.
Rhode Island. Phone: 401/277-2409.
South Carolina. Phone: 803/737-5870.
South Dakota. Phone: 605/773-3641.
Tennessee. Phone: 615/741-1820.
Texas. Phone: 512/463-2181.
Utah. Phone: 801/538-4400.
Vermont. Phone: 802/241-2319.
Virginia. Phone: 804/662-9629.
Washington. Phone: 206/586-3162.
West Virginia. Phone: 304/348-3780.
Wisconsin. Phone: 608/266-1175.
Wyoming. Phone: 307/777-7892.

Chapter 13

Education

PREPARING YOUR CHILD FOR SCHOOL SUCCESS

Free and Inexpensive Resources

Becoming Your Child's First Teacher. A guidebook for parents of preschoolers, explaining how they can help their children develop creativity, imagination, and communication skills before formal education begins. For a free copy, write Snyder Communications, 6903 Rockledge Drive, 15th Floor, Bethesda, Maryland 20817. Phone: 1/800-654-ROCK, ext. 51.

Help Your Young Child Learn at Home. This PTA (Parent Teacher Association) brochure offers guidelines for teaching young children at home. Included are ways to instill a love of learning, to motivate, and to help children succeed in school, as well as activities to make learning enjoyable. For a free copy, send a self-addressed, stamped, business-size envelope along with your request to the National PTA (see appendix I for contact information).

Helping Your Child Get Ready for School. By Nancy Paulu. U.S. Department of Education, Office of Educational Research and Improvement, 1992. 58 pages. One in a series of booklets on different education topics intended to help parents make the most of their child's natural curiosity. Describes the qualities and skills children need to get a good start in kindergarten; explains what to expect from preschoolers each year from birth to age five; suggests activities that can help preschoolers grow and develop; and offers advice on making the adjustment to kindergarten an easy one. (For information on ordering government publications, see appendix B.) Inquire about price. Request S/N 065-000-00522-1.

Helping Your Child Succeed in School. By Dorothy Rich. U.S. Department of Education, Office of Educational Research and Improvement, 1992. 48 pages. One in a series of booklets on different education topics intended to help parents make the most of their child's natural curiosity. Includes home learning activities for children ages five to eleven adapted from programs of the Home and Learning Institute (see listing under "Associations"). Talks about what's necessary for school success and explains when parents should talk to teachers and how to handle parent-teacher conferences. (For information on ordering government publications, see appendix B.) Inquire about price. Request S/N 065-000-00523-9.

The Little Things Make a Big Difference. A booklet containing tips on home activities that will help children be successful in school. For a free copy, send a self-addressed, stamped envelope to World Book Educational Products, Station 9/NAESP, 101 Northwest Point Boulevard, Elk Grove Village, Illinois 60007. Phone: 1/800-621-8202. (A videotape by the same name can be rented at Blockbuster video stores, free of charge. For more information on the video, see listing under "Videotapes.")

Your Home Is Your Child's First School. This brochure discusses the role of the parent as teacher and offers suggestions to help develop visual, listening, language, social, emotional, and intellectual skills in children. For a free copy, send a self-addressed, stamped envelope along with your request to the International Reading Association (see appendix I for contact information).

Books

Awakening Your Child's Natural Genius. By Thomas Armstrong, Ph.D. Jeremy P. Tarcher, 1991. 268 pages. Armstrong argues that every child is a genius, and explains how parents can help their child realize his or her true gifts. Discusses learning in the home, conventional school learning, the whole-language approach to reading and writing, hands-on science, math, history, play and toys, music, drawing, computers, television, "giftedness," alternatives to standardized testing, Montessori and Waldorf education, superlearning, and cooperative learning. Offers practical suggestions and activities to enhance learning. Resource listings are included at the end of each chapter.

Developing Talent in Young People. Edited by Benjamin S. Bloom. Ballantine, 1985. 558 pages. Reveals the results of a University of Chicago study to determine how and why 120 extraordinary men and women (including concert pianists, Olympic swimmers, and research neurologists) had achieved the highest levels of accomplishment in their chosen fields. Explores in detail each of the crucial stages of talent development and shows how the quality of support and instruction that children receive from their parents and teachers is central to the process. Raises questions about earlier views of special gifts and innate aptitudes as necessary prerequisites of talent development.

Don't Push Your Preschooler. By Louis Bates Ames and Juan Chase. Revised edition. Harper and Row, 1981. 214 pages. In this book, the authors recommend that parents relax and enjoy their preschoolers, rather than push them to learn faster. They point out that most young children learn to walk, talk, think—even read—without vast adult interference.

Educating the Infant and Toddler. By Burton White. Lexington Books, 1988. 361 pages. Recognizes the important role parents play in their children's development—as teachers.

Learning Begins at Home

From *A Leader's Guide to Parent and Family Involvement,* produced by the National PTA.

Parents can set the stage for learning in everyday activities at home: Here's how.

Set a good example by reading.

Read to your children, even after they can read independently. Set aside a family reading time. Take turns reading aloud to each other.

Take your children to the library regularly. Let them see you checking out books for yourself, too.

Build math and reasoning skills together. Have young children help sort laundry, measure ingredients for a recipe or keep track of rainfall for watering the lawn. Involve teens in research and planning for a family vacation or a household project, such as planting a garden or repainting a room.

Regulate the amount and content of the television your family watches. Read the weekly TV listing together and plan shows to watch.

Encourage discussions. Play family games. Show good sportsmanship.

Ask specific questions about school. Show your children that school is important to you so that it will be important to them.

Help your children, especially teens, manage time. Make a chart showing when chores need to be done and when assignments are due.

Volunteer. Build a sense of community and caring by giving your time. Choose projects in which children and teens can take part, too.

Focuses on the Parents as Teachers project in Missouri, a program to help parents guide the learning process of their children from birth to age three (for more information on this program, see listing under "Associations"). Discusses what is known (and not known) about children's early intellectual, social, and physical development. Includes an annotated list of resources, including books, magazines, and visual materials (films and videos) on early development and child care.

The Elementary School Handbook: Making the Most of Your Child's Education. By Joanne Oppenheim.

Pantheon, 1989. 297 pages. A Bank Street Complete Parent Guide to K-6, this book covers various aspects of the elementary school experience. Offers activities and suggestions parents can use at home to enrich their child's school experiences. Also talks about choosing a school, evaluating learning programs, dealing with school authorities, and solving children's problems during the elementary years.

Growing Up Confident: How to Make Your Child's Early Years Learning Years. By Melitta Cutright, Ph.D. Doubleday, 1992. 222 pages. From the National PTA, this book offers advice to help parents instill the love of learning in their child, build self-esteem, encourage self-discipline, and build the confidence necessary for school success. Talks about the parent as teacher, sex role stereotyping (and how to prevent it), finding quality child care, toddlerhood, the preschool years (including tips on finding the right preschool for your child), getting ready for kindergarten, and other topics.

Growing Up Creative: Nurturing a Lifetime of Creativity. By Teresa Amabile. Crown, 1989. 212 pages. Explains how to recognize and foster creativity in children. Describes techniques and hands-on exercises that can help parents and teachers keep creativity alive at home and at school. The author points out that, paradoxically, creativity is often destroyed when grown-ups attempt to foster it through reward and encouragement. Internal motivation is key, according to the author.

Growing Wisdom, Growing Wonder: Helping Your Child to Learn from Birth through Five Years. By Elizabeth Gregg and Judith Knotts. Macmillan, 1980. 289 pages. Encourages parents to use their own knowledge and ideas in making the everyday world richer for their children. Offers chapters in fourteen "areas of knowledge," including texture, size, shape, numbers, feelings, and relationships. In each chapter the authors explain how and when a child's understanding of a particular concept develops and how parents can help them grasp a concept more easily and thoroughly. Preface by T. Berry Brazelton, M.D.

In Their Own Way: Discovering and Encouraging Your Child's Personal Learning Style. By Thomas Armstrong, Ph.D. See listing under "Learning".

Learning All the Time. By John Holt. See listing under "Learning".

Making the Best of Schools: A Handbook for Parents, Teachers, and Policymakers. See listing under "Parent Involvement in Education."

MegaSkills®: In School and In Life—The Best Gift You Can Give Your Child. By Dorothy Rich. Revised and updated edition. Houghton Mifflin, 1992. 363 pages. Describes life skills that the author believes are essential for not only school success, but life in general. These "MegaSkills" include confidence, motivation, effort, responsibility, initiative, perseverance, caring, teamwork, common sense, and problem solving. Describes hundreds of how-to activities for teaching MegaSkills to children ages four through twelve. Also includes chapters on creativity and the "three Rs."

The National PTA Talks to Parents: How to Get the Best Education for Your Child. See listing under "Parent Involvement in Education."

The Ordinary Is Extraordinary. By Amy Laura Dombro and Leah Wallach. Simon and Schuster, 1988. 333 pages. Explains how ordinary routines give young children the chance to learn. The authors use scenes from the lives of three imaginary families to illustrate how children under the age of three learn physical, intellectual, emotional, and social skills by participating in everyday activities. Shows parents how they can make day-to-day life more fun and more educational for themselves and their children.

Parents' Guide to Raising Kids Who Love to Learn. Children's Television Workshop. Prentice-Hall, 1989. 214 pages. Part of the Children's Television Workshop's Family Living Series, this book suggests ways to promote your child's natural desire to learn. Describes child-focused activities to use at home and at school. Explains how to encourage children to learn without pushing or creating pressure. Offers strategies for selecting schools, handling learning problems, and evaluating test scores. Preface by David Elkind, author of *The Hurried Child* and *Miseducation: Preschoolers at Risk.*

The Passionate Mind: Bringing Up an Intelligent and Creative Child. By Michael Schulman. The Free Press, 1991. 352 pages. This book focuses on intellectual achievement in its broadest sense, encompassing curiosity, imagination, creativity, concentration, problem-solving ability, and aesthetic sensitivity. Concept learning, reading, computation, and test-taking skills are dealt with as part of a general program to support and stimulate a child's natural passion for learning. Offers practical ways to enhance abilities at every stage of development.

The Preschool Handbook: Making the Most of Your Child's Education. See listing under "Choosing a School."

The School-Smart Parent. See listing under "Parent Involvement in Education."

The Superbaby Syndrome: Escaping the Dangers of Hurrying Your Child. By Jean Grasso Fitzpatrick. Harcourt Brace, 1988. 203 pages. Reassures parents who have doubts about "programming" their children for success. Examines and critiques various early-learning programs and offers an alternative approach to educating and enjoying our children.

You Are Your Child's First Teacher. By Rahima Baldwin. Celestial Arts, 1989. 376 pages. Written by a Waldorf school teacher and childbirth educator, this book explains how parents can enhance their child's physical, emotional, intellectual, and spiritual development in the early years, without having negative effects later in life. Includes a resource listing.

Your Child's Growing Mind. By Jane Healy. Doubleday, 1987. 324 pages. Describes how children learn from birth to adolescence and how parents can help in the process. Discusses brain development, intelligence, memory, language development, and academic learning. Offers an indictment of early pressures to teach children to read.

Home Learning Programs

Home and School Institute. MegaSkills Education Center, 1201 Sixteenth Street, N.W. Washington, D.C. 20036. Phone: 202/466-3633. Offers programs and materials to help parents stimulate their children's learning in the home. Researches and designs home learning activities parents can use with their children; offers a series of workshops for parents sponsored by school systems in states across the country; and develops educational strategies emphasizing cooperation between families and schools, schools and the community, and families and businesses. Offers a variety of books on family learning and parent/community involvement in schools. [Note: The founder and president of the Home and School Institute, Dorothy Rich, is the author of *MegaSkills®*, a book describing ten skills that the author believes are essential not only to school success but life in general (see listing under "Books" for more information).]

The Home Instruction Program for Preschool Youngsters (HIPPY). 53 West Twenty-third Street, 6th Floor, New York, New York 10010. Phone:

212/645-2006. An international program offering parents information through home visits, literature, and recommended parent/child activities. Support and training for parents are given by paraprofessionals, who are themselves parents of young children from the communities served by the program. Designed primarily for parents with little formal schooling (approximately 10,000 economically disadvantaged families currently participate in 61 programs across the country). Will refer callers to local HIPPY programs (or, if none exist, similar programs in their area).

Parents as Teachers National Center. 9374 Olive Boulevard, St. Louis, Missouri 63132. Phone: 314/432-4330. Believes that parents are a child's most influential teachers and that the parent/school partnership should begin at birth. Stresses that children learn more during the first three years of life than ever again, and bases its programs on this belief. Pairs parents of infants and toddlers with local school district employees who meet with them regularly to offer free advice, information, and support. Participating parents can also attend monthly group sessions on child development. For parents who live in areas where the program is not available, the center offers a book, *Be Your Child's Best First Teacher,* which covers discipline, self-esteem, learning opportunities, and other areas of interest to parents. The book is available for $6.00.

Wings. Designed to help parents make a difference in their child's success in school. Provides games and activities that help teach basic learning and thinking skills to children ages three to six. For more information on Wings, call 1/800-KIDS-222 (extension 1200) (6 a.m. to 9 p.m., pacific standard time, seven days a week).

Videotapes

For Parents

Smart Start for Parents. This video learning program shows busy parents how to be partners in their child's education. Explains what today's schools are like, what is being taught, and how to turn everyday activities (including television viewing) into positive learning experiences. Two of the videotapes are designed for parents with children in kindergarten through second grade. The other two are geared toward parents with children in grades three through five. Developed by 21st Century Learning in cooperation with educators, child development experts, and media specialists. For more information, contact 21st Century Learning Corporation, 625 Third Street, 4th Floor, San Francisco, California 94107. Phone: 1/800-LETS-LEARN.

For Children

The following award-winning video series encourages preschoolers to develop confidence-building skills. Each features fun-loving preschoolers playing the role of teacher. Montessori-inspired, they use song, dance, and humor to help teach independence. Available from Hand in Hand (see chapter 27 for contact information).

Preschool Power! Concept Videos. Running time: 30 minutes. New York Film Festival Gold Medal Winner. A live-action musical video illustrating important life skills, including buttoning, zipping, washing, and room-cleaning. For children ages one to six.

More Preschool Power! Concept Videos. Running time: 30 minutes. Parents' Choice Gold Medal winner. Using songs, jokes, and shadow puppets, this video helps teach skills like tying shoelaces, brushing teeth, and making fruit salad. For children ages one to six.

Preschool Power III! Concept Videos. Running time: 30 minutes. More activities to learn, including cleaning up spills, putting on gloves, and baking French bread. Includes original

songs to sing along with. For children ages one to six.

Preschool Power IV! Concept Videos. Running time: 30 minutes. Includes more songs and activities like doing a somersault, making clay, and whipping up cinnamon toast. For children ages one to six.

COMPETITION

Books

Children of Fast-Track Parents: Raising Self-Sufficient and Confident Children in an Achievement-Oriented World. By Andree Aelion Brooks. Viking Penguin, 1990. 258 pages. Examines issues that arise in families when parents are unusually ambitious or highly accomplished. How to improve the child's self esteem—which may need substantial bolstering in light of parents' own accomplishments; how to know when pressure to succeed academically acts as a motivating force and when it can turn a child off; and the impact of a caregiver on a child's personality and skill development are all explored in this book.

The Hurried Child: Growing Up Too Fast Too Soon. By David Elkind. Revised edition. Addison-Wesley, 1988. 217 pages. Explains the burden of stress placed on children who are forced to grow up too soon. Offers insight and parental advice.

No Contest: The Case against Competition. By Alfie Kohn. Houghton Mifflin, 1986. 257 pages. Explains why we often lose in our race to win and why competition (in the classroom, sports, etc.) is so often counterproductive. Refutes common myths about competition (for example, that competition builds character) and offers cooperation as an alternative.

CHOOSING A SCHOOL

Database

SchoolMatch. A database developed by educators profiling all of America's public school systems, along with nearly eight thousand private, parochial, and overseas schools. Compares schools according to standardized test scores, teacher/student ratios, school size, teacher salaries, money spent per student, and the income levels of the school-system's residents. Many public and academic libraries offer public access to

this information service. Alternatively, parents can purchase customized reports directly from SchoolMatch. For more information, contact SchoolMatch, 5027 Pine Creek Drive, Westerville, Ohio 43081. Phone: 1/800-992-5323.

Free and Inexpensive Resources

Directory of Educational Consultants. Lists educational consultants who can provide parents with useful information on area schools. Available from the Independent Educational Consultants Association, Box 125, Forestdale, Massachusetts 02644. Phone: 508/477-2127.

How to Choose a Good Early Childhood Program. A brochure telling parents what to look for in a good program for their child. Available for 50¢ from the National Association for the Education of Young Children (see appendix I for contact information).

Books

Catholic Schools in America. Fisher Publishing in cooperation with the National Catholic Educational Association. Updated regularly. Produced in cooperation with the National Catholic Educational Association, this book includes the names, addresses, and phone numbers of Catholic schools in America (by state), as well as summary reports of basic school statistics.

The Elementary School Handbook: Making the Most of Your Child's Education. See listing under "Parent Involvement in Education."

The Handbook of Private Schools. Porter Sargent Publishers. Updated annually. This book includes profiles of private schools by region, as well as lists of schools by special category [schools offering ungraded curriculum, military programs, programs for students with learning differences (disabilities, gifts, talents), etc.]. Describes special features of each school, including information on summer programs.

How to Choose the Best School for Your Child. By Bud Howlett. Gulf Publishing, 1991. 226 pages. This book is designed to help parents choose the right public or private school for their child. Offers guidelines to help parents compare schools, recognize effective teachers and principals, perceive their child's educational needs, and define their own role in their child's education. Approved by Parents' Choice.

How to Pick a Perfect Private School. By Harlow G. Unger. Facts On File, 1993. 218 pages. Argues that there are extraordinary benefits to private education. Offers guidelines for evaluating schools; covers various categories of schools (country day schools, military academies, etc.); and contains a complete listing of member schools of the National Association of Independent Schools.

How to Get Your Child a "Private School" Education in a Public School. By Marty Nemko. Revised edition. Ten Speed Press, 1989. 191 pages. Explains how busy parents can help their child get the same quality of education in a public school that parents *hope* to find in a private school, even if they don't have time to be classroom volunteers or parent activists. Explains how to get your child enrolled in the public school of your choice (even if it's not in your assigned district), how to get your child assigned to the teacher of your choice, how to make the best use of a parent/teacher conference, and how to help your child be a self-sufficient learner.

Miseducation: Preschoolers at Risk. See listing under "Learning."

The Preschool Handbook: Making the Most of Your Child's Education. By Barbara Brenner. Pantheon, 1990. 276 pages. A Bank Street Complete Parent Guide, *The Preschool Handbook* helps parents decide whether or not their child would benefit from a preschool program, offers advice on choosing a school (includes a checklist for parents to take along with them when they visit preschool programs), and explains how to deal with the everyday routines of preschool life. Offers guidance in areas such as discipline, testing, emotional problems, and disabilities, and explores current educational issues.

Private Independent Schools. Bunting and Lyon. Published annually, this book lists and describes hundreds of private independent schools (day schools, as well as boarding schools) by state and country. Includes a section on summer programs. Also describes the Bunting and Lyon counseling service, which matches children with schools for a fee.

Public Schools USA: A Comparative Guide to School Districts. By Charles Harrison. Peterson's Guides, 1991. 483 pages. Provides information on 404 school districts in 41 major metropolitan areas. Includes guidelines for evaluating schools and information on trends in American education.

The School Book. See listing under "Parent Involvement in Education."

The School-Smart Parent. See listing under "Parent Involvement in Education."

Your Child's First School. By Diana Townsend-Butterworth. Walker and Company, 1992. 271 pages. Written by a former educator who conducts seminars on choosing schools, this book offers guidelines to help parents select a school that meets the individual needs of their child. Discusses educational options (public schools, private and independent schools, religious schools, traditional and nontraditional, competitive and noncompetitive, coed and single-sex, large and small, etc.). Also addresses school readiness, explains the admissions process, and offers guidelines to help parents make decisions about schools. Part III, "Your Role in Your Child's Education," offers sugges-

tions to help prepare children for school success and ways to help build strong parent/school partnerships. Includes bibliographies of books for parents and books for parents to read with their children, as well as listings of resource centers and organizations.

Associations

Christian Schools International. 3350 East Paris Avenue, S.E., Grand Rapids, Michigan 49512. Phone: 616/957-1070. Offers support services to reformed Christian elementary and secondary schools. Publishes an annual directory of Christian schools.

Committee on Boarding Schools. c/o National Association of Independent Schools, 1620 L Street, N.W., Washington, D.C. 20036. Phone: 202/973-9700. Provides information on boarding schools, including a videotape and an annual directory of schools with residential facilities.

Council for American Private Education. 1726 M Street, N.W., #1102, Washington, D.C. 20036. Phone: 202/659-0016. Fax: 202/659-0018. Coalition of national organizations serving the interests of private schools (kindergarten through twelfth grade). Seeks to stimulate the creation and effectiveness of private schools; formulates public policy concerning private schools; and promotes cooperation between private schools, public schools, and the government at the federal, state, and local levels. Identifies and works with private school advocates to build support for private education. Publishes *Outlook,* a monthly newsletter. Together with Market Data Retrieval, Inc., also publishes *Private Schools of the Unites States,* which is issued periodically.

Independent Educational Consultants Association. Box 125, Forestdale, MA 02644. Phone: 508/477-2127. Fax: 508/477-2127. A group of independent educational consultants who work with parents and students for a fee. Consultants test and evaluate students and recommend and contact schools meeting their client's requirements. Contact this organization for a free directory listing educational consultants who can provide you with information on schools in your area.

Jewish Education Service of North America. 730 Broadway, 2nd Floor, New York, New York 10003-9540. Phone: 212/529-2000. Oversees research on Jewish education. Maintains a roster of local central agencies that can provide information on Jewish schools in specific regions in North America. Publishes the *Jewish Education Directory* every three years.

National Association of Episcopal Schools. 815 Second Avenue, New York, New York 10017. Phone: 212/867-8400. An association of Episcopal church-related day schools and boarding schools. Works to strengthen school programs; develops teaching criteria and curriculum materials; and promotes the ministry of the Episcopal church. Publishes an annual directory of Episcopal church schools.

National Association of Independent Schools. 75 Federal Street, 5th Floor, Boston Massachusetts 02110. Phone: 617/451-2444. An association of more than nine hundred accredited, independent private schools (elementary and secondary).

National Catholic Educational Association. 1077 Thirtieth Street, N.W., Suite 100, Washington, D.C. 20007. Phone: 202/337-6232. Serves as a clearinghouse of information on Catholic education. Produces directories, reports, videotapes, and other resource materials for Catholic schools and religious education centers from elementary school through college, as well as for individuals with an interest in Catholic education.

Parents for Public Schools. See listing under "Parent Involvement In Education."

ALTERNATIVE EDUCATION

General

Free and Inexpensive Resources

Guide to Resources in Holistic Education. Holistic Education Press, 39 Pearl Street, Brandon, Vermont 05733-1007. Phone: 802/247-8312. Lists and describes organizations and publications from various movements, including Waldorf and Montessori. The introduction to the *Guide* says *Holistic education* is a comprehensive philosophy of learning and human development, which is today being applied by a growing number of educators in many kinds of schools and learning environments. There is no single type of "holistic" school, but a rich diversity of approaches that have at their core a deep respect for the unfolding experience of every learner.

Holistic Education Bibliography. An annotated bibliography, compiled by Dorothy Fadiman, for those interested in holistic/progressive/alternative education. Includes books on learning and teaching, approaches to education, education reform, and practical applications for change. Available from Holistic Education Press, 39 Pearl Street, Brandon, Vermont 05733-1007. Phone: 802/247-8312.

Book

Alternatives in Education: Choices and Options in Learning. By Mark Hegener and Helen Hegener. Home Education Press, 1992. 260 pages. This books includes information on alternative schools, Montessori and Waldorf, apprenticeships, learning exchanges, and other educational options. Available from the Alliance for Parental Involvement in Education, Inc., P.O. Box 59, East Chatham, New York 12060-0059. Phone: 518/392-6900.

Periodical

Holistic Education Review. Psychology Press/Holistic Education Press, 39 Pearl Street, Brandon, Vermont 05733-1007. Phone: 802/247-8312. Quarterly publication that covers innovative methods in teaching and learning as well as broader educational issues. Emphasizes the "wholeness" of the human/educational experience. For teachers, trainers, administrators, and parents.

Associations

National Coalition of Alternative Community Schools. 58 Schoolhouse Road, Summertown, Tennessee 38483. Phone: 615/964-3670. A coalition of regional and local alternative school associations. Supports educational systems that are controlled by parents, teachers, and students, and that discourage classism, racism, and sexism. Serves as an information clearinghouse on alternative schools. Offers consultation services. Publishes the *National Coalition of Alternative Community Schools Directory,* which lists alternative schools in the United States and abroad. Includes information on homeschooling.

Parents Rights Organization. 12571 Northwinds Drive, St. Louis, Missouri 63146. Phone: 314/434-4171. Members include parents seeking an alternative to public schools, as well as teachers, students, and school administrators seeking freedom of choice in education. Works to secure freedom of choice for parents in the education of their children, including an alternative to the government-established school system. Sponsors seminars, conferences, and workshops. Conducts research and undertakes and supports court action. Publishes the *Parents Rights Newsletter,* a quarterly offering news and views on parents' rights in education. Includes books reviews, research reports, coverage of legal developments, and home education resource listings.

Montessori

Books

Montessori Play and Learn. By Lesley Britton. Crown, 1992. 144 pages. A parents guide to purposeful play from two to six. Contains practical ideas and activities that fit into normal routines and supplement preschool learning. Based on Maria Montessori's beliefs that parents are the child's most important teacher and that work and play are synonymous.

The Secret of Childhood. By Maria Montessori. Ballantine, 1982. In this book, Maria Montessori clearly explains her philosophy and method of teaching, expressing the deep sense of reverence she held for the child. Other books by Montessori include *The Ab-*

sorbent Child (Dell, 1984) and *The Discovery of the Child* (Ballantine, 1986).

Teaching Montessori in the Home: The Pre-School Years. By Elizabeth G. Hainstock. NAL-Dutton, 1976. Explains how to make and use Montessori materials in the home to promote sensory awareness; task mastery; and reading, writing, and arithmetic skills. Includes clear instructions and exercises. See also the companion volume *Teaching Montessori in the Home: The School Years* (NAL-Dutton, 1989), which focuses on language and math activities.

Periodical

Children's House/Children's World. Children's House, Inc. P.O. Box 111, Caldwell, New Jersey 07006. Associated with the Montessori movement, this journal explores school-related topics such homework and the whole language approach to reading and writing. Brief articles offer common-sense advice for parents. Contains book reviews as well.

Mail Order Catalog

Nienhuis-Montessori USA. 320 Pioneer Way, Mountain View, California 94040. Phone: 415/964-2735. Mail order catalog of Montessori materials for use at home or school.

Associations

American Montessori Society. 150 Fifth Avenue, Suite 203, New York, New York 10011. Phone: 212/924-3209. A professional association formed in response to the growing interest in the Montessori approach to early learning. Certifies teachers in the Montessori method; provides information services; and maintains library and an exhibit of Montessori materials. Publishes *Montessori Life,* a quarterly magazine. Also produces an annual directory of Montessori schools, as well as books, papers, pamphlets, and other informational materials.

Association Montessori International—USA. P.O. Box 421390, San Francisco, California 94102-1390. Phone: 415/861-7113. A professional association that trains and certifies teachers in the traditional Montessori method.

North American Montessori Teacher's Association. 2859 Scarborough Road, Cleveland Heights, Ohio 44118. Phone: 216/371-1566. This association publishes a directory of Montessori schools across the country.

Waldorf Schools

Free and Inexpensive Resources

Waldorf Education. For more information about Waldorf education and Waldorf Schools in your area, write Association of Waldorf Schools of North America, Sacramento Waldorf School, 3750 Bannister Road, Fair Oaks, California 95628. (Enclose $1.00 for postage and handling.)

Books

The Four Temperaments. By Rudolf Steiner. Second revised edition. Anthroposophic Press, 1985. Steiner describes his theory of behavioral styles (temperaments)—and how these styles manifest themselves in children. Other books by Steiner include *Education as an Art* and *The Kingdom of Childhood.*

Waldorf Education
The following excerpt is from the *Hearthsong* catalog.

In 1919, at the request of the German Industrialist Emil Molt, Rudolf Steiner founded the first Waldorf school in Stuttgart, Germany. The curriculum and principles of Waldorf education, as outlined by Steiner, seek to educate the whole child: head, hands and heart. There are now more than 400 Waldorf schools worldwide, 80 in the U.S.A. alone, making Waldorf education the largest non-sectarian educational movement in the world today.

In Waldorf pre-schools and kindergartens, emphasis is put on the "will" forces of the child. Young children thrive on learning through doing and imitating. The focus is on imaginative play, coloring, painting, singing, dancing, cooking, baking, and other participatory activities.

In the primary grades the class teacher recognizes the "feeling" life of the child. The curriculum is rich with myths and legends, poetry, song, artistic activities and movement. When studying a period in history, for example, children draw, sing, dance and dramatize the historical period, and create their own handwritten, illustrated workbooks. There is also a strong emphasis on handwork skills such as knitting, sewing and wood carving.

Toward Wholeness: Rudolf Steiner's Education in America. By M. C. Richards. Wesleyan University Press, 1980. 222 pages. Offers an introduction to Rudolf Steiner's Waldorf educational approach, which emphasizes imagination and creativity. Includes a directory of major Waldorf schools and teacher training programs around the country.

The Waldorf Parenting Handbook. By Lois Cusick. Second revised edition. Rudolf Steiner College Publications, 1988. 119 pages. Explains how Waldorf education supports and nurtures the individual development of children. Answers questions commonly asked by parents interested in the Waldorf method of teaching and learning.

You Are Your Child's First Teacher. By Rahima Baldwin. See listing under "Preparing Your Child for School Success."

Mail Order Catalogs

Hearthsong. P.O. Box B, Sebastopol, California 95473-0601. Phone: 1/800-325-2502. Mail order catalog containing Waldorf-oriented toys, books, games, art supplies, musical instruments, and other items. A winner of the Parents' Choice Seal of Approval.

St. George Book Service. 9200 Fair Oaks Boulevard, Fair Oaks, California 95628. Phone: 916/961-8729. Offers a variety of books on Waldorf education. Includes titles for parents and teachers, as well as children. Write or call for a free mail order catalog.

Association

Association of Waldorf Schools of North America. 3750 Bannister Road, Fair Oaks, California 95628. Phone: 916/961-0927. Offers support services to Waldorf schools (also known as Steiner schools) and encourages the establishment of new schools. Provides information on teacher training programs and Steiner schools in the United States, Canada, and Mexico. Publishes a semiannual newsletter reporting on Waldorf schools and current issues in education. Produces other information materials as well.

Homeschooling

Free and Inexpensive Resources

Famous Homeschoolers. By Malcolm Plent. A twelve-page pamphlet that takes a look at famous people who were educated by their parents at home (Thomas Edison, Woodrow Wilson, and Noël Coward are included). Available for $2.00 from John Holt's Book and Music Store, Holt Associates, 2269 Massachusetts Avenue, Cambridge, Massachusetts 02140. Phone: 617/864-3100.

For New Homeschoolers. Home Education Press, 1992. An introduction to the issues of concern to new home educators, from the publishers of *Home Education Magazine*. Available for $2.00 from the Alliance for Parental Involvement in Education, Inc., P.O. Box 59, East Chatham, New York 12060-0059. Phone: 518/392-6900.

Learning Materials List. Includes more than 150 sources for books, games, magazines, and other materials for homeschoolers. Most were recommended in *Growing Without Schooling* (see listing under "Periodicals"). Available for $2.00 from John Holt's Book and Music Store, Holt Associates, 2269 Massachusetts Avenue, Cambridge, Massachusetts 02140. Phone: 617/864-3100.

Books

Family Matters: Why Homeschooling Makes Sense. By David Guterson. Harcourt Brace Jovanovich, 1992. 245 pages. The author of this book is a high school English teacher and a homeschooler of his own chil-dren. With one foot in each world, Guterson examines life at school and the opportunities offered learning outside it. Addresses commonly asked questions about homeschooling (socialization, legality, and costs are addressed, among other topics). Discusses the history of public schools, philosophies of education, and the academic successes of homeschooled children. Suggests proposals for cooperation between families and schools, and gives examples of successful programs already in place.

Homeschooling for Excellence: How to Take Charge of Your Child's Education and Why You Absolutely Must. By David and Micki Colfax. Warner Books, 1988. 128 pages. Written by parents who sent their own home-educated children to Harvard, this book offers information, guidance, and inspiration.

The Home School Manual. By Theodore E. Wade, Jr. Gazelle Publications, 1986. 318 pages. Provides how-to information for Christian homeschoolers. Twenty-two chapters cover a broad range of topics including the teaching of moral and spiritual values, keeping pace with school authorities, the social development of the homeschooled child, and the teaching of specific subjects (reading, math, science, etc.). Also lists additional sources of information such as books, support groups, and curriculum materials.

The Home School Source Book. By Donn Reed. Brook Farms Books,

1991. 265 pages. A source of inspiration and resources for home educators. Available from the Alliance for Parental Involvement in Education, Inc., P.O. Box 59, East Chatham, New York 12060-0059. Phone: 518/392-6900.

Home School: Taking the First Step. By Borg Hendrickson. Mountain Meadowpress, 1989. 323 pages. A basic guide for parents who have elected homeschooling, written by a former school teacher. Includes listings of support groups, services, publications, and other resources.

Schooling at Home: Parents, Kids, and Learning. Edited by Anne Pedersen and Peggy O'Mara. John Muir Publications, 1990. 258 pages. From *Mothering* magazine, this book is an anthology of articles presenting methods of teaching at home, philosophies of learning, legal issues involved in homeschooling, and personal accounts of part-time and full-time homeschooling. Contributors include John Holt, David Colfax, Patrick Farenga, and Raymond and Dorothy Moore.

Teach Your Own. By John Holt. Bantam Doubleday, 1981. 369 pages. An ardent advocate of homeschooling, the late John Holt builds a strong case for teaching children at home. Confronts the common objections to homeschooling and offers step-by-step guidance for taking—and keeping—children out of school.

Periodicals

Growing Without Schooling. Holt Associates, 2269 Massachusetts Avenue, Cambridge, Massachusetts 02140. Phone: 617/864-3100. Founded by the late John Holt, this bimonthly magazine contains news, stories, feature articles, and information about learning outside of school. Includes pen-pal listings, reviews of useful materials, and a directory of homeschooling families. Issued bimonthly.

Home Education Magazine. Home Education Press, P.O. Box 1083, Tonasket, Washington 98855. Phone: 509/486-1351. A national homeschooling magazine covering issues in the homeschooling movement and offering practical ideas for parents. Articles explore topics such as parental rights and curriculum development. Also contains book and product reviews. Issued six times annually.

Mail Order Catalogs

Home Education Press. P.O. Box 1083, Tonasket, WA 98855. Phone: 509/486-1351. This free catalog lists many books on homeschooling, including titles from the Home Education Press, as well as other publishers. The catalog also lists home education organizations, mail-order catalogs, and other resources for homeschoolers. Call or write for a free copy.

John Holt's Book and Music Store. Holt Associates, 2269 Massachusetts Avenue, Cambridge, Massachusetts 02140. Phone: 617/864-3100. This catalog offers books, cassettes, toys, and other materials for parents who choose to teach their children in the home.

Associations

Holt Associates. 2269 Massachusetts Avenue, Cambridge, Massachusetts 02140. Phone: 617/864-3100. Founded by the late John Holt, this organization promotes homeschooling, publishes a newsletter called *Growing Without Schooling* (see listing under "Periodicals"), and runs a mail-order service (see listing under "Mail Order Catalogs").

The National Center for Home Education. P.O. Box 125, Paeonian Springs, Virginia 22129. Phone: 703/882-4770. A division of the Home School Legal Defense Association, which provides legal counsel to families who educate their children at home. The center's parent group also monitors legal and legislative developments that affect what the group believes is a family's right to educate its children at home.

National Homeschool Association (NHA). P.O. Box 290, Hartland, Michigan 48353-0290. Phone: 313/632-5208. Promotes public awareness of home education and encourages the exchange of information and experience among families whose children are homeschooled.

STARTING SCHOOL

Free and Inexpensive Resources

Ready or Not: What Parents Should Know about School Readiness. Answers common questions about school readiness and offers tips to help parents prepare their children to succeed in school. Available for 50¢ from the National Association for the Education of Young Children, 1834 Connecticut Avenue, N.W., Washington, D.C. 20009-5786. Phone: 1/800-424-2460 or 202/232-8777. Fax: 202/328-1846.

Starting School: A Parent's Guide to the Kindergarten Year. By Judy Kechner. A booklet filled with tips on preparing children for kindergarten and guiding them through their first year. Begins in the months leading up to the first day and takes parents through the end of the school year. Copies are available for $1.95 each from Modern Learning Press/Programs for Education, P.O. Box 167, Department 323, Rosemont, New Jersey 08556. (For more information on Modern Learning Press, see listing under "Mail Order Catalogs.")

Understanding Your Child: A Parents Guide to Starting School. From the Gesell Institute of Human Development, this booklet offers guidelines to help parents make an informed decision on when their child should start kindergarten. Includes a developmental readiness checklist, answers to common questions parents ask, a description of developmentally appropriate classrooms, and information on the Gesell School Readiness Evaluation. For a copy of this booklet, contact the Gesell Institute of Human Development, 310 Prospect Street, New Haven, Connecticut 06511. Phone: 203/777-3481.

When Your Child Goes to School. A ten-page pamphlet for parents to read to their child. Produced by Family Communications, Inc., producers of "Mister Rogers' Neighborhood." For a copy, send a self-addressed, stamped envelope along with your request to Family Communications, Inc., 4802 Fifth Avenue, Pittsburgh, Pennsylvania 15213.

Book

Is Your Child Ready for School? A Parent's Guide to the Readiness Tests Required by Public and Private Primary Schools. By Jacqueline Robinson, M.S. Ed. Arco, 1990. 223 pages. Describes primary school entrance tests including Wechsler Intelligence Tests, the Stanford-Binet Intelligence Test, Gesell School Readiness Tests, and Metropolitan Readiness Tests. The author believes that parents can teach their children skills and concepts that will help them perform better on these tests. Describes "educational games" and activities accordingly.

Videotapes

Do You Know Where Your Child Is? What Every Parent Should Know about School Success. Running time: 43 minutes. Explains the readiness dilemma, addresses parents' concerns, and reassures parents that it is all right for a child to be developmentally young. This video can be purchased or rented from Modern Learning Press/Programs for Education, P.O. Box 167, Department 323, Rosemont, New Jersey 08556. Phone: 1/800-627-5867.

Worth Repeating. Running time: 15 minutes. Educator and author Jim Grant explains that retention can be very beneficial to a child who is overplaced and struggling to keep up. Available in two versions: Basic edition (for parents) and Teacher's edition. This video can be purchased or rented from Modern Learning Press/Programs for Education, P.O. Box 167, Department 323, Rosemont, New Jersey 08556. Phone: 1/800-627-5867.

[Note: A 195-page book by the same name is also available from Modern Learning Press.]

Associations

Gesell Institute of Human Development. 310 Prospect Street, New Haven, Connecticut 06511. Phone: 203/777-3481. The Gesell School Readiness Evaluation, which is performed by a trained professional, provides information related to a child's general level of maturity—separate from academic and intellectual abilities. Used together with parents' and teachers' observations, this evaluation is helpful in planning for a child's placement in school. The institute also offers a parents guide to starting school (see *Understanding Your Child,* under "Free and Inexpensive Resources"), as well as a variety of books on school readiness and developmental education, including *School Readiness* (a full explanation of developmental placement), *Is Your Child in the Wrong Grade?* (a handbook for determining whether a child is overplaced), and *Don't Push Your Preschooler.* These books can be purchased directly from the Gesell Institute or ordered from the Modern Learning Press and Programs for Education (see "Mail Order Catalogs" listed under "Teaching: Approaches and Techniques").

PARENT INVOLVEMENT IN EDUCATION

Free and Inexpensive Resources

The Busy Parent's Guide to Involvement in Education. A PTA booklet that tells how to motivate children to enjoy school and value education, how to get involved with your children's teachers, and how even a busy parent can get involved with the school and PTA. For a free copy, send a self-addressed, stamped, business-size envelope along with your request to the National PTA, 700 North Rush Street, Chicago, Illinois 60611.

Looking in on Your School: A Workbook for Improving Public Education. A guide for parents and PTAs who want to work with the school superintendent, school board, teachers, and other school staff to make their school the best it can be. Available for $3.00 from the National PTA, 700 North Rush Street, Chicago, Illinois 60611.

Making Parent-Teacher Conferences Work for Your Child. Offers tips on how parents can approach a conference with their child's teacher. Explains what parents can expect, what questions they should ask, and how to follow up with an action plan. A publication of the PTA and the National Education Association. For a free copy, send a self-addressed, stamped, business-size envelope along with your request to the National PTA, 700 North Rush Street, Chicago, Illinois 60611.

101 Things You Can Do to Help Education. A free booklet available from Campbell Soup Company. Contains ideas for parents, educators, government, business leaders, and others who want to help make a difference. Send a self-addressed, stamped, business-size envelope to "101 Things You Can Do to Help Education," Campbell Soup Company, Corporate Communication, Box 60G, Campbell Place, Camden, New Jersey 08103.

Books

The Elementary School Handbook: Making the Most of Your Child's Education. See listing under "Preparing Your Child for School Success."

Making the Best of Schools: A Handbook for Parents, Teachers, and Policymakers. By Jeannie Oakes and Martin Lipton. Yale University Press, 1990. 314 pages. Drawing on their own experience as educators and parents, as well as educational research findings, the authors define a set of schooling basics to help guide individual children and bring out the best in schools. Offers positive strategies for parent par-

ticipation in school learning. Discusses how children learn; what home conditions promote school success; how classrooms affect children's self-esteem; how grading, testing, tracking, and repeating a grade can be destructive to children; and how schools came to be the way they are and why they are so tough to change. Emphasizes active learning and mixed-ability groupings.

Making Schools Better. By Larry Martz. Times Books, 1992. 257 pages. Showcases successful new approaches to public education taking place across the country. Also provides practical recommendations to help readers create effective programs and encourage positive change in their own school system.

The National PTA Talks to Parents: How to Get the Best Education for Your Child. By Melitta J. Cutright. Doubleday, 1989. 291 pages. In this book, the PTA tells parents how they can help their child learn at home and how they can become more involved in their child's school. Topics explored include school readiness, standardized tests (explains what they can and cannot tell you), homework, health, self-esteem, nurturing a love of reading, and child-care options. Tells parents how they can encourage school reform and describes many imaginative ways that local PTAs have improved their schools.

101 Educational Conversations with Your Kindergartner-First Grader. By Vitro Perrone. Chelsea House, 1993. 80 pages. The first in a series of guidebooks designed to help parents play a more active role in their child's education. Offers an overview of kindergarten and first grade classrooms and curricula; contains 101 conversation starters and activities that will help parents assess their child's level of achievement and

What is Parent Involvement?

Parent involvement means becoming an active partner in the education of children and youth. It is more than attending a meeting, although it certainly can begin there. Three types of parent involvement are critical in a young person's education. The National PTA identifies them as follows:

- Parents as the first educators in the home.

- Parents as partners with the school.

- Parents as advocates for all children and youth in society

The National PTA describes parent involvement as the participation of parents in every facet of education and development of children from birth to adulthood, recognizing that parents are the primary influence in children's lives. Parent involvement takes many forms, including the parents' shared responsibilities in decisions about children's education, health and well-being, as well as the parents' participation in organizations that reflect the community's collaborative aspirations for all children. (National PTA, *A Leader's Guide to Parent and Family Involvement*)

better understand what their child is actually learning; and explains how parents and teachers can work together to create positive learning experiences for children. Also available: *101 Educational Conversations with Your 2nd Grader* and *101 Educational Conversations with Your 3rd Grader.*

Parenting Our Schools: A Hands-On Guide to Education Reform. See listing under "Education Reform."

A Parent's Guide to Innovative Education. By Anne Wescott Dodd. Nobel Press, 1992. 278 pages. Explains how parents can work with teachers, schools, and their children to promote real learning. Builds a strong case for school reform and provides parents with the information they need to help make it happen. Winner of *Child* magazine's Award for Excellence in Family Issues.

The Preschool Handbook: Making the Most of Your Child's Education. See listing under "Choosing a School."

Save Our Schools: 66 Things You Can Do to Improve Education. By Mary Susan Miller. HarperSanFrancisco, 1993. 163 pages. Describes easy and effective ways to enrich our schools (and our kids), based on real-life success stories involving parents, teachers, businesses, and community organizations across the country. Tells how to enable teachers to do a better job, enrich a watered-down curriculum, challenge quick learners and reinforce slower students, put parents on the teaching team, and involve the community.

The School Book. By Mary Susan Miller, Ph.D. St. Martin's Press, 1991. 382 pages. A guide for parents covering many issues related to their child's education from preschool through the eighth grade. Choosing a school, parent/teacher communication, grading, curriculum, health and safety, and the importance of play at home are among the topics discussed. Explains what parents can do when their child has school problems (for example, when your child cries when you leave her, refuses to do her homework, or gets picked on by the teacher). Shows parents how to help their children enjoy school and learning in general.

The School-Smart Parent. By Gene I. Maeroff. Times Books, 1989. 434 pages. Features lists of what your child should know at each stage of school from preschool through the sixth grade. Includes information and advice on choosing a school, reading with children, dealing with homework, turning television into a positive force, choosing toys that help children learn, overcoming math anxiety (and nourishing an interest in other subjects), teaching thinking skills, talking with teachers, how and when to get involved at school, and other school and learning-related topics.

___

Associations

Alliance for Parental Involvement in Education. P.O. Box 59, East Chatham, New York 12060-0059. Phone: 518/392-6900. A nonprofit organization that assists and encourages parental involvement in education, wherever that education takes place: in public school, in private school, or at home. Holds an annual conference, offers workshops, and publishes a book catalog, and a newsletter called *Options in Learning.*

Center on Families, Communities, Schools and Children's Learning. Johns Hopkins University, 3505 North Charles Street, Baltimore, Maryland 21218. Phone: 410/516-0370. Through research, evaluation, and policy analysis, this center works to produce new and useful knowledge about how families, schools, and communities influence student motivation, learning, and develop-

ment. A second important goal of the center is to improve the connections among these major social institutions. Two research programs guide the center's work: the Program on the Early Years of Childhood, covering children ages one to ten and the Program on the Years of Early and Late Adolescence, covering youngsters ages eleven to nineteen.

The center has developed TIPS (Teachers Involve Parents in Schoolwork), a prototype program designed by teachers to encourage parents' involvement in their child's schoolwork (TIPS activities require students to talk to someone at home about what they are learning in the classroom). The aim of TIPS is to build students' skills, increase the amount of supervised learning time, inform parents about their child's schoolwork, and encourage parents' support for the schools and appreciation of teachers. Write or call for more information. [Note: In addition to information on TIPS, the center provides a variety of research reports, guides, and other materials on parent involvement in education for under $10.00. Contact the center for a free listing.]

Designs for Change. 220 South State Street, Suite 1900, Chicago, Illinois 60604. Phone: 312/922-0317. Assists parent groups, teachers, students, and others working to improve public schools. Conducts research on school improvement at the local level. Provides information, consultation, training, and referral services. Produces handbooks such as *Helping Schools Change: Ideas for Assistance Groups* and *Standing Up for Children: Effective Child Advocacy in the Schools.* Also publishes a newsletter.

Educational Foundation Consultants. 147 South Putnum, Williamston, Michigan 48894. Phone: 517/655-4318. Provides information on setting up a private foundation to help your school raise money for items it could not otherwise afford, such as a new building, new equipment, or costly supplies.

Elementary School Center. 2 East 103rd Street, New York, New York 10029. Phone: 212/289-5929. Works to improve the quality of elementary- and middle-school education. Serves as an information center and acts as a national advocate for children and schools. Members include parents, educators, pediatricians, and others interested in the healthy development of children in elementary and middle schools. Sponsors seminars, study groups, and other educational activities. Holds an annual conference. Issues papers, monographs, conference proceedings, and a periodic newsletter called *Focus.*

Institute for Responsive Education. 605 Commonwealth Avenue, Boston, Massachusetts 02215. Phone: 617/353-3309. Fax: 617/353-8444. Fosters greater parental involvement in the schools, especially among poor and minority parents in urban areas. Offers assistance to those seeking school support within their community. Advises those who want to help their child succeed in school or learn how the schools can better serve African-American, Hispanic, and other minority children. Publishes *Equity and Choice,* a journal covering developments in bilingual education, desegregation, and choice in public schools. Published three times a year.

National Association of Partners in Education. 209 Madison Street, Suite 401, Alexandria, Virginia 22314. Phone: 703/836-4880. Promotes the value of school volunteer and partnership services and the involvement of citizens and businesses in schools. Assists school systems in starting or improving volunteer programs. Pub-

---

Get Your School Back on Track

For practical advice on improving your child's school, read "Get Your School Back on Track," by Anne Reeks, part two of a two-part series on America's public schools published in the February 1993 issue of *Parenting* magazine. Part one, "Fight or Flight?" by David Rubin, published in the December/January 1993 issue explains why some families opt for public education, while others choose alternatives. Many public libraries subscribe to this magazine (inquire about the availability of back issues).

---

lishes *Partners in Education,* a monthly newsletter. Also publishes guides, manuals, programs, and information packets, as well as a publications list.

National Coalition for Parent Involvement in Education. Box 39, 1201 Sixteenth Street, N.W., Washington, D.C. 20036. Dedicated to the development of strong family/school partnerships. Works to build broad community support for local schools. Offers information and resources primarily for teachers, administrators, and community leaders who wish to strengthen relationships between parents and schools.

National Coalition of Title I/Chapter I Parents. Edmonds School Building, Ninth and D Streets, N.W., Room 201, Washington, D.C. 20002. Phone: 202/547-9286. A coalition of parents, educators, administrators, and others who encourage and support community participation in the development of educational programs for disadvantaged children. (Title I is a federally subsidized program serving children who are disadvantaged in reading or math.) The coalition provides information, training, and technical assistance to Title I parents and other community groups, and exchanges information to enhance educational opportunities for disadvantaged students. The National Parent Center, established by the coalition, helps parents become actively involved in all aspects of their children's education. Publishes a bimonthly newsletter.

National Conference on Parent Involvement. 579 West Iroquois, Pontiac, Michigan 48341. Phone: 313/334-5887. The objective of this group (which consists of parents, teachers, and other interested individuals) is to hold an annual conference to bring together people who are advocates of parent involvement in the schools. Seeks to build partnerships and strengthen communication among schools, homes, and communities. Affiliated with the Center for the Study of Parent Involvement.

National PTA. 700 North Rush Street, Chicago, Illinois 60611-2571. Phone: 312/787-0977. Fax: 312/787-8342. Serves as national headquarters for the more than twenty-eight thousand local PTA chapters across the country. Seeks to unite home, school, and community in promoting the education, health, and safety of children, youth, and families. Among its various programs and activities, the National PTA works for legislation benefiting children and youth; bestows awards to outstanding educators; and sponsors an annual cultural arts award program for students in kindergarten through twelfth grade in literature, music, photography, and the visual arts. Offers information and advice to those who want to organize a PTA, assess their school's strengths and weaknesses, or improve parent-teacher communication. In addition to PTAs serving children in kindergarten through twelfth grade, the National PTA charters preschool PTAs. These groups provide educational and enrichment activities for parents and young children from birth to age five.

Produces educational materials for parents (including books, free brochures, videotapes, and kits) on a wide range of learning topics, including discipline, parent education, television's effects on children, school absenteeism, and relationships among parents, teachers, and school administrators. Periodicals include *PTA Today*, a magazine for parents, educators, and friends of children and youth featuring articles on education, parenting, health, and safety. Includes reviews of children's books, updates on federal legislation affecting children and youth, and program ideas for PTAs. Also publishes *What's Happening in Washington*, a bimonthly newsletter on current federal legislation. Books for parents include *The National PTA Talks to Parents* and *Growing Up Confident*. Produces a publications catalog as well. (Note: A list of state PTA offices can be found at the end of "Parent Involvement in Education.")

Parent Cooperative Elementary Program. Cedar Valley Elementary School, Edmonds School District 15, 20525 Fifty-second Avenue West, Lynnwood, Washington 98036. Offers guidelines and suggestions for starting a parent cooperative at your elementary school.

Parent Cooperative Pre-Schools International. c/o Kathy Mensel, P.O. Box 90410, Indianapolis, Indiana 46290. Phone: 317/849-0992. Provides information and research services to members, including individuals and groups interested in nonprofit preschools operated cooperatively by parents. Offers guidelines and suggestions to those interested in starting a parent cooperative preschool. Available publications include *How to Start a Co-Op; Health and Safety in the Preschool; Leadership Development–A Facilitators Handbook;* an index of relevant journal articles; and bulletins on parent programming, workshop planning, and other topics. Also publishes the *PCPI Directory,* an annual list of parent cooperative schools, and *Cooperatively Speaking,* a periodical issued three times a year.

Parents for Public Schools. P.O. Box 12807, Jackson, Mississippi 39263-2807. Phone: 601/982-1222 or 1/800-880-1222. Fax: 601/982-0002. Nonprofit, grass-roots organization comprised primarily of parents who believe their children receive the best available education in public schools and who actively recruit other parents to enroll their children in public schools. Promotes broad-based enrollment in public schools across America and convinces communities of the economic, social, and educational value of strong public schools. Aims to heal some of the racial and class divisiveness in America by promoting an appreciation and understanding of diversity among children. Chapters in states across the country. Publishes *Parent Press,* a periodic newsletter offering association coverage as well as news and information on current issues and events in public education.

Parents in Touch (PIT). Indianapolis Public Schools, 901 North Carrollton, Indianapolis, Indiana 46202. Phone: 317/226-4134. Parents in Touch offers the Parent Line/Communicator–a computerized telephone system that gives callers access to more than 140 tape-recorded mes-

sages on a variety of topics including school information, drug and alcohol abuse, and parenting skills (contact PIT for a list of topics; the hotline number is 317/631-4805). Parents in Touch also offers Dial-A-Teacher–a phone line that gives students and parents assistance with and information about homework. (Telephones are operated by a secretary who directs calls to teachers.) Contact PIT for more information on these and other programs and services, which can be duplicated in other school systems, using PIT's step-by-step guidelines.

PTA. See **National PTA**

United Parents-Teachers Association of Jewish Schools. 426 West Fifty-eighth Street, New York, New York 10019. Phone: 212/245-8200. Works to build a healthy partnership between the Jewish home and Jewish schools. Encourages parental involvement in Jewish education. Conducts seminars, workshops, and film forums. Produces a variety of informational brochures.

State Offices of the National PTA

Alabama Congress of Parents and Teachers, Inc. 470 South Union Street, Montgomery, Alabama 36104-4330. Phone: 205/834-2501. Fax: 205/834-2504.

Alaska Congress of Parents and Teachers. P.O. Box 201496, Anchorage, Alaska 99520-1496. Phone: 907/279-9345. (Note: Send packages to 619 East Fifth Avenue, Suite 203, Anchorage, Alaska 99501.)

Arizona Congress of Parents and Teachers, Inc. 2721 North Seventh Avenue, Phoenix, Arizona 85007-1102. Phone: 602/279-1811. Fax: 602/279-1814.

Arkansas Congress of Parents and Teachers, Inc. 2200 North Poplar Street, Suite 103, North Little Rock, Arkansas 72114-2322. Phone: 501/753-5247.

California Congress of Parents, Teachers, and Students, Inc. P.O. Box 15015, Los Angeles, California 90015-0100. Phone: 213/620-1100 Fax: 213/620-1411. (Note: Send packages to 930 Georgia Street, Los Angeles, California 90015.)

Colorado Congress of Parents and Teachers. 7251 West Thirty-eighth Avenue, Wheat Ridge, Colorado 80033-4840. Phone: 303/422-2213.

The Parent-Teacher Association of Connecticut, Inc. Wilbur Cross Commons, Building #11, 60 Connolly Parkway, Hamden, Connecticut 06514-2519. Phone: 203/281-6617.

Delaware Congress of Parents and Teachers. 92 South Gerald Drive, Newark, Delaware 19713-3299. Phone: 902/737-4646. (Note: Send packages to 116 Foxtail Circle, Hickory Woods, Bear, Delaware 19701.)

D.C. Congress of Parents and Teachers. J. O. Wilson Elementary School, 660 K Street, N.E., Washington, D.C. 20002-3530. Phone: 202/543-0333.

European Congress of American Parents, Teachers, and Students. 583 ABG, PSC 08, Box 4013, APO, AE 09109. Phone: 011/49/6543-9526.

Florida Congress of Parents and Teachers, Inc. 1747 Orlando Central Parkway, Orlando, Florida 32809-5757. Phone: 407/855-7604.

Georgia Congress of Parents and Teachers, Inc. 114 Baker Street, N.E., Atlanta, Georgia 30308-3366. Phone: 404/659-0214.

Hawaii Congress of Parents, Teachers, and Students. P.O. Box 10010, Hilo, Hawaii 96720-2663. Phone: 808/499-2663. Fax: 808/935-6227.

Idaho Congress of Parents and Teachers, Inc. 620 North Sixth Street, Boise, Idaho 83702-5553. Phone: 208/344-0851.

Illinois Congress of Parents and Teachers. 901 South Spring Street, Springfield, Illinois 62704-2790. Phone: 217/528-9617.

Indiana Congress of Parents and Teachers, Inc. 2150 Lafayette Road, Indianapolis, Indiana 46222-2394. Phone: 317/635-1733.

Iowa Congress of Parents and Teachers. 610 Merle Hay Towers, Des Moines, Iowa 50310-0121. Phone: 515/276-1019.

Kansas Congress of Parents and Teachers. 715 Southwest Tenth Street, Topeka, Kansas 66612-1686. Phone: 913/234-5782.

Kentucky Congress of Parents and Teachers. 148 Consumer Lane, Frankfort, Kentucky 40601. Phone: 502/564-4378.

Louisiana Parent-Teacher Association. One American Place, Suite 603, Baton Rouge, Louisiana 70825. Phone: 504/343-0386.

Maine Congress of Parents and Teachers, Inc. 16 Winthrop Street, Augusta, Maine 04330. Phone: 207/621-2782.

Maryland Congress of Parents and Teachers. 3121 St. Paul Street, Suite 25, Baltimore, Maryland 21218. Phone: 410/235-7290. Fax: 410/235-0357.

Massachusetts Parent-Teacher-Student Association. c/o Arlington High School, 869 Massachusetts Avenue, Arlington, Massachusetts 02174-4799. Phone: 617/646-6771.

Michigan Congress of Parents, Teachers, and Students. 1011 North Washington Avenue, Lansing, Michigan 48906-4897. Phone: 517/485-4345.

Minnesota Congress of Parents, Teachers, and Students. 1910 West County Road, B, Suite 105, Roseville, Minnesota 55113-5454. Phone: 612/631-1736.

Mississippi Congress of Parents and Teachers. P.O. Box 1937, Jackson, Mississippi 39215-1937. Phone: 601/352-7383. (Note: Send packages to 400 East South Street, Jackson, Mississippi 39201.)

Missouri Congress of Parents and Teachers. 2101 Burlington Street, Columbia, Missouri 65202-1997. Phone: 314/474-8631.

Montana Congress of Parents, Teachers, and Students, Inc. 1111 Eaton, Missoula, Montana 59801-3230. Phone: 406/728-6059.

Nebraska Congress of Parents and Teachers, Inc. 605 South Fourteenth, #412, Lincoln, Nebraska 68508-2712. Phone: 402/438-5140.

Nevada Parent-Teacher Association. 435 South Decatur Boulevard, Las Vegas, Nevada 89107. Phone: 702/258-7885. Fax: 702/258-7836.

New Hampshire Congress of Parents and Teachers. 33 Mount Vernon Road, Amhurst, New Hampshire 03031-3323. Phone: 603/673-4234.

New Jersey Congress of Parents and Teachers. 900 Berkeley Avenue, Trenton, New Jersey 08618-5322. Phone: 609/393-5004. Fax: 609/393-8471.

New Mexico Congress of Parents and Teachers. 1611 Bayita Lane, N.W., Albuquerque, New Mexico 87107. Phone: 505/344-2590. (Note: Send packages to 6001 M Lomas, N.E., Albuquerque, New Mexico 87110.)

New York State Congress of Parents and Teachers, Inc. 119 Washington Avenue, Albany, New York 12210-2282. Phone: 518/462-5326.

North Carolina Congress of Parents and Teachers. 3501 Glenwood Avenue, Raleigh, North Carolina 27612-4934. Phone: 919/787-0534.

North Dakota Congress of Parents and Teachers. 810 Divide Avenue East, Bismarck, North Dakota 58501-1899. Phone: 701/223-3578.

Ohio Congress of Parents and Teachers, Inc. 427 East Town Street, Columbus, Ohio 43215-4775. Phone: 614/221-4844.

Oklahoma Congress of Parents and Teachers, Inc. Moore Schools Administrative Annex, 224 S.E. Fourth Street, Moore, Oklahoma 73160-6102. Phone: 405/799-0026.

Oregon Congress of Parents and Teachers, Inc. 531 S.E. Fourteenth Avenue, Portland, Oregon 97214-2427. Phone: 503/234-3928.

Pennsylvania Congress of Parents and Teachers, Inc. P.O. Box 4384, 4804 Derry Street, Harrisburg, Pennsylvania 17111-0384. Phone: 717/564-8985. Fax: 717/564-9046.

Rhode Island Congress of Parents and Teachers. 1704 Broad Street, Cranston, Rhode Island 02905-2720. Phone: 401/785-1970.

South Carolina Congress of Parents and Teachers. 1826 Henderson Street, Columbia, South Carolina 29201-2619. Phone: 803/765-0806.

South Dakota Congress of Parents and Teachers. 411 East Capitol, Pierre, South Dakota 57501-3194. Phone: 605/224-0144.

Tennessee Congress of Parents and Teachers, Inc. 1905 Acklen Avenue, Nashville, Tennessee 37212-3788. Phone: 615/383-9740.

Texas Congress of Parents and Teachers. 408 West Eleventh Street, Austin, Texas 78701-2176. Phone: 512/476-6769.

Utah Congress of Parents and Teachers. 1037 East South Temple, Salt Lake City, Utah 84102-1578. Phone: 801/539-3875. Fax: 801/537-7827.

Vermont Congress of Parents and Teachers. P.O. Box 5, Washington, Vermont 05675-0005. Phone: 802/883-2226. (Note: Send packages to Route 110, Washington, Vermont 05675.)

Virginia Congress of Parents and Teachers. 3810 Augusta Avenue, Richmond, Virginia 23230-3999. Phone: 804/355-2816.

Washington Congress of Parents and Teachers. 2003 Sixty-fifth Avenue West, Tacoma, Washington 98466-6215. Phone: 206/565-2153.

West Virginia Congress of Parents and Teachers. P.O. Box 130, 708 Central Avenue, Barboursville, West Virginia 25504-0130. Phone: 304/736-4089.

Wisconsin Congress of Parents and Teachers, Inc. 4797 Hayes Road, Suite 2, Madison, Wisconsin 43704-3256. Phone: 608/244-1455.

Wyoming Congress of Parents and Teachers. 5030 East Seventeenth Street, Casper, Wyoming 82609. Phone: 307/265-2494.

HOMEWORK (HOW YOU CAN HELP)

Free Resources

Help Your Child Get the Most Out of Homework. Produced by the PTA and the National Education Association, this brochure offers advice to help parents improve their children's homework skills without having to nag. Written in question-and-answer format. For a free copy, send a self-addressed, stamped, business-size envelope along with your request to the National PTA (see appendix I for contact information).

Studying: A Key to Success. Discusses the importance of good study habits and explains ways that parents can help. For a free copy, send a self-addressed, stamped envelope along with your request to the International Reading Association (see appendix I for contact information).

Book

Taming the Homework Monster: How to Make Homework a Positive Learning Experience for Your Child. By Ellen Klavan. Poseidon Press, 1992. 201 pages. A guide for parents of elementary school children, *Taming the Homework Monster* offers step-by-step, grade-by-grade tips on motivating your child to do homework, helping your child get organized, creating a positive homework environment, and fostering good study habits. Offers advice on dealing with children who have trouble with homework (the procrastinator, the perfectionist, the forgetter, the obstinate refusenik); suggestions on how to help your child with math, science, reading, and other subjects; and guidelines for dealing with learning disabilities, gifted children, tutoring, and prolonged absences from school. Also offers lists of games, magazines, books, computer software, and activities to enhance your child's education and learning abilities.

TEACHING: APPROACHES AND TECHNIQUES

Inexpensive Resource

What Works: Research about Teaching and Learning. Written in easy-to-understand language, this eighty-six-page booklet discusses the importance of parent involvement in education, teaching and learning in the home, classroom approaches and techniques that work (according to various research findings), and schools that are effective (and why). Although some of the conclusions drawn from the research are controversial, the booklet has been highly praised for its clarity. Produced by the U.S. Department of Education, currently in its second edition. For a copy, write "What Works," Pueblo, Colorado 81009 (for price information, call the ordering desk at 202/783-3238). (Note: To learn more about the report, contact the U.S. Department of Education's Information Office, 555 New Jersey Avenue, Washington, D.C. 20208-1325. Phone: 1/800-424-1616. The Information Office is staffed with statisticians and education and information specialists who can answer questions about education statistics, research, technology, and practices.)

Books

Thousands of existing books explore teaching practices, approaches, techniques, curricula, and related topics. Good sources of information on such books include professional journals (which typically contain book reviews) and resource catalogs produced by professional associations. The following periodicals and mail order catalogs contain information that will be of interest to parents as well as educators. (For more resource listings on teaching approaches and techniques refer to Topics in Education, chapter 14.)

Periodicals

Childhood Education. Association for Childhood Education International, 11501 Georgia Avenue, Suite 315, Wheaton, Maryland 20902. Phone: 1/800-423-3563 or 301/942-2443. Covers various aspects of early childhood education, including recent teaching trends, child development, research findings, current issues affecting teachers and children, and the parent's role in the learning process. Reviews books, videotapes, and software. Written in a popular style suitable for parents as well as professionals involved in the education of children. Issued five times a year. $78.00 for an annual subscription (free to members of ACEI). Individual issues ($14.00 each), article reprints, and annual theme issues can also be ordered.

Reprints from *Childhood Education* (available to nonmembers for $2.75) include:

Children in a Changing Society: Frontiers of Challenge
The Physically Unattractive Child
When Parents of Kindergartners Ask "Why?"

Theme issues (with prices ranging from $6.50 to $14.00) include:

Are Schools Really for Kids?
The Child in the Community
Children and the Environment: Promoting Ecological Awareness in Young Children

Children in the Age of Microcomputers

Emerging Adolescents: Their Needs and Concerns

Pressures Abolishing Childhood

Public Policy Affecting Children

Teachers' Voices: Celebrating Excellence

Who Will Be Teaching the World's Children: A Global Perspective

Democracy and Education. Institute for Democracy in Education, Ohio University, College of Education, 119 McCracken Hall, Athens, Ohio 45701-2979. This quarterly journal explores democratic methods of teaching and learning. Contains articles that oppose standardized testing and other regimentation in the classroom. Encourages activities that develop self esteem and encourage individual initiative. Much of the material is written by teachers and targeted at parents.

Early Childhood Today. Scholastic, Inc., 730 Broadway, New York, New York 10003. Phone: 212/505-4900. Although this magazine is primarily for early childhood professionals, many of the articles will be of interest to parents. Includes articles on child development, techniques for dealing with behavioral problems, and innovative approaches to teaching young children. Issued eight times annually. (Individual copies can be purchased at larger newsstands.)

Education Today. The Educational Publishing Group, Inc., The Statler Building, Suite 1215, 20 Park Plaza, Boston, Massachusetts 02116. Phone: 1/800-927-6006. A newsletter for parents of school-aged children. Provides information on education trends and ways to help children succeed in school. Covers topics such as homework, resources for learning, parent/child communication, and parent involvement in education. Issued eight times annually. (A sample issue is available on request.)

Education Week. Editorial Projects in Education, 4301 Connecticut Avenue, N.W., Room 250, Washington, D.C. 20008. Phone: 202/686-0800. A newspaper covering recent developments in education from kindergarten through high school. Explores political and economic developments and the relationship between schools and society. Also covers unusual accomplishments of teachers and students. Issued forty times annually (weekly during the school year). $59.95 for an annual subscription.

Instructor. 730 Broadway, New York, New York 10003. Phone: 212/505-4900. A full-color magazine for teachers, with news and features that will interest involved parents as well. Offers innovative approaches and techniques for teaching science, math, writing, and other topics. Discusses literature connections, teaching with technology, and other ways to help children learn. Includes listings of free and inexpensive teaching tools.

Learning. Springhouse Corp., 111 Bethlehem Pike, Springhouse, Pennsylvania 19477. Phone: 215/646-8700. Contains creative ideas and educational insights for elementary school teachers. Although the projects and approaches described are intended for use in the classroom, parents might want to borrow ideas or adapt some of the material for home use. Issued nine times a year.

Parent and Preschooler Newsletter. Preschool Publications, Inc., P.O. Box 1851, Garden City, New York 11530-0816. Phone: 516/742-9557. Each issue of this four-page newsletter has a theme (separation anxiety, discipline, self-esteem, etc.), with a feature article written by an expert in the field. The newsletter also contains project ideas and activities, recipes, and recommended readings on the topic of focus. Of interest to parents and preschool teachers. Issued monthly. Back issues are available. [Note: For a listing of topics covered in back issues, request a copy of Preschool Publications' *Catalog of Resources for Early Childhood Professionals and Parents*. This catalog also describes *Guiding Your Preschooler . . . You Can Make a Difference*–a series of audiocassettes adapted from *Parent and Preschooler Newsletter*.]

Totline Newsletter. Warren Publishing House, Inc., P.O. Box 2255, Everett, Washington 98203. Phone: 1/800-334-4769. Each issue contains activity ideas, stories, songs, craft projects, and snack ideas. These could range from movement exercises, to the making of musical instruments from discarded household items, to making an art museum stimulating for a preschooler. For parents and teachers of preschool children. Twenty-four pages. Issued bimonthly.

Young Children. National Association for the Education of Young Children (NAEYC), 1509 Sixteenth Street, N.W., Washington, D.C. 20036-1426. Phone: 202/232-8777 or 1/800-424-2460. Fax: 202/328-1846. Professional journal of the National Association for the Education of Young Children exploring various aspects of early childhood education and young child development. Contains book reviews, summaries of current research, and articles of interest to those working with infants and toddlers, including child-care providers, early childhood educators, and parents.

Videotape

Why Do These Kids Love School? By Dorothy Fadiman/KTEH-TV San Jose. Pyramid Film and Video, 1990. Running time: 60 minutes. Shows some of the qualities that make for a good school, including innovative curricula; shared responsibility among parents, teachers, students, and administrators; and a willingness to allow teachers to experiment. This tape visits a number of schools—mostly public–in areas around the country. Comes with a twenty-eight-page study guide. $95.00 (plus $5.00 shipping and handling). Available from Pyramid Film and Video, Box 1048, Santa Monica, California 90406. Phone: 1/800-421-2304.

Mail Order Catalogs

Association for Childhood Education International, Publications Catalog. 11501 Georgia Avenue, Suite 315, Wheaton, Maryland 20902. Phone: 301/942-2443 or 1/800-423-3563. A catalog for those involved in the education of children from infancy through early adolescence. Among the many books offered for sale are *Toward Self Discipline: A Guide for Parents and Teachers; Learning Opportunities Beyond the School;* and *Learning from the Inside Out: A Guide to the Expressive Arts.* Position papers, reprints from ACEI's journal *Childhood Education* (see listing under "Periodicals"), videotapes, and audiocassettes are also described in the catalog.

Childhood Resources Catalog. National Association for the Education of Young Children (NAEYC), 1509 Sixteenth Street, N.W., Washington, D.C. 20036-1426. Phone: 202/232-8777 or 1/800-424-2460. Fax: 202/328-1846. Catalog describing books, brochures, videos, posters, information kits, and other materials for teachers, child care providers, parents, and others interested in early education programs. Brochures (available for

50¢) include *Appropriate Education in the Primary Grades, Good Teaching Practices for Older Preschoolers and Kindergartners,* and *Developmentally Appropriate Practice in Early Childhood Programs.* Book titles include *The Case for Mixed-Age Grouping in Early Education* and *The Child's Construction of Knowledge: Piaget for Teaching Children.*

Heinemann-Boyton/Cook Catalog.
361 Hanover Street, Portsmouth, New Hampshire 03801-3959. Phone: 603/431-7894. Offers a wide selection of books on teaching reading, writing, math, science, art, drama, and music to children. In recent years, Heinemann has developed its book list to include titles that extend the language arts across the curriculum into the areas of math, science, social studies, etc. Although most of the books are designed for use in the classroom, the catalog includes a section called "Books for Parents." (Specialty catalogs from Heinemann include *Art Education, Drama Education,* and *Math and Science.*)

Modern Learning Press and Programs for Education. P.O. Box 167, Department 323, Rosemont, New Jersey 08556. Phone: 1/800-627-5867. This catalog offers books and related resource materials based on the developmental principles of Dr. Arnold Gesell, founder of the Child Study Center at Yale University. Offerings explore various aspects of developmental education, including school readiness, developmentally appropriate curriculum, the whole language approach to reading and writing, art appreciation, discipline, and other topics. Titles include *Developmental Education in the 1990's, Miseducation: Preschoolers at Risk, Smart Kids with School Problems, Dialogues on Developmental Curriculum Pre-K-First, What's Best for Kids: A Guide to Developmentally Appropriate Practices for*

Teachers and Parents of Children Age 4-8, and many others. Although the catalog is designed for teachers, parents will be interested in many of the offerings as well. (For more information on this catalog, see listing under "Mail Order Catalogs" in chapter 1.)

Associations

Association for Childhood Education International (ACEI). 11501 Georgia Avenue, Suite 315, Wheaton, Maryland 20902. Phone: 301/942-2443 or 1/800-423-3563. A professional organization for those involved in the education of children from infancy through early adolescence. Advocates developmentally appropriate curricular materials. Works to promote the quality and availability of educational programs for children (infancy through adolescence). Promotes cooperation among individuals and groups concerned with children. Encourages professional growth of teachers. Informs the public about the needs of children.

Publishes books, booklets, monographs, reprints, and a variety of periodicals including *Childhood Education* (see listing under "Periodicals") and the *Journal of Research in Childhood Education,* an international journal of research on the education of children. Also produces a publications catalog (see listing under "Mail Order Catalogs"). Although ACEI's publications are targeted at education professionals, many of them are of interest to parents.

Bank Street College of Education.
610 West 112th Street, New York, New York 10025. Phone: 212/875-4400. Founded in 1916, the Bank Street College of Education conducts programs of research, consultation, and curriculum- and educational-materials development to benefit children. Bank Street College offers

graduate programs for educators and early-childhood specialists; operates a demonstration school for children ages three to thirteen, which serves as a working model of the college's approach to learning and teaching; and operates a nonprofit child-care center, which offers a training site for the college's graduate students studying infant/parent development, early childhood education, or special education. Bank Street College's approach to learning places emphasis on child development and individual learning styles; the importance of experiential learning; and the understanding that the emotional life of children is inseparable from their learning, interests, and motivation. Educators, psychologists, and child development experts are on staff.

In addition to videotapes, software, and curriculum guides, Bank Street College has produced a variety of books for children, as well as parents. Books for children include the Bank Street Ready-to-Read Series (published by Bantam); Bank Street Mind Builders (summer learning activity kits and books for children and parents, published by Cowles Educational Corporation); Bank Street Museum Books (including *Dinosaurium, Oceanarium, and Planetarium,* published by Bantam). Parent guides include *Kids and Play* and *Love and Discipline* (both published by Ballantine), as well as *Raising a Confident Child, The Preschool Handbook, The Elementary School Handbook, and Buy Me! Buy Me! The Bank Street Guide to Choosing Toys* (all published by Pantheon). In addition, the Child Study Children's Book Committee at Bank Street produces lists of recommended titles for children (see listing under "Choosing Children's Books," chapter 17).

[Note: For those within easy traveling distance, Bank Street College offers Saturday workshops for parents and children (science projects, cooking activities, tie-dye workshops, musical instrument making, etc.); workshops for parents only (positive discipline that works, choosing a school for your child, etc.); and performing arts programs for families (magic shows, storytelling, dance, and music).]

National Association for the Education of Young Children (NAEYC). 1509 Sixteenth Street, N.W., Washington, D.C. 20036-1426. Phone: 202/232-8777 or 1/800-424-2460. Fax: 202/328-1846. A nonprofit professional organization of more than eighty thousand members dedicated to improving the quality of services provided to young children and their families. Provides educational opportunities and resources to promote the professional development of those working for and with young children. Works to increase public knowledge and support for high quality early childhood programs (including those of preschools, primary schools, kindergartens, child care centers, cooperatives, church schools, and others). Advocates developmentally appropriate educational methods for young children. Operates a voluntary, national accreditation system for quality early childhood programs (you can write for a list of accredited schools within your state).

Publishes *Young Children,* a bimonthly journal (see listing under "Periodicals" for more information). Also publishes brochures, books, videos, posters, and information kits. While many of these publications are intended for teachers and child-care providers, others are directed at parents. Available publications are described in the NAEYC's appealing early childhood resources catalog.

National Education Association. 1201 Sixteenth Street, N.W., Washington, D.C. 20036. Phone: 202/833-

4000. This association's 2.1 million members include elementary and secondary school teachers, as well as administrators, principals, college professors, students, and others concerned with education. Provides a variety of services to its members, assisting them in lobbying, collective bargaining, research, training, legal services, organizational development, and communications. NEA's current efforts to revitalize American education are focused in its Center for Teaching and Learning, which helps fund reform initiatives designed and developed by local educators; establishes and supports experimental school renewal projects; and assists NEA affiliates in efforts to professionalize teaching, improve conditions in which teachers work and students learn, and promote self-governance of the profession. Among the NEA's periodicals are *Issues*, an annual magazine, and *NEA Today*, a paper covering news and events affecting public education (kindergarten to twelfth grade).

Quality Education for Minorities. 1818 N Street, N.W., Suite 350, Washington, D.C. 20036. Phone: 202/659-1818. Works to insure that minorities in the United States have equal access to educational opportunities. Assists local schools in carrying out educational programs to benefit minority children (African Americans, Mexican Americans, Native American Indians, Puerto Ricans, and others), particularly in the areas of math and science. Helps coordinates educational activities among organizations and institutions.

LEARNING

Inexpensive Resource

A Beginner's Bibliography. An annotated materials list for parents, teachers, and others who want to learn more about how young children learn and grow. Includes recent and classic books, brochures, and periodicals about early childhood education and child development. Among the book titles are *The Magic Years*, *The Learning Child*, and *Learning Opportunities Beyond the School*. Available for 50¢ from the National Association for the Education of Young Children (see appendix I for contract information).

Books

All Our Children Learning: A Primer for Parents, Teachers and Other Educators. By Benjamin S. Bloom. McGraw Hill, 1981. 275 pages. A collection of articles describing what can be done to help all children reach their full potential in school. Drawing on research findings, Bloom explores the effect of the home environment on children's school achievement, instruction and curriculum development, and evaluation procedures that help teachers teach and students learn.

How Children Learn. By John Holt. Revised edition. Delacorte Press/Seymour Lawrence, 1983. 303 pages. Shows how young children figure things out themselves (with little or no help) long before they are required (by schools) to learn under orders and rules, for praise and reward. Contains the text from the original edition (published in 1967), along with new material.

In Their Own Way: Discovering and Encouraging Your Child's Personal Learning Style. By Thomas Armstrong, Ph.D. Jeremy P. Tarcher,

1987. 211 pages. Shows how children are individuals with distinct personal learning styles (linguistic, logical-mathematical, spatial, musical, bodily-kinesthetic, interpersonal, and intrapersonal), and explains how parents and teachers can help them acquire knowledge according to these sometimes extraordinary aptitudes. Critical of formal testing, tracking, and teaching techniques that prevent children from developing their potential—from learning "in their own way." Includes a list of resources (publications and organizations) for each of the distinct styles of learning described in the book.

I Won't Learn from You! The Role of Assent in Learning. By Herbert Kohl. Milkweed Editions/Thistle Series, 1991. 47 pages. An essay that distinguishes between "failure" and a student's refusal to learn. The author introduces the reader to several capable young people who, for different reasons, decide they do not want to learn something. The author argues that we need to respect the truth behind the massive rejection of schooling by students. Recognizes that real learning must be voluntary.

Learning All the Time. By John Holt. Addison-Wesley, 1989. 169 pages. Describes how small children begin to read, write, count, and investigate the world without being taught. Discusses the many ways in which children are constantly learning about the world around them.

The Learning Child. By Dorothy Cohen. Schoken Books, 1988. 359 pages. Drawing on the findings of Piaget and other psychologists, as well as her own experiences as a child development teacher at Bank Street Col-

lege of Education, the author explains how parents can help turn their child's curiosity into a lifetime interest in learning. Talks about the importance of enhancing the child's self-concept and understanding individual differences in children.

Miseducation: Preschoolers at Risk. By David Elkind. Alfred A. Knopf, 1989. 221 pages. Elkind explains how a healthy education supports and encourages the spontaneous learning process through which young children explore and understand their immediate world, and how miseducation ignores it, attempting to teach the wrong things at the wrong times. He discusses the difference between the mind of a preschooler and the mind of a school-age child; explains which preschool programs are the most considerate of the individual child; and offers guidance to parents as they make early-on decisions concerning their children's education. Topics explored include testing, private schools (including Waldorf and Montessori), child's play, parenting styles, computers, and competition.

Association

New Horizons for Learning. P.O. Box 15329, Seattle, Washington 98115-0329. Phone: 206/547-7936. An international clearinghouse for information about new strategies in learning. Publishes a newsletter, *On the Beam,* which describes the latest research in learning and thinking skills. Issued three times a year. [Note: New Horizons for Learning is undergoing a transformation and will soon offer its newsletter via electronic network, rather than print.]

Cooperative Learning

Books

Circles of Learning. By David Johnson, Roger T. Johnson, and Edythe Johnson Holubec. Interaction Book Company, 1986. 88 pages. Offers an introduction to cooperative learning and compares it with competitive and individualistic approaches. For parents, teachers, and administrators.

Designing Groupwork. By Elizabeth Cohen. Teachers College Press, 1986. 189 pages. The author shows how students can more actively contribute, share, and learn when groupwork is part of their schooling. Combines easy-to-follow theory with examples and teaching strategies.

Associations

Cooperative Learning Center. University of Minnesota, 159 Pillsbury Drive, S.E., Minneapolis, Minnesota 55455. Phone: 612/624-7031. Center for research in cooperative learning. Write for information on available materials.

International Association for the Study of Cooperation in Education (IASCE). Box 1582, Santa Cruz, California 95061-1582. Phone: 408/426-7926. Promotes the study of cooperative learning at all levels of education. Maintains databases. Publishes *Cooperative Learning: A Resource Guide,* issued annually. Also publishes *Cooperative Learning Magazine,* a quarterly focusing on cooperative learning research and listing resources for practitioners.

Superlearning

Books

Accelerated Learning. By Colin Rose. Dell, 1987. 246 pages. This book combines Lozanov's approach to learning with other educational techniques. Written for adults, but offers guidelines on working with children.

The Centering Book: Awareness Activities for Children and Adults to Relax the Body and Mind and **The Second Centering Book.** By Gay Hendricks and Russel Wills. Prentice-Hall, 1989. These books teach relaxation techniques to help enhance creativity and learning. The first book covers yoga, imagery, dreams, and relaxation training. The second book covers feelings, intuition, fantasy, and meditation.

The Everyday Genius: Restoring Children's Natural Joy of Learning. By Peter Kline. Great Ocean Publishers, 1988. 274 pages. The author offers a personal account of his experience with superlearning methods. Includes suggestions to promote learning at home and in the classroom.

Superlearning™. By Sheila Ostrander and Lynn Schroeder. Delacorte Press, 1979. 342 pages. The best-selling introduction to Lozanov's method of learning. Describes a system that allows people to master facts, figures, and skills at a much faster pace. Includes techniques, practical exercises, and lists of musical selections to help enhance learning.

Unicorns Are Real: A Right-Brained Approach to Learning. By Barbara Meister Vitale. Warner, 1985. 240 pages. Offers guidelines to help parents and teachers determine a child's hemispheric dominance and use learning strategies that will help the individual child. Offers strategies for teaching math, reading, language, movement, and study skills at home and school.

Organizations

Barzak Educational Institute Inc. 88 Belvedere Street, Suite D, San Rafael, California 94901. Phone: 1/800-672-1717. In California, call 415/459-4474. Superlearning audio cassettes, guidebooks, and foreign language instruction kits for children are available by mail through this company, which also conducts seminars for educators and other professionals. Call or write for a product listing.

Society for Accelerative Learning and Teaching (SALT). Box 1216, Welch Station, Ames, IA 50010. Professional association of educators concerned with applying superlearning techniques in the classroom and other educational settings. Conducts research, sponsors conferences, and publishes a periodical and several books and pamphlets. Also produces an international resources directory

---

Is My Child "Gifted"?

If you elect to have your child tested for "giftedness," you can find a qualified tester in your area by contacting your school district or the National Association for Gifted Children, 1155 Fifteenth Street, N.W., No. 1002, Washington, D.C. 20005. 202/785-4268. See "Individual Differences" for more information on this association.

---

listing books, periodicals, workshops, and curriculum materials related to accelerated learning.

Superlearning Inc. 450 Seventh Avenue, New York, New York 10123. Phone: 212/279-8450. Supplier of tapes and other materials based on the best-selling book *Superlearning* (see listing under "Books").

TESTING

Taking Tests

Inexpensive Resource

Help Your Child Improve in Test-Taking. Offers techniques to help children at all grade levels avoid "test anxiety" and prepare for various types of tests. Published in 1985 by the Department of Education. For ordering information, request a copy of the free *Consumer Information Catalog*, available from the Consumer Information Center, P.O. Box 100, Pueblo, Colorado 81002.

Books

Is Your Child Ready for School? A Parent's Guide to the Readiness Tests Required by Public and Private Primary Schools. See listing under "Starting School."

Mental Measurements Yearbook. Buros Institute of Mental Measurements, University of Nebraska. Updated annually. A guide to standardized tests for children and adults. Includes reviews of recently released or revised tests. Also available from this publisher: *Tests in Print* (updated periodically). Both books are available in the reference sections of many public and academic libraries.

Testing and Your Child: What You Should Know about 150 of the Most Common Medical, Educational, and Psychological Tests. By Virginia E. McCullough. Penguin Books, 1992. 334 pages. This book includes descriptions of several dozen educational tests. Each entry includes information on who must administer the test (and under what conditions), what the test tests for and what it cannot reveal, what preparation is required, what affects scoring, and what follow-up testing might be recommended. Also includes full descriptions of developmental, psychological, and medical tests.

Criticism of and Alternatives to Standardized Testing

Free and Inexpensive Resources

On Standardized Testing. Position paper of the Association for Childhood Education International (ACEI), calling for a moratorium on standardized testing in the early years of schooling. Dedicated to seeking more constructive directions for assessment. 11 pages. Available for $2.50 from ACEI, 11501 Georgia Avenue, Suite 315, Wheaton, Maryland 20902-1924. Phone: 1/800-423-3563 or 301/942-2443.

Standardized Tests and Our Children: A Guide to Testing Reform. Fairtest, 1992. A booklet explaining what standardized tests are and how they work. Suggests better ways to evaluate students and explains what parents can do to help. Available for $3.00 from the Alliance for Parental Involvement in Education, Inc., P.O. Box 59, East Chatham, New York 12060-0059. Phone: 518/392-6900. (Specify national booklet or New York state booklet when ordering.)

Testing of Young Children: Concerns and Cautions. A brochure on standardized testing of children ages three through eight. Available for 50¢ from the National Association for the Education of Young Children (see appendix I for contact information).

Books

Achievement Testing in the Early Grades: The Games Grown-Ups Play. Edited by C. Kamii. National Association for the Education of Young Children, 1990. 182 pages. Explains how achievement tests fail to tell us what we need to know about children's progress, how they encourage bad teaching, and how they ultimately harm children. Available from the National Association for the Education of Young Children (see appendix I for contact information).

Degrading the Grading Myths: A Primer on Alternatives to Grades and Marks. Edited by Sidney Simon and James Bellanca. Association for Supervision and Curriculum Development, 1976. 151 pages. Prepared in cooperation with the National Center for Grading/Learning Alternatives, this book explores common myths about grading and compares the alternatives (contract methods, performance evaluation, etc.).

The Mismeasure of Man. By Stephen Jay Gould. Norton, 1981. 352 pages. Chronicles the rise of intelligence tests in the United States and describes how they have been used to legitimize racist, classist, and sexist policies.

None of the Above. By David Owen. Houghton Mifflin, 1985. 327 pages.

Although the book focuses on the Scholastic Aptitude Test (SAT) (it's a scam, the author convincingly argues), parents concerned about standardized testing in general will find this book insightful.

Testing for Learning: How New Approaches to Evaluation Can Improve American Schools. By Ruth Mitchell. The Free Press, 1992. The author argues that students should be asked to demonstrate their abilities to think and to apply their knowledge productively, rather than simply to regurgitate information. Explains how new approaches to evaluation can improve our schools.

The Testing Trap. By Andrew J. Strenio, Jr. Rawson, Wade Publishers, 1981. 328 pages. Reveals how tests that "measure" everything from intelligence to aptitude control the lives of all Americans, limit our hopes and accomplishments, and shape our futures in our jobs and professions. Examines what we can do to cope with them. Suggests changes to make tests fairer and more accurate. Aims to reduce society's obsessive dependence on testing.

Associations

Friends for Education. 600 Girard Boulevard, N.E., Albuquerque, New Mexico 87106. Phone: 505/260-1745. Works to establish and improve public school accountability systems. Has filed law suits against standardized tests publishers, who the group believes manipulated their tests to allow students to score higher than their abilities would justify. Claims that test results from all fifty states show students scoring above the national average. Publications include *The "Lake Woebegone" Report: How Public Educators Cheat on Standardized Achievement Tests* and *Nationally Normed Elementary Achievement Testing in America's Public Schools—How All Fifty States Are Above the National Average.*

National Center for Fair and Open Testing. 342 Broadway, Cambridge, Massachusetts 02139. Phone: 617/864-4810. Explores the problems and inequities in standardized testing. Seeks to ensure that standardized tests are fair; open; educationally sound; and free of racial, cultural, and sexual biases. Holds educational programs, seminars, and workshops. Publishes *Fairtest Examiner,* a newsletter focusing primarily on test reform. Explores the limits of—and alternatives to—standardized testing. Produces other publications on testing as well.

Education Reform

Books

Cultural Literacy: What Every American Needs to Know. By E. D. Hirsch, Jr. Houghton Mifflin, 1987. 251 pages. Argues that cultural literacy—the grasp of background information that writers and speakers assume their readers and listeners already have—is the hidden key to effective education in America. Outlines a plan for making cultural literacy our educational priority, which includes defining core knowledge, putting more of that information into school textbooks, and developing tests of core learning that can help students measure their progress. [Note: E. D. Hirsch, Jr., is also the editor of the Core Knowledge series, which includes *What Every First Grader Needs to Know, What Every Second Grader Needs to Know,* and so forth. For more information, call the Core Knowledge Foundation at 1/800-238-3233.]

Educating for Character: How Our Schools Can Teach Respect and Responsibility. By Thomas Lickona. Bantam, 1992. 478 pages. Offers advice to help parents and educators create a responsible, caring environment that promotes learning. Offers strategies designed to create a working coalition of parents, teachers, and others who care about young people.

Endangered Minds: Why Our Children Don't Think and What We Can Do about It. By Jane M. Healy, Ph.D. Simon and Schuster, 1990. 382 pages. The author argues that today's children, bombarded by a fast-paced media culture, have developed different "habits of mind" than those of previous decades. Particularly at risk are children's language-related learning abilities (reading, writing, analytic reasoning, oral expression), problem-solving skills, and attention spans). Healy explains how and why these changes are occurring, what can be done about them, and what they mean for the future. She believes parents and teachers can make a critical difference, helping children to become good learners not only during their school years but throughout their lifetimes.

Parenting Our Schools: A Hands-On Guide to Education Reform. By Jill Bloom. Little, Brown, 1992. 313 pages. For parents who want to know how they can make a difference, not just by getting their children the best education within the system, but also by changing the systems that clearly don't work. Offers parents hands-on guidance to education reform at the local, state, and national level. Discusses school budgets, the writing of legislation, and other relevant topics.

Savage Inequalities: Children in America's Schools. By Jonathan Kozol. HarperPerennial, 1991. 262 pages. A primer on why schooling inequity exists in America. Demonstrates how various forces—neighborhood segregation, corporate apathy, and elitism—contribute to the deterioration of school systems. Children trapped in neglected public schools are the innocent victims. Includes conversations with students, teachers, and administrators; documents the condition of schools in the inner cities; explores funding disparities; and explains how American politics imposes inequality in our schools. Argues that property tax-based funding provides children from affluent neighborhoods with a sound education while ensuring an impoverished future for poor students.

Schools that Work: America's Most Innovative Public Education Programs. By George H. Wood, Ph.D. Dutton, 1992. 290 pages. Describes "schools that work" and demonstrates what makes them effective. Takes readers into the classrooms and explains the various elements that help create healthy learning institutions.

Smart Schools, Smart Kids: Why Do Some Schools Work? By Edward B. Fiske. Simon and Schuster, 1991. 303 pages. Reports on the grass-roots revolution that is transforming America's classroom. Takes readers into pioneering schools where they can see what's taking place, what problems are encountered, and what results are achieved. Winner of the *Child* magazine Book Award for Excellence in Family Issues.

The Unschooled Mind: How Children Think and How Schools Should Teach. By Howard Gardner. Basic Books, 1991. 303 pages. Analyzes the American school system. Shows how ill-suited our minds and natural patterns of learning are to current educational materials, practices, and institutions. How can we help students move beyond rote learning to achieve genuine understanding? Gardner builds a strong case for restructuring our schools, finding clues for reform in the art of apprenticeship and in modern children's museum. The author argues that in both these settings genuine understanding occurs because learning takes place within a meaningful context.

U. S. Government Resources

Head Start. Department of Health and Human Services, Administration for Children and Families, 370 L'Enfant Promenade, S.W., Washington, D.C. 20447. Phone: 202/401-9215. Since its establishment in 1965, Head Start has served more than 13.1 million children and their families. This national program offers "comprehensive developmental services" for America's low-income preschool children ages three to five and social services for their families. Specific services focus on education, emotional and social development, physical and mental health, and nutrition. Parent involvement is an essential part of the program. Grants to conduct Head Start programs are awarded to local public or private nonprofit agencies through regional offices of the Administration for Children and Families and the Head Start Bureau's American Indian and Migrant Programs Branches. Twenty percent of the cost must be contributed by the community. Head Start programs operate in all fifty states, the District of Columbia, and the U.S. territories.

U.S. Department of Education. Office of Educational Research and Improvement, 555 New Jersey Avenue, N.W., Washington, D.C. 20208. Phone: 1/800-424-1616. Supports and conducts research on education, collects and analyzes education statistics, and disseminates information. Among its various programs, the Office of Educational Research and Improvement supports the Educational Resources Information Center (see listing under "Databases" for more information). Call the number listed above for department directory assistance, education statistics, or information on programs and publications of the U.S. Department of Education.

Database

Educational Resources Information Center (ERIC). Office of Educational Research and Improvement, 555 New Jersey Avenue, N.W., Washington, D.C. 20208. Phone: 202/219-2289 or 1/800-LET-ERIC (ACCESS ERIC). A national information system responsible for developing, maintaining, and providing access to the world's largest single source of information on education research and educational practices. The ERIC system includes a network of clearinghouses, each of which specializes in a different area of education. Within their subject areas, the ERIC clearinghouses acquire significant literature for the database, publish research summaries and other products, and provide free reference and referral services. Altogether, the databases now contain more than 750,000 documents and journal articles, with approximately 2,600 records added monthly. There are several ways to access ERIC documents (these are described in several free guides: *A Pocket Guide to ERIC, All About ERIC,* and *For Education Information . . . Call ACCESS ERIC.* Call or write for copies). ACCESS ERIC is a toll-free service offering information on the ERIC network and other education resources. ACCESS ERIC staff will answer questions, refer callers to education

"If you are a concerned parent who wants to be more involved in your child's education, ACCESS ERIC can help you identify important information about schools and gifted programs, send you a variety of pamphlets on questions commonly asked by parents about their child's education, and refer you to education information centers for additional publications and reference and referral services."

—From the free brochure, "For Education Information . . . Call ACCESS ERIC."

sources, and provide information about the ERIC network.

A Sampling of ERIC documents
The following documents are from the ERIC Clearinghouse on Elementary and Early Childhood Education, University of Illinois, 805 West Pennsylvania Avenue, Urbana, Illinois 61801-4897.

For Parents: An Introduction to Kindergarten. 1992. A fifteen-page booklet describing activities that take place in kindergarten classrooms and characteristics of kindergarten staff members. Describes how kindergarten activities and teachers help children develop and discusses the nature of children's learning and motivation in general.

For Parents' Sake: A Survival Kit for Parents and Kids. Edited by Linda C. Passmark. 1991. 32 pages. Describes the growth and developmental stages of children from birth through adolescence. Also offers

ways to help mothers and fathers deal with the stress of parenthood, including suggestions for relieving tension, developing support systems, and seeking professional help. An appendix lists agencies that provide information on parenting, child development, and parent support groups.

Increasing Parent Involvement in the Moral and Ethical Development of the Elementary Child to Decrease Acts of Violence in Preadolescent Children. By Beth L. Woodard. 1992. 41 pages. This paper reports on a ten-week program at an urban elementary school developed to addresses the problem of aggressive behavior among the student population. The objectives of the program were to increase parental supervision of children's media consumption, increase students' use of conflict resolution strategies, and to decrease the number of students referred because of aggressive behavior. The first two objectives were met; the third was not.

SOME TERMS IN EDUCATION (A GLOSSARY)

Charter Schools. Charter schools offer a way to broaden educational choices within the public school system. Parents or educators interested in establishing a new kind of school approach the local school district (or some other public body) for a contract under which they would establish an autonomous public school.

The new school might specialize in a particular learning method (Montessori, for example) or field of study (science, art, etc.), or in students of a particular age, type, or sort (at-risk children, for example). The school would agree to meet required learning objectives.

Cooperative Learning (Collaborative Learning). When students of mixed abilities work in pairs or small groups to learn a process, skill, or subject. The group might produce a newsletter, make a sun dial, design a building, or spell out words. Research shows that children learn well when they help each other.

Developmental Education. Takes into account predictable patterns that are discernible as children grow physically, mentally, emotionally, and socially. Emphasizing age-appropriate activities, projects, and materials. Unlike teacher-directed programs, developmental programs allow children to initiate activities (for example, painting, listening to tapes, or solving puzzles), with the teacher helping to make these experiences meaningful. In developmental programs, activities initiated by the teacher are age-appropriate.

Learning Centers. Classrooms with individual "learning centers" allow children to learn a particular lesson through a series of activities—perhaps listening to tapes, working on a computer, reading books, or performing experiments. An approach that takes into account individual styles of learning.

Magnet Schools. A public school (usually with a specialty such as science, language, or the arts) to which anyone in the district or school system (depending on the program) can apply. Entrance requirements can vary: some use a lottery system or admit students on a first-come, first-served basis; others hold auditions or evaluate previous grades and/or standardized test scores. To graduate, students must complete all of the courses required by the state.

Mixed-Age Grouping (Family Grouping). In mixed-age groupings, children stay with the same teacher for more than one year, thereby creating continuity. The children, who are encouraged to help one another, learn at their own pace and move on to a new area of learning after they have mastered a specific skill. Based on the belief that age-based groupings are illogical, given how widely normal development varies in the early grades. Opponents are concerned that precocious students may suffer academically if they are grouped with those at earlier levels of development.

Multiculturalism. An emphasis on a variety of cultures in teaching curricula. Seeks to create a better understanding and appreciation of ethnic differences in student populations. Some fear that multiculturalism will have the opposite effect—that it will push people apart, rather than bring them together. Others feel that classroom time would be better spent exploring other topics and bases of knowledge.

National Testing. Students in schools across the country would take the same standardized tests (determined at the national level). Advocates of national testing say it is necessary to provide accountability in schools across the country and to help parents select the best schools for their children, given their strengths and weaknesses. Critics say that such tests will encourage children to spit out facts, rather than learn how to genuinely think and solve problems.

School Choice. Existing school choice programs allow parents to select the public school their children attend as long as the school system's desired racial balance is maintained. Parents may select from among the schools in their school district or from schools in other districts as well, depending on the particular program. Advocates of school choice believe such programs improve the quality of education since schools must compete for students. Critics are concerned that schools in impoverished neighborhoods will suffer, since resources will be redirected to already successful schools. [According to a report entitled *School Choice,* by Ernest L. Boyer, president of the Carnegie Foundation for the Advancement of Teaching, less than 2 percent of parents in areas where school choice has been adopted actually participate in the program. The report also shows that 75 percent of parents with children in public schools are satisfied with their current public school arrangement. This information is based on national surveys; site visits to school districts with successful choice programs; and interviews with parents, students, teachers, and administrators.]

Superlearning. Based on the work of Georgi Lozanov, a Bulgarian psychiatrist, superlearning recognizes that people often learn best from relaxing, enjoyable experiences, rather than through concentrated effort. Background music and the power of suggestion are two superlearning techniques used to activate memory, ability, and motivation in learning.

Tracking. A system whereby students are mixed according to ability. Advocates of tracking fear that bright students will be slowed down if they are forced to learn along side less abled students; opponents say that tracking cheats many students out of a really good education.

STATE DEPARTMENTS OF EDUCATION

State Departments of Education or Public Instruction collect, compile, and disseminate information on students, teachers, school and district finances, demographics, etc. Upon request, many of these offices will conduct computer searches (some charge a fee) on student/staff ratios, drop-out rates, test scores, class size, teacher salaries, special programs, etc. This data is usually available by school, school district, county, region, or state. In addition, many departments offer listings of teachers' names and school addresses. Written requests are preferred.

Alabama State Department of Education. Gordon Persons Office Building, 50 North Ripley Street, Montgomery, Alabama 36130-3901. Phone: 205/242-9700.

Alaska Department of Education. 801 West Tenth Street, Suite 200, Juneau, Alaska 99801-1894. Phone: 907/465-2800.

Arizona State Department of Education. 1535 West Jefferson, Phoenix, Arizona 85007. Phone: 602/542-5460.

Arkansas State Department of Education. Four State Capitol Mall, Room 304 A, Little Rock, Arkansas 72201-1071. Phone: 501/682-4204.

California State Department of Education. 721 Capitol Mall, Sacramento, California 94814. Phone: 916/657-4585.

Colorado State Department of Education. 201 East Colfax Avenue, Denver, Colorado 80203-1799. Phone: 303/866-6600.

Connecticut State Department of Education. 165 Capitol Avenue, Room 305, State Office Building, Hartford, Connecticut 06106-1630. Phone: 203/566-5061.

Delaware State Department of Education. P.O. Box 1402, Townsend Building, #279, Federal and Lockerman Streets, Dover, Delaware 19903. Phone: 302/739-4601.

District of Columbia Public Schools. The Presidential Building, 415 Twelfth Street, N.W., Washington, D.C. 20004. Phone: 202/724-4222.

Florida State Department of Education. Capitol Building, Room PL 08, Tallahassee, Florida 32301. Phone: 904/487-1785.

Georgia State Department of Education. 2066 Twin Towers East, 205 Butler Street, Atlanta, Georgia 30334. Phone: 404/656-2800.

Hawaii Department of Education. 1390 Miller Street, #307, Honolulu, Hawaii 96813. Phone: 808/586-3310.

Idaho State Department of Education. Len B. Jordan Office Building, 650 West State Street, Boise, Idaho 83720. Phone: 208/334-3300.

Illinois State Board of Education. 100 North First Street, Springfield, Illinois 62777. Phone: 217/782-2221.

Indiana State Department of Education. State House, Room 229, Indianapolis, Indiana 46204-2798. Phone: 317/232-6665.

Iowa State Department of Education. Grimes State Office Building, East Fourteenth and Grand Streets, Des Moines, Iowa 50319-0146. Phone: 515/281-5294.

Kansas State Department of Education. 120 Southeast Tenth Avenue, Topeka, Kansas 66612-1182. Phone: 913/296-3202.

Kentucky State Department of Education. Capitol Plaza Tower, 500 Mero Street, Frankfort, Kentucky 40601. Phone: 502/564-3141.

Louisiana State Department of Education. P.O. Box 94064, 626 North Fourth Street, Baton Rouge, Louisiana 70804-9064. Phone: 504/342-3602.

Maine Department of Education. State House Station #23, Augusta, Maine 04333. Phone: 207/287-5800.

Maryland State Department of Education. 200 West Baltimore Street, Baltimore, Maryland 21201. Phone: 410/333-2200.

Massachusetts State Department of Education. 350 Main Street, Malden, Massachusetts 02148. Phone: 617/388-3300.

Michigan State Department of Education. P.O. Box 30008, 608 West Allegan Street, Lansing, Michigan 48909. Phone: 517/373-3354.

Minnesota State Department of Education. 712 Capitol Square Building, 550 Cedar Street, St. Paul, Minnesota 55101. Phone: 612/296-2358.

Mississippi State Department of Education. P.O. Box 771, 550 High Street, Room 501, Jackson, Mississippi 39205-0771. Phone: 601/359-3513.

Missouri Department of Elementary and Secondary Education. P.O. Box 480, 205 Jefferson Street, 6th Floor, Jefferson City, Missouri 65102. Phone: 314/751-4446.

Montana State Office of Public Instruction. 106 State Capitol, Helena, Montana 59620. Phone: 406/444-3680.

Nebraska State Department of Education. P.O. Box 94987, 301 Centennial Mall, South, Lincoln, Nebraska 68509. Phone: 402/471-5020.

Nevada State Department of Education. 400 West King Street, Capitol Complex, Carson City, Nevada 89710. Phone: 702/687-3100.

New Hampshire State Department of Education. 101 Pleasant Street, State Office Park South, Concord, New Hampshire 03301. Phone: 603/271-3144.

New Jersey State Department of Education. 225 East State Street, CN500, Trenton, New Jersey 08625-0500. Phone: 609/292-4450.

New Mexico State Department of Education. Education Building, 300 Don Gaspar, Santa Fe, New Mexico 87501-2786. Phone: 505/827-6516.

New York State Education Department. 111 Education Building, Washington Avenue, Albany, New York 12234. Phone: 518/474-5844.

North Carolina State Department of Public Instruction. Education Building, 301 North Wilmington Street, Raleigh, North Carolina 27601-2825. Phone: 919/715-1299.

North Dakota State Department of Public Instruction. State Capitol Building, 11th Floor, 600 Builevard Avenue East, Bismarck, North Dakota 58505-0440. Phone: 701/224-2261.

Ohio State Department of Education. 65 South Front Street, Room 808, Columbus, Ohio 43266-0308. Phone: 614/466-3304.

Oklahoma State Department of Education. Hodge Education Building, 2500 North Lincoln Boulevard, Oklahoma City, Oklahoma 73105-4599. Phone: 405/521-3301.

Oregon State Department of Education. 700 Pringle Parkway, S.E., Salem, Oregon 97310-0290. Phone: 503/378-3573.

Pennsylvania State Department of Education. 333 Market Street, 10th Floor, Harrisburg, Pennsylvania 17126-0333. Phone: 717/787-5820.

Rhode Island State Department of Education. 22 Hayes Street, Providence, Rhode Island 02908. Phone: 401/277-2031.

South Carolina State Department of Education. 1006 Rutledge Building, 1429 Senate Street, Columbia, South Carolina 29201. Phone: 803/734-8492.

South Dakota Department of Education and Cultural Affairs. 700 Governors Drive, Pierre, South Dakota 57501-2291. Phone: 605/773-3134.

Tennessee State Department of Education. 100 Cordell Hull Building, Nashville, Tennessee 37243-0375. Phone: 615/741-2731.

Texas Education Agency. William B. Travis Building, 1701 North Congress Avenue, Austin, Texas 78701-1494. Phone: 512/463-8985.

Utah State Office of Education. 250 East 500 South, Salt Lake City, Utah 84111. Phone: 801/538-7510.

Vermont State Department of Education. 120 State Street, Montpelier, Vermont 05620-2501. Phone: 802/828-3135.

Virginia State Department of Education. James Monroe Building, Fourteenth and Franklin Streets, Richmond, Virginia 23216-2120. Phone: 804/225-2755.

Washington State Department of Public Instruction. Old Capitol Building, Washington and Legion, P.O. Box 47200, Olympia, Washington 98504-7200. Phone: 206/586-6904.

West Virginia State Department of Education. 1900 Kanawha Boulevard, East, Building 6, Room B-358, Charleston, West Virginia 25305. Phone: 304/558-2681.

Wisconsin State Department of Public Instruction. 125 South Webster Street, P.O. Box 7841, Madison, Wisconsin 53707. Phone: 608/266-1771.

Wyoming State Department of Education. 2300 Capitol Avenue, 2nd Floor, Hathaway Building, Cheyenne, Wyoming 82002-0050. Phone: 307/777-7675.

Chapter 14

Topics in Education (School Subjects)

SOCIAL STUDIES

General Resources

Inexpensive Resource

Notable Children's Trade Books in the Field of Social Studies. An annotated listing of the year's best books in the field of social studies for children in kindergarten through grade eight. For a free copy of the most recent listing, send a 6" x 9" self-addressed, stamped envelope (85¢ postage) along with your request to the Children's Book Council, 568 Broadway, Suite 404, New York, New York 10012.

Association

National Council for the Social Studies. 3501 Newark Street, N.W., Washington, D.C. 20016. Phone: 202/966-7840. An association of teachers of elementary and secondary school social studies, including civics, history, geography, psychology, sociology, and anthropology.

Works to successfully integrate bodies of knowledge. Publishes *Social Studies and the Young Learner,* a quarterly journal covering research, theory, and creative classroom activities for social studies teaching in elementary school. Other periodicals include *Social Education,* a journal covering various aspects of social studies teaching and learning, and *The Social Studies Professional,* a tabloid covering council activities and news of the social studies profession.

Mail Order Catalog

Social Studies School Service. 10200 Jefferson Boulevard, P.O. Box 802, Culver City, California 90232-0802. Phone: 1/800-421-4246. Publishes a global education catalog containing multicultural materials appropriate for both school and home use.

Geography

Free and Inexpensive Resources

Catalog of Maps. To obtain a catalog of maps available from the U.S. Geological Survey, call its toll-free number: 1/800-USA-MAPS. The broad selection includes maps of U.S. cities, world maps, crop maps, and satellite-picture maps. Most maps cost between $2.00 and $4.00.

Helping Your Child Learn Geography. Produced by the U.S. Department of Education, this booklet contains fun learning activities for children. For ordering information, request a copy of the free *Consumer Information Catalog,* available from the Consumer Information Center, P.O. Box 100, Pueblo, Colorado 81002. (Note: You can also order this publication by contacting the U. S. Government Printing Office in Washington, D.C. See appendix B for more information.)

Map of the United States. This map shows the U.S. Wildlife Refuges and is available, free of charge, from the U.S. Fish and Wildlife Service, Division of Refuge, Eighteenth and C Streets, N.W., Washington, D.C. 20204.

In addition to the resources listed above, many state tourist agencies publish walking tour maps and guidebooks to area attractions. See listings of state tourist agencies in chapter 21.

Books

For Adults

The Map Catalog. Joel Makower, editor; Laura Bergheim, associate editor. Revised edition. Random House, 1990. 368 pages. A book that lists and describes hundreds of available maps, including many that are free or inexpensive.

For Children

Courage Children's Illustrated World Atlas. Edited by Brian Dicks. Running Press, 1989. 128 pages. An atlas for children, illustrated with more than five hundred maps and pictures. Begins with familiar environments (the child's house and neighborhood) and then broadens its perspective to encompass countries around the world. For grades one and up.

Maps and Globes. By Jack Knowlton. HarperCollins, 1985. 42 pages. *Maps and Globes* offers young readers a brief history of map making; includes clear descriptions of the various maps, atlases, and globes used today. A Reading Rainbow selection. For children in grades one through five.

My First Atlas. By Kate Petty. Illustrated by Colin King. Warner Juvenile Books, 1991. Contains maps, facts, and activities that introduce young children to the countries and regions of the world. For ages three to seven.

My World. By Ira Wolfman. Workman, 1991. 64 pages. A first book of geography filled with facts, maps, projects, and stickers. Comes with an inflatable globe, showing oceans, rivers, mountains, and continents. Children ages four and up will enjoy filling in the rest with the enclosed stickers.

Picture Atlas of the World. By the Rand McNally staff. Illustrated by Brian Delf. Rand McNally, 1991. 80 pages. Includes maps, famous landmarks, natural resources, flags, and descriptions of cultures around the globe. Maps include mountains, rivers, and major cities. For children ages six to twelve.

Rand McNally Giant Atlas of the USA. Illustrated by Stuart Brendon. Rand McNally, 1992. 14 pages. An oversized book featuring colorful maps of the United States. Includes picture keys, fact boxes, and two-page spreads of the states by region. Also shows the "history of the United States" (on a single map, with pictures and a timeline of important events in American history). Kids can spread this book out on the floor, read it (or just look at the pictures), and crawl around on the sturdy pages.

The Sierra Club Wayfinding Book. By Vicki McVey. Illustrated by Martha Weston. Little, Brown, 1989. 88 pages. Takes readers of all ages on a journey through the history of wayfinding and shows how we can become wayfinders ourselves, whether we're in the wilderness or in our daily environments. Includes activities such as making a compass, reading different kinds of maps, and playing animal tracking games.

The Viking Children's World Atlas. By Jacqueline Tivers and Michael Day. Viking, 1983. 47 pages. Features Sarah and Simon—two children who travel around the world. The atlas begins with an aerial view of Sarah and Simon's home, then widens its lens to encompass the young travelers' street, town, country, the world (and various countries in it), and the world of space. Includes diagrams and photographs of the things Sarah and Simon encounter on their journey.

Where on Earth: A Geografunny Guide to the Globe. By Paul Rosenthal. Alfred A. Knopf, 1992. 106 pages. A humorous introduction to various aspects of geography and how they affect life on the different continents. Combines simple text and cartoon-like drawings to make children laugh as they learn.

Videotapes

Tommy Tricker and the Stamp Travelers. FHE (distributed by Live Home Video). Running time: 101 minutes. In this action adventure film, a boy shrinks to the size of postage stamp and travels around the world on an envelope. For ages seven and up.

Where Do You Think You're Going, Christopher Columbus? Weston Woods. Running time: 35 minutes. In this videotape, Jean Fritz reads her version of Christopher Columbus' journeys. Combines new artwork with illustrations from the book *Where Do You Think You're Going* (Putnam, 1980). Shows maps of the Old World, as well as modern-day maps. For ages eight and up.

Where in the World: Kids Explore Mexico. Encounter Video. Running time: 30 minutes. One in a series of "Where in the World" videotapes, *Kids Explore Mexico* introduces children to this neighboring country using maps and film footage showing the land and its people. Highlights are noted by a group of children, who learn more about Mexico at their local library and by visiting museums, restaurants, and ethnic festivals. Other titles in the series explore Kenya, Alaska, and the United States' national parks.

Games

Mad Dash. ITOS Enterprises. Using colorful maps, playing cards, and a sand timer, players (ages eight and up) blaze trails across the United States. Also includes "State Secrets," a strategy game in which players uncover basic facts of U.S. geography. Winner of the 1992 Parents' Choice Award. Available from ITOS Enterprises, Department C, R.D. 3, Box 300, York, Pennsylvania 17402. Phone: 1/800-827-5725.

Where in the World. Aristoplay. A game that teaches children about the countries of the world, including their location, their capital, the languages spoken, religions practiced, and major imports and exports. Six games in one. For two to six players, ages eight and up. Available from Aristoplay (see chapter 27 for contact information).

Where in the World Is Carmen Sandiego? A boardgame designed to help teach children ages ten and up about world geography. Players answer geography questions, uncover secret hideouts, and try to get to Carmen and her crew before they steal priceless monuments. For two to four players. Available from Reader's Digest Kids Catalog (see chapter 27 for contact information).

Software

Where in the World Is Carmen Sandiego? Carmen and her crew lead young detectives to several dozen of the world's greatest cities. At each stop, players can search for clues to Carmen's whereabouts while learning about the cultures, architecture, and geography of the planet. For children ages seven and up. Comes in versions for use with Macintosh computers or IBM compatibles. Available from Music for Little People (see chapter 27 for contact information).

Associations

American Geographical Society. 156 Fifth Avenue, Suite 600, New York, New York 10010-7002. Phone: 212/242-0214. A society of geographers, educators, and others interested in all phases of geography. Sponsors research projects, as well as symposia and lectures. Disseminates geographic knowledge. Publishes *Focus*, a quarterly magazine of geographical interests. Sends businesspeople with geography degrees to eighth-grade classrooms to teach geography as an important business tool used in market research, selecting store and factory locations, and reducing transportation costs.

National Geographic Society. Seventeenth and M Streets, N.W., Washington, D.C. 20036. Phone: 202/857-7000 or 1/800-638-4077. A society for individuals interested in geography, natural history, archaeology, astronomy, ethnology, and oceanography. Conducts research, sponsors expeditions, and disseminates information. Maintains the National Geographic Society Geography Education Program to enhance geographic education in kindergarten through grade twelve. Houses Explorers Hall, a small museum with child-friendly exhibits. Produces maps, globes, books (including picture atlases, pop-ups, and other eye-appealing nonfiction for young audiences), monographs, and films. Periodicals include *National Geographic,* with its state-of-the-art photography and a circulation of ten million, and *National Geographic World,* a general interest magazine for children ages eight to fourteen. Produces book and video mail order catalogs as well, containing many items for children and families.

Mail Order Catalog

The George F. Cram Company, Inc. P.O. Box 426, Indianapolis, Indiana 46206. Phone: 317/635-5564. Fax: 317/635-2720. Makers of quality globes ranging from $31.00 to $700.00. Also publishes wall, desk, and children's wipe-off U.S./world maps. Write or call for a free catalog.

A Glossary of Terms

From *Helping Your Child Learn Geography,* produced by the U.S. Department of Education with courtesy, in part, from Hammond, Inc.

altitude. Distance above sea level.

atlas. A bound collection of maps.

archipelago. A group of islands or a sea studded with islands.

bay. A wide area of water extending into land from a sea or lake.

boundaries. Lines indicating the limits of countries, states, or other political jurisdictions.

canal. A man-made watercourse designed to carry goods or water.

canyon. A large but narrow gorge with steep sides.

cape (or point). A piece of land extending into water.

cartographer. A person who draws or makes maps or charts.

continent. One of the large, continuous areas of the Earth into which the land surface is divided.

degree. A unit of angular measure. A circle is divided into 360 degrees, represented by the symbol °. Degrees, when applied to the roughly spherical shape of the Earth for geographic and cartographic purposes, are each divided into 60 minutes, represented by the symbol '.

delta. The fan-shaped area at the mouth, or lower end, of a river, formed by eroded material that has been carried downstream and dropped in quantities larger than can be carried off by tides or currents.

desert. A land area so dry that little or no plant life can survive.

elevation. The altitude of an object, such as a celestial body, above the horizon; or the raising of a portion of the Earth's crust relative to its surroundings, as in a mountain range.

equator. An imaginary circle around the Earth halfway between the North Pole and the South Pole; the largest circumference of the Earth.

glacier. A large body of ice that moves slowly down a mountainside from highlands toward sea level.

gulf. A large arm of an ocean or sea extending into a land mass.

hemisphere. Half of the Earth, usually conceived as resulting from the division of the globe into two equal parts, north and south or east and west.

ice shelf. A thick mass of ice extending from a polar shore. The seaward edge is afloat and sometimes extends hundreds of miles out to sea.

international date line. An imaginary line of longitude generally 180 degrees east or west of the prime meridian. The date becomes one day earlier to the east of the line.

island. An area of land, smaller than a continent, completely surrounded by water.

isthmus. A narrow strip of land located between two bodies of water, connecting two large land areas.

lagoon. A shallow area of water separated from the ocean by a sandbank or by a strip of low land.

lake. A body of fresh or salt water entirely surrounded by land.

latitude. The angular distance north or south of the equator, measured in degrees.

legend. A listing which contains symbols and other information about a map.

longitude. The angular distance east or west of the prime meridian, measured in degrees.

mountain. A high point of land rising steeply above its surroundings.

oasis. A spot in a desert made fertile by water.

ocean. The salt water surrounding the great land masses, and divided by the land masses into several distinct portions, each of which is called an ocean.

peak. The highest point of a mountain.

peninsula. A piece of land extending into the sea almost surrounded by water.

physical feature. A land shape formed by nature.

plain. A large area of land, either level or gently rolling, usually at low elevation.

plateau (or tableland). An elevated area of mostly level land, sometimes containing deep canyons.

population. The number of people inhabiting a place.

prime meridian. An imaginary line running from north to south through Greenwich, England, used as the reference point for longitude.

range (or mountain range). A group or chain of high elevations.

reef. A chain of rocks, often coral, lying near the water surface.

Helping Your Child Learn Geography

From *Helping Your Child Learn Geography*, published by the U.S. Department of Education in cooperation with the Department of the Interior, U.S. Geological Survey.

Location: Position on the Earth's Surface

Look at a map. *Where are places located?* To determine location, geographers use a set of imaginary lines that crisscross the surface of the globe. Lines designating "latitude" tell us how far north or south of the equator a place is. Lines designating "longitude" measure distance east and west of the prime meridian—an imaginary line running between the North Pole and the South Pole through Greenwich, England. You can use latitude and longitude as you would a simple grid system on a state highway map. The point where the lines intersect is the "location"—or global address. For example, St. Louis, Missouri, is roughly at 39° (degrees) north latitude and 90° west longitude.

Why are things located in particular places and how do those places influence our lives? Location further describes how one place relates to another. St. Louis is where the Mississippi and the Missouri rivers meet about midway between Minneapolis—St. Paul and New Orleans. It developed as a trading center between east and west, north and south.

Directions

To help young children learn location, make sure they know the color and style of the building in which they live, the name of their town, and their street address. Then, when you talk about other places, they have something of their own with which to compare.

- Children need to understand positional words. Teach children words like "above" and "below" in a natural way when you talk with them or give them directions. When picking up toys to put away, say, "Please put your toy into the basket on the *right*" or, "Put the green washcloth *into* the drawer." Right and left are as much directional terms as north, south, east, and west. Other words that describe such features as color, size, and shape are also important.

- Show your children north, south, east, and west by using your home as a reference point. Perhaps you can see the sun rising in the morning through a bedroom window that faces east and setting at night through the westerly kitchen window.

- Reinforce their knowledge by playing games. Once children have their directional bearings, you can hide an object, for example, then give them directions to its location: "two steps to the north, three steps west . . . ."

- Use pictures from books and magazines to help your children associate words with visual images. A picture of a desert can stimulate conversation about the features of a desert—arid and barren. Work with your children to develop more complex descriptions of different natural and cultural features.

Maps

Put your child's natural curiosity to work. Even small children can learn to read simple maps of their school, neighborhood, and community. Here are some simple map activities you can do with your children.

- Go on a walk and collect natural materials such as acorns and leaves to use for an art project. Map the location where you found those items.

- Create a treasure map for children to find hidden treats in the back yard for inside your home. Treasure maps work especially well for birthday parties.

- Look for your city or town on a map. If you live in a large city or town, you may even be able to find your street. Point out where your relatives or your children's best friends live.

- Find the nearest park, lake, mountain, or other cultural or physical feature on a map. Then, talk about how these features affect your child's life. Living near the ocean may make your climate moderate, prairies may provide an open path for high winds, and mountains may block some weather fronts.

- By looking at a map, your children may learn why they go to a particular school. Perhaps the next nearest school is on the other side of a park, a busy street, or a large hill. Maps teach us about our surroundings by portraying them in relation to other places.

- Before taking a trip, show your children a map of where you are going and how you plan to get there. Look for other ways you could go, and talk about why you decided to use a particular route. Maybe they can suggest other routes.

- Encourage your children to make their own maps using legends with symbols. Older children can draw a layout of their street, or they can illustrate places or journeys they have read about. Some books, like *Winnie-the-Pooh* and *The Wizard of Oz*, contain fanciful maps. These can be models for children to create and plot their own stories.

- Keep a globe and a map of the United States near the television and use them to locate places talked about on television programs, or to follow the travels of your favorite sports team.

Additional Activities

Children use all of their senses to learn about the world. Objects that they can touch, see, smell, taste, and hear help them understand the link between a model and the real thing.

- Put together puzzles of the United States or the world. Through the placement of the puzzle pieces, children gain a tactile and visual sense of where one place is located in relation to others.

- Make a three-dimensional map of your home or neighborhood using milk cartons for buildings. Draw a map of the block on a piece of cardboard, then cut up the cartons (or any other three-dimensional item) and use them to represent buildings. Use bottle tops or smaller boxes to add interest to the map, but try to keep the scale relationships correct.

- Use popular board games like "Game of the States" or "Trip around the World" to teach your children about location, commerce, transportation, and the relationships among different countries and areas of the world. Some of these games are available at public libraries.

- Make papier-maché using strips of old newspaper and a paste made from flour and water. If children form balls by wrapping the strips of papier-maché around a balloon, they will develop a realistic understanding of the difficulties in making accurate globes. They can also use papier-maché to make models of hills and valleys.

Place: Physical and Human Characteristics

Every place has a personality. What makes a place special? What are the physical and cultural characteristics of your hometown? Is the soil sandy or rocky? Is the temperature warm or is it cold? If it has many characteristics, which are the most distinct?

How do these characteristics affect the people living there? People change the character of a place. They speak a particular language, have styles of government and architecture, and form patterns of business. How have people shaped the landscapes?

Investigate Your Neighborhood

- Walk around your neighborhood and look at what makes it unique. Point out differences from and similarities to other places. Can your children distinguish various types of homes and shops? Look at the buildings and talk about their uses. Are there features built to conform with the weather or topography? Do the shapes of some buildings indicate how they were used in the past or how they're used now? These observations help children understand the character of a place.

- Show your children the historical, recreational, or natural points of interest in your town. What animals and plants live in your neighborhood? If you live near a harbor, pay it a visit, and tour a docked boat. You can even look up the shipping schedule in your local newspaper. If you live near a national park, a lake, a river, or a stream, take your children there and spend time talking about its uses.

- Use songs to teach geography. "Home on the Range," "Red River Valley," and "This Land Is Your Land" conjure up images of place. Children enjoy folk songs of different countries like "Sur La Pont D'Avignon," "Guantanamara," and "London Bridge." When your children sing these songs, talk with them about the places they celebrate, locate them on the map, and discuss how the places are described.

Study the Weather

Weather has important geographic implications that affect the character of a place. The amount of sun or rain, heat or cold, the direction and strength of the wind, all determine such things as how people dress, how well crops grow, and the extent to which people will want to live in a particular spot.

- Watch the weather forecast on television or read the weather map in the newspaper. Save the maps for a month or more. You can see changes over time, and compare conditions over several weeks and seasons. Reading the weather map helps children observe changes in the local climate.

- Use a weather map to look up the temperatures of cities around the world and discover how hot each gets in the summer and how cold each gets in the winter. Ask your children if they can think of reasons why different locations have different temperatures. Compare these figures with your town. Some children enjoy finding the place that is the hottest or the coldest.

- Make simple weather-related devices such as barometers, pinwheels, weather vanes, and wind chimes. Watch cloud formations and make weather forecasts. Talk about how these describe the weather in your town.

Learn about Other Cultures

People shape the personality of their areas. The beliefs, languages, and customs distinguish one place from another.

- Make different ethnic foods, take your children to an ethnic restaurant, or treat them to ethnic snacks at a folk festival. Such an experience is an opportunity to talk about why people eat different foods. What ingredients in ethnic dishes are unique to a particular area? For example, why do the Japanese eat so much seafood? (If your children look for Japan on a map they will realize it is a country of many islands.)

- Read stories from or about other countries, and books that describe journeys. Many children's books provide colorful images of different places and a sense of what it would be like to live in them. Drawings or photographs of distant places or situations can arouse interest in other lands. *The Little House in the Big Woods, Holiday Tales of Sholem Aleichem,* and *The Polar Express* are examples of books with descriptions of place that have transported the imaginations of many young readers.

reservoir. A man-made lake where water is kept for future use.

river. A stream, larger than a creek, generally flowing to another stream, a lake, or to the ocean.

scale. The relationship of the length between two points as shown on a map and the distance between the same two points on the Earth.

sea level. The ocean surface; the mean level between high and low tides.

strait. A narrow body of water connecting two larger bodies of water.

swamp. A tract of permanently saturated low land, usually overgrown with vegetation. (A marsh is temporarily or periodically saturated.)

topography. The physical features of a place; or the study and depiction of physical features, including terrain relief.

valley. A relatively long, narrow land area lying between two areas of higher elevation, often containing a stream.

volcano. A vent in the Earth's crust caused by molten rock coming to the surface and being ejected, sometimes violently.

waterfall. A sudden drop of a stream from a high level to a much lower level.

History

Free and Inexpensive Resources

Helping Your Child Learn History. By Elaine Wrisley Reed. Offers guidelines to help parents encourage their children's natural interest in history. Includes a variety of activities to stimulate learning, as well as resource listings for additional reading and information. Published in 1993 by the U.S. Department of Education. For ordering information, request a copy of the free *Consumer Information Catalog,* available from the Consumer Information Center, P.O. Box 100, Pueblo, Colorado 81002. (Note: You can also order this publication directly from the U.S. Department of Education (phone: 1/800-424-1616) or from the U.S. Government Printing Office in Washington, D.C.—see appendix B.)

Books

Illustrated Atlas of World History. By Simon Adam, John Briquebec, and Ann Kramer. Random House, 1992. 160 pages. A geographical journey in maps and pictures from prehistoric times to the present day. Using this book, children discover that history is not just about dates, events, and empires, but about ordinary people and how they lived. For ages 10 and up.

My Backyard History Book. By David Weitzman. Little, Brown, 1975. 128 pages. Organized around the idea that learning about the past begins best at home. Recommends projects and activities—taking photographs, making rubbings in cemeteries, interviewing neighbors, etc.—intended to spark children's interest in their past. For children ages eight and up (parents are invited to join in the fun).

The Timetables of History: A Horizontal Linkage of People and Events. By Bernard Grun. Third edition. Simon and Schuster, 1991. 688 pages. A reference book that can be used to locate specific events in history. Chronicles events from 5000 B.C. to 1978. Includes easy-access charts with separate columns for the visual arts, history and politics, literature and theater, and other areas of interest.

Periodicals

Calliope. Cobblestone Publishing Company, 7 School Street, Peterborough, New Hampshire 03458. Phone: 603/924-7209. A children's magazine exploring world history. Each issues covers a single topic (famous battles, ancient cities, independence movements, etc.). Includes articles, short stories, activities, puzzles, and games related to the issue's central theme. For children ages nine to fifteen. Published five times annually.

Cobblestone. Cobblestone Publishing Company. 7 School Street, Peterborough, New Hampshire 03458. Phone: 603/924-7209. A history magazine for young people (ages nine to fifteen). Contains articles and occasional fiction on topics such as the Anti-Slavery movement, Duke Ellington, witchcraft, and the cultures of pre-Columbian North America. Includes descriptions of books to read and places to visit. Photographs, paintings, illustrations, and maps help make this magazine engaging. Issued ten times annually.

Videotape

Tell Me Why: Beginnings of Government and Civilization. Paramount. Running time: 30 minutes. Part of the "Tell Me Why" series, this videotape presents and answers questions about the beginning of civilization and government. Where was the first city? How was cooking discovered? Who built the first fire truck? Who wrote the first laws? This tape answers these questions, and many others. Also included in the series is *Tell Me Why: Americana* (When did the Vikings visit America? Why wasn't America named after Columbus? What is the Liberty Bell?).

Software

Time Riders in American History. The Learning Company. IBM, DOS. Equipped with maps, a timeline, and interviews with people who are making history, the user's job is to find out what really happened in history, before Dr. Dread alters the historical facts—and takes over the world! Approved by Parents' Choice. For children ages ten and up.

Time Traveler CD. New Media Schoolhouse. Macintosh, CD-ROM drive. Users pick a year—any year from 4000 B.C. to 1992—and then pull up maps, music, illustrations, and historical highlights of that period. For ages eight and up. Approved by Parents' Choice.

Games

American History Playing Card Deck. Aristoplay. A card deck illustrated with presidents, poets, scientists, and military leaders. Comes with a booklet describing their achievements. For two or more players, ages seven and up. Available from Aristoplay (see chapter 27 for contact information).

Made for Trade: A Game of Early American Life. Aristoplay. As settlers in colonial America, players go from store to store collecting the goods on their shopping list or trade with other settlers. Comes with replicas of colonial shillings. For two to four players, ages eight and up. Available from Aristoplay (see chapter 27 for contact information) [Note: Other history-related boardgames from Aristoplay include Pyramids and Mummies, Knights and Castles, Greek Myths and Legends, and Land Ho! (The Voyage to America Game, in both English and Spanish.) Call for a free catalog.]

Associations

American Association for State and Local History. 172 Second Avenue North, Suite 202, Nashville, Tennessee 37201. Phone: 615/255-2971. An association of historians, teachers, historical societies, and others interested in improving the study of state and local history. Maintains an extensive list of museums, historical sites, and historical societies. Publications include *The Living History Sourcebook,* by Jan Anderson, listing living history organizations, museums, and publications (updated periodically—last edition published in 1987).

American Historical Association. 400 A Street, S.E., Washington, D.C. 20003. Phone: 202/544-2422. Professional association of historians, educators, and others interested in promoting historical studies and the preservation of historical documents. Conducts research and educational programs. Publishes an annual directory of history departments and organization in the United States and Canada. Also publishes *American Historical Association—Perspectives* (an association newsletter) and *American Historical Review* (a scholarly journal).

Association for Living Historical Farms and Agricultural Museums. Route 14, Box 214, Santa Fe, New Mexico 87505. Phone: 505/471-2261. A central repository of information on the plants, animals, tools, and implements used in farming in the past. Accredits living historical farms and museums and works to maintain standards of historical accuracy. Publishes an annual membership list and a bimonthly bulletin entitled *Living Historical Farms.*

National Council for History Education. 26915 Westwood Road, Suite B2, Westlake, Ohio 44145-4656. 216/835-1776. Founded in 1990, the National Council for History Education is dedicated to the proposition that history is important to both the public and private lives of all citizens. Works to promote the study of history in the school curriculum, as well as *after* formal education. Believes that the social sciences and current issues, both domestic and global, are best studied in their historical contexts and perspectives. Speaks vigorously to policymakers about the importance of providing enough time in the curriculum for both world and U.S. history and adequate support for good teaching and materials. Encourages regular communication between those who teach history in the schools and those who promote history in the community. Publishes a monthly newsletter, *History Matters!,* which offers ideas, notes, and news about history. Offers members discount prices on new publications and materials developed by the council, as well as books and reports published by the Bradley Commission on History (predecessor to the National Council for History Education).

National Trust for Historic Preservation. 1785 Massachusetts Avenue, N.W., Washington, D.C. 20036. Phone: 202/673-4000. Works to "safeguard America's built heritage." Acts as a clearinghouse for information on preservation programs. Write to them for a list of preservation groups in your community (these groups often provide walking maps and offer special historical programs).

Organization of American Historians. 112 North Bryan Street, Bloomington, Indiana 47408. Phone: 812/855-7311. An organization of professional historians, including educators, students of history, and others in related fields. Concerned with American history as both an educational program and as a profes-

History in the Schools
From the message and mission statement of the National Council for History Education.

The National Council for History Education is pressing for all teachers to be given the chance to offer courses that:

1. Combine an analytical, chronological narrative with frequent pauses for studies in depth, neither of which can do without the insights of the other.

2. Deal constantly with the relation between fact and concept, neither of which educates without the other.

3. Carry significant, compelling themes and questions from the start of United States and world history down to the present day, frequently responding to the students' challenge: "So what?"

4. Demonstrate the interdependence of history and the social sciences, by teaching the concepts of the latter in dramatic historical context.

5. Demonstrate the interdependence of history and the humanities, by concurrent studies of literature, philosophy, and the arts.

6. Are pluralist, multicultural, inclusive of people of all kinds and conditions in whatever society is under study.

7. Provide a sophisticated understanding of the origins, the advances and defeats, the worldwide adventures of the democratic ideas that bind us together as one people.

8. Offer many chances for active learning, inquiry and the development of critical, historical habits of the mind.

9. Are taught by a wide diversity of pedagogical methods, of the teacher's own choice and design.

sion. Promotes historical research and study, and conducts educational programs. Publishes the *Magazine of History,* a quarterly containing news items, feature articles, and other material for teachers of history and social studies, as well as others with a serious interest in the topic.

Multiculturalism

Free and Inexpensive Resources

African American Literature for Young Children. A resource list developed by the National Black Child Development Institute. Includes literary works that provide accurate and realistic images of African Americans and reinforces the importance of African-American cultural traditions. Available for 50¢ from the National Association for the Education of Young Children (see appendix I for contact information).

Culturgrams. A series of brochures describing the customs, manners, general attitudes, and lifestyles of more than one hundred countries. Each describes the land and climate, economy, government, and history of a particular nation. $2.00 per copy. Available from the Brigham Young University, Kennedy Center for International Studies, Publication Services, 280 Herald R. Clark Building, Provo, Utah 84602-4538. Phone: 801/378-6528.

The Culturgram series includes the following:

Algeria
Argentina
Australia
Austria
Bangladesh
Barbados
Belgium
Bolivia
Brazil
Bulgaria
Cambodia
Cameroon
Canada (Atlantic)
Canada (Ontario and West)
Canada (Quebec)
Central African Republic
Chile
China
Colombia
Costa Rica
Czech and Slovak Republic
Denmark
Ecuador
Egypt
El Salvador
England
Ethiopia
Fiji
Finland
France
Gabon
Gambia
Germany
Ghana
Greece
Guatemala
Guinea-Bissau

Honduras
Hong Kong
Hungary
Iceland
India
Indonesia
Iran
Ireland
Israel
Italy
Jamaica
Japan
Jordan
Kenya
Korea, North
Korea, South
Laos
Lebanon
Lesotho
Luxembourg
Malaysia
Mali
Mauritius
Mexico
Mongolia
Morocco
Nepal
Netherlands
New Zealand
Nicaragua
Nigeria
Northern Ireland
Norway
Pakistan
Panama
Paraguay
Peru
Philippines
Poland
Portugal
Puerto Rico
Romania
Russia
Samoa
Saudi Arabia
Scotland
Senegal
Singapore
South Africa
Spain
Sri Lanka

Sudan
Sweden
Switzerland
Syria
Tahiti
Taiwan
Tanzania
Thailand
Tonga
Tunisia
Turkey
Uruguay
USA
Venezuela
Vietnam
Wales
West Bank and Gaza
Zaire
Zambia
Zimbabwe

Teaching Young Children to Resist Bias: What Parents Can Do. A brochure offering tips for parents and teachers to help children appreciate diversity and deal with the biases of others. Available for 50¢ from the National Association for the Education of Young Children (see appendix I for contact information).

What to Tell Your Child about Prejudice and Discrimination. This brochure offers advice for parents to help children live harmoniously in an increasingly multicultural and multi-racial society. A publication of the PTA and the Anti-Defamation League of B'nai B'rith. For a free copy, send a self-addressed, stamped business-size envelope along with your request to the National PTA, 700 North Rush Street, Chicago, IL 60611.

Books

All the Colors of the Race. By Arnold Adoff. Illustrated by John Steptoe. William Morrow, 1992. 80 pages. This collection of poems explores the color that lies beneath the surface—

the. one that's not reflected in the color of a person's skin. For ages six to twelve.

Art from Many Hands. By Jo Miles Schuman. Davis Publications, 1984. 256 pages. Contains art activities from cultures around the globe. Includes set-by-step instructions. For children in elementary through high school.

Bright Eyes, Brown Skin. By Cheryl Willis Hudson and B. G. Ford. Just Us Books, 1990. 24 pages. Combines simple rhyming text with paintings of bright, energetic, and enthusiastic brown-skinned children. *Booklist* says the book is "perfectly paced, brilliantly combines understatement and directness, giving a celebratory tone." For children ages two to six.

Discover the World: Helping Children Develop Respect for Themselves, Others, and the Earth. By Susan Hopkins and J. Winters. New Society Publications, 1990. 157 pages. Encourages respect for cultural diversity through art, music, science, language, and movement activities. Explains how to develop a child's sense of self-worth and self-esteem while becoming respectful and appreciative of others. Includes sections on African-American, Native-American, Asian-American, and other cultures. Activities are designed for children ages three to twelve.

Ethnic Information Sources of the United States. Paul Wasserman, editor. Gale Research. 1,400 pages. Updated periodically, this two-volume set lists print and nonprint sources of information on ethnic groups representing more than ninety countries, regions, and language groups. Includes listings of associations, fraternal and religious organizations, festivals, libraries, museums, periodicals, etc. (You'll want to check your local libraries, as the set is expensive.)

Families the World Over (series). Lerner Publications. 32 pages each. A series of books, each focusing on a family living in a different country (France, Nigeria, Saudi Arabia, etc.).

Family Pictures. By Carmen Lomas Garza. Children's Books Press, 1990. 32 pages. Takes a look at Hispanic family culture through a series of drawings from a family album. Going to a fair in Mexico and making tamales are among the activities celebrated in the book. Text in English and Spanish.

Hands around the World: 365 Creative Ways to Build Cultural Awareness and Global Respect. By Susan Milord. Williamson Publishing, 1992. 176 pages. Features projects (cooking, ornament making, etc.) that help children discover world cultures. Describes holiday customs, traditions, and celebrations around the globe. For children in grades one to eight.

Native People, Native Ways (series). By Gabriel Horn (White Deer of Autumn). Beyond Words Publishing. 85-88 pages. Books in this series shed light on Native Americans' history, traditions, beliefs, and ways of life. Titles include *The Native American Book of Knowledge* (investigating the origin of Native Americans), *The Native American Book of Life* (exploring the lives of Native-American children), *The Native American Book of Change* (focusing on the struggles of the Native Americans since the arrival of the Europeans, including modern-day prejudice and stereotyping), and *The Native American Book of Wisdom* (exploring traditional beliefs).

Our Family, Our Friends, Our World. By L. Miller-Lachmann. R. R. Bowker, 1992. 710 pages. An annotated guide to multicultural books for children and teenagers. Includes both fiction and nonfiction. For work with children ages three to eighteen.

People. By Peter Spier. Doubleday, 1980. 41 pages. This picture book shows how cultural differences make the world a fascinating place.

The People Atlas. Illustrated by Philip Steele. Oxford University Press, 1991. 64 pages. An atlas that emphasizes people rather than places. Explores the food, clothing, customs, and traditions of people all over the world.

Straight to the Heart: Children of the World. By Ethan Hubbard. Chelsea Green Publishing, 1992. 49 pages. Contains photographs of joyful children from various parts of the world (Peru, Nepal, New Zealand, Guatemala, etc.) taken by the author during his travels.

Periodicals

Faces: The Magazine about People. Cobblestone Publishing Company, 7 School Street, Peterborough, New Hampshire 03458. Phone: 603/924-7209. Published in cooperation with the American Museum of Natural History (New York), this magazine takes readers around the globe to places like South Africa, Haiti, and Egypt (old and new), exploring topics in archaeology, cultural anthropology, and natural history. Includes stories, articles, recipes, and crafts related to each issue's central theme. Also contains games and short reviews of books and videos. For children ages nine to fifteen. Issued ten times annually.

Skipping Stones: A Multi-Ethnic Children's Forum. 80574 Hazelton Road, Cottage Grove, Oregon 97424. A forum for communication among children from different parts of the globe. Written by and for children, this quarterly includes poetry, prose, drawings, photographs, and articles. Welcomes material written in any language (translations appear next to the originals.) For children ages seven to thirteen.

Mail Order Catalogs

The Children's Small Press Collection. 719 North Fourth Avenue, Ann Arbor, Michigan 48104. Phone: 313/668-8056 or 1/800-221-8056. This catalog contains a variety of children's fiction and nonfiction books exploring Hispanic, Asian, African, and Native-American customs and cultures.

Claudia's Caravan. P.O. Box 1582, Alameda, California 94501. Phone: 510/521-7871. This mail order catalog contains multicultural/multilingual materials for global education, multicultural studies, antibias curriculum, and bilingual/multilingual instruction. Includes books such as *Discover the World, Your Skin and Mine, Maps and Globes, Book of Black Heroes,* and dozens of cultural stories. Also contains dolls made by Native-American Indians, musical instruments from around the world, records celebrating music from distant lands, and aids (cassettes, games, and books) for teaching foreign languages. In addition, this catalog offers Asian, Latino, and African-American baby dolls, cultural games, and videotapes that encourage cultural understanding and promote world peace.

Association

Council on Interracial Books for Children. 1841 Broadway, New York, New York 10023. Phone: 212/757-5339. Promotes children's books and other learning materials that are free of bias, based on race, sex, age, or physical disability. Develops criteria for the evaluation of children's materials. Produces guidelines for selecting bias-free textbooks and storybooks. Publishes the *Interracial Books for Children Bulletin,* a newsletter containing articles and reviews on issues of sexism, racism, and other biases in children's literature. Issued eight times annually.

Toys and Other Learning Tools

Friends around the World. By Joan Walsh Anglund. In this game for ages five and up, players race their international friends toward world peace. A cooperative game where their is no single winner. Available from Aristoplay (see chapter 27 for contact information).

The Hip Hop Kids. Olmec. Twelve-inch, soft-bodied figures created by Puerto Rican rap artist Ricardo Rodriguez of the rap group Latin Empire. Available in black, white, and Hispanic versions. Six different figures available. Each comes with a message on the importance of staying in school and staying away from drugs.

Learning Kids. Olmec. Girl and boy dolls that let little fingers tie, snap, button, buckle, and zip. Available in black and Hispanic versions.

Little Sis and International Friends Dolls. H. Lee Toys, Inc. Fourteen-inch soft rag dolls. The American Ethnic Collection dolls have four different racial backgrounds—African-American, Asian, Hispanic, and Caucasian. Each comes with removable clothing.

"My World Colors." By Crayola crayons. A pack of sixteen crayons reflecting the different shades of skin, hair, and eye color in the world's population.

MATH

Free and Inexpensive Resources

Booklist from the Lawrence Hall of Science. University of California, Berkeley, California 94720. Phone: 510/642-1016. An annotated list of math and science books for children and educators from a reputable institution. Included on the list are the Brown Paper School series (including *The I Hate Mathematics! Book* and *Math for Smarty Pants*), *Anno's Math Games,* and *Games for Math: Playful Ways to Help Your Child Learn Math.* Although the books are produced by various publishers, each can be ordered directly from the Lawrence Hall of Science. (Be sure to request the "Educators' Booklist" when making your request.)

Math Matters. A PTA brochure designed to help parents build their children's math confidence and skills. Filled with fun activities for young children and their parents. For a free copy, send a self-addressed, stamped business-size envelope along with your request to the National PTA (see appendix I for contact information).

More than 1, 2, 3: The Real Basics of Mathematics. Recognizing that math is more than counting and worksheets, the author of this brochure, J. B. McCracken, offers tips on making math an exciting part of children's lives. Available for 50¢ from the National Association for the Education of Young Children (see appendix I for contact information).

Books

For Adults

Family Math. By Jean Stenmark, Virginia Thompson, and Ruth Cossey. 1986. Equals, Lawrence Hall of Science, University of California, Berkeley, California 94720. Phone: 510/642-1823. 304 pages. Contains over ninety challenging math activities for parents to do with children of all ages. Includes resource lists of mathematics materials. Available in English and Spanish. Can be ordered from Eureka! (see chapter 27 for contact information).

Games for Math: Playful Ways to Help Your Child Learn Math. By Peggy Kaye. Pantheon Books, 1988. 224 pages. Offers more than fifty ways to help children in kindergarten through third grade learn math (and have fun while doing it).

Garbage Pizza, Patchwork Quilts and Math Magic. By Susan Ohanian. W. H. Freeman, 1992. 248 pages. A collection of stories about teachers (kindergarten through grade three) who have a hands-on view of math and whose students love to learn. Individual chapters cover topics such as problem solving, evaluation, parents as partners, and the art of teaching. Includes recommended reading lists.

The I Hate Mathematics! Book. By Marilyn Burns. Little, Brown, 1975. 127 pages. Mathematics is a way of looking at the world, according to this book, and should not be confused with arithmetic. Contains several hundred math games, magic tricks, and experiments for children in grades four through eight (parents are invited to share in the fun). Also by Marilyn Burns: *Math for Smarty*

Pants (see separate listing) and *The Book of Think* (Little, Brown, 1976).

Innumeracy: Mathematical Illiteracy and Its Consequences. By John Allen Paulos, Ph.D. Vintage, 1988. 180 pages. Best-selling book lamenting Americans' lack of interest in mathematics. The author believes that everyone is capable of becoming mathematically literate and the knowledge of numbers is important in everyday life.

Math for Smarty Pants. By Marilyn Burns. Little, Brown, 1982. 128 pages. In addition to numbers, math involves shapes, logic, and creative problem solving. There are many ways to be smart when it comes to mathematics, according to this author, and her book tells children and grown-ups about them. Contains illustrated math activities and tricks to get children interested in math concepts, along with interesting historical tidbits and informational tastings. Also by Marilyn Burns: *The I Hate Mathematics! Book* (see separate listing).

Parents' Guide to Great Explorations in Math and Science. By Jacqueline Barber and Lincoln Bergman. 1991. Great Explorations in Math and Science (GEMS), Lawrence Hall of Science, University of California, Berkeley, California 94720. Phone: 510/642-7771. A fifty-five-page handbook for parents presenting activities to encourage a child's interest in math and science. Developed by the Lawrence Hall of Science, this teaching tool includes personal anecdotes from staff members describing practical and natural ways to bring the fun and excitement of math and science to children. Available from Eureka! (see chapter 27 for contact information).

The Wonderful World of Mathematics: A Critically Annotated List of Children's Books in Mathematics. Edited by Diane Thiessen and Margaret Matthias. National Council of Teachers of Mathematics, 1993. Reviews five hundred children's books and suggests math activities to do after reading each one. Available from the National Council of Teachers of Mathematics (phone: 1/800-235-7566).

For Children

Anno's Counting Book. By Mitsumasa Anno. T. Y. Crowell/HarperCollins, 1977. 28 pages. A counting book showing the growth in a village and surrounding countryside during twelve months. Children can count the roads, houses, plantings, and other items as the "story" unfolds. Each picture shows a succeeding month, as well as the time of day. For children ages three to seven. Also from Anno: *Anno's Counting House, Anno's Mysterious Multiplying Jar,* and *Anno's Math Games I, II, and III.*

Seventeen Kings and 42 Elephants. By Margaret Mahy. Dial Books, 1987. 26 pages. Seventeen kings and forty-two elephants romp with a variety of jungle animals during their journey through a wild, wet night. For children in preschool to grade three.

The Shapes Game. By Paul Rogers. Henry Holt, 1990. 26 pages. This book introduces children to basic shapes through simple riddle verse. For preschoolers through grade one.

Software

Elastic Lines: The Electronic Geoboard. Sunburst. Users can create geometric shapes and patterns, using "geoboards" with pegs and electronic rubber bands. Introduces children (ages seven to twelve) to mathematical concepts and encourages creativity. For use with the Apple II or IBM Tandy.

Millie's Math House. Edmark. IBM, Macintosh. This software package for preschoolers (ages three to seven) combines music and graphics with counting, problem solving, and other math-related play activities. Opening cash register drawers and decorating cookies with jellybeans are among the tasks tots perform with this 1992 Parents' Choice award winner.

Math Kit

Math Matters: Kids Are Counting on You. The National PTA and Mathematical Sciences Education Board, 1989. A kit containing a calculator, a videotape on the importance of math in the home, the "math matters" brochure (see listing under "Free and Inexpensive Resources") and math activities that parents and kids can do at home using inexpensive materials. Contact your local PTA for more information. The kit is also available through the National PTA (see appendix I for contact information).

Mail Order Catalogs

Creative Publications. 5040 West 111th Street, Oak Lawn, Illinois 60453. Phone: 1/800-624-0822 or 1/800-435-5843 (in Illinois). Produces a free catalog chock full of innovative math materials, including games, manipulatives, puzzles, kits, and books. The catalog is arranged by topic (money, math language, number concepts, measurement, geometry, and algebra for example). Some of the materials are appropriate for preschoolers; others are intended for children in elementary and high school. This full-color catalog is more than one hundred pages in length.

Cuisenaire: Materials for Learning Mathematics and Science. P.O. Box 5026, White Plains, New York 10602-5026. Phone: 1/800-237-3142. Fax: 1/800-551-RODS. The first portion of this catalog illustrates and describes

scores of books, manipulatives, games, and numerical models for children from kindergarten through ninth grade.

Eureka! Lawrence Hall of Science Publications Catalog. Lawrence Hall of Science, University of California, Berkeley, California 94720. Phone: 510/642-5133. This catalog lists and describes dozens of math and science books, curriculum guides, videotapes, software programs, and other teaching/learning tools for teachers, parents, and children. *Family Math* and *Parent's Guide to Great Explorations in Math and Science* (see individual listings under "Books") are among the book offerings. The catalog also explains the various math and science programs offered by the Lawrence Hall of Science at the University of California at Berkeley, and provides addresses and phone numbers for those seeking additional information.

Heinemann Math and Science. Heinemann, 361 Hanover Street, Portsmouth, New Hampshire 03801-3959. Phone: 1/800-541-2086. One of Heinemann's specialty catalogs, containing a variety of books on teaching math and science to children.

Associations

Association for Women in Mathematics. Wellesley College, Box 178, Wellesley, Massachusetts 02181. Phone: 617/237-7517. Seeks to make students aware of opportunities for women in the field of mathematics and improve the status of women in the mathematical profession.

Lawrence Hall of Science. University of California, Berkeley, California 94720. Phone: 510/642-5133. The public science center on the University of California at Berkeley campus. Serves as a center for teacher education, research, and development in mathematics and science education. In addition to books, videotapes, software, and curriculum guides, the center produces *The LHS Quarterly*, which describes current programs, events, exhibits, classes, films, and workshops at the center. Produces a free annotated book list (see "Booklist" under "Free and Inexpensive Resources") and the *Eureka!* publications catalog (see listing under "Mail Order Catalogs") as well. Math programs at the Lawrence Hall of Science include the following:

Equals. Phone: 510/642-1823. Promotes participation of students and adults in mathematics courses and encourages their interest and involvement in math-based fields of study and work. Offers a variety of publications for parents and teachers, including *Math for Girls and Other Problem Solvers* and *Parents, Kids, and Computers* (available through the Eureka! mail order catalog—see listing under "Mail Order Catalogs.").

Family Math Program. Phone: 510/642-1823. Teaches parents how to help their children with math at home. Also trains parents and teachers to offer family math courses—where parents and their children learn together—at schools, libraries, and community centers. Offers a videotape that shows how parents and children can work cooperatively on math activities. Also offers *Family Math*, a book containing the full curriculum for family math courses (see listing under "Books.").

Great Explorations in Math and Science (GEMS). Phone: 510/642-

7771. A publication series based on activities and exhibits that originated at the Lawrence Hall of Science, reflecting the "guided discovery" approach to math and science education. (GEMS publications can be ordered through the Eureka! mail order catalog—see separate listing under "Mail Order Catalogs.")

Mathematics Education Program. Phone: 510/642-3167. Provides hands-on mathematics experiences for people of all ages, using a problem-solving approach and integrating computer and off-line activities. Assists parents and teachers in creating exciting learning environments for children. Offers a variety of software packages exploring math concepts (these can be ordered through the Eureka! mail order catalog—see listing under "Mail Order Catalogs").

National Council of Teachers of Mathematics. 1906 Association Drive, Reston, Virginia 22091. Phone: 703/620-9840. Professional organization for mathematics teachers, primarily in elementary and high schools. Publishes a variety of journals, including *Arithmetic Teacher*, a monthly featuring articles on innovative methods of teaching arithmetic, as well as information on problem solving, math fundamentals, and new technologies. Other publications include the *Journal of Research in Mathematics Education*, which reports on research, studies, and theoretical analysis, and *The Wonderful World of Mathematics: A Critically Annotated List of Children's Books in Mathematics* (see listing under "Books").

SCIENCE

Free and Inexpensive Resources

Booklist from the Lawrence Hall of Science. University of California, Berkeley, California 94720. Phone: 510/642-1016. An annotated list of science and math books for children and educators from a reputable institution. Included on the list are the Eyewitness and Eyewitness Juniors series, the Brown Paper School series (including *Blood and Guts* and *Gee Whiz: How to Mix Art and Science*), the Magic School Bus series, and dozens of other titles. Although the books are produced by various publishers, each can be ordered directly from the Lawrence Hall of Science. (Be sure to request the "Educators' Booklist" when making your request.)

Helping Your Child Learn Science. Describes learning activities for children ages three to ten. Also lists resources for parents who want more help and information. 58 pages. Produced by the U.S. Department of Education's Office of Educational Research and Improvement. For ordering information, request a copy of the free *Consumer Information Catalog,* available from the Consumer Information Center, Box 100, Pueblo, Colorado 81002.

Outstanding Science Trade Books for Children. Each year, the National Science Teachers Association and the Children's Book Council cite outstanding science trade books for children in kindergarten through grade eight. For a free copy of the most recent annotated list, send a 6" x 9" self-addressed, stamped envelope (85¢ postage) along with your request to Children's Book Council, 568 Broadway, Suite 404, New York, New York 10012 (Attention: Outstanding Science Trade Books for Children).

Books

Children's Museum Activity Books (series). By Bernie Zubrowski. Little Brown, 1981. 64 pages. Books in this popular series includes *Messing around with Water Pumps and Siphons, Messing around with Baking Chemistry,* and *Messing around With Drinking Straw Construction.* For children in grades three through seven.

Early Childhood and Science. Compiled by Margaret McIntyre and the National Science Teachers Association. National Science Teachers Association, 1984. 136 pages. A collection of articles from *Science and Children* magazine, published by the National Science Teachers Association. Focuses on teaching science to young children (pre-kindergarten through second grade). Chapters explore topics such as ecology, pumpkin science, and learning about dirt.

Explorabook: A Kid's Science Museum in a Book. By John Cassidy and the Exploratorium. Klutz Press, 1991. 100 pages. Contains clear descriptions of hands-on science activities for children. Light filters, magnet experiments, bouncing light rays, and growing bacteria are among the projects included. Comes with required materials, including a mirror and a magnet.

Gee, Wiz! How to Mix Art and Science or The Art of Thinking Scientifically. By Linda Allison and David Katz. Little, Brown, 1983. 128 pages. Reminds young readers that science is an *art*–a special way of thinking about the world. Explores topics such as color, symmetry, and physics, and offers dozens of learning activities.

How Science Works. By Judith Hann. Reader's Digest, 1991. 192 pages. Suggests more than one hundred ways for parents and children to share science. Projects are designed to help children gain a clear understanding of scientific principles (speed, resonance, refraction, electricity, etc.). Fully illustrated. For children ages seven and up.

Mudpies to Magnets: A Preschool Science Curriculum. By Robert A. Williams, Robert E. Rockwell, and Elizabeth A. Sherwood. Gryphon House, 1987. 200 pages. Contains more than one hundred science-related activities for children (pre-kindergarten through second grade) using everyday materials. Various sections explore construction and measurement, health and nutrition, creativity and movement, outdoor science, and other areas of learning. Also available: *More Mudpies to Magnets: Science for Young Children.*

My First Science Book. By Angela Wilkes. Alfred A. Knopf, 1990. 48 pages. A guide to simple science experiments for children ages five to ten. Includes life-size photographs, clear directions, and listings of required materials.

Parents' Guide to Great Explorations in Math and Science. By Jacqueline Barber and Lincoln Bergman. 1991 Great Explorations in Math and Science (GEMS), Lawrence Hall of Science, University of California, Berkeley, California 94720. Phone: 510/642-7771. A fify-five-page handbook for parents presenting activities to encourage a child's interest in math and science. Developed by the Lawrence Hall of Science, this teaching tool includes personal anecdotes from staff members describing prac-

tical and natural ways to bring the fun and excitement of math and science to children. Available from Eureka! (see chapter 27 for contact information).

The Science Book. By Sara Stein. Workman, 1980. 285 pages. Provides answers to science questions (common and not-so-common), explaining why the honeybee dances, why your hair stands on end, why the sun appears before it rises, and why things work the way they do. For children in grades four through seven.

Science Experiments You Can Eat. By Vicki Cobb. HarperCollins, 1972. 127 pages. What makes popcorn pop? How does jelly jell? Why does bread rise? This book invites children ages ten to thirteen to experiment and find out the answers to these and other questions. Best of all, you can eat the results! Also available: *More Science Experiments You Can Eat.*

Science Fare: An Illustrated Guide and Catalog of Toys, Books, and Activities for Kids. By Wendy Saul, with Allan Newman. Harper and Row, 1986. 295 pages. Lists children's science books, magazines, and toys. Offers suggestions on purchasing equipment for science experiments. Contains safety recommendations as well.

Science for Every Kid (series). By Janice VanCleave. John Wiley. 225 pages. A five-volume series containing one hundred and one easy experiments introducing science concepts and terminology to children in grades three through nine. Books in the series include *Biology for Every Kid, Earth Science for Every Kid, Physics for Every Kid, Chemistry for Every Kid,* and *Astronomy for Every Kid.*

Scienceworks. By the Ontario Science Centre. Addison-Wesley, 1986. 86 pages. Contains sixty-five experi-

Choosing Science Books for Children

From *Helping Your Child Learn Science,* published by the Office of Educational Research and Improvement, U.S. Department of Education.

When selecting books, remember that recommended reading levels printed on the jackets or backs of books are not always helpful. After the third grade, what children read is usually based as much on interest as it is on reading level.

The National Science Teachers Association asks a range of questions when evaluating books for young people:

Is the author reliable? Does the author have a good background and reputation? Is the content interesting to children? Is the sequence of events logical? Is the material accurate? Is the format pleasant? Are the illustrations accurate, and do they match the text? Is the vocabulary appropriate? (Big words are OK as long as they are explained and used in context). Are the biases evident (biases against race, sex, or nationality)? Does the book glorify violence? Are controversies handled fairly?

Are the suggested activities safe? Practical?

If you need help in selecting books, consult a children's librarian or bookstore clerk.

ments that introduce basic (but amazing) concepts. Making butter, building paper houses, making a solar cooker, and experimenting with magnets are among the activities described. For children in grades two through seven. Also available from the Ontario Science Center: *Science Express,* which contains more science projects for children ages seven to twelve.

Teaching Children about Science. By Elaine Levenson. Prentice-Hall, 1986. 272 pages. Helps parents and teachers guide elementary-school age children through a wide range of scientific concepts, offering a variety of ideas and activities.

Vital Connections: Children, Science, and Books. Edited by Wendy Saul and S. A. Jagusch. Heinemann Educational Books, 1992. 176 pages. An outgrowth of a symposium sponsored by the Children's Literature Center of the Library of Congress, this book highlights issues surrounding the use of science trade books in classrooms and libraries. Presents the viewpoints of educators, editors, literature and science specialists, and well-known children's authors. For anyone interested in enhancing a child's comprehension and appreciation of the physical world.

Book Reviews

Appraisal: Science Books for Young People. Children's Science Book Review Committee, 36 Cummington Street, Boston University, Boston, Massachusetts 02215. A quarterly review of science and technology books for children and young adults. Each issue contains reviews of more than sixty books, providing recommended age levels and quality ratings.

Science and Children. National Science Teachers Association, 1742 Connecticut Avenue, N.W., Washington, D.C. 20009. A journal containing a children's book review column. Also reviews science-related nonprint materials (for more information see the National Science Teachers Association listed under "Associations").

Science Books and Films. American Association for the Advancement of Science, 1333 H Street, N.W., Washington, D.C. 20005. Reviews trade, reference, and evaluation books for students of science (all grades). Also reviews nonprint material, including films and videotapes (for more information see the American Association for the Advancement of Science, listed under "Associations").

Magazines for Children

Kids Discover. P.O. Box 54205, Boulder, Colorado 80322-4205. Phone: 212/242-5133. Each issue of this magazine explores a single topic (flight, glass, volcanoes, the weather, rain forests, et al.). Includes news items, articles, activities, and historical and scientific facts. Complete with full-color photos and illustrations. For children ages five to twelve. Issued ten times annually.

National Geographic World. National Geographic Society, Seventeenth and M Streets, N.W., Washington, D.C. 20036. Phone: 1/800-638-4077. Explores a wide variety of topics of interest to kids everywhere, including wildlife, the weather, inventions, ice cream, and outdoor adventure. Includes high quality photographs, illustrations, and interesting narratives. For children ages eight to thirteen. Issued monthly.

Odyssey. Cobblestone Publishing Company, 7 School Street, Peterborough, New Hampshire 03458. Phone: 603/924-7209. Covers "science that's out of this world," including astronomy, space exploration, and oceanography. Includes full-color photographs, illustrations, activities, news items,

articles, and profiles of people in the news. For children ages eight to fourteen. Issued monthly.

Owl. Young Naturalist Foundation, P.O. Box 11314, Des Moines, Iowa 50304 (editorial offices: The Young Naturalist Foundation, 56 The Esplanade, Toronto, Ontario, Canada M5E 1A7). A discovery magazine for children ages nine to twelve, presenting articles on wildlife, science, technology, and related topics. Includes full-color photographs, illustrations, cartoons, and projects. Issued monthly.

3-2-1 Contact. Children's Television Workshop, P.O. Box 53051, Boulder, Colorado 80322-3051. A publication of the Children's Television Workshop, this magazine explores a variety of science-related topics, including wildlife preservation, space exploration, and the science of sports. Includes puzzles, projects, and experiments. For children ages eight to fourteen. Issued ten times annually.

WonderScience. The American Chemical Society, 1155 Sixteenth Street, N.W., Washington, D.C. 20036. Phone: 202/452-2113. Produced by the American Chemical Society and the American Institute of Physics, this magazine features fun physical science activities for adults and children to do together. Published eight times a year.

Videotapes

Newton's Apple (series). This Emmy award-winning program as seen on PBS is available on videotape. Offers a kid's-eye view of the world of science, answering questions about plastic surgery, bulletproof glass, boomerangs, mummies, penguins, and scores of other topics. Each title in the series explores a handful of different topics: "Dinosaurs, Whales, Bulletproof Glass, etc."; "Boomerangs, Muscles, Bones, Bears, etc."; "Mummies, Tigers, Helium, etc."; and so forth. These and others are available from Schoolmasters Science (see chapter 27 for contact information).

NOVA (series). This award-winning television series is now available on videotape. Titles in the series include *The Case of the Flying Dinosaur* (are birds descendants of the dinosaurs?); *UFO's: Are We Alone?* (the truth behind UFO sightings); *Earthquake* (can we predict the world's most frightening natural occurrence?); *The Science of Murder* (a look at America's medical detectives); and *Signs of the Apes, Songs of the Whales* (a "conversation" with the animal kingdom). Available from Schoolmasters Science (see chapter 27 for contact information).

Tell Me Why (series). Paramount. Running time: 30 minutes each. Many of the tapes in the "Tell Me Why" collection explore topics in science. Each uses a question and answer format, providing interesting answers to common (and not-so-common) questions. Tapes in the series include *A Healthy Body, Anatomy and Genetics, How Things Work, Medicine, Flight, Water and Weather, Science, Sound and Energy,* and *Space, Earth, and Atmosphere.* Available from Schoolmasters Science (see chapter 27 for contact information).

Science-Kit Club

Things of Science. 1950 Landings Boulevard, Suite 202, Sarasota, Florida 34231. A science-kit club for children ages nine through fourteen. Every month members receive a new science kit containing materials and instructions for carrying out experiments in specific fields. Write for details.

Associations

American Association for the Advancement of Science. 1333 H Street, N.W., Washington, D.C. 20005. Phone: 202/326-6400. A membership organization representing all fields of science. Works to further the work of scientists, improve the effectiveness of science in the promotion of human welfare, and encourage the public to learn about science. Publishes *Science Books and Films,* a review of children's books, films, and videos on science, issued five times annually (a reference book based on the review called *Science Books and Films: Best Books for Children—1988-1991* is also available). Other publications include *Notes for Parents,* an irregular newsletter with articles on encouraging parents to teach science to girls and others, and *The Sourcebook for Science, Mathematics, and Technology Education,* which lists more than 2,500 programs, museums, research centers, government agencies, organizations, and others involved in science, mathematics, and technology education. Also produces *A Guide to Organizing a Community Public Science Day,* which is designed to help communities participate in Public Science Day (organized to help students in kindergarten through grade ten understand the increasing importance that science and technology play in their lives). (Public Science Day occurs each year in conjunction with the AAAS annual meeting.)

Association of Science-Technology Centers. 1025 Vermont Avenue, N.W., Suite #500, Washington, D.C. 20005. Phone: 202/783-7200. An association of science and technology museums. Operates a Teacher Educator's Network in which museum staff working with schools share ideas and resources; organizes and circulates hands-on science exhibitions to museums; and manages special projects to increase participation in science-museum activities. Maintains a directory of approximately three hundred national and one hundred international science museums and related institutions that welcome the public.

Lawrence Hall of Science. University of California, Berkeley, California 94720. Phone: 510/642-5133. The public science center on the University of California at Berkeley campus. Serves as a center for teacher education, research, and development in science and mathematics education. Science programs include Great Explorations in Math and Science (GEMS), a publication series reflecting the "guided discovery" approach to science and mathematics education, based on exhibits and hands-on activities originating at the Lawrence Hall of Science. Among the books offered by GEMS is the *Once Upon a GEMS Guide,* a handbook that connects children's literature with explorations in math and science. The Lawrence Hall of Science also publishes *The LHS Quarterly,* which describes current programs, events, exhibits, classes, films, and workshops at the center. Produces a free annotated book list (see "Booklist" under "Free and Inexpensive Resources") and the *Eureka!* publications catalog (see listing under "Mail Order Catalogs") as well.

National Academy of Sciences. Office of Public Information, 2101 Constitution Avenue, N.W., Washington, D.C. 20418. Phone: 202/334-2138. An honorary organization dedicated to the furtherance of science and engineering. Members are elected in recognition of their outstanding and continuing contributions to science or engineering. Together with the Smithsonian Institution, the National Academy of Sciences operates the National Science Resource Center (see separate listing).

National Center for Improving Science Education. c/o Senta A. Raizen, 2000 L Street, N.W., Suite 602, Washington, D.C. 20036. Phone: 202/467-0652. Gathers, organizes, and synthesizes current research in science education to promote positive changes in state and local policies and practices in science education. Works to improve science education, to better prepare teachers, and to create sound science curricula. Offers recommendations and reports, including *Getting Started in Science: A Blueprint for Elementary School Science Education.*

National Science Foundation. 1800 G Street, N.W., Room 520, Washington, D.C. 20550. Phone: 202/357-9498. An independent agency in the executive branch of the federal government that supports education and research in science and engineering. A participant in Project 2061, a joint effort to reform education in science and technology by the year Halley's comet makes its next trip around the sun. This plan envisions students studying a dozen or so topics (such as the atmosphere) from many perspectives over their thirteen school years from kindergarten to high school.

National Science Resource Center. Smithsonian Institution, National Academy of Sciences, Arts and Industry Building, Room 110, Washington, D.C. 20560. Operated by the Smithsonian Institution and the National Academy of Sciences, the center offers resources and assistance to schools in creating hands-on science programs in the classroom. Sponsors workshops featuring hands-on science curricula. Conducts a program called the National Elementary Science Leadership Initiative—a four-year effort to engage teams of educators and scientists from various school districts to improve elementary science teaching. Offers a directory called *Science and Children: Resources for Teachers* (recently updated). Also produces a newsletter.

National Science Teachers Association. 1742 Connecticut Avenue, N.W., Washington, D.C. 20009. Phone: 202/328-5800. Professional association of teachers seeking to encourage quality science teaching in the schools. Studies students and how they learn, science curriculum, teacher preparation, classroom procedures, and facilities for teaching science. Publishes *Science and Children,* a periodical reporting on innovative science teaching methods and techniques (see listing under "Book Reviews" for more information). Also publishes *Science Scope,* a professional journal reporting on innovative teaching methods and educational theory, and *Energy and Education Newsletter,* a bimonthly containing information on energy facts, trends, and energy education resources. Each year, the National Science Teachers Association and the Children's Book Council cite outstanding science trade books for children (see "Outstanding Science Trade Books" under "Free and Inexpensive Resources"). Produces a free publications catalog as well.

Mail Order Catalogs

American Science and Surplus. Jerryco, Inc., 601 Linden Place, Evanston, Illinois 60202. Phone: 708/475-8440. Illuminated pocket microscopes, paper binoculars, half periscopes, midget magnets, hydraulic pump components, and hundreds of other hard-to-find and unusual items are described in this catalog produced by Jerryco American Science Center. At warehouse prices,

parents can stock up on items for their children's science experiments and projects.

Cuisenaire: Materials for Learning Mathematics and Science. P.O. Box 5026, White Plains, New York 10602-5026. Phone: 1/800-237-3142. Fax: 1/800-551-RODS. The second portion of this catalog illustrates and describes books, science kits, microscopes, magnifiers, lab equipment, models, and other items to help children learn about earth, life, physical, and environmental science. Products are intended for children from kindergarten through ninth grade.

Edmund Scientific Co. 101 East Gloucester Pike, Barrington, New Jersey 07410. Phone: 609/547-3488 or 1/800-222-0224. This company's mail order catalog contains science kits, microscopes, telescopes, and other science-related products.

Eureka! Lawrence Hall of Science Publications Catalog. Lawrence Hall of Science, University of California, Berkeley, California 94720. Phone: 510/642-5133. This catalog lists and describes dozens of science and math books, curriculum guides, videotapes, software programs, and other teaching/learning tools for teachers, parents, and children. The catalog also describes the various science and math programs offered by the Lawrence Hall of Science at the University of California at Berkeley, and provides addresses and phone numbers for those seeking additional information.

Exploratorium to Go! 3601 Lyon Street, San Francisco, California 94123. Phone: 1/800-359-9899. This catalog contains gifts and learning tools from the Exploratorium store in San Francisco. Includes *Explorabook: A Kids' Science Museum in a Book; Paper Anew* (a recycled paper-making kit); an abacus/calculator combination; an ant farm; and the highly unusual *Owl Pellet Kit,* which contains fur, feathers, bones, and other pellets coughed up by owls after they swallow their prey. (The assignment is to identify the prey animals in each pellet. Yuck!) Books, videotapes, erector sets, and microscopes are among the other items offered.

Heinemann Math and Science. Heinemann, 361 Hanover Street, Portsmouth, New Hampshire 03801-3959. Phone: 1/800-541-2086. One of Heinemann's specialty catalogs, containing a variety of books on teaching science and math to children.

Hubbard Scientific, Inc. P.O. Box 760, Chippewa Falls, Wisconsin 54729-0760. Phone: 715/723-4427 or 1/800-323-8368. Offers catalogs of materials to help children learn about life, earth, environmental, and physical science. Relief maps, star finders and charts, aquariums and terrariums, anatomy and zoology models, science games, pulleys, and metric scales are among the offerings.

Schoolmasters Science. 745 State Circle, Box 1941, Ann Arbor, Michigan 48106. Phone: 313/761-5175 or 1/800-521-2832 (orders only). Among the many items featured in this catalog are microscopes, magnifiers, scales, anatomical models, indoor greenhouses, field guides, science activity books, science card sets, butterfly collecting materials, videotapes, and magnet kits. Nearly one hundred pages in length, this catalog contains items for exploring earth science (including dinosaurs and solar energy), astronomy, life science (including anatomy and biology), and physical science (including magnetism and electricity).

Science News Books. A division of Science Service, 1719 N Street, N.W., Washington, D.C. 20036. Phone: 1/800-544-4565. A catalog of science-related books for children and grownups alike. Includes Janice Van Cleave's science projects series (*Gravity, Molecules,* and *Animals*), books and kits for aspiring engineers and chemists, a variety of pictorial atlases, and more.

THE ARTS

Visual Art

Free and Inexpensive Resources
Your Child and the Visual Arts. One of five pamphlets contained in the *Children + Parents + Arts* informational packet produced in 1992 by the National Endowment for the Arts in cooperation with the National Art Education Association, the National Dance Association, the Teachers and Writers Collaborative, Music Educators National Conference, and the American Alliance for Theatre and Education. Contains creative ideas to help children develop their artistic skills in theatre, writing, music, dance, and the visual arts. For ordering information, request a copy of the free *Consumer Information Catalog,* available from the Consumer Information Center, P.O. Box 100, Pueblo, Colorado 81002.

Books
Art for Children (series). By Ernest Raboff. Harper and Row. 32 pages. A series of books containing biographies of famous artists, interpretations of their work, and reproductions of their art. Series features more than a dozen

Science Starts at Home: How You Can Help

From *Helping Your Child Learn Science*, published by the Office of Educational Research and Improvement, U.S. Department of Education.

Every day is filled with opportunities to learn science—without expensive chemistry sets or books. Children can easily be introduced to the natural world and encouraged to observe what goes on around them.

Together, parents and children can:

- See how long it takes for a dandelion or a rose to burst into full bloom; or
- Watch the moon as it appears to change shape over the course of a month, and record the changes; or
- Watch a kitten grow into a cat; or
- Bake a cake; or
- Guess why one of your plants is drooping; or
- Figure out how the spin cycle of the washing machine gets the water out of the clothes.

Learning to observe objects carefully is an important step leading to scientific explanations. Experiencing the world together and exchanging information about what we see are important, too.

A nasty head cold can even be turned into a chance to learn science. We can point out that there is no known cure for a cold, but that we do know how diseases are passed from person to person. Or we can teach some ways to stay healthy—such as washing our hands, not sharing forks, spoons, or glasses, and covering our nose and mouth when we sneeze or cough.

Finding the Right Activity for Your Child

Different children have different interests and need different science projects. A sand and rock collection that was a big hit with an 8-year-old daughter may not be a big hit with a 6-year-old son.

Fortunately, all types of children can find plenty of projects that are fun. If your child loves to cook, let him or her observe how sugar melts into caramel syrup or how vinegar curdles milk.

Knowing our children is the best way to find suitable activities. Here are some tips:

- Encourage activities that are neither too hard nor to easy. If in doubt, err on the easy side since something too difficult may give the idea that science itself is too hard.

- Age suggestions on book jackets or toy containers are just that—suggestions. They may not reflect the interest or ability of your child. A child who is interested in a subject can often handle materials for a higher age group, while a child who isn't interested in or hasn't been exposed to the subject may need to start with something for a younger age group.

- Consider a child's personality and social habits. Some projects are best done alone, others in a group; some require help, others require little or no supervision. Solitary activities may bore some, while group projects may frighten others.

- Select activities appropriate for the child's environment. A brightly lighted city isn't the best place for star-gazing, for example.

- Allow your children to help select the activities. If you don't know whether Sarah would rather collect shells or plant daffodils, ask her. When she picks something she wants to do, she'll learn more and have a better time doing it.

artists, including Van Gogh, Picasso, Renoir, Michelangelo, and Matisse. For ages five and up.

Artful Scribbles: The Significance of Children's Drawings. By Howard Gardner. Basic Books, 1980. 280 pages. Discusses the development of drawing ability in children from infancy through adolescence. Explores the relationships between the artwork of children and the intellectual and emotional development of the child. Chapter 7, "To Copy or Not," addresses the controversy over whether children should copy drawings from visual models.

Children and Their Art: Methods for the Elementary School. By Al Hurwitz and Michael Day. Fifth edition. Harcourt Brace Jovanovich, 1991. 530 pages. Discusses developments in art education, teaching methods, and classroom activities in art. The first edition, by Al Hurwitz and Charles D. Gaitskill, was published in 1958.

Children in Art. By Robin Richmond. Ideals Publishing Corp, 1992. 48 pages. Contains reproductions of dozens of famous paintings of children to help encourage an appreciation of fine art. For children of all ages.

Come Look with Me: Enjoying Art with Children. By Gladys S. Blizzard. Thomasson-Grant, 1991. 32 pages. Contains full-color reproductions of famous paintings (all with children in them), along with thought-provoking questions and brief biographies of the artists. For children ages six and up. Other books in the "Come Look with Me" series include *Exploring Landscape Art with Children* and *Animals in Art*.

The Creative Spirit. By Daniel Coleman, Paul Kaufman, and Michael Ray. Penguin Books, 1992. 185 pages. Creativity is not the exclusive domain of artists, poets, or a genius elite, according to this companion book to the PBS series. Rather, creativity can be cultivated by anyone—by children and adults, by companies, by whole communities. Explores the creative process—including the realms of intuition and the concept of "flow"—and offers a series of exercises to help liberate the creative spirit in each of us.

Encouraging the Artist in Your Child (Even if You Can't Draw). By Sally Warner. St. Martin's Press, 1989. 259 pages. Written by an artist and educator, this book explains how to share the joy of creating art with your child. Includes one hundred and one projects for kids ages two to ten in drawing, painting, sculpture, clay, and other visual media.

Getting to Know the World's Greatest Artists (series). By Mike Venezia. Children's Press. 32 pages. This series of books takes a light-hearted look at famous artists, their lives, and their masterpieces. Includes large text, humorous illustrations, and photographs of famous paintings. Books in the series include Da Vinci, Monet, Van Gogh, Hopper, Picasso, Rembrandt, Michelangelo, and Botticelli. Discusses their lives and their work. For children ages four to eight.

Great Painters. By Piero Ventura. G. P. Putnam's Sons, 1984. 160 pages. Combines reproductions of masterpieces with light-hearted illustrations and engaging text to help children better understand and appreciate fine art. For children ages eight and up.

I Spy: An Alphabet in Art. By Lucy Micklethwait. Greenwillow, 1992. Readers play the game "I spy with my little eye," searching for various items found in reproductions of famous paintings. Winner of a 1992 Parents' Choice Award. For children ages four to fourteen.

Let's Go to the Art Museum. By Virginia K. Levy. Harry N. Abrams, 1988. 34 pages. Discusses processes, materials, and mediums used in various art forms. Includes art-related questions intended to stimulate thinking and create interest. For children ages eight and up.

Linnea in Monet's Garden. By Christina Bjork and Lena Anderson. Farrar, Straus, Giroux, 1987. 56 pages. An introduction to impressionism through the eyes of a young girl visiting Monet's home in Giverny. Includes illustrations and colorful reproductions of Monet's masterpieces. For children in grades three through six.

A Parent's Guide to Teaching Art. By Donna Gray. Betterway Books, 1991. 184 pages. Offers guidelines for encouraging your child's artistic talent and ability.

Picture This: A First Introduction to Paintings. By Felicity Woolf. Doubleday, 1990. 40 pages. Introduces children to Western art. Explains how to use clues found in paintings to determine the lifestyles of the people in them—and figure out why the painter may have chosen a particular person, place, or subject. For children ages six and up.

Videotape

Don't Eat the Pictures: Sesame Street at the Metropolitan Museum of Art. Children's Television Workshop. Running time: 60 minutes. Young viewers can spend a night locked in an art museum with Big Bird, Cookie Monster, and the rest of the Sesame Street gang. Features the highlights of their adventure—the extraordinary artwork in particular. For ages three to six.

Games

Artdeck. The game of modern masters: impressionism to surrealism. A card game containing reproductions of masters such as Monet, Picasso, and Degas. Introduces children to the works, styles, and lives of influential artists. For two to six players, ages ten and up. Available from Aristoplay (see chapter 27 for contact information).

In the Picture. Intempo Toys. A boardgame featuring reproductions of masterpieces as well as pictures by children. Players tour a museum and try to solve the mystery of a missing painting. For ages six and up. Available at many art museum shops (or call Intempo Toys at 415/324-2502).

Mail Order Catalog

Art Education. Heinemann, 361 Hanover Street, Portsmouth, New Hampshire 03801-3959. Phone: 1/800-541-2086. One of Heinemann's specialty catalogs, containing a variety of books on teaching art to children.

Associations

Alliance for Arts Education. Education Department, Kennedy Center for the Performing Arts, Washington, D.C. 20566. Phone: 202/416-8845. Works to advance education in the arts. Gathers and disseminates information on arts education. Offers guidance in establishing school arts programs.

Children's Art Foundation. P.O. Box 83, Santa Cruz, California 95063. Phone: 408/426-5557. A foundation of individuals, schools, and libraries working to encourage American children to develop their artistic and literary potentials. Provides information on the artistic capabilities of young people. Conducts research on the differences between children's art in America and children's art in other countries. Maintains the Museum of Children's Art and publishes books and periodicals containing art by children. Publications include *Stone Soup: The Magazine by Children,* which contains fiction, poetry, and art created by children ages six to thirteen.

Getty Center for Education in the Arts. 401 Wilshire Boulevard, Suite 950, Santa Monica, California 90401. Phone: 310/395-6657. An operating program of the J. Paul Getty Trust dedicated to improving the quality and status of art education (primarily the visual arts) in the nation's public schools. Initiates and supports advocacy programs in five major program areas: advocacy for the value of art in education, professional development for teachers and administrators in schools and universities, theory development, demonstration programs, and curriculum development. Produces books, research reports, conference proceedings, videotapes, and a biannual newsletter. In collaboration with the National PTA, the center also has produced a kit called *Be Smart, Include Art,* which recommends ways parents can promote art education in school and at home. The kit comes with a guide, brochures, and the Center's advocacy video *Arts for Life* (available from the National PTA—see appendix I for contact information). The Getty Center produces a publications catalog as well.

National Art Education Association. 1916 Association Drive, Reston, Virginia 22901. Phone: 703/860-8000. Works to advance art education through professional development, services, leadership, and advancement of knowledge. Clearinghouse for information on art education programs, materials, and methods used in teaching art from kindergarten through college. Publishes *Art Education,* a bimonthly journal covering current issues, teaching strategies, and innovative programs in visual art education. Also publishes *Studies in Art Education,* a scholarly journal issued quarterly, as well as an association newsletter.

National Endowment for the Arts. Room 602, Nancy Hanks Center, 1100 Pennsylvania Avenue, N.W., Washington, D.C. 20506. Phone: 202/682-5426. An independent federal agency founded by Congress in 1965 to foster excellence in the arts throughout the United States, to help broaden the public's understanding of the arts, and to provide broader access to the nation's cultural resources. The NEA's Arts in Education Program focuses on increasing and improving arts programs in the nation's schools. Offers information on establishing school arts programs. Also provides updates on recent developments, including congressional arts education committee reports.

Young Audiences. 115 East Ninety-second Street, New York, New York 10128. Phone: 212/831-8110. Fax: 212/289-1202. A nonprofit organization with thirty-two chapters in states across the country (see listings below). Works to establish the arts as an essential part of young people's lives and education. Encourages community-wide collaborations on behalf of the arts and education. In many cases, Young Audiences' programs allow children not only to encounter, but also actively participate with, musicians, dancers, actors, and visual artists. Special projects include Family Festival of the Arts (performance programs by professional artists designed for family audiences in community settings), Arts Partners (an arts-in-education program for kindergarten through grade twelve), and Run for the Arts (a student jog-a-thon that helps schools raise funds for the arts in education). Some of the chapters offer the Young Audiences Arts Card, a wallet-sized card that allows children and all accompanying family members to receive discounts of up to 50 percent off admission at participating museums, performances, and other cultural events and establishments. Through its Resource Center, Young Audiences makes available books, reports, videotapes, artist training materials, curriculum materials, and a selected arts-in-education bibliography. Also publishes *Young Audiences News,* a periodic newsletter highlighting recent developments and new resources in arts education.

Following is a listing of Young Audiences chapters across the country:

Arizona

Santa Cruz County Young Audiences. P.O. Box 2484, Nogales, Arizona 85628. Phone: 602/287-3133.

Southern Arizona Young Audiences. P.O. Box 43606, Tucson, Arizona 85712. Phone: 602/322-6296.

California

Young Audiences of Kern County. P.O. Box 9983, Bakersfield, California 93389. Phone: 805/833-8414.

San Diego Chapter of Young Audiences. House of Hospitality, Balboa Park, 1549 El Prado, Suite 14, San Diego, California 92101. Phone: 619/232-2818.

Young Audiences of the Bay Area. 1182 Market Street, Suite 311, San Francisco, California 94102-4919. Phone: 415/863-1719.

Young Audiences of San Jose. 1211 Park Avenue, Suite 203, San Jose, California 95126-2951. Phone: 408/294-6991.

Colorado

Denver Area Chapter of Young Audiences. 1415 Larimer Street, Suite 304, Denver, Colorado 80202. Phone: 303/825-3465.

Connecticut

Young Audiences of Connecticut. 254 College Street, Suite 406, New Haven, Connecticut 06510-2403. Phone: 203/865-0600.

District of Columbia

Young Audiences of Washington, D.C. 1200 Twenty-ninth Street, N.W., Lower Level, Washington, D.C. 20007. Phone: 202/944-2790.

Georgia

Young Audiences of Atlanta. P.O. Box 420195, Atlanta, Georgia 30342. Phone: 404/589-0644.

Indiana

Young Audiences of Indiana. 3050 North Meridian Street, Indianapolis, Indiana 46208. Phone: 317/925-4043.

Louisiana

New Orleans Chapter of Young Audiences. 234 Loyola, Suite 302, New Orleans, Louisiana 70112. Phone: 504/523-3525.

Maryland

Young Audiences of Maryland. 927 North Calvert Street, Baltimore, Maryland 21202-3742. Phone: 410/837-7577.

Massachusetts

Young Audiences of Massachusetts. One Kendall Square, Building 200, Cambridge, Massachusetts 02139. Phone: 617/577-0570.

Michigan

Young Audiences of Michigan. P.O. Box 32-1014, Detroit, Michigan 48232. Phone: 313/843-6940.

Minnesota

Young Audiences of Minnesota.
1111 Nicollet Mall, Minneapolis, Minnesota 55403. Phone: 612/371-5655.

Missouri

Kansas City Chapter of Young Audiences. 4601 Madison Avenue, Kansas City, Missouri 64112. Phone: 816/531-4022.

St. Louis Chapter of Young Audiences. 5615 Pershing, Suite 27, St. Louis, Missouri 63112. Phone: 314/367-1400.

Montana

Young Audiences of Western Montana. P.O. Box 9096, Missoula, Montana 59807. Phone: 406/721-5924.

Nevada

Young Audiences of Northern Nevada. P.O. Box 471, Reno, Nevada 89504. Phone: 702/348-6316.

New Jersey

Young Audiences of New Jersey.
245 Nassau Street, Princeton, New Jersey 08540. Phone: 609/683-7966.

New York

Young Audiences/New York. One East Fifty-third Street, New York, New York 10022. Phone: 212/319-YANY (9269).

Young Audiences of Rochester. 935 East Avenue, Rochester, New York 14607. Phone: 716/271-4080.

Young Audiences of Western New York. 16 Linwood Avenue, Buffalo, New York 14209. Phone: 716/881-0917.

Ohio

Young Audiences of Greater Cleveland. 4614 Prospect Avenue, Suite 533, Cleveland, Ohio 44103-4314. Phone: 216/881-4651.

Oregon

Young Audiences of Oregon. 418 Southwest Washington, Room 202, Portland, Oregon 97204. Phone: 503/224-1412.

Pennsylvania

Young Audiences of Eastern Pennsylvania. 2400 Chestnut Street, #1410, Philadelphia, Pennsylvania 19103. Phone: 215/977-7707.

Texas

Young Audiences of Beaumont.
P.O. Box 5346, Beaumont, Texas 77726-5346. Phone: 409/835-3884.

Young Audiences of Greater Dallas. 4145 Travis Street, Suite 201, Dallas, Texas 75204-1809. Phone: 214/520-9988.

Young Audiences of Houston. 2515 West Main at Kirby, Suite 500, Houston, Texas 77098. Phone: 713/520-9264.

Utah

Young Audiences of Utah. Granite School District, 340 East 3545 South, Salt Lake City, Utah 84115. Phone: 801/268-8542.

Virginia

Young Audiences of Virginia. #5 Koger Center, Suite 216, Norfolk, Virginia 23502. Phone: 804/466-7555.

The Performing Arts

Dance

Free and Inexpensive Resources

Dance and Your Child. One of five pamphlets contained in the *Children + Parents + Arts* informational packet produced in 1992 by the National Endowment for the Arts in cooperation with the National Art Education Association, the National Dance Association, the Teachers and Writers

Collaborative, Music Educators National Conference, and the American Alliance for Theatre and Education. Contains creative ideas to help children develop their artistic skills in dance, music, theatre, writing, and the visual arts. For ordering information, request a copy of the free *Consumer Information Catalog,* published by the Consumer Information Center, P.O. Box 100, Pueblo, Colorado 81002.

Books

Black Dance in America: A History through Its People. By James Haskins. Thomas Y. Crowell, 1990. 232 pages. Shows the evolution of black dance in America, including dance forms like tap, jazz dancing, break dancing, and dance crazes like the Charleston, which came to us from the Ashanti people of Africa by way of the American South. Includes stories of extraordinary performers and creators, like Bill "Bojangles" Robinson, Katherine Dunham, and Arthur Mitchell. Although this book is most appropriate for older children (ages twelve and up), parents with younger children might read the book themselves, then pass along some of their insights. A companion volume to *Black Theater in America* and *Black Music in America.*

Dancer's Companion. By Teri Loren. Dial Press, 1978. 275 pages. A guide to deciding which kinds of dance to study, what to look for in a dance teacher, how often to take class, how to avoid injuries, and how to handle tension and competition. Although the book focuses on dancing for adults, several chapters contain information which will be of interest to parents. Chapter two, "The Questions of Age: Children, Adults, and Age Anxiety," talks about appropriate ages for beginning different types of dance, including ballet.

I Feel Like Dancing: A Year with Jacques d'Amboise and the National Dance Institute. By Steven Barboza. Photographs by Carolyn George d'Amboise. Crown, 1992. 44 pages. The story of how a thousand children from thirty schools discovered the magic of dance as members of Jacques d'Amboise's National Dance Institute.

Magic Slippers: Stories from the Ballet. By Gilda Berger. Illustrated by Vera Rosenberry. Doubleday, 1990. 126 pages. A collection of stories behind ten of the most popular ballets of all times, retold in language that children can understand. Included are *Romeo and Juliet, The Nutcracker, Cinderella, Swan Lake,* and *Sleeping Beauty.* For children ages eight and up.

Videotapes

Dance with Us: A Creative Movement Video for Children. Ezmiar Productions. Running time: 25 minutes. This videotape invites young children to dance along as they watch six enthusiastic young dancers move to the music of Carl Orff, the celebrated music educator. For children ages three to ten.

I Can Dance: An Introduction to the Ballet with Debra Maxwell. Running time: 29 minutes. This videotape is designed to help boys and girls become familiar with the world of ballet and the joys of dance. Shows the basic steps, accompanied by the sounds of classical piano. For children ages seven and up. Available from Music for Little People (see chapter 27 for contact information).

Put On Your Own Show. WGTE Home Video. Running time: 55 minutes. Former ballerina and dance/fitness instructor Susan Zaliouk takes

What You Can Do to Get Your Child Started in Dance

From *Dance and Your Child,* a pamphlet produced by the National Endowment for the Arts in cooperation with the National Dance Association.

As a parent, you can offer your child early exposure to the art of dance and movement through many activities:

- Encourage your child to experience movement. Ask questions like "How many ways can you balance yourself besides standing?" and "How many different ways can you move your head (arms, leg, upper body)?" Questions like these will help your child become aware of his body and its relationship to other people and the environment.

- Provide a place and times for your child to explore and invent movement. Have her tell a story by acting it out with body movements. Or, ask him to move with different types of walks (downhill, on parade, stiff, up stairs) or to pretend to use different kinds of vehicles (bicycle, skateboard, car, horse, etc.).

- Encourage the child to relate movement to rhythm. This can be as simple as getting a child to clap, rock or hop to music or a rhythmic beat. Your child may also enjoy moving or dancing to familiar songs and nursery rhymes. The goal is to get the child to experience movement as it relates to music or rhythm.

- Allow the child to experiment with basic movements. Walking, running, jumping, skipping and such are basic locomotor movements. Bending, stretching, twisting and swinging are non-locomotor movements. By varying the size, level and direction of these basics, children discover a large number of movements which can be combined to form basic dance steps.

young viewers from basic choreography and dance routines through the finishing touches of live dance performances. Includes simple lessons on props, staging, makeup, and costumes. For children ages eight to thirteen.

Associations

American Alliance for Health, Physical Education, Recreation and Dance. 1900 Association Drive, Reston, Virginia 22091-1502. Phone: 703/476-3436. An association of educators and students in the fields of health, physical education, recrea-

tion, and dance. Works to improve these fields of education. Offers leadership development programs and consultation services. Conducts research. Produces periodicals and special publications. Divisions include the National Dance Association (see separate listing).

Dance Educators of America. 85 Rockaway Avenue, Rockville Centre, New York 11570. Phone: 516/766-6615. An association of dance instructors who have passed an examination and met other membership requirements concerning ethics and advertising rules and regulations. Sponsors workshops, seminars, training sessions, and competitions. Engages in charitable activities; presents awards to individuals who have made outstanding contributions to musical theatre in America.

Dance Masters of America. P.O. Box 438, Independence, Missouri 64051-0438. An association of dance teachers. Works to further the art of teaching dance. Publishes a periodic membership roster. Also publishes a magazine and newsletter (both bimonthly).

National Dance Association. 1900 Association Drive, Reston, Virginia 22091-1502. Phone: 703/476-3436. Promotes quality dance and dance education for all ages, levels, populations, and cultures. Holds confer-

ences; conducts programs and special projects; offers symposia and workshops; and produces publications, including books, pamphlets, and periodicals such as *Spotlight on Dance,* a newsletter issued three times annually. Publications available for purchase include *Dance for the Young Child, Children's Dance, Guide to Creative Dance for the Young Child, Dance Resource Guide,* and *Dance Education—What Is It? Why Is It Important?* Also produces audio-visual materials. A division of the American Alliance for Health, Physical Education, Recreation and Dance (see separate listing).

National Endowment for the Arts. See listing under "Visual Art."

Young Audiences. See listing under "Visual Art."

Theatre and Drama

Free and Inexpensive Resources

The Theater and Your Child. One of five pamphlets contained in the *Children + Parents + Arts* informational packet produced in 1992 by the National Endowment for the Arts in cooperation with the National Art Education Association, the National Dance Association, the Teachers and Writers Collaborative, Music Educators National Conference, and the American Alliance for Theatre and Education. Contains creative ideas to help children develop their artistic skills in theatre, writing, music, dance, and the visual arts. For ordering information, request a copy of the free *Consumer Information Catalog,* available from the Consumer Information Center, P.O. Box 100, Pueblo, Colorado 81002.

Books

Playmaking: Children Writing and Performing Their Own Plays. By Daniel Judah Sklar. Teachers & Writers Collaborative, 1990. 184 pages. This book offers step-by-step guidelines to help children write, direct, and perform their own plays. Although the book is designed for teachers, it will appeal to others interested in theatre, children, and teaching. Includes an annotated bibliography and a glossary of theatre terms. Offers insights for working with children of all ages. Winner of the 1992 American Alliance for Theatre and Education's Distinguished Book Award.

Teaching Drama to Young Children. By M. Fox. Heinemann Educational Books, 1987. 128 pages. Offers instructions on how to set up activities in which young children can develop their imaginations, organizing abilities, confidence, and language.

Written for teachers working with children ages five to eight. (Also of interest to parents of aspiring young actors and actresses.)

Theater Magic: Behind the Scenes at a Children's Theater. By Cheryl Walsh Bellville. Carolrhoda Books, 1986. 48 pages. Takes readers behind the scenes at a children's theatre to show how makeup, costumes, sets, props, and special effects are used to create theatre magic.

Periodical

Plays: The Drama Magazine for Young People. Plays, Inc., 120 Boylston Street, Boston, Massachusetts 02116-4615. A magazine containing plays for children to read and/or perform in the middle and lower grades, as well as junior and senior high. Includes new plays, dramatized classics (*Alice in Wonderland*, for example), and puppet plays. Available at many libraries.

Mail Order Catalog

Drama Education. Heinemann, 361 Hanover Street, Portsmouth, New Hampshire 03801-3959. Phone: 1/800-541-2086. One of Heinemann's specialty catalogs, containing a variety of books on teaching drama to children.

Associations

American Alliance for Theatre and Education. Arizona State University, Theatre Department, Tempe, Arizona 85287-3411. Phone: 602/965-6064. An alliance of theatre teachers, theatre artists, playwrights, publishers, and other professionals interest in theatre for young people. Promotes standards of excellence in theatre and theatre education for youth. Provides advocacy, support services, resources, and access to programs that emphasize the importance of drama. Publications include the quarterly *Youth Theatre Journal;* a directory of professional theatre for young audiences, and an annual membership directory.

National Endowment for the Arts. See listing under "Visual Art."

Young Audiences. See listing under "Visual Art."

Music

Free and Inexpensive Resources

Music and Your Child's Education. One of five pamphlets contained in the *Children + Parents + Arts* informational packet produced in 1992 by the National Endowment for the Arts in cooperation with the National Art Education Association, the National Dance Association, the Teachers and Writers Collaborative, Music Educators National Conference, and the American Alliance for Theatre and Education. Contains creative ideas to help children develop their artistic skills in music, theater, writing, dance, and the visual arts. For ordering information, request a copy of the free *Consumer Information Catalog,* available from the Consumer Information Center, P.O. Box 100, Pueblo, Colorado 81002.

Books

Make Your Own Musical Instruments. By Margaret McLean. Lerner Publications, 1988. 32 pages. Provides easy-to-follow instructions for making dozens of musical instruments. For grades four through seven.

Music. By Neil Ardley. Alfred A. Knopf, 1989. 64 pages. Part of the Eyewitness series of books, *Music*

"Dramatic Play" and "Creative Drama"

From *The Theater and Children,* a pamphlet produced by the National Endowment for the Arts in cooperation with the American Alliance for Theatre and Education.

Children enter the world of make-believe first as toddlers when they discover the soul of theater by engaging in activities they see around them and by putting themselves in the places of others. This activity involves mind, body and imagination. It is *dramatic play,* what one educator calls "rehearsal for life." An extension of ordinary play, creative play—the root of theater—is essential to a child's full development.

As children grow older, their play develops structure. They act out favorite stories, create original situations from life experiences, and imagine themselves in fantasy worlds where anything is possible. If they are encouraged in this kind of play at home, they become ready for *creative drama* by the time they enter primary school. As essential as dramatic play is to a child's healthy development, creative drama is an art form, a socializing activity and a means of learning. At this point, guidance by an experienced teacher or leader is needed, someone to guide the drama, to help the young players deepen their experiences and express themselves more effectively.

Creative drama is not acting as adults think of it. It requires no script or memorized lines. It is improvised and centers on children as the participants. Older children often want to extend the process and present their work for an audience. This is fine, so long as the desire to "go public" comes from them, for it is the process rather than the product that is important for youngsters.

In middle school or junior high, many children become ready for what most people think of as the "theater arts" which involve a stage, actors and a play. This implies theater's formal elements: acting, directing, scene and costume design, as well as technical concerns such as stage management, set building, lighting, publicity, etc.

Besides creating theater in its many forms, children also benefit from seeing it. *Children's theater,* comprising an ever-growing diversity of companies and scripts, is an excellent introduction to lifelong enjoyment of theater. . . .

Benefits of Attending the Theater

Going to the theater has many benefits for children, among them:

- Appreciation of theater as an esthetic experience.

- Increased awareness of social and cultural values.

- Sharing in a communal art form.

- Increased knowledge of history and human events.

Elements of a Good Production

By attending children's theater regularly, both parent and child gain personal likes and dislikes and can grasp what is an excellent production as opposed to one that is poor or merely competent. If you have not attended children's theater regularly, here are some elements that characterize a good production, along with some questions concerning each element. Not every criterion will apply to every production.

- **A Good Story:** Children's theater today is wide-ranging, offering plays from traditional fairy tales to homelessness and drug abuse. Whatever the topic, a good production will clarify its subject. Did you learn something new or gain a new insight through the play?

- **Credible Characters:** A "willing suspension of disbelief" is necessary for viewing theater, but the characters should be believable. Did actions seem totally out-of-character for someone in the play? If so, did you lose interest in the action?

- **Excellent Performance Skills** (acting, dance, music, and any other skills called for such as juggling, fencing, etc.): Do the skills support the believability of the characters? Are they at a level befitting the expectations of the actors, both in terms of the amateur or professional status of the company and the actions of the characters?

- **Effective Visual Elements:** Do scenery, costumes, and lighting help transport you to the place and time of the play? Are they visually appealing? In cases where scenery and lighting are minimal or absent, did the production stimulate your imagination in other effective ways?

- **Challenging Ideas:** A good script can provoke thought, bring new ideas to light, perhaps help you look at a facet of life in a new or different way. Ask your child what he or she got from a performance. Try open-ended questions such as: What did you see on the stage? What was a particular character trying to do? What happened at the very beginning? The discussion you are likely to have may surprise you.

- **Insight into Other Cultures:** Theater can take us in time and place to other communities and cultures. Did the production help you to learn about cultural or ethnic traditions? If the play was in the present time, were there characters of culturally diverse backgrounds reflecting contemporary society?

- **Strong Emotional Response and Involvement in the Plot:** Were you moved by the action of the play? Tears or laughter are sure signs that the playwright and actors reached you. While emotions can't always be verbalized, a discussion with your child about his or her feelings about what happened can benefit both of you.

Children's theater includes a wide range of subject matter: folk and fairy tales; contemporary social issues; adventure stories; historical and biographical dramas. The form may be the straight dramatic play, the musical, documentary, or movement theater. In every case, however, the story line or theme should be clear and honestly presented and the production should be enjoyable.

shows how music is made—from the most primitive to the most modern of instruments. Contains photographs of string, brass, percussion, and other instruments; illustrations showing how they are used; and descriptive text. For children ages five and up.

Music and Child Development. By F. Wilson and F. Roehmann. MMB Music, 1988. Insightful proceedings of the 1987 Biology of Music Making Denver Conference on Music and Child Development. To order a copy, write: MMB Music, Inc., 10370 Page Industrial Boulevard, St. Louis, Missouri 63132.

Nurtured by Love. By S. Suzuki. Exposition Press, 1969. 121 pages. The founder of the Suzuki Talent Education Program describes his philosophy of learning. Presents evidence to substantiate the view that every child—even those who appear to be below average—is born with ability. This applies not only to musical talent but to all fields of learning. Suzuki relates meaningful experiences in his own musical career and the circumstances that brought about his creation of the Talent Education method.

A Parent's Guide to Teaching Music. By Jim Probasco. Betterway Publications, 1992. 136 pages. Offers guidance to parents on helping their children "make music" by singing or playing a musical instrument, teaching the basics of reading music, and developing a listening program to broaden the musical horizons of their offspring. Also offers information on teaching materials, including music-related supplies, games, and computer software. Discusses careers in music.

Sound Health: The Music and Sounds that Make Us Whole. By Steven Halpern and Savary Louis.

Harper San Francisco, 1985. 192 pages. Underlines the importance of music in promoting physical and emotional health. Good suggestions for using music as a background environmental enhancer. Currently out of print (check your library).

Audiocassettes

The Classical Child (series). A three-volume set of cassettes (30 minutes each) featuring simplified versions of classic works from Mozart, Handel, Beethoven, Bach, Mozart, Debussy, and other celebrated musicians. Each is gently orchestrated with a synthesizer. For newborns to seven years old. Available from Hand in Hand (see chapter 27 for contact information).

Mr. Bach Comes to Call. Classical Kids Collection. The Children's Group. Running time: 46 minutes. An American Library Association Notable Children's Recording featuring the Toronto Boys Choir and Studio Arts Orchestra. Blends drama, history, humor, and music to help children better understand and appreciate the genius of Bach. For children ages six and up. Other recordings in the series include *Beethoven Lives Upstairs* (see listing under "Videotapes"), *Mozart's Magic Fantasy,* and *Vivaldi's Ring of Mystery.* Available on cassette or compact disk from Music for Little People (see chapter 27 for contact information).

Videotapes

Beethoven Lives Upstairs. The Children's Group, Classical Kids. Running time: 52 minutes. This video tells the story of a special friendship between a ten-year-old boy and the great composer. Includes many excerpts from Beethoven's works. For ages six and up. Available from Alcazar (see chapter 27 for contact information).

Making and Playing Homemade Instruments. Homespun Video. Running time: 60 minutes. Shows how to make a banjo out of an oatmeal box, maracas out of tin cans, a bass out of a washtub, and more. Required materials are easy to come by and inexpensive.

The Orchestra Video. Mark Rubin Productions. Running time: 40 minutes. Narrated by Peter Ustinov. An enhanced video version of the award-winning recording. Using excerpts from the great classics, Peter Ustinov introduces children to musical composition and concepts. For all ages (especially children ages five to ten). Available from Alcazar (see chapter 27 for contact information).

Games

Music Maestro II. Winner of the Parents' Choice Award, this is a game that teaches children about musical instruments, past and present. Preschoolers discover the shapes of forty-eight instruments, while older children are challenged to recognize the instruments and their ensembles as well as their functions. Comes with a four-part puzzle board, three sets of instruments cards, and two cassette tapes featuring works performed by the Oberlin College Conservatory of Music. Available from Aristoplay (see chapter 27 for contact information).

Piccolo Park. Intempo Toys. Four music games in one. During a Piccolo Park "concert," children can identify the sounds of various instruments featured on a cassette tape, race players to the concert stage, and develop an appreciation for music. Comes with a game board, stage, cassette tape, playing cards, and a spin-

ner. Available form Chaselle (see chapter 27 for contact information).

Associations

American Orff-Schulwerk Association. P.O. Box 391089, Cleveland, Ohio 44115. Phone: 216/543-5366. The Orff-Schulwerk music program introduces children from preschool on up to elements of rhythm and melody through creativity and imagination. In group classes, children explore melody, percussion, movement, and other elements of music. The association offers information, encourages research on the Orff-Schulwerk method of musical learning, and assists in developing teacher training materials.

American Symphony Orchestra League. 777 Fourteenth Street, N.W., Suite 500, Washington, D.C. 20005. Phone: 202/628-0099. Through its Youth Orchestra Division, the league represents the interests, addresses the concerns, and helps meet the needs of youth orchestras. (For a state-by-state listing of youth orchestras, see appendix D.)

Music Educators National Conference. 1902 Association Drive, Reston, Virginia 22091. Phone: 703/860-4000. Association of public school music teachers, administrators, consultants, and music majors in college. Addresses all aspects of music education, including general music, band, chorus, orchestra, teacher education, and research. Works to ensure that students have access to well-balanced and comprehensive school music programs. Offers information on promoting music education in schools. Publishes a variety of periodicals, including *General Music Today,* the *Journal of Research in Music Education,* and *Music Educators Journal.* Other publications available through the National Conference include *Mu-*

sic in Today's Schools: Rationale and Commentary (explains why music is important in every child's education); *The School Music Program: Description and Standards* (guidelines for music curricula, kindergarten through twelfth grade); and *Action Kit for Music Education* (includes two videotapes, two books, including *Building Support for School Music,* and four brochures to help conduct a local advocacy campaign).

Music Resources International. Phone: 1/800-628-5687. Provides information on Kindermusik programs, which introduce children to elements of melody and rhythm through a combination of classes and at-home learning with a parent. The programs emphasize creativity and imagination in learning and are suitable for children from eighteen months to seven years old.

National Endowment for the Arts. See listing under "Visual Art."

Suzuki Association of the Americas. P.O. Box 17310, Boulder, Colorado 80308. Phone: 303/444-0948. An association of parents and teachers united to promote the Suzuki Method of music education for children, which advocates formal instruction training as early as age three and requires parents to attend classes and practice daily with their children. Offers information about Suzuki teachers across the country. Conducts workshops and camps that parents and children attend together.

Yamaha Corporation of America. Director of Education, 3445 East Paris Avenue, S.E., P.O. Box 899, Grand Rapids, Michigan 49512-0899. Developer of the Yamaha Primary Course in music instruction, which features two-octave electronic keyboards. In group classes, each child learns to play, read, and compose music at his individual keyboard.

Yamaha has also designed "Music in Education," a program for general music classrooms that enable students to develop at their own individual rates and encourage creativity and active participation.

Young Audiences. See listing under "Visual Art."

Mail Order Catalogs

Alcazar's Catalog of Children's Music. P.O. Box 429, Waterbury, Vermont 05676. Phone: 1/800-541-9904. A catalog containing two hundred audio and video recordings for children. Represents leading artists in the field as well as up-and-coming talents. Lullabies, folk music, swing, jazz, rock and roll, showtunes, classical music, and Disney movie soundtracks are among the many offerings.

Anyone Can Whistle. P.O. Box 4407, Kingston, New York 12401. Phone: 1/800-435-8863. "A catalog of musical discovery," containing quality instruments, music on cassette, children's books about music, and other items that promote an appreciation of music.

Homespun Tapes. Box 694, Woodstock, New York 12498-0694. Phone: 1/800-338-2737. Offers music instruction on video and audio cassette. Here, you'll find tapes on playing the piano, drums, banjo, and a variety of other instruments. Includes some tapes produced especially for kids.

Music for Little People. Box 1460, Redway, California 95560. Phone: 1/800-727-2233. Contains audiocassettes, videotapes, Compact disks, tape recorders, songbooks, and musical instruments—almost everything parents could possibly need to encourage a love of music in their children. This is also a catalog with a message: throughout, there are refer-

Music and Your Child's Education

From *Music and Your Child's Education,* a pamphlet produced by the National Endowment for the Arts in cooperation with the Music Educators National Conference.

What You Can Do

As a parent, you can encourage your child's love of music and nurture his or her musical talents in a number of ways: By listening to good music programs and recordings together, by attending musical events and making music as a family, by praising children for their musical activities and accomplishments. As a result of music-listening and music-making experiences, elementary school children can become better listeners and develop musical intelligence. They also develop pride and a sense of accomplishment as young musicians.

Suggested Activities

Listening to music, moving to music and playing musical games are best for small children and good for elementary students as well. By ages five to eight, many children are ready for one-on-one music lessons. You can help your child choose an instrument by consulting the school music teacher and by noticing what sounds your child most enjoys while listening to music. If you decide to supplement lessons offered at the school with private lessons, you can find a good teacher by asking the school music teacher or the music faculty at a local university for recommendations.

Group classes are particularly supportive for young children. In the early stages, a parent should be in the room with the child during at-home practice periods to offer encouragement and praise and to request specific songs ("That was really good! Would you play it again for me?") It is impossible to give any child too much encouragement. Success at music-making bolsters self-esteem.

When to Start

- Children can begin piano lessons whenever they can sit on a piano bench and concentrate.

- Stringed-instrument study can begin very early (if scaled-down instruments are used)—preferably by grade four.

- Study on wind instruments should begin by grade five.

ences to world peace, social responsibility, and environmental efforts.

Music in Motion. P.O. Box 833814, Richardson, Texas 75083-3814. Phone: 1/800-445-0649. A music education and gift catalog for all ages. This catalog contains hundreds of music-related items to help children and adults learn about, appreci-

ate, and celebrate music. Includes instruments for babies and toddlers; music games (including music domino, music listening bingo, and boardgames); keyboard/staff writing pads; folk tune story books; books about sound; books about musical instruments; audiocassettes featuring music from around the world; videotapes about music; and gifts galore featuring musical notes, clefs, and instruments.

NEMC's Band and Orchestra Instrument Catalog. National Educational Music Company, Ltd., 1181 Route 22, Box 1130, Mountainside, New Jersey 07092. Phone: 1/800-526-4593. Offers musical instruments at discount prices. Offers autoharps, clarinets, trumpets, trombones, violins, xylophones, and every band and orchestra instrument in between. Also sells reeds, cases, violin bows, strings, and other accessories.

READING AND WRITING

Free and Inexpensive Resources

Becoming a Nation of Readers: What Parents Can Do. A thirty-six-page booklet containing activities and techniques to help children of all ages build reading skills. Published by D.C. Heath and Company in cooperation with the Office of Educational Research and Improvement of the U.S. Department of Education. For ordering information, request a copy of the free *Consumer Information Catalog,* available from the Consumer Information Center, P.O. Box 100, Pueblo, Colorado 81002.

From Words to Stories. One of five pamphlets contained in the *Children + Parents + Arts* informational packet produced in 1992 by the National Endowment for the Arts in cooperation with the National Art Education Association, the National Dance Association, the Teachers and Writers Collaborative, Music Educators National Conference, and the American Alliance for Theatre and Education. Contains creative ideas to help children develop their artistic skills in writing, theatre, music, dance, and the visual arts. For ordering information, request a copy of the free *Consumer Information Catalog,* available from the Consumer Information Center, P.O. Box 100, Pueblo, Colorado 81002.

Helping Children Learn about Reading. This brochure briefly explains how to make learning to read a meaningful part of children's lives. Offers guidelines for parents of children from infancy through the school years. Available for 50¢ from the National Association for the Education of Young Children (see appendix I for contact information).

Helping Your Child Use the Library. Contains tips for getting children of all ages interested in books. For ordering information, request a copy of the free *Consumer Information Catalog,* available from the Consumer Information Center, P.O. Box 100, Pueblo, Colorado 81002.

Help Your Child Become a Good Reader. Explains how to help teach children reading fundamentals. Includes suggestions that center around everyday occurrences and readily available materials. Produced by the U.S. Department of Education. For ordering information, request a copy of the free *Consumer Information Catalog,* available from the Consumer Information Center, P.O. Box 100, Pueblo, Colorado 81002.

Help Your Child Learn to Write Well. Contains simple strategies for adults to help encourage children who are just learning to express their ideas through writing. Produced by the Office of Educational Research and Improvement, U.S. Department of Education. For ordering information, request a copy of the free *Consumer Information Catalog,* available from the Consumer Information Center, P.O. Box 100, Pueblo, Colorado 81002.

Help Your Young Child Become a Good Reader. A PTA guide full of ideas for parents to help their young children (ages three to six) become good readers. Offers tips on making reading activities fun and choosing books children will like. Explains the connection between reading and writing. For a free copy, send a self-addressed, stamped, business-size envelope along with your request to the National PTA (see appendix I for contact information).

Parent Booklets. The following parent booklets (sixteen to thirty-two pages each) are available for $1.75 from the International Reading Association (see appendix I for contact information).

You Can Help Your Young Child with Writing. By Marcia Baghban. 1989. Shows how parents can encourage and support preschoolers as they learn to write (available in English or Spanish).

Helping Your Child Become a Reader. By Nancy L. Roser. 1989. Encourages parents to trust their instincts and offers suggestions for parental involvement in children's learning.

How Can I Prepare My Young Child for Reading? By Paula C. Grinnel. 1989. Helps parents understand their role as the child's first teacher in the critical educational years from birth through kindergarten.

Beginning Literacy and Your Child. By Steven B. Silvern and Linda R. Silvern. 1990. Offers parents a wealth of ideas on how to foster those all-important first attempts at reading and writing.

Creating Readers and Writers. By Susan Mandel Glazer. 1990. Packed with ideas to help you help your child become a reader and writer.

Parent Brochures. The following brochures, available free of charge from the International Reading Association, focus on practical reading concerns of parents and on ways for parents to help their children develop reading skills and a lifetime reading habit. For single copies, send your request with along with a self-addressed, stamped, business-size envelope to the International Reading Association (see appendix I for contact information).

Good Books Make Reading Fun for Your Child. By Glenna Davis Sloan (available in French and English).

Summer Reading Is Important. By John Micklos, Jr. (available in French and English).

You Can Help Your Child Connect Reading to Writing. By Nicholas P. Criscuolo.

You Can Help Your Child in Reading by Using the Newspaper. By Nicholas P. Criscuolo (available in French and English).

You Can Prepare Your Child for Reading Tests. By Nicholas P. Criscuolo.

You Can Use Television to Stimulate Your Child's Reading Habits. By Nicholas P. Criscuolo (available in French, Spanish, and English).

Whole Language. Based on the theory that children learn to read and write best when language is not artificially broken into its component parts. Rather than use basal readers and phonics workbooks, whole language students read lively books that allow them to see words in context. The language arts are extended across the curriculum, demonstrating the relationships between reading, writing, and real life. The emphasis is on *meaning,* rather than grammar, spelling, and punctuation. Phonics is one part of the whole language approach to reading instruction.

Following are some good books on the whole language approach to reading and writing:

What's Whole in Whole Language? By Kenneth S. Goodman. Heinemann Educational Books, 1986. 80 pages. Describes the essence of the whole language movement. Provides criteria that parents and teachers can use in helping children to develop literacy, offers examples of whole language programs already at work, and suggests directions for building whole language programs and transforming existing programs.

The Whole Language Catalog. By Kenneth S. Goodman, Louis Bridges Bird, and Yetta M. Goodman. American School Publishers. 448 pages. A compendium of whole language ideas and resources. Includes explanations of language theories, ideas and teaching strategies, and information on more than five hundred publishers and mail order companies. Available from the Teachers and Writers Collaborative (see listing under "Associations").

Whole Language: What's the Difference? By Carole Edelsky, Bess Altwerger, and Barbara Flores. Heinemann Educational Books, 1990. 120 pages. A book for those who want to increase their understanding of the whole language trend in American education. Just what is whole language? Does the term have a core meaning? This book provides answers to such questions.

Books

Families Writing. By Peter R. Stillman. Writer's Digest Books, 1989. 189 pages. Describes more than sixty writing activities that can help bring families closer together. Constructing poetry, recording family stories, and making use of a home computer are examples.

Home: Where Reading and Writing Begin. By Mary W. Hill. Heinemann Educational Books, 1989. 120 pages. A book for parents who want to explore and reflect upon the role they have in their children's literacy development. Explains how reading has many purposes and extends beyond books and magazines to include "recipes, sewing patterns, road maps, tax forms, and directions for assembling tools or toys." Explains what makes a book hold a child's interest, why parents should listen to their children read (and read to them), and how to find time to read with children. Also offers insights on how children learn from their own writing.

Kids Have All the Write Stuff: Inspiring Your Children to Put Pencil to Paper. By Sharon A. Edwards and Robert W. Maloy. Penguin Books, 1992. 300 pages. Explains how parents can help spark a reluctant writer's enthusiasm. Offers dozens of activities to help make writing fun for children: creating a graffiti wall at home and organizing a treasure hunt (complete with maps and clues) are just two examples. Explains how to make writing an integral part of a child's day-to-day life. Also contains resource listings for parents and children and "A Young Writer's Bookcase" listing good books to add to your budding writer's shelf.

Lessons from a Child. By Lucy Calkins. Heinemann Educational Books, 1983. 192 pages. A story of one child's growth in writing, this book follows "Susie" from her introduction to the writing process, through her early efforts at revision and at writing for real audiences, to her becoming a committed writer. Explains how teachers can work with children, helping them to teach themselves and each other. Describes the sequences of writing development and growth.

Let's Do a Poem! Introducing Poetry to Children. By Nancy Larrick. Delacorte Press, 1991. 122 pages. A handbook on introducing poetry to children through singing, chanting, dancing, reading aloud, dramatization, and impromptu choral reading. Includes a directory of recommended poetry collections for children.

Literacy at Home and School: A Guide for Parents. Compiled by V. Nicoll and L. Wilkie. Heinemann Educational Books, 1991. 96 pages. Covers the foundations of literacy in the first five years of life; current approaches to teaching reading, writing, and spelling in Australian primary schools; and ways for parents to help children develop as readers and writers at home. Offers guidelines on choosing books to include in a family collection.

Literacy before Schooling. By Emilia Ferreiro and Ana Teberosky. Heinemann Educational Books, 1982. 304 pages. Explores literacy development in young children prior to school instruction in reading and writing.

On Learning to Read: The Child's Fascination with Meaning. By Bruno Bettelheim and Karen Zelan. Alfred A. Knopf, 1982. 306 pages. From the world-renowned child psychologist, in collaboration with a long-time associate, Karen Zelan, this book argues that true literacy goes beyond the ability to identify words—that it demands an inner attitude inspired by the intrinsic value to the reader of what is being read. The authors remind us that young children are literally enchanted by words. But all too often this enchantment is suffocated by the very methods used to teach reading. Suggests ways that reading can be made important and real to children.

Rainbow Writing. By Mary Furetig and Darlene Kreisberg. Dream Tree Press, 1990. A journal with activities for young writers. Presents monthly themes and suggests writing topics such as journeys and surprises. For children ages six to ten.

Read to Me: Raising Kids Who Love to Read. By Bernice E. Cullinan. Scholastic, 1992. 144 pages. Offers ideas for getting children interested in the printed word: keep books handy, make a daily reading date, and don't rush through a book—savor it.

Real Books for Reading: Learning to Read with Children's Literature. By Linda Hart-Hewins and Jan Wells. Heinemann Educational Books, 1990. 112 pages. A guide to selecting and using real books to nurture a love of reading and language in three- to eight-year-olds. Designed to help parents, teachers, and librarians evaluate books most appropriate for children at specific points in their development as readers.

Wishes, Lies, and Dreams: Teaching Children to Write Poetry. By Kenneth Koch. HarperPerennial, 1980. 310 pages. A highly acclaimed resource for parents as well as teachers, written by a poet. (Available from the Teachers and Writers Collaborative, listed under "Associations.")

Word Works: Why the Alphabet Is a Kid's Best Friend. By Cathryn Berger Kaye. Little, Brown, 1985. 128 pages. Explores the ways words are used in everyday life, in talking, writing, communicating and thinking, as well as in creating stories and poems, printing books, playing games, and programming computers.

Writing for Kids. By Carol Lea Benjamin. Harper and Row, 1985. 102 pages. An introduction to writing for children ages eight to twelve. Explains how to get ideas, how to express thoughts and feelings on paper, and how to work from sentence to paragraph to finished story or essay. Includes chapters on journal writing and notebook keeping.

A Young Person's Guide to Becoming a Writer. By Janet E. Grant. Shoe Tree Press/Betterway Publications, 1991. 152 pages. Offers inspiration and advice to young writers. Explains how they can build confidence and gain control over their writing.

Associations

International Reading Association. 800 Barksdale Road, P.O. Box 8139, Newark, Delaware 19714-8139. Phone: 302/731-1600 or 1/800-336-READ. Fax: 302/731-1057. Works to improve reading instruction, increase literacy levels, and promote lifetime reading habits. Serves as a clearinghouse for the dissemination of reading research through conferences, journals, and other publications. Periodicals include *Reading Teacher,* which offers information about how to teach reading at the preschool, primary, and elementary school levels. Also produces a variety of books on reading instruction (examples include *What Research Has to Say about Reading Instruction, Beginning to Read: Thinking and Learning about Print,* and *Developing a Whole Language Program for a Whole School*). Offers numerous free parent brochures on reading as well (see listings under "Free and Inexpensive Resources"). (For more information, see "Associations" listed in chapter 17.)

National Council of Teachers of English. 1111 Kenyon Road, Urbana, Illinois 61801. Phone: 217/328-3870. An association of teachers of English at all school levels. Works to increase the effectiveness of instruction in English language and literature. Publications include *Language Arts,* a monthly journal containing articles on reading, language development, literature in the classroom, etc. Includes "Books for Children," a section featuring reviews of new children's books.

Reading Is Fundamental (RIF). 600 Maryland Ave., S.W., Suite 500, Washington, D.C. 20024. Phone: 202/287-3220. Fax: 202/287-3196. Sponsors grass-roots reading motivation programs for 2.5 million children (preschool through high-school aged) nationwide. Involves youngsters in reading activities aimed at showing that reading is fun. Provides services to parents to help them encourage reading in the home. Publishes *RIF Newsletter,* a quarterly, and *Children's Bookshelf,* an annotated booklist (available for $1.00).

Teachers and Writers Collaborative. 5 Union Square West, New York, New York 10003-3306. Phone: 212/691-6590. Believes that all children are capable of producing complex, original written work when they are genuinely engaged. Publishes *Teachers and Writers* magazine, along with books on the teaching of writing in the schools. Offers a free book catalog as well as a parent brochure, "From Words to Stories," which gives advice to parents on how to help their kids with writing at home (the brochure is free with each order from the catalog).

Television

Ghostwriter. Produced by the Children's Television Workshop, this program was created to enhance the

American children do not spend much time reading independently at school or at home. In the average elementary school, for example, children spend just 7 to 8 minutes a day reading silently. At home, half of all fifth graders spend only 4 minutes a day reading. These same children spend an average of 130 minutes a day watching television. From *What Works: Research about Teaching and Learning,* produced by the U.S. Department of Education.

reading and writing skills of children in grade school (ages seven to ten, approximately). During each half-hour episode, six young actors solve mysteries with the help of an invisible character—the "Ghostwriter"—who is capable of communicating only through the written word. The Ghostwriter leaves written clues everywhere—on a wall of graffiti, on a computer screen, and everywhere in between. As the young actors unravel the mystery, they demonstrate opportunities to make good use of the written word. Airs on PBS (check local listings).

Mail Order Catalogs

Heinemann-Boyton/Cook Catalog. 361 Hanover Street, Portsmouth, New Hampshire 03801-3959. Phone: 603/431-7894. Offers a wide selection of books on teaching reading and writing to children, including many on the whole language approach. In recent years, Heinemann has developed its booklist to include titles that extend the language arts across the curriculum into the areas of math, science, the social studies, etc. Although most of the books are designed for use in the classroom, the catalog includes a section called "Books for Parents."

Teachers and Writers Collaborative. See listing under "Associations."

Magazines for (and by) Children

The following magazines accept submissions from young writers:

Boodle: By Kids for Kids. P.O. Box 1049, Portland, Indiana 47371. A quarterly magazine containing poetry, stories, and drawings by (and for) children ages six to twelve. Accepts roughly fifty contributions per issue.

Children's Express Quarterly. See listing under "A News Service by Children."

Creative Kids. P.O. Box 6448, Mobile, Alabama 36660. A literary magazine containing reviews, poems, stories, interviews, articles, and artwork. For (and by) children ages eight to eighteen.

Skipping Stones. 80574 Hazelton Road, Cottage Grove, Oregon 97424. A forum for communication among children (ages seven to thirteen) from different lands and backgrounds.

Stone Soup. P.O. Box 83, Santa Cruz, California 95063. Edited by the Children's Art Foundation (see "Associations" listed under "Visual Art"), this literary magazine publishes stories and poems by and for young writers ages six to thirteen.

A News Service by Children

Children's Express. 30 Cooper Square, 4th Floor, New York, New York 10003. Phone: 212/505-7777. A news service where children (ages eight to thirteen) are the reporters and teens (ages fourteen to eighteen) serve as their editors. Children's Express reports on serious issues affecting children, including violence, homelessness, and education. Currently has news bureaus in New York (Harlem and Cooper Square), Indianapolis, Washington, D.C., Oakland, Atlanta, Australia, and New Zealand. Anyone can become a member of Children's Express. Those who want to become a reporter or an editor attend a one day training session conducted by Children's Express teenagers. Application forms are available upon request.

Produces *Children's Express Quarterly*, the magazine of Children's

Express (sample copies are available for $1.00), and *CE News Service,* a weekly newspaper column written by children and syndicated in newspapers across the country. Has published a number of books as well, including *Voices from the Future* (voices of children across the country talking about violence and its impact on their lives). Also produces children's radio and television broadcast series (Children's Express won an Emmy and a George Foster Peabody Award for its coverage of the 1988 presidential campaign).

Making Books

Books

A Book of One's Own: Developing Literacy through Making Books. By Paul Johnson. Heinemann Educational Books, 1992. 119 pages. Offers examples and step-by-step instructions for making a variety of books, from simple folded paper books to hard cover Japanese side-bound volumes. The author shows how book making can help children develop a wide variety of skills and enhance many different areas of the school curriculum.

How to Make Books with Children. By Joy Evans and Jo Ellen Moore. Evan-Moor, 1991. 96 pages. Offers ideas,

tips, and techniques for making all kinds of books, including pop-ups. Appropriate for children ages six and up.

Illustory. By Chimeric, Inc. This book-making kit offers children ages six and up the opportunity to write and illustrate their own published story. After the child develops the narrative and drawings, a parent sends the story to the publisher, who turns it into a typeset, hard-bound book, complete with the title and author's name engraved in gold. The kit comes with water-based markers, paper, and a set of instructions. Available from PlayFair Toys (see chapter 27 for contact information).

Pen Pals

Inexpensive Resource

Hints on Successful Pen Friendships. A booklet available for $1.00 from Pen Friends, Department C, P.O. Box 220, Yamhill, Oregon 97148.

Pen Pal Networks

Some pen pal networks are free. Others charge a modest fee (usually no more than $5.00). Some link up children by age and/or special interest

(sports, cleaning up the environment, etc.). When requesting information, remember to write down names, addresses, and ages, and be sure to enclose a self-addressed, stamped envelope.

American Kids Pen Pal Club. P.O. Box 201, Imperial Beach, California 91933. For children ages seven to seventeen.

Information Center on Children's Cultures. U.S. Committee for UNICEF, 331 East Thirty-eighth Street, New York, New York 10016.

International Pen Friends. Department C-LM, P.O. Box 963, Pioneer, California 95666. For children ages eight and up.

Kids Meeting Kids Can Make a Difference. Box 8H, 380 Riverside Drive, New York, New York 10025. Phone: 212/662-2327.

Pen Friends. Department C, P.O. Box 220, Yamhill, Oregon 97148. For children of all ages.

Pen Pal Post. c/o Els Van Dam, 559 Pape Avenue, Toronto, Ontario, Canada M4K 3R5. For children ages six to thirteen.

Pen Pals for Peace. 747 Eighth Street, S.E., Washington, D.C. 20003.

Sports Pen Pals. P.O. Box 20103, Park West Station, New York, New York 10025. For children ages seven to seventeen.

Student Letter Exchange. R.R. 4, Box 109, Waseca, Minnesota 56093. For children ages nine to twenty.

World Pen Pals. 1694 Como Avenue, St. Paul, Minnesota 55108.

Kit

Passport to Friendship. Included in this kit is an activity book explaining how to get a pen pal, what to write about, etc. Also comes with a world map for charting travels, materials for starting an international stamp collection, and more. For children ages eight and up. Available from Discovery Toys (see listing under "Toys" in chapter 16).

Periodical

The Letter Exchange (Lex). P.O. Box 6218, Albany, California 94706. A magazine containing hundreds of listings from (and for) prospective pen pals (both children and adults). Each entry offers a description of the would-be pen pal (hobbies, interests, and other relevant tidbits). The cost for placing a pen-pal ad is 50¢ a word. Responding is free—simply send a letter, along with an extra stamp and envelope to a number at *The Letter Exchange*. A subscription to this publication, which is issued three times annually, is $18.00. For more information, write to the above address.

FOREIGN LANGUAGES

Books

Berlitz Jr. Macmillan. 64 pages (with accompanying 60-minute cassette tapes). Available in French, German, Italian, and Spanish, these book and cassette packages introduce children to four popular foreign languages. Offers phrases useful when going to school, playing on the playground, and making new friends. For chil-

dren ages three to seven, created by the editors of the adult Berlitz series.

First Hundred Words in French [English, Spanish, German]. Usborne Publishing, 1988. 32 pages. A series for beginners with humorous illustrations (by Stephen Cartwright) intended to make learning fun. Includes everyday words, along with a pronunciation guide. For children ages four to ten.

My First 100 Words in Spanish and English. Simon and Schuster, 1991. 24 pages. A "Pull the Tab Language Book," showing scenes of a store, home, town, park, and other common places. The adjacent page shows specific items from the scene in English/Spanish (pulling a single tab converts all the words to the other language). For children in preschool through grade three. Also available: *My First Phrases in Spanish and English,* another "pull the tab" book showing various scenes and activities (the seashore, making friends, school, etc.) and common phrases used in such situations.

Passport Books. This publisher offers a tape-and-book series for children in French, Italian, German, Spanish, and Japanese. Individual sets come with sixty-minute cassette tapes plus activity booklets containing activities, games, songs, and information about the culture.

Teach Me (series). By Judy Mahoney and Mary Cronin. Teach Me. 20 page booklets (with accompanying forty-five-minute cassettes). Popular book and tape sets designed to help teach young children foreign languages. The series includes *Teach Me German, Teach Me French, Teach Me Spanish, Teach Me Japanese,* and *Teach Me Hebrew.* Sequels are also available (*Teach Me More French,* etc.).

Software

Language Explorer. Nordic Software. This software program is designed to help children ages five and up build vocabulary in French, German, Spanish, and English. Includes more than five hundred animated picture tiles in forty-two topics. Users simply select a topic and a language. Five levels of difficulty. For more information, contact Nordic Software at 402/488-5086.

> Students are most likely to become fluent in a foreign language if they begin studying it in elementary school and continue studying it for 6 to 8 years. Although older students may learn foreign languages faster than younger ones, students who start early are likely to become more proficient and to speak with a near-native accent.
> From *What Works: Research about Teaching and Learning,* produced by the U.S. Department of Education.

Living Books (series). Broderbund. CD-ROM, Macintosh, IBM. This series of interactive animated books allows kids to explore the pages of Mercer Mayer's *Just Grandma and Me,* Marc Browns' *Arthur's Teacher Trouble,* and other fun titles. In addition to dozens of discovery "buttons" (click on a chimney and it puffs smoke, click on a nest and you wake the baby bird, etc.), young users can hear words spoken in different languages. *Just Grandma and Me* "speaks" English, Spanish, and Japanese (you choose which language you want with a simple click);" *Arthur's Teacher Trouble* includes complete Spanish translations for narration, dialogue, and text. For ages three and up. A CD-ROM drive required.

Vocabulary Games. Queue, Inc. Available in French, German, Spanish, Italian, and Latin, this software package contains seven popular word games—Hangman, for example—for children to play alone or with another budding bilinguist. Available in IBM and Apple II formats.

The percentage of high school students studying foreign language declined from 73 percent in 1915 to 15 percent in 1979. Some states and schools are beginning to emphasize foreign language study. However, even with this new emphasis, most students who take a foreign language study it for 2 years or less in high school and do not learn to communicate with it effectively.

From *What Works: Research about Teaching and Learning,* produced by the U.S. Department of Education.

Mail Order Catalog

Claudia's Caravan. P.O. Box 1582, Alameda, California 94501. Phone: 510/521-7871. A portion of this mail order catalog contains materials for bilingual/multilingual instruction, including books, cassettes, and games. Includes series such as *The First 1000 Words* (in French, German, Hebrew, Italian, Russian, and Spanish); *Count Your Way Through* (Canada, China, India, Italy, Japan, Korea, Mexico, and Russia); and the *Spot the Dog* series in Spanish (these are lift-the-flap books, for ages three to seven). Other items include "Language Lotto" kits including a game and bilingual cassette for teaching languages such as Farsi, Cantonese, Cambodian, Russian, and Spanish; "Teach Me" (German, Hebrew, Japanese, etc.) cassette tapes and accompanying read-along coloring books; and folktales from around the globe.

Associations

American Council on the Teaching of Foreign Languages. 6 Executive Plaza, Yonkers, New York 10701. Phone: 914/963-8830. An association of individuals interested in teaching foreign languages in American schools. The council's materials center produces inexpensive classroom and professional materials. Publishes an annual series on foreign language education, a quarterly newsletter, and a professional journal (*Foreign Language Annals*) covering teaching methods, research, and professional concerns.

Modern Language Association. 10 Astor Place, 5th Floor, New York, New York 10003. Phone: 212/475-9500. An association of college and university teachers of English and modern foreign languages. Seeks to advance all aspects of linguistic and literary study. Publications include the *MLA International Bibliography*—an annual list of books and articles on modern languages and literature.

Clearinghouse

ERIC Clearinghouse on Languages and Linguistics. Center for Applied Linguistics, 1118 Twenty-second Street, N.W., Washington, D.C. 20037. Phone: 202/429-9292. Gathers and disseminates information on bilingualism, bilingual education, cultural education, study abroad, and English as a second or foreign language. Materials are intended for specialists, as well as nonspecialists.

National Clearinghouse on Bilingual Education Helpline. Department of Education, 1118 Twenty-second Street, N.W., Washington, D.C. 20037. Phone: 1/800-321-NCBC or 202/467-0867. A resource and referral service. Will answer general questions having to do with bilingual education (including language immersion programs). Refers callers looking for specific information to relevant publications and language specialists.

Language Immersion Programs

Immersion programs, which typically begin in kindergarten and continue through the sixth grade, teach children to read, write, solve problems, and express their thoughts in a foreign language. Immersion programs can be "total" or "partial." In total immersion, all classes are taught in the second language from kindergarten through the second grade. Only after children have reached a certain level of fluency is English gradually phased in. Eventually, half the classes are taught in English and the other half in a foreign language. In "partial" immersion programs, children are taught reading and language arts in English, while other subjects are taught in a foreign language. Of course, there are variations at different schools. Some teachers, for example, may elect to alternate classes between the two languages. Immersion programs have gained popularity, and are offered in many elementary schools across the country in languages such as Spanish, Arabic, and Chinese.

Chapter 15

When School's Out

GENERAL RESOURCES

Books

School's Out. By Joan M. Bergstrom, E.D. Revised edition. Ten Speed Press, 1990. 330 pages. A resource to help elementary school children make good use of their out-of-school time. Helps parents identify their children's special interests and fill their free time creatively. Suggests ways for parents to provide practical help and guidance. Complete with checklists and resource listings. Also by Bergstrom: *School's Out–It's Summer* (Ten Speed Press, 1992), a ninety-six-page book containing suggestions for making kids' summer vacations fun, educational, and rewarding.

The Sierra Club Summer Book. By Linda Allison. Sierra Club Books, 1977. 160 pages. Offers ideas and projects to stimulate children during the summer months. Explains what summer is, offers information about the sun and the seasons, explains what makes us feel hot, and suggests ways to keep cool. Includes tips on favorite summer pastimes like hiking, camping, water sports, gardening, and car trips. Contains a section on first aid as well. For children ages eight to twelve.

Organizations for Boys and Girls

Boy Scouts of America. 1325 Walnut Hill Lane, P.O. Box 152079, Irving, Texas 75015. Phone: 214/580-2000. An educational program for boys ages six to eighteen geared toward character development, responsible citizenship, and mental and physical fitness. Operates local councils in more than four hundred communities. Periodicals include *Boys Life,* a monthly magazine covering Boy Scout activities and other information of interest to scouts, and *Exploring Magazine: The Journal for Explorers,* a quarterly magazine featuring articles on outdoor recreation, hobbies, careers, and entertainment. Also publishes handbooks and manuals for Boy Scouts and scout leaders.

Boys and Girls Clubs of America. 771 First Avenue, New York, New York 10017. Phone: 212/351-5900. A youth development organization offering services to disadvantaged youth. Local groups across the country conduct programs that emphasize health and fitness, career exploration, educational enrichment, leadership development, and drug prevention.

Camp Fire Boys and Girls. 4601 Madison Avenue, Kansas City, Missouri 64112-1278. Phone: 816/756-1950 or 1/800-373-4012. Offers a variety of programs to help boys and girls (ages seven and up) develop a positive self-image, an appreciation and respect for others, and a sense of responsibility. Informal educational activities encourage creativity and help participants learn planning, decision making, and problem-solving skills. Roughly two hundred and forty councils across the country offer camps, field trips, nature excursions, and other programs that help youngsters realize their potential.

4-H Program and Youth Development. U.S. Department of Agriculture, Extension Service, Washington, D.C. 20250. Phone: 202/447-5853. A nonformal, educational program for youth ages five to nineteen. Aims to assist all youth—rural and urban—to become productive citizens through practical training and involvement in such areas as food production, nutrition, family living, environmental education, science and technology, drug abuse education, health concerns, and other societal issues. The four H's stand for fourfold develop-

ment of youth through head, heart, hands, and health.

Girl Scouts of the USA. 830 Third Avenue, New York, New York 10022. Phone: 212/940-7500. Works to meet the special needs of girls, helping them to develop into happy, resourceful individuals who are willing to share their abilities with others. Local groups provide girls with opportunities to expand personal interests, learn new skills, and explore career possibilities. Programs encourage self awareness, interaction with others, development of values, and service to society. For ages five to seventeen.

Girls, Inc. 30 East Thirty-third Street, New York, New York 10016. Phone: 212/689-3700. Works to create an environment in which girls can learn and grow to their fullest potential. Groups across the country offer educational and recreational activities such as photography, cooking, and computer classes. Also conducts daily programs in sports, health and sexuality, life planning and careers, leadership and communication, life skills, and self-reliance. Represents girls on issues of equality. Conducts contests in writing, photography, citizenship, and scholarship at local, regional, and national levels. Maintains a national resource center that houses a database and a collection of resource materials on girls. Publishes *Girls Ink,* a newsletter containing information of interest to girls and young women (ages six to eighteen).

YMCA of the USA. 101 North Wacker Drive, Chicago, Illinois 60606. Phone: 312/977-0031. National council serving more than two thousand YMCAs across the country. Individual YMCAs are controlled locally and offer programs designed to meet the special needs of their communities. Among the offerings are parent/child programs, youth sports activities, informal education programs, camping programs, child-care services, and swimming facilities. Check with your local YMCA for details.

YWCA of the USA. 726 Broadway, New York, New York 10003. Phone: 212/614-2700. Community YWCAs provide a variety of service programs for women and girls. More than four hundred and fifty local groups offer recreational activities, clubs, and classes that promote physical and emotional health, self-improvement, educational enhancement, and responsible citizens. The YWCA of the USA can put you in touch with the community group in your area.

CAMPS FOR KIDS

Free and Inexpensive Resources

How to Choose a Camp for Your Child. Free brochure available from the American Camping Association. Send a self-addressed, stamped, envelope with your request to the American Camping Association (see listing under "Associations").

Questions to Ask the Camp Director. Free brochure available from the American Camping Association. Send a self-addressed, stamped, envelope with your request to the American Camping Association (see listing under "Associations").

Books

Choosing the Right Camp (1993-94 Edition): A Complete Guide to the Best Summer Camp for Your Child. By Richard C. Kennedy and Michael Kimball. Random House, 1992. 194 pages. Explains what to look for in a summer camp. Profiles a variety of camps across the country and groups them by location and specialty. Individual camp entries include addresses, phone numbers, cost, enrollment, and other data, along with text descriptions. Provides a variety of checklists and guidelines.

Guide to Accredited Camps. See American Camping Association under "Associations."

Smart Parents' Guide to Summer Camps. By Sheldon Silver, with Jeremy Solomon. Farrar, Straus and Giroux, 1991. 368 pages. Profiles more than one hundred and fifty summer camps. Individual entries include cost, activities included in the program, religious affiliation (where applicable), type of lodging provided, number of campers admitted, number of counselors, and other information. Organized by region and state (also lists some camps in Canada). Camps are also indexed by name and special needs served (such as physical and behavioral disabilities).

Summer Opportunities for Kids and Teenagers. By Terry Schneider and Vicki Young. Peterson's Guides. Regularly updated (ninth edition printed in 1992). Provides information on summer camps, academic programs, wilderness trips, programs in the arts, and more.

Associations

American Camping Association. 5000 State Road 67 North, Martinsville, Indiana 46151. Phone: 317/342-8456 or 1/800-428-CAMP. A nonprofit organization committed to continuing the values and benefits unique to camp. Works to enhance the quality of the camp experience for children and adults, promote high professional practices in camp administration, and to interpret the values of camp to the public. Offers camp accreditation and site approval programs, as well as certification programs for camp professionals. Publishes *Camping Magazine,* containing practical advice and camp programming ideas. Also produces the annual *Guide to Accredited Camps,* which lists and describes more than two thousand camps throughout the United States. The *Guide,* which is arranged alphabetically by state, includes fees, facilities, operating season, and the length of the camp session for each entry. Indexes for activities and special populations are included as well. ACA also offers a video, *Choosing Your Child's Summer Camp.* Provides free brochures as well (see listings under "Free and Inexpensive Resources"). Contact the association for a copy of their "Camp and Program Leader Catalog" (see listing under "Mail Order Catalog"), which describes these resources, along with scores of other camp-related materials.

The National Camp Association Camp Advisory Service. Phone: 1/800-966-CAMP. Recommends camps (the service is free).

Tips on Trips and Camps. Phone: 410/764-1660. Matches kids with camps. Has regional chapters that make camp suggestions.

Mail Order Catalog

Camp and Program Leader Catalog. American Camping Association, 5000 State Road 67 North, Martinsville, Indiana 46151-7902. Phone: 317/342-8456 or 1/800-428-CAMP. Although this catalog is targeted at camp counselors and program leaders, many of the items will be of interest to parents. Included is the periodic *Guide to Accredited Camps* and the videotape *Choosing Your Child's Summer Camp.* Also contains scores of books highlighting both indoor and outdoor learning opportunities and activities for kids. *Psychology for Kids, 50 Simple Things Kids Can Do to Save the Earth, Sharing the Joy of Nature, Tree Finder, Exploring the Sky, Making Wood Folk Instruments,* and *Campfire Tales* are just a small sampling. Arts and crafts, hiking, canoeing, and orienteering are among the areas of interest. All of the items in the catalog can be ordered by mail from the American Camping Association.

Chapter 16

Fun and Learning

PLAY

Inexpensive Resources

Play Is FUN-damental. A brochure explaining how parents and teachers can make play an enriching experience for children. Available for 50¢ from the National Association for the Education of Young Children (see appendix I for contact information).

Books

Helping Young Children Develop through Play. By J. K. Sawyers and C. S. Rogers. National Association for the Education of Young Children, 1988. 60 pages. Explains the importance of play to children's learning. Offers practical suggestions on how adults can foster play with infants, toddlers, preschoolers, and school-aged children. Available from the National Association for the Education of Young Children (see appendix I for contact information).

The House of Make Believe: Children's Play and the Developing Imagination. By Dorothy G. Singer, Ed.D., and Jerome L. Singer, Ph.D. Harvard University Press, 1990. 330 pages. A comprehensive book on play and imagination, based on research results and the authors' lifelong observations. Explores the connection between imaginative play in childhood and the development of long-term creativity in adults.

Play with a Purpose. By Dorothy Einon. Pantheon Books, 1985. 256 pages. Suggests play activities based on stages of development (from infancy through age ten). For each age group, the author explains what children are like, what interests them, and what activities will engage, entertain, and help them learn. Describes procedures for each activity, the value of the game or project (for example, teaching social or perceptual skills, self-awareness, muscular control, etc.), and variations on the idea.

The Power of Play. By Frank and Theresa Caplan. Anchor Press/Doubleday, 1973. 334 pages. Describes the many benefits of play. Includes a chapter on pioneering educators who contributed to our understanding of play.

Your Child at Play. By Marilyn Segal, Ph.D. Newmarket Press. 208-288 pages. A series of books exploring indoor and outdoor play through the various stages of a child's development. Filled with games, activities, and insights to help parents stay in close touch with their developing child and take advantage of her natural desire to learn. The series includes *Your Child at Play: Birth to One Year* (*One to Two Years; Two to Three Years;* and *Three to Five Years*). A starter kit, containing the first three volumes, is also available.

GAMES

Books

For Babies and Young Children

Baby Games: The Joyful Guide to Child's Play from Birth to Three Years. By Elaine Martin. Running Press, 1988. 184 pages. Contains creative activities (rhymes, songs, games, etc.) to help parents awaken their baby's awareness and establish a strong parent-child bond. Offers month-by-month suggestions for play, including quiet time diversions and outside activities. Fingerplays, water play, word games, and art projects are among the suggestions. Includes a section on toys for babies as well.

Hand Rhymes. By Marc Brown. Penguin USA, 1985. 32 pages. Includes more than a dozen hand rhymes and related illustrations. Clearly shows what to do with your hands while reciting the rhymes. For play with children ages six months to five years.

The Lap-Time Song and Play Book. Edited by Jane Yolen. Harcourt Brace Jovanovich, 1989. 32 pages. Includes songs to sing and fun games to play with a baby on your lap. Includes a brief history of each game/song, guidelines for lap play, and lyrics/music for accompanying songs. "Where Is Thumbkin?", "Here Is the Church," and "Down by the Station" are among the selections.

Pat-A-Cake and Other Play Rhymes. By Joanna Cole and Stephanie Calmenson. Morrow Junior Books, 1992. 46 pages. Dozens of rhymes to chant while tickling, bouncing, patting, or otherwise playing with your baby. Includes old favorites like "This Little Piggy," as well as a variety of less-familiar ditties and play ideas. Simple illustrations show parents how to play each game.

Pretend You're A Cat. By Jean Marzollo and Jerry Pinkney. Dial Books for Young Readers, 1990. 32 pages. Contains verse and pictures that encourage young children to act like their favorite animals (cats, birds, bears, and many others). For children ages two and up.

For Older Children

Backyard Games. By A. Cort Sinnes. Andrews and McMeel, 1993. 127 pages. A manual explaining how to set up and play more than fifty outdoor games. Includes the official rules for badminton, volleyball, croquet, horseshoes, shuffleboard, hide-and-seek, and others.

The Book of Classic Board Games. Collected by Sid Sackson and the editors of Klutz Press. Klutz Press, 1991. Fifteen classic boardgames printed on heavy-duty cardboard, complete with playing pieces. For two or more players, ages five and up.

Changing Kids' Games. By G. S. Don Morris and Jim Stiehl. Human Kinetics, 1989. 143 pages. Offers hundreds of new possibilities for traditional games, with an emphasis on fair play, cooperation, and fun. Presents the Games Design Model, which shows how to add challenging new twists to games. Offers guidelines for creating scores of variations of a single game.

The Cooperative Sports and Games Book: Challenge Without Competition. By Terry Orlick. Pantheon Books, 1978. 123 pages. Includes more than a hundred games for children and grown-ups that provide challenge while eliminating competition. By the same author: *The Second Cooperative Sports and Games Book,* which describes over two hundred more games for players of all ages and abilities.

Everybody Wins: 393 Noncompetitive Games for Young Children. By Jeffrey Sobel. Walker and Co., 1984. 137 pages. Contains cooperative games for children ages three to ten. Selections include variations on old favorites and well as new, noncompetitive games.

Everyone Wins! By Sambhava and Josette Luvmour. New Society Publishers, 1990. 100 pages. This book is for parents and teachers looking for alternatives to competitive games and activities. Offers 161 alternatives that are not only fun, but encourage cooperation and help build communication skills.

The New Games Book. Edited by Andrew Fluegelman. Doubleday, 1976. 196 pages. From the New Games Foundation, this collection features games created or adapted to encourage participation and cooperation and eliminate competition. Also available: *More New Games!,* which includes a resource guide to publications, organizations, and game equipment.

New Games for the Whole Family. By Dale N. LeFevre. Putnam, 1988. 175 pages. A handbook of cooperative games, full of personal anecdotes and humorous pictures. Presents games that are easy to play, require no special equipment, and allow no losers (everyone wins).

Playfair: Everybody's Guide to Noncompetitive Play. By Matt Winstein and Joel Goodman. Impact Publishers, 1980. 249 pages. Clearly describes cooperative games for both large and small groups of children of all ages. Includes detailed instructions for leaders.

The World's Best Street and Yard Games. By Glen Vecchione. Sterling, 1990. 128 pages. From traditional tag, to dress-up fun, to rough-house games, this book describes ways to entertain children everywhere. Includes an index of games according to age range.

Traditional Boardgames

Candy Land. Milton Bradley. A "first" boardgame for young children (ages three to six). Players try to work their way down the colorful path to the candy castle. For two to four players. Other boardgames from Milton Bradley include **Uncle Wiggily,** where players try to get Uncle Wiggily to Dr. Possum's House (for two to four players, ages four to seven) and **Chutes and Ladders**, a boardgame where young players work their way "up and down," from square #1 to square #100 (for two to four players, ages four to seven).

The Game of Life. Milton Bradley. Children get to pretend they're grownups, dodging bad luck (and making bucks) along the way. Updated for the nineties, board spaces now say things like "support your wildlife fund" and "recycle your trash." The cost of housing has gone up as well! Will you land a good job? Have children? Retire in style? Play and find out. For two to four players, ages nine and up.

Monopoly. Parker Brothers. Take a walk on the boardwalk, while your children learn all about money, acquisition, and debt (not to mention taking turns, playing fair, and being a good sport). For two to ten players, ages eight and up. Also available: **Monopoly Junior**, for ages five to eight.

"New Games"

The "new games" movement, which has been around for several years, aims to see competitive sports and games supplemented or replaced by cooperative sports and games where there is no clear winner or loser. "Most schools still teach physical education as though winning were all that mattered," writes Susan Perry in her book, *Playing Smart* (Free Spirit Publishing, 1990). "As you and your child will discover, game-changing can be a liberating experience.

Practitioners of this approach point out that among its many advantages, cooperative play makes it easier for children to ad-lib the rules, reinvent traditional games, and generally communicate more with each other. "You can change the rules of the games you play to meet the needs of the players," Perry writes. "Flexibility and creativity are the key words. As long as both players agree, anything goes (except making mistakes or losing on purpose, since children see through those ploys)." Perry believes that traditional, competitive games can often be both frustrating and boring for players who aren't well matched, with the older sibling or parent winning all the time and the younger or less skilled simply expecting to lose.

Some children initially resist a switch-over to cooperative sports, believing they are pointless without a winner. If this happens when you try to introduce the idea to your child, Perry suggests, "Play with them to show how it's done and how much fun it can be. Choose challenging games for older children used to competition. Suggest they simply try it to see if they like it, and don't push."

Parcheesi. Milton Bradley. An ancient game (it was played by royalty in India back in the 1500s) that hasn't lost its appeal. A race and chase game for home, where players encounter blockades, benefit from bonus moves, and enhance their travel with lucky doubles. Comes with an intriguing board, a dice roller, and rules that aren't too difficult to understand. For two to four players, ages seven and up.

Scrabble. Milton Bradley. A favorite family wordgame, where players try to connect letter tiles (up, down, and across the board) to create different crosswords. Comes with one hundred wooden letter tiles and holders. For two to four players, ages eight and up.

Also available: **Scrabble for Juniors,** for children ages five to eight).

Trivial Pursuit (Family Edition). Parker Brothers. An adaptation of the best-selling original, this version is designed for parents and children to play together. Comes with two boxes of questions—one for adults, one for kids (roughly ages eight to ten). Kid questions cover topics such as *Sesame Street*, Madonna, and skateboarding. For two to six players.

Cooperative Boardgames

Dam Builders Game. Animal Town. A cooperative way to learn about beavers—nature's master engineer. Acting as beavers, players move up and down the stream to collect branches for their dam. But hazards are lurking (wolves, forest fires, etc.). Will they succeed? For two to four players, ages eight to adult.

Fe, Fi, Fo, Fum. Animal Town. A children's fantasy game of cooperation and sharing. The grumpy old giant has taken the villagers' treasures and is now fast asleep at the top of the beanstalk. Players climb the stalk together to retrieve the stolen goods. Players share the treasures with each other—and leave some behind for the old grump (maybe he just had a bad day). For two to four players, ages four to seven. Available from Animal Town, P.O. Box 485, Healdsburg, California 95448. Phone: 1/800-445-8642.

Friends Around the World: A Game of World Peace. Aristoplay. Illustrated by Joan Walsh Anglund. A boardgame that teaches the benefits of cooperation. Players help each other race to bring sixteen friends—each from a different country—to the World Peace center before "the Blob" gets there. For two to four players, ages five and up. Available from Aristoplay, P.O. Box 7529, Ann Arbor, Michigan 48107. Phone: 1/800-634-7738.

Pyramids and Mummies. Aristoplay. Winner of the Parents' Choice Award, this unique three-dimensional board is actually two games in one. In the Pyramid game, players work together to build the pyramid by deciphering messages in rebus writing. Then explore the inner chambers and secret passages in the depths of the great pyramid. For two to four players, ages eight and up.

Card Games

The Book of Cards for Kids. By Gail MacCoil. Workman, 1992. An introduction to card playing for kids. From Crazy Eights, to Call Rummy, and Solitaire, this book offers easy-to-understand directions for thirty-five games. Comes with an over-sized deck of playing cards for small hands.

Playing Cards from Aristoplay. Aristoplay offers a variety of playing card decks exploring specific topics. Each comes with a complete set of instructions (some also come with an informational booklet). Card decks include:

> American History
> Baseball Legends
> Black History
> Fairytale Cards
> The Game of Authors
> Great Women
> Inventors, Explorers, and Scientists
> New Testament Stories
> Old Testament Stories
> Pioneers in Medicine

Available through the Aristoplay mail order catalog, P.O. Box 7529, Ann Arbor, Michigan 48107-7529. Phone: 1/800-634-7738.

TOYS

Free and Inexpensive Resources

Guide to Toys and Play. A free booklet produced by Toy Manufacturers of America. Offers guidelines on toy selection for children from infancy through adolescence. Also contains tips on safety and information on toy labeling. For a copy, send a postcard that includes your name and mailing address to "Toy Booklet," P.O. Box 866, Madison Square Station, New York 10159-0866 (or call 1/800-851-9955).

Toys: Tools for Learning. Offers tips for making wise, economical toy

Indoor/Outdoor Games
(That Cost Nothing and Have Withstood the Test of Time)

Flashlight Tag

A group divides up into two teams. One team tries to crawl, creep, tiptoe, or otherwise move across the dark lawn while the other team attempts to spot them with a flashlight beam. Anyone spotted is out. The team that gets the most players to the finish line is the winner. Teams reverse roles after each round of play.

Hot Potato

One person is "It." "It" stands outside a circle of children with her eyes closed while the kids quickly pass a "hot potato" (almost any small object—an apple, orange, cold potato, etc.—will do). When "It" yells "Stop!" and opens his or her eyes, the one caught holding the hot potato is out. The last one remaining is the winner.

Red Light, Green Light

Players form a line away from the child designated "It." "It" turns away from the line and shouts "green light," while the rest of the children quickly move up to try to touch her. "It" then yells "red light," counts to three, and turns around. Anyone she spots moving must go back. The first person to reach her is the winner.

Red Rover

Players are divided into two teams of equal size who face each other, holding hands. One team selects a player from the opposite team. (If it's "Michael," they chant "Red rover, red rover, let Michael come over.") Michael then leaves his own team and tries to break through the linked arms of the opposing team. If he breaks through, he's allowed to go back to his team. If he is "captured," he then joins that team. The largest team at the end of the game wins.

Sardines

One player hides while the other children count (usually to one hundred). Next, the players all search for the person in hiding. When a player finds this person, she quietly joins him while the rest continue to search. This goes on until all but one child has disappeared. The last person to find the group is "It" the next time around.

choices for children from birth through age eight. Includes a long chart explaining what children are like (and which types of toys and activities are appropriate) at the various stages of development. This brochure is available for 50¢ from the National Association for the Education of Young Children (see appendix I for contact information).

Which Toy for Which Child: A Consumer's Guide for Selecting Suitable Toys. Free booklets (one for children from infancy through age five, the other for ages six and up) available from the Consumer Product Safety

Commission, Office of Information and Public Affairs, 5401 West Bard Avenue, Bethesda, Maryland 20816. Phone: 301/504-0580.

Books

General

The Best Toys, Books and Videos for Kids. By Joanne Oppenheim and Stephanie Oppenheim. HarperCollins, 1993. 332 pages. Based on the acclaimed consumer newsletter, *The Oppenheim Toy Portfolio,* this guide tips parents off to the best toys, books, videotapes, and computer products for kids from infancy through age ten. Contains reviews of more than one thousand products. Shopping tips, manufacturers' toll-free numbers, and brand-name comparisons are also included.

Buy Me, Buy Me! The Bank Street Guide to Choosing Toys for Children. By Joanne Oppenheim. Pantheon Books, 1987. 311 pages. Filled with suggestions on how to help choose toys, whether the toy is as simple as a paint brush or as complex as an electronic teaching toy. The first portion of the book offers an overview of toyland; the second section recommends toys according to children's ages and stages of development. Part three is a directory to toy suppliers and organizations that can help parents enhance their child's play life.

Parents' Choice: A Sourcebook of the Very Best Products to Educate, Inform, and Entertain Children of all Ages. Selected by Diana Huss Green. Andrews and McMeel, 1993. 208 pages. Compiled by the founder and editor of *Parents' Choice* magazine, this sourcebook offers recommendations on the best toys, home videos, audio cassettes, computer programs, books, and magazines for

children. Each entry includes the name of the manufacturer or publisher, suggested retail price, recommended age range, and a full description to help parents decide if the product is right for their family. For parents with children of all ages.

The Toy Chest: A Sourcebook of Toys for Children. By Stevanne Auerbach. Lyle Stuart, 1986. 226 pages. Contains practical information on selecting appropriate toys for children of various ages and with different needs.

Making Toys (A Sampling of Available Titles on Toy-making)

Bear Book: How to Make Teddy Bears and a Few Close Friends. By Diana Deakin. Sterling, 1990. 150 pages.

Big Book of Stuffed Toy and Doll Making: Instructions and Full-Size Patterns for 45 Playthings. By Margaret Hutchings. Dover, 1983. 256 pages.

The Great All-American Wooden Toy Book: More than 40 Easy-to-Build Projects. By Bill Jones and Norm Marshall. Rodale Press, 1986. 224 pages.

Making Noah's Ark Toys in Wood. By Alan Bridgewater and Gill Bridgewater. Sterling, 1988. 164 pages.

Making Wooden Toys That Move. By Alan Bridgewater and Gill Bridgewater. TAB Books, 1989. 208 pages.

No Bored Babies: A Guide to Making Developmental Toys for Babies Birth-Age Two. By Jan F. Shea. Second edition. Bear Creek Publications, 1986. 64 pages.

Outdoor Playhouses and Toys: Projects and Plans. By the Workbench magazine staff. Sterling, 1985. 112 pages.

Paper Toy Making. By Margaret W. Campbell. Dover, 1975. 96 pages.

Steven Caney's Toy Book: More than 50 Toys to Make from Things You Already Have Around the House. By Steven Caney. Workman, 1972. 175 pages.

Teachables from Trashables: Home-Made Toys That Teach. By the Toys 'n Things Press staff. Redleaf Press, 1979. 180 pages.

Whirligigs for Children Young and Old. By Anders S. Lunde. Chilton, 1992. 150 pages.

Toy Reviews

The Oppenheim Toy Portfolio. 40 East Ninth Street, New York, New York 10003. Phone: 212/598-0502 or 1/800-544-TOYS. A quarterly newsletter that reviews toys, books, and videos for children of different ages. Recommends the most innovative products, including products for children with special needs.

Parents' Choice. A quarterly review of children's media including toys, games, books, movies, television programs, recordings, videotapes, and computer software. Contact Parents' Choice Foundation, P.O. Box 185, Waban, Massachusetts 02168. Phone: 617/965-5913. (See also listing for Parents' Choice Foundation under "Associations.")

Associations

Parents' Choice Foundation. P.O. Box 185, Waban, Massachusetts 02168. Phone: 617/965-5913. Serves as a central source of information on children's media (toys, games, books, movies, television programs, recordings, videotapes, and computer software) selected by parents, children, teachers, and other professionals. Presents the annual Parents' Choice awards which honor the year's best in children's media. Publishes the quarterly journal *Parents' Choice*, (see listing under "Periodicals").

Toy Manufacturers of America. 200 Fifth Avenue, Room 740, New York, New York 10010. A trade association for U.S. toy manufacturers and importers. Manages the annual American International Toy Fair. Compiles statistics and conducts safety, education, and public information programs. Publications include the *American International Toy Fair Official Directory* and the *Guide to Toys and Play*, a free booklet (see listing under "Free and Inexpensive Resources").

USA Toy Library Association. 2719 Broadway, Evanston, Illinois 60201. Phone: 708/864-3330. Promotes the importance of play and facilitates the development of toy lending libraries in schools, child care centers, medical facilities, etc. Publishes *Child's Play*, a quarterly newsletter covering toys and play, early childhood development, and events involving toy libraries. Will direct callers to the toy-lending library nearest their home. Also produces a directory of toy-lending libraries in the United States (there are more than 270 of them).

Mail Order Catalogs

The American Girls Collection. Pleasant Company, 8400 Fairway Place, P.O. Box 190, Middleton, Wisconsin 53562-0190. Phone: 1/800-845-0005. Contains dolls, doll clothes and accessories, furniture and equipment (fishing sets, cookware, school supplies, tea sets, camping gear, etc.) based on The American Girls Collection series of books. These books, which include stories about young girls such as Felicity, Kirsten, Samantha, and Molly, are designed to celebrate girlhood (past and present) and help explain what life was like for girls during the past two hundred years. Includes stories about girls growing up in colonial America, on the American frontier, during the Victorian era, and on the home front during World War Two. The catalog also contains "The New Baby Collection" of baby dolls, accessories, and accompanying books. *American Girl* magazine, for children ages seven and up, is also described in the catalog.

Animal Town. P.O. Box 485, Healdsburg, California 95448. Phone: 1/800-445-8642. This catalog contains cooperative and non-competitive games; outdoor playthings; children's tapes, books, and puzzles; and books for parents on cooperation and family activities. Includes a notable collection of boardgames that help teach children about the stars, animals, farming, friendship, and the environment.

Aristoplay. P.O. Box 7529, Ann Arbor, Michigan 48107. Phone: 1/800-634-7738. Contains "games for the best in fun and learning," including boardgames, card games, and puzzle games. Parents' Choice Award winners such as *Pyramids and Mummies, Music Maestro II,* and *Artdeck* are among the offerings. Other award-winners include *Alpha Animals* (an A-to-Z animal classification game), *Pollution Solution* (a pollution-solving game), and *Hail to the Chief* (a game designed to teach children about presidential elections). Also contains sets of specialized playing cards exploring black history, baseball legions, pioneers in medicine, great women, and other areas of interest.

Back to Basics Toys. 2707 Pittman Drive, Silver Spring, Maryland 20910. Phone: 1/800-356-5360. This catalog is full of toys that have been popular for decades. Included are Tinkertoys, Lincoln Logs, Colorforms, Raggedy Ann and Andy Dolls, wooden alphabet blocks, corrugated cardboard building blocks, erector sets, the original Radio Flyer wagon, race cars, and a solid maple easel. Also includes Brio toys such as the seventy-one-piece Brio-Mec Vehicle Kit and classic wooden train set; Playmobil Pirate fantasy sets; and many newer, Parents' Choice and other award-winners like the "Toy Cupboard" floor puzzle and the "Awesome Tower" race car set. An extensive collection of outdoor play equipment is offered through this catalog as well.

Bits and Pieces. 1 Puzzle Place, B8016, Stevens Point, Wisconsin 54481-7199. Phone: 1/800-JIGSAWS. A collection of puzzles and games for children and adults. "Easy" puzzles for the younger set include "Up by a Neck" (a family of wooden jigsaw giraffes), Fairy Tale and Number Blocks (four classic fairytales, along with numbers from one to sixteen), the Tropical Rainforest giant floor puzzle, Ninja Turtle floor puzzles, and the wooden alphabet turtle puzzle. Among the more challenging are a globe puzzle with magnetized pieces, the Purple Passion puzzle (with five hundred pieces of an identical color), and the "World's Most Difficult Jigsaw Puzzle" series, featuring the same picture on both sides, but rotated 90 degrees. This company will also turn one of your favorite photographs into a jigsaw.

Childcraft. P.O. Box 29149, Mission, Kansas 66201-9149. Phone: 1/800-631-5657. A catalog full of toys and learning tools for toddlers through preteens. Outdoor play equipment (balls, bats, pogo sticks, etc.), science equipment (microscopes, magnifiers, and nature books), gardening tools, art and building supplies, dress-up clothes, and bedroom furnishings are among the ever-changing inventory.

Childswork/Childsplay. Center for Applied Psychology, Inc., P.O. Box 1586, King of Prussia, Pennsylvania 19406. Phone: 1/800-962-1141. This catalog contains products developed by mental health professionals and educators that are designed to teach children values, coping skills, and self-confidence through play. Includes board games, toys, audiotapes, and books that teach social skills and help children understand their feelings.

Constructive Playthings. 1227 East 119th Street, Grandview, Missouri 64030-1117. 1/800-832-0572. Primarily for teachers, this catalog offers toys, books, manipulatives, play equipment, and other items to help teach young children social and motor skills, math and science concepts, language, social studies, and creative expression, among other areas of learning. Parents will be interested in many of the items as well.

Dover Children's Book Catalog. Dover Publications, Inc., 31 East Second Street, Mineola, New York 11501. Offers a large selection of inexpensive "cut and assemble" books for making toy theaters, buildings, vehicles, dollhouse furniture—even whole villages! Other toy-making kits from Dover include the "Easy-to-Make Train," "Easy-to-Make Lighthouse," "Easy-to-Make Pinwheel," and "Easy-to-Make Playtime Farm." Also offers dozens of paper dolls, activity books, fun-to-do mazes, make-your-own mask books, and theme-based coloring books. Write for a free catalog.

F.A.O. Schwarz. 767 Fifth Avenue, New York, New York 10153. Phone: 1/800-635-2451. In addition to electric ride-on vehicles (among the items this company is famous for), this catalog contains stuffed animals and dolls (including a near-life-size radio-controlled one!), toy trains, building

Bang! (A Word on Toy Guns)

Many parents ask themselves whether or not they should allow their children to play with toy guns. This issue is a very personal one. Many child-development experts agree that there should be ground rules for toy-gun play (when it is allowed). For example, parents might tell their children that they can't point their toy guns at *people,* but that they can practice target-shooting with them. They should also make sure their children understand the difference between play and real guns. Some parents decide not to purchase toy guns for their children, but don't forbid their children from making their own out of sticks or construction toys. Parents can explain to their children their objections to gun play ("there is enough violence in the world already," for example) so that the child understands the reasons behind their parents' lack of enthusiasm for war toys.

Who's Calling the Shots? How to Respond Effectively to Children's Fascination with War Toys.
By Nancy Carlsson-Paige and Diane E. Levin. New Society Publishers, 1990. 188 pages. In this book, two educators explain how many of today's Rambo-style toys actually undermine the potential value of aggressive play, which is often developmentally necessary in childhood. Offers creative alternatives to ill-conceived war toys.

blocks, high tech games, water guns, musical instruments, art and science kits, books, videotapes, and other products for children from infancy through the elementary years.

The Great Kids Company. P.O. Box 609, Lewisville, North Carolina 27023-0609. Phone: 1/800-533-2166. Offers toys and learning tools for kids. Musical instruments, construction toys (including Legos, Tinkertoys, and Erector sets), puzzles, art supplies (easles, chalk, modeling clay, etc.), and other tools for fun and learning fill this catalog.

Kids and Things. DEMCO, Box 7488, Madison, Wisconsin 53707. Phone: 608/241-1201 or 1/800-356-1200. Demco's *Kids and Things* catalog contains quality children's books, together with dolls, puppets, puzzles, kits, figurines, and other items that expand on the themes and characters found in the books. For example, the Three Little Pigs collection includes three versions of the classic children's book, "The Three Little Pigs Floor Puzzle," a trio of pig hand puppets, and a soft-sculptured doll house with a carrying handle (complete with stuffed, appliquéd pigs and a big, bad wolf). The Dinosaur collection includes various dinosaur books by notable authors and illustrators, along with dinosaur stickers, games, masks, posters, cassettes, videotapes, stuffed dinosaurs, and prehistoric figurines.

Learning Materials Workshop. 274 North Winookski, Burlington, Vermont 05401. Phone: 802/862-8399. A unique collection of maple and birch hardwood toys with modular, interchangeable units. As the child grows, so do the possibilities for these toys, which include several Parents' Choice Award winners such as "Arcobaleno" (a puzzle and construction toy in one) and "Cubes, Bobbins, Beams," an open-ended building and balancing toy. The various toys can be used in combination.

Lego Shop at Home Service. 555 Taylor Road, P.O. Box 1310, Enfield, Connecticut 06083. Phone: 203/763-4011. The Shop at Home Imagination Book contains Duplo and Lego play sets for children from ages one-and-a-half through the early teen years. In addition to the popular basic building sets, this catalog contains the advanced systems such as the technica control center for inventing remote controlled vehicles; pneumatic power sets that can lift, pull, and pick things up using compressed air controls; and the metroliner train set, complete with a working engine, passenger and steering wagons, and compartments with bunk beds, a restroom, and other details. For the very young, there is the six-piece "Little Skipper" boat for the bath, a Duplo Farm Animals set, and "Fire House #9" (complete with firefighters, engines, and fire alarm). For older children, there are pirate sets, space vehicles, castles, beach resorts, horse ranches, and dozens of others. Action figures, accessories, tracks, wheels, and other replacement/add-on pieces can be ordered through this catalog.

Lilly's Kids. Lillian Vernon Corporation, Virginia Beach, Virginia 23479-0002. Phone: 804/430-1500. A collection of toys that encourage creativity and spark the imagination, including a carpentry box (complete with hammer, nails, sandpaper, and precut wood), a marble shoot, blocks, puzzles, play cookware, art supplies, musical instruments, craft kits, costumes, construction toys, and a cardboard club house that can be colored. For the younger set, there are pull-toys, cuddly animals, rattles, and spinning tops.

The Perfectly Safe Catalog. 7245 Whipple Avenue, N.W., North Canton, Ohio 44720. Phone: 1/800-873-KIDS. Safe scissors that only cut paper, waffle blocks, non-toxic fingerpaints in unbreakable pots, peek-a-boo puppets, and a safety tricycle with a detachable guide bar for parents are among the offerings in this catalog containing items intended to keep babies and young children safe. Each item is pretested. (For more information on this catalog, see listing in chapter 7.)

PlayFair Toys. P.O. Box 18210, Boulder, Colorado 80308. Phone: 1/800-824-7255. Contains toys, games, and kits that stimulate learning and encourage creative expression. Among the offerings are the "Make My Own Fun" greeting card kit, a "Children of the World Wall Hanging," and the "Mad-Sad-Glad Game," which is designed to help kids get in touch with their feelings.

Reader's Digest Kids Catalog. Reader's Digest Association, Inc., Pleasantville, New York 00401. Phone: 1/800-458-3014. Contains toys, kits, games, puzzles, art supplies, books, videocassettes, and other items for children from infancy through the elementary school years. Includes time-tested favorites such as building blocks, Lincoln Logs, and Erector sets, as well as a wildlife hexagonal puzzle, pizza garden for kids, the *"Where in the World Is Carmen Sandiego"* boardgame. Other products include the Children's Theatre (complete with table top stage, backdrops, and characters), the Magna Shapes magnetic construction game, and a Singer sewing machine for children.

Sensational Beginnings. P.O. Box 2009, 300 Detroit, Suite E, Monroe, Michigan 48161. Phone: 1/800-444-2147. A collection of toys and learning tools for tots. Includes stuffed animals (Peter Rabbit, a lullaby lamb, and a Pat the Bunny gift set), dolls (Raggedy Ann and Andy, Madeleine, Linnea, and the complete set of Sesame Street characters), housekeeping and cooking toys, construction toys, riding toys, outdoor play equipment, stacking toys, and puzzles, as well as books and videotapes.

Toys to Grow On. P.O. Box 17, Long Beach, California 90801. Phone: 1/800-542-8338. Offers toys, crafts, games, and books that expand the imagination and encourage creativity and learning. Dolls, building sets, toy vehicles, garden tools, bath toys, and outdoor play equipment (tug or war rope and archery, dart, and tennis sets) are just some of the items offered. Others include a Victorian cardboard house to color and decorate, a bathtub scientist kit, a kid-safe makeup set, a veterinarian kit, a toy horse farm, an endangered animals set, and a collection of travel toys.

Troll Learn and Play. 100 Corporate Drive, Mahwah, New Jersey 07430. Phone: 1/800-247-6106. Art supplies, sports equipment, building blocks, infant toys, dress-up clothes, musical instruments, puzzles, toy vehicles, books, audiocassettes, and troll dolls are among the products offered for sale in this free catalog.

World Wide Games. P.O. Box 517, Colchester, Connecticut 06415-0517. Phone: 1/800-243-9232. A collection of games from around the world for both children and adults. A Paris street 3-D puzzle, a double wooden maze, a pine box full of one hundred target marbles, a marble roller, and a paper glider kit are among the items found in this unique catalog. Also contains chess sets, tic-tac-toe, pick-up sticks, and other timeless classics.

Other Toy Sources

For a list of toy manufacturers, see "Toys" in the "Product Listing by

Category" index to Juvenile Products, appendix A.

In addition to the toy sources described under "Mail Order Catalogs," Discovery Toys offers an impressive collection of fun, educational items for children from infancy through the elementary years:

Discovery Toys. Martinez, California 94553. 1/800-426-4777. Offers quality developmental toys, books, kits, and games through a growing network of Discovery Toy consultants (currently numbering twenty-five thousand). Produces a full-color toy catalog, containing many items you won't find at your local toy store (for example, Discovery Toy's own "Gearopolis" Builder set, containing gears, wheels, cranks, and other pieces for super inventions, and its highly acclaimed "Measure Up" cups, which can be stacked, nested, filled up, emptied out, or used to make animal prints). The catalog is available at Discovery Toy demonstrations. Check your local phone directory or contact the above number to receive the name of your nearest Discovery Toys consultant.

ACTIVITIES AND PROJECTS FOR KIDS

General Resources

Books

Child's Play. By Leslie Hamilton. Crown, 1989. 192 pages. Contains two hundred craft projects and engaging activities for preschoolers. Making hats out of newspapers, conducting scientific experiments, and playing musical instruments are among the activities described. Also available: *Child's Play 6-12* (for the slightly older set).

The Kid Fun Activity Book. By Sharla Feldscher with Susan Lieberman. Harper and Row, 1990. 246 pages. Describes more than 250 easy activities that require little or no equipment. Includes suggestions for bath time, bed time, car travel, and waiting. Also includes outdoor and seasonal activities, rainy-day activities, household chores (ways to make them interesting) ways to help cheer up sick children, and ideas to help make parties fun.

Kids' America. By Steven Caney. Workman, 1978. 414 pages. Packed with activities, projects, tales, and legends from across the country. Magic, tap dancing, frog jumping, weather forecasting, and panning for gold are among the offerings. (Note: Inspired by the book are innovative activity kits including *Teach Yourself Tap Dancing, Make Your Own Time Capsule,* and *Start Your Own Lemonade Stand.* All of these are available from Workman.)

Kids and Weekends: Creative Ways to Make Special Days. By Avery Hart and Paul Mantell. Williamson Publishing, 1992. 173 pages. Describes more than one hundred fun, low-cost activities for children ages five to twelve. Crafts, science, games, dancing, cooking, and garage sales are among the suggested ideas.

1001 Things to Do With Your Kids. By Caryl Waller Krueger. Abingdon, 1988. 320 pages. Written by a child development specialist, this book describes activities for parents and children to do at home, at the grocery store, in the library, in the car, and al-

Toys and Fun Games for Every Age

The toys and games recommended below are just a sampling to inspire your se-
lections. The suggestions for ages newborn to eight are based on those listed in
Toys: Tools for Learning, a brochure published by the National Association for the
Education of Young Children; the suggestions for ages nine to twelve come from
the Consumer Product Safety Commission's booklet, *Which Toy for Which Child?*
A Consumer's Guide for Selecting Suitable Toys.

Birth to Three Months

- rattles, squeeze toys
- tear-proof cardboard or vinyl books with high-contrast pictures
- brightly patterned sheets
- mobiles and bright pictures hung within baby's view
- lullabies, nursery rhymes

Four to Six Months
all of the above, plus

- soft dolls
- textured balls
- toys that make sounds when squeezed or hit
- measuring spoons
- teething toys
- cloth books with bright pictures to see, chew, and shake
- peek-a-boo
- simple songs

Seven Months to One Year
all of the above, plus

- baby dolls
- puppets and stuffed animals
- floating water toys
- containers filled with large beads
- nesting cups or bowls
- recording of voices, animal sounds, music
- wooden blocks
- large balls
- toy vehicles with wheels (be sure there are no removable parts
  to choke on)

One Year to Eighteen Months
all of the above, plus

- music box
- 2-to-6-piece puzzles
- pouring and measuring with sand or water
- miniature people, animals, preferably of wood or rubber
- kitchen cupboard filled with safe pots, pans, lids, and dull utensils
- a large cardboard box for hiding and tunneling
- picture books and recordings of short stories and rhymes
- a bench with pounding holes and child's tools
- thick nontoxic crayons and watercolor markers and large sheets of paper

Eighteen Months to Two Years
all of the above, plus

- soft clay or modeling compound
- large spools or beads with thread to string them
- small broom
- sorting trays
- small wagon, shopping cart
- steerable riding toy
- large picture books

Two Years to Three-and-a-Half Years
all of the above, plus

- stacking toys
- 4-to-20-piece wooden puzzles
- tempera paint, blunt scissors, white paste
- finger painting
- spare hats, shoes, shirts
- "dressing up" games
- soft wood, roofing nails, small hammer
- matching games with textures or sounds
- picture lotto
- music of all kinds

- wagon or wheelbarrow
- doll with clothes and doll bed
- sewing cards
- dominoes

Three-and-a-Half to Five Years

- flannel board
- easel, paint, and narrow brushes
- smaller beads
- sturdy tape recorder
- tape and other collage materials
- bigger puzzles
- realistic model vehicles
- woodworking outfit, with sandpaper, saw, etc.
- roller skates
- old tires
- maracas, tambourine, xylophone
- doll house, miniature airport, garage
- finger puppets
- bowling pins
- pail, shovel, egg beater and muffin tin for water and sand play
- child-size sink and stove

Five to Eight Years

- increasingly complex books to have read and to read
- bicycle
- harmonica
- hobby and craft materials, including fabric, stapler, yarn
- cash register
- jump rope
- basic science instruments, including magnets, magnifying glass
- Frisbee, tetherball
- card games

- team games, including board games
- recipe books for kids
- diaries to write in

Nine to Twelve Years

- books to read, including childhood classics, myths, and legends
- athletic and team sports of many kinds, including boating, basketball, baseball, swimming, skating, and skiing
- musical instruments and serious musical instruction
- science and other models requiring complex written instructions
- creating and acting original dramas, as well as marionette and puppet productions
- membership in clubs, group activities
- more paper and art materials
- jigsaw puzzles with more than 100 pieces
- motorized models
- simple working cameras
- quiz games
- sewing crafts kits and handlooms
- papier maché construction
- telescope, microscope, field binoculars
- stopwatch

most everywhere else. Offers guidelines on creating meaningful conversations, housework motivation tips—and 999 other suggestions.

Play Book. By Steven Caney. Workman, 1975. 240 pages. Describes more than seventy play projects and activities for children, including gardening in a bottle, boardgame making, paper hat construction, fingerprinting, and hand shadowing. Includes lists of materials and tools needed, directions, diagrams for construction, and rules of the game or guidelines for use. Also includes a list of suggested minimum ages for each activity.

Playing Smart. By Susan K. Perry. Free Spirit Publishing, 1990. 211 pages. Offers hundreds of fun, different, and enriching activities for children ages four to fourteen. From photography to psychology, cooking to cultural diversity, gardening to cooperative game playing—parents and children alike will learn to find adventure in ordinary places close to home. None of the activities are specially designed to make your child read more, write better, or score higher in math and science. But some of these might happen naturally when you and your child "play smart"—using the guidelines from this book.

Prime Time Together . . . with Kids. By Donna Erickson. Augsburg Fortress, 1989. 128 pages. Winner of a 1990 Parents' Choice Award. Offers dozens of creative suggestions to help make time spent together with children more rewarding (for example, taking apart an old machine, planting a tiny garden, or building a village out of graham crackers). Also offers ideas to help ease separation anxiety when a parent's work requires traveling (write a pretravel diary for your children, bring postcards from the cities you travel to, leave tape-recorded stories for your children to listen to at bedtime, etc.). Also by Donna Erickson: *More Prime Time Activities With Kids.*

SuperKids: Creative Learning Activities for Children 5-15. By Jean Marzollo. Harper and Row, 1981. 188 pages. Offers specific ideas for projects, along with instructions for carrying them out. Older children can do many of these projects themselves; young children will need adult supervision at times. Chapters include cooking, gardening, drama, making gifts, earning money, music, dance, woodworking, arts and crafts, and animals. Also by Jean Marzollo: *Supertots: Creative Learning Activities for Children One to Three (and Sympathetic Advice for Their Parents).*

Things to Do with Toddlers and Twos. By Karen Miller. Telshare, 1984. 168 pages. For grown-ups looking for interesting ways to spend time with tots, this book contains more than four hundred easy-to-do activities, techniques, and toy designs. Also by Karen Miller: *More Things to Do with Toddlers and Twos,* which offers over five hundred more ideas and activities, and *Ages and Stages,* which describes a variety of activities suitable for various stages of physical, emotional, and intellectual development.

365 TV-Free Activities You Can Do with Your Child. By Steve and Ruth Bennett. Bob Adams, 1991. 415 pages. Describes 365 engaging activities for parents and children, none of which necessitate the use of a television set. Includes Indoor Safari, Beanbag Olympics, and other clever ideas that can be adapted to match the interests and ages of children in individual families. All activities require little (if any) expense, and make use of household items or outdoor surroundings. Also available: *365 Outdoor Activities You Can Do with Your Child.*

Periodical

Family Fun. P.O. Box 10161, Des Moines, Iowa 50340-0161. Phone: 1/800-289-4849. A bimonthly magazine full of ideas, activities, and projects for family fun and learning. Included are things to do (inside and outside the home), places to go (nearby and far away), and books and videotapes not to miss.

Arts and Crafts

Books

Adventures in Art: Art and Craft Experiences for 7-14-Year-Olds. By Susan Milord. Williamson Publishing, 1990. 160 pages. Offers instructions for over one hundred arts and crafts projects for children that can be completed with minimal assistance. Puppets, pot holders, and handmade paper are among the activities described.

Good Earth Art: Environmental Art for Kids. By Mary Ann F. Kohl and Cindy Gainer. Bright Ring, 1991.

224 pages. Offers more than two hundred craft ideas using recycled (discarded) objects and materials from nature. Natural berry dye, car part sculpture, and homemade crayons are among the activities featured in this book.

Kids Create! By Laurie Carlson. Williamson Publishing, 1990. 159 pages. Offers more than one hundred arts and crafts activities using ordinary materials. Helpful tips, the amount of time required for completion, and the level of difficulty is given for each project. For children ages three to nine.

The Kids Encyclopedia of Things to Make and Do. By Richard Michael Rasmussen and Ronda Lea Rasmussen. Redleaf Press, 1989. 244 pages. A compendium of nearly two thousand craft and activity ideas, complete with illustrations. Arranged alphabetically by subject.

Making Things: The Hand Book of Creative Discovery. By Ann Wiseman. Little, Brown, 1973. 153 pages. Includes instructions for making over one hundred objects from paper, potatoes, leaves, tin cans, rope, etc.

My First Activity Book. By Angela Wilkes. Alfred A. Knopf, 1990. 48 pages. Using life-size photographs and simple text, this book provides instructions for a variety of projects, including party masks and papier maché plates. (See also *My First Activity Video*, under "Videotapes.")

Scribble Cookies: And Other Independent Creative Art Experiences for Children. By Mary Ann F. Kohl. Revised edition. Bright Ring, 1985. 130 pages. Chock full of art ideas, some familiar, many new, that stimulate creative thinking and encourage independent expression in children. Explains how to set up an art center and shows the value in allowing children to pursue their own tastes and interests.

Snips and Snails and Walnut Whales. By Phyllis Fiarotta. Workman, 1975. 280 pages. Using natural materials, this book describes more than one hundred craft projects for children and their families. Printing, stenciling, sand casting, and many other art forms are described. Includes detailed instructions, background information, and lists of materials needed for each craft.

Periodicals

Pack-O-Fun. Pack-O-Fun, P.O. Box 7522, Red Oak, Iowa 51591-0522. Phone: 1/800-444-0441. A bimonthly magazine containing family craft and activity ideas. Includes step-by-step instructions for children's crafts, beginner projects, gift ideas, and patterns.

Spark: Creative Fun for Kids. P.O. Box 5028, Harlan, Iowa 51593. Offers step-by-step instructions for dozens of art projects and language activities. Examples include making candy molds, recycling grocery bags into drawing paper, and creating letters of the alphabet out of favorite objects. Face painting, writing projects, and drawing exercises are some others. For work with children ages three and up. Issued nine times annually.

Videotape

My First Activity Video. Sony. Running time: 50 minutes. The "My First" series of videos are based on the best-selling "My First" books. This one calls on kids to use objects from around the house—paper clips, macaroni, beads, etc.—to create arts and crafts projects. Pasta jewelry and robot puppets are among the projects described.

Kit

Anytime, Anyplace Craft Case. A colorful case full of dozens of art supplies, including sequins, feathers, beads, markers, confetti, paint, glue, scissors, construction paper, and more. Available from Toys to Grow On, P.O. Box 17, Long Beach, California 90801. Phone: 1/800-542-8338.

Mail Order Catalogs

Nasco Arts and Crafts. 901 Janesville Avenue, P.O. Box 901, Fort Atkinson, Wisconsin 53538-0901. Phone: 1/800-558-9595. Nearly four hundred pages in length, this catalog features hundreds of arts and crafts supplies for painting, drawing, print making, woodworking, weaving, ceramic making, and other creative endeavors. Paint, palettes, brushes, easels, markers, pastels, paper, modeling clay, yarn, and fabric are just a handful of the items offered for sale. Also contains how-to books and videotapes on printmaking, origami, weaving, calligraphy, art apprecia-

In Your Own Backyard

Create a secret garden for your child's tea parties or transform a wooden deck into a performance stage. These are just two of the many ideas found in *In Your Own Backyard,* a book explaining how to create and enjoy your own private retreat (and turn your backyard into an exciting play area for children). Andrews and McMeel, 1992. 127 pages.

tion, etc. Includes items for children as well as adults.

Vanguard Crafts. P.O. Box 340170, Brooklyn, New York 11234. Phone: 718/377-5188 or 1/800-66-CRAFTS (to order). Between the covers of this catalog, you'll find supplies for needlework, basketry, beadwork, wood projects, rubber stamping, and other arts and crafts.

Drawing

Books

Drawing on the Right Side of the Brain. By Betty Edwards. Jeremy P. Tarcher, 1979. 207 pages. Offers numerous exercises for developing artistic perception based on right-left brain research, including copying upside-down pictures, drawing a common household object without taking one's eyes off it, and paying attention to the empty space between solid objects. The book includes sections on the stages of artistic development in children and advice on teaching children to draw.

Drawing with Children: A Creative Teaching and Learning Method That Works for Adults, Too. By Mona Brookes. Jeremy P. Tarcher,

1986. 211 pages. Offers step-by-step instructions for drawing, using five basic shapes: a dot, a circle, a straight line, a curved line, and an angle line. Also offers guidelines on creating a supportive environment, choosing the right supplies, selecting the appropriate starting level, and drawing in a wide variety of styles using different types of media.

Teaching Children to Draw: A Guide for Teachers and Parents. By Marjorie Wilson and Brent Wilson. Prentice-Hall, 1982. 173 pages. Explains the importance of drawing to childhood development and sets forth a program for increasing children's graphic skills and personal awareness. Distinguishes between *school art* and *spontaneous art*—the art that comes from the child's own desire to create.

Teach Your Child to Draw: Bringing Out Your Child's Talents and Appreciation for Art. By Mai Johnson. Lowell House, 1990. 152 pages. An illustrated assortment of drawing exercises developed to help children learn visual concepts such as point of view, proportion, shading, texture, and movement.

Videotape

Squiggles, Dots and Lines. Kidvidz (A Price Stern Sloan Video). Running time: 30 minutes. An award-winning video featuring Caldecott winner Ed Emberley, who presents a "drawing alphabet" kids can use to draw anything, from a fire truck to a fish. Using this video, kids can learn how to make cards, books, giant murals, and more. For ages five to twelve.

Painting

Books

Paint! By Kim Solga. North Light Books, 1991. 48 pages. Offers nearly a dozen painting projects that escape the boundaries of brush and paper. Shows children how to use stencils, marbles, and their fingers to paint on rocks, cloth, and foil. Explains how to use egg yolks and powdered drink mix to make paint. Helps teach children ages six and up about color, texture, and mixed media. One in a series of books, that also includes *Draw!*, *Make Prints!*, *Make Gifts!*, *Make Sculptures!*, and *Make Clothes Fun!*

Painting with Children. By Brunhild Muller. Floris Books, 1990. 48 pages. Shows how painting stimulates imagination and creativity (vital ingredients in the healthy development of a child).

Watercolor (for the Artistically Undiscovered). By Thacher Hurd and John Cassidy. Klutz Press, 1992. A how-to book on painting with watercolors plus a six-color set of paints and a #5 brush. Provides ideas and advice, examples, and information on color mixing, light and shadow, and perspective. For ages nine and up (including adults).

Software

Kid Pix. Broderbund. A painting software program that allows children to experiment with color, contrast, and shapes to create their own computer masterpieces. Complete with fun sound effects. Turns a computer into an art center for kids. For ages four and up. Macintosh and IBM compatibles available. Requires a hard disk drive and a mouse. Also available: *Kids Pix Companion Software,* which adds more patterns and paint options.

Fun with Paper

Books

The ABCs of Origami: Paper Folding for Children. By Claude Sarasus. Charles E Tuttle Company. 55 pages. A classic among origami books, complete with easy-to-follow diagrams, numerous items to create, and colorful illustrations by the author.

The Amazing Paper Book. By Paulette Gourgeous. Addison-Wesley,

1990. 79 pages. Offers a few dozen paper-related projects and activities, along with stories on the history and making of paper. For elementary school age children.

How to Make Pop-Ups. By Joan Irvine. Illustrated by Barbara Reid. William Morrow, 1987. 93 pages. Offers step-by-step instructions for making pop-up creations, including cards, invitations, and decorations.

Origami. By H. Sakata. Japan Publications USA, 1984. 66 pages. Offers instructions and step-by-step photographs for making boats, birds, flowers, and other paper patterns. For ages ten and up (younger with an adult's assistance).

The Paper Book: Fun Things to Make and Do with Paper. By Hannah Tofts. Simon and Schuster, 1990. 32 pages. Illustrates many paper activities, ranging from easy to more challenging. Includes photographs and easy-to-follow instructions. For children ages six and up. Also by Hannah Tofts: *The 3-D Paper Book.*

Paper Pets. By Seymour Chwast. Harry N. Abrams, 1993. A cut-and-assemble collection of animals with interlocking tabs, created by the director of a New York design firm. Includes three dogs, two cats, one rabbit, one parrot, and one monkey. For ages five to twelve.

Papier Maché for Kids. By Sheila McGraw. Firefly Books, 1991. 72 pages. Guides children through various papier mache projects—masks, vases, monsters, and much more can be made by children ages four through nine. Includes photographs and easy-to-understand text.

The World's Greatest Paper Airplane and Toy Book. By Keith R. Laux. TAB Books, 1987. 120 pages. For older children, this book offers forty differ-

Cardboard Boxes

There are endless possibilities for fun play with cardboard boxes. Large appliance or furniture boxes make perfect playhouses (or club houses); medium sized-boxes can be turned into race cars, doll houses (simply add dividers), or tables for toddlers. Cut a slot in a box and it becomes a post office; fill a box with jewelry or coins and it's a treasure chest. Other children might turn them into rocket ships, jack-in-the boxes, juke boxes, or other play items.

ent paper aircraft designs and includes illustrated, step-by-step instructions.

Videotape

Look What I Made: Paper Playthings and Gifts. Pacific Arts Video. Running time: 45 minutes. A school teacher demonstrates seven craft projects for children, including a piñata, paper hats, and a hammock made out of rolled up newspapers. Recipient of a Parents' Choice silver honor award.

Kit

Paper Anew. Chasley. With this kit, kids ages four and up can make paper using scraps from around the house (junk mail, old newspapers, egg cartons, etc.). Comes with a mold in the shape of a cherry sun-face, cotton linters, a sponge, and detailed instructions. Requires a blender. Available from Exploratorium to Go!, Exploratorium, 3601 Lyon Street, San Francisco, California 94123. Phone: 1/800-359-9899.

Modeling and Sculpting

Books

Mudworks: Creative Clay, Dough, and Modeling Experiences. By MaryAnn Kobl. Bright Ring, 1989. 150 pages. Includes scores of recipes for modeling materials (playdough, papier mache, bread dough, bead clay, stain glass dough, etc.) along with guidelines and suggestions for their use. Activities for ages four to ten.

Sand Castles Step-by-Step. By Lucinda Wierrenga with Walter McDonald. Meadowbrook Press, 1990. 96 pages. Explains how to sculpt sandcastles, step-by-step. Includes simple castles for younger kids, as well as more detailed structures for older children. Written by experienced sandcastle builders. For ages six and up.

Building Forts

Books

Children's Special Places: Exploring the Role of Forts, Dens, and Bush Houses in Middle Childhood. By David Sobel. Zephyr Press, 1993. 168 pages. Explores the den-building activities of children living in various parts of the world. Discusses the children's need for such places. Points out how schools can give children a chance to create special places during school hours and how these activities can be incorporated into the curriculum.

A Kids' Guide to Building Forts. By Tom Birdseye. Harbinger House, 1993. 61 pages. Offers basic building plans for a variety of forts and hideouts, using easy-to-find materials and simple tools. Includes plans for inside and outside forts.

Construction and Building

Materials and Tools

Architectural Blocks. A set of hard rock maple blocks for building projects. Comes in a large set of seventy pieces (thirteen shapes) or a small set of forty pieces (ten shapes). Available through the Hand in Hand mail order catalog, Catalogue Center, Route 26, R.R. I, Box 1425, Oxford, Maine 04270-9711. Phone: 1/800-872-9745.

Brio-Mec. BRIO Scanditoy. Similar to erector sets, only the plates and girders are made out of wood and the nuts and bolts are plastic. Comes with a wooden screwdriver. For ages four and up. Available at toy stores.

Erector Sets. Meccano, Inc. The starter set contains more than two hundred pieces (girders, wheels, nuts, bolts, tools, etc.), plus instructions for creating cranes, planes, trucks, helicopters, and other vehicles. The larger sets (for children ages nine and up) come with real motors, battery packs, and switches. Distributed through toy stores (also available through mail-order companies such as Back to Basics Toys, 2707 Pittman Drive, Silver Spring, Maryland 20910. Phone: 1/800-356-5360.

Gearopolis®. Available from Discovery Toys, this set of plastic gears, cranks, arrows, axels, and platforms is sure to inspire some imaginative construction work. The 80-piece Basic Builder set is for children ages five to twelve; the 212-piece advanced builder set is for children ages seven and up. (For information on obtaining Discovery Toys, see "Other Toy Sources" listed under "Toys.")

Lego Play Sets. In addition to basic building sets, Lego produces advanced systems such as the technic control center for inventing remote controlled vehicles; pneumatic power sets that can lift, pull, and pick things up using compressed air controls; and the metroliner train set, complete with a working engine, passenger and steering wagons, and compartments with bunk beds, a restroom, and other details. Offers sets for children from 1½ years through the early teens. Contact the company for a copy of their Shop at Home Imagination Book (Lego Shop at Home Service, 555 Taylor Road, P.O. Box 1310, Enfield, Connecticut 06083. Phone: 203/763-4011).

Lincoln Logs. Playskool. Designed by the son of architect Frank Lloyd Wright, these simple pine pieces can be used to create cabins, forts, farms, and other inspirations. The new twist: sets come with plastic chimneys, windows, and doors. Available at toy stores or from Back to Basics Toys, 2707 Pittman Drive, Silver Spring, Maryland 20910. Phone: 1/800-356-5360.

"No-Ends." These building sets come with plastic beams (straight and curved) plus six-sided connectors for building imaginative shapes and forms, including theatres, animals, and castles. The starter set has 80 pieces; the largest set has 150 pieces. Available from Back to Basics Toys, 2707 Pittman Drive, Silver Spring, Maryland 20910. Phone: 1/800-356-5360.

Tinkertoys. Playskool. A classic construction toy, now with colorful plastic sticks and spools. Comes in four different size sets, ranging from the Big Builder Set (thirty-five pieces) to the Colossal Construction Set (one hundred and fifteen pieces). Available at toy stores or from Back to Basics Toys, 2707 Pittman Drive, Silver Spring, Maryland 20910. Phone: 1/800-356-5360.

Carpentry

Book

Carpentry for Children. By Lester Walker. Overlook Press, 1985. 208 pages. Written by an architect, this book offers step-by-step plans for more than a dozen do-it-yourself carpentry projects. Includes more than three hundred and fifty photographs. For children ages eight and up (with supervision). Also by Lester Walker: *Housebuilding for Children,* which shows how a group of children ages seven to ten went about constructing their own playhouses.

Tools and Building Materials

Build-It-Yourself Woodworking Kit. A carpentry kit for kids, containing sandpaper, nails, a ruler, hammer, glue, and wood (pine) in all shapes and sizes (planks, dowels, etc.). For children ages five to twelve. Available from Toys to Grow On, P.O. Box 17, Long Beach, California 90801. Phone: 1/800-874-4242.

Children's Handy Tool Set. A twelve-piece set with tools made to fit small hands. A saw, wrench, screwdrivers, hammer, and more come in a sturdy wooden carrying case. For children ages eight and up. Available from Animal Town, P.O. Box 485, Healdsburg, California 95448. Phone: 1/800-445-8642.

Inventing

Books

How to Be an Inventor. By Harvey Weiss. Crowell, 1980. 95 pages. Discusses different types of inventors and their creations. Offers advice on becoming an inventor. For children in grades five and up.

Invention. By Lionel Bender. Alfred A. Knopf, 1991. 64 pages. Part of the Eyewitness series of award-winning books, *Invention* takes a look at man-made devices over the decades. Includes captivating photographs and informative captions. For children ages ten and up.

Inventors Workshop. By Alan J. McCormack. Fearon, 1981. 84 pages. Features more than two dozen challenging projects for children in grades three through eight. Among these are a bubble-making machine, a toothpaste dispenser, and a candle-powered steamboat.

Mistakes that Worked. By Charlotte Foltz Jones. Doubleday, 1991. 78 pages. Explains how various individuals discovered (or "invented") popular products by accident. Tea bags, Silly Putty, and chocolate chip cookies are among the serendipitous discoveries described. For children ages eight and up.

Steven Caney's Invention Book. By Steven Caney. Workman, 1985. 200 pages. An A-to-Z invention book for children ages eight and up. Includes stories about American inventions—from the Frisbee to chocolate chip cookies—plus at-home projects to stimulate creativity.

Contests

All the Best Contests for Kids. By Joan M. Bergstrom and Craig Bergstrom. Ten Speed Press, 1992. 288 pages. Updated periodically, this book offers details on more than one hundred contests for children ages six to twelve. Drawing, writing, and inventing are among the contest categories. Also explains how to submit work to children's magazines and how to sign up for national children's clubs.

Invent America. 1505 Powhatan Street, Alexandria, Virginia 22314. Phone: 703/684-1836. This program/contest is designed to encourage creativity and help develop children's problem-solving abilities at home and at school. Winning inventors are eligible for national awards and a free trip to Washington, D.C. Sample packet available for $2.95.

Gardening

Free and Inexpensive Resources

A Child's Garden Seed Collection. Samples of flower and vegetable seeds, available for $1.00 from Watch It Grow, 2560 Nickel Place, Hayward, California 94545. (Be sure to request "A Child's Garden Seed Collection.")

Growing Vegetables in the Home Garden. This forty-seven-page booklet explains how to plant and care for more than fifty kinds of herbs and vegetables, including basil, eggplant, cucumbers, peppers, and tomatoes. Produced by the U.S. Department of Agriculture. For ordering information, request a copy of the free *Consumer Information Catalog,* available from the Consumer Information Center, P.O. Box 100, Pueblo, Colorado 81002.

Out and About Town

Visit a bakery. Children love to peer into the cases and get a close-up look at the impressive array of cookies, cakes, muffins, pies, and breads found inside them. Allow your child to pick out one special item to go (find a pleasant place to eat it—on a bench, in a park, etc.)

Visit a cemetery. Here, children can compare tombstones; read names, dates, and epigraphs (and imagine the stories behind the individuals or families buried); do rubbings; and enjoy the trees, grass, flowers, or other forms of life commonly found in such places.

Visit a fire department. Often times, children get to climb on a fire truck, try on a hat, and see the poles that those lucky firefighters get to slide down.

Visit a hardware store. Toys from the hardware store (a plastic tool chest, measuring tape, putty knives, boards, nuts and bolts, etc.) can teach girls and boys alike to feel comfortable with tools. Have them "help" with a project around the house, using their own tools, or set them up with their own activity.

Books

Best Kids Garden Book. By the Sunset editors. Sunset Publishing, 1992. 95 pages. Tells children how to plant and care for their very own garden—large or small, in the ground or in pots, outdoors or indoors. Includes descriptions, pictures, and growing instructions for more than forty-five plants. Also discusses garden safety and garden-related activities and special projects—creating a garden journal, painting with leaves, and growing a jungle in a jar.

Grow It! By Erika Markmann. Random House, 1991. 48 pages. An indoor/outdoor gardening guide for kids. Offers easy-to-understand information on planning, planting, and tending a garden on a plot or in a pot. For ages seven to twelve.

A Kid's First Book of Gardening. By Derek Fell. Running Press, 1990. 96 pages. Packed with activities, experiments, and information for young gardeners. Comes with seed packets and a small, plastic greenhouse. For children in grades two and up.

Kids Gardening: A Kids' Guide to Messing Around in the Dirt. By Kevin Raftery and Kim Gilbert Raftery. Klutz Press, 1989. 87 pages. A spiral-bound book on indoor and outdoor gardening for children ages four and up. Comes with plant and flower seeds plus a shovel.

Let's Grow! 72 Gardening Adventures with Children. By Linda Tilgner. Storey Communications, 1988. 216 pages. Offers creative and unusual gardening projects and activities for children of all ages.

Linnea's Windowsill Garden. By Christina Bjork and Lena Anderson. Farrar, Straus and Giroux, 1988. 60 pages. A child-friendly book about indoor gardening, complete with recipes, tips on plant care, and garden-related projects. For ages five to twelve.

My First Garden Book. By Angela Wilkes. Alfred A. Knopf, 1992. 48 pages. A large-format guide for young gardeners, complete with life-sized photographs. For children in grades two and up.

Sunflower Houses: Garden Discoveries for Children of All Ages. By Sharon Lovejoy. Interweave, 1991. 144 pages. For parents to share with their children, this book talks about the various treasures found in the garden. Offers information, nature-related activities, and delicate illustrations intended to inspire.

Games and Kits

The Garden Box. This kit for kids contains seed packets and planting pots for every month of the year. Basil, broccoli, and tomatoes are among the items that can be grown using the instructions from this Nature Company product. Available by mail through the Nature Company Catalog, P.O. Box 188, Florence, Kentucky 41022. Phone: 1/800-227-1114.

Harvest Time. Available from Animal Town, this cooperative boardgame calls on young children to help one another harvest the peas, corn, carrots, and tomatoes before the frost sets in. For two to four players, ages three to seven. Contact: Animal Town, P.O. Box 485, Healdsburg, California 95448. Phone: 1/800-445-8642.

Indoor Hydroponic Garden. Using this kit, kids can grow herbs, vegetables, and flowers without soil. Set comes with a plastic tank and cover, nutrient supplements, seeds, and a complete set of instructions. For children in kindergarten through twelfth grade. Available through the Cuisenaire mail order catalog, P.O. Box 5026, White Plains, New York 10602-5026. Phone: 1/800-237-3142.

Pizza Garden for Kids. Using this kit, kids can create a garden full of ingredients for a pizza. Includes seed packets for basil, oregano, onions, green peppers, and cherry tomatoes. Comes with an instruction booklet. Available from Reader's Digest Kids Catalog, Reader's Digest Association, Inc., Pleasantville, New York 00401. Phone: 1/800-458-3014.

Associations

American Horticultural Society. 7931 East Boulevard Drive, Alexandria, Virginia 22308. Phone: 703/768-5700. A society of amateur and professional gardeners. Operates an information service, free seed exchange, and discount book service for members. Publishes books, calendars, and periodicals.

The Brooklyn Botanic Garden. 1000 Washington Avenue, Brooklyn, New York 11225. Offers a kit containing a videocassette called *Get Ready, Get Set, Grow!*, which explores gardening through the eyes of a child, describing the planting season from planning to harvest. Comes with two books offering tips on starting a garden. For children ages eight to fourteen.

National Gardening Association. 180 Flynn Avenue, Burlington, Vermont 05401. Phone: 802/863-1308. Seeks to help individuals be successful gardeners. Serves as an information clearinghouse for home and community gardening. Offers information on children's gardening books and resources. Publishes *NGA Guide to Kids Gardening* (available for $9.95 plus $3 shipping and handling). Also publishes periodicals, how-to books, and other materials.

Gardening Catalogs

Burpee Garden Catalog. Phone: 1/800-888-1447.

Johnny's Selected Seeds. Phone: 207/437-4301.

Park Seed. Phone: 1/800-845-3369.

Thompson and Morgan. Phone: 1/800-274-7333.

White Flower Farm. Phone: 203/567-0801.

Photography

Books

My First Camera Book. By Anne Kostick. Workman, 1989. 64 pages. This guide for children (ages four through eight) features a friendly bear who teaches basic photography techniques. Comes with a pocket-size camera and a twelve-page photo album.

Photography: Take Your Best Shot. By Terri Morgan. Lerner Publications, 1991. 72 pages. This book for young photographers explains how the camera works, how to see the way a camera sees, how to set up shots, capture action, and adjust for light. Also explains how to develop black-and-white film and print photographs. Illustrated with both black-and-white and color photographs. For children in grades five and up.

Kits

Fun with Photography. Creativity for Kids. This hands-on science kit comes with a real camera, the makings for a pinhole camera and a simple slide projector, and plenty of activity ideas and interesting facts on photography. For children ages nine and up (younger, with an adult's assistance).

Nature Print Paper. Pack of paper for making sun prints. The paper undergoes a chemical change when exposed to sunlight, with images appearing in minutes. Simply arrange small objects (leaves, shells, keys, buttons, etc.) on paper, expose it to sunlight for several minutes, then soak it in water. Also available: Nature Print Critters, featuring wildlife drawings to place on Nature Print Paper. Available from Nasco Arts and Crafts, 901 Janesville Avenue, P.O. Box 901, Fort Atkinson, Wisconsin 53538-0901. Phone: 1/800-558-9595.

Clowning Around

Books

Be a Clown! The Complete Guide to Instant Clowning. By Turk Pipkin. Workman, 1989. 112 pages. Offers an introduction to the art of clowning. Includes tricks and helpful tips. For children ages five and up.

Face Painting. By the editors of Klutz Press. Klutz Press, 1990. 63 pages. A how-to book that brings out the animal (clown, Halloween character, etc.) in children. Offers dozens of fun face-painting ideas that encourage dramatic play. Comes with a set of nontoxic paints and a brush.

Puppetry

Book

Puppetry in Early Childhood Education. By Tamara Hunt and Nancy Renfro. Renfro Studios, 1981. 264 pages. An inspirational sourcebook for parents, including instructions on making puppets and stages for small children.

Videotape

Introduction to Puppet Making. Jim Gamble Puppet Productions. Bogner Entertainment, Inc. (BEI). Running time: 30 minutes. Puppeteer Jim Gamble shows children how to make their own puppets using common household items. Also demonstrates how to create an elaborate marionette puppet. For ages three and up. Other videos in the Jim Gamble Puppet Production series include *The Nutcracker, Carnival of the Animals, Peter and the Wolf,* and *The Adventures of Peer Gynt.* These marionette productions features the puppetry of Jim Gamble and music by Prokofiev, Tchaikovsky, Saint-Saëns, and others.

Toys

Children's Theatre. Peleman-McLaughlin. A cardboard stage set, complete with backdrop, scripts, and stiff-paper puppets attached to sticks held from below. Sets include a grand ballroom and the cottage in Little Red Riding Hood. Winner of the 1992 Parents' Choice Award.

Friendly Finger Puppets. Zoo animal and Old McDonald Farm finger puppets that fit small fingers. Knitted with hand-washable acrylic. Each set (zoo or Old McDonald) contains five characters. Available from Animal Town, P.O. Box 485, Healdsburg, California 95448. Phone: 1/800-445-8642.

Puppet Pals. A collection of quality animal puppets, including a cricket, baby turtle, ladybug, spider, bug, mouse, baby black bear, dinosaur egg, and baby dragon. Also available: the reversible polliwog/frog puppet and the reversible caterpillar/ butterfly puppet. Prices range from $10 to $30. Available from Bookmates, Listening Library, One Park Avenue, Old Greenwich, Connecticut 06870. Phone: 1/800-243-4504.

Mail Order Catalogs

Bookmates. Listening Library, One Park Avenue, Old Greenwich, Connecticut 06870. Phone: 1/800-243-4504. This catalog contains "picture book pals," including hand puppets, stuffed animals, and dolls based on the characters in children's books. Curious George, Madeline, Babar, and Paddington Bear are among the available puppets. This catalog received the Parents' Choice seal of approval in 1991.

Kids and Things. DEMCO, Box 7488, Madison, Wisconsin 53707. Phone: 608/241-1201 or 1/800-356-1200. Demco's *Kids and Things* catalog contains a wide variety of hand puppets based on the central characters found in children's classics. Also offers collections of puppets such as the oceanic puppet collection (a seal, shark, octopus, etc.); the zoo puppet collection (a lion, kangaroo, crocodile, etc.); and the forest friends puppet collection (a frog, fox, tortoise, etc.). Puppet-theatre stages are sold through this catalog as well.

Association

National Association of Professional Puppeteers and Puppet Enthusiasts. Gayle C. Schluter, 15 Cricklewood Path, Pasadena, California 91107. Members include amateur and professional puppeteers, educators, children, and others interested in puppetry. Holds biennial puppetry festivals, presents awards, and maintains an audiovisual library. Can tell you how to contact a puppetry guild in your area that may provide event listings of nearby puppet shows for families.

Storytelling

Books

The Art of the Story Teller. By Marie L. Shedlock. Third edition revised. Dover, (1952). 291 pages. Describes how to tell stories successfully, how to captivate an audience, and how to recapture straying attention. Complete with eighteen good stories just waiting to be told.

Awakening the Hidden Storyteller: How to Build a Storytelling Tradition in Your Family. By Robin Moore. Shambhala Publications, 1991. 153 pages. A professional storyteller offers advice and encouragement for family tale-telling. Explains how to create stories and how to use gestures, body language, and the human voice to liven up story time.

The Family Storytelling Handbook. By Anne Pellowski. Macmillan, 1987. 160 pages. Offers inspirational tips on family storytelling, including the use of puppets to help dramatize fiction. Explains how to use stories, rhymes, handkerchiefs, paper, and other objects to enrich family traditions.

Hey! Listen to This: Stories to Read Aloud. Edited by Jim Trelease. Viking, 1992. 414 pages. Contains a variety of read-aloud stories, including folklore, fairytales, and famous stories from around the world.

Association

National Association for the Preservation and Perpetuation of Storytelling, P.O. Box 309, Jonesborough, Tennessee 37659. Phone: 615/753-2171. An association of individuals and organizations interested in the art of storytelling. Offers workshops and classes; supports story-telling activities at festivals and concerts. Offers books on the art of storytelling, recordings of accomplished storytellers, and information about story-telling events across the country. Publishes *Storytelling Magazine*, a quarterly.

OTHER THINGS THAT FASCINATE KIDS

Dinosaurs

Books

Digging Up Dinosaurs. By Aliki. Thomas Y. Crowell, 1981. 34 pages. Featured on the award-winning television series "Reading Rainbow," this book explains how and where dinosaur skeletons are found and how they are dug out of the ground. Describes what scientists can learn about these prehistoric giants from their fossil bones and how they put the bones together again. Filled with detailed drawings and easy-to-read text. Also by Aliki: *Dinosaurs Bones, Dinosaurs Are Different,* and *My Visit to the Dinosaurs.*

Dinosaur. By David Norman and Angela Miller. Alfred A. Knopf, 1989. 64 pages. Part of the award-winning Eyewitness series of books for children in grades five and up. Contains captivating photographs and informative captions.

Dinosaur Bones! By C. E. Thompson. Putnam, 1992. 27 pages. Explains how we came to know about the dinosaurs and offers an introduction to seven of them (Stegosaurus, Tyrannosaurus, Triceratops, etc.). Includes a glow-in-the-dark dinosaur mobile. For children in preschool through third grade.

Dinosaurs Walked Here and Other Stories Fossils Tell. By Patricia Lauber. Bradbury Press, 1987. 56 pages. Describes how plant and animal fossils reveal the characteristics of the prehistoric world. For children in grades two through four.

Dinotopia. By James Gurney. Turner, 1992. 159 pages. Imaginative artwork complements this fantasy of a shipwrecked professor and his son who find themselves on the island of Dinotopia where Man and Dinosaur coexist. For children ages seven and up.

The Great Dinosaur Atlas. By William Lindsay. Simon and Schuster, 1991. 64 pages. A pictorial guide to the prehistoric world, with lots of interesting dinosaur information for children in grades three and up. With this book, children can discover how and where dinosaurs lived, what the continents were like during the days of the dinosaurs, and which sites have been the richest sources of dinosaur fossil bones.

Patrick's Dinosaurs. By Carol Carrick. Clarion Books, 1987. 31 pages. When his older brother, Hank, talks about dinosaurs during a trip to the zoo, Patrick is afraid, until he discovers that the great beasts died millions of years ago. (Note: See also listings under "Videotapes" and "Kits and Games.")

What Happened to the Dinosaurs? By Franklyn Mansfield Branley. Illustrated by Marc Simont. Crowell, 1989. 30 pages. Examines various theories on the dinosaurs' disappearance, using easy-to-understand text and watercolor illustrations. For children ages five to nine.

Videotapes

Dinosaur! Vestron. Running time: 48 minutes. Narrated by Cristopher Reeve, this documentary explores

---

The Art and Science of Doing Nothing

Kids need time off—to daydream, kick back, unwind, relax. Often times, parents are in too much of a rush to have their children do something "worthwhile." Periods of inactivity are vital to a child's psychological growth and emotional well-being.

"dinosaur mania," along with recent scientific discoveries.

The Dinosaurs (series). PBS Home Video/Pacific Arts. Running time: 60 minutes each. Approved by Parent's Choice, this series combines graphics, animation, and sound effects with latest information on the popular prehistoric beasts. Titles in the series include "The Monsters Emerge," "Flesh on Bones," "Nature of the Beast," and "The Death of the Dinosaur." For ages eight and up.

Patrick's Dinosaurs. MCA/Universal. Running time: 25 minutes. As his older brother, Hank, talks about the dinosaurs, Patrick's imagination takes off—and dinosaurs spring up everywhere. Narrated by Martin Short. For children ages three to ten.

Kits and Games

Dinosaurs and Things. The game of dinosaurs from beginning to end. Young children can simply move along the colored path through the prehistoric world of dinosaurs. Older children answer challenging questions along the way. For two to four players, ages four to ten. Available through the Aristoplay mail order catalog, P.O. Box 7529, Ann Arbor, Michigan 48107. Phone: 1/800-634-7738.

Patrick's Dinosaurs (a literature-based theme packet). This packet contains giant footprint sponges, dinosaur stencils, self-inking stamps, a collection of mini-dinosaurs, and the book, *Patrick's Dinosaurs,* by Carol Carrick (together with a read-aloud cassette tape). Also comes with a teacher's guide loaded with activities and lessons. Available from Lake Shore Learning Materials, 2695 East Moninguez Street, Carson, California 90749. Phone: 1/800-421-5354.

Wooden Skeleton Kits. Using precision cut, laminated wood, children can assemble detailed models of Triceratops, Brontosaurus, Pteranodon, Stegosaurus, or Tyrannosaurus. For children in grades three and up. Each kit features a different dinosaur. Available through the Cuisenaire mail order catalog, P.O. Box 5026, White Plains, New York 10602-5026. Phone: 1/800-237-3142.

Association

The Academy of Natural Sciences. 1900 Benjamin Franklin Parkway, Philadelphia, Pennsylvania 19103-1195. Phone: 215/299-1000. Open 10 to 4:30 p.m. weekdays; 10 a.m. to 5 p.m. on weekends. The dinosaur exhibits in this museum are among the best. Includes hands-on displays where kids can operate levers to understand how dinosaurs once lived, a mechanical apatosaurus that really roars, a variety of dinosaur-inspired products, and a skeleton of a tyrannosaurus rex (the meat-eater kids seem to cherish most).

Vehicles (Things that Go)

Books

"Eye Openers" (series). A Dorling Kindersley book. Macmillan. 24 pages each. Included in this series are books for young children who are fascinated by things that go. Printed on heavy paper stock, each book offers colorful photographs and simple illustrations, together with simple descriptions (two or three sentences) and labels for vehicle parts. Titles include *Planes, Trucks, Ships and Boats, Cars,* and *Diggers and Dump Trucks.* For children ages one-and-a-half to five.

My First Look at Things That Go. First American edition. Random House, 1991. 20 pages. Contains full-color photographs of trucks, planes, boats, spaceships, and other "things that go" on farms, in the water, at construction sites, and in other places. Each item is labeled for easy identification. For children ages one to three.

See How It Works (series). By Tony Potter. Macmillan, 1989. 28 pages. This series provides see-through pages that show progressively more in-depth views of cars, planes, trucks, and earth movers (four separate books in the series). For children ages four to seven.

Favorite Authors

Anne Rockwell. This prolific children's book author and illustrator introduces young fact-finders to a variety of favorite vehicles. Her books feature brightly colored illustrations, simple words of explanation, and animals in place of people. *Bikes, Boats, Cars, Planes, Trains, Trucks, Big Wheels, Fire Engines,* and *Things That Go* are among the books that preschoolers adore. Check your local library for these titles—or purchase your own copies (published by E. P. Dutton; twenty-four pages each).

Gail Gibbons. Writes and illustrates colorful concept books, including many about vehicles and transportation. *Trains, Trucks,* and *Tunnels* are a hit with preschoolers. For slightly older children, check out *New Road!* and *From Path to Highway: The Story of the Boston Post Road.* Check your local library, or purchase copies of your own (published by HarperCollins; thirty-two pages each).

Videotapes

Big Rigs. Stage Fright Productions. Running time: 30 minutes. A wordless, live-action videotape showing a blue-and-white eighteen-wheeler as it travels along the highway each day, rain or shine, through city and countryside. Takes young viewers to a truck stop, a truck wash, and a service station as well. For ages one to five.

Here We Go. Running time: 30 minutes. Narrated by Lynn Redgrave, this videotape presents various vehicles in motion, including a steam locomotive, helicopter, hovercraft, blimp, and construction equipment. Winner of the Parents' Choice Award. Available from Constructive Playthings, 1227 East 119th Street, Grandview, Missouri 64030-1117. 1/800-448-1412.

Mike Mulligan and His Steam Shovel. Golden Book Video. Running time: 25 minutes. A fully animated musical version of Virginia Burton's classic, written more than fifty years ago. Narrated by Robert Klein, this video tells the story about the man who had faith in his trusty old steam shovel.

Moving Machines (Kids at Play; Big Machines at Work). Running time: 25 minutes. Shows boys and girls playing with their own toy trucks (filling them up, making vroom noises, etc.), as well as real bulldozers, cranes,

cement trucks, etc., at work. For preschoolers. Available from Chinaberry, 2780 Via Orange Way, Suite B, Spring Valley, California 91978. Phone: 1/800-776-2242.

Road Construction Ahead. Focus Video. Running time: 30 minutes. An action video that takes young viewers to an actual road construction site where they get to see bulldozers at work. No plot, but plenty of action.

Building Your Own Vehicles: Toys and Tools

Baufix Elements. These sets are designed to introduce young children to simple machine making. Each comes with wooden, easy-to-assemble components, connectors, nuts, screw bolts, wheel hubs, tires, girders, and a wrench/screwdriver tool. A descriptive pamphlet includes pictures of a variety of models (including an airplane, wheelbarrow, and scooter) so that reading is not a requirement. Alternately, kids can create their own machines. Large and small sets available. For children in pre-kindergarten through fourth grade. Available from Cuisenaire, P.O. Box 5026, White Plains, New York 10602-5026. Phone: 1/800-237-3142.

Brio-Mec Vehicle Kit. This wooden construction kit contains seventy-one pieces (girders, wheels, nuts, bolts, tools, and wooden passengers) plus instructions for building cars, airplanes, trains, motorcycles, and other vehicles. Comes in a nylon-canvas case for convenient carrying. Available from Back to Basics Toys, 2707 Pittman Drive, Silver Spring, Maryland 20910. Phone: 1/800-356-5360.)

Erector Sets. Meccano, Inc. The starter set contains more than two hundred pieces (girders, wheels, nuts, bolts, tools, etc.), plus instructions for creating planes, trucks, cranes, race cars, helicopters, and other vehicles. The larger sets (for children ages nine and up) come with real motors, battery packs, and switches. Distributed through toy stores. Also available through mail-order companies such as Back to Basics Toys, 2707 Pittman Drive, Silver Spring, Maryland 20910. Phone: 1/800-356-5360.

Lego Play Sets. In addition to basic building sets, Lego produces advanced systems such as the technic control center for inventing remote controlled vehicles; pneumatic power sets that can lift, pull, and pick things up using compressed air controls; and the metroliner train set, complete with a working engine, passenger and steering wagons, and compartments with bunk beds, a restroom, and other details. Offers sets for children from one-and-a-half years through the early teens. Contact the company for a copy of their Shop at Home Imagination Book (Lego Shop at Home Service, 555 Taylor Road, P.O. Box 1310, Enfield, Connecticut 06083. Phone: 203/763-4011).

Magic

Book

The Klutz Book of Magic. By Michael Stroud and John Cassidy. Klutz Press, 1989. 96 pages. A spiral-bound guide describing thirty-one magic tricks for children ages eight and up. Comes with several props for magic making.

Games and Kits

Amazing Illusions. Available from Animal House, this boardgame calls on players to perform various tricks and illusions (Water Torture, Death in a Coffin, etc.). Requires strategy and a cooperative spirit (players work together as a team). Contact Animal House, P.O. Box 485, Healdsburg, California 95448. Phone: 1/800-445-8642.

Box of Magic. Features props for twenty-four magic tricks plus a videotape that shows children how to perform them. Available from Back to Basics Toys, 2707 Pittman Drive, Silver Spring, Maryland 20910. Phone: 1/800-356-5360.

Videotape

101 Things for Kids to Do. Random House Home Video. Running time: 60 minutes. Shari Lewis presents dozens of things for kids to do, including many magic tricks and riddles. For children ages five to ten.

Mail Order Catalog

Magic, Inc. 5082 North Lincoln Avenue, Chicago, Illinois 60625. Offers a trick catalog, containing hundreds of packaged tricks, decks of cards, and other magic-making items. The cost of the catalog is $7.00.

Flight

Books

Flight: The Journey of Charles Lindbergh. By Robert Burleigh. Putnam, 1991. 32 pages. The story of Charles Lindbergh's flight across the Atlantic in the "Spirit of St. Louis." For children ages six to nine.

The Ultimate Kite Book. By Paul and Helene Morgan. Simon and Schuster, 1992. 80 pages. An illustrated encyclopedia showing every imaginable kind of kite, along with guidelines for flying them. Includes build-it-yourself kite models as well.

The World's Greatest Paper Airplane and Toy Book. By Keith R. Laux. TAB Books, 1987. 120 pages. For older children, this book offers forty different paper aircraft designs and includes illustrated, step-by-step instructions.

Kit

Flight and Aerodynamics Kit. The Nature Company's "Alliance for Science" Flight Kit, produced in cooperation with The Museum of Science in Boston, offers children a hands-on course on how things move through the air. Allows kids to build gliders, kites, helicopters, and parachutes. Available by mail through the Nature Company catalog, P.O. Box 188, Florence, Kentucky 41022. Phone: 1/800-227-1114.

Star, Sky, and Space Exploration

Free and Inexpensive Resources

A Look at the Planets. Produced by NASA. 8 pages. Contains full-color photographs and descriptions of the planets in the solar system. Also offers information on U.S. space exploration. For ordering information, write for a copy of the free *Consumer Information Catalog,* available from the Consumer Information Center, P.O. Box 100, Pueblo, Colorado 81002.

Stars in Your Eyes: A Guide to the Northern Skies. Produced by the U.S. Army Corps of Engineers. 23 pages. Offers helpful hints on finding the better known constellations (big dipper, little dipper, the northern crown, etc.) and explanations of how they were named. For ordering information, write for a copy of the free *Consumer Information Catalog,* available from the Consumer Information Center, P.O. Box 100, Pueblo, Colorado 81002.

Books

Earth, Moon, and Stars. By Cary Sneider and the Lawrence Hall of Science. Lawrence Hall of Science, 1986. 45 pages. Contains lessons on gravity, moon phases, eclipses, constellations, and related topics. For children in grades three through six.

The Glow-in-the-Dark Night Sky Book. By Clint Hatchett. Random House, 1988. 24 pages. Contains star maps, illustrations, and explanations of constellation origins.

The Magic School Bus Lost in the Solar System. By Joanna Cole. Illustrated by Bruce Degen. Scholastic, 1990. 40 pages. The eccentric Ms. Frizzle takes her class on another wacky field trip—this time through space. During their adventure, the teacher's tether line snaps, the magic school bus/rocket ship zooms out of control, and the kids get a bit too close to some of the gaseous planets. Nevertheless, the entire class, including the rescued teacher, eventually arrive safely back at school, having learned a great deal about gravity, planets, asteroids, and orbits along the way.

Seeing the Sky. By Fred Schaff. John Wiley, 1990. 212 pages. Filled with over one hundred projects, explorations, and daytime/nighttime activities in astronomy. Children in grades three through six can learn about stars, plants, meteors, and much more.

The Space Atlas. By Heather Cooper and Nigel Henbest. Harcourt Brace Jovanovich, 1991. 64 pages. With this large-format, pictorial atlas, children can discover how the moon was formed, what black holes are, what

Planetariums
From *Helping Your Child Learn Science* (U.S. Department of Education).

Planetariums have wonderful exhibits and activities for youngsters. There are about 1,000 planetariums in the United States, ranging from small ones that hold about 20 people to giant facilities with 300 or more seats. These facilities are particularly useful for children in urban areas, where metropolitan lights and pollution obstruct one's view of the solar system. Inside planetariums, children often can:

- Use telescopes to view the rings of Saturn;
- See the "sky" with vivid clarity from inside the planetarium's dome; and
- Step on scales to learn what they would weigh on the moon or on Mars.

To find the nearest planetarium, call the astronomy or physics department at a local college, your local science museum, or the science curriculum specialist or science teachers in your school district.

lies at the heart of a comet, and much more. For children ages eight and up.

Games and Other Learning Tools

Constellation Station. Aristoplay. A glow-in-the-dark night sky adventure game for ages ten and up (including adults). Helps children discover and identify more than fifty constellations. For two to six players, ages ten and up. Available through the Aristoplay mail order catalog, P.O. Box 7529, Ann Arbor, Michigan 48107. Phone: 1/800-634-7738.

Stellarscope. A scope-shaped map of the heavens that will reveal a labeled image of the night sky at any time of day, anywhere in the world (20 to 60 degrees north and south latitude). Simple rotations of the scope are all it takes. Available through the Exploratorium to Go! catalog, 3601 Lyon Street, San Francisco, California 94123. Phone: 1/800-359-9899.

Software

Stars and Planets. Advanced Ideas. This software program includes six games for young children (ages three to six), all having to do with stars, planets, and spaceships. In one game, moon rocks are collected by an on-screen astronaut (software users help him count the rocks). Games test basic math, logic, and early reading skills. For use with an Apple IIGS.

Association

Challenger Center for Space Science Education. 1550 West Bay Area Boulevard, Friendswood, Texas 77546. Phone: 713/488-6481. Designed as a living memorial to the crew that died on the space shuttle Challenger in 1986, this program promotes science and math education. At simulation centers scattered around the country (the network of sites is growing), children can take part in simulated space missions, familiarize themselves with space technology, and acquaint themselves with the science of the future. A home activities kit is also available. Contact the center for more information.

Mail Order Catalog

Orion Telescope Center. 2450 Seventeenth Avenue, P.O. Box 1158, Santa Cruz, California 95061-1158. Offers a wide variety of telescopes, binoculars, astronomy videos, stargazing software, reference guides to the stars, and related products.

Rocks and Minerals

Books

The Magic School Bus Inside the Earth. By Joanna Cole. Scholastic, 1987. 40 pages. Led by their eccentric teacher, Ms. Frizzle, a class full of elementary school kids goes on a field trip through the earth, learning about rocks along the way. Their means of transportation? The famous school bus, which magically sprouts a drill to penetrate through the earth's crust.

The Roadside Geology (series). Mountain Press. A series of books written for people who are interested in rocks, minerals, and the landscapes around them. Each book features a state (*Roadside Geology of Virginia, Roadside Geology of Pennsylvania,* etc.) and highlights good localities for family rock and mineral hunting. Written in language that nongeologists can understand.

Rocks and Minerals. By R. F. Symes and the Natural History Museum staff. Alfred A. Knopf, 1988. 64 pages. An Eyewitness book explaining where rocks and minerals come from, how they're formed, how to identify and collect them, and what they're used for. For grades five and up.

Kit

Minerals and Fossils Collection Kit. A kit featuring mineral and fossil specimens such as rose quartz, ame-thyst, fool's gold, and a dinosaur bone fragment. Explanatory labels help budding geologists identify specimens. Available through the Exploratorium to Go! catalog, 3601 Lyon Street, San Francisco, California 94123. Phone: 1/800-359-9899.

Periodical

Rock and Gem Magazine. Miller Magazines, Inc., 4880 Market Street, Ventura, California 93003-2888. Phone: 805/644-3824. For rock and mineral hobbyists, this monthly recommends areas for collecting; includes photo-essays on creating jewelry and other items; and contains a calendar of events listing, among other things, gem and mineral shows taking place across the country (there, parents can introduce their children to nature's dazzling formations).

Government Agency

United States Geological Survey. Sunrise Valley Drive, Reston, Virginia 22092. Phone: 703/648-4460. Responsible for collecting earth/science information. Oversees nationally owned public lands and natural resources. Produces a variety of maps covering a wide range of areas (see "Free and Inexpensive Resources," in chapter 14 for information on ordering a free catalog). At the visitors center in Reston, Virginia, children ages four and up can make maps, explore rocks and minerals, or use interactive computers. Alternatively, families can visit laboratories and the map-printing plant during guided tours, which last about an hour and a half. Tours take place during weekdays (call for hours).

Bubbles and Balloons

Books

Balloon Science. By Etta Kaner. Addison-Wesley, 1990. 96 pages. Contains more than fifty balloon activities and experiments. With help from this book, children can, for example, launch a balloon rocket or make a working model of the human lungs. Comes with a supply of balloons.

The Unbelievable Bubble Book. By John Cassidy and David Stein. Klutz Press, 1987. 79 pages. Contains bubble facts, how-tos on creating them, guidelines for solving bubble problems, and instructions for making mega-bubbles from the "bubble thing" that comes with the book.

Time

Books

My First Look at Time. A Dorling Kindersley book. First American edition. Random House, 1991. 20 pages. Introduces the concept of time using pictures of clocks and photographs of breakfast time, bathtime, bedtime, time to go shopping, and other times.

The Time Book (plus watch). By John Cassidy. Klutz Press, 1991. 29 pages. Contains questions and answers about time for preschoolers. Using this book, young kids will discover what their mom really means when she says, "I'll only be a minute" and why time sometimes flies, crawls, and comes to a complete stop (when you're at the dentist's office, for example).

Electricity and Electronics

Books

Electricity. By Philip Chapman. EDC Publishing, 1976. 32 pages. Part of the Usborne Young Scientist series, this book contains safe, simple experiments using inexpensive, accessible objects. Using Usborne's guidelines, children ages eight to fourteen can make electricity with a comb, build an electric motor, and complete other projects.

My First Batteries and Magnets Book. By Jack Challoner. Dorling Kindersley, 1992. 48 pages. Life-size photographs and step-by-step instructions help take the mystery out of electricity and magnetism, allowing children to create their own batteries, simple circuits, headlights for toy cars, fans, buzzers, and a working radio! For children ages eight and up.

Wires and Watts: Understanding and Using Electricity. By Irwin Math. Macmillan, 1989. 96 pages. Written for children, this book explains the basic principles of electricity. Also offers instructions for making electric-powered doorbells, dollhouse lamps, burglar alarms, and other items. For children ages eight to fourteen.

Kits

Build Your Own Radio. By Jim Becker and Andy Mayer. Running Press, 1992. This do-it-yourself kit takes kids step-by-step through the process of assembling an AM radio. Includes a preassembled circuit board, radio components, and color-coded wires. Runs on a 9-volt battery. The book is clearly illustrated and written in language children can understand.

Shaw Basic Electricity Set. This introductory set comes with batteries, test leads, and various electrical components mounted on connecting modules. A twenty-four-page booklet illustrates and describes a dozen electrical experiments that can be done with the kit. For children in grades four through eight. Available through the Cuisenaire mail order catalog, P.O. Box 5026, White Plains, New York 10602-5026. Phone: 1/800-237-3142.

Sight, Sound Kit. A kit that helps children learn electronic principles using a buzzer, push-button switches, lights, and a motor, all mounted onto hardwood blocks. Comes with a step-by-step instruction booklet explaining how to build circuits, create on-off switches, conduct Morse Code, and more. Available through the Animal Town mail order catalog, P.O. Box 485, Healdsburg, California 95448. Phone: 1/800-445-8642.

Magnets

Book

My First Batteries and Magnets Book. By Jack Challoner. Dorling Kindersley, 1992. 48 pages. Life-size photographs and step-by-step instructions help take the mystery out of electricity and magnetism, allowing children to create their own magnetic fields, electromagnets, clay refrigerator magnets, a turtle compass, a porcupine paper clip holder, and more. For children ages eight and up.

Toy

Super Magna Shapes. A magnetic construction game for children ages five and up. Contains 110 nickel-plated pieces in a variety of colors, two permanent magnets, two 3-D tangram sets, and a plastic base. Using these items, kids can create their own magnetic figures, shapes, and designs. Available through the Exploratorium to Go! catalog, 3601 Lyon Street, San Francisco, California 94123. Phone: 1/800-359-9899.

The Human Body

Books

Blood and Guts: A Working Guide to Your Own Insides. By Linda Allison. Little, Brown, 1976. 127 pages. Offers interesting facts and fun activities for exploring elements of the human body. Written for children ages nine and up.

The Bones Book and Skeleton. By Stephen Cumbaa. Workman, 1991. Includes a 64-page book explaining how the human skeleton works and the vital organs it protects. Includes fun facts and related projects. Comes with an assemble-it-yourself, plastic skeleton with movable joints.

The Magic School Bus Inside the Human Body. By Joanna Cole. Illustrated by Bruce Degen. Scholastic, 1989. 40 pages. Once again, Ms. Frizzle, the eccentric school teacher, takes her class on an unusual field trip, this time inside a human body (one of the classmates!). By the time the infamous magic school bus finally gets sneezed out, the children have learned the fundamentals of the human body's inside workings.

My Five Senses. By Aliki. Revised edition. HarperCollins, 1991. 32 pages. A Let's Read-and-Find-Out Book. Offers a simple presentation of the five senses, demonstrating some of the ways we use them. For children ages three to eight.

Outside-In. By Clare Smallman. Barron's, 1986. 32 pages. A lift-the-flap book for young children (ages four to eight), showing what's underneath their skin (muscles, bones, organs, etc.)

Game

Somebody. Aristoplay. A peel-off/press-on board game designed to introduce kids to human anatomy. Offers four different levels of play. For two to four players, ages six to ten. Available from Aristoplay, P.O. Box 7529, Ann Arbor, Michigan 48107. Phone: 1/800-634-7738.

Secret Codes

Books

The Cat's Elbow and Other Secret Languages. Collected by Alvin Schwartz. Farrar, Straus and Giroux, 1982. 96 pages. A children's guide to more than a dozen secret languages, including Ziph and Pig Latin. For ages eight and up.

Code Busters! By Burton Albert, Jr. Whitman, 1985. 32 pages. Filled with secret codes for kids ages eight to twelve.

Kids' Book of Secret Codes, Signals and Ciphers. By E. A. Grant. Running Press, 1989. 80 pages. Features dozens of ways to send messages using sign language, invisible ink, and other "secret" forms of communication. For children ages seven and up.

Visual Challenges

Books

I Spy: A Book of Picture Riddles. By Jean Marzollo. Photographed by Walter Wick. Scholastic, 1992. 48 pages. Each page presents life-sized photographs of familiar objects—baseballs, buttons, glasses, feathers, etc.—and challenges readers to find specific items in the various collections. For ages three and up.

Where's Waldo? By Martin Handford. Little, Brown, 1987. This runaway best-selling series challenges readers to find "Waldo" in various scenes (on a beach, in a museum, and in a railroad yard, for example). The fine details are interesting, and often comical—even to a grownup. Also available: *The Great Waldo Search, Find Waldo Now,* and other spin-offs.

Periodical

Highlights for Children. 803 Church Street, Homesdale, Pennsylvania 18431. Phone: 1/800-255-9517 (subscriptions). Contains rebus stories and the popular "Hidden Picture" pages, along with puzzles, riddles, recipes, craft ideas, fiction, and articles on science, sports, cultures, and other topics. For children ages two to twelve.

Mazes

Books

Amazing Mazes. By Rolf Heimann. Watermill Press, 1989. 32 pages. A colorful array of amazing mazes and mind-bending puzzles for ages six to one hundred.

Animaze! By Wendy Madgwick. Illustrated by Lorna Hussey. Alfred A. Knopf, 1992. A collection of amazing nature mazes for children ages four and up.

Mail Order Catalog

Dover Children's Book Catalog. Dover Publications, Inc., 31 East Second Street, Mineola, New York 11501. This catalog includes an impressive collection of maze books, including *Space Age Mazes, Monster Mazes, Storybook Mazes, Animal Mazes, Pirate Treasure Mazes,* and others. For younger children, there's the "Little Activity" book series, including a number of easy maze books.

Water

Books

Sink or Swim: The Science of Water. By Barbara Taylor. Random House, 1991. 40 pages. Part of the "Step into Science Series," for children in grades two through five.

Water Science. By Deborah Seed. Addison-Wesley, 1992. 104 pages. An illustrated guide to water experimentation for children in grades two through seven.

Toys and Other Learning Tools

Bathtub Scientist. A water science kit, complete with funnels, measuring cups, tubing, pump, toy boats, activity cards, and more, for hours of bathtub play. For children ages four to nine. Available from Toys to Grow On, P.O. Box 17, Long Beach, California 90801. Phone: 1/800-542-8338.

Tubtime Sea Creatures. A collection of exotic bathtub sea creatures, including a squirting squid, a humpback whale that blows bubbles, and an awesome octopus. Fourteen in all, plus a plastic storage bin. Available from Toys to Grow On, P.O. Box 17, Long Beach, California 90801. Phone: 1/800-542-8338.

String and Rope

Books

Cat's Cradle, Owl's Eyes: A Book of String Games. By Camilla Gryski. William Morrow, 1984. 78 pages. Provides directions and illustrations for a variety of string games.

Fun with String. By Joseph Leeming. Dover, 1974. 161 pages. Includes scores of string-related activities, including knot tying, weaving, and magic tricks.

The Klutz Book of Knots. By John Cassidy. Klutz Press, 1985. 24 pages. A young beginner's guide to tying knots, complete with cord and holes for practicing.

Building Construction

Books

Cathedral: The Story of Its Construction. By David Macaulay. Houghton Mifflin, 1973. 77 pages. Detailed illustrations and descriptive text tell the story of a great cathedral built in the thirteenth and fourteenth centuries in Chutreaux, France. From the planning stages through the final details, *Cathedral* shows the extraordinary effort involved in the making of a monumental building. For children in grades one and up. Other books by Macaulay include *Castle, Unbuilding, Underground, City,* and *How Things Work.*

Up Goes the Skyscraper! By Gail Gibbons. Four Winds, 1986. 32 pages. Shows how a skyscraper is built from the planning stages through the finishing touches. Written in clear language that preschoolers can understand. Grown-ups might learn a thing or two too!

Toys and Games

Architectural Blocks. A set of hard rock maple blocks for building projects. Comes in a large set of seventy pieces (thirteen shapes) or a small set of forty pieces (ten shapes). Available through the Hand in Hand mail order catalog, Catalogue Center, Route 26, R.R. 1, Box 1425, Oxford, Maine 04270-9711. Phone: 1/800-872-9745.

Building Houses Puzzle. A wooden puzzle containing five houses to be "built" in layers (the frame, roof and siding, etc.). For children ages three and up. Available from Animal House, P.O. Box 485, Healdsburg, California 95448. Phone: 1/800-445-8642.

Fun with Architecture. This set includes thirty-five rubber stamps showing various elements of architecture (columns, arches, etc.), along with an ink pad, an architectural chart, and a guidebook on architecture to help kids create familiar buildings or fantastic originals. For children ages eight and up. Available from PlayFair Toys, P.O. Box 18210, Boulder, Colorado 80308. Phone: 1/800-824-7255.

Good Old Houses Puzzle Game. With this puzzle game on historic American architecture, children can learn to recognize the features of a Queen Anne home, a bungalow, and six other architectural styles found across the United States. A fact sheet provides additional information on architectural details. For two to five players, ages eight and up. Available through the Aristoplay mail order catalog, P.O. Box 7529, Ann Arbor, Michigan 48107. Phone: 1/800-634-7738.

Renaissance Building Blocks. A forty-six-piece set of maple miniblocks, including Doric columns, Roman arches, a dome, and more. Using various pieces, children can become architects, creating their own unique structures. Available from World Wide Games, P.O. Box 517, Colchester, Connecticut 06415-0517. Phone: 1/800-243-9232.

Association

Center for Understanding the Built Environment. 5328 West Sixty-seventh Street, Prairie Village, Kansas 66208-1408. Phone: 913/262-0691. An organization of teachers, architects, and citizens working to increase awareness of the built environment. Offers a variety of toys, games, building materials, and other learning tools to help children understand architecture. Conducts workshops. Produces *ArchiNews,* a monthly newsletter. To receive a sample newsletter, a sales catalog of environmental materials, and a workshop listing, send $2.50 to "archiSources" (use the address listed above).

Nature

Books

Eyewitness Books (series). Alfred A. Knopf. This award-winning series contains lush photographs and lively captions. Subjects are divided into component parts to help children better understand the structure and workings of various topics. Among the topics explored are ponds and rivers, the seashore, plants and flowers, and shells (for more topics in the series, see "Animals.") For children ages ten and up. (Note: younger children often enjoy looking at the pictures.)

Hands-On Nature. By Jenepher Lingelbach. Vermont Institute of Natural Sciences, 1987. 235 pages. Full of information and activities for exploring the environment with children. Topics include "Forest Floor" and "Beaks, Feet, and Feathers." For children in grades three through six.

How Nature Works: 100 Ways Parents and Kids Can Share the Secrets of Nature. By David Burnie. Readers Digest, 1991. 192 pages. Offers step-by-step nature-related activities for children ages seven and up. Raising butterflies, building birdfeeders, and growing beansprouts are among the offerings.

The Kids' Nature Book. By Susan Milord. Williamson Publishing, 1989. 159 pages. Contains 365 indoor/outdoor activities and experiences for young children (pre-kindergarten through grade six). Arranged by month, activities include making snow cream and catching fireflies.

My First Nature Book. By Angela Wilkes. Alfred A. Knopf, 1990. 48 pages. One of many in a series of "My First" books, this handsomely photographed guide for children contains nature activities such as making tree prints and flower presses. Each activity includes photographs of materials needed and the finished product. For children ages six to ten.

Nature Crafts for Kids. By Gwen Diehn and Terry Krautwurst. Sterling, 1992. 144 pages. Contains fifty fantastic things to make with Mother Nature's help, including herb dolls, wildflower candles, apple puppets, and wind vanes. Includes color photographs and comprehensive descriptions. For grades four through eight. Also available: *Nature Crafts for Kids* book and kit, which includes the materials needed to complete the projects described, including sand, nontoxic paint, and a blank puzzle.

Nature for the Very Young: A Handbook of Indoor and Outdoor Activities. By Marcia Bowden. John Wiley, 1989. 232 pages. This book suggests a variety of nature activities for young children (pre-kindergarten through grade two) involving plants, animals, insects, and more.

Nature Search: A Hands-On Guide for Nature Sleuths. Readers Digest, 1992. Two separate books—*Nature Search: Rain Forest* and *Nature Search: Underwater*—allow children to uncover the mysteries of nature using a magnifier that come with each book. With this tool in hand, young nature-lovers can take a closer look, looking for camouflaged plants and animals illustrated in their natural habitats. For ages seven to twelve.

Naturewatch. By Adrienne Katz. Addison-Wesley, 1986. 128 pages. Offers dozens of ways to explore ecology, seasonal changes, animal behavior, and plant adaption. Poems, projects, and activities are all included. For children ages seven to twelve.

Nature with Children of All Ages: Adventures for Exploring, Learning, and Enjoying the World Around You. By Edith A. Sisson and the Massachusetts Audubon Society. Prentice-Hall, 1982. 195 pages. Nature games, facts, crafts, and photographs. Activities include lists of necessary materials and step-by-step instructions. For children of all ages.

Sharing the Joy of Nature. By Joseph Cornell. Dawn Publications, 1989. 168 pages. A treasury of nature activities for children of all ages. Animals, habitats, and plant life are among the topics included. (Note: See also listing under "Videotapes.")

Sharing Nature with Children. By Joseph Cornell. Dawn Publications, 1979. 143 pages. A guidebook to help parents and teachers create joyful nature experiences for children. Describes imaginative, noncompetitive activities to help children appreciate and enjoy their natural surroundings.

The Tree. By Pascale De Bourging. Scholastic, 1992. 24 pages. One in a series of First Discovery Books for young children. Layers of transparent pages allow children to see colorful images transform, revealing seasonal changes. Other books in the series include *Fruit, Weather, The Ladybug and Other Insects, Colors, Flowers, Birds, Bears, Cats, The Egg,* and *Earth and Sky.*

Whisper from the Woods. By Victoria Wirth. Illustrated by A. Scott Banfill. Simon and Schuster, 1991. 30 pages. Highly detailed illustrations complement this story of a tree that gives birth to new trees, nurtures its young, and eventually falls in a storm. Tells the tale of natural life cycles and reminds readers of the spe-cial qualities found in nature. For children ages five to eight.

Videotapes

Aunt Merriwether's Adventures in the Backyard. Nature Company/Sea Studios. Running time: 30 minutes. An ant's eye journey through the jungles of the backyard. Includes songs, live action, animation, and close-up photographs of backyard insects and animals. The Nature Company's version of "Roger Rabbit" and "Honey I Shrunk the Kids." A California Children's Video Award winner. For ages five through eight. Available by mail through the Nature Company Catalog, P.O. Box 188, Florence, Kentucky 41022. Phone: 1/800-227-1114.

Exploring Nature with Your Child. RMI Media Productions, Inc. Running time: 30 minutes. Part of the Parents' Point of View series designed to offer ideas and expert advice to parents of children from birth to age five.

My First Nature Video. Sony. Running time: 40 minutes. Based on the popular *My First Book* series, this video presents nature activities for children ages five and up. Following straightforward guidelines, kids can build a bird feeder, create a garden in a bottle, or complete other fun projects using materials found in the home.

Sharing the Joy of Nature. By Joseph Cornell, author of *Sharing Nature with Children.* Running time: 40 minutes. An award-winning video designed for anyone who enjoys the beauty of nature. Presents eight nature awareness activities and demonstrates nature games. Includes footage of the Sierra mountains and Yosemite National Park. Available from Schoolmasters Video, 745 State Circle, P.O. Box 1941, Ann Arbor, Michigan 48106. Phone: 313/761-

5175 (customer service) or 1/800-521-2832 (orders only).

Audiocassette

Nature Nuts. By Mary Miche. Song Trek Music. A musical celebration of outdoor life, including songs like "Dirt," "Romp in the Swamp," "Hey, Ms. Spider," and "Newts, Salamanders, and Frogs." For children ages three to eleven.

Toys

Amazing Changing Forest. Selected toy of the year for 1992 by *Parenting* magazine, this collection of nature stamps allows kids to create their own nature scenes using trees, clouds, rabbits, owls, deer, squirrels, birds, and other natural elements. Available by mail through the Nature Company Catalog, P.O. Box 188, Florence, Kentucky 41022. Phone: 1/800-227-1114.

Portable Microscope. Winner of the Parents' Choice Award, this durable microscope can go anywhere (even under water!). Comes with a holster and an indoor-outdoor activity guide. Available from Back to Basics Toys, 2707 Pittman Drive, Silver Spring, Maryland 20910. Phone: 1/800-356-5360.

Associations

National Audubon Society. 950 Third Avenue, New York, New York 10022. Phone: 212/979-3119. A society of individuals concerned with ecology, conservation, and restoration of natural resources (primarily water, soil, forests, wildlife, and wildlife habitats). Conducts research on endangered species and their habitats. Produces educational materials for school children. Many local groups also sponsor exploration and investigation sessions for children.

Publishes *Audubon Adventures*, a bimonthly children's newspaper. Also publishes *Audubon*, a bimonthly exploring wildlife topics, as well as *American Birds*, a bimonthly. Offers annual awards to outstanding nature writers, photographers, and artists.

The National Wildlife Federation. 1400 Sixteenth Street, N.W., Washington, D.C. 20036-2266. Phone: 202/797-6800. The largest conservation group in the United States. Educates the public about environmental issues. Among the federation's most innovative programs is the "Backyard Habitat Program," which encourages nature-lovers to turn their yards into wildlife preserves. Participants receive tailored instructions on how to attract butterflies, deer, or other forms of wildlife. Once the transformation is complete, the federation certifies the land as an official "Wildlife Habitat."

Members of the federation can also participate in conservation summits that provide families with week-long opportunities to explore mountains, canyons, or a seacoast (fees for these programs range from $1,000 to $1,700 per family).

Publishes a variety of periodicals, including two magazines for children: *Ranger Rick* and *Your Big Backyard*. *Ranger Rick*, a monthly for ages six to twelve, covers wildlife, outdoor adventures, and conservation. *Your Big Backyard*, for ages three to five, contains picture-oriented material (simple games, crafts, short stories, etc.) on animals, nature, and conservation. Other magazines include *National Wildlife* and *International Wildlife* (adults might want to share some of the photographs and stories in these publications with their children).

The National Wildlife Federation has also developed the Ranger Rick NatureScope series—curriculum guides covering topics such as insects, weather, tropical rain forests, wetlands, geology, and mammals. Each volume includes related outdoor activities plus lists of additional resources. For nature-related gifts (including subscriptions to the federation's magazines), request a copy of the nature gift catalog (see listing under "Mail Order Catalogs" for more information).

The Nature Conservancy. 1815 North Lynn Street, Arlington, Virginia 22209. Phone: 703/841-5300 or 1/800-628-6860. Works to protect natural areas and preserve biological diversity. Identifies and helps protect significant areas and provides long-term stewardship for preserves owned by the conservancy. Offers information on protecting plants and animals (and the spaces they live in). Sponsors tours of the U.S. preserves and international regions to study plant and animal life. Conducts an "Adopt an Acre" program in which families can help preserve rain forests. Publishes the *Nature Conservancy Magazine*, a bimonthly magazine containing articles on ecosystems and information on ecological tours and trips.

Sierra Club. 730 Polk Street, San Francisco, California 94109. Phone: 415/776-2211. Devoted to the study and protection of the earth's scenic and ecological resources—woodlands, wetlands, shores and rivers, deserts and plains. Some sixty chapters across the country schedule outings, exhibits, conferences, and lectures. Through its publishing programs for children, the Sierra Club offers fiction and nonfiction books for young people about the earth, its creatures, and the role of human beings living among them. Publishes *Si-*

erra, a bimonthly magazine covering conservation, the wilderness, environmental policy, and outdoor adventure. Also publishes a biweekly newsletter, along with books on environmental issues and outdoor activities.

Mail Order Catalogs

National Wildlife Nature Gift Catalog. National Wildlife Federation, 1400 Sixteenth Street, N.W., Washington, D.C. 20036-2266. Phone: 1/800-245-5484. A catalog containing nature-related gifts, including a hummingbird wallpaper border, tiger tee-shirts, and dancing dolphin wind chimes. Items for children include an unbreakable dinner set featuring pandas, giraffes, and zebras; a "math in the bath" play set (stick-on dinosaurs with push out numbers); an animal alphabet throw; a manatee and baby stuffed animals; an endangered species growth chart; a glow-in-the-dark star chart; and "my first microscope." The catalog also contains ordering information on the National Wildlife Federation's magazines, including *Ranger Rick* and *Your Big Backyard.*

The Nature Company Catalog. P.O. Box 188, Florence, Kentucky 41022. Phone: 1/800-227-1114. Offers a wide-range of nature-related products and services, many of them offered only through the Nature Company. The "Nature Explorer" Backpack (containing binoculars, a pocket microscope, magnifier, and a thirty-two-page activity book), Environmental Sounds (morning songbirds, thunder, and ocean sounds on cassette or compact disc), and Nature Company vacation adventures are among the offerings.

The Changing Seasons

Books

Changing Seasons (series). By Elaine W. Good. Good Books. 32 pages. Full-color illustrations and simply text convey the sights, sounds, smells, and common activities enjoyed during the various seasons. Written from a child's perspective, these books discuss the natural highlights (snow falling, buds appearing, etc.) as well as seasonal activities (sledding, marshmallow roasting, and preserve-making, for example). Books include *White Wonderful Winter, It's Summertime, That's What Happens When It's Spring!,* and *Fall Is Here! I Love It.* For children ages two to six.

A Field Guide to Your Own Backyard. By John Hanson Mitchell. W. W. Norton, 1986. 288 pages. Explains what families can find in their own backyards (bugs, birds, blossoms, etc.) during each of the four seasons.

Linnea's Almanac. By Christina Bjork and Lena Anderson. R & S Books, 1989. Guides children through each month of the year, describing all the changes that take place. Activities related to each season are included. For children ages seven to eleven.

Nature All Year Long. By Clare Walker Leslie. Greenwillow, 1991. 56 pages. Month-by-month, this book offers interesting facts, craft projects, and seasonal investigations. For ages seven and up.

The Reasons for Seasons. By Linda Allison. Little, Brown, 1975. 121 pages. This book is designed to help children better understand—and appreciate—the seasons of the year. Includes many project ideas. For ages nine and up.

The Weather

Books

How the Weather Works. By Peter Seymour. Macmillan, 1985. 10 pages. Combines straightforward text with pop-ups, pulldown tabs, and other devices to introduce children to the elements. For ages five and up.

Weather. By Brian Cosgrove. Alfred A. Knopf, 1991. 64 pages. Part of the award-winning Eyewitness series of books, containing appealing photographs and informative captions. For children in grades five and up.

Weather. By Jan Pienkowski. Simon and Schuster, 1990. A board-book with colorful illustrations and single-word captions for the preschool set.

Weather. By Howard E. Smith, Jr. Doubleday, 1990. 45 pages. A book about weather for the slightly older set (ages seven to eleven). Explores fog, flash floods, and other phenomena. Combines straightforward prose with dramatic illustrations.

The Weather Pop-Up Book. By Francis Wilson. Simon and Schuster, 1987. 10 pages. A full-color pop-up book exploring wind, rain, cyclones, heatwaves, hail, and other weather phenomena. For children ages ten and up.

Weatherwatch. By Valerie Wyatt. Addison-Wesley, 1990. 95 pages. Features two dozen weather projects, including preserving a snowflake, catching pollution, and making a rainbow. All the activities call for inexpensive and easily obtainable materials. For ages eight to twelve.

Kit

The Weather Tracker's Kit: Explore the Changing Forces of Nature. By Gregory C. Aaron. Running Press, 1991. A weather station in a box to help children chart cloud formations, wind direction, temperature, wind chill factor, and rainfall amounts. The accompanying book is eighty pages in length.

THE ANIMAL KINGDOM

General Resources

Books

Amazing Animal Senses. By Ron and Atie van der Meer. Little, Brown, 1990. Contains twenty-five tricks, tests, and movable parts that show how animals use their five senses to survive. Complete with lift up flaps and scratch-and-sniff patches. For children ages eight and up.

The Animal Atlas. By Barbara Taylor. Alfred A. Knopf, 1992. 64 pages. A Dorling Kindersley Book. Depicts different habitats and the animals that live there, including the Amazon, Himalayas, European woodlands, and the Rocky Mountains.

"Eye Openers" (series). A Dorling Kindersley book. Macmillan. 24 pages each. Included in this series are books for young animal lovers. Titles include *Pets, Farm Animals, Baby Animals,* and *Sea Animals.* Includes photographs plus accompanying illustrations and simple text. For children ages three to seven.

Eyewitness Books (series). Alfred A. Knopf. 64 pages. This award-winning series contains lush photographs and lively captions. Subjects are divided into component parts to help children better understand the structure and workings of various topics. Among the animal topics explored in the series are mammals, reptiles, fish, insects, cats, birds, butterflies, dinosaurs, and early humans. For children ages ten and up. (Note: younger children often enjoy looking at the pictures.)

Eyewitness Jrs. (series). Alfred A. Knopf. 32 pages. A nonfiction series for children ages six to ten. Filled with facts, illustrations, and lifelike photographs to help the younger set better understand the true behavior of animals. Books in the series explore bats, snakes, beetles, birds, cats, fish, frogs, mammals, monkeys, bears, lizards, spiders, poisonous animals, butterflies and moths, crocodiles and reptiles, animal disguises, and wolves, dogs, and foxes.

See How They Grow (series). By Jane Burton. Dutton. 24 pages. A series of books for preschoolers showing how baby animals grow up. Photographs capture the early stages of life, various stages of development, and the mischief baby animals are famous for. Books in the series include *Puppy, Kitten, Duck, Pig, Calf, Frog, Foal, Rabbit, Fox, Owl,* and *Butterfly.* Sturdy pages, for children ages three to six.

Magazines for Children

Dolphin Log. 930 West Twenty-first Street, Norfolk, Virginia 23517. From the Cousteau Society, this bimonthly magazine covers underwater life and exploration. Includes illustrations and articles on a variety of aquatic creatures, ecology, and marine biology. Also contains puzzles, quizzes, and other fun fillers. For children ages seven to fifteen. Issued bimonthly.

Owl. Young Naturalist Foundation, P.O. Box 11314, Des Moines, Iowa 50304. (Editorial offices: The Young Naturalist Foundation, 56 The Esplanade, Toronto, Ontario, Canada M5E1A7.) A discovery magazine for children ages nine to twelve, presenting articles on wildlife, science, technology, and related topics. Includes full-color photographs, illustrations, cartoons, and projects. Issued monthly. For younger children (ages three to eight), the Young Naturalist Foundation publishes *Chickadee,* a picture-oriented nature magazine, complete with animal stories, activities, games, puzzles, craft ideas, and short fiction (to be read to young children).

Ranger Rick. National Wildlife Federation, 1400 Sixteenth Street, N.W., Washington, D.C. 20036-2266. Phone: 1/800-432-6564. A monthly magazine containing high-quality photographs and short features on animals (both common and exotic), conservation, and outdoor adventure. Includes craft and activity ideas, cartoons, and letters from kids. For children ages six to twelve.

Your Big Backyard. National Wildlife Federation, 1400 Sixteenth Street, N.W., Washington, D.C. 20036-2266. Phone: 1/800-432-6564. For children ages three to six, this monthly magazine contains picture-oriented materials (simple games, crafts, short stories, and mini-articles) on animals, nature, and conservation.

Zoobooks. P.O. Box 85384, San Diego, California 92186-5384. Phone: 1/800-992-5034. Each issue of this magazine focuses on a different animal (sharks, eagles, wild cats, etc.). Includes photographs, illustrations, and informative text. For children ages six to ten. Issued ten times annually.

Videotapes

Animal Friends (series). Scholastic. Running time: 30 minutes each. These videos include live photography, songs, and stories about lovable, playful animals. Videos in the series include *Animal Babies in the Wild* and *Baby Animals Just Want to Have Fun.* Available from Reader's Digest Kids Catalog, Reader's Digest Association, Inc., Pleasantville, New York 00401. Phone: 1/800-458-3014. For children ages two to eight.

Carnival of Animals. Running time: 30 minutes. This award-winning video features live animals, live action, and the Mormon Youth Symphony orchestra. Verses by Ogden Nash. Available from Music in Motion, P.O. Box 833814, Richardson, Texas 75083-3814. Phone: 1/800-445-0649.

Cousteau (series). The Cousteau Society. Running times: 48-73 minutes. Jean-Michel Cousteau and his team take viewers on journeys under the sea and into exotic lands. Tapes in the series focus on marine life (and how industrialization, human carelessness, or lack of concern, are affecting it). Titles include *Bearing Sea, Alaska: Outrage at Valdez,* and *Haiti: Waters of Sorrow.* Available from Schoolmasters Video, 745 State Circle, P.O. Box 1941, Ann Arbor, Michigan 48106. Phone: 313/761-5175 (customer service) or 1/800-521-2832 (orders only).

Exploring the World of Birds. Sea World/Bush Gardens Video Treasures. Running time: 30 minutes. Young naturalists will learn more about the world of birds in this captivating video complete with songs, stories, animation, and dramatic

Visiting the Zoo

From *Helping Your Child Learn Science* (U.S. Department of Education, 1992).

A few suggestions to help make your visit worthwhile:

Discuss expectations with your children ahead of time. What do they think they'll find at the zoo? Very young children may go to the zoo with a more positive attitude if they are assured that it has food stands, water fountains, and bathrooms.

Don't try to see everything in one visit. Zoos are such busy places that they can overwhelm youngsters, particularly preschoolers and those in primary grades.

Try to visit zoos at off times or hours (in winter, for example, or very early on a Saturday morning). This provides some peace and quiet and gives children unobstructed views of the animals.

Look for special exhibits and facilities for children, such as "family learning labs" or petting zoos. Here, children can touch and examine animals and engage in projects specially designed for them. For example, at the HERPlab (derived from the word *herpetology*) at the National Zoo in Washington, D.C., visitors can learn about reptiles and amphibians by doing everything from assembling a turtle skeleton to locating the different parts of a snake.

Plan follow-up activities and projects. A child who particularly liked the flamingos and ducks may enjoy building a bird house for the back yard. One who liked the mud turtle may enjoy using a margarine tub as a base to a papier-maché turtle.

---

wildlife scenes. For children ages four to twelve. Available through the Music for Little People catalog. Box 1460, Redway, California 95560. Phone: 1/800-727-2233.

Exploring the World of Fish. Sea World/Bush Gardens Video Treasures. Running time: 30 minutes. Young viewers can explore the world of sharks, eels, and other members of the underwater animal kingdom. Includes stories, songs, animation, and dramatic wildlife scenes. For children ages four to twelve. Available through the Music for Little People catalog. Box 1460, Redway, California 95560. Phone: 1/800-727-2233.

Exploring the World of Mammals. Sea World/Bush Gardens Video Treasures. Running time: 30 minutes. Young viewers can visit lions, gorillas, monkeys, dolphins, and other members of the animal kingdom in their natural habitats. Includes dramatic wildlife scenes, along with stories, songs, and animation. For children ages four to twelve. Available through the Music for Little People catalog. Box 1460, Redway, California 95560. Phone: 1/800-727-2233.

Exploring the World of Reptiles. Sea World/Bush Gardens Video Treasures. Running time: 30 minutes. Learn more about snakes, turtles, crocodiles, and other reptiles

Aquariums

Aquariums enable youngsters to see everything from starfish to electric eels. Children particularly enjoy feeding times. Call ahead to find out when the penguins, sharks, and other creatures get to eat. And check for special shows with sea lions and dolphins. From *Helping Your Child Learn Science* (U.S. Department of Education, 1992).

through songs, stories, animation, and dramatic wildlife scenes. For children ages four to twelve. Available through the Music for Little People catalog. Box 1460, Redway, California 95560. Phone: 1/800-727-2233.

Meet Your Animal Friends. Kids Express. Running time: 52 minutes. Narrated by Lynn Redgrave, this musical videotape is made up of short film segments showing horses, cows, dogs, and other familiar animals. Winner of the Film Advisory Board's Award of Excellence. For children ages one to five. Available from Hand in Hand, Route 26, R.R. 1, Box 1425, Oxford, Maine 04270-9711. Phone: 1/800-872-9745.

National Geographic Video (series). National Geographic Society. Running time: 60 minutes each. This documentary series takes viewers around the globe, showing how wild animals live in their natural habitats. *Lions of the African Night, Land of the Tiger, Elephant, Gorilla and Strange Creatures of the Night* are some of the available titles. Available from Schoolmasters Video, 745 State Circle, P.O. Box 1941, Ann Arbor, Michigan 48106. Phone: 313/761-5175

(customer service) or 1/800-521-2832 (orders only).

Video Safaris (series). Children's Video Encyclopedia. Running time: 30 minutes each. In this series of videotapes, child narrators challenge viewers to "guess the secret animal," providing clues along the way such as physical characteristics, behavioral patterns, and natural habits. The identify of the animal is revealed at the end of each "video safari" segment. Titles in the series include: *The Search for Africa's Most Secret Animals, The Search for Australia's Most Secret Animals, The Search for the United States' Most Secret Animals, The Search for India's Most Secret Animals, The Search for China's Most Secret Animals,* and *The Search for Canada's Most Secret Animals.* Available from Pyramid School Products, 6510 North Fifty-fourth Street, Tampa, Florida 33610-1994. Phone: 1/800-792-2644.

Game

Alpha Animals. Aristoplay. An A-to-Z course in animal names and classifications. Beginning players take a safari through the alphabet, naming animals that begin with each letter along the way. Older folks must name animals within specific groups. Available from Aristoplay, P.O. Box 7529, Ann Arbor, Michigan 48107. Phone: 1/800-634-7738.

Associations

American Humane Association. Animal Protection Division, 63 East Inverness Drive, Englewood, Colorado 80112. Phone: 303/792-9900. The American Humane Association provides publications and educational materials to teachers, students, and pet owners on proper pet care, humane education lessons, and animal welfare and legislative issues.

Publishes *Advocate,* a quarterly membership magazine.

American Society for the Prevention of Cruelty to Animals. 441 East Ninety-second Street, New York, New York 10128. Phone: 212/876-7700. Promotes appreciation for and humane treatment of animals. Maintains shelters for stray, lost, or unwanted animals (cares for more than 100,000 dogs, cats, and other animals each year). Conducts education programs and provides information on animals for children and adults. Offers brochures, videotapes, and books on animals, animal rights, and pet care. Also publishes *ASPCA Report,* a magazine on animal welfare issues put out three times annually.

Animal Welfare Institute. P.O. Box 3650, Washington, D.C. 20007. Phone: 202/337-2333. Promotes humane treatment of animals. Among the institute's primary concerns are cruelty in the use of trapping devices, destruction of endangered species, and the mistreatment of animals used in lab experiments or raised for food. Publishes books, as well as a quarterly newsletter.

Humane Society of the United States. 2100 L Street, N.W., Washington, D.C. 20037. Phone: 202/452-1100. Promotes public education to foster respect, understanding, and compassion for all animals. Encourages responsible pet care, and seeks to eliminate cruelty to animals (in research and testing, hunting and trapping, zoos and pet shops, kennels, farming practices, etc.). Monitors and seeks to influence public policy regarding animal protection. Publications include *Animal Activist Alert,* a quarterly newsletter covering animal legislation.

Down on the Farm

Books

Farm Animals. A Dorling Kindersley book. Macmillan, 1991. 24 pages. Designed for young animal lovers, this book includes photographs plus accompanying illustrations and simple text. Part of the "Eye Openers" series of books. For children ages three to seven.

The Milk Makers. By Gail Gibbons. Macmillan, 1987. 32 pages. For children in kindergarten through grade three. Shows where the milk we drink comes from.

Our Animal Friends at Maple Hill Farm. By Alice and Martin Provensen. Random House, 1984. 56 pages. Describes animals on the authors' own farm in New York: dogs, horses, pigs, geese, cows, goats, cats, sheep, chickens, and others.

Pig. By Mary Ling. Dorling Kindersley, 1993. 24 pages. Part of the "See How They Grow" series of books for preschoolers, showing how baby animals grow up. Other farm animals in the series include *Calf, Duck,* and *Foal.* Sturdy pages, for children ages three to six.

Videotape

Farm Animals. Running time: 30 minutes. Shows farm animals in their natural habitat (the barnyard) doing their thing (grunting, quacking, rolling in the mud, etc.). For children ages one to five. Available from Chinaberry, 2780 Via Orange Way, Suite B, Spring Valley, California 91978. Phone: 1/800-776-2242.

Game

Back to the Farm. Animal Town. An organic-farm boardgame for children

Visiting a Farm

From *Helping Your Child Learn Science* (U.S. Department of Education, 1992).

A visit to a farm makes a wonderful field trip for elementary school youngsters. But parents can also arrange visits. If you don't know a farmer, call the closest 4-H Club for a referral. Consider dairy farms, as well as vegetable, poultry, hog, and tree farms.

On a dairy farm, see the cows close up, view silos, and learn what cows eat. Find out from the farmer:

- Up to what age do calves drink only milk?

- When do they add other items to their diets? What are they?

- Why are the various foods a cow eats nutritious?

A visit to a farm also enables children to identify the difference between calves, heifers, and cows; to watch the cows being milked; to see farm equipment; to sit on tractors; and to ask questions about how tractors work.

If you visit a vegetable farm, encourage your children to look at the crops and ask questions about how they grow. If your children grew up in an urban area, they may have no idea what potatoes or beans look like growing in a field.

ages eight and up. Players build their own farm by acquiring food, animals, and tools by trading, purchasing, and getting lucky. Helps teach the benefits of alternative energy sources (solar collectors and windmills) and pesticide-free farming. Many social, environmental, and economic lessons are integrated. Although there is a winner, players are encouraged to cooperate. For two to four players. Available from Animal Town, P.O. Box 485, Healdsburg, California 95448. Phone: 1/800-445-8642.

Birds

Books

Birdwatch: A Young Person's Guide to Birding. By Mary MacPherson. Sterling, 1989. 144 pages. An introduction to birdwatching, for children ages six and up. Includes listings of bird conservation societies.

Bird Wise. By Pamela M. Hickman. Addison-Wesley, 1989. 96 pages. "Forty fun feats for finding out about our feathered friends." Facts and bird-related activities galore. Projects for children in grades two through seven.

A Field Guide to the Birds Coloring Book. By Roger Tory Peterson and Peter Alden. Illustrated by John Sill. Houghton Mifflin, 1982. With this guide, children can color elaborate pictures while learning about their feathered friends.

A Kids First Book of Birdwatching (with Bird Song Audiocassette). By Scott Weidensaul. Running Press, 1990. 64 pages. An introduction to birdwatching, including easy-to-understand text, drawings, and photographs. Comes with a bird song audiocassette.

Backyard Bird Feeding

The following is from *Backyard Bird Feeding* (U.S. Fish and Wildlife Service, 1990).

Getting Started

No matter where you live, you can put food outside your door, and some creature, feathered or furred, will show its appreciation and make an appearance. That's all it takes. Once you get started, it's hard to stop.

Before you know it, you're learning bird names. After awhile, you'll start to recognize individuals and the messages in their behavior and song.

When you get to the point where you want to attract and "keep" a particular species, what you do will be determined by where you live, and the time of year. For example, on any winter day, you're likely to see a cardinal at a sunflower feeder in Virginia, a goldfinch at a thistle feeder in Massachusetts and hummingbirds at a nectar feeder in southern California.

How can you find out which birds to expect? A bird field identification book has pictures of different birds and will help you find the names for the birds you're likely to see.

Feeder Selection

When the ground is covered with snow and ice, it's hard to resist just tossing seed out the door. But it's healthier for the birds to get their "hand-outs" at a feeding station, off the ground.

Regardless of the season, food that sits on the ground for even a short time is exposed to potential contamination by dampness, mold, bacteria, animal droppings, law fertilizers and pesticides.

It's best, for the birds' sake, to use a feeder.

You can start simply with a piece of scrap wood, elevated a few inches above the ground. Add a few holes for drainage and you've built a platform feeder. It won't be long before the birds find it.

Whether you buy one or build one, eventually you'll find yourself looking at commercially manufactured feeders. There are literally hundreds to choose from. How do you make the "right" choice? What makes a feeder "good?"

First Consider Placement

Where do you want to watch your birds? From a kitchen window . . . a sliding glass door opening on to a deck, a second story window?

Pick a location that has year-round easy access. When the weather's bad and birds are most vulnerable, you may be reluctant to fill a feeder that isn't in a convenient spot near a door or accessible window.

Also consider the "mess" factor. Pick a location where discarded seed shells and bird droppings won't be a clean-up problem.

Put your feeder where the squirrels can't reach. Those cute little rodents seem to like sunflower and peanuts as much or more than acorns. Squirrels become a problem when they take over a bird feeder, scaring the birds away, and tossing seed all over.

What's worse . . . frustrated squirrels have been known to entertain themselves by chewing right through plastic and wooden feeders.

If you've seen squirrels in your neighborhood, it's safe to assume they will visit your feeder. Think long and hard before you hang anything from a tree limb. Squirrels are incredibly agile and any feeder hanging from a tree with or without a squirrel guard or baffle, is likely to become a squirrel feeder.

In the long run, a squirrel-proof feeder or any feeder on a pole with a baffle is the least aggravating solution. The most effective squirrel-proof feeder is the pole mounted metal "house" type.

If you must hang a feeder, select a tube protected with metal mesh. Most plastic "squirrel-proof" feeders, despite manufacturers' claims, may eventually succumb to rodent teeth.

If you have the "right" situation in your yard, a pole with a baffle should suffice. Any wood or plastic feeder can be effective when mounted on a pole with a plastic or metal baffle, if the pole is at least 10 feet or more from a tree limb or trunk.

Once you've determined where you're going to put your feeder, you're ready to go shopping. In addition to good looks, ask yourself these question:

- How durable is it?
- Will it keep the seeds dry?
- How easy is it to clean?
- How much seed will it hold?
- How many birds will it feed at one time?
- Which species will use it?

Kit

The Junior Birder's Fanny Pack. Available from the Nature Company, this kit comes with red plastic binoculars, a 100mm mini-camera, bird identification cards, and the Audubon bird call. Available by mail through the Nature Company catalog, P.O. Box 188, Florence, Kentucky 41022. Phone: 1/800-227-1114.

Association

National Audubon Society. Phone: 212/979-3119. Will put callers in touch with state societies that can help families locate hands-on bird programs in their area.

Bugs

Books

BugPlay. By Marlene Nachbar Hapai and Leon H. Burton. Addison-Wesley. 283 pages. Presents information on insects, together with simple, thought-provoking activities. Comes with a cassette of songs about bugs.

Bugs. By Nancy Winslow Parker and Joan Richards Wright. Greenwillow Books, 1987. 40 pages. An introduction to sixteen common insects. Includes general information, jokes, and brief descriptions of the physical characteristics, habitats, and natural environment. For children in grades one through four.

Bug Wise. By Pamela M. Hickman. Addison-Wesley, 1991. 96 pages Contains thirty insect investigations and arachnid activities, along with bug-related facts. Projects for children in grades two through seven.

Videotape

Bugs Don't Bug Us. Bo Peep Productions. Running time: 35 minutes. Winner of the Parents' Choice Award, this video features recognizable insects in action–and children interacting with them. Also shows how a caterpillar transforms into a butterfly. For ages two to seven. Available from Alcazar, P.O. Box 429, South Main Street, Waterbury, Vermont 05676. Phone: 1/800-541-9904.

Toys and Kits

The Bug Box. From Toys to Grow On, this box contains a set of realistic play bugs collected from around the world. Spiders, snakes, beetles, grasshoppers, and ants are among the seventy-plus assortment. Contact Toys to Grow On, P.O. Box 17, Long Beach, California 90801. Phone: 1/800-874-4242.

Insect Lore Products. Phone: 1/800-LIVE-BUG. Offers a variety of insect kits, including the popular "Ant Farm."

Butterflies

Kit

Butterfly Garden Set. Using this kit, kids can observe the amazing metamorphosis of a larvae into a Painted Lady butterfly. For grades two to nine. Large garden has thirty larvae; small garden has five larvae. Both sets are available through the Cuisenaire mail order catalog, P.O. Box 5026, White Plains, New York 10602-5026. Phone: 1/800-237-3142.

Pets

Books

ASPCA Pet Guides for Kids (series). By Mark Evans. Dorling Kindersley. 48 pages each. This series includes illustrated guides to help children care for their pet fish, hamster, bird, rabbit, kitten, puppy, or guinea pig. Includes general information on the animal and its behavior, along with guidelines on feeding, cleaning, playing with, and otherwise caring for and appreciating a pet. For ages seven and up.

Pets. A Dorling Kindersley book. Macmillan. 24 pages. Designed for young pet owners (or would-be pet owners), this book includes photographs plus accompanying illustrations and simple text. Part of the "Eye Openers" series of books. For children ages three to seven.

Videotape

Paws, Claws, Feathers and Fins. Kidsvidz (Price Stern Sloan Video). Running time: 30 minutes. A kids' guide to pets. Shows how being a responsible pet owner can be fun. For children ages four to twelve.

Associations

American Humane Association. Animal Protection Division, 63 East Inverness Drive, Englewood, Colorado 80112. Phone: 303/792-9900. The American Humane Association provides publications and educational materials to teachers, students, and pet owners on proper pet care, humane education lessons, and animal welfare and legislative issues. Publishes *Advocate,* a quarterly membership magazine.

American Pet Society. 406 South First Avenue, Carcadia, California 91006. Phone: 818/447-2222. Promotes responsible pet ownership. Offers educational programs, including services for children. Also sponsors charitable programs.

American Society for the Prevention of Cruelty to Animals. 441 East Ninety-second Street, New York, New York 10128. Phone: 212/876-7700. Promotes appreciation for and humane treatment of animals. Main-tains shelters for stray, lost, or unwanted animals (cares for more than 100,000 dogs, cats, and other animals each year). Conducts education programs and provides information on animals for children and adults. Offers brochures, videotapes, and books on animals, animal rights, and pet care. Also publishes *ASPCA Report,* a magazine on animal welfare issues issued three times annually.

Humane Society of the United States. 2100 L Street, N.W., Washington, D.C. 20037. Phone: 202/452-1100. Promotes public education to foster respect, understanding, and compassion for all animals. Encourages responsible pet care and seeks to eliminate cruelty to animals (in research and testing, hunting and trapping, zoos and pet shops, kennels, farming practices, etc.). Monitors and seeks to influence public policy regarding animal protection. Publications include *Animal Activist Alert,* a quarterly newsletter covering animal legislation.

MUSEUMS

Books

America on Display: A Guide to Unusual Museums and Collections in the United States and Canada. By Joyce Jurnovoy and David Jenness. Facts on File, 1988. 280 pages. Streetcar museums, firefighters' memorial museums, ethnic museums, musical instrument collections—they're all listed by region in this guide.

Children's Museums, Zoos, and Discovery Rooms: An International Reference Guide. Edited by Barbara Fleisher Zucker. Greenwood Press, 1987. 278 pages. Contains profiles of more than two hundred zoos, museums, and aquariums for chil-dren worldwide. Entries include name and location, descriptions of exhibits, facilities, and special programs, funding sources, and publications produced (if any).

Doing Children's Museums: A Guide to 165 Hands-On Museums. By Joanne Cleaver. Williamson Publishing, 1988. 229 pages. Offers detailed discussions of museums across the country, including admission fees, phone numbers, hours of operation, descriptions of exhibits, special programs and workshops, infant/toddler playspaces, and more. Also mentions nearby parks, child-friendly eating spots, and other side stops. Also offers guidelines on pre-

Should We Get a Pet?

The following suggestions are derived from the March/April 1992 issue of *Washington Parent*.

If you are deciding whether to buy a pet for your family, it may be useful to ask yourself the following questions:

1. How old and how mature are your children?
2. Will the pet's needs mesh with your family's work and home schedules?
3. Who will be the pet's main caretaker?
4. How much attention will the pet require?
5. How will the pet be attended to when the family is away on vacation?
6. Does anyone in the family have an allergy or other medical condition affected by pets?
7. Will the pet need any special training?
8. Are you planning to renovate your home or move to a new home?

paring children for museum visits and gaining maximum pleasure from such trips.

Minds in Motion. By Alan R. Gartenhaus. Caddo Gap Press, 1991. 128 pages. Explains how art, science, and history museums can expand creative thinking in children and adults. Includes an in-depth discussion of creativity; offers games, exercises, and guidelines to help museum-goers see beyond labels and objects. Includes an extensive bibliography and a list of worthwhile museums across the country.

Where's the ME in Museum. By Milde Waterfall and Sarah Grusin. Vandamere Press, 1989. 128 pages. A guide for museum-going with children to make the most of museums as centers for exploration and discovery. Includes chapters on art, science, history, and children's museums.

Association

American Association of Museums. 1225 Eye Street, N.W., Suite 200, Washington, D.C. 20005. Phone: 202/289-1818. An association of art, history, and science museums; art centers and associations; historical houses and societies; aquariums, planetariums, zoos, and botanical gardens; college and university museums; special museums; and others interested in the museum field. Offers a variety of publications, including the *Official Museum Directory* (a descriptive guide to museums in the United States) and *Museum News,* a bimonthly magazine offering information on museum trends and exhibits. Also includes reviews of books and exhibits.

Children's Museums (A Short List of Good Museums for Hands-on Learning)

Brooklyn Children's Museum. 145 Brooklyn Avenue, Brooklyn, New York 11213. Phone: 718/735-4400. Visitors enter this underground museum through a trolley car, then continue their journey by foot through a huge drainage tunnel. Among the highlights are cultural exhibits such as "Night Journeys: Home Is Where I Sleep," where children can try out a variety of beds and headrests used in Africa, Japan, and other countries. The museums contains four floors of exhibits, including "The Boneyard," which shows how bones grow and help us move and where kids can shake hands with a skeleton and play a pinball game that shows how the digestive system works.

Capital Children's Museum. 800 Third Street, N.E., Washington, D.C. 20002. Phone: 202/543-8600. One wing of this museum is devoted to the evolution of communication, from prehistoric times to the arrival of electronic telecommunications. Children can view primitive drawings inside a walk-in cave, examine movable type and make their own prints on a replica of a Franklin Press, use a Braille typewriter, and write their names in Morse code (among many other activities). International Hall offers exhibits and hands-on activities from featured countries such as Thailand and Mexico. Here, kids can make tortillas using traditional Mexican utensils, climb up into a Thai house built on stilts, or use Thai letter ink stamps to print their names (with the help of staff members). Another popular section of the museum explores the physical world, from the feeling of sliding down a fire pole, to the experience of climbing into a dentist's chair, to "cooking" soup in a play kitchen, and weighing objects on a real metric scale. Other highlights include a crawl-through maze and a fully equipped radio station.

Children's Museum of Boston. Museum Wharf, 300 Congress Street, Boston 02210. Phone: 617/426-8855. This museum serves as a model for museum directors and hands-on museum specialists around the world. Highlights include a rugged two-story climbing structure with wire mesh to keep kids from falling, thousands of Lego blocks for imaginative building projects, and an outdoor minigolf course where children can learn about the urban environment. Other popular exhibits include an underground network where visitors can see how things work under their feet; "Design of the Times," where older children can use design and draft equipment; and "Play Space," a developmental play area for infants and toddlers, complete with houses, castles, and plenty of crawling spaces.

The Children's Museum (Indianapolis, Indiana). 3000 North Meridian Street, Indianapolis, Indiana 46206. Phone: 317/924-KIDS. Thousands of exhibits in this children's museum (the largest in the world) engage parents as much as they do children. Here, kids can go on a flight-simulated mission to Mars, ride on an antique carousel, and play games popular in other cultures. Within this five-story building, children can play on climbing equipment, participate in a wide variety of hands-on activities, or enjoy looking at special collections behind glass.

The Children's Museum (St. Paul, Minnesota). 1217 North Bandana Boulevard North, St. Paul, Minnesota 55108. Phone: 612/644-3818. In this museum, kids can become instant T.V. stars by way of KOALA, the museum's closed-circuit television station. For babies and toddlers, there's an infant developmental center containing tunnels, jumbo blocks, and other safe, entertaining playthings. Boys and girls can learn more about automatic teller machines, pretend they're a patient (or doctor) at the children's clinic, or hop aboard a steam engine.

Los Angeles Children's Museum. 310 North Main Street, Los Angeles, California 90012. Phone: 213/687-8801. Located in the entertaining capital of the world, this museum offers television, recording, and animation studios where young museum-goers can record and play back tapes, capture themselves on videotape, or create animated cartoons. Other features include "Ethnic L.A.," where kids can learn about the cultural diversity in Los Angeles; a room filled with attachable foam building blocks, which can be used to create a "Sticky City;" and a series of city tours, that take families outside the museum walls to explore science centers, factories, and other interesting spots around town.

The Magic House. 516 South Kirkwood Road, St. Louis, Missouri 63122. Phone: 314/822-8900. Includes a special experiment center, complete with lab, kitchen, art studio, and workshop. Attractions include a electrostatic generator that makes your hair stand on end (literally), a three-story spiral slide, and a variety of exhibits for hands on physics and computer experiments. This museum is housed in a converted Victorian mansion.

Please Touch Museum. 210 North Twenty-first Street, Philadelphia, Pennsylvania 19103. Phone: 215/963-0667. The first museum in the country to cater to kids under age seven, Please Touch offers hands-on exhibits such as "Happily Ever After" where young museum-goers can dress up like characters in folk and fairytales; walk into art (enter a papier-maché cave or step into an impressionistic nightscape of Philadelphia created from shadows). Special exhibit for infants and toddlers are designed to stimulate their senses and mobilize their bodies. Here they can smells flowers, touch textures, and crawl through logs. The museum also contains a good bubble-making exhibit.

The Seattle Children's Museum. Seattle Center, 305 Harrison Street, Seattle, Washington 98109. Phone: 206/441-1767. Children love the gold-mining exhibit here, where they can board a nineteenth century steamship and make their way to a gold-mining town, where they can pan for gold, try on various costumes, and explore an old mine shaft. In "The Neighborhood," children can visit scaled-down stores and shops, and play the role of a bus driver, fireman, or family physician. The museum also contains an interactive exhibit on modern forms of communication, ranging from Morse code to cellular phones, and the "Playcenter," where babies and toddlers are free to explore interesting objects among safe play structures.

ZOOS AND AQUARIUMS

For a listing of zoos and aquariums around the country, see appendix F. For other resource listings, see "Animals" in this chapter.

Books

Where the Animals Are: A Guide to the Best Zoos, Aquariums, and Wildlife Sanctuaries in North America. By Tim O'Brien. Globe Pequot Press, 1992. 301 pages. Covers more than 250 sites in the United States and Canada, where you'll find animals that creep, crawl, burrow, swim, fly, walk, run, gallop, and flee. Each entry includes information on hours and seasons of operation, featured species and special animals (endangered, exotic, etc.), events, and entertainment, suggested length of stay, admission prices, food services, and nearby attractions. Includes a general index plus an index organized by state and province.

The Zoo Book: Fun for Everyone at America's Zoos. By Allen W. Nyhuis. Carousel Press, 1994. Written by a zoo-buff who has visited each and every zoo featured in this standout guide.

Associations

American Association of Museums. 1225 Eye Street, N.W., Suite 200, Washington, D.C. 20005. Phone: 202/289-1818. An association of art, history, and science museums; art centers and associations; historical houses and societies; aquariums, planetariums, zoos, and botanical gardens; college and university museums; special museums; and others interested in the museum field. Offers a variety of publications, including the *Official Museum Directory* (a descriptive guide that includes zoos, aquariums, wildlife refuges, bird sanctuaries, and nature centers in the United States).

American Association of Zoological Parks and Aquariums. Oglebay Park, Route 88, Wheeling, West Virginia 26003. Phone: 304/242-2160. An organization of individuals interested in promoting zoos and aquariums for public recreation, educational purposes, and scientific discovery. Publishes *Zoological Parks and Aquariums in the Americas,* a biennial directory.

Chapter 17

Choosing Children's Books

GENERAL RESOURCES

Free and Inexpensive Resources

Caldecott and Newbery Medal Bookmarks. These bookmarks explain the history of the awards, illustrate the medals, and list award recipients, past and present. Recent honor books are listed as well. Copies are free with a self-addressed, stamped enveloped. Write to the Children's Book Council, Inc., 568 Broadway, Suite 404, New York, New York 10012.

Choosing a Child's Book. This pamphlet, produced by the Children's Book Council, contains guidelines for parents on choosing children's books. Includes a short bibliography. For a free copy, send a self-addressed, stamped envelope along with your request to the Children's Book Council, Inc., 568 Broadway, Suite 404, New York, New York 10012.

Book Lists

The Black Experience in Children's Books. Titles with short descriptions, from the New York Public Library Office of Children's Services.

Also available from the Office of Children's Services: *Children's Books,* recommending one hundred titles. Each of these lists is available for $2.50 from the New York Public Library Office of Children's Services, Office of Branch Libraries, 455 Fifth Avenue, N.W., New York, New York 10016.

Caldecott Medal Books. A complete list of medal-winning picture books, published annually by the Association for Library Service to Children. For a free copy, send a self-addressed, stamped envelope along with your request to the Association for Library Service to Children (see appendix I for contact information).

Children's Books. The Library of Congress's annual listing of about two hundred books for children from preschool through junior high school, classified by theme. Can be ordered from the Superintendent of Documents, U.S. Government Printing Office, Washington, D.C. 20402. (For more information on ordering publications from the federal government, see appendix B.) Inquire about price; specify stock number SN 030-011-00094-0 when ordering.

Children's Bookshelf. Includes titles with short descriptions. Available for $1.00 from Reading Is Fundamental, Inc., P.O. Box 23444, Washington, D.C. 20026.

Children's Books of the Year. Lists more than six hundred titles, fiction and non-fiction, classified by age (preschool to fourteen) and genre. Includes hardcovers, paperbacks, reprints, and new editions of old favorites. Chosen from 4,500 books submitted. Contact the Child Study Children's Book Committee, Bank Street College, 610 West 112th Street, New York, N.Y. 10025. Phone: 212/222-6700. Inquire about price. (Note: Child Study Children's Book Committee also produces *Books to Read Aloud with Children through Age 8* and *Paperback Books for Children.*)

Children's Choices. An annotated list of books chosen by children. Single copy free with a stamped, self-addressed envelope. Allow for four ounces of postage. Write "Children's Choices," International Reading Association, 800 Barksdale Road, P.O. Box 8139, Newark, Delaware 19714-8139.

Children's Classics. A sixteen-page annotated and illustrated book-selection aid for parents of infants, toddlers, preschoolers, and school-aged children. Available for $3.00 from The Horn Book, Inc., 31 St. James Avenue, Boston, Massachusetts 02116.

Newbery Medal Books. A complete list of books awarded this medal for literature. Produced annually by the Association for Library Service to Children. For a free copy, send a self-addressed, stamped envelope along with your request to the Association for Library Service to Children (see appendix I for contact information).

Notable Children's Books. Lists books of commendable quality that encourage and reflect children's interests. Issued annually by the Association for Library Service to Children. For a free copy, send a self-addressed, stamped envelope along with your request to the Association for Library Service to Children (see appendix I for contact information).

Timeless Classics. Produced by the National Endowment for the Humanities, this four-page list includes nearly four hundred books published before 1960 for children of all ages. For ordering information on *Timeless Classics,* request the most recent issue of the free *Consumer Information Catalog,* available from the Consumer Information Center, P.O. Box 100, Pueblo, Colorado 81002.

Bookstores and Public Libraries. In addition to the lists mentioned above, children's bookstores and public libraries often produce their own age-appropriate listings of recommended titles. Many public libraries also sponsor special programs that stretch young imaginations and encourage kids to read. In addition, librarians will answer specific questions, offer informed suggestions, and otherwise assist patrons of all ages.

Book Reviews

Booklinks: Connecting Books, Libraries, and Classrooms. American Library Association, 50 East Huron Street, Chicago, Illinois 60611. (Subscription offices: 434 West Downer, Aurora, Illinois 60506. Phone: 708/892-7465.) An imprint of the American Library Association, this publication connects books, libraries, and classrooms. Each issue provides annotated listings of children's books, along with related activities, discussion questions, and ideas for linking topics and themes found in the featured books. Also contains interviews with authors and illustrators. Audience includes teachers, librarians, and parents.

Booklist. Reviews books for both children and adults, as well as nonprint material such as software. Issued semimonthly. Published by the American Library Association, 50 East Huron Street, Chicago, Illinois 60611. Phone: 312/944-6780 or 1/800-545-2433.

Bulletin of the Center for Children's Books. Edited by Betsy Hearne, this bulletin reviews more than eight hundred current books for children each year. Each review gives information on the book's content, strengths and weaknesses, and reading level, as well as suggestions for curricular use. Published eleven times annually by the University of Illinois Press. Subscription offices: University of Illinois Press, BCCB, 54 East Gregory Drive, Champaign, Illinois 61820. (To place credit card orders, call 217/333-8935.) [Note: Betsy Hearne is the author of *Choosing Books for Children* and coauthor of *The Best in Children's Books* (see listings under "Books").]

The Five Owls. A review of children's books for parents, teachers, librarians, and others personally and professionally involved in children's literature. Organized thematically. Highly selective (no negative reviews). Issued bimonthly. Available from The Five Owls, Inc., 2004 Sheridan Avenue, Minneapolis, Minnesota 55405. Phone: 612/377-2004.

Horn Book. A literary periodical published bimonthly with detailed reviews of new books for children and young adults in every issue. Reviews more than four hundred books a year. Also contains interviews with authors and articles on various aspects of children's literature. The Horn Book, Inc., 14 Beacon Street, Boston, Massachusetts 02108. Phone: 617/227-1555 or 1/800-325-1170.

Hungry Mind Review, Children's Book Supplement. A supplement to the *Hungry Mind Review,* this quarterly reviews all kinds of books for children, including picture books, fiction, nonfiction, and poetry. Also reviews some books for parents. Contains essays and interviews with children's book authors and artists. Contact *Hungry Mind Review,* 1628 Grand Avenue, St. Paul, Minnesota 44105. Phone: 612/699-2610.

Parents' Choice. A quarterly review of children's media including children's books, movies, television programs, toys, games, records, videos, and computer software. Contact Parents' Choice Foundation, P.O. Box

185, Waban, Massachusetts 02168. Phone: 617/965-5913.

Publishers Weekly. Reviews books of all kinds, including books for children. Twice a year (in the spring and fall), special children's book issues include listings of new titles from major publishers, as well as reviews of children's books. *Publishers Weekly* occasionally includes articles on children's books and publishing for children as well. Published weekly. Contact Bowker Magazine Group, Cahners Magazine Division, 249 West Seventeenth Street, New York, New York 10011. Phone: 212/463-6758 or 1/800-278-2991 (subscriptions).

School Library Journal. Contains reviews of new books for children and young adults. Reviews more than three thousand books annually. Published monthly. Contact School Library Journal, 249 West Seventeenth Street, New York, New York 10011. Phone: 212/463-6759 or 1/800-456-9409 (subscriptions).

Books

A to Zoo: Subject Access to Children's Picture Books. By Carolyn W. Lima and John A. Lima. Fourth edition. R. R. Bowker, 1993. 1,158 pages. A subject guide to picture books. Contains more than fourteen thousand titles (fiction and nonfiction) arranged under nearly eight hundred subject headings and indexed by title, author, and illustrator. For work with children ages three to seven.

Babies Need Books. By Dorothy Butler. Atheneum, 1982. 178 pages. Offers advice on how books can be used not only to entertain and to comfort, but to stimulate the imagination, to stir the emotions, and to help the early forging of relationships by "establishing the habit of verbal give-and-take." Advocates a long-term process in which children begin to become acquainted with the wonders of language and the many benefits of the written word.

Best Books for Children: Preschool through Grade 6. By John T. Gillespie and Corinne J. Haden. R. R. Bowker, 1990. 1,002 pages. An evaluative listing of 11,299 titles, each with two or three recommendations from leading review journals. Includes separate author, title, illustrator, and subject indexes. Reading level recommendations also included. For work with children ages three to fourteen.

The Best in Children's Books: The University of Chicago Guide to Children's Literature, 1985-1990. By Zena Sutherland, Betsy Hearne, and Roger Sutton. University of Chicago Press, 1991. 492 pages. This book brings together close to 1,500 reviews from those first published in the *Bulletin of the Center for Children's Books* (see listing under "Book Reviews"). Includes assessments of a wide range of American and British fiction and nonfiction for preschool to young adult readers. Organized alphabetically by author. Six indexes, including title, subject, type of literature, reading level, curricular use (school subject area), and developmental value (self-esteem, separation, etc.)

The Best of the Best. Edited by Denise Perry Donavin. Random House, 1992. 366 pages. This annotated guidebook from the American Library Association recommends hundreds of children's books, magazines, videotapes, audiocassettes, toys, and computer software. Selected items, chosen by professionals in children's media, are grouped according to age appropriateness and media format. "Connections" refer readers to related materials in other portions of the book.

Beyond Picture Books: A Guide to First Readers. By Barbara Barstow and Judith Riggle. R. R. Bowker, 1989. 354 pages. A companion to *A to Zoo* (see separate listing), this guide lists first readers for children ages four to seven. Books are listed by subject, then cross-referenced to the annotated bibliography where you'll find plot synopses, evaluations, and comments about the illustrations, along with the name of the publisher, ISBN, and other information. Includes a list of two hundred outstanding first readers.

Bibliography of Books for Children. Helen Sheldon, editor. The Association for Childhood Education International (ACEI), 1989. 128 pages. Updated triennially, this guide contains more than 1,500 annotated listings of children's books. Titles are listed under the following general headings: picture books, fiction, nonfiction, selected references for an elementary school library, and magazines and newspapers for young children and adolescents. Includes title and author indexes. Available from the Association for Childhood Education International, 11501 Georgia Avenue, Suite 315, Wheaton, Maryland 20902. Phone: 301/942-2443 or 1/800-423-3563.

Children and Books. By Zena Sutherland and May Hill Arbuthnot. Eighth edition. HarperCollins, 1991. 768 pages. Meant for all adults who are interested in bringing children and books together, but designed particularly for classes in children's literature. Explores the history of children's books; describes how books help meet the needs of children at various stages of development; discusses in detail the various types of literature (folk tales, fables, myths, epics, modern fantasy, information books, etc.); and offers guidelines on evaluating children's books

and guiding children's book selections. Includes an annotated list of resources to assist adults in selecting books for children, as well as listings of publishers and their addresses, children's book awards, and indexes by subject, author, illustrator, and title.

Children's Books in Print. Edited by R. R. Bowker staff. R. R. Bowker. Updated annually. Indexed by title, author, and illustrator, *Children's Books in Print* provides ordering information on more than sixty thousand children's fiction and nonfiction books. Includes current prices and publishers' addresses and phone numbers, along with page length and age level recommendations. Covers more than sixty-five thousand titles. Also includes an awards index (i.e., listings of award-winning books, authors, and illustrators, organized by award). Also available: *Subject Guide to Children's Books in Print*, which includes information by subject for most available fiction and nonfiction children's books in print. (These volumes can be found in most public libraries.)

Children's Literature in the Elementary School. By Charlotte S. Huck, Susan Hepler, and Janet Hickman. Fifth edition. Harcourt Brace Jovanovich College Publishers, 1993. 866 pages. A textbook that will appeal to parents who want to make good literature available to their children. Offers an historical overview of children's literature, guidelines for selecting materials, and an in-depth look at the various genres of children's literature. Part three focuses on literature as a tool for teaching and learning. Appendixes include children's book awards, book selection aids, and publishers' addresses.

Choosing Books for Children: A Commonsense Guide. By Betsy Hearne. Revised, expanded, and updated. Delacorte Press, Delta, 1990. 228 pages. Offers readers information on how to choose appropriate books for children at all stages of development. Includes hundreds of annotated listings of children's books.

Choosing Books for Kids: How to Choose the Right Book for the Right Child at the Right Time. A Bank Street Book by Joanne Oppenheim, Barbara Brenner, and Betty Goegehold. Ballantine Books, 1986. 345 pages. Offers guidelines on choosing appropriate books for children, and reviews more than 1,500 books. Also lists additional sources of information for parents, including associations, periodicals, and books.

Eyeopeners: How to Choose and Use Children's Books About Real People, Places, and Things. By Beverly Kobrin. Penguin Books, 1988. 317 pages. Shows you how to find—and make the most of—nonfiction books about real people, places, and things. Includes annotated listings of more than five hundred nonfiction books, indexed by subject. Also offers guidelines to help fuel curiosity and foster a love of reading, along with tips for book-based activities (examples include breadbaking and watching wildlife).

For Love of Reading: A Parent's Guide to Encouraging Young Readers from Infancy through Age 5. By Masha Kabakow Rudman, Ed.D., Anna Markus Pearce, Ed.D., and the editors of Consumer Reports Books. Consumers Union, 1988. 399 pages. For parents of young children, this guide was produced to help foster an appreciation of—and positive attitude about—reading. In addition to ideas, activities, and suggestions, *For Love of Reading* features an annotated bibliography of over one thousand classic, award-winning, and contemporary children's books. Includes lists of

child's book awards and book clubs, along with recommended reading for parents.

Mother Goose Comes First. By Lois Winkel and Sue Kimmel. Henry Holt, 1990. 194 pages. An annotated guide to books and recordings for preschool children (from infancy through age five). Describes over seven hundred books and recordings, categorized by subject and age level. Includes listings of nursery rhymes and lullabies, folktales, poetry, and contemporary classics, as well as books on the family, growing up, health, animals, transportation, the earth and outer space, holidays, seasons, and much more.

The New Read-Aloud Handbook. By Jim Trelease. Penguin Books, 1989. 290 pages. Explains how reading aloud awakens children's imaginations, improves their language skills, and opens new worlds of enjoyment. Explains *how* to begin reading aloud—and which books to choose (including an annotated listing of recommended books).

The New York Times Parent's Guide to the Best Books for Children. By Eden Ross Lipson. Revised and updated. Random House, 1991. 508 pages. Compiled by the children's book editor for the *New York Times*, this annotated volume recommends wordless books, picture books, story books, and books for early, middle, and young-adult readers. Multiple indexes help parents select books according to subject, their child's age, title, author, and illustrator. Read-aloud books are also highlighted.

A Parent's Guide to Children's Reading. By Nancy Larrick. Westminster John Knox, 1983. 284 pages. Guide designed to help parents encourage their children to read and learn. Suggests reading activities and strategies to reach children of different ages and with different interests.

The RIF Guide to Encouraging Young Readers. By Reading Is Fundamental (RIF). Edited by Ruth Graves. Doubleday, 1987. 324 pages. Describes more than two hundred activities to engage children in the fun of words and reading. This books contains an annotated list of more than two hundred recommended books, plus lists of helpful publications, organizations, and other resources.

Story Stretchers. By Shirley C. Raines and Robert J. Canady. Gryphon House, 1989. 250 pages. Contains hundreds of literature-based activities that expand on concepts and themes found in ninety popular children's books. Story extension ideas include activities in art, block building, cooking, music, movement, and science. Also available: *More Story Stretchers* and *Story Stretchers for the Primary Grades*. (Note: These books, along with many of the children's books highlighted within, are available from Demco's Kids and Things, Box 7488, Madison, Wisconsin 53707. Phone: 1/800-356-1200.)

Taking Books to Heart: How to Develop a Love of Reading in Your Child. By Paul Copperman. Addison-Wesley, 1986. 273 pages. Explains how parents can help their children become avid readers. Discusses how children are typically taught reading skills at school, and how families can encourage the love of reading at home. Includes lists of recommended books for each reading level.

The Uses of Enchantment: The Meaning and Importance of Fairy Tales. By Bruno Bettelheim. Vintage Books, 1989. 328 pages. Winner of the National Book Award and the National Book Critics Circle Award, this book shows how fairy tales provide a unique way for children to come to terms with the dilemmas of their inner lives. Explains how fairy stories represent, in imaginative form, what the process of healthy human development consists of, and shows how these stories make such development appealing to the child. Written by the renowned child psychologist Bruno Bettelheim.

Mail Order Catalogs

Books of Wonder News. 132 Seventh Avenue at Eighteenth Street, New York, New York 10011. Phone: 212/989-3270. From New York's largest children's bookstore, *Books of Wonder News* features new books by top-notch authors and illustrators, older gems that deserve attention, and children's classics (some with facelifts). Signed copies of books are available. Call or write if you'd like to be put on the mailing list.

The Children's Small Press Collection. 719 North Fourth Avenue, Ann Arbor, Michigan 48104. Phone: 313/668-8056 or 1/800-221-8056. This company represents more than one hundred small publishers of children's books and cassettes. Their catalog, which is organized thematically, includes both fiction and nonfiction for children (or work with children) from infancy through adolescence. Includes books on topics such as self-sufficiency, self-esteem, science and the environment, family structure and change, and cooperation and conflict resolution. Also offers multicultural and bilingual materials, classic children's stories on cassette, music on cassette, parenting books, and teaching materials.

Chinaberry Book Service. 2780 Via Orange Way, Suite B, Spring Valley, California 91978. Phone: 619/670-5200 or 1/800-776-2242. Each issue of this mail order catalog describes in detail dozens of books and audiocassettes for children (infants through adolescents). Includes fiction and nonfiction that is humorous, serious, soothing, enlightening, entertaining, educational, inspirational, or otherwise stimulating. Features award-winning books, authors, and illustrators, as well as lesser-known talent and children's treasures. Also offers a selected list of parenting books. More than one hundred pages in length. Includes a complete subject index.

Kids and Things. Demco, Box 7488, Madison, Wisconsin 53707. Phone: 608/241-1201 or 1/800-356-1200. Demco's *Kids and Things* catalog contains quality children's books, together with dolls, puppets, puzzles, kits, figurines, and other items that expand on the themes and characters found in the books. Also offers videotapes and stories on cassette. For example, the Three Little Pigs collection includes three versions of the classic children's book, "The Three Little Pigs Floor Puzzle," a trio of pig hand puppets, and a soft-sculptured doll house with a carrying handle (complete with stuffed, appliquéed pigs and a big, bad wolf). The Dinosaur collection includes various dinosaur books by notable authors and illustrators, along with dinosaur stickers, games, masks, posters, cassettes, videotapes, stuffed dinosaurs, and prehistoric figurines. Offers many of the book titles from *Story Stretchers* and *More Story Stretchers*. Also offers the complete set of "First Discovery" books; "My First" books and videos, "My First Look At" series, and the "Getting to Know the Worlds' Greatest Artists" book series.

Listening Library. One Park Avenue, Old Greenwich, Connecticut 06870-1727. Phone: 1/800-243-4504. The Listening Library catalog contains literature-based media for children and young adults (ages four to sixteen-plus), including award-winning

books, book and cassette packages, recorded books (unabridged classics on cassette), and cassette listening libraries. Listening Library also produces *Bookmates,* a catalog containing children's classics, award-winning books, and popular titles, together with dolls, stuffed animals, and puppets based on the characters in the books.

Recorded Books. 270 Skipjack Road, Prince Frederick, Maryland 20678. Phone: 1/800-638-1304. Offers a variety of unabridged books on cassette for children and young adults, including classics by Kipling, Twain, and Tolkien. Also offers contemporary authors such as Beverly Clearly and Robert Newton Peck. Most of the recordings are for children in upper elementary school (grades four to six) up through high school.

Associations

The American Library Association. 50 East Huron Street, Chicago, Illinois 60611. Phone: 312/944-6780 or 1/800-545-2433. Produces dozens of publications of interest to reading teachers, parents, media experts, and children's and young adults' librarians. Recommended reading lists, book selection guides, and periodicals (including *Booklist* and *Books Links*) are among the offerings. The Association for Library Service to Children is a division of the American Library Association (see following listing).

Association for Library Service to Children. 50 East Huron Street, Chicago, Illinois 60611. Phone: 312/944-6780. A division of the American Library Association. Works to improve and extend library services to children from preschool through junior high. Evaluates book and nonbook materials, including film, video, audio, and computer software. Presents Newbery, Caldecott, and other awards. Publishes book lists, including *Caldecott Medal Books, Newbery Medal Books,* and the annotated *Notable Children's Books* (these lists are free with stamped, self-addressed envelopes). Other publications include the *ALSC Newsletter* and the *Journal of Youth Services in Libraries.* Also publishes books, brochures, and monographs.

The Children's Book Council, Inc. 568 Broadway, Suite 404, New York, New York 10012. Phone: 212/966-1990. A nonprofit trade association made up of children's book publishers. Promotes the reading and enjoyment of children's books. Develops children's book programs. Maintains a library of professional reference works and recently published children's trade books. Publishes informational sheets, brochures, booklists, and other educational and promotional materials for parents, teachers, librarians, and booksellers. Also publishes *CBC Features,* a semiannual newsletter that includes listings of free and inexpensive materials from publishers, lists of award-winners, and discussions of new books.

The Children's Literature Center. Library of Congress, Washington, D.C. 20540. Established in 1963, the Children's Literature Center calls attention to issues concerning children's books. Organizes symposia. Produces guides to children's books housed in the Library of Congress as well as an annual, annotated guide to noteworthy children's books for that year. (See *Children's Books* under "Book Lists" for more information on this guide.)

Council on Interracial Books for Children. 1841 Broadway, New York, New York 10023. Phone: 212/757-5339. Promotes children's books and other learning materials that are free

of bias, based on race, sex, age, or physical disability. Develops criteria for the evaluation of children's materials. Produces guidelines for selecting bias-free textbooks and storybooks. Publishes the *Interracial Books for Children Bulletin,* a newsletter containing articles and reviews on issues of sexism, racism, and other biases in children's literature. Issued eight times annually.

Great Books Foundation. 35 East Wacker Drive, Suite 2300, Chicago, Illinois 60601-2298. Phone: 312/332-5870. Fosters the education of children and adults through reading and group discussion of acclaimed literary works. Conducts special courses throughout the United States on interpretive discussion methods for teachers and volunteers. Programs include the Junior Great Books Read Aloud Program (for children in grades kindergarten through one) and Junior Great Books (for children in grades two through nine).

International Reading Association. 800 Barksdale Road, P.O. Box 8139, Newark, Delaware 19714-8139. Phone: 302/731-1600 or 1/800-336-READ. Fax: 302/731-1057. Works to improve reading instruction, increase literacy levels, and promote a lifetime reading habit. Offers information on a variety of reading-related topics including literature for children and adolescents, computer technology and reading, early childhood and literacy development, parents and reading, and reading disabilities.

Serves as a clearinghouse for the dissemination of reading research through conferences, journals, and other publications. Periodicals include the *Journal of Reading, Reading Research Quarterly,* and *Reading Teacher,* which offers information about how to teach reading at the preschool, primary, and elementary school levels. Other available publications include *Children's Choices,* an annotated list of books chosen annually by children; *Teachers' Choices,* an annotated list of books chosen by teachers; and *Young Adults' Choices,* an annotated list of books chosen by students in middle, junior, and high school. A variety of books and free brochures (see "Free and Inexpensive Resources" under "Reading and Writing" in chapter 14) are available as well, all of which are described in the annual publications catalog (contact the association for a free copy).

Parents' Choice Foundation. Box 185, Waban, Massachusetts 02168. Phone: 617/965-5913. A nonprofit service organization offering "mothers and fathers information to help their children keep learning when day care or school lets out." Publishes the quarterly journal, *Parents' Choice,* (see listing under "Book Reviews") and presents the annual Parents' Choice awards which honor the year's best in children's media. Also offers press information services; and contributes books to deprived children via their school or neighborhood libraries. Searches out children's books in Spanish for use in public libraries, compiles lists of educational videos, and runs public service announcements promoting children's literacy.

Book Clubs for Kids

The Beginning Readers' Program. Division of Grolier Enterprises, Inc., P.O. Box 1772, Danbury, Connecticut 06815. Offers Dr. Seuss (Theodor S. Geisel) classics such as *The Cat in the Hat, Hop on Pop,* and *Green Eggs and Ham,* as well as other fun-to-read books by Dr. Seuss "friends" (Stan and Jan Berenstain, P. D. Eastman, et al.). Members receive two books each month.

Books of My Very Own. Book-of-the-Month Club, Inc., Time-Life Building, 1271 Avenue of the Americas, New York, New York 10020. Phone: 212/522-4200 or 1/800-233-1066. Offers classics and new titles in both hardcover and softcover for four different age groups, including infants and toddlers, "read-to-me" preschoolers, "I-can-read" beginners and "on-my-own" readers (for children up to ten years old).

Children's Book-of-the-Month Club. Division of Book-of-the-Month Club, Inc., Time-Life Building, 1271 Avenue of the Americas, New York, New York 10020. Phone: 212/522-4200 or 1/800-233-1066. A book club for five different age groups (under two, two to four, four to six, six to nine, and nine to twelve) Each month, the *Children's Book of the Month Club Review* highlights one selection for each age group plus alternate selections.

Children's Choice Book Club. Newbridge Communications, Inc., 333 East Thirty-eighth Street, New York, New York 10016. Phone: 212/455-5000 or 1/800-347-7829. Provides children ages three to seven with storybook classics and outstanding new hardcover books from major publishers.

Doubleday Children's Book Club. 6550 East Thirtieth Street, P.O. Box 6347, Indianapolis, Indiana 46206-6347. Phone: 1/800-688-4442. Along with new fiction and nonfiction titles, this club offers children's classics, arts and crafts books, poetry anthologies, and child-care books for parents. When joining, new members request either the five-and-under or five-and-over age group. Members can choose their own books from the club magazine (mailed fourteen times annually) or receive featured selections automatically.

Ideas for Families

- Read books aloud to each other
- Talk about the books you read
- Keep books and magazines around the home
- Give books and magazine subscriptions as gifts
- Encourage a child to get a library card
- Make regular family visits to the library
- Help a child compile and illustrate a book
- Reread a book you loved as a child, then share it with a child
- Make the bedtime story a regular family event
- Visit a bookstore with a child
- Help a child set up a personal library
- Help children choose books *they* want to read
- Use television and radio to encourage reading
- Talk about local events reported by the media
- Encourage a child to write—stories, a diary, letters to friends
- Plan a summer reading program
- Set family reading goals
- Give favorite books to other children
- Pack books for family trips
- Read together about travel destinations
- Visit a literary landmark

Recommendations from a brochure produced for "1989—the Year of the Young Reader," a joint project of the Center for the Book and the Children's Literature Center in the Library of Congress (made possible by a contribution from Pizza Hut, Inc., sponsor of The Book It® National Reading Incentive Program in America's Schools).

Early Start Book Club. Newbridge Communications, Inc., 333 East Thirty-eighth Street, New York, New York 10016. Phone: 212/455-5000 or 1/800-347-7829. Offers classic storybooks and board books that appeal to children ages six months to three years.

Gateway to Imagination Book Club. From Discovery Toys. Chooses books from all over the world. The selections offered through this club are chosen from around the world and appeal to preschoolers (ages two to five). Each order comes with a newsletter covering current issues in child development. (Alternatively, parents can order the entire book series all at once.) To receive the name of your nearest Discovery Toys and Book Club educational consultant, call 1/800-426-4777.

Parents Magazine Read Aloud Book Club. Division of Gruner and Jahr USA Publishing, 685 Third Avenue, New York, New York 10017. Phone: 212/878-8700. Offers hardcover books from Parents Magazine Press, specifically written and designed to be read aloud to children ages two to seven. Members receive two books each month along with the *Clown-Arounds' Activity Page* of games and puzzles, and a newsletter for parents filled with tips and information.

Scholastic, Inc., Book Clubs. 730 Broadway, New York, New York 10003. Phone: 212/505-3215. Scholastic clubs include the Firefly Book Club (for preschoolers—infants through age five); the See-Saw Book Club (for grades kindergarten through one); the Lucky Book Club (for grades two through three); and the Arrow Book Club (for grades four through six). Selections include paperbound reprints and originals at remarkably low prices. Offered only through schools.

Sesame Street Book Club. Golden Press, 120 Brighton Road, Clifton, New Jersey 07012-9805. Phone: 1/800-537-1517. This club offers hardcover books featuring the characters from the highly acclaimed *Sesame Street* television series. A joint effort of Golden Press, the Children's Television Workshop, and the creators of *Sesame Street*. For children ages two and a half to five.

Troll Book Clubs. 100 Corporate Drive, Mahwah, New Jersey 07430. Phone: 212/492-9595 or 1/800-526-5289. Offers mostly hardcover books (many with accompanying cassettes) for children ages two to twelve. In addition to new books and children's classics, Troll offers the "Question and Answer Library" series (for children ages six to ten) and the "Talking Picture Dictionary" series (for ages three to eight).

The Trumpet Club. Subsidiary of Bantam Doubleday Dell, 666 Fifth Avenue, New York, New York 10103. Phone: 212/492-9595 or 1/800-826-0110. Offers quality titles from many publishers on a wide variety of subjects. The "Early Years" club offers books for children ages three to six; the "Primary Years" club includes books for children ages six to eight; and the "Middle Years" club provides books for children ages nine to twelve.

The Weekly Reader Children's Book Clubs. 4343 Equity Drive, Columbus, Ohio 43216. Phone: 614/771-0006. Offers hardcover selections from various children's book publishers for three different age groups (four to seven; seven to nine; and nine to eleven). The "I Can Read Book Club," for children ages four to eight, features hardcover selections from Harper and Row's "I Can Read" series.

CALDECOTT MEDAL WINNERS

Each year, the Association for Library Service to Children presents the Caldecott Medal to the artist of an outstanding American picture book for children. The medal is named in honor of the nineteenth-century English illustrator Randolph Caldecott, whose work represents the "joyousness and beauty of picture books."

1994

Grandfather's Journey. By Allen Say.

Honor Books
Peppe the Lamplighter. By Elisa Bartone. Illustrated by Ted Lewin.
In the Small, Small Pond. By Denise Fleming.
Owen. By Kevin Henkes. Edited by Susan Hirschman.
Raven: A Trickster Tale from the Pacific Northwest. By Gerald McDermott.
Yo! Yes? By Chris Raschka. Edited by Richard Jackson.

1993

Mirette on the High Wire. By Emily Arnold McCully.

Honor Books
The Stinky Cheese Man. By Jon Scieszka. Illustrated by Lane Smith.
Working Cotton. By Sherley Anne Williams. Illustrated by Carole Byard.
Seven Blind Mice. By Ed Young.

1992

Tuesday. By David Wiesner.

Honor Book
Tar Beach. By Faith Ringgold.

1991

Black and White. By David Macaulay.

Honor Books
Puss in Boots. By Fred Marcellino.
"More, More, More," Said the Baby. By Vera B. Williams.

1990

Lon Po Po: A Red Riding Hood Story from China. Adapted and illustrated by Ed Young.

Honor Books
Color Zoo. By Lois Ehlert.
Hershel and the Hanukkah Goblins. By Eric Kimmel. Illustrated by Trina Schart Hyman.
Bill Peet: An Autobiography. By Bill Peet.
The Talking Eggs. By Robert D. San Souci. Illustrated by Jerry Pinkney.

1989

Song and Dance Man. By Karen Ackerman. Illustrated by Stephen Gammell.

Honor Books
Mirandy and Brother Wind. By Patricia C. McKissack. Illustrated by Jerry Pinkney.
Goldilocks and the Three Bears. Adapted and illustrated by James Marshall.
The Boy of the Three-Year Nap. By Diane Snyder. Illustrated by Allen Say.
Free Fall. By David Wiesner.

1988

Owl Moon. By Jane Yolen. Illustrated by John Schoenherr.

Honor Book
Mufaro's Beautiful Daughters: An African Tale. By John Steptoe.

1987

Hey, Al. By Arthur Yorinks. Illustrated by Richard Egielski.

Honor Books
The Village of Round and Square Houses. By Ann Grifalconi.
Alphabatics. By Suse MacDonald.
Rumpelstiltskin. By Paul O. Zelinsky.

1986

The Polar Express. By Chris Van Allsburg.

Honor Books
The Relatives Came. By Cynthia Rylant. Illustrated by Stephen Gammell.
King Bidgood's in the Bathtub. By Audry Wood. Illustrated by Don Wood.

1985

St. George and the Dragon. Retold by Margaret Hodges. Illustrated by Trina Schart Hyman.

Honor Books
Hansel and Gretel. By Rika Lesser. Illustrated by Paul O. Zelinsky.
The Story of Jumping Mouse. By John Steptoe.
Have You Seen My Duckling? By Nancy Tafuri.

1984

The Glorious Flight: Across the Channel with Louis Blériot. By Alice and Martin Provensen.

Honor Books
Ten, Nine, Eight. By Molly Bang.
Little Red Riding Hood. By Trina Schart Hyman.

1983

Shadow. By Blaise Cendrars. Translated and illustrated by Marcia Brown.

Honor Books
When I Was Young in the Mountains. By Cynthia Rylant. Illustrated by Diane Goode.
A Chair for My Mother. By Vera B. Williams.

1982

Jumanji. By Chris Van Allsburg.

Honor Books
Where the Buffaloes Began. By Olaf Baker. Illustrated by Stephen Gammel.

On Market Street. By Arnold Lobel. Illustrated by Anita Lobel.
Outside Over There. By Maurice Sendak.
A Visit to William Blake's Inn: Poems for Innocent and Experienced Travelers. By Nancy Willard. Illustrated by Alice and Martin Provensen.

1981

Fables. By Arnold Lobel.

Honor Books
The Grey Lady and the Strawberry Snatcher. By Molly Bang.
Truck. By Donald Crews.
Mice Twice. By Joseph Low.
The Bremen-Town Musicians. By Ilse Plume.

1980

Ox-Cart Man. By Donald Hall. Pictures by Barbara Cooney.

Honor Books
Ben's Trumpet. By Rachel Isadora.
The Treasure. By Uri Shulevitz.
The Garden of Abdul Gasazi. By Chris Van Allsburg.

1979

The Girl Who Loved Wild Horses. By Paul Goble.

Honor Books
The Way to Start a Day. By Byrd Baylor. Illustrated by Peter Parnall.
Freight Train. By Donald Crews.

1978

Noah's Ark. By Peter Spier.

Honor Books
Castle. By David Macaulay.
It Could Always Be Worse. By Margot Zemach.

1977

Ashanti to Zulu: African Traditions. By Margaret Musgrove. Pictures by Leo and Diane Dillon.

Honor Books
Hawk, I'm Your Brother. By Byrd Baylor. Illustrated by Peter Parnall.
Fish for Supper. By M. B. Goffstein.
The Contest. By Nonny Hogrogian.
The Golem. By Beverly Brodsky McDermott.
The Amazing Bone. By William Steig.

1976

Why Mosquitoes Buzz in People's Ears. Retold by Verna Aardema. Pictures by Leo and Diane Dillon.

Honor Books
The Desert Is Theirs. By Byrd Baylor. Illustrated by Peter Parnall.
Strega Nona. Retold and illustrated by Tomie de Paola.

1975

Arrow to the Sun. By Gerald McDermott.

Honor Book
Jambo Means Hello: Swahili Alphabet Book. By Muriel Feelings. Illustrated by Tom Feelings.

1974

Duffy and the Devil. Retold by Harve Zemach. Pictures by Margot Zemach.

Honor Books
Three Jovial Huntsmen. By Susan Jeffers.
Cathedral. By David Macaulay.

1973

The Funny Little Woman. Retold by Arlene Mosel. Illustrated by Blair Lent.

Honor Books
Hosie's Alphabet. By Hosea Baskin, Tobias Baskin, and Lisa Baskin. Illustrated by Leonard Baskin.
When Clay Sings. By Byrd Baylor. Illustrated by Tom Bahti.
Snow-White and the Seven Dwarfs. By the Brothers Grimm. Translated by Randall Jarrell. Illustrated by Nancy Ekholm Burkert.
Anansi the Spider. By Gerald McDermott.

1972

One Fine Day. By Nonny Hogrogian.

Honor Books
If All the Seas Were One Sea. By Janina Domanska.
Moja Means One: Swahili Counting Book. By Muriel Feelings. Illustrated by Tom Feelings.
Hildilid's Night. By Cheli Duran Ryan. Illustrated by Arnold Lobel.

1971

A Story A Story. Retold and illustrated by Gail E. Haley.

Honor Books
Frog and Toad Are Friends. By Arnold Lobel.
In the Night Kitchen. By Maurice Sendak.
The Angry Moon. Retold by William Sleator. Illustrated by Blair Lent.

1970

Sylvester and the Magic Pebble. By William Steig.

Honor Books
Goggles. By Ezra Jack Keats.
Alexander and the Wind-up Mouse. By Leo Lionni.

Pop Corn and Ma Goodness. By Edna
   Mitchell Preston. Illustrated by
   Robert Andrew Parker.
The Friend, Obadiah. By Brinton
   Turkle.
The Judge. By Harve Zemach.
   Illustrated by Margot Zemack.

1969

**The Fool of the World and the
Flying Ship.** Retold by Arthur
   Ransome. Illustrated by Uri
   Shulevitz.

Honor Book
*Why the Sun and the Moon Live in the
Sky.* By Elphinstone Dayrell.
   Illustrated by Blair Lent.

1968

Drummer Hoff. Adapted by
   Barbara Emberley. Illustrated by
   Ed Emberley.

Honor Books
Frederick. By Leo Lionni.
Seashore Story. By Taro Yaskima.
The Emperor and the Kite. By Jane
   Yolen. Illustrated by Ed Young.

1967

Sam, Bangs and Moonshine. By
   Evaline Ness.

Honor Book
One Wide River to Cross. By Barbara
   Emberley. Illustrated by Ed
   Emberley.

1966

Always Room for One More. By
   Sorche Nic Leodhas. Illustrated
   by Nonny Hogrogian.

Honor Books
Just Me. By Marie Hall Ets.
Tom Tit Tot. Edited by Joseph Jacobs.
   Illustrated by Evaline Ness.
Hide and Seek Fog. By Alvin Tresselt.
   Illustrated by Roger Duvoisin.

1965

May I Bring a Friend? By Beatrice
   Schenk de Regniers. Illustrated
   by Beni Montresor.

Honor Books
A Pocketful of Cricket. By Rebecca
   Caudill. Illustrated by Evaline
   Ness.
The Wave. By Margaret Hodges.
   Illustrated by Blair Lent.
Rain Makes Applesauce. By Julian
   Scheer. Illustrated by Marvin
   Bileck.

1964

Where the Wild Things Are. By
   Maurice Sendak.

Honor Books
All in the Morning Early. By Sorche
   Nic Leodhas. Illustrated by
   Evaline Ness.
Swimmy. By Leo Lionni.
Mother Goose and Nursery Rhymes.
   By Philip Reed.

1963

The Snowy Day. By Ezra Jack
   Keats.

Honor Books
The Sun Is a Golden Earring. By
   Natalia Belting. Illustrated by
   Bernarda Bryson.
Mr. Rabbit and the Lovely Present. By
   Charlotte Zolotow. Illustrated by
   Maurice Sendak.

1962

Once A Mouse. By Marcia Brown.

Honor Books
The Day We Saw the Sun Come Up.
   By Alice Goudey. Illustrated by
   Adrienne Adams.
Little Bear's Visit. By Else Minarik.
   Illustrated by Maurice Sendak.
The Fox Went Out on a Chilly Night.
   By Peter Spier.

1961

Baboushka and the Three Kings.
By Ruth Robbins. Illustrated by
Nicolas Sidjakov.

Honor Book
Inch by Inch. By Leo Lionni.

1960

Nine Days to Christmas. By Marie
Hall Ets and Aurora Labastida.

Honor Books
Houses from the Sea. By Alice E.
Goudey. Illustrated by Adrienne
Adams.
The Moon Jumpers. By Janice May
Udry. Illustrated by Maurice
Sendak.

1959

Chanticleer and the Fox. Edited
and illustrated by Barbara
Cooney.

Honor Books
The House that Jack Built. By
Antonio Frasconi.
What Do You Say, Dear? By Sesyle
Joslin. Illustrated by Maurice
Sendak.
Umbrella. By Taro Yashima.

1958

Time of Wonder. By Robert
McCloskey.

Honor Books
Fly High, Fly Low. By Don Freeman.
Anatole and the Cat. By Eve Titus.
Illustrated by Paul Galdone.

1957

A Tree Is Nice. By Janice Udry.
Illustrated by Marc Simont.

Honor Books
Lion. By William Pène du Bois.

Gillespie and the Guards. By
Benjamin Elkin. Illustrated by
James Daugherty.
Mr. Penny's Race Horse. By Marie
Hall Ets.
Anatole. By Eve Titus. Illustrated by
Paul Galdone.
1 Is One. By Tasha Tudor.

1956

Frog Went A-Courtin'. Retold by
John Langstaff. Illustrated by
Feodor Rojankovsky.

Honor Books
Play with Me. By Marie Hall Ets.
Crow Boy. By Taro Yashima.

1955

Cinderella. Illustrated and retold
from Charles Perrault by Marcia
Brown.

Honor Books
*Book of Nursery and Mother Goose
Rhymes.* Compiled and
illustrated by Marguerite de
Angeli.
Wheel on the Chimney. By Margaret
Wise Brown. Illustrated by Tibor
Gergely.

1954

Madeline's Rescue. By Ludwig
Bemelmans.

Honor Books
Green Eyes. By Abe Birnbaum.
The Steadfast Tin Soldier. Translated
by M. R. James. Adapted from
Hans Christian Andersen.
Illustrated by Marcia Brown.
A Very Special House. By Ruth
Krauss. Illustrated by Maurice
Sendak.
Journey Cake, Ho! By Ruth Sawyer.
Illustrated by Robert McCloskey.
When Will the World Be Mine? By
Mariam Schlein. Illustrated by
Jean Charlot.

1953

The Biggest Bear. By Lynd Ward.

Honor Books
Puss in Boots. Illustrated and translated from Charles Perrault by Marcia Brown.
Ape in a Cape. By Fritz Eichenberg.
Five Little Monkeys. By Juliet Kepes.
One Morning in Maine. By Robert McCloskey.
The Storm Book. By Charlotte Zolotow. Illustrated by Margaret Bloy Graham.

1952

Finders Keepers. By Will Lipkind. Illustrated by Nicolas Mordvinoff.

Honor Books
Bear Party. By William Pène du Bois.
Skipper John's Cook. By Marcia Brown.
Mr. T. W. Anthony Woo. By Marie Hall Ets.
Feather Mountain. By Elizabeth Olds.
All Falling Down. By Gene Zion. Illustrated by Margaret Bloy Graham.

1951

The Egg Tree. By Katherine Milhous.

Honor Books
Dick Whittington and His Cat. Retold and illustrated by Marcia Brown.
If I Ran the Zoo. By Theodor S. Geisel (Dr. Seuss).
The Two Reds. By William Lipkind. Illustrated by Nicolas Mordvinoff.
The Most Wonderful Doll in the World. By Phyllis McGinley. Illustrated by Helen Stone.
T-Bone the Baby-Sitter. By Clare Turlay Newberry.

1950

Song of the Swallows. By Leo Politi.

Honor Books
Henry-Fisherman. By Marcia Brown.
The Wild Birthday Cake. By Lavinia R. Davis. Illustrated by Hildegard Woodward.
Bartholomew and the Oobleck. By Theodor S. Geisel (Dr. Seuss).
America's Ethan Allen. By Stewart Holbrook. Illustrated by Lynd Ward.
Happy Day. By Ruth Krauss. Illustrated by Marc Simont.

1949

The Big Snow. By Berta Hader and Elmer Hader

Honor Books
Blueberries for Sal. By Robert McCloskey.
All Around the Town. By Phyllis McGinley. Illustrated by Helen Stone.
Juanita. By Leo Politi.
Fish in the Air. By Kurt Wiese.

1948

White Snow, Bright Snow. By Alvin Tresselt. Illustrated by Roger Duvoisin.

Honor Books
Stone Soup. Told and illustrated by Marcia Brown.
Roger and the Fox. By Lavinia R. Davis. Illustrated by Hildegard Woodward.
McElligot's Pool. By Theodor S. Geisel (Dr. Seuss).
Song of Robin Hood. Edited by Anne Malcolmson. Illustrated by Virginia Lee Burton.
Bambino the Clown. By George Schreiber.

1947

The Little Island. By Golden MacDonald. Illustrated by Leonard Weisgard.

Honor Books
Boats on the River. By Marjorie Flack. Illustrated by Jay Hyde Barnum.
Timothy Turtle. By Al Graham. Illustrated by Tony Palazzo.
Pedro, Angel of Olvera Street. By Leo Politi.
Rain Drop Splash. By Alvin R. Tresselt. Illustrated by Leonard Weisgard.
Sing in Praise. By Opal Wheeler. Illustrated by Marjorie Torrey.

1946

The Rooster Crows. By Maude Petersham and Miska Petersham.

Honor Books
Little Lost Lamb. By Margaret Wise Brown. Illustrated by Leonard Weisgard.
My Mother Is the Most Beautiful Woman in the World. By Becky Reyher. Illustrated by Ruth C. Gannett.
Sing Mother Goose. Music by Opal Wheeler. Illustrated by Marjorie Torrey.
You Can Write Chinese. By Kurt Wiese.

1945

Prayer for a Child. By Rachel Field. Illustrated by Elizabeth Orton Jones.

Honor Books
Yonie Wondernose. By Marguerite de Angeli.
In the Forest. By Marie Hall Ets.
The Christmas Anna Angel. By Ruth Sawyer. Illustrated by Kate Seredy.
Mother Goose. Compiled and illustrated by Tasha Tudor.

1944

Many Moons. By James Thurber. Illustrated by Louis Slobodkin.

Honor Books
A Child's Good Night Book. By Margaret Wise Brown. Illustrated by Jean Charlot.
Good-Luck Horse. By Chih-Yi Chan. Illustrated by Plato Chan.
Mighty Hunter. By Berta Hader and Elmer Hader.
Small Rain. Text arranged from the Bible by Jessie Orton Jones. Illustrated by Elizabeth Orton Jones.
Pierre Pidgeon. By Lee Kingman. Illustrated by Arnold Edwin Bare.

1943

The Little House. By Virginia Lee Burton.

Honor Books
Dash and Dart. By Mary Buff and Conrad Buff.
Marshmallow. By Clare Turlay Newberry.

1942

Make Way for Ducklings. By Robert McCloskey.

Honor Books
In My Mother's House. By Ann Nolan Clark. Illustrated by Velino Herrera.
Nothing at All. By Wanda Gág.
Paddle-to-the-Sea. By Holling Clancy Holling.
An American ABC. By Maud Petersham and Miska Petersham.

1941

They Were Strong and Good. By Robert Lawson.

Honor Book
April's Kittens. By Clare Turlay Newberry.

1940

Abraham Lincoln. By Ingri d'Aulaire and Edgar Parin d'Aulaire.

Honor Books
Madeline. By Ludwig Bemelmans.
The Ageless Story. By Lauren Ford.
Cock-a-Doodle-Doo. By Berta Hader and Elmer Hader.

1939

Mei Li. By Thomas Handforth.

Honor Books
The Forest Pool. By Laura Adams Armer.
Andy and the Lion. By James Daugherty.

Snow White and the Seven Dwarfs. Translated and illustrated by Wanda Gág.
Wee Gillis. By Munro Leaf. Illustrated by Robert Lawson.
Barkis. By Clare Turlay Newberry.

1938

Animals of the Bible. Text selected by Helen Dean Fish. Illustrated by Dorothy P. Lathrop.

Honor Books
Seven Simeons. By Boris Artzybasheff.
Four and Twenty Blackbirds. Compiled by Helen Dean Fish. Illustrated by Robert Lawson.

NEWBERY MEDAL WINNERS

Each year, the Association for Library Service to Children presents the Newbery Medal to "the author of the most distinguished contribution to American literature for children." The medal is named after John Newbery, the eighteenth-century British publisher and bookseller.

1994

The Giver. By Lois Lowry.

Honor Books
Crazy Lady. By Jane Leslie Conly.
Eleanor Roosevelt: A Life of Discovery. By Russell Freedman.
Dragon's Gate. By Laurence Yep.

1993

Missing May. By Cynthia Rylant.

Honor Books
What Hearts. By Bruce Brooks.
The Dark-Thirty: Southern Tales of the Supernatural. By Patricia C. McKissack.
Somewhere in the Darkness. By Walter Dean Myers.

1992

Shiloh. By Phyllis Reynolds Naylor.

Honor Books
Nothing but the Truth. By Avi.
The Wright Brothers: How They Invented the Airplane. By Russell Freedman.

1991

Maniac Magee. By Jerry Spinelli.

Honor Book
The True Confessions of Charlotte Doyle. By Avi.

1990

Number the Stars. By Lois Lowry.

Honor Books
Afternoon of the Elves. By Janet Taylor Lisle.

The Winter Room. By Gary Paulsen.
Shabanu, Daughter of the Wind. By Suzanne Fisher Staples.

1989

Joyful Noise: Poems for Two Voices. By Paul Fleischman.

Honor Books
In the Beginning: Creation Stories from Around the World. By Virginia Hamilton.
Scorpions. By Walter Dean Myers.

1988

Lincoln: A Photobiography. By Russell Freedman.

Honor Books
After the Rain. By Norma Fox Mazer.
Hatchet. By Gary Paulsen.

1987

The Whipping Boy. By Sid Fleischman.

Honor Books
On My Honor. By Marion Bauer.
Volcano. By Patricia Lauber.
A Fine White Dust. By Cynthia Rylant.

1986

Sarah, Plain and Tall. By Patricia MacLachlan.

Honor Books
Commodore Perry in the Land of the Shogun. By Rhoda Blumberg.
Dogsong. By Gary Paulson.

1985

The Hero and the Crown. By Robin McKinley.

Honor Books
The Moves Make the Man. By Bruce Brooks.
One-Eyed Cat. By Paula Fox.
Like Jake and Me. By Mavis Jukes

1984

Dear Mr. Henshaw. By Beverly Cleary.

Honor Books
The Wish-Giver. By Bill Brittain.
Sugaring Time. By Kathryn Lasky.
The Sign of the Beaver. By Elizabeth George Speare.
A Solitary Blue. By Cynthia Voigt.

1983

Dicey's Song. By Cynthia Voigt.

Honor Books
Graven Images. By Paul Fleischman.
Homesick: My Own Story. By Jean Fritz.
Sweet Whispers, Brother Rush. By Virginia Hamilton.
The Blue Sword. By Robin McKinley.
Doctor De Soto. By William Steig.

1982

A Visit to William Blake's Inn: Poems for Innocent and Experienced Travelers. By Nancy Willard.

Honor Books
Ramona Quimby, Age 8. By Beverly Cleary.
Upon the Head of the Goat: A Childhood in Hungary, 1939-1944. By Aranka Siegal.

1981

Jacob Have I Loved. By Katherine Paterson.

Honor Books
The Fledgling. By Jane Langton.
A Ring of Endless Light. By Madeleine L'Engle.

1980

A Gathering of Days: A New England Girl's Journal, 1830-32. By Joan W. Blos.

Honor Books
The Road from Home: The Story of an American Girl. By David Kherdian.

1979

The Westing Game. By Ellen Raskin.

Honor Book
The Great Gilly Hopkins. By Katherine Paterson.

1978

Bridge to Terabithia. By Katherine Paterson.

Honor Books
Ramona and Her Father. By Beverly Cleary.
Anpao: An American Indian Odyssey. By Jamake Highwater.

1977

Roll of Thunder, Hear My Cry. By Mildred Taylor.

Honor Books
A String in the Harp. By Nancy Bond.
Abel's Island. By William Steig.

1976

The Grey King. By Susan Cooper.

Honor Books
The Hundred Penny Box. By Sharon Mathis.
Dragonwings. By Laurence Yep.

1975

M. C. Higgins, the Great. By Virginia Hamilton.

Honor Books
My Brother Sam Is Dead. By James Collier and Christopher Collier.
Philip Hall Likes Me, I Reckon Maybe. By Bette Greene.
The Perilous Gard. By Elizabeth Pope.

Figgs and Phantoms. By Ellen Raskin.

1974

The Slave Dancer. By Paula Fox.

Honor Book
The Dark Is Rising. By Susan Cooper.

1973

Julie of the Wolves. By Jean Craighead George.

Honor Books
Frog and Toad Together. By Arnold Lobel.
The Upstairs Room. By Johanna Reiss.
The Witches of Worm. By Zilpha Keatley Snyder.

1972

Mrs. Frisby and the Rats of NIMH. By Robert C. O'Brien.

Honor Books
Incident at Hawk's Hill. By Allan W. Eckert.
The Planet of Junior Brown. By Virginia Hamilton.
The Tombs of Atuan. By Ursula K. LeGuin.
Annie and the Old One. By Miska Miles.
The Headless Cupid. By Zilpha Keatley Snyder.

1971

Summer of the Swans. By Betsy C. Byars.

Honor Books
Kneeknock Rise. By Natalie Babbitt.
Enchantress from the Stars. By Sylvia Louise Engdahl.
Sing Down the Moon. By Scott O'Dell.

1970

Sounder. By William Armstrong.

Honor Books
Our Eddie. By Sulamith Ish-Kishor.

The Many Ways of Seeing: An Introduction to the Pleasures of Art. By Janet Gaylord Moore.
Journey Outside. By Mary Q. Steele.

1969

The High King. By Lloyd Alexander.

Honor Books
To Be a Slave. By Julius Lester.
When Shlemiel Went to Warsaw and Other Stories. By Isaac Bashevis Singer.

1968

From the Mixed-Up Files of Mrs. Basil E. Frankweiler. By E. L. Konigsburg.

Honor Books
Jennifer, Hecate, Macbeth, William McKinley, and Me, Elizabeth. By E. L. Konigsburg.
The Black Pearl. By Scott O'Dell.
The Fearsome Inn. By Isaac Bashevis Singer.
The Egypt Game. By Zilpha Keatley Snyder.

1967

Up a Road Slowly. By Irene Hunt.

Honor Books
The King's Fifth. By Scott O'Dell.
Zlateh the Goat and Other Stories. By Isaac Bashevis Singer.
The Jazz Man. By Mary Hays Weik.

1966

I, Juan De Pareja. By Elizabeth Borton de Trevino.

Honor Books
The Black Cauldron. By Lloyd Alexander.
The Animal Family. By Randall Jarrell.
The Noonday Friends. By Mary Stolz.

1965

Shadow of a Bull. By Maia Wojciechowska.

Honor Book
Across Five Aprils. By Irene Hunt.

1964

It's Like This, Cat. By Emily Neville.

Honor Books
Rascal. By Sterling North.
The Loner. By Ester Wier.

1963

A Wrinkle in Time. By Madeleine L'Engle.

Honor Books
Men of Athens. By Olivia Coolidge.
Thistle and Thyme. By Sorche Nic Leodhas.

1962

The Bronze Bow. By Elizabeth George Speare.

Honor Books
The Golden Goblet. By Eloise J. McGraw.
Belling the Tiger. By Mary Stolz.
Frontier Living. By Edwin Tunis.

1961

Island of the Blue Dolphins. By Scott O'Dell.

Honor Books
America Moves Forward. By Gerald Johnson.
Old Ramon. By Jack Schaefer.
The Cricket in Times Square. By George Selden.

1960

Onion John. By Joseph Krumgold.

Honor Books
My Side of the Mountain. By Jean George.

America Is Born. By Gerald Johnson.
The Gammage Cup. By Carol Kendall.

1959

The Witch of Blackbird Pond. By Elizabeth George Speare.

Honor Books
The Family under the Bridge. By Natalie S. Carlson.
Along Came a Dog. By Meindert DeJong.
Chucaro. By Francis Kalnay.
The Perilous Road. By William O. Steele.

1958

Rifles for Watie. By Harold Keith.

Honor Books
Gone-away Lake. By Elizabeth Enright.
Tom Paine, Freedom's Apostle. By Leo Gurko.
The Great Wheel. By Robert Lawson.
The Horsecatcher. By Mari Sandoz.

1957

Miracles on Maple Hill. By Virginia Sorensen.

Honor Books
The Black Fox of Lorne. By Marguerite de Angeli.
The House of Sixty Fathers. By Meindert DeJong.
Old Yeller. By Fred Gipson.
Mr. Justice Holmes. By Clara I. Judson.
The Corn Grows Ripe. By Dorothy Rhoads.

1956

Carry on, Mr. Bowditch. By Jean Lee Latham.

Honor Books
The Secret River. By Marjorie Kinnan.
The Golden Name Day. By Jennie D. Lindquist.

Men, Microscopes and Living Things. By Katherine B. Shippen.

1955

The Wheel of the School. By Meindert DeJong.

Honor Books
The Courage of Sarah Noble. By Alice Dalgliesh.
Banner in the Sky. By James Ramsey Ullman.

1954

And Now Miguel. By Joseph Krumgold.

Honor Books
All Alone. By Clarie Huchet Bishop.
Magic Maize. By Mary Buff.
Shadrach. By Meindert DeJong.
Hurry Home, Candy. By Meindert DeJong.
Theodore Roosevelt, Fighting Patriot. By Clara I. Judson.

1953

Secret of the Andes. By Ann Nolan Clark.

Honor Books
The Bears on Hemlock Mountain. By Alice Dalgliesh.
Birthdays of Freedom. By Genevieve Foster.
Moccasin Trail. By Eloise J. McGraw.
Red Sails for Capri. By Ann Weil.
Charlotte's Web. By E. B. White.

1952

Ginger Pye. By Eleanor Estes.

Honor Books
Americans Before Columbus. By Elizabeth Chesley Baity.
The Apple and the Arrow. By Mary Buff.
Minn of the Mississippi. By Holling Clancy Holling.

The Defender. By Nicholas
    Kalashnikoff.
The Light at Tern Rock. By Julia L.
    Sauer.

1951

Amos Fortune, Free Man. By
    Elizabeth Yates.

Honor Books
Gandhi, Fighter without a Sword. By
    Jeanette Eaton.
Better Known as Johnny Appleseed.
    By Mabel Leigh Hunt.
*Abraham Lincoln, Friend of the
    People.* By Clara I. Judson.
The Story of Appleby Capple. By
    Anne Parrish.

1950

The Door in the Wall. By
    Marguerite de Angeli.

Honor Books
Tree of Freedom. By Rebecca Caudill.
Blue Cat of Castle Town. By
    Catherine Coblentz.
George Washington. By Genevieve
    Foster.
Song of the Pines. By Walter
    Havighurst and Marion
    Havighurst.
Kildee House. By Rutherford
    Montgomery.

1949

King of the Wind. By Marguerite
    Henry.

Honor Books
Story of the Negro. By Arna Bontemps.
My Father's Dragon. By Ruth S.
    Gannett.
Seabird. By Holling Clancy Holling.
Daughter of the Mountains. By
    Louise Rankin.

1948

The Twenty-One Balloons. By
    William Pène du Bois.

Honor Books
*The Quaint and Curious Quest of
    Johnny Longfoot.* By Catherine
    Besterman.
Pancakes-Paris. By Claire Hucher
    Bishop.
The Cow-Tail Switch. By Harold
    Courlander and George Herzog.
Misty of Chincoteague. By
    Marguerite Henry.
Li Lun, Lad of Courage. By Carolyn
    Treffinger.

1947

Miss Hickory. By Carolyn Bailey.

Honor Books
The Wonderful Year. By Nancy
    Barnes.
Big Tree. By Mary Buff and Conrad
    Buff.
The Avion My Uncle Flew. By Cyrus
    Fisher.
The Hidden Treasure of Glaston. By
    Eleanore M. Jewett.
The Heavenly Tenants. By William
    Maxwell.

1946

Strawberry Girl. By Lois Lenski.

Honor Books
Justin Morgan Had a Horse. By
    Marguerite Henry.
The Moved-Outers. By Florence
    Crannel Means.
New Found World. By Katherine B.
    Shippen.
Bhimsa, the Dancing Bear. By
    Christine Weston.

1945

Rabbit Hill. By Robert Lawson.

Honor Books
The Silver Pencil. By Alice Dalgliesh.
Lone Journey. By Jeanette Eaton.
The Hundred Dresses. By Eleanor
    Estes.

Abraham Lincoln's World. By Genevieve Foster.

1944

Johnny Tremain. By Esther Forbes.

Honor Books
Rufus M. By Eleanor Estes.
Fog Magic. By Julia L. Sauer.
These Happy Golden Years. By Laura Ingalls Wilder.
Mountain Born. By Elizabeth Yates.

1943

Adam of the Road. By Elizabeth Gray.

Honor Books
The Middle Moffat. By Eleanor Estes.
"Have You Seen Tom Thumb?" By Mabel Leigh Hunt.

1942

The Matchlock Gun. By Walter Edmonds.

Honor Books
George Washington's World. By G. Foster.
Indian Captive. By Lois Lenski.
Down Ryton Water. By E. R. Gaggin.
Little Town on the Prairie. By Laura Ingalls Wilder.

1941

Call It Courage. By Armstrong Sperry.

Honor Books
Young Mac of Fort Vancouver. By Mary Jane Carr.
Blue Willow. By Doris Gates.
Nansen. By Anne Gertrude Hall.
The Long Winter. By Laura Ingalls Wilder.

1940

Daniel Boone. By James Daugherty.

Honor Books
Boy with a Pack. By Stephen W. Meader.

Runner of the Mountain Tops. By Mabel L. Robinson.
The Winging Tree. By Kate Seredy.
By the Shores of Silver Lake. By Laura Ingalls Wilder.

1939

Thimble Summer. By Elizabeth Enright.

Honor Books
Nino. By Valenti Angelo.
Mr. Popper's Penguins. By Richard and Florence Atwater.
"Hello, the Boat!" By Phyllis Crawford.
Leader by Destiny. By Jeanette Eaton.
Penn. By Elizabeth Janet Gray.

1938

The White Stag. By Kate Seredy.

Honor Books
Pecos Bill. By James Cloyd Bowman.
Bright Island. By Mabel L. Robinson.
On the Banks of Plum Creek. By Laura Ingalls Wilder.

1937

Roller Skates. By Ruth Sawyer.

Honor Books
The Golden Basket. By Ludwig Bemelmans.
Winterbound. By Margery Bianco.
The Codfish Musket. By Agnes D. Hewes.
Whistler's Van. By Idwal Jones.
Phoebe Fairchild: Her Book. By Lois Lenski.
Audubon. By Constance Rourke.

1936

Caddie Woodlawn. By Carol Brink.

Honor Books
Young Walter Scott. By Elizabeth Janet Gray.
The Good Master. By Kate Seredy.
All Sail Set. By Armstrong Sperry.
Honk the Moose. By Phil Stong.

1935

Dobry. By Monica Shannon.

Honor Books
Davy Crockett. By Constance Rourke.
The Pageant of Chinese History. By Elizabeth Seeger.
A Day on Skates. By Hilda Van Stockum.

1934

Invincible Louisa. By Cornelia Meigs.

Honor Books
Winged Girl of Knossos. By Erick Berry.
ABC Bunny. By Wanda Gág.
Apprentices of Florence. By Anne Kyle.
New Land. By Sarah L. Schmidt.
Swords of Steel. By Elsie Singmaster.
Forgotten Daughter. By Caroline Dale Snedeker.

1933

Young Fu of the Upper Yangtze. By Elizabeth Lewis.

Honor Books
Children of the Soil. By Nora Burglon.
Swift Rivers. By Cornelia Meigs.
The Railroad to Freedom. By Hildegarde Swift.

1932

Waterless Mountain. By Laura Armer.

Honor Books
Jane's Island. By Marjorie Hill Alee.
Truce of the Wolf. By Mary Gould Davis.
Calico Bush. By Rachel Field.
The Fairy Circus. By Dorothy Lathrop.
Out of the Flame. By Eloise Lounsbery.
Boy of the South Seas. By Eunice Tietjens.

1931

The Cat Who Went to Heaven. By Elizabeth Coatsworth.

Honor Books
Mountains Are Free. By Julia Davis Adams.
Meggy McIntosh. By Elizabeth Janet Gray.
Spice and the Devil's Cave. By Agnes D. Hewes.
Queer Person. By Ralph Hubbard.
The Dark Star of Itza. By Alida Malkus.
Floating Island. By Anne Parrish.

1930

Hitty, Her First Hundred Years. By Rachel Field.

Honor Books
A Daughter of the Seine. By Jeanette Eaton.
The Jumping-Off Place. By Marian Hurd McNeely.
Pran of Albania. By Elizabeth C. Miller.

1929

The Trumpeter of Krakow. By Eric P. Kelly.

Honor Books
The Pigtail of Ah Lee Ben Loo. By John Bennett.
Millions of Cats. By Wanda Gág.
The Boy Who Was. By Grace T. Hallock.
Clearing Weather. By Cornelia Meigs.
The Runaway Papoose. By Grace P. Moon.
Tod of the Fens. By Eleanor Whitney.

1928

Gay Neck, the Story of a Pigeon. By Dhan Mukerji.

Honor Books
Downright Dencey. By Caroline Dale Snedeker.
The Wonder-Smith and His Son. By Ella Young.

1927

Smoky, the Cowhorse. By Will James.

1926

Shen of the Sea. By Arthur Chrisman.

Honor Book
The Voyagers. By Padraic Colum.

1925

Tales from Silver Lands. By
   Charles Finger.

Honor Books
Nicholas. By Anne Carroll Moore.
Dream Coach. By Anne and Dillwyn
   Parrish.

1924

The Dark Frigate. By Charles
   Hawes.

1923

The Voyages of Doctor Dolittle.
   By Hugh Lofting.

1922

The Story of Mankind. By Henrik
   Van Loon.

Honor Books
The Old Tobacco Shop. By William
   Bowen.
The Golden Fleece. By Padraic Colum.
The Great Quest. By Charles
   Boardman Hawes.
Cedric the Forester. By Bernard G.
   Marshall.
Windy Hill. By Cornelia Meigs.

OTHER AWARDS

Laura Ingalls Wilder Award

This award is presented every three
years to an author or illustrator
whose books (published in the
United States) have made a significant and lasting contribution to literature for children. Established in
1954, the award is given by the Association for Library Service to Children. Following is a list of the
award-winners.

1954	Laura Ingalls Wilder
1960	Clara Ingram Judson
1965	Ruth Sawyer
1970	E. B. White
1975	Beverly Cleary
1980	Theodor S. Geisel (Dr. Seuss)
1983	Maurice Sendak
1986	Jean Fritz
1989	Elizabeth George Speare
1992	Marcia Brown

The Hans Christian Andersen Prize

An international children's book
award established in 1956 by the International Board on Books for
Young People. At first, only outstanding authors were awarded; later (in
1966), the award was expanded to
honor outstanding illustrators as
well. Winners are selected by an international committee composed of
judges from different countries. Recommendations come from the board,
as well as library associations. The
following is a list of authors and illustrators (from 1966 on) who have
been awarded this prestigious prize.

1966
   Tove Jansson (author from Fin-
      land)
   Alois Carigiet (illustrator from
      Switzerland)

1968
    James Kruss (author from Germany)
    Jose Maria Sanchez-Silva (author from Spain)
    Jiri Trnka (illustrator from Czechoslovakia)
1970
    Gianni Rodari (author from Italy)
    Maurice Sendak (illustrator from the United States)
1972
    Scott O'Dell (author from the United States)
    Ib Spang Olsen (illustrator from Denmark)
1974
    Maria Gripe (author from Sweden)
    Farshid Mesghali (illustrator from Iran)
1976
    Cecil Bodker (author from Denmark)
    Tatjana Mawrina (illustrator from the U.S.S.R.)
1978
    Paula Fox (author from the United States)
    Svend Otto (illustrator from Denmark)
1980
    Bohumil Riha (author from Czechoslovakia)
    Suekichi Akaba (illustrator from Japan)
1982
    Lygia Bojunga Nunes (author from Brazil)
    Zibigniew Rychlicki (illustrator from Poland)

1984
    Christine Nostlinger (author from Austria)
    Mitsumasa Anno (illustrator from Japan)
1986
    Patricia Wrightson (author from Australia)
    Robert Ingpen (illustrator from Australia)
1988
    Annie M. G. Schmidt (author from the Netherlands)
    Dusan Kallay (illustrator from Yugoslavia)
1990
    Tormod Haugen (author from Norway)
    Lisbeth Zwerger (illustrator from Austria)
1992
    Virginia Hamilton (author from the United States)
    Kveta Pacovska (illustrator from Czechoslovakia)

Other Books Awards

In addition to the preceding awards, many others are given to help honor and celebrate outstanding authors, illustrators, and books for children. Many of these are described (along with listings of current winners) in *Children's Books in Print* (see listing under "Books"). Another good source of information on awards is *Children's Books: Awards and Prizes*, which includes 125 major U.S., British Commonwealth, and International awards (published by the Children's Books Council, 568 Broadway, Suite 404, New York, New York 10012. Phone: 212/966-1990).

Chapter 18

Magazines for Children

GENERAL RESOURCES

Magazine Selection Tools

Children's Magazine Guide. R. R. Bowker, P.O. Box 7247-8599, Philadelphia, Pennsylvania 19170-8599. Phone: 1/800-521-8110. A subject guide to articles appearing in more than forty children's magazines. Each citation includes the name of the article, magazine, author, issue date, and number of pages. Points parents, teachers, and children to articles on science, sports, current events, popular culture, and more. Issued nine times annually. Includes a complete listing of indexed magazines, along with their addresses and phone numbers. For work with children ages eight to twelve.

Children's Magazine List. An annotated list of children's magazines, produced by the Educational Press Association of America. Individual entries include a description, recommended age level, frequency, ordering information, and more. Revised edition published in December 1993. For a copy, contact the Educational Press Association of America, Glassboro State College Communications Department, Glassboro, New Jersey 08028. Phone: 609/863-7349.

Magazines for Children: A Guide for Parents, Teachers, and Librarians. Edited by Selma K. Richardson. Second edition. American Library Association, 1991. 139 pages. A guide to magazines for children of all ages. Each entry includes a highly detailed description, recommended age range, frequency, and editorial and subscription offices.

Magazines for Young People. By Bill Katz and Linda Sternberg Katz. Second edition. R. R. Bowker, 1991 (updated triennially). 361 pages. Describes and evaluates more than one thousand magazines, newsletters, and journals for young people (ages three and up). Featured periodicals cover seventy-four different subject areas, including geography and travel, health, pets, religion, birds, boats, and sports.

Other Selection Guides

The Best of the Best. Edited by Denise Perry Donavin. Random House, 1992. 366 pages. This annotated guidebook from the American Library Association includes recommended magazines for children of all ages (toddlers through teenagers). Individual entries offer informative descriptions, recommended age ranges, frequency, and editorial and subscription addresses.

The Best Toys, Books and Videos for Kids. By Joanne Oppenheim and Stephanie Oppenheim. HarperCollins, 1993. 332 pages. Don't let the title of this book fool you. Also included are recommendations for kids' software programs, audio recordings, and magazines. The magazine section lists and describes sixteen quality publications for preschool and school-aged children.

Parents' Choice: A Sourcebook of the Very Best Products to Educate, Inform, and Entertain Children of All Ages. Selected by Diana Huss Green. Andrews and McMeel, 1993. 208 pages. Included in this sourcebook, compiled by the founder and editor of *Parents' Choice* magazine, is a detailed listing of recommended magazines for children (from preschool through the early teen years). Includes a separate list of magazine addresses and phone numbers.

QUALITY MAGAZINES FOR KIDS

American Girl. Pleasant Company, 8400 Fairway Place, P.O. Box 620190, Middleton, Wisconsin 53562-0190. Phone: 1/800-845-0005 (for subscriptions). For ages seven to twelve. See Gender Differences, Individual Differences in Children.

Boodle: By Kids for Kids. P.O. Box 1049, Portland, Indiana 47371. For ages six to twelve. See Reading and Writing, Education.

Boomerang. (Audiomagazine for Kids). Listen and Learn Home Education, Box 261, La Honda, California 94020. For elementary-school age children. Phone: 1/800-333-7858. See Quality Recordings, Audio for Children.

Boys Life. Boy Scouts of America, 1325 West Walnut Hill Lane, P.O. Box 152079, Irving, Texas 75015-2079. For ages eight to sixteen. See Gender Differences, Individual Differences in Children.

Calliope. Cobblestone Publishing Company, 7 School Street, Peterborough, New Hampshire 03458. Phone: 603/924-7209. For ages nine to fifteen. See History, Education.

Chickadee. Young Naturalist Foundation. P.O. Box 11314, Des Moines, Iowa 50304. Editorial offices: 56 The Esplanade, Toronto, Ontario, Canada M5E 1A7. For ages three to eight. See *Owl* magazine, The Animal Kingdom, Fun and Learning.

Children's Express. (A News Service by Children). 30 Cooper Square, 4th Floor, New York, New York 10003. Phone: 212/505-7777. For ages eight to thirteen. See Reading and Writing, Education.

Club KidSoft. (Software Magazine for Kids). 718 University Avenue, Los Gatos, California 95030. Phone: 1/800-354-6150. For ages four to twelve. See Kids and Computers.

Cobblestone. Cobblestone Publishing Company, 7 School Street, Peterborough, New Hampshire 03458.

You'll find a wide selection of fine children's magazines described under specific topic headings in *The Parents' Resource Almanac* (the list below tells you where to turn). The following four (which didn't find their way into other portions of the book) also receive accolades for their exceptional quality.

Cricket. P.O. Box 387, Mt. Morris, Illinois 61054-7904. Phone: 1/800-888-6995. No children's magazine receives more praise than this one. The quality of the stories and articles, the range of topics explored, and the appealing illustrations leave an impression. In 1993, *Cricket* celebrated its twentieth birthday. For children ages six to twelve. Published monthly.

Ladybug. Box 592, Mt. Morris, Illinois 61054-7665. Phone: 1/800-827-0227. For the preschool set, this well-designed magazine offers quality stories and poems, along with games, activities, cartoon strips, and plenty of full-color illustrations. Includes "Tom and Pippo" stories for toddlers, as well as fiction that can be read aloud to five and six year olds. Carefully conceived and visually appealing. An informative little parent's guide is stapled inside each issue. Published monthly.

Sesame Street Magazine. Children's Television Workshop, P.O. Box 52000, Boulder, Colorado 80322-2000. Phone: 1/800-678-0613. In this magazine, preschoolers (ages two to six) find the same popular characters they see on TV, along with visual puzzles, games, activities, stories, poems, and more. Although *Sesame Street Magazine* can be found on newsstands, parents who subscribe for their children receive the *Parents' Guide,* the award-winning supplement magazine, with each issue. Published ten times annually. (For *Sesame Street* graduates (ages six to ten), Children's Television Workshop publishes *Kid City,* with word games, puzzles, stories, projects, and features designed to make reading, language skills, and learning fun.)

Spider. Box 639, Mt. Morris, Illinois 61054-0639. Phone: 1/800-888-6995. Launched in 1993, this attractive magazine features stories, games, poems, jokes, fun facts, and activities for children who are just getting excited about reading on their own. From the publishers of *Cricket* and *Ladybug.* Issued monthly. For ages six to nine.

Phone: 603/924-7209. For ages nine to fifteen. See History, Education.

Creative Kids. P.O. Box 6448, Mobile, Alabama 36660. For ages eight to eighteen. See Creativity, Talent, and Giftedness, Individual Differences in Children; Reading and Writing, Education.

Dolphin Log. 930 West Twenty-first Street, Norfolk, Virginia 23517. For ages seven to fifteen. See The Animal Kingdom, Fun and Learning.

Faces: The Magazine About People. Cobblestone Publishing Company, 7 School Street, Peterborough, New Hampshire 03458. Phone: 603/924-7209. For ages nine to fifteen. See Multiculturalism, Education.

Highlights for Children. 803 Church Street, Homesdale, Pennsylvania 18431. Phone: 1/800-255-9517 (subscriptions). For ages two to twelve. See Visual Challenges, Fun and Learning.

Hopscotch: The Magazine for Girls. P.O. Box 1292, Saratoga Springs, New York 12866. For ages six to twelve. See Gender Differences, Individual Differences in Children.

Kid City. P.O. Box 52000, Boulder, Colorado 80322-2000. Phone: 1/800/678-0613. For ages six to ten. See *Sesame Street Magazine* in the introduction to listings.

Kids Discover. P.O. Box 54205, Boulder, Colorado 80322-4205. Phone: 212/242-5133. For ages five to twelve. See Science, Education.

KidSports. P.O. Box 8488, Coral Springs, Florida 33075. Phone: 1/800-938-5588. For ages eight to fourteen. See Fitness, Exercise, and Sports.

National Geographic World. National Geographic Society, Seventeenth and M Streets, N.W., Washington, D.C. 20036. Phone: 1/800-638-4077. For ages eight to thirteen. See Science, Education.

New Moon: The Magazine for Girls and Their Dreams. P.O. Box 3587, Duluth, Minnesota 55803-3587. Phone: 218/728-5507. See Gender Differences, Individual Differences in Children.

Odyssey. Cobblestone Publishing Company, 7 School Street, Peterborough, New Hampshire 03458. Phone: 603/924-7209. For ages eight to fourteen. See Science, Education.

Owl. Young Naturalist Foundation, P.O. Box 11314, Des Moines, Iowa 50304. Editorial offices: 56 The Esplanade, Toronto, Ontario, Canada M5E 1A7. For ages nine to twelve. See Science, Education; The Animal Kingdom, Fun and Learning

Plays: The Drama Magazine for Young People. Plays, Inc., 120 Boylston Street, Boston, Massachusetts 02116-4615. See Theatre and Drama, Education.

Ranger Rick. National Wildlife Federation, 1400 Sixteenth Street, N.W., Washington, D.C. 20036-2266. Phone: 1/800-432-6564. For ages six to twelve. See The Animal Kingdom, Fun and Learning; The Environment.

Skipping Stones: A Multi-ethnic Children's Forum. 80574 Hazelton Road, Cottage Grove, Oregon 97424. For ages seven to thirteen. See Multiculturalism, Education; Reading and Writing, Education.

Soccer Jr. P.O. Box 420442, Palm Coast, Florida 32142-9744. Phone: 1/800-829-5382. For ages eight to fourteen. See Fitness, Exercise, and Sports.

Spark: Creative Fun for Kids. P.O. Box 5028, Harlan, Iowa 51593. For work with ages three and up. See Arts and Crafts, Fun and Learning.

Sports Illustrated for Kids. P.O. Box 830609, Birmingham, Alabama 35283-0609. Phone: 1/800-992-0196. For ages seven to twelve. See Fitness, Exercise, and Sports.

Stone Soup. P.O. Box 83, Santa Cruz, California 95063. For ages six to thirteen. See Reading and Writing, Education.

3-2-1 Contact. Children's Television Workshop, P.O. Box 53051, Boulder, Colorado 80322-3051. For ages eight to fourteen. See Science, Education.

WonderScience. The American Chemical Society, 1155 Sixteenth Street, N.W., Washington, D.C. 20036. Phone: 202/452-2113. See Science, Education.

World. See *National Geographic World*

Your Big Backyard. National Wildlife Federation, 1400 Sixteenth Street, N.W., Washington, D.C. 20036-2266. Phone: 1/800-432-6564. For ages three to six. See The Animal Kingdom, Fun and Learning; The Environment.

Zillions. Consumers Union, Box 54861, Boulder, Colorado 80322-4861. Phone: 1/800-288-7898. For ages eight to fourteen. Dollars and Sense.

Zoobooks. P.O. Box 85384, San Diego, California 92186-5384. Phone: 1/800-992-5034. For ages six to ten. See The Animal Kingdom, Fun and Learning.

Chapter 19

Kids and Computers

Free and Inexpensive Resources

Girls and Computers. The Women's Action Alliance offers two brochures designed to encourage girls to become and remain computer-skilled. *Does Your Daughter Say "No Thanks" to the Computer?* explains what parents can do to encourage their daughter's computer use. *Do Your Female Students Say "No Thanks" to the Computer?* introduces computer equity for girls to teachers and administrators, and explains how the computer gender gap can be closed. Each of these eight-page brochures is available for $1.00 from the Women's Action Alliance, Inc., 370 Lexington Avenue, Suite 603, New York, New York 10017. Phone: 212/532-8330.

Notable Films/Videos, Recordings and Microcomputer Software. A listing of quality recordings, films, videotapes, and computer software for young people through age fourteen. Compiled annually by three committees of the Association for Library Service to Children of the American Library Association. In making their selections, the committees consider the aesthetics and technical quality (i.e., the effective use of

What Is "Multimedia Technology"?

This state-of-the-art computer technology combines text, animation, graphic images, lifelike voices, and stereo sound effects, resulting in a multi-sensory experience for computer users of all ages. Imagine a cross between a computer, a videogame, a television set, and a compact disc player, and you'll get a feel for multimedia technology. CD-ROM is the most popular multimedia computer system.

narration, sound effects, music, and visuals). For a free copy, send a self-addressed, stamped envelope along with your request to the Association of Library Service to Children, 50 East Huron Street, Chicago, Illinois 60611.

Parent's Guide to Educational Software. Early learning experts provide information on software for young children in this free pamphlet from Edmark Corporation. For a copy, write "Parent's Guide," Edmark Corporation, P.O. Box 3218, Redmond, Washington 98073-3218. Phone: 206/556-8484.

___

Books

General

Kids and Computers: A Parent's Handbook. By Judy Salpeter. Sams/Prentice-Hall, 1991. 275 pages. Explains how to work with your child at the computer and how to use home computers to enhance school instruction. Includes detailed descriptions

of dozens of educational and entertaining software programs for kids.

Parents, Kids and Computers. By Robin Raskin and Carol Ellison. Random House Electronic Publishing, 1992. 390 pages. A guide for parents who want to help their children use computers at home (and learn more about them themselves). Includes guidelines on shopping for a computer and suggestions for hands-on computer activities. Showcases kid-tested software programs.

Software Selection Guides

The Best of the Best. Edited by Denise Perry Donavin. Random House, 1992. 366 pages. This annotated guidebook from the American Library Association includes recommended computer software programs for children (toddlers through teenagers). Each entry offers a description of the program, the name of the producer/distributor, recommended age range, format, and price. Includes a complete listing of companies that sell the products (names, addresses, and telephone numbers).

The Best Toys, Books and Videos for Kids. By Joanne Oppenheim and Stephanie Oppenheim. HarperCollins, 1993. 332 pages. In addition to toys, books, and videotapes, this guide recommends computer software/CD-ROM for children. Based on the consumer newsletter *The Oppenheim Toy Portfolio.*

High/Scope Buyer's Guide to Children's Software. By Warren Buckleitner. High/Scope Press. Published annually, this guide describes and rates software programs for young children (ages three to six). Includes recommended age range, format, producer/distributor, and price. Designed for parents and early childhood educators.

Only the Best: Annual Guide to Highest Rated Software/Multimedia (Preschool-Grade 12). By Shirley B. Neill and George W. Neill. Education News Service. Published annually. A guide to educational software and multimedia programs for children (preschool through grade twelve), based on thirty-one evaluation efforts in the United States and Canada. Each entry includes a brief description, including subject area and system compatibility; grade level recommendations and usage tips; and price and ordering information.

Parents' Choice: A Sourcebook of the Very Best Products to Educate, Inform, and Entertain Children of all Ages. Selected by Diana Huss Green. Andrews and McMeel, 1993. 208 pages. Compiled by the founder and editor of *Parent's Choice* magazine, this sourcebook offers recommendations on home video, audiocassettes, computer programs, and other products for children. Includes informative descriptions of the software, recommended age range, format, distributor, and suggested retail price. Also included is an alphabetical list of companies that sell the products, including their addresses and phone numbers. For parents with children of all ages.

The Parent's Guide to Educational Software. By Marion Blank and Laura Berlin. Microsoft Press, 1991. 405 pages. Evaluates more than two hundred educational software programs for children. Describes curriculum objectives, the software's strengths and weaknesses, and equipment requirements for use. Also offers advice on evaluating programs and setting up a home computer.

Prides' Guide to Educational Software. By Bill and Mary Pride. Crossway/Good News, 1992. 408 pages. Offers reviews (including ratings) of more than 750 educational software programs for computer-users of all ages (preschool through adult).

What Is a CD-ROM?

CD-ROMs look like the compact discs you stick in your audio CD player. But they're designed for computers, and you need a CD-ROM drive to use them. They can store much more information than a floppy disk (including massive quantities of text, animated pictures, and music and digitized speech) but require a larger investment. In addition to the CD-ROM drive, you may need to add memory capacity and purchase an audio card. A hard disk drive is required (ask your computer dealer for more details).

For Children

My First Computer Book. By David Schiller. Workman, 1991. 64 pages. An introduction to the computer for children ages four through eight. Explains what's inside the computer and how it works. Comes with a floppy disk containing five programs (painting, solving a mystery, etc.). IBM-compatible or Apple II-compatible versions available. Requires a color monitor.

The Ultimate Collection of Computer Facts and Fun. By C. Tison and Mary Jo Woodside. Sams/Prentice-Hall, 1991. 100 pages. Full of games, puzzles, activities, and graphics designed to help children better understand how computers work.

Periodicals

For Adults

Booklist. American Library Association, 50 East Huron Street, Chicago, Illinois 60611. Phone: 1/800-545-2433. Reviews new software for children and adults, in addition to books, films, videotapes, and audiocassettes.

Family Fun. Family Fun, P.O. Box 10161, Des Moines, Iowa 50340-0161. Phone: 1/800-289-4849. Each issue of the monthly magazine includes a feature called "Family Computing." Includes tips on choosing hardware and software for kids of all ages. Offers software reviews and specific program recommendations as well. Available on newsstands or by subscription.

Kids and Computers. Ziff-Davis Publishing Company, 13 Chaparral Court, Suite 260, Anaheim Hills, California 92808. Phone: 1/800-827-4450. Designed for parents, this magazine features articles on family computing, profiles of new products and technology, and "Kids' View," a department containing computer ideas and tips mailed in by kids. Issued six times annually.

The Oppenheim Toy Portfolio. 40 East Ninth Street, New York, New York 10003. Phone: 212/598-0502 or 1/800-544-TOYS. In addition to toys, books, and videos, this quarterly publication reviews innovative software and CD-ROM programs for children.

Parents' Choice. Parents' Choice Foundation, P.O. Box 185, Waban, Massachusetts 02168. Phone: 617/965-5913. A quarterly review of children's media, including software and CD-ROM programs (Apple, Macintosh, and IBM-compatibles).

School Library Journal. 249 West Seventeenth Street, New York, New York 10011. Phone: 212/463-6759 or 1/800-456-9409 (subscriptions). Reviews software for children and young adults, along with books, films, videotapes, and recordings.

SoftWorlds for Children: Report on Macintosh Software for Fun and Learning. P.O. Box 219, Edmonds, Washington 98020. Phone: 206/672-2107. Contains reviews of Macintosh software, along with articles on the use of computers in education. For parents and teachers. Issued bimonthly.

Technology and Learning. Peter Li, Inc., 2451 East River Road, Dayton, Ohio 45439. Published monthly during the school year, this publication regularly reviews educational software. Publishes an "Only the Best" list once a year.

For Children

Club KidSoft. 718 University Avenue, Los Gatos, California 95030. Phone: 1/800-354-6150. A software magazine for children ages four to twelve. Colorful, oversized issues include clever games, activities, and reviews of software programs for PC and Macintosh systems. Included in each issue is a catalog of kid- and parent-tested disk and CD-ROM software titles, all of which can be ordered from Club KidSoft (see listing under "Mail Order Catalogs" for more details). Issued four times annually.

Mail Order Catalogs

General

Broderbund Software Catalog. P.O. Box 6125, Novato, California 94948-6125. Phone: 1/800-521-6263. The Broderbund catalog describes the company's high-quality and award-winning software and CD-ROM programs for kids ages three and up. Also contains information on the Kids Club (members receive newsletters, reports on new software and upgrades, and a package full of surprises, toys, and gifts).

Club KidSoft. 718 University Avenue, Los Gatos, California 95030. Phone: 1/800-354-6150. A software magazine and catalog rolled into one, for children ages four to twelve. The catalog portion describes a variety of kid- and parent-tested software titles (available on disk or CD-ROM), including interactive books, publishing software, educational programs, and games for PC or Macintosh systems. In fact, if you have a CD-ROM drive, you can begin using some programs immediately (they're already loaded onto a free CD that comes with each issue; you simply call to find out how to unlock the program and charge your purchase over the phone). The magazine/catalog is issued four times annually. (For more information on the magazine, see listing under "Magazines.")

CompUSA. Phone: 1/800-451-7638. This superstore offers hundreds of computer products (hardware, software, accessories, books, etc.) by mail. (You can also visit one of their stores, located in cities across the country.)

Educational Resources. 1550 Executive Drive, Elgin, Illinois 60123. Phone: 1/800-624-2926. Offers educational software for children at discounted prices.

MacWarehouse. 1720 Oak Street, P.O. Box 3031, Lakewood, New Jersey 08701. Phone: 1/800-255-6227. Offers a wide selection of products for Macintosh users, including quality software programs for kids.

The Mac Zone. The PC Zone, 17411 Northeast Union Hill Road, Suite 140, Redmond, Washington 98052-6716. Phone: 1/800-436-8000. Catalog superstore for Macintosh products.

What Is "Shareware"?

Answer: Computer programs that you can preview for a small fee (typically $5 to $8). If you like the program and decide to use it, you must register and pay a fee to the program's author. Even with the registration fees, shareware users pay less than they would to purchase the program outright.

The PC Zone. 17411 Northeast Union Hill Road, Suite 140, Redmond, Washington 98052-6716. Phone: 1/800-252-0386. Each issue of this catalog lists over two thousand software and hardware products for PC users.

Shareware Catalogs

Educorp. Phone: 1/800-843-9497. Offers shareware for Macintosh users (both children and adults). Each quarterly catalog lists thousands of available disks.

Familyware. Phone: 1/800-827-KIDS or 813/933-6625. Offers easy-to-use shareware for children on IBM-formatted disks.

Associations

Center for Children and Technology/Center for Technology in Education. Education Development Center, 96 Morton Street, 7th Floor, New York, New York 10014. Phone: 212/875-4560. Investigates the roles technology does and can play in children's lives in general and in the classroom in particular. Has undertaken a wide program of basic and applied research, as well as the design and development of prototypical software that supports engaged, active learning. Issues a quarterly newsletter. Founded at the Bank Street College of Education in 1981.

The Computer Learning Foundation. P.O. Box 60007, Palo Alto, California 94306-0007. A nonprofit organization promoting computer literacy and education. For more information on the foundation's programs and materials, request a copy of *Computer Learning,* free with a self-addressed envelope and 52¢ postage.

High/Scope Educational Research Foundation. 600 North River Street, Ypsilanti, Michigan 48198-2898. Phone: 313/485-2000. Works to develop practical alternatives to the traditional methods of educating children. Explores the use of computers with young children (ages three to six), and has been integrating computer technology into the early childhood curriculum at its demonstration school in Ypsilanti, Michigan. Produces a variety of publications, including a newsletter and a magazine. Write or call for information about their work with young children.

Museum

The Computer Museum. Located in Boston, the Computer Museum offers children an opportunity to walk through a working model of a computer (it's two stories high!); produce a video commercial; and write on a wall with an enormous, laser-guided pen. An exhibit called "Tools and Toys: The Amazing Personal Computer" includes three-dozen interactive displays that introduce museum-goers to the latest technology. For more information, call 617/423-6758 (if you prefer speaking to a human being, call 617/426-2800).

Chapter 20

Tuning In: Audio, Radio, Video, and Television

AUDIO FOR CHILDREN

Free Resource

Notable Films/Videos, Recordings and Microcomputer Software. A listing of quality recordings, films, videotapes, and computer software for young people through age fourteen. Compiled annually by three committees of the Association for Library Service to Children of the American Library Association. In making their selections, the committees consider the esthetic and technical quality (i.e., the effective use of narration, sound effects, music, and visuals). For a free copy, send a self-addressed, stamped envelope along with your request to the Association for Library Service to Children, 50 East Huron Street, Chicago, Illinois 60611.

Books

General

All Ears: How to Choose and Use Recorded Music for Children. By Jill Jarnow. Penguin, 1991. 210 pages. The author profiles more than seventy-five artists and highlights more than two hundred recordings. Also explains the powerful role music plays in children's lives, how to make well-informed music selections for children from birth to age ten, and where to find what you're looking for. Includes a state-by-state listing of radio programs for kids.

The Best of the Best. Edited by Denise Perry Donavin. Random House, 1992. 366 pages. This annotated guidebook from the American Library Association recommends hundreds of children's books, magazines, videotapes, audiocassettes, toys, and computer software. Selected items, chosen by professionals in children's media, are grouped according to age appropriateness and media format. "Connections" refer readers to related materials in other portions of the book.

The Best Toys, Books and Videos for Kids. By Joanne Oppenheim and Stephanie Oppenheim. HarperCollins, 1993. 332 pages. In addition to toys, books, and videotapes, the guide recommends musical recordings and stories on cassette for kids from infancy through age ten. Based on the consumer newsletter, *The Oppenheim Toy Portfolio.*

Growing Up with Music. By Laurie Sale. Avon Books, 1992. 294 pages. A descriptive guide to top-quality recordings for children (from infancy through age ten).

Mother Goose Comes First. By Lois Winkel and Sue Kimmel. Henry Holt, 1990. 194 pages. An annotated guide to books and recordings for preschool children from infancy through age five, categorized by subject and age level. Includes books on tape, read-along kits, and musical recordings for kids. Subject areas include the family, growing up, health, animals, transportation, the earth and outer space, holidays, seasons, and many others.

Parents' Choice: A Sourcebook of the Very Best Products to Educate, Inform, and Entertain Children of all Ages. Selected by Diana Huss Green. Andrews and McMeel, 1993. 208 pages. Compiled by the founder and editor of *Parents' Choice* magazine, this sourcebook offers recommendations on the best toys, home video, audiocassettes, computer programs, books, and magazines for children. Each entry includes the suggested retail price, recommended age range, and a full description to help parents decide if the product is right for their family. Also included is a list of companies that produce/distribute the products. For parents with children of all ages.

Play, Learn, and Grow. By James L. Thomas. R. R. Bowker, 1992. 352 pages. An evaluative guide to videotapes, audiocassettes, magazines, and books for very young children (up to age five). Each entry includes a brief description, recommended age level, bibliographic information, and a "priority of purchase" ranking. Material is indexed by author, subject, age range, and purchase priority. Also lists publishers, producers, and organizations adults can consult for guidance.

Standard Library Directories

AV Market Place. R. R. Bowker. Updated annually, this comprehensive directory puts people in touch with more than sixty-three thousand companies that create, supply, or distribute audio/visual materials, including films, videotapes, and recordings. A good source for current names, addresses, and phone numbers.

Words on Cassette. R. R. Bowker. Issued annually. Over 2,000 pages. Covers more than fifty thousand audiocassettes, including fiction and nonfiction for children. Individual entries include a content summary, running time, reader's name, price, and more. Includes names, addresses, and telephone numbers of producers and distributors.

Reviews

Booklist. American Library Association, 50 East Huron Street, Chicago, Illinois 60611. Phone: 1/800-545-2433. In addition to book reviews, *Booklist* also contains reviews of audiobooks, videotapes, and filmstrips for children and adults. Issued semimonthly.

Family Fun. Each issue of the monthly magazine includes reviews of cassettes and compact discs for kids. Available on newsstands or by subscription (P.O. Box 10161, Des Moines, Iowa 50340-0161. Phone: 1/800-289-4849).

The Oppenheim Toy Portfolio. 40 East Ninth Street, New York, New York 10003. Phone: 212/598-0502 or 1/800-544-TOYS. In addition to toys, books, and videos, this quarterly reviews musical recordings and stories on cassette or compact disc for children.

Parents' Choice. A quarterly review of children's media including children's books, movies, television programs, videotapes, and audio recordings. Contact Parents' Choice Foundation, P.O. Box 185, Waban, Massachusetts 02168. Phone: 617/965-5913.

School Library Journal. Contains reviews of new books, recordings, and videotapes for children and young adults. Published monthly. Contact School Library Journal, 249 West Seventeenth Street, New York, New York 10011. Phone: 212/463-6759 or 1/800-456-9409 (subscriptions).

Computerized Clearinghouse

KIDSNET. A national nonprofit computerized clearinghouse devoted to children's audio, video, radio, and television programming. Those who subscribe to the electronic database have access to detailed information on more than twenty thousand video and audiocassette programs. (For more information, see "Computerized Clearinghouse" listed under "Television.")

Mail Order Catalogs

Musical Recordings

Alcazar's Catalog of Children's Music. P.O. Box 429, Waterbury, Vermont 05676. Phone: 1/800-541-9904. A catalog containing two hundred audio and video recordings for children. Represents leading artists in the field as well as up-and-coming talents. Lullabies, folk music, swing, jazz, rock and roll, showtunes, classical music, and Disney movie soundtracks are among the the the many offerings.

Educational Record Center. 3233 Burnt Mill Drive, Suite 100, Wilmington, North Carolina 28403-2655. Phone: 919/251-1235. Children's favorite recording artists available on compact disc include Joanie Bartels, Fred Penner, Hap Palmer, Ella Jenkins, and Sharon, Lois and Bram. Also offers a variety of award-winning musical recordings on cassette and videotape.

A Gentle Wind. Box 3103, Albany, New York 12203. Phone: 518/436-

0391. Music and stories for children on tape, including winners of the Parents' Choice Award, the Oppenheim Gold Seal Best Audio Award, and American Library Association Notable Children's Recordings.

Music for Little People. Box 1460, Redway, California 95560. Phone: 1/800-727-2233. Lullabies, reggae, classical, folk music, rock for tots—you name it, it's available here on audiocassette, compact disc, and/or videotape.

Wireless Audio Collection. P.O. Box 64422, St. Paul, Minnesota 55164-0422. Phone: 1/800-733-3369. "For Fans and Friends of Public Radio," this catalog includes a wide variety of musical recordings, including a handful of quality productions for children. *Raffi in Concert with the Rise and Shine Band, American Folksongs for Children*, and *Arthur Fiedler and the Boston Pops: Classics for Children* are among the offerings.

Stories on Cassette

Alcazar's Catalog of Children's Music. P.O. Box 429, Waterbury, Vermont 05676. Phone: 1/800-541-9904. This catalog includes many award-winning stories on cassette and compact disc.

Educational Record Center. 3233 Burnt Mill Drive, Suite 100, Wilmington, North Carolina 28403-2655. Phone: 919/251-1235. Offers a wide variety of read-along sets (book and cassette), including *Madeline, Goodnight Moon, Lyle, Lyle Crocodile, Cloudy with a Chance of Meatballs*, and Beatrix Potter books and tapes.

A Gentle Wind. Box 3103, Albany, New York 12203. Phone: 518/436-0391. Music and stories for children on tape, including winners of the Parents' Choice Award, the Oppenheim Gold Seal Best Audio Award, and American Library Association Notable Children's Recordings.

Listening Library. One Park Avenue, Old Greenwich, Connecticut 06870-1727. Phone: 1/800-243-4504. The Listening Library catalog contains literature-based media for children and young adults (ages four to sixteen-plus), including award-winning books, book and cassette packages, recorded books (unabridged classics on cassette), and cassette listening libraries.

The Mind's Eye. Box 1060, Petaluma, California 94953. Phone: 1/800-227-2020. Offers stories on cassette for listeners of all ages. For children, their are the "Fantastic Adventures" (*Pinocchio, Peter Pan*, and *The Wind in the Willows* on six cassettes); bilingual fables (first read in French or Spanish, then in English); *The Complete Winnie-the-Pooh* (in a collection of nine cassettes plus four books); the "Junior Cassette Library" (*Frog and Toad, Little Bear*, and *Amelia Bedelia* on six cassettes); and many other audio titles. Performed by various readers (some are dramatized, others are simply read).

Music for Little People. Box 1460, Redway, California 95560. Phone: 1/800-727-2233. In addition to audio and video musical recordings, this catalog features a handful of award-winning stories on cassette/compact disc.

Recorded Books. 270 Skipjack Road, Prince Frederick, Maryland 20678. Phone: 1/800-638-1304. Offers a variety of unabridged books on cassette for children and young adults, including classics by Kipling, Twain, and Tolkien. Also offers contemporary authors such as Beverly Cleary and Robert Newton Peck. Most of the recordings are for children in upper elementary school (grades four to six), up through high school.

Wireless Audio Collection. P.O. Box 64422, St. Paul, Minnesota 55164-0422. Phone: 1/800-733-3369. This catalog includes a small collection of stories on cassette for children, including titles like *The Teddy Bears' Picnic* (winner of the Children's Choice Award), *Charlotte's Web* (read by E. B. White himself), and *The Tale of Peter Rabbit and Other Stories by Beatrix Potter* (read by Meryl Streep).

Quality Recordings for Kids

In addition to the acclaimed and/or award-winning recordings listed here, you'll find other audiocassettes/compact discs featured under specific topics in *The Parents' Resource Almanac*. Refer to the section on Music, listed under "The Arts" (Education, chapter 14), for a select list of other quality musical recordings for kids.

Musical Recordings

All for Freedom. Sweet Honey in the Rock's first children's album, featuring folk songs and traditional spirituals rooted in the African-American experience. Includes jazz, blues, gospel, and contemporary music. An ALA Notable Children's Recording and winner of a Parents' Choice Gold Award. For ages four and up. Available on cassette and compact disc. Distributed by Music for Little People.

Animal Folk Songs for Children and Other People. Rounder Records. Songs sung and played by Mike, Peggy, Barbara, and Penny Seeger, together with their children. Includes fifty-eight cuts celebrating possums, 'gators, squirrels, ground hogs, and doodlebugs, among many others. On two cassettes or two compact discs.

Bahamas Pajamas. Joe Scruggs performs a collection of songs that teach, entertain, and excite. Titles include "Star Sun," "Humpty Dumpty," and the title song "Bahamas Pajamas." For ages four to eight. Cassette. Distributed by Alcazar.

Billy the Squid. Tom Chapin. Sony Kids Music. This recording includes fourteen original songs to entertain and delight, including "City Lights" and "Billy the Squid." Cassette and compact disc. Other quality recordings by Chapin include "Family Tree," "Moonboat," and "Mother Earth."

A Child's Celebration of Showtunes. Music for Little People. Introduces young listeners to show tunes such as *Oliver!*, *Peter Pan*, *The Sound of Music*, and *Fiddler on the Roof*, sung by the Broadway stars who made them famous. Comes with a family activity book. Cassette or compact disc.

Hello Everybody! By Rachel Buchman. A Gentle Wind. Features a cheerful collection of playsongs, rhymes, and lullabies for toddlers. Titles include "Little Red Wagon," "Pussy Willow Riddle," and "A Tickling Rhyme."

I'm Just a Kid! Rory. Sony Kids Music. Rory presents ten zestful songs for kids (people she obviously understands and cares about). Titles include "The Ballad of Mr. Toad" and "The Best You Can Be Is You." For ages five to eight. Cassette.

Lullaby Berceuse. Oak Street Music. On this award-winning cassette, you'll here Connie Kaldor and Carmen Campagne perform a collection of beautiful sleep songs in English and French.

Lullaby Magic. Joanie Bartels. Discovery Music. On one side of this tape, you'll hear the pure voice of Joanie Bartels; the flip side features instrumental versions of the same songs (contemporary and traditional lullabies, including gems from James Taylor, Elvis Presley, and Brahms). Cassette. Also highly recommended: *Morning Magic* and *Dancin' Magic* by Joanie Bartels.

Singable Songs for the Very Young. By Raffi. MCA. Great songs for young listeners (ages one to five), including "Peanut Butter Sandwich," "Down by the Bay," "Bumping Up and Down," and "Going to the Zoo." Cassette or compact disc. Other recordings by Raffi include: *More Singable Songs, The Corner Grocery Store, One Light, One Sun, Everything Grows, Evergreen Everblue, Raffi In Concert, Raffi's Christmas Album, Rise and Shine,* and *Baby Beluga.*

Uh-Oh! Rosenshontz. Lightyear Entertainment. Twelve fun tunes, enthusiastically performed by Gary Rosen and Bill Shontz. A host of children join in the fun. For ages five to nine. Cassette or compact disc.

Woody's 20 Grow Big Songs. Warner Brothers. Inspired by the discovery of a long-lost children's songbook by Woody Guthrie, this recording mixes the voices of Arlo and other Guthrie kin with Woody's original recordings (accomplished by overdubbing). For ages two and up. Cassette (ten songs on two separate tapes) or compact disc (all twenty songs).

Stories/Words on Tape

Anansi. Rabbit Ears. Oscar-winner Denzel Washington narrates the tale of the clever spider Anansi (from traditional African folklore), who outwits the prideful Snake and wins possession of all the stories in the jungle. The story is set in the sugarcane fields of Jamaica; UB40 provides the reggae background music. For ages five to ten. Book and tape set or cassette only. Distributed by Alcazar.

Blueberries for Sal. Puffin Books. Robert McCloskey's story of the mother bear and cub who become separated (temporarily). Set includes paperback and audiocassette. Flip side of tape offers theme-related activities. For ages three to seven.

Boomerang. An award-winning monthly audiomagazine for elementary-school age kids. Narrated by children, each issue includes news, regular columns, special features, and fun (jokes, word quizzes, etc.). Offers "interviews" with historic figures (Thomas Edison, for example), coverage of current events such as rain forests and gun control, a column on money, and more. Each cassette is seventy minutes in length. *The Best of Boomerang,* a four-volume collection pulled together by the producers, is also available, as are *More Best of Boomerang, The Best of the Best of Boomerang,* and *The Rest of the Best of Boomerang.* Contact Listen and Learn Home Education, Box 261, La Honda, California 94020. Phone: 1/800-333-7858.

Chicka Chicka Boom Boom. Simon and Schuster. Ray Charles does two different readings of the rhyme about the alphabet in the coconut tree, by Bill Martin, Jr., and John Archambault. Also included is a rap version by kids. For ages three and up. Book and audiotape set. Distributed by Educational Record Center.

Frog and Toad Tales. Caedmon. The author himself, Arnold Lobel, tells tales about two amphibious friends. Two cassettes. For ages two to five.

Horton Hatches the Egg. Billy Crystal's word-for-word reading of the Dr. Seuss classic, along with original music and fun sound effects. For ages three and up. Book and cassette. Distributed by Educational Record Center.

Noah's Ark. Penguin USA. James Earl Jones reads two different versions of the story of Noah and the flood. For ages eight and up. Cassette and book set (the accompanying book, by Peter Spier, won a Caldecott Medal).

Roald Dahl Audio Collection. Caedmon. Running time: 4 hours. Performed by the author. Four cassettes feature *Charlie and the Chocolate Factory, James and the Giant Peach, Fantastic Mr. Fox,* and *The Enormous Crocodile.* For ages eight to twelve.

The Snow Queen. Lightyear Entertainment. Narrated by Sigourney Weaver, this tape features the story of brave young Gerta, who overcomes many obstacles in her quest to rescue a lost friend from the Snow Queen's palace. Music by Jason Miles. For ages five and up. Cassette, compact disc, or video.

The Velveteen Rabbit. Rabbit Ears. Meryl Streep reads Margery Williams' classic tale about the meaning of "real." A fine tape, for listeners of all ages, with music by George Winston. Cassette or compact disc. Distributed by Alcazar.

Producers and Distributors

Alcazar. P.O. Box 429, Waterbury, Vermont 05676. Phone: 1/800-541-9904.

Caedmon/Harper Audio. 1995 Broadway, New York, New York 10023. Phone: 212/207-7000.

Discovery Music. 5554 Calhoun Avenue, Van Nuys, California 91401. Phone: 1/800-451-5175.

Educational Record Center. 3233 Burnt Mill Drive, Suite 100, Wilmington, North Carolina 28403-2655. Phone: 919/251-1235.

A Gentle Wind. Box 3103, Albany, New York 12203. Phone: 518/436-0391.

Lightyear Entertainment. Empire State Building, 350 Fifth Avenue, Suite 5101, New York, New York 10118. Phone: 212/563-4610.

MCA Records. 70 Universal City Plaza, Universal City, California 91608. Phone: 818/777-4000.

Music for Little People. P.O. Box 1460, Redway, California 95560. Phone: 1/800-727-2233.

Oak Street Music. 93 Lombard Avenue, Suite 108, Winnipeg, Manitoba, Canada R3B 3B1. Phone: 204/957-0085.

Penguin USA. 375 Hudson Street, New York, New York 10012. Phone: 212/366-2000.

Puffin Books. 375 Hudson Street, New York, New York 10014. Phone: 212/366-2000.

Rounder Records. P.O. Box 154, Cambridge, Massachusetts 02140. Phone: 1/800-443-4727.

Sony Kids Music. 550 Madison Avenue, 21st Floor, New York, New York 10101. Phone: 1/800-336-0248 or 212/833-4231.

Warner Brothers. 400 Warner Boulevard, Burbank, California 91522. Phone: 818/945-6000.

Other Audio Sources
Purchasing
- Specialty children's book and toy stores
- Record and tape shops
- Mail order catalogs (refer to listings in this chapter)
- Directly from the producer/distributor. You can find current addresses and phone numbers in standard library directories

such as *AV Market Place* and *Words On Cassette* (see listings under "Books"). Sourcebooks such as *The Best of the Best* and *Parents' Choice* include lists of distributors for every recommended audio recording (see listings under "Books" for more information on these titles).

Borrowing or Renting
- Your local library
- Books-on-Tape rental stores.

CHILDREN'S RADIO

You probably don't realize it, but chances are you live within the broadcast range of a children's radio program. More than three hundred stations currently run broadcasts aimed at the ears of kids from preschoolers to preteeners, from the Arctic Circle (Barrow, Alaska) to the tip of Florida, and indications are that such programs are expanding. One of the newest developments is full-time, commercial children's radio: when this book went to press, the city of St. Louis had two such stations. If one counts satellite affiliates and public stations, day-long children's radio can now be heard in a dozen major cities. Many shorter programs are extending their reach as well, syndicated over satellite networks or broadcast locally from prerecorded tapes.

Not so new but no less vital are the many live, locally produced and broadcast weekly kids' shows, some of which have been riding the airwaves for a decade now. A number of them have proven their lasting value and garnered prestigious broadcasting awards. Consider WNYC's "New York Kids," a weekly two-hour show filled with young voices live from the studio or calling in on the phone and featuring not only ethnically diverse music but—appropriately for New York City—book and film reviews. Then there is "Kids and Classics" from KOHM in Lubbock, Texas, which concentrates on classical music, while in Provincetown (Cape Cod), Massachusetts, WOMR offers weekend shows hosted and produced entirely by local elementary and high school students—including fourteen-year-old DJs whose rock and rap show is called "Vicious Variety." In Alamo, New Mexico, KABR offers shows for Navajo youngsters five days a week, including bilingual broadcasts, a service not uncommon among Native American community stations. Locally produced programs, in short, are especially attuned to their listeners' interests. Many of them offer newsletters for fans, allow call-in requests, and include special events calendars for children and their families.

Children's Radio Directory. Because it can be difficult to learn about programs even in your own listening area, a nationwide Children's Radio Directory is included at the end of this section. Space does not allow descriptions of individual programs within the directory, though syndicated shows are described. Every station listed was actively airing (or about to begin airing) shows for children as of Spring 1994. Bear in mind that because most radio stations add and drop programs every year, the directory is best used as a jumping-off point. For up-to-the-minute program and scheduling details, you can call the stations directly or write to the syndicated shows that interest you.

Popular Syndicated Shows

Many of the best children's shows on the air are independently produced at small radio stations and heard only by those with nearby antennas. But several programs of very high quality are syndicated across the country. Since one of these syndicated shows may be available in your listening area, they warrant a brief description.

Pickleberry Pie. If Alvin's Chipmunks had cool vegetarian cousins in California, they might be the Pickleberries. These green pie-dwelling creatures star in a rib-tickling weekly half-hour show geared toward the preschool set and carried on selected National Public Radio stations (more than fifty of them, at last count). Young studio guests join in shaping each show, which includes original music by Linda Arnold, a well-known children's performer. Shows often take a hands-on approach to real-world issues, such as recycling trash at home or baking an English muffin pizza. The Pickleberries have been on the air since 1986 and have won broadcasting awards from Parents' Choice and the Corporation for Public Broadcasting. For an up-to-the-minute station listing, write: P.J. Swift, Pickleberry Pie, 305 Dickens Way, Santa Cruz, California 95064.

We Like Kids. Also a weekly half-hour show, "We Like Kids" features a mixture of quality music recordings and storytelling, each program tied together by a theme introduced by Professor Sphagnum Moss (the show is produced in Alaska). "Horses," "Freedom," "The Body Show," and "Fables and Fairy Tales" have been a few of the featured themes. A regular newsletter is mailed out to fans and educators, including listings of all the songs broadcast (and where to order tapes), organized by theme. Two songbooks based on the show have also been published, and are available through GoodYear Books (phone: 1/800-628-4480). Winner of a Parents' Choice Award, "We Like Kids" is now carried throughout Alaska and on over thirty stations elsewhere. For an up-to-the-minute station listing, write: Jeff Brown, We Like Kids, KTOO-FM, 224 Fourth St., Juneau, Alaska 99801.

Rabbit Ears Radio. Premiering in the summer of 1994, this weekly storytelling series is being carried on many Public Radio International (formerly American Public Radio) affiliate stations nationwide. Actor Mel Gibson introduces each prerecorded classic tale, which is narrated by a Hollywood veteran with outstanding musical accompaniment. Two of the recordings won Grammy awards: "The Velveteen Rabbit" by Margery Williams, read by Meryl Streep with piano accompaniment by George Winston; and Rudyard Kipling's "The Elephant's Child," read by Jack Nicholson with vocal "instrumentals" by Bobby McFerrin. For more information about this program, call Public Radio International (612/338-5000) or Rabbit Ears (203/857-3760).

Kinetic City Supercrew. This new science-adventure show, scheduled to begin airing in the fall of 1994, will feature a crew of youngsters who seek answers to science mysteries as they chug along on their imaginary train, the Kinetic City Express. Weekly half-hour segments make up the series. No station listing was available when this book went to press; to obtain the latest listing of stations, write: John Keefe, Senior Producer, Kinetic City Supercrew, American Association for the Advancement of Science, 1333 H Street NW, Washington, D.C. 20005.

Full-Time Children's Stations

Detroit, Michigan: WDTR 90.9 fm. Phone: 313/596-3507. On the air twelve hours a day, WDTR includes children's programming as part of its community-oriented mix. It broadcasts a number of storytelling and music shows, including "Tall Tales," read by students, and "Griot Tales from Under the Baobob Tree," read by storyteller Katherine Blackwell. Students figure in other programs as well; including segments on science and cultural enrichment. Prerecorded material includes "Pickleberry Pie." WDTR is owned by the Detroit Board of Education.

Minneapolis, Minnesota: WWTC, "Radio Aahs," 1280 am. Phone: 1-800/552-2470. "Radio Aahs," which is on the air twenty four hours a day, seven days a week, has made full-time children's radio a commercial success, and its music programming reflects that polish. The songs—from those by Raffi to Little Richard—are flipped by live DJs who are kids themselves, and the station carries regular news and talk segments. The station's most loyal audience seems to fall within the four to nine year-old range.

In early 1993, "Aahs" began to fan out across the country by satellite, and as of Spring 1994, it counted fourteen affiliated satellite stations. At present, most of these stations rebroadcast the Minneapolis-produced material (some full day, some part-time) with little or no local programming. However, as they become better established (and endowed), the affiliates are likely to liven up their menu with local activity. The current "Radio Aahs" affiliates are:

Baltimore—WKDB
Dallas—KAHZ
Denver—KKYD
Eau Claire, Wisconsin—WEIO
Grand Rapids—WISZ
Los Angeles—KPLS
Manassas, Virginia—WKDV
Phoenix—KIDR
Salt Lake City—KKDS
San Luis Obispo, California—KIID
Spokane—KAZZ
St. Louis—KLZE
Ventura, California—KCTQ
Washington, D.C.—WKDL

New York, New York: WNYE 91.5 fm. Phone: 718/935-4480. WNYE runs its kids' programming during regular school hours, but the shows have leaned more toward the creative and entertaining than toward traditional instruction. As of Spring 1994, the programming was in transition, but if its track record is maintained, listeners can expect to hear excellent children's music and storytelling broadcasts. WNYE is a public station owned by the New York City Board of Education.

Portland, Oregon: KBPS 1450 am. Phone: 503/280-5828. KBPS airs educational and entertainment shows for children and teens weekdays from 10 a.m. to 3 p.m., with roughly ten hours per week for the under-twelve set. Features include a children's music show hosted by teenage DJs. Students also participate on the air in panel debates and radio dramas. KBPS is a public station licensed by the Portland Public Schools.

St. Louis, Missouri: WFUN 95.5 fm. Phone: 314/291-9386. WFUN, whose radio signal reaches parts of Illinois as well as St. Louis, is commercially supported and runs twenty-four hours a day, seven days a week. Kids can make calls on the air. The music programming is punctuated during rush-hour travel time with riddle and game segments, and the comments of "The Weatherdude."

Seattle, Washington: KidStar 1250 am. Phone: 206/625-1250. Like "Radio Aahs," KidStar is a fully commercial children's station. It has only been operating since May 1993, but its eighteen-hour-a-day schedule and glossy quarterly fan magazine suggest that it intends to be around for a while. Young listeners can dial a special toll-free number in order to have their comments prerecorded and later aired. The magazine is cleverly designed to entertain while challenging the mind, all of it tied into the show. Most of the broadcast day is filled with music; the remainder includes news, information, interviews, and roving reportage.

Springfield, Missouri: KIDS 1340 am. Phone: 417/864-KIDS. Running twelve hours a day, KIDS is an independent, commercially supported kids' station. Shows feature music and stories, and the station has a "Green" policy of running at least one song about the environment every hour.

Radio for the Visually Impaired

Children who are visually impaired or have some other severe reading disability should also know about Radio Reading Services, essentially radio stations specializing in reading news, fiction, and other material over the airwaves. Listeners usually need to have special radio adapters hooked up in their homes in order to receive these programs, which are broadcast locally from some fifty locations around the country. Each Radio Reading Service runs its own programming, so it is not possible to provide a blanket description here. Nevertheless, many do include storytelling and other material especially for children (for example, the Radio Reading Service of Western New England, based in Springfield, Massachusetts, carries "Pickleberry Pie"). To find out whether such a service is available in your area, write The Association of Radio Reading Services, 4200 Wisconsin Avenue, N.W., Suite 106-346, Washington, D.C. 20036.

Radio for the Holidays

During the Thanksgiving New Year holiday season, listeners can tune in to "Mrs. Bush's Story Time," which at last count was carried on more than seventy stations across the country. Featuring extended readings by the former First Lady accompanied by such big names as Whitney Houston, Mel Gibson, and Minnie Mouse, the series is coproduced by the Children's Literacy Initiative and the ABC Radio Networks. To find out if it is carried on a station near you, contact the Children's Literacy Initiative, 320 Walnut Street, 2nd Floor, Philadelphia, Pennsylvania 19106.

CHILDREN'S RADIO DIRECTORY, 1994

ALASKA

Anchorage	KRUA 88.1 fm	907/786-1077	"We Like Kids"
Anchorage	KSKA 91.1 fm	907/561-1161	"We Like Kids," "Pickleberry Pie," "Rabbit Ears"
Barrow	KBRW 680 am	907/852-6811	"We Like Kids"
Bethel	KYUK 640 am	907/543-3131	"We Like Kids," "Pickleberry Pie," "Rabbit Ears"

Chevak	KCUK 88.1 fm	907/858-7014	"We Like Kids"
Dillingham	KDLG 670 am	907/842-5281	"We Like Kids," "Rabbit Ears"
Fairbanks	KUAC 104.7 fm	907/474-7491	"Rabbit Ears"
Galena	KIYU 910 am	907/656-1488	"We Like Kids," "Rabbit Ears"
Haines	KHNS 102.3 fm	907/766-2020	"We Like Kids"
Homer	KBBI 890 am	907/235-7721	"We Like Kids," "Rabbit Ears"
Juneau	KTOO 104.3 fm	907/586-1670	"We Like Kids"
Kenai	KCZP 91.9 fm	907/776-5225	"Rabbit Ears"
Kodiak	KMXT 100.1 fm	907/486-3181	"We Like Kids"
Kotzebue	KOTZ 720 am	907/442-3435	"We Like Kids"
McGrath	KSKO 870 am	907/524-3001	"We Like Kids," "Rabbit Ears"
Petersburg	KFSK 100.9 fm	907/772-3808	"We Like Kids"
Sand Point	KSDP 840 am	907/383-5737	"We Like Kids," "Rabbit Ears"
St. Paul Island	KUHB 91.9 fm	907/546-2254	"We Like Kids," "Rabbit Ears"
Talkeetna	KTNA 88.9 fm	907/733-1045	"Rabbit Ears"
Unalaska	KIAL 1450 am	907/581-1888	"We Like Kids," "Rabbit Ears"
Unalakleet	KNSA 930 am	907/624-3101	"We Like Kids," "Rabbit Ears"
Valdez	KCHU 88.1 fm	907/835-4665	"We Like Kids," "Pickleberry Pie"
Wrangell	KSTK 101.7 fm	907/874-2345	"Rabbit Ears"

ALABAMA

Birmingham	WGIB 91.9 fm	205/323-1516	religious
Dothan	WRWA 88.7 fm	205/670-3268	"Rabbit Ears"
Huntsville	WLRH 89.3 fm	205/895-9574	"Rabbit Ears"
Mobile	WHIL 91.3 fm	205/460-2395	"Rabbit Ears"
Mussel Shoals	WQPR 88.7 fm	205/348-6644	"Rabbit Ears"
Troy	WTSU 89.9 fm	205/670-3268	"Rabbit Ears"
Tuscaloosa	WUAL 91.5 fm	205/348-6644	"Rabbit Ears"

ARIZONA

Phoenix	KIDR 740 am	602/279-5577	full-time "Radio Aahs" satellite station
White River	KNNB 88.1 fm	602/338-5229	occasional programs

ARKANSAS

Conway	KUCA 91.3 fm	501/450-5555	eleven hours per week, "We Like Kids," "Pickleberry Pie"
Little Rock	KUAR 89.1 fm	501/569-8485	"Rabbit Ears"

CALIFORNIA

Arcata	KHSU 90.5 fm	707/826-4807	"We Like Kids"

Bakersfield	KPRX 89.1 fm	209/275-0764	"Rabbit Ears"
Claremont	KSPC 88.7 fm	714/621-8157	
Cupertino	KKUP 91.5 fm	408/253-0303	
El Centro	KUBO 88.7 fm	619/337-8051	"Pickleberry Pie"
Fresno	KVPR 89.3 fm	209/275-0764	"Rabbit Ears"
Garberville	KMUD 91.1 fm	707/923-2513	
Hayward	KCRH 89.9 fm	510/786-6954	"Pickleberry Pie"
Los Angeles area:			
(Los Angeles)	KUSC 91.5 fm	213/743-5872	"Rabbit Ears"
(North Hollywood)	KPFK 90.7 fm	818/985-2711	
(North Hollywood)	KWNK 670 am	818/763-4226	
(Orange)	KPLS 830 am	714/282-8300	full-time "Radio Aahs" satellite station
Nevada City	KVMR 89.5 fm	916/265-9073	three hours per week
Northridge	KCSN 88.5 fm	818/885-3089	"Pickleberry Pie"
Palm Springs	KPSC 88.5 fm	213/743-5872	"Rabbit Ears"
San Bernardino	KVCR 91.9 fm	909/888-6511	"Rabbit Ears"
San Clemente	KWVE 107.9 fm	714/492-9800	three hours per week, religious
San Francisco	KUSF 90.3 fm	415/386-5873	daily, "Pickleberry Pie"
San Francisco	KALW 91.7 fm	415/695-5740	"Rabbit Ears"
San Luis Obispo	KCBX 90.1 fm	805/781-3020	"Pickleberry Pie," "We Like Kids"
San Luis Obispo	KIID 1400 am	805/543-9400	full-time "Radio Aahs" satellite station
Santa Barbara	KCSB 91.9 fm	805/961-3757	
Santa Barbara	KFAC 88.7 fm	213/743-5872	"Rabbit Ears"
Santa Cruz	KUSP 88.9 fm	408/476-2800	
Thousand Oaks	KCTQ 850 am	805/495-6251	full-time "Radio Aahs" satellite station
Thousand Oaks	KCPB 91.1 fm	213/743-5872	"Rabbit Ears"
Ventura	KNJO 92.7 fm	805/497-8511	

COLORADO

Alamosa	KRZA 88.7 fm	719/589-9057	"We Like Kids"
Carbondale	KDNK 90.5 fm	303/963-2976	"Pickleberry Pie"
Cortez	KSJD 91.5 fm	303/565-8457	"Rabbit Ears"
Denver	KKYD 1340 am	303/989-1340	full-time "Radio Aahs" satellite station
Fort Collins	KCSU 90.5 fm	303/491-7611	"We Like Kids," "Pickleberry Pie"

| Ignacio | KSUT 91.3 fm | 303/247-4900 | "We Like Kids," "Pickleberry Pie," "Rabbit Ears" |
| Lamar | KANZ 98.3 fm | 316/275-7444 | "We Like Kids," "Rabbit Ears" |

CONNECTICUT

Hartford	WPKT 90.5 fm	203/527-0905	"Rabbit Ears"
Norwich	WNPR 89.1 fm	203/527-0905	"Rabbit Ears"
Stamford	WEDW 88.5 fm	203/527-0905	"Rabbit Ears"
Storrs	WHUS 91.7 fm	203/486-4007	"Pickleberry Pie"

DELAWARE

| Newark | WVUD 91.3 fm | 302/831-2701 | |

DISTRICT OF COLUMBIA

Washington D.C. WPFW 89.3 fm   202/783-3100

See also Silver Spring, Maryland (WKDL), and Manassas, Virginia (WKDV).

FLORIDA

Fort Pierce	WQCS 88.9 fm	407/468-4744	"Rabbit Ears"
Jacksonville	WJCT 89.9 fm	904/353-7770	"Rabbit Ears"
Miami	WDNA 88.9 fm	305/662-8889	"Rabbit Ears"
Ocala	WTMC 1290 am	904/629-7400	
Panama City	WKGC 90.7 fm	904/769-5241	"Pickleberry Pie," "We Like Kids," "Rabbit Ears"
Pensacola	WUWF 88.1 fm	904/474-2327	"Rabbit Ears"
Tallahassee	WFSU 88.9 fm	904/487-3086	"Rabbit Ears"
Tampa	WMNF 88.5 fm	813/238-8001	

GEORGIA

Albany	WUNV 91.7 fm	404/756-4730	"Rabbit Ears"
Athens	WUGA 91.7 fm	706/542-9842	"Rabbit Ears"
Augusta	WACG 90.7 fm	706/737-1661	"Rabbit Ears"
Brunswick	WWIO 89.1 fm	404/756-4730	"Rabbit Ears"
Columbus	WJSP 88.1 fm	404/756-4730	"Rabbit Ears"
Fort Gaines	WJWV 90.9 fm	404/756-4730	"Rabbit Ears"
Macon	WDCO 89.7 fm	404/656-5961	"Rabbit Ears"
Savannah	WSVH 91.1 fm	912/238-0911	"Rabbit Ears"
Tifton	WABR 91.1 fm	912/386-3964	"Rabbit Ears"
Valdosta	WWET 91.7 fm	404/756-4730	"Rabbit Ears"
Waycross	WXVS 90.1 fm	404/756-4730	"Rabbit Ears"

HAWAII

Honolulu	KIPO 89.3 fm	808/955-8821	"Rabbit Ears"

IDAHO

Rexburg	KRIC 100.5 fm	208/356-2907	"Rabbit Ears"

ILLINOIS

Carbondale	WSIU 91.9 fm	618/453-4343	"Rabbit Ears"
Chicago	WXAV 88.3 fm	312/779-9858	"Pickleberry Pie"
Chicago	WBEZ 91.5 fm	312/460-9150	"Rabbit Ears
Chicago	WLUP 1000 am	312/447-5270	
Eureka	WCRI 98.5 fm	309/467-5555	
Galesburg	WVKC 90.5 fm	309/343-9940	"Pickleberry Pie"
Glen Ellyn	WDCB 90.9 fm	708/858-5196	
Olney	WUSI 90.3 fm	618/395-3422	"Rabbit Ears"
Peoria	WCBU 89.9 fm	309/677-3690	"Rabbit Ears
Quincy	WWQC 90.3 fm	217/228-5409	
Urbana	WEFT 90.1 fm	217/359-9338	"Pickleberry Pie," "We Like Kids"
Urbana	WILL 90.9 fm	217/356-2400	"We Like Kids," "Rabbit Ears"

INDIANA

Columbia City	WJHS 91.5 fm	219/248-8915	"Pickleberry Pie"
Evansville	WPSR 90.7 fm	812/465-8241	"Pickleberry Pie"
Fort Wayne	WBNI 89.1 fm	219/423-1629	"Rabbit Ears"
Gary	WGVE 88.7 fm	219/962-7571	"Pickleberry Pie"
Indianapolis	WFYI 90.1 fm	317/636-2020	
Muncie	WBST 92.1 fm	317/285-5888	"Rabbit Ears"
Pendleton	WEEM 91.7 fm	317/778-2161	"Pickleberry Pie"
Richmond	WVXR 89.3 fm	513/731-9898	"Rabbit Ears"
West Lafayette	WBAA 920 am	317/494-5920	"Rabbit Ears"

IOWA

Ames	WOI 640 am	515/294-2025	"Rabbit Ears"
Des Moines	KDPS 88.1 fm	515/242-7723	

KANSAS

Ashland	KANZ 98.3 fm	316/275-7444	"We Like Kids," "Rabbit Ears"
Atwood	KANZ 95.3 fm	316/275-7444	"We Like Kids," "Rabbit Ears"
Colby	KANZ 88.9 fm	316/275-7444	"We Like Kids," "Rabbit Ears"
Dodge City	KANZ 96.3 fm	316/275-7444	"We Like Kids," "Rabbit Ears"
Elkhart	KANZ 98.3 fm	316/275-7444	"We Like Kids," "Rabbit Ears"

Garden City	KANZ 91.1 fm	316/275-7444	"We Like Kids," "Rabbit Ears"
Goodland	KANZ 91.7 fm	316/275-7444	"We Like Kids," "Rabbit Ears"
Hays	KANZ 98.3 fm	316/275-7444	"We Like Kids," "Rabbit Ears"
Herndon	KANZ 91.3 fm	316/275-7444	"We Like Kids," "Rabbit Ears"
Liberal	KANZ 98.3 fm	316/275-7444	"We Like Kids," "Rabbit Ears"
McDonald	KANZ 91.3 fm	316/275-7444	"We Like Kids," "Rabbit Ears"
Ness City	KANZ 98.3 fm	316/275-7444	"We Like Kids," "Rabbit Ears"
St. Francis	KANZ 99.3 fm	316/275-7444	"We Like Kids," "Rabbit Ears"
Sharon Springs	KANZ 90.7 fm	316/275-7444	"We Like Kids," "Rabbit Ears"
Topeka	KJTY 88 fm	913/357-8888	five hours per week
Tribune	KANZ 98.3 fm	316/275-7444	"We Like Kids," "Rabbit Ears"

KENTUCKY

Bowling Green	WKYU 88.9 fm	502/745-5489	"Pickleberry Pie," "We Like Kids"
Elizabethtown	WKUE 90.9 fm	502/745-5489	"Pickleberry Pie," "We Like Kids"
Henderson-Owensboro	WKPB 89.5 fm	502/745-5489	"Pickleberry Pie," "We Like Kids"
Murray	WKMS 91.3 fm	502/762-4359	"Rabbit Ears"
Somerset	WDCL 89.7 fm	502/745-5489	"Pickleberry Pie," "We Like Kids"
Versailles	WJMM 106.3 fm	502/873-8096	religious

LOUISIANA

Hammond	KSLU 90.9 fm	504/549-5758	"Rabbit Ears"
Monroe	KEDM 90.3 fm	318/342-5556	"Rabbit Ears"
New Orleans	WRBH 88.3 fm	504/899-1144	

MAINE

Bangor	WMEH 90.9 fm	207/941-1010	"Rabbit Ears"
Blue Hill	WERU 89.9 fm	207/374-2313	
Calais	WMED 89.7 fm	207/941-1010	"Rabbit Ears"
Fort Kent	WMEF 106.5 fm	207/941-1010	"Rabbit Ears"
Portland	WMPG 90.9 fm	207/780-4974	"We Like Kids"
Portland	WMEA 90.1 fm	207/941-1010	"Rabbit Ears"
Presque Isle	WMEM 106.1 fm	207/941-1010	"Rabbit Ears"
Waterville	WMEW 91.5 fm	207/941-1010	"Rabbit Ears"

MARYLAND

Baltimore	WBGR 860 am	410/367-7773	
Baltimore	WRBS 95.1 fm	410/247-4100	
Baltimore	WKDB 1570 am	1-800/552-2470	full-time "Radio Aahs" satellite station

| Silver Spring | WKDL 1050 am | 301/588-1050 | full-time "Radio Aahs" satellite station |

MASSACHUSETTS
Boston area:

(Boston)	WBZ 1030 am	617/787-7000	
(Boston)	WGBH 89.7 fm	617/492-2777	"Rabbit Ears"
(Boston)	WUMB 91.9 fm	617/287-6900	
(Cambridge)	WMBR 88.1 fm	617/253-8810	
(Waltham)	WCRB 102.5 fm	617/893-7080	
(Waltham)	WBRS 100.1 fm	617/736-4785	twelve hours per week, "Pickleberry Pie"
(Waltham)	WRCA 1330 am	617/492-3300	
Concord	WADN 1120 am	508/371-3200	
Provincetown	WOMR 91.9 fm	508/487-2106	four hours per week

MICHIGAN

Ann Arbor	WUOM 91.7 fm	313/764-9210	"Rabbit Ears"
Ann Arbor	WVGR 104.1 fm	616/956-7711	"Rabbit Ears"
Detroit	WDTR 90.9 fm	313/596-3507	full-time children's station
Flint	WFBE 95.1 fm	313/760-1148	"We Like Kids," "Rabbit Ears
Flint	WFUM 91.1 fm	313/764-9210	"Rabbit Ears"
Grand Rapids	WGVU 88.5 fm	616/771-6666	"Rabbit Ears"
Grand Rapids	WGVU 1480 am	616/771-6666	"Rabbit Ears"
Grand Rapids	WISZ 640 am	616/949-8585	full-time "Radio Aahs" satellite station
Interlochen	WIAA 88.7 fm	616/276-6171	"Rabbit Ears"
Lansing	WVFN 730 am	517/487-5986	
Marquette	WNMU 90.1 fm	906/227-2600	"Rabbit Ears"
Spring Arbor	KTGG 1540 am	517/750-6540	daily, religious
Traverse City	WNMC 90.9 fm	616/922-1091	"We Like Kids"

MINNESOTA

| Grand Rapids | KAXE 91.7 fm | 218/326-1234 | "We Like Kids" |
| Minneapolis | WWTC 1280 am | 612/926-1280 | full-time, flagship "Radio Aahs" station |

MISSISSIPPI

| Holly Springs | WURC 88.1 fm | 601/252-5881 | "Pickleberry Pie" |
| Senatobia | WKNA 88.9 fm | 901/458-2521 | "Rabbit Ears" |

MISSOURI

Columbia	KOPN 89.5 fm	314/874-5676	"Pickleberry Pie," "We Like Kids," "Rabbit Ears"
St. Joseph	KGNM 1270 am	816/233-2577	eight hours per week, religious
St. Louis	WFUN 95.5 fm	314/291-9386	full-time children's station
St. Louis	KLZE 95.3 fm	314/437-6121	full-time "Radio Aahs" satellite station
Springfield	KIDS 1340 am	417/864-KIDS	full-time children's station
Springfield	KSMU 91.1 fm	417/836-5878	"Pickleberry Pie," "We Like Kids"

MONTANA

Missoula	KUFM 89.1 fm	406/243-4931	daily

NEBRASKA

Alliance	KTNE 91.1 fm	402/472-3611	"Rabbit Ears"
Bassett	KMNE 90.3 fm	402/472-3611	"Rabbit Ears"
Chadron	KCNE 91.9 fm	402/472-3611	"Rabbit Ears"
Hastings	KHNE 89.1 fm	402/472-3611	"Rabbit Ears"
Lexington	KLNE 88.7 fm	402/472-3611	"Rabbit Ears"
Lincoln	KZUM 89.3 fm	402/474-5086	
Lincoln	KUCV 90.9 fm	402/472-3611	"Rabbit Ears"
Merriman	KRNE 91.5 fm	402/472-3611	"Rabbit Ears"
Norfolk	KXNE 89.3 fm	402/472-3611	"Rabbit Ears"
North Platte	KPNE 91.7 fm	402/472-3611	"Rabbit Ears"
Omaha	KIOS 91.5 fm	402/554-2777	"Rabbit Ears"

NEVADA

Reno	KUNR 88.7 fm	702/784-6591	"Rabbit Ears"
Elko	KNCC 91.5 fm	702/738-8493	"Rabbit Ears"

NEW HAMPSHIRE

Concord	WEVO 89.1 fm	603/228-8910	"Pickleberry Pie"
Keene	WKNH 91.3 fm	603/358-2417	"Pickleberry Pie"

NEW JERSEY

Atlantic City	WFPG 1450 am	609/348-4646	
Cherry Hill	WEEE 89.5 fm	609/424-8981	religious
Teaneck	WFDU 89.1 fm	201/692-2806	"Pickleberry Pie"

NEW MEXICO

Alamo	KABR 1500 am	505/854-2632	twelve hours per week, "Pickleberry Pie," "We Like Kids"
Albuquerque	KUNM 89.9 fm	505/277-4806	"Pickleberry Pie"

Albuquerque	KANW 89.1 fm	505/242-7163	"We Like Kids," "Rabbit Ears"
Dulce	KCIE 90.5 fm	505/759-3681	
Gallup	KGLP 91.7 fm	505/863-7625	"We Like Kids," "Rabbit Ears"
Pine Hill	KTDB 89.7 fm	505/775-3215	"Pickleberry Pie"

NEW YORK STATE

Albany	WAMC 90.3 fm	518/465-5233	"Rabbit Ears"
Albany	WCAN 93.3 fm	518/465-5233	"Rabbit Ears"
Alexandria Bay	N.C.P.R.* 91.3 fm	315/379-5356	"Rabbit Ears"
Brockport	WBSU 88.9 fm	716/395-5626	"Pickleberry Pie"
Brookville	WCWP 88.1 fm	516/299-2626	
Canton	WSLU 89.5 fm	315/379-5356	"Rabbit Ears"
Geneva	WEOS 89.7 fm	315/781-3456	"Rabbit Ears"
Hempstead	WRHU 88.7 fm	516/463-5668	
Jeffersonville	WJFF 90.5 fm	914/482-4141	"Rabbit Ears"
Kingston	WAMK 90.9 fm	518/465-5233	"Rabbit Ears"
Lake Placid	N.C.P.R.* 91.7 fm	315/379-5356	"Rabbit Ears"
Long Lake	N.C.P.R.* 91.7 fm	315/379-5356	"Rabbit Ears"
Malone	WSLO 90.9 fm	315/379-5356	"Rabbit Ears"
Middletown	WOSR 91.7 fm	518/465-5233	"Rabbit Ears"
New York City	WBAI 99.5 fm	212/279-0707	
New York City	WNCN 104.3 fm	212/730-9626	
New York City	WNYC 93.9 fm	212/669-7800	"Rabbit Ears"
New York City	WNYU 89.1 fm	212/998-1660	
New York City	WNYE 91.5 fm	718/935-4480	full-time children's station, "Pickleberry Pie," "We Like Kids"
Oswego	WNYO 88.9 fm	315/341-2907	"Pickleberry Pie," "We Like Kids"
Oswego	WRVO 89.9 fm	315/341-3690	"Rabbit Ears"
Peru	WXLU 88.3 fm	315/379-5356	"Rabbit Ears"
Plattsburgh	WCFE 91.9 fm	518/563-9770	"Pickleberry Pie," "We Like Kids"; "Rabbit Ears"
Rochester	WXXI 91.5 fm	716/325-7500	"Rabbit Ears"
Saranac Lake	WSLL 90.5 fm	315/379-5356	"Rabbit Ears"
Southampton	WPBX 91.3 fm	516/283-8555	"Rabbit Ears"
Ticonderoga	WANC 103.9 fm	518/465-5233	"Rabbit Ears"
Tupper Lake	N.C.P.R.* 91.7 fm	315/379-5356	"Rabbit Ears"
Utica	WRNV 91.9 fm	315/341-3690	"Rabbit Ears"
Watertown	WRVJ 91.7 fm	315/341-3690	"Rabbit Ears"
Watertown	WSLJ 88.9 fm	315/379-5350	"Rabbit Ears"

White Plains   WFAS 1230 am   914/693-2400
* *North Country Public Radio*

NORTH CAROLINA

Fayetteville	WFSS 89.1 fm	919/486-1381	"Pickleberry Pie," "We Like Kids"
Spindale	WNCW 88.7 fm	704/287-8000	"We Like Kids"

NORTH DAKOTA

Belcourt	KEYA 88.5 fm	701/477-5686	
Bismark	KNDR 104.7 fm	701/663-2345	
Fargo	KFNW 1200 am	701/282-5910	religious
Minot	KHRT 1320 am	701/852-3789	religious

OHIO

Cincinnati	WVXC 89.3 fm	513/731-9898	"Rabbit Ears"
Cincinnati	WGRR 103.5 fm	513/321-8900	
Cincinnati	WXVU 91.7 fm	513/731-9898	"Rabbit Ears"
Cleveland	WCLV 95.5 fm	216/464-0900	
Cleveland	WRUW 91.1 fm	216/368-2207	
Columbus	WCBE 90.5 fm	614/365-5555	
DeGraff	WDEQ 103.3 fm	513/585-5981	"Pickleberry Pie"
Oberlin	WOBC 91.5 fm	216/775-8107	
Toledo	WSPD 1370 am	419/244-8321	
West Union	WVXM 89.5 fm	513/731-9898	"Rabbit Ears"
Yellow Springs	WYSO 91.3 fm	513/767-6422	"We Like Kids"
Youngstown	WYSU 88.5 fm	216/742-3363	"Rabbit Ears"

OKLAHOMA

Guymon	KANZ 88.9 fm	316/275-7444	"We Like Kids," "Rabbit Ears"
Stillwater	KSPI 780 am	405/372-7800	
Tulsa	KWGS 89.5 fm	918/631-2577	"Rabbit Ears"

OREGON

Astoria	KMUN 91.9 fm	503/325-0010	"We Like Kids"
Corvallis	KOAC 550 am	503/737-4311	"Rabbit Ears"
Pendleton	KRBM 90.0 fm	503/244-9900	"Rabbit Ears"
Portland	KBPS 1450 am	503/280-5828	daily
Portland	KBPS 89.9 fm	503/280-5828	three hours per week, "We Like Kids"
Portland	KOAB 91.3 fm	503/244-9900	"Rabbit Ears"

PENNSYLVANIA

Clarion	WCUC 91.7 fm	814/226-2330	"Pickleberry Pie"
Corry	WWCB 1370 am	814/664-8694	
East Stroudsburg	WESS 90.3 fm	717/424-3134	"We Like Kids"
Philadelphia	WPEB 88.1 fm	215/386-3800	daily
Philadelphia	WXPN 88.5 fm	215/898-6677	
Scranton	WVIA 89.9 fm	717/655-2808	"Rabbit Ears"
Shiremanstown	WWII 720 am	717/737-9944	religious
Stroudsburg	WVPO 840 am	717/421-2100	
University Park	WPSU 91.1 fm	814/865-9191	
Warminster	WRDV 89.3 fm	215/674-8002	
Williamsport	WRLC 91.7 fm	717/321-4054	three hours per week
York	WVYC 88.1 fm	717/845-7413	

RHODE ISLAND

Newport	WADK 1540 am	401/846-1540

SOUTH CAROLINA

Charleston	WSCI 89.3 fm	803/881-1160
Columbia	WLTR 91.3 fm	803/737-3420
Columbia	WMHK 89.7 fm	803/754-5400

SOUTH DAKOTA

St. Francis	KINI 96.1 fm	605/747-2291	"Pickleberry Pie"
Porcupine	KILI 90.1 fm	605/867-5002	

TENNESSEE

Collegedale	WSMC 90.5 fm	615/238-2905	"Rabbit Ears"
Dyersburg	WKNQ 90.7 fm	901/458-2521	"Rabbit Ears"
Jackson	WKNP 90.1 fm	901/458-2521	"Rabbit Ears"
Johnson City	WETS 89.5 fm	615/929-6440	"Rabbit Ears"
Memphis	WYPL 89.3 fm	901/725-8833	"Pickleberry Pie"
Memphis	WKNO 91.1 fm	901/458-2521	"Rabbit Ears"

TEXAS

Alvin	KACC 89.7 fm	713/388-4675	"Pickleberry Pie"
Dallas	KAHZ 1360 am	817/589-1100	full-time "Radio Aahs" satellite station
Houston	KPFT 90.1 fm	713/526-4000	"Rabbit Ears"
Killeen	KNCT 91.3 fm	817/526-1176	"We Like Kids," "Rabbit Ears"
Lubbock	KOHM 89.1 fm	806/742-3100	

| Texarkana | KTXK 91.5 fm | 903/838-4541 | "Rabbit Ears" |

UTAH

| Salt Lake City | KKDS 1060 am | 801/262-5624 | full-time children's station, both local and "Radio Aahs" satellite |

VERMONT

Plainfield	WGDR 91.9 fm	802/454-7762	
Waterbury	WDEV 550 am	802/244-7321	
White River Junction	WKXE 95.3 fm	802/295-5850	

VIRGINIA

Blacksburg	WUVT 90.7 fm	703/282-4975	
Harrisonburg	WMRA 90.7 fm	703/568-6221	"Rabbit Ears"
Lexington	WMRL 89.9 fm	703/568-6221	"Rabbit Ears"
Manassas	WKDV 1460 am	703/503-1460	full-time "Radio Aahs" satellite station
Norfolk	WHRV 89.5 fm	804/489-9476	"Rabbit Ears"
Radford	WVRU 89.9 fm	703/831-5171	"Pickleberry Pie"
Richmond	WCVE 88.9 fm	804/320-1301	

WASHINGTON

Bellevue	KBCS 91.3 fm	206/641-2427	
Bellingham	KZAZ 91.3 fm	206/738-9170	"Rabbit Ears"
Lynnwood	KSER 90.7 fm	206/742-4541	daily, "Pickleberry Pie," "We Like Kids"
Olympia	KAOS 89.3 fm	206/866-6893	
Seattle	KidStar 1250 am	206/625-1250	full-time children's station
Seattle	KNHC 89.5 fm	206/281-6215	
Seattle	KUOW 94.9 fm	206/543-2710	"Rabbit Ears"
Spokane	KAZZ 107.1 fm	509/276-8816	full-time "Radio Aahs" satellite station

WASHINGTON, DC

See District of Columbia; Silver Spring, Maryland; and Manassas, Virginia.

WEST VIRGINIA

Beckley	WVPB 91.7 fm	304/558-3000	
Charleston	WVPN 88.5 fm	304/558-3000	
Clarksburg (Buckhannon-Weston)	WVPW 88.9 fm	304/558-3000	
Huntington	WVWV 89.9 fm	304/558-3000	

Martinsburg	WVEP 88.9 fm	304/558-3000	
Morgantown	WVPM 90.0 fm	304/558-3000	
Parkersburg	WVPG 90.3 fm	304/558-3000	
Philippi	WQAB 91.3 fm	304/457-2916	"Pickleberry Pie"
Wheeling	WVNP 89.9 fm	304/558-3000	

WISCONSIN

Appleton	WLFM 91.1 fm	414/465-2444	"Rabbit Ears"
Eau Claire	WEIO 1050 am	715/836-0123	full-time "Radio Aahs" satellite station
Green Bay	WGBW 91.5 fm	414/465-2444	"Rabbit Ears"
Hayward	WOJB 88.9 fm	715/634-2100	
LaCrosse	WHLA 90.3 fm	715/839-3868	"Rabbit Ears"
Madison	WHHI 91.3 fm	608/263-3970	"Rabbit Ears"
Madison	WHA 970 am	608/263-3970	"Rabbit Ears"
Madison	WORT 89.9 fm	608/256-2695	
Menomonie	WHWC 88.3 fm	715/839-3868	"Rabbit Ears"
Milwaukee	WYMS 88.9 fm	414/475-8389	"We Like Kids"
Milwaukee	WHAD 90.7 fm	414/271-8686	"Rabbit Ears"
Oshkosh	WRST 90.3 fm	414/465-2444	"Rabbit Ears"
Park Falls	WHBM 90.3 fm	715/394-8531	"Rabbit Ears"
Stevens Point	WLBL 930 am	715/839-3868	"Rabbit Ears"
Superior	KUWS 91.3 fm	715/394-8531	"Rabbit Ears"
Whitewater	WSUW 91.7 fm	414/472-1317	

VIDEO FOR CHILDREN

Free Resource

Notable Films/Videos, Recordings and Microcomputer Software. A listing of quality recordings, films, videotapes, and computer software for young people through age fourteen. Compiled annually by three committees of the Association for Library Service to Children of the American Library Association. In making their selections, the committees consider the esthetic and technical quality (i.e., the effective use of narration, sound effects, music, and visuals). For a free copy, send a self-addressed, stamped envelope along with your request to the Association of Library Service to Children, 50 East Huron Street, Chicago, Illinois 60611.

Books

General

The Best of the Best. Edited by Denise Perry Donavin. Random House, 1992. 366 pages. This annotated guidebook from the American Library Association recommends hundreds of children's books, magazines, videotapes, audiocassettes, toys, and computer software. Selected items, chosen by professionals in children's media, are grouped according to age appropriateness and media format. "Connections" refer readers to related materials in other portions of the book.

The Best Toys, Books and Videos for Kids. By Joanne Oppenheim and Stephanie Oppenheim. HarperCollins, 1993. 332 pages. Based on the consumer newsletter *The Oppenheim Toy Portfolio*, this guide tips parents off to the best toys, books, videotapes, audiocassettes, and computer products for kids from infancy through age ten. Contains reviews of more than one thousand products. Shopping tips, manufacturers' toll-free numbers, and brand-name comparisons are also included.

Great Videos for Kids: A Parent's Guide to Choosing the Best. By Catherine Cella. Carol Publishing Group, 1992. 157 pages. Offers informative reviews of videos for children of all ages. Each entry includes a synopsis, critical commentary, running time, recommended viewing age, and the production company. The very best are highlighted with a gold star. Arranged by category (music, folk, and fairy tales, etc.). Includes a foreword by Shelly Duvall.

Parents' Choice: A Sourcebook of the Very Best Products to Educate, Inform, and Entertain Children of All Ages. Selected by Diana Huss Green. Andrews and McMeel, 1993. 208 pages. Compiled by the founder and editor of *Parents' Choice* magazine, this sourcebook offers recommendations on the best toys, home videos, audiocassettes, computer programs, books, and magazines for children. Each entry includes the suggested retail price, recommended age range, and a full description to help parents decide if the product is right for their family. Also included is a list of companies that produce/distribute the products. For parents with children of all ages.

Play, Learn, and Grow. By James L. Thomas. R. R. Bowker, 1992. 352 pages. An evaluative guide to videotapes, audiocassettes, magazines, and books for very young children (up to age five). Each entry includes a brief description, recommended age level, bibliographic information, and a "priority of purchase" ranking. Material is indexed by author, subject, age range, and purchase priority. Also lists publishers, producers, and organizations adults can consult for guidance.

Family Viewing Guides

The Family Video Guide: Over 300 Movies to Share with Your Children. By Terry and Catherine Catchpole. Williamson Publishing, 1992. 242 pages. Offers tips on family video watching, including advice on choosing a video store, determining age appropriateness, and selecting videotapes for younger children. Includes reviews of movies organized by theme, plus a list of good flicks for the very young.

Leonard Maltin's Movie and Video Guide. By Leonard Maltin. Penguin Group. Published annually. 1,500+ pages. Reviews more than nineteen thousand movies, videotapes, and laser discs; includes ratings, running time, and other pertinent information for each. Arranged alphabetically.

Movies on TV and Videocassette. By Steven Scheuer. Bantam. Published every two years. 1,300+ pages. This comprehensive guide contains reviews and ratings for cable programs, movies on television, and videocassettes. Entries are arranged alphabetically. Includes indexes to stars and directors.

Roger Ebert's Video Companion.
By Roger Ebert. Andrews and
McMeel, 1993 (1994 edition). 880
pages. The Pulitzer Prize-winning
film critic reviews more than twelve
hundred films. Also included are essays and interviews with movie stars
and directors (Robert Redford, Al
Pacino, Spike Lee, etc.).

**Viewer's Choice Guide to Movies
on Video.** By the editors of Consumer Reports Books and Joe Blade.
Consumer Reports Books, 1991. 416
pages. A guide to movies on videocassette for the selective viewer.

Standard Library Directories

AV Market Place. R. R. Bowker. Updated annually, this comprehensive
directory puts people in touch with
more than sixty-three thousand companies that create, supply, or distribute audio-visual materials, including
films, videotapes, and recordings. A
good source for current names, addresses, and phone numbers.

**Bowker's Complete Video Direc-
tory.** R. R. Bowker. Updated annually,
this two-volume reference covers
more than seventy-five thousand videos. Intended for use as a selection
guide. Includes content summaries,
ordering information and acquisition
assistance. Volume 1 covers entertainment; volume 2 covers educa-
tion/special interest. Check your
local library.

The Video Source Book. Gale Research. Published annually. A massive, two-volume guide to more than
130,000 videos, including feature
films, children's programs, documentaries, instructional guides, travel
guides, and more. Each entry includes a description, targeted audience and purpose, format, price, and
distributor. Arranged alphabetically,
with a subject index plus a listing of
hundreds of program distributors

(including their addresses and phone
numbers).

Video on Video

**Choosing the Best in Children's
Video.** Produced by Joshua Greene
for ALA Video. Christopher Reeve
hosts this thirty-five-minute tour
through some of the best live-action
and animated videotapes available.
Explains how to select and locate
quality viewing (fiction and nonfiction) for children from infancy
through age twelve. Available from
the American Library Association, 50
East Huron Street, Chicago, Illinois
60611. Phone: 312/944-6780 or
1/800-545-2433.

Reviews and Guides

Booklist. American Library Association, 50 East Huron Street, Chicago,
Illinois 60611. Phone: 1/800-545-
2433. In addition to book reviews,
Booklist provides reviews of videotapes, filmstrips, and audiobooks
for children and adults.

Children's Video Report. 390 Court
Street, #76, Brooklyn, New York
11231-4331. Phone: 718/935-0600.
An independent review of children's
videotapes. Includes descriptions,
commentary, ratings (from four stars
to no stars), running time, recommended age-level, price, and distributor. Each issue has a theme (the
environment, fantasy and science fiction, tapes that teach, tapes for toddlers, etc.). Back issues are available.
Issued eight times annually.

Entertainment Weekly. P.O. Box
60001, Tampa, Florida 33612. Phone:
1/800-828-6882. This weekly includes a supplement called *Kids Entertainment Extra*, a guide for parents
from the editors of *Entertainment
Weekly* and *Parenting* magazine
(you'll find this supplement in *Parenting* as well). *Kids Entertainment Extra*

includes reviews of movies, videotapes, videogames, books, and theme-related products for children.

The Oppenheim Toy Portfolio. 40 East Ninth Street, New York, New York 10003. Phone: 212/598-0502 or 1/800-544-TOYS. A quarterly newsletter that reviews toys, books, and videos for children of different ages. Recommends the most innovative products, including products for children with special needs.

Parents' Choice. A quarterly review of children's media, including books, movies, television programs, videotapes, and audio recordings. Contact Parents' Choice Foundation, P.O. Box 185, Waban, Massachusetts 02168. Phone: 617/965-5913.

School Library Journal. Contains reviews of new books, recordings, and videocassettes for children and young adults. Published monthly. Contact School Library Journal, 249 West Seventeenth Street, New York, New York 10011. Phone: 212/463-6759 or 1/800-456-9409 (subscriptions).

Video Librarian. Box 2725, Bremerton, Washington 98310. Phone: 206/377-2231. Offers news, features, and reviews of videos, including books and magazines on video. A good source for information on recent releases. Available at many libraries. Issued bimonthly.

The following parenting magazines regularly review children's videotapes:

Child. Section called "KidsMedia" includes television and video recommendations. Available on newsstands or by subscription (P.O. Box 3176, Harlan, Iowa 51593-0367. Phone: 1/800-777-0222).

Family Fun. Each issue includes reviews of audio and video for kids. Available on newsstands or by subscription (P.O. Box 10161, Des

---

How to Guard Your VCR
Find any spoons in your VCR lately? If so, you may want to guard your VCR slot from your curious George or Georgette with a VCR slot guard, a one-piece shield that blocks the front opening when the machine is not in use. Manufactured by Playskool Baby, Inc., and available in baby-product and department stores nationwide for around $3.00.

Moines, Iowa 50340-0161. Phone: 1/800-289-4849).

Parenting. Includes *Kids Entertainment Extra*, a pull-out review of videotapes, videogames, books, and theme-related products. Available on newsstands or by subscription (Time, Inc., Ventures, 301 Howard Street, 17th Floor, San Francisco, California 94105. Phone: 1/800-635-2665).

Parents. "Reviews and News" section offers a roundup of new books, recordings, and videos for children. Available on newsstands or by subscription (685 Third Avenue, New York, New York 10017. Phone: 1/800-727-3682).

Hotline

Child Magazine's MediaKids Hotline. Phone: 1/900-407-4KID (95¢ per call). Each week, *Child* magazine picks what it considers to be the best movie, videotape, and television program for children and then makes this information available through its MediaKids Hotline. Callers can choose weekly recommendations for children ages two to six or age seven and up. New media selections for the week begin every Tuesday morning at

9:00 a.m. eastern standard time. (Note: *Child* magazine contains a regular feature called "MediaKids," where you'll also find descriptions of quality movies, videotapes, and television shows for kids.)

Computerized Clearinghouse

KIDSNET. A national nonprofit computerized clearinghouse devoted to children's audio, video, radio, and television programming. Those who subscribe to the electronic database have access to detailed information on more than twenty thousand video and audiocassette programs. (For more information, see "Computerized Clearinghouse" listed under "Television.")

Mail Order Catalogs

Alcazar's Catalog of Children's Music. P.O. Box 429, Waterbury, Vermont 05676. Phone: 1/800-541-9904. In addition to audio recordings for children, this catalog includes some of the finest videotapes available. Offers music on video, animated versions of classic tales, and award-winning fiction and nonfiction titles.

Bookmates/Listening Library. One Park Avenue, Old Greenwich, Connecticut 06870-1727. Phone: 1/800-243-4504. *Bookmates* contains a number of quality videotapes based on children's classics, including *Madeline, Whistle for Willie, Lyle, Lyle, Crocodile,* and *Curious George.* Also contains dolls, stuffed animals, and puppets based on the characters in the books.

Educational Record Center. 3233 Burnt Mill Drive, Suite 100, Wilmington, North Carolina 28403-2655. Phone: 919/251-1235. Offers a selection of award-winning videotapes, including musical recordings and animated children's classics. Many quality nonfiction titles are offered as well.

Kids First! Catalog. From the Coalition for Quality Children's Videos, this mail order catalog features forty quality videotapes, selected for their outstanding content and their ability to stimulate kids' intellects and imaginations. For a free copy, call 1/800-331-6197.

Music for Little People. Box 1460, Redway, California 95560. Phone: 1/800-727-2233. Offers a choice selection of videos for children, including the *Madeline* series, Rabbit Ears' folk tales, Shari Lewis and Lamb Chop tapes, the animated Shakespeare tales, and classics like *The Red Balloon.*

The Video Catalog. P.O. Box 64267, St. Paul, Minnesota 55164-0428. Phone: 1/800-733-6656. The "Family" section of this fifty-plus page catalog includes animated tales such as *Watership Down,* classics like *Sarah, Plain and Tall* and Disney's *Tales from Avonlea.* Also available are Reading Rainbow tapes, highlights from the long-running *Waltons* series, television specials such as *Roots* and *Lonesome Dove,* a variety of acclaimed documentaries, and holiday specials. British drama, comedy, and performing arts tapes can be found here as well.

Videos for Kids. Schoolmasters Video, 745 State Circle, P.O. Box 1941, Ann Arbor, Michigan 48106. Phone: 313/761-5175 or 1/800-521-2832 (orders only). In this catalog, you'll find fiction and nonfiction videos for kids of all ages. Educational offerings include the *Newton's Apple* and *Tell Me Why* science series; *National Geographic* and Jacques Cousteau collections; and videos about safety, history, space exploration, travel, the environment, dinosaurs, money, and other topics. Also included are children's classics, including Dr. Seuss, *Madeline*, *Babar*, and the Rabbit Ears collection of famous tales narrated by famous people. Disney videos, Shelly Duvall's *Bedtime Stories*, and Shakespeare animated tales (as seen on HBO) are among the other choice offerings.

Don't forget to check out the audio and video collections at your public library!

HIGHLY RECOMMENDED VIDEOTAPES (A SHORT LIST)

Below is a listing of highly recommended and/or award-winning videos for children. For descriptions of other videotapes for young viewers, refer to listings under specific topics (Friendship, Science, Animals, etc.) in other chapters of *The Parents' Resource Almanac*.

Baby's Bedtime and **Baby's Morningtime.** Lightyear Entertainment. Running time: 25 minutes each. Judy Collins' soothing voice, combined with animation based on Kay Chorao's award-winning artwork. For ages two to five.

Baby Songs and **More Baby Songs.** Hi-Tops Video. Running time: 30 minutes each. These award-winning videos feature toddlers in action, animation, puppetry, and catchy tunes. For ages one-and-a-half to five. *Even More Baby Songs* , *Super Baby Songs*, and other spin-offs are available as well.

The Dingles (and Three Other Titles for Family Enjoyment). Smarty Pants. Running time: 30 minutes. Using highly stylized animation, the title piece tells the tale of an off-beat woman and her family (three wacky cats). Other stories include *Little Red Riding Hood, The Lion and the Mouse,* and *The Boy and the Snow Goose*. Nominated for an Academy Award; produced by the National Film Board of Canada. For children ages three to eight.

Don't Wake Your Mom! A&M Video. Running time: 47 minutes. While Mom snoozes, young viewers are encouraged to play along with Shari Lewis and her puppets Lamb Chop, Charlie Horse, and Hush Puppy. Stories, magic, and jokes make this tape good fun for children ages one-and-a-half to five (older kids like to watch too).

Ezra Jack Keats Library. Children's Circle. Running time: 45 minutes. A collection of classic stories, including *The Snowy Day, Peter's Chair*, and *Whistle for Willie*. For ages three and up.

Harold and the Purple Crayon and Other Harold Stories. Children's Circle. Running time: 27 minutes. In addition to the imaginative stories themselves, this video includes a segment showing how the pictures were animated. For ages four to eight.

Madeline's Rescue. Golden Book Video. Running time: 30 minutes. Narrated by Christopher Plumber, this video presents the charming tale of Madeline and the dog who saves her life. An animated, musical version of the book that won Ludwig Bemelmans a Caldecott Medal back in 1954.

Maurice Sendak Library. Children's Circle. Running time: 35 minutes. A collection of timeless Sendak tales, including *Where the Wild Things Are* and *In the Night Kitchen*. Includes music by Carol King and an interview with the author himself. For ages five to eight.

Max's Chocolate Chicken (and Other Stories for the Very Young). Children's Circle. Running time: 30 minutes. Does Max play by the rules when he and his big sister compete for the chocolate chicken by collecting the most eggs? Young viewers find out during this five-minute animated film. Also on this tape are the stories *Each Peach Pear Plum, The Circus Baby,* and *Picnic* (an American Library Association Notable Video). For ages two to five.

Pegasus. Lightyear. Running time: 25 minutes. The myth of Pegasus, the winged horse, narrated by Mia Farrow. For ages seven and up.

The Pigs' Wedding. Children's Circle. Running time: 39 minutes. The music and animation set just the right tone for the feature title, about two pigs in love. Other stories on the tape include *A Letter to Amy* and *The Owl and the Pussy-Cat.* For ages two and up.

This Pretty Planet: Tom Chapin Live in Concert. Sony. Running time: 50 minutes. Chapin performs more than a dozen of his best songs. For all ages.

Raffi in Concert. A&M Video. Running time: 50 minutes. A quality performance by the mega-popular musician. For ages two and up. *Raffi's Young Children's Concert* is highly recommended as well.

Reading Rainbow (series). GPN. Running time: 25 minutes each. All the programs from the award-winning television series are available on videocassette. Among the best are *Arthur's Eyes, The Magic School Bus Inside the Earth,* and *The Robbery at the Diamond Dog Diner.* For elementary-school age children. An annotated listing of approximately one hundred programs is available from GPN, P.O. Box 80669, Lincoln, Nebraska 68501. Phone: 1/800-228-4630. (See listing under "Television" for more information on the series.)

The Red Balloon. New Line Home Video. Running time: 34 minutes. The Academy Award-winning film about a little boy and the balloon he befriends. For ages five and up.

The Red Shoes. Family Home Entertainment. Running time: 30 minutes. A story about friendship and an important pair of shoes, adapted from the Hans Christian Andersen fairy tale. For ages six and up.

The Secret Garden. CBS/Fox. Running time: 107 minutes. The BBC version of the classic story. For ages seven and up.

Shari Lewis Presents 101 Things for Kids to Do. Random House Home Video. Running time: 60 minutes. Shari Lewis, together with Lamb Chop, Hush Puppy, and Charlie Horse, demonstrates simple crafts and tricks using everyday items such as coins, pencils, and paper. For ages three to eight.

Shelley Duvall's Bedtime Stories. MCA/Universal Home Video. Running time: 25 minutes each. A collection of animated stories from the award-winning television program (Showtime). See listing under "Television" for more information.

The Snowman. Children's Circle. Running time: 26 minutes. A nonverbal winter tale about a young boy's adventures with a snowman. A classic, for ages four and up.

Stories from the Black Tradition. Children's Circle. Running time: 52 minutes. This multiple award-winning tape features folk and fairy tales from Africa, along with one story from the inner-city. For ages five and up.

We All Have Tall Tales (series). Rabbit Ears Productions. A collection of videotapes featuring folk tales from around the world, narrated by famous actors (Robin Williams and Jack Nicholson, for example). For ages five to nine. Also available in storybook/audio sets.

Producers and Distributors

A & M Video. 1416 North Labrea Avenue, Hollywood, California 90028. Phone: 213/469-2411.

Alcazar. P.O. Box 429, Waterbury, Vermont 05676. Phone: 1/800/541-9904.

CBS/Fox. 1330 Avenue of the Americas, 5th Floor, New York, New York 10019. Phone: 1/800-800-2369.

Children's Circle. Division of Weston Woods, CC Studios, Inc., Weston, Connecticut 06883. Phone: 1/800-543-7843 or 203/222-0002.

Family Home Entertainment. P.O. Box 10124, Van Nuys, California 91410. Phone: 818/778-3823.

Golden Book Video. 1220 Mound Avenue, Racine, Wisconsin 53401. Phone: 414/633-2431.

GPN. P.O. Box 80669, Lincoln, Nebraska 68501. Phone: 1/800-228-4630 or 402/472-1785.

Hi-Tops/Media Home Entertainment. 5730 Buckingham Way, Culver City, California 90230. Phone: 213/216-7900.

Lightyear Entertainment. Empire State Building, 350 Fifth Avenue, Suite 5101, New York, New York 10118. Phone: 212/563-4610.

MCA/Universal Home Video. 70 Universal City Plaza, Universal City, California 91608. Phone: 818/985-3894.

Music for Little People. P.O. Box 1460, Redway, California 95560. Phone: 1/800-727-2233.

New Line Home Video. Columbia Tristar/Home Video Distribution, 3400 Riverside, Burbank, California 91505-4627. Phone: 818/972-8090.

Rabbit Ears Productions. Distributed by UNI, 5 South Sylvan Road, Westport, Connecticut 06880. Phone: 203/857-3760.

Random House Home Video. 400 Hanh Road, Westminster, Maryland 21157. Phone: 1/800-733-3000.

Smarty Pants. 15104 Detroit Avenue, Suite #2, Lakewood, Ohio 44107. Phone: 216/221-5300.

Sony Kids' Video. 1700 Broadway, New York, New York 10019. Phone: 212/689-8897.

Other Video Sources

Purchasing

- Specialty children's book and toy stores,
- Video departments in larger general-merchandise stores
- Video stores/rental companies (many will special order)
- Mail order catalogs (refer to listings in this chapter)
- Directly from the producer/distributor. You can find current addresses and phone numbers in standard library directories such as *Bowker's Complete Video Directory*, *AV Market Place*, and *The Video Source Book* (see listings under "Books"). Sourcebooks such as *The Best of the Best* and *Parents' Choice* include lists of distributors for every recommended videotape (see listings under "Books" for more information on these titles).

Borrowing or Renting

- Your local library
- Video rental shops
- Some distributors offer both videotape rentals and sales (typically when their prices are very high).

VIDEOGAMES

Books

Game Over: How Nintendo Zapped an American Industry, Captured Your Dollars and Enslaved Your Children. By David Sheff. Random House, 1993. 445 pages. The success of the Nintendo invasion, according to the author, is one of remarkable invention, skillful marketing, and ruthlessness. Fads have come and gone before, but this one is different. The intensity with which kids play videogames and with which they submerge themselves in the Nintendo culture is noticeably different from the attention they pay to television. This book, based on two years of extensive research, offers insights.

Mind and Media: The Effects of Television, Video Games and Computers. By Patricia Marks Greenfield. Harvard University Press, 1984. 210 pages. Explains how the various media (television, video games, and computers) can be used to promote social growth and thinking skills. Offers practical suggestions for helping children thrive in a technological world.

A Parent's Guide to Video Games. By Jason R. Rich. DMS, 1991. 120 pages. A practical guide to selecting and managing home video games. Contains reviews of more than forty popular videogames. Each entry includes a description of the game; targeted age group; and a discussion of the positive lessons, knowledge, and/or skills a child can acquire from playing the game.

Video Kids: Making Sense of Nintendo. By Eugene F. Provenzo, Jr. Harvard University Press, 1991. 184 pages. Explores the role of videogames within American culture. The author argues that videogame technology is neither neutral nor trivial—that videogames reflect and pass on the particular values of mainstream culture. But to ensure a creative educational environment for all young learners, videogames must be freed of the violent and sexist messages that currently pervade the medium.

Videogame Review

Kids Entertainment Extra. From the editors of *Entertainment Weekly* and *Parenting*, this review column includes reviews and ratings of videogames for kids. Look for this pull-out guide in either magazine, available on newsstands or by subscription (*Parenting*, Time, Inc., Ventures, 301 Howard Street, 17th Floor, San Francisco, California 94105. Phone: 1/800-635-2665. *Entertainment Weekly*, P.O. Box 60001, Tampa, Florida 33612. Phone: 1/800-828-6882).

A Few Good Videogame Choices

Ariel: The Little Mermaid. Sega Genesis. This game features detailed graphics, music from the hit movie, and a heroine (as opposed to a hero). The player's mission is to help Ariel, Sebastian, and other friends save the sea creatures from the wicked Ursula. For ages seven and up.

Mickey's Safari in Letterland. Nintendo Entertainment System. Young viewers travel around the world with Mickey Mouse in search of the ancient alphabet tablets. Developed to enhance letter recognition. For ages three to seven.

Super Mario Paint and Mouse. Super Nintendo Entertainment System.

With this game, players can create animated drawings, complete with music and sound effects. Designed to encourage creativity and stretch children's imaginations. For ages seven and up.

Yoshi. Nintendo Entertainment System and Nintendo Game Boy. A challenging puzzle game for children ages eight and up.

TELEVISION

Children's television viewing continues to be highly controversial. There are those who advocate eliminating television altogether; others believe that television can be used as a learning tool; and some say the programming needs to be improved and that commercials should be curtailed. The resources listed in this section reflect the many differing opinions. Included are listings of television reviews and other resources designed to help parents and children select quality cable and broadcast programs.

Free and Inexpensive Resources

Children and Television. This brochure offers parents tips on how they can teach their children TV viewing skills. Includes what parents can do about time spent watching TV and the effects of violence and advertising on children. Produced by the PTA/Boys Town. For a free copy, send a self-addressed, stamped, business-size envelope along with your request to the National PTA. (See appendix I for contact information.)

Media Violence and Children: A Guide for Parents. Provides information about the effects associated with children's repeated viewing of television violence and offers guidelines for parents. Available for 50¢ from the National Association for the Education of Young Children. (See appendix I for contact information.)

Television and the Family. From the American Academy of Pediatrics, this free brochure offers guidelines for parents on children's television viewing. For a free copy, send a self-addressed, stamped, business-size envelope to "Television and the Family," Department C, American Academy of Pediatrics. (See appendix I for contact information.)

TV with Books Completes the Picture. This brochure suggests ways in which TV and video can serve as companions to reading. Includes additional resource listings. For ordering information, request a copy of the free *Consumer Information Catalog*, available from the Consumer Information Center, P.O. Box 100, Pueblo, Colorado 81002.

You Can Use Television to Stimulate Your Child's Reading Habits. A parent brochure available from the International Reading Association. Available in French, Spanish, and English. For a free copy, send a written request along with a self-addressed, stamped, business-size envelope to the International Reading Association. (See appendix I for contact information.)

Books

Television as a Learning Tool
Mind and Media: The Effects of Television, Video Games and Computers. By Patricia Marks Green-

field. See "Books" listed under "Videogames."

Taking Advantage of Media: A Manual for Parents and Teachers. By Laurene K. Brown. Routledge, 1986. 208 pages. The author answers questions that worried parents and teachers ask when they see their children preferring videos to books or spending their time watching too much television.

Use TV to Your Child's Advantage. By Dorothy G. Singer. Acropolis Books, 1990. 154 pages. Offers discussion ideas and activities to help parents and children make good use of television. Covers TV violence, stereotyping, commercials, and other important topics. Reviews the research on children and television.

What's Wrong With TV

The Beast, the Eunuch, and the Glass-Eyed Child: Television in the 80s and Beyond. By Ron Powers. Harcourt Brace, 1990. 382 pages. A series of essays by a Pulitzer Prize-winning critic. Wittily, and often scathingly, presents serious thoughts on television, including programs targeted at kids.

Endangered Minds: Why Children Don't Think and What We Can Do About It. By Jane M. Healy, Ph.D. Touchstone, 1991. 382 pages. According to the author of this book, too much television viewing and videogame playing may actually alter the structure of the growing brain, leading to reduced abilities to sustain attention independently, stick to problems actively, listen intelligently, read with understanding, and use language effectively. Advises parents to limit television and video use, participate with children whenever possible, and talk with their child about television content and methods of audience manipulation. A chapter called "*Sesame Street* and Death of Reading" describes how this popular program, which stands as a symbol of "good" programming, contains developmentally inappropriate material, manipulates children's senses, and gives young viewers an erroneous idea of what to expect from the printed page. "Words in books do not jump about, transform before one's eyes, or call attention to themselves," the author writes.

Four Arguments for the Elimination of Television. By Jerry Mander. Quill, 1978. 371 pages. Drawing on research and his own personal experiences, the author argues that the problems inherent in television technology itself are a threat to our mental and physical health, the environment, and to the democratic process. Since the medium cannot be reformed, Mander proposes that television be eliminated entirely.

The Plug-In Drug. By Marie Winn. Revised edition. Penguin Books, 1985. 288 pages. Explains how television viewing disrupts family life and steals precious time away from more valuable activities (playing, reading, conversing, developing skills, etc.). The author argues that it's the act of watching, not what your child watches, that matters.

Associations

Campaign for Kids' TV. See Center for Media Education.

Children's Television Workshop. One Lincoln Plaza, New York, New York 10023. Phone: 212/595-3456. This research and development laboratory explores new uses of television and related communications media. Has created and produced a variety of acclaimed educational television series, including *Sesame Street, The Electric Company, 3-2-1-Contact,* and

Square One TV. Produces books and magazines and maintains a library as well. Periodicals include *Kid City*, a magazine full of stories, poems, crafts, puzzles, and hands-on activities, and magazines based on *Sesame Street* and *3-2-1 Contact.*

Center for Media and Values. 1962 South Shenandoah Street, Los Angeles, California 90034. Phone: 310/559-2944. The center has developed workshop kits for use by parents, teachers, and youth leaders who work with various age groups. These kits are designed to help children view television and other media with a critical eye. (Call for current price and ordering information.) Also publishes a quarterly magazine, *Media and Values.*

Center for Media Education. P.O. Box 33039, Washington, D.C. 20033. Phone: 202/628-2620. A Washington-based consumer group that monitors children's TV. Conducts the Campaign for Kids' TV, which advocates better programming for children. Monitors compliance with—and works to maximize the impact of—the Children's Television Act of 1990, which requires broadcasters to offer more educational and informational programming for kids. Offers a parent's action guide and a videotape on monitoring the Children's Television Act.

Federal Communications Commission. 1919 M Street, N.W., Washington, D.C. 20554. Phone: 202/632-7048 (complaint branch). Renews licenses for television stations (for renewal, stations must comply with the Children's Television Act (CTA) of 1990, which requires broadcasters to offer more educational and informational children's programs). You can call the complaint branch to protest noncompliance with the CTA.

Video Tie-In

On Television: Teach the Children. Hosted by journalist Edwin Newman, this hour-long documentary examines the role of television as an educational tool. Explores the relationship between television and learning, and takes a look at the history of educational television (including clips from children's programs spanning the past forty years). Shows parents and teachers how to teach critical viewing skills to youngsters. The videotape comes with a free study guide. For more information, contact On Television Limited, 338 Broadway, New York, New York 10013. Phone: 212/925-5289.

National Coalition on Television Violence. P.O. Box 2157, Champaign, Illinois 61825. Phone: 217/384-1920. A research and educational organization working to decrease the amount of violence shown on television and in films. Rates television programs, movies, and musical videotapes. Sponsors seminars on violent entertainment and public action, and organizes programs on nonviolence in schools. Publishes research reports, bibliographies, educational materials, *NCTV News* (a newsletter), and a list of the best and worst shows on television.

National PTA. 700 North Rush Street, Chicago, Illinois 60611. Phone: 312/787-0977. Actively campaigning for better programming. Offers a publication called *The Children's Television Act: What Your PTA Can Do to Improve TV Program-*

ming. Also offers information on Channel One, a highly controversial video news program interspersed with advertising for fast food, sneakers, and other products for kids. The program is designed for use in the classroom and is distributed to schools (along with free video equipment for those who agree to use it) by Whittle Communication.

Yale University Family Television Research and Consultation Center. Department of Psychology, P.O. Box 11A, Yale Station, New Haven, Connecticut 06520. Phone: 203/432-7172. Researches the influence of television on children of all ages, including the uses of selective viewing in the development of creativity and imaginative play, and the influence of television viewing patterns on behavior and language development in young children. Dorothy G. Singer, Ed.D., is the codirector.

Selecting Quality Programs: Guides and Reviews

"MediaKids" (*Child* magazine). A review section featured in *Child* magazine. Highlights quality television programs, videotapes, and books for children. Available on newsstands or by subscription (*Child*, P.O. Box 3176, Harlan, Iowa 51593-0367. Phone: 1/800-777-0222).

Parents' Choice. A quarterly review of children's media, including books, movies, television programs, videotapes, and audio recordings. Contact Parents' Choice Foundation, P.O. Box 185, Waban, Massachusetts 02168. Phone: 617/965-5913.

TV Guide. P.O. Box 400, Radnor, Pennsylvania 19088. The weekly *TV Guide* puts out a special parents' issue at the start of the new season. This special issue highlights quality

TV programs for children (toddlers through teens), offering descriptions of new and continuing series, brief articles, and interviews with experts like T. Berry Brazelton and Shelley Duvall. Parents can also use this guide throughout the year to learn about programs worth watching. Available at most newsstands.

Hotline

Child Magazine's MediaKids Hotline. Phone: 1/900-407-4KID (95¢ per call). Each week, *Child* magazine picks what it considers to be the best movie, videotape, and television program for children and then makes this information available through its MediaKids Hotline. Callers can choose weekly recommendations for children ages two to six or age seven and up. New media selections for the week begin every Tuesday morning at 9:00 a.m. eastern standard time. (Note: *Child* magazine contains a regular feature called MediaKids, where you'll also find listings of quality movies, videotapes, and television shows for kids.)

Computerized Clearinghouse

KIDSNET. 6856 Eastern Avenue, N.W., Suite 208, Washington, D.C. 20012. Phone: 202/291-1400. A national nonprofit computerized clearinghouse devoted to children's audio, video, radio, and television programming. Those who subscribe to the electronic database (the cost ranges from $435 to $585) have access to detailed information on more than twenty thousand video and audiocassette programs and five thousand current children's programs and public service announcements on television and radio. The database can be searched by grade level, subject area, or special needs. Those without access to a computer and modem can use KIDSNET's toll-free services instead (requests are taken and entered into the computer for you). In addition, the clearinghouse produces *The KIDSNET Future Bulletin*, a monthly publication detailing upcoming broadcast programs, along with programs currently being developed. Individual entries in the bulletin include a full description; air-date; subject area; grade level; off-air taping rights; supplemental materials (viewing guides, curriculum materials, etc.); and other information. *The KIDSNET Calendar*, issued quarterly, lists events, publications, research and public service projects, relevant legislation, regulations, and U.S. and international media awards and competitions. A subscription to the *Future Bulletin* and *Calendar* costs $260.00. Write or call KIDSNET for more information on products and services.

Television Programs for Kids

The following programs are among those frequently recommended for children (check your local and cable listings for times):

Adventures in Wonderland. The Disney Channel. Based on Lewis Carroll's classic books, this fantasy series combines fun word play, original songs, and a cast of Broadway performers dressed up as Wonderland characters (Walrus, Red Queen, and others). Designed to help children from kindergarten through grade three build language and vocabulary skills. To catch this half-hour program, tune in to the Disney Channel.

Ghostwriter. PBS. Produced by Children's Television Workshop, this program was created to enhance the reading and writing skills of children in grade school (ages seven to ten, approximately). During each half-hour episode, six young actors solve mysteries with the help of an invisible character—the Ghostwriter—who is capable of communicating only through the written word. The Ghostwriter leaves written clues everywhere—on a wall of graffiti, on a computer screen, and anywhere in between. As the young actors unfold the mystery, they demonstrate opportunities to make good use of the written word.

Lamb Chop's Play-Along. PBS. Ventriloquist Shari Lewis and her puppet Lamb Chop encourage viewers to join in the fun (play games, sing songs, perform magic tricks, tell jokes, and make things). Lewis's energy is inspiring and her material is clever. An award-winning half-hour program for children ages one to eight.

Mr. Rogers' Neighborhood. PBS. Offers preschoolers encouragement, reassurance, gentle words of wisdom, and an opportunity to share new experiences. Unlike most other children's programs, the pace of *Mr. Rogers' Neighborhood* comes close to matching real life. The jazz pianist's timing is impeccable.

Newton's Apple. PBS. Viewers learn about science with host David Heil and a variety of guest experts. The range of topics explored is impressive (psychology, archaeology, sports physiology, and so on) and the teaching approach is hands-on. For children in elementary school through junior high.

Reading Rainbow. PBS. This Emmy Award-winning program, hosted by LeVar Burton, offers a wide variety of reading adventures for young viewers (ages five through nine). The featured books are among the best available, and the theme-related segments help children see how reading can relate to real life. Each half-hour program includes several book reviews by children.

Sesame Street. PBS. After twenty-five seasons, *Sesame Street* continues to delight preschoolers with its colorful cast of characters, its respect for children's feelings and individual differences, and its sheer cleverness. Although many question the show's emphasis on teaching the alphabet (believing this to be developmentally inappropriate for preschoolers), few will deny the program's appeal. Parents are tempted to tune in too (and often do).

Sharon, Lois and Bram's Elephant Show. Nickelodeon. This series features a fun-loving elephant, enthusiastic kids, and the folk music of the popular North American trio, Sharon, Lois and Bram. Each half-hour program explores a new theme.

Shelley Duvall's Bedtime Stories. Showtime. This award-winning program introduces young viewers to a wonderful collection of fully animated tales, carefully crafted to evoke the feeling of the books from which they came. *Choo Choo, Bill and Pete, Elbert's Bad Word, There's a Nightmare in My Closet,* and *Amos, The Story of an Old Dog and His Couch* are among the stories presented. Another Duvall production, *Mrs. Piggle Wiggle,* a thirteen-part series based on the books by Betty MacDonald, was in development at the time of this writing.

Shining Time Station. PBS. Thomas the Tank Engine and the other talking trains featured in this popular program have distinct personalities and faces that clearly express human emotions. At the station, children join the conductor (played by George Carlin), the perky station manager, and "Schemer" for a series of mishaps, adventures, and life lessons.

3-2-1 Contact. PBS. Introduces science and technology to elementary-school aged children.

Some Other Worthwhile Programs

Avonlea. The Disney Channel.
Babar. HBO.
Clarissa Explains It All. Nickelodeon.
Doug. Nickelodeon.
Eureeka's Castle. Nickelodeon.
Long Ago and Far Away. PBS.
National Geographic Explorer. TBS.
Nick News. Nickelodeon.
Real News for Kids. Syndicated; TBS.
Rugrats. Nickelodeon.
Shakespeare: The Animated Tales. HBO.
Where in the World Is Carmen Sandiego? PBS.
WonderWorks, PBS.
The Wonder Years. Syndicated.
The World of Peter Rabbit and Friends. Family Channel.

Mail Order Catalog

Signals. WGBH Educational Foundation, P.O. Box 64428, St. Paul, Minnesota 55164-0428. Phone: 1/800-669-5225 (customer service); 1/800-669-9696 (to place an order). "For Fans and Friends of Public Television," this catalog offers videotapes of award-winning TV specials and series, along with theme-related products (books, clothing, audio recordings, etc.). Includes items such as plush animals, dolls, slippers, and tableware based on popular characters in children's public television programs.

Alternatives to TV

Books

365 T.V.-Free Activities You Can Do with Your Child. By Steve and Ruth Bennet. Bob Adams, 1991. 415 pages. Describes 365 engaging activities for parents and children, none of which necessitate the use of a television set. Includes Indoor Safari, Beanbag

Good Television Habits

From *Helping Your Child Get Ready for School*, by Nancy Paulu, published in 1992 by the U.S. Department of Education, Office of Educational Research and Improvement.

Children in the United States have watched an average of 4,000 hours of television by the time they begin school. Most experts agree that this is too much. But banning television isn't the answer, because good television can spark curiosity and open up new worlds to children. Monitoring how much and what television children watch helps them, starting at an early age, to develop good viewing habits.

Too much television can be harmful because

- It can expose children to too much sex and violence;
- Children can be unduly influenced by junk-food and toy commercials;
- It can give children a poor model for good behavior before they have developed a clear idea of right and wrong;
- Young children do not have the experience and wisdom to understand complicated plots or scary scenes; and
- Sitting passively in front of the set for extended periods of time can slow young children's social and intellectual development.

Here are some tips to help children develop good television-viewing habits.

Keep a record of how many hours of TV your children watch, and what they watch. Generally, it's good to limit the amount to 2 hours or less a day, although you can make exceptions for special programs.

Learn about current TV programs and videos and select good ones. As parents, you know your children best. So, select TV programs and videos that are meaningful to your family.

Parents who would like help in finding good TV programs for children can subscribe to *Parents' Choice*, a quarterly review of children's media which includes television programs and home video materials. [For more information on *Parents' Choice*, see listing under "Selecting Quality Programs: Guides and Reviews."]

You can also read about programs in TV columns in newspapers and magazines. Cable subscribers and public broadcasting contributors can check monthly program guides for information.

Plan with your children (starting at age 3) what programs to watch. After selecting programs appropriate for your children, help them decide which ones to watch. Turn the TV on when these shows start, and turn the set off when they are over.

Watch television with your children so you can answer questions and talk about what they see. Pay special attention to how they respond so you can help them understand what they're seeing, if that's needed.

Follow-up TV viewing with activities or games. You might have your child tell you a new word he learned on television that you can look up together in the dictionary. Or you might have him make up his own story about one of his favorite TV characters.

Include the whole family in discussion and activities or games that relate to television programs. Older siblings, aunts, uncles, and grandparents can all contribute.

Make certain that television isn't regularly used as a babysitter. Instead, try to balance good television with other fun activities for your child.

Olympics, and other clever ideas that can be adapted to match the interests and ages of children in individual families. Also available: *365 Outdoor Activities You Can Do with Your Child.*

What To Do After You Turn Off the TV. By Frances Moore Lappe and family. Ballantine, 1985. 197 pages. Describes two hundred engaging activities developed as alternatives to watching television. Ideas come not only from the author and her children, but dozens of other families as well. Includes activities for toddlers, older children, and for the whole family.

For more ideas on TV-free activities, see resource listings under "Activities and Projects for Kids" in chapter 16.

Chapter 21

Family Travel

GENERAL RESOURCES

Free and Inexpensive Resources

General

Discover America: A Listing of State and Territorial Travel Offices of the United States. Use this list to order free vacation information including maps, calendars of events, travel guides, and more. Published by the Department of the Interior. For ordering information, request a copy of the free *Consumer Information Catalog*, available from the Consumer Information Center, P.O. Box 100, Pueblo, Colorado 81002.

Family Vacations. A booklet from Visa designed to help families plan their vacations. Full of advice and tips on traveling with children. For a free copy, call 1/800-VISA-511.

Happy Highways. A thirty-minute car-travel cassette featuring songs by the Vocal Jazz Ensemble of the University of Texas at Arlington. Describes car games for children ages six and up, and offers travel safety tips as well. Available by writing Hampton Inn Happy Highways Tape, 2828 Routh Street, Suite 680, Dallas, Texas 75201. Enclose a check for $1.50 for postage and handling, made payable to Hampton Inn Happy Highways.

Information Please. Provides the phone numbers (800 numbers when available) for the Visitors Bureaus in all fifty states, plus numbers for major domestic hotel chains, airlines, and car rental agencies. Available from Family Travel Guides Catalogue, P.O. Box 6061, Albany, California 94706-0061. Phone: 510/527-5849.

Merrily We Roll Along. This brochure explains how to help keep children happy while they are buckled up in their safety seats. Available for 50¢ from the National Association for the Education of Young Children, 1509 Sixteenth Street, N.W., Washington, D.C. 20036-1426. Phone: 202/232-8777 or 1/800-424-2460. Fax: 202/328-1846.

Travel Papers. Brief, information-packed articles about specific destinations and modes of travel, available from Family Travel Guides Catalogue, P.O. Box 6061, Albany, California 94706-0061. Phone: 510/527-5849. Prices range from $1.00 to $4.00. Here is a small sampling of available titles [for a complete listing of available Travel Papers, request a free copy of the Family Travel Guides Catalogue (see listing under "Mail Order Catalogs")]:

> Bermuda: The Family Island
> Budget Family Vacations in Northern California
> Club Med for Family
> Cruising Guidelines for Families
> Disneyland
> Family River Trips
> Flying Solo
> Fun in New York City . . . with the Kids
> Germany's Fairy Tale Road
> Restaurant Hints and Games
> Rome for Children
> Spend a Free Weekend in Philly
> Taking the Kids on Amtrak
> Traveling by Car with Pets
> Vacationing with Grandchildren

Travel Abroad

Background Notes. Brief, factual pamphlets, one for each country of the world and some for selected international organizations. The approximately 170 *Notes* contain information on each country's culture, people, history, geography, government, economy, and political conditions. *Background Notes* also include a reading list, travel notes, and maps. Single copies are available from the U.S. Government Printing Office [see appendix B for ordering information].

Foreign Entry Requirements. Lists the addresses of embassies and consulates in over two hundred countries where visas may be obtained, along with any special requirements. Published by the State Department. 16 pages. For ordering information, request a copy of the free *Consumer Information Catalog*, available from the Consumer Information Center, P.O. Box 100, Pueblo, Colorado 81002.

Tips for Travelers. These pamphlets provide advice prepared by the State Department's Bureau of Consular Affairs on travel to specific areas of the world. Depending on the region discussed, a tips pamphlet will cover such topics as currency and customs regulations, entry requirements, import and export controls, vaccination requirements, restrictions on use of photography, and other information. Single copies of the following tips pamphlets are available from the U.S. Government Printing Office [see appendix B for ordering information]:

Tips for Travelers to the Caribbean
Tips for Travelers to Central and
    South America
Tips for Travelers to Eastern Europe
Tips for Travelers to Mexico
Tips for Travelers to the Middle
    East and North Africa
Tips for Travelers to the People's
    Republic of China
Tips for Travelers to South Asia
Tips for Travelers to Sub-Saharan
    Africa
Tips for Travelers to the USSR

Your Trip Abroad. This handy guide provides the information needed for a carefree and relaxing trip overseas.

Information Packets for Travel Abroad

Travel-Health Packets. If you're traveling abroad, Travel-Health International, Inc., can send you a packet containing information on visa requirements, health risks, suggested immunizations, weather information, travel tips, and background information on your destination country. The charge is $9.95 for the first country and $4.00 for each additional country. For more information, call Travel-Health International, Inc., at 1/800-659-7361.

Includes information on things to do before you go, legal tips, shopping suggestions, how to deal with the unexpected while traveling, how to get help from American consuls, and what to do when you return. Also lists additional sources of information. Produced by the U.S. Department of State, Bureau of Consular Affairs. For ordering information, request a copy of the free *Consumer Information Catalog*, available from the Consumer Information Center, P.O. Box 100, Pueblo, Colorado 81002.

Kids and Air Travel

Kids and Teens and Flight. For this free pamphlet on air travel and children, call 202/366-2220 or write U.S. Department of Transportation, Consumer Affairs, I-25, Washington, D.C. 20590.

When Kids Fly. This free consumer guide from Boston's Logan Airport is designed for air travelers flying with toddlers, children, and teenagers. Includes information on safety seats, airline policies, special meals, and stress-control, along with ideas for in-flight games and entertainment. For a copy, write Public Affairs Department, Massport, Ten Park Plaza, Boston, Massachusetts 02116-3971.

Books

General

Adventuring with Children: The Family Pack-Along Guide to the Outdoors and the World. By Nan Jeffrey with Kevin Jeffrey. Foghorn Press, 1992. 328 pages. This guide offers information and advice on all kinds of outdoor adventures, including camping, biking, sailing and canoeing. Offers guidelines on packing and tips on adjusting when you find yourself in unfamiliar territory.

The Best Bargain Family Vacations in the U.S.A. By Laura Sutherland and Valerie Wolf Deutsch. St. Martin's Press, 1993. 342 pages. Describes more than two hundred affordable family vacation spots across the country, including resorts, camps, parks, and dude ranches. Travel tips plus listings of budget hotel chains and travel information centers are included.

Best Places to Stay (series). Various authors. Houghton Mifflin. Describes quality lodgings (guest houses, small and large hotels, etc.) in regions of the United States (Hawaii, the Mid-Atlantic States, the Midwest, the Pacific Northwest, Rocky Mountain States, the Southwest, and other places), as well as other countries.

The Family Travel Guide. Edited by Carole Terwilliger Meyers. Carousel Press, forthcoming. A colossal collection of family-oriented travel articles by various authors.

Fly There for Less. By Bob Martin. Third edition. Teakwood Press, 1992. 336 pages. Explains how to slash the cost of air travel worldwide.

Frommers Family Travel Guides (series). Various authors. Prentice-Hall. Guides to Los Angeles, New York, California, San Francisco, and Washington, D.C., highlight family-friendly places, accommodations, and children's activities. Ice cream parlors, puppet shows, and other kid-pleasers are featured throughout these guides.

Going Places: A Guide to Travel Guides. By Greg Hayes and Joan Wright. The Harvard Common Press, 1988. 772 pages. Lists and describes guides ranging in subject from gourmet tours to family vacations to safari adventures. Organized by region and country. Includes self-published and hard-to-find guides unknown to bookstores, as well as standard, familiar series. Appendixes list names and addresses of travel bookstores, travel guide publishers, travel magazines, and newsletters.

Great Vacations with Your Kids. By Dorothy Jordon and Marjorie Cohen. Revised edition. NAL-Dutton, 1990. 384 pages. A complete guide to family vacations in the United States. For those traveling with children of all ages (from infants to teenagers).

Innocents Abroad: Traveling with Kids in Europe. By Valerie Wolf Deutsch. Plume, 1991. 508 pages. Concentrates on attractions in countries such as France, Italy, Belgium, Germany, Switzerland, Great Britain, and the Netherlands. Also includes information on food and lodging.

Miles of Smiles. By Carole Terwilliger Meyers. Carousel Press, 1993. 123 pages. Filled with games and activities to help eliminate back seat squabbling and make the most of family travel time. For children ages four and up.

Places to Go with Children (series). Various authors. Chronicle

Books. Describes attractions that appeal to both children and adults in places around the country. Books in the series include *Places to Go with Children in Miami [New England, Northern California, Orlando and Central Florida, Southern California, the Delaware Valley, the Southwest, Washington, D.C.,* and *Around Puget Sound]*.

Recommended Family Inns of America. Cary Schuler Hall, editor. Globe Pequot Press, 1989. 304 pages. Highlights more than one hundred of the best inns for families, including farm inns, inns with cabins, and inns with hiking and cross-country ski trails.

Recommended Family Resorts. By Jane Wilford with Janet Tice. Globe Pequot Press, 1990. 280 pages. Recommends one hundred family resorts, mostly in the United States, the rest in Canada and the Caribbean. Each resort is described in detail, including information on baby-sitting services and recreational activities for children and adults.

Super Family Vacations: Resort and Adventure Guide. By Martha Shirk and Nancy Klepper. Revised edition. HarperPerennial, 1992. 493 pages. Recommends more than one hundred vacation spots for families. For each destination (in the United States, Canada, or the Caribbean), the authors highlight places to eat and sleep, local happenings, and other useful details.

Take Your Kids to Europe. By Cynthia W. Harrison. Mason-Grant, 1991. 236 pages. Explains how to find inexpensive lodgings, good family restaurants, and worthwhile sights in France, Italy, Greece, Switzerland, and other European countries. Compiled by two travel-savvy families who spent weeks exploring the continent with their kids.

Travel Games for Kids! By Andrew Langley. Revised edition. Berkshire House, 1992. 108 pages. Describes more than one hundred games for kids en route. Word play, puzzles, and hand games are among the suggestions. For ages four to fourteen.

Traveling with Children and Enjoying It. Globe Pequot Press, 1991. 306 pages. A complete guide to family travel by car, plane, and train. Explains how to plan your trip, adjust when you return home, and make the most of what's in between. Offers guidelines on packing, finding quality services at affordable prices, and eliminating family conflicts. A variety of checklists are included.

Travel with Children. By Maureen Wheeler. Lonely Planet Books, 1990. 160 pages. The authors give advice on traveling with children of all ages, mainly to Third World countries. The authors discuss trips to Nepal, Sri Lanka, Indonesia, the Cook Islands, the Australian Outback, and other interesting spots on the planet.

Trouble-Free Travel with Children: Helpful Hints for Parents on the Go. By Vicki Lansky. Second revised edition. The Book Peddlers, 1991. 156 pages. This compact paperback offers handy advice on family travel, including medical tips and packing checklists. Written by Vicki Lansky, parent and author of other child-related nonfiction.

Special Attractions

AAA Guide to North America's Theme Parks. By the American Automobile Association (AAA) staff, edited by Doreen Russo. Second edition. Macmillan, 1992. 256 pages. A guide to theme parks in the United States and Canada, compiled by AAA travel experts.

The Amusement Park Guide. By Tim O'Brien. Globe Pequot Press,

1991. 248 pages. Features descriptions of more than 250 amusement and theme parks in the United States and Canada.

Disney World and Beyond: The Ultimate Family Guidebook. By Stacy Ritz. Ulysses Press, 1992. 266 pages. A family guide to rides and attractions at Disney World, EPCOT Center, Disney/MGM Studios, Universal Studios, and Sea World. Includes listings of hotels, motels, restaurants, and campsites. Suggests side-trips to nearby towns and attractions as well.

Steel, Smoke and Steam. By Margery Read. Country Roads, 1992. 128 pages. An illustrated guide to restored railways in the United States and Canada.

FOR KIDS ON THE GO

Books

Air Travel Games. By Moira Butterfield. EDC Publishing, 1986. 32 pages. This book is designed to help keep airborne youngsters occupied. Also available: *The Usborne Book of Car Travel Games* by Tony Potter. For children in grades three and up.

Are We There Yet? Travel Games for Kids. By Richard Salter. Crown, 1991. 90 pages. Describes more than fifty fun travel games for children ages six and up. Playing requires nothing more than a pencil and paper and a good eye for picking out letters, numbers, signs, and clues from the vehicles, signs, and sights around you.

Dinosaur's Travel: A Guide for Families on the Go. By Laurie Brown and Marc C. Brown. Little, Brown, 1988. 32 pages. Dinosaur characters illustrate the pleasures and practicalities of travel from packing up and taking off to returning home again. For preschoolers through grade three.

Kidding Around (series). Various authors. John Muir. Written for children, these easy-to-read books give information on history and sightseeing highlights, family-friendly restaurants, stores of interest to young shoppers, and a calendar of special events. Books in the series include *Kidding around Atlanta [Boston, Chicago, London, Los Angeles, New York City, Paris, Philadelphia, San Diego, Santa Fe, Seattle, San Francisco, Spain, the Hawaiian Islands, National Parks of the Southwest,* and *Washington, D.C.*]. For children ages eight and up.

Let's Go Traveling. By Robin Rector Krupp. Morrow Junior Books, 1992. A guide for young travelers (ages five and up). Narrated by a child who travels to the pyramids of Egypt, the Great Wall of China, and other historical places. Excerpts from the young explorer's travel diary can be found throughout the book, along with pictures of what she encountered along the way.

My Family Vacation. By Dayal Kaur Khalso. C. N. Potter (distributed by Crown), 1988. 24 pages. An enthusiastic young girl takes her first trip away from home when the family goes on a vacation in Florida. The adventures that she and her brother have in Miami bring them to a better understanding of each other.

Audiocassettes

A Car Full of Songs. By Tom Paxton. Sony Kids' Music. Paxton's upbeat music will help keep boredom at bay. "Dad's Not Lost" and "I've Gotta Go" are among the highlights. For ages four to eight.

Games for the Road. Running time: 40 minutes. Your kids can take a funny road trip with the Fairy Game Mother, working their way through nearly two-dozen fun and educational games. Also available: *More Games for the Road* (40 minutes) and *More Games for the Road Activity Book* (a twenty-page book full of mazes, hidden pictures, and other activity pages). Available from Valentine Productions, 3856 Grand Forest Drive, Norcross, Georgia 20092. Phone: 404/368-9017 or 1/800-544-8322.

Hopping Around from Place to Place. By Ella Jenkins. Educational Activities, Inc. Features original tunes about international voyages, giving kids a feel for other cultures and places. Among the instruments played are the ukulele, accordion, and guitar. For ages four to seven.

Traffic Jams. By Joe Scruggs. Shadow Play Records. A collection of original, fun songs for kids ages three to ten. Begins with "Buckle Up" and ends with the "Evening Breeze" lullaby. In the middle are tunes like "Speed Bump Blues," "Car Seat Exercise," "Big Toe Truck," and others to help put your kids in a cheerful mood. Comes with a lyric sheet. Available from the Family Travel Guides Catalogue, P.O. Box 6061, Albany, California 94706-0061. Phone: 510/527-5849.

Videotapes

International Video Network Video Catalog. See listing under "Mail Order Catalogs."

Traveling the World via Video. This issue of the *Children's Video Report* contains reviews of thirty videos that teach children about other places and foreign cultures. Includes selections such as *Big Bird Goes to China, The Grand Canyon*, and a variety of language tapes. Single copies are available for $5.00. Contact *Children's Video Report*, 370 Court Street, #76, Brooklyn, New York 11231-4331. Phone: 718/935-0600. (Request issue #1 in volume 4.)

Travel Toys

Busy Baby Car Seat Toys. Four colorful toys for tots attached to twenty bright plastic links. Designed to keep infants and toddlers (six months to two years) entertained while mom or dad does the driving. Available from Toys to Grow On, P.O. Box 17, Long Beach, California 90801. Phone: 1/800-874-4242.

Miles of Smiles Travel Tote. A carry-along tote packed with activity books, a two-sided chalkboard, chalk, eraser, and twenty-four crayons. For children ages five to twelve. Available from Toys to Grow On, P.O. Box 17, Long Beach, California 90801. Phone: 1/800-874-4242.

The Puzzle Box. Six challenging puzzle-games, packed in a take-along box. For children ages five and up. Available from Toys to Grow On, P.O. Box 17, Long Beach, California 90801. Phone: 1/800-874-4242.

6-in-1 Travel Magnetic Games. By Pressman. A compact, magnetic toy chest containing pieces for six traditional games, including chess, checkers, backgammon, and snakes and ladders. A sliding screen presents the various playing boards, while a side drawer stores the game pieces. Available at toy stores.

Sticker Games for the Road. Young travelers can spend hours spotting various trucks, road signs, and license plates with these travel sticker games. Each of the three games (License Plate Games, Truck Games, and Road Sign Games, all sold separately) comes with an instruction booklet and scoring card, stickers, and a heavy stock folder to attach them to. Along the lines of car bingo. Available from Chinaberry, 2780 Via Orange Way, Suite B, Spring Valley, California 91978. Phone: 1/800-776-2242.

Travel Ghost Writer. By Ohio Art. From the makers of Etch-a-Sketch, this scaled down Ghost Writer comes with a fat pen that small hands can easily control, plus a magic board to draw on (shake and your child's pictures disappear). Available at toy stores.

Traveling Art Show. This portable art case comes with thin-line and jumbo markers, crayons, paints, and brush, all packed in a handy carrying case that doubles as a lapboard. For ages four and up. Available from Toys to Grow On, P.O. Box 17, Long Beach, California 90801. Phone: 1/800-874-4242.

Mail Order Catalogs

Family Travel Guides Catalogue. Located in Albany, California, this clearinghouse offers travel books for children and grown-ups alike. Offers general travel guides; how-to books; guides to specific regions in the United States and abroad; and guides to amusement parks, museums, zoos, and other attractions. Also offers travel games and activity books, audiocassettes for kids, and low-cost "travel papers" (see separate listing under "Free and Inexpensive Resources"). For a free copy of their catalog, send a self-addressed envelope with 52¢ postage to Family Travel Guides Catalogue, P.O. Box 6061, Albany, California 94706-0061. Phone: 510/527-5849.

International Video Network Video Catalog. International Video Network, 2242 Camino Ramon, San Ramon, California 94583. Phone: 1/800-669-4486. Offers a wide selection of travel videos covering regions in the Americas, Europe, Asia, Africa, the South Pacific, and other fascinating places. Includes videos produced by Fodor's Video, Rand McNally, and others.

Periodicals

Family Travel

Family Fun. P.O. Box 10161, Des Moines, Iowa 50340-0161. Phone: 1/800-289-4849. Regularly features exciting places to go and things to do with kids. Covers amusement parks, zoos, aquariums, museums, outdoor adventure, and travel destinations. Full of vacation ideas, including beach trips, dude ranch and camping adventures, annual festivals, and family tours. Each issue includes "Family Traveler," a guide to good deals, new attractions, and vacation news for families on the go.

Family Travel Times. 80 Eighth Avenue, New York, New York 10011. Phone: 212/206-0688. A newsletter full of travel ideas, including where to go and how to get there. Published ten times a year. A subscription also entitles readers to free travel advice from the publisher.

General Travel

Conde Nast Traveler. Box 57018, Boulder, Colorado 80322-7018. Phone: 1/800-777-0700. Slick monthly magazine covering travel and travel destinations in the United States and abroad. Charting the coast of Maine, secrets of the Seine, Polynesia (living the dream), and the Sphinx (clues to a lost civilization) have been among the magazine's features.

Consumer Reports Travel Letter. 256 Washington Street, Mount Vernon, New York 10553. Phone: 1/800-999-

7959. This monthly newsletter features great bargains and travel tips.

National Geographic Traveler. 1145 Seventeenth Street, N.W., Washington, D.C. 20036. Phone: 1/800-636-4077. From the publishers of *National Geographic*, this magazine features spectacular photography and informative text. Articles have focused on the Guadalupe mountains, national parks, Lake Superior, Atlanta (Georgia), Geneva, Prague, and hundreds of other interesting destinations.

Travel and Leisure. 1120 Avenue of the Americas, New York, New York 10036. Phone: 1/800-888-8728 (for subscription inquiries and requests for back issues and indexes). Explores domestic and international travel opportunities. Feature articles have covered Paris hotels, American cities, Portugal's castle country, and England's best walks.

Travel/Holiday. P.O. Box 2036, Marion, Ohio 43305. Issued monthly, this magazine highlights travel destinations around the globe, including many in the United States. Montana, Germany's castle country, the Yangtze river, and America's local flavors are examples of the varied features.

Club Med for Kids

Club Med Mini Clubs offer children ages two to eleven a chance to enjoy the company of other small fries, leaving parents free to be adults. Scuba diving, tennis, acrobatics, sailing, and swimming are just a few of the activities open to kids. At the end of their action-packed days, kids can sit down in their own dining room and choose meals from a special kids menu. Club Med also has a baby club for four- to twenty-four-month-olds. For more information, see your travel agent or contact Club Med Sales, 7975 North Hayden Road, Scottsdale, Arizona 85258. Phone: 1/800-CLUB-MED.

Associations

Access America. 600 Third Avenue, 4th Floor, New York, New York 10016. Phone: 1/800-284-8300. A for-profit service for travelers and travel organizations. Maintains a message center through which subscribers can receive airline schedules, updates on national political situations worldwide, and other travel information. Operates a ticket replacement service for travelers who are forced to reschedule their trips on short notice and thereby forfeit reimbursement. Offers life and health insurance for travelers. Provides emergency medical and legal services.

American Automobile Association. 1000 AAA Drive, Heathrow, Florida 32746-5063. Phone: 407/444-7000. A federation of automobile clubs (with one thousand offices) providing domestic and foreign travel services, emergency road services, and insurance. Upon request, members receive free maps, travel routes, and destination guides complete with listings of hotels, motels, restaurants, and special attractions.

American Society of Travel Agents. 1101 King Street, Alexandria, Virginia 22314. Phone: 703/739-2782. Promotes travel and encourages the use of professional travel agents worldwide. Serves as an information resource for the travel industry worldwide. Can tell you if there is a complaint record on a specific company offering tour packages or charter flights.

American Youth Hostels. P.O. Box 37613, Washington, D.C. 20013-7613. Phone: 202/783-6161. A nonprofit organization that runs a network of inexpensive lodging facilities in the United States and abroad. Members of this nonprofit organization can choose among more than six thousand hostels (including farms, log cabins, even tree houses!). Fees are extremely affordable (generally between $5 and $15 per person, per night). Members receive a free guidebook called *Hosteling North America* (the cost is $7.00 for nonmembers), which includes a map and a list of U.S. and Canadian hostels. Other publications include the annual *AYH Discovery Tours* and a budget travel catalog.

International Cruise Passengers Association. 1521 Alton Road, Suite 350, Miami Beach, Florida 33139-3301. Phone: 305/374-2224. An association of cruise passengers and ship enthusiasts in countries around the globe. Promotes cruise vacationing and passenger ship travel. Offers up-to-date rating reports on cruise ships currently in service. Publishes *Cruise Digest Reports*, a bimonthly magazine. Also produces the annual *Berlitz Complete Guide to Cruising and Cruise Ships*.

National Bed-and-Breakfast Association. P.O. Box 332, Norwalk, Connecticut 06852. Phone: 203/847-6196. An association of innkeepers of bed-and-breakfast lodgings and family-owned and operated inns. Publishes the *Bed and Breakfast Guide for the U.S., Canada, and the Caribbean.*

National Travel Club. 28 West Twenty-third Street, 10th Floor, New York, New York 10010. Phone: 212/366-8644. This for-profit service offers subscribers travel information, travel insurance, and car rental discounts. Call or write for more information.

Travel Agents and Trip Organizers

Backroads. Phone: 510/527-1555 or 1/800-462-2848. Organizes family bicycling, walking, and hiking trips. Call for more information on trip packages.

The Cruise Line, Inc. Phone: 1/800-777-0707. Based in Miami, Florida, this discount company can help families find good deals on cruise lines that welcome children.

Families Welcome. Phone: 1/800-326-0724. Family vacation packages include trips to Paris, London, and New York. Participants receive a welcome kit on sightseeing in these popular cities.

Family Faire. Phone: 1/800-677-4FUN. This organization specializes in family trips to California and the Hawaiian islands.

Grandtravel. Phone: 1/800-247-7651. Located in Chevy Chase, Maryland, this travel agency specializes in trips for grandparents and grandchildren. Washington, D.C., colonial Williamsburg, and the coast of Maine are among their domestic destinations.

International Family Adventures. Phone: 1/800-972-3842. Travel packages include exotic destinations such as Kenya and the Galapagos.

Mountain Travel– Sobek. Phone: 510/527-8100. This travel firm offers a wide variety of outdoor adventure packages, including trekking in Nepal, rafting the Zambezi River in Africa, and cruising worldwide. The company's *Adventure Annual* (available for $10.00) features more than one hundred adventure travel destinations worldwide. A photo-CD version of the catalog is also available.

1-800-FLY-CHEAP. Both the name and number of a national travel company specializing in finding inexpensive air fair for its customers. This company also books hotels.

Rascals in Paradise. Phone: 1/800-872-7225. This family-friendly travel agency offers unique vacation packages (bike expeditions in the Rocky Mountains and barging adventurers in France are two examples). Their "Family Weeks" program allows families to spend time in Jamaica, Mexico, and other exciting places, accompanied by an escort who, among other things, creates fun activities for the kids.

South Florida Cruises. Phone: 1/800-327-7447. Offers discounts on cruises for families who are willing to make last-minute plans.

Travel Avenue. Phone: 1/800-333-3335. A "no-frills" travel agency offering significant savings on flights for families.

Vistatours. Phone: 1/800-248-4782. Offers trips for grandparents and grandchildren. Destinations include Nevada, New England, and South Dakota.

Wilderness Threshold Trips. Phone: 415/776-2211. A division of the Sierra Club, this travel service offers nature treks and educational adventures for parents and children alike.

Family University: Where Kids and Parents Come Together to Learn. At Cornell University in Ithaca, New York, families are coming together to learn. During the summer, parents can spend their days attending classes and seminars taught by university faculty, while children participate in recreational activities, science seminars, writing programs, and other events. At night, families sleep in campus dormitories. The cost of the week-long program is around $750 for adults and $300 for children. Infants and toddlers are free (there is a charge for day-care services, however). For more information, phone 607/255-6260.

Costa Cruises. Phone: 1/800-322-8263.
Cunard. Phone: 1/800-221-4770
Norwegian Cruise Line. Phone: 1/800-262-4NCL.
Premier Cruise Lines. Phone: 1/800-888-6759.
Princess Cruises. Phone: 1/800-765-0888.
Royal Caribbean Cruise Line. Phone: 1/800-327-6700 (in Florida, call 1/800-432-6559.

Cruise Lines that Accommodate Kids

The following cruise lines offer special programs for kids on board:

American Hawaii Cruises. Phone: 1/800-765-7000.
Carnival Cruise Lines. Phone: 1/800-327-7276.
Chandris Fantasy Cruises/Celebrity Cruises. Phone: 1/800-621-3446.

Family-Friendly Hotel Chains

Many hotel and motel chains offer special family services. These often include free or discounted meals and lodging for children, special activity programs for kids, and baby-sitting services. Some even deliver milk and cookies at bedtime! Not all chains have system-wide policies, so you'll want to call in advance.

Here's a list of some of the

chains that make special arrangements for traveling families:

Days Inn. Phone: 1/800-325-2525.
Embassy Suites. Phone: 1/800-EM-BASSY.
Four Seasons. Phone: 1/800-268-6282.
Hilton Hotels. Phone: 1/800-445-8667.
Holiday Inn. Phone: 1/800-HOLI-DAY.
Hyatt Hotels. Phone: 1/800-233-1234.
Loews. Phone: 1/800-23-LOEWS.
The Ritz-Carlton: 1/800-241-3333.
Sonesta. Phone: 1/800-SONESTA.
Stouffer. Phone: 1/800-HOTELS-1.
Westin. Phone: 1/800-228-3000.

Other hotel chains for families:

Best Western. Phone: 1/800-528-1234.
Choice. Phone: 1/800-221-2222.
Hampton Inn. Phone: 1/800-426-7866
Howard Johnson. Phone: 1/800-654-2000.
Motel 6. Phone: 505/891-6161.
Ramada. Phone: 1/800-272-6232
Red Roof Inn. Phone: 1/800-THE-ROOF.

Hotel Room Reservation Services

The following reservation services offer hotel room discounts at 10 to 50 percent savings.

Central Reservation Service. Phone: 1/800-950-0232. Works with about one hundred fifty hotels in New Orleans, New York, San Francisco, Miami, and Orlando.

Hotel Reservations Network. Phone: 1/800-964-6835. Callers can choose from about one thousand hotels, including many medium-priced chains, in New York, Boston, Chicago, Orlando, New Orleans, Washington, San Francisco, Los Angeles, Maui and Oahu, London, and Paris.

Quikbook. Phone: 1/800-221-3531. Works with more than one thousand hotels in major cities, including Atlanta, Boston, Chicago, Dallas, Denver, Los Angeles, and Washington, D.C.

Travel Hotlines

Advice on Travel to Foreign Countries. U.S. State Department. Phone: 202/647-5225. The State Department issues advisories on traveling abroad, including whether or not a country is safe to visit (health problems or civil uprisings would be cause for words of caution). You can also receive information on customs regulations and inconveniences such as traffic problems within the destination country.

Airline Complaint Line. U.S. Department of Transportation. Phone: 202/366-2220. Call this number to register complaints against airlines. If you get bumped from a flight against your will or if you're dissatisfied with the airline's handling in an emergency situation (lost tickets or luggage, for example), operators at the U.S. Department of Transportation can offer guidance.

International Traveler's Hotline. Phone: 404/332-4559. A service of the Centers for Disease Control, this hotline allows callers to punch in their destination on a push-button phone and receive vital health information in return: required shots, disease risks for that region, and preventive measures you should take before embarking on your journey.

Your Trip Abroad

From *Your Trip Abroad*, a guide produced by the U.S. Department of State Bureau of Consular Affairs.

Learn about the Places You Will Visit

- A travel agent can provide brochures and tourist information about the countries you plan to visit.

- Your travel agent should also be able to provide you with the Department of State travel advisory for any country you plan to visit, *if* an advisory has been issued for the country. If your travel agent cannot provide travel advisories, you can obtain them 24 hours a day by calling 202/647-5225.

- Look in your local bookstore and public library for books on foreign travel.

- Many countries have tourist information offices in large cities that can give you brochures and, in some cases, maps. International airlines may also supply you with travel brochures on the countries they serve.

- Foreign embassies or consulates in the United States can provide up-to-date information on their countries. Addresses and telephone numbers of the embassies of foreign governments are listed in the *Congressional Directory*, available at most public libraries. In addition to their embassies, some countries also have consulates in major U.S. cities. Look for their addresses in your local telephone directory, or find them in the publication, *Foreign Consular Offices in the United States*, available in many public libraries.

Arrange Ahead

Lodging

Reserve in Advance. Many travelers wait until they reach their destination before making hotel reservations. Some train stations and airports have travel desks to assist you in finding lodging. However, when you arrive, you may be tired and unfamiliar with your surroundings, and could have difficulty locating a hotel to meet your needs. Therefore, when possible, reserve your lodging in advance and reconfirm your reservations along the way. During peak tourist season, it is important to have a hotel reservation for at least the first night you arrive in a foreign city.

An alternative to hotels is the youth hostel system, offering travelers of all ages clean, inexpensive, overnight accommodations in more than 6,000 locations in over 70 countries worldwide. Some hostels have family rooms that can be reserved in advance. Curfews are often imposed and membership is often required. You may write to: American Youth Hostels, P.O. Box 37613, Washington, D.C. 20013-7613.

Organized Programs

The majority of private programs for vacation, study, or work abroad are reputable and financially sound. However, some charge exorbitant fees, use deliberately false "educational" claims, and provide working conditions far different from those advertised. Even programs of legitimate organizations can be poorly administered. Be cautious. Before committing yourself or your finances, find out about the organization and what it offers.

Transportation

Charter Flights and Airlines

There have been occasions when airlines or companies that sell charter flights or tour packages have gone out of business with little warning, stranding passengers overseas. If you know from the media or from your travel agent that an airline is in financial difficulty, ask your travel agent or the airlines what recourse you would have if the airline ceased to operate. Some airlines may honor the tickets of a defunct airlines, but they usually do so with restrictions.

Before you purchase a charter flight or tour package, read the contract carefully. Unless it guarantees they will deliver services promised or give a full refund, consider purchasing trip insurance. If you are unsure of the reputation of a charter company or tour operator, consult your local Better Business Bureau or the American Society of Travel Agents at 1101 King Street, Alexandria, Virginia 22314 (phone 703/739-2782) to learn if the company has a complaint record.

While You Are Overseas

How to Deal with the Unexpected

If you change your travel plans, miss your return flight, or extend your trip, be sure to notify relatives or friends back home. Should you find yourself in an area of civil unrest or natural disaster, let them know as soon as you can that you are safe. In addition, contact the nearest U.S. embassy or consulate to register your presence and to keep the U.S. consul informed of your whereabouts.

Safeguard Your Passport

Carelessness is the main cause for losing a passport or having it stolen. You may find that you have to carry your passport with you because either you need to show it when you cash travelers checks or the country you are in requires you to carry it as an identity document. When you must carry your passport, hide it securely on your person. Do not leave it in a handbag or an exposed pocket. Whenever possible, leave your passport in the hotel safe, not in an empty hotel room or packed in your luggage. One family member should not carry all the passports for the entire family.

Currency

Local banks usually offer better rates of exchange than hotels, restaurants, or stores. Rates are often posted in windows. Above all, avoid private currency transactions. In some countries, you risk more than being swindled or stuck with counterfeit currency—you risk arrest. Avoid the black market—learn and obey the local currency laws wherever you go.

When You Return

Reconfirm your return reservation at least 72 hours before departure. Whenever possible, obtain a written confirmation. If you do it by phone, record the time, day, and the agent's name who took the call. If your name does not appear on the reservations list, you have no recourse and may find yourself stranded.

STATE TRAVEL OFFICES

Your can write or call the following offices for free vacation information:

Alabama Bureau of Tourism and Travel. P.O. Box 4309, Department TIA, Montgomery, Alabama 36103-4309. Phone: 205/242-4169 or 1/800-ALABAMA.

Alaska Division of Tourism. P.O. Box 110801, TIA, Juneau, Alaska 99811-0801. Phone: 907/465-2010.

Arizona Office of Tourism. 1100 West Washington, Phoenix, Arizona 85007. Phone: 602/542-8687.

Arkansas Tourism Office. One Capitol Mall, Department 7701, Little Rock, Arkansas 72201. Phone: 501/682-7777 or 1/800-NATURAL.

California Office of Tourism. P.O. Box 9278, Department TIA, Van Nuys, California 91409. Phone: 916/322-2881 or 1/800-TO-CALIF.

Colorado Tourism Board. P.O. Box 38700, Denver, Colorado 80238. Phone: 303/592-5410 or 1/800-COLORADO.

Connecticut Department of Economic Development. Tourism Division, 865 Brook Street, Rocky Hill, Connecticut 06067. Phone: 203/258-4355 or 1/800-CT-BOUND.

Delaware Tourism Office. 99 Kings Highway, Box 1401, Department TIA, Dover, Delaware 19903. Phone: 302/739-4271 or 1/800-441-8846.

District of Columbia Convention and Visitors Association. 1212 New York Avenue, N.W., Washington, D.C. 20005. Phone: 202/789-7000.

Florida Division of Tourism. 126 West Van Buren Street, FLDA, Tallahassee, Florida 32301. Phone: 904/487-1462.

Georgia Department of Industry, Trade and Tourism. P.O. Box 1776, Department TIA, Atlanta, Georgia 30301. Phone: 404/656-3590 or 1/800-VISIT-GA.

Hawaii State of Department of Business, Economic Development and Tourism. P.O. Box 2359, Honolulu, Hawaii 96804. Phone: 808/586-2423.

Idaho Division of Tourism Development. 700 West State Street, Department C, Boise, Idaho 83720.

Phone: 208/334-2470 or 1/800-635-7820.

Illinois Bureau of Tourism. 100 West Randolph, Suite 3-400, Chicago, Illinois 60601. Phone: 312/814-4732 or 1/800-223-0121.

Indiana Department of Commerce/Tourism and Film Development Division. One North Capitol, Suite 700, Indianapolis, Indiana 46204-2288. Phone: 317/232-8860 or 1/800-289-6646.

Iowa Division of Tourism. 200 East Grand, TIA, Des Moines, Iowa 50309. Phone: 515/242-4705 or 1/800-345-IOWA.

Kansas Travel and Tourism Division. 400 West 8th Street, 5th Floor, Department DIS, Topeka, Kansas 66603-3957. Phone: 913/296-3009 or 1/800-252-6727.

Kentucky Department of Travel Development. 2200 Capitol Plaza Tower, Department DA, Frankfort, Kentucky 40601. Phone: 502/564-4930 or 1/800-225-TRIP.

Louisiana Office of Tourism. Inquiry Department, P.O. Box 94291, LOT, Baton Rouge, Louisiana 70804-9291. Phone: 504/342-8119 or 1/800-33-GUMBO.

Maine Office of Tourism. 189 State Street, Augusta, Maine 04333. Phone: 207/289-5711 or 1/800-533-9595.

Maryland Office of Tourism Development. 217 East Redwood Street, 9th Floor, Baltimore, Maryland 21202. Phone: 410/333-6611 or 1/800-543-1036.

Massachusetts Office of Travel and Tourism. 100 Cambridge Street, 13th Floor, Boston, Massachusetts 02202. Phone: 617/727-3201 or 1/800-447-MASS (for ordering vacation kit only).

Michigan Travel Bureau. P.O. Box 30226, Lansing, Michigan 48909. Phone: 517/373-0670 or 1/800-5432-YES.

Minnesota Office of Tourism. 375 Jackson Street, 250 Skyway Level, St. Paul, Minnesota 55101. Phone: 612/296-5029 or 1/800-657-3700.

Mississippi Division of Tourism. P.O. Box 22825, Jackson, Mississippi 39205. Phone: 601/359-3297 or 1/800-647-2290.

Missouri Division of Tourism. P.O. Box 1055, Department TIA, Jefferson City, Missouri 65102. Phone: 314/751-4133 or 1/800-877-1234.

Travel Montana. Room 259, Deer Lodge, Montana 59722. Phone: 406/444-2654 or 1/800-541-1447.

Nebraska Division of Travel and Tourism. 301 Centennial Mall South, Room 88937, Lincoln, Nebraska 68509. Phone: 402/471-3796 or 1/800-228-4307.

Nevada Commission of Tourism. Capitol Complex, Department TIA, Carson City, Nevada 89710. Phone: 702/687-4322 or 1/800-NEVADA-8.

New Hampshire Office of Travel and Tourism Development. P.O. Box 856, Department TIA, Concord, New Hampshire 03302. Phone: 603/271-2343.

New Jersey Division of Travel and Tourism. 20 West State Street, CN 826, Department TIA, Trenton, New Jersey 08625. Phone: 609/292-2470 or 1/800-JERSEY-7.

New Mexico Department of Tourism. 1100 St. Francis Drive, Joseph Montoya Building, Santa Fe, New Mexico 87503. Phone: 505/827-0291 or 1/800-545-2040.

New York State Department of Economic Development. One Commerce Plaza, Albany, New York

12245. Phone: 518/474-4116 or 1/800-CALL-NYS.

North Carolina Division of Travel and Tourism. 430 North Salisbury Street, Raleigh, North Carolina 27603. Phone: 919/733-4171 or 1/800-VISIT-NC.

North Dakota Tourism Promotion. Liberty Memorial Building, Capitol Grounds, Bismarck, North Dakota 58505. Phone: 701/224-2525 or 1/800-HELLO-ND.

Ohio Division of Travel and Tourism. P.O. Box 1001, Department TIA, Columbus, Ohio 43211-0101. Phone: 614/466-8844 or 1/800-BUCKEYE.

Oklahoma Tourism and Recreation Department Travel and Tourism Division. 500 Will Rogers Building, DA92, Oklahoma City, Oklahoma 73105-4492. Phone: 405/521-3981 or 1/800-652-6552 (information requests only).

Oregon Economic Development Department. Tourism Division, 775 Summer Street, N.E., Salem, Oregon 97310. Phone: 503/373-1270 or 1/800-547-7842.

Pennsylvania Bureau of Travel Marketing. 130 Commonwealth Drive, Warrendale, Pennsylvania 15086. Phone: 717/787-5453 or 1/800-VISIT-PA.

Rhode Island Tourism Division. 7 Jackson Walkway, Department TIA, Providence, Rhode Island 02903. Phone: 401/277-2601 or 1/800-556-2484.

South Carolina Division of Tourism. Box 71, Room 902, Columbia, South Carolina 29202. Phone: 803/734-0235.

South Dakota Department of Tourism. 711 East Wells Avenue, Pierre, South Dakota 57501-3369. Phone: 605/773-3301 or 1/800-843-1930.

Tennessee Department of Tourism Development. P.O. Box 23170, TNDA, Nashville, Tennessee 37202. Phone: 615/741-2158.

Texas Department of Commerce. Tourism Division, P.O. Box 12728, Austin, Texas 78711-2728. Phone: 512/462-9191 or 1/800-8888-TEX.

Utah Travel Council. Council Hall/Capitol Hill, Department TIA, Salt Lake City, Utah 84114. Phone: 801/538-1030.

Vermont Travel Division. 134 State Street, Department TIA, Montpelier, Vermont 05602. Phone: 802/828-3236.

Virginia Tourism. 1021 East Cary Street, Department VT, Richmond, Virginia 23219. Phone: 804/786-4484 or 1/800-VISIT-VA.

Washington State Tourism Development Division. P.O. Box 42513, Olympia, Washington 98504-2513. Phone: 206/586-2088 or 206/586-2012 or 1/800-544-1800.

West Virginia Division of Tourism and Parks. 2101 Washington Street East, Charleston, West Virginia 25305. Phone: 304/348-2286 or 1/800-225-5982.

Wisconsin Division of Tourism. P.O. Box 7606, Madison, Wisconsin 53707. Phone: 608/266-2161 or 1/800-432-TRIP or 1/800-372-2737 (in state).

Wyoming Division of Tourism. I-25 at College Drive, Department WY, Cheyenne, Wyoming 82002. Phone: 307/777-7777 or 1/800-225-5996.

Chapter 22

Camping and Hiking

Hotline

L. L. Bean Hotline. Phone: 1/800-341-4341, ext. 3100. Call for free advice on equipment and outdoor pursuits such as hiking, canoeing, and cross-country skiing.

Free and Inexpensive Resources

A Guide to Your National Forests. A map showing each national forest plus addresses and phone numbers of information offices to help you plan your visit. Published by the U.S. Department of Agriculture. For ordering information, request a copy of the free *Consumer Information Catalog*, available from the Consumer Information Center, P.O. Box 100, Pueblo, Colorado 81002.

Lesser Known Areas of the National Park System. Contains state-by-state listings of more than 170 national parks, including locations, accommodations, and historical significance. 48 pages. Published in 1989 by the Department of the Interior. For ordering information, re-

quest a copy of the free *Consumer Information Catalog*, available from the Consumer Information Center, P.O. Box 100, Pueblo, Colorado 81002.

National Park System Map and Guide. A fold-out map with lists of activities at over three hundred parks, monuments, and historic sites. Published in 1992 by the Department of the Interior. For ordering information, request a copy of the free *Consumer Information Catalog*, available from the Consumer Information Center, P.O. Box 100, Pueblo, Colorado 81002.

National Trails System Map and Guide. Fold-out map describing eight National Scenic Trails and nine National Historic Trails. Published in 1992 by the Department of the Interior. For ordering information, request a copy of the free *Consumer Information Catalog*, available from the Consumer Information Center, P.O. Box 100, Pueblo, Colorado 81002.

National Wildlife Refuges. A fold-out map listing the facilities and best viewing seasons at over three hundred wildlife refuges nationwide. Published in 1991 by the Department of the Interior. For ordering information, request a copy of the free *Consumer Information Catalog*, available from the Consumer Information Center, P.O. Box 100, Pueblo, Colorado 81002.

Books

Backpacking with Babies and Small Children. By Goldie Silverman. Wilderness Press, 1986. 122 pages. Written by an experienced family camper, this book offers information on planning, packing, setting up camp, making meals, and making the most of your camping experience on rainy days (among other topics).

Best Hikes with Children (series). Mountaineers. A series of books describing hikes that the whole family can enjoy. Each suggested hike lists the level of difficulty, total hiking distance, elevation, and admission fees (if any). Maps and photographs help complete the picture. Also includes health and safety precautions to take and tips on food, clothing, emergency supplies, and gear to take along on a trip. Books cover Colorado, Connecticut, the Catskills, Oregon, New Jersey, Vermont, New Hampshire, Maine, Rhode Island, San Francisco, and the state of Washington.

Camping with Kids. By Don Wright and Pam Wright. Cottage Publications (distributed by Career Press), 1992. 192 pages. Explains how to plan a trip the whole family will enjoy.

Take a Hike! The Sierra Club Kid's Guide to Hiking and Backpacking. By Lynne Foster. Little, Brown, 1991. 176 pages. Written for young hikers by a seasoned backpacker, this book explains how to get in shape for the trail, how to plan for the trip and

bring along the right gear, how to read the weather, and how *not* to get lost, among other things. Offers guidelines to help young hikers notice and enjoy the trees, rocks, flowers, and animals they'll see along the way.

The 2 Oz. Backpacker. By Robert S. Wood. Ten Speed Press, 1982. 127 pages. A brief question and answer book for problem solving in the wilds. Discusses planning, camping, cooking, navigating, tents, first-aid techniques, and more.

Wilderness with Children: A Parent's Guide to Fun Family Outings. By Michael Hodgson. Stackpole, 1992. 144 pages. Explains how to introduce children to the joys of nature. Offers guidelines on making outings a fun adventure and including children in the entire trip process (including planning). Covers first aid and safety, necessary equipment, and specific outdoor adventures such as biking, canoeing, and cross-country skiing. Includes recommended reading lists, the names and addresses of equipment suppliers, and places to write for information on destinations.

Kit

The Pathfinder's Adventure Kit. By Christine Kennedy. Random House, 1993. Contains everything kids need to become skilled pathfinders—people who can find their way anywhere and never get lost. Comes with a working compass and *The Pathfinder's Handbook* (56 pages), plus a map and pathfinding markers for scavenger hunts and pathfinding games. For children ages eight and up.

Associations

American Hiking Society. P.O. Box 20160, Washington, D.C. 20041-2160. Phone: 703/385-3252. Encourages the use of foot trails and educates the public on the pleasures of walking. Works to protect the interests of hikers. Encourages hikers to build and maintain footpaths. Publications include *Pathways across America*, a quarterly newsletter containing information on long distance trails, and *American Hiker*, a quarterly magazine.

Backroads. Phone: 510/527-1555 or 1/800-462-2848. This travel service offers family bicycling, walking, and hiking trips. Call for information on Backroads trip packages.

National Campers and Hikers Association. 4804 Transit Road, Building 2, Depew, New York 14043. Phone: 716/668-6242. An association of campers, hikers, and others interested in conservation and the great outdoors. Through regional information centers, the association provides updated reports on local trails and campsites. Also provides an exchange for camping and hiking equipment. Publishes *Camping Today*, a monthly magazine offering discount information and a calendar of events. Through state and local groups (there are more than two thousand nationwide), members exchange information on routes, campsites, equipment, and related issues.

Rails-to-Trails Conservancy. 1400 Sixteenth Street, N.W., Suite 300, Washington, D.C. 20036. Phone: 202/797-5400. A nonprofit organization that has helped transform more than five thousand miles of old, unused railroad tracks into a national network of bicycle, hiking, and cross-country ski trails. Publishes a periodic directory listing converted railways serving as trails. Also publishes *Trailblazer*, a quarterly newsletter exploring issues, trends, and legislation dealing with the conversion of railroad lines into trails. Contact this organization to find the nearest trail or help out in this family-friendly cause.

U.S. Orienteering Federation. P.O. Box 1444, Forest Park, Georgia 30051. A federation of individuals interested in the sport of orienteering (finding one's way in the outdoors using maps and a compass). Promotes orienteering activities and establishes guidelines for orienteering competitions. Provides maps. Also rents compasses for a modest fee ($1.00 to $3.00 apiece).

Mail Order Catalogs

Camp and Program Leader Catalog. American Camping Association, 5000 State Road 67 North, Martinsville, Indiana 46151-7902. Phone: 317/342-8456. Although this catalog is targeted at camp counselors and program leaders, many of the items will be of interest to family campers. Included are scores of books and videotapes exploring outdoor activities such as hiking, canoeing, orienteering, tying knots, backpacking, and plant and animal identification. All of the items in the catalog can be ordered by mail from the American Camping Association.

Campmor. 810 Route 17 North, P.O. Box 997-J, Paramus, New Jersey 07653-0997. Phone: 201/445-5000 (for catalog) or 1/800-526-4784 (to order). Offers a large selection of camping equipment—tents, sleeping bags, backpacks, cookware, first-aid kits, flashlights, inflatable rafts, coolers, and hundreds of other basic items. All of Campmor's products are listed and described in an unpretentious, newsprint catalog, available for free.

L. L. Bean. Freeport, Maine 04033. Phone: 1/800-341-4341. L. L. Bean's full-color winter sporting catalog contains outdoor sports and camping gear (tents, sleeping bags, back-packs, lanterns, and much more). L. L. Bean also offers a line of clothing for kids (sizes range from infants through children's 16), including jackets, over-alls, hats, and boots. Sports equipment and accessories are available in chil-dren's sizes as well.

Tough Traveler. 1012 State Street, Schenectady, New York 12307. Phone: 518/377-8526. This company offers durable front and back carriers for carting infants and toddlers on hiking trips (and other potentially ex-hausting expeditions, including trips around town), as well light-weight packs that kids themselves can carry. "The Ranger" is an internal frame backpack that can be worn by nine to fourteen year olds; "The Camper" can be worn by kids ages five to eleven; and the "Kiddy Pack" can be worn by toddlers and preschoolers. Also sells flight bags and duffel bags for kids.

Chapter 23

The Environment

Books

For Parents and Teachers

E for Environment. By Patti K. Sinclair. R. R. Bowker, 1992. 292 pages. An annotated bibliography of children's books providing descriptive and bibliographic information on more than five hundred trade books with environmental themes (energy, pollution, recycling, protecting endangered species, etc.). Includes title, author, and subject indexes, along with a short list of "Environmental Classics." For work with children ages three through fourteen.

Earth Child: Games, Stories, Activities, Experiments and Ideas. By Kathryn Sheehan and Mary Waidner, Ph.D. Council Oak Books, 1992. 327 pages. Describes hundreds of hands-on activities to improve children's understanding of the interconnectedness of all living things. Each chapter includes a bibliography and additional resources for children and adults. For work with children ages four through nine.

Earthways: Simple Environmental Activities for Young Children. By Carol Petrash. Gryphon House, 1992. 220 pages Arranged by season, this book describes nature crafts and activities to help promote environmental awareness in young children.

Environmental Literacy. By H. Steven Dashefsky. Random House. 298 pages. An encyclopedia of environmental terminology. Describes dozens of words, ranging from the commonly used (acid rain) to the comical (Zoo Doo), to science-specific (oology). Describes organizations as well.

Good Earth Art: Environmental Art for Kids. By Mary Ann F. Kohl and Cindy Gainer. Bright Ring Publishing, 1991. 224 pages. Offers more than two hundred craft ideas using recycled (discarded) objects and materials from nature. Natural berry dye, car-part sculptures, and homemade crayons are among the activities featured. For work with ages four and up.

Likeable Recylables. By Linda Schwartz. Learning Works, 1992. 128 pages. Contains creative ideas for reusing all kinds of everyday items (bags, boxes, cartons, cans, etc.). Parents and teachers can show kids how to make an egg carton zoo, tin can totem poles, and many other fun items. Each project is illustrated and described in easy-to-understand terms.

The Nature Directory: A Guide to Environmental Organizations. By Susan D. Lanier-Graham. Walker, 1991. 190 pages. Lists and describes more than one hundred environ-

mental groups. Explains how individuals can become members, volunteer, contribute, and get more information.

Raising an Earth Friendly Child: The Keys to Your Child's Happy, Healthy Future. By Debbie J. Tilsworth. Raven Press, 1991. 216 pages. This guidebook includes more than fifty games, puzzles, stories, songs, and activities to help children ages three to twelve become more environmentally conscious. The activities, which are designed for parents and kids to do together, explore topics such as acid rain, global warming, and polluted rivers.

Teaching Kids to Love the Earth. By Marina Herman, Joseph Passineau, Ann Schimpf, and Paul Treuer. Pfeifer-Hamilton Publishers, 1991. 192 pages. The authors offer 186 outdoor activities for families who care about the earth, based on their experiences as teachers of family-centered nature workshops. Also contains a collection of stories related to the activities, along with additional resource listings. For children ages four and up.

This Planet Is Mine: Teaching Environmental Awareness and Appreciation to Children. By C. Whittaker and M. Metzger. Simon and Schuster, 1991. 256 pages. Using easy-to-understand language, the authors describe various environmental issues and problems and explain how parents and children can help "make a difference." Includes dozens of creative learning activities for use at home or in the classroom. Includes a glossary of terms, as well as a resource list for parents.

Major Reference Work

Beacham's Guide to Environmental Issues and Sources. Beacham Publishing, 1993. 3,335 pages. A five-volume guide to thousands of environmental resources, extracted from a variety of databases and catalogs, grouped by category and type (books, articles, videotapes, and other information sources). Although the set is designed primarily for researchers, it includes a variety of listings of interest to concerned parents and other inhabitants of the earth (including young people).

For Children

Come Back, Salmon. By Molly Cone with photographs by Sidnee Wheelwright. Sierra Club, 1992. 48 pages. Describes how a group of dedicated elementary school children adopted Pigeon Creek (once a spawning ground for salmon) and brought it back to life. Contains forty full-color photographs that help tell the story. For children ages eight through twelve.

Earth Book for Kids: Activities to Help Heal the Environment. By Linda Schwartz. The Learning Works, 1990. 184 pages. An illustrated book full of facts, activities, experiments, and explanations to help young children gain a better understanding of environmental problems. Kids can learn how to test the effects of pollution, compare phosphate levels in detergents, make paper, create sculptures out of trash, and more. Includes a listing of environmental resources. For children ages eight to twelve.

50 Simple Things Kids Can Do to Save the Earth. By John Javna. Andrews and McMeel, 1990. 156 pages. By the Earth Works group, this book describes everyday things kids can do to improve the environment, including recycling, re-using, and speaking out. For ages eight and up.

Going Green: A Kids' Handbook to Saving the Planet. By John Elkington, Julia Hailes, Douglas Hill, and Joel Makower. Viking Child Books, 1990. 96 pages. Discusses environmental issues in easy-to-understand language. Also offers guidelines for getting involved in the green movement. For ages eight and up.

The Great Kapok Tree: A Tale of the Amazon Rain Forest. By Lynne Cherry. Harcourt Brace, 1990. 32 pages. Illustrates the natural beauty and richness of the Amazon rain forest and conveys an important message about the importance of each tree. Written and illustrated by Lynne Cherry, who spent time in the Amazon rain forest researching the story. For ages four to none.

The Lorax (book and cassette). By Dr. Seuss. Random House, 1992. 64 pages. A tale about a greedy entrepreneur who wacks down an entire forest of Truffula trees in the process of making more and more "thneeds" (and more and more money). The Lorax—who speaks for the trees (as well as the birds, fish, and other inhabitants of the forest)—tries to make him stop, but the message falls on deaf ears. In the end, the repentant "Once-ler," who is sad and lonely having chopped down the very last tree, bequeaths to a young boy the last Truffula seed, urging him to plant it and cultivate a new forest: "Then the Lorax and all of his friends may come back." The accompanying cassette features a reading by Ted Danson. For children ages four and up.

My First Green Book. By Angela Wilkes. Alfred A. Knopf, 1991. 48 pages. Offers easy-to-follow instructions for experiments that help kids understand pollution, acid rain, and other aspects of ecology. Includes full-color, life-size photographs. For children ages six to ten.

Recycle! By Gail Gibbons. Little, Brown, 1992. 32 pages. A handbook for kids explaining the process of recycling from start to finish. Focuses on the paths of five different types of garbage—glass, paper, aluminum cans, plastic, and polystyrene. Shows how each of these can be recycled into new products.

Walk When the Moon Is Full. By Frances Hamerstrom. The Crossing Press, 1975. 64 pages. An illustrated story about a real family living on a 240-acre farm in Wisconsin and their magical, nighttime explorations "when the moon is full." For children ages eight through fourteen.

Periodicals

For Parents and Teachers

E: The Environmental Magazine. Subscription Department, P.O. Box 667, Syracuse, New York 13217-7934. (Editorial offices: Earth Action Network, Inc., 28 Knight Street, Norwalk, Connecticut 06851. Phone: 203/854-5559.) A bimonthly environmental magazine containing articles, interviews, news, and reviews. The "Green Marketplace" lists and describes a collection of ecologically oriented products, services, catalogs, and publications.

Garbage: The Practical Journal for the Environment. Dovetale Publishers, The Blackburn Tavern, 2 Main Street, Gloucester, Massachusetts 01930. Phone: 508/283-3200. Articles in this bimonthly journal explore topics such as lead poisoning, environmentally sound gardening, the fresh-water wetlands, and trash disposal. Includes news, reviews, and regular columns as well.

"Promoting Ecological Awareness." Published in 1992, this special theme issue of *Childhood Education*, the journal of the Association for Childhood Education International, looks at ecological teaching on an international scale. Various writers describe community-wide

programs for children, as well as classroom and family-oriented activities. Includes an annotated bibliography and resource guide. Available for $14.00 from the Association for Childhood Education International, 11501 Georgia Avenue, Suite 315, Wheaton, Maryland 20902. Phone: 1/800-423-3563 or 301/942-2443.

For Children

Ranger Rick. National Wildlife Federation, 1400 Sixteenth Street, N.W., Washington, D.C. 20036-2266. Phone: 1/800-432-6564. This monthly magazine, for children ages six to twelve, covers wildlife, outdoor adventure, and conservation. Includes stunning photographs, puzzles, quizzes, articles, and "The Adventures of Ranger Rick" stories. For younger children (ages three to six), the National Wildlife Federation publishes *Your Big Backyard*, containing picture-oriented material (simple games, crafts, short stories, etc.) on animals, nature, and conservation.

TerraTopia Times. Kids for Nature Club, The Nature Company, 750 Hearst Avenue, Berkeley, California 94710. Phone: 1/800-227-1114. A quarterly newsletter designed to help kids appreciate and care for the natural world and have fun in their own backyards. Contains articles, jokes, fun facts, and an activity section called "To The Rescue," which encourages kids to recycle and reuse products. For ages eight and up. Included in membership to the Kids For Nature Club (see listing under "Organizations for Kids").

Audiocassettes and Compact Discs

Evergreen, Everblue. Winner of the Parents' Choice Gold Award, this Raffi recording celebrates the earth and its natural wonders. Contains Raffi originals such as "Clear Rain,"

"Evergreen," "Everblue," and "We Are Not Alone." Comes with a fifty-four-page songbook including music for piano and guitar. For ages five and up. On cassette and compact disc. Available from Music for Little People, Box 1460, Redway, California 95560. Phone: 1/800-727-2233.

A Kid's Eye View of the Environment. By Michael Mish. Mish Mash Music. Running time: 35 minutes. This children's artist combines lively tunes and a top-notch children's chorus to address ecological concerns. "Recycle It," "Trash in the River," and "My Electric Car" are among the songs featured in styles that range from rap to rock and roll.

Put On Your Green Shoes: An All-star Album Dedicated to Healing the Planet. Includes more than a dozen songs containing messages about ecology in styles ranging from folk and blues to rap and rock and roll. Artists include Cyndi Lauper, Tom Chapin, Olivia Newton-John, Richie Havens, and Rockapella, among many others. All profits donated to environmental groups and family programs around the world. Available on cassette or compact disc. Available from Music for Little People, Box 1460, Redway, California 95560. Phone: 1/800-727-2233.

Save the Animals, Save the Earth. Lois Skiera-Zucek offers a varied collection of songs about endangered animals and the planet earth. Includes titles like "The Rainforest," "The Animal Alphabet Song," and "What Can I Do?" in rap, polka, calypso, and other styles. Comes with a lyric sheet. For ages four to nine. Available on record or cassette from Kimbo Educational, P.O. Box 477, Long Branch, New Jersey 07740-0477. Phone: 1/800-631-2187.

Videotapes

Earth to Kids: A Guide to Products for a Healthy Planet. Films, Inc. Running time: 27 minutes. A family documentary showing children and parents the types of products they should (and shouldn't) use to help protect/clean up the environment. This tape was awarded a blue ribbon by the American Film and Video Association.

Samson and Sally. Just for Kids Home Video. Running time: 70 minutes. An award-winning video about the search for a whale who might one day save all the whales from dangers caused by man. Teaches children about conservation in a light-handed way.

Sing-Along Earth Songs. Children's Television Workshop. Running time: 30 minutes. Features "Sesame Street" characters on a hike in Monster State Park, where they learn lessons about protecting the environment. Includes a dozen sing-along ecology tunes, including the "Box City Recycling Rap" and "Every Bit o' Litter Hurts."

Teaching Environmental Concepts with Video. This issue of the *Children's Video Report* contains reviews of twenty-nine videos that introduce young children to environmental concepts. Single copies are available for $5.00. Contact *Children's Video Report*, 370 Court Street, #76, Brooklyn, New York 11231-4331. Phone: 718/935-0600. (Request issue #6 in volume 4.)

Software

Davidson's Zoo Keeper. Davidson and Associates. MS-DOS, Macintosh. In addition to feeding the animals, kids can learn where they come from (by calling up a map), protect those that are being mistreated, and return endangered animals to their natural habitats (if they choose). For ages six and up.

Earthquest 2.0. Earthquest, Inc. IBM, Macintosh Plus (and higher). A mini-encyclopedia offering a detailed history of the earth and planets through maps, animated graphics, and games. Includes a section called "Environment," exploring environmental issues and ways to protect the planet. For ages ten and up.

Eco-Adventures in the Rainforest. Chariot. IBM, Macintosh. Users learn interesting facts while exploring a rainforest (climbing trees, crossing rivers, and charting courses). For children ages ten to fifteen.

Eco-Saurus. First Byte/Davidson and Associates. IBM, Macintosh. An ecological fantasy game, where kids help a dinosaur collect and sort the trash on Eco Island and use it to rebuild an extraterrestrial's spaceship, which has crash-landed. For ages four to nine.

Kits and Games

A Beautiful Place. A cooperative boardgame where players work together to restore the natural beauty of the land (planting a tree, recycling paper, etc.). Pollution vanishes, and a beautiful place is created. For two to four players, ages five to eight. Available from Animal Town, P.O. Box 485, Healdsburg, California 95448. Phone: 1/800-445-8642.

Bottles and Bins (When We Recycle Everyone Wins). In this cooperative boardgame from Ravensburger, players work together to sort their "garbage" (glass, paper, food scraps, etc.) before the recycling and garbage trucks come to haul it away. Everyone wins if all the trash is put in its proper place. For two to four players, ages five to eight. Available from Animal Town, P.O. Box 485, Healdsburg, California 95448. Phone: 1/800-445-8642.

Pollution Solution: The Game of Environmental Impact. A problem-solving game that challenges children to "solve" pollution problems and keep a section of a township map environmentally sound. Comes with a booklet addressing various pollution problems. For two to six players, ages ten and up. Available from Aristoplay, P.O. Box 7529, Ann Arbor, Michigan 48107. Phone: 1/800-634-7738.

Replay. With this unusual kit, kids can learn about recycling while creating imaginative works of art. Includes more than seventy different reclaimed manufacturing components along with sticky-tape. All the materials are non-toxic and safe for home use. Available from Exploratorium to Go!, Exploratorium, 3601 Lyon Street, San Francisco, California 94123. Phone: 1/800-359-9899.

Save the Whales. In this cooperative boardgame, players work together to save eight great whales as oil spills, fishing nets, and waste materials move them toward extinction. Whale playing pieces are made of shiny cast metal. For two to six players, ages eight to adult. Available from Animal Town, P.O. Box 485, Healdsburg, California 95448. Phone: 1/800/445-8642.

Smithsonian Environmental Test Kit. Allows kids to examine acid rain, air pollution, contaminated water, and other environmental hazards. For ordering information, call 1/800-322-0344.

William's Tree. By Deb Hannigan. Mommymade, 1990. This tree-planting kit comes with a storybook about young William and the tree that was planted the day he was born. Includes a variety of seeds and a map of recommended climate zones for the continental United States. Available from Patagonia, 1609 West Babcock Street, P.O. Box 8900, Bozeman, Montana 59715. Phone: 1/800-336-

9090 (for catalog request); 1/800-638-6464 (to order).

Mail Order Catalogs

General

Animal Town. P.O. Box 485, Healdsburg, California 95448. Phone: 1/800-445-8642. Animal Town offers a collection of environmental boardgames, including *Save the Whales, A Beautiful Place, Eyes of the Jungle,* and *Back to the Farm.* Also offers books and tapes that celebrate the earth and help children appreciate and respect the environment.

Music for Little People. Box 1460, Redway, California 95560. Phone: 1/800-727-2233. Printed on recycled paper, the Music for Little People catalog contains a variety of cassettes, compact discs, videotapes, and other items that teach kids about the environment and help them appreciate their planet. Check out the "Peaceful Planet" section.

The Nature Company Catalog. P.O. Box 188, Florence, Kentucky 41002. Phone: 1/800-227-1114. Note cards and wrapping paper printed on recycled paper, children's nature books, backyard birdfeeders, sounds from nature (on cassette or compact disc), nature activity kits, endangered animal cookies, and a solar-powered AM/FM radio are just some of the items featured in this quality catalog.

Patagonia Kids. 1609 West Babcock Street, P.O. Box 8900, Bozeman, Montana 59715. Phone: 1/800-336-9090 (for catalog request); 1/800-638-6464 (to order). The Patagonia Kids catalog, printed on recycled paper, features durable clothing for active kids (sizes range from 6 months to children's 14), along with a selection of environmental books for parents and children. The company is well-known for it's unique fabrics (re-

cently, Patagonia rolled out a new line of sweaters made from 80 percent recycled bottles). The company pledges 1 percent of all sales to the preservation and restoration of the natural environment (for information on the groups the company supports, write the Patagonia Environmental Program, Box 150, Ventura, California 93002).

Soundprints. 165 Water Street, P.O. Box 679, Norwalk, Connecticut 06856. Phone: 1/800-228-7839. Soundprints offers the "Adventures of Ranger Rick" series of books and audiocassettes, featuring Ranger Rick and the gang as they explore environmental concerns. Stuffed animals based on characters in the books are featured in the catalog as well. Also featured in the catalog is the Smithsonian Wild Heritage Collection of books and audiocassettes exploring animals' habits and habitats.

Other Earth-Friendly Catalogs

Earth Care Paper, Inc. P.O. Box 7070, Madison, Wisconsin 53707-7070. Phone: 608/223-4000. Specializes in 100 percent recycled paper products, including coloring books, rolls of drawing paper, and gift wrap.

Heart of Vermont. The Old Schoolhouse, Route 132, P.O. Box 183, Sharon, Vermont 05065. Phone: 802/763-2720 or 1/800-639-4123 (to order). Offers "products for the chemically sensitive and environmentally concerned," including organic cotton bedding and bath items, natural wood furniture (beds, chairs, benches, and end tables), and books on the environmentally sound home.

The Natural Choice. 1365 Rufina Circle, Santa Fe, New Mexico 87501. Phone: 505/438-3448. A catalog of healthy home products, including natural, nontoxic cleansers, all-natural paints and wood finishes, thinner, hypo-allergenic body-care products, nontoxic art supplies, organic seeds, and more.

Real Goods. Real Goods, 966 Mazzoni Street, Ukiah, California 95482. Phone: 1/800-762-7325. Offers environmentally friendly products for the home, including recycling bins, reusable lunch bags, and environmental games.

Seventh Generation. Colchester, Vermont 05446-1672. Phone: 1/800-456-1177. Offers "products for a healthy planet," including cloth diapers, recycled paper products, earth-friendly cleansers, baby products and accessories, and organic cotton bedding, towels, and clothing, among dozens of other products.

Associations

For Adults

Alliance for Environmental Education. P.O. Box 368, 51 Main Street, The Plains, Virginia 22171. Phone: 703/253-5812. Works to advance both formal and informal environmental education. Provides information on environmental centers across the country that use a hands-on approach to teaching children about the environment.

Center for Children's Environmental Literature. P.O. Box 28, Edgewater, Maryland 20137-0028. Phone: 301/261-4190. Publishes *Nature's Course*, a newsletter for teachers (interested parents, too) who want to use children's books for environmental education. Encourages publishers to adopt environmentally sound publishing practices. Founded by Lynne Cherry, author of the best-selling children's books *The Great Kapok Tree* (see listing under "Books") and *A River Ran Wild*.

Center for Marine Conservation. 1725 De Sales Street, N.W., Suite 500, Washington, D.C. 20036. Phone: 202/429-5609. Dedicated to the conservation and protection of the oceans and the life contained within, especially marine mammals such as whales and sea turtles. Promotes public awareness and education. Organizes the International Coastal Cleanup, a beach clean-up project (contact the center for more information and a free beach cleanup guide). Publishes books, reports, and periodicals, including *Marine Conservation News*, a quarterly newsletter covering recent developments in the conservation of marine species and their habitats.

The Cousteau Society, Inc. 930 West Twenty-first Street, Norfolk, Virginia 23517. Phone: 804/523-9335. This environmental organization perpetuates the oceanic preservation and exploration of Jacques Cousteau through research, education, and evaluation of man/nature interrelationships. Publishes *Dolphin Log*, a bimonthly magazine exploring the world's water system (for ages seven to fifteen). Also produces books, films, and other materials.

Earth Day USA. 2 Elm Street, Box 470, Peterborough, New Hampshire 03458. Phone: 603/924-7720. Organizes annual Earth Day activities and events, designed to focus public attention on environmental issues. Publishes a periodic newsletter. Offers a listing of children's environmental programs.

Global Action Network. 575 Soquel Avenue, Santa Cruz, California 95062. Gathers and disseminates information on environmental issues and legislation. Maintains a database. Encourages public advocacy to protect the environment. Publishes a manual called *Action Guide*, along with periodic alerts and reports.

Global ReLeaf. c/o American Forests, P.O. Box 2000, Washington, D.C. 20013. Phone: 202/667-3300. Encourages and sponsors tree-planting projects in an effort to prevent global warming. Write for information on planting trees in your community.

Greenpeace USA, Inc. 1436 U Street, N.W., Washington, D.C. 20009. Phone: 202/462-1177. An association of conservationists working to aid endangered species and clean up the environment. Monitors environmental concerns such as the greenhouse effect and toxic waste dumping. Stages non-violent protests in order to draw attention to specific causes (saving whales and seals, for example). Publishes *The Kids Alert*, a quarterly newsletter exploring environmental issues from children's perspectives.

International Wildlife Coalition. 70 East Falmouth Highway, P.O. Box 388, North Falmouth, Massachusetts 02536. Phone: 508/548-8328. Works to preserve wildlife and wildlife habitats. The coalition's "Whale Adoption Project" allows children to purchase "partial ownership" in one of fifty humpback whales spotted off the Massachusetts coast. Adoption kits come with a biographic sketch of your family's newly adopted pet, a photograph of the whale, and a subscription to *Whalewatch*, a quarterly newsletter. Adoption fee contributions are used to help rescue and protect whales.

Izaak Walton League of America. 1401 Wilson Boulevard, Level B, Arlington, Virginia 22209. Phone: 703/528-1818. An environmental conservation and recreation organization. Works to educate the public on conserving, protecting, and restoring the natural resources of the United States. Promotes the enjoyment and wholesome use of these resources. Sponsors the "Save Our Streams Program," similar to the one described in *Come Back, Salmon* (see listing under "Books"), to help teach children and their parents to monitor water quality in local waterways ("Save Our Streams" kits are available from the league). Publishes *Outdoor America*, a quarterly magazine focusing on conservation and outdoor recreation.

National Audubon Society. 950 Third Avenue, New York, New York 10022. Phone: 212/979-3119. A society of individuals concerned with ecology, conservation, and restoration of natural resources (primarily water, soil, forests, wildlife, and wildlife habitats). Conducts research on endangered species and their habitats. Produces curricula for kindergarten through twelfth grade; offers *Audubon Adventures*, a classroom program for grades three through six (students receive *Audubon Adventures*, a bimonthly newspaper). Also publishes *American Birds*, a bimonthly magazine. Offers annual awards to outstanding nature writers, photographers, and artists. Many local groups also sponsor exploration and investigation sessions for children.

National Center for Environmental Health Strategies. 1100 Rural Avenue, Voorhees, New Jersey 08043. Phone: 609/429-5358. Gathers information and compiles statistics on indoor and outdoor pollutants and promotes public awareness of health problems caused by them. Encourages the development of programs and policies to prevent future public health problems. Publishes The *Delicate Balance*, a quarterly newsletter covering environmental issues and illnesses, including legislation and policy. Offers a free information packet.

The National Wildlife Federation. 1400 Sixteenth Street, N.W., Washington, D.C. 20036-2266. Phone:

202/797-6800. Promotes appreciation for the earth's life-sustaining resources and encourages the responsible management of them. Among the federation's most innovative programs is the "Backyard Habitat Program," which encourages nature-lovers to turn their yards into wildlife preserves. Participants receive tailored instructions on how to attract butterflies, deer, and other forms of wildlife. Once the transformation is complete, the federation certifies the land as an official "Wildlife Habitat." Members of the federation can also participate in conservation summits that provide families with week-long opportunities to explore mountains, canyons, or a seacoast (fees for these programs range from $1,000 to $1,700 per family).

Publishes a variety of magazines, including two for children. *Ranger Rick*, a monthly for kids ages six to twelve, covers wildlife, outdoor adventure, and conservation. *Your Big Backyard*, for ages three to five, contains picture-oriented material (simple games, crafts, short stories, etc.) on animals, nature, and conservation. Other magazines include *National Wildlife* and *International Wildlife* (adults might want to share some of the photographs and stories in these publications with their children). The National Wildlife Federation has also developed the "Ranger Rick NatureScope Series"—curriculum guides covering topics such as insects, weather, tropical rain forests, wetlands, geology, and mammals. Each volume includes related outdoor activities plus lists of additional resources.

The Nature Conservancy. 1815 North Lynn Street, Arlington, Virginia 22209. Phone: 703/841-5300 or 1/800-628-6860. Works to protect natural areas and preserve biological diversity. Identifies and helps protect significant natural areas and provides long-term stewardship for preserves owned by the conservancy. Offers information on protecting plants and animals (and the spaces they live in). Sponsors tours of U.S. preserves and international regions to study plant and animal life. Conducts an "Adopt an Acre" program, which calls on families to help preserve rain forests. Publishes the *Nature Conservancy Magazine*, which contains articles on the ecosystems and information on ecological tours and trips.

Rainforest Action Network. 450 Sansome Street, Suite 700, San Francisco, California 94111. Phone: 415/398-4404. An activist organization seeking to preserve the world's rain forests. Promotes ecologically sound plantations to restore misused land and educates the public on the effects of tropical logging. Publishes *Action Alert*, a monthly bulletin on issues requiring public action, as well as the quarterly *World Rainforest Report*.

Rainforest Alliance. 270 Lafayette Street, Suite 512, New York, New York 10012. Phone: 212/941-1900. Works to protect tropical rain forests. Promotes alternatives to tropical deforestation and works to expand awareness of the role the United States plays in the fate of tropical forests. Encourages sound policies and attitudes. Publishes The *Canopy*, a quarterly newsletter.

Sierra Club. 730 Polk Street, San Francisco, California 94109. Phone: 415/776-2211. Devoted to the study and protection of the earth's scenic and ecological resources—woodlands, wetlands, shores and rivers, and deserts and plains. Educates others on the need to preserve and restore the quality of the environment. Attempts to influence public policy at all levels of government. Chapters in states across the country schedule outings, exhibits, conferences, and lectures. Through its publishing programs for children, the Sierra Club offers fiction and nonfiction books for young people about the earth, its creatures, and the role of human beings living among them. Publishes *Sierra*, a bimonthly magazine covering conservation, the wilderness, environmental policy, and outdoor adventure. Also publishes a biweekly newsletter, along with books and guides for adults on environmental issues and outdoor activities. Offers a free sourcebook listing educational materials, including a suggested reading list.

The Wilderness Society. 900 Seventeenth Street, N.W., Washington, D.C. 20006. Phone: 202/833-2300. Seeks to preserve and protect areas of wilderness (and the life in them) through grass-roots organizing, lobbying, research, and public education. Publishes fact sheets, reports, brochures, and a quarterly magazine called *Wilderness.*

Women's Environmental Network USA. P.O. Box 4560, Chicago, Illinois 60680-4560. Phone: 312/666-1401. A nonprofit organization working to inform and empower women who care about the environment and its effect on women's health (and the health of their families). Among its studies are the effects of disposable diapers on the environment (and on the children who wear them). Works to ensure that consumers have access to reliable information.

World Wildlife Fund. 1250 Twenty-fourth Street, N.W., Washington, D.C. 20037. Phone: 202/293-4800. Seeks to preserve endangered and threatened species of plants and wildlife and the habitats in which they live. Focuses on scientifically based conservation measures and provides

models for effective management practices and policies. Publishes a bimonthly newsletter, a catalog, and other materials.

For Kids

Children for Old Growth. P.O. Box 1090, Redway, California 95560. A children's environmental group dedicated to preserving what remains of ancient American rain forests. Works to halt the clearcutting of forests (helped save more than one thousand acres over a two-year period!) and has purchased two redwood groves near its home in Northern California. Members receive an annual newsletter and a poster to color.

The Children's Rainforest. P.O. Box 936, Lewiston, Maine 04240. Works to preserve rain forests in Costa Rica. Send a self-addressed, stamped envelope for more information.

Global Kidz Fund. 4880 Lower Roswell Road, Suite 630, Marietta, Georgia 30067. An international nonprofit organization that taps children's self-esteem for the good of the plant, using the motto "The Earth Matters, and So Do I." Promotes family activities, neighborhood events (such as tree-plantings), and a pen-pal network. Publishes a newsletter for members called *The Seed.* Contact Global Kidz Fund for information on starting up (or joining) a program in your area.

Kids against Pollution. c/o Tenakill School, 275 High Street, Closter, New Jersey 07624. A grass-roots lobbying group with chapters across the country. Has been instrumental in setting up recycling programs and banning the use of plastic foam packaging in some schools. Organizes letter-writing campaigns and produces a biannual newsletter, which provides information on environmental issues, including current clean-up efforts. Includes information on how to start up a local chapter (there are more than five hundred across the country).

Kids for a Clean Environment (Kids F.A.C.E.). P.O. Box 158254, Nashville, Tennessee 37215. Phone: 615/331-7381 or 1/800-952-FACE. Conducts a variety of programs aimed at cleaning up the environment and helping children appreciate their natural surroundings. For example, Kids F.A.C.E. launched a signature drive urging that a small, but significant, portion of each national park and forest be set aside exclusively for young people. It costs nothing to join, and members receive a certificate and a bimonthly environmental newsletter.

Kids for Nature Club. The Nature Company, 750 Hearst Avenue, Berkeley, California 94710. Phone: 1/800-227-1114. This club is designed to help children learn more about the natural world and how to take care of it (and have fun in the process). From The Nature Company, the annual membership kit comes with a compass, bug-box, flashlight, magnifying glass, and a secret decoder pen. Members also receive the quarterly *TerraTopia Times* (see listing under "Periodicals"), along with postcard updates on the secret, magical island of TerraTopia (and our own world). Recommended for ages eight and up.

Kids for Saving Earth. P.O. Box 47247, Plymouth, Minnesota 55447-0247. Phone: 612/525-0002. A nonprofit organization working to educate and empower children to take positive, peaceful action to help protect the environment. Thousands of clubs around the globe (run by kids with the help of parents and school teachers) promote environmental awareness through a variety of programs and activities. Offers *The KSE Action Guide* (free to members), which includes tips on conserving, recycling, and protecting animals and forests. Write for information on joining or starting up a club.

YES (Youth for Environmental Sanity). 706 Frederick Street, Santa Cruz, California 95062. Phone: 408/459-9344. Encourages young people to get involved in the environmental movement. Offers a publication called the *Student Action Guide*.

Government Resources

Environmental Protection Agency (EPA) Hotlines

Asbestos Ombudsman Clearinghouse/Hotline. Phone: 1/800/368-5888 or 703/305-5938 (8 a.m. to 4:30 p.m., eastern standard time, Monday to Friday). Provides information to the public, including individual citizens, on the handling and abatement of asbestos in schools, the home, and the work place.

General Information on Environmental Issues. Phone: 303/293-1603 (7:30 a.m. to 4:30 p.m., central standard time, Monday to Friday). This hotline provides general information on environmental issues.

National Pesticides Telecommunications Network. Phone: 1/800-858-7378 (8:00 a.m. to 6:00 p.m., central standard time, Monday to Friday). Provides the general public with information on pesticides, including health and environmental effects, product and safety information, and clean-up and disposal procedures.

National Radon Hotline. Phone: 1/800-767-7236 (8:00 a.m. to 5:00 p.m., eastern standard time, Monday to Friday). Provides information on the National Radon Program. Will send callers a free radon brochure.

Pollution Prevention Information Clearinghouse. Phone: 202/260-1023 (10 a.m. to 4:00 p.m., eastern standard time, Monday to Friday). A pollution-prevention reference and referral service. Can help callers select relevant EPA fact sheets and documents.

Safe Drinking Water Hotline. Phone: 1/800-426-4791 (8:30 a.m. to 5:00 p.m., eastern standard time, Monday to Friday). Provides information to the public on the regulations and programs developed in response to the Safe Drinking Water Act Amendments.

Stratospheric Ozone Information Hotline. Phone: 1/800-296-1996 (10:00 a.m. to 4:00 p.m., eastern standard time, Monday to Friday). Acts as a distribution center and point of referral for information on stratospheric ozone protection and depletion.

Superfund Hotline. Phone: 1/800-424-9346 (8:30 a.m. to 7:30 p.m., eastern standard time, Monay to Friday). Answers question about Superfunds (federal funds reserved to clean up hazardous-waste sights); underground storage tank issues; and the federally mandated Emergency Planning and Community Right-to-Know Act (EPCRA), which has established state and local committees to determine what chemicals are being stored in neighborhoods across the country. You can also order EPA documents by calling this number.

Wetlands Protection Hotline. Phone: 1/800-832-7828 (9 a.m. to 5:30 p.m., eastern standard time, Monday to Friday). Provides answers to questions about the value and function of wetlands and options for their protection. Callers are referred elsewhere when necessary.

Other

Consumer Information Center. P.O. Box 100, Pueblo, Colorado 81002. Offers free and inexpensive pamphlets and booklets on environmental safety, preservation, and conservation. Produced by various government agencies, titles include *Tips for Energy Savers, Why Save Endangered Species?, "Green" Advertising Claims, Homebuyer's Guide to Environmental Hazards, Citizen's Guide to Pesticides,* and *Biological Pollutants in Your Home,* among others. Also offers guides to national wildlife refuges, trails, and parks. For ordering information on these and other publications, request a copy of the free *Consumer Information Catalog.*

Chapter 24

Social Responsibility and World Peace

SOCIAL RESPONSIBILITY

Books for Children

The Kids Can Help Book. By Suzanne Logan. Perigee, 1992. 123 pages. A guide for young volunteers, *The Kids Can Help Book* is full of ideas on how to help the hungry and homeless, the elderly, other children, the sick, the disabled, and the environment. Includes stories about suc-cessful kids' projects, insightful anec-dotes, and listings of national organi-zations.

Kids Ending Hunger: What Can We Do? By Tracy A. Howard and Sage A. Howard. Andrews and McMeel, 1992. 224 pages. A get-into-action book for children and their parents and teachers. Offers many ideas on what kids themselves can do.

The Kid's Guide to Social Action: How to Solve the Social Problems You Choose—and Turn Creative Thinking into Positive Action. By Barbara A. Lewis. Free Spirit Publishing, 1992. 185 pages. This guide urges young people to help solve social problems and turn creative thinking into positive action. Offers strategies for raising money, writing letters, and working cooperatively, among other things. Selected "A Children's Book of Distinction" for 1992 by *Hungry Mind Review*.

Kids with Courage: True Stories About Young People Making a Difference. By Barbara A. Lewis. Free Spirit Publishing, 1992. 175 pages. These stories tell of young people all across the country who are active members of their communities and catalysts for positive change. Organized into four sections—Heroic Kids, Kids Fighting Crime, Kids Taking Social Action, and Kids Saving the Environment. For children ages eleven and up.

Association

Educators for Social Responsibility. 23 Garden Street, Cambridge, Massachusetts 02138. Phone: 617/492-1764. A group of educators, parents, and concerned individuals working to encourage students to think critically about global issues, develop a sense of community, and actively participate in a democratic society. Develops curriculum materials and sponsors school and community-based education projects.

Charitable Giving and Voluntarism

Books

Every Kid Counts. By Margaret Brodkin and Coleman Advocates for Children and Youth. HarperSanFrancisco, 1993. 205 pages. Describes a variety of things families can do to help children in need. For example, they can help feed a hungry child, befriend a homeless family, and help fight childhood poverty. Each chapter includes useful resource listings (charities, associations, research groups, hotlines, and books for parents and children). (Note: For more information on *Every Kid Counts*, see "Books" listed in chapter 25.]

Volunteer USA. By Andrew Carroll. Fawcett Columbine, 1991. 397 pages. For families interested in volunteering, this book offers information on specific social issues, including hunger and the environment. Includes lists of daily activities—sponsoring a hungry child, using nontoxic cleansers, etc.—that can help make the planet a more hospitable and inhabitable place. Lists national nonprofit organizations as well.

Associations

For Adults

National Charities Information Bureau. 19 Union Square, West, 6th Floor, New York, New York 10003-3395. Phone: 212/929-6300. Provides reports on national and international nonprofit organizations that solicit contributions from the public, including their various purposes, programs, and finances (according to a set of basic standards). Publishes the *Wise Giving Guide* (three times annually), as well as the periodic *Reports about Individual Agencies*. Also offers *Before You Give: A Contributor's Checklist*.

Points of Light Foundation. 1737 H Street, N.W., Washington, D.C. 20006. Phone: 202/223-9186 or 1/800-879-5400. Serves as a major clearinghouse for information on volunteer services and opportunities. Encourages more Americans to become volunteers and works to strengthen volunteer programs. Has more than four hundred affiliates nationwide. Ask how you can contact organizations in your community that need volunteers.

For Children

Kids for Kids. c/o Childreach, 155 Plan Way, Warwick, Rhode Island 02886. Phone: 1/800-556-7918. A sponsorship program that matches children from the United States with needy children around the world. In return for a $22 per month sponsorship fee, young participants are given an opportunity to learn more about other cultures. They receive a photograph and profile of the child they're sponsoring; a monthly newsletter focusing on a participating country (complete with native recipes, games, and facts about the region); and a membership kit containing a certificate, stickers, coloring books, and more.

Citizenship

Close-Up Foundation. 44 Canal Center Plaza, Alexandria, Virginia 22314. 703/706-3300. Encourages responsible participation in the democratic process by citizens of all ages and backgrounds. Promotes increased civic awareness, involvement, and achievement through a variety of educational programs, including the Civic Achievement Award Program (CAAP) for students in grades five through eight. CAAP is designed to help young people better understand what it means to be a citizen of the United States and to learn more about their country. The program includes a *Student Resource Guide*, which explains in easy-to-understand language terms such as economics, cultural diversity, current events, and civics issues. Participants receive an award certificate.

WORLD PEACE

Books for Children

Fighting the Invisible Enemy: Understanding the Effects of Conditioning. By Terrence Webster-Doyle. Atrium Publications, 1990. 164 pages. Explains how war is created by the way we think and how conditioning can make individuals act like robots. Offers creative, nonviolent alternatives to fighting. For children ages ten and up.

Peace Tales: World Folktales to Talk About. By Margaret Read MacDonald. Shoe String, 1992. 116 pages. A collection of folktales from around the globe that invite young readers to think about the possibilities if we were to achieve peace (and how they can help make it a reality). For ages ten and up (can also be read to younger children).

Talking Walls. By Margy Burns Knight. Tilbury House, 1992. 40 pages. Young readers learn about the Berlin Wall, the Great Wall of China, and other barriers, including their impact on the people who built them and their effects on those who are divided or unified by them. Includes pastel drawings showing how children today live with the walls. For ages six and up.

Tug of War: Peace through Understanding Conflict. By Terrence Webster-Doyle. Atrium Publications, 1990. 106 pages. Teaches what the roots of war are and how we create "the enemy." Includes stories and activities that teach practical skills to cope with violence and resolve conflict peacefully. For children ages ten and up.

Young Peacemakers Project Book. By Kathleen Fry-Miller and Judith Myers-Walls. Brethren, 1988. 116 pages. This book describes activities and projects that convey messages about the environment, respect for others, cultural diversity, and peace-making. Includes a resource list and suggested scripture verses (*Peace Works: Young Peacemakers Project Book II* offers similar types of activities, but omits the scripture references). For work with children in preschool through the elementary years.

Game

Friends around the World: A Game of World Peace. Illustrated by Joan Walsh Anglund. Aristoplay. A board game that teaches the benefits of co-operation. Players help each other race to bring sixteen friends—each from a different country—to the World Peace center before "the Blob" gets there. Available from Aristoplay, P.O. Box 7529, Ann Arbor, Michigan 48107. Phone: 1/800-634-7738.

Mail Order Catalogs

Animal Town. P.O. Box 485, Healdsburg, California 95448. Phone: 1/800-445-8642. This catalog promotes cooperation, friendship, and cultural understanding. Includes a wide variety of cooperative and noncompetitive games; children's tapes, books, and puzzles; and books on cooperation and family activities.

Chinaberry. 2780 Via Orange Way, Suite B, Spring Valley, California 91978. Many selections in this book and tape catalog celebrate cultural

differences and promote global peace and understanding. Includes book titles like *Peace Tales: World Folktales to Talk About*, and audiocassettes such as *Till Their Eyes Shine*, a collection of lullabies by well-known artists (proceeds from this cassette benefit children at risk in countries torn by war).

Music for Little People. P.O. Box 1460, Redway, California 95560. Phone: 1/800-727-2233. Offers a variety of recordings on cassette, compact disc, and video that celebrate cultural diversity and promote world peace.

Periodical

Parenting for Peace and Justice Newsletter. Institute for Peace and Justice, 4144 Lindell Boulevard, #122, St. Louis, MO 63108. Phone: 314/533-4445. Contains articles for parents on nonviolent conflict resolution, social concerns (peace, hunger, racial attitudes, stereotypes), and consumerism. Recommends family-oriented resources and activities related to these topics. Also discusses outreach strategies for families, church groups, programs, and organizations. Issued bimonthly.

Associations

General

Children as the Peacemakers. 1591 Shrader Street, San Francisco, California 94117. Phone: 415/731-2757. A group of individuals interested in fostering world peace through cultural exchange. Arranges for children to speak to world leaders about peace and to meet with each other to discuss global issues and problems. Offers peace education programs.

Children's Creative Response to Conflict Program. c/o Fellowship of Reconciliation, 523 North Broadway, Box 271, Nyack, New York 10960. Phone: 914/358-4601. The program's goal is to help children learn to live peacefully with others and to acquire the skills necessary to resolve conflict. Offers publications, activities, workshops, and courses to help teachers and children learn skills of cooperation, communication, and conflict resolution.

Consortium on Peace Research, Education, and Development. George Mason University, 4400 University Drive, Fairfax, Virginia 22030. Phone: 703/993-3639. A consortium of academic institutions, organizations, foundations, and individuals associated with national and international peace education and research efforts. Produces the *Directory of Peace Studies Programs*, a bimonthly newsletter, and a variety of peace education/research materials.

Global Education Associates. 475 Riverside Drive, Suite 456, New York, New York 10115. Phone: 212/870-3209. Advocates cross-cultural understanding and explores alternative solutions to international conflicts. Seeks to achieve international cooperation through education. Produces a list of publications and audiovisual materials. Publishes a quarterly magazine called *Breakthrough*.

International Association of Educators for World Peace. Box 3282, Mastin Lake Station, Huntsville, Alabama 35810-0282. Phone: 205/534-5501. An association of teachers, students, and other individuals working to improve international relations and achieve world peace through education. Promotes improved curricula and methods of instruction in the schools. Publishes *Peace Education*, a semiannual journal, as well as other publications.

Martin Luther King, Jr., Center for Nonviolent Social Change, Inc. 449 Auburn Avenue, N.E., Atlanta, Georgia 30312. Phone: 404/524-8969. En-

The Community Playground

Perhaps one of the last, great places to get to know your neighbors is the community playground. Here, parents can still swap information, talk politics, share jokes, and exchange recipes—while their children learn valuable lessons about sharing, friendship, and the law of gravity. If you don't have a playground in your community, you might consider building one. It's a big job, but it's do-able, and the rewards are immeasurable. One group that helps communities design and build their own playgrounds is Robert S. Leathers and Associates (phone: 607/277-1650). They offer fundraising guidelines as well.

courages the nonviolent settlement of disputes. Works to continue the work of Reverend Martin Luther King, Jr., through education, research, and constructive action. Offers curriculum materials for students (elementary school through senior high).

Peace Links. 747 Eighth Street, S.E., Washington, D.C. 20003. Phone: 202/544-0805. Dedicated to public education about peace and nuclear issues. Offers informational packets for parents, teachers, and children. Sponsors exchanges and other programs. Publishes a newsletter.

Perhaps Kids Meeting Kids Can Make a Difference. 380 Riverside Drive, New York, New York 10025. Phone: 212/662-2327. Works for peace and social justice, and advocates children's rights around the world. Conducts a children's exchange program. Sponsors a letter-writing project and a computer information exchange. Issues a periodic newsletter.

Handgun Violence

Center to Prevent Handgun Violence. 1225 Eye Street, N.W., Suite 1100, Washington, D.C. 20005. Phone: 202/289-7319. Works to educate the American public about the risks of handgun ownership. Sponsors programs for school-aged students (junior and senior high), including discussions on the role of the handgun in society. Conducts research and compiles statistics on handgun-related crimes, injuries, and deaths. Offers a variety of free educational materials on children and guns.

The Educational Fund to End Handgun Violence. 110 Maryland Avenue, N.E., Box 72, Washington, D.C. 20002. Phone: 202/544-7227. Examines and offers public education on handgun violence in the United States, particularly as it relates to children. Participates in the development of gun-education materials and programs for schools. Publications include *Kids and Guns*, an in-depth report.

Mad Dads (Men Against Destruction—Defending Against Drugs and Social [disorder]). Eddie Staton, president. 221 North Twenty-fourth Street, Omaha, Nebraska 68110. An organization of concerned fathers and mothers working to prevent street violence and make their communities safer for their children. Conducts antiviolence campaigns, and works to prevent drug dealing and social disorder. Sponsors community beautification projects and encourages young people to get involved in the MAD DAD cause. The message is spreading, and chapters are opening in cities and towns across the country.

Chapter 25

Child Advocacy and Public Policy

Hotlines

Legislative Hotline. Phone: 202/662-3678 (twenty-four-hours-a-day, seven-days-a-week). Run by the Children's Defense Fund, this hotline provides updates on legislative action at the federal level related to children's issues. Prerecorded messages explain what is happening, what is needed, and what callers can do to help.

Project Vote Smart. Phone: 1/800-622-7627. Will provide callers with free information on the voting record of any senator or representative on family issues, among other topics.

Make Your Voice Heard!

Congress. U.S. Senate and House of Representatives, Washington, D.C. 20515-0001. Phone: 202/224-3121 (Capitol switchboard). The Capitol switchboard can connect you with the office of your elected senators and representatives, where you can voice your opinion.

President of the United States. 1600 Pennsylvania Avenue, Washington, D.C. 20500. Phone: 202/456-1111 (White House opinion line).

Free and Inexpensive Resources

Guiding Principles for the Development, Analysis, and Implementation of Early Childhood Legislation. Position statement of the National Association for the Education of Young Children that can be used as a tool for advocacy at the federal, state, and local level. Available for 50¢ from the National Association for the Education of Young Children (for contact information, see appendix I).

U.S. Congress: A Guide to Making Your Voice Heard. A resource packet available from Parent Action, the National Association of Parents. For a copy of "U.S. Congress," send $3.75 along with your request to Parent Action, (see listing under "Associations").

Books

Childhood's Future. By Richard Louv. Houghton Mifflin, 1991. 420 pages. Based on interviews with parents, educators, children, and others, the author concludes that the ties that used to bind neighbors, communities, learning institutions, and government with children are gone. Louv's goal is to "reweave the web," to reconnect young and old, schools and families, and so forth. Challenges government to encourage family-friendly workplaces and counsels parents to reach out to other parents for support. Emphasizes the importance of children in our society's future.

Every Kid Counts: 31 Ways to Save Our Children. By Margaret Brodkin and Coleman Advocates for Children and Youth. HarperCollins, 1993. 204 pages. A collection of ideas and strategies to help parents and others make a positive difference in the lives of children. Suggestions range from easy-to-do (donate a used toy to a homeless shelter) to the more complex (organize a candidates' forum). Each chapter concludes with additional resource listings.

"Public Networking: Influencing Public Policy." A chapter from *Staying Home Instead: Alternatives to the Two-Paycheck Family*, by Christine Davidson (Macmillan, 1992). This portion of the book offers advice to parents who believe they can make a difference. Includes a listing of advocacy groups. (For more information on *Staying Home Instead*, see "Books" listed under "Mothers at Home" in chapter 11.)

So You Want to Make a Difference: A Key to Advocacy. By Nancy Amidei. OMB Watch, 1991. 62 pages. A primer on becoming an advocate. To order a copy of this book, contact OMB Watch, 1731 Connecticut Avenue, N.W., 4th Floor, Washington, D.C. 20009-1146. Phone: 202/234-8494.

When the Bough Breaks: The Cost of Neglecting Our Children. By Sylvia Ann Hewlett. HarperCollins, 1991. 346 pages. Presents evidence showing that American children—rich and poor—are the victims of a level of both public and private neglect that is unique among developed nations. Documents a parenting deficit, fueled by the increase in divorce rates and the involuntary increase in the hours parents work. Outlines a multifaceted action plan encompassing child-care policy, parenting leave, tax reform, and family-friendly workplaces. Describes cost-effective private programs that have helped families and children.

You Can Change America. By the Earth Works Group. Earth Works Press, 1992. A handbook on political involvement.

Associations

Center for Policy Alternatives. 1875 Connecticut Avenue, N.W., Suite 710, Washington, D.C. 20009. Phone: 202/387-6030. Acts as a national clearinghouse and forum for the exchange of ideas on progressive public policy. Offers assistance to individuals and groups in developing model legislation. Disseminates information. Publishes books, monographs, reports, and a newsletter called *Alternatives*.

Center for the Study of Social Policy. 1250 Eye Street, N.W., Suite 503, Washington, D.C. 20005-3922. Phone: 202/371-1565. Analyzes contemporary policy issues, including those affecting children, youth, and families. Makes research findings available to both public and private sectors. Participated in a joint, nationwide study with the Annie E. Casey Foundation in Greenwich, Connecticut, called *Kids Count*, which shows that children in 1992 lead less safe, less healthy, and less privileged lives than children in 1980.

Child Care Action Campaign. 330 Seventh Avenue, 17th Floor, New

York, New York 10001. Phone: 212/239-0138. A national advocacy organization working to increase and improve child care services across the country. Analyzes existing services and identifies gaps. Works with communities in developing plans for quality child care programs. Alerts the public on legislative action and child care regulations in various states. Publishes *Child Care ActioNews*, a bimonthly newsletter on innovations in the field of child care for working parents. Also publishes a variety of guides (for more information, see listing in chapter 11).

Child Care Employee Project. 6536 Telegraph Avenue, Suite A201, Oakland, California 94609. Phone: 510/653-9889. An advocacy group that seeks to improve salaries, working conditions, and status of childcare providers. Is conducting the "Worthy Wage Campaign," a five-year initiative to secure decent wages for child care workers. Encourages parental involvement in this cause. Offers a packet of materials about the campaign and information about community efforts across the country.

Child Welfare League of America. 440 First Street, N.W., Suite 310, Washington, D.C. 20001-2085. Phone: 202/638-2952. Works to bring greater visibility to the needs of abused, neglected, and vulnerable children and their families. Runs the Children's Campaign, a grass-roots advocacy network of individuals committed to acting on behalf of children. Sponsors "Volunteer for Kids," a group that can put individuals in touch with children's agencies across the country that need volunteers (for more information, call 1/800-950-3453). Disseminates information on legislative action (including specific information on who to lobby when a bill is scheduled for immediate action). Offers consultation and conducts research. Works with agencies that provide foster-care services and residential programs for children. Publishes books, monographs, and a variety of periodicals, including *Children's Voice*, a quarterly magazine covering program and policy development in child welfare services.

Children's Defense Fund. 25 East Street, N.W., Washington, D.C. 20001. Phone: 202/628-8787 or 202/662-3678 (legislative hotline). A nonprofit organization advocating children's rights in public policy through research, legislation, litigation, public education, and community organizing. Works to change policies and practices resulting in neglect or mistreatment of children. Seeks to make existing programs and services more accessible and to create new programs where necessary. Deals primarily with child health, welfare, education, child care, juvenile justice, homelessness, and adolescent-pregnancy prevention. Releases information on individual legislators' voting records. Publishes *CDF Reports*, a monthly newsletter covering issues relating to children and adolescents. Also produces the annual *State of America's Children* report, which examines the current status of America's children and families. Issues books, handbooks, and state-specific fact sheets about children and child advocacy as well. Runs a legislative hotline (see listing under "Hotlines").

Coalition for America's Children. 1710 Rhode Island Avenue, N.W., 4th Floor, Washington, D.C. 20036. Phone: 202/857-7829. An organization concerned with the welfare of children. Lobbies for improved health, safety, security, and educational legislation. Offers information and materials to help parents and others campaign for pro-child candidates.

Coleman Advocates for Children and Youth. 2601 Mission Street, #804, San Francisco, California 94110. Phone: 415/641-4362. Provides information on starting local child advocacy organizations and initiatives. Offers videotapes, bumperstickers ("I'm for Kids and I Vote"), information kits, and a book called *Every Kid Counts* (see listing under "Books").

Family Research Council. 700 Thirteenth Street, Suite 500, Washington, D.C. 20005. Phone: 202/393-2100. An independent, nonprofit organization offering information and expertise on family issues, including the impact of parental absence on children, community support for single parents, and the effects of the tax system on families. Publishes *Family Policy*, a bimonthly magazine containing policy analyses, and *Washington Watch*, a monthly newsletter.

FEMALE (Formerly Employed Mothers at the Leading Edge). P.O. Box 31, Elmhurst, Illinois 60126. Phone: 708/941-3553. An advocacy group concerned with changing society's perceptions of—and public policies on—families with mothers at home. (For more information on FEMALE, see "Associations" listed under "Mothers at Home" in chapter 11.)

Institute for American Values. 1841 Broadway, Suite 211, New York, New York 10023. Phone: 212/246-3942. A nonpartisan, nonprofit policy organization concerned with issues affecting the well-being of the American family. Conducts research. Currently working to establish a national family agenda. Publishes *Family Affairs*, a quarterly newsletter.

Mothers at Home. 8310-A Old Courthouse Road, Vienna, Virginia 22182. Phone: 703/827-5903. Works to influence public policy on families with mothers at home. Provides in-

formation at congressional hearings. (For more information on Mothers at Home see "Associations" listed under "Mothers at Home" in chapter 11.)

National Association of Child Advocates. 1625 K Street, N.W., Suite 510, Washington, D.C. 20006. Phone: 202/828-6950. Offers services to child advocacy organizations. Directs individuals who would like to become involved locally to an advocacy group in their state or community.

National Black Child Development Institute. 1023 Fifteenth Street, N.W., Suite 600, Washington, D.C. 20005. Phone: 202/387-1281. Fax: 202/234-1738. Works to improve the quality of life for black children and youth. Holds conferences. Conducts seminars. Analyzes legislation, regulations, and policy decisions as they relate to black children and youth. Publishes *Black Child Advocate*, a quarterly newsletter containing updates on legislation and public policy, as well as information on local service programs. Also publishes *Child Health Talk*, a quarterly covering child behavior, childhood stress, nutrition and exercise, and other health topics. Call or write for an information packet and contact with a local affiliate.

National League of Cities. 1301 Pennsylvania Avenue, N.W., Suite 600, Washington, D.C. 20004. Phone: 202/626-3150. Shares information on innovative children's projects in cities across the country. Offers a booklet called *Making Government Work for Your City's Kids*, which shows how government programs affect families; how communities can help shape local, state, and national agendas; and how local officials can become advocates for children and families.

National PTA. 700 North Rush Street, Chicago, Illinois 60611.

Phone: 312/787-0977. Publishes *What's Happening in Washington*, a newsletter covering current federal legislation that affects the health, safety, education, and protection of children and youth, and that addresses PTA concerns. Also offers *A Voice for Children and Youth*, a practical guide describing the PTA's role in federal legislative activities, including strategies to help PTAs become more effective child advocates at the national level.

Parent Action, The National Association of Parents. 2 North Charles Street, Suite 960, Baltimore, Maryland 21201. Phone: 410/727-3687. Fax: 410/752-1793. Formed in 1989 by Dr. T. Berry Brazelton, Bernice Weissbourd, and Susan DeConcini, this association represents the special interests of parents. Advocates parents' concerns at all levels of government and promotes sound family policy. Offers referrals and provides information on topics of concern to parents. Publishes *Parent Post*, a quarterly newsletter reporting on current issues that affect families. Also offers inexpensive resource packets for parents covering topics such as child care, separation and divorce, education, moving, self-esteem, and advocacy. Produces a book and video list as well (items on the list can be ordered at discounts through Parent Action). Members are also eligible for discounts on a variety of products and services, including health products, hotel rates, theme parks, and magazine subscriptions. Annual membership costs only $10.00.

United Nations Children's Fund (UNICEF). 3 United Nations Plaza, New York, New York 10017. Phone: 212/922-2537. Dedicated to addressing the needs of children around the globe. Provides information on the state of the world's youth. Involved with lobbying and fund-raising for children. Publishes annually the *State of the World's Children*, which contains facts and figures about children around the world (issued in five languages).

The following organizations will be of interest to mothers who choose to support female candidates, promote "women's" issues (despite progress in recent years, research shows that mothers are still largely responsible for child care–including the arrangement of it when they work outside the home), or simply want to join other women in working toward a common goal. Many mothers agree that women can better represent their needs and interests.

Congressional Caucus for Women's Issues. 2471 Rayburn House Office Building, Washington, D.C. 20515. Phone: 202/225-6740. Promotes women's issues through the national legislative process.

League of Women Voters of the United States. 1730 M Street, N.W., Washington, D.C. 20036. Phone: 202/429-1965. A nonpartisan organization promoting political responsibility and informed participation for all citizens (men and women). Lobbies on a wide variety of local and national issues. The league sponsors the presidential debates and initiates candidate forums as well. During the 1992 presidential campaign, the league included child-care centers in their national week-long voter registration drive.

National Organization for Women. 1000 Sixteenth Street, N.W., Suite 700, Washington, D.C. 20036. Phone: 202/331-0066. Participates in political and legislative activities that promote women's equality in the political arena, in the workplace, and elsewhere. Works to increase the number of women elected to public office.

National Women's Political Caucus. 1275 K Street, N.W., Suite 750, Washington, D.C. 20005. Phone: 202/898-1100. A multipartisan caucus seeking to gain an equal voice and place for women in the political process at all levels of government. Raises women's issues during elections and seeks to ensure that women hold policy-making positions in political parties. Also raises money for women candidates. Issues *Women's Political Times*, a quarterly newsletter covering political issues from a feminist viewpoint.

Women's Campaign Fund. 120 Maryland Avenue, N.E., Washington, D.C. 20002. Phone: 202/544-4484. A bipartisan, pro-choice political action committee dedicated to getting more women into office. Raises funds and makes direct contributions to the campaigns of WCF-endorsed candidates. Promotes public awareness of the need for more women in public office.

Chapter 26

Dollars and Sense: Purchasing Savvy, Advertising Gimmicks, Consumer Complaints, Money Management, and More (Including Free Stuff for Kids to Send Away For)

RESOURCES FOR ADULTS

Free and Inexpensive Resources

Consumer's Resource Handbook. Produced by the U.S. Office of Consumer Affairs, this ninety-six-page guide lists corporate, federal, state, and local offices to contact if you have a question or need to resolve a complaint. Includes consumer tips and product safety information. For ordering information, request a copy of the free *Consumer Information Catalog*, available from the Consumer Information Center, P.O. Box 100, Pueblo, Colorado 81002.

A Parent's Guide: Advertising and Your Child. This guide is available from the Children's Advertising Review Unit, a division of the Council of Better Business Bureaus, Inc. (CBBB). For a copy, send $1 to CARU Parent's Guide, CBBB, Department 023, Washington, D.C. 20042-0023.

Staying Healthy and Whole. A ten-page consumer guide to product safety recalls, produced by the U.S. Office of Consumer Affairs. Lists products regulated by eight federal agencies (their addresses and phone numbers are included). For ordering information, request a copy of the free *Consumer Information Catalog*, available from the Consumer Information Center, P.O. Box 100, Pueblo, Colorado 81002.

Books

General

The Childwise Catalog. By Jack Gillis and Mary Ellen R. Fise. Third edition, revised and expanded. HarperCollins, 1993. 470 pages. A consumer's guide to buying the safest and best products for your children.

Includes sections on products and equipment, food and diet, family travel, child safety (including products that have been recalled), a brand-specific "best and worst" section on toys, and information on selecting a pediatrician, child care, preschool, and other "services." Includes money-saving consumer tips, the latest information on child safety, and extensive resource listings. (For more information on *The Childwise Catalog*, see listing under "Books" in chapter 7.)

Guide to Baby Products: Consumer Reports Books. By Sandy Jones with Werner Freitag and the Editors of Consumer Reports Books. Third revised edition. Consumers Union, 1991. 334 pages. Offers advice on buying a wide variety of baby products, including backpacks, clothing, baby foods, and nursery accessories. Also contains brand-name ratings, safety and recall information, and price guidelines. (For more information on *Guide to Baby Products*, see listing under "Books" in chapter 7.)

Teaching Children about Money

Kids, Money and Values: Creative Ways to Teach Your Kids About Money. By Patricia Shiff Estess and Irving Barocas. Betterway Books, 1994. 133 pages. A book to help parents teach their kids sound money values using activities, games, and projects. Offers guidance to help children distinguish "wants" from "needs," become wise shoppers, and learn the art of giving.

Money Doesn't Grow on Trees: A Parent's Guide to Raising Financially Responsible Children. By Neale S. Godfrey and Carolina Edwards. Simon and Schuster, 1993.

175 pages. This book is designed to help parents teach their children how to earn, save, and spend money wisely, and in the process, pass along important family values.

Associations

Consumer Product Safety Commission. See listing under "Government Agencies" in chapter 7.

Consumers Union. Phone: 914/378-2000 or 1/800-288-7898 (for subscriptions to Consumers Union publications). Provides consumers with information and advice on consumer products and services Produces a variety of publications to assist consumers in purchasing reliable products at reasonable prices, including *Consumer Reports* magazine, *Zillions: Consumer Reports for Children, Consumer Reports on Health*, and the *Travel Letter*. Also publishes special reports and books on particular fields of consumer interest. Consumer Reports Television produces television series and specials for cable TV, including the three-part series, "Buy Me That!/Buy Me That Too!/Buy Me That 3!" (designed to help children understand advertising). Other programs include a half-hour special called "Zillions" (based on the magazine), for kids ages seven to thirteen.

Council of Better Business Bureaus, Inc. See "Better Business Bureaus" listing at the end of this chapter.

National Consumers League. 815 Fifteenth Street, N.W., Suite 928, Washington, D.C. 20005. Phone: 202/639-8140. Conducts research and develops educational and advocacy programs on consumer issues, including product safety and standards. Encourages citizens to participate in government and industry decision making. Publishes consumer guides, quarterlies, information sheets, and manuals.

Public Citizen. P.O. Box 19404, Washington, D.C. 20036. Phone: 202/833-3000. Founded by Ralph Nader in 1971, this nonprofit organization addresses a variety of consumer, health, and environmental issues, including consumer rights in the marketplace, product safety, and government accountability. Publishes *Public Citizen*, a bimonthly magazine covering consumer issues, and *Health Letter*, a monthly newsletter covering drugs, medical devices, and other health issues. Publishes books, reports, and policy papers as well.

RESOURCES FOR CHILDREN

Books

General

The Kids' Money Book. By Neale Godfrey. Checkerboard Press, 1991. 128 pages. This handbook for kids explains the history of money and offers tips on saving it and spending it. For grades three and up.

Making Cents: Every Kid's Guide to Money: How to Make It, What to Do with It. By Elizabeth Wilkinson. Little, Brown, 1989. 128 pages. Explores the concept f money and illustrates ways to make it. For children ages nine to fourteen.

My First Look at Shopping. Random House, 1991. First American edition. 20 pages. Includes simple text and photographs depicting different things we shop for in supermarkets, toy stores, drugstores, and other places. For children ages one to three.

Making Money

Better Than a Lemonade Stand! Small Business Ideas for Kids. By Daryl Bernstein. Beyond Words Publishing, 1992. 125 pages. Written by a fifteen-year-old who has been making money since he was eight, this book describes more than fifty small business ventures for kids ages ten and up. Offers information and tips on supplies, time required, what to charge, and how to attract customers. For children in grades two and up.

Jobs for Kids. By Carol Barkin and Elizabeth James. Lothrop, Lee, and Shepard Books, 1990. 112 pages. Offers tips to help children make money doing what they enjoy. Dog-walking, lawn work, paper work, and teaching younger children sports or computer skills are some examples. Includes advice on selling, setting prices, and working with a partner. For children in grades five through nine.

Making Sense: Every Kid's Guide to Money. See "General Books."

Games and Kits

The Allowance Game. As players move around the board, they earn and spend an allowance. Washing the car earns a player $1.30; forgetting to do homework means losing a turn. Designed to teach children how to handle money. Comes with play bills and coins. Available from Toys to Grow On (for contact information, see chapter 27).

BanKit: The Home Checking Account and Money Management System for Kids. This kit is designed to teach children responsible money management, savings savvy, and check balancing skills. Comes with a kid's manual, a banker's manual (for mom or dad), deposit slips, checks, savings envelopes, and more. For children ages eight and up (together with their parents). Available from Discovery Toys (see listing under "Toys" in chapter 16).

The Money Machine. A unique money-storing device complete with wheels and cranks that spring to life when kids drop in nickels, dimes, pennies, and quarters. Also stores bills. Available from Exploratorium to Go! (for contact information, see chapter 27).

Periodical

Zillions. Consumers Union, Box 54861, Boulder, Colorado 80322-4861. Phone: 1/800-288-7898. Billed as "the *Consumer Reports* for kids," this magazine is designed to help children become wise consumers. Compares videogames, toys, sports equipment, allowances, etc. For children ages eight to fourteen. Issued six times annually.

Videotapes

Buy Me That! A Kids' Survival Guide to TV Advertising. Films, Inc. Running time: 30 minutes. Films, Inc. Drawing from the kids' magazine, *Zillions*, this video exposes deceptive television advertising practices. Highlights a variety of misleading commercials featuring toys with critical parts "sold separately," toys that are supposed to go (but instead stand still), and play items that require hours and hours of assembly work. The host of this video, Jim Fyfe, leads a discussion among children, who have much to say about this advertising trickery. Produced by Consumer Reports Television and HBO. For children ages six to ten. To order a copy of the videotape, contact Films, Inc., 5547 Ravenswood Avenue, Chicago, Illinois 60640-1199. Phone: 1/800-323-4222. (Note: Discussion guides are available from Consumer Reports Television, 101

Truman Avenue, Yonkers, New York 10703-1057. Phone: 914/378-2492.)

Piggy Banks to Money Markets. Kidvidz (distributed by Price Stern Sloan, Inc.) Running time: 30 min-utes. A kid's video guide to dollars and sense. For children ages five to twelve. Comes with an activity guide. To order a copy, contact Price Stern Sloan, Inc. (Phone: 1/800-421-0892).

FREE THINGS TO SEND AWAY FOR

Book

Free Stuff for Kids. By the Free Stuff editors. Meadowbrook Press. Updated annually. Lists, describes, and provides ordering information for more than three hundred free and very low-cost items for kids. Garden seeds, stamps, stickers, posters, ball-point pens, and activity books are among the offer-ings. Intended for use by children, with easy-to-understand text.

Periodical

Freebies. P.O. Box 20283, Santa Barbara, California 93120. A magazine listing dozens of mail order bargains. Includes a special section for kids. Issued five times annually. Sample copies available for $2.50.

BETTER BUSINESS BUREAUS

National Headquarters
Council of Better Business Bureaus, Inc. 4200 Wilson Boulevard, Arlington, Virginia 22203. Phone: 703/276-0100.

Local Bureaus
Alabama
P.O. Box 55268, Birmingham, Alabama 35255-5268. Phone: 205/558-2222.

118 Woodburn Street, Dothan, Alabama 36301. Phone: 205/792-3804.

P.O. Box 383, Huntsville, Alabama 35801. Phone: 205/533-1640.

707 Van Antwerp Building, Mobile, Alabama 36602. Phone: 205/433-5494 or 5495.

Commerce Street, Suite 806, Montgomery, Alabama 36104. Phone: 205/262-5606.

Alaska
3380 C Street, Suite 103, Anchorage, Alaska 99503. Phone: 907/562-0704.

Arizona
4428 North Twelfth Street, Phoenix, Arizona 85014-4585. Phone: 602/264-1721.

50 West Brachman Street, Suite 103, Tucson, Arizona 85705. Phone: 602/622-7651 (inquiries); 602/622-7654 (complaints).

Arkansas
1415 South University, Little Rock, Arizona 72204. Phone: 501/664-7274.

California
705 Eighteenth Street, Bakersfield, California 93301-4882. Phone: 805/322-2074.

P.O. Box 970, Colton, California 92324-0522. Phone: 714/825-7280.

Better Business Bureaus (BBBs) are non-profit organizations sponsored by local businesses. BBBs offer a variety of consumer services. For example, they can provide consumer education materials, answer consumer questions, mediate and arbitrate complaints, and provide general information on companies' consumer complaint records.

Each BBB has its own policy about reporting information. It might or might not tell you the nature of the complaint against a business, but all will tell you if a complaint has been registered. Many of the BBBs accept written complaints and will contact a firm on your behalf. BBBs do not judge or rate individual products or brands, handle complaints concerning the prices of goods or services, or give legal advice. However, many bureaus do offer binding arbitration, a form of dispute resolution, to those who ask for it. If you need help with a consumer question or complaint, call your local BBB to ask about their services.

From the *Consumer's Resource Handbook*, published by the United States Office of Consumer Affairs (1992 edition).

6101 Ball Road, Suite 309, Cypress, California 90630. Phone: 714/527-0680.

1398 West Indianapolis, Suite 102, Fresno, California 93705. Phone: 209/222-8111.

494 Alvarado Street, Suite C, Monterey, California 93940. Phone: 408/372-3149.

510 Sixteenth Street, Oakland, California 94612. Phone: 415/839-5900.

400 S Street, Sacramento, California 95814. Phone: 916/443-6843.

3111 Camino del Rio, North, Suite 600, San Diego, California 92108-1729. Phone: 619/281-6422.

33 New Montgomery Street Tower, San Francisco, California 94105. Phone: 415/243-9999.

1505 Meridian Avenue, San Jose, California 95125. Phone: 408/978-8700.

P.O. Box 294, San Mateo, California 94401. Phone: 415/696-1240.

P.O. Box 746, Santa Barbara, California 93102. Phone: 805/963-8657.

300 B Street, Santa Rosa, California 95401. Phone: 707/577-0300.

1111 North Center Street, Stockton, California 95202-1383. Phone: 209/948-4880 or 4881.

Colorado

P.O. Box 7970, Colorado Springs, Colorado 80933. Phone: 719/636-1155.

1780 South Bellaire, Suite 700, Denver, Colorado 80222. Phone: 303/758-2100 (inquiries); 303/758-2212 (complaints).

1730 South College Avenue, Suite 303, Fort Collins, Colorado 80525. Phone: 303/484-1348.

119 West Sixth Street, Suite 203, Pueblo, Colorado 81003-3119. Phone: 719/542-6464.

Connecticut

2345 Black Rock Turnpike, Fairfield, Connecticut 06430. Phone: 203/374-6161.

2080 Silas Deane Highway, Rocky Hill, Connecticut 06067-2311. Phone: 203/529-3575.

100 South Turnpike Road, Wallingford, Connecticut 06492-4395. Phone: 203/269-2700 (inquiries); 203/269-4457 (complaints).

Delaware
2055 Limestone Road, Suite 200, Wilmington, Delaware 19808. Phone: 302/996-9200.

District of Columbia
1012 Fourteenth Street, N.W., 14th Floor, Washington, D.C. 20005-3410. Phone: 202/393-8000.

Florida
In addition to the Better Business Bureaus, Florida has a number of Better Business Councils that are affiliated with local Chambers of Commerce throughout the state. The Better Business Councils are listed following the Better Business Bureaus.

Better Business Bureaus

P.O. Box 7950, Clearwater, Florida 34618-7950. Phone: 813/535-5522.

2976-E Cleveland Avenue, Fort Myers, Florida 33901. Phone: 813/334-7331.

3100 University Boulevard, South, Suite 239, Jacksonville, Florida 32216. Phone: 904/721-2288.

2605 Maitland Center Parkway, Maitland, Florida 32751-7147. Phone: 407/660-9500.

16291 Northwest Fifty-seventh Avenue, Miami, Florida 33014-6709, Inquiries for Dade County, Phone: 305/625-0307. Complaints for Dade County, Phone: 305/625-1302. Inquiries for Broward County, Phone: 305/524-2803. Complaints for Broward County, Phone: 305/527-1643.

P.O. Box 1511, Pensacola, Florida 32597-1511. Phone: 904/433-6111.

1950 Southeast Port Street, Lucie Boulevard, Suite 211, Port St. Lucie, Florida 34952. Phone: 407/878-2010; 407/337-2083 (Martin County).

2247 Palm Beach Lakes Boulevard, Suite 211, West Palm Beach, Florida 33409. Phone: 407/686-2200.

Better Business Councils

P.O. Box 321, Bradenton, Florida 34206-0321. Phone: 813/748-1325 (Manatee County).

P.O. Box 3607, Lakeland, Florida 33802-3607. Phone: 813/680-1030 (Polk County).

P.O. Box 492426, Leesburg, Florida 32749-2426. Phone: 904/326-0770 (Lake County).

400 Fortenberry Road, Merritt Island, Florida 32952. Phone: 407/452-8869 (Central Brevard County).

13000 South Tamiami Trail, Suite 111, North Port, Florida 34287. Phone: 813/426-8744.

4100 Dixie Highway, N.E., Palm Bay, Florida 32905. Phone: 407/984-8454 (South Brevard County).

1819 Main Street, Suite 240, Sarasota, Florida 34236. Phone: 813/366-3144.

P.O. Drawer 2767, Titusville, Florida 32781-2767. Phone: 407/268-2822 (North Brevard County).

257 Tamiami Trail, North, Venice, Florida 34285-1534. Phone: 813/485-3510.

Georgia
1319-B Dawson Road, Albany, Georgia 31707. Phone: 912/883-0744.

100 Edgewood Avenue, Suite 1012, Atlanta, Georgia 30303. Phone: 404/688-4910.

P.O. Box 2085, Augusta, Georgia 30903. Phone: 404/722-1574.

P.O. Box 2587, Columbus, Georgia 31902. Phone: 404/324-0712.

1765 Shurling Drive, Macon, Georgia 31211. Phone: 912/742-7999.

P.O. Box 13956, Savannah, Georgia 31416-0956. Phone: 912/354-7521.

Hawaii
1600 Kapiolani Boulevard, Suite 714, Honolulu, Hawaii 96814. Phone: 808/942-2355.

Idaho
1333 West Jefferson, Boise, Idaho 83702. Phone: 208/342-4649; 208/467-5547 (Canyon County).

545 Shoup Avenue, Suite 210, Idaho Falls, Idaho 83402. Phone: 208/523-9754.

Illinois
211 West Wacker Drive, Chicago, Illinois 60606. Phone: 312/444-1188 (inquiries); 312/346-3313 (complaints).

3024 West Lake, Peoria, Illinois 61615. Phone: 309/688-3741.

810 East State Street, 3rd Floor, Rockford, Illinois 61104. Phone: 815/963-2222.

Indiana
P.O. Box 405, Elkhart, Indiana 46515-0405. Phone: 219/262-8996.

4004 Morgan Avenue, Suite 201, Evansville, Indiana 47715. Phone: 812/473-0202.

1203 Webster Street, Fort Wayne, Indiana 46802. Phone: 219/423-4433.

4231 Cleveland Street, Gary, Indiana 46408. Phone: 219/980-1511.

Victoria Centre, 22 East Washington Street, Suite 200, Indianapolis, Indiana 46204. Phone: 317/637-0197.

Marion, Indiana. Phone: 1/800-552-4631 (toll-free in Indiana).

Consumer Education Council (non-BBB), Ball State University, WB 150, Muncie, Indiana 47306. Phone: 317/747-8108.

52303 Emmons Road, Suite 9, South Bend, Indiana 46637. Phone: 219/277-9121.

Iowa
852 Middle Road, Suite 290, Bettendorf, Iowa 52722-4100. Phone: 319/355-6344.

615 Insurance Exchange Building, Des Moines, Iowa 50309. Phone: 515/243-8137.

318 Badgerow Building, Sioux City, Iowa 51101. Phone: 712/252-4501.

Kansas
501 Jefferson, Suite 24, Topeka, Kansas 66607-1190. Phone: 913/232-0454.

300 Kaufman Building, Wichita, Kansas 67202. Phone: 316/263-3146.

Kentucky
311 West Short Street, Lexington, Kentucky 40507. Phone: 606/259-1008.

844 South Fourth Street, Louisville, Kentucky 40203-2186. Phone: 502/583-6546.

Louisiana
1605 Murray Street, Suite 117, Alexandria, Louisiana 71301. Phone: 318/473-4494.

2055 Wooddale Boulevard, Baton Rouge, Louisiana 70806-1519. Phone: 504/926-3010.

501 East Main Street, Houma, Louisiana 70360. Phone: 504/868-3456.

P.O. Box 30297, Lafayette, Louisiana 70593-0297. Phone: 318/981-3497.

P.O. Box 1681, Lake Charles, Louisiana 70602. Phone: 318/433-1633.

141 De Siard Street, Suite 808, Monroe, Louisiana 71201-7380. Phone: 318/387-4600 or 8421.

1539 Jackson Avenue, New Orleans, Louisiana 70130-3400. Phone: 504/581-6222.

1401 North Market Street, Shreveport, Louisiana 71107-6525. Phone: 318/221-8352.

Maine
812 Stevens Avenue, Portland, Maine 04103. Phone: 207/878-2715.

Maryland
2100 Huntingdon Avenue, Baltimore, Maryland 21211-3215. Phone: 410/347-3990.

Massachusetts
20 Park Plaza, Suite 820, Boston, Massachusetts 02116-4404. Phone: 617/426-9000.

Framingham, Massachusetts. Phone: 1/800-422-2811, (toll-free in Massachusetts).

78 North Street, Suite 1, Hyannis, Massachusetts 02601-3808. Phone: 508/771-3022.

Lawrence, Massachusetts. Phone: 1/800-422-2811 (toll-free in Massachusetts).

293 Bridge Street, Suite 320, Springfield, Massachusetts 01103. Phone: 413/734-3114.

P.O. Box 379, Worcester, Massachusetts 01601. Phone: 508/755-2548.

Michigan
620 Trust Building, Grand Rapids, Michigan 49503. Phone: 616/774-8236.

30555 Southfield Road, Suite 200, Southfield, Michigan 48076-7751. Phone: 313/644-1012 (inquiries); 313/644-9136 (complaints); 313/644-9152 (auto line); 1/800-955-5100 (toll-free nationwide auto line).

Minnesota
2706 Gannon Road, St. Paul, Minnesota 55116. Phone: 612/699-1111.

Mississippi
460 Briarwood Drive, Suite 340, Jackson, Mississippi 39206-3088. Phone: 601/956-8282; 1/800-274-7222 (toll-free in Mississippi); 601/957-2886 (automotive complaints only).

Missouri
306 East Twelfth Street, Suite 1024, Kansas City, Missouri 64106-2418. Phone: 816/421-7800.

5100 Oakland Avenue, Suite 200, St. Louis, Missouri 63110. Phone: 314/531-3300.

205 Park Central East, Suite 509, Springfield, Missouri 65806. Phone: 417/862-9231.

Nebraska
719 North Forty-eighth Street, Lincoln, Nebraska 68504-3491. Phone: 402/467-5261.

1613 Farnam Street, Room 417, Omaha, Nebraska 68102-2158. Phone: 402/346-3033.

Nevada
1022 East Sahara Avenue, Las Vegas, Nevada 89104-1515. Phone: 702/735-6900 or 1969.

P.O. Box 21269, Reno, Nevada 89515-1269. Phone: 712/322-0657.

New Hampshire
410 South Main Street, Concord, New Hampshire 03301. Phone: 603/224-1991.

New Jersey
494 Broad Street, Newark, New Jersey 07102. Phone: 201/642-INFO.

2 Forest Avenue, Paramus, New Jersey 07652. Phone: 201/845-4044.

1721 Route 37, East, Toms River, New Jersey 08753-8239. Phone: 201/270-5577.

1700 Whitehorse, Hamilton Square, Suite D-5, Trenton, New Jersey 08690. Phone: 609/588-0808 (Mercer County).

P.O. Box 303, Westmont, New Jersey 08108-0303. Phone: 609/854-8467.

New Mexico
4600-A Montgomery, N.E., Suite 200, Albuquerque, New Mexico 87109. Phone: 505/884-0500; 1/800-445-1461 (toll-free in New Mexico).

308 North Locke, Farmington, New Mexico 87401. Phone: 505/326-6501.

2407 West Picacho, Suite B-2, Las Cruces, New Mexico 88005. Phone: 505/524-3130.

New York
346 Delaware Avenue, Buffalo, New York 14202. Phone: 716/856-7180.

266 Main Street, Farmingdale, New York 11735. Phone: 516/420-0500; 1/800-955-5100 (toll-free auto line).

257 Park Avenue South, New York, New York 10010. Phone: 1/900-463-6222 (85¢ per minute).

1122 Sibley Tower, Rochester, New York 14604-1084. Phone: 716/546-6776.

847 James Street, Suite 200, Syracuse, New York 13203. Phone: 315/479-6635.

1211 Route 9, Wappingers Falls, New York 12590. Phone: 914/297-6550; 1/800-955-5100 (toll-free auto line).

30 Glenn Street, White Plains, New York 10603. Phone: 914/428-1230 or 1231; 1/800-955-5100 (toll-free auto line).

North Carolina
801 BB&T Building, Asheville, North Carolina 28801. Phone: 704/253-2392.

1130 East Third Street, Suite 400, Charlotte, North Carolina 28204-2626. Phone: 704/332-7151.

3608 West Friendly Avenue, Greensboro, North Carolina 27410. Phone: 919/852-4240 or 4241 or 4242.

P.O. Box 1882, Hickory, North Carolina 28603. Phone: 704/464-0372.

3120 Poplarwood Court, Suite 101, Raleigh, North Carolina 27604-1080. Phone: 919/872-9240.

2110 Cloverdale Avenue, Suite 2-B, Winston-Salem, North Carolina 27103. Phone: 919/725-8348.

Ohio
222 West Market Street, Akron, Ohio 44303-2111. Phone: 216/253-4590.

1434 Cleveland Avenue, N.W., Canton, Ohio 44703. Phone: 216/454-9401.

898 Walnut Street, Cincinnati, Ohio 45202. Phone: 513/421-3015.

2217 East Ninth Street, Suite 200, Cleveland, Ohio 44115-1299. Phone: 216/241-7678.

527 South High Street, Columbus, Ohio 43215. Phone: 614/221-6336.

40 West Fourth Street, Suite 1250, Dayton, Ohio 45402. Phone: 513/222-5825; 1/800-521-5357 (toll-free in Ohio).

P.O. Box 269, Lima, Ohio 45802. Phone: 419/223-7010.

130 West Second Street, Mansfield, Ohio 44902-1915. Phone: 419/522-1700.

425 Jefferson Avenue, Suite 909, Toledo, Ohio 43604-1055. Phone: 419/241-6276.

345 North Market, Suite 202, Wooster, Ohio 44691. Phone: 216/263-6444.

P.O. Box 1495, Youngstown, Ohio 44501-1495. Phone: 216/744-3111.

Oklahoma

17 South Dewey, Oklahoma City, Oklahoma 73102. Phone: 405/239-6860 or 6081 (inquiries); 405/239-6083 (complaints).

6711 South Yale, Suite 230, Tulsa, Oklahoma 74136-3327. Phone: 918/492-1266.

Oregon

610 Southwest Adler Street, Suite 615, Portland, Oregon 97205. Phone: 503/226-3981. Phone: 1/800-226-3981 (toll-free in Oregon).

Pennsylvania

528 North New Street, Bethlehem, Pennsylvania 18018. Phone: 215/866-8780.

6 Marion Court, Lancaster, Pennsylvania 17602. Phone: 717/291-1151; 717/323-2800 (Harrisburg); 717/846-2700 (York County); 717/394-9318 (auto line).

P.O. Box 2297, Philadelphia, Pennsylvania 19103-0297. Phone: 215/496-1000.

610 Smithfield Street, Pittsburgh, Pennsylvania 15222. Phone: 412/456-2700.

P.O. Box 993, Scranton, Pennsylvania 18501. Phone: 717/342-9129 or 717/655-0445.

Rhode Island

Bureau Park, P.O. Box 1300, Warwick, Rhode Island 02887-1300. Phone: 401/785-1212 (inquiries); 401/785-1213 (complaints).

South Carolina

1830 Bull Street, Columbus, South Carolina 29201. Phone: 803/254-2525.

311 Pettigru Street, Greenville, South Carolina 29601. Phone: 803/242-5052.

1310-G Azalea Court, Myrtle Beach, South Carolina 92577. Phone: 803/497-8667.

Tennessee

P.O. Box 1178 TCAS, Blountville, Tennessee 37617. Phone: 615/323-6311.

1010 Market Street, Suite 200, Chattanooga, Tennessee 37402-2614. Phone: 615/266-6144 (also serves Whitfield and Murray counties in Georgia); 615/479-6096 (Bradley County only).

900 East Hill Avenue, Suite 165, Knoxville, Tennessee 37915-2525. Phone: 615/522-2552.

P.O. Box 750704, Memphis, Tennessee 38175-0704. Phone: 901/795-8771.

Sovran Plaza, Suite 1830, Nashville, Tennessee 37239. Phone: 615/254-5872.

Texas

3300 South Fourteenth Street, Suite 307, Abilene, Texas 79605. Phone: 915/691-1533.

P.O. Box 1905, Amarillo, Texas 79105-1905. Phone: 806/379-6222.

708 Colorado, Suite 720, Austin, Texas 78701-3028. Phone: 512/476-1616.

P.O. Box 2988, Beaumont, Texas 77704-2988. Phone: 409/835-5348.

202 Varisco Building, Bryan, Texas 77803. Phone: 409/823-8148 or 8149.

4535 South Padre Island Drive, Suite 28, Corpus Christi, Texas 78411. Phone: 512/854-2892.

2001 Bryan Street, Suite 850, Dallas, Texas 75201. Phone: 214/220-2000; 1/800-442-1456 (toll-free in Texas).

5160 Montana, Lower Level, El Paso, Texas 79903. Phone: 915/772-2727.

512 Main Street, Suite 807, Fort Worth, Texas 76102. Phone: 817/332-7585.

2707 North Loop West, Suite 900, Houston, Texas 77008. Phone: 713/868-9500.

P.O. Box 1178, Lubbock, Texas 79408-1178. Phone: 806/763-0459.

P.O. Box 60206, Midland, Texas 79711-0206. Phone: 915/563-1880; 1/800-592-4433 (toll-free in 915 area code).

P.O. Box 3366, San Angelo, Texas 76902-3366. Phone: 915/949-2989.

1800 Northeast Loop 410, Suite 400, San Antonio, Texas 78217. Phone: 512/828-9441.

P.O. Box 6652, Tyler, Texas 75711-6652. Phone: 903/581-5704.

P.O. Box 7203, Waco, Texas 76714-7203. Phone: 817/772-7530.

P.O. Box 69, Weslaco, Texas 78596-0069. Phone: 512/968-3678.

1106 Brook Street, Wichita Falls, Texas 76301-5079. Phone: 817/723-5526.

Utah

1588 South Main Street, Salt Lake City, Utah 84115. Phone: 801/487-4656.

Virginia

4022B Plank Road, Fredericksburg, Virginia 22407. Phone: 703/786-8397.

3608 Tidewater Drive, Norfolk, Virginia 23509-1499. Phone: 804/627-5651.

701 East Franklin Street, Suite 712, Richmond, Virginia 23219. Phone: 804/648-0016.

31 West Campbell Avenue, Roanoke, Virginia 24011-1301. Phone: 703/342-3455.

Washington

127 West Canal Drive, Kennewick, Washington 99336-3819. Phone: 519/582-0222.

2200 Sixth Avenue, Suite 828, Seattle, Washington 98121-1857. Phone: 206/448-8888; 206/448-6222 (24-hour business reporting system).

South 176 Stevens, Spokane, Washington 99204-1393. Phone: 509/747-1155.

P.O. Box 1274, Tacoma, Washington 98401-1274. Phone: 206/383-5561.

P.O. Box 1584, Yakima, Washington 98907-1584. Phone: 509/248-1326.

Wisconsin

740 North Plankinton Avenue, Milwaukee, Wisconsin 53203. Phone: 414/273-1600 (inquiries); 414/273-0123 (complaints).

Wyoming

BBB/Fort Collins, (serves all other Wyoming counties), 1730 South College Avenue, Suite 303, Fort Collins, Colorado 80525. Phone: 1/800/873-3222 (toll-free in Wyoming).

BBB/Idaho Falls, (serves Teton, Park and Lincoln counties in Wyoming), 545 Shoup Avenue, Suite 210, Idaho Falls, Idaho 83402. Phone: 208/523-9754.

Chapter 27

Mail Order Catalogs

GENERAL RESOURCES

Books

Bargains-By-Mail For Baby and You. By Dawn Hardy. Prima Publishing, 1992. 413 pages. Describes hundreds of mail order companies where parents can purchase products for children (many at discount prices). Includes companies that sell safety devices, clothing, furniture, toys and games, educational products, and resources for children with special needs, among other offerings. Also explains how to navigate the mail order maze.

The Catalog of Catalogs III. By Edward L. Palder. Woobine House, 1993. 550 pages. A guide to mail order catalogs of all kinds, arranged by subject. Includes an alphabetical source index as well.

Great Buys for Kids. By Sue Goldstein. Penguin Books, 1992. 351 pages. Designed to save parents money and time, this book describes hundreds of places that offer products, services, and programs for kids. Included are a variety of companies that offer mail order catalogs and brochures. Sports equipment, clothing, toys, diapers, and baby gear are among the order-by-mail products featured. The book also lists and describes associations, museums, travel companies, camps, and clubs.

The Kids' Catalog Collection. By Jane Smolik. Globe Pequot Press, 1990. 276 pages. A selective guide to more than five hundred catalogs full of toys, books, clothing, sports equipment, and other items that children of all ages want or need. Chapters include "Clothing," "Music," "Party Supplies," "Health and Safety Products," "Science and Nature," "Sports Equipment," "Educational Materials," "Books," "Toys," "Videos," and "Computers and Computer Software," among others. Includes a company index, plus an "Interest Index" listing specific products and interest areas (puzzles, biking, diapering needs, etc.).

The Wholesale-by-Mail Catalog. Edited by Prudence McCullough. HarperCollins. Updated annually, this catalog offers information on over five hundred carefully chosen companies that sell products of all kinds. Consumers can shop by mail or telephone and save 30 to 90 percent off the list price.

MAIL ORDER CATALOGS, A TO Z

Most of the catalogs listed below are described in detail under specific topics in *The Parents' Resource Almanac*. The last line in each of the following entries tells you the section and then chapter, to turn to for additional information on the catalog.

Adoption Book Catalog. Tapestry Books, P.O. Box 359, Ringoes, New Jersey 08551-0359. Phone: 908/806-6695 or 1/800-765-2367. See chapter 12.

After the Stork. 1501 Twelfth Street, N.W., Albuquerque, Mew Mexico 87104. Phone: 1/800/333-KIDS. See Chapter 10.

Alcazar's Catalog of Children's Music. P.O. Box 429, Waterbury, Vermont 05676. Phone: 1/800-541-9904. See chapter 14 and 20.

The American Girls Collection. Pleasant Company, 8400 Fairway Place, P.O. Box 190, Middleton, Wisconsin 53562-0190. Phone: 1/800-845-0005. See chapter 16.

American Science and Surplus. Jerryco, Inc., 601 Linden Place, Evanston, Illinois 60202. Phone: 708/475-8440. See chapters 13 and 14.

Animal Town. P.O. Box 485, Healdsburg, California 95448. Phone: 1/800-445-8642. See Toys, chapters 16, 23, and 24.

Anyone Can Whistle. (A Catalog of Musical Discovery.) P.O. Box 4407, Kingston, New York 12401. Phone: 1/800-435-8863. See chapters 13 and 14.

Aristoplay. P.O. Box 7529, Ann Arbor, Michigan 48107. Phone: 1/800-634-7738. See chapter 16.

Art Education. Heinemann, 361 Hanover Street, Portsmouth, New Hampshire 03801-3959. Phone: 1/800-541-2086. See chapter 14.

Association for Childhood Education International, Publications Catalog. 11501 Georgia Avenue, Suite 315, Wheaton, Maryland 20902. Phone: 1/800-423-3563 or 301/942-2443. See chapter 13.

Baby Basics. 4809 Avenue N, Brooklyn, New York 11234. Phone: 718/531-3992. See chapter 3.

Baby Bunz and Co. P.O. Box 1717, Sebastopol, California 95473. Phone: 707/829-5347 or 1/800-676-4559. See chapter 3.

Babyworks. 11725 Northwest West Road #2, Portland, Oregon 97229. Phone: 503/645-4349 or 1/800-422-2910. See chapter 3.

Back to Basics Toys. 2707 Pittman Drive, Silver Spring, Maryland 20910. Phone: 1/800-356-5360. See chapters 9 and 16.

Biobottoms. P.O. Box 6009, Petaluma, California 94953. Phone: 1/800-766-1254. See chapters 3 and 10.

Bits and Pieces. One Puzzle Place, B8016, Stevens Point, Wisconsin 54481-7199. Phone: 1/800-JIGSAWS. See chapter 16.

Bookmates. Listening Library, One Park Avenue, Old Greenwich, Connecticut 06870-1727. Phone: 1/800-243-4504. See chapters 16 and 20.

Books of Wonder. 132 Seventh Avenue at Eighteenth Street, New York, New York 10011. Phone: 212/989-3270. See chapter 17.

Brights Creek. Bay Point, Hampton, Virginia 23653. Phone: 1/800-285-4300. Fax: 1/800-677-8687. See chapter 10.

Broderbund Software Catalog. P.O. Box 6125, Novato, California 94948-6125. Phone: 1/800-521-6263. See chapter 19.

Burpy Garden Catalog. Phone: 1/800-888-1447. See chapter 16.

Cambridge Parenting and Family Life. Cambridge Parenting, P.O. Box 2153, Department PA5, Charleston, West Virginia 25328-2153. Phone: 1/800-468-4227. See chapter 3.

Camp and Program Leader Catalog. American Camping Association, 5000 State Road 67 North, Martinsville, Indiana 46151-7902. Phone: 317/342-8456 or 1/800-428-CAMP. See chapters 15 and 22.

Campmor. 810 Route 17 North, P.O. Box 997-J, Paramus, New Jersey 07653-0997. Phone: 201/445-5000 (for catalog) or 1/800-526-4784 (to order). See chapter 22.

Catalog of Creative Resources. Creative Education Foundation, 1050 Union Road, Buffalo, New York 14224. Phone: 716/675-3181. Fax: 716/675-3209. See chapter 2.

* Chasselle/The Book of Early Learning. Chaselle, Inc. , 9645 Gerwig Lane, Columbia, Maryland 21046-1503. Phone: 410/381-5407 or 1/800-242-7355 (to order).

Childcraft. P.O. Box 29149, Mission, Kansas 66201-9149. Phone: 1/800-631-5657. See chapters 9 and 16.

Childhood Resources Catalog. National Association for the Education of Young Children, 1509 Sixteenth Street, N.W., Washington, D.C. 20036-1426. Phone: 202/232-8777 or 1/800-424-2460. Fax: 202/328-1846. See chapter 13.

The Children's Small Press Collection. 719 North Fourth Avenue, Ann Arbor, Michigan 48104. Phone: 313/668-8056 or 1/800-221-8056. See chapters 14 and 17.

Children's Wear Digest. 31333 Agoura Road, Westlake Village, California 91361-4639. Phone: 1/800-242-KIDS. See chapter 10.

Childswork/Childsplay. Center for Applied Psychology, Inc., P.O. Box 1586, King of Prussia, Pennsylvania 19406. Phone: 1/800-962-1141. See chapters 2, 3, and 16.

Chinaberry Book Service. 2780 Via Orange Way, Suite B, Spring Valley, California 91978. Phone: 619/670-5200 or 1/800-776-2242. See chapters 17 and 24.

Claudia's Caravan, P.O. Box 1582, Alameda, California 94501. Phone: 510/521-7871. See chapter 14.

Club KidSoft. 718 University Avenue, Los Gatos, California 95030. Phone: 1/800-354-6150. See chapter 19.

CompUSA. Phone: 1/800-451-7638. See chapter 19.

Constructive Playthings. 1227 East 119th Street, Grandview, Missouri 64030-1117, 1/800-832-0572 or 816/761-5900. See chapters 9 and 16.

Creative Parenting. Parenting Press, Inc., P.O. Box 75267, Seattle, Washington 98125. Phone: 1/800-992-6657. See chapter 3.

* A catalog for early-childhood educators, containing a wide range of products designed to enhance motor skills, encourage creative expression, and teach young children concepts in math, science, social studies, and the language arts. Includes indoor and outdoor play equipment, toys, games, books, arts and crafts supplies, and other tools for learning.

Creative Publications. 5040 West 111th Street, Oak Lawn, Illinois 60453. Phone: 1/800-624-0822 or 1/800-435-5843 (in Illinois). See chapter 14.

Cuisenaire: Materials for Learning Mathematics and Science. P.O. Box 5026, White Plains, New York 10602-5026. Phone: 1/800-237-3142. Fax: 1/800-551-RODS. See chapter 14.

CW. One Clifford Way, Asheville, North Carolina 28810-1000. Phone: 1/800-633-3485. See chapter 10.

Demco. See chapter 16.

Descriptive Video Service (DVS) Home Video. WGBH, 125 Western Avenue, Boston, Massachusetts 02134. Phone: 617/492-2777. See chapter 2.

Diaperaps. P.O. Box 3050, Granada Hills, California 91344. Phone: 1/800-477-3424. See chapter 3.

Dover Children's Book Catalog. Dover Publications, Inc., 31 East Second Street, Mineola, New York 11501. See chapter 16.

Drama Education. Heinemann, 361 Hanover Street, Portsmouth, New Hampshire 03801-3959. Phone: 1/800-541-2086. See chapter 14.

Dr. Possum. P.O. Box 4183, Mountain View, California 94040. Phone: 1/800-827-4086. See chapter 6.

Earth Care Paper, Inc. P.O. Box 7070, Madison, Wisconsin 53707-7070. Phone: 608/223-4000. See chapter 23.

Edmund Scientific Co. 101 East Gloucester Pike, Barrington, New Jersey 07410. Phone: 609/547-3488 or 1/800-222-0224. See chapter 14.

Educational Record Center. 3233 Burnt Mill Drive, Suite 100, Wilmington, North Carolina 28403-2655. Phone: 919/251-1235. See chapter 20.

Educational Resources. 1550 Executive Drive, Elgin, Illinois 60123. Phone: 1/800-624-2926. See chapter 19.

Educorp. Phone: 1/800-843-9497. See chapter 17.

*   Environments. Environments, Inc., P.O. Box 1348, Beaufort Industrial Park, Beaufort, South Carolina 29901-1348. Phone: 803/846-8155 or 1/800-342-4453.

Eureka! Lawrence Hall of Science Publications Catalog. Lawrence Hall of Science, University of California, Berkeley, California 94720. Phone: 510/642-5133. See chapter 14.

Exploratorium to Go! 3601 Lyon Street, San Francisco, California 94123. Phone: 1/800-359-9899. See chapter 14.

Family Clubhouse. 6 Chiles Avenue, Asheville, North Carolina 28803. Phone: 1/800-876-1574. See chapter 3.

Family Communications. 4802 Fifth Avenue, Pittsburgh, Pennsylvania 15213. Phone: 412/687-2990. Fax: 412/687-1226. See chapter 3.

Family Travel Guides Catalogue. P.O. Box 6061, Albany, California 94706-0061. Phone: 510/527-5849. See chapter 21.

Familyware. Phone: 1/800-827-KIDS or 813/933-6625. See chapter 19.

---

* A catalog for early-childhood educators, containing a wide range of products designed to enhance motor skills, encourage creative expression, and teach young children concepts in math, science, social studies, and the language arts. Includes indoor and outdoor play equipment, toys, games, books, arts and crafts supplies, and other tools for learning.

F.A.O. Schwarz. 767 Fifth Avenue, New York, New York 10153. Phone: 1/800-635-2451. See chapter 16.

Funtastic Therapy Catalog. Phone: 1/800-531-3176. See chapter 2.

A Gentle Wind. Box 3103, Albany, New York 12203. Phone: 518/436-0391. See chapter 20.

The George F. Cram Company, Inc. P.O. Box 426, Indianapolis, Indiana 46206. Phone: 317/635-5564. Fax: 317/635-2720. See chapter 14.

The Gifted Child Today Catalog. GCT, Inc., 314-350 Weinacker Avenue, P.O. Box 6448, Mobile, Alabama 36660-0448. See chapter 2.

The Great Kids Company. P.O. Box 609, Lewisville, North Carolina 27023-0609. Phone: 1/800-533-2166. See chapter 16.

Hand in Hand. Catalogue Center, Route 26, R.R. 1, Box 1425, Oxford, Maine 04270-9711. Phone: 1/800-872-9745. See chapter 3.

Hanna Andersson. 1010 Northwest Flanders, Portland, Oregon 97209. Phone: 1/800-222-0544. See chapter 10.

Hearthsong. P.O. Box B, Sebastopol, California 95473-0601. Phone: 1/800-325-2502. See chapter 14.

Heart of Vermont. The Old Schoolhouse, Route 132, P.O. Box 183, Sharon, Vermont 05065. Phone: 802/763-2720 or 1/800-639-4123 (to order). See chapter 23.

Heinemann-Boynton/Cook Catalog. 361 Hanover Street, Portsmouth, New Hampshire 03801-3959. Phone: 603/431-7894. See chapter 13.

Heinemann Math and Science. Heinemann, 361 Hanover Street, Portsmouth, New Hampshire 03801-3959. Phone: 1/800-541-2086. See chapter 14.

Home Education Press. P.O. Box 1083, Tonasket, Washington 98855. Phone: 509/486-1351. See chapter 13.

Homeopathy. Homeopathic Educational Services, 2124 Kittredge Street, Berkeley, California 94704. Phone: 510/649-0294 or 1/800-359-9051. See chapter 6.

Homespun Tapes. Box 694, Woodstock, New York 12498-0694. Phone: 1/800-338-2737. See chapter 14.

Hubbard Scientific Inc. P.O. Box 760, Chippewa Falls, Wisconsin 54729-0760. Phone: 715/723-4427 or 1/800-323-8368. See chapter 14.

Imprints. Birth and Life Bookstore, 7001 Alonzo Avenue, N.W., P.O. Box 70625, Seattle, Washington 98107-0625. Phone: 206/789-4444 or 1/800-736-0631 (orders only). See chapters 8 and 13.

International Video Network Video Catalog. International Video Network, 2242 Camino Ramon, San Ramon, California 94583. Phone: 1/800-669-4486. See chapter 21.

Jesana Ltd., A Very Special Catalogue. Phone: 1/800-443-4728. See chapter 2.

John Holt's Book and Music Store. Holt Associates, 2269 Massachusetts Avenue, Cambridge, Massachusetts 02140. Phone: 617/864-3100. See chapter 13.

Johnny's Selected Seeds. Phone: 207/437-4301. See chapter 16.

Just for Kids. P.O. Box 29141, Shawnee, Kansas 66201-9141. Phone: 1/800-654-6963. See chapters 9 and 10.

Kapable Kids. P.O. Box 250, Bohemia, New York 11716. Phone: 1/800-356-1564. See chapter 2.

Kids and Things. DEMCO, Box 7488, Madison, Wisconsin 53707.

Phone: 608/241-1201 or 1/800-356-1200. See chapters 16 and 17.

Kids First! Catalog. Coalition for Quality Children's Videos. Phone: 1/800-331-6197. See chapter 20.

Lakeshore Learning Materials. 2695 East Dominquez Street, Carson, California 90749. Phone: 1/800-421-5354 or 310/537-8600. See chapter 9.

Learning Materials Workshop. 274 North Winookski, Burlington, Vermont 05401. Phone: 802/862-8399. See chapter 16.

Lego Shop at Home Service. 555 Taylor Road, P.O. Box 1310, Enfield, Connecticut 06083. Phone: 203/763-4011. See chapter 16.

Lilly's Kids. Lillian Vernon Corporation, Virginia Beach, Virginia 23479-0002. Phone: 804/430-1500. See chapter 16.

Listening Library, One Park Avenue, Old Greenwich, Connecticut 06870-1727. Phone: 1/800-243-4504. See chapters 17 and 20.

L. L. Bean. Freeport, Maine 04033. Phone: 1/800-341-4341. See chapter 22.

Love Publishing Company/Catalog of Books. 1777 South Bellaire Street, Denver, Colorado 80222. Phone: 303/757-2579 or 303/757-6912. See chapter 2.

MacWarehouse. 1720 Oak Street, P.O. Box 3031, Lakewood, New Jersey 08701. Phone: 1/800-255-6227. See chapter 19.

The Mac Zone. The PC Zone, 17411 Northeast Union Hill Road, Suite 140, Redmond, Washington 98052-6716. Phone: 1/800-436-8000. See chapter 19.

Magic, Inc. 5082 North Lincoln Avenue, Chicago, Illinois 60625. See chapter 16.

The Mind's Eye. Box 1060, Petaluma, California 94953. Phone: 1/800-227-2020. See chapter 20.

Modern Learning Press. Programs for Education, P.O. Box 167, Department 323, Rosemont, New Jersey 08556. Phone: 1/800-627-5867. See chapters 1 and 13.

Moonflower Natural Parenting Catalog. 2810 Wilderness Place, #D, Boulder, Colorado 80301. Phone: 303/440-5566 or 1/800-462-4784. See chapter 3.

Music for Little People. Box 1460, Redway, California 95560. Phone: 800/727-2233. See chapters 14, 20, 23, and 24.

Music in Motion. P.O. Box 833814, Richardson, Texas 75083-3814. Phone: 1/800-445-0649. See chapter 14.

Nasco Arts and Crafts. 901 Janesville Avenue, P.O. Box 901, Fort Atkinson, Wisconsin 53538-0901. Phone: 1/800-558-9595. See chapter 16.

National Wildlife Nature Gift Catalog. National Wildlife Federation, 1400 Sixteenth Street, N.W., Washington, D.C. 20036-2266. Phone: 1/800-245-5484. See chapter 16.

The Natural Baby Catalog. 114 West Franklin, Suite S, Pennington, New Jersey 08534. Phone: 609/737-2895. See chapters 3 and 6.

The Natural Choice. 1365 Rufina Circle, Santa Fe, New Mexico 87501. Phone: 505/438-3448. See chapter 23.

The Nature Company Catalog. P.O. Box 188, Florence, Kentucky 41022. Phone: 1/800-227-1114. See chapters 16 and 23.

NEMC's Band and Orchestra Instrument Catalog. National Educational Music Company, Ltd., 1181 Route 22, Box 1130, Mountainside, New Jersey 07092. Phone: 800/526-4593. See chapter 14.

Nienhuis-Montessori USA. 320 Pioneer Way, Mountain View, California 94040. Phone: 415/964-2735. See chapter 13.

One Step Ahead. P.O. Box 517, Lake Bluff, Illinois 60044. Phone: 1/800-274-8440. See chapters 3 and 7.

Orion Telescope Center. 2450 Seventeenth Avenue, P.O. Box 1158, Santa Cruz, California 95061-1158. See chapter 16.

Park Seed. Phone: 1/800-845-3369. See chapter 16.

Passon's Sports. P.O. Box 49, Jenkintown, Pennsylvania 19046. Phone: 1/800-523-1557. See chapter 9.

Patagonia Kids. 1609 West Babcock Street, P.O. Box 8900, Bozeman, Montana 59715. Phone: 1/800-336-9090. See chapters 10 and 23.

The PC Zone. 17411 Northeast Union Hill Road, Suite 140, Redmond, Washington 98052-6716. Phone: 1/800-252-0386. See chapter 19.

The Perfectly Safe Catalog. 7245 Whipple Avenue, N.W., North Canton, Ohio 44720. Phone: 1/800-873-KIDS. See chapters 7 and 16.

PlayFair Toys. P.O. Box 18210, Boulder, Colorado 80308. Phone: 1/800-824-7255. See chapter 16.

Practical Parenting Catalogue: Vicki Lansky's Books by Mail. Practical Parenting, 18326 Minnetonka Boulevard, Deephaven, Minnesota 55391. Phone: 1/800-255-3379 or 612/475-3527 (customer service). Fax: 612/475-1505. See chapter 3.

* Pyramid School Products. 6510 North Fifty-fourth Street, Tampa, Florida 33610-1994. Phone: 813/621-6446 or 1/800-792-2644.

The R. Duck Company, Inc. 650 Ward Drive, Suite H, Santa Barbara, California 93111. Phone: 1/800-422-DUCK (3825). See chapter 3.

Reader's Digest Kids Catalog. Reader's Digest Association, Inc., Pleasantville, New York 00401. Phone: 1/800-458-3014. See chapter 16.

Real Goods. 966 Mazzoni Street, Ukiah, California 95482. Phone: 1/800-762-7325. See chapter 23.

Recorded Books. 270 Skipjack Road, Prince Frederick, Maryland 20678. Phone: 800/638-1304. See chapters 17 and 20.

Richman Cotton Company. 529 Fifth Street, Santa Rosa, California 95401. Phone: 707/575-8924 or 1/800-992-8924. See chapter 10.

The Right Start. Right Start Plaza, 5334 Sterling Center Drive, Westlake Village, California 91361. Phone: 1/800-548-8531. See chapters 3 and 7.

Sassy. 1534 College Southeast, Grand Rapids, Michigan 49507. Phone: 616/243-0767. Fax: 616/243-1042. See chapter 3.

Schoolmasters Science. 745 State Circle, Box 1941, Ann Arbor, Michigan 48106. Phone: 1/800-521-2832 (orders only) or 313/761-5175. See chapter 14.

Science News Books. A division of Science Service, 1719 N Street, N.W., Washington, D.C. 20036. Phone: 1/800-544-4565. See chapter 14.

Self Care Catalog. 5850 Shellmound Street, Emeryville, California 94662-

---

* A catalog for early-childhood educators, containing a wide range of products designed to enhance motor skills, encourage creative expression, and teach young children concepts in math, science, social studies, and the language arts. Includes indoor and outdoor play equipment, toys, games, books, arts and crafts supplies, and other tools for learning.

0813. Phone: 1/800-345-3371. See chapter 6.

Sensational Beginnings. P.O. Box 2009, 300 Detroit, Suite E, Monroe, Michigan 48161. Phone: 1/800-444-2147. See chapter 16.

Seventh Generation. Colchester, Vermont 05446-1672. Phone: 1/800-456-1177. See chapter 23.

Signals. WGBH Educational Foundation, P.O. Box 64428, St. Paul, Minnesota 55164-0428. Phone: 1/800-669-5225 (customer service) or 1/800-669-9696 (to place an order). See chapter 20.

Social Studies School Service. 10200 Jefferson Boulevard, P.O. Box 802, Culver City, California 90232-0802. Phone: 1/800-421-4246. See chapter 14.

Soundprints. 165 Water Street, P.O. Box 679, Norwalk, Connecticut 06856. Phone: 1/800-228-7839. See chapter 23.

Special Clothes for Special Children. P.O. Box 4220, Alexandria, Virginia 22303. Phone: 703/683-7343. See chapter 2.

Teachers and Writers Collaborative. 5 Union Square West, New York, New York 10003-3306. Phone: 212/691-6590. See chapter 14.

Thompson and Morgan. Phone: 1/800-274-7333. See chapter 16.

Tough Traveler. 1012 State Street, Schenectady, New York 12307. Phone: 518/377-8526. See chapter 22.

Toys to Grow On. P.O. Box 17, Long Beach, California 90801. Phone: 1/800-542-8338 (ordering); 1/800-874-4242 (customer service); or 310/603-8890. See chapters 9 and 16.

Troll Learn and Play. 100 Corporate Drive, Mahwah, New Jersey 07430. Phone: 1/800-247-6106. See chapter 16.

Vanguard Crafts. P.O. Box 340170, Brooklyn, New York 11234. Phone: 718/377-5188 or 1/800-66-CRAFTS (to order). See chapter 16.

The Video Catalog. P.O. Box 64267, St. Paul, Minnesota 55164-0428. Phone: 1/800-733-6656. See chapter 20.

Videos for Kids. Schoolmasters Video, 745 State Circle, P.O. Box 1941, Ann Arbor, Michigan 48106. Phone: 313/761-5175 or 1/800-521-2832 (orders only). See chapter 20.

White Flower Farm. Phone: 203/567-0801. See chapter 16.

Wireless Audio Collection. P.O. Box 64422, St. Paul, Minnesota 55164-0422. Phone: 1/800-733-3369. See chapter 20.

Woodbine House. 5615 Fishers Lane, Rockville, Maryland 20852. Phone: 301/468-8800 or 1/800-843-7323. See chapter 2.

World Wide Games. P.O. Box 517, Colchester, Connecticut 06415-0517. Phone: 1/800-243-9232. See chapter 16.

Zephyr Press. 3316 North Chapel Avenue, P.O. Box 66006, Tucson, Arizona 85728-6006. Phone: 602/322-5090. See chapter 2.

Appendix A

Juvenile Products:
An A-to-Z Guide to Companies that Sell Products for Kids

ADI Lamps. P.O. Box 6357, Phoenix, Arizona 85005. Phone: 602/253-4548 or 602/395-1471. Fax: 602/252-9078. Product: Lamps.

Adorable Baby Company. 307 Canal Street, Lemont, Illinois 60439. Phone: 708/257-8786. Fax: 708/257-8735. Products: Audiocassettes, videotapes, infant feeding items, toys, liquid filled high chair placemats, playmats.

All Our Kids. 1540 Beach Street, Montebello, California 90640. Phone: 1/800-545-3265, 213/887-6161. Fax: 213/728-5238. Products: Gates, strollers, walkers, car seats.

Alma's Designs. 948 Hunakai Street, Honolulu, Hawaii 96816. Phone: 1/800-826-5627 or 808/734-8775. Fax: 808/943-1689. Products, Books, bassinets, bumper guards, comforters/quilts, pillows, toys, wall hangings/pictures, crib organizers, crib bedding ensembles.

American Baby Concepts. P.O. Box 217, Wheatland, Iowa 52777. Phone: 1/800-537-7181, 319/374-1231. Fax: 319/374-1806. Products: Audiocassettes, videotapes, bath aids/toys, bibs, booties/footwear, decorative items, diaper bags, infant feeding items, mattress covers/pads, pacifiers, play yard pads, safety items, switch plates, thermometers, toilet training items, car seat pillows, stroller bags, pacifier clips, scented drawer liners, nursing pillows, tote bags, bottles, organizers.

American Fiber and Finishing, Inc. 6 New England Executive Park, Burlington, Massachusetts 01803. Phone: 1/800-323-7724 or 617/270-9350. Fax: 617/270-0116. Products: Cotton products, diapers.

American Pacific. 70 West Fortieth Street, New York, New York 10018. Phone: 212/944-6799. Fax: 212/944-7042. Products: Bumper guards, comforters/quilts, blankets, rugs.

Americare Products. 3950-A Nebraska Street, Newportville, Pennsylvania 19056. Phone: 1/800-220-CARE or 215/781-0430. Fax: 215/781-0432. Products: Bibs, carriage and stroller pads, mattress covers/pads, play yard pads, floor mats, smocks, changing pads, changing table pads, diapers (cloth).

ANSA Company, Inc. P.O. Box 2758, 1200 South Main, Muskogee, Oklahoma 74402. Phone: 918/687-1664. Fax: 918/682-3420. Products: Infant feeding items.

Aprica U.S.A. 1200 Howell Avenue, Anaheim, California 92805. Phone: 714/634-0402. Fax: 714/634-1630. Products: Carriages, carriage and stroller pads, diaper bags, highchairs, strollers, ride-on toys.

Artsana of America, Inc. 200 Fifth Avenue, Room 910, New York, New York 10010. Phone: 1/800-336-8697, 212/255-6977. Fax: 212/645-7143. Products: Canopies, carriages, highchairs, highchair pads, play yards (playpens), rattles, strollers, toys, walkers.

Avent. 5161 Thatcher Road, Downers Grove, Illinois 60515. Phone: 1/800-54A-AVENT, 708/769-1700. Fax: 708/769-0300. Products: Breast pumps, nursing pads and shields, infant feeding items, pacifiers, microwave and electric steam vaporizers, bottle warmers, bottles.

Babi Bags by Romar International. 112 West Thirty-fourth Street, New York, New York 10120. Phone: 1/800-828-6546, 212/736-9555. Fax: 212/967-4819. Products: Diaper bags, gift sets, infant feeding items, rattles, toys.

Babies Alley. 20 West Thirty-third Street, New York, New York 10001. Phone: 212/563-1414. Fax: 212/563-3396. Products: Baby/child carriers, carriage and stroller pads, diaper bags, bottle holders, cooler bags.

Babies Are #1. P.O. Box 11905, Daytona Beach, Florida 32114. Phone: 904/252-2473. Products: Bottles, infant feeding items, rattles, sipper cups.

The Baby Bag Company. P.O. Box 566, Cumberland, Maine 04021. Phone: 1/800-866-2247 or 207/829-5037. Fax: 207/829-5946. Product: Buntings.

Baby Buddies, Inc. 615 Jasmine Avenue North, Suite 1, Tarpon Springs, Florida 34689. Phone: 813/934-3359. Fax: 813/934-8385. Products: Infant feeding items, safety items, pacifier holders, shopping cart accessories.

Baby Doll Infants Wear Co., Inc. 300 Monroe Street, Passaic, New Jersey 07055. Phone: 1/800-622-2702 or 201/473-3730. Fax: 201/473-6137. Products: Bassinet liners/skirts, bumper guards, comforters/quilts, crib sheets, diaper bags, pillows, crib accessories.

Baby Dreams by Bibb. 237 Coliseum Drive, Macon, Georgia 31201. Phone: 912/752-6700. Fax: 912/752-6808. Products: Bumper guards, comforters/quilts, crib sheets, diaper stackers, dust ruffles, gift sets, receiving blankets, toddler bedding.

Baby Duckies. 9927 Venice Boulevard, Los Angeles, California 90034. Phone: 310/559-2229. Fax: 310/559-1121. Products: Bumper guards, car seat covers, comforters/quilts, dust ruffles, pillows, receiving blankets, rockers.

Baby Face Bedding. 740-K Sierra Vista, Mountain View, California 94043. Phone: 415/390-0657. Fax: 415/390-0659. Products: Bumper guards, canopies, comforters/quilts, crib sheets, curtains/draperies, diaper stackers, dust ruffles, lamps, pillows, sheets, wall hangings/pictures, crib bedding ensembles, toddler bedding, twin bedding.

Babygund. 1 Runyons Lane, Edison, New Jersey 08818. Phone: 908/248-1500. Fax: 908/248-1968. Products: Bath aids/toys, books, mobiles, rattles, plush toys.

Baby Optics. 273 North Bluff, St. George, Utah 84770. Phone: 1/800-962-6874 or 801/673-8066. Fax: 801/673-8159. Products: Baby sunglasses and accessories.

Baby Trend, Inc. 1928 West Holt Avenue, Pomona, California 91768. Phone: 1/800-328-7363 or 714/469-1188. Fax: 714/469-1194. Products: Carriages, highchairs, hook-on chairs, play yards (playpens), strollers, walkers.

Baby World Company, Inc. Pike Street, Grafton, West Virginia 26354. Phone: 1/800-545-2800 or 304/265-2120. Fax: 304/265-2123. Products: Baby baths, baby/child carriers, bath aids/toys, bibs, books, diaper pails, gift sets, infant feeding items, mobiles, pacifiers, rattles, safety items, thermometers, toilet training items, toys.

Badger Basket Company. 111 Lions Drive, Suite 220, Barrington, Illinois 60010. Phone: 708/381-6200. Fax: 708/361-6218. Products: Baby/child carriers, basket pads, bassinets, bassinet liners/skirts, changing/dressing tables, comforters/quilts, cradles, hampers, toy chests, handwoven bassinets, youth/teen furniture.

Bambineto Products International. 9285 Chesapeake Drive, Suite B, San Diego, California 92123. Phone: 1/800-736-7603 or 619/576-7225. Fax: 619/576-7227. Products: Baby/child carriers, bassinets, buntings, diaper bags, diaper stackers, sheets, crib bedding ensembles.

Bandaks Emmaljunga, Inc. 737 South Vinewood, Escondido, California 92029. Phone: 1/800-232-4411 or 619/739-8911. Fax: 619/739-0643. Products: Bassinets, carriages, carriage and stroller pads, strollers, bassinet stands.

Banix Corporation. 11835 Carmel Mountain Road, Suite 1304, San Diego, California 92128. Phone: 619/673-1863. Fax: 619/487-5733. Products: Safety items.

Bantam Collections, Inc. 131 West Thirty-third Street, Suite 1703, New York, New York 10001. Phone: 1/800-647-7784 or 212/567-6750. Fax: 212/268-5284. Products: Mobiles, rattles, toys, dolls, clowns, musical plush toys, musical pull toys, chime toys.

Basic Comfort, Inc. 12 Broadway, Denver, Colorado 80203. Phone: 1/800-456-8687 or 303/778-7535. Fax: 303/778-0143. Products: Baby/child carriers, baby carrier covers, basket pads, bassinet liners/skirts, buntings, car seat covers, carriage and stroller pads, highchair pads, infant feeding items, mattress covers/pads, pillows, play yard (playpen) pads, walkers, swing bumper guards, maternity support garments, baby toothbrushes, day-care/preschool pads, bath towels/cloths, robes, head supports, organizers, twin bedding.

Bassett Furniture Industries, Inc. Main Street, Bassett, Virginia 24055. Phone: 703/629-6000. Fax: 703/629-6333. Products: Case goods/dressers, changing/dressing tables, cribs, rockers.

Bathtime Baby Products. Craig Industrial Park, Building One, Selma, Alabama 36701. Phone: 1/800-762-5229 or 305/942-7990. Fax: 305/942-1929. Products: Bibs, booties/footwear, decorative items, gift sets, bath towels/cloths/robes.

Battat Inc. 2 Industrial Boulevard West Circle, Plattsburgh, New York 12901. Phone: 1/800-247-6144 or 518/562-2200. Fax: 518/562-2203. Product: Toys.

Beacon Manufacturing Company. 202 Whitson Avenue, Swannanoa, North Carolina 28778. Phone: 704/686-3861. Fax: 704/686-5137. Products: Buntings, receiving blankets, wall hangings/pictures, crib mattress pads, blankets.

Beautiful Baby. 2807 West Marshall Avenue, Longview, Texas 75601.

Phone: 903/295-2229. Fax: 903/295-2232. Products: Bumper guards, canopies, car seat covers, carriage and stroller pads, comforters/quilts, crib sheets, curtains/draperies, diaper bags, diaper stackers, dust ruffles, highchair pads, receiving blankets, sheets, wall hangings/pictures, blankets, crib bedding ensembles, organizers, toddler beds, toddler bedding, twin bedding.

Bebe Chic. 115 River Road, Suite 303, Edgewater, New Jersey 07020. Phone: 1/800-354-4519 or 201/941-5414. Fax: 201/941-3834. Products: Baby carrier covers, bibs, bumper guards, buntings, car seat covers, carriage and stroller pads, comforters/quilts, crib sheets, diaper bags, diaper stackers, dust ruffles, pillows, play yard pads, sheets, bonnets, toweling, twin bedding, bath towels/cloths/robes, blankets, toddler bedding, twin bedding.

Bebegoes, Inc. 1115 St. Amour, Ville St. Laurent, Quebec, Canada H4S 1T4. Phone: 514/956-8362. Fax: 514/624-6202, Product: Strollers.

Bedtime Originals. 5978 Bowcroft Street, Los Angeles, California 90016. Phone: 1/800-345-2627 or 310/839-5155. Fax: 310/839-0767. Products: Bumper guards, comforters/quilts, crib sheets, diaper stackers, dust ruffles, pillows, sheets, wall hangings/pictures, blankets, crib bedding ensembles.

Betlar, Inc. 30971 San Benito Court, Hayward, California 94544. Phone: 1/800-323-8527 or 510/429-8070. Fax: 510/429-0769. Products: Gift sets, lamps, baby skin and hair care products, bookends.

Binky Griptight, Inc. 519-523 Paterson Avenue, Wallington, New Jersey 07057. Phone: 201/935-4580. Fax: 201/935-4585. Products: Baby baths, baby/child carriers, bath aids/toys, bibs, books, diaper pails, infant feeding items, mirrors, pacifiers, rattles, thermometers, toilet training items, toys.

Bo Peep Nursery Products. 1399 Kennedy Road, Unit #22, Toronto, Ontario, Canada M1P 2L6. Phone: 416/285-7525. Fax: 416/285-7658. Products: Crib mattresses, safety items.

Boston Bag Co. of N.Y./Cutie Pie Diaper Bag. 10 West Thirty-third Street, New York, New York 10001. Phone: 212/279-0022. Fax: 212/213-4813. Products: Diaper bags, layettes, bottle bags, stroller bags, backpacks, knapsacks, toddler bags.

Brandee Danielle, Inc. 3211 South Maple Street, Santa Ana, California 92707. Phone: 1/800-748-6531 or 714/557-4006. Fax: 714/557-4320. Products: Baby carrier covers, bumper guards, canopies, car seat covers, carriage and stroller pads, changing/dressing tables, comforters/quilts, crib sheets, diaper stackers, dust ruffles, highchair pads, lamps, mobiles, pillows, sheets, wall hangings/pictures, wallpaper and borders, portable cribs, towel sets, head supports.

Brooks Furniture Manufacturing, Inc. P.O. Box 199, Tazewell, Tennessee 37879. Phone: 615/626-1111. Fax: 615/626-8346. Product: Rockers.

Bumkins Family Products. 1945 East Watkins, Phoenix, Arizona 85034. Phone: 1/800-553-9302 or 602/254-2626. Fax: 602/252-2286. Products: Bibs, receiving blankets, bath towels/cloths/robes, blankets, diapers, diaper covers/wraps.

Burlington Basket Company. P.O. Box 808, Burlington, Iowa 52601. Phone: 1/800-553-2300 or 319/754-6508. Fax: 319/754-5991. Products: Bassinets, changing/dressing tables, hampers.

Calico Cottage, Inc. 12920 Southwest 132nd Court, Miami, Florida 33186. Phone: 305/233-1404. Fax: 305/233-5014. Products: Baby carrier covers, bumper guards, car seat covers, carriage and stroller pads, comforters/quilts, crib sheets, curtains/draperies, diaper bags, diaper stackers, dust ruffles, pillows, receiving blankets, wall hangings/pictures.

California Feather and Down. 11842 South Alameda Street, Lynwood, California 90262. Phone: 310/898-1900. Fax: 310/898-1201. Products: Comforters/quilts, pillows, tri-channel feather bed.

California Kids. 621 Old County Road, San Carlos, California 94070. Phone: 1/800-548-5214, 415/637-9054. Fax: 415/637-0810. Products: Bassinet liners/skirts, bumper guards, canopies, comforters/quilts, crib sheets, diaper stackers, dust ruffles, pillows, toddler bedding, twin bedding.

Camp Kazoo. 602 Park Point Drive, Suite 150, Golden, Colorado 80401. Phone: 303/526-2626. Fax: 303/526-5470. Products: Bottles, head supports, toddler bedding.

C and T International, Inc. 170 Roosevelt Place, Palisades Park, New Jersey 07650. Phone: 201/461-9444. Fax: 201/461-9213. Products: Case goods/dressers, changing/dressing tables, cradles, cribs, highchairs, play yards (playpens), walkers, car beds, youth/teen furniture.

Canwood Furniture, Inc. 955 Timmins Street, Pentieton, British Columbia, Canada V2A 5V3. Phone: 604/493-5656. Fax: 604/493-4405. Products: Bunk beds, base goods/dressers, tables and chairs, twin beds.

Capaz Enterprises. P.O. Box 93451, Lubbock, Texas 79493. Phone: 806/791-3568. Products: Growth charts, toys, kid calendars, activity charts, family organizers.

Carlson Children's Products, Inc. 122 Kirkland Circle, Oswego, Illinois 60543. Phone: 1/800-933-3309, 708/851-3366. Fax: 708/851-3401. Products: Play yards (playpens), strollers, swings.

The Carousel. 159 Friendship, Pilot Point, Texas 76258. Phone: 817/365-9863. Products: Bumper guards, canopies, comforters/quilts, crib sheets, curtains/draperies, decorative items, diaper stackers, dust ruffles, pillows, sheets, wall hangings/pictures, crib bedding ensembles.

Carousel Designs, Ltd. 4519 Bankhead Highway, Douglasville, Georgia 30134. Phone: 1/800-662-2236 or 404/949-2123. Fax: 404/920-1987. Products: Bumper guards, canopies, comforters/quilts, crib sheets, diaper stackers, dust ruffles, highchair pads, lamps, pillows, sheets, wall hangings/pictures, cradle sets, portable crib sets, adult rocking chair pads, dressing table covers, crib bedding ensembles.

Celebrations by Brandi Patton. P.O. Box 4497, Oceanside, California 92502-4497. Phone: 1/800-341-7789 or 619/967-1131. Fax: 619/967-6747. Products: Bumper guards, canopies, comforters/quilts, crib sheets, decorative items, diaper stackers, dust ruffles, sheets, wall hangings/pictures.

Century Products Company. 9600 Valley View Road, Macedonia, Ohio 44056. Phone: 216/468-2000. Fax: 216/650-2875. Products: Baby baths, baby/child carriers, bath aids/toys, booster seats, car seats, car seat covers, carriages, gates, highchairs, mobiles, play yards (playpens), strollers, swings, toilet training items, toys, walkers.

Charles D. Owen Manufacturing. 875 Warren Willson Road, Swannanoa, North Carolina 28778. Phone: 704/298-6802. Fax: 704/298-4788. Products: Bumper guards, comforters/quilts, crib sheets, dust ruffles, gift sets, pillows, receiving blankets, blankets, crib bedding ensembles, toddler bedding.

Cherubs Collection. 700 Fairfield Avenue, Stamford, Connecticut 06904. Phone: 203/356-8000. Fax: 203/356-8448. Products: Bibs, gift sets, infant feeding items, pacifiers, bottles.

Child Craft. P.O. Box 444, Salem, Indiana 47167. Phone: 812/883-3111. Fax: 812/883-1819. Products: Bunk beds, canopies, case goods/dressers, changing/dressing tables, cribs, crib mattresses, highchairs, mirrors, rockers, toy chests, toddler beds, twin beds, youth/teen furniture.

Children On the Go. 1670 South Wolf Road, Wheeling, Illinois 60090. Phone: 1/800-537-2684 or 708/537-3797. Fax: 708/537-3961. Products: Baby/child carriers, gift sets, safety items, toilet training items, bottle accessories, infant seats, stroller accessories, automotive accessories.

The Children's Factory. 505 North Kirkwood Road, St. Louis, Missouri 63122. Phone: 314/821-1441. Fax: 314/821-3916. Products: Crib sheets, decorative items, growth charts, play yards (playpens), receiving blankets, toys, wall hangings/pictures, wallpaper and borders, soft indoor play items, blankets.

Clinton Prints. Division of the C. R. Gibson Co., 20 Carter Drive, Guilford, Connecticut 06437. Phone: 203/847-4543. Fax: 203/847-7613. Products: Growth charts, picture frames, baby record books, photo albums.

Clothworks. 1822 Ridge Avenue, Evanston, Illinois 60201. Phone: 1/800-783-1750 or 708/864-5750. Fax: 708/864-6093. Products: Bumper guards, canopies, comforters/quilts, crib sheets, diaper stackers, dust ruffles, highchair pads, lamps, pillows, sheets, wall hangings/pictures, wallpaper and borders, crib bedding ensembles, rugs.

Colgate Mattress Atlanta Corporation/Colgate Juvenile Products. 712 Ponce De Leon Place N.E., Atlanta, Georgia 30306. Phone: 404/892-0862. Fax: 404/875-2479. Products: Basket pads, bumper guards, crib mattresses, highchair pads, mattress covers/pads, play yard (playpen) pads, portable crib bumpers and mattresses, dressing table pads, cradle bumpers, mattresses.

Combi International Corporation. 1471 North Wood Dale Road, Wood Dale, Illinois 60191. Phone: 1/800-992-6624, 708/350-0101. Fax: 708/350-0402. Products: Carriages, strollers, toys.

Comfort Silkie Company, Inc. P.O. Box A.E., Sunland, California 91040. Phone: 1/800-266-BABY or 818/352-0601. Fax: 818/951-3667. Products: Baskets, bath aids/toys, booties/footwear, buntings, comforters/quilts, gift sets, layettes, receiving blankets, parent education. Products, newborn comfort/care items, blankets.

Conant Ball. Division of Shermag, Inc., 2007 Tiffany Place, Greensboro, North Carolina 27408. Phone: 919/282-9525. Fax: 919/545-0280, Product: Rockers.

Continental Quilting Co., Inc. 6201 Fifteenth Avenue, Brooklyn, New York 11219. Phone: 718/259-3131. Fax: 718/234-0494. Products: Quilted baby pads, waterproof pads, playpen pad covers, mattress covers.

Convenience Kits International, Ltd. 366 Pearsall Avenue, Suite 7, Cedarhurst, New York 11516. Phone: 1/800-255-5436 or 516/239-9290.

Fax: 516/239-6934. Products: Bath aids/toys, gift sets, rattles.

Cosco Inc. A Dorel Company, 2525 State Street, Columbus, Indiana 47201. Phone: 812/372-0141. Fax: 812/372-0911. Products: Baby baths, baby/child carriers, bed guards, booster seats, bunk beds, car seats, case goods/dressers, changing/dressing tables, cradles, cribs, crib mattresses, highchairs, jumpers, lamps, monitors/intercoms, step stools, strollers, swings, tables and chairs, toilet training items, toy chests, walkers, juvenile furniture, desks, toddler beds, twin beds, youth/teen furniture.

Cotton Tale Designs, Inc. 4030 Chandler Avenue, Santa Ana, California 92704. Phone: 1/800-628-2621 or 714/435-9558. Products: Bumper guards, buntings, canopies, car seat covers, comforters/quilts, crib sheets, curtains/draperies, decorative items, diaper bags, diaper stackers, dust ruffles, lamps, mobiles, pillows, wall hangings/pictures, wallpaper and borders, glider rocker covers, crib bedding ensembles.

Country Carver. 1632 West Thirty-first Place, Hialeah, Florida 33012. Phone: 305/828-1880. Products: Decorative items, wall hangings/pictures.

Couristan, Inc. Two Executive Drive, Fort Lee, New Jersey 07024. Phone: 1/800-223-6186 or 201/585-8500. Fax: 201/585-8552. Product: Juvenile rugs.

Creative Playthings, Ltd. 33 Loring Drive, Framingham, Massachusetts 01701. Phone: 1/800-444-0901 or 508/620-0900. Fax: 508/872-3120. Products: Booster seats, bunk beds, highchairs.

The C. R. Gibson Company. 32 Knight Street, Norwalk, Connecticut 06856. Phone: 1/800-247-2340 or 203/847-4543. Fax: 203/847-7613. Products: Books, growth charts, picture frames, gift wrap, calendars, paper tableware, invitations/announcements, baby record books, photo albums.

Crib Critters. 185 Drennen Road, Suite 341, Orlando, Florida 32806. Phone: 407/851-2360. Products: Bibs, booties/footwear, crib sheets, dust ruffles, receiving blankets, sheets, bath towels, blankets.

Cuddle Time by Triboro. 172 South Broadway, White Plains, New York 10605. Phone: 914/428-7551. Fax: 914/428-0610. Products: Bumper guards, comforters/quilts, crib sheets, dust ruffles, gift sets, layettes, pillows, receiving blankets, hooded towels, blanket sleepers, pramsuits, sleep and play baby garments, blankets.

Cudlie Diaper Bags. One East Thirty-third Street, 7th Floor, New York, New York 10016. Phone: 212/689-3508. Fax: 212/683-0703. Products: Carriage and stroller pads, decorative items, diaper bags, gift sets, stroller organizers, bottles, organizers.

Daisy Kingdom, Inc. 134 Northwest Eighth Street, Portland, Oregon 97209. Phone: 1/800-288-6004 or 503/222-9033. Fax: 503/222-9120. Products: Bibs, bumper guards, canopies, car seat covers, comforters/quilts, crib sheets, decorative items, diaper stackers, dust ruffles, lamps, mobiles, pillows, wall hangings/pictures, rugs, toddler bedding.

Dakin, Inc. 1649 Adrian Road, Burlingame, California 94010. Phone: 1/800-227-6598 or 415/692-1555. Fax: 415/259-2525. Products: Bath aids/toys, decorative items, mobiles, rattles, toys, wall hangings/pictures, musicals, plush animals.

Danara International, Ltd. 14 Central Boulevard, South Hackensack, New Jersey 07606. Phone: 1/800-526-7048 or 201/641-4350. Fax: 201/641-0421. Products: Bath aids/toys, bibs, books, diaper bags, gift sets, infant feeding items, pacifiers, rattles, safety items, thermometers, toys, bottles, juice boxes/holders/accessories, organizers.

Dandelion. 4030 Chandler Avenue, Santa Ana, California 92704. Phone: 1/800-358-4911 or 714/755-3677. Fax: 714/755-4990. Products: Bumper guards, comforters/quilts, sheets, wall hangings/pictures.

D and F Wicker/Rattan Imports. 1050 Route 46, P.O. Box 430, Ledgewood, New Jersey 07852. Phone: 201/927-8530. Fax: 201/584-7446. Products: Baby/child carriers, baskets, bassinets, cradles, hampers, lamps, toy chests, youth/teen furniture.

Daust Juvenile Products/Apollo. 401 Marcy Avenue, Brooklyn, New York 11206. Phone: 1/800-662-3883 or 718/384-3200. Fax: 718/384-3906. Products: Carriages, cribs, strollers, walkers, doll strollers.

Delta Enterprise Corporation. 175 Liberty Avenue, Brooklyn, New York 11212. Phone: 718/385-1000. Fax: 718/385-8455. Products: Baby/child carriers, bassinets, bed guards, bumper guards, buntings, canopies, carriages, carriage and stroller pads, case goods/dressers, changing/dressing tables, comforters/quilts, cradles, cribs, crib mattresses, crib sheets, decorative items, dust ruffles, highchairs, mattress covers/pads, pillows, play yards (playpens), rockers, sheets, strollers, tables and chairs, toilet training items, toy chests, walkers, crib bedding ensembles, mattresses, toddler beds, twin beds, twin bedding, youth/teen furniture.

Devilbiss Health Care, Inc. 1200 East Main Street, Somerset, Pennsylvania 15501. Phone: 1/800-DEV-1988 or 814/443-4881. Fax: 1/800-345-2202. Products: Humidifier/vaporizer and accessories.

Diplomat Juvenile Corporation. 25 Kay Fries Drive, Stony Point, New York 10980. Phone: 1/800-247-9063 or 914/786-5552. Fax: 914/786-8727. Products: Baby carrier covers, bassinet liners/skirts, bath aids/toys, bumper guards, car seat covers, carriage and stroller pads, comforters/quilts, crib sheets, curtains/draperies, decorative items, diaper stackers, dust ruffles, gift sets, highchair pads, layettes, mattress covers/pads, play yard (playpen) pads, receiving blankets, safety items, sheets, toilet training items, wall hangings/pictures, one-piece underwear, training pants, crib bedding ensembles, diapers (cloth), diaper covers/wraps, head supports, toddler bedding, twin bedding, wipes and accessories.

Direct Connect International, Inc. 700 Godwin Avenue, Suite 110, Midland Park, New Jersey 07432. Phone: 201/445-2101. Fax: 201/445-3839. Products: Bath aids/toys, gift sets, rattles, toys.

Disney Infant and Preschool Toys by Mattel. 333 Continental Boulevard, El Segundo, California 90245-5012. Phone: 213/524-2000. Fax: 213/524-2042. Product: Toys.

Dolly, Inc. 320 North Fourth Street, Tipp City, Ohio 45371. Phone: 513/667-5711. Fax: 513/667-5328. Products: Booster seats, decorative items, diaper bags, lamps, mobiles.

Dundee Mills, Inc./Fisher-Price Bedding and Underwear. 111 West Fortieth Street, New York, New York 10018. Phone: 212/840-7200. Fax: 212/840-3980. Products: Bumper guards, comforters/quilts, crib sheets, curtains/draperies, diaper stackers, dust ruffles, gift sets, layettes, receiving blankets, underwear/layette, hooded baby towels, knit caps and booties, crib bedding ensembles, toddler bedding.

Dutailier, Inc. 298 Chaput, St-Pie, Quebec, Canada J0H 1W0. Phone: 1/800-363-9817 or 514/772-2403. Fax: 514/772-5055. Product: Rockers (adult/child/glider).

Eagle Affiliates, Inc. 101-01 Avenue D, Brooklyn, New York 11236. Phone: 1/800-221-0988 or 718/649-8007. Fax: 718/649-1718. Products: Gift sets, children's tableware.

Eastwood Products, Inc. 53 Advance Road, Toronto, Ontario, Canada M82 2S6. Products: Children's sofa set, bath towels/cloths/robes, youth/teen furniture.

Ecology Kids. c/o Diplomat Juvenile Corporation, 25 Kay Fries Drive, Stony Point, New York 10980. Phone: 1/800-247-9063 or 914/786-5552. Fax: 914/786-8727. Products: Crib sheets, curtains/draperies, diaper stackers, dust ruffles, gift sets, layettes, mattress covers/pads, pillows, receiving blankets, safety items, sheets, wall hangings/pictures, crib bedding ensembles, diapers (cloth), diaper covers/wraps, head supports, toddler bedding, twin bedding, wipes and accessories.

Eden Toys, Inc. 112 West Thirty-fourth Street, Suite 2208, New York, New York 10120. Phone: 1/800-443-4275 or 212/947-4400. Fax: 212/239-9616. Products: Books, gift sets, mobiles, picture frames, rattles, toys.

Evenflo Juvenile Furniture Company. 1801 Commerce Drive, Piqua, Ohio 45356. Phone: 1/800-543-8954 or 513/773-3971. Fax: 513/773-4751. Products: Baby/child carriers, basket pads, bumper guards, car seats, changing/dressing tables, cradles, cribs, crib mattresses, highchairs, highchair pads, jumpers, play yards (playpens), play yard (playpen) pads, rockers, step stools, swings, toilet training items, toddler beds.

Evenflo Products Company. 771 North Freedom Street, Ravenna, Ohio 44266. Phone: 1/800-432-4453 or 216/296-3465. Fax: 216/296-8588. Products: Bibs, breast bumps/nursing pads and shields, gift sets, infant feeding items, pacifiers, rattles, safety items, toys, nipples, disposable bottle feeding systems, bottle carriers, automobile bottle warmers, bottles.

Family Home Products. 1147 Sixty-first Street, Brooklyn, New York 11219. Phone: 718/851-2700. Fax: 718/851-0655. Product: Rockers.

Fan Fair Toys, Inc. 131 West Thirty-third Street, Suite 1703, New York, New York 10001. Phone: 1/800-647-7784 or 212/564-1626. Fax: 212/268-5284. Products: Rattles, toys, dolls.

Fantasy Bed Manufacturing Co. 711 East Fifty-ninth Street, Los Angeles, California 90001. Phone: 1/800-422-3441 or 213/234-3441. Products: Bassinets, bed guards, bunk beds, canopies, changing/dressing tables, cradles, cribs, toddler canopy beds, toddler day beds, toddler beds, twin beds, youth/teen furniture.

FBS, Inc./Renolux. 1071 Batesville Road, Greer, South Carolina 29650. Phone: 1/800-476-5273 or 803/848-0569. Fax: 803/877-6671. Product: Car seats.

Fieldcrest Cannon. 1271 Avenue of the Americas, New York, New York 10020. Phone: 212/957-3310. Fax: 212/957-3385. Product: Blankets.

Fine Art Pillow and Special Ties Corporation. 601 West Twenty-sixth Street, New York, New York 10001. Phone: 212/929-0229. Fax: 212/645-5921. Products: Basket pads, bumper guards, comforters/quilts, crib sheets, dust ruffles.

The First Years/Kiddie Products, Inc. 1 Kiddie Drive, Avon, Massachusetts 02322. Phone: 1/800-225-0382 or 508/588-1220. Fax: 508/583-9067. Products: Baby baths, bath aids/toys, booties/footwear, car seat covers, diaper pails, gift sets, infant feeding items, pacifiers, rattles, safety items, toilet training items, health items.

Fisher-Price, Inc. 636 Girard Avenue, East Aurora, New York 14052. Phone: 1/800-828-4000 or 716/687-3000. Fax: 716/687-3667. Products: Baby baths, bassinets, bath aids/toys, bed guards, booster seats, car seats, crib mattresses, diaper pails, gates, highchairs, infant feeding items, jumpers, lamps, mirrors, mobiles, monitors/intercoms, play yards (playpens), rattles, step stools, swings, tables and chairs, toilet training items, toys, toy chests, walkers, youth beds, youth bed underdrawers.

Flap Happy. 3516 Centinela Avenue, Los Angeles, California 90066. Phone: 1/800-234-3527 or 310/398-3516. Fax: 310/822-7522. Products: Headwear, sun protection gear, clothing.

Flexible Flyer Co. 10 Tubb Avenue, West Point, Mississippi 39773. Phone: 601/494-4732. Products: Swings, thermometers, toy chests, rotocast plastic toys, outdoor play equipment, spring horses, snow items.

Forecees. 14320 South Portage Road, P.O. Box 153, Vicksburg, Michigan 49097. Phone: 616/649-2900. Fax: 616/649-3427. Products: Audiocassettes, videotapes, toys, educational manipulatives (used in preschool and elementary schools).

Frank and Son, Inc. P.O. Box 1252, Conway, South Carolina 29526. Phone: 803/347-3155. Product: Rockers.

Fun Designs, Inc. P.O. Box 2837, Duxbury, Massachusetts 02331. Phone: 617/934-7136. Fax: 617/934-7519. Products: Tote bags, juice boxes/holders, accessories.

Gerber Childrenswear, Inc. 531 South Main Street, Greenville, South Carolina 29601. Phone: 803/240-2840. Fax: 803/232-3335. Products: Bibs, booties/footwear, bumper guards, comforters/quilts, crib sheets, curtains/draperies, diaper stackers, dust ruffles, gift sets, layettes, receiving blankets, sheets, wall hangings/pictures, wallpaper and borders, pillow cases, bassinet sheets, training pants, infant hosiery, bath towels/cloths/robes, blankets, crib bedding ensembles, diapers, diaper covers/wraps, toddler bedding.

Gerber Products Company. 445 State Street, Fremont, Michigan 49413. Phone: 616/928-2550. Fax: 616/928-2972. Products: Bath aids/toys, bibs, booties/footwear, breast bumps/nursing pads and shields, gift sets, hampers, infant feeding items, mirrors, monitors/intercoms, pacifiers, rattles, safety items, switch plates, thermometers, toys, bottles, juice boxes/holders/accessories.

Gerry Baby Products Company. (Gerry, Snugli, and Nu-line), 12520 Grant Drive, Denver, Colorado 80241. Phone: 1/800-525-2472 or 303/457-0926. Fax: 303/450-9542. Products: Baby baths, baby/child carriers, bath aids/toys, bed guards, booster seats, car seats, changing/dressing tables, cradles, cribs, crib mattresses, crib sheets, diaper pails, gates, gift sets, highchairs, mattress covers/pads, monitors/intercoms, play yards (playpens), play yard (playpen) pads, strollers, swings, toilet training items, crib/night lights, portable beds, bath towels/cloths/robes.

G. L. Bowron and Co. Ltd. P.O. Box 151, Bellingham, Massachusetts 02019. Phone: 1/800-9BO-WRON or 508/966-1400. Fax: 508/966-3063.

Product: Lambskins approved for infant care.

Glenna Jean Manufacturing. 230 North Sycamore Street, Petersburg, Virginia 23803. Phone: 1/800-446-6018 or 804/861-0687. Fax: 800/772-8912. Products: Baby carrier covers, bumper guards, canopies, comforters/quilts, crib sheets, curtains/draperies, diaper stackers, dust ruffles, highchair pads, mobiles, pillows, wall hangings/pictures, wallpaper and borders, portable crib sets, cradle sets, stroller covers, 100 percent cotton towels, rocking chair pads, blankets.

Gold Bug. 4999 Oakland Street, Denver, Colorado 80239. Phone: 303/371-2535. Fax: 303/371-2880. Products: Baby carrier covers, booties/footwear, car seat covers, head supports.

Graco Children's Products, Inc. Route 23, Main Street, Elverson, Pennsylvania 19520. Phone: 215/286-5951. Fax: 215/286-2894. Products: Baby/child carriers, highchairs, hook-on chairs, jumpers, play yards (playpens), strollers, swings, walkers, travelyards.

Graham-Field, Inc. 400 Rabro Drive, Hauppauge, New York 11788. Phone: 516/582-5900. Products: Books, breast pumps/nursing pads and shields, infant feeding items, thermometers.

Great Idea Products. 5521 Highway 21, House Springs, Missouri 63051. Phone: 314/948-2215. Products: Battery operated portable fans.

Greenleaf, Inc. 200 Winding Way, Spartanburg, South Carolina 29301. Phone: 1/800-533-1214 or 803/573-7341. Fax: 803/573-7373. Products: Bumper guards, canopies, comforters/quilts, crib sheets, dust ruffles, layettes, pillows, receiving blankets, sheets, blankets, crib bedding ensembles.

Guri-USA, Inc. 2201 Barren Hill Road, Conshohocken, Pennsylvania 19428. Phone: 1/800-688-GURI or 215/832-1166. Fax: 215/828-2362. Products: Decorative items, monitors/intercoms, toilet training items, wall hangings/pictures, electronic crib rockers, nursery clock, nursery room thermometer, toddler bedding, wipes and accessories, videotapes, audiocassettes.

G. W. DMKA, Inc. 168 East Main Street, Prospect Park, New Jersey 07508. Phone: 201/595-5599. Fax: 201/595-0095. Products: Baby baths, bath aids/toys, bed guards, breast pumps/nursing pads and shields, case goods/dressers, changing/dressing tables, cradles, cribs, diaper pails, gift sets, monitors/intercoms, safety items, step stools, tables and chairs, toilet training items, toy chests, intercom, crib rocker, bottle holder, youth/teen furniture.

Hamco, Inc. 16131 Highway 44 North, Prairieville, Louisiana 70769. Phone: 1/800-433-9560 or 504/622-1877. Fax: 504/622-3654. Products: Bibs, gift sets, receiving blankets, bath towels/cloths/robes.

Handy Chair—Remond for Babies. 6105 Portal Way, Ferndale, Washington 98248. Phone: 1/800-426-9244 or 206/384-0466. Fax: 206/384-0544. Products: Baby/child carriers, bath aids/toys, bibs, breast pumps/nursing pads and shields, gift sets, hook-on chairs, infant feeding items, mattress covers/pads, pacifiers, rattles, safety items, thermometers, toys, diapers (cloth), diaper covers/wraps.

Hanseatic Overseas Trading, Inc. 212 South Magnolia Avenue, Tampa, Florida 33606. Phone: 813/251-2342. Fax: 813/251-1621. Products: Carriages, carriage and stroller pads, strollers.

Harper Design Co., Inc. P.O. Box 37, Camden, South Carolina 29020. Phone: 803/432-6367. Fax: 803/425-4517. Products: Bunk beds, lamps, tables and chairs, coat trees, bookshelves, peg racks, corkboards, chalkboards, headboards, bookends, twin beds, youth/teen furniture.

Health-Tex by Triboro. 172 South Broadway, White Plains, New York 10605. Phone: 914/428-7551. Fax: 914/428-0610. Products: Bumper guards, comforters/quilts, crib sheets, dust ruffles, gift sets, layettes, pillows, receiving blankets, hooded towels, blanket sleepers, pramsuits, blankets.

Hoopla, Inc. 1250 Addison Street, Suite 112, Berkeley, California 94702. Phone: 415/649-8547. Products: Baby carrier covers, bibs, books, booties/footwear, bumper guards, car seat covers, comforters/quilts, diaper bags, highchair pads, toys, bath towels/cloths/robes, blankets, toddler bedding.

House of Hatten, Inc. 2200 Denton Drive, Suite 110, Austin, Texas 78758. Phone: 1/800-938-4467 or 512/837-4467. Fax: 512/835-7012. Products: Bibs, bumper guards, comforters/quilts, crib sheets, decorative items, diaper bags, diaper stackers, dust ruffles, gift sets, layettes, mobiles, picture frames, rattles, sheets, toys, bath towels/cloths/robes, crib bedding ensembles.

HR Haslett Fine Woodworking. 9820 Bell Ranch Drive, Suite 102, Santa Fe Springs, California 90670. Phone: 1/800-732-8649 or 310/946-9221. Products: Toy chests, comforter/quilt/blanket stands, animal shapes (for holding quilts/blankets/bedding), chairs.

Impressions Imports, Inc. 1100 Trend Drive, Carrollton, Texas 75006. Phone: 214/418-5414. Fax: 214/418-5130. Product: Comforters/quilts.

Infantino, Inc. 650 Arizona Street, Chula Vista, California 91911. Phone: 1/800-365-8182. Fax: 619/420-0836. Products: Baby baths, baby/child carriers, comforters/quilts, high chairs, mirrors, mobiles, monitors/intercoms, wall hangings/pictures, toddler sleeping bags, crib lights.

Infant Technologies, Inc. 3200 Ash Street, Palo Alto, California 94306. Phone: 1/800-322-7638 or 415/424-0900. Fax: 415/424-0743. Products: Wipes and accessories.

Infinitely Infants. 319 Manley Street, West Bridgewater, Massachusetts 02379. Phone: 1/800-445-5905 or 508/588-5555. Fax: 508/588-3838. Products: Baskets, bibs, booties/footwear, gift sets, infant feeding items, picture frames, rattles, receiving blankets, toys, quilted and applique bottle covers, combs, brushes, teethers, bath towels/cloths/robes, bottles.

Infinity Corp. 5812 East Burnside Street, Portland, Oregon 97215. Phone: 1/800-762-5229 or 305/942-7990. Fax: 305/942-1929, Product: Infant safety cushion.

Inglesina Baby. 1190 Stirling Road, Dania, Florida 33004. Phone: 305/922-6991. Fax: 305/922-7007. Products: Bassinets, carriages, carriage and stroller pads, diaper bags.

Inmon Enterprises, Inc. DBA Country Pleasures, 8825-D Kenneth, Nixa, Missouri 65714. Phone: 417/725-2894. Fax: 417/725-2567. Products: Decorative items, lamps, wall hangings/pictures, bookends.

Instant Products, Inc. P.O. Box 33068, Louisville, Kentucky 40232. Phone: 502/367-2266. Products: Rockers, doll cradles.

International Playthings, Inc. 120 Riverdale Road, Riverdale, New Jersey 07457. Phone: 1/800-631-1272 or 201/831-1400. Fax: 201/831-8643. Product: Toys.

J. E. Morgan Knitting Mills. 120 West Forty-fifth Street, 15th Floor, New York, New York 10036. Phone: 212/768-8080. Fax: 212/382-2450. Products: Receiving blankets, infant and toddler thermal underwear, bath towels/cloths/robes, blankets.

J. L. Childress Co., Inc. 552 North Waverly Street, Orange, California 92667. Phone: 714/997-4534. Fax: 714/997-0153. Products: Diaper bags, breastfeeding tote, bottle bags, gift sachets, insulated hot/cold bags, reusable ice packs, stroller bags, changing pads, juice boxes/holders/accessories.

J. Mason Products. 27756 Avenue Mentry, Santa Clarita, California 91355. Phone: 1/800-242-1922 or 805/295-5100. Fax: 805/295-5800. Products: Baby/child carriers, carriages, changing/dressing tables, cribs, play yards (playpens), strollers, walkers, bouncers, toddler beds.

Jolly Jumper, Inc. P.O. Box M, Woonsocket, Rhode Island 02895. Phone: 1/800-628-5168 or 401/765-5950. Fax: 401/766-7103. Products: Carriages, jumpers, lamps, mobiles, strollers, toys, toddler car seat cushion, bouncers.

Jonica Distributors, Inc. 3719 Polk Street, Houston, Texas 77003. Phone: 713/222-2103. Fax: 713/222-2104. Products: Changing/dressing tables, cradles, cribs, highchairs, rockers.

JTG of Nashville. 1024C Eighteenth Avenue South, Nashville, Tennessee 37212. Phone: 1/800-222-2JTG or 615/329-3036. Fax: 615/329-4028. Products: Toys, puzzles, books, musical keyboard books, videotapes, audiocassettes.

Judi's Originals. 7722 East Gray Road, Scottsdale, Arizona 85260. Phone: 1/800-421-9433 or 602/991-5885. Fax: 602/948-7403. Products: Audiocassettes, videotapes, bumper guards, canopies, car seat covers, comforters/quilts, crib sheets, curtains/draperies, diaper stackers, dust ruffles, high chair pads, lamps, mobiles, pillows, sheets, switch plates, wall hangings/pictures, wallpaper and borders, quick change bedding, portable crib accessories, cradle accessories, car seat shield, crib bedding ensembles, head supports, toddler bedding.

Kalencom Corporation. 740 Clouet Street, New Orleans, Louisiana 70117. Phone: 1/800-344-6699 or 504/943-0123. Fax: 504/943-5333. Products: Baby carrier covers, car seat covers, carriage and stroller pads, diaper bags, head supports.

Keeper's Kidstuff. 35 Skyline Drive, Intervale, New Hampshire 03845-0750. Phone: 1/800-252-3377 or 603/356-5239. Fax: 603/356-3393. Products: Decorative items, growth charts, frameable birth certificates (English and Spanish), greeting cards, birth announcements, baby show invitations, thank you notes.

Kel-Gar, Inc. P.O. Box 796934, Dallas, Texas 75379-6934. Phone: 214/250-3838. Fax: 214/250-3805. Products: Bath aids/toys, stroller/feeding/other accessories.

Kiddie Lites and Accessories, Too! 202 Main Street, Roxbury, New York 12474. Phone: 607/326-4923. Products: Decorative items, lamps, picture frames, switch plates, wall hangings/pictures, wallpaper and borders, bookends, piggy banks, musical boxes, nightlights, clocks.

Kidentials/Infants Specialty Co. 7101 East Slauson Avenue, Commerce, California 90040. Phone:

1/800-762-6872 or 213/723-1026. Fax: 213/728-0036. Products: Bath aids/toys, booties/footwear, breast pumps/nursing pads and shields, gift sets, infant feeding items, mobiles, rattles, safety items, toys.

Kid Kraft, Inc. 5952 South Kline Street, Littleton, Colorado 80127. Phone: 303/973-0612. Fax: 303/933-0372. Products: Tables and chairs, toy chests, desks, toddler beds.

Kids Basics. Box 3202 R.S., Stamford, Connecticut 06905. Phone: 203/325-1117. Fax: 203/358-0165. Products: Basket pads, carriage and stroller pads, crib mattresses, gates, highchair pads, mirrors, play yard (playpen) pads, portable dressing table pads, carriage and stroller nets, mattresses (not crib).

Kidsline, Inc. 6800 Avalon Boulevard, Los Angeles, California 90003. Phone: 213/758-6096. Products: Baby carrier covers, baskets, bassinets, bassinet liners/skirts, bumper guards, canopies, car seat covers, carriage and stroller pads, comforters/quilts, crib sheets, curtains/draperies, diaper stackers, dust ruffles, highchairs, mattress covers/pads, pillows, wall hangings/pictures, rocking chair pads, cradle bedding sets, parasols, bassinet stands, crib bedding ensembles, head supports, toddler bedding, twin bedding.

Kidstuff Pals, Inc. 5416 West Crenshaw Street, Tampa, Florida 33634. Phone: 813/888-7408. Fax: 813/884-0505. Products: Canopies, comforters/quilts, decorative items, dust ruffles, pillows, wall hangings/pictures, twin bedding.

Kinderkids Ltd., Inc. 4115 Northwest 132nd Street, Opa Locka, Florida 33054. Phone: 1/800-741-8567 or 305/681-0406. Fax: 305/769-1076. Products: Baby/child carriers, bas-

kets, basket pads, bassinets, buntings, canopies, carriages, cradles, highchairs, strollers, bouncers.

Kolcraft Juvenile Products, Inc. 3455 West Thirty-first Place, Chicago, Illinois 60623. Phone: 312/247-4494. Fax: 312/376-7972. Products: Baby/child carriers, basket pads, booster seats, car seats, carriages, crib mattresses, highchairs, play yards (playpens), play yard (playpen) pads, strollers, swings, walkers, toddler beds.

Koolkids (Division of KKC Inc.). 1421 Champion Drive, #311, Carrollton, Texas 75006. Phone: 1/800-348-5665 or 214/241-5200. Fax: 214/241-7240. Products: Baby/child carriers, bath aids/toys, changing/dressing tables, cribs, crib sheets, gift sets, safety items, pregnancy pillows, bouncers.

Kooshies Diapers International, Inc. 132 West High Street, Wills Point, Texas 75169. Phone: 1/800-872-2581 or 903/873-2581. Fax: 903/873-2682. Products: Bibs, breast pumps/nursing pads and shields, receiving blankets, sheets, waterproof pads, diapers (cloth), diaper covers/wraps.

Kubla Crafts. P.O. Box 771, Hampton Bays, New York 11946. Phone: 1/800-645-1116 or 516/288-0222. Fax: 803/724-3411. Products: Bibs, comforters/quilts, decorative items, growth charts, picture frames, toys, wall hangings/pictures.

Lambs and Ivy, Inc. 5978 Bowcroft Street, Los Angeles, California 90016. Phone: 1/800-345-2627 or 310/839-5155. Fax: 310/839-0767. Products: Baby carrier covers, bumper guards, canopies, car seat covers, carriage and stroller pads, comforters/quilts, crib sheets, diaper stackers, dust ruffles, highchair pads, lamps, mobiles, pillows, play yard (playpen) pads, sheets, switch plates, wall hangings/pictures, wallpaper and borders, blankets, crib bedding ensembles, head supports, organizers.

Lamby Nursery Collection. 305 Grover Street, Lynden, Washington 98264. Phone: 1/800-669-0527 or 206/354-6719. Fax: 206/354-6513. Products: Bath aids/toys, booties/footwear, car seat covers, carriage and stroller pads, pillows, lambskin cuddle rugs, car seat strap covers, blankets.

Lauri. P.O. Box F, Avon Valley Road, Phillips-Avon, Maine 04966. Phone: 1/800-451-0520 or 207/639-2000. Fax: 207/639-3555. Products: Mirrors, toys, toothbrush holders, wall racks.

Leachco, Inc. 130 East Tenth Street, Ada, Oklahoma 74820. Phone: 1/800-525-1050 or 405/436-1142. Fax: 405/332-7549. Products: Baby/child carriers, bath aids/toys, bumper guards, car seat covers, crib sheets, gift sets, highchair pads, infant feeding items, safety items, toys, head supports.

Lea Industries. A Ladd Furniture, Inc., Co., 1 Plaza Center, P.O. Box HP-3, High Point, North Carolina 27261. Phone: 919/889-0333. Fax: 919/888-6490. Products: Case goods/dressers, cribs, youth/teen furniture.

Lean on Me. 10 Arkansas Street, Suite 1, San Francisco, California 94107. Phone: 510/527-9400. Fax: 510/528-9022. Products: Bumper guards, infant feeding items.

Lear Siegler Seymour Corp. 885 North Chestnut Street, Seymour, Indiana 47274. Phone: 1/800-457-9881 or 812/522-5130. Fax: 812/522-5294. Product: Gates.

Le Clair Furniture Co. 12951 Forty-ninth Street, Clearwater, Florida 34622. Phone: 813/572-7188. Fax: 813/572-9022. Products: Bunk beds, case goods/dressers, mirrors, desks, youth/teen furniture.

Lepine Furniture USA. 2625 Rossmoor Drive, Pittsburgh, Pennsylvania 15241. Phone: 1/800-326-2121. Fax: 412/942-3581. Products: Bed guards, case goods/dressers, changing/dressing tables, cribs, highchairs, mirrors, rockers, desks, twin beds, youth/teen furniture.

Li'l Partners/Tamara's Exclusive. 6363 Santa Monica Boulevard, Hollywood, California 90038-1619. Phone: 1/800-235-4222 or 213/957-7850. Fax: 213/962-8222. Products: Bassinet liners/skirts, bumper guards, canopies, carriage and stroller pads, comforters/quilts, crib sheets, diaper bags, diaper stackers, dust ruffles, pillows, receiving blankets, wall hangings/pictures, rocker covers.

Little Bedding. Division of Red Calliope, 13003 South Figueroa Street, Los Angeles, California 90061. Phone: 1/800-421-0526 or 310/516-6100. Fax: 1/800-338-7170. Products: Bumper guards, car seat covers, comforters/quilts, crib sheets, diaper stackers, dust ruffles, lamps, mobiles, wall hangings/pictures, wallpaper and borders, head supports.

Little Colorado, Inc. 15866 West Seventh Avenue, Golden, Colorado 80401. Phone: 1/800-776-7337 or 303/278-2451. Fax: 303/278-4245. Products: Cradles, lamps, rockers, step stools, tables and chairs, toys, toy chests, rocking horses, bookcases, benches, headboards, coat trees, wall shelves, doll house and furniture sets, doll cradles, wooden kitchen sets, toddler beds, twin beds, youth/teen furniture.

Little Kids, Inc. 2757 Pawtucket Avenue, East Providence, Rhode Island 02914. Phone: 1/800-545-5437 or 401/435-4120. Fax: 401/438-0665.

Products: Infant feeding items, toys, toddler feeding. Products, video accessories, juice boxes/holders/accessories.

The Little Tikes Company. 2180 Barlow Road, Hudson, Ohio 44236. Phone: 216/650-3000. Fax: 216/650-3109. Products: Booster seats, case goods/dressers, changing/dressing tables, diaper pails, highchairs, rattles, rockers, step stools, swings, tables and chairs, toilet training items, toys, toy chests, youth/teen furniture.

Little Vikings, Ltd. 395 Park Street, P.O. Box 644, Housatonic, Massachusetts 01236. Phone: 1/800-333-VIKI or 413/274-3538. Products: Bumper guards, canopies, carriage and stroller pads, comforters/quilts, crib sheets, diaper stackers, dust ruffles, highchair pads, pillows, sheets, wall hangings/pictures, twin comforters, pillow cases, pillow shams.

L.M.W. Designs. 333 Harrison #8, Riverside, California 92503. Phone: 714/352-2429. Products: Wall hangings/pictures, palm trees, room decor.

The Loose Goose. 927 Auburnview Drive, Cincinnati, Ohio 45206. Phone: 513/221-4961. Product: Wall hangings/pictures.

Lullabye. 1017 Third Street, Stevens Point, Wisconsin 54481-2761. Phone: 1/800-236-2742 or 715/344-2742. Fax: 715/344-6929. Products: Canopies, case goods/dressers, changing/dressing tables, cribs, mirrors.

Lundy Look. 2601 Frontier, Midland, Texas 79705. Phone: 915/682-3154. Products: Crib bedding ensembles, toddler bedding, twin bedding.

Luv N' Care. 112 West Thirty-fourth Street, Room 618, New York, New York 10120. Phone: 1/800-256-2399 or 212/594-4780. Fax: 212/629-6196. Products: Baby baths, bath aids/toys, bibs, booties/footwear, decorative items, diaper stackers, gift sets, infant feeding items, layettes, mobiles, monitors/intercoms, pacifiers, pillows, rattles, receiving blankets, safety items, switch plates, thermometers, toilet training items, toys, pacifier holders, jar sets, training pants, hooded towels, bath towels/cloths/robes, blankets, bottles, head supports.

Luv Stuff. 2809 Industrial Lane, Garland, Texas 75041. Phone: 1/800-835-BABY or 214/278-BABY. Fax: 214/271-3272. Products: Baby carrier covers, bed guards, bumper guards, canopies, car seat covers, carriage and stroller pads, comforters/quilts, crib sheets, curtains/draperies, decorative items, diaper bags, diaper stackers, dust ruffles, mobiles, pillows, receiving blankets, sheets, wall hangings/pictures, teething rail covers, rocker cushions, toy bags, blankets, crib bedding ensembles, twin bedding.

Marshall Baby Products. A Division of Omron Healthcare, 300 Lakeview Parkway, Vernon Hills, Illinois 60061. Phone: 1/800-922-2959 or 708/680-6200. Fax: 708/680-6269. Products: Baskets, basket pads, breast pumps/nursing pads and shields, canopies, carriages, highchairs, infant feeding items, strollers, tables and chairs, thermometers, toy chests, doll carriages, rocking horses, wipes and accessories.

The Maya Group, Inc. 15621 Graham Street, Huntington Beach, California 92649. Phone: 714/898-0807. Fax: 714/898-7487. Products: Infant feeding items, illuminated wall clock.

Medela, Inc. 4610 Prime Parkway, McHenry, Illinois 60050. Phone: 1/800-435-8316 or 815/363-1246. Products: Audiocassettes, videotapes, baby/child carriers, books, breast bumps/nursing pads and shields, infant feeding items, thermometers.

Meg, Inc. 808 Guimond Street, Longueuil, Quebec, Canada J4G 1T5. Phone: 514/442-2577. Fax: 514/442-1580. Products: Case goods/dressers, changing/dressing tables, cribs, crib mattresses, youth/teen furniture.

Mericon Child Safety Products. 24355 Capitol Avenue, Redford, Michigan 48239. Phone: 1/800-753-SAFE or 313/255-6700. Products: Baby baths, highchair pads, safety items.

Merri-Tots/Sheridan Infant Products, Inc. 699 Hertel Avenue, Buffalo, New York 14207. Phone: 1/800-225-5215 or 716/871-2400. Fax: 716/871-2402. Products: Bibs, gift sets, infant feeding items, pacifiers, rattles, toys, novelty teethers, shoe accessories, sunglasses (infant-to-thirty-six months), bottles.

Michael Friedman Corp. (Crib Mates). 650 Fountain Avenue, Brooklyn, New York 11208. Phone: 1/800-431-3166 or 718/257-7800. Fax: 718/257-7808. Products: Specializes in baby gift sets, silverplate, decorated bottles, layette gift accessories, teethers. Also produces baby baths, bath aids/toys, bibs, decorative items, diaper pails, infant feeding items, pacifiers, picture frames, rattles, safety items, thermometers, toys.

Miller Enterprises. 11446 Northeast Fremont Court, Portland, Oregon 97220. Phone: 503/257-3633. Products: Bibs, lap pads, laundry sacks.

Million Dollar Baby. 855 Washington Boulevard, Montebello, California 90640. Phone: 1/800-282-3886 or 213/722-2288. Fax: 213/728-2228. Products: Case goods/dressers, changing/dressing tables, cradles, cribs, highchairs, rockers.

Mini Togs/Panda Knits. 112 West Thirty-fourth Street, Room 618, New York, New York 10120. Phone: 1/800-256-2399 or 212/594-4780. Fax: 212/629-6196. Products: Baby baths, bath aids/toys, bibs, books, booties/footwear, decorative items, diaper stackers, gift sets, infant feeding items, layettes, mobiles, monitors/intercoms, pacifiers, pillows, rattles, receiving blankets, safety items, switch plates, thermometers, toilet training items, toys, training pants, underwear, pacifier holders, bath towels/cloths/robes, blankets, bottles, diaper covers/wraps, head supports.

MM's Designs, Inc. 1555 West Sam Houston Parkway North, Houston, Texas 77043. Phone: 1/800-444-4090 or 713/461-2600. Fax: 713/827-7071. Products: Baskets, bibs, growth charts, lamps, picture frames, step stools, switch plates, tables and chairs, wall hangings/pictures, rugs.

Mommy's Helper, Inc. P.O. Box 780838, Wichita, Kansas 67278-0838. Phone: 316/636-9512. Fax: 316/634-2783. Products: Infant feeding items, toilet training items, juice boxes/holders/accessories.

Morigeau Furniture USA. 2625 Rossmoor Drive, Pittsburgh, Pennsylvania 15241. Phone: 1/800-326-2121. Fax: 412/942-3581. Products: Bed guards, bunk beds, case goods/dressers, changing/dressing tables, cribs, highchairs, mirrors, rockers, toy chests, desks, twin beds, youth/teen furniture.

Mother's Love, Inc. 11693 San Vicente Boulevard, Suite 376, Los Angeles, California 90049. Phone: 1/800-846-0059. Fax: 310/447-9680. Product: Natural audio pacifier.

Munchkin Bottling, Inc. 7535 Woodman Place, Van Nuys, California 91405-6343. Phone: 1/800-344-2229 or 818/786-2229. Fax: 818/786-6343. Products: Bibs, bottles.

Nava's Designs. 16742 Stagg Street #106, Van Nuys, California 91406. Phone: 818/988-9050. Fax: 818/780-6988. Products: Bassinet liners/skirts, bumper guards, comforters/quilts, crib sheets, decorative items, diaper bags, diaper stackers, dust ruffles, pillows, sheets, wall hangings/pictures, blankets, crib bedding ensembles.

Nelson Juvenile Products, Inc. 805 Tate Drive, Dothan, Alabama 36302. Phone: 1/800-736-1140 or 205/792-1144. Fax: 205/794-2251. Products: Carriages, case goods/dressers, changing/dressing tables, cradles, cribs, highchairs, hook-on chairs, rockers, strollers, walkers, youth/teen furniture.

New Age Concepts, Inc. Department 339, P.O. Box 4172, Woodland Hills, California 91365-4172. Phone: 818/999-5192. Product: Baby sleeper.

New Spring Company. 7760 Coral Way, Dublin, California 94568. Phone: 510/833-0766. Fax: 510/833-0766. Products: Comforters/quilts, pillows, toddler sleeping bags.

Nikky/Family Clubhouse. 6 Chiles Avenue, Asheville, North Carolina 28803. Phone: 704/254-9236. Fax: 704/258-9052. Product: Diapers (cloth).

Nogatco International, Inc. 86 Lackawanna Avenue, West Paterson, New Jersey 07424. Phone: 1/800-922-0938 or 201/785-4907. Fax: 201/785-2314. Products: Baby/child carriers, carriages, cribs, strollers, walkers, doll strollers, youth/teen furniture.

NoJo (Noel Joanna, Inc.). 22942 Arroyo Vista, Rancho Santa Margarita, California 92688. Phone: 1/800-854-8760 or 714/858-9717. Fax: 714/858-4930. Products: Baby/child carriers, bumper guards, canopies, car seat covers, carriage and stroller pads, comforters/quilts, crib sheets, decorative items, diaper bags, diaper stackers, dust ruffles, highchair pads, lamps, mattress covers/pads, mobiles, pillows, receiving blankets, sheets, wall hangings/pictures, wallpaper and borders, bath towels/cloths/robes, blankets, crib bedding ensembles, toddler bedding.

North States Industries Inc. 1200 Mendelssohn Avenue, Suite 210, Minneapolis, Minnesota 55427. Phone: 612/541-9101. Fax: 612/541-9026. Products: Gates, play yards (playpens).

Nursery Needs by Sanitoy, Inc. 1 Nursery Lane, Fitchburg, Massachusetts 01420. Phone: 1/800-726-4869 or 508/345-7571. Fax: 508/342-5887. Products: Baby baths, baby/child carriers, baskets, bath aids/toys, bibs, books, booster seats, diaper pails, gift sets, infant feeding items, pacifiers, rattles, safety items, step stools, toilet training items, toys, comb and brush sets, juice boxes/holders/accessories, organizers, youth/teen furniture.

Ocean Shore Toys, Inc. 3 Terraza Del Mar, Dana Point, California 92629. Phone: 1/800-422-8810 or 714/493-9600. Fax: 714/493-2039. Products: Infant feeding items, talking spoon and fork, singing tooth brush.

Offspring. 3345 East Miraloma Avenue, Suite 133, Anaheim, California 92807. Phone: 1/800-637-7713 or 714/993-1897. Fax: 714/993-3579. Products: Decorative items, step stools, tables and chairs, toy chests, toddler beds, twin beds.

OFNA Baby Products. 18 Technology, Suite #159, Irvine, California 92718. Phone: 714/586-2910. Product: Safety items.

Okla Homer Smith Furniture Mfg. Co. 416 South Fifth Street, Fort Smith, Arkansas 72901. Phone: 501/783-6191. Fax: 501/783-5767. Products: Bumper guards, changing/dressing tables, cradles, cribs, crib mattresses, chests, dressers, toddler beds.

Once Upon a Whimsy. Division of the Nursery Collection, 5974 Taylor Road, Naples, Florida 33942. Phone: 1/800-338-1184 or 813/597-1744. Fax: 813/597-2040. Products: Baby carrier covers, bumper guards, canopies, car seat covers, carriage and stroller pads, comforters/quilts, crib sheets, decorative items, diaper bags, diaper stackers, dust ruffles, gift sets, pillows, receiving blankets, sheets, wall hangings/pictures, wallpaper and borders, crib bedding ensembles.

Palais Royal. 1725 Broadway, Charlottesville, Virginia 22901. Phone: 1/800-322-3911 or 804/979-3911. Fax: 804/977-8962. Products: Bibs, bumper guards, buntings, comforters/quilts, crib sheets, decorative items, diaper bags, diaper stackers, pillows, sheets, bath towels/cloths/robes, crib bedding ensembles, twin bedding.

Pali Spa/R. Levine Distributor. 107 East Farnham, Wheaton, Illinois 60187. Phone: 708/690-6926. Fax: 708/894-7974. Products: Case goods/dressers, cradles, cribs.

Pansy Ellen Products, Inc. 1245 Old Alpharetta Road, Alpharetta, Georgia 30202. Phone: 404/751-0442. Fax: 404/751-0543. Products: Baby baths, bath aids/toys, booster seats, car seat covers, comforters/quilts, decorative items, gift sets, infant feeding items, mobiles, monitors/intercoms, rattles, safety items, toy organizers, laundry bags, car seat cushions.

PatchKraft, Inc. 70 Outwater Lane, Garfield, New Jersey 07026. Phone: 201/340-3300. Fax: 1/800-882-3552. Products: Bibs, bumper guards, canopies, carriage and stroller pads, comforters/quilts, crib sheets, curtains/draperies, decorative items, diaper bags, diaper stackers, dust ruffles, gift sets, highchair pads, mobiles, pillows, play yard (playpen) pads, sheets (crib/juvenile), wall hangings/pictures, blankets, crib bedding ensembles.

Pat Higdon Industries, Inc. South Roberts Street, Quincy, Florida 32351. Phone: 1/800-874-8181 or 904/627-9524. Fax: 904/627-9525. Products: Case goods/dressers, changing/dressing tables, cradles, cribs.

Patsy Aiken Designs. 3222-J Wellington Court, Raleigh, North Carolina 27615. Phone: 1/800-828-2351 or 919/872-8789. Fax: 919/872-9731. Products: Baby carrier covers, canopies, comforters/quilts, crib sheets, diaper bags, diaper stackers, dust ruffles, lamps, layettes, mobiles, picture frames, pillows, sheets, switch plates, wall hangings/pictures.

Pecoware. 13620 Benson Avenue, Chino, California 91710. Phone: 1/800-456-7326 or 714/590-3399. Fax: 714/590-4800. Products: Gift sets, infant feeding items, children's dinnerware and plastic accessories, back-to-school products.

Peg Perego U.S.A., Inc. 3625 Independence Drive, Ft. Wayne, Indiana 46808. Phone: 219/482-8191. Fax: 219/484-2940. Products: Baby baths, baby/child carriers, bassinets, carriages, changing/dressing tables, highchairs, strollers, walkers, youth/teen furniture.

Perine Lowe Enterprises; Child to Cherish. 555 West Lambert, Unit 0, Brea, California 92621. Phone: 1/800-776-7002 or 714/990-1590. Products: Picture frames, keepsake items, hangers (padded), drawer liners.

Pieces of Dreams. 5154 Edith Northeast, Albuquerque, New Mexico 87102. Phone: 505/345-5656. Fax: 505/345-5127. Products: Bunk beds, case goods/dressers, cradles, dust ruffles, growth charts, rockers, tables and chairs, toddler furniture, toddler beds, toddler bedding, twin beds, youth/teen furniture.

Pine Creek Bedding. 21030 Highway 99E, Aurora, Colorado 97002. Phone: 503/678-2517. Fax: 503/678-2519. Products: Bumper guards, comforters/quilts, dust ruffles, pillows, receiving blankets, crib bedding ensembles.

Pinky Baby Products. 8450 Westpark #104, Houston, Texas 77063. Phone: 713/781-9200. Fax: 713/781-5624. Products: Bath aids/toys, bibs, infant feeding items, safety items, baby cabanas, highchair safety items, diaper covers/wraps.

Pippen Hill, Inc. 76 Eden Valley Road, Rome, Georgia 30161. Phone: 1/800-736-1591 or 404/235-3846. Fax: 404/232-3280. Products: Decorative items, growth charts, lamps, mirrors, rockers, step stools, bookends, coat racks, wall hangers, youth/teen furniture.

Playmobil U.S.A., Inc. 11E Nicholas Court, Dayton, New Jersey 08810. Phone: 908/274-0101. Fax: 908/274-0110. Product: Toys.

Playskool Baby, Inc. 108 Fairway Court, Northvale, New Jersey 07647. Phone: 1/800-777-0371 or 201/767-0900. Fax: 201/767-4392. Products: Baby baths, baby/child carriers, bath aids/toys, bibs, books, booster seats, booties/footwear, diaper bags, gift sets, infant feeding items, monitors/intercoms, pacifiers, rattles, safety items, step stools, thermometers, toilet training items, toys, clothing, night lights, juvenile furniture.

Playtech, Inc. 139 Harristown Road, Glen Rock, New Jersey 07452. Phone: 201/670-1655. Fax: 201/670-4967. Products: Infant feeding items, monitors/intercoms, rattles, toys, night lights.

Playtex Family Products Corp. 700 Fairfield Avenue, Stamford, Connecticut 06904. Phone: 203/356-8000. Fax: 203/356-8448. Products: Gift sets, infant feeding items, pacifiers, juice cups, bottles.

Pockets of Learning Ltd. 31-G Union Avenue, Sudbury, Massachusetts 01776. Phone: 1/800-635-2994 or 508/443-5808. Fax: 508/443-5812. Products: Books, decorative items, toys, wall hangings/pictures, play and sleep mats, advent calendars.

Powell Company. 8631 Hayden Place, Culver City, California 90232-1408. Phone: 1/800-622-4456 or 310/204-2224. Fax: 310/837-6223. Products: Bunk beds, case goods/dressers, decorative items, gift sets, lamps, rockers, toy chests, wall hangings/pictures, desks, twin beds, youth/teen furniture.

Prelude Designs. 1 Hayes Street, Elmsford, New York 10523. Phone: 1/800-229-4566. Products: Wall hangings/pictures, wallpaper and borders.

Prestige Toy Corp. 131 West Thirty-third Street, Room 606, New York, New York 10001. Phone: 212/736-8977. Fax: 212/239-4841. Products: Rattles, toilet training items.

Preston International Corporation. 4930 Holland-Sylvania Road, Sylvania, Ohio 43560. Phone: 419/882-4816. Fax: 419/882-3747. Products: Bassinets, case goods/dressers, changing/dressing tables, cribs.

Pride-Trimble. P.O. Box 2231, Weber CIty, Virginia 24290. Phone: 703/386-2959. Fax: 703/386-2938. Products: Bed guards, booster seats, car seats, changing/dressing tables, hampers, highchairs, play yards (playpens), play yard (playpen) pads, toilet training items.

Prince Lionheart. 2421 South Westgate Road, Santa Maria, California 93455. Phone: 1/800-544-1132 or 805/922-2250. Fax: 805/922-9442. Products: Bath aids/toys, decorative items, gift sets, infant feeding items, mirrors, safety items, auto upholstery protectors, floor protection mats, storage carousel, dishwasher basket, bottles, organizers.

Priss Prints, Inc. 3960 Broadway Boulevard, Suite 105, Garland, Texas 75043. Phone: 1/800-543-4971 or 214/278-5600. Fax: 214/278-8327. Products: Decorative items, growth charts, wall hangings/pictures, wallpaper and borders.

Proteus Design Group, Inc. 28300 White Road, Perrysburg, Ohio 43551. Phone: 419/874-0902. Fax: 419/893-4871. Product: Diaper bags.

Quiltcraft Kids. 1233 Levee Street, Dallas, Texas 75207. Phone: 1/800-462-2805 or 214/741-1662. Fax: 214/748-1521. Products: Bumper guards, comforters/quilts, crib sheets, curtains/draperies, diaper stackers, dust ruffles, pillows, sheets, shams, headboards, toddler/twin/full comforters, twin/full sheets sets, European pillows.

The Quiltex Company. 100 West Thirty-third Street, New York, New York 10001. Phone: 1/800-237-3636 or 212/594-2205. Fax: 212/594-1401. Products: Bibs, bumper guards, buntings, canopies, comforters/quilts, crib sheets, decorative items, diaper stackers, dust ruffles, gift sets, layettes, mobiles, picture frames, pillows, receiving blankets, sheets, wall hangings/pictures.

Quiltown Collection. P.O. Box 260672, Plano, Texas 75026-0672. Phone: 214/238-2183. Product: Toys.

Racing Strollers, Inc. 2609 River Road, Yakima, Washington 98902.

Phone: 509/457-0925. Fax: 509/453-7732. Products: Canopies, strollers.

Railnet Corp./Networks, Inc. 806 West Spruce Street, Missoula, Montana 59802. Phone: 406/721-7775. Fax: 406/721-9969. Products: Bath aids/toys, bibs, diaper bags, gates, play yards (playpens), safety items, toy chests, stroller bags, auto seat bags, toy bags, stuffed animal hammocks, organizers.

Rainbow Mountain, Inc. 751 North Frontenac Road, Naperville, Illinois 60563. Phone: 1/800-253-5410 or 708/416-7877. Fax: 708/416-7880. Products: Changing/dressing tables, cradles, cribs, highchairs, lamps, mobiles, picture frames, rockers.

Red Calliope and Associates Inc. 13003 South Figueroa Street, Los Angeles, California 90061. Phone: 1/800-421-0526 or 310/516-6100. Fax: 800/338-5989. Products: Bumper guards, canopies, car seat covers, comforters/quilts, crib sheets, curtains/draperies, diaper stackers, dust ruffles, lamps, mobiles, sheets, switch plates, wall hangings/pictures, wallpaper and borders, cradle sets, portable crib sets, head supports, toddler bedding.

Redmon. 200 Harrison Avenue, Peru, Indiana 46970. Phone: 317/473-6683. Fax: 317/473-6686. Products: Bassinets, bassinet liners/skirts, changing/dressing tables, decorative items, hampers, picture frames, tables and chairs, toy chests.

Reflections Fine Bedding Attire. 2950-A Jefferson Street, Riverside, California 92504. Phone: 818/508-8512. Fax: 818/508-1238. Products: Bumper guards, comforters/quilts, crib sheets, curtains/draperies, dust ruffles, pillows, sheets, crib bedding ensembles, toddler bedding, twin bedding.

Regal Lager, Inc./Baby Bjorn. 1506 Waynesboro Court, Marietta, Georgia 30062. Phone: 1/800-593-5522 or 404/565-5522. Fax: 404/565-5721. Products: Baby baths, baby/child carriers, bibs, booster seats, changing/dressing tables, diaper bags, highchairs, step stools, toilet training items, toys, infant carry bags, portable beds, bouncers.

Regent Baby Products Corp./ Babyking. 43-21 Fifty-second Street, P.O. Box 473, Woodside, New York 11377. Phone: 1/800-424-BABY or 718/458-5855. Fax: 718/478-2709. Products: Baby baths, baby/child carriers, bath aids/toys, bibs, books, booties/footwear, diaper bags, gift sets, infant feeding items, mirrors, pacifiers, rattles, safety items, toys, bath towels/cloths/robes, bottles.

Remco Baby, Inc. 1107 Broadway, New York, New York 10010. Phone: 212/675-3427. Fax: 212/243-4271. Products: Bibs, gift sets, infant feeding items, mobiles, rattles, toys, bottles.

Rev-A-Shelf, Inc. 2409 Plantside Drive, Jeffersontown, Kentucky 40299. Phone: 1/800-762-9030 or 502/499-5835. Fax: 502/491-2215. Products: Safety items, drawer and cabinet lock.

Riegel—CPD; Mount Vernon Mills, Inc. 1 Riegel Road, Johnston, South Carolina 29832. Phone: 1/800-845-3251 or 803/275-2541. Fax: 803/275-2541. Products: Bumper guards, comforters/quilts, crib sheets, curtains/draperies, diaper stackers, dust ruffles, gift sets, layettes, pillows, receiving blankets, sheets, lap pads, mattress pads, blankets, crib bedding ensembles, toddler bedding.

Rochelle Furniture. P.O. Box 8, Duncannon, Pennsylvania 17020. Phone: 717/834-3031. Fax: 717/834-5561. Products: Cradles, highchairs, rockers, tables and chairs.

Rock A Bye Baby, Inc. 1404 Southwest 13 Court, Pompano Beach, Florida 33069. Phone: 800/762-5229, 305/942-7990. Fax: 305/942-1929. Products: Bath aids/toys, bibs, booties/footwear, gift sets, infant feeding items, safety items, toilet training items, toys, natural audio pacifiers, children's clocks, shopping cart safety seats, infant safety cushions, bath towels/cloths/robes, head supports, wipes and accessories.

Rosalina Baby Collections, Inc. 1017 Pecten Court, Milpitas, California 95035. Phone: 1/800-846-1215 or 408/956-8056. Fax: 408/956-9020. Products: Baby carrier covers, bibs, bumper guards, carriage and stroller pads, comforters/quilts, crib sheets, diaper stackers, dust ruffles, growth charts, picture frames, pillows, rattles, sheets, wall hangings/pictures, fabric bottle warmers, soft educational toys, play bags, tooth fairy pillows, cradle set covers.

Safeline Children's Products Company. 5335 West Forty-eighth Avenue, Suite 300, Denver, Colorado 80212. Phone: 1/800-829-1625 or 303/455-8335. Fax: 303/455-6502. Products: Sit and stroll (a combination carseat/ stroller).

Safety 1st, Inc. 210 Boylston Street, Chestnut Hill, Massachusetts 02167. Phone: 1/800-962-7233 or 617/964-7744. Fax: 617/332-0125. Products: Bath aids/toys, books, booster seats, gates, gift sets, infant feeding items, monitors/intercoms, pacifiers, safety items, toys, head supports, organizers.

Sandbox Industries. P.O. Box 477, Tenafly, New Jersey 07670. Phone: 1/800-451-6636 or 201/567-5696. Fax: 201/567-1455. Products: Bumper guards, car seat covers, carriage and stroller pads, crib sheets, diaper bags, highchair pads, covers for changing table pads and play yard (playpen) pads, rocker covers, sheet protectors.

Sarah's Baby Safety Crib Sheets. P.O. Box 571, Jackson, New Hampshire 03846. Phone: 603/356-9475. Fax: 603/356-6449. Products: Bumper guards, crib sheets, safety items, sheets.

Sassy, Inc. 1534 College S.E., Grand Rapids, Michigan 49507. Phone: 616/243-0767. Fax: 616/243-1042. Products: Baby baths, breast pumps/nursing pads and shields, hook-on chairs, infant feeding items, pacifiers, toilet training items, bouncers.

Sauder Woodworking Co. 502 Middle Street, Archbold, Ohio 43502. Phone: 419/446-2711. Products: Case goods/dressers, toy chests, desks, twin beds.

Selfix, Inc. 4501 West Forty-seventh Street, Chicago, Illinois 60632. Phone: 1/800-327-3534 or 312/890-1010. Fax: 312/890-0523. Products: Decorative items, toy chests, children's hangers, organizers.

Shades of Jade, Inc. 720 Fessey Park Road, Nashville, Tennessee 37204. Phone: 615/298-4056. Fax: 615/298-4081. Products: Decorative items, diaper pails, hampers, lamps, mirrors, rockers, step stools, switch plates, tables and chairs, toy chests, rocking horses, clothes trees, shelves, potty chairs, doll furniture, decorative hats, upholstered stools, youth/teen furniture.

Sherry's Lamps & Etc. 16635 Gemini Lane, Huntington Beach, California 92647. Phone: 714/847-1183. Fax: 714/842-2282. Products: Lamps, switch plates, clocks, nightlights.

Simmons Juvenile Products Co., Inc. 613 East Beacon Avenue, New London, Wisconsin 54961. Phone: 414/982-2140. Fax: 414/982-5052. Products: Baby carrier covers, basket pads, bassinet liners/skirts, bumper guards, bunk beds, canopies, car seat covers, carriage and stroller pads, case goods/dressers, changing/dressing tables, comforters/quilts, cribs, crib mattresses, crib sheets, curtains/draperies, decorative items, diaper stackers, dust ruffles, highchairs, highchair pads, lamps, mattress covers/pads, mirrors, pillows, play yard (playpen) pads, receiving blankets, sheets, wall hangings/pictures, wallpaper and borders, desks, toddler bedding, twin beds, twin bedding, youth/teen furniture.

Simplicity, Inc. 8101 Washington Lane, Wyncote, Pennsylvania 19095. Phone: 1/800-858-8323 or 215/887-7608. Fax: 215/887-6612. Product: Cribs.

Small Potatoes, Inc. 2505 Stone Creek Drive, Plano, Texas 75075. Phone: 214/596-5027. Products: Step stools, tables and chairs.

Small World Toys. 5711 Buckingham Parkway, Culver City, California 90230-6515. Phone: 1/800-421-4153 or 310/645-9680. Fax: 310/410-9606. Products: Bath aids/toys, books, decorative items, mobiles, rockers, toys.

Smile Tote, Inc. 12979 Culver Boulevard, Los Angeles, California 90066. Phone: 1/800-826-6130 or 310/827-0156. Fax: 301/827-2576. Products: Infant feeding items, infant dispensing traveling juice cups, easy-to-hold sippers, toddler tumblers, nipple stoppers, juice boxes/holders/accessories.

Snap Ups. 131 West Thirty-third Street, 5th Floor, New York, New York 10001. Phone: 212/244-6440. Fax: 212/239-0696. Products: Bibs, booties/footwear, diaper bags, gift sets, infant feeding items, layettes, pacifiers, rattles, receiving blankets, toys, socks, 100 percent cotton coordinates, hats, bath towels/cloths/ robes.

The Softer Image. 1155B Chess Drive, Unit G, Foster City, California 94404. Phone: 1/800-528-8887 or 415/571-6606. Fax: 415/571-1948. Products: Breast pumps/nursing pads and shields, infant feeding items, bottles.

Spartus Home Furnishings. 3250 North Arlington Heights Road, Arlington Heights, Illinois 60004. Phone: 708/870-7777. Fax: 708/870-9914. Products: Lamps, wall and alarm clocks, clock radios, night lamps.

Spectrum Juvenile Products, Inc. 1974 Ohio Street, Lisle, Illinois 60532. Phone: 1/800-343-4945 or 708/852-9585. Fax: 708/852-9794. Products: Baby/child carriers, bed guards, carriages, diaper bags, infant feeding items, mobiles, strollers, toys, walkers, bouncers.

Stork Craft. 11511 #5 Road, Richmond, British Columbia, Canada V7A 4E8. Phone: 604/274-5121. Fax: 604/274-9727. Products: Changing/dressing tables, cradles, cribs, toddler beds.

Strolee. 6430 Variel Avenue, Suite 105, Woodland Hills, California 91367. Phone: 1/800-829-4488 or 818/346-5200. Fax: 818/346-5700. Products: Baby/child carriers, carriages, gates, highchairs, hook-on chairs, monitors/intercoms, strollers, walkers.

Sumersault, Ltd. P.O. Box 269, Scarsdale, New York 10583. Phone: 1/800-232-3006 or 201/768-7890. Fax: 201/768-4909. Products: Bumper guards, comforters/quilts, crib sheets, diaper stackers, dust ruffles, pillows, sheets, wall hangings/pictures, wallpaper and borders, bunk covers/sheets/pillowcases/dust ruffles, decorative and floor cushions,

laundry bags, crib bedding ensembles, toddler bedding, twin bedding.

Summer Infant Products, Inc. 33 Meeting Street, Cumberland, Rhode Island 02864. Phone: 401/725-8286. Fax: 401/725-7019. Products: Baby/child carriers, toys, infant bouncer seats with accessories, baby teething toys, bouncers.

Super Plastic, Inc. 5790 West Washington Boulevard, Culver City, California 90232. Phone: 1/800-545-7438 or 213/965-5590. Fax: 213/965-5592. Products: Gift sets, pacifiers, bottles.

Surya Carpet, Inc. 1000 Castle Road, Secaucus, New Jersey 07094. Phone: 1/800-397-4499 or 201/864-1772. Fax: 201/864-0171. Product: Rugs.

Sweetpea of California. P.O. Box 90756, Pasadena, California 91109-0756. Phone: 818/578-0866. Fax: 818/304-0864. Products: Bumper guards, canopies, car seat covers, carriage and stroller pads, comforters/quilts, crib sheets, decorative items, diaper bags, diaper stackers, dust ruffles, highchair pads, pillows, receiving blankets, sheets, toy bags, stuffed animals, tablecloths, glider/rocker covers, blankets, crib bedding ensembles, toddler bedding, twin bedding.

Tabor Designs. 8220 West Thirtieth Court, Hialeah, Florida 33016. Phone: 1/800-822-6748 or 305/557-1481. Fax: 305/362-7884. Products: Case goods/dressers, changing/dressing tables, cradles, cribs, decorative items, rockers, tables and chairs, toy chests, youth/teen furniture.

Tailored Baby, Inc. 19351 Londelius Street, Northridge, California 91324. Phone: 818/727-9024. Fax: 818/727-0206. Products: Baby carrier covers, bassinet liners/skirts, bibs, bumper guards, car seat covers, carriage and stroller pads, comforters/quilts, crib sheets, diaper bags, diaper stackers, dust ruffles, gift sets, highchair pads, mattress covers/pads, pillows, play yard (playpen) pads, receiving blankets, safety items, sheets, washcloths, crib netting, sheet savers, diaper covers/wraps, head supports.

Tennessee Woolen Mills. 2451 Atrium Way, Suite 209, Nashville, Tennessee 37214. Phone: 1/800-950-9665 or 615/391-4235. Fax: 615/391-4250. Products: Buntings, baby warmers, blankets.

Terraillon Corporation 700 Canal Street, Stamford, Connecticut 06902. Phone: 203/328-3715. Fax: 203/328-3716, Product: Scales.

Texas Instruments 7800 Banner Drive, Dallas, Texas 75265. Phone: 1/800-842-2737 or 806/741-4812. Product: Toys.

3 Marthas, Inc. 159 Cole Street, Dallas, Texas 75207. Phone: 1/800-553-8058 or 214/747-0022. Fax: 214/742-1110. Products: Bath aids/toys, bibs, buntings, receiving blankets, bath aprons, changing pads, burp pads, slippers, bath towels/cloths/robes, diaper covers/wraps.

The Three Weavers. 150 Bennington Street, Suite A, Houston, Texas 77022. Phone: 1/800-526-5929 or 713/697-3995. Fax: 713/697-9548. Products: Buntings, comforters/quilts, handwoven baby blankets, blankets.

TL Care, Inc. P.O. Box 77087, San Francisco, California 94107. Phone: 415/626-3127. Fax: 415/626-2983. Products: Bibs, booties/footwear, breast pumps/nursing pads and shields, gift sets, layettes, toilet training items, diaper pants, diaper doublers, bath towels/cloths/robes, diapers (cloth), diaper covers/wraps.

Today's Kids. 13630 Neutron Road, Dallas, Texas 75244. Phone: 214/404-9335. Fax: 214/404-9227. Products: Swings, toys.

Toddler Bobbler Products Inc. 1035 Toy Avenue, Unit #16, Pickering, Ontario, Canada L1W 3N9. Phone: 416/619-1600. Fax: 416/619-1603. Product: Exercisers.

Tot, Inc. 2139 Wisconsin Avenue, N.W., P.O. Box 32239, Washington, D.C. 20007. Phone: 202/337-1177. Fax: 202/337-1007. Products: Bibs, decorative items, mirrors, mobiles, picture frames, rattles, toys.

Totally Toddler (Division of Out! International, Inc.). P.O. Box 227215, Dallas, Texas 75222-7215. Phone: 1/800-527-9919 or 214/438-0157. Fax: 213/438-0959. Products: Nursery cleaning products, nursery deodorizers, nursery stain and odor removers and air fresheners.

Tots in Mind, Inc. 290 Broadway, Suite 405, Methuen, Massachusetts 01844. Phone: 1/800-626-0339 or 508/688-4684. Fax: 508/794-9628. Product: Safety items.

Towne Square Furniture, Inc. P.O. Box 419, 402 Hawkins Street, Hillsboro, Texas 76645. Phone: 1/800-356-1663 or 817/582-7444. Product: Rockers (adult/child/glider).

Tracers Furniture, Inc. 30 Warren Place, Mount Vernon, New York 10550. Phone: 914/668-9372. Fax: 914/668-9368. Products: Bibs, bunk beds, case goods/dressers, changing/dressing tables, cradles, cribs, youth/teen furniture.

Treetop Collection. 614 East Purl Street, Goshen, Indiana 46526. Phone: 219/534-5080. Fax: 219/533-4017. Products: Rockers, tables and chairs, toy chests, desks, toddler beds, youth/teen furniture.

Triboro Quilt Manufacturing Corp. 172 South Broadway, White

Plains, New York 10605. Phone: 914/428-7551. Fax: 914/428-0610. Products: Bumper guards, comforters/quilts, crib sheets, dust ruffles, gift sets, layettes, pillows, receiving blankets, hooded towels, blankets, blanket sleepers, pramsuits, sleep and play baby garments.

TRI Industries, Inc. 7401 Washington Avenue South, Edina, Minnesota 55439. Phone: 1/800-242-6110 or 612/944-5198. Fax: 612/944-5093. Products: Strollers, jogging strollers, bicycle trailer and jogging stroller combinations.

Two Little Girls Inc. 617 Huntington Avenue, San Bruno, California 94066. Phone: 1/800-437-2229 or 415/873-2229. Fax: 417/873-0498. Products: Sun protection products, all-weather gear.

Tyke Corporation. 3838 West Fifty-first Street, Chicago, Illinois 60632. Phone: 1/800-533-8953 or 312/284-5660. Fax: 312/284-8644. Products: Bibs, books, booster seats, diaper bags, rockers, tables and chairs, toys, toy chests, easels, dinner ware, luggage, lunch boxes, slippers, bath towels/cloths/robes.

Unisar, Inc. 151 West Nineteenth Street, New York, New York 10011. Phone: 212/989-5219. Fax: 212/691-1318. Products: Audiocassettes, monitors/intercoms, prenatal listening kits, videotapes.

Up and Adam, Inc. P.O. Box 2953, 3 Pierce Street, Framingham, Massachusetts 01701. Phone: 508/626-2439. Fax: 508/879-9737. Products: Infant feeding items, plastic and nylon lunch bags, insulated drink carriers, juice boxes/holders/accessories.

Vencor International, Inc. 2768 Loker Avenue West, Suite #100, Carlsbad, California 92008. Phone: 619/438-1701. Fax: 619/438-4552. Products: Bibs, diaper stackers, gift sets, diapers (cloth), diaper covers/wraps, head supports.

Weebok (Reebok International). 11835 West Olympic Boulevard, Suite 350, Los Angeles, California 90064. Phone: 310/312-8004. Products: Booties/footwear, diaper bags, layettes, strollers, infant/toddler clothing, caps, baby wraps.

Welcome to the World. 319 Manley Street, West Bridgewater, Massachusetts 02379. Phone: 508/588-5555. Fax: 508/588-3838. Products: Baskets, bibs, booties/footwear, gift sets, infant feeding items, picture frames, rattles, receiving blankets, toys, quilted and appliqued bottle covers, combs, brushes, teethers, bath towels/cloths/robes, bottles.

Welsh Company. 1535 South Eighth Street, St. Louis, Missouri 63104. Phone: 314/231-8822. Fax: 314/231-7108. Products: Bed guards, carriages, case goods/dressers, cradles, cribs, crib mattresses, highchairs, play yards (playpens), rockers, strollers, tables and chairs, toy chests, walkers.

Westech U.S.A. Inc. 575 Morgan Boulevard, Baie D'Urfe, Quebec, Canada H9X 3T6. Phone: 1/800-934-4646 or 514/457-0099. Fax: 514/457-7525. Products: Safety items, car shoulder belt relocation devices.

White Wicker Company. 4400 Southwestern Boulevard, Dallas, Texas 75225. Phone: 214/368-4811. Products: Decorative items, highchairs, rockers, tables and chairs, toy chests.

Wimmer-Ferguson Child Products, Inc. P.O. Box 100427, Denver, Colorado 80250. Phone: 1/800-747-2454 or 303/733-0848. Fax: 303/777-1510. High-contrast black and white toys for infants.

Wood Model Shop. 330 Main Street, Scandinavia, Wisconsin 54977. Phone: 1/800-344-6493 or 715/467-2780. Fax: 715/467-2704. Products: Bunk beds, case goods/dressers, mirrors, toy chests, desks, twin beds, youth/teen furniture.

Zak Designs, Inc. 2010 West Sixty-second Street, Los Angeles, California 90047-1345. Phone: 1/800-331-1089 or 213/751-1575. Fax: 213/751-0717. Products: Infant feeding items, children melamine dinnerware, flatware, placemats, acrylic tumblers, infant/toddler drinkware, dinnerware.

Zoptics Sunglasses. 723 East Patapsco Avenue, Baltimore, Maryland 21225. Phone: 1/800-533-7050 or 410/355-7050. Fax: 410/355-3527, Product: Sunglasses.

PRODUCT LISTINGS BY CATEGORY

Baby Baths

Baby World
Binky Griptight
Century
Cosco
First Years
Fisher-Price
Gerry Baby
G. W. DMKA
Infantino
Luv N' Care
Mericon
Michael Friedman
Mini Togs/Panda Knits
Nursery Needs by Sanitoy
Pansy Ellen
Peg Perego
Playskool Baby
Regal Lager
Regent Baby
Sassy

Baby Carrier Covers

Basic Comfort
Bebe Chic
Brandee Danielle
Calico Cottage
Diplomat
Glenna Jean
Gold Bug
Hoopla
Kalencom
Kidsline
Lambs and Ivy
Luv Stuff
Once Upon a Whimsy
Patsy Aiken Designs
Rosalina Baby
Simmons
Tailored Baby

Baby/Child Carriers

Babies Alley
Baby World
Badger Basket
Bambineto
Basic Comfort
Binky Griptight
Century
Children on the Go
Cosco
D and F Wicker
Delta
Evenflo Furniture
Gerry Baby
Graco
Handy Chair
Infantino
J. Mason
Kinderkids
Kolcraft
Koolkids
Leachco
Medela
Nogatco
NoJo
Nursery Needs by Sanitoy
Peg Perego
Playskool Baby

Regal Lager
Regent Baby
Spectrum
Strolee
Summer Infant

Basket Pads

Badger Basket
Basic Comfort
Colgate Mattress
Evenflo Furniture
Fine Art Pillow
Kids Basics
Kinderkids
Kolcraft
Marshall Baby
Simmons

Baskets

Comfort Silkie
D and F Wicker
Infinitely Infants
Kidsline
Kinderkids
Marshall Baby
MM's Designs
Nursery Needs by Sanitoy
Welcome to the World

Bassinet Liners/Skirts

Baby Doll Infants Wear
Badger Basket
Basic Comfort
California Kids
Diplomat
Kidsline
Li'l Partners
Nava's Designs
Redmon
Simmons
Tailored Baby

Bassinets

Alma's Designs
Badger Basket
Bambineto
Bandaks Emmaljunga

Burlington Basket
D and F Wicker
Delta
Fantasy Bed
Fisher-Price
Inglesina
Kidsline
Kinderkids
Peg Perego
Preston International
Redmon

Bath Aids/Toys

American Baby Concepts
Baby World
Babygund
Binky Griptight
Century
Comfort Silkie
Convenience Kits
Dakin
Danara
Diplomat
Direct Connect
First Years
Fisher-Price
Gerber Products
Gerry Baby
G. W. DMKA
Handy Chair
Kel-Gar
Kidentials
Koolkids
Lamby Nursery
Leachco
Luv N' Care
Michael Friedman
Mini Togs/Panda Knits
Nursery Needs by Sanitoy
Pansy Ellen
Pinky Baby
Playskool Baby
Prince Lionheart
Railnet
Regent Baby
Rock A Bye Baby
Safety 1st
Small World Toys
3 Marthas

Bath Towels/Cloths/Robes

Basic Comfort
Bathtime Baby
Bebe Chic
Bumkins
Crib Critters
Eastwood
Gerber Childrenswear
Gerry Baby
Hamco
Hoopla
House of Hatten
Infinitely Infants
J. E. Morgan
Luv N' Care
Mini Togs/Panda Knits
NoJo
Palais Royal
Regent Baby
Rock A Bye Baby
Snap Ups
3 Marthas
TL Care
Tyke
Welcome to the World

Bed Guards

Cosco
Delta
Fantasy Bed
Fisher-Price
Gerry Baby
G. W. DMKA
Lepine Furniture
Luv Stuff
Morigeau
Pride-Trimble
Spectrum
Welsh

Bibs

American Baby Concepts
Americare
Baby World
Bathtime Baby
Bebe Chic
Binky Griptight
Bumkins

Cherubs Collection
Crib Critters
Daisy Kingdom
Danara
Evenflo Products
Gerber Childrenswear
Gerber Products
Hamco
Handy Chair
Hoopla
House of Hatten
Infinitely Infants
Kooshies
Kubla Crafts
Luv N' Care
Merri-Tots
Michael Friedman
Miller Enterprises
Mini Togs/Panda Knits
MM's Designs
Munchkin
Nursery Needs by Sanitoy
Palais Royal
PatchKraft
Pinky Baby
Playskool Baby
Quiltex
Railnet
Regal Lager
Regent Baby
Remco Baby
Rock A Bye Baby
Rosalina Baby
Snap Ups
Tailored Baby
3 Marthas
TL Care
Tot, Inc.
Tracers
Tyke
Vencor
Welcome to the World

Blankets (Crib/Juvenile)

American Pacific
Beacon
Beautiful Baby
Bebe Chic
Bedtime Originals

Bumkins
Charles Owen
Children's Factory
Comfort Silkie
Crib Critters
Cuddle Time
Dundee
Fieldcrest
Gerber Childrenswear
Glenna Jean
Greenleaf
Health-Tex
Hoopla
J. E. Morgan
Lambs and Ivy
Lamby Nursery
Luv N' Care
Luv Stuff
Mini Togs/Panda Knits
Nava's Designs
NoJo
PatchKraft
Riegel
Sweetpea
Tennessee Woolen
The Three Weavers

Booster Seats

Century
Cosco
Creative Playthings
Dolly
Fisher-Price
Gerry Baby
Kolcraft
Little Tikes
Nursery Needs by Sanitoy
Pansy Ellen
Playskool Baby
Pride-Trimble
Regal Lager
Safety 1st
Tyke

Booties/Footwear

American Baby Concepts
Bathtime Baby
Comfort Silkie
Crib Critters

Dundee
First Years
Gerber Childrenswear
Gerber Products
Gold Bug
Hoopla
Infinitely Infants
Kidentials
Lamby Nursery
Luv N' Care
Mini Togs/Panda Knits
Playskool Baby
Regent Baby
Rock A Bye Baby
Snap Ups
TL Care
Weebok
Welcome to the World

Bottles

American Baby Concepts
Avent
Babies Are #1
Camp Kazoo
Cherubs Collection
Cudlie
Danara
Evenflo Products
Gerber Products
Infinitely Infants
Luv N' Care
Merri-Tots
Mini Togs/Panda Knits
Munchkin
Playtex
Prince Lionheart
Regent Baby
Remco Baby
Softer Image
Super Plastic
Welcome to the World

Bouncers

J. Mason
Jolly Jumper
Kinderkids
Koolkids
Regal Lager
Sassy

Spectrum
Summer Infant

Breast Pumps/Nursing Pads and Shields

Avent
Evenflo Products
Gerber Products
Graham-Field
G. W. DMKA
Handy Chair
Kidentials
Kooshies
Marshall Baby
Medela
Sassy
Softer Image
TL Care

Bumper Guards

Alma's Designs
American Pacific
Baby Doll Infants Wear
Baby Dreams
Baby Duckies
Baby Face
Beautiful Baby
Bebe Chic
Bedtime Originals
Brandee Danielle
Calico Cottage
California Kids
The Carousel
Carousel Designs
Celebrations
Charles Owen
Clothworks
Colgate Mattress
Cotton Tale Designs
Cuddle Time
Daisy Kingdom
Dandelion
Delta
Diplomat
Dundee Mills/Fisher-Price
Evenflo Furniture
Fine Art Pillow
Gerber Childrenswear
Glenna Jean

Greenleaf
Health-Tex
Hoopla
House of Hatten
Judi's Originals
Kidsline
Lambs and Ivy
Leachco
Lean on Me
Li'l Partners
Little Bedding
Little Vikings
Luv Stuff
Nava's Designs
NoJo
Okla Homer Smith
Once Upon a Whimsy
Palais Royal
PatchKraft
Pine Creek
Quiltcraft Kids
Quiltex
Red Calliope
Reflections
Riegel
Rosalina Baby
Sandbox
Sarah's Safety Sheets
Simmons
Sumersault
Sweetpea
Tailored Baby
Triboro Quilt

Bunk Beds

Canwood
Child Craft
Cosco
Creative Playthings
Fantasy Bed
Harper Design
Le Clair
Morigeau
Pieces of Dreams
Powell
Simmons
Tracers
Wood Model

Buntings

Baby Bag
Bambineto
Basic Comfort
Beacon
Bebe Chic
Comfort Silkie
Cotton Tale Designs
Delta
Kinderkids
Palais Royal
Quiltex
Tennessee Woolen
3 Marthas
The Three Weavers

Canopies

Artsana of America
Baby Face
Beautiful Baby
Brandee Danielle
California Kids
The Carousel
Carousel Designs
Celebrations
Child Craft
Clothworks
Cotton Tale Designs
Daisy Kingdom
Delta
Fantasy Bed
Glenna Jean
Greenleaf
Judi's Originals
Kidsline
Kidstuff Pals
Kinderkids
Lambs and Ivy
Li'l Partners
Little Vikings
Lullabye
Luv Stuff
Marshall Baby
NoJo
Once Upon a Whimsy
PatchKraft
Patsy Aiken Designs
Quiltex

Racing Strollers
Red Calliope
Simmons
Sweetpea

Carriage and Stroller Pads

Americare
Aprica
Babies Alley
Bandaks Emmaljunga
Basic Comfort
Beautiful Baby
Bebe Chic
Brandee Danielle
Calico Cottage
Cudlie
Delta
Diplomat
Hanseatic
Inglesina
Kalencom
Kids Basics
Kidsline
Lambs and Ivy
Lamby Nursery
Li'l Partners
Little Vikings
Luv Stuff
NoJo
Once Upon a Whimsy
PatchKraft
Rosalina Baby
Sandbox
Simmons
Sweetpea
Tailored Baby

Carriages

Aprica
Artsana of America
Baby Trend
Bandaks Emmaljunga
Century
Combi
Daust
Delta
Hanseatic
Inglesina
J. Mason

Jolly Jumper
Kinderkids
Kolcraft
Marshall Baby
Nelson Juvenile
Nogatco
Peg Perego
Spectrum
Strolee
Welsh

Car Seat Covers

Baby Duckies
Basic Comfort
Beautiful Baby
Bebe Chic
Brandee Danielle
Calico Cottage
Century
Cotton Tale Designs
Daisy Kingdom
Diplomat
First Years
Gold Bug
Hoopla
Judi's Originals
Kalencom
Kidsline
Lambs and Ivy
Lamby Nursery
Leachco
Little Bedding
Luv Stuff
NoJo
Once Upon a Whimsy
Pansy Ellen
Red Calliope
Sandbox
Simmons
Sweetpea
Tailored Baby

Car Seats

All Our Kids
Century
Cosco
Evenflo Furniture
FBS/Renolux
Fisher-Price

Gerry Baby
Kolcraft
Pride-Trimble
Safeline

Case Goods/Dressers

Bassett
C and T International
Canwood
Child Craft
Cosco
Delta
G. W. DMKA
Lea Industries
Le Clair
Lepine Furniture
Little Tikes
Lullabye
Meg
Million Dollar Baby
Morigeau
Nelson Juvenile
Pali
Pat Higdon
Pieces of Dreams
Powell
Preston International
Sauder Woodworking
Simmons
Tabor
Tracers
Welsh
Wood Model Shop

Changing/Dressing Tables

Badger Basket
Bassett
Brandee Danielle
Burlington Basket
C and T International
Child Craft
Cosco
Delta
Evenflo Furniture
Fantasy Bed
Gerry Baby
G. W. DMKA
J. Mason
Jonica

Koolkids
Lepine Furniture
Little Tikes
Lullabye
Meg
Million Dollar Baby
Morigeau
Nelson Juvenile
Okla Homer Smith
Pat Higdon
Peg Perego
Preston International
Pride-Trimble
Rainbow Mountain
Redmon
Regal Lager
Simmons
Stork Craft
Tabor
Tracers

Comforters/Quilts

Alma's Designs
American Pacific
Baby Doll Infants Wear
Baby Dreams
Baby Duckies
Baby Face
Badger Basket
Beautiful Baby
Bebe Chic
Bedtime Originals
Brandee Danielle
Calico Cottage
California Feather
California Kids
The Carousel
Carousel Designs
Celebrations
Charles Owen
Clothworks
Comfort Silkie
Cotton Tale Designs
Cuddle Time
Daisy Kingdom
Dandelion
Delta
Diplomat
Dundee Mills/Fisher-Price

Fine Art Pillow
Gerber Childrenswear
Glenna Jean
Greenleaf
Health-Tex
Hoopla
House of Hatten
Impressions
Infantino
Judi's Originals
Kidsline
Kidstuff Pals
Kubla Crafts
Lambs and Ivy
Li'l Partners
Little Bedding
Little Vikings
Luv Stuff
Nava's Designs
New Spring
NoJo
Once Upon a Whimsy
Palais Royal
Pansy Ellen
PatchKraft
Patsy Aiken Designs
Pine Creek
Quiltcraft Kids
Quiltex
Red Calliope
Reflections
Riegel
Rosalina Baby
Simmons
Sumersault
Sweetpea
Tailored Baby
The Three Weavers
Triboro Quilt

Cradles

Badger Basket
C and T International
Cosco
D and F Wicker
Delta
Evenflo Furniture
Fantasy Bed
Gerry Baby

G. W. DMKA
Jonica
Kinderkids
Little Colorado
Million Dollar Baby
Nelson Juvenile
Okla Homer Smith
Pali
Pat Higdon
Pieces of Dreams
Rainbow Mountain
Rochelle Furniture
Stork Craft
Tabor
Tracers
Welsh

Crib Bedding Ensembles

Alma's Designs
Baby Face
Bambineto
Beautiful Baby
Bedtime Originals
The Carousel
Carousel Designs
Charles Owen
Clothworks
Cotton Tale Designs
Delta
Diplomat
Dundee Mills/Fisher-Price
Ecology Kids
Gerber Childrenswear
Greenleaf
House of Hatten
Judi's Originals
Kidsline
Lambs and Ivy
Lundy Look
Luv Stuff
Nava's Designs
NoJo
Once Upon a Whimsy
Palais Royal
PatchKraft
Pine Creek
Reflections
Riegel
Sumersault
Sweetpea

Crib Mattresses

Bo Peep
Child Craft
Colgate Mattress
Cosco
Delta
Evenflo Furniture
Fisher-Price
Gerry Baby
Kids Basics
Kolcraft
Meg
Okla Homer Smith
Simmons
Welsh

Cribs

Bassett
C and T International
Child Craft
Cosco
Daust
Delta
Evenflo Furniture
Fantasy Bed
Gerry Baby
G. W. DMKA
J. Mason
Jonica
Koolkids
Lea Industries
Lepine Furniture
Lullabye
Meg
Million Dollar Baby
Morigeau
Nelson Juvenile
Nogatco
Okla Homer Smith
Pali
Pat Higdon
Preston International
Rainbow Mountain
Simmons
Simplicity
Stork Craft
Tabor
Tracers
Welsh

Crib Sheets

Baby Doll Infants Wear
Baby Dreams
Baby Face
Beautiful Baby
Bebe Chic
Bedtime Originals
Brandee Danielle
Calico Cottage
California Kids
The Carousel
Carousel Designs
Celebrations
Charles Owens
Children's Factory
Clothworks
Cotton Tale Designs
Crib Critters
Cuddle Time
Daisy Kingdom
Delta
Diplomat
Dundee Mills/Fisher-Price
Ecology Kids
Fine Art Pillow
Gerber Childrenswear
Gerry Baby
Glenna Jean
Greenleaf
Health-Tex
House of Hatten
Judi's Originals
Kidsline
Koolkids
Lambs and Ivy
Leachco
Li'l Partners
Little Bedding
Little Vikings
Luv Stuff
Nava's Designs
NoJo
Once Upon a Whimsy
Palais Royal
PatchKraft
Patsy Aiken Designs
Quiltcraft Kids
Quiltex
Red Calliope

Reflections
Riegel
Rosalina Baby
Sandbox
Sarah's Safety Sheets
Simmons
Sumersault
Sweetpea
Tailored Baby
Triboro Quilt

Curtains/Draperies

Baby Face
Beautiful Baby
Calico Cottage
The Carousel
Cotton Tale Designs
Diplomat
Dundee Mills/Fisher-Price
Ecology Kids
Gerber Childrenswear
Glenna Jean
Judi's Originals
Kidsline
Luv Stuff
PatchKraft
Quiltcraft Kids
Red Calliope
Reflections
Riegel
Simmons

Decorative Items

American Baby Concepts
Bathtime Baby
The Carousel
Celebrations
Children's Factory
Cotton Tale Designs
Country Carver
Cudlie
Daisy Kingdom
Dakin
Delta
Diplomat
Dolly
Guri
House of Hatten
Inmon Enterprises

Keeper's Kidstuff
Kiddie Lites
Kidstuff Pals
Kubla Crafts
Luv N' Care
Luv Stuff
Michael Friedman
Mini Togs/Panda Knits
Nava's Designs
NoJo
Offspring
Once Upon a Whimsy
Palais Royal
Pansy Ellen
PatchKraft
Pippen Hill
Pockets of Learning
Powell
Prince Lionheart
Priss Prints
Quiltex
Redmon
Selfix
Shades of Jade
Simmons
Small World Toys
Sweetpea
Tabor
Tot, Inc.
White Wicker

Desks

Cosco
Kid Craft
Le Clair
Lepine Furniture
Morigeau
Powell
Sauder Woodworking
Simmons
Treetop
Wood Model

Diaper Bags

American Baby Concepts
Aprica
Babi Bags by Romar
Babies Alley
Baby Doll Infants Wear

Bambineto
Beautiful Baby
Bebe Chic
Boston Bag
Calico Cottage
Cotton Tale Designs
Cudlie
Danara
Dolly
Hoopla
House of Hatten
Inglesina
J. L. Childress
Kalencom
Li'l Partners
Luv Stuff
Nava's Designs
NoJo
Once Upon a Whimsy
Palais Royal
PatchKraft
Patsy Aiken Designs
Playskool Baby
Proteus
Railnet
Regal Lager
Regent Baby
Sandbox
Snap Ups
Spectrum
Sweetpea
Tailored Baby
Tyke
Weebok

Diaper Covers/Wraps

Bumkins
Diplomat
Ecology Kids
Gerber Childrenswear
Handy Chair
Kooshies
Mini Togs/Panda Knits
Pinky Baby
Tailored Baby
3 Marthas
TL Care
Vencor

Diaper Pails

Baby World
Binky Griptight
First Years
Fisher-Price
Gerry Baby
G. W. DMKA
Little Tikes
Michael Friedman
Nursery Needs by Sanitoy
Shades of Jade

Diapers (Cloth)

American Fiber
Americare
Bumkins
Diplomat
Ecology Kids
Gerber Childrenswear
Handy Chair
Kooshies
Nikky
TL Care
Vencor

Diaper Stackers

Baby Dreams
Baby Face
Bambineto
Beautiful Baby
Bebe Chic
Bedtime Originals
Brandee Danielle
Calico Cottage
California Kids
The Carousel
Carousel Designs
Celebrations
Clothworks
Cotton Tale Designs
Daisy Kingdom
Diplomat
Dundee Mills/Fisher-Price
Ecology Kids
Gerber Childrenswear
Glenna Jean
House of Hatten
Judi's Originals

Kidsline
Lambs and Ivy
Li'l Partners
Little Bedding
Little Vikings
Luv N' Care
Luv Stuff
Mini Togs/Panda Knits
Nava's Designs
NoJo
Once Upon a Whimsy
Palais Royal
PatchKraft
Patsy Aiken Designs
Quiltcraft Kids
Quiltex
Red Calliope
Riegel
Rosalina Baby
Simmons
Sumersault
Sweetpea
Tailored Baby
Vencor

Dust Ruffles

Baby Dreams
Baby Duckies
Baby Face
Beautiful Baby
Bebe Chic
Bedtime Originals
Brandee Danielle
Calico Cottage
California Kids
The Carousel
Carousel Designs
Celebrations
Charles Owen
Clothworks
Cotton Tale Designs
Crib Critters
Cuddle Time
Daisy Kingdom
Delta
Diplomat
Dundee Mills/Fisher-Price
Ecology Kids
Fine Art Pillow

Gerber Childrenswear
Glenna Jean
Greenleaf
Health-Tex
House of Hatten
Judi's Originals
Kidsline
Kidstuff Pals
Lambs and Ivy
Li'l Partners
Little Bedding
Little Vikings
Luv Stuff
Nava's Designs
NoJo
Once Upon a Whimsy
PatchKraft
Patsy Aiken Designs
Pieces of Dreams
Pine Creek
Quiltcraft Kids
Quiltex
Red Calliope
Reflections
Riegel
Rosalina Baby
Simmons
Sumersault
Sweetpea
Tailored Baby
Triboro Quilt

Gates

All Our Kids
Century
Fisher-Price
Gerry Baby
Kids Basics
Lear Siegler
North States
Railnet
Safety 1st
Strolee

Gift Sets

Babi Bags by Romar
Baby Dreams
Baby World
Bathtime Baby

Betlar
Charles Owen
Cherubs Collection
Children on the Go
Comfort Silkie
Convenience Kits
Cuddle Time
Cudlie
Danara
Diplomat
Direct Connect
Dundee Mills/Fisher-Price
Eagle Affiliates
Ecology Kids
Eden Toys
Evenflo Products
First Years
Gerber Childrenswear
Gerber Products
Gerry Baby
G. W. DMKA
Hamco
Handy Chair
Health-Tex
House of Hatten
Infinitely Infants
Kidentials
Koolkids
Leachco
Luv N' Care
Merri-Tots
Mini Togs/Panda Knits
Nursery Needs by Sanitoy
Once Upon a Whimsy
Pansy Ellen
PatchKraft
Pecoware
Playskool Baby
Playtex
Powell
Prince Lionheart
Quiltex
Regent Baby
Remco Baby
Riegel
Rock A Bye Baby
Safety 1st
Snap Ups
Super Plastic
Tailored Baby

TL Care
Triboro Quilt
Vencor
Welcome to the World

Growth Charts

Capaz
Children's Factory
Clinton Prints
C. R. Gibson
Keeper's KidStuff
Kubla Crafts
MM's Designs
Pieces of Dreams
Pippen Hill
Priss Prints
Rosalina Baby

Hampers

Badger Basket
Burlington Basket
D and F Wicker
Gerber Products
Pride-Trimble
Redmon
Shades of Jade

Head Supports

Basic Comfort
Brandee Danielle
Camp Kazoo
Diplomat
Ecology Kids
Gold Bug
Judi's Originals
Kalencom
Kidsline
Lambs and Ivy
Leachco
Little Bedding
Luv N' Care
Mini Togs/Panda Knits
Red Calliope
Rock A Bye Baby
Safety 1st
Tailored Baby
Vencor

Highchair Pads

Artsana of America
Basic Comfort
Beautiful Baby
Brandee Danielle
Carousel Designs
Clothworks
Colgate Mattress
Diplomat
Evenflo Furniture
Glenna Jean
Hoopla
Judi's Originals
Kids Basics
Lambs and Ivy
Leachco
Little Vikings
Mericon
NoJo
PatchKraft
Sandbox
Simmons
Sweetpea
Tailored Baby

Highchairs

Aprica
Artsana of America
Baby Trend
C and T International
Century
Child Craft
Cosco
Creative Playthings
Delta
Evenflo Furniture
Fisher-Price
Gerry Baby
Graco
Infantino
Jonica
Kidsline
Kinderkids
Kolcraft
Lepine Furniture
Little Tikes
Marshall Baby
Million Dollar Baby

Morigeau
Nelson Juvenile
Peg Perego
Pride-Trimble
Rainbow Mountain
Regal Lager
Rochelle Furniture
Simmons
Strolee
Welsh
White Wicker

Hook-On Chairs

Baby Trend
Graco
Handy Chair
Nelson Juvenile
Sassy
Strolee

Humidifier/Vaporizer and Accessories

Avent
DeVilbiss

Infant Feeding Items

Adorable Baby
American Baby Concepts
Ansa
Avent
Babi Bags by Romar
Babies Are #1
Baby Buddies
Baby World
Basic Comfort
Binky Griptight
Cherubs Collection
Danara
Evenflo Products
First Years
Fisher-Price
Gerber Products
Graham-Field
Handy Chair
Infinitely Infants
Kidentials
Leachco
Lean on Me

Little Kids
Luv N' Care
Marshall Baby
Maya
Medela
Merri-Tots
Michael Friedman
Mini Togs/Panda Knits
Mommy's Helper
Nursery Needs by Sanitoy
Ocean Shore
Pansy Ellen
Pecoware
Pinky Baby
Playskool Baby
Playtech
Playtex
Prince Lionheart
Regent Baby
Remco Baby
Rock A Bye Baby
Safety 1st
Sassy
Smile Tote
Snap Ups
Softer Image
Spectrum
Up and Adam
Welcome to the World
Zak

Juice Boxes/Holders/Accessories

Danara
Fun Designs
Gerber Products
J. L. Childress
Little Kids
Mommy's Helper
Smile Tote
Up and Adam

Jumpers

Cosco
Evenflo Furniture
Fisher-Price
Graco
Jolly Jumper

Lamps

ADI Lamps
Baby Face
Betlar
Brandee Danielle
Carousel Designs
Clothworks
Cosco
Cotton Tale Designs
Daisy Kingdom
D and F Wicker
Dolly
Fisher-Price
Harper Design
Inmon Enterprises
Jolly Jumper
Judi's Originals
Kiddie Lites
Lambs and Ivy
Little Bedding
Little Colorado
MM's Designs
NoJo
Patsy Aiken Designs
Pippen Hill
Powell
Rainbow Mountain
Red Calliope
Shades of Jade
Sherry's Lamps
Simmons
Spartus

Layettes

Boston Bag
Comfort Silkie
Cuddle Time
Diplomat
Dundee Mills/Fisher-Price
Ecology Kids
Gerber Childrenswear
Greenleaf
Health-Tex
House of Hatten
Luv N' Care
Mini Togs/Panda Knits
Patsy Aiken Designs
Quiltex

Riegel
Snap Ups
TL Care
Triboro Quilt
Weebok

Mattress Covers/Pads

American Baby Concepts
Americare
Basic Comfort
Colgate Mattress
Delta
Diplomat
Ecology Kids
Gerry Baby
Handy Chair
Kidsline
NoJo
Simmons
Tailored Baby

Mattresses (Other Than Crib)

Colgate Mattress
Delta
Kids Basics

Mirrors

Binky Griptight
Child Craft
Fisher-Price
Gerber Products
Infantino
Kids Basics
Lauri
Le Clair
Lepine Furniture
Lullabye
Morigeau
Pippen Hill
Prince Lionheart
Regent Baby
Shades of Jade
Simmons
Tot, Inc.
Wimmer-Ferguson
Wood Model

Mobiles

Babygund
Baby World
Bantam Collections
Brandee Danielle
Century
Cotton Tale Designs
Daisy Kingdom
Dakin
Dolly
Eden Toys
Fisher-Price
Glenna Jean
House of Hatten
Infantino
Jolly Jumper
Judi's Originals
Kidentials
Lambs and Ivy
Little Bedding
Luv N' Care
Luv Stuff
Mini Togs/Panda Knits
NoJo
Pansy Ellen
PatchKraft
Patsy Aiken Designs
Quiltex
Rainbow Mountain
Red Calliope
Remco Baby
Small World Toys
Spectrum
Tot, Inc.
Wimmer-Ferguson

Monitors/Intercoms

Cosco
Fisher-Price
Gerber Products
Gerry Baby
Guri
G. W. DMKA
Infantino
Luv N' Care
Mini Togs/Panda Knits
Pansy Ellen
Playskool Baby

Playtech
Safety 1st
Strolee
Unisar

Organizers

American Baby Concepts
Basic Comfort
Beautiful Baby
Cudlie
Danara
Lambs and Ivy
Nursery Needs by Sanitoy
Prince Lionheart
Railnet
Safety 1st
Selfix

Pacifiers

American Baby Concepts
Avent
Baby World
Binky Griptight
Cherubs Collection
Danara
Evenflo Products
First Years
Gerber Products
Handy Chair
Luv N' Care
Merri-Tots
Michael Friedman
Mini Togs/Panda Knits
Nursery Needs by Sanitoy
Playskool Baby
Playtex
Regent Baby
Safety 1st
Sassy
Snap Ups
Super Plastic

Picture Frames

Clinton Prints
C. R. Gibson
Eden Toys
House of Hatten
Infinitely Infants

Kiddie Lites
Kubla Crafts
Michael Friedman
MM's Designs
Patsy Aiken Designs
Perine Lowe
Quiltex
Rainbow Mountain
Redmon
Rosalina Baby
Tot, Inc.
Welcome to the World

Pillows

Alma's Designs
Baby Doll Infants Wear
Baby Duckies
Baby Face
Basic Comfort
Bebe Chic
Bedtime Originals
Brandee Danielle
Calico Cottage
California Feather
California Kids
The Carousel
Carousel Designs
Charles Owen
Clothworks
Cotton Tale Designs
Cuddle Time
Daisy Kingdom
Delta
Ecology Kids
Glenna Jean
Greenleaf
Health-Tex
Judi's Originals
Kidsline
Kidstuff Pals
Lambs and Ivy
Lamby Nursery
Li'l Partners
Little Vikings
Luv N' Care
Luv Stuff
Mini Togs/Panda Knits
Nava's Designs
New Spring

NoJo
Once Upon a Whimsy
Palais Royal
PatchKraft
Patsy Aiken Designs
Pine Creek
Quiltcraft Kids
Quiltex
Reflections
Riegel
Rosalina Baby
Simmons
Sumersault
Sweetpea
Tailored Baby
Triboro Quilt

Play Yard (Playpen) Pads

American Baby Concepts
Americare
Basic Comfort
Bebe Chic
Colgate Mattress
Diplomat
Evenflo Furniture
Gerry Baby
Kids Basics
Kolcraft
Lambs and Ivy
PatchKraft
Pride-Trimble
Simmons
Tailored Baby

Play Yards (Playpens)

Artsana of America
Baby Trend
C and T International
Carlson Children's Products
Century
Childrens' Factory
Delta
Evenflo Furniture
Fisher-Price
Gerry Baby
Graco
J. Mason
Kolcraft
North States

Pride-Trimble
Railnet
Welsh

Rattles

Artsana of America
Babi Bags by Romar
Babies Are #1
Babygund
Baby World
Bantam Collections
Binky Griptight
Convenience Kits
Dakin
Danara
Direct Connect
Eden Toys
Evenflo Products
Fan Fair Toys
First Years
Fisher-Price
Gerber Products
Handy Chair
House of Hatten
Infinitely Infants
Kidentials
Little Tikes
Luv N' Care
Merri-Tots
Michael Friedman
Mini Togs/Panda Knits
Nursery Needs by Sanitoy
Pansy Ellen
Playskool Baby
Playtech
Prestige Toy
Regent Baby
Remco Baby
Rosalina Baby
Snap Ups
Tot, Inc.
Welcome to the World

Receiving Blankets

Baby Dreams
Baby Duckies
Beacon
Beautiful Baby
Bumkins

Calico Cottage
Charles Owen
Children's Factory
Comfort Silkie
Crib Critters
Cuddle Time
Diplomat
Dundee Mills/Fisher-Price
Ecology Kids
Gerber Childrenswear
Greenleaf
Hamco
Health-Tex
Infinitely Infants
J. E. Morgan
Kooshies
Li'l Partners
Luv N' Care
Luv Stuff
Mini Togs/Panda Knits
NoJo
Once Upon a Whimsy
Pine Creek
Quiltex
Riegel
Simmons
Snap Ups
Sweetpea
Tailored Baby
3 Marthas
Triboro Quilt
Welcome to the World

Rockers (Adult/Child/Glider)

Baby Duckies
Bassett
Brooks Furniture
Child Craft
Conant Ball
Delta
Dutailier
Evenflo Furniture
Family Home
Frank and Son
Instant Products
Jonica
Lepine Furniture
Little Colorado
Little Tikes

Million Dollar Baby
Morigeau
Nelson Juvenile
Pieces of Dreams
Pippen Hill
Powell
Rainbow Mountain
Rochelle Furniture
Shades of Jade
Small World Toys
Tabor
Towne Square
Treetop
Tyke
Welsh
White Wicker

Rugs

American Pacific
Clothworks
Daisy Kingdom
MM's Designs
Surya Carpet

Safety Items

American Baby Concepts
Baby Buddies
Baby World
Banix
Bo Peep
Children on the Go
Danara
Diplomat
Ecology Kids
Evenflo Products
First Years
Gerber Products
G. W. DMKA
Handy Chair
Kidentials
Koolkids
Leachco
Luv N' Care
Mericon
Michael Friedman
Mini Togs/Panda Knits
Nursery Needs by Sanitoy
OFNA
Pansy Ellen

Pinky Baby
Playskool Baby
Prince Lionheart
Railnet
Regent Baby
Rev-A-Shelf
Rock A Bye Baby
Safety 1st
Sarah's Safety Sheets
Tailored Baby
Tots in Mind
Westech

Scales

Terraillon

Sheets

Baby Face
Bambineto
Beautiful Baby
Bebe Chic
Bedtime Originals
Brandee Danielle
The Carousel
Carousel Designs
Celebrations
Clothworks
Crib Critters
Dandelion
Delta
Diplomat
Ecology Kids
Gerber Childrenswear
Greenleaf
House of Hatten
Judi's Originals
Kidsline
Kooshies
Lambs and Ivy
Little Vikings
Luv Stuff
Nava's Designs
NoJo
Once Upon a Whimsy
Palais Royal
PatchKraft
Patsy Aiken Designs
Quiltcraft Kids
Quiltex

Red Calliope
Reflections
Riegel
Rosalina Baby
Sarah's Safety Sheets
Simmons
Sumersault
Sweetpea
Tailored Baby

Step Stools

Cosco
Evenflo Furniture
Fisher-Price
G. W. DMKA
Little Colorado
Little Tikes
MM's Designs
Nursery Needs by Sanitoy
Offspring
Pippen Hill
Playskool Baby
Regal Lager
Shades of Jade
Small Potatoes

Strollers

All Our Kids
Aprica
Artsana of America
Baby Trend
Bandaks Emmaljunga
Bebegoes
Carlson Children's
Century
Combi
Cosco
Daust
Delta
Gerry Baby
Graco
J. Mason
Jolly Jumper
Kinderkids
Kolcraft
Marshall Baby
Nelson Juvenile
Nogatco
Peg Perego

Racing Strollers
Safeline
Spectrum
Strolee
TRI
Weebok
Welsh

Swings

Carlson Children's
Century
Cosco
Evenflo Furniture
Fisher-Price
Flexible Flyer
Gerry Baby
Graco
Kolcraft
Little Tikes
Today's Kids

Switch Plates

American Baby Concepts
Gerber Products
Judi's Originals
Kiddie Lites
Lambs and Ivy
Luv N' Care
Mini Togs/Panda Knits
MM's Designs
Patsy Aiken Designs
Red Calliope
Shades of Jade
Sherry's Lamps

Tables and Chairs

Canwood
Cosco
Delta
Fisher-Price
G. W. DMKA
Harper Design
Kid Kraft
Little Colorado
Little Tikes
Marshall Baby
MM's Design
Offspring

Pieces of Dreams
Redmon
Rochelle Furniture
Shades of Jade
Small Potatoes
Tabor
Treetop
Tyke
Welsh
White Wicker

Thermometers

American Baby Concepts
Baby World
Binky Griptight
Danara
Flexible Flyer
Gerber Products
Graham-Field
Handy Chair
Luv N' Care
Marshall Baby
Medela
Michael Friedman
Mini Togs/Panda Knits
Playskool Baby

Toddler Bedding

Baby Dreams
Baby Face
Beautiful Baby
Bebe Chic
California Kids
Camp Kazoo
Charles Owen
Daisy Kingdom
Diplomat
Dundee Mills/Fisher-Price
Ecology Kids
Gerber Childrenswear
Guri
Hoopla
Judi's Originals
Kidsline
Lundy Look
NoJo
Pieces of Dreams
Red Calliope
Reflections

Riegel
Simmons
Sumersault
Sweetpea

Toddler Beds

Beautiful Baby
Child Craft
Cosco
Delta
Evenflo Furniture
Fantasy Bed
J. Mason
Kid Kraft
Kolcraft
Little Colorado
Offspring
Pieces of Dreams
Stork Craft
Treetop

Toilet Training Items

American Baby Concepts
Baby World
Binky Griptight
Century
Children on the Go
Cosco
Delta
Diplomat
Evenflo Furniture
First Years
Fisher-Price
Gerry Baby
Guri
G. W. DMKA
Little Tikes
Luv N' Care
Mini Togs/Panda Knits
Nursery Needs by Sanitoy
Playskool Baby
Prestige Toy
Pride-Trimble
Regal Lager
Rock A Bye Baby
Sassy
TL Care

Toy Chests

Badger Basket
Child Craft
Cosco
D and F Wicker
Delta
Fisher-Price
Flexible Flyer
G. W. DMKA
Kid Kraft
Little Colorado
Little Tikes
Marshall Baby
Morigeau
Offspring
Powell
Railnet
Redmon
Sauder Woodworking
Selfix
Shades of Jade
Tabor
Treetop
Tyke
Welsh
White Wicker
Wood Model

Toys

Adorable Baby
Alma's Designs
Artsana of America
Babi Bags by Romar
Babygund
Baby World
Bantam Collections
Battat
Binky Griptight
Capaz
Century
Children's Factory
Combi
Dakin
Danara
Direct Connect
Disney
Eden Toys
Evenflo Products

Fan Fair Toys
Fisher-Price
Forecees
Gerber Products
Handy Chair
Hoopla
House of Hatten
Infinitely Infants
International Playthings
Jolly Jumper
JTG
Kidentials
Kubla Craft
Lauri
Leachco
Little Colorado
Little Kids
Little Tikes
Luv N' Care
Merri-Tots
Michael Friedman
Mini Togs/Panda Knits
Playmobil
Playskool Baby
Playtech
Pockets of Learning
Quiltown
Regal Lager
Regent Baby
Remco Baby
Rock A Bye Baby
Safety 1st
Small World Toys
Snap Ups
Spectrum
Summer Infant
Texas Instruments
Today's Kids
Tot, Inc.
Tyke
Welcome to the World
Wimmer-Ferguson

Twin Bedding

Baby Face
Basic Comfort
Beautiful Baby
Bebe Chic
California Kids

Delta
Diplomat
Ecology Kids
Kidsline
Kidstuff Pals
Lundy Look
Luv Stuff
Palais Royal
Reflections
Simmons
Sumersault
Sweetpea

Twin Beds

Canwood
Child Craft
Cosco
Delta
Fantasy Bed
Harper Design
Lepine Furniture
Little Colorado
Morigeau
Offspring
Pieces of Dreams
Powell
Sauder Woodworking
Simmons
Wood Model

Walkers

All Our Kids
Artsana of America
Baby Trend
Basic Comfort
C and T International
Century
Cosco
Daust
Delta
Fisher-Price
Graco
J. Mason
Kolcraft
Nelson Juvenile
Nogatco
Peg Perego
Spectrum
Strolee
Welsh

Wall Hangings/Pictures

Alma's Designs
Baby Face
Beacon
Beautiful Baby
Bedtime Originals
Brandee Danielle
Calico Cottage
The Carousel
Carousel Designs
Celebrations
Children's Factory
Clothworks
Cotton Tale Designs
Country Carver
Daisy Kingdom
Dakin
Dandelion
Diplomat
Ecology Kids
Gerber Childrenswear
Glenna Jean
Guri
Infantino
Inmon Enterprises
Judi's Originals
Kiddie Lites
Kidsline
Kidstuff Pals
Kubla Crafts
Lambs and Ivy
Li'l Partners
Little Bedding
Little Vikings
L. M. W. Designs
Loose Goose
Luv Stuff
MM's Designs
Nava's Designs
NoJo
Once Upon a Whimsy
PatchKraft
Patsy Aiken Designs
Pockets of Learning
Powell
Prelude Designs
Priss Prints
Quiltex
Red Calliope

Rosalina Baby
Simmons
Sumersault

Wallpaper and Borders

Brandee Danielle
Children's Factory
Clothworks
Cotton Tale Designs
Gerber Childrenswear
Glenna Jean
Judi's Originals
Kiddie Lites
Lambs and Ivy
Little Bedding
NoJo
Once Upon a Whimsy
Prelude Designs
Priss Prints
Red Calliope
Simmons
Sumersault

Wipes and Accessories

Diplomat
Ecology Kids
Guri
Infant Technologies
Marshall Baby
Rock A Bye Baby

Youth/Teen Furniture

Badger Basket
C and T International
Child Craft
Cosco
D and F Wicker
Delta
Eastwood
Fantasy Bed
G. W. DMKA
Harper Design
Lea Industries
Le Clair
Lepine Furniture
Little Colorado
Little Tikes
Meg
Morigeau
Nelson Juvenile
Nogatco
Nursery Needs by Sanitoy
Peg Perego
Pieces of Dreams
Pippen Hill
Powell
Shades of Jade
Simmons
Tabor
Tracers
Treetop
White Wicker
Wood Model

Appendix B

Ordering U.S. Government Publications

Most of the government publications mentioned in *The Parents' Resource Almanac* can be ordered directly from the Government Printing Office in Washington, D.C. To inquire about availability and prices, call 202/783-3238 between the hours of 8 a.m. and 4 p.m. (eastern standard time). It helps if you know the S/N number, but the telephone "technicians" will look it up if you don't have it. If the publication you're looking for is in stock (and the price is right), you can simply charge your order over the phone (VISA and MasterCard accepted).

Alternatively, you can purchase government publications from your nearest government bookstore.

U.S. GOVERNMENT BOOKSTORES

The Government Printing Office operates U.S. government bookstores around the country where customers are free to browse through shelves full of books, directories, pamphlets, brochures, posters, and periodicals. These stores don't stock all of the titles in Uncle Sam's inventory (there are more than twelve thousand), but they do carry the ones you're most likely to be looking for. And they'll order any government book currently offered for sale and have it shipped directly to you. All of these bookstores accept VISA and MasterCard.

The government bookstores, arranged alphabetically by city (Note: Government bookstores do relocate. If you have trouble reaching one of the bookstores listed below, check your yellow pages.)

Atlanta. 275 Peachtree Street, N.E., Room 100, P.O. Box 56445, Atlanta, Georgia 30343. Phone: 404/331-6947. Fax: 404/331-1787.

Birmingham. O'Neill Building, 2021 Third Avenue, North, Birmingham, Alabama 35203. Phone: 205/731-1056. Fax: 205/731-3444.

Boston. Thomas P. O'Neill Building, Room 169, 10 Causeway Street, Boston, Massachusetts 02222. Phone: 617/720-4180. Fax: 617/720-5753.

Chicago. One Congress Center, 401 South State Street, Suite 124, Chicago, Illinois 60605. Phone: 312/353-5133. Fax: 312/353-1590.

Cleveland. Room 1653, Federal Building, 1240 East Ninth Street, Cleveland, Ohio 44199. Phone: 216/522-4922. Fax: 216/522-4714.

Columbus. Room 207, Federal Building, 200 North High Street, Columbus, Ohio 43215. Phone: 614/469-6956. Fax: 614/469-5374.

Dallas. Room IC46, Federal Building, 1100 Commerce Street, Dallas, Texas 75242. Phone: 214/767-0076. Fax: 214/767-3239.

Denver. Room 117, Federal Building, 1961 Stout Street, Denver, Colorado 80294. Phone: 303/844-3964. Fax: 303/844-4000.

Detroit. Suite 160, Federal Building, 477 Michigan Avenue, Detroit, Michigan 48226. Phone: 313/226-7816. Fax: 313/226-4698.

Houston. Texas Crude Building, 801 Travis Street, Suite 120, Houston, Texas 77002. Phone: 713/228-1187. Fax: 713/228-1186.

Jacksonville. 100 West Bay Street, Suite 100, Jacksonville, FLorida 32202. Phone: 904/353-0569. Fax: 904/353-1280.

Kansas City. 120 Bannister Mall, 5600 East Bannister Road, Kansas City, Missouri 64137. Phone: 816/765-2256. Fax: 816/767-8233.

Laurel. U.S. Government Printing Office, Warehouse Sales Outlet, 8660 Cherry Lane, Laurel, Maryland 20707. Phone: 301/953-7974 or 301/792-0262. Fax: 301/498-9107.

Los Angeles. ARCO Plaza, C-Level, 505 South Flower Street, Los Angeles, California 90071. Phone: 213/239-9844. Fax: 213/239-9848.

Milwaukee. Room 190, Federal Building, 517 East Wisconsin Avenue, Milwaukee, Wisconsin 53202. Phone: 414/297-1304. Fax: 414/297-1300.

New York. Room 110, Federal Building, 26 Federal Plaza, New York, New York 10278. Phone: 212/264-3825. Fax: 212/264-9318.

Philadelphia. Robert Morris Building, 100 North Seventeenth Street, Philadelphia, Pennsylvania 19103. Phone: 215/597-0677. Fax: 215/597-4548.

Pittsburgh. Room 118, Federal Building, 1000 Liberty Avenue, Pittsburgh, Pennsylvania 15222. Phone: 412/644-2721. Fax: 412/644-4547.

Portland. 1305 Southwest First Avenue, Portland, Oregon 97201-5801. Phone: 503/221-6217. Fax: 503/225-0563.

Pueblo. World Savings Building, 720 North Main Street, Pueblo, Colorado 81003. Phone: 719/544-3142. Fax: 719/544-6719.

San Francisco. Room 1023, Federal Building, 450 Golden Gate Avenue, San Francisco, California 94102. Phone: 415/252-5334. Fax: 415/252-5339.

Seattle. Room 194, Federal Building, 915 Second Avenue, Seattle, Washington 98174. Phone: 206/553-4270. Fax: 206/553-6717.

Washington, D.C. U.S. Government Printing Office, 710 North Capitol Street, N.W., Washington, D.C. 20401. Phone: 202/512-0132. Fax: 202/512-1355.

1510 H Street, N.W., Washington, D.C. 20005. Phone: 202/653-5075. Fax: 202/376-5055.

Appendix C

Children's Book Publishers

Below is a listing of many of the more prominent children's book publishers. Information on others can be found in *Literary Marketplace*, published annually by R. R. Bowker and available at most libraries. Another good source is *Books in Print* (publishers volume), also published by R. R. Bowker. In addition, the Children's Book Council, Inc., maintains a Members List, which includes information on many publishers of children's books. For an updated Members List, contact the Children's Book Council, Inc., 568 Broadway, Suite 404, New York, New York 10012. Phone: 212/966-1990.

Aladdin Books. (An imprint of the Macmillan Children's Book Group.) 866 Third Avenue, New York, New York 10022. Phone: 212/702-2000. Publishes paperback books for children (preschoolers through young adults), including picture books, fiction, and nonfiction. Also publishes hardcover books for children, including board books, concept books, and novelty items. Publishes about seventy titles a year.

Arcade Publishing. (A subsidiary of Little, Brown.) 141 Fifth Avenue, New York, New York 10010. Phone: 212/475-2633. Publishes hardcover books for children (preschoolers through young adults), including picture books, fiction, and nonfiction. Publishes about twelve to fifteen titles a year.

Atheneum Publishers. (An imprint of the Macmillan Children's Book Group.) 866 Third Avenue, New York, New York 10022. Phone: 212/702-2000. Publishes hardcover trade books for children (preschool through young adult), including picture books, fiction, and nonfiction. Publishes science fiction and fantasy for older readers. Releases about sixty titles a year.

Avon Books. 1350 Avenue of the Americas, New York, New York 10019. Phone: 212/261-6800. Publishes two lines of paperback books: Camelot Books for children in grades four through six and Avon Flare Books for young adults. Publishes approximately eighty-five titles a year.

Bantam Books. 666 Fifth Avenue, New York, New York 10103. Phone: 212/765-6500. Publishes books for readers ages three through young adult. Bantam Little Rooster Books are illustrated picture books, beginning readers, fiction, and nonfiction for ages three to eight. Other series include Bantam Skylark Hardcovers (for children ages six to twelve); Sweet Valley Kids (for ages six to nine); Sweet Valley Twins (for ages eight to twelve); The Saddle Club (for ages eight to eleven); The Fabulous Five (for ages nine to thirteen); and Choose Your Own Adventure (multiple path interactive books for ages ten to fourteen).

Barron's Educational Series, Inc. 250 Wireless Boulevard, P.O. Box 8040, Hauppauge, New York 11788. Phone: 516/434-3311. Publishes hardcover and paperback books for children (preschool through young adult). Emphasis is on picture books, easy reading books, and nonfiction. Also publishes some novelty books, concept books, and pop-ups. Publishes about seventy-five titles a year.

Boyd's Mills Press. 4 Hubbell Mountain Road, Sherman, Connecticut 06784. Phone: 203/355-9498. Publishes hardcover and softcover trade books for children (preschool through young adult), including fiction and nonfiction, picture books, board books, and craft and activity books, as well as quality books of literary merit. Offers original publications, as well as reissued titles. Publishes about eighty titles a year.

Bradbury Press. (An affiliate of Macmillan, Inc.) 866 Third Avenue, New York, New York 10022. Phone: 212/702-9809. Publishes hardcover trade books for children (preschool through young adult). The primary emphasis is on picture books and fiction, with occasional nonfiction. Publishes about forty titles a year.

Carolrhoda Books, Inc. 241 First Avenue North, Minneapolis, Minnesota 55401. Phone: 612/332-3344. Publishes hardcover books for children (preschool through grade six). Primary emphasis is on picture books and illustrated fiction and nonfiction. Lines include On My Own Beginning Readers, Creative Minds Biographies, Photo Essay Books, Nature Watch and Earth Watch Science Books, and the Trailblazers Biographies. Publishes thirty-five to forty titles a year.

Clarion Books. (Imprint of Houghton Mifflin Co.) 215 Park Avenue South, New York, New York 10003. Phone: 212/420-5800. Publishes hardcover trade books for children (preschool through young adult), including picture books, fiction, and nonfiction. Also releases some simultaneous paperback publications and reprints of backlist titles. Publishes fifty titles a year.

Cobblehill Books. (An affiliate of Dutton Children's Books/Penguin USA.) 375 Hudson Street, New York, New York 10014. Phone: 212/366-2628. Publishes hardcover trade books for children (preschool to young adult), including picture books, fiction, and nonfiction. Releases approximately twenty to twenty-five titles a year.

Crown Publishers. 225 Park Avenue South, New York, New York 10003. Phone: 212/254-1600. Publishes hardcover and trade paperback for children (preschool through young adult). Primary emphasis is on picture books, fiction, and nonfiction titles. Publishes around forty titles a year. Affiliated with (and distributed by) Random House.

Delacorte/Doubleday Books for Young Readers. 666 Fifth Avenue, New York, New York 10103. Phone: 212/765-6500. Publishes hardcover fiction and nonfiction books for readers ages ten to sixteen under the Delacorte imprint. Hardcover and paperback picture books and illustrated books for children (preschool through fifth grade) are published as Doubleday Books for Young Readers. Doubleday titles are published by Delacorte Press, the hardcover imprint of Dell Publishing, a member of the Bantam Doubleday Dell Publishing Group, Inc.

Dell Publishing. 666 Fifth Avenue, New York, New York 10103. Phone:

212/765-6500. Publishing lines for children include Picture Yearling books for ages two to six; Young Yearling books for ages four to seven; Yearling books for readers up to eleven; Laurel Leaf books for readers ten and up; and Yearling Classics for all ages. These imprints publish about 250 reprints and original titles a year. Affiliated with Delacorte/Doubleday Books for Young Readers, a member of the Bantam Doubleday Dell Publishing Group, Inc.

Dial Books for Young Readers. (A division of Penguin USA.) 375 Hudson Street, New York, New York 10014. Phone: 212/366-2800. Publishes hardcover trade books for children (preschool through young adult). Primary emphasis is on picture books and fiction. Publishes Very First Books for toddlers and Easy-to-Read Books for primary readers. Also publishes a line of paperbacks called Pied Piper Books (mainly reprints of Dial hardcover picture books).

Disney Press. (An imprint of Walt Disney Book Publishing Group, Inc.) 114 Fifth Avenue, New York, New York 10011. Phone: 212/633-4400. Publishes hardcover and paperback trade books for children, including both fiction and nonfiction based on characters from Disney films and television. Primary emphasis is on picture books and retellings of the classic films, as well as board books, pop-ups, and books from the Disney Archives. Publishes approximately forty titles a year. Distributed by Little, Brown and Warner Books.

Dorling Kindersley, Inc. 232 Madison Avenue, New York, New York 10016. Phone: 212/684-0404. Publishes hardcover originals for children (preschool through young adult). Primary emphasis on nonfiction, including natural history, science, zoology, and anatomy. Also offers some fiction titles in picture-book and beginning-reader formats. Releases approximately seventy-five titles per year. Publishes calendars and posters as well.

Dutton Children's Books. (A division of Penguin USA.) 375 Hudson Street, New York, New York 10014. Phone: 212/366-2600. Publishes hardcover trade books for children (preschool to young adult). Primary emphasis is on picture books and fiction; some nonfiction. Unicorn Paperbacks are reprints of picture books, Dutton Easy Readers are full-color books for beginning readers, and Dutton Speedsters are transitional beginning reader/chapter books. Also publishes some pop-ups and other novelty books. Publishes approximately seventy to eight titles a year.

Enslow Publishers, Inc. Bloy Street and Ramsey Avenue, Box 777, Hillside, New Jersey 07205. Phone: 201/964-4116. Publishes hardcover and paperback children's and young adult nonfiction books on all topics. Releases about forty titles a year.

Farrar, Straus and Giroux, Inc. 19 Union Square West, New York, New York 10003. Phone: 212/741-6900. Publishes hardcover trade books for children (preschool through young adult). Primary emphasis is on fiction, picture books, and nonfiction. Also publishes a paperback line, Sunburst Books, for children, which includes picture books and fiction from Farrar's backlist.

Four Winds Press. (An imprint of the Macmillan Children's Book Group.) 866 Third Avenue, New York, New York 10022. Phone: 212/702-2000. Publishes picture books, nonfiction from younger grades through middle grades, and some fiction for middle grades. Releases about twenty-five titles a year.

Franklin Watts, Inc. 95 Madison Avenue, New York, New York 10016. Phone: 212/447-7788. Publishes hardcover books in library bindings for children (kindergarten through young adult). Emphasis is on nonfiction in the areas of social studies, science, and technology for grades four to twelve. Publishes approximately one hundred titles a year.

Frederick Warne and Co., Inc. (A division of Penguin USA.) 375 Hudson Street, New York, New York 10014. Phone: 212/366-2000. An imprint of Penguin USA. Publishes books by and about Beatrix Potter and such classic children's authors as Kathleen Hale and Cicely Mary Barker. Offers hardcover, paperbacks, pop-ups, and novelty books for all ages. Publishes thirty titles a year.

Good Books. Main Street, P.O. Box 419, Intercourse, Pennsylvania 17534. Phone: 717/768-7171. Publishes hardcover and paperback books for children (ages three to six and four to ten). Primary emphasis is on picture books and fiction, with occasional how-to books. Publishes two to four titles a year.

Greenwillow Books. 1350 Avenue of the Americas, New York, New York 10019. Phone: 212/261-6500. Publishes hardcover trade books for children (preschool through young adult). Primary emphasis is on picture books and fiction. Publishes about sixty titles a year.

Grosset and Dunlap, Inc. (The Putnam and Grosset Book Group.) 200 Madison Avenue, New York, New York 10016. Phone: 212/951-8700. Publishes hardcover and paperback mass market books for children ages two to twelve. Emphasis is on inexpensive series, novelty formats, and preschool board books. Nonfiction is included. Publishes approximately seventy titles a year.

Gulliver Books. (An imprint of Harcourt Brace Jovanovich, Inc.) 1250 Sixth Avenue, San Diego, California 92101. Phone: 619/699-6810. Publishes hardcover trade books for children (preschool through young adult). Emphasis is on picture books, historical fiction, and nonfiction with some middle grade and young adult fiction. Publishes about twenty-five books a year.

Harcourt Brace Jovanovich, Inc. 1250 Sixth Avenue, San Diego, California 92101. Phone: 619/699-6810. Publishes hardcover trade books for children (preschool through young adult). Emphasis is on picture books and middle grade fiction, with some young adult fiction and some nonfiction titles. Includes Voyager and Odyssey paperbacks, the Jane Yolen Books publishing programs, and the Gulliver Books imprint. Publishes about seventy-five titles a year.

HarperCollins Children's Books. 10 East Fifty-third Street, New York, New York 10022. Phone: 212/207-7044. Publishes trade books for children (preschool through young adult), including picture books, fiction, and nonfiction. Hardcover books also published as Michael di Capua Books, Willa Perlman Books, and Laura Geringer Books. Publishes some pop-up and other novelty books as well. Publishes about one hundred forty titles a year.

Harper Trophy Paperbacks. (HarperCollins Children's Books.) 10 East Fifty-third Street, New York, New York 10022. Phone: 212/207-7044. Publishes paperback books for children and young adults reprinted from the hardcover HarperCollins list or acquired from other publishers. Also publishes picture books, fiction, and nonfiction. Put out around ninety titles a year.

Henry Holt and Company, Inc. 115 West Eighteenth Street, New York, New York 10011. Phone: 212/886-9200. Publishes hardcover trade books for children (preschool through junior high), including picture books, middle grade and young adult fiction, and nonfiction for all ages. Occasionally publishes paperback titles. Releases approximately seventy-five titles a year.

Holiday House. 425 Madison Avenue, New York, New York 10017. Phone: 212/688-0085. Publishes hardcover and paperback trade books for children (preschool through young adult). Primary emphasis on picture books and fiction. Also publishes nonfiction titles. Publishes about fifty titles a year.

Houghton Mifflin Co. 222 Berkeley Street, Boston, Massachusetts 02116. Phone: 617/351-5000. Publishes hardcover and paperback trade books for children (preschool through young adult). Publishes around fifty titles a year.

Hyperion Books for Children. (An imprint of Walt Disney Book Publishing Group, Inc.) 114 Fifth Avenue, New York, New York 10011. Phone: 212/633-4400. Publishes hardcover and paperback trade books for children (preschool through young adult), including picture books, fiction, and nonfiction. Also publishes some pop-up and other novelty books. Publishes around fifty titles a year. Distributed by Little, Brown and Warner Books.

Jewish Publication Society. 2112 Broadway, New York, New York 10023. Phone: 212/873-8399. Publishes hardcover and paperback trade books for children (preschool through young adult), including a biography series for younger readers and fiction and nonfiction for older readers all relating to Jewish life, culture, and history. Publishes six to eight titles a year.

Joy Street Books. (An imprint of Little, Brown.) 34 Beacon Street, Boston, Massachusetts 02108. Phone: 617/227-0730. Publishes hardcover trade books for children (preschool through young adult), with occasional original paperbacks. Primary emphasis is on picture books and fiction, with increasing interest in picture book nonfiction and nonfiction for eight to twelve year olds. Publishes about thirty titles a year.

Klutz Press. 2121 Staunton Court, Palo Alto, California 94306. Phone: 415/857-0888. Publishes trade paperbacks, including how-to, cooking, music, sports, humor, and game books. Specializes in books for kids that come with game pieces, simple tools, or materials called for in the text. Publishes three titles a year. Twenty-seven titles in print.

Alfred A. Knopf, Inc. 225 Park Avenue South, New York, New York 10003. Phone: 212/254-1600. Publishes hardcover and paperback trade books for children (preschool through young adult). Primary emphasis is on picture books and fiction; occasional nonfiction titles. (As of 1986, Pantheon's Books for Young Readers was merged with the Knopf children's book list). Affiliated with and distributed by Random House.

Lerner Publications Company. 241 First Avenue North, Minneapolis, Minnesota 55401. Phone: 612/332-3344. Publishes hardcover books for children (primary grades through young adult). Primary emphasis is on nonfiction (including sports, science, history, and geography), with occasional fiction titles. Publishes around seventy-five titles a year.

Little, Brown and Co. 34 Beacon Street, Boston, Massachusetts 02108.

Phone: 617/227-0730. Publishes hardcover and paperback trade books for children (preschool through young adult). Emphasis on picture books, fiction, and nonfiction titles. Publishes around eighty titles a year.

Lodestar Books. (An affiliate of Dutton's Children Books/Penguin USA.) 375 Hudson Street, New York, New York 10014. Phone: 212/366-2627. Publishes hardcover trade books for children (principally for middle schoolers and young adults). Also publishes picture books. Releases thirty titles a year.

Lothrop, Lee and Shepard Books. 1350 Avenue of the Americas, New York, New York 10019. Phone: 212/261-6641. Publishes hardcover trade books for children from infancy to young adult. Primary emphasis is on picture books for ages three to eight and novels for ages seven to twelve. Also publishes nonfiction for children of all ages. Releases about sixty books a year.

Macmillan Publishing Co. 866 Third Avenue, New York, New York 10022. Phone: 212/702-2000. Publishes hardcover books for children and young adults (preschool through high school), including picture books, fiction, and nonfiction. Publishes about sixty-five titles a year.

Margaret K. McElderry Books. (An imprint of the Macmillan Children's Book Group.) 866 Third Avenue, New York, New York 10022. Phone: 212/702-7855. Publishes hardcover trade books for children (preschool through young adult). Emphasis is on picture books, easy reading books, fiction, and special nonfiction titles. Publishes about twenty-five titles a year.

Meadowbrook Press. 18318 Minnetonka Boulevard, Deephaven, Minnesota 55391. Phone: 1/800-338-2232, or 612/473-5400. Publishes chil-

dren's activity books, including *Free Stuff for Kids* and *More Free Stuff for Kids*. Also publishes books on child care, parenting, and party planning. Publishes about eight titles a year.

Millbrook Press, Inc. 2 Old New Milford Road, Brookfield, Connecticut 06804. Phone: 203/740-2220. Publishes hardcover and paperback school and library books for children (preschool through young adult). Primarily nonfiction, including picture books and reference works. Publishes more than one hundred titles a year.

Milliken Publishing Company. 1100 Research Boulevard, P.O. Box 21579, St. Louis, Missouri 63132-0579. Phone: 314/991-4220 or 1/800-325-4136. Publishes softcover trade books for children (preschool through grade three). Emphasis is on picture books, fiction, and educational self-directed activity books. Publishes about fifteen titles a year.

Morrow Junior Books. 1350 Avenue of the Americas, New York, New York 10019. Phone: 212/261-6691. Publishers hardcover trade books for children (preschool through young adult). Equal emphasis on picture books, fiction, and nonfiction. Publishes approximately sixty titles a year.

Mulberry Books. 1350 Avenue of the Americas, New York, New York 10019. Phone: 212/261-6500. Publishes paperback reprints of picture books, both fiction and nonfiction. Releases approximately forty titles a year.

North-South Books. 1133 Broadway, Suite 1016, New York, New York 10010. Phone: 212/463-9736. Publishes hardcover children's picture books, with occasional children's nonfiction titles. North-South Books is the English-language imprint of Nord-Sud Verlag, Switzerland, but the U.S. office also acquires books for the imprint. Releases about twenty-five titles a year.

Orchard Books. 387 Park Avenue South, New York, New York 10016. Phone: 212/686-7070. Publishes hardcover trade books for children (preschool through young adult). Emphasis is on picture books and fiction, with occasional nonfiction for the picture book age group and photo essays for all ages. Publishes about sixty titles per year.

Pelican Publishing Company, Inc. 1101 Monroe Street, P.O. Box 189, Gretna, Louisiana 70054. Phone: 504/368-1175. Publishes hardcover and paperback trade books for children (lower elementary to junior high), but with an increasing interest in young adult books. Strong regional interests. Publishes about thirteen to fifteen titles a year.

Philomel Books. (The Putnam and Grosset Book Group), 200 Madison Avenue, New York, New York 10016. Phone: 212/951-8700. Publishes hardcover trade books for children (preschool through young adult). Primary emphasis on picture books, and middle and teenage fiction, with occasional nonfiction titles. At times, publishes paperbacks of own backlist titles. Releases around forty titles a year.

Pleasant Company. 8400 Fairway Place, P.O. Box 991, Middleton, Wisconsin 53562. Phone: 1/800-233-0264. Publishes The American Girls Collection, a series of twenty-four hardcover and paperback books for girls seven to ten years old. Each title portrays a girl's life within a historical context, e.g., 1774, 1854, 1904, 1944, and includes a nonfiction photo essay. Portfolio of Pastimes includes six activity books (diary, cookbook, album, paper dolls, theater, and games) featuring activities from the past for girls of today. Our New Baby is an interactive pop-up book line that shows preschoolers how to care for newborns.

Puffin Books. (A division of Penguin USA.) 375 Hudson Street, New York, New York 10014. Phone: 212/366-2000. Puffin Books is the paperback children's imprint of Penguin USA. Publishes books for children in preschool through junior high. Emphasis is on picture books and middle grade fiction. Also publishes some series, nonfiction, activity, and novelty books. Offers reprints of books from many publishers, as well as some originals. Releases more than one hundred books a year.

G. P. Putnam's Sons. (The Putnam and Grosset Book Group.) 200 Madison Avenue, New York, New York 10016. Phone: 212/951-8700. Publishes hardcover trade books for children. Emphasis on books for preschoolers, picture books, fiction, and novelty books. Also publishes some nonfiction.

Random House. 225 Park Avenue South, New York, New York 10003. Phone: 212/254-1600. Publishes hardcover and paperback children's trade books, as well as library bound books for children in preschool through elementary school. Emphasis is on picture books, fiction, nonfiction, and novelty books. Publishes about two hundred titles a year.

Rizzoli International Publications, Inc. 300 Park Avenue South, New York, New York 10010. Phone: 212/387-3400.

Scholastic Hardcover. 730 Broadway, New York, New York 10003. Phone: 212/505-3000. Publishes hardcover trade books for children (preschool through young adult), including fiction and nonfiction. Publishes around fifty to sixty titles a year.

Scholastic, Inc. 730 Broadway, New York, New York 10003. Phone: 212/

505-3000. Publishes paperback originals and reprints, as well as some hardcover books for children (preschool through young adult). Emphasis on fiction; some nonfiction. Includes the following imprints: Little Apple® books (for readers ages seven to nine), Apple Paperbacks (for readers eight to thirteen). Point Books (for readers ages twelve and up), and Blue Ribbon® (reprints of classic picture books by award-winning authors and/or illustrators). Publishes around three hundred titles a year.

Charles Scribner's Sons. (An imprint of the Macmillan Children's Book Group.) 866 Third Avenue, New York, New York 10022. Phone: 212/702-7885. Publishes hardcover trade books for children (preschool through young adult). Emphasis is on fiction and nonfiction for intermediate readers. Also publishes some picture books. Releases about twenty titles a year.

Sierra Club Books for Children and Young Adults. 100 Bush Street, 13th Floor, San Francisco, California 94104. Phone: 415/291-1600. Publishes children's fiction, nonfiction, and picture books with an emphasis on nature, outdoor activities, and the environment. More than thirty-two titles in print.

Simon and Schuster Books for Young Readers. 15 Columbus Circle, New York, New York 10023. Phone: 212/373-8424. Publishes fiction and nonfiction for children ages one to fourteen. Emphasis is on picture books illustrated with original art or photography, as well as anthologies and classic tales. Also publishes middle group fiction, nonfiction, informational books, high interest reference, and science and natural history books. Publishes one hundred hardcover and sixty paperbacks (new books, as well as reprints) a year. Imprint includes backlist titles of Prentice-Hall Books for Young Readers.

Stemmer House Publishers, Inc. 2627 Caves Road, Owings Mills, Maryland 21117. Phone: 301/363-3690. Publishes hardcover and paperbound trade books for children (preschool through young adult), emphasizing full-color illustrations Publishes about three children's titles a year. Audiocassette readings of some children's titles published by Stemmer House are produced by its division, BEDE Productions.

Stewart, Tabori and Chang. 575 Broadway, New York, New York 10012. Phone: 212/941-2955. Publishes hardcover picture books for children, crossover picture books for children, and crossover photographic books for young adults. Titles include fiction, nonfiction, and classics. Emphasis is on high quality production. Publishes approximately eight to ten titles a year.

Tambourine Books. 1350 Avenue of the Americas, New York, New York 10019. Phone: 212/261-6500. Publishes hardcover trade books for children (preschool through young adult). Primary emphasis is on picture books and fiction. Publishes about fifty titles a year.

Viking. (A division of Penguin USA.) 375 Hudson Street, New York, New York 10014. Phone: 212/366-2000. A hardcover children's imprint of Penguin USA. Publishes trade books for toddlers, preschoolers, and young adults. Booklist includes board books, picture books, series (including the Women of Our Time™ series, the Once upon America series, and the Hello Reading! series for beginning readers), pop-ups, and novelty books. Publishes both fiction and nonfiction. Releases about seventy-five titles a year.

Walker and Company. 720 Fifth Avenue, New York, New York 10019. Phone: 212/265-3632. Publishes hardcover and paperback books for children (preschool through young adult). Primary emphasis is on non-fiction, with occasional picture books and fiction. Publishes about forty titles a year.

Williamson Publishing Co. Church Hill Road, P.O. Box 185, Charlotte, Vermont 05445. Phone: 802/425-2102 or 1/800-234-8791. Publishes quality trade books, including kids' activity books and parenting guides. Publishes twelve titles a year. Forty-five titles in print.

Appendix D

Youth Orchestras

The following youth orchestras are members of the American Symphony Orchestra League's Youth Orchestra Division. For more information on the league and its services, please contact the American Symphony Orchestra League, Youth Orchestra Division, 777 Fourteenth Street, N.W., Suite 500, Washington, D.C. 20005. Phone: 202/628-0099.

Alabama

Alabama Youth Symphony. P.O. Box 2125, Birmingham, Alabama 35203. Phone: 205/326-0100.

Huntsville Youth Orchestra. P.O. Box 7223, Huntsville, Alabama 35807. Phone: 205/880-0622.

Metropolitan Youth Orchestra of Huntsville. P.O. Box 912, Huntsville, Alabama 35804. Phone: 205/880-6234.

Alaska

Anchorage Youth Symphony. P.O. Box 240541, Anchorage, Alaska 99524-0541. Phone: 907/243-0690.

Fairbanks Youth Symphony. P.O. Box 82104, Fairbanks, Alaska 99708. Phone: 907/479-3407.

Arizona

Metropolitan Youth Symphony. P.O. Box 41852, Mesa, Arizona 85274-1852. Phone: 602/838-0741.

Phoenix Symphony Guild Youth Orchestra. P.O. Box 15150, Phoenix, Arizona 85060. Phone: 602/277-7013.

Tucson Philharmonic Youth Orchestra. P.O. Box 41882, Tucson, Arizona 85717. Phone: 602/326-2793.

Arkansas

Arkansas Youth Orchestra. UALR Fine Arts Building, Room 164, 2801 South University Avenue, Little Rock, Arkansas 72204. Phone: 501/569-8779.

California

American Youth Symphony. 343 Church Lane, Los Angels, California 90049. Phone: 213/476-2825.

California Youth Symphony. P.O. Box 1441, Palo Alto, California 94302. Phone: 415/325-6666.

Claremont Young Musicians Orchestras. P.O. Box 722, Claremont, California 91711. Phone: 714/624-9553.

CSUN Youth Orchestra Academy Orchestra. CSUN Music Building, Room 149, 18111 Nordhoff Street, Northridge, California 91330. Phone: 818/885-3074.

El Camino Youth Symphony. 1345 Martin Avenue, Palo Alto, California 94301. Phone: 415/327-3369.

Glendale Youth Orchestra. P.O. Box 4401, Glendale, California 91222-0401.

Modesto Symphony Stanislaus Youth Orchestra. c/o Music Department CSU, Stanislaus, 801 West Monte Viste Avenue, Turlock, California 95380. Phone: 209/668-9173.

Oakland Youth Orchestra. P.O. Box 30274, Oakland, California 94604. Phone: 510/420-8666.

Orange County Youth Symphony Junior Orchestra. P.O. Box 18692, Anaheim Hills, California 92817. Phone: 714/278-1713.

Pasadena Young Musicians Orchestra. P.O. Box 50386, Pasadena, California 91105. Phone: 818/793-0701.

Sacramento Youth Symphony. 8031-B Fruitridge Road, Sacramento, California 95820. Phone: 916/388-5777.

San Diego Youth Symphony. San Diego City Park and Recreation Department, Casa Del Prado, Balboa Park, San Diego, California 92101. Phone: 619/233-3232.

San Francisco Symphony Youth Orchestra. Davies Symphony Hall, San Francisco, California 94102. Phone: 415/552-8011.

Santa Cruz County Youth Symphony. 143 Laurent Street, Santa Cruz, California 95060. Phone: 408/458-9013.

Sonoma County Junior Symphony. P.O. Box 9261, Santa Rosa, California 95405. Phone: 707/528-8884.

Young Artists Symphony Orchestra. P.O. Box 4849, Walnut Creek, California 94596. Phone: 510/687-8029.

Young Musicians Foundation Debut Orchestra. Suite 400, 195 South Beverly Drive, Beverly Hills, California 90212. Phone: 310/859-7668.

Young People's Symphony Orchestra. P.O. Box 7010, Berkeley, California 94707. Phone: 510/843-3053.

Youth Music Monterey. Youth and Honors Orchestra of Monterey, 2959 Monterey-Salinas Highway, Monterey, California 93940. Phone: 408/375-1992.

Youth Orchestra of South Alameda County. P.O. Box 3970, Hayward, California 94540. Phone: 510/278-1413.

Colorado

Colorado Springs Youth Symphony. P.O. Box 25478, Colorado Springs, Colorado 80936. Phone: 719/634-5623.

Denver Young Artists Orchestra. 1415 Larimer Street, Denver, Colorado 80202. Phone: 303/571-1935.

Front Range Youth Symphony. 6901 Wadsworth Boulevard, Arvada, Colorado 80003. Phone: 303/431-3080.

Connecticut

Greater Bridgeport Youth Orchestra. P.O. Box 645, Fairfield, Connecticut 06430. Phone: 203/227-6695.

Norwalk Youth Symphony. P.O. Box 73, Norwalk, Connecticut 06856-0073. Phone: 203/226-6562.

Young Artists Philharmonic. P.O. Box 3301, Ridgeway Station, Stamford, Connecticut 06905. Phone: 203/532-1278.

District of Columbia

D.C. Youth Orchestra. P.O. Box 56198, Washington, D.C. 20011. Phone: 202/723-1612.

Washington Conservatory Orchestra. 5144 Massachusetts Avenue, P.O. Box 5758, Washington, D.C. 20016. Phone: 301/320-2770.

Florida

Brevard Symphony Youth Orchestra. 3865 North Wickham Road, Melbourne, Florida 32935. Phone: 305/254-9583.

Florida Symphony Youth Orchestra. P.O. Box 2328, Winter Park, Florida 32790. Phone: 407/657-8889.

Florida West Coast Symphony Youth Orchestra. 709 North Tamiami Trail, Sarasota, Florida 34236. Phone: 813/953-4252.

Greater Miami Youth Symphony. P.O. Box 431125, Miami, Florida 33143. Phone: 305/263-8699.

Pinellas Youth Symphony. P.O. Box 40044, Saint Petersburg, Florida 33743-0044. Phone: 813/822-5342.

South Florida Youth Symphony. 555 Northwest 152 Street, Miami, Florida 33169. Phone: 305/681-6406.

Tampa Bay Youth Orchestras. Tampa Bay Performing Arts Center, P.O. Box 518, Tampa, Florida 33601. Phone: 813/222-1085.

Youth Orchestra of Florida. 1708 North 40 Avenue, Hollywood, Florida 33021. Phone: 305/963-5575.

Georgia

Albany Area Youth Symphony. P.O. Box 70065, Albany, Georgia 31708-0002. Phone: 912/888-8799.

Atlanta Symphony Youth Orchestra. Suite 300, 1293 Peachtree Street, N.E., Atlanta, Georgia 30309. Phone: 404/898-9572.

Hawaii

Hawaii Youth Symphony Association. 1110 University Avenue, #202, Honolulu, Hawaii 96826. Phone: 808/941-9706.

Idaho

Treasure Valley Youth Symphony. Suite C, 516 South Ninth, Boise, Idaho 83702. Phone: 208/338-7840.

Illinois

Central Illinois Youth Symphony. P.O. Box 3736, Peoria, Illinois 61612-3736. Phone: 309/822-8775.

Chicago Youth Symphony Orchestra. 410 South Michigan Avenue, Suite 922, Chicago, Illinois 60605. Phone: 312/939-2207.

Civic Orchestra of Chicago. 220 South Michigan Avenue, Chicago, Illinois 60604. Phone: 312/435-8159.

Classical Symphony Orchestra. Fine Arts Building, Suite 730, 410 South Michigan Avenue, Chicago, Illinois 60605. Phone: 312/341-1521.

McHenry County Youth Orchestras. 64 East Crystal Lake Avenue, Crystal Lake, Illinois 60014-6137. Phone: 815/356-6296.

Midwest Youth Orchestra. 2520 Cowper Avenue, Evanston, Illinois 60201. Phone: 708/328-9998.

North Shore Youth Orchestra. Music Center of the North Shore, 300 Green Bay Road, Winnetka, Illinois 60093. Phone: 708/446-3822.

Schaumburg Youth Orchestra. c/o Prairie Center for the Arts, 201 Schaumburg Court, Schaumburg, Illinois 60193. Phone: 708/894-3600.

Suburban Youth Symphony Orchestra. P.O. Box 1411, Homewood, Illinois 60430-0411. Phone: 312/799-4826.

Indiana

East Central Indiana Youth Orchestra. Ball State University, School of Music, Muncie, Indiana 47306-0410. Phone: 317/285-5400.

Iowa

Quad City Youth Symphony Orchestra. P.O. Box 1144, Davenport, Iowa 52805-1144. Phone: 319/322-0931.

Kansas

Wichita Youth Orchestras. 225 West Douglas, Suite 207, Wichita, Kansas 67202. Phone: 316/267-5259.

Youth Symphony of Kansas City. P.O. Box 9477, Shawnee Mission, Kansas 66201-2177. Phone: 913/722-6810.

Kentucky

Central Kentucky Youth Orchestras. ArtsPlace, 161 North Mill Street, Lexington, Kentucky 40507. Phone: 606/254-0796.

Kentucky Youth Chamber Orchestra. 117 Millstone Drive, Richmond, Kentucky 40475. Phone: 502/535-6906.

Louisville Youth Orchestra. 623 West Main Street, Louisville, Kentucky 40202. Phone: 502/582-0135.

Owensboro Youth and Cadet Symphony. 122 East Eighteenth Street, Owensboro, Kentucky 42301. Phone: 502/684-0661.

Louisiana

Louisiana Youth Orchestra. One American Place, Suite 620, Baton Rouge, Louisiana 70808. Phone: 504/387-2776.

Maine

Portland Symphony Youth Ensembles. P.O. Box 3573, Portland, Maine 04104. Phone: 207/773-6128.

Maryland

Chesapeake Youth Symphony Orchestra. P.O. Box 863, Arnold, Maryland 21012. Phone: 410/647-7494.

Greater Baltimore Youth Orchestra. Essex Community College, 7201 Rossville Boulevard, Baltimore, Maryland 21237. Phone: 410/821-5783.

Maryland Youth Symphony Orchestra. P.O. Box 27, Glenwood, Maryland 21738. Phone: 410/442-5645.

Montgomery County Youth Orchestras. P.O. Box 30036, Bethesda, Maryland 20814. Phone: 301/654-2018.

Massachusetts

Boston University/Tanglewood Youth Artists Orchestra. 855 Commonwealth Avenue, Boston, Massachusetts 02215. Phone: 617/353-3386.

Greater Boston Youth Symphony Orchestra. 855 Commonwealth Avenue, Boston, Massachusetts 02215. Phone: 617/353-3348.

New England Conservatory Youth Philharmonic Orchestra. 290 Huntington Avenue, Boston, Massachusetts 02115. Phone: 617/262-1120.

Western Massachusetts Youth Orchestras. 1391 Main Street, Springfield, Massachusetts 01103. Phone: 413/733-0636.

Worcester Youth Symphony Orchestra. 29 High Street, Worcester, Massachusetts 01608-1814. Phone: 508/755-8246.

Michigan

Detroit Symphony Civic Orchestra. 3711 Woodward, Detroit, Michigan 48201. Phone: 313/833-3362.

Flint Youth Symphony. 1025 East Kearsley, Flint, Michigan 48503. Phone: 313/238-9651.

Grand Rapids Youth Symphony. 220 Lyon Northwest, Suite 415, Grand Rapids, Michigan 49503. Phone: 616/454-9451.

Holland Area Youth Orchestra. 25 West Eighth Street, Holland, Michigan 49423. Phone: 616/396-3278.

Interlochen Arts Academy Orchestra. Interlochen Center for the Arts, Interlochen, Michigan 49643. Phone: 616/276-9221.

Kalamazoo Junior Symphony. 714 South Westnedge Avenue, Kalamazoo, Michigan 49007. Phone: 616/349-7557.

Metropolitan Youth Symphony. P.O. Box 244, Southfield, Michigan 48037-0244.

Saginaw Symphony Youth Orchestra. P.O. Box 415, Saginaw, Michigan 48606. Phone: 517/755-6471.

West Shore Youth Symphony Orchestra. Suite 406, Frauenthal Building, 425 West Western Avenue, Muskegon, Michigan 49440. Phone: 616/726-3231.

Minnesota

Greater Twin Cities Youth Symphonies. 420 Oak Grove Street, Suite 205, Minneapolis, Minnesota 55403. Phone: 612/870-7611.

Minnesota Youth Symphonies. Suite 203, 790 Cleveland Avenue South, St. Paul, Minnesota 55116. Phone: 612/699-5811.

Southeastern Minnesota Youth Orchestra. Wellington Square, 214 First Avenue, S.W., Rochester, Minnesota 55902-3129. Phone: 507/282-1718.

Missouri

Saint Louis Symphony Youth Orchestra. Powell Symphony Hall, 718 North Grand Boulevard, St. Louis, Missouri 63103. Phone: 314/286-4132.

Nebraska

Lincoln Youth Symphony. Public School Administration Building, P.O. Box 82889, Lincoln, Nebraska 68501. Phone: 402/436-1000.

Omaha Area Youth Orchestra. P.O. Box 24813, Omaha, Nebraska 68124-0813. Phone: 402/553-7655.

New Hampshire

New Hampshire Youth Orchestra. P.O. Box 1031, Lebanon, New Hampshire 03766. Phone: 802/649-5349.

New Jersey

Bergen Youth Orchestra. 41 Joyce Road, Tenafly, New Jersey 07670. Phone: 201/569-1625.

Greater Princeton Youth Orchestra. c/o Hillier Group, 500 Alexander Park, Princeton, New Jersey 08543. Phone: 609/452-8332.

New Jersey Youth Symphony. P.O. Box 477, Summit, New Jersey 07902-0477. Phone: 908/771-5544.

New Mexico

Albuquerque Youth Symphony. Music Department, University of New Mexico, Albuquerque, New Mexico 87131. Phone: 505/277-2126.

New York

Binghamton Youth Symphony. P.O. Box 1152, Binghamton, New York 13902. Phone: 607/722-7150.

Camerata Youth Orchestra. 71 Woodland Avenue, Rockville Centre, New York 11570. Phone: 516/766-5405.

Empire State Youth Orchestra. 432 State Street, Suite 230, Schenectady, New York 12305. Phone: 518/382-7581.

Gemini Youth Symphony. P.O. Box 705, Melville, New York 11747-0705. Phone: 516/277-0591.

Greater Westchester Youth Orchestras. 21 Shaw Lane, Irvington, New York 10533.

InterSchool Orchestras of New York. 207 East Eighty-fifth Street, New York, New York 10028. Phone: 212/288-0763.

Long Island Youth Orchestra. 316 Littleworth Lane, Sea Cliff, New York 11579. Phone: 516/627-8873.

New York Youth Symphony. Carnegie Hall 504, 881 Seventh Avenue, New York, New York 10019. Phone: 212/581-5933.

Rochester Philharmonic Youth Orchestra. 108 East Avenue, Rochester, New York 14604. Phone: 716/454-2620.

Rockland Youth Philharmonic. P.O. Box 161, Tallman, New York 10982. Phone: 914/357-7011.

Syracuse Symphony Youth Orchestra. Civic Center, Suite 40, 411 Montgomery Street, Syracuse, New York 13202. Phone: 315/424-8222.

North Carolina

Brevard Music Center. P.O. Box 592, Brevard, North Carolina 28712. Phone: 704/884-2011.

Charlotte Symphony Youth Orchestra. P.O. Box 35547, Charlotte, North Carolina 28235. Phone: 704/332-0468.

Greensboro Symphony Youth Orchestra. P.O. Box 20303, Greensboro, North Carolina 27420. Phone: 919/333-7490.

Ohio

Akron Youth Symphony. 17 North Broadway, Akron, Ohio 44308. Phone: 216/535-8131.

Canton Youth Symphony. 1001 Market Avenue, North, Canton, Ohio 44072. Phone: 216/452-3434.

Cincinnati Symphony Youth Orchestra. Music Hall, 1241 Elm Street, Cincinnati, Ohio 45210. Phone: 513/621-1919.

Cleveland Institute of Music Youth Orchestra. 11021 East Boulevard, Cleveland, Ohio 44106. Phone: 216/791-5165.

Cleveland Orchestra Youth Orchestra. Severance Hall, 11001 Euclid Avenue, Cleveland, Ohio 44106. Phone: 216/231-7300.

Columbus Symphony Youth Orchestras. 55 East State Street, Columbus, Ohio 43215. Phone: 614/224-5281.

Dayton Philharmonic Youth Orchestra. Montgomery County's Memorial Hall, 125 East First Street, Dayton, Ohio 45402. Phone: 513/224-3521.

Mansfield Symphony Youth Orchestra. 142 Park Avenue West, Mansfield, Ohio 44902. Phone: 419/524-5927.

Northern Ohio Youth Orchestras. P.O. Box 427, Oberlin, Ohio 44074. Phone: 216/775-0716.

Oklahoma

Oklahoma City Junior Symphony. P.O. Box 92, Oklahoma City, Oklahoma 73101. Phone: 405/841-8549.

Oklahoma Youth Orchestra. P.O. Box 60408, Oklahoma City, Oklahoma 73146. Phone: 405/232-1199.

Tulsa Youth Symphony Orchestra. 2901 South Harvard Avenue, Tulsa, Oklahoma 74114-6119. Phone: 918/747-7473.

Oregon

Argonauts Salem Youth Symphony. 1320 Capitol Street, N.E., Salem, Oregon 97303. Phone: 503/399-0153.

Corvallis Youth Symphony. P.O. Box 857, Corvallis, Oregon 97339-0857. Phone: 503/757-6181.

Eugene Youth Symphony Association. P.O. Box 306, Eugene, Oregon 97440. Phone: 503/484-0473.

Portland Youth Philharmonic. 1119 South West Park Avenue, Portland, Oregon 97205-2495. Phone: 503/223-5939.

Youth Symphony of Southern Oregon. 322 Bridge Street, Ashland, Oregon 97520. Phone: 503/482-2040.

Pennsylvania

Erie Junior Philharmonic Orchestra. 1001 State Street, #924, Erie, Pennsylvania 16502-1878. Phone: 814/455-1375.

Erie Youth Orchestra. 501 East Thirty-eighth Street, Erie, Pennsylvania 16546. Phone: 814/833-0877.

Johnstown Youth Symphony. 809 Franco Avenue, Johnstown, Pennsylvania 15905. Phone: 814/255-2033.

Philadelphia Youth Orchestra. P.O. Box 41810, Philadelphia, Pennsylvania 19101-1810. Phone: 215/765-8485.

Pittsburgh Youth Symphony Orchestra. Heinz Hall, 600 Penn Avenue, Pittsburgh, Pennsylvania 15222. Phone: 412/392-4872.

South Hills Junior Orchestra. P.O. Box 12642, Upper St. Clair, Pennsylvania 15241. Phone: 412/833-1600.

Three Rivers Young People's Orchestras. 711 Penn Avenue, Suite 400, Pittsburgh, Pennsylvania 15222. Phone: 412/391-0526.

York Junior Symphony Orchestra. 2518 Stanford Drive, York, Pennsylvania 17402. Phone: 717/757-3787.

York Youth Symphony. 1732 Crescent Road, York, Pennsylvania 17403. Phone: 717/846-4188.

Youth Orchestra of Bucks County. c/o Gimbel Associates, 130 Almshouse Road, Suite 406, Richboro, Pennsylvnaia 18954. Phone: 215/357-8830.

Rhode Island

Rhode Island Philharmonic Youth Orchestra. Suite 112, 222 Richmond Street, Providence, Rhode Island 02903. Phone: 401/831-3123.

Young Peoples Symphony of Rhode Island. 131 Washington Street, Providence, Rhode Island 02903. Phone: 401/421-0460.

South Carolina

Carolina Youth Symphony. P.O. Box 6401, Suite B-117, Koger Executive Center, Greenville, South Carolina 29606. Phone: 803/675-0375.

Columbia Youth Orchestra. P.O. Box 5703, Columbia, South Carolina 29250. Phone: 803/733-3381.

Greenville County Youth Orchestra. Fine Arts Center, 1613 West Washington Road, Greenville, South Carolina 29601. Phone: 803/241-3327.

Tennessee

Knoxville Symphony Youth Orchestra. 708 Gay Street, Knoxville, Tennessee 37902. Phone: 615/523-1178.

Memphis Youth Symphony Orchestra. 3100 Walnut Grove Road, Suite 501, Memphis, Tennessee 38111. Phone: 901/324-3627.

Nashville Youth Symphony. Blair School of Music, 2400 Blakemore Avenue, Nashville, Tennessee 37212. Phone: 615/343-3165.

Texas

Greater Dallas Youth Orchestra. Sammons Arts Center, Suite 406, 3630 Harry Hines Boulevard, Dallas, Texas 75219. Phone: 214/528-7747.

Houston Youth Symphony and Ballet. P.O. Box 56104, Houston, Texas 77256. Phone: 713/621-2411.

Huntsville Youth Orchestra. SHSU Department of Music, Huntsville, Texas 77341. Phone: 409/294-3595.

Lubbock Youth Symphony Orchestra. Suite 204, 8200 Nashville, Lubbock, Texas 79423. Phone: 806/794-7175.

Tyler Youth Orchestra. P.O. Box 130694, Tyler, Texas 75713. Phone: 903/593-1711.

Youth Orchestra of Greater Fort Worth. 4401 Trail Lake Drive, Fort Worth, Texas 76109. Phone: 817/923-3121.

Youth Orchestras of San Antonio. 950 East Hildebrand, San Antonio, Texas 78212. Phone: 512/737-0097.

Utah

Utah Valley Youth Symphony Orchestra. P.O. Box 1235, Provo, Utah 84603. Phone: 801/377-1184.

Utah Youth Symphony. 203 Gardner Hall, University of Utah, Salt Lake City, Utah 84112. Phone: 801/485-5252.

Vermont

Lakes Region Youth Orchestra. Fine Arts Center, Castleton State College, Castleton, Vermont 05735. Phone: 802/468-5611.

Vermont Youth Orchestra. P.O. Box 905, Burlington, Vermont 05402-0905. Phone: 802/658-3199.

Virginia

Bay Youth Symphony of Virginia. 710 Round Bay Road, Norfolk, Virginia 23502. Phone: 804/461-8834.

Northern Virginia Youth Symphony Association. 4026 Hummer Road, Annandale, Virginia 22003. Phone: 703/642-0862.

Youth Orchestra of Charlottesville-Albemarle. P.O. Box 4845, Charlottesville, Virginia 22905. Phone: 804/974-6242.

Youth Orchestras of Prince William. P.O. Box 2127, Woodbridge, Virginia 22193. Phone: 703/590-7083.

Washington

Capital Area Youth Symphony. P.O. Box 676, Olympia, Washington 98507. Phone: 206/956-1892.

Seattle Youth Symphony Orchestras. 11065 Fifth N.E., Suite E, Seattle, Washington 98125. Phone: 206/362-2300.

Tacoma Youth Symphony. P.O. Box 660, Tacoma, Washington 98401. Phone: 206/627-2792.

West Virginia

Ovations Youth Orchestra. 410 Washington Avenue, Wheeling, West Virginia 26003. Phone: 304/233-0772.

West Virginia Youth Symphony. P.O. Box 2292, Charleston, West Virginia 25328. Phone: 304/342-0151.

Wisconsin

La Crosse Youth Symphony. P.O. Box 2511, La Crosse, Wisconsin 54601. Phone: 608/788-0159.

Milwaukee Youth Symphony Orchestra. 929 North Water Street, Milwaukee, Wisconsin 53202. Phone: 414/272-8540.

Wisconsin Youth Symphony Orchestras. 1621 C Humanities Building, 455 North Park Street, Madison, Wisconsin 53706. Phone: 608/263-3320.

Appendix E

Children's Museums, Science and Technology Centers, and Other Places that Promote Hands-On Learning

Alabama

Alabama Museum of Natural History. Smith Hall, University of Alabama, Tuscaloosa, Alabama 35487-0340. Phone: 205/348-7550.

Anniston Museum of Natural History. 4301 McClellan Boulevard, P.O. Box 1587, Anniston, Alabama 36202-1587. Phone: 205/237-6766.

Center for Cultural Arts. 501 Broad Street, P.O. Box 1507, Gadsden, Alabama 35901. Phone: 205/543-2787.

Discovery 2000. 1320 South Twenty-second Street, Birmingham, Alabama 35205. Phone: 205/939-1177.

Exploreum. 1906 Springhill Avenue, Mobile, Alabama 36607. Phone: 205/471-5923.

North Alabama Science Center, Inc. P.O. Box 18831, Huntsville, Alabama 35804. Phone: 205/882-4640.

Southern Museum of Flight. 4343 Seventy-third Street North, Birmingham, Alabama 35206. Phone: 205/833-8226.

U.S. Space and Rocket Center. Tranquility Base, Huntsville, Alabama 35807. Phone: 205/837-3400.

Alaska

Imaginarium. 725 West Fifth Avenue, Anchorage, Alaska 99501. Phone: 907/276-3179.

University of Alaska Museum. 907 Yukon Drive, Fairbanks, Alaska 99775-1200. Phone: 907/474-6939.

Arizona

Arizona Museum for Youth. 35 North Robson, Mesa, Arizona 85201. Phone: 602/644-2467.

Arizona Museum of Science and Technology. 147 East Adams Street, Phoenix, Arizona 85004-2331. Phone: 602/258-7250.

Flandrau Science Center and Planetarium. Planetarium Building #91, University of Arizona, Tucson, Arizona 85721. Phone: 602/621-4515.

Kitt Peak Museum. 950 North Cherry Avenue, P.O. Box 26732, Tucson, Arizona 85726-6732. Phone: 602/740-2426.

Tucson Children's Museum. 200 South Sixth Street, Tucson, Arizona 85701. Phone: 602/792-9985.

Arkansas

Arkansas Museum of Science and History. MacArthur Park, Little Rock, Arkansas 72202. Phone: 501/324-9231.

Mid-America Museum. 400 Mid-America Boulevard, Hot Springs, Arkansas 71913. Phone: 501/767-3461.

California

California Academy of Sciences. Golden Gate Park, San Francisco, California 94118. Phone: 415/221-5100.

California Museum of Science and Industry. 700 State Drive, Los Angeles, California 90037. Phone: 213/744-7400.

Carter House Natural Science Center. 48 Quartz Hill, Redding, California 96003. Phone: 916/225-4125.

Children's Discovery Museum of San Jose. 180 Woz Way, San Jose, California 95110-2780. Phone: 408/298-5437.

Children's Museum at La Habra. 301 South Euclid, La Habra, California 90631. Phone: 310/691-4464.

The Discovery Center. 1944 North Winery Avenue, Fresno, California 93703. Phone: 209/251-5533.

Discovery Museum of Orange County. 3101 West Harvard Street, Santa Ana, California 92704. Phone: 714/540-0404.

Discovery Pavilion. 10 Universal City Plaza, #1950, Universal City, California 91608. Phone: 818/752-2250.

Exploratorium. 3601 Lyon Street, San Francisco, California 94123. Phone: 415/563-7337.

EXPLORIT! Science Center. 3141 Fifth Street, Davis, California 95616. Phone: 916/756-0191.

Fresno Metropolitan Museum. 1515 Van Ness Avenue, Fresno, California 93721. Phone: 209/441-1444.

Kidspace, A Participatory Museum. 390 South El Molino, Pasadena, California 91101. Phone: 818/449-9143.

Lawrence Hall of Science. University of California, Centennial Drive, Berkeley, California 94720. Phone: 510/642-4193.

Lawrence Livermore National Laboratory. Visitor Center, P.O. Box 808, L-790, Livermore, California 94550. Phone: 415/422-9797.

Lori Brock Children's Museum. 3803 Chester Avenue, Bakersfield, California 93301. Phone: 805/395-1201.

Los Angeles Children's Museum. 310 North Main Street, Los Angeles, California 90012. Phone: 213/687-8801.

Natural History Museum of LA County. 900 Exposition Boulevard, Los Angeles, California 90007. Phone: 213/744-3543.

Oakland Museum. 1000 Oak Street, Oakland, California 94607. Phone: 510/238-3401.

Palo Alto Junior Museum. 1451 Middlefield Road, Palo Alto, California 94301. Phone: 415/329-2111.

Pasadena Hall of Science. 1150 Foot Hill Boulevard, Suite E, La Canada, California 91011. Phone: 818/952-4022.

Rancho Santa Ana Botanic Garden. 1500 North College Avenue, Claremont, California 91711. Phone: 714/625-8767.

Reuben H. Fleet Space Theater. 1875 El Prado, P.O. Box 33303, San Diego, California 92103. Phone: 619/238-1233.

Sacramento Science Center. 3615 Auburn Boulevard, Sacramento, California 95821. Phone: 916/277-6180.

San Francisco Bay Model Visitor Center. 2100 Bridgeway, Sausalito, California 94965. Phone: 415/332-3871.

Santa Barbara Botanic Garden. 1212 Mission Canyon Road, Santa Barbara, California 93105. Phone: 805/682-4726.

Santa Barbara Museum of Natural History. 2559 Puesta del Sol Road, Santa Barbara, California 93105. Phone: 805/682-4711.

The Tech Museum of Innovation. 145 West San Carlos Street, San Jose, California 95113. Phone: 408/279-7150.

Colorado

Children's Museum of Denver. 2121 Children's Museum Drive, Denver, Colorado 80211-5221. Phone: 303/433-7444.

Denver Museum of Natural History. 2001 Colorado Boulevard, Denver, Colorado 80205. Phone: 303/333-6387.

Discovery Center. P.O. Box 301, Fort Collins, Colorado 80522. Phone: 303/493-2182.

National Center for Atmospheric Research. P.O. Box 3000, Boulder, Colorado 80307-3000. Phone: 303/497-8603.

National Renewable Energy Laboratory. 1617 Cole Boulevard, Golden, Colorado 80401. Phone: 303/231-1000.

Connecticut

The Discovery Museum. 4450 Park Avenue, Bridgeport, Connecticut 06604. Phone: 203/372-3521.

Eli Whitney Museum. 915 Whitney Avenue, Hamden, Connecticut 06517-4001. Phone: 203/777-1833.

New Britain Youth Museum. 30 High Street, New Britain, Connecticut 06051. Phone: 203/225-3020.

Science Museum of Connecticut. 950 Trout Brook Drive, West Hartford, Connecticut 06119. Phone: 203/236-2961.

Thames Science Center. Gallows Lane, New London, Connecticut 06320. Phone: 203/442-0391.

Delaware

Delaware Art Museum. 2301 Kentmere Parkway, Wilmington, Delaware 19806. Phone: 302/571-9590.

Delaware Museum of Natural History. 4840 Kennett Pike, Wilmington, Delaware 19807. Phone: 302/658-9111.

District of Columbia

Capital Children's Museum. 800 Third Street, N.E., Washington, D.C. 20002. Phone: 202/543-8600.

Explorers Hall, National Geographic Society. Seventeenth and M Streets, N.W., Washington, D.C. 20036. Phone: 202/857-7455.

National Air and Space Museum. Sixth Street and Independence Avenue, S.W., Washington, D.C. 20560. Phone: 202/357-1663.

National Museum of American History. Fourteenth Street and Constitution Avenue, N.W., Washington, D.C. 20560. Phone: 202/357-2510.

National Museum of Natural History. Tenth Street and Constitution Avenue, N.W., Washington, D.C. 20560. Phone: 202/786-2604.

Florida

Children's Museum of Tampa.
7550 North Boulevard, Tampa, Florida 33604. Phone: 813/935-8441.

The Children's Science Center. P.O.
Box 151381, Cape Coral, Florida 33915-1381. Phone: 813/772-4466.

Children's Science Explorium. 131
Mizner Boulevard, Suite 15, Boca Raton, Florida 33432. Phone: 407/395-8401.

Collier Automotive Museum. 2500
South Horseshoe Drive, Naples, Florida 33942. Phone: 813/643-5252.

Discovery Science Center. 50 South
Magnolia Avenue, Ocala, Florida 34474-4153. Phone: 904/368-2710.

**Great Explorations, The Hands-On
Museum.** 1120 Fourth Street South, St. Petersburg, Florida 33701. Phone: 813/821-8992.

Gulf Coast World of Science. 717
North Tamiami Trail, Sarasota, Florida 34236-4047. Phone: 813/957-4969.

Imaginarium Group. P.O. Box 2217,
Ft. Myers, Florida 33902. Phone: 813/332-6666.

**Miami Museum of Science and
Space Transit Planetarium.** 3280 South Miami Avenue, Miami, Florida 33129. Phone: 305/854-4247.

Museum of Discovery and Science.
401 Southwest Second Street, Ft. Lauderdale, Florida 33312-1707. Phone: 305/467-6637.

**Museum of Science and History of
Jacksonville.** 1025 Museum Circle, Jacksonville, Florida 32207. Phone: 904/396-7062.

Museum of Science and Industry.
4801 East Fowler Avenue, Tampa, Florida 33617. Phone: 813/987-6300.

Odyssey—Tallahassee Science Center. P.O. Box 13355, Tallahassee, Florida 32317-3355. Phone: 904/893-2998.

Orlando Science Center. 810 East
Rollins Street, Orlando, Florida 32803-1291. Phone: 407/896-7151.

South Florida Science Museum.
4801 Dreher Trail North, West Palm Beach, Florida 33405. Phone: 305/832-1988.

Space Coast Science Center. 1510
Highland Avenue, Melbourne, Florida 32935. Phone: 407/259-5572.

**Tallahassee Museum of History
and Natural Science.** 3945 Museum Drive, Tallahassee, Florida 32310. Phone: 904/576-1636.

Georgia

Fernbank Science Center. 156 Heaton Park Drive, N.E., Atlanta, Georgia 30307-1398. Phone: 404/378-4311.

Georgia Southern Museum. Landrum Box 8061, Statesboro, Georgia 30460-8061. Phone: 912/681-5444.

High Museum of Art. 1280
Peachtree Street, N.E., Atlanta, Georgia 30309. Phone: 404/892-3600.

The Museum of Arts and Sciences.
4182 Forsyth Road, Macon, Georgia 31210. Phone: 912/477-3232.

National Science Center. ATZH-NSC-D, Fort Gordon, Georgia 30905-5689. Phone: 706/791-3912.

Savannah Science Museum. 4405
Paulsen Street, Savannah, Georgia 31405. Phone: 912/355-6705.

**SciTrek, Science and Technology
Museum of Atlanta.** 395 Piedmont Avenue, N.E., Atlanta, Georgia 30308. Phone: 404/522-5500.

Hawaii

Astronaut Ellison S. Onizuka Space Center. P.O. Box 833, Kailua-Kona, Hawaii 96745. Phone: 808/329-3441.

Bishop Museum. 1525 Bernice Street, P.O. Box 19000-A, Honolulu, Hawaii 96817-0916. Phone: 808/847-3511.

Idaho

Discovery Center of Idaho. P.O. Box 192, Boise, Idaho 83701. Phone: 208/343-9895.

The Herett Museum. 315 Falls Avenue, College of Southern Idaho, Twin Falls, Idaho 83303. Phone: 208/733-9554.

Idaho Museum of Natural History. Box 8096, Pocatello, Idaho 83209. Phone: 208/236-3168.

Illinois

The Adler Planetarium. 1300 South Lake Shore Drive, Chicago, Illinois 60605. Phone: 312/322-0304.

Art Institute of Chicago. Michigan Avenue and Adams Street, Chicago, Illinois 60603. Phone: 312/443-3600.

Chicago Academy of Sciences. 2001 North Clark Street, Chicago, Illinois 60614. Phone: 312/549-0607.

Chicago Botanic Garden. 1000 Lake Cook Road, P.O. Box 400, Glencoe, Illinois 60022. Phone: 708/835-5440.

Chicago Children's Museum. 435 East Illinois, Suite 370, Chicago, Illinois 60611. Phone: 312/527-1000.

Chicago Historical Society. Clark Street at North Avenue, Chicago, Illinois 60614. Phone: 312/642-4600.

Discovery Center Museum. 711 North Main Street, Rockford, Illinois 61103. Phone: 815/963-6769.

Fermi National Lab-Science Education Center. P.O. Box 500, MS 777, Batavia, Illinois 60510. Phone: 312/840-3092.

Field Museum of Natural History. Roosevelt Road at Lake Shore Drive, Chicago, Illinois 60605. Phone: 312/922-9410.

International Museum of Surgical Science. 1524 North Lake Shore Drive, Chicago, Illinois 60610. Phone: 312/642-6502.

Kohl Children's Museum. 165 Green Bay Road, Wilmette, Illinois 60091. Phone: 708/256-6056.

Lakeview Museum of Arts and Sciences. 1125 West Lake Avenue, Peoria, Illinois 61614. Phone: 309/686-7000.

Museum of Science and Industry. Fifty-seventh Street and Lake Shore Drive, Chicago, Illinois 60637-2093. Phone: 312/684-1414.

SciTech, Science and Technology Interactive Center. 18 West Benton, Aurora, Illinois 60506. Phone: 312/898-8235.

Indiana

Children's Museum of Indianapolis. 3000 North Meridian Street, Indianapolis, Indiana 46208. Phone: 317/924-KIDS.

Children's Science and Technology Museum of Terre Haute. 523 Wabash Avenue, Terre Haute, Indiana 47802. Phone: 812/235-5548.

Evansville Museum of Arts and Science. 411 Southeast Riverside Drive, Evansville, Indiana 47713. Phone: 812/425-2406.

Hannah Lindahl Children's Museum. 1402 South Main Street, Mishawaka, Indiana 46544. Phone: 219/258-3056.

Muncie Children's Museum. P.O. Box 544, 306 South Walnut Plaza, Muncie, Indiana 47308. Phone: 317/286-1660.

Science Central. 1950 North Clinton, Fort Wayne, Indiana 46805-4049. Phone: 219/424-2413.

Iowa

Children's Museum. 533 Sixteenth Street, Bettendorf, Iowa 52722. Phone: 319/344-4106.

Grout Museums: Bluedorn Science Imaginarium. 503 South Street, Waterloo, Iowa 50701. Phone: 319/234-6357.

Science Center of Iowa. 4500 Grand Avenue, Des Moines, Iowa 50312. Phone: 515/274-6868.

The Science Station. 427 First Street, S.E., Cedar Rapids, Iowa 52401. Phone: 319/366-0968.

Kansas

Children's Museum of Wichita. 435 South Water, Wichita, Kansas 67208. Phone: 316/267-2281.

Museum of Natural History. University of Kansas, 602 Dyche Hall, Lawrence, Kansas 66045. Phone: 913/864-4540.

Old Cowtown Museum. 1871 Sim Park Drive, Wichita, Kansas 67203. Phone: 316/264-0671.

Omnisphere and Science Center. 220 South Main Street, Wichita, Kansas 67202. Phone: 316/264-3174.

Wichita Art Museum. 619 Stackman Drive, Wichita Drive, Wichita, Kansas 67203. Phone: 316/268-4921.

Kentucky

Museum of History and Science. 727 West Main Street, Louisville, Kentucky 40202. Phone: 502/561-6103.

Louisiana

Audubon Institute. 111 Rue Iberville, New Orleans, Louisiana 70130. Phone: 504/565-3020.

Lafayette Natural History Museum and Planetarium. 637 Girard Park Drive, Lafayette, Louisiana 70503-2896. Phone: 318/268-5544.

Louisiana Arts and Science Center. 100 South River Road, Baton Rouge, Louisiana 70802. Phone: 504/344-9463.

Louisiana Children's Museum. 428 Julia Street, New Orleans, Louisiana 70130. Phone: 504/523-1357.

Louisiana Nature and Science Center. Nature Center Drive, P.O. Box 870610, New Orleans, Louisiana 70187-0610. Phone: 504/246-5672.

LSU Museum of Natural Science. Louisiana State University, 119 Foster Hall. Baton Rouge, Louisiana 70803. Phone: 504/388-2855.

Sci-Port Discovery Center. 101 Milam Street, Shreveport, Louisiana 71101. Phone: 318/424-3466.

Maine

The Children's Museum of Maine. 746 Stevens Avenue, Portland, Maine 04103. Phone: 207/828-1234.

Maryland

Baltimore City Life Museums. 800 East Lombard Street, Baltimore, Maryland 21202-4523. Phone: 410/396-3523.

Christopher Columbus Center of Marine Research and Exploration. 111 Marketplace, Suite 300, Baltimore, Maryland 21202. Phone: 410/547-8727.

Cloisters Children's Museum. 10440 Falls Road, Brooklandville, Maryland 21022. Phone: 410/823-2551.

Draketail Maritime Science Center. P.O. Box 595, Churchton, Maryland 20723. Phone: 410/867-2722.

Maryland Science Center. 601 Light Street, Baltimore, Maryland 21230. Phone: 410/685-2370.

Massachusetts

Children's Museum at Holyoke. 444 Dwight Street, Holyoke, Massachusetts 01040. Phone: 413/536-5437.

The Children's Museum of Boston. Museum Wharf, 300 Congress Street, Boston, Massachusetts 02210-1034. Phone: 617/426-8855.

Children's Museum of Dartmouth. 276 Gulf Road, South Dartmouth, Massachusetts 02748. Phone: 617/993-3361.

Computer Museum. 300 Congress Street, Boston, Massachusetts 02210. Phone: 617/426-2800.

The Discovery Museums. 177 Main Street, Acton, Massachusetts 07120. Phone: 508/264-4201.

Museum of Science. Science Park, Boston, Massachusetts 02114-1099. Phone: 617/589-0100.

National Plastics Center and Museum. P.O. Box 639, Leominster, Massachusetts 01453. Phone: 508/534-4961.

New England Science Center. 222 Harrington Way, Worcester, Massachusetts 01604. Phone: 508/791-9211.

Springfield Science Museum. 236 State Street, Springfield, Massachusetts 01103. Phone: 414/733-1194.

Woods Hole Oceanographic Institution. Co-Op Building, Woods Hole, Massachusetts 02543. Phone: 508/457-2000.

Michigan

Aldred P. Sloan Museum. 1221 East Kearsley Street, Flint, Michigan 48503. Phone: 313/760-1169.

Ann Arbor Hands-On Museum. 219 East Huron Street, Ann Arbor, Michigan 48104. Phone: 313/995-5439.

Children's Museum/Detroit Public Schools. 67 East Kirby, Detroit, Michigan 48202. Phone: 313/494-1210.

Cranbrook Institute of Science. 1221 North Woodward Avenue, Box 801, Bloomfield Hills, Michigan 48303-0801. Phone: 313/645-3230.

Detroit Science Center. 5020 John R. Street, Detroit, Michigan 48202. Phone: 313/577-8400.

The Flint Children's Museum. 1602 West Third Avenue, Flint, Michigan 48504. Phone: 313/238-6900.

Hall of Ideas, Midland Center for the Arts. 1801 West St. Andrews Road, Midland, Michigan 48640-2695. Phone: 517/631-5930.

Henry Ford Museum and Greenfield Village. 20900 Oakwood Boulevard, Dearborn, Michigan 48121. Phone: 313/271-1620.

Impression 5 Science Museum. 200 Museum Drive, Lansing, Michigan 48933-1905. Phone: 517/485-8116.

Kalamazoo Public Museum. 315 South Rose Street, Kalamazoo, Michigan 49007. Phone: 616/345-7092.

Kingman Museum of Natural History. West Michigan Avenue at Twentieth Street, Battle Creek, Michigan 49017. Phone: 616/965-5117.

Southwestern Michigan College Museum. Southwestern Michigan College, 58900 Cherry Grove Road, Dowagiac, Michigan 49047. Phone: 616/782-5113.

Minnesota

The Bakken: A Library and Museum of Electricity in Life. 3537 Zenith Avenue South, Minneapolis, Minnesota 55416. Phone: 612/927-6508.

Children's Museum. 1217 Bandana Boulevard, North, St. Paul, Minnesota 55108. Phone: 612/622-5305.

Headwaters Science Center. P.O. Box 1176, Bemidji, Minnesota 56601. Phone: 218/751-1110.

James Ford Bell Museum of Natural History. 100 Ecology Building, University of Minnesota, 1987 Upper Bufford Circle, St. Paul, Minnesota 55108-6097. Phone: 612/624-4112.

Science Museum of Minnesota. 30 East Tenth Street, St. Paul, Minnesota 55101. Phone: 612/221-9488.

Mississippi

Mississippi Museum of Natural Science. 111 North Jefferson Street, Jackson, Mississippi 39202. Phone: 601/354-7303.

Missouri

Discovery Center of Springfield. P.O. Box 50162, Springfield, Missouri 65805. Phone: 417/831-1800.

Kansas City Museum. 3218 Gladstone Boulevard, Kansas City, Missouri 64123. Phone: 816/483-8300.

Magic House — St. Louis Children's Museum. 516 South Kirkwood Road, St. Louis, Missouri 63122. Phone: 314/822-8900.

Missouri Botanical Garden. 4344 Shaw Boulevard, St. Louis, Missouri 63110. Phone: 314/577-5140.

St. Louis Science Center. 5050 Oakland Avenue, St. Louis, Missouri 63110. Phone: 314/289-4400.

Montana

Museum of the Rockies. Montana State University, Bozeman, Montana 59717. Phone: 406/994-5283.

Nebraska

Edgerton Educational Center. c/o Hamilton Telephone Co., 1001 Twelfth Street, Aurora, Nebraska 68818. Phone: 402/694-5101.

Omaha Children's Museum. 500 South Twentieth Street, Omaha, Nebraska 68102. Phone: 402/342-6164.

University of Nebraska State Museum. 307 Morrill Hall, Lincoln, Nebraska 68588-0338. Phone: 402/-472-6365.

Western Heritage Museum. 801 South Tenth Street, Omaha, Nebraska 68108. Phone: 402/444-5071.

Nevada

Lied Discovery Children's Museum. 833 Las Vegas Boulevard North, Las Vegas, Nevada 89101. Phone: 702/382-3445.

Nevada Science Center. c/o Nuclear Waste Repository Office, P.O. Box 1767, Tonopah, Nevada 89049. Phone: 702/482-8181.

New Hampshire

The Children's Museum of Portsmouth. 280 Mancy Street, Portsmouth, New Hampshire 03801. Phone: 603/436-3853.

Science Enrichment Encounters. 324 Commercial Street, Manchester, New Hampshire 03101. Phone: 603/669-0400.

New Jersey

Invention Factory. 714 South Clinton Avenue, Trenton, New Jersey 08611. Phone: 609/396-1818.

Liberty Science Center and Hall of Technology. 251 Phillips Street, Jersey City, New Jersey 07304. Phone: 201/451-0006.

Monmouth County Historical Association. 70 Court Street, Freehold, New Jersey 07728. Phone: 908/462-1466.

The Newark Museum. 49 Washington Street, P.O. Box 540, Newark, New Jersey 07101-0540. Phone: 201/596-6550.

New Mexico

Bradbury Science Museum. Los Alamos National Laboratory MS-M897, Los Alamos, New Mexico 87545. Phone: 505/667-4444.

Explora Science Center Foundation. P.O. Box 27616, Albuquerque, New Mexico 87125. Phone: 505/266-7045.

Las Cruces Natural History Museum. Mesilla Valley Mall, Las Cruces, New Mexico 88001. Phone: 505/522-3120.

New Mexico Museum of Natural History. 1801 Mountain Road, N.W., P.O. Box 7010, Albuquerque, New Mexico 87194. Phone: 505/841-8837.

Space Center. Top of New Mexico Highway 2001, P.O. Box 533, Alamogordo, New Mexico 88311-0533. Phone: 505/437-2840.

New York

American Museum of Natural History. Central Park West at Seventy-ninth Street, New York, New York 10024. Phone: 212/769-5000.

The Brooklyn Children's Museum. 145 Brooklyn Avenue, Brooklyn, New York 11213. Phone: 718/735-4400.

Buffalo Museum of Science and Tifft Nature Preserve. 1020 Humbolt Parkway, Buffalo, New York 14211-1293. Phone: 716/896-5200.

Children's Museum at Utica, New York. 311 Main Street, Utica, New York 13501. Phone: 315/724-6128.

DNA Learning Center. 334 Main Street, Cold Spring Harbor, New York 11724. Phone: 516/367-7240.

Exhibit Center/Science Museum. Brookhaven National Laboratory, Upton, New York 11973. Phone: 516/282-4049.

Friends of LIMSAT. 14 Stafford Drive, Huntington Station, New York 11746. Phone: 516/427-5804.

Hudson River Museum of Westchester. 511 Warburton Avenue, Yonkers, New York 10701. Phone: 914/963-4550.

International Museum of Photography at George Eastman House. 900 East Avenue, Rochester, New York 14607. Phone: 716/271-3361.

Museum of Science and Technology. 500 South Franklin, Syracuse, New York 13202. Phone: 315/425-9068.

New York Botanical Garden. 200th Street and Southern Boulevard, Bronx, New York 10458-5126. Phone: 212/220-8700.

New York Hall of Science. 47-01 111th Street, Flushing Meadows, Corona Park, New York 11368. Phone: 718/699-0005.

New York State Museum. Room 9852, CEC, Albany, New York 12230. Phone: 518/474-5801.

New York Transit Museum. 130 Livingston Street, Brooklyn, New York 11201. Phone: 718/694-5102.

Ontario County Historical Society. 55 North Main Street, Canandaigua, New York 14424. Phone: 716/394-4975.

Petrified Creatures Museum of Natural History. R.D. #2, Route 20, Richfield Springs, New York 13439. Phone: 315/858-2868.

Roberson Museum and Science Center. 30 Front Street, Binghamton, New York 13905. Phone: 607/772-0660.

Rochester Museum and Science Center. 657 East Avenue, P.O. Box 1480, Rochester, New York 14603-1480. Phone: 716/271-4320.

Schenectady Museum and Planetarium. Nott Terrace Heights, Schenectady, New York 12308. Phone: 518/382-7890.

Science Discovery Center of Oneonta. State University College, PS-B-11, Oneonta, New York 13820-4015. Phone: 607/436-2011.

Science Museum. Shoreham-Wading River Schools, Shoreham, New York 11786. Phone: 516/821-5860.

Sciencenter. P.O. Box 6697, Ithaca, New York 14851. Phone: 607/272-0350.

SciencePort. Playland Parkway, Rye, New York 10580. Phone: 914/967-5312.

Staten Island Children's Museum. 1000 Richmond Terrace, Staten Island, New York 10301. Phone: 718/273-2060.

The Vanderbilt Museum. 180 Little Neck Road, Centerport, New York 11721. Phone: 516/262-7800.

North Carolina

Arts and Science Center. 1335 Museum Road, Statesville, North Carolina 28677. Phone: 704/873-4734.

Catawba Science Center. 243 Third Avenue, N.E., P.O. Box 2431, Hickory, North Carolina 28601. Phone: 704/322-8169.

Harris Visitors Center. Route 1, Box 327, New Hill, North Carolina 27526. Phone: 919/362-3263.

The Health Adventure. P.O. Box 180, 2 South Pack Square, Asheville, North Carolina 28802-0180. Phone: 704/254-6373.

Imagination Station. P.O. Box 2127, 224 East Nash Street, Wilson, North Carolina 27893. Phone: 919/291-5113.

Natural Science Center of Greensboro. 4301 Lawndale Drive, Greensboro, North Carolina 27408-1899. Phone: 919/288-3769.

North Carolina Museum of Life and Science. 433 Murray Avenue, P.O. Box 15190. Durham, North Carolina 27704. Phone: 919/220-5429.

North Carolina State Museum of Natural Sciences. P.O. Box 27647, Raleigh, North Carolina 27611. Phone: 919/733-7450.

Rocky Mount Children's Museum. 1610 Gay Street, Rocky Mount, North Carolina 27801. Phone: 919/972-1167.

Schiele Museum of Natural History and Planetarium. 1500 East Garrison Boulevard, P.O. Box 953, Gastonia, North Carolina 28054. Phone: 704/865-6131.

Science Museums of Charlotte. 301 North Tryon Street, Charlotte, North Carolina 28202. Phone: 704/372-6261.

SciWorks, The Science Center and Environmental Park. 400 Hanes Mill Road, Winston-Salem, North Carolina 27105. Phone: 919/767-6734.

Ohio

Cincinnati Art Museum. Eden Park, Cincinnati, Ohio 45202-1596. Phone: 513/721-5204.

Cincinnati Museum of Natural History. 1301 Western Avenue, Cincinnati, Ohio 45203. Phone: 513/287-7020.

Cleveland Children's Museum. 10730 Euclid Avenue, Cleveland, Ohio 44106. Phone: 216/791-7114.

Cleveland Health Education Museum. 8911 Euclid Avenue, Cleveland, Ohio 44106. Phone: 216/231-5010.

COSI, Ohio's Center of Science and Industry. 280 East Broad Street, Columbus, Ohio 43215-3773. Phone: 614/228-2674.

COSI/Toledo. c/o Toledo Edison, 300 Madison Avenue, Toledo, Ohio 43652. Phone: 419/249-5222.

Dayton Museum of Natural History. 2629 Ridge Avenue, Dayton, Ohio 45414. Phone: 513/275-7431.

Great Lakes Museum of Science, Environment, and Technology. 1590 North Point Tower, 1001 Lakeside Avenue, Cleveland, Ohio 44114. Phone: 216/736-7900.

McKinley Museum of History, Science, and Industry. 800 McKinley Monument Drive, N.W., Canton, Ohio 44708. Phone: 216/455-7043.

National Invention Center. 80 West Bowery Street, Akron, Ohio 44308. Phone: 216/668-6596.

SciMaTec—The University of Toledo. 1260 SWAC, 2801 West Bancroft Street, Toledo, Ohio 43606. Phone: 419/537-3915.

Oklahoma

Harmon Science Center. P.O. Box 52568, Tulsa, Oklahoma 74152-0568. Phone: 918/743-6191.

Omniplex Science Museum. 2100 Northeast Fifty-second Street, Oklahoma City, Oklahoma 73111. Phone: 405/424-5545.

Tyke Museum. 23 West Fourth Street, Suite 800, Tulsa, Oklahoma 74103. Phone: 918/582-5039.

Oregon

Children's Museum of Portland, Oregon. 3037 Southwest Second Avenue, Portland, Oregon 97201. Phone: 503/823-2230.

The High Desert Museum. 59800 South Highway 97, Bend, Oregon 97702. Phone: 503/382-4754.

Oregon Museum of Science and Industry. 1945 Southeast Water Avenue, Portland, Oregon 97214-3354. Phone: 503/797-4000.

Southern Oregon Historical Society. 106 North Central Avenue, Medford, Oregon 97501-5926. Phone: 503/773-6536.

WISTEC, Willamette Science and Technology Center. 2300 Leo Harris Parkway, Eugene, Oregon 97401. Phone: 503/687-3619.

Wonder Works, A Children's Museum. 419 East Second, The Dalles, Oregon 97058. Phone: 503/296-2444.

Pennsylvania

Academy of Natural Sciences. Nineteenth Street and the Parkway, Philadelphia, Pennsylvania 19103-1195. Phone: 215/299-1000.

The Carnegie Science Center. One Allegheny Avenue, Pittsburgh, Pennsylvania 15212-5363. Phone: 412/237-3400.

Franklin Institute Science Museum. Twentieth Street and the Parkway, Philadelphia, Pennsylvania 19103. Phone: 215/448-1208.

Museum of Scientific Discovery. Strawberry Square, P.O. Box 934, Harrisburg, Pennsylvania 17108-0934. Phone: 717/233-7969.

The Pittsburgh Children's Museum. One Landmarks Square, Pittsburgh, Pennsylvania 15212-5242. Phone: 412/322-5059.

Please Touch Museum. 210 North Twenty-first Street, Philadelphia, Pennsylvania 19103. Phone: 215/963-0667.

Quiet Valley Living Historical Farm. 1000 Turkey Hill Road, Stroudsburg, Pennsylvania 18360. Phone: 717/992-6161.

Reading Public Museum and Art Gallery. 500 Museum Road, Reading, Pennsylvania 19611-1425. Phone: 215/371-5838.

Rhode Island

Children's Museum of Rhode Island. 58 Walcott Street, Pawtucket, Rhode Island 02860. Phone: 401/726-2591.

South Carolina

Roper Mountain Science Center. 504 Roper Mountain Road, Greenville, South Carolina 29615. Phone: 803/297-0232.

South Carolina State Museum. 301 Gervais Street, Columbia, South Carolina 29201. Phone: 803/734-9020.

South Dakota

South Dakota Discovery Center and Aquarium. 805 West Sioux Avenue, P.O. Box 1054, Pierre, South Dakota 57501. Phone: 605/224-8295.

Tennessee

American Museum of Science and Energy. 300 South Tulane Avenue, Oak Ridge, Tennessee 37830. Phone: 615/576-3200.

Children's Museum of Memphis. 2525 Central Avenue, Memphis, Tennessee 38104. Phone: 901/458-2678.

Children's Museum of Oak Ridge. 461 West Outer Drive, Oak Ridge, Tennessee 37830. Phone: 615/482-1074.

The Creative Discovery Museum. 702 Tallan Building, Chattanooga, Tennessee 37402. Phone: 615/756-0611.

Cumberland Science Museum. 800 Ridley Boulevard, Nashville, Tennessee 37203. Phone: 615/862-5160.

East Tennessee Discovery Center. 516 Beaman Street, P.O. Box 6204, Knoxville, Tennessee 37914. Phone: 615/637-1121.

Hands On! Regional Museum. 315 East Main Street, Johnson City, Tennessee 37601. Phone: 615/928-6508.

Memphis Pink Palace Museum. 3050 Central Avenue, Memphis, Tennessee 38111-3399. Phone: 901/320-6320.

Sequoyah Energy Connection. 2000 Igou Ferry Road, Soddy-Daisy, Tennessee 37379. Phone: 615/843-4100.

Texas

Austin Children's Museum. 1501 West Fifth Street, Austin, Texas 78703. Phone: 512/472-2499.

Children's Museum of Houston. 1500 Binz, Houston, Texas 77004-7112. Phone: 713/522-1138.

Dallas Museum of Natural History. P.O. Box 150433, Fair Park Station. Dallas, Texas 75315. Phone: 214/670-8457.

Don Harrington Discovery Center. 1200 Streit Drive, Amarillo, Texas 79106. Phone: 806/355-9547.

Fort Worth Museum of Science and History. 1501 Montgomery Street, Fort Worth, Texas 76107. Phone: 817/732-1631.

Foundation for the Museum of Medical Science. 1133 M. D. Anderson Boulevard, #400, Houston, Texas 77030-2896. Phone: 713/790-1838.

Houston Museum of Natural Science. One Herman Circle Drive, Houston, Texas 77030-1799. Phone: 713/639-4660.

Insights/El Paso Science Center. 303 North Oregon Street, El Paso, Texas 79901. Phone: 915/542-2990.

McAllen International Museum. 1900 Nolana, McAllen, Texas 78504. Phone: 512/682-1564.

McDonald Observatory. RLM 15.308, Austin, Texas 78712. Phone: 512/471-5285.

Museum of the Southwest. 1705 West Missouri Street, Midland, Texas 79701. Phone: 915/683-2882.

San Antonio Museum of Art. 200 West Jones Avenue, San Antonio, Texas 78215. Phone: 512/978-8100.

The Science Place. P.O. Box 151469, Dallas, Texas 75315-1469. Phone: 214/428-7200.

Science Spectrum. 2579 South Loop 289, Suite 250, Lubbock, Texas 79423. Phone: 806/797-1676.

Site Foundation of Garland. P.O. Box 460242, Garland, Texas 75046-0242. Phone: 214/494-7483.

Space Center Houston. 1601 NASA Road One, Houston, Texas 77058-3696. Phone: 713/244-2105.

Wichita Falls Museum and Art Center. 2 Eureka Circle, Wichita Falls, Texas 76308. Phone: 817/692-0923.

Witte Museum. San Antonio Museum Association, 3801 Broadway, San Antonio, Texas 78209. Phone: 512/978-8100.

Utah

The Children's Museum of Utah. 840 North 300th West, Salt Lake City, Utah 84103. Phone: 801/328-3383.

Hansen Planetarium. 15 South State Street, Salt Lake City, Utah 84111. Phone: 801/538-2104.

Utah Museum of Natural History. University of Utah, Salt Lake City, Utah 84112. Phone: 801/581-6927.

Vermont

Montshire Museum of Science. P.O. Box 770, Montshire Road, Norwich, Vermont 05055. Phone: 802/649-2200.

Shelburne Museum. U.S. Route 7, Shelburne, Vermont 05482. Phone: 802/985-3346.

Virginia

Challenger Center for Space and Science Education. 1055 North Fairfax Street, Suite 100, Alexandria, Virginia 22314. Phone: 703/683-9740.

Portsmouth Museums. 420 High Street, Portsmouth, Virginia 23704. Phone: 804/393-8983.

Richmond Children's Museum. 740 North Sixth Street, Richmond, Virginia 23219. Phone: 804/788-4949.

Science Museum of Virginia. 2500 West Broad Street, Richmond, Virginia 23220. Phone: 804/367-1013.

Science Museum of Western Virginia. One Market Square, Roanoke, Virginia 24011. Phone: 703/342-5710.

Virginia Air and Space Center. 600 Settlers Landing Road, Hampton, Virginia 23669. Phone: 804/727-0800.

Virginia Discovery Museum. East Downtown Mall, P.O. Box 1128, Charlottesville, Virginia 22902. Phone: 804/293-5528.

Virginia Living Museum. 524 J. Clyde Morris Boulevard, Newport News, Virginia 23601. Phone: 804/595-1900.

Virginia Museum of Natural History. 1001 Douglas Avenue, Martinsville, Virginia 24112. Phone: 703/666-8600.

Washington

The Children's Museum of Seattle. 305 Harrison, Seattle, Washington 98109. Phone: 206/441-1767.

Hanford Science Center. 825 Jadwin Avenue, P.O. Box 1970 A1-60, Richland, Washington 99352. Phone: 509/376-6826.

Life Trek, Northwest Museum of Health and Science. North 14 Howard, Suite 323, Spokane, Washington 99201. Phone: 509/459-0444.

Marine Science Society of the Pacific Northwest. P.O. Box 10512, Bainbridge Island, Washington 98110. Phone: 206/842-5883.

Pacific Science Center. 200 Second Avenue North, Seattle, Washington 98109. Phone: 206/443-2001.

West Virginia

Carnegie Hall. 105 Church Street, Lewisburg, West Virginia 24901. Phone: 304/645-7917.

Sunrise Museum. 746 Myrtle Road, Charleston, West Virginia 25314. Phone: 304/344-8035.

Wisconsin

Discovery World. 818 West Wisconsin Avenue, Milwaukee, Wisconsin 53233. Phone: 414/765-9966.

Madison Children's Museum. 100 State Street, Madison, Wisconsin 53703. Phone: 608/256-6446.

Milwaukee Public Museum. 800 West Wells Street, Milwaukee, Wisconsin 53233. Phone: 414/278-2702.

Wyoming

Children's Discovery Foundation. 1017 Ford Circle, Rock Springs, Wyoming 82901. Phone: 307/362-4685.

Teton Science School. P.O. Box 68, Kelly, Wyoming 83011. Phone: 307/733-4765.

Appendix F

Zoos and Aquariums

The addresses below are street addresses, not mailing addresses, which frequently are different.

Alabama

Birmingham Zoo. 2630 Cahaba Road, Birmingham, Alabama. Phone: 205/879-0409.

Montgomery Zoo. 329 Vandiver Boulevard, Montgomery, Alabama. Phone: 205/240-4900.

Tom Mann's Fish World Aquarium. Route 431, Eufaula, Alabama. Phone: 205/687-3655.

Alaska

Alaska Zoo. 4731 O'Malley Road, Anchorage, Alaska. Phone: 907/346-2133.

Arizona

Arizona-Sonora Desert Museum. 2021 North Kinney Road, Tucson, Arizona. Phone: 602/883-1380.

Phoenix Zoo. 5810 East Van Buren Street, Phoenix, Arizona. Phone: 602/273-1341.

Reid Park Zoo. 1100 South Randolph Way, Tucson, Arizona. Phone: 602/791-3204.

Wildlife World Zoo. 16501 West Northern Avenue, Litchfield Park, Arizona. Phone: 602/935-WILD.

Arkansas

Educated Animal Zoo. 380 Whittington Avenue, Hot Springs, Arizona. Phone: 501/623-4311.

Little Rock Zoological Gardens. One Jonesboro Drive, Little Rock, Arizona. Phone: 501/666-2406.

California

Applegate Park Zoo. Twenty-fifth and R Streets, Merced, California. Phone: 209/385-6840.

Chaffee Zoological Gardens of Fresno. Roeding Park, 894 West Belmont Avenue, Fresno, California. Phone: 209/488-1549.

Living Desert. 47900 Portola Avenue, Palm Desert, California. Phone: 619/346-5694.

Los Angeles Zoo. 5333 Zoo Drive, Los Angeles, California. Phone: 213/666-4650.

Marine World-Africa USA. Marine World Parkway, Vallejo, California. Phone: 707/644-4000.

Monterey Bay Aquarium. 886 Cannery Row, Monterey, California. Phone: 408/648-4802.

Oakland Zoo in Knowland Park. 9777 Golf Links Road, Oakland, California. Phone: 510/632-9525.

Sacramento Zoo. 3930 West Land Park Drive, Sacramento, California. Phone: 916/449-5166 or 916/449-5885 (recording).

San Diego Wild Animal Park. 15500 San Pasqual Valley Road, Escondido, California. Phone: 619/747-8702.

San Diego Zoo. 2920 Zoo Drive, San Diego, California. Phone: 619/231-1515.

San Francisco Zoological Gardens. One Zoo Road, San Francisco, California. Phone: 415/753-7080.

Santa Ana Zoo. 1801 East Chestnut Avenue, Santa Ana, California. Phone: 714/436-4000.

Santa Barbara Zoological Gardens. 500 Ninos Drive, Santa Barbara, California. Phone: 805/962-5339.

Sea World. 1720 South Shores Road, San Diego, California. Phone: 619/222-6363.

Stephen Birch Aquarium. Scripps Institution of Oceanography, 2300 Expedition Way, La Jolla, California. Phone: 619/534-4086.

Colorado

Cheyenne Mountain Zoological Park. 4250 Cheyenne Mountain Zoo Road, Colorado Springs, Colorado. Phone: 719/633-0917.

Denver Zoological Gardens. City Park, Denver, Colorado. Phone: 303/331-4100.

Connecticut

Beardsley Zoo. 1875 Noble Avenue, Bridgeport, Connecticut. Phone: 203/331-1557.

The Maritime Center at Norwalk. 10 North Water Street, Norwalk, Connecticut. Phone: 203/852-0700.

Mystic Marinelife Aquarium. 55 Coogan Boulevard, Mystic, Connecticut. Phone: 203/536-9631.

Delaware

Brandywine Zoo. Brandywine Park, 1001 North Park Drive, Wilmington, Delaware. Phone: 302/571-7788.

District of Columbia

National Aquarium. Department of Commerce Building, Fourteenth Street and Constitution Avenue, N.W., Washington, D.C. Phone: 202/482-2825.

National Zoological Park. Smithsonian Institution, 3000 Connecticut Avenue, N.W., Washington, D.C. Phone: 202/673-4800.

Florida

Central Florida Zoological Park. U.S. Highway 17/92 (at Interstate 4), Monroe, Florida. Phone: 407/323-4450.

Dreher Park Zoo. 1301 Summit Boulevard, West Palm Beach, Florida. Phone: 407/533-0887.

Jacksonville Zoological Park. 8605 Zoo Road, Jacksonville, Florida. Phone: 904/757-4463.

Jungle Larry's Zoological Park. 1590 Goodlette Road, Naples, Florida. Phone: 813/262-5409.

Lowry Park Zoo. 7530 North Boulevard, Tampa, Florida. Phone: 813/935-8552.

Marineland. 9507 Ocean Shore Boulevard, Marineland, Florida. Phone: 904/471-1111.

Miami Metrozoo. 12400 Southwest 152nd Street, Miami, Florida. Phone: 305/251-0400.

Miami Seaquarium. 4400 Rickenbacker Causeway, Miami, Florida. Phone: 305/361-5705.

Monkey Jungle. 14805 Southwest 216th Street, Miami, Florida. Phone: 305/235-1611.

Santa Fe Teaching Zoo. 3000 Northwest Eighty-third Street, Gainesville, Florida. Phone: 904/395-5604.

Sea World of Florida. 7007 Sea World Drive, Orlando, Florida. Phone: 407/351-3600.

The Zoo. 5701 Gulf Breeze Parkway, Gulf Breeze, Florida. Phone: 904/932-2229.

Georgia

Aquarium of the University of Georgia. McWhorter Road (located on Skidaway Island), Savannah, Georgia. Phone: 912/598-2496.

Zoo Atlanta. 800 Cherokee Avenue, Atlanta, Georgia. Phone: 404/624-5600.

Hawaii

Honolulu Zoo. 151 Kapahula Avenue, Honolulu, Hawaii. Phone: 808/971-7175 or 808/971-7171 (recording).

Sea Life Park Hawaii. Makapu'u Point, Oahu, Waimanalo, Hawaii. Phone: 808/259-7933.

Waikiki Aquarium. 2777 Kalakausa Avenue, Honolulu, Hawaii. Phone: 808/923-9741.

Idaho

Zoo Boise. Julia Davis Park, Capitol Boulevard, Boise, Idaho. Phone: 208/384-4260.

Illinois

Brookfield Zoo (Chicago Zoological Park). 8400 Thirty-first Street, Brookfield, Illinois. Phone: 708/485-0263.

Glen Oak Zoo. 2218 North Prospect Road, Peoria, Illinois. Phone: 309/686-3365.

Henson-Robinson Zoo. 1100 East Lake Drive, Springfield, Illinois. Phone: 217/529-2097.

Lincoln Park Zoological Gardens. 2200 North Cannon Drive, Chicago, Illinois. Phone: 312/294-4662.

John G. Shedd Aquarium. 1200 South Lake Shore Drive, Chicago, Illinois. Phone: 312/939-2438.

Indiana

Columbian Park Zoo. 1915 Scott Street, Lafayette, Indiana. Phone: 317/447-9353.

Fort Wayne Children's Zoo. 3411 Sherman Boulevard, Fort Wayne, Indiana. Phone: 219/482-4610.

Indianapolis Zoo. 1200 West Washington Street, Indianapolis, Indiana. Phone: 317/630-2001.

Mesker Park Zoo. 2421 Bement Avenue, Evansville, Indiana. Phone: 812/428-0715.

Potawatomi Zoo. 500 South Greenlawn Boulevard, South Bend, Indiana. Phone: 219/284-9800.

Washington Park Zoological Gardens. Lakefront, Michigan City, Indiana. Phone: 219/873-1510.

Iowa

Blank Park Zoo of Des Moines. 7401 Southwest Ninth Street, Des Moines, Iowa. Phone: 515/285-4722.

Greater Iowa Aquarium. 501 East Thirtieth Street, Des Moines, Iowa. Phone: 515/263-0612.

Kansas

Emporia Zoo. South Commercial and Soden's Roads, Emporia, Kansas. Phone: 316/342-5105.

Lee Richardson Zoo. Finnup Park, Garden City, Kansas. Phone: 316/276-1250.

Sedgwick County Zoo and Botanical Garden. 5555 Zoo Boulevard, Wichita, Kansas. Phone: 316/942-2213.

Sunset Zoological Park. 2333 Oak Street, Manhattan, Kansas. Phone: 913/587-2737.

Topeka Zoological Park. 635 Southwest Gage Boulevard, Topeka, Kansas. Phone: 913/272-5821.

Kentucky

Louisville Zoological Garden. 1100 Trevilian Way, Louisville, Kentucky. Phone: 502/459-2181.

Louisiana

Alexandria Zoological Park. Bringhurst Park, City Park Boulevard, Alexandria, Louisiana. Phone: 318/473-1385.

Aquarium of the Americas. 111 Iberville Street, New Orleans, Louisiana. Phone: 504/595-3474.

Audubon Park and Zoological Garden. 6500 Magazine Avenue, New Orleans, Louisiana. Phone: 504/861-5108.

Greater Baton Rouge Zoo. 3601 Thomas Road, Baker, Louisiana. Phone: 504/775-3877.

Maine

Mount Desert Oceanarium. Clark Point Boulevard, Southwest Harbor, Maine. Phone: 207/244-7330.

Old Orchard Beach Aquarium. End of Pier, Old Orchard Beach, Maine. Phone: 207/934-2344.

York's Wild Kingdom Zoo and Amusement Park. Route 1, York Beach, Maine. Phone: 1/800-456-4911.

Maryland

Baltimore Zoo. Druid Hill Park, Baltimore, Maryland. Phone: 410/396-7102.

Catoctin Mountain Zoological Park. Route 15, Thurmont, Maryland. Phone: 301/271-7488.

National Aquarium in Baltimore. 501 East Pratt Street, Pier 3, Baltimore, Maryland. Phone: 410/576-3800.

Salisbury Zoological Park. 755 South Park Drive, Salisbury, Maryland. Phone: 410/548-3188.

Massachusetts

Cape Cod Aquarium. 281 Route 6A, Brewster, Massachusetts. Phone: 508/385-9252.

Franklin Park Zoo. Franklin Park Road, Dorchester, Boston, Massachusetts. Phone: 617/442-2815.

New England Aquarium. Central Wharf, Boston, Massachusetts. Phone: 617/973-5220.

Michigan

Belle Isle Aquarium and Belle Isle Zoo. Belle Isle (Detroit River), Detroit, Michigan. Phone: 313/267-7159 (aquarium); 313/267-7160 (zoo).

Binder Park Zoo. 7400 Division Drive, Battle Creek, Michigan. Phone: 616/979-1351.

Detroit Zoo. 8450 West Ten Mile Road, Royal Oak, Michigan. Phone: 313/398-0903.

John Ball Zoological Garden. 1300 West Fulton Street Northwest, Grand Rapids, Michigan. Phone: 616/776-2591.

Potter Park Zoo. 1301 South Pennsylvania Avenue, Lansing, Michigan. Phone: 517/483-4221.

Saginaw Children's Zoo. 1730 South Washington, Saginaw, Michigan. Phone: 517/759-1657.

Minnesota

Como Zoo. Midway Parkway and Kaufman Drive, St. Paul, Minnesota. Phone: 612/488-4041.

Lake Superior Zoological Gardens. Fairmont Park, 7210 Freemont Street, Duluth, Minnesota. Phone: 218/723-3747.

Minnesota Zoo. 13000 Zoo Boulevard, Apple Valley, Minnesota. Phone: 612/431-9200.

Mississippi

Jackson Zoological Park. 2918 West Capitol Street, Jackson, Mississippi. Phone: 601/352-2585.

Missouri

Dickerson Park Zoo. 3043 North Fort, Springfield, Missouri. Phone: 417/833-1570.

Kansas City Zoological Gardens. 6700 Zoo Drive, Kansas City, Missouri. Phone: 816/333-7406.

St. Louis Zoological Park. Forest Park, St. Louis, Missouri. Phone: 314/781-0900.

Nebraska

Ak-Sar-Ben Aquarium. Schramm Park State Recreation Area, 21502 West Highway 31, Gretna, Nebraska. Phone: 402/332-3901.

Folsom Children's Zoo and Botanical Garden. 1222 South Twenty-seventh Street, Lincoln, Nebraska. Phone: 402/475-6741.

Henry Doorly Zoo. 3701 South Tenth Street, Omaha, Nebraska. Phone: 402/733-8401.

Riverside Park Zoo. 1600 South Beltline Highway West, Scottsbluff, Nebraska. Phone: 308/630-6236.

New Jersey

Bergen County Zoological Park. 216 Forest Avenue, Paramus, New Jersey. Phone: 201/262-3771.

Cape May County Park Zoo. Route 9 and Pine Lane, Cape May Court House, New Jersey. Phone: 609/465-5271.

Cohanzick Zoo. City Park, Mayor Aitken Drive, Bridgeton, New Jersey. Phone: 609/455-3230.

New Jersey State Aquarium at Camden. One Riverside Drive, Camden, New Jersey. Phone: 609/365-3300.

Popcorn Park Zoo. Humane Way, Forked River, New Jersey. Phone: 609/693-1900.

New Mexico

Alameda Park Zoo. 1321 North White Sands Boulevard, Alamogondo, New Mexico. Phone: 505/437-8430.

Living Desert State Park. Skyline Drive, Carlsbad, New Mexico. Phone: 505/887-5516.

Rio Grande Zoological Park. 903 Tenth Street, S.W., Albuquerque, New Mexico. Phone: 505/843-7413.

Spring River Park and Zoo. College and Atkinson Streets, Roswell, New Mexico. Phone: 505/624-6760.

New York

Aquarium for Wildlife Conservation. West Eighth Street and Surf Avenue, Brooklyn (Coney Island), New York. Phone: 718/265-FISH.

Aquarium of Niagara Falls. 701 Whirlpool Street, Niagara Falls, New York. Phone: 716/285-3575.

The Bronx Zoo. Bronx River Parkway and Fordham Road, Bronx, New York. Phone: 718/367-1010.

Buffalo Zoological Gardens. Delaware Park, Buffalo, New York. Phone: 716/837-3900.

Burnet Park Zoo. 500 Burnet Park Drive, Syracuse, New York. Phone: 315/435-8511.

Central Park Zoo. 830 Fifth Avenue, New York, New York. Phone: 212/861-6030.

Ross Park Zoo. Morgan Road, Binghamton, New York. Phone: 607/724-5461.

Seneca Park Zoo. 2222 St. Paul Street, Rochester, New York. Phone: 716/342-2744.

Utica Zoo. Roscoe Conkling Park, Steele Hill Road, Utica, New York. Phone: 315/738-0475.

North Carolina

North Carolina Aquarium. Fort Fisher, 2201 Fort Fisher Boulevard, South Kure Beach, North Carolina. Phone: 919/458-8257.

North Carolina Aquarium on Pine Knoll Shores. Route 58, Atlantic Beach, North Carolina. Phone: 919/247-4003.

North Carolina Aquarium on Roanoke Island. Airport Road, Ronaoke Island, North Carolina. Phone: 919/473-3494.

North Carolina Zoological Park. Zoo Parkway (Route 4), Asheboro, North Carolina. Phone: 919/879-7000.

North Dakota

Dakota Zoo. Sertoma Park Road, Bismarck, North Dakota. Phone: 701/223-7543.

Roosevelt Park Zoo. 1215 Burdick Expressway East, Minot, North Dakota. Phone: 701/852-2751.

Ohio

Akron Zoological Park. 50 Edgewood Avenue, Akron, Ohio. Phone: 216/434-8645.

Cincinnati Zoo and Botanical Garden. 3400 Vine Street, Cincinnati, Ohio. Phone: 513/281-4701.

Cleveland Metroparks Zoo. 3900 Brookside Park Drive, Cleveland, Ohio. Phone: 216/661-6500.

Columbus Zoological Park. 9990 Riverside Drive, Powell, Ohio. Phone: 614/645-3400.

Sea World of Ohio. 1100 Sea World Drive, Aurora, Ohio. Phone: 216/995-2121.

Toledo Zoological Gardens and Museum of Science. 2700 Broadway, Toledo, Ohio. Phone: 419/385-5721.

Oklahoma

Oklahoma City Zoological Park. 2101 Northeast Fiftieth Street, Oklahoma City, Oklahoma. Phone: 405/424-3344.

Tulsa Zoological Park. 5701 East Thirty-sixth Street, North, Tulsa, Oklahoma. Phone: 918/596-2400.

Oregon

Hatfield Marine Science Center Aquarium. 2030 Marine Science Drive, Newport, Oregon. Phone: 503/867-0226.

Metro Washington Park Zoo. 4001 Southwest Canyon Road, Portland, Oregon. Phone: 503/226-1561.

Oregon Coast Aquarium. Newport, Oregon. Phone: 503/867-3123.

Pennsylvania

Erie Zoological Gardens. Glenwood Park, 423 West Thirty-eighth Street, Erie, Pennsylvania. Phone: 814/864-4093.

Philadelphia Zoo. 3400 West Girard Avenue, Philadelphia, Pennsylvania. Phone: 215/243-1100.

Pittsburgh Zoo. Highland Park, Pittsburgh, Pennsylvania. Phone: 412/665-3639.

ZooAmerica North America Wildlife Park. Route 743, Hershey, Pennsylvania. Phone: 717/534-3860.

Rhode Island

Roger Williams Park Zoo. 1000 Elmwood Avenue, Providence, Rhode Island. Phone: 401/785-3510.

South Carolina

Brookgreen Gardens. U.S. Highway 17 South, Murrells Inlet, South Carolina. Phone: 803/237-4218.

Riverbanks Zoological Park. 50 Wildlife Parkway, Columbia, South Carolina. Phone: 803/779-8717.

South Dakota

Bear Country USA. Route 16, Rapid City, South Dakota. Phone: 605/343-2290.

Gavins Point Fish Hatchery Aquarium. Highway 52, Yankton, South Dakota. Phone: 605/665-3352.

Great Plains Zoo. 805 South Kiwanis Avenue, Sioux Falls, South Dakota. Phone: 605/339-7059.

Reptile Gardens. Mt. Rushmore Road (U.S. Highway 16), Rapid City, South Dakota. Phone: 605/342-5873.

South Dakota Discovery Center and Aquarium. 805 West Sioux Avenue, P.O. Box 1054, Pierre, South Dakota. Phone: 605/224-8295.

Tennessee

Grassmere Wildlife Park. 3777 Nolensville Road, Nashville, Tennessee. Phone: 615/833-1534.

Knoxville Zoological Gardens. 3333 Woodbine Avenue, Knoxville, Tennessee. Phone: 615/637-5331.

Memphis Zoo and Aquarium. Overton Park, 2000 Galloway Avenue, Memphis, Tennessee. Phone: 901/726-4787.

Nashville Zoo. 1710 Ridge Road Circle, Joelton, Tennessee. Phone: 615/370-3333.

Tennessee Aquarium. 101 West Second Street, Chattanooga, Tennessee. Phone: 615/265-0695.

Texas

Abilene Zoological Gardens. 1800 East South Eleventh Street, Abilene, Texas. Phone: 915/676-6222 or 915/672-9771 (recording).

Caldwell Zoo. 2203 Martin Luther King Boulevard, Tyler, Texas. Phone: 903/593-0121.

Central Texas Zoological Park. 3601 Zoo Park Road, Waco, Texas. Phone: 817/750-5976.

Dallas Aquarium. Fair Park, First Avenue and Martin Luther King Boulevard, Dallas, Texas. Phone: 214/670-8453 or 214/670-8443 (recording).

Dallas Zoo. Marsalis Park, 620 East Clarendon Drive, Dallas, Texas. Phone: 214/670-6825.

El Paso Zoo. 400 East Paisano, El Paso, Texas. Phone: 915/521-1850.

Fort Worth Zoological Park. 1989 Colonial Parkway, Fort Worth, Texas. Phone: 817/871-7050.

Gladys Porter Zoo. 500 Ringgold Street, Brownsville, Texas. Phone: 512/546-7187.

Houston Zoological Gardens. Hermann Park, 1513 North Macgregor, Houston, Texas. Phone: 713/525-3300.

San Antonio Zoological Gardens and Aquarium. Brackenridge Park, 3903 North Saint Mary's Street, San Antonio, Texas. Phone: 512/734-7184 or 512/734-7183 (recording).

Sea World of Texas. 10500 Sea World Drive, San Antonio, Texas. Phone: 512/523-3600.

Texas State Aquarium. One Shoreline Plaza, Corpus Christi, Texas. Phone: 1/800-477-4853 or 512/881-1300.

Texas Zoo. Riverside Park, 110 Memorial Drive, Victoria, Texas. Phone: 512/573-7681.

Utah

Hogle Zoological Garden. 2600 East Sunnyside Avenue, Salt Lake City, Utah. Phone: 801/582-1632.

Virginia

Chincoteague National Wildlife Refuge. Tom Cove Visitors Center, Chincoteague, Virginia. Phone: 804/336-6122.

Virginia Zoological Park. 350 Granby Street, Norfolk, Virginia. Phone: 804/441-2374 or 804/441-2706 (recording).

Washington

Point Defiance Zoo and Aquarium. 5400 North Pearl Street, Tacoma, Washington. Phone: 206/591-5337.

Seattle Aquarium. Pier 59, Waterfront Park, Seattle, Washington. Phone: 206/386-4320.

Woodland Park Zoological Gardens. 5500 Phinney Avenue North, Seattle, Washington. Phone: 206/684-4800.

West Virginia

Good Children's Zoo. Oglebay Park, Wheeling, West Virginia. Phone: 304/243-4030.

Wisconsin

Henry Vilas Park Zoo. 702 South Randall Avenue, Madison, Wisconsin. Phone: 608/266-4732.

Lincoln Park Zoo. North Eighth Street, Manitowoc, Wisconsin. Phone: 414/683-4537.

Milwaukee County Zoological Gardens. 10001 West Bluemound Road, Milwaukee, Wisconsin. Phone: 414/771-3040.

Racine Zoological Gardens. 2131 North Main Street, Racine, Wisconsin. Phone: 414/636-9189.

Appendix G

National Forests

The following information on national forests (including contact offices for each) is from *A Guide to Your National Forests*, produced by the U.S. Department of Agriculture. For ordering information on this inexpensive guide, request a copy of the free *Consumer Information Catalog*, available from the Consumer Information Center, P.O. Box 100, Pueblo, Colorado 81002.

More than 150 national forests cover an area about the size of Oregon, Washington, and California combined and stretch from Alaska to Puerto Rico. Hiking, camping, fishing, biking, and skiing are among the activities families can enjoy together on the more than one hundred thousand miles of trails and ten thousand recreational sites these forests have to offer. Most likely, you'll be able to reach at least one of the following sites within a day's drive:

Northern Region

Follow the route of the Lewis and Clark Expedition through the Bitterroot Mountains, catch your limit of trout at a pristine alpine lake, or camp under the stars and listen to the howl of the wolf. Whether you're looking for the rigors of a wilderness trek or an easy drive along a scenic byway, you'll find it here in the National Forests of the Northern Region.

Idaho

Clearwater National Forest. 12730 Highway 12, Orofino, Idaho 83544. Phone: 208/476-4541.

Idaho Panhandle National Forests: Coeur d'Alene, Kaniksu, and St. Joe National Forests. 1201 Ironwood Drive, Coeur d'Alene, Idaho 83814. Phone: 208/765-7223.

Nez Perce National Forest. East U.S. Highway 13, Route 2, P.O. Box 475, Grangeville, Idaho 83530. Phone: 208/983-1950.

Montana

Beaverhead National Forest. 610 North Montana Street, Dillon, Montana 59725. Phone: 406/683-3900.

Bitterroot National Forest. 316 North Third Street, Hamilton, Montana 59840. Phone: 406/363-3131.

Custer National Forest. 2602 First Avenue North, Billings, Montana 59103. Phone: 406/657-6361.

Deerlodge National Forest. Federal Building, Corner of Cooper and Main Streets, P.O. Box 400, Butte, Montana 59703. Phone: 406/496-3400.

Flathead National Forest. 1935 Third Avenue East, Kalispell, Montana 59901. Phone: 406/755-5401.

Gallatin National Forest. Federal Building, 10 East Babcock Street, P.O. Box 130, Bozeman, Montana 59771. Phone: 406/587-6701.

Helena National Forest. Federal Building, 301 South Park, Room 328, Drawer 10014, Helena, Montana 59626. Phone: 406/449-5201.

Kootenai National Forest. 506 U.S. Highway 2 West, Libby, Montana 59923. Phone: 406/293-6211.

Lewis and Clark National Forest. 1101 Fifteenth Street North, P.O. Box 871, Great Falls, Montana 59403. Phone: 406/791-7700.

Lolo National Forest. Building 24, Fort Missoula, Missoula, Montana 59801. Phone: 406/329-3750.

Rocky Mountain Region

Enjoy the quiet beauty of a mountain meadow, or hike through aspen groves and rugged mountains on well-maintained trails. Challenge yourself on some of the world's finest ski slopes, or relax by a fireplace in a friendly mountain resort. You'll find yourself wanting to return often once you discover the refreshing change of pace awaiting you in the Rocky Mountain Region.

Colorado

Arapaho and Roosevelt National Forests. 240 West Prospect Road, Fort Collins, Colorado 80526. Phone: 303/224-1100.

Grand Mesa, Gunnison, and Uncompagre National Forests. 2250 U.S. Highway 50, Delta, Colorado 81416. Phone: 303/874-7691.

Pike and San Isabel National Forests. 1920 Valley Drive, Pueblo, Colorado 81008. Phone: 719/545-8737.

Rio Grande National Forest. 1803 West U.S. Highway 160, Monte Vista, Colorado 81144. Phone: 719/852-5941.

Routt National Forest. 29587 West U.S. Highway 40, Suite 20, Steamboat Springs, Colorado 80487. Phone: 303/879-1722.

San Juan National Forest. 701 Camino Del Rio, Durango, Colorado 81301. Phone: 303/247-4874.

White River National Forest. Old Federal Building, Ninth Street and Grand Avenue, P.O. Box 948, Glenwood Springs, Colorado 81602. Phone: 303/945-2521.

Nebraska

Nebraska National Forest. 270 Pine Street, Chadron, Nebraska 69337. Phone: 308/432-3367.

South Dakota

Black Hills National Forest. Highway 385 North, Route 2, P.O. Box 200, Custer, South Dakota 57730. Phone: 605/673-2251.

Wyoming

Bighorn National Forest. 1969 South Sheridan Avenue, Sheridan, Wyoming 82801. Phone: 307/672-0751.

Medicine Bow National Forest. 605 Skyline Drive, Laramie, Wyoming 82070. Phone: 307/745-8971.

Shoshone National Forest. 225 West Yellowstone Avenue, P. O. Box 2140, Cody, Wyoming 82414. Phone: 307/527-6241.

Southwestern Region

If exploring a labyrinth of canyons and mesa, floating in an inner tube down the Salt River past sandstone cliffs, or visiting the fascinating Ghost Ranch Living Museum with its live animal displays sounds like a fun way to relax, then the national forests of the Southwestern Region are just what you're looking for. Whether you decide to visit the magnificent mountains or colorful desert—or both— you'll find it easy to travel by foot, horseback, or road.

Arizona

Apache-Sitgreaves National Forest. Federal Building, 309 South Mountain Avenue, P.O. Box 640, Springerville, Arizona 85938. Phone: 602/333-4301.

Coconino National Forest. 2323 East Greenlaw Lane, Flagstaff, Arizona 86004. Phone: 602/527-7400.

Coronado National Forest. 300 West Congress Street, 6th Floor, Tucson, Arizona 85701. Phone: 602/629-6483.

Kaibab National Forest. 800 South Sixth Street, Williams, Arizona 86046. Phone: 602/635-2681.

Prescott National Forest. 344 South Cortez, Prescott, Arizona 86303. Phone: 602/445-1762.

Tonto National Forest. 2324 East McDowell Road, P.O. Box 5348, Phoeniz, Arizona 85010. Phone: 602/225-5200.

New Mexico

Carson National Forest. Forest Service Building, 208 Cruz Alta Road, P.O. Box 558, Taos, New Mexico 87571. Phone: 505/758-6200.

Cibola National Forest. 10308 Canderlaria Northeast, Albuquerque, New Mexico 87112. Phone: 505/275-5207.

Gila National Forest. 2610 North Silver Street, Silver City, New Mexico 88061. Phone: 505/388-8201.

Lincoln National Forest. Federal Building, Eleventh Street and New York Avenue, Alamogordo, New Mexico 88310. Phone: 505/437-6030.

Santa Fe National Forest. Pinon Building, 1220 St. Francis Drive, P.O. Box 1689, Santa Fe, New Mexico 87504. Phone: 505/988-6940.

Intermountain Region

Colorful wildflowers carpet alpine meadows during summer, while winter brings powder snow, sought by skiers from around the world. Here you'll find a land of contrasts—from deep red canyons to tall mountains wrapped with pine and fir. Opportunities for sightseeing, camping, and whitewater rafting abound. A visit of a lifetime awaits you in the national forests of the Intermountain Region.

Idaho

Boise National Forest. 1750 Front Street, Boise, Idaho 83702. Phone: 208/334-1516.

Caribou National Forest. Federal Building, Suite 282, 250 South Fourth Avenue, Pocatello, Idaho 83201. Phone: 208/236-6700.

Challis National Forest. Forest Service Building, U.S. Highway 93 North, P.O. Box 404, Challis, Idaho 83226. Phone: 208/879-2285.

Payette National Forest. 106 West Park Street, P.O. Box 1026, McCall, Idaho 83638. Phone: 208/634-8151.

Salmon National Forest. U.S. Highway 93 North, P.O. Box 729, Salmon, Idaho 83467. Phone: 208/756-2215.

Sawtooth National Forest. 2647 Kimberly Road East, Twin Falls, Idaho 83301. Phone: 208/737-3200.

Targhee National Forest. 420 North Bridge Street, P.O. Box 208, St. Anthony, Idaho 83445. Phone: 208/624-3151.

Nevada

Humboldt National Forest. 976 Mountain City Highway, Elko, Nevada 89801. Phone: 702/738-5171.

Toiyabe National Forest. 1200 Franklin Way, Sparks, Nevada 89431. Phone: 702/355-5301.

Utah

Ashley National Forest. Ashton Energy Center, 355 North Vernal Avenue, Vernal, Utah 84078. Phone: 801/789-1181.

Dixie National Forest. 82 North 100 East, P.O. Box 580, Cedar City, Utah 84720. Phone: 801/586-2421.

Fishlake National Forest. 115 East 900 North, Richfield, Utah 84701. Phone: 801/896-4491.

Manti-LaSal National Forest. 599 West Price River Drive, Price, Utah 84501. Phone: 801/637-2817.

Uinta National Forest. 88 West 100 North, Provo, Utah 84601. Phone: 801/377-5780.

Wasatch-Cache National Forest. 8230 Federal Building, 125 South State Street, Salt Lake City, Utah 84138. Phone: 801/524-5030.

Wyoming

Bridger-Teton National Forest. Forest Service Building, 340 North Cache, P.O. Box 1888, Jackson, Wyoming 83001. Phone: 307/733-2752.

Pacific Southwest Region

Here is a place where you can use words like "tallest" and "oldest" without exaggerating. See the coastal redwood (the tallest) or the bristlecone pine (the oldest trees on earth). Enjoy a picnic by a cool rushing stream, or discover mountain meadows filled with delicate spring wildflowers. Camp among the pine-encircled granite peaks of the Sierra Nevada Mountains, or climb a sleeping volcano—Mount Shasta. You'll find recreation opportunities for everyone in the national forests of the Pacific Southwest Region.

California

Angeles National Forest. 701 North Santa Anita Avenue, Arcadia, California 91006. Phone: 818/574-1613.

Cleveland National Forest. 880 Front Street, Room 5-N-14, San Diego, California 92188. Phone: 619/557-5050.

Eldorado National Forest. 100 Forni Road, Placerville, California 95667. Phone: 916/644-6048.

Inyo National Forest. 873 North Main Street, Bishop, California 93514. Phone: 619/873-5841.

Klamath National Forest. 1312 Fairlane Road, Yreka, California 96097. Phone: 916/842-6131.

Lake Tahoe Basin Mangement Unit. 870 Emerald Bay Road, P.O. Box 731002, South Lake Tahoe, California 95731. Phone: 916/573-2600.

Lassen National Forest. 55 South Sacramento Street, Susanville, California 96130. Phone: 916/257-2151.

Los Padres National Forest. 6144 Calle Real, Goleta, California 93117. Phone: 805/683-6711.

Mendocino National Forest. 420 East Laurel Street, Willows, California 95988. Phone: 916/934-3316.

Modoc National Forest. 441 North Main Street, Alturas, California 96101. Phone: 916/233-5811.

Plumas National Forest. 159 Lawrence Street, P.O. Box 11500, Quincy, California 95971. Phone: 916/283-2050.

San Bernardino National Forest.
1824 South Commercenter Circle,
San Bernardino, California 92408.
Phone: 714/383-5588.

Sequoia National Forest. 900 West
Grand Avenue, Porterville, California
93257. Phone: 209/784-1500.

Shasta-Trinity National Forests.
2400 Washington Avenue, Redding,
California 96001. Phone: 916/246-
5222.

Sierra National Forest. 1130 O
Street, Room 3009, Fresno, California 93721. Phone: 209/487-5155.

Six Rivers National Forest. 507 F
Street, Eureka, California 95501.
Phone: 707/442-1721.

Stanislaus National Forest. 19777
Greenley Road, Sonora, California
95370. Phone: 209/532-3671.

Tahoe National Forest. Highway 49
and Coyote Street, Nevada City, California 95959. Phone: 916/265-4531.

Pacific Northwest Region

Float the Snake River through the
deepest gorge in North America, or
enjoy a scenic drive around snow-
capped Mount Hood. Explore a rain
forest of spruce and fir growing beside glacier-fed rivers, or enjoy a forest interpreter's program at Mount St.
Helens National Volcanic Monument.
From high alpine meadows and craggy
peaks to surf-splashed coastlines, the
national forests of the Pacific Northwest Region offer unlimited opportunities for outdoor recreation.

Oregon

**Columbia River Gorge National
Scenic Area.** Waucoma Center, Suite
200, 902 Wasco Avenue, Hood River,
Oregon 97031. Phone: 503/386-2333.

Deschutes National Forest. 1645
U.S. Highway 20 East, Bend, Oregon
97701. Phone: 503/388-2715.

Fremont National Forest. 524
North G Street, Lakeview, Oregon
97630. Phone: 503/947-2151.

Malheur National Forest. 139 N.E.
Dayton Street, John Day, Oregon
97845. Phone: 503/575-1731.

Mount Hood National Forest. 2955
Northwest Division Street, Gresham,
Oregon 97030. Phone: 503/666-0700.

Ochoco National Forest. 155 North
Court Street, P.O. Box 490,
Prineville, Oregon 97754. Phone:
503/447-6247.

Rogue River National Forest. Federal Building, 333 West Eighth Street,
P.O. Box 520, Medford, Oregon
97501. Phone: 503/776-3600.

Siskiyou National Forest. 200
Northeast Greenfield Road, P.O. Box
440, Grants Pass, Oregon 97526.
Phone: 503/479-5301.

Siuslaw National Forest. 4077
Southwest Research Way, Corvallis,
Oregon 97339. Phone: 503/757-4480.

Umatilla National Forest. 2517
Southwest Hailey Avenue, Pendleton,
Oregon 97801. Phone: 503/276-3811.

Umpqua National Forest. 2900
Northwest Stewart Parkway, P.O. Box
1008, Roseburg, Oregon 97470.
Phone: 503/672-6601.

Wallowa-Whitman National Forest. 1550 Dewey Avenue, P.O. Box
907, Baker, Oregon 97814. Phone:
503/523-6391.

Willamette National Forest. 211
East Seventh Avenue, P.O. Box 10607,
Eugene, Oregon 97440. Phone:
503/687-6521.

Winema National Forest. 2819
Dahlia Street, Klamath Falls, Oregon
97601. Phone: 503/883-6714.

Washington

Colville National Forest. 695 South Main Street, Colville, Washington 99114. Phone: 509/684-3711.

Gifford Pinchot National Forest. 6926 East Fourth Plain Boulevard, P.O. Box 8944, Vancouver, Washington 98668. Phone: 206/696-7500.

Mount Baker-Snoqualmie National Forests. 1022 First Avenue, Seattle, Washington 98104. Phone: 206/442-5400.

Okanogan National Forest. 1240 South Second Avenue, P.O. Box 950, Okanogan, Washington 98840. Phone: 509/422-2704.

Olympic National Forest. 801 Capital Way, P.O. Box 2288, Olympia, Washington 98507. Phone: 206/753-9534.

Wenatchee National Forest. 301 Yakima Street, P.O. Box 811, Wenatchee, Washington 98801. Phone: 509/662-4335.

Southern Region

Enjoy a refreshing swim in a cool stream, join a tour of the magical Blanchard Springs Caverns, or hike along the famous Appalachian Trail. Explore the exotic beauty of a tropical rain forest, or picnic along the breathtaking Talimena Scenic Drive. The scenery varies as much as the recreation—from cypress swamps and mountain meadows to pine and hardwood forests. Plan an adventure to your national forests of the Southern Region.

Alabama

National Forests in Alabama: William B. Bankhead, Conecuh, Talladega, and Tuskegee National Forests. 1765 Highland Avenue, Montgomery, Alabama 36107. Phone: 205/832-4470.

Arkansas

Ouachita National Forest. Federal Building, 100 Reserve Street, P.O. Box 1270, Hot Springs National Park, Arkansas 71902. Phone: 501/321-5202.

Ozark–St. Francis National Forest. 605 West Main Street, P.O. Box 1008, Russellville, Arkansas 72801. Phone: 501/968-2354.

Florida

National Forests in Florida: Apalchicola, Ocala, and Osceola National Forests. USDA Forest Service, 227 North Bronough Street, Suite 4061, Tallahassee, Florida 32301. Phone: 904/681-7265.

Georgia

Chattahoochee-Oconee National Forests. 508 Oak Street, N.W., Gainesville, Georgia 30501. Phone: 404/536-0541.

Kentucky

Daniel Boone National Forest. 100 Vaught Road, Winchester, Kentucky 40391. Phone: 606/745-3100.

Louisiana

Kisatchie National Forest. 2500 Shreveport Highway, P.O. Box 5500, Pineville, Louisiana 71360. Phone: 318/473-7160.

Mississippi

National Forests in Mississippi: Bienville, Delta, DeSoto, Holly Springs, Homochitto, and Tombigbee National Forests. 100 West Capitol Street, Suite 1141, Jackson, Mississippi 39269. Phone: 601/965-4391.

North Carolina

National Forests in North Carolina: Croatan, Nantahala, Pisgah, and Uwharrie National Forests. 100 Otis Street, P.O. Box 2750, Asheville, North Carolina 28802. Phone: 704/257-4200.

South Carolina

Francis Marion-Sumter National Forests. 1835 Assembly Street, P.O. Box 2227, Columbia, South Carolina 29202. Phone: 803/765-5222.

Tennessee

Cherokee National Forest. 2800 North Ocoee Street, N.W., P.O. Box 2010, Cleveland, Tennessee 37320. Phone: 615/476-9700.

Texas

National Forests in Texas: Angelina, Davy Crockett, Sabine, and Sam Houston National Forests. Homer Garrison Federal Building, 701 North First Street, Lufkin, Texas 75901. Phone: 409/639-8501.

Virginia

George Washington National Forest. 101 North Main Street, P.O. Box 233, Harrison Plaza, Harrisonburg, Virginia 22801. Phone: 703/433-2491.

Jefferson National Forest. 210 Franklin Road Southwest, Roanoke, Virginia 24001. Phone: 703/982-6270.

Eastern Region

Each season offers special opportunities to enjoy your national forests of the Eastern Region. In the winter, you can cross-country ski along winter trails. In spring and summer, paddle through the Boundary Waters Canoe Area and listen for the call of the loon. In the fall, driving along winding roads through the hardwood forest (in all their autumn splendor) should be at the top of your list.

Illinois

Shawnee National Forest. 901 South Commercial Street, Harrisburg, Illinois 62946. Phone: 618/253-7114.

Indiana and Ohio

Wayne-Hoosier National Forests. 811 Constitution Avenue, Bedford, Indiana 47421. Phone: 812/275-5987.

Michigan

Hiawatha National Forest. 2727 North Lincoln Road, Escanaba, Michigan 49829. Phone: 906/786-4062.

Huron-Manistee National Forests. 421 South Mitchell Street, Cadillac, Michigan 49601. Phone: 616/775-2421.

Ottawa National Forest. East U.S. Highway 2, Ironwood, Michigan 49938. Phone: 906/932-1330.

Minnesota

Chippewa National Forest. Route 3, P.O. Box 244, Cass Lake, Minnesota 56633. Phone: 218/335-2226.

Superior National Forest. 515 West First Street, P.O. Box 338, Duluth, Minnesota 55801. Phone: 218/720-5324.

Missouri

Mark Twain National Forest. 401 Fairgrounds Road, Rolla, Missouri 65401. Phone: 314/364-4621.

New Hampshire and Maine

White Mountain National Forest. Federal Building, 719 North Main Street, P.O. Box 638, Laconia, New Hampshire 03247. Phone: 603/524-6450.

Pennsylvania

Allegheny National Forest. Spiridon Building, 222 Liberty Street, P.O. Box 847, Warren, Pennsylvania 16365. Phone: 814/723-5150.

Vermont

Green Mountain and Finger Lakes National Forests. Federal Building, 151 West Street, P.O. Box 519, Rutland, Vermont 05701. Phone: 802/773-0300.

West Virginia

Monongahela National Forest.
USDA Building, 200 Sycamore Street,
Elkins, West Virginia 26241. Phone:
304/636-1800.

Wisconsin

Chequamegon National Forest.
1170 Fourth Avenue South, Park
Falls, Wisconsin 54552. Phone:
715/762-2461.

Nicolet National Forest. Federal
Building, 68 South Stevens Street,
Rhinelander, Wisconsin 54501.
Phone: 715/362-3415.

Alaska Region

North to Alaska! Evergreen forests
blanket rugged snow-capped mountains, rushing streams teem with
salmon, and glaciers calve icebergs
the size of office buildings. Camp
along historic gold rush trails, watch
eagles soar above forests from the
comfort of a passenger ship, or kayak
the shoreline of a quiet fiord. Your
national forests in Alaska are a special reason to visit America's "Last
Frontier."

Chugach National Forest. 201 East
Ninth Avenue, Suite 206, Anchorage,
Alaska 99501. Phone: 907/271-2500.

Ketchikan Area. Federal Building,
Ketchikan, Akaska 99901. Phone:
907/225-3101.

Sitkine Area. 201 Twelfth Street, P.O.
Box 309, Petersburg, Alaska 99833.
Phone: 907/772-3841.

Tongass National Forest. Chatham
Area, 204 Siginaka Way, Sitka, Alaska
99835. Phone: 907/747-6671.

Appendix H

National Parks

The following information on national parks (including mailing addresses for each) is from the *National Park System Map and Guide*, produced by the Department of the Interior. For ordering information on this inexpensive publication, request a copy of the free *Consumer Information Catalog*, available from the Consumer Information Center, P.O. Box 100, Pueblo, Colorado 81002.

Alabama

Horseshoe Bend National Military Park. Route 1, Box 103, Daviston, Alabama 36256. Visitor center, museum/exhibit, guided tours, self-guiding tour/trail, picnic area, hiking, boating, boat ramp, fishing, campsites, restrooms.

Russell Cave National Monument. Route 1, Box 175, Bridgeport, Alabama 35740. Visitor center, museum/exhibit, self-guiding tour/trail, picnic area, hiking, horseback riding, restrooms.

Tuskegee Institute National Historic Site. P.O. Drawer 10, Tuskegee, Alabama 36088. Visitor center, museum/exhibit, guided tours, self-guiding tour/trail, restrooms.

Alaska

Aniakchak National Monument and Preserve. P.O. Box 7, King Salmon, Alaska 99613. Hiking, boating, fishing, hunting.

Bering Land Bridge National Preserve. P.O. Box 220, Nome, Alaska 99762. Hiking, fishing, hunting, snowmobile route.

Cape Krusenstern National Monument. P.O. Box 1029, Kotzebue, Alaska 99752. Visitor center, guide for hire, hiking, mountain climbing, boating, fishing, snowmobile route, lodging.

Denali National Park and Preserve. P.O. Box 9, McKinley Park, Alaska 99755. Visitor center, guided tours, self-guiding tour/trail, guide for hire, campground, campsites, hiking, mountain climbing, fishing, lodging, groceries/ice, restaurant/snacks, restrooms. Entrance fee.

Gates of the Arctic National Park and Preserve. P.O. Box 74680, Fairbanks, Alaska 99707. Guide for hire, hiking, mountain climbing, boating, fishing, hunting.

Glacier Bay National Park and Preserve. Gustavus, Alaska 99826. Guided tours, campground, group campsites, hiking, mountain climbing, boating, fishing, off-road vehicle trail, lodging, restaurant/snacks.

Katmai National Park and Preserve. P.O. Box 7, King Salmon, Alaska 99613. Visitor center, guided tours, self-guiding tour/trail, guide for hire, picnic area, campground, hiking, mountain climbing, boating, boat rental, boat ramp, fishing, hunting, lodging, groceries/ice, restaurant/snacks.

Kenai Fjords National Park. P.O. Box 1727, Seward, Alaska 99664. Visitor center, guided tours, picnic area, hiking, mountain climbing, boating, fishing, snowmobile route, cross-country ski trail.

Klondike Gold Rush National Historical Park. P.O. Box 517, Skagway, Alaska 99840. Visitor center, museum/exhibit, guided tours, self-guiding tour/trail, guide for hire, picnic area, campground, hiking, fishing, hunting, lodging, groceries/ice, restaurant/snacks.

Kobuk Valley National Park. P.O. Box 1029, Kotzebue, Alaska 99752. Visitor center, guide for hire, hiking, mountain climbing, boating, fishing, snowmobile trail, lodging.

Lake Clark National Park and Preserve. 701 C Street, P.O. Box 61, Anchorage, Alaska 99513. Guide for hire, hiking, mountain climbing, boating, fishing, hunting, snowmobile route, cross-country ski trail, cabin rentals, other lodging, restaurant/snacks.

Noatak National Preserve. P.O. Box 1029, Kotzebue, Alaska 99752. Visitor center, guide for hire, hiking, mountain climbing, boating, fishing, hunting, snowmobile route, lodging.

Sitka National Historical Park. P.O. Box 738, Sitka, Alaska 99835. Visitor center, museum/exhibit, guided tours, self-guiding tour/trail, picnic area, hiking, fishing.

Wrangell–St. Elias National Park and Preserve. P.O. Box 29, Glennallen, Alaska 99588. Visitor center, guide for hire, hiking, mountain climbing, horseback riding, boating, boat rental,

fishing, hunting, off-road vehicle trail, snowmobile route, lodging.

Yukon-Charley Rivers National Preserve. P.O. Box 64, Eagle, Alaska 99738. Visitor center, guide for hire, hiking, mountain climbing, boating, fishing, hunting.

Arizona

Canyon de Chelly National Monument. P.O. Box 588, Chinle, Arizona 86503. Visitor center, museum/exhibit, guided tours, self-guiding tour/trail, guide for hire, picnic area, campground, group campsite, hiking, horseback riding, lodging, groceries/ice, restaurant/snacks.

Casa Grande National Monument. P.O. Box 518, Coolidge, Arizona 85228. Visitor center, museum/exhibit, guided tours, self-guiding tour/trail, picnic area, restrooms. Entrance fee.

Chiricahua National Monument. Dos Cabezas Route, Box 6500, Wilcox, Arizona 85643. Visitor center, museum/exhibit, guided tours, self guiding tour/trail, picnic area, campground, group campsites, hiking, restrooms. Entrance fee.

Coronado National Memorial. R.R. 2, Box 126, Hereford, Arizona 85615. Visitor center, museum/exhibit, self-guiding tour/trail, picnic area, hiking, restrooms.

Fort Bowie National Historic Site. P.O. Box 158, Bowie, Arizona 85605. Museum/exhibit, self-guiding tour/trail, hiking, restrooms.

Grand Canyon National Park. P.O. Box 129, Grand Canyon, Arizona 86023. Visitor center/museum/exhibit, guided tours, self guiding tour/trail, guide for hire, picnic area, campground, campsites, hiking, horseback riding, fishing, cabin rentals, other lodging, groceries/ice, restaurant/snacks, restrooms. Entrance fee.

Hubbell Trading Post National Historic Site. P.O. Box 150, Ganado, Arizona 86505. Visitor center, museum/exhibit, guided tours, self-guiding tour/trail, picnic area, groceries/ice, restrooms.

Montezuma Castle National Monument. P.O. Box 219, Camp Verde, Arizona 86322. Visitor center, museum/exhibit, self-guiding tour/trail, picnic area, restrooms. Entrance fee.

Navajo National Monument. H.C. 71, Box 3, Tonalea, Arizona 86044-9704. Visitor center, museum/exhibit, guided tours, self-guiding tour/trail, picnic area, campground, campsites, horseback riding, restrooms.

Organ Pipe Cactus National Monument. Route 1, Box 100, Ajo, Arizona 85321. Visitor center, museum/exhibit, guided tours, self-guiding tour/trail, picnic area, campground, campsites, hiking, restrooms. Entrance fee.

Petrified Forest National Park. Petrified Forest National Park, Arizona 86028. Visitor center, museum/exhibit, self-guiding tour/trail, guide for hire, picnic area, hiking, restaurant/snacks, restrooms. Entrance fee.

Pipe Spring National Monument. Moccasin, Arizona 86002. Visitor center, museum/exhibit, guided tours, self-guiding tour/trail, restaurant/snacks, restrooms. Entrance fee.

Saguaro National Monument. 3693 South Old Spanish Trail, Tucson, Arizona 85730-5699. Visitor center, museum/exhibit, guided tours, self-guiding tour/trail, picnic area, hiking, restrooms. Entrance fee.

Sunset Crater National Monument. Route 3, Box 149, Flagstaff, Arizona 86004. Visitor center, museum/exhibit, guided tours, self-guiding tour/trail, picnic area, campground, campsites, hiking, restrooms. Entrance fee.

Tonto National Monument. P.O. Box 707, Roosevelt, Arizona 85545. Visitor center, museum/exhibit, guided tours, self-guiding tour/trail, picnic area, restrooms. Entrance fee.

Tumacacori National Monument. P.O. Box 67, Tumacacori, Arizona 85640. Visitor center, museum/exhibit, guided tours, self-guiding tour/trail, picnic area, restrooms. Entrance fee.

Tuzigoot National Monument. Clarkdale, Arizona 86324. Visitor center, museum/exhibit, self-guiding tour/trail, restrooms. Entrance fee.

Walnut Canyon National Monument. Walnut Canyon Road, Flagstaff, Arizona 86004-9705. Visitor center, museum/exhibit, self-guiding tour/trail, picnic area, restrooms. Entrance fee.

Wupatki National Monument. H.C. 33, Box 444A, Flagstaff, Arizona 86004. Visitor center, museum/exhibit, guided tours, self-guiding tour/trail, picnic area, hiking. Entrance fee.

Arkansas

Arkansas Post National Memorial. Route 1, Box 16, Gillett, Arkansas 72055. Visitor center, museum/exhibit, guided tours, self-guiding tour/trail, picnic area, hiking, fishing, bicycle trail, restrooms.

Buffalo National River. P.O. Box 1173, Harrison, Arkansas 72601. Visitor center, museum/exhibit, guided tours, self-guiding tour/trail, guide for hire, picnic area, campground, campsites, hiking, horseback riding, swimming, boating, boat rental, boat ramp, fishing, hunting, cabin rental, restaurant/snacks, restrooms.

Fort Smith National Historic Site. P.O. Box 1406, Fort Smith, Arkansas 72902. Visitor center, museum/exhibit, guided tours, self-guiding tour/trail, picnic area. Entrance fee.

Hot Springs National Park. P.O. Box 1860, Hot Springs, Arkansas 71902. Visitor center, museum/exhibit, guided tours, self-guiding tour/trail, picnic area, campground, campsites, hiking, horseback riding, bathhouse, restrooms.

Pea Ridge National Military Park. Pea Ridge, Arkansas 72751. Visitor center, museum/exhibit, self-guiding tour/trail, picnic area, hiking.

California

Cabrillo National Monument. P.O. Box 6670, San Diego, California 92106. Visitor center, museum/exhibit, guided tours, self-guiding tour/trail, hiking, fishing, restrooms. Entrance fee.

Channel Islands National Park. 1901 Spinnaker Drive, Ventura, California 93001. Visitor center, museum/exhibit, guided tours, self-guiding tour/trail, picnic area, campground, group campsites, hiking, swimming, boating, fishing, restrooms.

Death Valley National Monument. (California, Nevada.) Death Valley, California 92328. Visitor center, museum/exhibit, guided tours, self-guiding tour/trail, guide for hire, picnic area, campground, campsites, hiking, horseback riding, swimming, bathhouse, bicycle trail, cabin rental, other lodging, groceries/ice, restaurant/snacks, restrooms. Entrance fee.

Devils Postpile National Monument. c/o Sequoia and Kings Canyon National Parks, Three Rivers, California 93271. Visitor center, guided tours, picnic area, camp-ground, hiking, horseback riding, swimming, fishing.

Fort Point National Historic Site. P.O. Box 29333, Presidio of San Francisco, California 94129. Visitor center, museum/exhibit, guided tours, picnic area, fishing, restrooms.

Golden Gate National Recreation Area. Fort Mason Building 201, San Francisco, California 94123. Visitor center, museum/exhibit, guided tours, self-guiding tour/trail, picnic area, campground, campsites, hiking, horseback riding, swimming, bathhouse, fishing, bicycle trail, restaurant/snacks, restrooms.

John Muir National Historic Site. 4202 Alhambra Avenue, Martinez, California 94553. Visitor center, museum/exhibit, guided tours, self-guiding tour/trail, picnic area, restrooms. Entrance fee.

Joshua Tree National Monument. 74485 National Monument Drive, Twentynine Palms, California 92277. Visitor center, museum/exhibit, guided tours, self-guiding tour/trail, picnic area, campground, campsites, hiking, mountain climbing, horseback riding, restrooms. Entrance fee.

Kings Canyon National Park. Three Rivers, California 93271. Visitor center, museum/exhibit, guided tours, self-guiding tour/trail, guide for hire, picnic area, campground, campsites, hiking, mountain climbing, horseback riding, fishing, cross-country ski trail, cabin rental, other lodging, groceries/ice, restaurant, restrooms. Entrance fee.

Lassen Volcanic National Park. P.O. Box 100, Mineral, California 96063. Visitor center, guided tours, self-guiding tour/trail, picnic area, campground, campsites, hiking, mountain climbing, horseback riding, swimming, boating, boat ramp, fishing, cross-country ski trail, cabin rental, groceries/ice, restaurant/ snacks, restrooms. Entrance fee.

Lava Beds National Monument. P.O. Box 867, Tulelake, California 96134. Visitor center, museum/exhibit, guided tours, self-guiding tour/trail, picnic area, campground, campsites, hiking, restrooms. Entrance fee.

Muir Woods National Monument. Mill Valley, California 94941. Visitor center, museum/exhibit, guided tours, self-guiding tour/trail, hiking, restaurant/snacks, restrooms.

Pinnacles National Monument. Paicines, California 95043. Visitor center, museum/exhibit, self-guiding tour/trail, picnic area, campground, campsites, hiking, mountain climbing, restrooms. Entrance fee.

Point Reyes National Seashore. Point Reyes, California 94956. Visitor center, museum/exhibit, guided tours, self-guiding tour/trail, picnic area, campground, group campsite, hiking, horseback riding, swimming, fishing, bicycle trail, restaurant/snacks, restrooms.

Redwood National Park. 1111 Second Street, Crescent City, California 95531. Visitor center, museum/exhibit, guided tours, self-guiding tour/trail, picnic area, campground, group campsite, hiking, horseback riding, swimming, fishing, restrooms.

Santa Monica Mountains National Recreation Area. 22900 Ventura Boulevard, Suite 140, Woodland Hills, California 91364. Visitor center, museum/exhibit, guided tours, self-guiding tour/trail, picnic area, campground, campsites, hiking, horseback riding, swimming, boating, fishing, bicycle trail, groceries/ice, restaurant/snacks, restrooms.

Sequoia National Park. Three Rivers, California 93271. Visitor center, museum/exhibit, guided tours, self-guiding tours, guide for hire, picnic area, campground, campsites, hiking, mountain climbing, horseback riding, fishing, cross-country ski trail, cabin rental, other lodging, groceries/ice, restaurant, restrooms. Entrance fee.

Whiskeytown-Shasta-Trinity National Recreation Area. P.O. Box 188, Whiskeytown, California 96095. Visitor center, guided tours, self-guiding tour/trail, picnic area, campground, campsites, hiking, horseback riding, swimming, bathhouse, boating, boat rental, boat ramp, fishing, hunting, groceries/ice, restaurant/snacks, restrooms.

Yosemite National Park. P.O. Box 577, Yosemite National Park, California 95389. Visitor center, museum/exhibit, guided tours, self-guiding tour/trail, guide for hire, picnic area, campground, campsites, hiking, mountain climbing, horseback riding, swimming, bathhouse, boating, boat rental, boat ramp, fishing, bicycle trail, cross-country ski trail, cabin rental, other lodging, groceries/ice, restaurant/snacks, restrooms. Entrance fee.

Colorado

Bent's Old Fort National Historic Site. 35110 Highway 194 East, La Junta, Colorado 81050-9523. Museum/exhibit, guided tours, self-guiding tour/trail, picnic area, restrooms. Entrance fee.

Black Canyon of the Gunnison National Monument. P.O. Box 1648, Montrose, Colorado 81402. Visitor center, museum/exhibit, guided tours, self-guiding tour/trail, picnic area, campground, campsites, hiking, mountain climbing, fishing, cross-country ski trail, restaurant/snacks, restrooms. Entrance fee.

Colorado National Monument. Fruita, Colorado 81521. Visitor center, museum/exhibit, guided tours, self-guiding tour/trail, picnic area, campground, hiking, mountain climbing, horseback riding, bicycle trail, cross-country ski trail, restrooms. Entrance fee.

Curecanti National Recreation Area. 102 Elk Creek, Gunnison, Colorado 81230. Visitor center, museum/exhibit, guided tours, self-guiding tour/trail, guide for hire, picnic area, campground, campsites, hiking, swimming, boating, boat rental, boat ramp, fishing, hunting, snowmobile route, cross-country ski trail, groceries/ice, restaurant/snacks, restrooms.

Dinosaur National Monument. (Colorado, Utah.) P.O. Box 210, Dinosaur, Colorado 81610. Visitor center, museum/exhibit, guided tours, self-guiding tour/trail, picnic area, campground, hiking, boating, fishing, restrooms. Entrance fee.

Florissant Fossil Beds National Monument. P.O. Box 185, Florissant, Colorado 80816. Visitor center, museum/exhibit, guided tours, self-guiding tour/trail, picnic area, hiking, cross-country ski trail, restrooms. Entrance fee.

Great Sand Dunes National Monument. Mosca, Colorado 81146. Visitor center, museum/exhibit, guided tours, self-guiding tour/trail, picnic area, campground, campsites, hiking, fishing, groceries/ice, restrooms. Entrance fee.

Hovenweep National Monument. (Colorado, Utah.) c/o Mesa Verde National Park, Mesa Verde National Park, Colorado 81330. Visitor center, museum/exhibit, self-guiding tour/trail, picnic area, campground, restrooms.

Mesa Verde National Park. Mesa Verde National Park, Colorado 81330. Visitor center, museum/ex-

hibit, guided tours, self-guiding tour/trail, guide for hire, picnic area, campground, campsites, lodging, groceries/ice, restaurant/snacks, restrooms. Entrance fee.

Rocky Mountain National Park. Estes Park, Colorado 80517. Visitor center, museum/exhibit, guided tours, self-guiding tour/trail, guide for hire, picnic area, campground, campsites, hiking, mountain climbing, horseback riding, fishing, snowmobile route, cross-country ski trail, restaurant/snacks, restrooms. Entrance fee.

District of Columbia

Constitution Gardens. c/o NCP—Central, 900 Ohio Drive, S.W., Washington, D.C. 20242. Picnic area, restrooms.

Ford's Theatre National Historic Site. c/o NCP—Central, 900 Ohio Drive, S.W., Washington, D.C. 20242. Visitor center, museum/exhibit, guided tours, self-guiding tour.

Frederick Douglass National Historic Site. 1411 W Street, S.E., Washington, D.C. 20020. Visitor center, museum/exhibit, guided tours, self-guiding tour, picnic area, bicycle trail, restrooms.

John F. Kennedy Center for the Performing Arts. National Park Service, 2700 F Street, N.W., Washington, D.C. 20566. Visitor center, guided tours, self-guiding tour, restaurant/snacks, restrooms.

Lincoln Memorial. c/o NCP—Central, 900 Ohio Drive, S.W., Washington, D.C. 20242. Guided tours, self-guiding tour, restrooms.

Lyndon B. Johnson Memorial Grove on the Potomac. c/o George Washington Memorial Parkway, Turkey Run Park, McLean, Virginia 22101. Picnic area, boating, boat ramp, fishing, groceries/ice, restrooms.

Rock Creek Park. 5000 Glover Road, N.W., Washington, D.C. 20015. Visitor center, museum/exhibit, guided tours, self-guiding tour, picnic area, hiking, horseback riding, fishing, restrooms.

Theodore Roosevelt Island. c/o George Washington Memorial Parkway, Turkey Run Park, McLean, Virginia 22101. Guided tours, self-guiding tour/trail, hiking, horseback riding, fishing, restrooms.

Thomas Jefferson Memorial and Tidal Basin. c/o NCP—Central, 900 Ohio Drive, S.W., Washington, D.C. 20242. Visitor center, museum/exhibit, guided tours, self-guiding tour, restrooms.

Vietnam Veterans Memorial. c/o NCP—Central, 900 Ohio Drive, S.W., Washington, D.C. 20242. Restrooms.

Washington Monument. c/o NCP—Central, 900 Ohio Drive, S.W., Washington, D.C. 20242. Museum/exhibit, guided tours, self-guiding tour, bicycle trail, restaurant/snacks, restrooms.

White House. c/o NCR, National Park Service, 1100 Ohio Drive, S.W., Washington, D.C. 20242. Guided and self-guided tours, restrooms.

Florida

Big Cypress National Preserve. Star Route, Box 110, Ochopee, Florida 33943. Visitor center, museum/exhibit, guide for hire, picnic area, campground, hiking, fishing, hunting, off-road vehicle trail, groceries/ice, restrooms.

Biscayne National Park. P.O. Box 1369, Homestead, Florida 33090. Visitor center, museum/exhibit, guided tours, self-guiding tour/trail, picnic area, campground, group campsites, hiking, swimming, boating, fishing, restrooms.

Canaveral National Seashore. P.O. Box 6447, Titusville, Florida 32782. Visitor center, museum/exhibit, guided tours, self-guiding tour/trail, picnic area, hiking, swimming, boating, boat ramp, fishing, restrooms.

Castillo de San Marcos National Monument. One Castillo Drive, St. Augustine, Florida 32084. Museum/exhibit, guided tours, self-guiding tour/trail, restrooms. Entrance fee.

DeSoto National Memorial. Seventy-fifth Street, N.W., Bradenton, Florida 33529. Visitor center, museum/exhibit, self-guiding tour/trail, fishing. Entrance fee.

Everglades National Park. P.O. Box 279, Homestead, Florida 33030. Visitor center, museum/exhibit, guided tours, self-guiding tour/trail, picnic area, campground, campsites, hiking, boating, boat rental, boat ramp, fishing, bicycle trail, cabin rental, other lodging, groceries/ice, restaurant/snacks, restrooms. Entrance fee.

Fort Caroline National Memorial. 12713 Fort Caroline Road, Jacksonville, Florida 32225. Visitor center, museum/exhibit, guided tours, self-guiding tour/trail, picnic area, hiking, restrooms.

Fort Jefferson National Monument. c/o Everglades National Park, P.O. Box 279, Homestead, Florida 33030. Visitor center, museum/exhibit, self-guiding tour/trail, picnic area, campground, campsites, swimming, boating, fishing, restrooms.

Fort Matanzas National Monument. c/o Castillo de San Marcos National Monument, One Castillo Drive, St. Augustine, Florida 32084. Visitor center, museum/exhibit, guided tours, self-guiding tour/trail, swimming, fishing.

Gulf Islands National Seashore.
1801 Gulf Breeze Parkway, Gulf
Breeze, Florida 32561. Visitor center,
museum/exhibit, guided tours, self-
guiding tour/trail, picnic area, campground, group campsite, hiking,
swimming, bathhouse, boating, fishing, bicycle trail, groceries/ice, res-
taurant/snacks, restrooms. Entrance
fee.

Georgia

**Andersonville National Historic
Site.** Route 1, Box 85, Andersonville,
Georgia 31711. Visitor center, mu-
seum/exhibit, guided tours, self-
guiding tour/trail, picnic area,
restrooms. Entrance fee.

**Chattahoochee River National Rec-
reation Area.** 1978 Island Ford Parkway, Dunwoody, Georgia 30350.
Self-guiding tour/trail, picnic area,
hiking, boating, boat rental, boat
ramp, fishing, restaurant/snacks,
restrooms.

**Chickamauga and Chattanooga
National Military Park.** (Georgia,
Tennessee.) P.O. Box 2128, Fort
Oglethorpe, Georgia 30742. Visitor
center, museum/exhibit, self-guiding
tour/trail, picnic area, hiking, horseback riding, restrooms. Entrance fee.

**Cumberland Island National Sea-
shore.** P.O. Box 806, St. Marys, Georgia 31558. Visitor center,
museum/exhibit, guided tours, self-
guiding tour/trail, picnic area, campground, group campsite, hiking,
swimming, bathhouse, fishing,
restrooms.

**Fort Frederica National Monu-
ment.** Route 9, Box 286C, St. Simons
Island, Georgia 31522. Visitor center,
museum/exhibit, guided tours, self-
guiding tour/trail, restrooms. Entrance fee.

Fort Pulaski National Monument.
P.O. Box 98, Tybee Island, Georgia

31328. Visitor center, museum/ex-
hibit, guided tours, self-guiding
tour/trail, picnic area, group campsite, hiking, boating, boat ramp, fishing, restrooms. Entrance fee.

**Kennesaw Mountain National Bat-
tlefield Park.** P.O. Box 1167,
Marietta, Georgia 30061. Visitor center, museum/exhibit, self-guiding
tour/trail, picnic area, hiking, horseback riding, restrooms.

**Martin Luther King, Jr., National
Historic Site.** 522 Auburn Avenue,
N.E., Atlanta, Georgia 30312. Visitor
center, museum/exhibit, guided
tours, self-guiding tour/trail.

Ocmulgee National Monument.
1207 Emery Highway, Macon, Georgia 31201. Visitor center, museum/ex-
hibit, guided tours, self-guiding
tour/trail, picnic area, hiking, fishing, restrooms. Entrance fee.

Hawaii

Haleakala National Park. P.O. Box
369, Makawao, Hawaii 96768. Visitor
center, museum/exhibit, self-guiding
tour/trail, picnic area, campground,
group campsite, hiking, horseback
riding, hunting, cabin rental,
restrooms. Entrance fee.

Hawaii Volcanoes National Park.
Hawaii National Park, Hawaii 96718.
Visitor center, museum/exhibit, self-
guiding tour/trail, picnic area, campground, campsites, hiking, mountain
climbing, cabin rentals, other lodging, groceries/ice, restaurant/snacks,
restrooms. Entrance fee.

**Kalaupapa National Historical
Park.** Kalaupapa, Hawaii 96742. Mu-
seum/exhibit, guide for hire.

**Pu'uhonua o Honaunau National
Historical Park.** P.O. Box 128,
Honaunau, Kona, Hawaii 96726. Visitor center, museum/exhibit, self-
guiding tour/trail, picnic area,

hiking, swimming, bathhouse, fishing. Entrance fee.

Puukohola Heiau National Historic Site. P.O. Box 4963, Kawaihae, Hawaii 96743. Visitor center, guided tours, self-guiding tour/trail, restrooms.

USS Arizona Memorial. One Arizona Memorial Place, Honolulu, Hawaii 96818. Visitor center, museum/exhibit, guided tours, restaurant/snacks, restrooms.

Idaho

Craters of the Moon National Monument. P.O. Box 29, Arco, Idaho 83213. Visitor center, museum/exhibit, guided tours, self-guiding tour/trail, picnic area, campground, group campsite, hiking, cross-country ski trail, restrooms. Entrance fee.

Nez Perce National Historical Park. P.O. Box 93, Spalding, Idaho 83551. Visitor center, museum/exhibit, self-guiding tour/trail, picnic area, fishing, restrooms.

Illinois

Lincoln Home National Historic Site. 426 South Seventh Street, Springfield, Illinois 62701. Visitor center, museum/exhibit, guided tours, self-guiding tour/trail, picnic area, restrooms.

Indiana

George Rogers Clark National Historical Park. 401 South Second Street, Vincennes, Indiana 47591. Visitor center, museum/exhibit, restrooms. Entrance fee.

Indiana Dunes National Lakeshore. 1100 North Mineral Springs Road, Porter, Indiana 46304. Visitor center, museum/exhibit, guided tours, self-guiding tour/trail, picnic area, hiking, horseback riding, swimming, bathhouse, boating, fishing, bicycle trail, cross-country ski trail, restaurant/snacks, restrooms.

Lincoln Boyhood National Memorial. Lincoln City, Indiana 47552. Visitor center, museum/exhibit, guided tours, self-guiding tour/trail, hiking, restrooms. Entrance fee.

Iowa

Effigy Mounds National Monument. R.R. 1, Box 25A, Harpers Ferry, Iowa 52146. Visitor center, museum/exhibit, guided tours, self-guiding tour/trail, hiking, cross- country ski trail, restrooms. Entrance fee.

Herbert Hoover National Historic Site. P.O. Box 607, West Branch, Iowa 52358. Visitor center, museum/exhibit, guided tours, self-guiding tour/trail, picnic area, hiking, cross-country ski trail, restrooms. Entrance fee.

Kansas

Fort Larned National Historic Site. Route 3, Larned, Kansas 67550. Visitor center, museum/exhibit, guided tours, self-guiding tour/trail, picnic area, fishing, restrooms. Entrance fee.

Fort Scott National Historic Site. Old Fort Boulevard, Fort Scott, Kansas 66701. Visitor center, museum/exhibit, guided tours, self-guiding tour/trail, picnic area, restrooms. Entrance fee.

Kentucky

Abraham Lincoln Birthplace National Historic Site. R.F.D. 1, Hodgenville, Kentucky 42748. Visitor center, museum/exhibit, self-guiding tour/trail, picnic area, hiking, restrooms.

Cumberland Gap National Historical Park. (Kentucky, Tennessee, Virginia.) P.O. Box 1848, Middlesboro, Kentucky 40965. Visitor center, museum/exhibit, picnic area, campground, campsites, hiking, restrooms.

Mammoth Cave National Park.
Mammoth Cave, Kentucky 42259.
Visitor center, museum/exhibit,
guided tour, self-guiding tour/trail,
picnic area, campground, campsites,
hiking, horseback riding, boating,
fishing, cabin rental, other lodging,
groceries/ice, restaurant/snacks,
restrooms.

Louisiana

**Jean Lafitte National Historical
Park and Preserve.** 423 Canal
Street, Room 210, New Orleans, Lou-
isiana 70130-2341.

Maine

Acadia National Park. P.O. Box 177,
Bar Harbor, Maine 04609. Visitor
center, museum/exhibit, self-guiding
tour/trail, picnic area, campground,
campsites, hiking, mountain climbing, horseback riding, swimming,
boating, boat rental, boat ramp, fishing, bicycle trail, snowmobile route,
cross-country skiing, lodging, grocer-
ies/ice, restaurant/snacks, restrooms.
Entrance fee.

**Saint Croix Island International
Historic Site.** c/o Acadia National
Park, P.O. Box 177, Bar Harbor,
Maine 04609. Picnic area, hiking,
boat ramp.

Maryland

Antietam National Battlefield. Box
158, Sharpsburg, Maryland 21782.
Visitor center, museum/exhibit, self-
guiding tour/trail, campsites, hiking,
fishing, bicycle trail, restrooms. Entrance fee.

**Assateague Island National Sea-
shore.** (Maryland, Virginia.) Route 2,
Box 294, Berlin, Maryland 21811.
Visitor center, museum/exhibit,
guided tours, self-guiding tour/trail,
picnic area, campground, campsites,
hiking, swimming, bathhouse, boating, fishing, hunting, off-road vehicle
trail, restrooms. Entrance fee.

Catoctin Mountain Park. 6602
Foxville Road, Thurmont, Maryland
21788. Visitor center, museum/ex-
hibit, guided tours, self-guiding
tour/trail, picnic area, campground,
campsites, hiking, mountain climbing, fishing, cross-country ski trail,
cabin rental, restrooms.

**Chesapeake and Ohio Canal Na-
tional Historical Park.** (Maryland,
West Virginia, District of Columbia.)
P.O. Box 4, Sharpsburg, Maryland
21782. Visitor center, museum/ex-
hibit, guided tours, self-guiding
tour/trail, picnic area, campground,
group campsite, hiking, horseback
riding, boating, boat rental, boat
ramp, fishing, restaurant/snacks,
restrooms.

**Clara Barton National Historic
Site.** 5801 Oxford Road, Glen Echo,
Maryland 20812. Visitor center, mu-
seum/exhibit, guided tours, self-
guiding tour/trail, bicycle trail.

**Fort McHenry National Monument
and Historic Shrine.** End of East
Fort Avenue, Baltimore, Maryland
21230-5393. Visitor center, mu-
seum/exhibit, guided tours, self-
guiding tour/trail, picnic area,
restrooms. Entrance fee.

Fort Washington Park. NCP–East,
1900 Anacostia Drive, S.E., Washington, D.C. 20020. Visitor center, mu-
seum/exhibit, guided tours,
self-guiding tour/trail, picnic area,
hiking, fishing, bicycle trail. Entrance
fee.

Greenbelt Park. 6565 Greenbelt
Road, Greenbelt, Maryland 20770.
Guided tours, self-guiding tour/trail,
picnic area, campground, campsites,
hiking, restrooms.

Hampton National Historic Site. 535
Hampton Lane, Towson, Maryland
21204. Visitor center, museum/exhibit,
guided tours, self-guiding tour/trail,
restaurant/snacks.

Piscataway Park. c/o NCP–East, 1900 Anacostia Drive, S.E., Washington, D.C. 20019. Picnic area, hiking, fishing, campsites.

Massachusetts

Adams National Historic Site. P.O. Box 531, 135 Adams Street, Quincy, Massachusetts 02269-0531. Museum/exhibit, guided tours. Entrance fee.

Boston National Historical Park. Charlestown Navy Yard, Boston, Massachusetts 02129. Visitor center, museum/exhibit, guided tours, self-guiding tour/trail, picnic area, restaurant/snacks, restrooms.

Cape Cod National Seashore. South Wellfleet, Massachusetts 02663. Visitor center, museum/exhibit, guided tours, self-guiding tour/trail, guide for hire, picnic area, hiking, horseback riding, swimming, bathhouse, fishing, hunting, off-road vehicle trail, bicycle trail, lodging, restaurant/snacks, restrooms. Entrance fee.

Frederick Law Olmsted National Historic Site. 99 Warren Street, Brookline, Massachusetts 02146. Museum/exhibit, guided tour, self-guiding tour/trail.

John Fitzgerald Kennedy National Historic Site. 83 Beals Street, Brookline, Massachusetts 02146. Visitor center, museum/exhibit, guided tours. Entrance fee.

Longfellow National Historic Site. 105 Brattle Street, Cambridge, Massachusetts 02138. Visitor center, museum/exhibit, guided tours. Entrance fee.

Lowell National Historical Park. 169 Merrimack Street, Lowell, Massachusetts 01852. Visitor center, museum/exhibit, guided tour, self-guiding tour/trail, picnic area, boating, boat ramp, fishing, lodging,

groceries/ice, restaurant/snacks, restrooms.

Minute Man National Historical Park. P.O. Box 160, 174 Liberty Street, Concord, Massachusetts 01742. Visitor center, museum/exhibit, guided tours, self-guiding tour/trail, restrooms. Entrance fee.

Salem Maritime National Historic Site. Custom House, 174 Derby Street, Salem, Massachusetts 01970. Visitor center, museum/exhibit, guided tours, self-guiding tour/trail, picnic area, hiking, boating, fishing, bicycle trail, restaurant/snacks.

Saugus Iron Works National Historic Site. 244 Central Street, Saugus, Massachusetts 01906. Visitor center, museum/exhibit, guided tours, self-guiding tour/trail, picnic area, restrooms.

Springfield Armory National Historic Site. One Armory Square, Springfield, Massachusetts 01105. Museum/exhibit, self-guiding tour/trail, restrooms.

Michigan

Isle Royale National Park. 87 North Ripley Street, Houghton, Michigan 49931. Visitor center, guided tours, self-guiding tour/trail, picnic area, campground, group campsite, hiking, swimming, boating, boat rental, fishing, cabin rental, other lodging, groceries/ice, restaurant/snacks, restrooms.

Pictured Rocks National Lakeshore. P.O. Box 40, Munising, Michigan 49862. Visitor center, museum/exhibit, self-guiding tour/trail, picnic area, campground, campsites, hiking, swimming, boating, boat ramp, fishing, hunting, snowmobile route, cross-country ski trail, restrooms.

Sleeping Bear Dunes National Lakeshore. P.O. Box 277, 9922 Front Street, Empire, Michigan 49630. Visitor center, museum/exhibit, guided tours, self-guiding tour/trail, picnic area, campground, campsites, hiking, swimming, bathhouse, boating, boat rental, boat ramp, fishing, hunting, cross-country ski trail, restaurant/snacks.

Minnesota

Grand Portage National Monument. P.O. Box 666, Grand Marais, Minnesota 55604. Visitor center, museum/exhibit, guided tours, self-guiding tour/trail, picnic area, hiking, fishing, cross-country ski trail, restrooms. Entrance fee.

Pipestone National Monument. P.O. Box 727, Pipestone, Minnesota 56164. Visitor center, museum/exhibit, self-guiding tour/trail, picnic area, restrooms. Entrance fee.

Voyageurs National Park. P.O. Box 50, International Falls, Minnesota 56649. Visitor center, museum/exhibit, guided tours, self-guiding tour/trail, guide for hire, picnic area, campground, group campsite, hiking, swimming, boating, boat rental, boat ramp, fishing, snowmobile route, cross-country ski trail, cabin rental, other lodging, groceries/ice, restaurant/snacks, restrooms.

Mississippi

Brices Cross Roads National Battlefield Site. c/o Natchez Trace Parkway, R.R. 1, NT-143, Tupelo, Mississippi 38801. Museum/exhibit.

Gulf Islands National Seashore. 3500 Park Road, Ocean Springs, Mississippi 39564. Visitor center, museum/exhibit, guided tours, self-guiding tour/trail, picnic area, campground, campsite, hiking, swimming, bathhouse, boating, boat ramp, fishing, restrooms. Entrance fee.

Natchez Trace Parkway. (Mississippi, Alabama, Tennessee.) R.R. 1,

NT-143, Tupelo, Mississippi 38801. Visitor center, museum/exhibit, self-guiding tour/trail, picnic area, campground, campsites, hiking, horseback riding, swimming, boating, boat ramp, fishing, groceries/ice, restrooms.

Tupelo National Battlefield. c/o Natchez Trace Parkway, R.R. 1, NT-143, Tupelo, Mississippi 38801. Museum/exhibit.

Vicksburg National Military Park. 3201 Clay Street, Vicksburg, Mississippi 39180. Visitor center, museum/exhibit, self-guiding tour/trail, guide for hire, picnic area, restrooms. Entrance fee.

Missouri

George Washington Carver National Monument. P.O. Box 38, Diamond, Missouri 64840. Visitor center, museum/exhibit, guided tours, self-guiding tour/trail, picnic area, restrooms. Entrance fee.

Harry S Truman National Historic Site. 223 North Main Street, Independence, Missouri 64050. Visitor center, museum/exhibit, guided tours, restrooms. Entrance fee.

Jefferson National Expansion Memorial. 11 North Fourth Street, St. Louis, Missouri 63102. Visitor center, museum/exhibit, guided tours, restrooms. Entrance fee.

Ozark National Scenic Riverways. P.O. Box 490, Van Buren, Missouri 63965. Museum/exhibit, guided tour, picnic area, campground, campsites, hiking, horseback riding, swimming, boating, boat rental, boat ramp, fishing, hunting, cabin rental, groceries/ice, restaurant/snacks, restrooms.

Wilson's Creek National Battlefield. Postal Drawer C, Republic, Missouri 65738. Visitor center, museum/exhibit, self-guiding tour/trail, picnic area, hiking, horseback riding, fishing, bicycle trail, restrooms. Entrance fee.

Montana

Big Hole National Battlefield. P.O. Box 237, Wisdom, Montana 59761. Visitor center, museum/exhibit, self-guiding tour/trail, picnic area, fishing. Entrance fee.

Bighorn Canyon National Recreation Area. (Montana, Wyoming), P.O. Box 458, Fort Smith, Montana 59035. Visitor center, museum/exhibit, guided tours, self-guiding tour/trail, picnic area, campground, campsites, hiking, swimming, boating, boat rental, boat ramp, fishing, hunting, snowmobile route, groceries/ice, restrooms.

Custer Battlefield National Monument. P.O. Box 39, Crow Agency, Montana 59022. Visitor center, museum/exhibit, guided tours, self-guiding tour/trail, restrooms. Entrance fee.

Glacier National Park. West Glacier, Montana 59936. Visitor center, museum/exhibit, guided tours, self-guiding tour/trail, guide for hire, picnic area, campground, campsites, hiking, mountain climbing, horseback riding, swimming, boating, boat rental, boat ramp, fishing, cross-country ski trail, cabin rental, other lodging, groceries/ice, restaurant/snacks, restrooms. Entrance fee.

Grant-Kohrs Ranch National Historic Site. P.O. Box 790, Deer Lodge, Montana 59722. Visitor center, museum/exhibit, guided tours, self-guiding tour/trail, restrooms. Entrance fee.

Nebraska

Agate Fossil Beds National Monument. P.O. Box 427, Gering, Nebraska 69341. Visitor center, museum/ exhibit, self-guiding tour/ trail, picnic area, hiking, fishing, restrooms.

Homestead National Monument of America. Route 3, Box 47, Beatrice, Nebraska 68310. Visitor center, museum/exhibit, self-guiding tour/trail, picnic area, hiking, cross-country ski trail, restrooms.

Scotts Bluff National Monument. P.O. Box 427, Gering, Nebraska 69341. Visitor center, museum/exhibit, self-guiding tour/trail, hiking, bicycle trail, restrooms. Entrance fee.

Nevada

Great Basin National Park. Baker, Nevada 89311. Visitor center, museum/exhibit, guided tours, self-guiding tour/trail, picnic area, campground, campsites, hiking, mountain climbing, horseback riding, fishing, cross-country ski trail, restaurant/snacks, restrooms.

Lake Mead National Recreation Area. (Nevada, Arizona.) Nevada Highway, Boulder City, Nevada 89005-2426. Visitor center, museum/exhibit, self-guiding tour/trail, guide for hire, picnic area, campground, campsites, hiking, swimming, bathhouse, boating, boat rental, boat ramp, fishing, hunting, lodging, groceries/ice, restaurant/snacks, restrooms.

New Hampshire

Saint-Gaudens National Site. R.R. 2, Box 73, Cornish, New Hampshire 03745-9704. Museum/exhibit, guided tours, self-guiding tour/trail, picnic area, hiking, cross-country ski trail, restrooms. Entrance fee.

New Jersey

Edison National Historic Site. Main Street and Lakeside Avenue, West Orange, New Jersey 07052. Visitor center, museum/exhibit, guided tours, restrooms. Entrance fee.

Morristown National Historical Park. Washington Place, Morristown, New Jersey 07960. Visitor center, museum/exhibit, guided tours, self-guiding tour/trail, hiking, cross-country ski trail, restrooms. Entrance fee.

New Mexico

Aztec Ruins National Monument. P.O. Box 640, Aztec, New Mexico 87410. Visitor center, museum/exhibit, self-guiding tour/trail, picnic area. Entrance fee.

Bandelier National Monument. Los Alamos, New Mexico 87544. Visitor center, museum/exhibit, guided tours, self-guiding tour/trail, picnic area, campground, campsites, hiking, fishing, groceries/ice, restaurant/snacks, restrooms. Entrance fee.

Capulin Volcano National Monument. Capulin, New Mexico 88414. Visitor center, museum/exhibit, self-guiding tour/trail, picnic area, hiking, restrooms. Entrance fee.

Carlsbad Caverns National Park. 3225 National Parks Highway, Carlsbad, New Mexico 88220. Visitor center, museum/exhibit, guided tours, self-guiding tour/trail, picnic area, hiking, restaurant/snacks, restrooms.

Chaco Culture National Historical Park. Star Route 4, Box 6500, Bloomfield, New Mexico 87413. Visitor center, museum/exhibit, guided tours, self-guiding tour/trail, picnic area, campground, campsites, hiking, bicycle trail, restrooms. Entrance fee.

El Malpais National Monument. c/o Southwest Regional Office, NPS, P.O. Box 728, Santa Fe, New Mexico 87504. Visitor center, self-guiding tour/trail, hiking.

El Morro National Monument. Ramah, New Mexico 87321. Visitor center, museum/exhibit, self-guiding tour/trail, picnic area, campground, campsites, hiking, restrooms. Entrance fee.

Fort Union National Monument. Watrous, New Mexico 87753. Visitor center, museum/exhibit, self-guiding tour/trail, picnic area, restrooms. Entrance fee.

Gila Cliff Dwellings National Monument. Route 11, Box 100, Silver City, New Mexico 88061. Visitor center, museum/exhibit, self-guiding tour/trail, fishing, restrooms.

Pecos National Historical Park. P.O. Drawer 11, Pecos, New Mexico 87552. Visitor center, museum/exhibit, guided tours, self-guiding tour/trail, picnic area, restrooms. Entrance fee.

Salinas National Monument. P.O. Box 496, Mountainair, New Mexico 87036. Visitor center, museum/exhibit, guided tours, self-guiding tour/trail, picnic area, restrooms. Entrance fee.

White Sands National Monument. P.O. Box 458, Alamogordo, New Mexico 88310. Visitor center, museum/exhibit, guided tours, self-guiding tour/trail, picnic area, hiking, restrooms. Entrance fee.

New York

Castle Clinton National Monument. Manhattan Sites, 26 Wall Street, New York, New York 10005. Visitor center, museum/exhibit, guided tours, self-guiding tour/trail, restrooms.

Eleanor Roosevelt National Historic Site. 249 Albany Post Road, Hyde Park, New York 12538. Museum/exhibit, guided tours, restrooms.

Federal Hall National Memorial. Manhattan Sites, 26 Wall Street, New York, New York 10005. Visitor center, guided tours, restrooms.

Fire Island National Seashore. 120 Laurel Street, Patchogue, New York 11772. Visitor center, museum/exhibit, guided tours, self-guiding tour/trail, picnic area, campground, campsites, hiking, swimming, bathhouse, boating, fishing, hunting, groceries/ice, restaurant/snacks, restrooms.

Fort Stanwix National Monument. 112 East Park Street, Rome, New York 13440. Visitor center, museum/exhibit, guided tours, restrooms. Entrance fee.

Gateway National Recreation Area. (New York, New Jersey), Floyd Bennett Field, Building 69, Brooklyn, New York 11234. Visitor center, museum/exhibit, guided tours, self-guiding tour/trail, picnic area, group campsites, hiking, horseback riding, swimming, bathhouse, boating, boat ramp, fishing, bicycle trail, cross-country ski trail, restaurant/snacks, restrooms.

General Grant National Memorial. 122nd Street and Riverside Drive, New York, New York 10027. Visitor center, guided tours.

Hamilton Grange National Memorial. 287 Convent Avenue, New York, New York 10031. Visitor center, museum/exhibit, guided tours, self-guiding tour, restrooms.

Home of Franklin D. Roosevelt National Historic Site. 249 Albany Post Road, Hyde Park, New York 12538. Visitor center, museum/exhibit, self-guiding tour/trail, picnic area, restrooms.

Martin Van Buren National Historic Site. P.O. Box 545, Route 9H, Kinderhook, New York 12106. Visitor center, museum/exhibit, guided tours. Entrance fee.

Sagamore Hill National Historic Site. 20 Sagamore Hill Road, Oyster Bay, New York 11771-1899. Visitor center, museum/exhibit, self-guiding tour/trail, restrooms. Entrance fee.

Saint Paul's Church National Historic Site. 897 South Columbus Avenue, Mount Vernon, New York 10550. Visitor center, museum/exhibit, guided tours, restrooms.

Saratoga National Historical Park. R.D. 2, Box 33, Stillwater, New York 12170. Visitor center, museum/exhibit, guided tours, self-guiding tour/trail, picnic area, hiking, bicycle trail, cross-country ski trail, restrooms. Entrance fee.

Statue of Liberty National Monument. (New York, New Jersey.) Liberty Island, New York, New York 10004. Visitor center, museum/exhibit, guided tours, self-guiding tour, restaurant/snacks, restrooms.

Theodore Roosevelt Birthplace National Historic Site. 28 East Twentieth Street, New York, New York 10003. Museum/exhibit, guided tours. Entrance fee.

Theodore Roosevelt Inaugural National Historic Site. 641 Delaware Avenue, Buffalo, New York 14202. Visitor center, museum/exhibit, guided tours.

Vanderbilt Mansion National Historic Site. 249 Albany Post Road, Hyde Park, New York 12538. Visitor center, museum/exhibit, guided tours, picnic area. Entrance fee.

Women's Rights National Historical Park. P.O. Box 70, Seneca Falls, New York 13148. Visitor center, museum/exhibit, guided tours, self-guiding tour/trail, restrooms.

North Carolina

Blue Ridge Parkway. (North Carolina, Virginia), 700 Northwestern Plaza, Asheville, North Carolina 28801. Visitor center, museum/exhibit, guided tours, self-guiding tour/trail, picnic area, campground, campsites, hiking, horseback riding, boating, boat rental, fishing, snowmobile route, cross-country ski trail, cabin rental, other lodging, groceries/ice, restaurant/snacks, restrooms.

Cape Hatteras National Seashore. Route 1, Box 675, Manteo, North Carolina 27954. Visitor center, museum/exhibit, guided tours, self-guiding tour/trail, picnic area, campground, group campsite, hiking, swimming, bathhouse, boating, boat ramp, fishing, hunting, off-road vehicle trail, groceries/ice, restrooms.

Cape Lookout National Seashore. P.O. Box 690, Beaufort, North Carolina 28516. Visitor center, museum/exhibit, guided tours, picnic area, hiking, swimming, boating, fishing, hunting, off-road vehicle trail, cabin rental.

Carl Sandburg Home National Historic Site. P.O. Box 395, Flat Rock, North Carolina 28731. Visitor center, museum/exhibit, guided tours, hiking, restrooms. Entrance fee.

Fort Raleigh National Historic Site. Cape Hatteras Group, Route 1, Box 675, Manteo, North Carolina 27954. Visitor center, museum/exhibit, guided tours, self-guiding tour/trail, restrooms.

Guilford Courthouse National Military Park. P.O. Box 9806, Greensboro, North Carolina 27429. Visitor center, museum/exhibit, self-guiding tour/trail, bicycle trail, restrooms.

Moores Creek National Battlefield. P.O. Box 69, Currie, North Carolina 28435. Visitor center, museum/exhibit, self-guiding tour/trail, picnic area, fishing, restrooms.

Wright Brothers National Memorial. Cape Hatteras Group, Route 1, Box 675 Manteo, North Carolina 27954. Visitor center, museum/exhibit, guided tours, self-guiding tour/trail, restrooms. Entrance fee.

North Dakota

Fort Union Trading Post National Historic Site. (North Dakota, Montana), Buford Route, Williston, North Dakota 58801. Visitor center, museum/exhibit, guided tours, self-guiding tour/trail, hiking, fishing, cross-country ski trail, restrooms.

Knife River Indian Villages National Historic Site. R.R. 1, Box 168, Stanton, North Dakota 58571. Visitor center, museum/exhibit, guided tours, self-guiding tour/trail, picnic area, hiking, fishing, cross-country ski trail, restrooms.

Theodore Roosevelt National Park. P.O. Box 7, Medora, North Dakota 58645. Visitor center, museum/exhibit, guided tours, self-guiding tour/trail, picnic area, campground, group campsite, hiking, horseback riding, boating, fishing, snowmobile route, restrooms. Entrance fee.

Ohio

Cuyahoga Valley National Recreation Area. 15610 Vaughn Road, Brecksville, Ohio 44141. Visitor center, museum/exhibit, guided tours, self-guiding tour/trail, hiking, horseback riding, swimming, fishing, bicycle trail, cross-country ski trail, lodging, restrooms.

James A. Garfield National Historic Site. Lawnfield, 8095 Mentor Avenue, Mentor, Ohio 44060. Visitor center, museum/exhibit, guided tour, self-guiding tour/trail, picnic area.

Mound City Group National Monument. 16062 State Route 104, Chillicothe, Ohio 45601. Visitor center, museum/exhibit, guided tours, self-guiding tour/trail, picnic area, hiking, fishing, restrooms. Entrance fee.

Perry's Victory and International Peace Memorial. P.O. Box 549, 93 Delaware Avenue, Put-in-Bay, Ohio

43456. Museum/exhibit, guided tours, fishing, snowmobile route, restrooms. Entrance fee.

William Howard Taft National Historic Site. 2038 Auburn Avenue, Cincinnati, Ohio 45219. Visitor center, museum/exhibit, guided tour, self-guiding tour/trail, restrooms.

Oklahoma

Chickasaw National Recreation Area. P.O. Box 201, Sulphur, Oklahoma 73086. Visitor center, museum/exhibit, guided tours, self-guiding tour/trail, picnic area, campground, campsites, hiking, swimming, boating, boat ramp, fishing, hunting, restrooms.

Oregon

Crater Lake National Park. P.O. Box 7, Crater Lake, Oregon 97604. Visitor center, museum/exhibit, guided tours, self-guiding tour/trail, picnic area, campground, campsites, hiking, fishing, snowmobile route, cross-country ski trail, cabin rental, lodging, groceries/ice, restaurant/snacks, restrooms. Entrance fee.

Fort Clatsop National Memorial. Route 3, Box 604-FC, Astoria, Oregon 97103. Visitor center, museum/exhibit, guided tours, self-guiding tour/trail, picnic area, restrooms. Entrance fee.

John Day Fossil Beds National Monument. 420 West Main Street, John Day, Oregon 97845. Visitor center, museum/exhibit, self-guiding tour/trail, picnic area, hiking, fishing, restrooms.

Oregon Caves National Monument. 19000 Caves Highway, Cave Junction, Oregon 97523. Self-guiding tour/trail, picnic area, hiking, lodging, restaurant/snacks.

Pennsylvania

Allegheny Portage Railroad National Historic Site. P.O. Box 247, Cresson, Pennsylvania 16630. Visitor center, museum/exhibit, guided tours, self-guiding tour/trail, picnic area, hiking, cross-country ski trail, restrooms.

Delaware Water Gap National Recreation Area. (Pennsylvania, New Jersey.) Bushkill, Pennsylvania 18324. Visitor center, museum/exhibit, guided tours, self-guiding tour/trail, picnic area, campground, group campsite, hiking, mountain climbing, swimming, boating, boat rental, boat ramp, fishing, hunting, snowmobile route, cross-country ski trail, restrooms.

Edgar Allan Poe National Historic Site. c/o Independence NHP, 313 Walnut Street, Philadelphia, Pennsylvania 19106. Museum/exhibit, guided tours, self-guiding tour/trail.

Eisenhower National Historic Site. Gettysburg, Pennsylvania 17325. Visitor center, museum/exhibit, guided tours, self-guiding tour/trail, restrooms. Entrance fee.

Fort Necessity National Battlefield. The National Pike, R.D. 2, Box 528, Farmington, Pennsylvania 15437. Visitor center, museum/exhibit, guided tours, self-guiding tour/trail, picnic area, group campsite, hiking, cross-country ski trail, restrooms. Entrance fee.

Friendship Hill National Historic Site. c/o Fort Necessity National Battlefield, R.D. 2, Box 528, Farmington, Pennsylvania 15437. Visitor center, museum/exhibit, guided tours, self-guiding tour/trail, picnic area, hiking, fishing, cross-country ski trail, restrooms.

Gettysburg National Military Park. Gettysburg, Pennsylvania

17325. Visitor center, museum/exhibit, guided tours, self-guiding tour/trail, guide for hire, picnic area, group campsite, bicycle trail, restrooms.

Hopewell Furnace National Historic Site. R.D. 1, Box 345, Elverson, Pennsylvania 19520. Visitor center, museum/exhibit, self-guiding tour/trail, hiking, restrooms. Entrance fee.

Independence National Historical Park. 313 Walnut Street, Philadelphia, Pennsylvania 19106. Visitor center, museum/exhibit, guided tours, self-guiding tour/trail, restaurant/snacks, restrooms.

Johnstown Flood National Memorial. c/o Allegheny Portage Railroad NHS, P.O. Box 247, Cresson, Pennsylvania 16630. Visitor center, museum/exhibit, guided tours, self-guiding tour/trail, picnic area, hiking.

Thaddeus Kosciuszko National Memorial. c/o Independence National Historic Park, 313 Walnut Street, Philadelphia, Pennsylvania 19106. Museum/exhibit, self-guiding tour/trail.

Upper Delaware Scenic and Recreational River. (Pennsylvania, New York.) P.O. Box C, Narrowsburg, New York 12764. Visitor center, museum/exhibit, guided tours, campground, group campsite, horseback riding, swimming, boating, boat rental, boat ramp, fishing, hunting, cabin rental, other lodging, groceries/ice, restaurant/snacks, restrooms.

Valley Forge National Historical Park. Valley Forge, Pennsylvania 19481. Visitor center, museum/exhibit, self-guiding tour/trail, picnic area, hiking, horseback riding, boating, boat ramp, fishing, bicycle trail, cross-country ski trail, restaurant/snacks, restrooms. Entrance fee.

Puerto Rico

San Juan National Historic Site. P.O. Box 712, Old San Juan, Puerto Rico 00902. Visitor center, museum/exhibit, guided tours.

Rhode Island

Roger Williams National Memorial. P.O. Box 367, Annex Station, Providence, Rhode Island 02901. Visitor center, museum/exhibit, restrooms.

South Carolina

Congaree Swamp National Monument. Suite 607, 1835 Assembly Street, Columbia, South Carolina 29201. Visitor center, museum/exhibit, self-guiding tour/trail, campsites, hiking, boating, fishing, restrooms.

Cowpens National Battlefield. P.O. Box 308, Chesnee, South Carolina 29323. Visitor center, museum/exhibit, guided tours, self-guiding tour/trail, picnic area, hiking, bicycle trail, restrooms. Entrance fee.

Fort Sumter National Monument. 1214 Middle Street, Sullivans Island, South Carolina 29482. Visitor center, museum/exhibit, guided tours, self-guiding tour/trail, fishing, restrooms.

Kings Mountain National Military Park. P.O. Box 40, Kings Mountain, North Carolina 28086. Visitor center, museum/exhibit, self-guiding tour/trail, hiking, horseback riding, restrooms.

Ninety Six National Historic Site. P.O. Box 496, Ninety Six, South Carolina 29666. Visitor center, museum/exhibit, guided tours, self-guiding tour/trail, picnic area, hiking, horseback riding, fishing, restrooms.

South Dakota

Badlands National Park. P.O. Box 6, Interior, South Dakota 57750. Visitor center, museum/exhibit, guided tours, self-guiding tour/trail, picnic area, campground, group campsite, hiking, cabin rental, restaurant/snacks. Entrance fee.

Jewel Cave National Monument. R.R. 1, Box 60AA, Custer, South Dakota 57730. Visitor center, museum/exhibit, guided tours, picnic area, restrooms.

Mount Rushmore National Memorial. P.O. Box 268, Keystone, South Dakota 57751. Visitor center, museum/exhibit, restaurant/snacks, restrooms.

Wind Cave National Park. Hot Springs, South Dakota 57747. Visitor center, museum/exhibit, guided tours, self-guiding tour/trail, picnic area, campground, campsites, hiking, restaurant/snacks, restrooms.

Tennessee

Andrew Johnson National Historic Site. P.O. Box 1088, Greeneville, Tennessee 37744. Visitor center, museum/exhibit, self-guiding tour/trail, restrooms. Entrance fee.

Big South Fork National River and Recreation Area. (Tennessee, Kentucky.) P.O. Drawer 630, Oneida, Tennessee 37841. Visitor center, museum/exhibit, picnic area, campground, campsites, hiking, swimming, boating, boat ramp, fishing, hunting, restrooms.

Fort Donelson National Battlefield. P.O. Box 434, Dover, Tennessee 37058-0434. Visitor center, museum/exhibit, self-guiding tour/trail, picnic area, group campsite, hiking, restrooms. Entrance fee.

Great Smoky Mountains National Park. (Tennessee, North Carolina.) Gatlinburg, Tennessee 37738. Visitor center, museum/exhibit, guided tours, self-guiding tour/trail, picnic area, campground, campsites, hiking,

horseback riding, fishing, bicycle trail, cabin rental, other lodging, groceries/ice, restrooms.

Obed Wild and Scenic River. P.O. Box 429, Wartburg, Tennessee 37887. Visitor center, museum/exhibit, picnic area, swimming, boating, fishing, hunting, restrooms.

Shiloh National Military Park. P.O. Box 61, Shiloh, Tennessee 38376. Visitor center, museum/exhibit, guided tours, self-guiding tour/trail, picnic area, bicycle trail, restrooms. Entrance fee.

Stones River National Battlefield. Route 10, Box 495, Old Nashville Highway, Murfreesboro, Tennessee 37130. Visitor center, museum/exhibit, guided tours, self-guiding tour/trail, picnic area, hiking, bicycle trail, restrooms. Entrance fee.

Texas

Alibates Flint Quarries National Monument. c/o Lake Meredith Recreation Area, P.O. Box 1438, Fritch, Texas 79036. Museum/exhibit, guided tours.

Amistad Recreation Area. P.O. Box 420367, Del Rio, Texas 78842-0367. Self-guiding tour/trail, guide for hire, picnic area, campground, campsites, hiking, horseback riding, swimming, boating, boat rental, boat ramp, fishing, hunting, groceries/ice, restaurant/snacks, restrooms.

Big Bend National Park. Big Bend National Park, Texas 79834. Visitor center, museum/exhibit, guided tours, self-guiding tour/trail, picnic area, campground, group campsite, hiking, horseback riding, boating, fishing, lodging, groceries/ice, restaurant/snacks, restrooms. Entrance fee.

Big Thicket National Preserve. 3785 Milam, Beaumont, Texas 77701. Visitor center, guided tours, self-guiding tour/trail, picnic area, hiking, boating, boat ramp, fishing, hunting, restrooms.

Chamizal National Memorial. c/o Federal Building, 700 East San Antonio, Suite D-301, El Paso, Texas 79901. Visitor center, museum/exhibit, guided tours, self-guiding tour/trail, picnic area, restrooms.

Fort Davis National Historic Site. P.O. Box 1456, Fort Davis, Texas 79734. Visitor center, museum/exhibit, self-guiding tour/trail, picnic area, hiking, restrooms. Entrance fee.

Guadalupe Mountains National Park. N.C. 60, Box 400, Salt Flat, Texas 79847-9400. Visitor center, museum/exhibit, guided tours, self-guiding tour/trail, picnic area, campground, campsites, hiking, off-road vehicle trail, restrooms.

Lake Meredith Recreation Area. P.O. Box 1438, Fritch, Texas 79036. Museum/exhibit, picnic area, campground, swimming, boating, boat ramp, fishing, hunting, off-road vehicle trail, groceries/ice.

Lyndon B. Johnson National Historical Park. P.O. Box 329, Johnson City, Texas 78636. Visitor center, museum/exhibit, guided tours, self-guiding tour/trail, restrooms.

Padre Island National Seashore. 9405 South Padre Island Drive, Corpus Christi, Texas 78418-5597. Visitor center, museum/exhibit, self-guiding tour/trail, campground, campsites, hiking, horseback riding, swimming, bathhouse, boating, boat ramp, fishing, hunting, restrooms. Entrance fee.

San Antonio Missions National Historical Park. 2202 Roosevelt Avenue, San Antonio, Texas 78210-4919. Museum/exhibit, guided tours, self-guiding tour/trail, hiking, bicycle trail.

Utah

Arches National Park. P.O. Box 907, Moab, Utah 84532. Visitor center, museum/exhibit, guided tours, self-guiding tour/trail, picnic area, campground, campsites, hiking, restrooms. Entrance fee.

Bryce Canyon National Park. Bryce Canyon, Utah 84717. Visitor center, museum/exhibit, guided tours, self-guiding tour/trail, picnic area, campground, campsites, hiking, horseback riding, cross-country ski trail, cabin rental, other lodging, groceries/ice, restaurant/snacks, restrooms. Entrance fee.

Canyonlands National Park. 125 West 200 South, Moab, Utah 84532. Visitor center, guided tours, self-guiding tour/trail, guide for hire, picnic area, campground, campsites, hiking, horseback riding, boating, off-road vehicle trail, restrooms. Entrance fee.

Capitol Reef National Park. Torrey, Utah 84775. Visitor center, museum/exhibit, guided tours, self-guiding tour/trail, picnic area, campground, group campsite, hiking, mountain climbing, horseback riding, restrooms. Entrance fee.

Cedar Breaks National Monument. P.O. Box 749, Cedar City, Utah 84720. Visitor center, museum/exhibit, guided tours, self-guiding tour/trail, picnic area, campground, group campsite, hiking, snowmobile route, cross-country ski trail, restrooms. Entrance fee.

Glen Canyon National Recreation Area. (Utah, Arizona.) P.O. Box 1507, Page, Arizona 86040. Visitor center, museum/exhibit, guided tours, self-guiding tour/trail, guide for hire, picnic area, campground, group campsite, hiking, swimming, boating, boat rental, boat ramp, fishing, hunting, lodging, groceries/ice, restaurant/snacks.

Golden Spike National Historic Site. P.O. Box W, Brigham City, Utah 84302. Visitor center, museum/exhibit, self-guiding tour/trail, picnic area. Entrance fee.

Natural Bridges National Monument. Box 1, Lake Powell, Utah 84533. Visitor center, museum/exhibit, self-guiding tour/trail, picnic area, campground, group campsites, hiking, restrooms. Entrance fee.

Rainbow Bridge National Monument. c/o Glenn Canyon National Recreation Area, P.O. Box 1507, Page, Arizona 86040. Self-guiding tour/trail, guide for hire, hiking, swimming, boating, fishing.

Timpanogos Cave National Monument. R.R. 3, Box 200, American Fork, Utah 84003. Visitor center, museum/exhibit, guided tours, self-guiding tour/trail, picnic area, restaurant/snacks.

Zion National Park. Springdale, Utah 84767-1099. Visitor center, museum/exhibit, guided tours, self-guiding tour/trail, picnic area, campground, campsites, hiking, mountain climbing, horseback riding, snowmobile route, cross-country ski trail, cabin rental, other lodging, restaurant/snacks, restrooms.

Virginia

Appomattox Court House National Historical Park. P.O. Box 218, Appomattox, Virginia 24522. Visitor center, museum/exhibit, guided tours, self-guiding tour/trail, picnic area, hiking, restrooms. Entrance fee.

Arlington House. The Robert E. Lee Memorial, c/o George Washington Memorial Parkway, Turkey Run Park, McLean, Virginia 22101. Visitor center, museum/exhibit, guided tours, bicycle trail, restrooms.

Booker T. Washington National Monument. Route 1, Box 195, Hardy, Virginia 24101. Visitor center, museum/exhibit, guided tours, self-guiding tour/trail, picnic area, group campsites, hiking. Entrance fee.

Colonial National Historical Park. P.O. Box 210, Yorktown, Virginia 23690. Visitor center, museum/exhibit, guided tours, self-guiding tour/trail, picnic area, hiking, bicycle trail, restrooms. Entrance fee.

Fredericksburg and Spotsylvania National Military Park. P.O. Box 679, Fredericksburg, Virginia 22404. Visitor center, museum/exhibit, guided tours, self-guiding tour/trail, picnic area, hiking, fishing, bicycle trail, lodging, groceries/ice, restaurant/snacks, restrooms.

George Washington Birthplace National Monument. R.R. 1, Box 717, Washington's Birthplace, Virginia 22575. Visitor center, museum/exhibit, guided tours, self-guiding tour/trail, picnic area, hiking, fishing, restrooms. Entrance fee.

George Washington Memorial Parkway. (Virginia, Maryland.) Turkey Run Park, McLean, Virginia 22101. Visitor center, museum/exhibit, guided tours, self-guiding tour/trail, picnic area, hiking, horseback riding, boating, boat ramp, fishing, bicycle trail, restaurant/snacks, restrooms.

Great Falls Park. 9200 Old Dominion Drive, Great Falls, Virginia 22066. Visitor center, museum/exhibit, guided tours, self-guiding tour/trail, picnic area, hiking, mountain climbing, fishing, cross-country ski trail, restaurant/snacks. Entrance fee.

Maggie L. Walker National Historic Site. c/o Richmond NBP, 3215 East Broad Street, Richmond, Virginia 23223. Museum/exhibit, guided tours.

Manassas National Battlefield Park. P.O. Box 1830, Manassas, Virginia 22110. Visitor center, museum/exhibit, guided tours, self-guiding tour/trail, picnic area, hiking, horseback riding, fishing, restrooms. Entrance fee.

Petersburg National Battlefield. P.O. Box 549, Route 36 East, Petersburg, Virginia 23804. Visitor center, museum/exhibit, guided tours, self-guiding tour/trail, picnic area, hiking, horseback riding, bicycle trail. Entrance fee.

Prince William Forest Park. P.O. Box 209, Triangle, Virginia 22172. Visitor center, museum/exhibit, guided tours, self-guiding tour/trail, picnic area, campground, group campsite, hiking, fishing, bicycle trail, cabin rental, restrooms. Entrance fee.

Richmond National Battlefield Park. 3215 East Broad Street, Richmond, Virginia 23223. Visitor center, museum/exhibit, self-guiding tour/trail, picnic area.

Shenandoah National Park. Route 4, Box 348, Luray, Virginia 22835. Visitor center, museum/exhibit, guided tours, self-guiding tour/trail, picnic area, campground, campsites, hiking, mountain climbing, horseback riding, fishing, cross-country ski trail, cabin rental, other lodging, groceries/ice, restaurant/snacks, restrooms. Entrance fee.

Wolf Trap Farm Park for the Performing Arts. 1551 Trap Road, Vienna, Virginia 22180. Guided tours, self-guiding tour/trail, picnic area, restaurant/snacks, restrooms.

Washington

Coulee Dam National Recreation Area. P.O. Box 37, Coulee Dam, Washington 99116. Visitor center, museum/exhibit, guided tours, self-guiding tour/trail, picnic area, campground, campsites, swimming, bathhouse, boating, boat ramp, fishing, hunting, restrooms.

Fort Vancouver National Historic Site. 612 East Reserve Street, Vancouver, Washington 98661-3897. Visitor center, museum/exhibit, guided tours, picnic area, restrooms. Entrance fee.

Klondike Gold Rush National Historical Park. 117 South Main Street, Seattle, Washington 98104. Visitor center, museum/exhibit, restrooms.

Lake Chelan National Recreation Area. 2105 Highway 20, Sedro, Wooley, Washington 98284. Visitor center, guided tours, self-guiding tour/trail, picnic area, campground, group campsite, hiking, mountain climbing, horseback riding, boating, boat rental, fishing, hunting, cross-country ski trail, cabin rental, other lodging, groceries/ice, restaurant/snacks.

Mount Rainier National Park. Tahoma Woods, Star Route, Ashford, Washington 98304. Visitor center, museum/exhibit, guided tours, self-guiding tour/trail, guide for hire, picnic area, campground, group campsite, hiking, mountain climbing, fishing, snowmobile route, cross-country ski trail, lodging, groceries/ice, restaurant/snacks, restrooms. Entrance fee.

North Cascades National Park. 2105 Highway 20, Sedro Wooley, Washington 98284. Group campsite, hiking, mountain climbing, horseback riding, fishing.

Olympic National Park. 600 East Park Avenue, Port Angeles, Washington 98362. Visitor center, museum/exhibit, guided tours, self-guiding tour/trail, guide for hire, picnic area, campground, campsites, hiking, mountain climbing, horseback riding, swimming, bathhouse, boating, boat rental, boat ramp, fishing, cross-country ski trail, cabin rental, lodging, groceries/ice, restaurant/snacks, restrooms. Entrance fee.

Ross Lake National Recreation Area. 2105 Highway 20, Sedro Woolley, Washington 98284. Guided tours, self-guiding tour/trail, picnic area, campground, campsites, hiking, mountain climbing, horseback riding, boating, boat rental, boat ramp, fishing, hunting, snowmobile route, cabin rental, groceries/ice, restaurant/snacks, restrooms.

San Juan Island National Historical Park. P.O. Box 429, Friday Harbor, Washington 98250. Visitor center, museum/exhibit, guided tours, self-guiding tour/trail, picnic area, hiking, restrooms.

Whitman Mission National Historic Site. Route 2, Box 247, Walla Walla, Washington 99362. Visitor center, museum/exhibit, self-guiding tour/trail, picnic area, restrooms. Entrance fee.

West Virginia

Appalachian National Scenic Trail. (Maine to Georgia.) P.O. Box 807, Harpers Ferry, West Virginia 25425. Visitor center, museum/exhibit, self-guiding tour/trail, picnic area, campground, hiking, mountain climbing, cabin rental, groceries/ice.

Harpers Ferry National Historical Park. (West Virginia, Maryland, Virginia.) P.O. Box 65, Harpers Ferry, West Virginia 25425. Visitor center, museum/exhibit, guided tours, self-guiding tour/trail, hiking, mountain climbing, fishing, restrooms. Entrance fee.

New River Gorge National River. P.O. Box 1189, Oak Hill, West Virginia 25901. Visitor center, museum/exhibit, picnic area, campground, hiking,

horseback riding, swimming, boating, fishing, hunting, cabin rental, restrooms.

Wisconsin

Apostle Islands National Lakeshore. Route 1, Box 4, Bayfield, Wisconsin 54814. Visitor center, museum/exhibit, guided tours, self-guiding tour/trail, picnic area, campground, group campsite, hiking, swimming, boating, fishing, hunting, restrooms.

St. Croix and Lower St. Croix National Scenic Riverways. (Wisconsin, Minnesota.) P.O. Box 708, St. Croix Falls, Wisconsin 54024. Visitor center, museum/exhibit, self-guiding tour/trail, picnic area, campground, campsites, hiking, swimming, boating, boat rental, boat ramp, fishing, hunting, cross-country ski trail, cabin rental, other lodging, groceries/ice, restaurant/snacks, restrooms.

Wyoming

Devils Tower National Monument. Devils Tower, Wyoming 82714. Visitor center, museum/exhibit, guided tours, self-guiding tour/trail, picnic area, campground, campsites, hiking, mountain climbing, fishing, restrooms. Entrance fee.

Fort Laramie National Historic Site. Fort Laramie, Wyoming 82212. Visitor center, museum/exhibit, guided tours, self-guiding tour/trail, picnic area, fishing, restrooms. Entrance fee.

Fossil Butte National Monument. P.O. Box 527, Kemmerer, Wyoming 83101. Visitor center, museum/exhibit, guided tours, self-guiding tour/trail, picnic area, hiking, horseback riding.

Grand Teton National Park. P.O. Drawer 170, Moose, Wyoming 83012. Visitor center, museum/exhibit, guided tours, self-guiding tour/trail, guide for hire, picnic area, campground, campsites, hiking, mountain climbing, horseback riding, swimming, boating, boat rental, boat ramp, fishing, snowmobile route, cross-country ski trail, cabin rental, other lodging, groceries/ice, restaurant/snacks, restrooms. Entrance fee.

John D. Rockefeller, Jr., Memorial Parkway. c/o Grand Teton National Park, P.O. Drawer 170, Moose, Wyoming 83012. Guided tours, self-guiding tour/trail, guide for hire, campground, campsites, hiking, horseback riding, boating, fishing, hunting, snowmobile route, cross-country ski trail, cabin rental, other lodging, groceries/ice, restaurant/snacks, restrooms.

Yellowstone National Park. (Wyoming, Idaho, Montana.) P.O. Box 168, Yellowstone National Park, Wyoming\ 82190. Visitor center, museum/exhibit, guided tours, self-guiding tours/trail, guide for hire, picnic area, campground, campsites, hiking, horseback riding, boating, boat rental, boat ramp, fishing, snowmobile route, cross-country ski trail, cabin rental, other lodging, groceries/ice, restaurant/snacks, restrooms. Entrance fee.

Appendix I

Frequently Mentioned Associations

Alliance for Parental Involvement in Education. P.O. Box 59, East Chatham, New York 12060. Phone: 518/392-6900.

American Academy of Pediatrics. 141 Northwest Point Boulevard, P.O. Box 927, Elk Grove Village, Illinois 60009-0927. Phone: 708/228-5005 or 1/800-433-9016. When requesting a free brochure by mail, be sure to include the name of the brochure on the envelope. (The academy regrets that it cannot fulfill requests that do not include a return envelope.)

Association for Library Service to Children. American Library Association, 50 East Huron Road, Chicago, Illinois 60611. Phone: 312/944-6780.

Family Resource Coalition. 200 South Michigan Avenue, Suite 1520, Chicago, Illinois 60604. Phone: 312/341-0900. Fax: 312/341-9361.

International Reading Association. 800 Barksdale Road, P.O. Box 8139, Newark, Delaware 19714-8139. Phone: 302/731-1600 or 1/800-336-READ. Fax: 302/731-1057.

La Leche League International. 9616 Minneapolis Avenue, P.O. Box 1209, Franklin Park, Illinois 60131-8209. Phone: 708/455-7730. Hotline: 1/800-LA-LECHE.

National Association for the Education of Young Children. 1509 Sixteenth Street, N.W., Washington, D.C. 20036-1426. Phone: 202/232-8777 or 1/800-424-2460. Fax: 202/328-1846.

National PTA. 700 North Rush Street, Chicago, Illinois 60611-2571. Phone: 312/787-0977. Fax: 312/787-8342.

Index

A note on the index: Listed here are organizations, publications, and other specific items referenced in this book. For information on subject categories, please see the table of contents.